enVision™ Algebra 2
Student Edition

SAVVAS
LEARNING COMPANY

ISBN-13: 978-0-328-93156-9
ISBN-10:   0-328-93156-X

13 21

Contents in Brief

enVision Algebra 2

Reviewers & Consultants

Mathematicians

David Bressoud, Ph.D.
Professor Emeritus of Mathematics
Macalester College
St. Paul, MN

Karen Edwards, Ph.D.
Mathematics Lecturer
Harvard University
Cambridge, MA

Teacher Reviewers

Jennifer Barkey
K-12 Math Supervisor
Gateway School District
Monroeville, PA

Miesha Beck
Math Teacher/Department Chair
Blackfoot School District
Blackfoot, ID

Joseph Brandell, Ph.D.
West Bloomfield High School
West Bloomfield Public Schools
West Bloomfield, MI

Andrea Coles
Mathematics Teacher
Mountain View Middle School
Blackfoot, ID

Julie Johnson
Mathematics/CS teacher (9–12)
Williamsville Central Schools
Williamsville, NY

Tamar McPherson
Plum Sr HS/Math Teacher
Plum School District
Pittsburgh, PA

Melisa Rice
Math Department Chairperson
Shawnee Public Schools
Shawnee, OK

Erin Zitka
6–12 Math Coordinator
Forsyth County
Cumming, GA

Jeff Ziegler
Teacher
Pittsburgh City Schools
Pittsburgh, PA

About the Authors

Authors

Dan Kennedy, Ph.D

- Classroom teacher and the Lupton Distinguished Professor of Mathematics at the Baylor School in Chattanooga, TN
- Co-author of textbooks *Precalculus: Graphical, Numerical, Algebraic* and *Calculus: Graphical, Numerical, Algebraic, AP Edition*
- Past chair of the College Board's AP Calculus Development Committee.
- Previous Tandy Technology Scholar and Presidential Award winner

Eric Milou, Ed.D

- Professor of Mathematics, Rowan University, Glassboro, NJ
- Member of the author team for Savvas' **enVision**math**2.0** 6-8
- Member of National Council of Teachers of Mathematics (NCTM) feedback/advisory team for the Common Core State Standards
- Author of *Teaching Mathematics to Middle School Students*

Christine D. Thomas, Ph.D

- Professor of Mathematics Education at Georgia State University, Atlanta, GA
- Past-President of the Association of Mathematics Teacher Educators (AMTE)
- Past NCTM Board of Directors Member
- Past member of the editorial panel of the NCTM journal *Mathematics Teacher*
- Past co-chair of the steering committee of the North American chapter of the International Group of the Psychology of Mathematics Education

Rose Mary Zbiek, Ph.D

- Professor of Mathematics Education, Pennsylvania State University, College Park, PA
- Series editor for the NCTM *Essential Understanding* project

Contributing Author

Al Cuoco, Ph.D

- Lead author of CME Project, a National Science Foundation (NSF)-funded high school curriculum
- Team member to revise the Conference Board of the Mathematical Sciences (CBMS) recommendations for teacher preparation and professional development
- Co-author of several books published by the Mathematical Association of America and the American Mathematical Society
- Consultant to the writers of the Common Core State Standards for Mathematics and the PARCC Content Frameworks for high school mathematics

enVision™ Algebra 2 offers a carefully constructed lesson design to help you succeed in math.

Step 1 At the start of each lesson, you and your classmates will work together to come up with a solution strategy for the problem or task posed. After a class discussion, you'll be asked to reflect back on the processes and strategies you used in solving the problem.

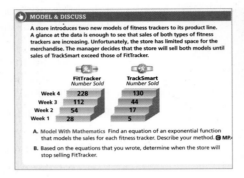

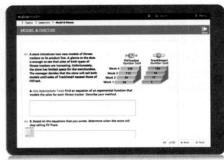

Step 2 Next, your teacher will guide you through new concepts and skills for the lesson.

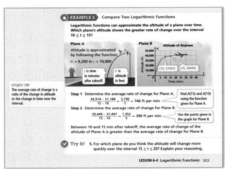

After each example, you work out a problem called the **Try It!** to solidify your understanding of these concepts.

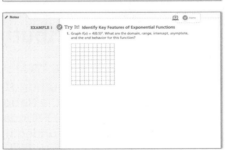

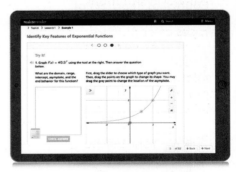

In addition, you will periodically answer **Habits of Mind** questions to refine your thinking and problem-solving skills.

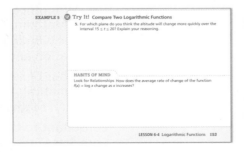

This part of the lesson concludes with a Lesson Check that helps you to know how well you are understanding the new content presented in the lesson. With the exercises in the **Do You Understand?** and **Do You Know How?**, you can gauge your understanding of the lesson concepts.

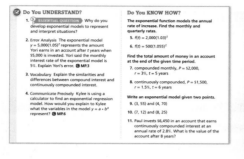

Step 3 In Step 3, you will find a balanced exercise set with **Understand** exercises that focus on conceptual understanding, **Practice** exercises that target procedural fluency, and **Apply** exercises for which you apply concept and skills to real-world situations. The **Assessment Practice** exercises offer practice for high stakes assessments. Your teacher may have you complete the assignment in print or online at SavvasRealize.com

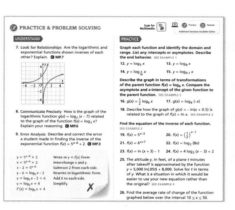

Step 4 Your teacher may have you take the Lesson Quiz after each lesson. You can take the quiz online or in print. To do your best on the quiz, review the lesson problems in that lesson.

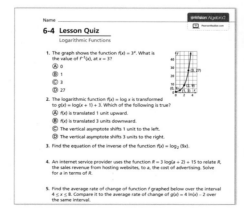

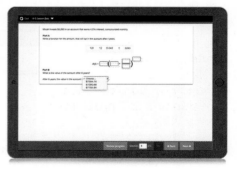

Digital Resources

Everything you need for math, anytime, anywhere.

SavvasRealize.com is your gateway to all of the digital resources for
enVision™ Algebra 2. Log in to access your interactive student edition, called Realize Reader.

In SavvasRealize, you can:

Activities Complete Explore & Reason, Model & Discuss, Critique & Explain activities.

Animation View and interact with real-world applications.

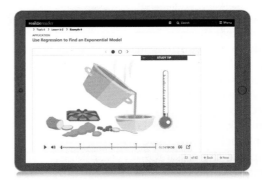

Activities Interact with Examples and Try Its.

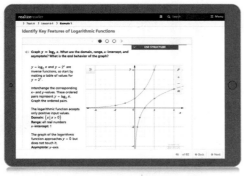

Practice Practice what you've learned.

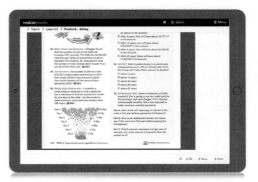

Videos Watch clips to support Mathematical Modeling in 3 Acts Lessons and enVision™ STEM Projects.

Assessment Show what you've learned.

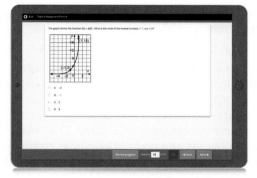

Tutorials Get help from Virtual Nerd, right when you need it.

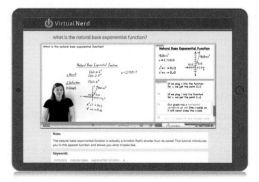

Concept Sumary Review key lesson content through multiple representations.

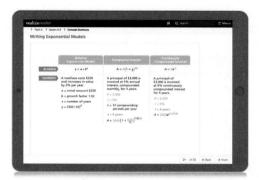

Glossary Read and listen to English and Spanish definitions.

Math Tools Explore math with digital tools and manipulatives.

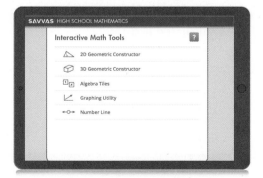

Making Sense of and Solving Problems

Make sense of problems and persevere in solving them.

Proficient math thinkers read through a problem situation and can put together a workable solution path to solve the problem posed. They analyze the information provided and identify constraints and dependencies. They identify multiple entries to a problem solution and choose an efficient and effective entry point.

Consider these questions to help you make sense of problems.

- What am I asked to find?
- What are the quantities and variables? The dependencies and the constraints? How do they relate?
- What are some possible strategies to solve the problem?

Attend to precision.

Proficient math thinkers communicate clearly and precisely the approach they are using. They identify the meaning of symbols that they use and always remember to specify units of measure and to label graphical models accurately. They use mathematical terms precisely and express their answers with the appropriate degree of accuracy.

Consider these questions to help you attend to precision.

- Have I stated the meaning of the variables and symbols I am using?
- Have I specified the units of measure I am using?
- Have I calculated accurately?

Reasoning and Communicating

Reason abstractly and quantitatively.

Proficient math thinkers make sense of quantities in problem situations. They represent a problem situation using symbols or equations and explain what the symbols or equation represent in relationship to a problem situation. As they model a situation symbolically or mathematically, they explain the meaning of the quantities.

Consider these questions to help you reason abstractly and quantitatively.

- How can I represent this problem situation using equations or formulas?
- What do the numbers, variables, and symbols in the equation or formula represent?

Construct viable arguments and critique the reasoning of others.

Proficient math thinkers and problem solvers communicate their problem solutions clearly and convincingly. They construct sound mathematical arguments and develop and defend conjectures to explain mathematical situations. They make use of examples and counterexamples to support their arguments and justify their conclusions. When asked, they respond clearly and logically to the positions and conclusions of others, and compare two arguments, identifying any flaws in logic or reasoning that the arguments may contain. They ask questions to clarify or improve the position of a classmate.

Consider these questions to help you construct mathematical arguments.

- What assumptions can I make when constructing an argument?
- What conjectures can I make about the solution to the problem?
- What arguments can I present to defend my conjectures?

Representing and Connecting

Model with mathematics.

Proficient math thinkers use mathematics to represent a problem situation and make connections between a real-world problem situation and mathematics. They see the applicability of mathematics to solve every-day problems and explain how geometry can be used to solve a carpentry problem or algebra to solve a proportional relationship problem. They define and map relationships among quantities in a problem, using appropriate tools. They analyze the relationships and draw conclusions about the solutions.

Consider these questions to help you model with mathematics.

- What representations can I use to show the relationship among quantities or variables?
- What assumptions can I make about the problem situation to simplify the problem?

Use appropriate tools strategically.

Proficient math thinkers strategize about which tools are more helpful to solve a problem situation. They consider all tools, from paper and pencil to protractors and rulers, to calculators and software applications. They articulate the appropriateness of different tools and recognize which would best serve the needs for a given problem. They are especially insightful about technological tools and use them in ways that deepen or extend their understanding of concepts. They also make use of mental tools, such as estimation, to determine the appropriateness of a solution.

Consider these questions to help you use appropriate tools.

- What tool can I use to help me solve the problem?
- How can technology help me solve the problem?

Seeing Structure and Generalizing

Look for and make use of structure.

Proficient math thinkers see the structure of mathematics in the problems they are solving and generalize mathematics principles from this structure. They see complicated expressions or equations as single objects composed of many parts.

Consider these questions to help you see structure.

- Can I see a pattern or structure in the problem or solution strategy?
- How can I use the pattern or structure I see to help me solve the problem?

Look for and express regularity in repeated reasoning.

Proficient math thinkers notice when calculations are repeated and can uncover both general methods and shortcuts for solving similar problems.

Consider these questions to help you look for regularity in repeated reasoning.

- Do I notice any repeated calculations or steps?
- Are there general methods that I can use to solve the problem?
- What can I generalize from one problem to another?
- How reasonable are the results that I am getting?

STANDARDS FOR MATHEMATICAL PRACTICE

Standards for Mathematical Content in Algebra 2

Number and Quantity

The Real Number System

Extend the properties of exponents to rational exponents

HSN.RN.A.1 Explain how the definition of the meaning of rational exponents follows from extending the properties of integer exponents to those values, allowing for a notation for radicals in terms of rational exponents.

HSN.RN.A.2 Rewrite expressions involving radicals and rational exponents using the properties of exponents.

Quantities*

Reason quantitatively and use units to solve problems

HSN.Q.A.2 Define appropriate quantities for the purpose of descriptive modeling.

The Complex Number System

Perform arithmetic operations with complex numbers

HSN.CN.A.1 Know there is a complex number i such that $i^2 = -1$, and every complex number has the form $a + bi$ with a and b real.

HSN.CN.A.2 Use the relation $i^2 = -1$ and the commutative, associative, and distributive properties to add, subtract, and multiply complex numbers.

HSN.CN.A.3 (+) Find the conjugate of a complex number; use conjugates to find moduli and quotients of complex numbers.

Represent complex numbers and their operations on the complex plane

HSN.CN.B.4 (+) Represent complex numbers on the complex plane in rectangular and polar form (including real and imaginary numbers), and explain why the rectangular and polar forms of a given complex number represent the same number.

HSN.CN.B.5 (+) Represent addition, subtraction, multiplication, and conjugation of complex numbers geometrically on the complex plane; use properties of this representation for computation.

HSN.CN.B.6 (+) Calculate the distance between numbers in the complex plane as the modulus of the difference, and the midpoint of a segment as the average of the numbers at its endpoints.

Use complex numbers in polynomial identities and equations

HSN.CN.C.7 Solve quadratic equations with real coefficients that have complex solutions.

HSN.CN.C.8 (+) Extend polynomial identities to the complex numbers.

HSN.CN.C.9 (+) Know the Fundamental Theorem of Algebra; show that it is true for quadratic polynomials.

Vector and Matrix Quantities

Represent and model with vector quantities

HSN.VM.A.1 (+) Recognize vector quantities as having both magnitude and direction. Represent vector quantities by directed line segments, and use appropriate symbols for vectors and their magnitudes (e.g., v, $|v|$, $\|v\|$, v).

HSN.VM.A.2 (+) Find the components of a vector by subtracting the coordinates of an initial point from the coordinates of a terminal point.

HSN.VM.A.3 (+) Solve problems involving velocity and other quantities that can be represented by vectors.

Perform operations on vectors

HSN.VM.B.4 (+) Add and subtract vectors.

HSN.VM.B.4.A Add vectors end-to-end, component-wise, and by the parallelogram rule. Understand that the magnitude of a sum of two vectors is typically not the sum of the magnitudes.

HSN.VM.B.4.B Given two vectors in magnitude and direction form, determine the magnitude and direction of their sum.

HSN.VM.B.4.C Understand vector subtraction $v - w$ as $v + (-w)$, where $-w$ is the additive inverse of w, with the same magnitude as w and pointing in the opposite direction. Represent vector subtraction graphically by connecting the tips in the appropriate order, and perform vector subtraction component-wise.

HSN.VM.B.5 (+) Multiply a vector by a scalar.

HSN.VM.B.5.A Represent scalar multiplication graphically by scaling vectors and possibly reversing their direction; perform scalar multiplication component-wise, e.g., as $c(v_x, v_y) = (cv_x, cv_y)$.

HSN.VM.B.5.B Compute the magnitude of a scalar multiple cv using $\|cv\| = |c|v$. Compute the direction of cv knowing that when $|c|v \neq 0$, the direction of cv is either along v (for $c > 0$) or against v (for $c < 0$).

Perform operations on matrices and use matrices in applications

HSN.VM.C.6 (+) Use matrices to represent and manipulate data, e.g., to represent payoffs or incidence relationships in a network.

HSN.VM.C.7 (+) Multiply matrices by scalars to produce new matrices, e.g., as when all of the payoffs in a game are doubled.

HSN.VM.C.8 (+) Add, subtract, and multiply matrices of appropriate dimensions.

HSN.VM.C.9 (+) Understand that, unlike multiplication of numbers, matrix multiplication for square matrices is not a commutative operation, but still satisfies the associative and distributive properties.

HSN.VM.C.10 (+) Understand that the zero and identity matrices play a role in matrix addition and multiplication similar to the role of 0 and 1 in the real numbers. The determinant of a square matrix is nonzero if and only if the matrix has a multiplicative inverse.

HSN.VM.C.11 (+) Multiply a vector (regarded as a matrix with one column) by a matrix of suitable dimensions to produce another vector. Work with matrices as transformations of vectors.

HSN.VM.C.12 (+) Work with 2×2 matrices as transformations of the plane, and interpret the absolute value of the determinant in terms of area.

Algebra

Seeing Structure in Expressions

Interpret the structure of expressions

HSA.SSE.A.1 Interpret expressions that represent a quantity in terms of its context.*

HSA.SSE.A.1.A Interpret parts of an expression, such as terms, factors, and coefficients.

HSA.SSE.A.1.B Interpret complicated expressions by viewing one or more of their parts as a single entity.

HSA.SSE.A.2 Use the structure of an expression to identify ways to rewrite it.

Write expressions in equivalent forms to solve problems

HSA.SSE.B.3 Choose and produce an equivalent form of an expression to reveal and explain properties of the quantity represented by the expression.*

HSA.SSE.B.3.A Factor a quadratic expression to reveal the zeros of the function it defines.

HSA.SSE.B.3.C Use the properties of exponents to transform expressions for exponential functions.

HSA.SSE.B.4 Derive the formula for the sum of a finite geometric series (when the common ratio is not 1), and use the formula to solve problems.*

Arithmetic with Polynomials and Rational Expressions

Perform arithmetic operations on polynomials

HSA.APR.A.1 Understand that polynomials form a system analogous to the integers, namely, they are closed under the operations of addition, subtraction, and multiplication; add, subtract, and multiply polynomials.

Understand the relationship between zeros and factors of polynomials

HSA.APR.B.2 Know and apply the Remainder Theorem: For a polynomial $p(x)$ and a number a, the remainder on division by $x - a$ is $p(a)$, so $p(a) = 0$ if and only if $(x - a)$ is a factor of $p(x)$.

HSA.APR.B.3 Identify zeros of polynomials when suitable factorizations are available, and use the zeros to construct a rough graph of the function defined by the polynomial.

Use polynomial identities to solve problems

HSA.APR.C.4 Prove polynomial identities and use them to describe numerical relationships.

HSA.APR.C.5 (+) Know and apply the Binomial Theorem for the expansion of $(x + y)^n$ in powers of x and y for a positive integer n, where x and y are any numbers, with coefficients determined for example by Pascal's Triangle.

Rewrite rational expressions

HSA.APR.D.6 Rewrite simple rational expressions in different forms; write $\frac{a(x)}{b(x)}$ in the form $q(x) + \frac{r(x)}{b(x)}$, where $a(x)$, $b(x)$, $q(x)$, and $r(x)$ are polynomials with the degree of $r(x)$ less than the degree of $b(x)$, using inspection, long division, or, for the more complicated examples, a computer algebra system.

HSA.APR.D.7 (+) Understand that rational expressions form a system analogous to the rational numbers, closed under addition, subtraction, multiplication, and division by a nonzero rational expression; add, subtract, multiply, and divide rational expressions.

Creating Equations*

Create equations that describe numbers or relationships

HSA.CED.A.1 Create equations and inequalities in one variable and use them to solve problems. Include equations arising from linear and quadratic functions, and simple rational and exponential functions.

HSA.CED.A.2 Create equations in two or more variables to represent relationships between quantities; graph equations on coordinate axes with labels and scales.

COMMON CORE STATE STANDARDS

Standards for Mathematical Content in Algebra 2

HAS.CED.A.2 Represent constraints by equations or inequalities, and by systems of equations and/or inequalities, and interpret solutions as viable or nonviable options in a modeling context.

HSA.CED.A.4 Rearrange formulas to highlight a quantity of interest, using the same reasoning as in solving equations.

Reasoning with Equations and Inequalities

Understand solving equations as a process of reasoning and explain the reasoning

HSA.REI.A.1 Explain each step in solving a simple equation as following from the equality of numbers asserted at the previous step, starting from the assumption that the original equation has a solution. Construct a viable argument to justify a solution method.

HSA.REI.A.2 Solve simple rational and radical equations in one variable, and give examples showing how extraneous solutions may arise.

Solve equations and Inequalities in one variable

HSA.REI.B.4 Solve quadratic equations in one variable.

HSA.REI.B.4.A Use the method of completing the square to transform any quadratic equation in x into an equation of the form $(x - p)^2 = q$ that has the same solutions. Derive the quadratic formula from this form.

HSA.REI.B.4.B Solve quadratic equations by inspection (e.g., for $x^2 = 49$), taking square roots, completing the square, the quadratic formula and factoring, as appropriate to the initial form of the equation. Recognize when the quadratic formula gives complex solutions and write them as $a \pm bi$ for real numbers a and b.

Solve systems of equations

HSA.REI.C.6 Solve systems of linear equations exactly and approximately (e.g., with graphs), focusing on pairs of linear equations in two variables.

HSA.REI.C.7 Solve a simple system consisting of a linear equation and a quadratic equation in two variables algebraically and graphically.

HSA.REI.C.8 (+) Represent a system of linear equations as a single matrix equation in a vector variable.

HSA.REI.C.9 (+) Find the inverse of a matrix if it exists and use it to solve systems of linear equations (using technology for matrices of dimension 3×3 or greater).

Represent and solve equations and inequalities graphically

HSA.REI.D.11 Explain why the x-coordinates of the points where the graphs of the equations $y = f(x)$ and $y = g(x)$ intersect are the solutions of the equation $f(x) = g(x)$; find the solutions approximately, e.g., using technology to graph the functions, make tables of values, or find successive approximations. Include cases where $f(x)$ and/or $g(x)$ are linear, polynomial, rational, absolute value, exponential, and logarithmic functions.*

Functions

Interpreting Functions

Understand the concept of a function and use function notation

HSF.IF.A.3 Recognize that sequences are functions, sometimes defined recursively, whose domain is a subset of the integers.

Interpret functions that arise in applications in terms of the context

HSF.IF.B.4 For a function that models a relationship between two quantities, interpret key features of graphs and tables in terms of the quantities, and sketch graphs showing key features given a verbal description of the relationship.*

HSF.IF.B.5 Relate the domain of a function to its graph and, where applicable, to the quantitative relationship it describes.*

HSF.IF.B.6 Calculate and interpret the average rate of change of a function (presented symbolically or as a table) over a specified interval. Estimate the rate of change from a graph.*

Analyze functions using different representations

HSF.IF.C.7 Graph functions expressed symbolically and show key features of the graph, by hand in simple cases and using technology for more complicated cases.*

HSF.IF.C.7.B Graph square root, cube root, and piecewise-defined functions, including step functions and absolute value functions.

HSF.IF.C.7.C Graph polynomial functions, identifying zeros when suitable factorizations are available, and showing end behavior.

HSF.IF.C.7.D (+) Graph rational functions, identifying zeros and asymptotes when suitable factorizations are available, and showing end behavior.

HSF.IF.C.7.E Graph exponential and logarithmic functions, showing intercepts and end behavior, and trigonometric functions, showing period, midline, and amplitude.

HSF.IF.C.8 Write a function defined by an expression in different but equivalent forms to reveal and explain different properties of the function.

HSF.IF.C.8.B Use the properties of exponents to interpret expressions for exponential functions.

HSF.IF.C.9 Compare properties of two functions each represented in a different way (algebraically, graphically, numerically in tables, or by verbal descriptions).

Building Functions

Build a function that models a relationship between two quantities

HSF.BF.A.1 Write a function that describes a relationship between two quantities.*

HSF.BF.A.1.A Determine an explicit expression, a recursive process, or steps for calculation from a context.

HSF.BF.A.1.B Combine standard function types using arithmetic operations.

HSF.BF.A.1.C (+) Compose functions.

HSF.BF.A.2 Write arithmetic and geometric sequences both recursively and with an explicit formula, use them to model situations, and translate between the two forms.*

Build new functions from existing functions

HSF.BF.B.3 Identify the effect on the graph of replacing $f(x)$ by $f(x) + k$, $kf(x)$, $f(kx)$, and $f(x + k)$ for specific values of k (both positive and negative); find the value of k given the graphs. Experiment with cases and illustrate an explanation of the effects on the graph using technology. Include recognizing even and odd functions from their graphs and algebraic expressions for them.

HSF.BF.B.4 Find inverse functions.

HSF.BF.B.4.A Solve an equation of the form $f(x) = c$ for a simple function f that has an inverse and write an expression for the inverse.

HSF.BF.B.4.B (+) Verify by composition that one function is the inverse of another.

HSF.BF.B.4.C (+) Read values of an inverse function from a graph or a table, given that the function has an inverse.

HSF.BF.B.4.D (+) Produce an invertible function from a non-invertible function by restricting the domain.

HSF.BF.B.5 (+) Understand the inverse relationship between exponents and logarithms and use this relationship to solve problems involving logarithms and exponents.

Linear, Quadratic, and Exponential Models*

Construct and compare linear, quadratic, and exponential models and solve problems

HSF.LE.A.2 Construct linear and exponential functions, including arithmetic and geometric sequences, given a graph, a description of a relationship, or two input-output pairs (include reading these from a table).

HSF.LE.A.4 For exponential models, express as a logarithm the solution to $ab^{ct} = d$ where a, c, and d are numbers and the base b is 2, 10, or e; evaluate the logarithm using technology.

Interpret expressions for functions in terms of the situation they model

HSF.LE.B.5 Interpret the parameters in a linear or exponential function in terms of a context.

Trigonometric Functions

Extend the domain of trigonometric functions using the unit circle

HSF.TF.A.1 Understand radian measure of an angle as the length of the arc on the unit circle subtended by the angle.

HSF.TF.A.2 Explain how the unit circle in the coordinate plane enables the extension of trigonometric functions to all real numbers, interpreted as radian measures of angles traversed counterclockwise around the unit circle.

HSF.TF.A.3 (+) Use special triangles to determine geometrically the values of sine, cosine, tangent for $\frac{\pi}{3}$, $\frac{\pi}{4}$ and $\frac{\pi}{6}$, and use the unit circle to express the values of sine, cosine, and tangent for $\pi - x$, $\pi + x$, and $2\pi - x$ in terms of their values for x, where x is any real number.

HSF.TF.A.4 (+) Use the unit circle to explain symmetry (odd and even) and periodicity of trigonometric functions.

Model periodic phenomena with trigonometric functions

HSF.TF.B.5 Choose trigonometric functions to model periodic phenomena with specified amplitude, frequency, and midline.*

HSF.TF.B.6 (+) Understand that restricting a trigonometric function to a domain on which it is always increasing or always decreasing allows its inverse to be constructed.

Standards for Mathematical Content in Algebra 2

HSF.TF.B.7 (+) Use inverse functions to solve trigonometric equations that arise in modeling contexts; evaluate the solutions using technology, and interpret them in terms of the context.*

Prove and apply trigonometric identities

HSF.TF.C.8 Prove the Pythagorean identity $\sin^2(\theta) + \cos^2(\theta) = 1$ and use it to find $\sin(\theta)$, $\cos(\theta)$, or $\tan(\theta)$ given $\sin(\theta)$, $\cos(\theta)$, or $\tan(\theta)$ and the quadrant of the angle.

HSF.TF.C.9 (+) Prove the addition and subtraction formulas for sine, cosine, and tangent and use them to solve problems.

Geometry

Similarity, Right Triangles, & Trigonometry

Apply trigonometry to general triangles

HSG.SRT.D.10 (+) Prove the Laws of Sines and Cosines and use them to solve problems.

HSG.SRT.D.11 (+) Understand and apply the Law of Sines and the Law of Cosines to find unknown measurements in right and non-right triangles (e.g., surveying problems, resultant forces).

Expressing Geometric Properties with Equations

Translate between the geometric description and the equation for a conic section

HSG.GPE.A.1 Derive the equation of a circle of given center and radius using the Pythagorean Theorem; complete the square to find the center and radius of a circle given by an equation.

HSG.GPE.A.2 Derive the equation of a parabola given a focus and directrix.

HSG.GPE.A.3 (+) Derive the equations of ellipses and hyperbolas given the foci, using the fact that the sum or difference of distances from the foci is constant.

Statistics and Probability

Interpreting Categorical and Quantitative Data

Summarize, represent, and interpret data on a single count or measurement variable

HSS.ID.A.2 Use statistics appropriate to the shape of the data distribution to compare center (median, mean) and spread (interquartile range, standard deviation) of two or more different data sets.

HSS.ID.A.4 Use the mean and standard deviation of a data set to fit it to a normal distribution and to estimate population percentages. Recognize that there are data sets for which such a procedure is not appropriate. Use calculators, spreadsheets, and tables to estimate areas under the normal curve.

Summarize, represent, and interpret data on two categorical and quantitative variables

HSS.ID.B.6 Represent data on two quantitative variables on a scatter plot, and describe how the variables are related.

HSS.ID.B.6.A Fit a function to the data; use functions fitted to data to solve problems in the context of the data. Use given functions or choose a function suggested by the context. Emphasize linear, quadratic, and exponential models.

Making Inferences & Justifying Conclusions

Understand and evaluate random processes underlying statistical experiments

HSS.IC.A.1 Understand statistics as a process for making inferences about population parameters based on a random sample from that population.

HSS.IC.A.2 Decide if a specified model is consistent with results from a given data-generating process, e.g., using simulation.

Make inferences and justify conclusions from sample surveys, experiments, and observational studies

HSS.IC.B.3 Recognize the purposes of and differences among sample surveys, experiments, and observational studies; explain how randomization relates to each.

HSS.IC.B.4 Use data from a sample survey to estimate a population mean or proportion; develop a margin of error through the use of simulation models for random sampling.

HSS.IC.B.5 Use data from a randomized experiment to compare two treatments; use simulations to decide if differences between parameters are significant.

HSS.IC.B.6 Evaluate reports based on data.

Conditional Probability & the Rules of Probability

Understand independence and conditional probability and use them to interpret data

HSS.CP.A.1 Describe events as subsets of a sample space (the set of outcomes) using characteristics (or categories) of the outcomes, or as unions, intersections, or complements of other events ("or," "and," "not").

HSS.CP.A.2 Understand that two events A and B are independent if the probability of A and B occurring together is the product of their probabilities, and use this characterization to determine if they are independent.

HSS.CP.A.3 Understand the conditional probability of A given B as $\frac{P(A \text{ and } B)}{P(B)}$, and interpret independence of A and B as saying that the conditional probability of A given B is the same as the probability of A, and the conditional probability of B given A is the same as the probability of B.

HSS.CP.A.4 Construct and interpret two-way frequency tables of data when two categories are associated with each object being classified. Use the two-way table as a sample space to decide if events are independent and to approximate conditional probabilities.

HSS.CP.A.5 Recognize and explain the concepts of conditional probability and independence in everyday language and everyday situations.

Use the rules of probability to compute probabilities of compound events

HSS.CP.B.6 Find the conditional probability of A given B as the fraction of B's outcomes that also belong to A, and interpret the answer in terms of the model.

HSS.CP.B.7 Apply the Addition Rule, $P(A \text{ or } B) = P(A) + P(B) - P(A \text{ and } B)$, and interpret the answer in terms of the model.

HSS.CP.B.8 (+) Apply the general Multiplication Rule in a uniform probability model, $P(A \text{ and } B) = P(A)P(B|A) = P(B)P(A|B)$, and interpret the answer in terms of the model.

HSS.CP.B.9 (+) Use permutations and combinations to compute probabilities of compound events and solve problems.

Using Probability to Make Decisions

Calculate expected values and use them to solve problems

HSS.MD.A.1 (+) Define a random variable for a quantity of interest by assigning a numerical value to each event in a sample space; graph the corresponding probability distribution using the same graphical displays as for data distributions.

HSS.MD.A.2 (+) Calculate the expected value of a random variable; interpret it as the mean of the probability distribution.

HSS.MD.A.3 (+) Develop a probability distribution for a random variable defined for a sample space in which theoretical probabilities can be calculated; find the expected value.

HSS.MD.A.4 (+) Develop a probability distribution for a random variable defined for a sample space in which probabilities are assigned empirically; find the expected value.

Use probability to evaluate outcomes of decisions

HSS.MD.B.5 (+) Weigh the possible outcomes of a decision by assigning probabilities to payoff values and finding expected values.

HSS.MD.B.5.A Find the expected payoff for a game of chance.

HSS.MD.B.5.B Evaluate and compare strategies on the basis of expected values.

HSS.MD.B.6 (+) Use probabilities to make fair decisions (e.g., drawing by lots, using a random number generator).

HSS.MD.B.7 (+) Analyze decisions and strategies using probability concepts (e.g., product testing, medical testing, pulling a hockey goalie at the end of a game).

COMMON CORE STATE STANDARDS

Algebra

Creating Equations

- Create equations that describe numbers or relationships.

Reasoning with Equations and Inequalities

- Solve systems of equations.
- Represent and solve equations and inequalities graphically.

Functions

Interpreting Functions

- Interpret functions that arise in applications in terms of the context.
- Analyze functions using different representations.

Building Functions

- Build a function that models a relationship between two quantities.
- Build new functions from existing functions.

Linear, Quadratic, & Exponential Models

- Construct and compare linear, quadratic, and exponential models and solve problems.

Number and Quantity

The Complex Number System

- Perform arithmetic operations with complex numbers.
- Use complex numbers in polynomial identities and equations.

Algebra

Seeing Structure in Expressions

- Interpret the structure of expressions.

- Write expressions in equivalent forms to solve problems.

Creating Equations

- Create equations that describe numbers or relationships.

Reasoning with Equations and Inequalities

- Solve equations and inequalities in one variable.
- Solve systems of equations.
- Represent and solve equations and inequalities graphically.

Functions

Interpreting Functions

- Interpret functions that arise in applications in terms of the context.

Building Functions

- Build a function that models a relationship between two quantities.
- Build new functions from existing functions.

TOPIC 3

Polynomial Functions

Number and Quantity

The Complex Number System

- Use complex numbers in polynomial identities and equations.

Algebra

Arithmetic with Polynomials & Rational Expressions

- Perform arithmetic operations on polynomials.
- Understand the relationship between zeros and factors of polynomials.
- Use polynomial identities to solve problems.
- Rewrite rational expressions.

Functions

Interpreting Functions

- Interpret functions that arise in applications in terms of the context.
- Analyze functions using different representations.

Building Functions

- Build a function that models a relationship between two quantities.
- Build new functions from existing functions.

Go Online | SavvasRealize.com

TOPIC 4

Rational Functions

Algebra

Seeing Structure in Expressions
- Interpret the structure of expressions.

Arithmetic with Polynomials & Rational Expressions
- Rewrite rational expressions.

Creating Equations
- Create equations that describe numbers or relationships.

Reasoning with Equations and Inequalities
- Understand solving equations as a process of reasoning and explain the reasoning.
- Solve equations and inequalities in one variable.
- Represent and solve equations and inequalities graphically.

Functions

Interpreting Functions
- Analyze functions using different representations.

Building Functions
- Build new functions from existing functions.

TOPIC 5

Rational Exponents and Radical Functions

Number and Quantity

The Real Number System

- Extend the properties of exponents to rational exponents.

Algebra

Seeing Structure in Expressions

- Interpret the structure of expressions.

Creating Equations

- Create equations that describe numbers or relationships.

Reasoning with Equations and Inequalities

- Understand solving equations as a process of reasoning and explain the reasoning.

Functions

Interpreting Functions

- Interpret functions that arise in applications in terms of the context.
- Analyze functions using different representations.

Building Functions

- Build a function that models a relationship between two quantities.
- Build new functions from existing functions.

Go Online | SavvasRealize.com

Algebra

Seeing Structure in Expressions

- Interpret the structure of expressions.
- Write expressions in equivalent forms to solve problems.

Creating Equations

- Create equations that describe numbers or relationships.

Functions

Interpreting Functions

- Understand the concept of a function and use function notation.
- Interpret functions that arise in applications in terms of the context.
- Analyze functions using different representations.

Building Functions

- Build new functions from existing functions.

Linear, Quadratic, & Exponential Models

- Interpret expressions for functions in terms of the situation they model.

Statistics & Probability

Interpreting Categorical & Quantitative Data

- Summarize, represent, and interpret data on two categorical and quantitative variables.

TOPIC 7

Trigonometric Functions

Functions

Interpreting Functions

- Interpret functions that arise in applications in terms of the context.
- Analyze functions using different representations.

Building Functions

- Build new functions from existing functions.

Trigonometric Functions

- Extend the domain of trigonometric functions using the unit circle.
- Model periodic phenomena with trigonometric functions.
- Prove and apply trigonometric identities.

Go Online | SavvasRealize.com

Number and Quantity

The Complex Number System

- Perform arithmetic operations with complex numbers.
- Represent complex numbers and their operations on the complex plane.

Algebra

Seeing Structure in Expressions

- Interpret the structure of expressions.

Functions

Building Functions

- Build new functions from existing functions.

Trigonometric Functions

- Extend the domain of trigonometric functions using the unit circle.
- Model periodic phenomena with trigonometric functions.
- Prove and apply trigonometric identities.

Geometry

Similarity, Right Triangles, & Trigonometry

- Apply trigonometry to general triangles.

Conic Sections

Algebra

Seeing Structure in Expressions
- Interpret the structure of expressions.
- Write expressions in equivalent forms to solve problems.

Reasoning with Equations and Inequalities
- Solve systems of equations.

Geometry

Expressing Geometric Properties with Equations
- Translate between the geometric description and the equation for a conic section.

Go Online | SavvasRealize.com

Number

Vector & Matrix Quantities

- Represent and model with vector quantities.
- Perform operations on vectors.
- Perform operations on matrices and use matrices in applications.

Algebra

Creating Equations

- Create equations that describe numbers or relationships.

Reasoning with Equations and Inequalities

- Solve systems of equations.

Number and Quantity

Quantities

- Reason quantitatively and use units to solve problems.

Statistics

Interpreting Categorical & Quantitative Data

- Summarize, represent, and interpret data on a single count or measurement variable.

Making Inferences & Justifying Conclusions

- Understand and evaluate random processes underlying statistical experiments.

- Make inferences and justify conclusions from sample surveys, experiments, and observational studies.

Statistics & Probability

Conditional Probability & the Rules of Probability

- Understand independence and conditional probability and use them to interpret data.
- Use the rules of probability to compute probabilities of compound events.

Using Probability to Make Decisions

- Calculate expected values and use them to solve problems.
- Use probability to evaluate outcomes of decisions.

TOPIC 1

Linear Functions and Systems

? TOPIC ESSENTIAL QUESTION

What are the ways in which functions can be used to represent and solve problems involving quantities?

Topic Overview

enVision™ STEM Project:
Fuel Efficiency

1-1 Key Features of Functions

1-2 Transformations of Functions

1-3 Piecewise-Defined Functions

1-4 Arithmetic Sequences and Series

1-5 Solving Equations and Inequalities by Graphing

1-6 Linear Systems

Mathematical Modeling in 3 Acts:
Current Events

1-7 Solving Linear Systems Using Matrices

Topic Vocabulary

- arithmetic sequence
- arithmetic series
- augmented matrix
- average rate of change
- coefficient matrix
- common difference
- compression
- dimensions
- explicit definition
- inconsistent system
- interval notation
- matrix
- maximum
- minimum
- piecewise-defined function
- recursive definition
- reduced row echelon form
- reflection
- sequence
- series
- set-builder notation
- sigma notation
- solution of a system of linear equations
- step function
- stretch
- system of linear equations
- system of linear inequalities
- transformation
- translation
- zero of a function

Digital Experience

 INTERACTIVE STUDENT EDITION Access online or offline.

 ACTIVITIES Complete *Explore & Reason, Model & Discuss*, and *Critique & Explain* activities. Interact with Examples and Try Its.

 ANIMATION View and interact with real-world applications.

 PRACTICE Practice what you've learned.

 Go online | SavvasRealize.com

▶ Current Events

You might say that someone who loses their temper has "blown a fuse." However, it's rare to hear about electrical fuses blowing these days. That's because most fuses have been replaced by circuit breakers. A fuse must be replaced once it's blown, but a circuit breaker can be reset.

Ask for permission to look at the electrical panel in your home. If there is a series of switches inside, each of those is a circuit breaker, designed to interrupt the circuit when the electrical current inside is too dangerous. How much electricity does it take to trip a circuit breaker? Think about this question during the Mathematical Modeling in 3-Acts lesson.

TOPIC 1

VIDEOS Watch clips to support *Mathematical Modeling in 3 Acts Lessons* and **enVision™** *STEM Projects.*

CONCEPT SUMMARY Review key lesson content through multiple representations.

ASSESSMENT Show what you've learned.

GLOSSARY Read and listen to English and Spanish definitions.

TUTORIALS Get help from *Virtual Nerd*, right when you need it.

MATH TOOLS Explore math with digital tools and manipulatives.

Video

Did You Know?

Carbon dioxide (CO_2) is composed of 1 atom of carbon and 2 atoms of oxygen. A gas that occurs naturally on Earth, CO_2 also produced by burning fossil fuels. In its solid form, CO_2 is commonly called "dry ice."

 This hybrid hatchback averages **59 mpg** in the city.

 This large SUV averages **10 mpg** in the city.

 In the United States, each state determines the **tax rate** on gasoline, so the state in which you buy your gas determines how much it costs to fill your tank.

How much **crude oil** do you use when filling up your car?

2 full tanks

10-gal.   10-gal.

19 gallons of gasoline

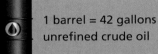
1 barrel = 42 gallons unrefined crude oil

▶ Your Task: Fuel Efficiency

You and your classmates will analyze cars' fuel efficiency. If you were designing a car to come out in 2024, what gas mileage would you target?

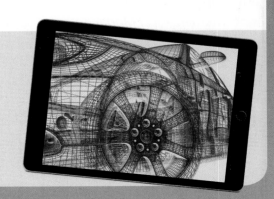

© **Common Core State Standards** HSF.IF.B.4, HSF.IF.C.7, HSF.IF.B.6, MP.3, MP.4, MP.6

  Activity  Assess

👆 **EXPLORE & REASON**

SavvasRealize.com

I CAN... interpret key features of linear, quadratic, and absolute value functions given an equation or a graph.

VOCABULARY
- average rate of change
- interval notation
- maximum
- minimum
- set-builder notation
- zero of a function

A diver is going through ocean search-and-rescue training. The graph shows the relationship between her depth and the time in seconds since starting her dive.

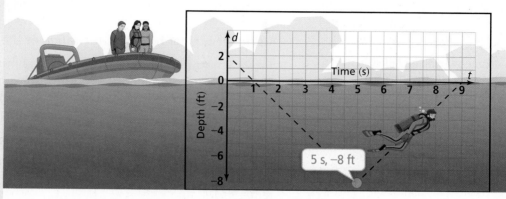

5 s, −8 ft

A. What details can you determine about the dive from the coordinates of the point (5, −8)?

B. What is the average speed of the diver in the water? How can you tell from the graph?

C. Which point on the graph shows the starting location of the diver? Explain.

D. **Communicate Precisely** What does the V-shape of the graph tell you about the dive? What information does it not tell you about the dive? © **MP.6**

? **ESSENTIAL QUESTION** How do graphs and equations reveal information about a relationship between two quantities?

👆 **EXAMPLE 1** Understand Domain and Range

A. What are the domain and range of the function defined by $y = x^2 - 3$?

The set of all possible inputs for a relation is called the *domain*.

You can square any real number, so any number can be input for x.

The square of a real number is greater than or equal to 0. So the minimum value of $y = x^2 - 3$ is $0 - 3$, or -3.

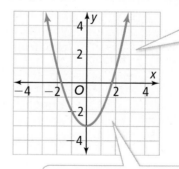

This graph represents a *function* because each input has exactly one output.

The set of all possible outputs for a relation is called the *range*.

CONSTRUCT ARGUMENTS
Consider this explanation of the function's minimum value. How do you know that the function has no maximum value? © **MP.3**

There are two notations used to represent intervals of numbers like domain and range.

Set-Builder Notation uses a verbal description or an inequality to describe the numbers.

CONTINUED ON THE NEXT PAGE

EXAMPLE 1 CONTINUED

Using set-builder notation, the domain of this function is
{x | x is a real number}.

> This is read "*The set of all x such that x is a real number.*"

> This is read "*The set of all y such that y is greater than or equal to −3.*"

Using set-builder notation, the range of the function is {y | y ≥ −3}.

Interval notation represents a set of real numbers by the pair of values that are its left (minimum) and right (maximum) boundaries. Using interval notation, the domain of the function is (−∞, ∞).

Using interval notation, the range is [−3, ∞).

To summarize the ways in which we can indicate intervals of numbers, refer to the table below.

STUDY TIP
An interval with excluded boundary points is called "open" and is represented by open circle end points on the graph. An interval with included boundary points is called "closed" and is represented by solid end points.

Interval Notation	Words	Set Notation
[3, 4]	All real numbers that are greater or equal to 3 and less than or equal to 4	$\{x \mid 3 \leq x \leq 4\}$
(3, 4]	All real numbers that are greater than 3 and less than or equal to 4	$\{x \mid 3 < x \leq 4\}$
[3, 4)	All real numbers that are greater than or equal to 3 and less than 4	$\{x \mid 3 \leq x < 4\}$
(3, 4)	All real numbers that are greater than 3 and less than 4	$\{x \mid 3 < x < 4\}$
[3, ∞)	All real numbers greater than or equal to 3	$\{x \mid 3 \leq x < \infty\}$
(−∞, 3]	All real numbers less than or equal to 3	$\{x \mid -\infty < x \leq 3\}$
(−∞, ∞)	All real numbers	$\{x \mid -\infty < x < \infty\}$

B. **An airtanker flies over forest fires and drops water at a constant rate until its tank is empty. What are the domain and range of the function that represents the volume of water the airtanker can drop in *x* seconds?**

400 gal/s

8,000 gal

The function is $f(x) = 400x$. The airtanker cannot drop water for a negative number of seconds, so $x \geq 0$. The tanker can drop water for a maximum of $\frac{8,000}{400} = 20$ s before running out of water, so $x \leq 20$.

The domain is {x | 0 ≤ x ≤ 20}, or [0, 20].

The airtanker cannot drop a negative number of gallons, and its maximum capacity is 8,000 gal.

The range is {y | 0 ≤ y ≤ 8,000}, or [0, 8,000].

 Try It! 1. What are the domain and range of each function? Write the domain and range in set-builder notation and interval notation.

a. $y = |x - 4|$

b. $y = 6x - 2x^2$

APPLICATION

EXAMPLE 2 Find *x*- and *y*-intercepts

A. A car starts a journey with a full tank of gas. The equation $y = 16 - 0.05x$ relates the number of gallons of gas, *y*, left in the tank to the number of miles the car has traveled, *x*. What are the *x*- and *y*-intercepts of the graph of this equation, and what do they represent about the situation?

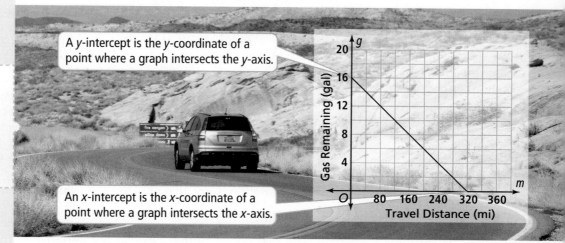

A *y*-intercept is the *y*-coordinate of a point where a graph intersects the *y*-axis.

An *x*-intercept is the *x*-coordinate of a point where a graph intersects the *x*-axis.

STUDY TIP
Depending on the situation modeled by a function, the intercept(s) may not be in the domain of the function, and may not represent anything important in the situation.

The graph above intersects the *x*-axis at (320, 0), so the *x*-intercept is 320. This means that the car can travel 320 mi before it runs out of gas.

The graph intersects the *y*-axis at (0, 16), so the *y*-intercept is 16. This means the car has 16 gal of gas when it starts its trip.

B. What are the *x*- and *y*-intercepts of the graph of $y = |x| - 3$?

Find the *x*-intercept(s) algebraically:

The *y*-coordinate of an *x*-intercept is 0.

$$y = |x| - 3$$
$$0 = |x| - 3$$
$$3 = |x|$$
$$x = \pm 3$$

Both 3 and −3 are 3 units away from 0, so they both have an absolute value of 3.

The *x*-intercepts of the graph of $y = |x| - 3$ are −3 and 3. The *x*-intercepts are also the **zeros of the function** because they are the input values that result in a function output value of 0.

Find the *y*-intercept algebraically:

$$y = |x| - 3$$
$$y = |0| - 3$$
$$y = 0 - 3$$
$$y = -3$$

The *x*-coordinate at the *y*-intercept is 0.

The *y*-intercept of the graph of $y = |x| - 3$ is −3.

 Try It! 2. What are the *x*- and *y*-intercepts of $g(x) = 4 - x^2$?

👆 **EXAMPLE 3** **Identify Positive or Negative Intervals**

For what intervals is $f(x) = x^2 - 9$ positive? For what intervals is the function negative?

Use technology to graph the function:

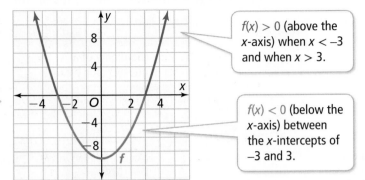

> $f(x) > 0$ (above the x-axis) when $x < -3$ and when $x > 3$.

> $f(x) < 0$ (below the x-axis) between the x-intercepts of -3 and 3.

COMMON ERROR
Be careful not to confuse a positive function value and a positive rate of change. A positive rate of change means the y-values of the function are increasing but are not necessarily greater than 0.

The function is positive at $(-\infty, -3)$ and $(3, \infty)$.

> Parentheses indicate that a boundary point is not included.

The function is negative at $(-3, 3)$.

The function is neither positive nor negative at the x-intercepts of -3 and 3.

☑ **Try It!** **3. a.** For what interval(s) is $h(x) = 2x + 10$ positive?

b. For what interval(s) is the function negative?

👆 **EXAMPLE 4** **Identify Where a Function Increases or Decreases**

For what values of x is $g(x) = 2 - |x|$ increasing? For what values is it decreasing?

Construct a table and sketch a graph to represent the function.

x	$g(x)$
-3	-1
-2	0
-1	1
0	2
1	1
2	0
3	-1

$g(x)$ is increasing from $-\infty$ to 0.

$g(x)$ is decreasing from 0 to ∞.

> The greatest value a function attains is the **maximum** of the function.
> The least value a function attains is the **minimum**.

The values of $g(x)$ are increasing on the interval $(-\infty, 0)$.

The values of $g(x)$ are decreasing on the interval $(0, \infty)$.

☑ **Try It!** **4.** For what values of x is each function increasing? For what values of x is it decreasing?

a. $f(x) = x^2 - 4x$ **b.** $f(x) = -2x - 3$

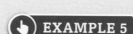
CONCEPTUAL
UNDERSTANDING

EXAMPLE 5 Understand Average Rate of Change Over an Interval

A. What is the average rate of change of a function $y = f(x)$ over the interval $[a, b]$?

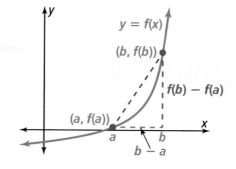

The interval starts at a value of $f(a)$ when $x = a$ and ends at a value of $f(b)$ when $x = b$.

The total change in the function values is $f(b) - f(a)$.

The length of the interval is $b - a$.

The **average rate of change** is the ratio $\frac{f(b) - f(a)}{b - a}$. This is the same as the slope of the line segment between the points $(a, f(a))$ and $(b, f(b))$.

B. What do the average rates of change over the intervals $[-2, 0]$, $[0, 3]$, and $[-2, 3]$ indicate about the given functions?

$$f(x) = 1 \qquad g(x) = \tfrac{1}{2}x - 1 \qquad h(x) = x^2$$

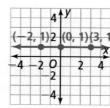
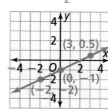
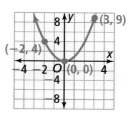

LOOK FOR RELATIONSHIPS
If (x_1, y_1) and (x_2, y_2) are points on the graph of the linear function $y = mx + b$, then the average rate of change in the interval $[x_1, x_2]$ is $m = \frac{y_2 - y_1}{x_2 - x_1}$. **MP.7**

$[-2, 0]$	$\frac{1-1}{0-(-2)} = 0$	$\frac{-1-(-2)}{0-(-2)} = \frac{1}{2}$	$\frac{0-4}{0-(-2)} = -2$
$[0, 3]$	$\frac{1-1}{3-0} = 0$	$\frac{0.5-(-1)}{3-0} = \frac{1}{2}$	$\frac{9-0}{3-0} = 3$
$[-2, 3]$	$\frac{1-1}{3-(-2)} = 0$	$\frac{0.5-(-2)}{3-(-2)} = \frac{1}{2}$	$\frac{9-4}{3-(-2)} = 1$

$f(x) = 1$ has the same rate of change, 0, over every interval $[a, b]$. This means it is a constant function.

$g(x) = \tfrac{1}{2}x - 1$ has a constant rate of change, $\tfrac{1}{2}$, over every interval $[a, b]$. This means it is a linear function.

$h(x) = x^2$ does not have a constant rate of change over every interval $[a, b]$. This means it is a nonlinear function.

 Try It! 5. What do the average rates of change of the function $y = |x| + 2$ over the intervals $[-2, 0]$, $[0, 3]$, and $[-2, 3]$ indicate about the function?

🔍 CONCEPT SUMMARY Some Functions With Key Features

FUNCTION	Linear $y = x$	Quadratic $y = x^2$	Absolute Value $y = |x|$	Constant $y = 1$
GRAPH	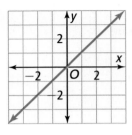	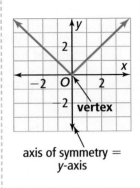 axis of symmetry = y-axis	vertex axis of symmetry = y-axis	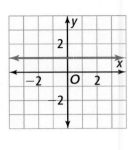
KEY FEATURES	Domain: $(-\infty, \infty)$ Range: $(-\infty, \infty)$ Increasing: $(-\infty, \infty)$	Domain: $(-\infty, \infty)$ Range: $[0, \infty)$ Increasing: $(0, \infty)$ Decreasing: $(-\infty, 0)$	Domain: $(-\infty, \infty)$ Range: $[0, \infty)$ Increasing: $(0, \infty)$ Decreasing: $(-\infty, 0)$	Domain: $(-\infty, \infty)$ Range: $\{y \mid y = 1\}$
INTERCEPTS	The x-intercept is 0. The y-intercept is 0.	The x-intercept is 0. The y-intercept is 0.	The x-intercept is 0. The y-intercept is 0.	There is no x-intercept. The y-intercept is 1.

☑ Do You UNDERSTAND?

1. **ESSENTIAL QUESTION** How do graphs and equations reveal information about a relationship between two quantities?

2. **Vocabulary** Define the term *zero of a function* in your own words.

3. **Error Analysis** Lonzell said the function shown in the graph is positive on the interval $(-1, 5)$ and negative on the interval $(-5, -1)$. Identify and correct Lonzell's error. © MP.3

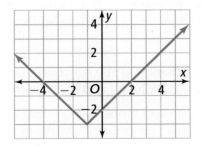

Do You KNOW HOW?

Find each key feature.

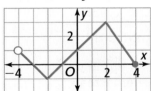

4. domain

5. range

6. x-intercept(s)

7. y-intercept(s)

8. interval(s) where the graph is positive

9. interval(s) where the graph is decreasing

10. interval(s) where the graph is increasing

11. rate of change on $[-1, 4]$

12. Reason The graph of $y = -\frac{1}{2}x + 2$ is negative over the interval $(4, \infty)$ and positive over the interval $(-\infty, 4)$. What happens on the graph when $x = 4$? Explain. © **MP.2**

13. Error Analysis Describe and correct the error a student made in finding the interval(s) over which the function is positive and negative. © **MP.3**

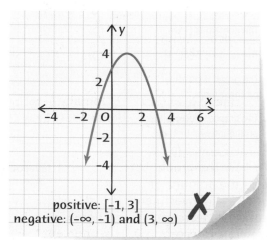

positive: $[-1, 3]$
negative: $(-\infty, -1)$ and $(3, \infty)$ ✗

14. Use Structure Sketch a graph given the following key features. © **MP.7**

domain: $(-4, 4)$ range: $(-4, 6]$

increasing: $(-4, 1)$ decreasing: $(1, 4)$

x-intercepts: $(-2, 0), (3, 0)$ y-intercept: $(0, 4)$

negative: $(-4, -2)$ and $(3, 4)$ positive: $(-2, 3)$

15. Construct Arguments A student says that all linear functions are either increasing or decreasing. Do you agree? Explain. © **MP.3**

16. Higher Order Thinking A relative maximum of a function occurs at the highest point on a graph over a certain interval. A relative minimum of a function occurs at the lowest point on a graph over a certain interval. Explain how to identify a relative maximum and a relative minimum of a function using key features.

17. Model With Mathematics For a graph of speed in miles per hour as a function of time in hours, what does it mean when the function is increasing? Decreasing? © **MP.4**

Use the graph of the function for Exercises 18–22.

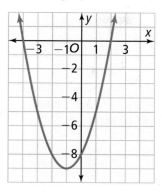

18. Identify the domain and range of the function. SEE EXAMPLE 1

19. Identify the x- and y-intercepts of the function. SEE EXAMPLE 2

20. On what intervals is the function positive? On what intervals is it negative? SEE EXAMPLE 3

21. On what intervals is the function increasing? On what intervals is it decreasing? SEE EXAMPLE 4

22. What is the average rate of change over the interval $(-3, 2)$? SEE EXAMPLE 5

Use the graph of the function for Exercises 23–27.

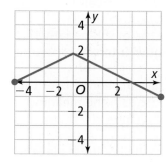

23. Identify the domain and range of the function. SEE EXAMPLE 1

24. Identify the x- and y-intercepts of the function. SEE EXAMPLE 2

25. Determine over what interval the function is positive or negative. SEE EXAMPLE 3

26. Determine over what interval the function is increasing or decreasing. SEE EXAMPLE 4

27. What is the average rate of change over the interval $(-1, 5)$? SEE EXAMPLE 5

APPLY

28. Communicate Precisely Kathryn is filling an empty 100 ft³ container with sand at a rate of 1.25 ft³/min. Describe the key features of the graph of the amount of sand inside the container. **© MP.6**

29. Make Sense and Persevere The graph shows a jumper's height, *y*, in feet *x* seconds after getting onto a trampoline. **© MP.1**

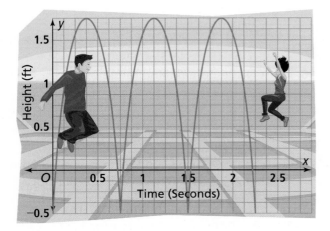

a. What are the *x*- and *y*-intercepts? Explain what the *x*- and *y*-intercepts represent.

b. Over what intervals is the graph positive? Explain what the positive intervals represent.

c. Over what intervals is the graph negative? Explain what the negative intervals represent.

d. What is the average rate of change over the interval [0.75, 1.125]? Explain the meaning of the average rate of change.

30. Model With Mathematics Bailey starts playing a game on her cell phone with the battery fully charged, and plays until the phone battery dies. While playing the game, the charge in Bailey's battery decreases by half a percent per minute. **© MP.4**

a. Write a function for the percent charge in the battery while Bailey is playing the game.

b. What is the domain and range of the function?

c. How long can Bailey play the game?

ASSESSMENT PRACTICE

31. Given the graph, select yes or no for each statement.

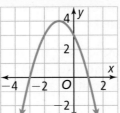

	Yes	No
a. The domain is $(-\infty, 4]$.	○	○
b. The range is $(-\infty, 4]$.	○	○
c. The graph is positive on the interval $(0, \infty)$.	○	○
d. The graph is decreasing on the interval $(-1, \infty)$.	○	○

32. SAT/ACT The graph shows the amount of money in an investment account. Which statement is true?

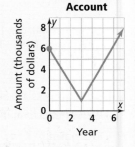

Investment Account

Ⓐ $6,000 was initially invested in the account.

Ⓑ $1,000 was initially invested in the account.

Ⓒ At Year 3, there was $0 in the account.

Ⓓ At Year 7, there was $0 in the account.

33. Performance Task The graph shows the amount of water in a water tank over several hours.

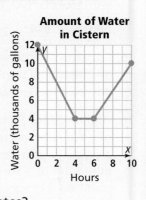

Amount of Water in Cistern

Part A What is the average rate of change on the interval [0, 4] and on the interval [6, 10]? What is a possible explanation for what each rate of change indicates?

Part B What is a possible explanation for what occurred between 4 and 6 h?

Part C What is the average rate of change on the interval [0, 10]? What does the rate of change mean? Does this rate of change give a good indication as to what is happening with the water in the cistern from 0 h to 10 h? Explain.

1-2
Transformations of Functions

I CAN... apply transformations to graph functions and write equations.

VOCABULARY
- compression
- reflection
- stretch
- transformation
- translation

LOOK FOR RELATIONSHIPS
This type of transformation slides the graph up or down. You could perform a transformation like this to a non-vertical line and produce a parallel line. © **MP.7**

👆 **EXPLORE & REASON**

The graph of the function $f(x) = |x|$ is shown.

A. Graph the function $g(x) = |x + c|$ several times with different values for c (any value from -5 to 5).

B. **Look for Relationships** Predict what will happen to the graph if c is a number greater than 100. What if c is a number between 0 and $\frac{1}{2}$? © **MP.7**

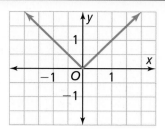

❓ **ESSENTIAL QUESTION**

What do the differences between the equation of a function and the equation of its parent function tell you about the differences in the graphs of the two functions?

👆 **EXAMPLE 1**   **Translate a Function**

A. Graph the function $f(x) = x^2$ for the domain $[-2, 2]$. The graph of g is the graph of f after a translation of 3 units down. How are the equations, domains, and ranges of f and g related?

Every point on the graph of g is 3 units below a corresponding point on the graph of f.

$$(x, f(x)) \rightarrow (x, f(x) - 3) = (x, g(x))$$

$$g(x) = f(x) - 3$$

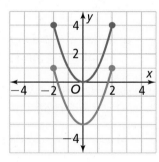

The domains of f and g are the same: $[-2, 2]$. The range values of g are 3 units less than the range values of f. The range of f is $[0, 4]$ and the range of g is $[-3, 1]$.

A **translation** like this one is a particular kind of transformation of a function, one that shifts each point on a graph the same distance and direction.

In general, if $g(x) = f(x) + k$, then the graph of g is a vertical translation of the graph of f by k units.

> Other kinds of **transformations** of a function may reflect its graph across an axis, or stretch or compress its graph.

CONTINUED ON THE NEXT PAGE

EXAMPLE 1 CONTINUED

B. Graph the function $f(x) = x^2$ for the domain [−2, 2]. The graph of the function g is the graph of f after a translation 3 units to the right. How are the equations, domains, and ranges of f and g related?

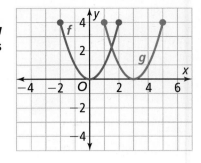

Every point on the graph of g is 3 units to the right of the corresponding point on the graph of f.

$$(x, f(x)) \rightarrow (x, g(x + 3))$$

The translation of the graph of f to the graph of g can be described as $g(x + 3) = f(x)$, or $g(x) = f(x − 3)$.

The range values of f and g are the same: [0, 4]. The domain values of g are 3 units more than the domain values of f. The domain of f is [−2, 2] and the domain of g is [1, 5].

In general, if $g(x) = f(x − h)$, then the graph of g is a horizontal translation of the graph of f by h units.

✓ **Try It!**   **1. a.** How did the transformation of f to g in part (a) affect the intercepts?

b. How did the transformation of f to g in part (b) affect the intercepts?

👆 **EXAMPLE 2**   **Reflect a Function Across the x- or y-Axis**

VOCABULARY
Recall that a **reflection** is a transformation that maps each point to a new point across a given line, called the *line of reflection*. The line of reflection is the perpendicular bisector of the segment between the point and its image.

A. Graph $f(x) = 2x − 6$ and the function g, whose graph is the reflection of the graph of f across the x-axis. How are their equations related?

Graph f. Then graph g by reflecting each point of the graph of f across the x-axis. For each point (x, y) on the graph of f, plot the point $(x, −y)$ to get the graph of g.

The y-intercept of g, 6, is the opposite of the y-intercept of f, −6.

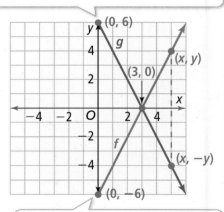

Since the y-values of the new function have the opposite sign, $g(x) = −f(x)$.

From the graph, you can see that $g(x) = −2x + 6$.

You can check that $g(x) = −f(x)$ by substituting for $f(x)$.

$$g(x) = −f(x)$$
$$= −(2x − 6)$$
$$g(x) = −2x + 6$$

The expression that defines g is the opposite of the expression that defines f.

The slope of the graph of f is 2, while the slope of the graph of g is −2.

CONTINUED ON THE NEXT PAGE

EXAMPLE 2 CONTINUED

B. Graph $f(x) = 2x - 6$ and the function h, whose graph is the reflection of the graph of f across the y-axis. How are their equations related?

Graph f. Then reflect every point on the graph of f over the y-axis to produce the graph of h.

From the graph, you can see that $h(x) = -2x - 6$.

You can check that $h(x) = f(-x)$ by substituting for $f(-x)$.

$$h(x) = f(-x)$$
$$= 2(-x) - 6$$
$$h(x) = -2x - 6$$

> The slope of the graph of f is 2, and the slope of the graph of h is –2.

The function h has a slope that is the opposite of the slope of f but with the same y-intercept.

> For any point (x, y) on the graph of f, there is a reflected point $(-x, y)$ on the graph of h, so $h(x) = f(-x)$. The x-intercept of h, -3, is the opposite of the x-intercept of f, 3.

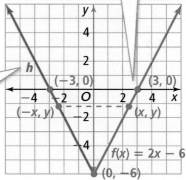

USE STRUCTURE
Why does $g(x) = -f(x)$ affect the y-coordinate of each point and $g(x) = f(-x)$ affect the x-coordinate of each point? © **MP.7**

 Try It! **2.** What is an equation for the reflected graph? Check by graphing.

    a. the graph of $f(x) = x^2 - 2$ reflected across the x-axis

    b. the graph of $f(x) = x^2 - 2$ reflected across the y-axis

CONCEPTUAL UNDERSTANDING

EXAMPLE 3   **Understand Stretches and Compressions**

A. Graph $f(x) = |x|$ with domain $[-4, 4]$ and $g(x) = 2 \cdot f(x)$. How are the domains and ranges related?

Use a table to find points on the graph of g.

x	$f(x)$	$g(x) = 2 \cdot f(x)$	$(x, g(x))$
-4	4	$2 \cdot f(-4) = 2(4) = 8$	$(-4, 8)$
-2	2	$2 \cdot f(-2) = 2(2) = 4$	$(-2, 4)$
0	0	$2 \cdot f(0) = 2(0) = 0$	$(0, 0)$
2	2	$2 \cdot f(2) = 2(2) = 4$	$(2, 4)$
4	4	$2 \cdot f(4) = 2(4) = 8$	$(4, 8)$

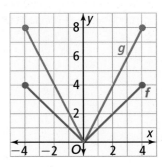

The domains of f and g are the same. Each y-value is multiplied by 2, so for the function with the given domain, the range of f, $[0, 4]$, is doubled for g to $[0, 8]$.

A transformation that increases the distance between the points of a graph and a given line by the same factor is called a **stretch**. The graph of g is a vertical stretch of the graph of f by a factor of 2.

CONTINUED ON THE NEXT PAGE

EXAMPLE 3 CONTINUED

B. Graph $f(x) = |x|$ with domain $[-4, 4]$ and $h(x) = f(2x)$. How are the domains and ranges related?

Use a table to find points on the graph of h.

x	$f(x)$	$h = f(2x)$	$(x, h(x))$
-2	2	$f(2(-2)) = f(-4) = 4$	$(-2, 4)$
-1	1	$f(2(-1)) = f(-2) = 2$	$(-1, 2)$
0	0	$f(2(0)) = f(0) = 0$	$(0, 0)$
1	1	$f(2(1)) = f(2) = 2$	$(1, 2)$
2	2	$f(2(2)) = f(4) = 4$	$(2, 4)$

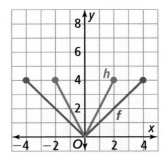

> **COMMON ERROR**
> Be careful not to assume that the domain of a transformed function is the same as the domain of the original function. Notice that $h(-4)$ would equal $f(-8)$, which is outside the domain of f, $[-4, 4]$.

For each corresponding output, the value of the input for h is half the value of the input for f. The two functions have the same range, but the values in the domain of h, $[-2, 2]$, are half as large as the values in the domain of f, $[-4, 4]$.

A transformation that decreases the distance between the points of a graph and a given line by the same factor is called a **compression**. The graph of h is a horizontal compression of the graph of f by a factor of 2.

 Try It! **3.** Show that $j(x) = f\left(\frac{1}{2}x\right)$ is a horizontal stretch of the graph of f.

CONCEPT Stretches and Compressions

Vertical	**Horizontal**
$g(x) = k \cdot f(x)$	$h(x) = f(kx)$

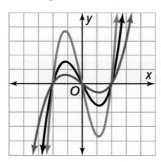

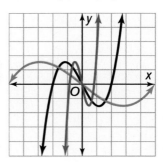

• stretch when $k > 1$
• compression when $0 < k < 1$

• stretch when $0 < k < 1$
• compression when $k > 1$

Go Online | SavvasRealize.com

EXAMPLE 4 **Graph a Combination of Transformations**

The graph represents $y = f(x)$. Using $y = f(x)$, how can you graph a combination of transformations?

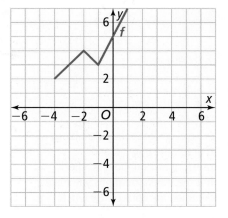

A. Graph $y = -f(x + 2)$.

Graph $g(x) = f(x + 2)$, which is a translation of f left 2 units.

Graph $h(x) = -f(x + 2)$, which is a reflection of g across the x-axis.

The graph of h is a translation of f left 2 units followed by a reflection across the x-axis.

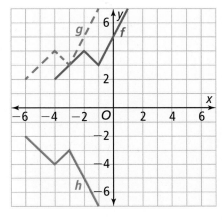

B. Graph $y = \frac{1}{2} f(x) + 3$.

Graph $g(x) = \frac{1}{2} f(x)$, which is a vertical compression of f by the factor $\frac{1}{2}$.

Graph $h(x) = \frac{1}{2} f(x) + 3$, which is a translation of g up 3 units.

The graph of h is a vertical compression of f by the factor $\frac{1}{2}$ followed by a translation 3 units up.

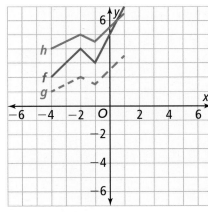

 Try It! **4.** Using the graph of f above, graph each equation.

    a. $y = f(2x) - 4$　　　　　**b.** $y = f(2x - 3) - 2$

EXAMPLE 5   **Identify Transformations From an Equation**

What transformations of $f(x) = x^2$ result in the graph of the function g?

A. $g(x) = -\left(\frac{1}{3}x\right)^2$

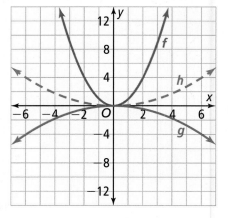

$h(x) = f\left(\frac{1}{3}x\right) = \left(\frac{1}{3}x\right)^2$ represents a horizontal stretch of the graph of f by the factor $\frac{1}{3}$.

$g(x) = -h(x) = -f\left(\frac{1}{3}x\right) = -\left(\frac{1}{3}x\right)^2$ represents a reflection across the x-axis of $f\left(\frac{1}{3}x\right)$.

The graph of g is a horizontal stretch by the factor $\frac{1}{3}$ and a reflection across the x-axis of the graph of f.

> **USE APPROPRIATE TOOLS**
> You can use graphing technology to graph the original and transformed equations to check that the transformations you have identified are correct. **© MP.5**

B. $g(x) = (x - 4)^2 + 5$

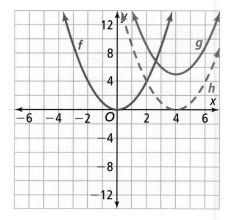

$h(x) = f(x - 4) = (x - 4)^2$ represents a translation 4 units to the right of the graph of f.

$g(x) = h(x) + 5 = f(x - 4) + 5 = (x - 4)^2 + 5$ represents a translation 5 units up of the graph of $f(x - 4)$.

The graph of g is a translation 4 units right and 5 units up of the graph of f.

✓ **Try It!**   **5.** What transformations of the graph of $f(x) = |x|$ are applied to graph the function g?

a. $g(x) = \frac{1}{2}|x + 3|$ **b.** $g(x) = -|x| + 2$

APPLICATION

🖐 **EXAMPLE 6**   **Write an Equation From a Graph**

A scenic train ride makes trips on an old mining line. The graph shows the distance *y* in kilometers of the train from the station *x* minutes after the ride begins. What equation represents the distance from the station as a function of time? What is its domain?

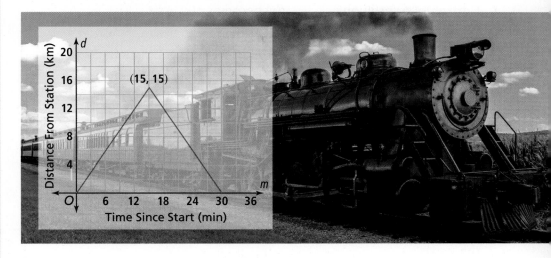

The graph shows a reflection of an absolute value graph across the *x*-axis and a translation upward and to the right. The general form of this absolute value function is $y = -a|x - h| + k$, where the point (h, k) represents the vertex and $-a$ indicates that the graph opens downward.

Substituting the point of the vertex (15, 15) for (h, k) gives the equation $y = -a|x - 15| + 15$.

To solve for *a*, you can use any point on the graph. Using the point (0, 0) to substitute for (x, y) in the equation simplifies the computation:

$$y = -a|x - 15| + 15$$
$$0 = -a|0 - 15| + 15$$
$$0 = -15a + 15$$
$$-15 = -15a$$
$$a = 1$$

STUDY TIP
Solving algebraically is only one method for determining a stretch or compression factor.

Now you can write the equation for distance as a function of time:

$$y = -|x - 15| + 15.$$

According to the graph, the train returns to its station after 30 minutes, so the function's domain is [0, 30].

 Try It!   **6.** How would the graph and equation be affected if the train traveled twice as far in the same amount of time?

For a function $f(x)$, the graph of $f(x) = a \cdot f[b(x - h)] + k$ represents a transformation of the graph of that function by translation, reflection, or stretching.

WORDS	EQUATIONS	GRAPHS
Horizontal translation of *f* right 2 units (altering *h*)	$f(x)$ becomes $g(x) = f(x - 2)$ $f(x) = x^2 + x$ $g(x) = (x - 2)^2 + (x - 2) = x^2 - 3x + 2$	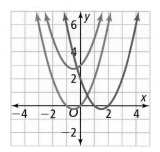
Vertical translation of *f* up 3 units (altering *k*)	$f(x)$ becomes $h(x) = f(x) + 3$ $f(x) = x^2 + x$ $h(x) = x^2 + x + 3$	
Reflection of *f* across the *x*-axis (altering *a*)	$f(x)$ becomes $-f(x)$ $f(x) = x^2 + x$ $-f(x) = -(x^2 + x) = -x^2 - x$	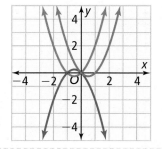
Reflection of *f* across the *y*-axis (altering *b*)	$f(x)$ becomes $f(-x)$ $f(x) = x^2 + x$ $f(-x) = (-x)^2 + (-x) = x^2 - x$	
Horizontal stretch of *f* by the factor $\frac{1}{2}$ (altering *b*)	$f(x)$ becomes $f\left(\frac{1}{2}x\right)$ $f(x) = x^2 + x$ $f\left(\frac{1}{2}x\right) = \left(\frac{1}{2}x\right)^2 + \frac{1}{2}x = \frac{1}{4}x^2 + \frac{1}{2}x$	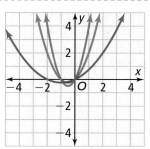
Vertical stretch of *f* by the factor 2 (altering *a*)	$f(x)$ becomes $2f(x)$ $f(x) = x^2 + x$ $2f(x) = 2(x^2 + x) = 2x^2 + 2x$	

✓ Do You UNDERSTAND?

1. ❓ **ESSENTIAL QUESTION** What do the differences between the equation of a function and the equation of its parent function tell you about the differences in the graphs of the two functions?

2. **Reason** Do *k* and *h* affect the input or output for $g(x) = f(x) + k$ and $g(x) = f(x - h)$? Explain. Ⓒ **MP.2**

3. **Error Analysis** Margo is comparing the functions $f(x) = |x|$ and $g(x) = |x + 1| - 5$. She said the graph of *g* is a vertical translation of the graph of *f* 5 units down and a horizontal translation of the graph of *f* 1 unit right. What is Margo's error? Ⓒ **MP.3**

Do You KNOW HOW?

Graph each function and its parent function.

4. $g(x) = |x| - 1$

5. $g(x) = (x - 3)^2$

6. $g(x) = -|x|$

7. $g(x) = -x$

8. $g(x) = x^2 - 2$

9. $g(x) = \frac{1}{2}|x|$

10. $g(x) = 4x$

11. $g(x) = |5x|$

12. Which types of transformations in Exercises 4–11 do not change the shape of a graph? Which types of transformations change the shape of a graph? Explain.

UNDERSTAND

13. Use Structure Write a function g with the parent function $f(x) = x^2$ that has a vertex at $(3, -6)$. **MP.7**

14. Error Analysis Describe and correct the error a student made in graphing $g(x) = f(-x)$ as a reflection across the y-axis of the graph of $f(x) = |x + 2| + 1$. **MP.3**

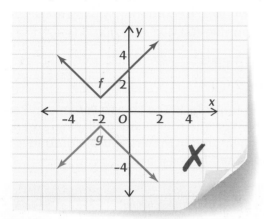

15. Higher Order Thinking Describe the transformation g of $f(x) = |x|$ as a stretch and as a compression. Then write two equations to represent the function. What can you conclude? Explain.

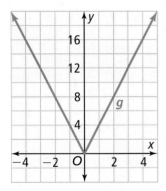

16. Use Structure The graph of the parent function $f(x) = x^2$ is reflected across the y-axis. Write an equation for the function g after the reflection. Show your work. Based on your equation, what happens to the graph? Explain. **MP.7**

17. Error Analysis Monisha is comparing $f(x) = |x|$ and $g(x) = |2x - 4|$. She said the graph of g is a horizontal translation of the graph of f 4 units to the right and a horizontal compression of the graph of f by a factor of 2. What is Monisha's error? **MP.3**

PRACTICE

Graph each function as a translation of its parent function, f. How did the transformation affect the domain and range? SEE EXAMPLE 1

18. $g(x) = |x| - 5$

19. $g(x) = (x + 1)^2$

20. $g(x) = |x - 3|$

21. $g(x) = x^2 + 2$

What is the equation for the image graph? Check by graphing. SEE EXAMPLE 2

22. Reflect $f(x) = x^2 + 1$ across the x-axis.

23. Reflect $f(x) = x^2 + 1$ across the y-axis.

Graph each function as a vertical stretch or compression of its parent function. SEE EXAMPLE 3

24. $g(x) = 0.25|x|$

25. $g(x) = 3x^2$

26. $g(x) = 1.5|x|$

27. $g(x) = 0.75x^2$

28. Use the graph of $f(x)$ to graph $y = f(x + 1) + 2$. SEE EXAMPLE 4

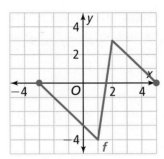

What transformations of $f(x) = x^2$ are applied to the function g? SEE EXAMPLE 5

29. $g(x) = 2(x + 1)^2$

30. $g(x) = (x - 3)^2 + 5$

31. $g(x) = -x^2 - 6$

32. $g(x) = 4(x - 7)^2 - 9$

33. The graph shows the height y in feet of a flying insect x seconds after taking off from the ground. Write an equation that represents the height of the insect as a function of time.
SEE EXAMPLE 6

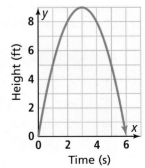

APPLY

34. Model With Mathematics Chiang walks to school each day. She passes the library halfway on her walk to school. She walks at a rate of 1 block per minute. The graph shows the distance Chiang is from the library as she walks to school. © MP.4

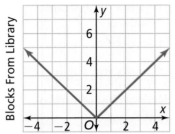

Minutes Before Passing Library   Minutes After Passing Library

a. Write a function, f, to model the distance Chiang is from the library when she walks to school.

b. If Chiang jogs to school, she travels at a rate of 2.5 blocks per minute. Write a function, g, to model the distance Chiang is from the library when she jogs to school.

c. Graph the function, g, that models the distance Chiang is from the library when she jogs to school.

35. Model With Mathematics The archer fish spits water at flying insects to knock them into the water. The path of the water is shown with x and y distances in feet. Write an equation to represent the path of the water in relation to the coordinate grid. Then determine the coordinates of the point of maximum height of the water. © MP.4

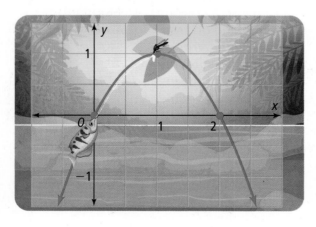

ASSESSMENT PRACTICE

36. Match each equation on the left to an equation on the right that has the same translation of $y = |x|$.

A. $y = |x| - 1$ D. $y = |x + 1| - 1$

B. $y = -|x + 1|$ E. $y = 2|x| - 1$

C. $y = -|x + 1| - 1$ F. $y = |x + 1|$

37. SAT/ACT Which translation is part of transforming $f(x) = x^2$ into $h(x) = (x + 4)^2 - 2$?

Ⓐ left 4 units   Ⓒ right 2 units

Ⓑ left 2 units   Ⓓ right 4 units

38. Performance Task The Louvre Pyramid in Paris is shown on the coordinate grid, where x and y are measured in meters and the ground is represented by the x-axis.

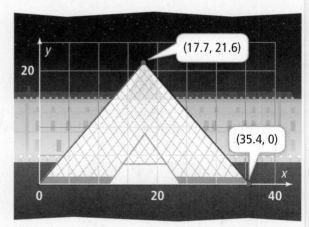

(17.7, 21.6)

(35.4, 0)

Part A The outline of the Pyramid is a transformation of the function $f(x) = |x|$. Write a function g to model the outline of the Pyramid.

Part B What is the domain and range of the function that models the outline of the Pyramid? What do the domain and range represent?

Activity Assess

1-3
Piecewise-Defined Functions

 SavvasRealize.com

I CAN... graph and interpret piecewise-defined functions.

VOCABULARY
- piecewise-defined function
- step function

MODEL & DISCUSS

A music teacher needs to buy guitar strings for her class. At store A, the guitar strings cost $6 each. At store B, the guitar strings are $20 for a pack of 4.

A. Make graphs that show the income each store receives if the teacher needs 1–20 guitar strings

B. Describe the shape of the graph for store A. Describe the shape of the graph for store B. Why are the graphs different?

C. **Communicate Precisely** Compare the graphs for stores A and B. For what numbers of guitar strings is it cheaper to buy from store B? Explain how you know. **ⓒ MP.6**

? ESSENTIAL QUESTION

How do you model a situation in which a function behaves differently over different parts of its domain?

CONCEPTUAL UNDERSTANDING

EXAMPLE 1 Model With a Piecewise-Defined Function

Alani has a summer job as a lifeguard. She makes $8/h for up to 40 h each week. If she works more than 40 h, she makes 1.5 times her hourly pay, or $12/h, for each hour over 40 h. How could you make a graph and write a function that shows Alani's weekly earnings based on the number of hours she worked?

Step 1 Make a table of values and a graph.

STUDY TIP
Remember that Alani makes $8/h for the first 40 h and $12/h for any additional hours after that.

Hours Worked	Pay
20	160
25	200
30	240
35	280
40	320
45	380
50	440
55	500

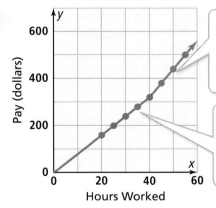

When $x > 40$, Alani's pay is $P(x) = (\$8)(40) + (\$12)(x - 40)$, or $P(x) = 12x - 160$.

When $0 \leq x \leq 40$, Alani's pay $P(x)$ is $8/h times the number of hours worked, or $8x$.

Step 2 Notice that the plot contains two linear segments with a slope that changes slightly at $x = 40$. A function that has different rules for different parts of its domain is called a **piecewise-defined function**.

USE STRUCTURE
This notation is used for piecewise-defined functions to indicate the different functions at different parts of the domain. **ⓒ MP.7**

Step 3 Write an equation for each piece of the graph.

$$P(x) = \begin{cases} 8x, & 0 \leq x \leq 40 \\ 12x - 160, & x > 40 \end{cases}$$

CONTINUED ON THE NEXT PAGE

EXAMPLE 1 CONTINUED

 Activity Assess

 Try It! **1.** How much will Alani earn if she works:

a. 37 hours? **b.** 43 hours?

 EXAMPLE 2 **Graph a Piecewise-Defined Function**

How do you graph a piecewise defined function?

$$f(x) = \begin{cases} 4x + 11, & -10 \le x < -2 \\ x^2 - 1, & -2 \le x \le 2 \\ x + 1, & 2 < x \le 10 \end{cases}$$

What are the domain and range? Over what intervals is the function increasing or decreasing?

Sketch the graph of $y = 4x + 11$ for values of x between -10 and -2.

Sketch the graph of $y = x^2 - 1$ for values of x between -2 and 2.

Sketch the graph of $y = x + 1$ for values between 2 and 10.

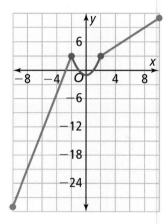

To determine the range, calculate the y-values that correspond to the minimum and maximum x-values on the graph. For this graph, these values occur at the endpoints of the domain of the piecewise function, $-10 \le x \le 10$.

> **COMMON ERROR**
> The values of -2 and 2 are only included in one piece of the graph. If they were included in more than one piece and had different values for different pieces, this would not be a function.

Evaluate $y = 4x + 11$ for $x = -10$ Evaluate $y = x + 1$ for $x = 10$

$y = 4(-10) + 11$ $y = 10 + 1$

$y = -29$ $y = 11$

The range is $-29 \le y \le 11$.

The domain is $\{x | -10 \le x \le 10\}$. The range is $\{y \mid -29 \le y \le 11\}$. The function is increasing when $-10 < x < -2$ and $0 < x < 10$. The function is decreasing when $-2 < x < 0$.

 Try It! **2.** Graph the piecewise-defined function. What are the domain and range? Over what intervals is the function increasing or decreasing?

a. $f(x) = \begin{cases} 2x + 5, & -6 \le x \le -2 \\ 2x^2 - 7, & -2 < x < 1 \\ -4 - x, & 1 \le x \le 3 \end{cases}$ **b.** $f(x) = \begin{cases} 3, & -4 < x \le -1 \\ -x, & 0 \le x \le 2 \\ 3 - x, & 2 < x < 4 \end{cases}$

EXAMPLE 3 Write a Piecewise-Defined Rule From a Graph

STUDY TIP
A closed circle on the graph means the coordinates of the point are included in the domain and range of the function. An open circle indicates they are not included.

What is the rule that describes the piecewise-defined function shown in the graph?

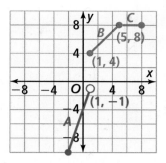

Step 1 Notice three separate linear pieces that make up the function.

Step 2 Determine the domain of each segment.

Step 3 For each segment, use the graph to locate points on the line and to find the slope.

Step 4 You can use the slope-intercept form of a linear function, $f(x) = mx + b$, to define the function for each segment.

Segment A	Segment B	Segment C
Domain: $-2 \leq x < 1$	Domain: $1 \leq x \leq 5$	Domain: $5 < x \leq 8$
$(1, -1)$, slope = 3	$(1, 4)$, slope = 1	$(5, 8)$, slope = 0
$y = mx + b$ $-1 = (3)(1) + b$ $b = -4$	$y = mx + b$ $4 = (1)(1) + b$ $b = 3$	$y = mx + b$ $8 = (0)(5) + b$ $b = 8$
$f(x) = 3x - 4$	$f(x) = x + 3$	$f(x) = 8$

The rule for this function is:

$$f(x) = \begin{cases} 3x - 4, & -2 \leq x < 1 \\ x + 3, & 1 \leq x \leq 5 \\ 8, & 5 < x \leq 8 \end{cases}$$

 Try It! 3. What rule defines the function in each of the following graphs?

a.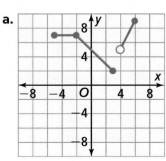

b.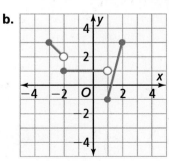

EXAMPLE 4 **Write a Rule for an Absolute Value Function**

How can you rewrite the function $f(x) = |6x + 18|$ as a piecewise-defined fuction?

Step 1 Write the function in the form $f(x) = a|x - h| + k$ to find the vertex of the function.

$$f(x) = |6x + 18|$$
$$= |6(x + 3)|$$
$$= 6|x - (-3)| + 0$$

$k = 0$

$h = -3$

The vertex is $(h, k) = (-3, 0)$. The graph has two linear pieces, one to the left of $x = -3$, and one to the right of $x = -3$.

Step 2 Determine the slope and equation of each piece of the function by testing x-values on either side of -3.

	Choose a point so that $x < -3$: let $x = -4$	Choose a point so that $x > -3$: let $x = 0$
Point	$(-4, 6)$	$(0, 18)$
Slope to $(-3, 0)$	-6	6
Equation	$y = -6x - 18$	$y = 6x + 18$

GENERALIZE

The parent absolute value function $f(x) = |x|$ is a piecewise-defined function:

$$f(x) = \begin{cases} x, & x \geq 0 \\ -x, & x < 0 \end{cases}$$ **Ⓒ MP.8**

Step 3 Write the piecewise-defined function.

The absolute value function $f(x) = |6x + 18|$ can be written as the piecewise-defined function:

$$f(x) = \begin{cases} -6x - 18, & x < -3 \\ 6x + 18, & x \geq -3 \end{cases}$$

Step 4 Confirm by graphing.

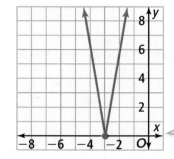

The vertex is $(-3, 0)$.

 Try It! **4.** How can you rewrite each function as a piecewise-defined function?

a. $f(x) = |-5x - 10|$ **b.** $f(x) = -|x| + 3$

APPLICATION

EXAMPLE 5   Graph a Step Function

The shipping cost of items purchased from an online store is dependent on the weight of the items. The table represents shipping costs _y_ based on the weight _x_. Graph the function. What are the domain and range of the function? What are the maximum and minimum values?

Weight of Items	$0 < x \le 2$ lb	$2 < x \le 4$ lb	$4 < x \le 6$ lb	$6 < x \le 8$ lb
Shipping Cost	$5	$8	$11	$14

The graph of the function looks like the steps of a staircase. This is called a **step function** since it pairs every input in an interval with the same output value.

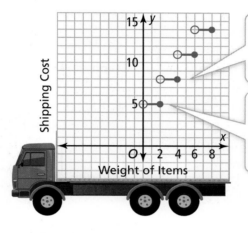

Each _y_-value goes with a set interval of _x_-values. For example, $y = 5$ for $0 < x \le 2$ and $y = 8$ for $2 < x \le 4$.

A closed circle means that the _x_-value is included in that domain, and the $\le$ or $\ge$ sign is used. An open circle means it is not included.

COMMON ERROR
You might think that the range of this function would be the interval [5, 14], but only the values 5, 8, 11, and 14 are possible outputs.

Domain: $\{x \mid 0 < x \le 8\}$

Range: $\{5, 8, 11, 14\}$

This function has a minimum of 5 and a maximum of 14.

Try It!   **5.** The table below represents fees for a parking lot. Graph the function. What are the domain and range of the function? What are the maximum and minimum values?

Time	$0 < t \le 3$h	$3 < t \le 6$h	$6 < t \le 9$h	$9 < t \le 12$h
Cost	$10	$15	$20	$25

CONCEPT SUMMARY Piecewise-Defined Functions

WORDS	ALGEBRA	GRAPH
A piecewise function has different rules for different parts of its domain.	$f(x) = \begin{cases} 7, & -5 \leq x \leq -2 \\ 5 - x, & -2 < x \leq 3 \\ 2x - 3, & 4 < x \leq 6 \end{cases}$	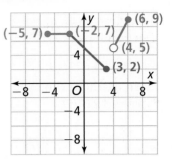

Do You UNDERSTAND?

1. **ESSENTIAL QUESTION** How do you model a situation in which a function behaves differently over different parts of its domain?

2. **Vocabulary** How do piecewise-defined functions differ from step functions?

3. **Error Analysis** Given the function
$f(x) = \begin{cases} 2x + 5, & -2 < x \leq 4 \\ -4x - 7, & 4 < x \leq 9 \end{cases}$
Rebecca says there is an open circle at $x = 4$ for both pieces of the function. Explain her error. ⓒ **MP.3**

4. **Communicate Precisely** What steps do you follow when graphing a piecewise-defined function? ⓒ **MP.6**

5. **Make Sense and Persevere** Is the relation defined by the following piecewise rule a function? Explain. ⓒ **MP.1**
$y = \begin{cases} 7x - 4, & x < 2 \\ -x + 5, & x \geq -2 \end{cases}$

Do You KNOW HOW?

Graph the function.

6. $f(x) = \begin{cases} -x + 1, & -10 \leq x < -3 \\ x^2 - 9, & -3 \leq x \leq 3 \\ 2x + 1, & 3 < x < 5 \end{cases}$

7. $g(x) = \begin{cases} 1, & 0 \leq x < 2 \\ 3, & 2 \leq x < 4 \\ 5, & 4 \leq x < 6 \\ 7, & 6 \leq x < 8 \end{cases}$

8. Given the function
$f(x) = \begin{cases} -2x + 4, & 0 \leq x < 8 \\ -5x + 11, & x \geq 8 \end{cases}$
is the function increasing or decreasing over the interval [2, 7]? Find the rate of change over this interval.

9. What is the rule that defines the function shown in the graph?

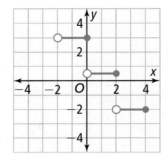

PRACTICE & PROBLEM SOLVING

UNDERSTAND

10. Communicate Precisely What do closed circles and open circles on the graph of a step function indicate? Ⓖ **MP.6**

11. Error Analysis What error did Damian make when defining the domain of the graph? Explain. Ⓖ **MP.3**

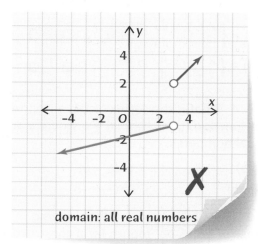

domain: all real numbers

12. Communicate Precisely For what values of x is the function $f(x) = \begin{cases} -3x + 4, & -2 < x \le 3 \\ 2x + 1, & 4 \le x < 9 \end{cases}$ defined? Ⓖ **MP.6**

13. Mathematical Connections For the piecewise-defined function $f(x) = \begin{cases} 7, & x > 3 \\ 5x - 3, & x \le 3 \end{cases}$ find two x-values that have the same y-value and the sum of the x-values is 10.

14. Higher Order Thinking The function $f(x) = \lfloor x \rfloor$ is called the greatest integer function because the output returned is the greatest integer less than or equal to x. For example, $f(3.2) = \lfloor 3.2 \rfloor = 3$ and $f(0.975) = \lfloor 0.975 \rfloor = 0$. Graph the function $f(x) = \lfloor x \rfloor$. What type of graph does this look like?

PRACTICE

15. A phone company offers a monthly cellular phone plan for $25. The plan includes 250 anytime minutes, and charges $0.20 per minute above 250 min. Write a piecewise-defined function for $C(x)$, the cost for using x minutes in a month. SEE EXAMPLE 1

16. Graph the piecewise-defined function. State the domain and range. Identify whether the function is increasing, constant, or decreasing on each interval of the domain. SEE EXAMPLE 2

$$f(x) = \begin{cases} \frac{1}{4}x + 3, & -2 < x \le 0 \\ 2, & 0 < x \le 4 \\ 3 - x, & 4 < x \le 7 \end{cases}$$

17. Write the rule that defines the function in the following graph. SEE EXAMPLE 3

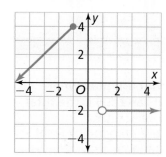

Write each absolute value function as a piecewise-defined function. SEE EXAMPLE 4

18. $f(x) = |3x + 1|$ **19.** $g(x) = |-2x - 6|$

Graph the step function. SEE EXAMPLE 5

20. $f(x) = \begin{cases} 2, & -3 \le x < 1 \\ 5, & 1 \le x < 4 \\ 8, & 4 \le x < 6 \\ 9, & 6 \le x < 10 \end{cases}$

21. The parking rates for a parking garage are shown. Graph the function for the cost of parking rates at the garage. SEE EXAMPLE 5

Parking Rates

$4 per half hour

$20 maximum for 12 hours

APPLY

22. **Model With Mathematics** If Kyle works more than 40 h per week, his hourly wage for the extra hour(s) is 1.5 times the normal hourly wage of $10 per hour. Write a piecewise-defined function that gives Kyle's weekly pay P in terms of the number h of hours he works. Determine how much Kyle will get paid if he works 45 h. © **MP.4**

23. **Model With Mathematics** Text message plans offered at a phone company, along with overage charges, are shown. © **MP.4**

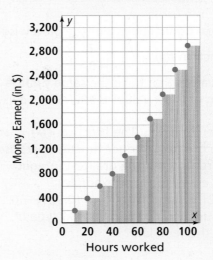

NO Message Plan — $0.10/text

500 Message Plan — $7.99/month — $0.10/text over 500

1,200 Message Plan — $13.99/month — $0.10/text over 1,200

UNLIMITED Message Plan — $24.99/month

   a. Write a function for each plan where x is the number of texts and $f(x)$ is the total monthly cost.

   b. Sarah uses approximately 1,500 texts per month. What is the monthly cost under each text message plan?

   c. Write an interval for the number of text messages that would make each plan the best one to purchase.

24. **Reason** The cost C (in dollars) of sending next-day mail depends on the weight x (in ounces) of a package. The cost of packages, up to 5 lb, is given by the function below. What are the domain and range of the function? © **MP.2**

$$f(x) = \begin{cases} 12.25, & 0 < x \le 8 \\ 16.75, & 8 < x \le 32 \\ 19.50, & 32 < x \le 48 \\ 23.50, & 48 < x \le 64 \\ 25.25, & 64 < x \le 80 \end{cases}$$

25. Does the function have a range of $(-\infty, 4)$? Write **yes** or **no**.

		Yes	No
a. $f(x) = \begin{cases} x - 3, & \text{if } x < -2 \\ 5 - x, & \text{if } x > 1 \end{cases}$		❏	❏
b. $h(x) = \begin{cases} x - 1, & \text{if } x < -1 \\ 3 - x, & \text{if } x > 2 \end{cases}$		❏	❏
c. $g(x) = \begin{cases} x + 5, & \text{if } x < -1 \\ -x - 5, & \text{if } x > 1 \end{cases}$		❏	❏
d. $k(x) = \begin{cases} x + 2, & \text{if } x < -2 \\ x + 4, & \text{if } x > 1 \end{cases}$		❏	❏

26. **SAT/ACT** What is the vertex of the absolute value function $f(x) = -|x - a| + b$ where a and b are real numbers?

Ⓐ (a, b) Ⓒ $(a, -b)$

Ⓑ $(-a, b)$ Ⓓ $(-a, -b)$

27. **Performance Task** Yama works a varying number of hours per month for a construction company. The following scatter plot shows how much money he earns for each number of hours he works. Write the piecewise-defined function that represents Yama's earnings as a function of his hours worked.

1-4

Arithmetic Sequences and Series

 SavvasRealize.com

I CAN... interpret arithmetic sequences and series.

VOCABULARY

- arithmetic sequence
- arithmetic series
- common difference
- explicit definition
- recursive definition
- sequence
- series
- sigma notation

CRITIQUE & EXPLAIN

Yumiko and Hugo are looking at the table of data.

Yumiko writes $f(1) = 1 + 4 = 5$,

$$f(2) = f(1) + 4 = 5 + 4 = 9,$$
$$f(3) = f(2) + 4 = 9 + 4 = 13,$$
$$f(4) = f(3) + 4 = 13 + 4 = 17.$$

Hugo writes $g(x) = 1 + 4x$.

Input	Output
0	1
1	5
2	9
3	13
4	17

A. Describe the pattern Yumiko found for finding an output value.

B. Describe the pattern Hugo found for finding an output value.

C. Use Structure Compare the two methods. Which method would be more useful in finding the 100th number in the list? Why? © **MP.7**

? ESSENTIAL QUESTION   **What is an arithmetic sequence, and how do you represent and find its terms and their sums?**

CONCEPTUAL UNDERSTANDING

👆 EXAMPLE 1   **Understand Arithmetic Sequences**

A. Is the sequence arithmetic? If so, what is the common difference? What is the next term in the sequence?

3, 8, 13, 18, 23, …

This is a **sequence**, a function whose domain is the Natural numbers.

Create a table that shows the term number, or domain, and the term, or range.

COMMON ERROR
The common difference is always calculated by subtracting a term from the next term; $d = a_n - a_{n-1}$.

Term Number	Term
1	3
2	8
3	13
4	18
5	23
6	?

$\big)$ +5
$\big)$ +5
$\big)$ +5
$\big)$ +5
$\big)$ +5

The difference between consecutive numbers in the range is 5.

An **arithmetic sequence** is a sequence with a constant difference between consecutive terms. This difference is known as the **common difference,** or d.

This sequence is an arithmetic sequence with the common difference, $d = 5$. The next term in the sequence is $23 + 5$, or 28.

CONTINUED ON THE NEXT PAGE

EXAMPLE 1 CONTINUED

B. How could you write a formula for finding the next term in the sequence?

Each term can be represented by $f(n)$ where n represents the number of the term.

So, for $n = 1$, $f(1) = 3$.

If $n > 1$, each term is the sum of the previous term and 5.

$f(2) = f(1) + 5$

$f(3) = f(2) + 5$

$f(n) = f(n - 1) + 5$

Write the general rule for an arithmetic sequence as a piecewise-defined function:

$$f(n) = \begin{cases} f(1), \, n = 1 \\ f(n - 1) + d, \, n > 1 \end{cases}$$

This is the **recursive definition** for an arithmetic sequence. Each term is defined by operations on the previous term.

Another way to write a recursive definition is to use subscript notation.

$$a_n = \begin{cases} a_1, \, n = 1 \\ a_{n - 1} + d, \, n > 1 \end{cases}$$

With the notation, the subscript shows the number of the term.

C. Is the sequence 4, 7, 10, 13, 16, ... arithmetic? If so, write the recursive definition for the sequence.

$a_1 = 4$ ➤ 4, 7, 10, 13, 16 ◄ The common difference, d, is 3, so this is an arithmetic sequence.

The recursive definition for this sequence is

$$a_n = \begin{cases} 4, \, n = 1 \\ a_{n - 1} + 3, \, n > 1. \end{cases}$$

 Try It! **1.** Are the following sequences arithmetic? If so, what is the recursive definition, and what is the next term in the sequence?

a. 25, 20, 15, 10, ...   **b.** 2, 4, 7, 12, 13, ...

STUDY TIP
An arithmetic sequence is a function, so you can write the terms using function notation.

 EXAMPLE 2 **Translate Between Recursive and Explicit Forms**

A. Given the recursive definition $a_n = \begin{cases} 3, n = 1 \\ a_{n-1} + 0.5, n > 1 \end{cases}$

what is an explicit definition for the sequence?

An **explicit definition**, also written as $a_n = a_1 + d(n-1)$, allows you to find any term in the sequence without knowing the previous term.

> **USE STRUCTURE**
> Since $a_2 = a_1 + 0.5$, use substitution to simplify the expression. **©** **MP.7**

Use the recursive definition to find a pattern:

$a_1 = 3$

$a_2 = 3 + 0.5$

$a_3 = a_2 + 0.5 = [3 + 0.5] + 0.5 = 3 + 2(0.5)$

$a_4 = a_3 + 0.5 = [3 + 2(0.5)] + 0.5 = 3 + 3(0.5)$

> The first term has 0 common differences added. The second term has 1 common difference added to the first term. The third term has 2 common differences added, and so on.

So the explicit definition is $a_n = 3 + (n-1)(0.5)$.

In general, the explicit definition of an arithmetic sequence is $a_n = a_1 + d(n-1)$.

B. Given the explicit definition $a_n = 16 - 3(n-1)$, what is the recursive definition for the arithmetic sequence?

The common difference d is -3 and $a_1 = 16$.

The recursive definition is $a_n = \begin{cases} 16, n = 1 \\ a_{n-1} - 3, n > 1. \end{cases}$

✔ **Try It!** **2. a.** For the recursive definition $a_n = \begin{cases} 45, n = 1 \\ a_{n-1} - 2, n > 1, \end{cases}$ what is the explicit definition?

b. For the explicit definition $a_n = 1 + 7(n-1)$, what is the recursive definition?

APPLICATION → **EXAMPLE 3** **Solve Problems With Arithmetic Sequences**

A high school auditorium has 18 seats in the first row and 26 seats in the fifth row. The number of seats in each row forms an arithmetic sequence.

A. What is the explicit definition for the sequence?

The problem states that $a_1 = 18$, $n = 5$, and $a_5 = 26$.

$a_n = a_1 + d(n-1)$ ·········· Write the general explicit formula.

$26 = 18 + d(5-1)$ ·········· Substitute.

$26 = 18 + 4d$ ·········· Simplify.

$8 = 4d$ ·········· Simplify.

$2 = d$ ·········· Solve.

Each row has two more seats than the previous row.

The explicit definition is $a_n = 18 + 2(n-1)$.

CONTINUED ON THE NEXT PAGE

EXAMPLE 3 CONTINUED

B. How many seats are in the twelfth row?

$$a_n = 18 + 2(n - 1)$$ ·········· Write the explicit formula.

$$a_{12} = 18 + 2(12 - 1)$$ ·········· Substitute 12 for n.

$$a_{12} = 40$$ ·········· Simplify.

The twelfth row has 40 seats.

 **Try It!**   **3.** Samantha is training for a race. The distances of her training runs form an arithmetic sequence. She runs 1 mi the first day and 2 mi the seventh day.

 a. What is the explicit definition for this sequence?

 b. How far does she run on day 19?

EXAMPLE 4   **Find the Sum of an Arithmetic Series**

A. What is the sum of the terms in the arithmetic sequence 1, 4, 7, 10, 13? What is a general formula for an arithmetic series?

A finite **series** is the sum of the terms in a finite sequence. A finite **arithmetic series** is the sum of the terms in an arithmetic sequence. For the sum of n numbers in a sequence, you can use a recursive formula, or simply add the terms.

$$S_n = a_1 + a_2 + a_3 + a_4 + \cdots + a_n$$

$$1 + 4 + 7 + 10 + 13 = 35$$

> This represents a partial sum of a series because it is the sum of a finite number of terms, n, in the series.

To find the sum of a series with many terms, you can use an explicit definition.

Step 1 To find the explicit definition for the sum, use the Commutative Property of Addition and reverse the order of the terms in the recursive series.

$$S_5 = 13 + 10 + 7 + 4 + 1$$

> Substitute the values from the series.

Step 2 Add the two expressions for the series, so you are adding the first term to the last term and the second term to the second-to-last term, and so on.

$$
\begin{array}{r}
S_5 = 1 + 4 + 7 + 10 + 13 \\
+\, S_5 = 13 + 10 + 7 + 4 + 1 \\
\hline
2S_5 = 14 + 14 + 14 + 14 + 14
\end{array}
$$

Step 3 Simplify.

$$2 \cdot S_5 = 5(14)$$

$$S_5 = \frac{5(1 + 13)}{2}$$

> Notice that 14 is the sum of the first and last terms, or $a_1 + a_5$.

Step 4 Write the general formula.

$$S_n = \frac{n(a_1 + a_n)}{2}$$

CONTINUED ON THE NEXT PAGE

EXAMPLE 4 CONTINUED

B. What is the sum of the following arithmetic sequence?
2, 6, 10, 14, 18, 22

$$n = 6 \qquad a_1 = 2 \qquad a_n = 22$$

Use the general formula to find the sum.

$$S_n = \frac{n(a_1 + a_n)}{2} \qquad S_n = \frac{6(2 + 22)}{2} = \frac{144}{2} = 72$$

The sum of the terms in the sequence is 72.

✅ **Try It!** **4.** Find the sum of each arithmetic series.

a. series with 12 terms, $a_1 = 3$ and $a_{12} = 25$

b. $5 + 11 + 17 + 23 + 29 + 35 + 41$

CONCEPT Sigma Notation

The sum of n terms of a sequence can be written using **sigma notation:**

$$\sum_{i=1}^{n} a_i$$

The index i counts through the terms in the partial sum. Here it takes the values from 1 up to n, the last term in the partial series. The value of the ith term is a_i. You can use the explicit formula for the sequence in place of a_i.

👆 **EXAMPLE 5**   **Use Sigma Notation**

A. What is $\sum\limits_{i=1}^{9} 2i - 6$?

Find the sum by writing out all of the terms in the series.

$$a_1 = 2(1) - 6 = -4 \qquad a_4 = 2(4) - 6 = 2 \qquad a_7 = 2(7) - 6 = 8$$

$$a_2 = 2(2) - 6 = -2 \qquad a_5 = 2(5) - 6 = 4 \qquad a_8 = 2(8) - 6 = 10$$

$$a_3 = 2(3) - 6 = 0 \qquad a_6 = 2(6) - 6 = 6 \qquad a_9 = 2(9) - 6 = 12$$

$$\sum_{i=1}^{9} 2i - 6 = S_9 = -4 - 2 + 0 + 2 + 4 + 6 + 8 + 10 + 12 = 36$$

LOOK FOR RELATIONSHIPS
You can quickly see that the common difference in this series is 2. Ⓒ **MP.7**

B. How can you write the series $2 + 9 + 16 + \cdots + 79$ using sigma notation? What is the sum?

Step 1 Solve for n to find the number of terms in the series: $a_1 = 2$, $d = 7$, and $a_n = 79$.

$a_n = a_1 + d(n - 1)$	Write the explicit formula.
$79 = 2 + (7)(n - 1)$	Substitute a_n, a_1, and d.
$77 = (7)(n - 1)$	Simplify.
$11 = n - 1$	Simplify.
$n = 12$	Solve.

There are 12 terms in the series.

CONTINUED ON THE NEXT PAGE

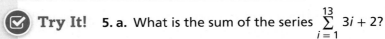
EXAMPLE 5 CONTINUED

Step 2 Write the explicit formula for the series.

$$a_n = 2 + 7(n - 1) = 7n - 5$$

Step 3 Write using sigma notation.

The index i will count from 1 to $n = 12$.

The explicit definition gives $a_i = 7i - 5$.

$$\sum_{i=1}^{12} 7i - 5$$

Step 4 Find the sum of the series.

$$S_n = \frac{n(a_1 + a_n)}{2}$$

$$S_{12} = \frac{12(2 + 79)}{2} = 486$$

So the series can be written $\sum_{i=1}^{12} 7i - 5$ in sigma notation. The sum of the series is 486.

 **Try It!** **5. a.** What is the sum of the series $\sum_{i=1}^{13} 3i + 2$?

b. How can you write the series $8 + 13 + 18 + \ldots + 43$ using sigma notation? What is the sum?

APPLICATION   **EXAMPLE 6** **Use a Finite Arithmetic Series**

A pyramid of cans is on display in a supermarket. The top row has 1 can, the second row has 2 cans, and the third row has 3 cans. If there are 10 rows of cans, how many total cans were used to make the pyramid?

This is an arithmetic series where the common difference is 1.

Step 1 Find a_1 and a_{10}.

$$a_1 = 1$$
$$a_{10} = a_1 + d(n - 1)$$
$$= 1 + 1(10 - 1)$$
$$= 10$$

STUDY TIP
Since you know n, a_1, and a_{10}, you can use the explicit formula to find the sum of the series efficiently.

Step 2 Use the explicit formula for finding the sum of a series.

$$S_n = \frac{n(a_1 + a_n)}{2}$$

$$S_n = \frac{10(1 + 10)}{2} = 55$$

There are 55 cans in the display.

 Try It! **6.** A flight of stairs gets wider as it descends. The top stair is 15 bricks across, the second stair is 17 bricks across, and the third stair is 19 bricks across. What is the total number of bricks used in all 16 stairs?

CONCEPT SUMMARY Arithmetic Sequences and Series

In an arithmetic sequence, each term is equal to the previous term plus a constant d, the common difference.

	Recursive Formula	Explicit Formula	Arithmetic Series
ALGEBRA	$a_n = \begin{cases} a_1, & n = 1 \\ a_{n-1} + d, & n > 1 \end{cases}$	$a_n = a_1 + d(n - 1)$	$S_n = \dfrac{n(a_1 + a_n)}{2}$
NUMBERS	For $a_1 = 1$ and $d = 7$, $a_2 = 1 + 7 = 8$ $a_3 = 8 + 7 = 15$ $a_4 = 15 + 7 = 22$ ....and so on	For $a_1 = 90$ and $d = -4$, $a_2 = 90 + 1(-4) = 86$ $a_3 = 90 + 2(-4) = 82$ $a_4 = 90 + 3(-4) = 78$ ....and so on	$\displaystyle\sum_{i=1}^{8} 5i - 2$ $3 + 8 + 13 + 18 + 23 + 28 + 33 + 38 = 164$ or $S_8 = \dfrac{8(3 + 38)}{2} = 164$

 Do You UNDERSTAND?

1. **ESSENTIAL QUESTION** What is an arithmetic sequence, and how do you represent and find its terms and their sums?

2. **Vocabulary** How do arithmetic sequences differ from arithmetic series?

3. **Error Analysis** A student claims the sequence 0, 1, 3, 6, … is an arithmetic sequence, and the next number is 10. What error did the student make? **ⓒ MP.3**

4. **Communicate Precisely** How would you tell someone how to calculate $\displaystyle\sum_{n=1}^{5} (2n + 1)$? **ⓒ MP.6**

Do You KNOW HOW?

Find the common difference and the next three terms of each arithmetic sequence.

5. $\dfrac{1}{4}, \dfrac{1}{2}, \dfrac{3}{4}, 1, \dfrac{5}{4}, \ldots$

6. $6, 1, -4, -9, -14, \ldots$

7. $215, 227, 239, 251, \ldots$

8. $-4, -5, -6, -7, \ldots$

9. $4.1, 6.3, 8.5, 10.7, \ldots$

10. $-17, -9, -1, 7, 15, \ldots$

11. In June, you start a holiday savings account with a deposit of $30. You increase each monthly deposit by $4 until the end of the year. How much money will you have saved by the end of December?

PRACTICE & PROBLEM SOLVING

UNDERSTAND

12. Use Structure Write an arithmetic sequence with at least four terms, and describe it using both an explicit and recursive definition. ⓒ **MP.7**

13. Error Analysis Alex says the common difference for an arithmetic sequence is always negative because of the definition of *difference*. Why is he wrong? Write an arithmetic sequence to show he is wrong. ⓒ **MP.3**

14. Use Structure A company will pay Becky $120 for her first sale. For each sale after that, they will pay an extra $31.50 per sale. So, she will make $151.50 for the second sale, $183 for the third sale, and so on. How many sales will Becky have to make to earn at least $2,000? ⓒ **MP.7**

15. Higher Order Thinking Felipe and Gregory are given the arithmetic sequence $-1, 6, 13, \ldots$. Gregory wrote the explicit definition $a_n = -1 + 7(n - 1)$ for the sequence. Felipe wrote the definition as $a_n = 7n - 8$. Which one of them is correct? Explain.

16. Model With Mathematics Suppose you are building 10 steps with 8 concrete blocks in the top step and 80 blocks in the bottom step. If the number of blocks in each step forms an arithmetic sequence, find the total number of concrete blocks needed to build the steps. ⓒ **MP.4**

17. Model With Mathematics With her half-marathon quickly approaching, Talisa decides to train every day up to the day of the race. She plans to run 2 mi the first day and 3.2 mi the fifth day. ⓒ **MP.4**

a. What is the explicit definition for this sequence?

b. Which day of training will she run the distance of a half-marathon (13.1 mi)?

PRACTICE

Are the following sequences arithmetic? If so, what is the common difference? What is the next term in the sequence? SEE EXAMPLE 1

18. 10, 20, 30, 40, . . .   **19.** 97, 86, 75, 64, . . .

20. 1, 4, 9, 16, . . .   **21.** 3, 7, 11, 15, . . .

Translate between the recursive and explicit definitions for each sequence. SEE EXAMPLE 2

22. $a_n = \begin{cases} 2, n = 1 \\ a_{n-1} + 2, n > 1 \end{cases}$

23. $a_n = -2 + 7(n - 1)$ **24.** $a_n = \frac{1}{8}(n - 1)$

25. $a_n = \begin{cases} -4, n = 1 \\ a_{n-1} - 4, n > 1 \end{cases}$

26. The members of a school's color guard begin their performance in a pyramid formation. The first row has 1 member, and the third row has 5 members. SEE EXAMPLE 3

a. What is the explicit definition for this sequence?

b. How many members are in the eighth row?

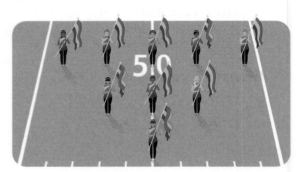

Find the sum of an arithmetic series with the given number of terms, a_1, and a_n. SEE EXAMPLE 4

27. 10 terms, $a_1 = 4$, $a_{10} = 31$

28. 15 terms, $a_1 = 17$, $a_{15} = 129$

What is the sum of each of the following series? SEE EXAMPLE 5

29. $\sum_{n=1}^{11} (3 + 2n)$ **30.** $\sum_{n=1}^{12} \left(\frac{n}{2} - 9\right)$

31. The number of seats in each row of an auditorium increases as you go back from the stage. The front row has 24 seats, the second row has 29 seats, and the third row has 34 seats. If there are 35 rows, how many seats are in the auditorium? SEE EXAMPLE 6

APPLY

32. Make Sense and Persevere A piece of tile artwork is in the shape of a triangle. The top row has 1 tile, the second row has 2 tiles, and the third row has 3 tiles. If there are 14 rows of tiles, how many tiles were used to make the artwork? ⓒ MP.1

33. Model With Mathematics A race car driver travels 34 ft in the first second of a race. If the driver travels 3.5 additional feet each subsequent second, how many feet did the driver travel in 52 s? ⓒ MP.4

34. Construct Arguments A school board committee has decided to spend its annual technology budget this year on 90 student laptops and plans to buy 40 new laptops each year from now on. ⓒ MP.3

   a. The school board decided that each student in the school should have access to a laptop in the next ten years. If there are 500 students, will the technology coordinator meet this goal? Explain.

   b. What are some pros and cons of buying student laptops in this manner? If you could change the plan, would you? If so, how would you change it?

35. Make Sense and Persevere On October 1, Nadia starts a push-up challenge by doing 18 push-ups. On October 2, she does 21 push-ups. On October 3, she does 24 push-ups. She continues until October 16, when she does the final push-ups in the challenge. ⓒ MP.1

   a. Write an explicit definition to model the number of push-ups Nadia does each day.

   b. Write a recursive definition to model the number of push-ups Nadia does each day.

   c. How many push-ups will Nadia do on October 16?

   d. What is the total number of push-ups Nadia does from October 1 to October 16?

16-Day Push-Up Challenge	
Day 1	18 push-ups
Day 2	21 push-ups
Day 3	24 push-ups

ⓒ ASSESSMENT PRACTICE

36. Which of the following are also numbers in the arithmetic sequence 4, 11, 18, 25, 32, . . . ? Write the numbers in the correct box.

60   68   75   39   81

In the sequence	Not in the sequence

37. SAT/ACT Tamika is selling magazines door to door. On her first day, she sells 12 magazines, and she intends to sell 5 more magazines per day than on the previous day. If she meets her goal and sells magazines for a total of 10 days, how many magazines would she sell?

  Ⓐ 314   Ⓑ 345   Ⓒ 415   Ⓓ 474   Ⓔ 505

38. Performance Task The chart shows the population of Edgar's beehive over the first four weeks. Assume the population will continue to grow at the same rate.

WEEK 1	175
WEEK 2	203
WEEK 3	231
WEEK 4	259

Part A Write an explicit definition for the sequence.

Part B If Edgar's bees have a mass of 1.5 g each, what will the total mass of all his bees be in 12 wk?

Part C When the colony reaches 1,015 bees, Edgar's beehive will not be big enough for all of them. In how many weeks will the bee population be too large?

1-5

Solving Equations and Inequalities by Graphing

SavvasRealize.com

I CAN... use graphs and tables to approximate solutions to algebraic equations and inequalities.

👆 Activity   ✓ Assess

👆 **MODEL & DISCUSS**

A homeowner has 32 feet of fencing to build three sides of a rectangular chicken run.

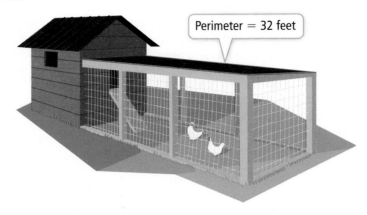

Perimeter = 32 feet

A. Make a table of values for the length, width, and area of different rectangular chicken runs that will utilize 32 feet of fencing. Then write a function for the area, in terms of width, of a rectangular run using this much fencing.

B. Graph your function.

C. Reason Explain what happens where the graph intersects the x-axis. © **MP.2**

❓ **ESSENTIAL QUESTION**   **How can you solve an equation or inequality by graphing?**

CONCEPTUAL UNDERSTANDING

👆 **EXAMPLE 1**   **Use a Graph to Solve an Equation**

How can you use a graph to solve an equation?

A. Solve −3x + 20 = 5 by graphing.

An equation is a statement that two expressions are equal. The values of x that make the equation true are the solutions.

To solve an equation by graphing, write two new equations by setting y equal to each in the original equation.

$$-3x + 20 = 5$$
$$y = -3x + 20 \qquad y = 5$$

Graph the two equations and identify the points of intersection. These points will have x-values that produce the same y-values for both expressions. Each of the x-values is a solution to the original equation.

Graph $y = -3x + 20$ and $y = 5$.

LOOK FOR RELATIONSHIPS
This method is similar to solving an equation by finding the x-intercept, where the solution is the intersection of the line and the line y = 0. © **MP.7**

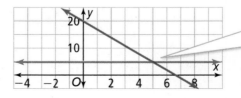

It appears that $y = -3x + 20$ and $y = 5$ intersect at $x = 5$. By substituting this value into the original equation, you can verify the result.

So $-3x + 20 = 5$ when $x = 5$. This is the only point on the graph where the value of the functions $y = -3x + 20$ and $y = 5$ are equal.

CONTINUED ON THE NEXT PAGE

EXAMPLE 1 CONTINUED

B. Solve $|x - 4| = \frac{1}{2}x + 1$ **by graphing.**

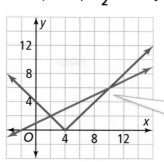

To solve $|x - 4| = \frac{1}{2}x + 1$, write two equations $y = |x - 4|$ and $y = \frac{1}{2}x + 1$, and graph.

> It appears that $y = |x - 4|$ and $y = \frac{1}{2}x + 1$ intersect at $x = 2$ and $x = 10$.

The solutions to the equation $|x - 4| = \frac{1}{2}x + 1$ are $x = 2$ and $x = 10$. You can verify these values by substituting them back into the original equation.

Try It!   **1. Use a graph to solve the equation.**

   a. $5x - 12 = 3$ **b.** $-|x - 2| = -\frac{1}{2}x - 2$

APPLICATION

EXAMPLE 2   **Solve a One-Variable Inequality by Graphing**

How can you use a graph to solve an inequality?

A. Solve $x^2 - 4 > 0$.

To solve the inequality, identify the values of x that make the value of the expression $x^2 - 4$ greater than 0. Graph the equation $y = x^2 - 4$ by translating the parent function $y = x^2$ down 4 units.

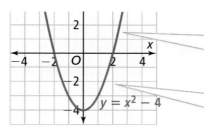

> Look for the points on the graph where the value of the function is positive.

> The intercepts appear to be $x = 2$ and $x = -2$.

COMMON ERROR
You may think that you need to find interval(s) where $x > 0$. However, you need to find where $x^2 - 4 > 0$, so you are looking for interval(s) where $y > 0$.

The graph of the function is positive over the intervals $(-\infty, -2)$ and $(2, \infty)$. So $x^2 - 4 > 0$ when $x < -2$ or $x > 2$.

B. A motorcycle is 40 mi ahead of a car. The motorcycle travels at an average rate of 40 mph. The car travels at a rate of 60 mph. When will the car be ahead of the motorcycle?

Let x represent the number of hours since the car started traveling. The expression $60x$ represents the distance the car travels in x hours. The expression $40x$ represents the distance the motorcycle travels in x hours.

40 mph

60 mph

CONTINUED ON THE NEXT PAGE

EXAMPLE 2 CONTINUED

To solve, we need to determine when the number of miles the car travels exceeds the number of miles the motorcycle travels.

Solve $60x > 40x + 40$.

Set $y = 60x$ and $y = 40x + 40$, and then graph both equations.

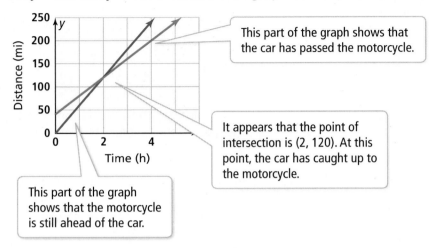

This part of the graph shows that the car has passed the motorcycle.

It appears that the point of intersection is (2, 120). At this point, the car has caught up to the motorcycle.

This part of the graph shows that the motorcycle is still ahead of the car.

The car will be ahead of the motorcycle any time after 2 h. You can verify the solution by selecting any number greater than 2 and substituting it into the original inequality.

 Try It! 2. Use a graph to solve each inequality.

a. $x^2 + 6x + 5 \geq 0$ **b.** $x + 3 > 7 - 3x$

EXAMPLE 3   **Use a Table to Solve an Equation**

Use a graph and tables to solve the equation $x^2 - 4x + 1 = x - 2$.

Sketch the graphs of $y = x^2 - 4x + 1$ and $y = x - 2$. Identify the points of intersection to find initial estimate(s) of the solution value(s).

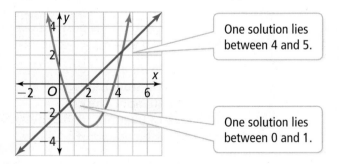

One solution lies between 4 and 5.

One solution lies between 0 and 1.

Neither solution appears to correspond to a grid point. You can use a table to get more accurate estimates for the solutions.

CONTINUED ON THE NEXT PAGE

EXAMPLE 3 CONTINUED

x	$x - 2$	$x^2 - 4x + 1$
0.5	−1.5	−0.75
0.6	−1.4	−1.04
0.7	−1.3	−1.31
0.8	−1.2	−1.56
0.9	−1.1	−1.79
1	−1	−2

x	$x - 2$	$x^2 - 4x + 1$
0.65	−1.35	−1.1775
0.66	−1.34	−1.2044
0.67	−1.33	−1.2311
0.68	−1.32	−1.2576
0.69	−1.31	−1.2839
0.7	−1.3	−1.31

x	$x - 2$	$x^2 - 4x + 1$
0.69	−1.31	−1.2839
0.691	−1.309	−1.28652
0.692	−1.308	−1.28914
0.693	−1.307	−1.29175
0.694	−1.306	−1.29436
0.695	−1.305	−1.29698
0.696	−1.304	−1.29958
0.697	−1.303	−1.30219
0.698	−1.302	−1.30480

If $x \leq 0.6$, then
$x^2 - 4x + 1 > x - 2$.
If $x \geq 0.7$, then
$x^2 - 4x + 1 < x - 2$.

Look for values where graphs will cross. Use these values to "zoom in," finding better and better approximations.

Choose the x-value with the smallest difference in the function values.

One solution is approximately $x = 0.697$.

You can use a similar method to approximate the second solution.

☑ **Try It!** **3.** The equation $x^2 - 4x + 1 = x - 2$ has a second solution in the interval $4 < x < 5$. Use a spreadsheet to approximate this solution to the nearest thousandth.

EXAMPLE 4 **Use Graphing Technology to Solve Equations**

Use graphing technology to approximate the solutions of the equation $-x^2 + 8x - 13 = |x - 4|$ to the nearest tenth.

Graph $y = -x^2 + 8x - 13$ and $y = |x - 4|$.

Use the INTERSECT feature to find the approximate solutions.

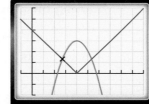

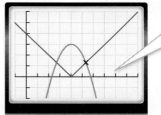

Remember that you are looking for the values of x where the graphs intersect.

$x = 2.6972244$ $y = 1.3027756$ $x = 5.3027756$ $y = 1.3027756$

The INTERSECT feature shows that the equation has solutions $x \approx 2.7$ and $x \approx 5.3$.

☑ **Try It!** **4.** Use graphing technology to approximate the solutions of the equation $x^2 + 2x - 1 = |x + 2| + 2$ to the nearest tenth.

CONCEPT SUMMARY Solving Equations and Inequalities by Graphing

Solve $|3x + 5| = \frac{1}{3}x + 5$.

Let $f(x) = |3x + 5|$ and $g(x) = \frac{1}{3}x + 5$

GRAPHS Graph each function, and identify the x-coordinates of the points of intersection.

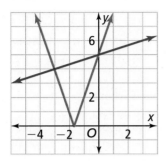

One solution appears to be 0. The second solution appears to be −3.

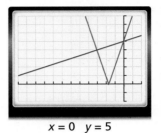

$x = 0 \quad y = 5$

When graphing with technology, use the INTERSECT feature to find the exact solution(s).

TABLE Graphs may not always yield integer results. Tables may be used to find solutions.

x	f(x)	g(x)
−3.3	4.9	3.9
−3.2	4.6	3.9333
−3.1	4.3	3.9667
−3.0	4	4
−2.9	3.7	4.0333

☑ Do You UNDERSTAND?

1. **ESSENTIAL QUESTION** How can you solve an equation or inequality by graphing?

2. **Communicate Precisely** What is an advantage of solving an equation graphically by finding the points of intersection? ⓒ MP.6

3. **Error Analysis** Ben said the graph of the inequality $-x^2 + 9 > 0$ shows the solution is $x < -3$ or $x > 3$. Is Ben correct? Explain. ⓒ MP.3

Do You KNOW HOW?

4. Using the graph below, what is the solution to $-2x + 4 = -2$? How can you tell?

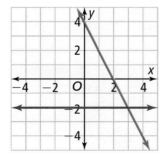

PRACTICE & PROBLEM SOLVING

UNDERSTAND

5. Construct Arguments Use a graph to solve the equation $3x - 5 = 2 + 3x$. How can you use algebra to confirm that your graph shows the correct solution? **MP.3**

6. Error Analysis Victor graphed the equation $x^2 + 2x - 5 = -0.6x + 1$. He used the INTERSECT feature on his graphing calculator to find the solution. Victor said one of the solutions is $x \approx 0.116$. Describe and correct the error Victor made. **MP.3**

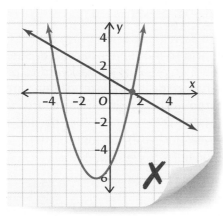

7. Higher Order Thinking Sadie used a graph to solve an equation. What equation did Sadie solve? Explain how to verify your equation is correct.

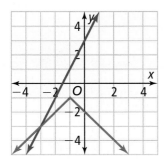

8. Communicate Precisely Explain how to use the table to find the approximate solution to the equation $f(x) = g(x)$. **MP.6**

x	f(x)	g(x)
1.1426	1.8556	1.857175
1.1427	1.8562	1.8571625
1.1428	1.8568	1.85715
1.1429	1.8574	1.8571375
1.1430	1.858	1.857125

PRACTICE

Use a graph to solve each equation. SEE EXAMPLE 1

9. $-x + 4 = 2$

10. $|x - 4| - 4 = \frac{1}{2}x$

11. $3x + 2 = x + 4$

12. $-\frac{1}{4}x + 6 = \frac{1}{2}x + 3$

13. $\frac{3}{4}x = 2x - 10$

14. $|x + 8| = |x - 2|$

Use a graph to solve each inequality. SEE EXAMPLE 2

15. $x^2 - 7x - 8 > 0$

16. $x - 5 > -2x + 4$

17. $x^2 + x - 6 < 0$

18. $x^2 + 2x - 8 \leq 0$

19. $-x^2 - 2x + 15 \leq 0$

20. $-x + 5 < \frac{1}{2}x - 1$

21. Cindy is longboarding 6 mi ahead of Tamira. Cindy is traveling at an average rate of 2 mph. Tamira is traveling at a rate of 4 mph. Let x represent the number of hours since Tamira started longboarding. When will Tamira be ahead of Cindy? Write an inequality to represent this situation.

Cindy, 2 mph

Tamira, 4 mph

Use a graph and tables to solve the equation.
SEE EXAMPLE 3

22. $x^2 - 8x + 5 = x + 3$

23. $\frac{1}{4}x + 3 = x^2 - x + 2$

24. $2x^2 - 5 = -x^2 + 2x - 1$

25. $3x - 4 = \frac{1}{2}|x - 5|$

Use graphing technology to approximate the solutions of the equation to the nearest tenth.
SEE EXAMPLE 4

26. $x^2 + 6x - 8 = |x - 1| + 3$

27. $|x + 2| - 6 = x^2 - 7x - 2$

28. $\frac{1}{5}|x + 2| - 3 = -|x - 1| + 5$

29. $x^2 + 3x - 7 = -2x^2 - 6x + 9$

PRACTICE & PROBLEM SOLVING

APPLY

30. Reason Jack is running 2.45 mi ahead of Zhang. Jack is running at an average rate of 5.5 mph. Zhang is running at a rate of 7.75 mph. Let x represent the number of hours since Zhang started jogging. **© MP.2**

a. Write an inequality to represent this situation.

b. Use graphing technology to find when Zhang will be ahead of Jack. Round to the nearest hundredth.

31. Use Structure In a kickball game, a ball is kicked and travels along a parabolic path. The height h, in feet, of the kickball t seconds after the kick can be modeled by the equation $h(t) = -16t^2 + 24t$. **© MP.7**

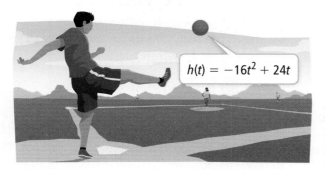

$$h(t) = -16t^2 + 24t$$

a. A fielder runs a route that will allow him to catch the kickball at about 3 ft above the ground. Write an equation that can be used to find when the fielder will catch the ball.

b. Use graphing technology to find out how long the kickball has been in the air when the fielder catches it on its descent. Round to the nearest hundredth.

32. Make Sense and Persevere The amount, in millions of dollars, that a company earns in revenue for selling x items, in thousands, is $R = -2x^2 + 18x - 2$. The expenses, in millions of dollars, for selling x items, in thousands, is $E = -0.25x + 6$. **© MP.1**

a. The profit P, in millions of dollars, for selling x items, in thousands, is the difference between the revenues and the expenses. Write an inequality that models the company earning a profit.

b. Use graphing technology to find how many items the company must sell to earn a profit. Round to the nearest item.

ASSESSMENT PRACTICE

33. Graph the equation $x^2 - 3 = x + 3$. What are the solutions to the equation?

34. SAT/ACT A graph shows the solution to the equation $-\frac{1}{2}x + \frac{7}{2} = -x + a$ is $x = -1$. What is the value of a?

Ⓐ −3

Ⓑ −2

Ⓒ 1

Ⓓ 2

Ⓔ 3

35. Performance Task Deondra is using a coordinate grid to model her backyard. She wants to mark an area in her backyard to plant a garden. She decides the center of her garden will be located at the origin on her coordinate grid. She models the outline of her garden on the coordinate grid with the inequalities $-\frac{1}{2}|x| + 5 \geq y$ and $y \leq \frac{1}{2}|x| - 5$.

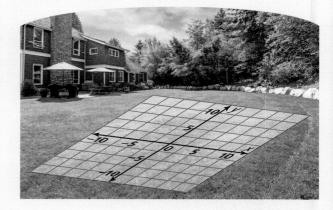

Part A Graph the inequalities that model the area of Deondra's garden on the coordinate grid.

Part B What shape is Deondra's garden?

Part C Deondra wants to cover her garden with garden soil. She wants the soil to be $\frac{1}{2}$ ft deep. If each unit on the coordinate grid represents 1 ft^2, how much garden soil will Deondra need?

Activity  Assess

1-6
Linear Systems

 SavvasRealize.com

I CAN... use a variety of tools to solve systems of linear equations and inequalities.

VOCABULARY
- augmented matrix
- coefficient matrix
- dimensions
- inconsistent system
- matrix
- solution of a system of linear equations
- system of linear equations
- system of linear inequalities

👆 **EXPLORE & REASON**

The graph shows two lines that intersect at one point.

A. What are the approximate coordinates of the point of intersection?

B. How could you verify whether the coordinates you estimated are, in fact, the solution? Is the point the solution to the equations of both lines?

C. **Make Sense and Persevere** Use your result to refine your approximation, and try again. Can you find the point of intersection this way? Is there a more efficient way? Ⓒ **MP.1**

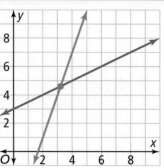

❓ **ESSENTIAL QUESTION**

How can you find and represent solutions of systems of linear equations and inequalities?

👆 **EXAMPLE 1** Solve a System of Linear Equations

What is the solution of the system of linear equations $\begin{cases} x + 2y = 3 \\ x - 2y = 4 \end{cases}$?

A **system of linear equations** is a set of two or more equations using the same variables. The **solution of a system of linear equations** is the set of all ordered coordinates that simultaneously make all equations in the system true.

Sketch the graph of each equation to estimate the solutions. Then solve algebraically.

GENERALIZE
Recall that there are three possible outcomes when solving a system of two linear equations: no solution, one solution, or an infinite number of solutions. Ⓒ **MP.8**

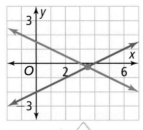

The *x*-coordinate of the solution is between 3 and 4, and the *y*-coordinate of the solution is between −1 and 0.

$$x + 2y = 3 \implies x = 3 - 2y$$
$$x - 2y = 4 \implies x = 4 + 2y$$

⇓

Substitute for *x* in both equations and solve.

$$3 - 2y = 4 + 2y$$
$$-1 = 4y$$
$$-\frac{1}{4} = y$$

Substitute the value for *y* into either original equation to find the value of *x*.

$$x = 3 - 2\left(-\frac{1}{4}\right)$$
$$x = \frac{7}{2}$$

The solution is $\left(\frac{7}{2}, -\frac{1}{4}\right)$. These values are close to the estimate made from the graph. You can check to confirm that these values satisfy both equations.

 Try It! **1.** Solve each system of equations.

a. $\begin{cases} 2x + y = -1 \\ 5y - 6x = 7 \end{cases}$

b. $\begin{cases} 3x + 2y = 5 \\ 6x + 4y = 3 \end{cases}$

APPLICATION  **EXAMPLE 2** **Solve a System of Linear Inequalities**

Malcolm earns $20 per hour mowing lawns and $10 per hour walking dogs. His goal is to earn at least $200 each week, but he can work a maximum of 20 h per week. Malcolm must spend at least 5 h per week walking his neighbors' dogs. For how many hours should Malcolm work at each job in order to meet his goals?

$20 per hour $10 per hour

A **system of linear inequalities** is a set of two or more inequalities using the same variables.

Step 1 Define the variables.

x = number of hours spent mowing lawns

y = number of hours spent walking dogs

Step 2 Write inequalities to model the constraints.

Malcolm wants to earn at least $200 each week at $20 per hour mowing lawns and $10 per hour walking dogs: $20x + 10y \geq 200$.

Malcolm cannot work more than 20 h each week: $x + y \leq 20$.

Malcolm must spend at least 5 h walking dogs each week: $y \geq 5$.

Step 3 Solve each inequality for y, then graph the inequalities on the same coordinate plane.

$y \geq 20 - 2x$

$y \leq 20 - x$

$y \geq 5$

Use arrows to show the region of the graph that satisfies each inequality.

Shade the region that satisfies all three inequalities.

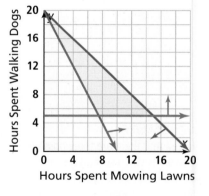

STUDY TIP
Using color to sketch graphs of equations or inequalities can make the graph easier to analyze.

Any point in the shaded region, such as (12, 7), is a solution to the system of inequalities. So if Malcolm spends 12 h mowing lawns and 7 h walking dogs, he will have met his goals.

 Try It! **2.** Sketch the graph of the set of all points that solve this system of linear inequalities.

$$\begin{cases} 2x + y \leq 14 \\ x + 2y \leq 10 \\ x \geq 0 \\ y \geq 0 \end{cases}$$

EXAMPLE 3   Solve a System of Equations in Three Variables

How can you solve a system of equations in three variables?

A. What is the solution of this system?
$$\begin{cases} 2x + y - z = -10 \\ -x + 2y + z = 3 \\ x + 2y + 3z = 13 \end{cases}$$

$2x + y - z = -10$ (A)	
$-x + 2y + z = 3$ (B)	
$x + 2y + 3z = 13$ (C)	

$x + 3y = -7$ (D)	(D) = (A) + (B)
$3x - 6y - 3z = -9$ (E)	(E) = $-3 \times$ (B)
$x + 2y + 3z = 13$ (F)	(F) = (C)

$x + 3y = -7$ (G)	(G) = (D)
$4x - 4y = 4$ (H)	(H) = (E) + (F)
$x + 2y + 3z = 13$ (J)	(J) = (F)

$x + 3y = -7$ (K)	(K) = (G)
$-x + y = -1$ (L)	(L) = (H) ÷ (−4)
$x + 2y + 3z = 13$ (M)	(M) = (J)

$4y = -8$ (N)	(N) = (K) + (L)
$-x + y = -1$ (P)	(P) = (L)
$x + 2y + 3z = 13$ (Q)	(Q) = (M)

LOOK FOR RELATIONSHIPS
The following actions do not change the solutions of a system of equations:

- rearranging the order of the list

- multiplying an equation by a nonzero number

- adding one equation to another and replacing one of these equations with the sum © MP.7

From equation (N):   Substituting into (P):   Substituting into (A):
$y = -2$ $-x + (-2) = -1$ $2(-1) + (-2) - z = -10$
                    $x = -1$ $z = 6$

The solution is $(-1, -2, 6)$.

B. What is the solution of this system of equations?
$$\begin{cases} 2x - y + z = 3 \\ x + y + z = 5 \\ -4x + 2y - 2z = 0 \end{cases}$$

$2x - y + z = 3$ (A)	
$x + y + z = 5$ (B)	
$-4x + 2y - 2z = 0$ (C)	

$3x + 2z = 8$ (D)	(D) = (A) + (B)
$x + y + z = 5$ (E)	(E) = (B)
$-6x - 4z = -10$ (F)	(F) = −2(B) + (C)

$3x + 2z = 8$ (G)	(G) = (D)
$x + y + z = 5$ (H)	(H) = (E)
$0 = 6$ (J)	(J) = 2(D) + (F)

Equation (J) is not true. There is no solution for this system of equations; it is an **inconsistent system**.

CONTINUED ON THE NEXT PAGE

EXAMPLE 3 CONTINUED   Activity Assess

 Try It! **3.** Solve the following systems of equations.

a. $\begin{cases} x + y + z = 3 \\ x - y + z = 1 \\ x + y - z = 2 \end{cases}$ **b.** $\begin{cases} 2x + y - 2z = 3 \\ x - 2y + 7z = 12 \\ 3x - y + 5z = 10 \end{cases}$

CONCEPTUAL UNDERSTANDING

EXAMPLE 4 **Write a System of Equations as a Matrix**

How can a matrix represent a system of linear equations?

USE APPROPRIATE TOOLS
A matrix allows you to keep track of the coefficients and constants in a system of equations without writing the variables. © MP.5

A. How can you represent $\begin{cases} 3y = 1 - 2x \\ 4x = 10 + 2y \end{cases}$ **using a matrix?**

A **matrix** is a rectangular array of values. To use a matrix to represent a linear system of equations, the equations must first be written in standard form.

$$\begin{cases} ax + by = c \\ dx + ey = f \end{cases} \qquad \begin{cases} 2x + 3y = 1 \\ 4x - 2y = 10 \end{cases}$$

A **coefficient matrix** shows the coefficients of the variables in the system of equations.

$$\begin{bmatrix} a & b \\ d & e \end{bmatrix} \qquad \begin{bmatrix} 2 & 3 \\ 4 & -2 \end{bmatrix}$$

An **augmented matrix** shows all coefficients and constants in the system of equations. A dotted line separates the variable terms from the constant terms.

COMMON ERROR
The system of equations cannot be set up as an augmented matrix until both equations are written in standard form.

$$\begin{bmatrix} a & b & \vdots & c \\ d & e & \vdots & f \end{bmatrix} \qquad \begin{bmatrix} 2 & 3 & \vdots & 1 \\ 4 & -2 & \vdots & 10 \end{bmatrix}$$

The **dimensions** of a matrix is $r \times c$, where r is the number of rows and c is the number of columns. This is a 2×3 matrix.

x-coefficients   *y*-coefficients   constants

The system $\begin{cases} 3y = 1 - 2x \\ 4x = 10 + 2y \end{cases}$ can be represented by the matrix $\begin{bmatrix} 2 & 3 & \vdots & 1 \\ 4 & -2 & \vdots & 10 \end{bmatrix}$.

B. How can you represent this system of equations of three variables and three equations with a matrix?

$$\begin{cases} x + 2y = 2 \\ x - y + 3z = 5 \\ 2x + y - 4z = 10 \end{cases}$$

Write each equation in standard form. Include all three variables in each equation.

$1x + 2y + 0z = 2$
$1x + (-1)y + 3z = 5$
$2x + 1y + (-4)z = 10$

Identify coefficients and constant terms. The coefficient of z in the first equation is 0.

CONTINUED ON THE NEXT PAGE

 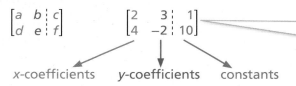

EXAMPLE 4 CONTINUED

Record the coefficients in matrix form.

$$\begin{bmatrix} 1 & 2 & 0 & | & 2 \\ 1 & -1 & 3 & | & 5 \\ 2 & 1 & -4 & | & 10 \end{bmatrix}$$

Create the augmented matrix.

Try It! **4.** Write the matrix for the system of equations or the system of equations for the matrix.

a. $\begin{cases} 3x - y = 4 \\ -2x + 7y = 20 \end{cases}$

b. $\begin{bmatrix} 0 & 2 & 3 & | & 4 \\ 8 & -1 & -2 & | & 5 \\ 2 & 0 & 1 & | & 9 \end{bmatrix}$

APPLICATION

EXAMPLE 5 **Relate Systems of Equations and Matrices**

An algebra teacher creates the matrix shown to describe an exam, where x represents the number of 2-point questions and y shows the number of 5-point questions.

The augmented matrix shows two equations with two variables.

A. Write the corresponding system of equations. What does each equation represent?

$1x + 1y = 19$ ⋯⋯⋯ x is the number of 2-point questions, and y is the number of 5-point questions. There are 19 questions on the exam.

$2x + 5y = 50$ ⋯⋯⋯ $2x$ is the number of points available from 2-points questions, and $5y$ is the number of points available from 5-point questions.. The exam is worth 50 points.

STUDY TIP
A matrix with 1s along the diagonal and 0s elsewhere translates into equations of the form $x = a$, $y = b$, which gives the solution of the system of equations.

B. What does the matrix $\begin{bmatrix} 1 & 0 & | & 15 \\ 0 & 1 & | & 4 \end{bmatrix}$ mean in terms of this context?

Recall that x represents the number of two-point questions on the test, and y represents the number of five-point questions. So the matrix means that there are 15 two-point questions and 4 five-point questions on the exam. Check that these values satisfy the original system of equations:

$1(15) + 1(4) = 19$
$2(15) + 5(4) = 30 + 20 = 50.$

Try It! **5. a.** Write the system of equations described by the augmented matrix. Describe a real-world situation that could be modeled by the system. $\begin{bmatrix} 1 & 1 & | & 10 \\ 3 & 2 & | & 80 \end{bmatrix}$

b. What would the matrix $\begin{bmatrix} 1 & 0 & | & 20 \\ 0 & 1 & | & 10 \end{bmatrix}$ represent in terms of your real–world situation?

CONCEPT SUMMARY Linear Systems

	System of linear equations	System of linear inequalities
WORDS	a set of two or more equations using the same variables	a set of two or more inequalities using the same variables
ALGEBRA	$\begin{cases} 4x - 3y = 4 \\ -x + 2y = 5 \end{cases}$ or $\begin{bmatrix} 4 & -3 & 4 \\ -1 & 2 & 5 \end{bmatrix}$	$\begin{cases} y \geq 16 - 2x \\ y \leq 16 - x \\ y \geq 6 \end{cases}$
GRAPHS	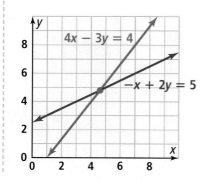	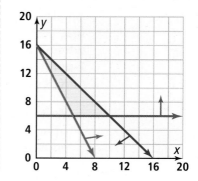

Do You UNDERSTAND?

1. **ESSENTIAL QUESTION** How can you find and represent solutions of systems of linear equations and inequalities?

2. **Error Analysis** Shandra said the solution of the system of equations $\begin{cases} 2x + y = 3 \\ -x + 4y = -6 \end{cases}$ is $(-1, 2)$. Is she correct? Explain. Ⓒ **MP.3**

3. **Communicate Precisely** Why is a system of linear inequalities often solved graphically? Ⓒ **MP.6**

4. **Make Sense and Persevere** How does knowing how to solve a system of two equations in two variables help you to solve a system of three equations in three variables? Ⓒ **MP.1**

5. **Vocabulary** What is the difference between a coefficient matrix and an augmented matrix?

Do You KNOW HOW?

6. Solve the following system of equations.
$\begin{cases} 2x + 2y = 10 \\ x + 5y = 13 \end{cases}$

7. Graph the following system of inequalities.
$\begin{cases} -x + 2y < 1 \\ x \geq 0 \\ y \geq 0 \end{cases}$

8. Write the system of equations represented by the matrix $\begin{bmatrix} 1 & -2 & 2 \\ -4 & 3 & -5 \end{bmatrix}$.

9. Equations with two variables that are raised only to the first power represent lines. There are three possible outcomes for the intersections of two lines. Describe the outcomes.

Scan for Multimedia

Practice   Tutorial

Additional Exercises Available Online

UNDERSTAND

10. Communicate Precisely What is represented by each row in a matrix representing a system of equations? **© MP.6**

11. Error Analysis Describe and correct the error a student made in solving the system of equations. **© MP.3**

$$2x + 4y = 0 \quad \Rightarrow \quad 2x + 4y = 0$$
$$3x - 2y = -24 \quad \Rightarrow \quad 6x - 4y = -24$$
$$\Downarrow$$
$$8x = -24$$
$$x = -3$$
$$\Downarrow$$
$$2(-3) + 4y = 0$$
$$-6 + 4y = 0$$
$$4y = 6$$
$$y = \frac{3}{2} \quad \text{✗}$$

12. Higher Order Thinking When solving a system of two equations using matrices, what does it mean graphically when the determinant is equal to zero? (*Hint:* The determinant is ($ae - bd$) for the coefficient matrix in the form $\begin{bmatrix} a & b \\ d & e \end{bmatrix}$.)

13. Use Structure Write a system of equations in three variables with integer solutions. Give the solution. Explain your process. **© MP.7**

14. Make Sense and Persevere Write a system of inequalities for the shaded region. **© MP.1**

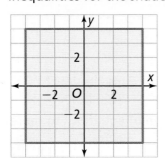

15. Mathematical Connections Find a solution to the following system of equations.

$$\begin{cases} x = 5 - 3y \\ y = -2x \end{cases}$$

What is a matrix that could represent the solution that you found?

PRACTICE

Solve the following systems of equations. SEE EXAMPLE 1

16. $\begin{cases} x = 2y - 5 \\ 3x - y = 5 \end{cases}$ **17.** $\begin{cases} y = 2x + 3 \\ 2y - x = 12 \end{cases}$

18. $\begin{cases} x - 3y = 1 \\ 2x - y = 7 \end{cases}$ **19.** $\begin{cases} x + 2y = -4 \\ 3x - y = -5 \end{cases}$

Sketch the graph of the set of all points that solve each system of linear inequalities. SEE EXAMPLE 2

20. $\begin{cases} 0 < x \le 125 \\ x \ge 2y > 0 \\ 2x + 2y \le 300 \end{cases}$ **21.** $\begin{cases} y + 2x < 10 \\ x - 2y < 8 \\ x > 0 \\ y > 0 \end{cases}$

Solve the following systems of equations. SEE EXAMPLE 3

22. $\begin{cases} 2x - y - 3z = 20 \\ 3x + y + 6z = 4 \\ x + 2y + 9z = -16 \end{cases}$ **23.** $\begin{cases} 2x + 5y - 3z = 14 \\ x - 2y + 4z = -12 \\ -x + 3y - 2z = 13 \end{cases}$

Write the augmented matrix for each system of equations. SEE EXAMPLE 4

24. $\begin{cases} x + y = 2 \\ x - 2y = 17 \end{cases}$ **25.** $\begin{cases} y = 2x \\ 4x - y = 9 \end{cases}$

26. $\begin{cases} 10a - 5b = 3 \\ a = -\frac{1}{2}b \end{cases}$ **27.** $\begin{cases} m = 7n - 1 \\ 1 - n = m \end{cases}$

Write the system of equations described by each augmented matrix. SEE EXAMPLE 4

28. $\begin{bmatrix} 2 & -2 & 4 \\ 1 & 2 & 11 \end{bmatrix}$ **29.** $\begin{bmatrix} 0.5 & 1 & 0 \\ -1 & 4 & 2 \end{bmatrix}$

30. Charles has a collection of dimes and quarters worth $1.25. He has 8 coins. What are a system of equations and an augmented matrix that can represent this situation? SEE EXAMPLE 5

31. A set of triangular and square tiles contains 50 pieces and 170 sides. Write a system of equations and an augmented matrix to represent this situation. SEE EXAMPLE 5

APPLY

32. Model With Mathematics In basketball, a successful free throw is worth 1 point, a basket made from inside the 3-point arc is worth 2 points, and a basket made from outside the 3-point arc basket is worth 3 points. How many of each type of basket did Pilar make? **MP.4**

SPORTS
PILAR SCORED
26 POINTS!
She made 2 more free throws than 2-point baskets. She also made 4 times as many free throws as 3-point baskets.

33. Reason Raul is paid $75 per week plus $5 for each new gym membership he sells. He may switch to a gym that pays $50 per week and $7.50 for each new membership. How many memberships per week does Raul have to sell for the new gym to be a better deal for him? **MP.2**

34. Reason Keisha is designing a rectangular giraffe enclosure with a length of at most 125 m. The animal sanctuary can afford at most 300 m of fencing, and the length of the enclosure must be at least double the width. **MP.2**

$y \leq 125$ m

a. Write inequalities to represent each constraint where $x =$ width and $y =$ length.

b. Graph and solve the linear system of inequalities.

c. What does the solution mean?

35. Make Sense and Persevere Ramona needs 10 mL of a 30% saline solution. She has a 50% saline solution and a 25% saline solution. How many milliliters of each solution does she need to create the 30% solution? **MP.1**

ASSESSMENT PRACTICE

36. One equation in a system of equations with one solution is $4x + 2y = 14$. Determine if each equation could be the second equation in the system. Select **Yes** or **No.**

a. $2x + y = 7$ ○ Yes   ○ No

b. $3x - 6y = -12$ ○ Yes   ○ No

c. $2x + 6y = 32$ ○ Yes   ○ No

d. $-3x + 10y = 1$ ○ Yes   ○ No

e. $2x + y = 5$ ○ Yes   ○ No

37. SAT/ACT What value of a gives $(-1, 1)$ as the solution of the system $\begin{cases} 3x + 5y = 2 \\ ax + 8y = 14 \end{cases}$?

Ⓐ −22   Ⓑ −6   Ⓒ 0   Ⓓ 6   Ⓔ 22

38. Performance Task Each Sophomore, Junior, and Senior at a high school collected aluminum cans and plastic bottles. The table shows the average number of cans and bottles collected per student, by grade level during a 3 week recyling drive.

Week 1
2,319
cans and bottles

Week 3
3,785
cans and bottles

Week 2
2,290
cans and bottles

	Sophomores	Juniors	Seniors
Week 1	3	4	4
Week 2	4	4	3
Week 3	5	6	7

Part A Write a system of equations to represent the situation.

Part B Find the solution of the system of equations you found in Part A.

Part C What does your solution to part B represent in terms of this scenario?

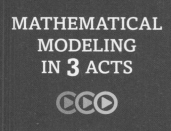
Ⓒ **Common Core State Standards** HSA.REI.C.6, HSA.CED.A.2, HSA.CED.A.3, MP.4

▶ Video

▶ Current Events

You might say that someone who loses their temper has "blown a fuse." However, it's rare to hear about electrical fuses blowing these days. That's because most fuses have been replaced by circuit breakers. A fuse must be replaced once it's blown, but a circuit breaker can be reset.

Ask for permission to look at the electrical panel in your home. If there is a series of switches inside, each of those is a circuit breaker, designed to interrupt the circuit when the electrical current inside is too dangerous. How much electricity does it take to trip a circuit breaker? Think about this question during the Mathematical Modeling in 3-Acts lesson.

Scan for Multimedia

ACT 1 ▸ Identify the Problem

1. What is the first question that comes to mind after watching the video?

2. Write down the main question you will answer about what you saw in the video.

3. Make an initial conjecture that answers this main question.

4. Explain how you arrived at your conjecture.

5. What information will be useful to know to answer the main question? How can you get it? How will you use that information?

ACT 2 ▸ Develop a Model

6. Use the math that you have learned in this Topic to refine your conjecture.

ACT 3 ▸ Interpret the Results

7. Did your refined conjecture match the actual answer exactly? If not, what might explain the difference?

1-7

Solving Linear Systems Using Matrices

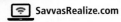 SavvasRealize.com

I CAN... solve systems of equations using matrices.

VOCABULARY
• reduced row echelon form

CRITIQUE & EXPLAIN

Alejandro and Emaan each set up an augmented matrix to represent a system of equations.

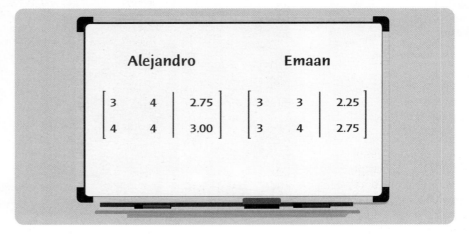

Alejandro
$$\begin{bmatrix} 3 & 4 & | & 2.75 \\ 4 & 4 & | & 3.00 \end{bmatrix}$$

Emaan
$$\begin{bmatrix} 3 & 3 & | & 2.25 \\ 3 & 4 & | & 2.75 \end{bmatrix}$$

A. Write a system of equations that represents each student's matrix.

B. How are Alejandro's and Emaan's matrices alike? How are they different?

C. **Use Structure** Simplify the equation in each system in which the coefficients for *x* and *y* are the same. How does this change your understanding of the two systems of equations? **© MP.7**

? ESSENTIAL QUESTION

How can matrix row operations be used to solve a system of linear equations?

CONCEPT Matrix Row Operations

Row operations can be applied to a matrix to create an equivalent matrix. There are three basic row operations:

Switching rows allows you to switch a row with another row.

$$\begin{bmatrix} a & b & | & c \\ d & e & | & f \end{bmatrix} \rightarrow \begin{bmatrix} d & e & | & f \\ a & b & | & c \end{bmatrix}$$ .... Switch the first row with the second row.

Multiply or divide elements of a row by a nonzero constant.

$$\begin{bmatrix} a & b & | & c \\ d & e & | & f \end{bmatrix} \rightarrow \begin{bmatrix} 3a & 3b & | & 3c \\ \frac{1}{2}d & \frac{1}{2}e & | & \frac{1}{2}f \end{bmatrix}$$ .... Multiply the first row by 3.

Multiply the second row by $\frac{1}{2}$, which is equivalent to dividing by 2.

Add elements of a row to (or **subtract** them from) elements of another row. This produces a new row, which you can use to replace one of the two rows you just combined.

$$\begin{bmatrix} a & b & | & c \\ d & e & | & f \end{bmatrix} \rightarrow \begin{bmatrix} a-d & b-e & | & c-f \\ d & e & | & f \end{bmatrix}$$ .... Subtract the second row from the first row, replacing the first row with the difference.

CONCEPTUAL
UNDERSTANDING

EXAMPLE 1   **Understand Row Operations on a Matrix**

What is the solution of the system of linear equations? $\begin{cases} 3x - 2y = 25 \\ 2x + 5y = 4 \end{cases}$

Solve using equations:	Row operations applied:	Solve using matrices:
$3x - 2y = 25$ $2x + 5y = 4$	Each equation corresponds to a matrix row.	$\begin{bmatrix} 3 & -2 & \vdots & 25 \\ 2 & 5 & \vdots & 4 \end{bmatrix}$
$6x - 4y = 50$ $6x + 15y = 12$	Multiply first row, row_1, by 2 and second row, row_2, by 3.	$\begin{bmatrix} 6 & -4 & \vdots & 50 \\ 6 & 15 & \vdots & 12 \end{bmatrix}$
$0x - 19y = 38$ $2x + 5y = 4$	Replace row_1 with $row_1 - row_2$. Divide row_2 by 3.	$\begin{bmatrix} 0 & -19 & \vdots & 38 \\ 2 & 5 & \vdots & 4 \end{bmatrix}$
$0x + 1y = -2$ $2x + 5y = 4$	Divide row_1 by -19.	$\begin{bmatrix} 0 & 1 & \vdots & -2 \\ 2 & 5 & \vdots & 4 \end{bmatrix}$
$0x - 5y = 10$ $2x + 5y = 4$	Multiply row_1 by -5.	$\begin{bmatrix} 0 & -5 & \vdots & 10 \\ 2 & 5 & \vdots & 4 \end{bmatrix}$
$0x - 5y = 10$ $2x + 0y = 14$	Replace row_2 with $row_1 + row_2$.	$\begin{bmatrix} 0 & -5 & \vdots & 10 \\ 2 & 0 & \vdots & 14 \end{bmatrix}$
$0x + 1y = -2$ $1x + 0y = 7$	Divide row_1 by -5 and row_2 by 2.	$\begin{bmatrix} 0 & 1 & \vdots & -2 \\ 1 & 0 & \vdots & 7 \end{bmatrix}$
$x = 7$ $y = -2$	Switch row_1 and row_2. This form of the matrix allows you to find the values of x and y.	$\begin{bmatrix} 1 & 0 & \vdots & 7 \\ 0 & 1 & \vdots & -2 \end{bmatrix}$

USE STRUCTURE
You have used properties of equality to write equivalent equations. Multiplying both sides of an equation by a constant and subtracting equal quantities from both sides should be familiar. ⓒ **MP.7**

Check that the values $x = 7$ and $y = -2$ satisfy both equations.

$$3x - 2y = 25 \qquad\qquad 2x + 5y = 4$$
$$3(7) - 2(-2) \stackrel{?}{=} 25 \qquad 2(7) + 5(-2) \stackrel{?}{=} 4$$
$$21 + 4 \stackrel{?}{=} 25 \qquad\qquad 14 - 10 \stackrel{?}{=} 4$$
$$25 = 25 \checkmark \qquad\qquad 4 = 4 \checkmark$$

The solution of the system of linear equations is $(7, -2)$.

Try It!   **1.** What is the solution of each system of linear equations?

a. $\begin{cases} 2x - 5y = 11 \\ 4x + 3y = 9 \end{cases}$

b. $\begin{cases} 3x - 4y = -18 \\ -4x + 8y = 32 \end{cases}$

EXAMPLE 2   **Solve a Linear System of Equations Using Matrices**

What is the solution of the linear system of equations?
$$\begin{cases} x + y + 2z = 13 \\ 2y + z = 5 \\ 2x - y = 6 \end{cases}$$

The process of solving a linear system of equations using matrices involves using row operations, as was done in the previous example, to write the matrix in **reduced row echelon form.** In this form, the matrix represents the solutions of the equations in the system.

$$\begin{bmatrix} 1 & 0 & 0 & a \\ 0 & 1 & 0 & b \\ 0 & 0 & 1 & c \end{bmatrix}$$

This is a matrix in reduced row echelon form. It is a 3×3 system with a unique solution.

This matrix translates to an equivalent system of equations that tells you the solution of the system: $\begin{cases} x = a \\ y = b \\ z = c \end{cases}$ You can also write the solution as (a, b, c).

$$\begin{aligned} x + y + 2z &= 13 \\ 0x + 2y + z &= 5 \\ 2x - 1y + 0z &= 6 \end{aligned}$$

First rewrite the equations so the variable terms are aligned.

$$\begin{bmatrix} 1 & 1 & 2 & 13 \\ 0 & 2 & 1 & 5 \\ 2 & -1 & 0 & 6 \end{bmatrix} \begin{matrix} (A) \\ \\ (B) \end{matrix}$$

Write a matrix representation of the system of equations.

To solve a linear system of equations using a matrix, analyze and apply the necessary row operations to transform the matrix into its reduced row echelon form.

$$\begin{bmatrix} 1 & 1 & 2 & 13 \\ 0 & 2 & 1 & 5 \\ 0 & -3 & -4 & -20 \end{bmatrix} \begin{matrix} \\ (C) \\ (D) \end{matrix}$$

(B) − 2(A) becomes (D).

$$\begin{bmatrix} 1 & 1 & 2 & 13 \\ 0 & 2 & 1 & 5 \\ 0 & 5 & 0 & 0 \end{bmatrix} \begin{matrix} \\ \\ (E) \end{matrix}$$

(D) + 4(C) becomes (E).

$$\begin{bmatrix} 1 & 1 & 2 & 13 \\ 0 & 2 & 1 & 5 \\ 0 & 1 & 0 & 0 \end{bmatrix} \begin{matrix} \\ (F) \\ (G) \end{matrix}$$

(E) divided by 5 becomes (G).

$$\begin{bmatrix} 1 & 1 & 2 & 13 \\ 0 & 1 & 0 & 0 \\ 0 & 2 & 1 & 5 \end{bmatrix} \begin{matrix} \\ (H) \\ (I) \end{matrix}$$

Switch (G) and (F). (H) now matches reduced row echelon form.

$$\begin{bmatrix} 1 & 1 & 2 & 13 \\ 0 & 1 & 0 & 0 \\ 0 & 0 & -1 & -5 \end{bmatrix} \begin{matrix} \\ \\ (J) \end{matrix}$$

2(H) − (I) becomes (J).

$$\begin{bmatrix} 1 & 1 & 2 & 13 \\ 0 & 1 & 0 & 0 \\ 0 & 0 & 1 & 5 \end{bmatrix} \begin{matrix} (K) \\ (L) \\ (M) \end{matrix}$$

Multiply (J) by −1. (M) now matches the desired form.

$$\begin{bmatrix} 1 & 0 & 2 & 13 \\ 0 & 1 & 0 & 0 \\ 0 & 0 & 1 & 5 \end{bmatrix} \begin{matrix} (N) \\ \\ (O) \end{matrix}$$

(K) − (L) becomes (N).

$$\begin{bmatrix} 1 & 0 & 0 & 3 \\ 0 & 1 & 0 & 0 \\ 0 & 0 & 1 & 5 \end{bmatrix} \begin{matrix} (P) \\ \\ \end{matrix}$$

(N) − 2(O) becomes (P). The entire matrix now matches the desired form.

STUDY TIP
Keep your goal in mind, and choose row operations that bring you closer to reduced row echelon form. Notice that the first column already matches the goal matrix.

CONTINUED ON THE NEXT PAGE

EXAMPLE 2 CONTINUED

The matrix shows that $x = 3$, $y = 0$, and $z = 5$.

Check the values in the original linear system of equations.

$$x + y + 2z = 13 \qquad\qquad 2y + z = 5 \qquad\qquad 2x - y = 6$$
$$(3) + (0) + 2(5) \overset{?}{=} 13 \qquad 2(0) + (5) \overset{?}{=} 5 \qquad 2(3) - (0) \overset{?}{=} 6$$
$$3 + 0 + 10 \overset{?}{=} 13 \qquad\qquad 0 + 5 \overset{?}{=} 5 \qquad\qquad 6 - 0 \overset{?}{=} 6$$
$$13 = 13 \checkmark \qquad\qquad 5 = 5 \checkmark \qquad\qquad 6 = 6 \checkmark$$

The solution of the linear system of equations is (3, 0, 5).

✅ **Try It!** **2.** What is the solution to each linear system of equations? Write the matrix in reduced row echelon form to solve.

a. $\begin{cases} x + y + z = 13 \\ y - z = 3 \\ z = 2x \end{cases}$
  b. $\begin{cases} x - y + z = 5 \\ 4x - z = 3 \\ y = -1 \end{cases}$

👆 **EXAMPLE 3** **Use Technology With Matrices**

What is the solution of the system of equations? $\begin{cases} x - y = z \\ 4x + 3y + 2z = 6 \\ 2y - x - 3z = 13 \end{cases}$

COMMON ERROR
Be careful with signs when rearranging equations to align like terms.

Start by representing the system of equations as a matrix.

$$\begin{aligned} x - y - z &= 0 \\ 4x + 3y + 2z &= 6 \\ -x + 2y - 3z &= 13 \end{aligned} \longrightarrow \left[\begin{array}{ccc|c} 1 & -1 & -1 & 0 \\ 4 & 3 & 2 & 6 \\ -1 & 2 & -3 & 13 \end{array}\right]$$

This matrix has dimension 3×4. You will need to enter the dimensions into your calculator to get the correct size and number of entries.

MATRIX[A] 3×4

[1	−1	−1	0]
[4	3	2	6]
[−1	2	−3	13]

Use graphing technology with a matrix function to input the system matrix. Sometimes a calculator cannot display the entire matrix on the screen.

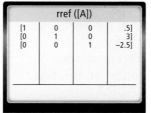

rref ([A])

[1	0	0	.5]
[0	1	0	3]
[0	0	1	−2.5]

Compute the reduced row echelon form (rref) of the matrix using the function rref.

Check your answer by substituting the solution back into the original system of equations:

$\begin{cases} x - y = z \\ 4x + 3y + 2z = 6 \\ 2y - x - 3z = 13 \end{cases}$
$\quad\begin{aligned} 0.5 - 3 &= -2.5 \\ 4(0.5) + 3(3) + 2(-2.5) &= 6 \quad\checkmark \\ 2(3) - 0.5 - 3(-2.5) &= 13 \end{aligned}$

The solution of the system of equations is (0.5, 3, −2.5).

CONTINUED ON THE NEXT PAGE

 Try It!   3. What is the solution of the linear system of equations?

a. $\begin{cases} x + y + z = 55 \\ 2x - y - z = -7 \\ x + 2y - 2z = 10 \end{cases}$
b. $\begin{cases} x + y + z = 1.8 \\ z = 2x + 0.1 \\ 3x + y - z = 0.8 \end{cases}$

Example 4   **Interpret the Reduced Row Echelon Form**

What is the solution of the system of equations?

$$\begin{aligned} 2x + 4y - 6z &= 8 \\ -4x + y + 12z &= -16 \\ x + 0y - 3z &= 4 \end{aligned} \quad \longrightarrow \quad \begin{bmatrix} 2 & 4 & -6 & | & 8 \\ -4 & 1 & 12 & | & -16 \\ 1 & 0 & -3 & | & 4 \end{bmatrix}$$

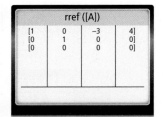

Notice that the output matrix from the rref function on your calculator is

not in the form $\begin{bmatrix} 1 & 0 & 0 & | & x_1 \\ 0 & 1 & 0 & | & y_1 \\ 0 & 0 & 1 & | & z_1 \end{bmatrix}$. The reduced row echelon form of this matrix

represents $\begin{cases} x - 3z = 4 \\ y = 0 \\ 0 = 0 \end{cases}$.

This set of equations has infinitely many solutions. Thinking geometrically, the equations $x - 3z = 4$ and $y = 0$ each represent a plane. The equation $0 = 0$ is true for all points.

The graph shows that the two planes intersect in a line. That means that all three equations are true for every point on this line.

There are infinitely many solutions of this system.

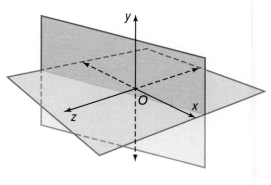

STUDY TIP
The intersection of three planes can be a point, line, or plane. A line or plane has infinitely many points. If the three planes do not intersect, then there are no solutions to the system of equations.

 Try It!   4. What is the solution of each system of equations?

a. $\begin{cases} x - 2y + z = 8 \\ -2x + 4y - 2z = 16 \\ x + 2y - z = -8 \end{cases}$
b. $\begin{cases} 0.9x - 0.3y + 0.6z = 4.2 \\ 2y + 28 = 6x + 4z \\ 3x - y + 2z = 14 \end{cases}$

 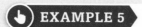

APPLICATION   **EXAMPLE 5**   **Apply a Linear System With Three Variables**

A party planner charges customers based on hours, guests, and tables. A record of the invoices for the last three customers is shown. What is the per unit charge for each element?

J. Powell Birthday	
Hours:	**3**
Guests:	**20**
Tables:	**4**
Total Charges:	**$370**

E. McMann Retirement	
Hours:	**4**
Guests:	**35**
Tables:	**2**
Total Charges:	**$560**

F. Patel Wedding	
Hours:	**6**
Guests:	**75**
Tables:	**16**
Total Charges:	**$1,130**

Formulate ◀   Let h represent the hourly charge, g represent the charge per guest, and t represent the charge per table:

$$\begin{aligned} 3h + 20g + 4t &= 370 \\ 6h + 75g + 16t &= 1{,}130 \\ 4h + 35g + 2t &= 560 \end{aligned} \longrightarrow \begin{bmatrix} 3 & 20 & 4 & 370 \\ 6 & 75 & 16 & 1{,}130 \\ 4 & 35 & 2 & 560 \end{bmatrix}$$

Compute ◀   Use a calculator to determine reduced row echelon form of the 3 × 4 matrix:

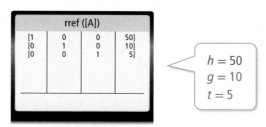

rref ([A])

$$\begin{bmatrix} 1 & 0 & 0 & 50 \\ 0 & 1 & 0 & 10 \\ 0 & 0 & 1 & 5 \end{bmatrix}$$

$h = 50$
$g = 10$
$t = 5$

Check the values in the original system.

$3h + 20g + 4t = 370$	$6h + 75g + 16t = 1{,}130$	$4h + 35g + 2t = 560$
$3(50) + 20(10) + 4(5) \stackrel{?}{=} 370$	$6(50) + 75(10) + 16(5) \stackrel{?}{=} 1{,}130$	$4(50) + 35(10) + 2(5) \stackrel{?}{=} 560$
$150 + 200 + 20 \stackrel{?}{=} 370$	$300 + 750 + 80 \stackrel{?}{=} 1{,}130$	$200 + 350 + 10 \stackrel{?}{=} 560$
$370 = 370 \checkmark$	$1{,}130 = 1{,}130 \checkmark$	$560 = 560 \checkmark$

Interpret ◀   The hourly charge is $50, the charge per guest is $10, and the charge per table is $5.

☑ **Try It!**   **5.** A student has $128 in a savings account. If she were to withdraw the money and was only given one-, five-, and twenty-dollar bills, how many bills of each denomination would she have? Assume she has a total of 28 bills, and she has 3 times as many one-dollar bills as she does five-dollar bills.

CONCEPT SUMMARY Use Matrices to Solve Linear Systems

	WORDS	**NUMBERS**
Switch Rows	You can change the order of the rows in a matrix.	switch row_1 and row_2 $$\begin{bmatrix} 2 & 3 & \vdots & 7 \\ 5 & 2 & \vdots & 9 \end{bmatrix} \rightarrow \begin{bmatrix} 5 & 2 & \vdots & 9 \\ 2 & 3 & \vdots & 7 \end{bmatrix}$$
Multiply Rows by a Nonzero Constant	You can multiply any row by a constant.	$2 \times \text{row}_2$ $$\begin{bmatrix} 2 & 3 & \vdots & 7 \\ 5 & 2 & \vdots & 9 \end{bmatrix} \rightarrow \begin{bmatrix} 2 & 3 & \vdots & 7 \\ 10 & 4 & \vdots & 18 \end{bmatrix}$$
Add or Subtract One Row From Another	You can add any two rows and replace one of those rows with the result.	$\text{row}_1 + \text{row}_2$ replaces row_2 $$\begin{bmatrix} 2 & 3 & \vdots & 7 \\ 5 & 2 & \vdots & 9 \end{bmatrix} \rightarrow \begin{bmatrix} 2 & 3 & \vdots & 7 \\ 7 & 5 & \vdots & 16 \end{bmatrix}$$
Reduced Row Echelon Form	The reduced row echelon form (rref) of a matrix represents the solution to a system of equations.	$$\begin{bmatrix} 1 & 0 & 0 & \vdots & -4 \\ 0 & 1 & 0 & \vdots & 2 \\ 0 & 0 & 1 & \vdots & 7 \end{bmatrix} \rightarrow \begin{cases} x = -4 \\ y = 2 \\ z = 7 \end{cases} \rightarrow (-4, 2, 7)$$

☑ Do You UNDERSTAND?

1. **ESSENTIAL QUESTION** How can matrix row operations be used to solve a system of linear equations?

2. **Vocabulary** The number of rows in a matrix representing a system of equations will be equal to the number of unique variables in the system of equations. True or False? Explain.

3. **Error Analysis** Dwayne was reducing a matrix into reduced row echelon form. He used row operations to get a matrix with a bottom row that was all zeros. He then added the first row to the bottom row to get a 1 in the bottom row. What error did Dwayne make? Ⓖ MP.3

4. **Use Appropriate Tools** Explain how to use technology to find the solution to a system of equations with three variables. Ⓖ MP.5

☑ Do You KNOW HOW?

Solve each system of equations using a matrix.

5. $\begin{cases} -x + 2y = -2 \\ x = 6y \end{cases}$

6. $\begin{cases} 2x + 2y = 50 \\ x + y - z = 0 \\ z = 2y - 5 \end{cases}$

Find the reduced row echelon form of each matrix.

7. $\begin{bmatrix} -3 & 2 & \vdots & 10 \\ 1 & -3 & \vdots & -22 \end{bmatrix}$

8. $\begin{bmatrix} 0 & 2 & 5 & \vdots & 5 \\ 2 & 2 & 1 & \vdots & -1 \\ -1 & 0 & 3 & \vdots & 2 \end{bmatrix}$

9. Find the reduced row echelon form of $\begin{bmatrix} 0 & -1 \\ 1 & 2 \\ 0 & 3 \end{bmatrix}$.

PRACTICE & PROBLEM SOLVING

Scan for Multimedia

Practice   Tutorial

Additional Exercises Available Online

UNDERSTAND

10. **Generalize** Is the series of row operations performed on a matrix to get it into reduced row echelon form unique? Is the reduced row echelon matrix unique? Explain. **Ⓒ MP.8**

11. **Construct Arguments** Would a matrix be useful to calculate the point of intersection of two linear functions $f(x)$ and $g(x)$? Explain your reasoning. **Ⓒ MP.3**

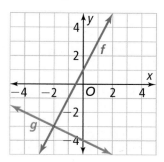

12. **Error Analysis** Dylan used a matrix to solve the system of equations below. What error did Dylan make? **Ⓒ MP.3**

$$\begin{cases} 5x + 4y = 2 \\ y = x + 5 \end{cases}$$

$$\text{rref} \begin{bmatrix} 5 & 4 & | & 2 \\ 1 & 1 & | & 5 \end{bmatrix} = \begin{bmatrix} 1 & 0 & | & -18 \\ 0 & 1 & | & 23 \end{bmatrix}$$

13. **Communicate Precisely** How is the process of using row operations to transform a matrix into rref form similar to the process of performing operations on equations in order to find a solution? **Ⓒ MP.6**

14. **Higher Order Thinking** What would be the result of applying row operations to a matrix representing a system of equations for parallel lines?

15. **Use Appropriate Tools** What characteristics of a system of equations would lead you to use technology to find a reduced row echelon form of a matrix representing the system of equations? **Ⓒ MP.5**

16. **Mathematical Connections** What is a system of two equations with two unknowns that would result in the following matrix in reduced row echelon form?

$$\begin{bmatrix} 1 & 0 & | & 2 \\ 0 & 1 & | & -3 \end{bmatrix}$$

PRACTICE

Solve each linear system of equations as a matrix. SEE EXAMPLES 1 AND 2

17. $\begin{cases} 2x + 3y = 1 \\ -x = 2y + 1 \end{cases}$

18. $\begin{cases} \frac{1}{2}x + y = 4 \\ -\frac{1}{4}x - 2y = -5 \end{cases}$

19. $\begin{cases} x + y + z = 3 \\ -y = x \\ 2z + 3y = 0 \end{cases}$

20. $\begin{cases} z = -4x \\ 2x + y = -3 \\ x - y + z = 5.5 \end{cases}$

Find the reduced row echelon form of each augmented matrix using technology. SEE EXAMPLE 3

21. $\begin{bmatrix} 4 & -1 & | & 8 \\ 0 & 2 & | & 16 \end{bmatrix}$

22. $\begin{bmatrix} 0.25 & 4 & | & 8 \\ 2 & 6 & | & 12 \end{bmatrix}$

23. $\begin{bmatrix} -1 & 1 & -2 & | & 18 \\ 3 & 0 & -1 & | & 0 \\ 0 & 6 & 3 & | & 6 \end{bmatrix}$

24. $\begin{bmatrix} 1 & 1 & 1 & | & 17 \\ 1 & 0 & 1 & | & 1 \\ 1 & -1 & 1 & | & 3 \end{bmatrix}$

Solve each system of equations using technology with matrices. SEE EXAMPLE 4

25. $\begin{cases} 2x + 2y + 2z = 4 \\ -x - y - z = -2 \\ 4z = -4x - 4y + 8 \end{cases}$

26. $\begin{cases} 2x - 2y - 4z = 8 \\ 8x - 8y - 4z = 4 \\ -2x + 2y + 4z = -3 \end{cases}$

27. Write a matrix to represent the system of equations showing the relationships between angles of the triangle. Then use technology to find the reduced row echelon form of the matrix and identify the measures of each angle. SEE EXAMPLES 5

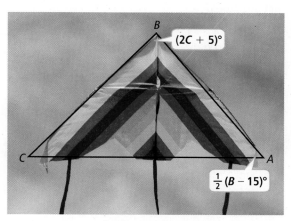

$$\begin{cases} A + B + C = 180 \\ B = 2C + 5 \\ 2A = B - 15 \end{cases}$$

PRACTICE & PROBLEM SOLVING

APPLY

28. Reason Talisha receives a $25 gift card to a digital application store. Each game download costs $3, and each song download costs $1. Talisha downloads 1 more song than games and uses all of the $25. How many of each application did Talisha download? Ⓒ **MP.2**

29. Model With Mathematics Noemi, Ines, Deondra, and Carla attend a concert. Noemi purchases 2 posters, 1 shirt, and 1 CD for $35. Ines purchases 1 shirt, 1 poster, and 2 CDs for $43. Deondra purchases 2 shirts and 1 poster for $34. How much will Carla pay if she buys the items shown? Ⓒ **MP.4**

$??? $???

30. Make Sense and Persevere An art supply store orders a total of 80 items of a single color at a time. Colored pencils cost the store $0.75 each, markers cost $2.50 each, and acrylic paints cost $4.00 each. The store budgets $161.25 per color. The matrix below represents the store manager's information for ordering blue art supplies.

$$\begin{bmatrix} 1 & 1 & 1 & \vdots & 80 \\ 0.75 & 2.5 & 4 & \vdots & 161.25 \\ 0 & 1 & -2 & \vdots & 0 \end{bmatrix}$$

$4.00 each

$0.75 each

$2.50 each

What is the relationship between the number of markers and the number of acrylic paints, based on the third row of the matrix? Ⓒ **MP.1**

ASSESSMENT PRACTICE

31. Complete the table to write matrix A in reduced row echelon form.

$$A = \begin{bmatrix} 2 & 3 & -1 & \vdots & -6 \\ -1 & 2 & 3 & \vdots & -5 \\ 3 & 4 & 2 & \vdots & -4 \end{bmatrix}$$

1	0	0	
0	1	0	
0	0	1	

32. SAT/ACT Which matrix represents the reduced row echelon form of matrix X?

$$X = \begin{bmatrix} 2 & 1 & \vdots & -1 \\ 1 & -5 & \vdots & -4 \end{bmatrix}$$

Ⓐ $\begin{bmatrix} 1 & 0 & | & \frac{9}{11} \\ 0 & 1 & | & -\frac{7}{11} \end{bmatrix}$ Ⓒ $\begin{bmatrix} 1 & 0 & | & \frac{7}{11} \\ 0 & 1 & | & -\frac{9}{11} \end{bmatrix}$

Ⓑ $\begin{bmatrix} 1 & 0 & | & -\frac{9}{11} \\ 0 & 1 & | & \frac{7}{11} \end{bmatrix}$ Ⓓ $\begin{bmatrix} 1 & 0 & | & -\frac{7}{11} \\ 0 & 1 & | & \frac{9}{11} \end{bmatrix}$

33. Performance Task The triangle has a perimeter of 30 cm, and y is twice the length of x.

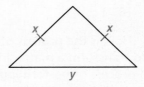

Part A Write a system of equations to represent this situation.

Part B Write a matrix to represent the system of equations you wrote in part (a).

Part C Find the reduced row echelon form of the matrix you wrote in part (b).

Part D What does the third column of the matrix you found in part (c) represent?

Topic Review

? TOPIC ESSENTIAL QUESTION

1. What are different ways in which functions can be used to represent and solve problems involving quantities?

Vocabulary Review

Choose the correct term to complete each sentence.

2. The _____ pairs every input in an interval with the same output value.

3. The point at which a function changes from increasing to decreasing is the _____ of the function.

4. A _____ of a function $y = af(x - h) + k$ is a change made to at least one of the values a, h, and k.

5. A _____ is the value of x when $y = 0$.

6. A _____ is defined by two or more functions, each over a different interval.

- step function
- piecewise-defined function
- minimum
- maximum
- system of linear equations
- transformation
- zero of the function

Concepts & Skills Review

LESSON 1-1 ▶ Key Features of Functions

Quick Review

The domain of a function is the set of input values, or x-values. The range of a function is the set of output values, or y-values. These sets can be described using **interval notation** or **set-builder notation**.

A y-intercept is a point on the graph of a function where $x = 0$. An x-intercept is a point on the graph where $y = 0$. An x-intercept may also be a **zero of a function**.

Example

Find the zeros of the function. Then determine over what domain the function is positive or negative.

The point where the line crosses the x-axis is $(1, 0)$, so $x = 1$ is a zero of the function. The function is positive on the interval $(-\infty, 1)$ and negative on the interval $(1, \infty)$.

Practice & Problem Solving

Identify the domain and range of the function in interval notation. Find the zeros of the function. Then determine for which values of x the function is positive and for which it is negative.

7.

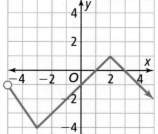

8.

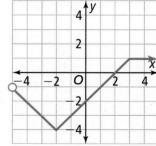

9. **Use Structure** Sketch a graph given the following key features. © **MP.7**

   domain: $(-5, 5)$; decreasing: $(-3, 1)$; x-intercepts: -4, -2; positive: $(-4, -2)$

10. **Communicate Precisely** Jeffrey is emptying a 50 ft³ container filled with water at a rate of 0.5 ft³/min. Find and interpret the key features for this situation. © **MP.6**

Quick Review

There are different types of **transformations** that change the graph of the parent function. A **translation** shifts each point on a graph the same distance and direction. A **reflection** maps each point to a new point across a given line. A **stretch** or a **compression** increases or decreases the distance between the points of a graph and a given line by the same factor.

Example

Graph the parent function $f(x) = |x|$ and $g(x) = -|x + 2| - 1$. Describe the transformation.

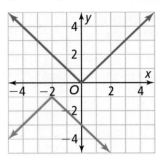

Multiplying the absolute value expression by -1 indicates a reflection over the x-axis.

Adding 2 to x indicates a translation 2 units to the left and subtracting 1 from the absolute value expression indicates a translation 1 unit down.

So the graph of g is a reflection of the graph of the parent function f over the x-axis, and then a translation 2 units left and 1 unit down.

Practice & Problem Solving

Graph each function as a translation of its parent function, f.

11. $g(x) = |x| - 7$ **12.** $g(x) = x^2 + 5$

Graph the function, g, as a reflection of the graph of f across the given axis.

13. across the x-axis   **14.** across the y-axis

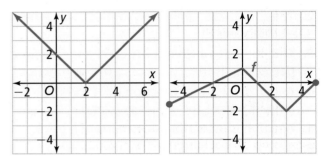

15. Look for Relationships Describe the effect of a vertical stretch by a factor greater than 1 on the graph of the absolute value function. How is that different from the effect of a horizontal stretch by the same factor? ⓒ **MP.7**

16. Use Structure Graph the function that is a vertical stretch by a factor of 3.5 of the parent function $f(x) = |x|$. ⓒ **MP.7**

17. Use Structure Graph the function that is a horizontal translation 1 unit to the right of the parent function $f(x) = x^2$. ⓒ **MP.7**

Piecewise-Defined Functions

Quick Review

A **piecewise-defined function** is a function defined by two or more function rules over different intervals. A **step function** pairs every number in an interval with a single value. The graph of a step function can look like the steps of a staircase.

Example

Graph the function.

$$y = \begin{cases} -3, \text{ if } -5 \leq x < -2 \\ x + 1, \text{ if } -2 < x < 2 \\ -x + 2, \text{ if } 2 \leq x < 5 \end{cases}$$

State the domain and range. Identify whether the function is increasing, constant, or decreasing on each interval of the domain.

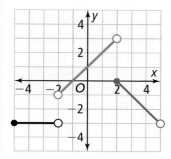

Graph the function.

Domain: $-5 \leq x < -2$ and $-2 < x < 5$

Range: $-3 \leq y < 3$

Increasing when $-2 < x < 3$

Constant when $-5 < x < -2$

Decreasing when $2 < x < 5$

Practice & Problem Solving

Graph each function.

18. $y = \begin{cases} -3, \text{ if } -4 \leq x < -2 \\ -1, \text{ if } -2 \leq x < 0 \\ 1, \text{ if } 0 \leq x < 2 \\ 3, \text{ if } 2 \leq x < 4 \end{cases}$

19. $y = \begin{cases} 2x + 5, \text{ if } x < -3 \\ -x - 2, \text{ if } -3 \leq x < 1 \\ x - 3, \text{ if } x \geq 1 \end{cases}$

20. What rule defines the function in the following graph?

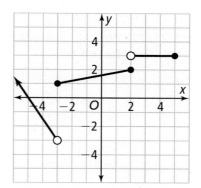

21. **Generalize** Can every transformation of the absolute value function also be written as a piecewise-defined function? Explain. Ⓒ **MP.8**

22. **Model With Mathematics** A coach is trying to decide how many new uniforms to purchase for a softball team. If the coach orders more than 10 uniforms, the cost for the extra uniforms is 0.75 times the normal cost per uniform of $120. Write a piecewise-defined function that gives the cost C, in dollars, in terms of the number of uniforms n the coach purchases. Determine how much the coach will pay for 18 uniforms. Ⓒ **MP.4**

LESSON 1-4   Arithmetic Sequences and Series

Quick Review

An **arithmetic sequence** is a sequence with a constant difference between consecutive terms. This difference is known as the **common difference**.

recursive definition: $a_n = \begin{cases} a_1, & \text{if } n = 1 \\ a_{n-1} + d, & \text{if } n > 1 \end{cases}$

explicit definition: $a_n = a_1 + (n - 1)d$

A **finite arithmetic series** is the sum of all the numbers in an arithmetic sequence.

Example

Given the sequence 22, 17, 12, 7, ..., write the explicit formula. Then find the 6th term.

$d = -5$ ·················· Find the common difference.

$a_n = 22 + (n - 1)(-5)$ ····· Substitute 22 for a_1 and -5 for d.

$a_n = 22 - 5(n - 1)$ ········· Simplify.

$a_6 = 22 - 5(6 - 1)$ ········· Substitute 6 for n.

$a_6 = -3$ ················· Solve for the 6th term.

Practice & Problem Solving

What is the common difference and the next term in the arithmetic sequence?

23. 3, 15, 27, 39, ...   **24.** 19, 13, 7, 1, ...

What are the recursive and explicit functions for each sequence?

25. 5, 9, 13, 17, 21, ...   **26.** 25, 18, 11, 4, −3, ...

Find the sum of an arithmetic sequence with the given number of terms and values of a_1 and a_n.

27. 8 terms, $a_1 = 2$, $a_8 = 74$

28. 12 terms, $a_1 = 87$, $a_{12} = 10$

What is the value of each of the following series?

29. $\sum_{n=1}^{9} (1 + 3n)$ **30.** $\sum_{n=1}^{6} (5n - 2)$

31. Make Sense and Persevere Cubes are stacked in the shape of a pyramid. The top row has 1 cube, the second row has 3, and the third row has 5. If there are 9 rows of cubes, how many cubes were used to make the front of the pyramid? **Ⓒ MP.1**

LESSON 1-5   Solving Equations and Inequalities by Graphing

Quick Review

To solve an equation by graphing, write two new equations by setting y equal to each expression in the original equation. Approximate coordinates of any points of intersection. The x-values of these points are the solutions to the equation. You can also solve equations using tables or graphing technology.

Example

Solve $|x + 3| - 5 = \frac{1}{2}x - 2$ by graphing.

Graph $y = |x + 3| - 5$ and $y = \frac{1}{2}x - 2$.

It appears that $x = -4$ and $x = 0$ are solutions.

Confirm the solutions by substituting into the original equation.

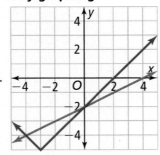

Practice & Problem Solving

Use a graph to solve each equation.

32. $-x + 2 = x^2$ **33.** $\frac{1}{4}|x + 3| = 2$

Use a graph to solve each inequality.

34. $x^2 + 2x - 3 > 0$ **35.** $x^2 - 7x - 8 < 0$

36. Construct Arguments Is graphing always the most convenient method for solving an equation? Why or why not? **Ⓒ MP.3**

37. Model With Mathematics A truck is traveling 30 mi ahead of a car at an average rate of 55 mph. The car is traveling at a rate of 63 mph. Let x represent the number of hours that the car and truck travel. Write an inequality to determine at what times the car will be ahead of the truck and graph the inequality to solve. **Ⓒ MP.4**

Quick Review

A **system of linear equations** is a set of two or more equations using the same variables. The **solution of a system of linear equations** is the set of all ordered coordinates that simultaneously make all equations in the system true. A **system of linear inequalities** is a set of two or more inequalities using the same variables.

Example

Solve the system. $\begin{cases} -4x + 4y = 16 \\ -x + 2y = 10 \end{cases}$

$x = 2y - 10$ ················· Solve the second equation for x.

$-4(2y - 10) + 4y = 16$ ····· Substitute $2y - 10$ for x. Solve
$y = 6$ for y.

$x = 2(6) - 10$ ············ Substitute 6 for y in the
$x = 2$ equation $x = 2y - 10$.

Practice & Problem Solving

Solve each system of equations.

38. $\begin{cases} y = 2x + 5 \\ 2x + 4y = 10 \end{cases}$ **39.** $\begin{cases} y = 2x - 6 \\ 6x + y = 10 \end{cases}$

40. Use Structure Write a linear system in two variables that has infinitely many solutions. Ⓒ **MP.7**

41. Model With Mathematics It takes Leo 12 h to make a table and 20 h to make a chair. In 8 wk, Leo wants to make at least 5 tables and 8 chairs to display in his new shop. Leo works 40 h a week. Write a system of linear inequalities relating the number of tables x and the number of chairs y Leo will be able to make. List two different combinations of tables and chairs Leo could have to display at the opening of his new shop. Ⓒ **MP.4**

Quick Review

You can solve systems with matrices. A matrix is a rectangular array of numbers, usually shown inside square brackets. Row operations can be applied to a matrix to create an equivalent matrix and can be used to write the matrix in **reduced row echelon form**.

Example

Solve the system $\begin{cases} -2x + 8y = 10 \\ 4x - 3y = 6 \end{cases}$ **using a matrix.**

$\begin{bmatrix} -2 & 8 & | & 10 \\ 4 & -3 & | & 6 \end{bmatrix}$ ······· Write the system in matrix form.

$\begin{bmatrix} 1 & -4 & | & -5 \\ 4 & -3 & | & 6 \end{bmatrix}$ ······· Divide row$_1$ by -2.

$\begin{bmatrix} 1 & -4 & | & -5 \\ 0 & 13 & | & 26 \end{bmatrix}$ ······· Multiply row$_1$ by -4, and add to row$_2$.

$\begin{bmatrix} 1 & -4 & | & -5 \\ 0 & 1 & | & 2 \end{bmatrix}$ ······· Divide row$_2$ by 13.

$\begin{bmatrix} 1 & 0 & | & 3 \\ 0 & 1 & | & 2 \end{bmatrix}$ ······· Multiply row$_2$ by 4, and add to row$_1$.

The solution to the system of linear equations is $x = 3$ and $y = 2$.

Practice & Problem Solving

42. Write the matrix that represents the system of equations and find the reduced row echelon form. $\begin{cases} 4x + 8y = 12 \\ -2x - 6y = 32 \end{cases}$

43. Write a system of equations represented by the matrix. $\begin{bmatrix} 5 & 2 & | & 6 \\ 6 & -7 & | & -4 \end{bmatrix}$

44. Communicate Precisely Why is it important to write equations in standard form before entering the coefficients into a matrix? Ⓒ **MP.6**

45. Model With Mathematics A trivia game consists of three types of questions in three different colors: red, white, and blue. Each type of question is worth a different number of points. Holly answered 4 red, 1 white, and 1 blue question correctly and earned 23 points. Jung answered 5 white and 1 blue question correctly and earned 35 points. Rochelle answered 2 red and 3 white questions, and earned 19 points. How many points is each color worth? Ⓒ **MP.4**

TOPIC 2

Quadratic Functions and Equations

? TOPIC ESSENTIAL QUESTION

How do you use quadratic functions to model situations and solve problems?

Topic Overview

Topic Vocabulary

- completing the square
- complex conjugates
- complex number
- discriminant
- imaginary number
- imaginary unit i
- parabola
- Quadratic Formula
- quadratic function
- standard form of a quadratic function
- vertex form of a quadratic function
- Zero Product Property

Digital Experience

 INTERACTIVE STUDENT EDITION Access online or offline.

 ACTIVITIES Complete *Explore & Reason, Model & Discuss,* and *Critique & Explain* activities. Interact with Examples and Try Its.

 ANIMATION View and interact with real-world applications.

 PRACTICE Practice what you've learned.

 Go online | **SavvasRealize.com**

▶ Swift Kick

Whether you call it soccer, football, or fùtbol, it's the most popular sport in the world by far. Even if you don't play soccer, you probably know several people who do.

There are many ways to kick a soccer ball: you can use any part of either foot. If you want the ball to end up in the goal, you also need to try different amounts of spin and power. You'll see one person's effort in the Mathematical Modeling in 3-Acts lesson.

▶ **VIDEOS** Watch clips to support *Mathematical Modeling in 3 Acts Lessons* and **enVision™ STEM Projects.**

CONCEPT SUMMARY Review key lesson content through multiple representations.

☑ **ASSESSMENT** Show what you've learned.

A-Z **GLOSSARY** Read and listen to English and Spanish definitions.

TUTORIALS Get help from *Virtual Nerd*, right when you need it.

🔧 **MATH TOOLS** Explore math with digital tools and manipulatives.

enVision™ STEM

Video

Did You Know?

Cameras and RADAR precisely track everything that happens in a professional baseball game, including the speed and launch angle of every batted ball.

If a baseball player hits a **90-mph** pitch with more than **8,000 pounds of force**, the ball leaves the bat at a speed of 110 mph.

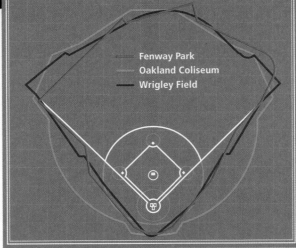

- — Fenway Park
- — Oakland Coliseum
- — Wrigley Field

Each baseball park has **unique features** that help determine whether a hit will be a home run.

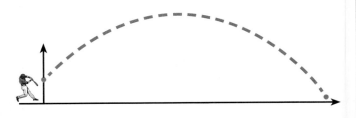

You can model the flight of a hit baseball with a **parabola**. The initial vertical and horizontal speed of the ball can be found using **right triangle trigonometry** and the **launch angle of the hit**.

▶ Your Task: Hit a Home Run

You and your classmates will design a ballpark and determine what it would take to hit a home run at that park.

© Common Core State Standards HSA.CED.A.2, HSF.BF.B.3, HSF.IF.B.4, MP.1, MP.3, MP.7

2-1

Vertex Form of a Quadratic Function

 SavvasRealize.com

I CAN... identify key features of quadratic functions.

VOCABULARY

- parabola
- quadratic function
- vertex form of a quadratic function

👆 EXPLORE & REASON

The table represents $A(x)$, the area of a square as a function of side length x units, where x is a positive real number.

Side Length (units)	x	1	2	3	4
Model					
Area (sq. units)	$A(x)$	1	4	9	16

A. Consider the function where the areas in the table are doubled. Write the equation of a function that represents this.

B. Look for Relationships Graph the ordered pairs for both $A(x)$ and your new function. How would you describe the differences in the locations of these points? **© MP.7**

C. Find the equation for a function whose x-values are the same as $A(x)$ but whose y-values are 2 units greater than each y-value in $A(x)$.

❓ ESSENTIAL QUESTION

How does the equation of a quadratic function in vertex form highlight key features of the function's graph?

CONCEPT Representations of Quadratic Functions

A function is a **quadratic function** if its equation can be written in the form $f(x) = ax^2 + bx + c$, with $a \neq 0$.

All quadratic functions are transformations of the parent function defined by $f(x) = x^2$.

The graph of a quadratic function is called a **parabola**.

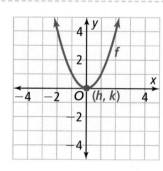

The **vertex form of a quadratic function** is $f(x) = a(x - h)^2 + k$ where (h, k) is the vertex of the parabola. Vertex form is useful because it highlights the vertex of the graph of the quadratic function.

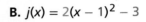

CONCEPTUAL
UNDERSTANDING ▶ 👆 **EXAMPLE 1** **Transform a Quadratic Function**

How are transformations of the graph of $f(x) = x^2$ related to an equation representing another quadratic function?

Vertex form shows three different ways in which the graph of the function $f(x) = x^2$ may be transformed.

$$f(x) = a(x - h)^2 + k$$

The value of a determines the direction the parabola opens and whether the graph is stretched or compressed.

The value of h determines the horizontal translation.

The value of k determines the vertical translation.

A. $g(x) = -\frac{1}{2}(x + 2)^2$

The equation shows that the graph is to be translated 2 units left, will open downward, and will be vertically compressed.

B. $j(x) = 2(x - 1)^2 - 3$

The equation shows that the graph is to be translated 1 unit right, vertically stretched, down 3 units. It will open upward.

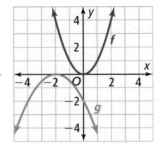

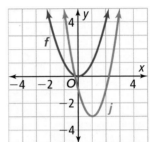

STUDY TIP
Recall that a vertical stretch makes the graph narrower and that a vertical compression makes the graph wider. To see the effects easily, use the same axes or units for all graphs.

When $a > 0$ the parabola opens upward. When $a < 0$, the parabola opens downward. When $|a| > 1$, the graph is stretched, and when $0 < |a| < 1$, the graph is compressed.

 Try It! **1.** Describe the transformations of the parent function $f(x) = x^2$. Then graph the function.

    a. $g(x) = -(x + 2)^2$ **b.** $g(x) = (x - 1)^2 + 2$

👆 **EXAMPLE 2** **Determine Key Features of a Quadratic Function**

What are the key features of the quadratic function $f(x) = 2(x - 3)^2 + 4$?

The graph represents $f(x) = 2(x - 3)^2 + 4$.

The 2 indicates that the graph opens upward and is vertically stretched.

The range is $y \geq 4$. There are no restrictions on the value of x, so the domain is all real numbers.

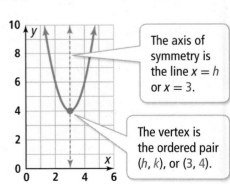

The axis of symmetry is the line $x = h$ or $x = 3$.

The vertex is the ordered pair (h, k), or $(3, 4)$.

 Try It! **2.** Identify the vertex, axis of symmetry, minimum or maximum, domain, and range of the function $f(x) = -(x + 4)^2 - 5$.

EXAMPLE 3   Write an Equation of a Parabola

What is the equation of a quadratic function with vertex (−2, 3) and y-intercept −1?

Step 1 Substitute the coordinates of the vertex for h and k in the vertex form of a quadratic function.

$(h, k) = (-2, 3)$, so $y = a(x - (-2))^2 + 3$

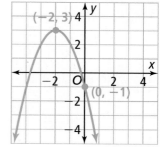

COMMON ERROR
Be careful to not switch the coordinate values when substituting them into the equation.

Step 2 Substitute the values of x and y from the y-intercept, and then solve for a.

$(x, y) = (0, -1)$, so $-1 = a(0 + 2)^2 + 3$

$-4 = a(2)^2$

$-4 = 4a$

$a = -1$

Step 3 Substitute the value of a into the vertex form of a quadratic function.

$a = -1$ so $y = -(x + 2)^2 + 3$

The equation of the parabola is $y = -(x + 2)^2 + 3$.

✓ **Try It!**   **3.** What is the equation of a parabola with a vertex of (1, −4) and which passes through (−2, −1)?

APPLICATION

EXAMPLE 4   Write an Equation of a Parabola Given the Graph

The height of a thrown ball is a quadratic function of the time it has been in the air. The graph of the quadratic function is the parabolic path of the ball. The vertex of the graph is (1, 20) and the path of the ball includes the point (0, 4). What is an expression that defines this function? Write the quadratic equation in vertex form and in the form $y = ax^2 + bx + c$.

$y = ax^2 + bx + c$

LOOK FOR RELATIONSHIPS
By converting vertex form into standard form, you can see how h and k relate to the coefficients of the equation. ⓒ MP.7

$y = a(x - h)^2 + k$

$4 = a(0 - 1)^2 + 20$

$4 = a(-1)^2 + 20$

$4 = a + 20$

$-16 = a$

> Find a by substituting the vertex and a given point.

$y = -16(x - 1)^2 + 20$

$y = -16(x^2 - 2x + 1) + 20$

$y = -16x^2 + 32x + 4$

The equation of the parabola in vertex form is $y = -16(x - 1)^2 + 20$.

In the form $y = ax^2 + bx + c$, the equation is $y = -16x^2 + 32x + 4$.

CONTINUED ON THE NEXT PAGE

EXAMPLE 4 CONTINUED

☑ **Try It!** **4.** The graph shows the height of the flying disk with respect to time. What is the equation of the function? Write the equation in vertex form. Then write the equation in the form $y = ax^2 + bx + c$.

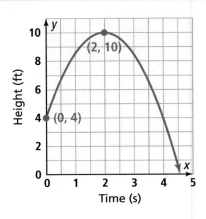

 EXAMPLE 5 ▶ **Write an Equation of a Transformed Function**

The function g is a translation of the parent function f 1 unit left and 3 units up. What is the equation of g? Write the quadratic equation in vertex form and in the form $f(x) = ax^2 + bx + c$.

Translate the graph of $f(x)$ left 1 unit to locate the graph of $f(x + 1)$, then translate the graph of $f(x + 1)$ up 3 units to locate the graph of $f(x + 1) + 3$.

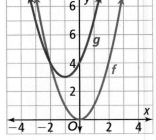

$g(x) = f(x + 1) + 3$

$g(x) = a(x + 1)^2 + 3$

From the graph, the point (0, 4) appears to be on g. Use the point (0, 4) to find a.

$4 = a(0 + 1)^2 + 3$

$4 = a + 3$

$1 = a$

Substituting $a = 1$, the equation is

$g(x) = a(x + 1)^2 + 3$

$g(x) = (x + 1)^2 + 3$

$g(x) = x^2 + 2x + 1 + 3$

$g(x) = x^2 + 2x + 4$

In vertex form, $g(x) = (x + 1)^2 + 3$ and in the form $y = ax^2 + bx + c$, the equation is $g(x) = x^2 + 2x + 4$.

☑ **Try It!** **5.** What is the equation of j? Write the equation in vertex form and in the form $y = ax^2 + bx + c$.

   a. Let j be a quadratic function whose graph is a translation 2 units right and 5 units down of the graph of f.

   b. Let j be a quadratic function whose graph is a reflection of the graph of f in the x-axis followed by a translation 1 unit down.

Go Online | SavvasRealize.com

CONCEPT SUMMARY Vertex Form of a Quadratic Function

WORDS ▸ The graph of a quadratic function is called a parabola.

A quadratic function can be represented by an equation in vertex form $y = a(x - h)^2 + k$. Vertex form shows the different ways in which the graph of the parent function $f(x) = x^2$ can be transformed.

ALGEBRA ▸ $f(x) = x^2$
vertex $(0, 0)$
axis of symmetry $x = 0$
opens upward
minimum $y = 0$
domain $(-\infty, \infty)$
range $[0, \infty)$

$y = a(x - h)^2 + k$
$a \neq 0$
vertex (h, k)
axis of symmetry $x = h$
domain: $(-\infty, \infty)$

If $a > 0$:
opens upward
minimum $y = k$
range: $[k, \infty)$

if $a < 0$:
opens downward
maximum $y = k$
range: $(-\infty, k]$

NUMBERS ▸ $g(x) = -\frac{1}{2}(x + 2)^2 + 3$
vertex $(-2, 3)$
axis of symmetry $x = -2$
opens downward
maximum $y = 3$
domain $(-\infty, \infty)$
range $(-\infty, 3]$

GRAPH ▸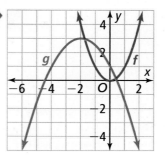

Do You UNDERSTAND?

1. **ESSENTIAL QUESTION** How does the equation of a quadratic function in vertex form highlight key features of the function's graph?

2. **Error Analysis** Given the function $g(x) = (x + 3)^2$, Martin says the graph should be translated right 3 units from the parent graph $f(x) = x^2$. Explain his error. ⒸMP.3

3. **Vocabulary** What shape does a quadratic function have when graphed?

4. **Communicate Precisely** How are the graphs of $f(x) = x^2$ and $g(x) = -(x + 2)^2 - 4$ related? ⒸMP.6

Do You KNOW HOW?

Describe the transformation of the parent function $f(x) = x^2$.

5. $g(x) = -(x + 5)^2 + 2$

6. $h(x) = (x + 2)^2 - 7$

Write the equation of each parabola in vertex form.

7. Vertex: $(-3, 7)$; Point: $(-2, -5)$

8. Vertex: $(1, 3)$; Point: $(2, 5)$

9. Vertex: $(-4, 6)$; Point: $(-2, -2)$

10. Vertex: $(7, 4)$; Point: $(5, 16)$

UNDERSTAND

11. Use Structure The graph of the function $f(x) = x^2$ will be translated 3 units up and 1 unit left. What is the resulting function $g(x)$? Ⓒ **MP.7**

12. Error Analysis A classmate said that the vertex of $g(x) = -5(x + 2)^2 - 4$ is (2, 4). Is your classmate correct? If not, what is the correct vertex? Ⓒ **MP.3**

13. Higher Order Thinking The graph below is a transformation of the graph of the parent function. Write the quadratic function to model the graph.

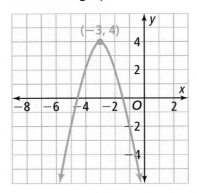

14. Construct Arguments Explain why the graph of the equation $g(x) = -(x + 1)^2 - 3$ would be a parabola opening downward. Ⓒ **MP.3**

15. Use Structure Amaya is standing 30 ft from a volleyball net. The net is 8 ft high. Amaya serves the ball. The path of the ball is modeled by the equation $y = -0.02(x - 18)^2 + 12$, where x is the ball's horizontal distance in feet from Amaya's position and y is the distance in feet from the ground to the ball.

a. How far away is the ball from Amaya when it is at its maximum height? Explain.

b. Describe how you would find the ball's height when it crosses the net at $x = 30$. Ⓒ **MP.7**

PRACTICE

Describe the transformation of the parent function $f(x) = x^2$. Then graph the transformed function. SEE EXAMPLE 1

16. $f(x) = (x - 1)^2 + 3$ **17.** $y = (x + 1)^2 - 3$

18. $g(x) = 2x^2$ **19.** $f(x) = -(x - 1)^2 + 7$

20. $y = -2(x + 1)^2 + 1$ **21.** $f(x) = \frac{1}{2}(x - 2)^2 + 3$

Identify the vertex, axis of symmetry, maximum or minimum, domain, and range of each function. SEE EXAMPLE 2

22. $y = 2(x - 2)^2 + 5$ **23.** $f(x) = -(x - 1)^2 + 2$

24. $g(x) = -(x + 4)^2$ **25.** $y = \frac{1}{3}(x + 2)^2 - 1$

Write the equation of each parabola in vertex form. SEE EXAMPLE 3

26. Vertex: (1, 2); Point: (2, −5)

27. Vertex: (3, 6); y-intercept: 2

28. Vertex: (0, 5); Point: (1, −2)

Write the equation of the function represented by the parabola in vertex form and in the form $y = ax^2 + bx + c$. SEE EXAMPLE 4

29.

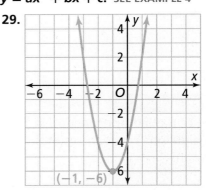

Write the equation $g(x)$ in vertex form of a quadratic function for the transformations given the function $f(x) = x^2$. SEE EXAMPLE 5

30. Let $g(x)$ be the function whose graph is a translation 4 units left and 1 unit up of the graph of $f(x)$.

31. Let $g(x)$ be the function whose graph is a reflection in the x-axis and translated 3 units right of the graph of $f(x)$.

32. Look for Relationships The height, in inches, that a person can jump while wearing a pair of jumping shoes is based on the time, x, in seconds, from the start of the jump. Beth is testing out Max Jumps and Jumpsters to determine which shoes she likes better. Compare the maximum heights on the two sets of shoes. © MP.7

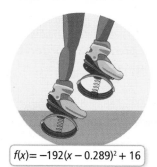

| $f(x) = -192(x - 0.289)^2 + 16$ | $g(x) = -192(x - 0.445)^2 + 38$ |

33. Make Sense and Persevere Find three additional points on the parabola that has vertex (1, −2) and passes through (0, −5). © MP.1

34. Make Sense and Persevere The curvature of the Tacoma Narrows Bridge in Washington is in the shape of a parabola.

$f(x) = -0.016 (x - 52.5)^2 + 45$

In the given function, x represents the horizontal distance (in meters) from the arch's left end and $f(x)$ represents the distance (in meters) from the base of the arch. What is the width of the arch? © MP.1

35. Model With Mathematics An object is thrown from a height of 5 in. After 2 s, the object reaches a maximum height of 9 in., and then it lands back on the ground 5 s after it was thrown. Write the vertex form of the quadratic equation that models the object's path, and draw the graph. © MP.4

36. The graph of $g(x) = 3(x - 2)^2$ is a transformation of the graph of $f(x) = x^2$. Are the following transformations of f that map to g? Select *yes* or *no*.

	Yes	No
Translation left	❑	❑
Translation right	❑	❑
Translation up	❑	❑
Translation down	❑	❑
Vertical Compression	❑	❑
Vertical Stretch	❑	❑

37. SAT/ACT Which of the following functions represents a parabola with a vertex at (−3, 4) and that passes through the point (−1, −4)?

Ⓐ $f(x) = x^2 - 5$

Ⓒ $f(x) = 2(x + 1)^2 - 4$

Ⓑ $f(x) = -2(x + 3)^2 + 4$

Ⓓ $f(x) = 2(x - 3)^2 - 32$

38. Performance Task The Bluebird Bakery sells more cookies when it lowers its prices, but this also changes profits.

$0.75 each
40¢ ea.

The profit function for the cookies is $f(x) = -500(x - 0.45)^2 + 400$. This function represents the profit earned when the price of a cookie is x dollars. The bakery wants to maximize their profits.

Part A What is the domain of the function?

Part B Find the daily profits for selling cookies for $0.40 each and for $0.75 each.

Part C What price should the bakery charge to maximize their profits from selling cookies?

Part D What is the maximum profit?

2-2

Standard Form of a Quadratic Function

SavvasRealize.com

I CAN... write and graph quadratic functions in standard form.

VOCABULARY
• standard form of a quadratic function

👆 CRITIQUE & EXPLAIN

Jordan and Emery are rewriting the vertex form of the quadratic function $y = 2(x - 4)^2 + 5$ in the form $y = ax^2 + bx + c$.

Jordan	Emery
$y = 2(x - 4)^2 + 5$	$y = 2(x - 4)^2 + 5$
$= (2x - 8)^2 + 5$	$= 2(x^2 - 16) + 5$
$= 4x^2 - 32x + 64 + 5$	$= 2x^2 - 32 + 5$
$= 4x^2 - 32x + 69$	$= 2x^2 - 27$

A. Communicate Precisely Did Jordan rewrite the equation correctly? Did Emery? Explain. © **MP.6**

B. Without rewriting the equation, how could you prove that Jordan or Emery's equations are not equivalent to the original?

❓ ESSENTIAL QUESTION

What key features can you determine about a quadratic function from an equation in standard form?

CONCEPTUAL UNDERSTANDING

👆 **EXAMPLE 1** Find the Vertex of a Quadratic Function in Standard Form

How can you find the vertex of a quadratic function written in standard form?

A. What is the x-coordinate of the vertex of $f(x) = ax^2 + bx + c$?

The **standard form of a quadratic function** is $y = ax^2 + bx + c$ where a, b, and c are real numbers, and $a \neq 0$. Use vertex form to derive standard form.

LOOK FOR RELATIONSHIPS
By converting vertex form into standard form, you can see how h and k relate to the coefficients of the equation. © **MP.7**

$y = a(x - h)^2 + k$ .... Write the vertex form of a quadratic equation.

$y = a(x^2 - 2xh + h^2) + k$ .... Square the binomial.

$y = ax^2 - 2ahx + ah^2 + k$ .... Simplify.

The equation $y = ax^2 - 2ahx + ah^2 + k$ is a *quadratic function* in standard form with $a = a$, $b = -2ah$, and $c = ah^2 + k$.

The vertex of a quadratic function is (h, k), so to determine the x-coordinate of the vertex, solve $b = -2ah$ for h.

$b = -2ah$

$-\dfrac{b}{2a} = h$

> Since h is the x-coordinate of the vertex, you can use this value to find the y-value, k, of the vertex.

B. What is the vertex of the function $f(x) = x^2 - 6x + 10$?

Step 1 Identify the coefficients a, b, and c.

$a = 1$, $b = -6$, and $c = 10$

Step 2 Solve for h, the x-coordinate of the vertex.

$h = -\dfrac{b}{2a} = -\dfrac{(-6)}{2(1)} = 3$

CONTINUED ON THE NEXT PAGE

EXAMPLE 1 CONTINUED

Step 3 **Substitute the value of *h* into the equation for *x* to find *k*, the *y*-coordinate of the vertex.**

$$f(3) = (3)^2 - 6(3) + 10$$
$$= 9 - 18 + 10$$
$$= 1$$

The vertex of the function is $(h, k) = (3, 1)$.

✓ **Try It!** **1.** What is the vertex of the graph of the function $f(x) = x^2 - 8x + 5$?

👆 **EXAMPLE 2** **Graph a Quadratic Function in Standard Form**

How can you use key features to graph $f(x) = x^2 - 4x + 8$?

For $f(x)$, identify *a*, *b*, and *c*: $a = 1$, $b = -4$, and $c = 8$.

Step 1 **Find the vertex and the axis of symmetry of the quadratic function.**

The *x*-coordinate of the vertex and the axis of symmetry can be determined by:

$$h = -\frac{b}{2a} = -\frac{(-4)}{2(1)} = 2$$

Substitute the value of *h* for *x* into the equation to find the *y*-coordinate of the vertex, *k*:

$$f(2) = (2)^2 - 4(2) + 8 = 4$$

The vertex is (2, 4), and the axis of symmetry is $x = 2$.

Step 2 **Find the y-intercept of the quadratic function.**

The *y*-intercept occurs at

$$f(0) = (0)^2 - 4(0) + 8 = 8.$$

> If the *y*-intercept is the same as the vertex, choose a different point here.

USE STRUCTURE

The *y*-intercept of a quadratic function in standard form is given by the ordered pair (0, *c*). Verify this by substituting $x = 0$ into the standard form equation. ⓒ **MP.7**

Step 3 **Find a point symmetric to the y-intercept across the axis of symmetry.**

Since (0, 8) is a point on the parabola 2 units to the left of the axis of symmetry, $x = 2$, (4, 8) will be a point on the parabola 2 units to the right of the axis of symmetry.

Step 4 **Sketch the graph.**

Once you have three points associated with the quadratic function, you can sketch the parabola based on your knowledge of its general shape.

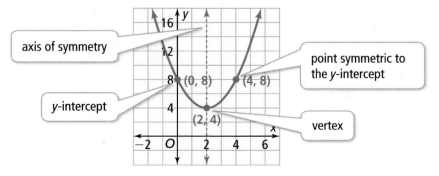

✓ **Try It!** **2.** Use the key features to graph the function $f(x) = x^2 - 6x - 1$.

APPLICATION   👆 **EXAMPLE 3**   Interpret the Graph of a Quadratic Function

The graph of the function $f(x) = -10x^2 + 700x - 6,000$ shows the profit a company earns for selling headphones at different prices. What is the maximum profit the company can expect to earn?

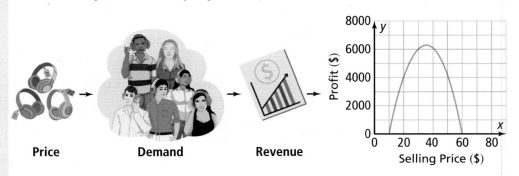

Price   Demand   Revenue

Formulate ◀   The x-axis shows selling price and the y-axis shows the profit. The maximum y-value of the profit function occurs at the vertex of its parabola. Find the vertex of the parabola.

Compute ◀   Use the function to find the x- and y-coordinates of the vertex.

Find the x-coordinate of the vertex.

$h = -\dfrac{b}{2a}$ ⋯⋯⋯⋯⋯ Use the formula to find the x-coordinate of the vertex.

$h = -\dfrac{700}{2(-10)}$ ⋯⋯⋯⋯ Substitute -10 for a and 700 for b.

$h = 35$ ⋯⋯⋯⋯⋯⋯ Simplify.

> **COMMON ERROR**
> Be careful with the negative signs; there is a negative in the formula and a negative value for a.

Find the y-coordinate of the vertex.

$y = -10x^2 + 700x - 6,000$ ⋯⋯⋯⋯ Write the original function.

$y = -10(35)^2 + 700(35) - 6,000$ ⋯⋯⋯ Substitute 35 for x.

$y = 6,250$ ⋯⋯⋯⋯⋯⋯⋯⋯⋯ Simplify.

The vertex is (35, 6,250).

Interpret ◀   The selling price of $35 per item gives the maximum profit of $6,250.

 Try It!   **3.** A water balloon was thrown from a window. The height of the water balloon over time can be modeled by the function $y = -16x^2 + 160x + 50$. What was the maximum height of the water balloon after it was thrown?

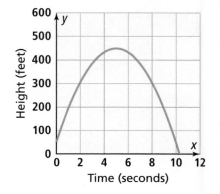

👆 **EXAMPLE 4**   **Write the Equation of a Parabola Given Three Points**

What is the equation of a parabola that passes through the points (−2, 32), (1, 5), and (3, 17)?

Step 1 Write three equations by substituting the given x- and y-values into the standard form of a parabola equation, $y = ax^2 + bx + c$.

(−2, 32) $32 = a(-2)^2 + b(-2) + c$

(1, 5) $5 = a(1)^2 + b(1) + c$
            $5 = 1a + 1b + c$

(3, 17) $17 = a(3)^2 + b(3) + c$
            $17 = 9a + 3b + c$

$$\begin{cases} 32 = 4a - 2b + c \\ 5 = 1a + 1b + c \\ 17 = 9a + 3b + c \end{cases}$$

STUDY TIP
You can also solve a linear system of three equations in three variables by hand, using elimination or substitution.

Step 2 Solve the system.

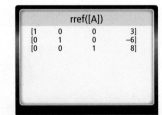

So the solution to the system is $a = 3$, $b = -6$, and $c = 8$.

Step 3 Substitute 3 for a, −6 for b, and 8 for c in the standard form of a quadratic equation.

$$y = 3x^2 - 6x + 8$$

Step 4 Confirm that the graph of the equation passes through the three given points.

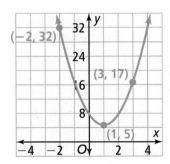

 Try It!   **4. What is the equation of a parabola that passes through the points (2, −12), (−1, −15), and (−4, −90)?**

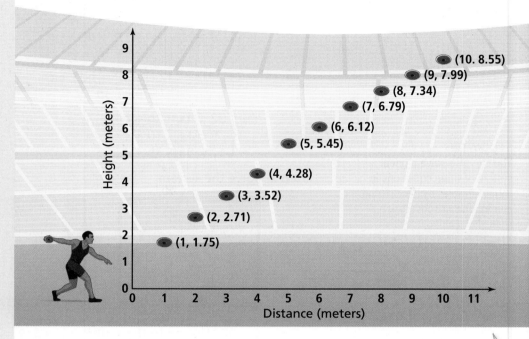

👆 EXAMPLE 5   Use Quadratic Regression

Esteban is training for the discus throw. His coach recorded the horizontal distance and height of one of Esteban's discus throws. The graph shows the horizontal distance the discus traveled, in meters, and the height of the discus, in meters. What will be the height of the discus when it has traveled 15 meters from Esteban?

Use graphing technology to perform quadratic regression with the data.

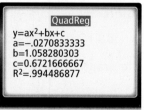

QuadReg
$y = ax^2 + bx + c$
$a = -.0270833333$
$b = 1.058280303$
$c = 0.6721666667$
$R^2 = .994486877$

The data show the discus only rising, but the model will resemble a parabola as the discus returns to the ground.

COMMON ERROR
Remember that once you use a regression equation, you are approximating values. Regression is used to make predictions, not to find exact values of variables.

$y \approx -0.027x^2 + 1.058x + 0.672$ ·········· Write the regression model.

$y \approx -0.027(15)^2 + 1.058(15) + 0.672$ ·········· Substitute 15 for x.

$y \approx 10.467$ ·········· Simplify.

Based on this model, when the discus is 15 meters away from Esteban, it will be at a height of approximately 10.5 meters.

✅ Try It!   5.

A fan threw a souvenir football into the air from the top of the bleachers toward the bottom of the bleachers. The table shows the height of the football, in feet, above the ground at various times, in seconds. If the football was not touched by anyone on its way to the ground, about how long did it take the football to reach the ground after it was thrown?

Time (s)	0	0.2	0.4	0.6	0.8	1.0
Height (ft)	10	11.76	12.24	11.44	9.36	6.0

CONCEPT SUMMARY Standard Form of a Quadratic Function

STANDARD FORM

$y = ax^2 + bx + c$

$y = -2x^2 - 8x + 1$

KEY FEATURES

Vertex x-coordinate of vertex: $h = -\dfrac{b}{2a}$

Substitute h for x and solve for y to find the y-coordinate of the vertex.

$h = -\dfrac{(-8)}{2(-2)} = -2$

$y = -2(-2)^2 - 8(-2) + 1$

$= -8 + 16 + 1$

$= 9$

The vertex is $(-2, 9)$.

Axis of Symmetry $x = -\dfrac{b}{2a}$

$x = -2$

y-intercept $(0, c)$

$(0, 1)$

GRAPHS

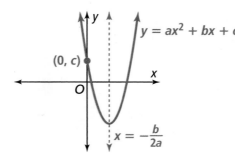

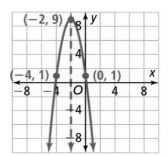

✓ Do You UNDERSTAND?

1. **? ESSENTIAL QUESTION** What key features can you determine about a quadratic function from an equation in standard form?

2. **Error Analysis** Cameron said that the y-intercept of a quadratic function always tells the maximum value of that function. Explain Cameron's error. © MP.3

3. **Vocabulary** Write a quadratic function in standard form.

4. **Make Sense and Persevere** Why do you need at least three points to graph a quadratic function when not given an equation? © MP.1

Do You KNOW HOW?

Find the vertex and y-intercept of the quadratic function.

5. $y = 3x^2 - 12x + 40$
6. $y = -x^2 + 4x + 7$

For 7 and 8, find the maximum or minimum of the parabola.

7. $y = -2x^2 - 16x + 20$
8. $y = x^2 + 12x - 15$

9. Find the equation in standard form of the parabola that passes through the points $(0, 6)$, $(-3, 15)$, and $(-6, 6)$.

Graph the parabola.

10. $y = 3x^2 + 6x - 2$

11. $y = -2x^2 + 4x + 1$

UNDERSTAND

12. Construct Arguments Devin found the parabola that fits the three points in the table to be $y = 0.345x^2 - 0.57x - 2.78$. Is Devin correct? Explain. ⓒ **MP.3**

x	−4	0.6	9
y	5	−3	20

13. Generalize How can you find the maximum or minimum value of a quadratic function? ⓒ **MP.8**

14. Higher Order Thinking The quadratic function whose graph is shown represents a cereal bowl. Its equation is $y = 0.32x^2 - 1.6x + 2$. Describe how you could use the function to find the diameter of the cereal bowl if you know its depth.

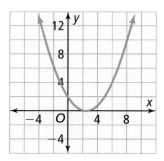

15. Error Analysis Micah found the vertex for the function $y = -9.5x^2 - 47.5x + 63$ as shown.

$$x = -\frac{b}{2a}$$

$$x = -\frac{47.5}{2(-9.5)}$$

$$x = -\frac{47.5}{-19}$$

$$x = -(-2.5)$$

$$x = 2.5$$

$$y = -9.5(2.5)^2 - 47.5(2.5) + 63$$

$$y = -59.375 - 118.75 + 63$$

$$y = -115.125$$

Find and correct Micah's error. ⓒ **MP.3**

PRACTICE

Find the vertex of each parabola. SEE EXAMPLE 1

16. $y = -x^2 + 6x + 30$

17. $y = 3x^2 + 12x - 5$

Find the vertex and y-intercept of the quadratic function, and use them to graph the function. SEE EXAMPLES 1 AND 2

18. $y = -x^2 + 6x - 8$ **19.** $y = x^2 - 8x + 11$

20. $y = 3x^2 + 18x + 10$ **21.** $y = -2x^2 - 12x - 5$

22. A rocket is launched into the air. The path of the rocket is modeled by the equation $y = -10x^2 + 160x - 100$. What is the maximum height reached by the rocket, in feet? SEE EXAMPLE 3

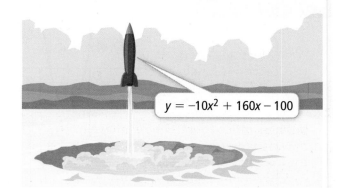

$y = -10x^2 + 160x - 100$

Write the equation of a quadratic function in standard form for the parabola that passes through the given points. SEE EXAMPLE 4

23. (−1, 5), (4, 0), (5, −7)

24. (−2, 2), (1, 8), (4, 50)

Use quadratic regression to find the equation of a quadratic function that fits the given points. SEE EXAMPLE 5

25.

x	0	0.5	1	1.5	2
y	35	36	29	14	−9

APPLY

26. Model With Mathematics The height of Amelia's mid-section was measured three times during a long jump.

Time in seconds, x	0	0.5	1
Height in meters, y	0.7	1.5	0.55

$h = 1.5$ meters

Write the equation of a quadratic function that describes Amelia's height as a function of time. Ⓒ **MP.4**

27. Make Sense and Persevere A college's business office found the relationship between the number of admissions counselors they employ and the college's profit from tuition could be modeled by the function $y = -10x^2 + 1,500x - 35,000$. Ⓒ **MP.1**

a. Graph the function.

b. How many admissions counselors should the college employ to maximize its profit?

c. What is the maximum amount of profit the college can make?

28. Mathematical Connections A rectangular tile has a perimeter of 48 inches.

a. The graph shows the relationship between the **width** of the tile and the **area** of the tile. What function describes this relationship?

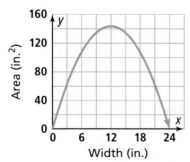

b. What is the maximum area? What length and width give the maximum area?

29. Consider the quadratic function $y = 5x^2 - 50x - 100$. Which of the following are true? Select all that apply.

Ⓐ Its vertex is (5, −225).

Ⓑ Its y-intercept is (0, 100).

Ⓒ It passes through the point (−1, −45).

Ⓓ The minimum height occurs when $x = 5$.

Ⓔ The maximum height occurs when $x = 5$.

30. SAT/ACT Which quadratic equation contains the three points (−4, 12), (2, 42), and (3, 40)?

Ⓐ $y = -x^2 + 3x + 42$

Ⓑ $y = 1.7x^2 - 10x - 55.2$

Ⓒ $y = -1.7x^2 + 10x + 55.2$

Ⓓ $y = x^2 - 3x - 40$

Ⓔ $y = -x^2 + 3x + 40$

31. Performance Task A diver jumped from a diving platform. The image shows her height above the water at several different times after leaving the platform.

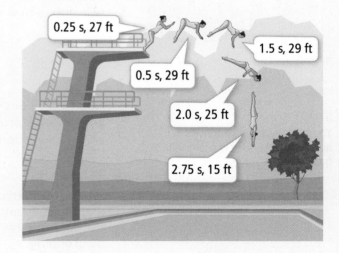

0.25 s, 27 ft

0.5 s, 29 ft

1.5 s, 29 ft

2.0 s, 25 ft

2.75 s, 15 ft

Part A Find the equation of the quadratic function that describes the relationship between the diver's time and height. Round to the nearest tenth.

Part B How high is the platform the diver jumped from? What is the maximum height reached?

Part C From the maximum height, how long does it take the diver to get halfway down? Which part of the dive is faster, from the top to the halfway point, or from the halfway point to the water? Explain.

I CAN... find the zeros of quadratic functions.

VOCABULARY
• Zero Product Property

Common Core State Standards HSA.SSE.A.2, HSA.SSE.B.3.A, HSA.APR.B.3, MP.1, MP.3, MP.7

 Activity   Assess

CRITIQUE & EXPLAIN

Corey wrote an equation in factored form, $y = (x + 8)(x - 2)$, to represent a quadratic function. Kimberly wrote the equation $y = x^2 + 6x - 16$, and Joshua wrote the equation $y = (x + 3)^2 - 25$.

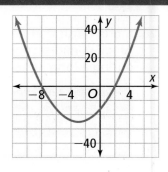

A. Reason Do all three equations represent the same function? If not, whose is different? Explain algebraically. © **MP.2**

B. How else could you determine if all three equations represent the same function?

C. What information can Corey's form help you find that is more difficult to find using Kimberly's or Joshua's form?

ESSENTIAL QUESTION

How is the factored form helpful in solving quadratic equations?

 EXAMPLE 1 Factor a Quadratic Expression

Factor the expression.

A. $x^2 + 7x + 12$

Recall that using the Distributive Property, $(x + m)(x + n) = x^2 + (m + n)x + mn$.

$$x^2 + 7x + 12$$

| $m + n$ | mn |

Add factor pairs of 12 to find the numbers that add to 7. The numbers 3 and 4 have a product of 12 and a sum of 7. Therefore, the factored form of the expression $x^2 + 7x + 12$ is $(x + 3)(x + 4)$.

B. $2x^2 - 5x - 3$

When the leading coefficient is not 1, multiply the leading coefficient and the constant. Look for factors of this product that add to the middle coefficient. Rewrite the middle term using these factors, then factor by grouping.

$2x^2 - 5x - 3$ ⟵ The factors of −6 that have a sum of −5 are 1 and −6.

$2x^2 + x - 6x - 3$ ⟵ Rewrite −5x as x − 6x.

$x(2x + 1) - 3(2x + 1)$

$(2x + 1)(x - 3)$

The factored form of the expression $2x^2 - 5x - 3$ is $(2x + 1)(x - 3)$.

> **STUDY TIP**
> You can check your work by multiplying the factors using the Distributive Property.

Try It! **1.** Factor the expression.

a. $x^2 - 9$ **b.** $3x^2 - 7x + 2$

CONCEPTUAL UNDERSTANDING

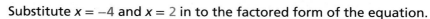 **EXAMPLE 2** Relate Factors to Zeros of a Function

The graph shows the function defined by $y = x^2 + 2x - 8$. How do the zeros of the function relate to the factors of the expression $x^2 + 2x - 8$?

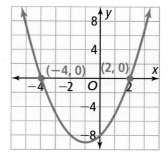

The expression $x^2 + 2x - 8$ can be represented as a product of two factors. The factors of -8 that have a sum of 2 are 4 and -2.

$$y = x^2 + 2x - 8 \qquad \rightarrow \qquad y = (x + 4)(x - 2)$$

The x-intercepts of the graph are -4 and 2, so the zeros of the function are $x = -4$ and $x = 2$.

Substitute $x = -4$ and $x = 2$ in to the factored form of the equation.

$$y = (-4 + 4)(-4 - 2) = 0(-6) = 0$$
$$y = (2 + 4)(2 - 2) = 6(0) = 0$$

The factors, $(x + 4)$ and $(x - 2)$, are related to the zeros $x = -4$ and $x = 2$ since each of the zeros makes one of the factors 0.

Try It! **2.** The graph shows the function $y = x^2 - 9x + 20$. Identify the zeros of the function. How do the zeros relate to the factors of $x^2 - 9x + 20$?

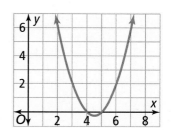

CONCEPT Zero Product Property

The **Zero Product Property** states that if a product of real-number factors is 0, then at least one of the factors must be 0.

In the case of two factors, if $ab = 0$, then either $a = 0$ or $b = 0$, or both.

To use the Zero Product Property, rewrite the equation so that it is an expression equal to 0, then factor and solve.

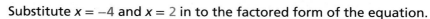 **EXAMPLE 3** Solve Quadratic Equations by Factoring

Solve the equation.

A. $x^2 + x = 42$

$$x^2 + x - 42 = 0 \quad \cdots\cdots\cdots\cdots\cdots\cdots \text{Set equation equal to 0.}$$

$$(x + 7)(x - 6) = 0 \quad \cdots\cdots\cdots\cdots\cdots \text{Factor.}$$

$$x + 7 = 0 \quad \text{or} \quad x - 6 = 0 \quad \cdots\cdots\cdots \text{Use the Zero Product Property.}$$

$$x = -7 \quad \text{or} \quad x = 6 \quad \cdots\cdots\cdots \text{Solve.}$$

CONTINUED ON THE NEXT PAGE

MAKE SENSE AND PERSEVERE
If you can write an expression in factored form, you can find the value of the variable that makes each factor 0. These values are the zeros of the function. **MP.1**

EXAMPLE 3 CONTINUED

B. $2x^2 = -9x + 5$

$2x^2 + 9x - 5 = 0$ .... Rewrite as equation equal to 0.

$2x^2 - x + 10x - 5 = 0$ .... Factor by grouping.

$x(2x - 1) + 5(2x - 1) = 0$

$(x + 5)(2x - 1) = 0$

$x + 5 = 0$ or $2x - 1 = 0$ .... Use the Zero Product Property.

$x = -5$ or $x = \dfrac{1}{2}$ .... Solve.

> **STUDY TIP**
> Check your work algebraically, by plugging the solutions in to the original equation. Or check graphically by confirming that your solutions are the *x*-intercepts of the graph.

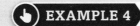 **Try It!** **3.** Solve the equation by factoring.

  a. $x^2 + 8x = 20$ **b.** $2x^2 = 3x + 2$

APPLICATION   **EXAMPLE 4**   **Find the Zeros of a Quadratic Function**

A multilevel driving range has three levels. Marco hits golf balls from the second level, which is 32 ft high. The height of a ball *x* seconds after Marco hits it is modeled by the function $h(x) = -16x^2 + 16x + 32$. When does the ball hit the ground?

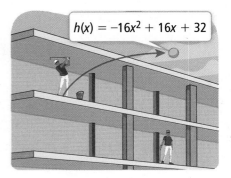

$h(x) = -16x^2 + 16x + 32$

The ball hits the ground when the height, $h(x)$, is 0.

$0 = -16x^2 + 16x + 32$ ..... Substitute 0 for $h(x)$.

$0 = -16(x^2 - x - 2)$ .... Factor out the GCF, -16.

$0 = -16(x + 1)(x - 2)$ ..... Factor.

$x + 1 = 0$ or $x - 2 = 0$ ... Use the Zero Product Property.

$x = -1$ or $x = 2$ .... Solve.

> **COMMUNICATE PRECISELY**
> Zeros of the function
> $h(x) = -16x^2 + 16x + 32$
> are solutions of the equation
> $0 = -16x^2 + 16x + 32$. Ⓒ **MP.6**

The zeros of the function are at $x = -1$ and $x = 2$.

Since time has to be positive, $x = 2$ is the only solution that makes sense.

This means that after 2 seconds, the golf ball will hit the ground.

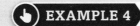 **Try It!** **4.** A baseball is thrown from the upper deck of a stadium, 128 ft above the ground. The function $h(x) = -16x^2 + 32x + 128$ gives the height of the ball *x* seconds after it is thrown. How long will it take the ball to reach the ground?

EXAMPLE 5   Determine Positive or Negative Intervals

Identify the interval(s) on which the function $y = x^2 - 2x - 3$ is positive.

The y-values of a quadratic function can only turn from positive to negative or from negative to positive when the graph crosses the x-axis. Find the zeros of the function to identify these points.

$$0 = x^2 - 2x - 3 \quad \text{..........} \quad \text{Set expression equal to 0.}$$
$$0 = (x - 3)(x + 1) \quad \text{..........} \quad \text{Factor.}$$
$$x - 3 = 0 \quad \text{or} \quad x + 1 = 0 \quad \text{..........} \quad \text{Zero Product Property}$$
$$x = 3 \quad \text{or} \quad x = -1 \quad \text{..........} \quad \text{Solve.}$$

Two zeros create three intervals. Choose an x-value to test in each interval. Substitute the x-value into the original expression to determine if the corresponding y-value is positive or negative.

LOOK FOR RELATIONSHIPS
The sign of the y-value of the test point is the same as for the y-value of any other point over the entire interval you are testing. ⒸⒸ **MP.7**

$x < -1$	$-1 < x < 3$	$x > 3$
Choose $x = -3$. $(-3)^2 - 2(-3) - 3$ $= 9 + 6 - 3$ $= 12$	Choose $x = 1$. $(1)^2 - 2(1) - 3$ $= 1 - 2 - 3$ $= -4$	Choose $x = 6$. $(6)^2 - 2(6) - 3$ $= 36 - 12 - 3$ $= 21$
Positive	Negative	Positive

Graph the function to verify where the function is positive or negative.

The function is positive when the graph is above the x-axis, or on the intervals $x < -1$ and $x > 3$.

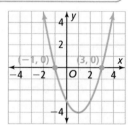

Try It!   **5.** Identify the interval(s) on which the function $y = x^2 - 4x - 21$ is negative.

EXAMPLE 6   Write the Equation of a Parabola in Factored Form

Write an equation of a parabola with x-intercepts at $(-2, 0)$ and $(-1, 0)$ and which passes through the point $(-3, 20)$.

$$y = a(x - p)(x - q) \quad \text{..........} \quad \text{Write the general form of a factored equation.}$$
$$y = a(x - (-2))(x - (-1)) \quad \text{..........} \quad \text{Substitute} -1 \text{ and } -2 \text{ for zeros.}$$
$$y = a(x + 2)(x + 1) \quad \text{..........} \quad \text{Simplify.}$$
$$20 = a(-3 + 2)(-3 + 1) \quad \text{..........} \quad \text{Substitute} -3 \text{ for } x \text{ and } 20 \text{ for } y.$$
$$20 = 2a \quad \text{..........} \quad \text{Simplify.}$$
$$10 = a \quad \text{..........} \quad \text{Solve.}$$
$$y = 10(x + 2)(x + 1) \quad \text{..........} \quad \text{Subsitute } 10 \text{ for } a.$$

COMMON ERROR
If $x = -2$ is an x-intercept, then $x + 2$ is the factor, not $x - 2$.

Try It!   **6.** Write an equation of a parabola with x-intercepts at $(3, 0)$ and $(-3, 0)$ and which passes through the point $(1, 2)$.

CONCEPT SUMMARY Factored Form of a Quadratic Function

FACTORED FORM $y = ax^2 + bx + c$ can be written as $0 = a(x - p)(x - q)$, where p and q are the zeros of the function. The x-intercepts of the graph correspond to the zeros of the function. Two zeros denote 3 intervals of x values.

GRAPH For the function $y = 2x^2 + 3x - 14$, write the equation $0 = 2x^2 + 3x - 14$ in factored form to identify the zeros.

$0 = 2x^2 + 3x - 14$

$0 = (2x + 7)(x - 2)$

The zeros of the function are $x = -\frac{7}{2}$ and $x = 2$.

intervals where function values are positive:
$x < -\frac{7}{2}$, and $x > 2$

interval where function values are negative: $-\frac{7}{2} < x < 2$

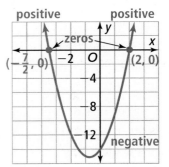

✅ Do You UNDERSTAND?

1. **ESSENTIAL QUESTION** How is the factored form helpful in solving quadratic equations?

2. **Error Analysis** Amir says the graph of $y = x^2 + 16$ has -4 as a zero. Is Amir correct? Explain. **ⓒ MP.3**

3. **Vocabulary** How does the factored form of a quadratic equation relate to the Zero Product Property?

4. **Generalize** How does knowing the zeros of a function help determine where a function is positive? **ⓒ MP.8**

Do You KNOW HOW?

Factor each expression.

5. $x^2 - 5x - 24$ 6. $5x^2 + 3x - 2$

Solve each equation.

7. $x^2 = 12x - 20$ 8. $4x^2 - 5x = 6$

9. The height, in feet, of a t-shirt launched from a t-shirt cannon high in the stands at a football stadium is given by $h(x) = -16x^2 + 64x + 80$, where x is the time in seconds after the t-shirt is launched. How long will it take before the t-shirt reaches the ground?

PRACTICE & PROBLEM SOLVING

UNDERSTAND

10. Generalize Can you write the equation of a quadratic function knowing its zeros and its non-zero y-intercept? If so, describe the process. If not, explain why. ⒸMP.8

11. Error Analysis Describe and correct the error a student made in solving a quadratic equation. ⒸMP.3

$$0 = 2x^2 + 7x + 5$$
$$0 = 2x^2 + 2x + 5x + 5$$
$$0 = 2x(x + 1) + 5(x + 1)$$
$$0 = 2x, 0 = x + 1, 0 \neq 5$$
$$0 = x, -1 = x$$
✗

12. Model With Mathematics Use the graph of the function to write the equation in factored form. ⒸMP.4

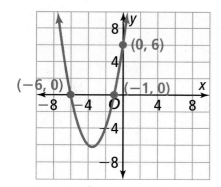

13. Generalize For what values of x is the expression $(x - 4)^2 > 0$? ⒸMP.8

14. Error Analysis A student says that the zeros of $y = (x - 2)(x + 7)$ are -2 and 7. Is the student correct? If not, describe and correct the error the student made. ⒸMP.3

15. Construct Arguments Explain why $x^2 + 25$ is not equal to $(x + 5)^2$. ⒸMP.3

16. Mathematical Connections Describe how factoring can help you find the x-intercepts of the graph of the quadratic function $y = x^2 - 4x + 3$.

PRACTICE

Factor each quadratic expression. SEE EXAMPLE 1

17. $x^2 - 3x - 10$ **18.** $3x^2 - 5x - 12$

19. $x^2 + 15x + 56$ **20.** $2x^2 + 7x - 15$

21. $3x^2 - 18x - 48$ **22.** $4x^2 - 11x - 3$

23. What are the zeros of the quadratic function $y = 3(x - 5)(x + 4)$? SEE EXAMPLE 2

Solve each quadratic equation. SEE EXAMPLE 3

24. $x^2 - 5x - 14 = 0$ **25.** $x^2 = 5x - 6$

26. $3x^2 - 60 = 3x$ **27.** $5x^2 + 12x = 9$

28. $4x^2 + 3x - 7 = 0$ **29.** $6x^2 = 5x + 6$

30. A penny is dropped from the top of a new building. Its height in feet can be modeled by the equation $y = 256 - 16x^2$, where x is the time in seconds since the penny was dropped. How long does it take for the penny to reach the ground? SEE EXAMPLE 4

Identify the interval(s) on which each quadratic function is positive. SEE EXAMPLE 5

31. $y = x^2 + 9x + 18$ **32.** $y = x^2 + 2x - 8$

33. $y = x^2 - 5x - 24$ **34.** $y = -x^2 + 4x + 12$

35. $y = 2x^2 + 12x + 18$ **36.** $y = 5x^2 - 3x - 8$

Write an equation for each parabola. SEE EXAMPLE 6

37. A parabola with x-intercepts at $(-1, 0)$ and $(3, 0)$ which passes through the point $(1, -8)$

38. A parabola with x-intercepts at 0 and 1 and which passes through the point $(2, -2)$

39. A snorkeler dives for a shell on a reef. After entering the water, the diver descends $\frac{11}{3}$ ft in one second. Write an equation that models the diver's position with respect to time.

APPLY

40. Make Sense and Persevere Rectangular apartments are 12 ft longer than they are wide. Each apartment has 1,053 ft² of floor space. What are the dimensions of an apartment? Explain. ⓒ **MP.1**

41. Use Structure The height of a drone, in meters, above its launching platform that is 5 m above the ground, is modeled by $y = 0.1x^2 - 1.5x + 5$, where x is the time in seconds. The drone leaves the launch pad, flies down into a canyon, and then it flies back up again. ⓒ **MP.7**

$y = 0.1x^2 - 1.5x + 5$

a. What is the factored form of the equation for the height of the drone?

b. After how many seconds will the drone be at ground level?

c. After how many seconds will the drone come back to the height of its platform?

42. Higher Order Thinking LaTanya is designing a rectangular garden with a uniform walkway around its border. LaTanya has 140 m² of material to build the walkway.

a. Write an equation for the dimensions of the garden and the surrounding walkway.

b. How wide is the walkway? Explain.

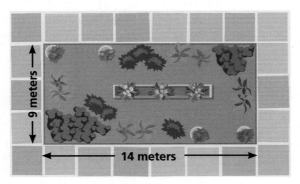

9 meters

14 meters

43. Which of the following are solutions to the equation $-11x = 2x^2 + 15$? Select all that apply.

Ⓐ -5 Ⓓ $\frac{5}{2}$

Ⓑ -3 Ⓔ 3

Ⓒ $-\frac{5}{2}$ Ⓕ 5

44. SAT/ACT What is the sum of the zeros of the function $y = x^2 - 9x - 10$?

Ⓐ -10 Ⓑ -9 Ⓒ 0 Ⓓ 9 Ⓔ 10

45. Performance Task A pumpkin is launched from the ground into the air and lands 4.5 s later.

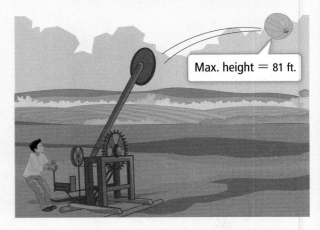

Max. height = 81 ft.

Part A Write a quadratic function that models the height, in feet, of the pumpkin x seconds after it is launched. Explain how you found the function.

Part B A second pumpkin is launched from the ground. After 1 second, it is 64 feet high. The pumpkin lands after 5 seconds. What is the maximum height of the pumpkin? Explain.

2-4

Complex Numbers and Operations

SavvasRealize.com

I CAN... solve problems with complex numbers.

VOCABULARY

• complex conjugates
• complex number
• imaginary number
• imaginary unit i

EXPLORE & REASON

A math class played a game called "Solve It, You're Out." At the start of each round, students chose a card from a deck marked with integers from −5 to 5. When an equation is shown, any student whose card states the solution to the equation is eliminated. Five students remain.

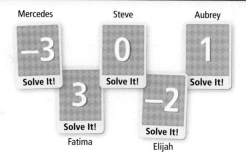

Mercedes Steve Aubrey
−3 0 1
Solve It! Solve It! Solve It!
3 −2
Solve It! Solve It!
Fatima Elijah

A. The next equation presented was $x^2 = 9$. Which student(s) was eliminated? Explain.

B. Construct Arguments In the next round, the equation presented was $x^2 = -4$. Elijah thought he was eliminated, but this is not the case. Explain why Elijah was incorrect. © **MP.3**

C. What is true about solutions to $x^2 = a$ when a is a positive number? When a is a negative number? What about when $a = 0$?

? **ESSENTIAL QUESTION**   How can you represent and operate on numbers that are not on the real number line?

EXAMPLE 1   Solve a Quadratic Equation Using Square Roots

How can you use square roots to solve each equation?

A. $x^2 = 16$

Notice that each side of the equation involves a perfect square.

$x^2 = 16$

$x = \pm\sqrt{16}$

What numbers can you square that result in 16?

$= \pm 4$

The solutions of the equation $x^2 = 16$ are 4 and −4.

STUDY TIP
You can also solve this equation by subtracting 16 from both sides, then factoring the expression.

B. $x^2 = -9$

There are no real numbers that you can square that result in −9. However, you can simplify the expression by extending the properties of radicals.

$x^2 = -9$

$x = \pm\sqrt{-9}$

$x = \pm\sqrt{9}\sqrt{-1}$

$x = \pm 3\sqrt{-1}$

The solutions of the equation $x^2 = -9$ are not real numbers but are part of a number system called the complex numbers. The number $\sqrt{-1}$ is called the **imaginary unit i**. Replacing $\sqrt{-1}$ with i allows you to write the solutions to the equation $x^2 = -9$ as $3i$ and $-3i$.

 Try It!   **1.** Use square roots to solve each equation. Write your solutions using the imaginary unit, i.

a. $x^2 = -5$ **b.** $x^2 = -72$

CONCEPT Complex Numbers

The imaginary unit, *i*, is the principal square root of −1. Then $i^2 = -1$.

An **imaginary number** is any number, *bi*, where *b* is a non-zero real number and *i* is the square root of −1.

Complex numbers are numbers that can be written in the form *a* + *bi*, where *a* and *b* are real numbers and *i* is the square root of −1. They include all real and imaginary numbers, as well as the sum of real and imaginary numbers.

For example:

$-6 + 4i$	$(a = -6, b = 4)$
$7 - i\sqrt{2}$	$(a = 7, b = -\sqrt{2})$
$0.5i$	$(a = 0, b = 0.5)$

 EXAMPLE 2 **Add and Subtract Complex Numbers**

How can you add and subtract complex numbers?

A. What is the sum of (4 − 7*i*) and (−11 + 9*i*)?

When adding (or subtracting) two numbers in the form *a* + *bi*, combine the real parts and then combine the imaginary parts. The sum (or difference) may include both a real and imaginary part and can be written in the form *a* + *bi*.

$$(4 - 7i) + (-11 + 9i) = (4 + -11) + (-7i + 9i)$$
$$= -7 + 2i$$

> **STUDY TIP**
> Combine real parts and imaginary parts of complex numbers as you would combine like terms.

B. What is the difference of (6 + 8*i*) and (2 − 5*i*)?

$$(6 + 8i) - (2 - 5i) = (6 + 8i) + (-2 + 5i)$$

> Remember to distribute the negative over the complex number.

$$= (6 + -2) + (8i + 5i)$$
$$= 4 + 13i$$

✓ **Try It!** **2.** Find the sum or difference.

    a. $(-4 + 6i) + (-2 - 9i)$

    b. $(3 - 2i) - (-4 + i)$

EXAMPLE 3 **Multiply Complex Numbers**

How can you write each product in the form $a + bi$?

A. $-2.5i(8 - 9i)$

$$-2.5i(8 - 9i) = -2.5i(8) - 2.5i(-9i)$$ .... Use the Distributive Property.

$$= -20i + 22.5i^2$$ .... Multiply.

$$= -20i + 22.5(-1)$$ .... Simplify using the definition of i^2.

$$= -22.5 - 20i$$ .... Write in the form $a + bi$.

The product is $-22.5 - 20i$.

B. $(3 - 2i)(3 + 2i)$

$$(3 - 2i)(3 + 2i) = 3(3 + 2i) - 2i(3 + 2i)$$ .... Use the Distributive Property.

$$= 9 + 6i - 6i - 4i^2$$ .... Use the Distributive Property.

$$= 9 + 6i - 6i - 4(-1)$$ .... Simplify using the definition of i^2.

$$= 13$$ .... Simplify.

The product is 13.

COMMON ERROR
Recall that $i^2 = -1$, so the product of 22.5 and i^2 is -22.5, not 22.5.

✓ **Try It!** **3.** Write each product in the form $a + bi$.

a. $\frac{2}{5}i\left(10 - \frac{5}{2}i\right)$

b. $\left(\frac{1}{2} + 2i\right)\left(\frac{1}{2} - 2i\right)$

CONCEPT Complex Conjugates

Complex conjugates are complex numbers with equivalent real parts and opposite imaginary parts. Their product is a real number.

For example:

$7 - 8i$, $7 + 8i$ $-2 + i$, $-2 - i$

$(a + bi)(a - bi)$

$a^2 - abi + abi - b^2i^2$

$a^2 - b^2(-1)$

$a^2 + b^2$

 EXAMPLE 4 **Simplify a Quotient With Complex Numbers**

How can you write the quotient $\frac{10}{2 - i}$ in the form $a + bi$?

When the denominator has an imaginary component, you can create an equivalent fraction with a real denominator by multiplying by its complex conjugate.

$$\frac{10}{2 - i} = \frac{10}{2 - i} \times \frac{2 + i}{2 + i}$$ .... Use the complex conjugate of the denominator to multiply by 1.

$$= \frac{10(2 + i)}{4 + 2i - 2i - i^2}$$ .... Use the Distributive Property.

$$= \frac{10(2 + i)}{4 + 2i - 2i - (-1)}$$ .... Simplify using the definition of i^2.

$$= \frac{10(2 + i)}{5}$$ .... Simplify.

$$= 2(2 + i)$$ .... Simplify.

$$= 4 + 2i$$ .... Write in the form $a + bi$.

STUDY TIP
Multiplying the denominator by its complex conjugate will result in a new denominator that is a real number.

CONTINUED ON THE NEXT PAGE

EXAMPLE 4 CONTINUED

 Try It! **4.** Write each quotient in the form $a + bi$.

    a. $\dfrac{80}{2 - 6i}$ **b.** $\dfrac{4 - 3i}{-1 + 2i}$

CONCEPTUAL UNDERSTANDING 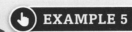 **EXAMPLE 5**   Factor a Sum of Squares

How can you use complex numbers to factor the sum of two squares?

A. How can you factor the expression $x^2 + y^2$?

Rewrite $x^2 + y^2$ as a difference of two squares: $x^2 - (-y^2)$.

You can think of $(-y^2)$ as $(-1)(y^2)$.

> How can $(-y^2)$ be a perfect square?

Since $-1 = i^2$, $(-1)(y^2) = (i^2)(y^2) = (yi)^2$.

So $x^2 + y^2 = x^2 - (yi)^2$

$= (x + yi)(x - yi)$

> Factor as the difference of two squares.

The factors of $x^2 + y^2$ are $(x + yi)$ and $(x - yi)$.

STUDY TIP
The product of complex conjugates $(a + bi)$ and $(a - bi)$ will always be equal to $a^2 + b^2$, which is the sum of two squares.

B. How can you factor the expression $12x^2 + 3$?

$12x^2 + 3 = 3(4x^2 + 1)$ ·········· Factor out the GCF.

$= 3(4x^2 - i^2)$ ·········· Rewrite as a difference of squares.

$= 3(2x + i)(2x - i)$ ·········· Factor the difference of squares.

The factors of $12x^2 + 3$ are 3, $(2x + i)$, and $(2x - i)$.

 Try It! **5.** Factor each expression.

    a. $4x^2 + 25$ **b.** $8y^2 + 18$

 EXAMPLE 6   Solve a Quadratic Equation With Complex Solutions

How can you solve $x^2 + 4 = 0$ using factoring?

    $x^2 + 4 = 0$ ·········· Write the original equation.

    $x^2 - (2i)^2 = 0$ ·········· Rewrite as a difference of squares.

$(x + 2i)(x - 2i) = 0$ ·········· Factor the difference of squares.

$x + 2i = 0$ $x - 2i = 0$ ·········· Set each factor equal to 0.

$x = -2i$ $x = 2i$ ·········· Solve.

The solutions are $x = -2i$ and $x = 2i$.

LOOK FOR RELATIONSHIPS
In Example 1, you solved a similar problem by taking the square root of both sides. This example provides an alternative method that utilizes factoring. Ⓒ **MP.7**

 Try It! **6.** Find the value(s) of x that will solve each equation.

    a. $x^2 + 49 = 0$ **b.** $9x^2 + 25 = 0$

CONCEPT SUMMARY Complex Numbers and Operations

The imaginary unit i is the number whose square is equal to -1: $\sqrt{-1} = i$, so $i^2 = -1$.

Complex numbers are written in the form $a + bi.$

real numbers   imaginary unit

The four basic operations can be applied to complex numbers, such as $2 + 3i$ and $5 - i$.

ADDITION

Add as you would with binomials with like terms.

$(2 + 3i) + (5 - i) = 7 + 2i$

SUBTRACTION

Subtract as you would with binomials with like terms.

$(2 + 3i) - (5 - i) = -3 + 4i$

MULTIPLICATION

Distribute as you would with binomials.

$(2 + 3i)(5 - i) = 10 - 2i + 15i - 3i^2 = 13 + 13i$

DIVISION

Simplify so that the denominator is a real number. Multiply the numerator and denominator by the conjugate of the denominator.

$\dfrac{2 + 3i}{5 - i} = \dfrac{(2 + 3i)(5 + i)}{(5 - i)(5 + i)} = \dfrac{7 + 17i}{26} = \dfrac{7}{26} + \dfrac{17}{26}i$

Do You UNDERSTAND?

1. **ESSENTIAL QUESTION** How can you represent and operate on numbers that are not on the real number line?

2. **Vocabulary** How do you form the *complex conjugate* of a complex number $a + bi$?

3. **Error Analysis** Helena was asked to write the quotient $\dfrac{4}{3 - i}$ in the form $a + bi$. She began this way: $\dfrac{4}{3 - i} \times \dfrac{3 - i}{3 - i} = \dfrac{4(3 - i)}{3^2 + 1^2} = \dfrac{12 - 4i}{10}$. Explain the error Helena made. ⓒ **MP.3**

4. **Look for Relationships** The quadratic equation $x^2 + 9 = 0$ has solutions $x = 3i$ and $x = -3i$. How many times will the graph of $f(x) = x^2 + 9$ cross the x-axis? Explain. ⓒ **MP.7**

Do You KNOW HOW?

Write each of the following in the form $a + bi$.

5. $(2 + 5i) - (-6 + i)$

6. $(2i)(6 + 3i)$

Solve each equation.

7. $x^2 + 16 = 0$

8. $y^2 = -25$

9. **Model With Mathematics** The total source voltage in the circuit is $6 - 3i$ V. What is the voltage at the middle source?

$(2 + 6i)V$ E_1

$(a + bi)V$ E_2

$(2 - 5i)V$ E_3

PRACTICE & PROBLEM SOLVING

UNDERSTAND

10. Construct Arguments Tamara says that raising the number i to any integer power results in either -1 or 1 as the result, since $i^2 = -1$. Do you agree with Tamara? Explain. ⒸMP.3

11. Error Analysis Describe and correct the error a student made when dividing complex numbers. ⒸMP.3

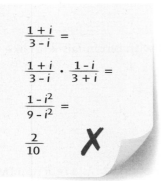

$$\frac{1+i}{3-i} =$$

$$\frac{1+i}{3-i} \cdot \frac{1-i}{3+i} =$$

$$\frac{1-i^2}{9-i^2} =$$

$$\frac{2}{10} \quad \text{✗}$$

12. Higher Order Thinking Label the diagram with the following sets of numbers:

1. complex numbers
2. real numbers
3. imaginary numbers
4. integers
5. rational numbers

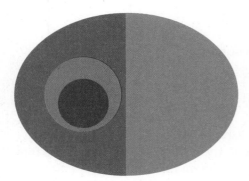

Include an example of each type of number in the diagram.

13. Generalize Write an explicit formula, in standard form, to find the quotient of two complex numbers. Use the numbers $a + bi$ and $c + di$. ⒸMP.8

PRACTICE

Use square roots to solve each equation over the complex numbers. SEE EXAMPLE 1

14. $x^2 = -5$

15. $x^2 = -0.01$

16. $x^2 = -18$

17. $x^2 = (-1)^2$

Add or subtract. Write the answer in the form $a + bi$. SEE EXAMPLE 2

18. $(3 - 2i) - (-9 + i)$

19. $(5 + 1.2i) + (-6 + 0.8i)$

20. $(2i) - (2i - 11)$

21. $13 + 2i - 4 - 8i$

22. $\frac{3-i}{4} - \frac{2+i}{3}$

23. $4.5i - 4.5 + 3.5i + 2.5$

Write each product in the form $a + bi$. SEE EXAMPLE 3

24. $(11i)(3i)$

25. $(3i)(5 - 4i)$

26. $(5 - 2i)(5 + 2i)$

27. $(8 + 3i)(8 + 3i)$

28. $\frac{1}{3}i(3 + 6i)$

29. $(-2i + 7)(7 + 2i)$

Write each quotient in the form $a + bi$. SEE EXAMPLE 4

30. $\frac{12}{1-i}$

31. $\frac{5}{6+2i}$

32. $\frac{6+12i}{3i}$

33. $\frac{4-4i}{1+3i}$

Factor the sums of two squares. SEE EXAMPLE 5

34. $4x^2 + 49$

35. $x^2 + 1$

36. $36 + 100a^2$

37. $18y^2 + 8$

38. $\frac{1}{4}b^2 + 25$

39. $x^2 + y^2$

Solve each equation. SEE EXAMPLE 6

40. $x^2 + 81 = 0$

41. $25x^2 + 9 = 0$

42. $x^2 = -16$

43. $4 + 49y^2 = 0$

44. $y^2 + 1 = 0$

45. $x^2 + \frac{1}{4} = 0$

APPLY

46. Model With Mathematics The two resistors shown in the circuit are referred to as *in parallel.* The total resistance of the resistors is given by the formula $\frac{1}{R_T} = \frac{1}{R_1} + \frac{1}{R_2}$. © **MP.4**

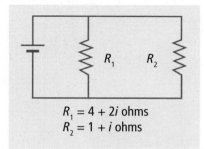

$R_1 = 4 + 2i$ ohms
$R_2 = 1 + i$ ohms

a. Find the total resistance. Write your answer in the form $a + bi$.

b. Show that the total resistance is equivalent to the expression $\frac{R_1 R_2}{R_1 + R_2}$.

c. Change the value of R_2 so that the total resistance is a real number. Explain how you chose the value.

47. Use Structure The complex number $a + bi$ can be represented on a coordinate plane as the point (a, b). You can use multiplication by i to rotate a point about the origin in the coordinate plane. © **MP.7**

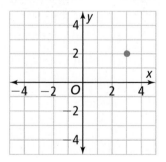

a. Write the point (x, y) on the graph as the complex number $x + yi$.

b. Multiply the complex number by i. Interpret the new value as a new point in the plane.

c. Repeat the steps above for two other points. How does multiplication by i rotate a point?

© **ASSESSMENT PRACTICE**

48. Complete the table by classifying each number as real, imaginary, or complex. Use the most specific classification. For example, all real numbers are also complex numbers, so it is more specific to classify a number as real.

Number	R, I, C
$2 + i$	C
$5 - 0i$	R
$2i$	I
$(3 - i)^2$	
$i^2 + 1$	
$3i$	
$(3 - i)(3 + i)$	
$(3 + i) - (2 + i)$	
$\sqrt{-14}$	
$i(4 + i) - 3i$	

49. SAT/ACT Which of the following is a solution to the equation $3x^2 = -12$?

Ⓐ $-4i$ Ⓑ $-2i$ Ⓒ -2 Ⓓ 2 Ⓔ $4i$

50. Performance Task Abby wants to write the square root of i in the form $a + bi$. She begins by writing the equation $\sqrt{i} = a + bi$.

Part A Square both sides of the equation. Then use the fact that the real part and imaginary part on each side of the equation are equal to write a system of equations involving the variables a and b.

Part B Solve the system to find b. Then find a.

Part C List the possible solutions for a and b.

Part D Square each of the possible solutions. What are the two square roots of i?

MATHEMATICAL MODELING IN 3 ACTS

© **Common Core State Standards** HSF.BF.A.1.A, HSF.IF.B.4, HSA.CED.A.2, MP.4

▶ Video

▶ Swift Kick

Whether you call it soccer, football, or fùtbol, it's the most popular sport in the world by far. Even if you don't play soccer, you probably know several people who do.

There are many ways to kick a soccer ball: you can use any part of either foot. If you want the ball to end up in the goal, you also need to try different amounts of spin and power. You'll see one person's effort in the Mathematical Modeling in 3-Acts lesson.

Scan for Multimedia

ACT 1 **Identify the Problem**

1. What is the first question that comes to mind after watching the video?

2. Write down the main question you will answer about what you saw in the video.

3. Make an initial conjecture that answers this main question.

4. Explain how you arrived at your conjecture.

5. What information will be useful to know to answer the main question? How can you get it? How will you use that information?

ACT 2 **Develop a Model**

6. Use the math that you have learned in this Topic to refine your conjecture.

ACT 3 **Interpret the Results**

7. Did your refined conjecture match the actual answer exactly? If not, what might explain the difference?

2-5

Completing the Square

 SavvasRealize.com

I CAN... solve quadratic equations by completing the square.

VOCABULARY

• completing the square

 Common Core State Standards HSN.CN.C.7, HSA.REI.B.4, HSA.REI.B.4.A, HSA.REI.B.4.B, MP.3, MP.6, MP.7

Activity Assess

CRITIQUE & EXPLAIN

Hana and Enrique used different methods to solve the equation $x^2 - 6x + 9 = 16$.

Hana

$$x^2 - 6x + 9 = 16$$
$$x^2 - 6x - 7 = 0$$
$$(x - 7)(x + 1) = 0$$
$$x - 7 = 0 \ \text{OR} \ x + 1 = 0$$
$$x = 7 \ \text{OR} \quad x = -1$$

The solutions are 7 and -1.

Enrique

$$x^2 - 6x + 9 = 16$$
$$(x - 3)^2 = 16$$

I can square 4 or -4 to get 16.

$$x - 3 = 4 \ \text{OR} \ x - 3 = -4$$
$$x = 7 \ \text{OR} \quad x = -1$$

The solutions are 7 and -1.

A. Does Hana's method work? If her method is valid, explain the reasoning she used. If her method is not valid, explain why not.

B. Does Enrique's method work? If his method is valid, explain the reasoning he used. If his method is not valid, explain why not.

C. Use Structure Can you use either Hana's or Enrique's method to solve the equation $x^2 + 10x + 25 = 3$? Explain. **MP.7**

ESSENTIAL QUESTION

How can you solve a quadratic equation by completing the square?

EXAMPLE 1   Use Square Roots to Solve Quadratic Equations

What are the solution(s) of $25 = x^2 + 14x + 49$?

Previously, you solved a simple quadratic equation by finding the square root of both sides. You can use a similar method to solve more complicated quadratic equations.

$25 = x^2 + 14x + 49$ · · · · · · · · · Write the original equation.

$25 = x^2 + 2(7)x + 7^2$ · · · · · · · · Recognize that the quadratic expression is a perfect square trinomial.

$25 = (x + 7)^2$ · · · · · · · · · Factor the perfect square trinomial.

$\sqrt{25} = \sqrt{(x + 7)^2}$ · · · · · · · · · Take the square root of each side of the equation.

$5 = |x + 7|$ · · · · · · · · · Apply the definition of principal square root.

$\pm 5 = x + 7$ · · · · · · · · · Apply the definition of absolute value.

COMMUNICATE PRECISELY
The principal square root returns only positive values, but you can square either 5 or -5 to get 25. How does the absolute value account for this? **MP.6**

$5 = x + 7$ or $-5 = x + 7$

$-2 = x$ or $-12 = x$

The solutions of $25 = x^2 + 14x + 49$ are $x = -2$ and $x = -12$.

Try It!   **1.** Find the solution(s) to the equations.

     a. $81 = x^2 + 12x + 36$ **b.** $9 = x^2 - 16x + 64$

CONCEPTUAL
UNDERSTANDING

EXAMPLE 2 ▸ Understand the Process of Completing the Square

How can you complete the square to write an expression as a perfect square?

A. How can you rewrite the expression $x^2 + bx$ in the form $(x + p)^2$?

Not every quadratic expression is a perfect square trinomial. **Completing the square** is the process of finding the constant to add to $x^2 + bx$ to create a perfect square trinomial.

The model below depicts the process of completing the square.

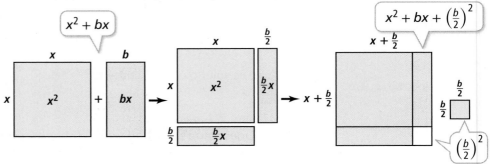

To create a perfect square trinomial, add $\left(\frac{b}{2}\right)^2$ to the variable expression.

$$x^2 + bx + \left(\frac{b}{2}\right)^2 = \left(x + \frac{b}{2}\right)^2$$

B. Write $x^2 + 8x + 5 = 0$ in the form $(x + p)^2 = q$

$x^2 + 8x + 5 = 0$	Write the original equation.
$x^2 + 8x = -5$	Isolate the variable expression.
$x^2 + 8x + 16 = -5 + 16$	Determine the constant needed to complete the square: $\left(\frac{b}{2}\right)^2 = \left(\frac{8}{2}\right)^2 = 16$.
$(x + 4)^2 = 11$	Write the left side of the equation as a perfect square.

The equation $x^2 + 8x + 5 = 0$ can be rewritten as $(x + 4)^2 = 11$.

✓ **Try It!** **2.** How can you write the equation $x^2 - 6x - 11 = 0$ in the form $(x - p)^2 = q$?

EXAMPLE 3 ▸ Solve a Quadratic Equation by Completing the Square

How can you solve $0 = x^2 - 2x + 3$ by completing the square?

$0 = x^2 - 2x + 3$	Write the original equation.
$-3 = x^2 - 2x$	Subtract 3 from each side.
$-3 + 1 = x^2 - 2x + 1$	Add $\left(\frac{-2}{2}\right)^2$ to both sides of the equation.
$-2 = (x - 1)^2$	Write the right side of the equation as a perfect square.
$\pm i\sqrt{2} = x - 1$	Take the square root of each side of the equation.
$1 \pm i\sqrt{2} = x$	Solve.

The solutions of $0 = x^2 - 2x + 3$ are $x = 1 + i\sqrt{2}$ and $x = 1 - i\sqrt{2}$.

CONTINUED ON THE NEXT PAGE

EXAMPLE 3 CONTINUED

 Activity Assess

 Try It! **3.** Solve the following equations by completing the square.

a. $0 = x^2 + 4x + 8$ **b.** $0 = x^2 - 8x + 17$

APPLICATION **EXAMPLE 4** **Complete the Square to Solve a Real-World Problem**

Libby plans to create a rectangular pasturing enclosure. She has 340 m of fencing available for the enclosure's perimeter and wants it to have an area of 6,000 m². What dimensions should Libby use?

6,000 m²
w
ℓ

Formulate ◀ Let ℓ and w represent the length and width of the enclosure.

The perimeter is $2\ell + 2w = 340$, so:

$$2w = 340 - 2\ell$$
$$w = 170 - \ell$$

Libby wants the area to be 6,000 m². Write this as an equation:

$$A = \ell w$$
$$6,000 = \ell(170 - \ell)$$

> Substitute for A and w.

Compute ◀
$$6,000 = 170\ell - \ell^2$$
$$\ell^2 - 170\ell = -6,000$$
$$\ell^2 - 170\ell + 7,225 = -6,000 + 7,225$$

> Find the number to complete the square: $\frac{-170}{2} = -85$ and $(-85)^2 = 7,225$.

$$(\ell - 85)^2 = 1,225$$
$$\ell - 85 = \pm 35$$
$$\ell = 85 \pm 35$$
$$\ell = 120 \text{ or } \ell = 50$$

Interpret ◀ When $\ell = 120$, then $w = 170 - 120$, or 50.

When $\ell = 50$, then $w = 170 - 50$, or 120.

In each case, there is $2(120) + 2(50)$, or 340 m, of fencing used.

Likewise, the area is $(120)(50)$, or 6,000 m².

Libby should make two sides of the enclosure 120 m long and the other two sides 50 m long.

CONTINUED ON THE NEXT PAGE

EXAMPLE 4 CONTINUED

 Try It! **4.** The relationship between the time since a ball was thrown and its height can be modeled by the equation $h = 32t - 16t^2 + 4$, where h is the height of the ball after t seconds. Complete the square to find how long it will take the ball to reach a height of 20 ft.

 EXAMPLE 5 **Write a Quadratic Equation in Vertex Form**

Write the equation $y = -2x^2 + 10x + 1$ in vertex form and graph it. What is the maximum or minimum value of the graph of the equation?

$$y = -2x^2 + 10x + 1$$ .... Write the original equation.

$$y - 1 = -2x^2 + 10x$$ .... Subtract 1 from each side.

$$y - 1 = -2(x^2 - 5x)$$ .... Factor out the x^2 coefficient, -2.

$$y - 1 - (2)(6.25) = -2(x^2 - 5x + 6.25)$$ .... Complete the square: $\left(\frac{b}{2}\right)^2 = \left(\frac{-5}{2}\right)^2 = 6.25.$

$$y - 13.5 = -2(x - 2.5)^2$$ .... Simplify and factor.

$$y = -2(x - 2.5)^2 + 13.5$$ .... Write in vertex form.

COMMON ERROR
You may think that you have to add 6.25 to both sides; on the right side, 6.25 was added **with −2 already factored out**. So add −2(6.25), or −12.5, to the left side of the equation.

The vertex of the parabola is (2.5, 13.5).

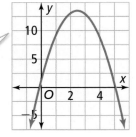

The graph of this equation is a parabola that opens downward, so it has a maximum of $y = 13.5$, at $x = 2.5$.

 Try It! **5.** Write each equation in vertex form. Identify the maximum or minimum value of the graph of each equation.

a. $y = -3x^2 - 9x + 7$ **b.** $y = 2x^2 + 12x + 9$

CONCEPT SUMMARY Key Features of Completing the Square

GEOMETRIC MODEL ▶ The rectangles showing $x^2 + 10x$ are arranged into a square.

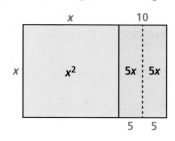

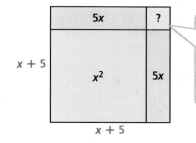

The green section represents the part of the square that has to be added in order to "complete" the square.

The square has side length $x + 5$, so the number needed to complete the square is 25.

ALGEBRAIC MODEL ▶ The number needed to complete the square is half the coefficient of the middle term, squared: the middle term coefficient is 10, half of 10 is 5, and $5^2 = 25$.

To solve $x^2 + 10x = 3$, add 25 to both sides of the equation, take the square root of both sides and solve for x:

$$x^2 + 10x + 25 = 3 + 25$$
$$(x + 5)^2 = 28$$
$$x + 5 = \pm 2\sqrt{7}$$
$$x = -5 \pm 2\sqrt{7}$$

☑ Do You UNDERSTAND?

1. **ESSENTIAL QUESTION** How can you solve a quadratic equation by completing the square?

2. **Error Analysis** Paula said that only quadratic equations with leading coefficients of 1 can be solved by completing the square. Is Paula correct? Explain. Ⓖ **MP.3**

3. **Generalize** Given the expression $x^2 + bx$, describe how to find c so that $x^2 + bx + c$ is a perfect square trinomial. Ⓖ **MP.8**

4. **Make Sense and Persevere** How can you complete the square to find the vertex of a parabola? Ⓖ **MP.1**

Do You KNOW HOW?

Solve each equation by completing the square.

5. $0 = x^2 + 12x + 11$

6. $27 = 3x^2 + 12x$

7. $0 = 2x^2 + 6x - 14$

Write the equation in vertex form, and identify the maximum or minimum point of the graph of the function.

8. $y = x^2 + 6x - 6$

9. $y = -2x^2 + 20x - 42$

10. The daily profit, P, for a company is modeled by the function $p(x) = -0.5x^2 + 40x - 300$, where x is the number of units sold. How many units does the company need to sell each day to maximize profits?

UNDERSTAND

11. **Use Appropriate Tools** How could you use a graphing calculator to determine whether you have correctly solved a quadratic equation by completing the square? ⓒ **MP.5**

12. **Error Analysis** Describe and correct the error a student made in solving a quadratic equation by completing the square. ⓒ **MP.3**

$$0 = x^2 + 16x - 5$$
$$5 = x^2 + 16x + 64$$
$$5 = (x + 8)^2$$
$$x = -8 \pm \sqrt{5} \quad \textbf{✗}$$

13. **Higher Order Thinking** What number do you need to add to $x^2 + \frac{7}{2}x$ in order to create a perfect square trinomial? Explain.

14. **Reason** Does the geometric model hold for finding the number that completes the square of the expression $x^2 - 12x$? Explain. ⓒ **MP.2**

15. **Error Analysis** When given the equation $-23 = x^2 + 8x$, a student says that you can add 64 to each side of the equation to complete the square. Is the student correct? If not, describe and correct the error. ⓒ **MP.3**

16. **Construct Arguments** Explain why you should not try to complete the square when solving $0 = x^2 - 4$. ⓒ **MP.3**

17. **Use Structure** Jacob completed the square to rewrite the equation $f(x) = -2x^2 + 12x - 13$ as $f(x) = -2(x - 3)^2 + 5$. Which form of the equation is more helpful for identifying the key features of the graph? Explain. ⓒ **MP.7**

PRACTICE

Use square roots to solve the quadratic equations.
SEE EXAMPLE 1

18. $9 = x^2 + 2x + 1$ 19. $16 = x^2 - 10x + 25$

20. $50 = 2x^2 + 16x + 32$ 21. $5 = 3x^2 - 36x + 108$

22. $7 = x^2 + 4x + 4$ 23. $-4 = x^2 + 14x + 49$

Rewrite the equations in the form $(x - p)^2 = q$.
SEE EXAMPLE 2

24. $0 = x^2 - 18x + 64$ 25. $x^2 + 22x + 120.5 = 0$

26. $x^2 + 3x - \frac{27}{4} = 0$ 27. $0 = 4x^2 + 4x - 14$

28. $0 = x^2 - \frac{3}{2}x - \frac{70}{8}$ 29. $x^2 + 0.6x - 19.1 = 0$

Solve the following quadratic equations by completing the square. SEE EXAMPLES 3 AND 4

30. $x^2 + 8x + 60 = 0$ 31. $x^2 + 14x = 51$

32 $4x^2 + 16x - 65 = 0$ 33. $7x^2 + 56x - 22 = 0$

34. $3x^2 - 6x + 13 = 0$ 35. $x^2 - 0.4x - 1.2 = 0$

36. $x^2 + 6x = 59$ 37. $8x^2 + 16x = 42$

38. $5x^2 - 25 = 10x$ 39. $-2x^2 - 12x + 18 = 0$

40. $-3x^2 - 24x - 19 = 0$ 41. $17 - x^2 - 18x = 0$

42. What is the length and width of the skate park?

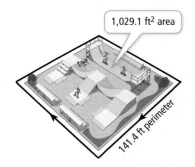

1,029.1 ft² area

141.4 ft perimeter

Write the equation in vertex form. Identify the maximum or minimum value of the graph of the equation. SEE EXAMPLE 5

43. $y = x^2 + 4x - 13$ 44. $y = x^2 - 14x + 71$

45. $y = -2x^2 - 20x - 58$ 46. $y = -3x^2 + 36x - 93$

47. $y = 6x^2 - 42x + 74.5$ 48. $y = 0.5x^2 + 0.5x + 2.125$

APPLY

49. Make Sense and Persevere Keenan launches a model helicopter. The height of the helicopter, in feet, is given by the equation $h = -16t^2 + 64t + 190$, where t is the time in seconds. To the nearest hundredth, how many seconds will it take the helicopter to hit the ground? What is the maximum height of the helicopter? © **MP.1**

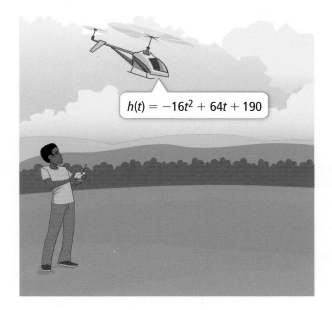

$h(t) = -16t^2 + 64t + 190$

50. Use Structure The decreasing population, p, of owls in a national park is being monitored by ecologists and is modeled by the equation $p = -0.4 t^2 + 128t + 1,200$, where t is the number of months since the ecologists started observing the owls.

a. If this model is accurate, when will the population reach its maximum?

b. What is the maximum population? Round to the nearest whole number.

c. Use the equation to determine in how many months the population of owls will disappear. © **MP.7**

51. Make Sense and Persevere Between 2000 and 2005, the number of skateboarders s in the United States, in millions, can be approximated by the equation $s = 0.33t^2 + 2.27t + 3.96$, where t represents the number of years since 2000. If this model is accurate, in what year did 9.8 million people skateboard? © **MP.1**

© ASSESSMENT PRACTICE

52. The roots of $f(x) = -2x^2 + 8x + 13$ are _____ and _____. The vertex of the parabola is at _____.

53. SAT/ACT Solve $x^2 + 2x - 5 = 0$.

Ⓐ −5, 1

Ⓑ $-1 \pm \sqrt{5}$

Ⓒ $-1 \pm \sqrt{6}$

Ⓓ $1 \pm \sqrt{5}$

Ⓔ −3, 1

54. Performance Task Yumiko has a rectangular-shaped patio. She wants to double the area of the patio by increasing the length and width by the same amount.

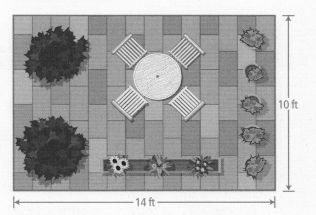

10 ft

14 ft

Part A Write a function to calculate the number of feet Yumiko would need to add to the length and width. Explain your reasoning.

Part B To the nearest hundredth, what are the new dimensions of the patio?

2-6

The Quadratic Formula

 SavvasRealize.com

I CAN... solve quadratic equations using the Quadratic Formula.

VOCABULARY

- discriminant
- Quadratic Formula

 EXPLORE & REASON

You can complete the square to solve the general quadratic equation, $ax^2 + bx + c = 0$.

A. Construct Arguments Justify each step in this general solution. © **MP.3**

B. What must be true of the value of $b^2 - 4ac$ if the equation $ax^2 + bx + c = 0$ has two non-real solutions? If it has just one solution?

$$ax^2 + bx + c = 0$$

$$ax^2 + bx = -c$$

$$x^2 + \left(\frac{b}{a}\right)x = -\frac{c}{a}$$

$$x^2 + \left(\frac{b}{a}\right)x + \left(\frac{b}{2a}\right)^2 = -\frac{c}{a} + \left(\frac{b}{2a}\right)^2$$

$$\left(x + \frac{b}{2a}\right)^2 = \frac{b^2}{4a^2} - \frac{c}{a}$$

$$\left(x + \frac{b}{2a}\right)^2 = \frac{b^2 - 4ac}{4a^2}$$

$$x + \frac{b}{2a} = \pm\sqrt{\frac{b^2 - 4ac}{4a^2}}$$

$$x = \frac{-b \pm \sqrt{b^2 - 4ac}}{2a}$$

? **ESSENTIAL QUESTION** How can you use the Quadratic Formula to solve quadratic equations or to predict the nature of their solutions?

 EXAMPLE 1 Solve Quadratic Equations

USE APPROPRIATE TOOLS
The Quadratic Formula is a useful tool for finding solutions, particularly when an equation cannot be easily factored. © **MP.5**

What are the solutions to the equation?

A. $3x^2 - 4x - 9 = 0$

The **Quadratic Formula**, $x = \frac{-b \pm \sqrt{b^2 - 4ac}}{2a}$, provides the solutions of the quadratic equation $ax^2 + bx + c = 0$, for $a \neq 0$.

$$x = \frac{-b \pm \sqrt{b^2 - 4ac}}{2a}$$ .... Write the Quadratic Formula.

$$= \frac{-(-4) \pm \sqrt{(-4)^2 - 4(3)(-9)}}{2(3)}$$ .... Substitute 3 for a, -4 for b, and -9 for c.

$$= \frac{4 \pm \sqrt{124}}{6}$$ .... Simplify.

$$= \frac{4 \pm 2\sqrt{31}}{6}$$

$$= \frac{2 \pm \sqrt{31}}{3}$$

The solutions are

$$x = \frac{2 + \sqrt{31}}{3} \text{ and } x = \frac{2 - \sqrt{31}}{3}.$$

CONTINUED ON THE NEXT PAGE

EXAMPLE 1 CONTINUED

B. How can you use the Quadratic Formula to solve $x^2 - 9x + 27 = 0$?

$$x = \frac{-b \pm \sqrt{b^2 - 4ac}}{2a} \quad \text{Write the Quadratic Formula.}$$

$$= \frac{-(-9) \pm \sqrt{(-9)^2 - 4(1)(27)}}{2(1)} \quad \text{Substitute 1 for } a, -9 \text{ for } b,$$
$$\text{and 27 for } c.$$

$$= \frac{9 \pm \sqrt{-27}}{2} \quad \text{Simplify.}$$

$$= \frac{9 \pm i\sqrt{27}}{2} \quad \sqrt{-1} = i$$

$$= \frac{9 \pm 3i\sqrt{3}}{2} \quad \text{Simplify.}$$

The solutions are $x = \frac{9 + 3i\sqrt{3}}{2}$ and $x = \frac{9 - 3i\sqrt{3}}{2}$.

GENERALIZE
Look for relationships between the coefficients of a quadratic equation and its solutions. If $a = 1$, then the sum of the solutions is the opposite of the x-coefficient, b, and their product is the constant coefficient, c. Ⓒ **MP.8**

 Try It! **1.** Solve using the Quadratic Formula.

    a. $2x^2 + 6x + 3 = 0$ **b.** $3x^2 - 2x + 7 = 0$

 EXAMPLE 2   **Choose a Solution Method**

STUDY TIP
When you substitute a negative number into a formula, such as the Quadratic Formula, use parentheses to help keep track of the effect of the sign.

Solve the equation $6x^2 - 7x - 20 = 0$ using two different methods. Which do you prefer and why?

Using the Quadratic Formula: Factoring by Grouping:

Let $a = 6$, $b = -7$, and $c = -20$ $6x^2 - 7x - 20 = 0$

$$x = \frac{-(-7) \pm \sqrt{(-7)^2 - 4(6)(-20)}}{2(6)} \qquad 6x^2 - 15x + 8x - 20 = 0$$

$$= \frac{7 \pm \sqrt{49 + 480}}{12} \qquad\qquad 3x(2x - 5) + 4(2x - 5) = 0$$

$$= \frac{7 \pm \sqrt{529}}{12} \qquad\qquad (3x + 4)(2x - 5) = 0$$

$$= \frac{7 \pm 23}{12} \qquad\qquad x = -\frac{4}{3} \text{ and } x = \frac{5}{2}$$

$$x = \frac{7 + 23}{12} = \frac{30}{12} = \frac{5}{2}, \text{ and}$$

$$x = \frac{7 - 23}{12} = -\frac{16}{12} = -\frac{4}{3}$$

> You may also find the factorization through trial and error.

Both solution methods give the same result. Factoring may be more efficient, but the Quadratic Formula *always works*, regardless of whether the function has real or imaginary roots.

 Try It! **2.** Solve the equation $6x^2 + x - 15 = 0$ using the Quadratic Formula and another method.

CONCEPTUAL
UNDERSTANDING

EXAMPLE 3 Identify the Number of Real-Number Solutions

How can you determine the number and type of roots for a quadratic equation?

Graph each equation. Then use the quadratic formula to find the roots.

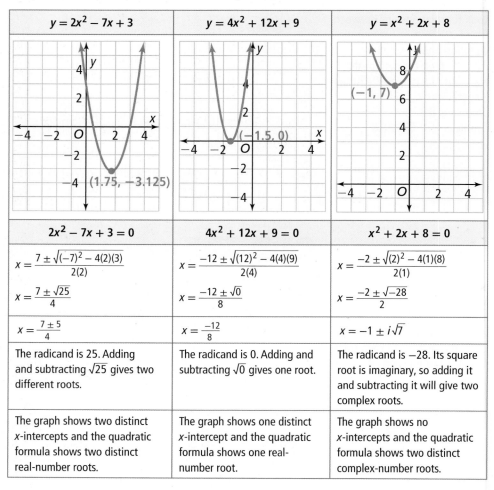

$y = 2x^2 - 7x + 3$	$y = 4x^2 + 12x + 9$	$y = x^2 + 2x + 8$
(1.75, −3.125)	(−1.5, 0)	(−1, 7)
$2x^2 - 7x + 3 = 0$	$4x^2 + 12x + 9 = 0$	$x^2 + 2x + 8 = 0$
$x = \dfrac{7 \pm \sqrt{(-7)^2 - 4(2)(3)}}{2(2)}$	$x = \dfrac{-12 \pm \sqrt{(12)^2 - 4(4)(9)}}{2(4)}$	$x = \dfrac{-2 \pm \sqrt{(2)^2 - 4(1)(8)}}{2(1)}$
$x = \dfrac{7 \pm \sqrt{25}}{4}$	$x = \dfrac{-12 \pm \sqrt{0}}{8}$	$x = \dfrac{-2 \pm \sqrt{-28}}{2}$
$x = \dfrac{7 \pm 5}{4}$	$x = \dfrac{-12}{8}$	$x = -1 \pm i\sqrt{7}$
The radicand is 25. Adding and subtracting $\sqrt{25}$ gives two different roots.	The radicand is 0. Adding and subtracting $\sqrt{0}$ gives one root.	The radicand is −28. Its square root is imaginary, so adding it and subtracting it will give two complex roots.
The graph shows two distinct x-intercepts and the quadratic formula shows two distinct real-number roots.	The graph shows one distinct x-intercept and the quadratic formula shows one real-number root.	The graph shows no x-intercepts and the quadratic formula shows two distinct complex-number roots.

The radicand in the quadratic formula is what determines the nature of the roots.

The **discriminant** of a quadratic equation in the form $ax^2 + bx + c = 0$ is the value of the radicand, $b^2 - 4ac$.

If $b^2 - 4ac > 0$, then $ax^2 + bx + c = 0$ has two real roots.

If $b^2 - 4ac = 0$, then $ax^2 + bx + c = 0$ has one real root.

If $b^2 - 4ac < 0$, then $ax^2 + bx + c = 0$ has two non-real roots.

Try It! 3. Describe the nature of the solutions for each equation.

    a. $16x^2 + 8x + 1 = 0$ **b.** $2x^2 - 5x + 6 = 0$

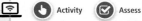
APPLICATION

 EXAMPLE 4 Interpret the Discriminant

Rachel is about to serve and tosses a tennis ball straight up into the air. The height, h, of the ball, in meters, at time t, in seconds is given by $h(t) = -5t^2 + 5t + 2$. Will the ball reach a height of 4 meters?

$h = -5t^2 + 5t + 2$

To see if $h = 4$ for some value of t, set the quadratic expression for h equal to 4, and solve.

$$-5t^2 + 5t + 2 = 4$$

Rewrite the equation in standard form:

$$-5t^2 + 5t - 2 = 0$$

$$a = -5, b = 5, c = -2$$

The discriminant is: $(5)^2 - 4(-5)(-2)$
$$= 25 - 40$$

$$25 - 40 = -15$$

$$-15 < 0$$

So the equation $h = 4$ does not have a real solution. Therefore, the ball does not reach 4 m.

 Try It! 4. According to the model of Rachel's serve, will the ball reach a height of 3 meters?

 EXAMPLE 5 Use the Discriminant to Find a Particular Equation

What value(s) of b will cause $2x^2 + bx + 18 = 0$ to have one real solution?

For this equation, $a = 2$ and $c = 18$.

The equation will have a single rational solution when the discriminant is equal to 0.

$$b^2 - 4ac = 0$$

$$b^2 - 4(2)(18) = 0$$

$$b^2 - 144 = 0$$

$$b^2 = 144$$

$$b = \pm 12$$

There are two possible equations: $2x^2 + 12x + 18 = 0$ and $2x^2 - 12x + 18 = 0$.

STUDY TIP
Note that the equation $2x^2 + bx + 18 = 0$ will have two real solutions if $b > 12$ or $b < -12$. It will have two non-real solutions if $-12 < b < 12$.

 Try It! 5. Determine the value(s) of b that ensure $5x^2 + bx + 5 = 0$ has two non-real solutions.

CONCEPT SUMMARY Key Features of the Quadratic Formula

QUADRATIC FORMULA

$$x = \frac{-b \pm \sqrt{b^2 - 4ac}}{2a}$$

This formula is used to solve any quadratic equation: $ax^2 + bx + c = 0$, where $a \neq 0$.

USING THE DISCRIMINANT

Predict the number and type of solutions using the discriminant, $b^2 - 4ac$.

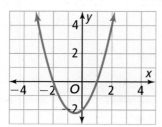

$x^2 + x - 2 = 0$

$b^2 - 4ac > 0$

Two real solutions

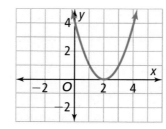

$x^2 - 4x + 4 = 0$

$b^2 - 4ac = 0$

One real solution

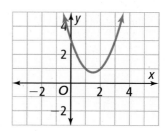

$x^2 - 3x + 3 = 0$

$b^2 - 4ac < 0$

Two non-real solutions

☑ Do You UNDERSTAND?

1. ❓ **ESSENTIAL QUESTION** How can you use the Quadratic Formula to solve quadratic equations or to predict the nature of their solutions?

2. **Vocabulary** Why is the discriminant a useful tool to use when solving quadratic equations?

3. **Error Analysis** Rick claims that the equation $x^2 + 5x + 9 = 0$ has no solution. Jenny claims that there are two solutions. Explain how Rick could be correct, and explain how Jenny could be correct. © **MP.3**

4. **Use Appropriate Tools** What methods can you use to solve quadratic equations? © **MP.5**

Do You KNOW HOW?

5. Describe the number and type of solutions of the equation $2x^2 + 7x + 11 = 0$.

6. Use the Quadratic Formula to solve the equation $x^2 + 6x - 10 = 0$.

7. At time t seconds, the height, h, of a ball thrown vertically upward is modeled by the equation $h = -5t^2 + 33t + 4$. About how long will it take for the ball to hit the ground?

8. Use the Quadratic Formula to solve the equation $x^2 - 8x + 16 = 0$. Is this the only way to solve this equation? Explain.

UNDERSTAND

9. Look for Relationships How can you use the Quadratic Formula to factor a quadratic equation? © MP.7

10. Error Analysis Describe and correct the error a student made in solving an equation. © MP.3

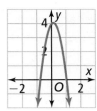

$x^2 - 5x + 5 = 0$

$a = 1, b = -5, c = 5$

$x = \dfrac{-5 \pm \sqrt{(-5)^2 - 4(1)(5)}}{2(1)}$

$= \dfrac{-5 \pm \sqrt{25 - 20}}{2}$

$= \dfrac{-5}{2} \pm \dfrac{\sqrt{5}}{2}$ ✗

11. Mathematical Connections What does the Quadratic Formula tell you about the graph of a quadratic function?

12. Communicate Precisely Explain your process for choosing a method for solving quadratic equations. © MP.6

13. Higher Order Thinking Kelsey wants to use the Quadratic Formula to solve the equation $x^4 + 5x^2 - 5 = 0$. Is this possible? If so, describe the steps she should follow.

14. Construct Arguments Explain why the graph of the quadratic function $f(x) = x^2 + x + 5$ crosses the y-axis but does not cross the x-axis. © MP.3

15. Construct Arguments Sage said that the Quadratic Formula does not always work. Sage used it to solve the equation $x^2 - 3x - 2 = -4$, with $a = 1$, $b = -3$, and $c = -2$. The formula gave $x = \dfrac{3 \pm \sqrt{17}}{2}$ as the solutions to the equation. When Sage checked, neither one of them satisfied the equation. How could you convince Sage that the Quadratic Formula does always work? © MP.3

PRACTICE

Use the Quadratic Formula to solve each equation. SEE EXAMPLE 1

16. $x^2 - 10x + 25 = 0$ **17.** $x^2 + 2x + 2 = 0$

18. $5x^2 - 8x + 4 = 0$ **19.** $x^2 + 9x - 1 = 3x - 10$

20. $3x^2 - 20x - 7 = 0$ **21.** $-x^2 + 3x - 8 = 0$

Use the discriminant to identify the number and type of solutions for each equation. SEE EXAMPLE 3

22. $25x^2 - 20x + 4 = 0$ **23.** $x^2 + 7x + 11 = 0$

24. $3x^2 - 8x - 10 = 0$ **25.** $2x^2 + 9x + 14 = 0$

Deon throws a ball into the air. The height, h, of the ball, in meters, at time t seconds is modeled by the function $h(t) = -5t^2 + t + 4$. SEE EXAMPLE 4

26. When will the ball hit the ground?

27. Will the ball reach a height of 5 meters?

Use any method to solve the equation. SEE EXAMPLE 2

28. $4x^2 + 7x - 11 = 0$ **29.** $x^2 + 4x + 4 = 100$

30. $3x^2 + x + 7 = x^2 + 10$ **31.** $6x^2 + 2x + 3 = 0$

Find the value(s) of k that will cause the equation to have the given number and type of solutions. SEE EXAMPLE 5

32. $5x^2 + kx + 5 = 0$, 1 real solution

33. $3x^2 + 12x + k = 0$, 2 real solutions

34. $kx^2 - 3x + 4 = 0$, 2 real solutions

APPLY

35. Model With Mathematics The table shows the average cost of tuition and fees at a public four-year college for an in-state student in recent years. © **MP.4**

Academic Year	Tuition and Fees
2012–13	$9,006
2013–14	$9,077
2014–15	$9,161
2015–16	$9,410

a. Write an equation that can be used to find the average cost, C, of tuition after x years.

b. Use the model to predict when tuition will exceed $10,000.

36. Make Sense and Persevere The first astronaut on Mars tosses a rock straight up. The height, h, measured in feet after t seconds, is given by the function $h(t) = -6t^2 + 24t + 6$. © **MP.1**

$h(t) = -6t^2 + 24t + 6$

a. After how many seconds will the rock be 30 feet above the surface?

b. After how many seconds will the rock be 10 feet above the surface?

c. How many seconds will it take for the rock to return to the surface?

d. The same action on Earth is modeled by the equation $g(t) = -16t^2 + 24t + 6$. On Earth, how many seconds would it take for the rock to hit the ground?

ASSESSMENT PRACTICE

37. Which of the following equations has two real solutions? Select *Yes* or *No*.

	Yes	No
a. $x^2 - 8x - 2 = 0$	❑	❑
b. $2x^2 + 10x + 17 = 0$	❑	❑
c. $4x^2 - 28x + 49 = 0$	❑	❑
d. $x^2 + 10x - 25 = 4x + 2$	❑	❑
e. $2x^2 + x + 10 = 5 - 4x - x^2$	❑	❑

38. SAT/ACT Which expression can be simplified to find the solution(s) of the equation $2x^2 - x - 15 = 0$?

Ⓐ $-1 \pm \dfrac{\sqrt{1 - 4(2)(-15)}}{2(2)}$

Ⓑ $\dfrac{1 \pm \sqrt{1 - 4(2)(-15)}}{2(2)}$

Ⓒ $\dfrac{1 \pm \sqrt{-1 - 4(2)(-15)}}{2(2)}$

Ⓓ $\dfrac{1 \pm \sqrt{1 - 4(2)(15)}}{2(2)}$

Ⓔ $\dfrac{1 \pm \sqrt{1 + 4(2)(-15)}}{2(2)}$

39. Performance Task Four congruent squares are cut from a rectangular piece of cardboard.

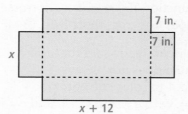

7 in.

7 in.

x

$x + 12$

Part A. If the resulting flaps are folded up and taped together to make a box, write a function to represent the volume of the box in terms of the width of the original piece of cardboard.

Part B. What are the dimensions of the original cardboard, to the nearest tenth, if the volume of the box is 434 in.³

2-7

Linear-Quadratic Systems

SavvasRealize.com

I CAN... solve linear-quadratic systems.

EXPLORE & REASON

Draw a rough sketch of a parabola and a line on the coordinate plane.

A. Count the number of points of intersection between the two graphs.

B. Sketch another parabola on a coordinate plane. Use a straightedge to investigate the different ways that a line and a parabola intersect. What conjectures can you make?

C. Construct Arguments How many different numbers of intersection points are possible between a quadratic function and a linear function? Justify that you have found all of the possibilities. **© MP.3**

? ESSENTIAL QUESTION How can you solve a system of two equations or inequalities in which one is linear and one is quadratic?

CONCEPTUAL UNDERSTANDING

EXAMPLE 1 Determine the Number of Solutions

How many solutions can there be for a linear-quadratic system?

COMMUNICATE PRECISELY
A solution to a system of equations is an ordered pair that produces a true statement in all the equations of the system. In the graph, the solutions are the coordinates of the intersection points. **© MP.6**

A. How many real solutions does the system $\begin{cases} y = x^2 \\ y = 2x \end{cases}$ have?

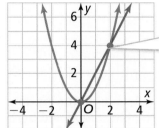

The graph seems to show that the quadratic function and linear function intersect at two points.

This system has two real solutions.

B. How does modifying the linear function in the system $\begin{cases} y = x^2 \\ y = 2x + b \end{cases}$ affect the number of solutions?

Test values for b to determine when the system has different numbers of solutions.

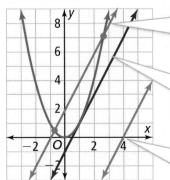

When $b = 2$, there are two solutions. The graphs intersect at two points.

When $b = -1$, there is one solution. The graph of $y = 2x - 1$ is tangent to the graph of $y = x^2$.

When $b = -8$, there are no solutions. The graph of $y = 2x - 8$ does not intersect the graph of $y = x^2$.

Visually inspecting the graph suggests that there is no way for a line to cross a parabola more than twice. Thus, the system of a linear function and a quadratic function may have 0, 1, or 2 solutions.

 Try It! **1.** Determine the number of real solutions of the system $\begin{cases} y = 3x^2 \\ y = 3x - 2 \end{cases}$.

EXAMPLE 2 **Solve a Linear-Quadratic System Using Substitution**

USE STRUCTURE
As with a system of linear equations, you can use substitution and elimination to find the values of x and y that make the system true. In this case, substitution yields a new quadratic equation to solve.

ⓒ **MP.7**

How can you use substitution to solve this system? $\begin{cases} y = 3x^2 + 3x - 5 \\ 2x - y = 3 \end{cases}$

The first equation provides an expression for y in terms of x. Substitute this expression in the second equation.

$2x - (3x^2 + 3x - 5) = 3$ ·········· Substitute $3x^2 + 3x - 5$ for y in the second equation.

$2x - 3x^2 - 3x + 5 = 3$ ·········· Distribute -1 to remove parentheses.

$3x^2 + x - 2 = 0$ ·········· Simplify.

$(x + 1)(3x - 2) = 0$ ·········· Factor.

So $x = -1$ and $x = \frac{2}{3}$ are solutions of this quadratic equation.

> If the graphs of the equations have two solutions, there are two points of intersection for the graphs of the equations.

When $x = -1$, $y = 2(-1) - 3$, or -5. When $x = \frac{2}{3}$, $y = 2\left(\frac{2}{3}\right) - 3$, or $-\frac{5}{3}$.

The solutions of the system are $(-1, -5)$ and $\left(\frac{2}{3}, -\frac{5}{3}\right)$.

✓ **Try It!** **2.** Solve each system by substitution.

a. $\begin{cases} y = 2x^2 - 6x - 8 \\ 2x - y = 16 \end{cases}$

b. $\begin{cases} y = -3x^2 + x + 4 \\ 4x - y = 2 \end{cases}$

APPLICATION

  EXAMPLE 3 **Applying a Linear-Quadratic System**

Andrew kicks a ball up a hill for his dog, Laika, to chase. The hill is modeled by a line through the origin. The path of the ball is modeled by the quadratic function shown. How far does the ball travel horizontally? How far must Laika run up the hill to catch it?

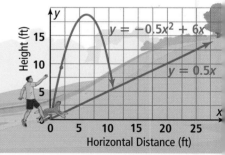

Create a system of equations and determine where the path of the ball intersects the hill.

$\begin{cases} y = -0.5x^2 + 6x \\ y = 0.5x \end{cases}$

$0.5x = -0.5x^2 + 6x$ ·········· Substitute for y.

$0 = -0.5x^2 + 5.5x$ ·········· Subtract $0.5x$ from both sides.

$0 = -0.5x(x - 11)$ ·········· Factor.

$-0.5x = 0$ and $x - 11 = 0$ ·········· Set each factor equal to 0 and solve.

$x = 0$ and $x = 11$

CONTINUED ON THE NEXT PAGE

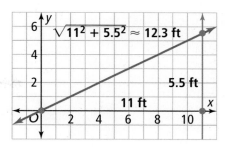

EXAMPLE 3 CONTINUED

COMMON ERROR
Make sure to answer every part of the question. After solving this equation, you still need to find the distance that Laika ran.

The solution $x = 0$ represents the horizontal distance, in feet, when Andrew kicks the ball. The solution $x = 11$ represents the horizontal distance, in feet, when the ball lands on the hill. So the ball travels 11 ft horizontally.

The route Laika runs can be modeled as the hypotenuse of a right triangle.

So Laika runs approximately 12.3 ft to get the ball.

$\sqrt{11^2 + 5.5^2} \approx 12.3$ ft

5.5 ft

11 ft

✓ **Try It!** 3. Revenue for the high school band concert is given by the function $y = -30x^2 + 250x$, where x is the ticket price, in dollars. The cost of the concert is given by the function $y = 490 - 30x$. At what ticket price will the band make enough revenue to cover their costs?

EXAMPLE 4 Solve a Linear-Quadratic System of Inequalities

How can you solve this system of inequalities? $\begin{cases} y < -2x^2 + 12x - 10 \\ 4x + y > 4 \end{cases}$

Graphing an inequality is similar to graphing an equation. You start in the same manner, but later you have to consider whether to sketch the graph as a solid or dotted and how to shade the graph.

Graph the quadratic inequality:

Complete the square to write the inequality in vertex form.

$$y + 10 < -2(x^2 - 6x)$$
$$y + 10 - 18 < -2(x^2 - 6x + 9)$$
$$y - 8 < -2(x - 3)^2$$
$$y < -2(x - 3)^2 + 8$$

The parabola has vertex $(3, 8)$.

Graph the linear inequality:

Solve the inequality for y to write in slope-intercept form:

Sketch the graph of the linear inequality using the slope and y-intercept.

$$y > -4x + 4$$

Find two symmetric points on either side of the vertex:

$x = 2, y = 6 \rightarrow (2, 6)$ $x = 4, y = 6 \rightarrow (4, 6)$

Sketch the graph of the quadratic inequality using these three points.

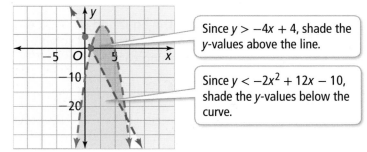

Since $y > -4x + 4$, shade the y-values above the line.

Since $y < -2x^2 + 12x - 10$, shade the y-values below the curve.

The region where the two shaded areas overlap holds the solutions to the system.

CONTINUED ON THE NEXT PAGE

EXAMPLE 4 CONTINUED

  Activity Assess

 Try It! **4.** Solve the system of inequalities $\begin{cases} y > x^2 + 6x - 12 \\ 3x - y \geq -8 \end{cases}$ using shading.

 EXAMPLE 5 **Using a System to Solve an Equation**

Solve the equation $x^2 + 9x - 5 = 4 - 3x$ by writing a linear-quadratic system and using the intersection feature of a graphing calculator to solve it.

Graph the system $\begin{cases} y = x^2 + 9x - 5 \\ y = 4 - 3x \end{cases}$.

The graphing calculator shows the curve and line intersect at $x \approx 0.71$ and $x \approx -12.71$.

STUDY TIP
If you graph both of these equations on your calculator, you can use the TRACE or INTERSECTION function to approximate the solution as a check.

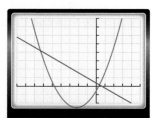

x scale: 2   y scale: 10

Check: Substitute the values into the original equation to verify the solutions. Because the values are approximations, one side of the equation should be approximately equal to the other.

$$x^2 + 9x - 5 = 4 - 3x$$
$$(0.71)^2 + 9(0.71) - 5 \stackrel{?}{=} 4 - 3(0.71)$$
$$0.5041 + 6.39 - 5 \stackrel{?}{=} 4 - 2.13$$
$$1.8941 \approx 1.87$$

$$x^2 + 9x - 5 = 4 - 3x$$
$$(-12.71)^2 + 9(-12.71) - 5 \stackrel{?}{=} 4 - 3(-12.71)$$
$$161.5441 - 114.39 - 5 \stackrel{?}{=} 4 + 38.13$$
$$42.1541 \approx 42.13$$

The equations show that the approximate solutions are reasonable.

 Try It! **5.** Solve the equation $3x^2 - 7x + 4 = 9 - 2x$ by writing a linear-quadratic system and solving using the intersection feature of a graphing calculator.

CONCEPT SUMMARY Key Features of Linear-Quadratic Systems

Linear-Quadratic Systems of Equations

WORDS Use substitution or elimination to solve the system.

GRAPHS

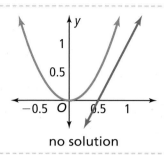

no solution

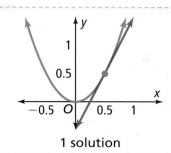

1 solution

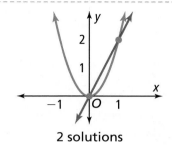

2 solutions

Linear-Quadratic Systems of Inequalities

WORDS Graph linear and quadratic inequalities, considering whether the graph is solid or dotted. Use shading to identify the solution region.

GRAPH

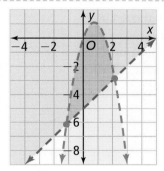

Do You UNDERSTAND?

1. **? ESSENTIAL QUESTION** How can you solve a system of two equations or inequalities in which one is linear and one is quadratic?

2. **Error Analysis** Dyani was asked to use substitution to solve this system:
$$\begin{cases} y = 2x^2 - 6x + 4 \\ x - y = 7 \end{cases}$$
She began as follows, to find the x-coordinate(s) to the solution(s) of the system:

$x + 2x^2 - 6x + 4 = 7$	Substitute for y.
$2x^2 - 5x - 3 = 0$	Simplify.
$(2x + 1)(x - 3) = 0$	Factor.
$x = -\frac{1}{2}, x = 3$	Set each factor equal to 0, solve for x. ✗

But Dyani has already made an error. What was her mistake? **© MP.3**

Do You KNOW HOW?

Determine the number of solutions for the system of equations.

3. $\begin{cases} y = \frac{2}{5}x^2 \\ y = x - 2 \end{cases}$

4. $\begin{cases} y = -x - 1 \\ 3x^2 + 2y = 4 \end{cases}$

Use substitution to solve the system of equations.

5. $\begin{cases} y = 3x^2 + 7x - 10 \\ y - 19x = 22 \end{cases}$

6. $\begin{cases} y = 3x^2 \\ y - 3x = -2 \end{cases}$

UNDERSTAND

7. **Construct Arguments** Nora and William are asked to solve the system of equations
$$\begin{cases} y - 1 = 3x \\ y = 2x^2 - 4x + 9 \end{cases}$$ without graphing.

Nora wants to use substitution, inserting $2x^2 - 4x + 9$ in place of y in the upper equation and solving. William wants to rewrite $y - 1 = 3x$ as $y = 3x + 1$ and begin by setting $3x + 1$ equal to $2x^2 - 4x + 9$, and then solving. Which student is correct, and why? ⓒ **MP.3**

8. **Error Analysis** Chris was given the system of equations $$\begin{cases} y = -x^2 \\ y = 2x + b \end{cases}$$ and asked to use graphing to test the number of solutions of the system for different values of b. He graphed the system as shown, and concluded that the system could have one solution or no solutions depending on the value of b. What was Chris's error? ⓒ **MP.3**

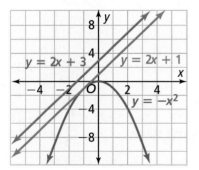

9. **Reason** You are given the following system of equations: $$\begin{cases} y = x^2 \\ y = -1 \end{cases}$$. Without graphing or performing any substitutions, can you see how many solutions the system must have? Describe your reasoning. ⓒ **MP.2**

10. **Construct Arguments** Can a system of equations with one linear and one quadratic equation have more than two solutions? Give at least two arguments for your answer. ⓒ **MP.3**

PRACTICE

Determine how many solutions each system of equations has by graphing them. SEE EXAMPLE 1

11. $$\begin{cases} y = 3 \\ y = x^2 - 4x + 7 \end{cases}$$

12. $$\begin{cases} y = 3x^2 - 2x + 7 \\ y + 5 = \frac{1}{2}x \end{cases}$$

Consider the system of equations $$\begin{cases} y = x^2 \\ y = mx + b \end{cases}$$.
SEE EXAMPLE 1

13. Find values for m and b so that the system has two solutions.

14. Find values for m and b so that the system has no solutions.

15. Find values for m and b so that the system has one solution.

Use substitution to solve the system of equations.
SEE EXAMPLE 2

16. $$\begin{cases} y = 5 \\ y = 2x^2 - 16x + 29 \end{cases}$$

17. $$\begin{cases} y = 3x^2 - 4x \\ 27 + y = 14x \end{cases}$$

18. LaToya throws a ball from the top of a bridge. Her throw is modeled by the equation $y = -0.5x^2 + 3x + 10$, and the bridge is modeled by the equation $y = -0.2x + 7$. About how far does the ball travel horizontally before its first bounce? SEE EXAMPLE 3

Solve each system of inequalities using shading.
SEE EXAMPLE 4

19. $$\begin{cases} y > x^2 \\ 5 > y \end{cases}$$

20. $$\begin{cases} -5 < y - x \\ y < -3x^2 + 6x + 1 \end{cases}$$

Solve each equation by writing a linear-quadratic system and solving using the intersection feature of a graphing calculator. SEE EXAMPLE 5

21. $6x^2 - 15x + 8 = 17 - 4x$

22. $7x^2 - 28x + 32 = 4$

23. $-\frac{5}{2}x - 10 = -2x^2 - x - 3$

PRACTICE & PROBLEM SOLVING

APPLY

24. **Model With Mathematics** A boulder is flung out of the top of a 3,000 m tall volcano. The boulder's height, y, in meters, is a function of the horizontal distance it travels, x, in meters. The slope of the line representing the volcano's hillside is $-\frac{5}{3}$. At what height above the ground will the boulder strike the hillside? How far will it have traveled horizontally when it crashes? © **MP.4**

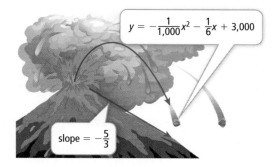

$$y = -\frac{1}{1,000}x^2 - \frac{1}{6}x + 3,000$$

$$\text{slope} = -\frac{5}{3}$$

25. **Use Structure** You are given the system of equations:

$$\begin{cases} y = x + 1 \\ y^2 + x^2 = 25 \end{cases}$$

Solve the system using any of the methods you have learned in this lesson. Explain why you selected the method you used. © **MP.7**

26. **Reason** A football player punts the football, whose path is modeled by the equation $h = -4.9t^2 + 18.24t + 0.8$ for h, in meters, and t, in seconds. The height of a blocker's hands for the same time, t, is modeled as $h = -1.43t + 4.26$. Is it possible for the blocker to knock down the ball? What else would you have to know to be sure? © **MP.2**

$$h = -4.9t^2 + 18.24t + 0.8$$

$$h = -1.43t + 4.26$$

27. Classify each function as having *exactly one* or *no* points of intersection with the function $y = x^2 + 8x + 11$.

    a. $y = 2x - 12$

    b. $y = 12x + 7$

    c. $y = -5$

    d. $y = 11 + 8x$

    e. $y = -6$

28. **SAT/ACT** How many solutions does the following system of equations have?

$$\begin{cases} y = 16x - 19 \\ y = 3x^2 + 4x - 7 \end{cases}$$

    Ⓐ two solutions

    Ⓑ no solutions

    Ⓒ an infinite number of solutions

    Ⓓ one solution

    Ⓔ The number of solutions cannot be determined.

29. **Performance Task** A golfer accidentally hits a ball toward a water hazard that is downhill from her current position on the fairway. The hill can be modeled by a line through the origin with slope $-\frac{1}{8}$. The path of the ball can be modeled by the function $y = -\frac{1}{100}x^2 + \frac{3}{2}x$.

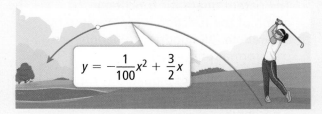

$$y = -\frac{1}{100}x^2 + \frac{3}{2}x$$

Part A If the golfer stands at the origin, and the water hazard is 180 yd away, will the golfer's ball bounce or splash?

Part B How far did the ball land from the edge of the water hazard?

Part C Does it matter whether you measure the 180 yd horizontally or along the hill? Explain.

? TOPIC ESSENTIAL QUESTION

1. How do you use quadratic functions to model situations and solve problems?

Vocabulary Review

Choose the correct term to complete each sentence.

2. According to the _____, a product is 0 only if one (or more) of its factors is 0.

3. The _____ of a quadratic function is $y = a(x - h)^2 + k$.

4. The _____ of a quadratic function is the value of the radicand, $b^2 - 4ac$.

5. A number with both real and imaginary parts is called a _____.

6. The _____ of a quadratic function is $y = ax^2 + bx + c$.

7. _____ is a method used to rewrite an equation as a perfect square trinomial equal to a constant.

- completing the square
- complex number
- discriminant
- imaginary number
- parabola
- quadratic function
- standard form
- vertex form
- Zero Product Property

Concepts & Skills Review

| LESSON 2-1 | Vertex Form of a Quadratic Function |

Quick Review

The parent **quadratic function** is $f(x) = x^2$. The graph of the function is represented by a **parabola**. All quadratic functions are transformations of $f(x) = x^2$.

The vertex form of a quadratic function is $y = a(x - h)^2 + k$, where (h, k) is the vertex of a parabola.

Example

What is the equation of a parabola with vertex (3, 1) and y-intercept 10?

$y = a(x - 3)^2 + 1$ ········· Substitute $(h, k) = (2, 3)$.

$10 = a(0 - 3)^2 + 1$ ········· Substitute y-intercept $(0, 10)$.

$9 = a(-3)^2$ ········· Simplify.

$9 = 9a$

$a = 1$ ········· Solve for a.

$y = 1(x - 3)^2 + 1$ ········· Substitute a.

The equation of the parabola is $y = (x - 3)^2 + 1$.

Practice & Problem Solving

Describe the transformation of the parent function $f(x) = x^2$. Then graph the given function.

8. $g(x) = (x + 2)^2 - 4$ 9. $h(x) = -2(x - 1)^2 + 5$

Identify the vertex, axis of symmetry, maximum or minimum, domain, and range of each function.

10. $g(x) = -(x + 3)^2 + 2$ 11. $h(x) = 3(x - 4)^2 - 3$

Write the equation of each quadratic function in vertex form.

12. Vertex: (2, 1); Point (0, 4)

13. Vertex: (1, 5); Point (3, −1)

14. **Use Structure** The graph of the function $f(x) = x^2$ will be translated 4 units down and 2 units right. What is the resulting function $g(x)$? Ⓒ MP.7

15. **Make Sense and Persevere** Find three additional points on the parabola that has vertex (5, 3) and passes through (2, 21). Ⓒ MP.1

Standard Form of a Quadratic Function

Quick Review

The **standard form of a quadratic function** is $y = ax^2 + bx + c$ where a, b, and c are real numbers, and $a \neq 0$. Use the formula $h = -\frac{b}{2a}$ to find the x-coordinate of the vertex and the axis of symmetry. Substitue 0 for x to find the y-intercept of the quadratic function.

Example

The function $y = -8x^2 + 880x - 5,000$ can be used to predict the profits for a company that sells eBook readers for a certain price, x. What is the maximum profit the company can expect to earn?

The maximum value of a quadratic function occurs at the vertex of a parabola. Use the formula $h = -\frac{b}{2a}$ to find the x-coordinate of the vertex.

$h = -\dfrac{880}{2(-8)}$ .... Substitute -8 for a and 880 for b.

$h = 55$ .... Simplify.

$x = 55$ .... Substitute h for x.

$y = -8(55)^2 + 880(55) - 5,000$ ··· Substitute 55 for x.

$y = 19,200$ ············ Simplify.

The vertex is (55, 19,200). The selling price of $55 per item gives the maximum profit of $19,200.

Practice & Problem Solving

Find the vertex and y-intercept of the quadratic function, and use them to graph the function.

16. $y = x^2 - 6x + 15$ **17.** $y = 4x^2 - 15x + 9$

Write an equation in standard form for the parabola that passes through the given points.

18. (1, 5), (3, 7), (6, 25)

19. (−2, 64), (3, −16), (7, 28)

20. Higher Order Thinking A golfer is on a hill that is 60 meters above the hole. The path of the ball can be modeled by the equation $y = -5x^2 + 40x + 60$, where x is the horizontal and y the vertical distance traveled by the ball in meters. How would you use the function to find the horizontal distance traveled by the ball and its maximum height?

21. Make Sense and Persevere The number of issues sold per month of a new magazine (in thousands) and its profit (in thousands of dollars) could be modeled by the function $y = -6x^2 + 36x + 50$. Determine the maximum profit. Ⓒ **MP.1**

Factored Form of a Quadratic Function

Quick Review

Factor a quadratic equation by first setting the quadratic expression equal to 0. Then factor and use the **Zero Product Property** to solve. According to the Zero Product Property, if $ab = 0$, then $a = 0$ or $b = 0$ (or $a = 0$ and $b = 0$).

Example

Solve the equation $x^2 + x = 72$.

$x^2 + x - 72 = 0$ ············ Set equation equal to 0.

$(x + 9)(x - 8)$ ············ Factor.

$x + 9 = 0$ or $x - 8 = 0$ ············ Zero Product Property.

$x = -9$ or $x = 8$ ············ Solve.

The solutions for equation $x^2 + x = 72$ are $x = -9$ or $x = 8$.

Practice & Problem Solving

Solve each quadratic equation.

22. $x^2 - 6x - 27 = 0$ **23.** $x^2 = 7x - 10$

24. $4x^2 + 4x = 3$ **25.** $5x^2 - 19x = -12$

Identify the interval(s) on which each function is positive.

26. $y = x^2 - x - 30$ **27.** $y = x^2 + 11x + 28$

28. Generalize For what values of x is the expression $(x + 6)^2 > 0$?

29. Model With Mathematics A prairie dog burrow has openings to the surface which, if they were graphed, correspond to points (2.5, 0) and (8, 0). What equation models the burrow if, at its deepest, it passes through point (5, −15)? Ⓒ **MP.4**

Quick Review

The **imaginary unit** i is the number whose square is equal to -1. An **imaginary number** bi is the product of any real number b and the imaginary unit i. A **complex number** is a number that may be written in the form $a + bi$. **Complex conjugates** are complex numbers with equivalent real parts and opposite imaginary parts.

Example

Write the product of $3.5i(4 - 6i)$ in the form $a + bi$.

$3.5i(4 - 6i)$

$= 3.5i(4) + 3.5i(-6i)$ ········· Distribute.

$= 14i - 21i^2$ ················· Simplify.

$= 14i - 21(-1)$ ············· Substitute -1 for i.

$= 14i + 21$ ················· Write in the form $a + bi$.

The product is $14i + 21$.

Practice & Problem Solving

Write each product in the form $a + bi$.

30. $(5 - 3i)(2 + i)$ **31.** $(-3 + 2i)(2 - 3i)$

Divide. Write the answer in the form $a + bi$.

32. $\dfrac{5}{3 + i}$ **33.** $\dfrac{2 - 3i}{1 + 2i}$

34. Error Analysis Describe and correct the error a student made when multiplying complex numbers. Ⓒ **MP.3**

$(2 - 3i)(4 + i) = 2(4) + 2(i) - 3i(4) - 3i(i)$
$= 8 + 2i - 12i - 3i^2$
$= 8 - 10i - 3i^2$

35. Model With Mathematics The formula $E = IZ$ is used to calculate voltage, where E is voltage, I is current, and Z is impedance. If the voltage in a circuit is $35 + 10i$ volts and the impedance is $4 + 4i$ ohms, what is the current (in amps)? Write your answer in the form $a + bi$. Ⓒ **MP.4**

Quick Review

Completing the square is a method used to rewrite a quadratic equation as a perfect square trinomial equal to a constant. A perfect square trinomial with the coefficient of x^2 equal to 1 has the form $(x - p)^2$ which is equivalent to $x^2 - 2px + p^2$.

Example

Solve the equation $0 = x^2 - 2x + 4$ by completing the square.

$0 = x^2 - 2x + 4$ ··· Write the original equation.

$-4 = x^2 - 2x$ ········ Subtract 4 from both sides of the equation.

$1 - 4 = x^2 - 2x + 1$ ··· Complete the square

$-3 = (x - 1)^2$ ········ Write the right side of the equation as a perfect square.

$\pm\sqrt{-3} = x - 1$ ········ Take the square root of each side of the equation.

$1 \pm \sqrt{-3} = x$ ········ Add 1 to each side of the equation.

The solutions are $x = 1 \pm \sqrt{-3}$.

Practice & Problem Solving

Rewrite the equations in the form $(x - p)^2 = q$.

36. $0 = x^2 - 16x + 36$ **37.** $0 = 4x^2 - 28x - 42$

Solve the following quadratic equations by completing the square.

38. $x^2 - 24x - 82 = 0$ **39.** $-3x^2 - 42x = 18$

40. $4x^2 = 16x + 25$ **41.** $12 + x^2 = 15x$

42. Reason The height, in meters, of a punted football with respect to time is modeled using the function $f(x) = -4.9x^2 + 24.5x + 1$, where x is time in seconds. You determine that the roots of the function $f(x) = -4.9x^2 + 24.5x + 1$ are approximately -0.04 and 5.04. When does the ball hit the ground? Explain. Ⓒ **MP.2**

43. Make Sense and Persevere A bike manufacturer can predict profits, P, from a new sports bike using the quadratic function $P(x) = -100x^2 + 46,000x - 2,100,000$, where x is the price of the bike. At what prices will the company make $0 in profit? Ⓒ **MP.1**

The Quadratic Formula

Quick Review

The **Quadratic Formula**, $x = \dfrac{-b \pm \sqrt{b^2 - 4ac}}{2a}$, provides the solutions of the quadratic equation $ax^2 + bx + c = 0$ for $a \neq 0$. You can calculate the **discriminant** of a quadratic equation to determine the number of real roots.

$b^2 - 4ac > 0$: $ax^2 + bx + c = 0$ has 2 real roots.

$b^2 - 4ac = 0$: $ax^2 + bx + c = 0$ has 1 real root.

$b^2 - 4ac < 0$: $ax^2 + bx + c = 0$ has 2 non-real roots.

Example

How many real roots does $3x^2 - 8x + 1 = 0$ have?

Find the discriminant.

$$b^2 - 4ac = (-8)^2 - 4(3)(1)$$
$$= 64 - 12$$
$$= 52$$

Since $52 > 0$, the equation has two real roots.

Practice & Problem Solving

Use the Quadratic Formula to solve the equation.

44. $x^2 - 16x + 24 = 0$ **45.** $x^2 + 5x + 2 = 0$

46. $2x^2 - 18x + 5 = 0$ **47.** $3x^2 - 5x - 19 = 0$

Use the discriminant to identify the number and type of solutions for each equation.

48. $x^2 - 24x + 19 = 0$ **49.** $3x^2 - 8x + 12 = 0$

50. Find the value(s) of k that will cause the equation $4x^2 - kx + 4 = 0$ to have one real solution.

51. Construct Arguments Why does the graph of the quadratic function $f(x) = x^2 + 4x + 5$ cross the y-axis but not the x-axis? Ⓒ **MP.3**

52. Model With Mathematics The function $C(x) = 0.0045x^2 - 0.47x + 139$ models the cost per hour of running a bus between two cities, where x is the speed in kilometers per hour. At what speeds will the cost of running the bus exceed \$130? Ⓒ **MP.4**

Linear-Quadratic Systems

Quick Review

Solutions to a system of equations are points that produces a true statement for all the equations of the system. The solutions on a graph are the coordinates of the intersection points.

Example

Use substitution to solve the system of equations.

$$\begin{cases} y = 2x^2 - 5x + 4 \\ 5x - y = 4 \end{cases}$$

Substitute $2x^2 - 5x + 4$ for y in the second equation.

$$5x - (2x^2 - 5x + 4) = 4$$
$$-2x^2 + 10x - 8 = 0$$

Factor: $-2(x - 1)(x - 4) = 0$

So $x = 1$ and $x = 4$ are solutions.

When $x = 1$, $y = 2(1)^2 - 5(1) + 4 = 1$.

When $x = 4$, $y = 2(4)^2 - 5(4) + 4 = 16$.

The solutions of the system are $(1, 1)$ and $(4, 16)$.

Practice & Problem Solving

Determine the number of solutions of each system of equations.

53. $\begin{cases} y = x^2 - 5x + 9 \\ y = 3 \end{cases}$ **54.** $\begin{cases} y = 3x^2 + 4x + 5 \\ y - 4 = 2x \end{cases}$

Solve each system of equations.

55. $\begin{cases} y = x^2 + 4x + 3 \\ y - 2x = 6 \end{cases}$ **56.** $\begin{cases} y = x^2 + 2x + 7 \\ y = 7 + x \end{cases}$

57. Model With Mathematics An archer shoots an arrow to a height (meters) given by the equation $y = -5t^2 + 18t - 0.25$, where t is the time in seconds. A target sits on a hill represented by the equation $y = 0.75x - 1$. At what height will the arrow strike the target, and how long will it take? Ⓒ **MP.4**

TOPIC 2 REVIEW

TOPIC 3

Polynomial Functions

? TOPIC ESSENTIAL QUESTION

What can the rule for a polynomial function reveal about its graph, and what can the graphs of polynomial functions reveal about the solutions of polynomial equations?

Topic Overview

enVision™ STEM Project
   Design a Stadium

3-1   Graphing Polynomial Functions

3-2   Adding, Subtracting, and Multiplying Polynomials

3-3   Polynomial Identities

3-4   Dividing Polynomials

3-5   Zeros of Polynomial Functions

Mathematical Modeling in 3 Acts: What Are the Rules?

3-6   Theorems About Roots of Polynomial Equations

3-7   Transformations of Polynomial Functions

Topic Vocabulary

- Binomial Theorem
- degree of a polynomial
- end behavior
- even function
- identity
- leading coefficient
- multiplicity of a zero
- odd function
- Pascal's triangle
- polynomial function
- relative maximum
- relative minimum
- Rational Root Theorem
- Remainder Theorem
- standard form of a polynomial
- synthetic division
- turning point

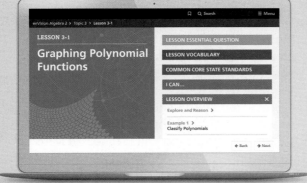

Digital Experience

INTERACTIVE STUDENT EDITION Access online or offline.

ACTIVITIES Complete *Explore & Reason, Model & Discuss,* and *Critique & Explain* activities. Interact with Examples and Try Its.

ANIMATION View and interact with real-world applications.

PRACTICE Practice what you've learned.

 Go online | SavvasRealize.com

▶ What Are the Rules?

All games have rules about how to play the game. The rules outline such things as when a ball is in or out, how a player scores points, and how many points a player gets for each winning shot.

If you didn't alreay know how to play tennis, or some other game, could you figure out what the rules were just by watching? What clues would help you understand the game? Think about this during the Mathematical Modeling in 3 Acts lesson.

VIDEOS Watch clips to support **Mathematical Modeling in 3 Acts Lessons** and **enVision™ STEM Projects.**

CONCEPT SUMMARY Review key lesson content through multiple representations.

ASSESSMENT Show what you've learned.

GLOSSARY Read and listen to English and Spanish definitions.

TUTORIALS Get help from *Virtual Nerd*, right when you need it.

MATH TOOLS Explore math with digital tools and manipulatives.

e̊nVision STEM

Video

Did You Know?

In a 2013–2015 overhaul, Texas A&M's football stadium increased its seating from 80,600 to 102,512. The renovation cost $450 million and included lowering the field and adding overhangs to two sides.

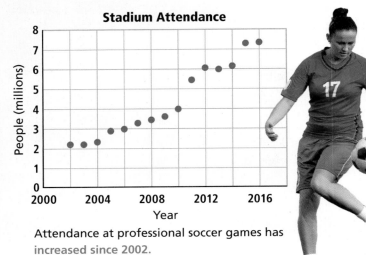

Stadium Attendance

Attendance at professional soccer games has increased since 2002.

The new home of the Minnesota Vikings, opened in Minneapolis in July 2016, includes approximately 1.6 million square feet of space. The stadium seats 66,200 spectators for most events but can expand to seat 73,000. The first row of seats is 41 feet from the sideline.

▶ Your Task: Design a Stadium

You and your classmates will plan the seating at a new stadium. You will explore attendance at the current stadium and use fitted curves to support your predictions of future attendance.

3-1
Graphing Polynomial Functions

SavvasRealize.com

I CAN... predict the behavior of polynomial functions.

VOCABULARY
- degree of a polynomial
- leading coefficient
- polynomial function
- relative maximum
- relative minimum
- standard form of a polynomial
- turning point

© **Common Core State Standards** HSF.IF.B.4, HSF.IF.B.6, HSF.IF.C.7.C, MP.2, MP.5, MP.7

  Activity Assess

EXPLORE & REASON

Consider functions of the form $f(x) = x^n$, where n is a positive integer.

A. Graph $f(x) = x^n$ for $n = 1$, 3, and 5. Look at the graphs in Quadrant I. As the exponent increases, what is happening to the graphs? Which quadrants do the graphs pass through?

B. **Look for Relationships** Now graph $f(x) = x^n$ for $n = 2$, 4, and 6. What happens to these graphs in Quadrant I as the exponent increases? Which quadrants do the graphs pass through? © **MP.7**

C. Write two equations in the form $f(x) = x^n$ with graphs that you predict are in Quadrants I and II. Write two equations with graphs that you predict are in Quadrants I and III. Use graphing technology to test your predictions.

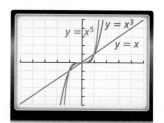

ESSENTIAL QUESTION

How do the key features of a polynomial function help you sketch its graph?

EXAMPLE 1 Classify Polynomials

How can you write a polynomial in standard form and use it to identify the leading coefficient, the degree, and the number of terms?

$$-4x + 9 + 2x^3$$

Recall that a polynomial is a monomial or the sum of one or more monomials, called terms. The degree of a term with one variable is the exponent of that variable.

Degree of $-4x$: 1   Degree of 9: 0   Degree of $2x^3$: 3

Standard form of a polynomial shows any like terms combined and the terms by degree in descending numerical order.

Standard form of this polynomial is:

USE STRUCTURE
Note that there is no x^2-term in the polynomial $2x^3 - 4x + 9$. In some cases, it may be useful to write the polynomial as $2x^3 + 0x^2 - 4x + 9$. © **MP.7**

The **leading coefficient** refers to the non-zero factor that is multiplied by the greatest power of x. The leading coefficient of this polynomial is 2.

$2x^3 - 4x + 9$

The polynomial has three terms, so it is called a *trinomial*.

The **degree of a polynomial** is the greatest degree of any of the terms. This is a polynomial of degree 3, also known as a *cubic polynomial*.

 Try It! **1.** What is each polynomial in standard form and what are the leading coefficient, the degree, and the number of terms of each?

a. $2x - 3x^4 + 6 - 5x^3$

b. $x^5 + 2x^6 - 3x^4 - 8x + 4x^3$

CONCEPTUAL
UNDERSTANDING ➔   ✊ **EXAMPLE 2** ▷ **Understand End Behavior of Polynomial Functions**

How do the sign of the leading coefficient and the degree of a polynomial affect the end behavior of the graph of a polynomial function?

A **polynomial function** is a function whose rule is a polynomial. The **end behavior** of a graph describes what happens to the function values as x approaches positive and negative infinity.

LOOK FOR RELATIONSHIPS
Though a polynomial function may have many terms, the leading term determines the end behavior because it has the greatest exponent and therefore the greatest impact on function values when x is very large or very small. Ⓒ **MP.7**

Odd Degree Positive Leading Coefficient	Even Degree Positive Leading Coefficient
$f(x) = x$; degree 1 $g(x) = 0.5x^3 - x^2 + 3$; degree 3 $h(x) = 2x^5 - x^2 - x - 2$; degree 5 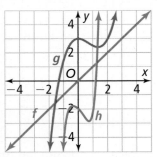	$f(x) = x^2$; degree 2 $g(x) = 0.9x^4 - 2x^3 + x^2 - 2x$; degree 4 $h(x) = 2x^6 + x^2 - 2$; degree 6 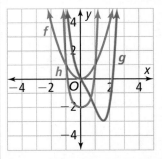
End behavior is similar to the linear parent function $f(x) = x$.	End is behavior similar to the quadratic parent function $f(x) = x^2$.

Recall that a reflection of a function across the x-axis occurs when the function is negated: $f(x)$ becomes $-f(x)$. The end behavior of a function is similarly affected when the leading coefficient is negative.

Odd Degree Negative Leading Coefficient	Even Degree Negative Leading Coefficient
$f(x) = -x$; degree 1 $g(x) = -0.5x^3 - x^2 - 3$; degree 3 $h(x) = -2x^5 + x^2 + x + 2$; degree 5 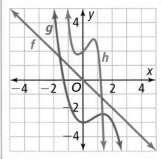	$f(x) = -x^2$; degree 2 $g(x) = -0.9x^4 + 2x^3 - x^2 + 2x$; degree 4 $h(x) = -2x^6 - x^2 + 2$; degree 6 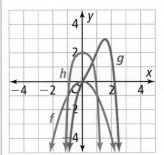
End behavior is similar to $f(x) = -x$.	End behavior is similar to $f(x) = -x^2$.

 Try It!   **2.** Use the leading coefficient and degree of the polynomial function to determine the end behavior of each graph.

    a. $f(x) = 2x^6 - 5x^5 + 6x^4 - x^3 + 4x^2 - x + 1$

    b. $g(x) = -5x^3 + 8x + 4$

EXAMPLE 3 Graph a Polynomial Function

Consider the polynomial function $f(x) = -0.5x^4 + 3x^2 + 2$.

A. How can you use a table of values to identify key features and sketch a graph of the function?

Make a table of values and identify intervals where the function is increasing and decreasing.

<table>
<tr><th>x</th><th>f(x)</th></tr>
<tr><td>−3</td><td>−11.5</td></tr>
<tr><td>−2</td><td>6</td></tr>
<tr><td>−1</td><td>4.5</td></tr>
<tr><td>0</td><td>2</td></tr>
<tr><td>1</td><td>4.5</td></tr>
<tr><td>2</td><td>6</td></tr>
<tr><td>3</td><td>−11.5</td></tr>
</table>

increasing

decreasing

increasing

decreasing

Points where the function values change from increasing to decreasing, or vice-versa, are **turning points**. This function has approximate turning points when the value of x is between −2 and −1, −1 and 0, and 1 and 2.

> **USE APPROPRIATE TOOLS**
> It can be very difficult to locate the precise turning points and zeros of polynomial functions. Graphing technology can help identify these points. © **MP.5**

This is a polynomial function with an even degree and a negative leading coefficient, so both ends of the graph will trend toward −∞.

Plot the points and sketch the graph with a smooth curve.

A point where the function has the least value over an interval is a **relative minimum**. This function has a relative minimum near (0, 2).

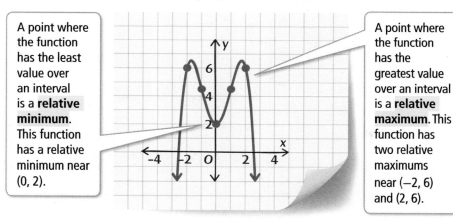

A point where the function has the greatest value over an interval is a **relative maximum**. This function has two relative maximums near (−2, 6) and (2, 6).

B. How can you use the graph to estimate the average rate of change over the interval [−2, 0]?

Recall that the average rate of change is $\frac{f(b) - f(a)}{b - a}$ for two points on a graph $(a, f(a))$ and $(b, f(b))$.

Average rate of change $= \dfrac{f(b) - f(a)}{b - a}$

$= \dfrac{2 - 6}{0 - (-2)}$

$= -2$

Substitute (−2, 6) and (0, 2).

The average rate of change over the interval [−2, 0] is −2.

✓ **Try It!** **3.** Consider the polynomial function $f(x) = x^5 + 18x^2 + 10x + 1$.

    a. Make a table of values to identify key features and sketch a graph of the function.

    b. Find the average rate of change over the interval [0, 2].

👆 **EXAMPLE 4**   Sketch the Graph from a Verbal Description

How can you sketch a graph of the polynomial function *f* from a verbal description?

- *f*(*x*) is positive on the intervals (−∞, −4) and (−1, 4).
- *f*(*x*) is negative on the intervals (−4, −1) and (4, ∞).
- *f*(*x*) is decreasing on the intervals (−∞, −2.67) and (2, ∞).
- *f*(*x*) is increasing on the interval (−2.67, 2).

Step 1: Identify or estimate *x*-intercepts. The function values change signs at *x* = −4, *x* = −1, and *x* = 4.

Step 2: Identify or estimate turning points. The function changes direction at *x* = −2.67 and *x* = 2.
- There is a relative minimum at *x* = −2.67.
- There is a relative maximum at *x* = 2.

Step 3: Evaluate end behavior.

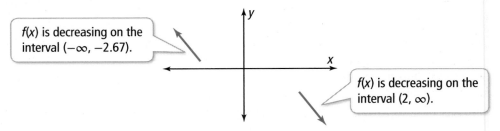

f(*x*) is decreasing on the interval (−∞, −2.67).

f(*x*) is decreasing on the interval (2, ∞).

Step 4: Sketch the graph.

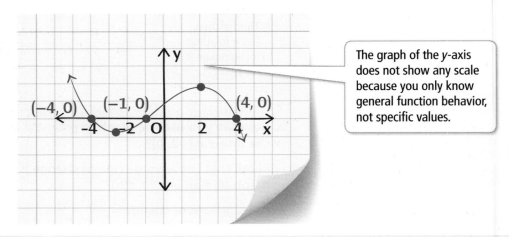

The graph of the *y*-axis does not show any scale because you only know general function behavior, not specific values.

 Try It!   **4.** Use the information below to sketch a graph of the polynomial function *y* = *f*(*x*).
- *f*(*x*) is positive on the intervals (−2, −1) and (1, 2).
- *f*(*x*) is negative on the intervals (−∞, −2), (−1, 1), and (2, ∞).
- *f*(*x*) is increasing on the interval (−∞, −1.5) and (0, 1.5).
- *f*(*x*) is decreasing on the intervals (−1.5, 0) and (1.5, ∞).

APPLICATION

EXAMPLE 5 Interpret a Polynomial Model

In science class, Abby mixes a fixed amount of baking soda with different amounts of vinegar in a bottle capped by a balloon. She records the amount of time it takes the gases produced by the reaction to inflate the balloon.

From her data, Abby created a function to model the situation. For x quarter-cups of vinegar, it takes $t(x) = -0.12x^3 + x^2 - 3.38x + 13.16$ seconds to inflate the balloon.

A. How long would it take to inflate the balloon with 5 quarter-cups of vinegar?

Use technology to sketch the graph.

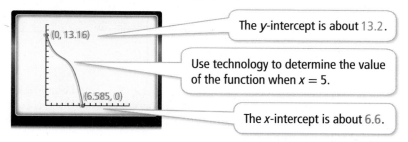

(0, 13.16)

(6.585, 0)

The y-intercept is about 13.2.

Use technology to determine the value of the function when $x = 5$.

The x-intercept is about 6.6.

STUDY TIP
Recall that when you are using a graph in a real-world context, you need to consider the context when thinking about domain and range. Does it make sense for x to be negative? Does it make sense for y to be negative?

When $x = 5$, the value of the function is about 6.3. This means that if Abby uses 5 quarter-cups of vinegar, the balloon will inflate in approximately 6.3 seconds.

B. What do the x- and y-intercepts of the graph mean in this context? Do those values make sense?

The x-intercept is approximately 6.6 which means that if 6.6 cups of vinegar are used, the balloon would inflate in 0 seconds.

The y-intercept is approximately 13.2, which means that if no vinegar is used, the balloon will inflate in 13.2 seconds.

Neither the x- nor the y-intercept make sense in this context. Therefore, we must limit the domain and range when considering this model.

 Try It! 5. Danielle is engineering a new brand of shoes. For x shoes sold, in thousands, a profit of $p(x) = -3x^4 + 4x^3 - 2x^2 + 5x + 10$ dollars, in ten thousands, will be earned.

   a. How much will be earned in profit for selling 1,000 shoes?

   b. What do the x- and y-intercepts of the graph mean in this context? Do those values make sense?

CONCEPT SUMMARY Graphing Polynomial Functions

> **WORDS** ▶ A **polynomial function** is a function whose rule is either a monomial or a sum of monomials.

> **KEY FEATURES** ▶ **Turning points** – function values change from increasing to decreasing, or vice-versa
>
> **Relative minimum** – changes from decreasing to increasing
>
> **Relative maximum** – changes from increasing to decreasing

> **GRAPHS** ▶ End behavior depends on the degree of the polynomial and the sign of its leading coefficient.

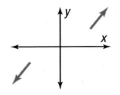   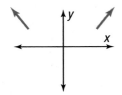   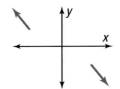   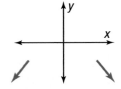

Degree: odd   Degree: even   Degree: odd   Degree: even
Leading Coefficient: +   Leading Coefficient: +   Leading Coefficient: −   Leading Coefficient: −

☑ Do You UNDERSTAND?

1. **❓ ESSENTIAL QUESTION** How do the key features of a polynomial function help you sketch its graph?

2. **Error Analysis** Allie said the degree of the polynomial function $f(x) = x^5 + 2x^4 + 3x^3 - 2x^6 - 9x^2 - 6x + 4$ is 5. Explain and correct Allie's error. ⒸMP.3

3. **Vocabulary** Explain how to determine the leading coefficient of a polynomial function.

4. **Look for Relationships** What is the relationship between the degree and leading coefficient of a polynomial function and the end behavior of the polynomial? ⒸMP.7

Do You KNOW HOW?

The graph shows the function $f(x) = x^4 + 2x^3 - 13x^2 - 14x + 24$. **Find the following.**

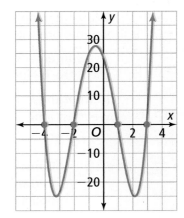

5. number of terms   6. degree

7. leading coefficient   8. end behavior

9. turning point(s)   10. x-intercept(s)

11. relative minimum(s)

12. relative maximum(s)

UNDERSTAND

13. Make Sense and Persevere The table shows some values of a polynomial function. Deshawn says there are turning points between the x-values -3 and -2 and between 0 and 1. He also says there is a relative minimum between the x-values -3 and -2, and a relative maximum between 0 and 1. Sketch a graph that shows how Deshawn could be correct and another graph that shows how Deshawn could be incorrect. © **MP.1**

x	-5	-4	-3	-2	-1	0	1	2
$f(x)$	-1004	129	220	85	12	1	4	165

14. Higher Order Thinking Use the information below about a polynomial function in standard form to write a possible polynomial function. Explain how you determined your function and graph it to verify that it satisfies the criteria.

• 6 terms

• y-intercept at 1

• end behavior: As $x \rightarrow -\infty$, $y \rightarrow +\infty$.
 As $x \rightarrow +\infty$, $y \rightarrow -\infty$.

15. Reason An analyst for a new company used the first three years of revenue data to project future revenue for the company. The analyst predicts the function $f(x) = -2x^5 + 6x^4 - x^3 + 5x^2 + 6x + 50$ will give the revenue after x years. Should the CEO expect the company to be successful? Explain. © **MP.2**

16. Look for Relationships Sketch a graph of each of the functions described below. © **MP.7**

• a cubic function with one x-intercept

• a cubic function with 2 x-intercepts

• a cubic function with 3 x-intercepts

17. Make Sense and Persevere Compare the rate of change for the function $f(x) = x^3 - 2x^2 + x + 1$ over the intervals $[0, 2]$ and $[2, 4]$. © **MP.1**

PRACTICE

Write each polynomial function in standard form. For each function, find the degree, number of terms, and leading coefficient. SEE EXAMPLE 1

18. $f(x) = -3x^3 + 2x^5 + x + 8x^3 - 6 + x^4 - 3x^2$

19. $f(x) = 8x^2 + 10x^7 - 7x^3 - x^4$

20. $f(x) = -x^3 + 9x + 12 - x^4 + 5x^2$

Use the leading coefficient and degree of the polynomial function to determine the end behavior of the graph. SEE EXAMPLE 2

21. $f(x) = -x^5 + 2x^4 + 3x^3 + 2x^2 - 8x + 9$

22. $f(x) = 7x^4 - 4x^3 + 7x^2 + 10x - 15$

23. $f(x) = -x^6 + 7x^5 - x^4 + 2x^3 + 9x^2 - 8x - 2$

Use a table of values to estimate the intercepts and turning points of the function. Then graph the function. SEE EXAMPLE 3

24. $f(x) = x^3 + 2x^2 - 5x - 6$

25. $f(x) = x^4 - x^3 - 21x^2 + x + 20$

26. Use the information below to sketch a graph of the polynomial function $y = f(x)$. SEE EXAMPLE 4

• $f(x)$ is positive on the intervals $(-\infty, -3)$, $(-2, 0)$, and $(2, 3)$.

• $f(x)$ is negative on the intervals $(-3, -2)$, $(0, 2)$, and $(3, \infty)$.

• $f(x)$ is increasing on the interval $(-2.67, -1)$ and $(1, 2.5)$.

• $f(x)$ is decreasing on the intervals $(-\infty, -2.67)$, $(-1, 1)$, and $(2.5, \infty)$.

27. The equation shown models the average depth y, in feet, of a lake, x years after 2016, where $0 < x < 6$. Use technology to graph the function. In what year does this model predict a relative minimum value for the depth? SEE EXAMPLE 5

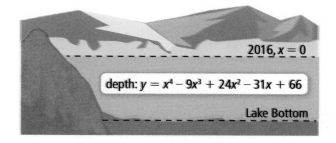

2016, $x = 0$

depth: $y = x^4 - 9x^3 + 24x^2 - 31x + 66$

Lake Bottom

APPLY

28. Reason Allie has a piece of construction paper that she wants to use to make an open rectangular prism. She will cut a square with side length x from each corner of the paper, so the length and width is decreased by $2x$ as shown in the diagram. **© MP.2**

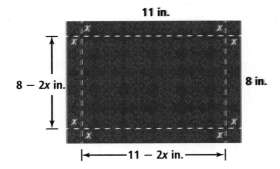

11 in.

8 − 2x in.   8 in.

|←——— 11 − 2x in. ———→|

a. Write a function that models the volume of the rectangular prism.

b. Graph the function and identify a reasonable domain.

c. What do the x-intercepts of the graph mean in this context?

d. If Allie wants to maximize the volume of the box, what is the side length of the squares that should be cut from each corner of the piece of construction paper? Explain.

29. Make Sense and Persevere Alberto is designing a container in the shape of a rectangular prism to ship electronic devices. The length of the container is 10 inches longer than the height. The sum of the length, width, and height is 25 inches. The volume of the container, in terms of height x, is shown. Use a graphing calculator to graph the function. What do the x-intercepts of the graph mean in this context? What dimensions of the container will maximize the volume? **© MP.1**

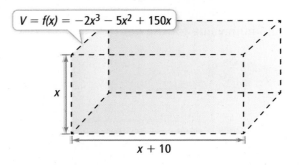

$V = f(x) = -2x^3 - 5x^2 + 150x$

x

x + 10

ASSESSMENT PRACTICE

30. Copy and complete the table to give the leading coefficient of each polynomial function.

Polynomial Function	Leading coefficient
$f(x) = 3x^3 + 2x^2 + 9x - 6$	
$f(x) = -3x^4 + 8x^2 - 2x + 7x^5$	
$f(x) = -3x^5 + 7x^3 + 6x^2 - 2$	
$f(x) = 3x^2 - 12x^4 - 3x^6 - 3x^3$	
$f(x) = 6x^3 + 9x^2 - 5x - 3$	

31. SAT/ACT What is the maximum number of terms a fourth-degree polynomial function in standard form can have?

Ⓐ 1   Ⓑ 2   Ⓒ 3   Ⓓ 4   Ⓔ 5

32. Performance Task In the year 2000, a demographer predicted the estimated population of a city, which can be modeled by the function $f(x) = 5x^4 - 4x^3 + 25x + 8,000$. Several years later, a statistician, using data from the U.S. Census Bureau, modeled the actual population with the function $P(x) = 7x^4 - 6x^3 + 5x + 8,000$. The graphs of the functions are shown.

Predicted vs. Actual Populations

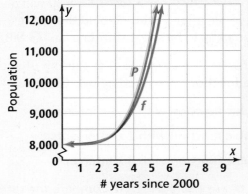

years since 2000

Part A What is the y-intercept of each function, and what does it represent?

Part B Identify the end behaviors of f and P.

Part C Compare the average rates of change of f and P from 2003 to 2005.

3-2

Adding, Subtracting, and Multiplying Polynomials

 SavvasRealize.com

I CAN... add, subtract, and multiply polynomials.

  ○ Activity   ○ Assess

◻ EXPLORE & REASON

Let *S* be the set of expressions that can be written as *ax* + *b* where *a* and *b* are real numbers.

A. Describe the Associative Property, Commutative Property, and the Distributive Property. Then, explain the role of each in simplifying the sum $(3x + 2) + (7x − 4)$. Identify the leading coefficient and the constant term in the result.

B. Is the sum you found in part A a member of *S*? Explain.

C. **Construct Arguments** Is the product of two expressions in *S* also a member of *S*? Explain why or produce a counterexample. ● **MP.3**

? ESSENTIAL QUESTION ▷   How do you add, subtract, and multiply polynomials?

◻ EXAMPLE 1   Add and Subtract Polynomials

How do you add or subtract the polynomials?

To add and subtract polynomials, use the Commutative and Associative Properties to group like terms. Then combine like terms.

A. $(6x^3 + 4x + x^2 − 7) + (2x^3 − 8x^2 + 3)$

$= (6x^3 + 2x^3) + 4x + (x^2 − 8x^2) + (−7 + 3)$ ········· Apply the Commutative and Associative Properties.

$= 8x^3 + 4x − 7x^2 − 4$ ·············· Combine like terms.

$= 8x^3 − 7x^2 + 4x − 4$ ·············· Write in standard form.

> **USE STRUCTURE**
> In order for terms to be *like terms*, the variables and their corresponding exponents must be identical. ● **MP.7**

B. $(3x^2y^2 + 2xy^2 + 6x^2) − (2x^2y^2 + 3xy^2 − 2x^2)$

$= 3x^2y^2 + 2xy^2 + 6x^2 − 2x^2y^2 − 3xy^2 + 2x^2$

$= (3x^2y^2 − 2x^2y^2) + (2xy^2 − 3xy^2) + (6x^2 + 2x^2)$

> Distribute the factor of −1.

$= x^2y^2 − xy^2 + 8x^2$

> The degree of a multi-variable polynomial is the greatest sum of powers in any term.

◻ Try It!   1. Add or subtract the polynomials.

a. $(4a^4 − 6a^3 − 3a^2 + a + 1) + (5a^3 + 7a^2 + 2a − 2)$

b. $(2a^2b^2 + 3ab^2 − 5a^2b) − (3a^2b^2 − 9a^2b + 7ab^2)$

EXAMPLE 2 Multiply Polynomials

How do you multiply the polynomials?

To multiply polynomials, use the Distributive Property, then group like terms and combine.

A. $(2m + 5)(3m^2 - 4m + 2)$

$= 2m(3m^2 - 4m + 2) + 5(3m^2 - 4m + 2)$ .... Use the Distributive Property.

$= 6m^3 - 8m^2 + 4m + 15m^2 - 20m + 10$ .... Use the Distributive Property.

$= 6m^3 + (-8m^2 + 15m^2) + (4m - 20m) + 10$ .... Group like terms.

$= 6m^3 + 7m^2 - 16m + 10$ .... Combine like terms.

B. $(mn + 1)(mn - 2)(mn + 4)$

$= [(mn + 1)(mn - 2)](mn + 4)$ .... Multiply two binomials first.

$= (m^2n^2 - 2mn + mn - 2)(mn + 4)$ .... Use the Distributive Property.

$= (m^2n^2 - mn - 2)(mn + 4)$ .... Combine like terms.

$= m^2n^2(mn + 4) + (-mn)(mn + 4) + (-2)(mn + 4)$ .... Use the Distributive Property.

$= m^3n^3 + 4m^2n^2 - m^2n^2 - 4mn - 2mn - 8$ .... Use the Distributive Property.

$= m^3n^3 + (4m^2n^2 - m^2n^2) + (-4mn - 2mn) - 8$ .... Group like terms.

$= m^3n^3 + 3m^2n^2 - 6mn - 8$ .... Combine like terms.

Try It! 2. Multiply the polynomials.

a. $(6n^2 - 7)(n^2 + n + 3)$ **b.** $(mn + 1)(m^2n - 1)(mn^2 + 2)$

CONCEPTUAL UNDERSTANDING

EXAMPLE 3 Understand Closure

Is the set of polynomials closed under addition and subtraction? Explain.

The set of real numbers is closed under addition: if a and b are real and $a + b = c$, then c is also real.

COMMUNICATE PRECISELY
Can you think of two real numbers such that when you add them, the result is NOT a real number? ● MP.6

Add two polynomials:

> Adding like terms does not change the variable factor(s) of the terms, only the coefficient: $-3x^2y^2 + 9x^2y^2 = 6x^2y^2$.

$(a_nx^n + a_{n-1}x^{n-1} + \ldots + a_2x^2 + a_1x + a_0)$

$+ (b_nx^n + b_{n-1}x^{n-1} + \ldots + b_2x^2 + b_1x + b_0)$

$(a_n + b_n)x^n + (a_{n-1} + b_{n-1})x^{n-1} + \ldots + (a_2 + b_2)x^2 + (a_1 + b_1)x + (a_0 + b_0)$

Since a and b are real, $(a + b)$ is also real. The exponents are unchanged. The sum is still a polynomial, so the set of polynomials is closed under addition.

Using the same logic, you can determine that the set of polynomials is closed under subtraction.

Try It! 3. Is the set of monomials closed under multiplication? Explain.

APPLICATION   **EXAMPLE 4** Write a Polynomial Function

Carolina makes wind chimes to sell at the local street market.

As Carolina produces a greater number of wind chimes, she can lower the price per unit. The function $v(x) = 48 - 2x$ relates the price v to the number produced x. The cost c of making x wind chimes can be represented with the function $c(x) = 12x + 64$.

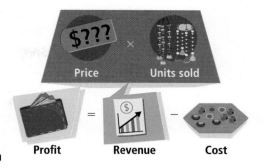

$$\$??? \times$$

Price   Units sold

$$= -$$

Profit   Revenue   Cost

How many wind chimes should Carolina sell each week to maximize her profit P?

Formulate ◀ Write a function for revenue R by multiplying the price $v(x) = 48 - 2x$ of each item by the number sold x.

$$R(x) = (48 - 2x)x$$

Then write the function for profit P.

$$P(x) = R(x) - c(x) \quad\cdots\cdots\cdots\cdots \text{Profit = Revenue − Cost}$$

$$= (48 - 2x)x - (12x + 64). \quad\cdots\cdots \text{Substitute for } R(x) \text{ and } c(x).$$

Compute ◀ Simplify the function.

$$P(x) = (48 - 2x)x - (12x + 64) \quad\cdots\cdots\cdots\cdots \text{Write the profit function.}$$

$$= (48x - 2x^2) - (12x + 64) \quad\cdots\cdots\cdots\cdots \text{Use the Distributive Property.}$$

$$= 48x - 2x^2 - 12x - 64 \quad\cdots\cdots\cdots\cdots \text{Distribute the factor of −1.}$$

$$= -2x^2 + 36x - 64 \quad\cdots\cdots\cdots\cdots \text{Combine like terms.}$$

Carolina's profit function is $P(x) = -2x^2 + 36x - 64$.

Interpret ◀ Carolina's profit is modeled by a quadratic function. The domain of the function is the set of whole numbers. Her maximum profit corresponds to the vertex of the graph.

Carolina's best business plan is to produce and sell 9 wind chimes per week, for a weekly profit of $98.

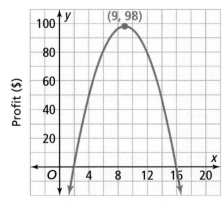

Try It! 4. The cost of Carolina's materials changes so that her new cost function is $c(x) = 4x + 42$.

Find the new profit function. Then find the quantity that maximizes profit and calculate the profit.

APPLICATION → **EXAMPLE 5** ▸ **Compare Two Polynomial Functions**

Carolina's profit function, $y = P(x)$ is represented by the graph. Kiyo's profit from selling x flowerpots can be modeled by the function shown.

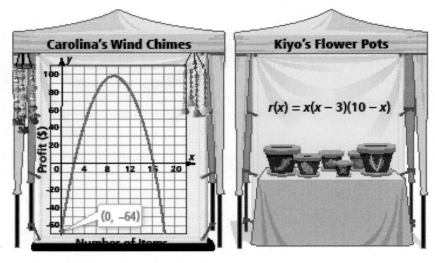

Carolina's Wind Chimes

Kiyo's Flower Pots

$r(x) = x(x - 3)(10 - x)$

A. **Find the y-intercept of each function. Who would lose more money if neither person sold any items?**

The y-intercept of $P(x)$ is -64. If Carolina does not sell any wind chimes this week, she will lose $64.

> Carolina has startup costs, which she pays whether she sells any items or not.

Substitute 0 for x in r to find the y-intercept.

$r(0) = 0(0 - 3)(10 - 0)$ ⋯⋯ Substitute 0 for x.

$= 0$ ⋯⋯⋯⋯⋯⋯ Simplify.

> Kiyo has no startup costs.

The y-intercept of r is 0. If Kiyo does not sell any flowerpots, he will not lose any money. So, Carolina loses more money by not making any sales.

B. **Interpret the end behavior of the functions.**

The domain of each function includes only non-negative values.

The graph of $P(x)$ shows that the end behavior, as $x \to \infty$, is $y \to -\infty$.

Rewrite the function r in standard form to identify end behavior.

$r(x) = x(x - 3)(10 - x)$

$= (x^2 - 3x)(10 - x)$ ⋯⋯⋯⋯⋯⋯ Use the Distributive Property.

$= -x^3 + 13x^2 - 30x$ ⋯⋯⋯⋯⋯ Combine like terms.

Because the leading coefficient is negative, we know that as $x \to \infty$, $y \to -\infty$.

USE STRUCTURE
As x approaches positive infinity or negative infinity, the leading term of the polynomial determines the end behavior of the graph of the function. ● MP.7

Kiyo and Carolina each have a finite number of items they should sell to maximize profits.

⬤ **Try It!** 5. Compare the profit functions of two additional market sellers modeled by the graph of f and the equation $g(x) = (x + 1)(5 - x)$. Compare and interpret the y-intercepts of these functions and their end behavior.

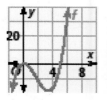 Go Online | SavvasRealize.com

CONCEPT SUMMARY Adding, Subtracting, and Multiplying Polynomials

ADD To add polynomials, use the Associative and Commutative Properties to group like terms. Then use the Distributive Property to combine like terms.

$$(2x^2 + 5x - 7) + (3x^2 - 9x + 12)$$
$$= (2x^2 + 3x^2) + (5x - 9x) + (-7 + 12)$$
$$= 5x^2 - 4x + 5$$

SUBTRACT To subtract polynomials, distribute the factor of -1. Then, group and combine like terms.

$$(6x^3 + 2x^2 + 14) - (4x^3 + 4x^2 - 8)$$
$$= 6x^3 + 2x^2 + 14 - 4x^3 - 4x^2 + 8$$
$$= (6x^3 - 4x^3) + (2x^2 - 4x^2) + (14 + 8)$$
$$= 2x^3 - 2x^2 + 22$$

Distribute the factor of -1 to each term.

MULTIPLY To multiply polynomials, use the Distributive Property. Then, group and combine like terms.

$$(x + 5)(3x^2 - 2x + 4)$$
$$= x(3x^2 - 2x + 4) + 5(3x^2 - 2x + 4)$$
$$= 3x^3 - 2x^2 + 4x + 15x^2 - 10x + 20$$
$$= 3x^3 + (-2x^2 + 15x^2) + (4x - 10x) + 20$$
$$= 3x^3 + 13x^2 - 6x + 20$$

Do You UNDERSTAND?

1. **ESSENTIAL QUESTION** How do you add, subtract, and multiply polynomials?

2. **Error Analysis** Chen subtracted two polynomials as shown. Explain Chen's error. **MP.3**

$$p^2 + 7mp + 4 - (-2p^2 - mp + 1)$$
$$p^2 + 2p^2 + 7mp - mp + 4 + 1$$
$$3p^2 + 6mp + 5 \quad \large\times$$

3. **Communicate Precisely** Why do we often write the results of polynomial calculations in standard form? **MP.6**

4. **Construct Arguments** Is the set of whole numbers closed under subtraction? Explain why you think so, or provide a counterexample. **MP.3**

Do You KNOW HOW?

Add or subtract the polynomials.

5. $(-3a^3 + 2a^2 - 4) + (a^3 - 3a^2 - 5a + 7)$

6. $(7x^2y^2 - 6x^3 + xy) - (5x^2y^2 - x^3 + xy + x)$

Multiply the polynomials.

7. $(7a + 2)(2a^2 - 5a + 3)$

8. $(xy - 1)(xy + 6)(xy - 8)$

9. The length of a rectangular speaker is three times its width, and the height is four more than the width. Write an expression for the volume V of the rectangular prism in terms of its width w.

UNDERSTAND

UNDERSTAND

10. **Generalize** Explain two methods by which $(2m^3 + 4n^2)^2$ can be simplified. Which method do you prefer and why? ● **MP.8**

11. **Use Structure** Polynomial function P is the sum of two polynomial functions, one with degree 2 and a positive leading coefficient and one with degree 3 and a negative leading coefficient. Describe the end behavior of P. Write an example of two polynomial functions and their sum, P, to justify your description. ● **MP.7**

12. **Generalize** Multiply the polynomials $(a + b)$ $(a + b)(a + b)$ to develop a general formula for cubing a binomial, $(a + b)^3$. ● **MP.8**

13. **Reason** Polynomial function R is the difference of two degree-two polynomial functions. What are the possible degrees for R? Explain. ● **MP.2**

14. **Error Analysis** Describe and correct the error a student made in multiplying the polynomials. ● **MP.3**

$$(y - 2)(3y^2 - y - 7)$$
$$= y(3y^2 - y - 7) - 2(3y^2 - y - 7)$$
$$= 3y^3 - y^2 - 7y + (-6y^2) + (-2y) - 14$$
$$= 3y^3 - 7y^2 - 9y - 14 \quad ✗$$

15. **Higher Order Thinking** Do you think polynomials are closed under division? Explain why you think so, or provide a counterexample.

16. **Construct Arguments** Explain why the expression $9x^3 + \frac{1}{2}x^2 + 3x^{-1}$ is not a polynomial. ● **MP.3**

17. **Communicate Precisely** Explain the difference between the graphs of polynomial functions with a degree of 3 that have a positive leading coefficient and the graphs of those with a negative leading coefficient. ● **MP.6**

PRACTICE

Add or subtract the polynomials. SEE EXAMPLE 1

18. $(2x^3 + 3x^2 + 4) + (6x^3 - x^2 - 5x)$

19. $(5y^4 + 3y^3 - 6y^2 + 14) - (-y^4 + y^2 - 7y - 1)$

20. $(4p^2q^2 + 2p^2q - 7pq) - (9p^2q^2 + 5pq^2 - 11pq)$

Multiply the polynomials. SEE EXAMPLE 2

21. $-4xy(5x^2 - 9xy - y^2)$

22. $(3c - 4)(2c^2 - 5c + 7)$

23. $(z + 5)(z - 9)(1 - z)$

24. Is the set of monomials closed under addition? Explain why you think so, or provide a counterexample. SEE EXAMPLE 3

25. An online shopping club has 13,500 members when it charges $8 per month for membership. For each $1 monthly increase in membership fee, the club loses approximately 500 of its existing members.

Write and simplify a function R to represent the monthly revenue received by the club when x represents the price increase.

Hint Monthly revenue = # members • monthly fee SEE EXAMPLE 4

26. The graph shows a polynomial function f. Polynomial function g is defined by $g(x) = x^2(6 - x)$. Compare the maximum values and the end behavior of the functions f and g when $x > 0$.
SEE EXAMPLE 5

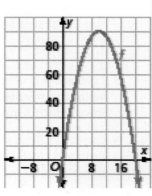

PRACTICE & PROBLEM SOLVING

APPLY

Use this information for 27 and 28. A foundry manufactures aluminum trays from pieces of sheet metal as shown.

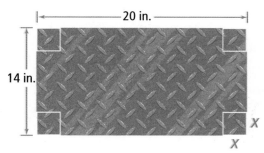

20 in.

14 in.

X

X

27. Model With Mathematics Let *x* represent the side length of each square. © **MP.4**

a. Write expressions for the length, width, and height of the metal tray.

b. Write and simplify a polynomial function *V* to represent the volume of the tray.

c. Using the graph of the function *V*, explain what the marked relative maximum represents.

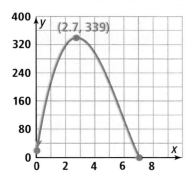

28. Reason Suppose the foundry manufacturer has a new design where the squares cut from the corners have sides that are half the length of the squares in the previous design. © **MP.2**

a. Write expressions for the length, width, and height of this tray.

b. Write and simplify the polynomial function *v*(*x*), to represent the volume of the new tray.

c. Write the function *D*(*x*) that represents the difference, *V*(*x*) − *v*(*x*).

29. Make Sense and Persevere Jacy has $1,000 to invest in a fund that pays approximately 4.6% per year or in a savings account with an annual interest rate of 1.8%. Write a polynomial function *S*(*x*) to represent the interest Jacy will earn in 1 year by investing *x* dollars in the fund and the remainder in the savings account. © **MP.1**

ASSESSMENT PRACTICE

30. Are polynomials open or closed under each operation? Classify each operation as *open* or *closed*.

  a. addition

  b. subtraction

  c. multiplication

  d. division

31. SAT/ACT Which of the following functions is NOT a polynomial function?

  Ⓐ $2y^2 + 9y - 8$

  Ⓑ $-\frac{1}{2}x^3 + 8$

  Ⓒ $(x - 1)(5 - x)(x + 4)$

  Ⓓ $9z^4 + 2z + \frac{1}{z}$

32. Performance Task Consider the polynomial functions $P(x) = x^2 - 4$ and $R(x) = -x^2 - 2x$.

Part A Write and simplify a polynomial function $T(x)$ that is the product of *P* and *R*.

Part B Copy and complete the table of values for all three functions.

x	P(x)	R(x)	T(x)
−3			
−2			
−1			
0			
1			
2			
3			

Part C Graph the functions on the same coordinate grid.

Part D How do the zeros of *T* relate to the zeros of *P* and *R*?

Part E Explain how you can identify the intervals in which *T* is positive by analyzing the *R* and *P*.

3-3

Polynomial Identities

 SavvasRealize.com

I CAN... prove and use polynomial identities.

VOCABULARY
- Binomial Theorem
- identity
- Pascal's Triangle

👆 **EXPLORE & REASON**

Look at the following triangle.

Each number is the sum of the two numbers diagonally above. If there is not a second number, think of it as 0.

A. Write the numbers in the next three rows.

B. **Look for Relationships** What other patterns do you see? © **MP.7**

C. Find the sum of the numbers in each row of the triangle. Write a formula for the sum of the numbers in the nth row.

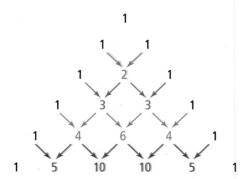

? **ESSENTIAL QUESTION**   How can you use polynomial identities to rewrite expressions efficiently?

CONCEPT Polynomial Identities

A mathematical statement that equates two polynomial expressions is an **identity** if one side can be transformed into the other side using mathematical operations. These polynomial identities are helpful tools used to multiply and factor polynomials.

Difference of Squares
$a^2 - b^2 = (a + b)(a - b)$

Example: $25x^2 - 36y^2$
Substitute $5x$ for a and $6y$ for b.
$25x^2 - 36y^2 = (5x + 6y)(5x - 6y)$

Square of a Sum
$(a + b)^2 = a^2 + 2ab + b^2$

Example: $(3x + 4y)^2$
Substitute $3x$ for a and $4y$ for b.
$(3x + 4y)^2 = (3x)^2 + 2(3x)(4y) + (4y)^2$
$= 9x^2 + 24xy + 16y^2$

Difference of Cubes
$a^3 - b^3 = (a - b)(a^2 + ab + b^2)$

Example: $8m^3 - 27$
Substitute $2m$ for a and 3 for b.
$8m^3 - 27 = (2m - 3)[(2m)^2 + (2m)(3) + 3^2]$
$= (2m - 3)(4m^2 + 6m + 9)$

Sum of Cubes
$a^3 + b^3 = (a + b)(a^2 - ab + b^2)$

Example: $g^3 + 64h^3$
Substitute g for a and $4h$ for b.
$g^3 + 64h^3 = (g + 4h)[g^2 - (g)(4h) + (4h)^2]$
$= (g + 4h)(g^2 - 4gh + 16h^2)$

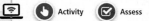
 EXAMPLE 1 ▶ **Prove a Polynomial Identity**

How can you prove the Sum of Cubes Identity, $a^3 + b^3 = (a + b)(a^2 - ab + b^2)$?

To prove an identity, start with the expression on one side of the equation and use properties of operations on polynomials to transform it into the expression on the other side.

USE STRUCTURE
Another way to establish the identity is to multiply each term of the second factor by $(a + b)$, and then combine like terms. © **MP.7**

$(a + b)(a^2 - ab + b^2)$

$= a(a^2 - ab + b^2) + b(a^2 - ab + b^2)$ ·········· Use the Distributive Property.

$= a^3 - a^2b + ab^2 + a^2b - ab^2 + b^3$ ·········· Use the Distributive Property.

$= a^3 + (-a^2b + a^2b) + (ab^2 - ab^2) + b^3$ ·········· Group like terms.

$= a^3 + b^3$ ·········· Combine like terms.

So, $a^3 + b^3 = (a + b)(a^2 - ab + b^2)$.

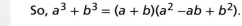 **Try It!** **1.** Prove the Difference of Cubes Identity.

 EXAMPLE 2 ▶ **Use Polynomial Identities to Multiply**

How can you use polynomial identities to multiply expressions?

A. $(2x^2 + y^3)^2$ — The sum is a binomial, and the entire sum is being raised to the second power.

COMMON ERROR
When finding $(a + b)^2$, recall that it is not sufficient to square the first term and square the second term. You must distribute the two binomials.

Use the Square of a Sum Identity to find the product:

$(a + b)^2 = a^2 + 2ab + b^2$

$(2x^2 + y^3)^2 = (2x^2)^2 + 2(2x^2)(y^3) + (y^3)^2$ ·········· Substitute $2x^2$ for a and y^3 for b.

$= 4x^4 + 4x^2y^3 + y^6$ ·········· Simplify.

So, $(2x^2 + y^3)^2 = 4x^4 + 4x^2y^3 + y^6$.

B. $41 \cdot 39$

Rewrite the expression in terms of a and b.

$41 \cdot 39 = (a + b)(a - b)$

$= (40 + 1)(40 - 1)$

Use the Difference of Squares Identity:

$(40 + 1)(40 - 1) = 40^2 - 1^2$

$= 1,600 - 1$

$= 1,599$

So $41 \cdot 39 = 1,599$.

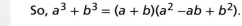 **Try It!** **2.** Use polynomial identities to multiply the expressions.

a. $(3x^2 + 5y^3)(3x^2 - 5y^3)$ **b.** $(12 + 15)^2$

👆 **EXAMPLE 3** **Use Polynomial Identities to Factor and Simplify**

How can you use polynomial identities to factor polynomials and simplify numerical expressions?

A. $9m^4 - 25n^6$

$9m^4$ and $25n^6$ are both perfect squares.

> A square term includes an even exponent, not necessarily an exponent that is a perfect square.

$$9m^4 = (3m^2)^2$$
$$25n^6 = (5n^3)^2$$

Use the Difference of Squares Identity: $a^2 - b^2 = (a + b)(a - b)$.

$9m^4 - 25n^6 = (3m^2)^2 - (5n^3)^2$ ·········· Express each term as a square.

$= (3m^2 + 5n^3)(3m^2 - 5n^3)$ ········ Write the factors.

So, $9m^4 - 25n^6 = (3m^2 + 5n^3)(3m^2 - 5n^3)$.

B. $x^3 - 216$

x^3 and 216 are both perfect cubes.

$$x^3 = (x)^3$$
$$216 = 6^3$$

Use the Difference of Cubes Identity: $a^3 - b^3 = (a - b)(a^2 + ab + b^2)$.

$x^3 - 216 = (x)^3 - (6)^3$ ························· Express each term as a cube.

$= (x - 6)(x^2 + 6x + 36)$ ·········· Write the factors.

So, $x^3 - 216 = (x - 6)(x^2 + 6x + 36)$.

COMMON ERROR
The second factor is *almost* a Square of a Sum. Remember that the middle term of the Difference of Cubes Identity is the product ab, not $2ab$.

C. $11^3 + 5^3$

Use the Sum of Cubes Identity: $a^3 + b^3 = (a + b)(a^2 - ab + b^2)$.

$11^3 + 5^3 = (11 + 5)(11^2 - 11(5) + 5^2)$

$= (16)(121 - 55 + 25)$

$= 16(91)$

$= 1,456$

So, $11^3 + 5^3 = 1,456$.

 Try It! 3. Use polynomial identities to factor each polynomial.

    a. $m^8 - 9n^{10}$ **b.** $27x^9 - 343y^6$ **c.** $12^3 + 2^3$

CONCEPTUAL UNDERSTANDING

 EXAMPLE 4 Expand a Power of a Binomial

How is $(x + y)^n$ obtained from $(x + y)^{n-1}$?

A. What are $(x + y)^3$ and $(x + y)^4$?

$$(x + y)^3 = (x + y)(x + y)^2$$
$$= (x + y)(x^2 + 2xy + y^2)$$

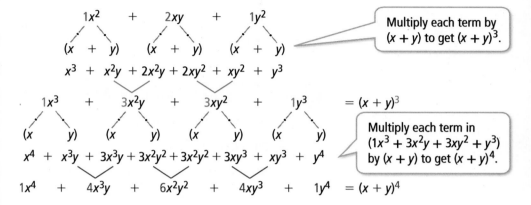

> Multiply each term by $(x + y)$ to get $(x + y)^3$.

$1x^2 \quad + \quad 2xy \quad + \quad 1y^2$

$(x + y) \quad (x + y) \quad (x + y)$

$x^3 + x^2y + 2x^2y + 2xy^2 + xy^2 + y^3$

$1x^3 \quad + \quad 3x^2y \quad + \quad 3xy^2 \quad + \quad 1y^3 \qquad = (x + y)^3$

$(x \quad y) \quad (x \quad y) \quad (x \quad y) \quad (x \quad y)$

> Multiply each term in $(1x^3 + 3x^2y + 3xy^2 + y^3)$ by $(x + y)$ to get $(x + y)^4$.

$x^4 + x^3y + 3x^3y + 3x^2y^2 + 3x^2y^2 + 3xy^3 + xy^3 + y^4$

$1x^4 \quad + \quad 4x^3y \quad + \quad 6x^2y^2 \quad + \quad 4xy^3 \quad + \quad 1y^4 \quad = (x + y)^4$

The coefficients of $(x + y)^n$ are produced by adding the coefficients of $(x + y)^{n-1}$, producing an array known as Pascal's Triangle. **Pascal's Triangle** is the triangular pattern of numbers where each number is the sum of the two numbers diagonally above it. If there is not a second number diagonally above in the triangle, think of the missing number as 0.

Row 0				1			1			$(x + y)^0$
Row 1			1		1		$1x + 1y$			$(x + y)^1$
Row 2		1		2		1	$1x^2 + 2xy + 1y^2$			$(x + y)^2$
Row 3	1		3		3	1	$1x^3 + 3x^2y + 3xy^2 + 1y^3$			$(x + y)^3$
Row 4	1	4		6	4	1	$1x^4 + 4x^3y + 6x^2y^2 + 4xy^3 + 1y^4$			$(x + y)^4$

STUDY TIP
Notice the patterns of the powers. The powers of x decrease from n to 0 and the powers of y increase from 0 to n when reading the terms from left to right.

You can obtain $(x + y)^n$ by adding adjacent pairs of coefficients from $(x + y)^{n-1}$.

B. Use Pascal's Triangle to expand $(x + y)^5$.

Add pairs of coefficients from Row 4 to complete Row 5.

Row 4   1   4   6   4   1

Row 5   1   5   10   10   5   1

Write the expansion. Use the coefficients from Row 5 with powers of x starting at 5 and decreasing to 0 and with powers of y starting at 0 and increasing to 5.

> The sum of the exponents in each term is equal to the exponent on the original binomial.

$$(x + y)^5 = 1x^5 + 5x^4y + 10x^3y^2 + 10x^2y^3 + 5xy^4 + 1y^5$$

☑ **Try It!** **4.** Use Pascal's Triangle to expand $(x + y)^6$.

CONCEPT Binomial Theorem

The **Binomial Theorem** states that, for every positive integer n,

$$(a + b)^n = C_0 a^n + C_1 a^{n-1}b + C_2 a^{n-2}b^2 + \ldots + C_{n-1}ab^{n-1} + C_n b^n.$$

The coefficients $C_0, C_1, C_2, \ldots, C_{n-1}, C_n$ are the numbers in Row n of Pascal's Triangle.

Notice that the powers of a are decreasing while the powers of b are increasing, and that the sum of the powers of a and b in each term is always n.

 EXAMPLE 5 Apply the Binomial Theorem

Use the Binomial Theorem to expand the expressions.

A. Find $(x - 3)^4$.

Step 1 Use the Binomial Theorem to write the expansion when $n = 4$.

$$C_0 a^4 + C_1 a^3 b + C_2 a^2 b^2 + C_3 ab^3 + C_4 b^4$$

Step 2 Use Row 4 in Pascal's Triangle to write the coefficients.

$$a^4 + 4a^3 b + 6a^2 b^2 + 4ab^3 + b^4$$

Step 3 Identify a and b.

$$a = x \text{ and } b = -3$$

Pascal's Triangle
1
1   1
1   2   1
1   3   3   1
1   4   6   4   1
1   5   10   10   5

> **COMMON ERROR**
> Remember that the base of $(a + b)^n$ in the Binomial Theorem is $(a + b)$. If the terms are being subtracted, use the opposite of b in the expansion.

Step 4 Substitute x for a and -3 for b in the pattern. Then simplify.

$$x^4 + 4x^3(-3) + 6x^2(-3)^2 + 4x(-3)^3 + (-3)^4$$

$$x^4 - 12x^3 + 54x^2 - 108x + 81$$

So $(x - 3)^4 = x^4 - 12x^3 + 54x^2 - 108x + 81$.

B. Find $(s^2 + 3)^5$.

The expansion of $(a + b)^5$ is $a^5 + 5a^4 b + 10a^3 b^2 + 10a^2 b^3 + 5ab^4 + b^5$.

Since $a = s^2$ and $b = 3$, the expansion is:

$$(s^2 + 3)^5 = (s^2)^5 + 5(s^2)^4(3) + 10(s^2)^3(3)^2 + 10(s^2)^2(3)^3 + 5(s^2)(3)^4 + (3)^5$$

$$= s^{10} + 15s^8 + 90s^6 + 270s^4 + 405s^2 + 243$$

So $(s^2 + 3)^5 = s^{10} + 15s^8 + 90s^6 + 270s^4 + 405s^2 + 243$.

☑ **Try It!** **5.** Use the Binomial Theorem to expand each expression.

a. $(x - 1)^7$ **b.** $(2c + d)^6$

🔑 CONCEPT SUMMARY Polynomial Identities

POLYNOMIAL IDENTITIES

Special polynomial identities can be used to multiply and factor polynomials.

Difference of Squares

$a^2 - b^2 = (a + b)(a - b)$

Difference of Cubes

$a^3 - b^3 = (a - b)(a^2 + ab + b^2)$

Square of a Sum

$(a + b)^2 = a^2 + 2ab + b^2$

Sum of Cubes

$a^3 + b^3 = (a + b)(a^2 - ab + b^2)$

BINOMIAL EXPANSION

The binomial expansion of $(a + b)^n$ has the following properties:

1) The expansion contains $n + 1$ terms.

2) The coefficients of each term are numbers from the nth row of Pascal's Triangle.

3) The exponent of a is n in the first term and decreases by 1 in each successive term.

4) The exponent of b is 0 in the first term and increases by 1 in each successive term.

5) The sum of the exponents in any term is n.

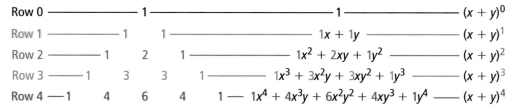

Row 0				1		1	$(x + y)^0$
Row 1		1	1		$1x + 1y$		$(x + y)^1$
Row 2	1	2	1		$1x^2 + 2xy + 1y^2$		$(x + y)^2$
Row 3	1	3	3	1	$1x^3 + 3x^2y + 3xy^2 + 1y^3$		$(x + y)^3$
Row 4	1	4	6	4	1	$1x^4 + 4x^3y + 6x^2y^2 + 4xy^3 + 1y^4$	$(x + y)^4$

☑ Do You UNDERSTAND?

1. **❓ ESSENTIAL QUESTION** How can you use polynomial identities to rewrite expressions efficiently?

2. **Reason** Explain why the middle term of $(x + 5)^2$ is $10x$. Ⓒ **MP.2**

3. **Communicate Precisely** How are Pascal's Triangle and a binomial expansion, such as $(a + b)^5$, related? Ⓒ **MP.6**

4. **Use Structure** Explain how to use a polynomial identity to factor $8x^6 - 27y^3$. Ⓒ **MP.7**

5. **Make Sense and Persevere** What number does C_3 represent in the expansion $C_0a^5 + C_1a^4b + C_2a^3b^2 + C_3a^2b^3 + C_4ab^4 + C_5b^5$? Explain. Ⓒ **MP.1**

6. **Error Analysis** Dakota said the third term of the expansion of $(2g + 3h)^4$ is $36g^2h^2$. Explain Dakota's error. Then correct the error. Ⓒ **MP.3**

Do You KNOW HOW?

Use polynomial identities to multiply each expression.

7. $(2x + 8y)(2x - 8y)$

8. $(x + 3y^3)^2$

Use polynomial identities to factor each polynomial.

9. $36a^6 - 4b^2$

10. $8x^6 - y^3$

11. $m^9 + 27n^6$

Find the term of the binomial expansion.

12. fifth term of $(x + y)^5$

13. third term of $(a - 3)^6$

Use Pascal's Triangle to expand each expression.

14. $(x + 1)^5$

15. $(a - b)^6$

Use the Binomial Theorem to expand each expression.

16. $(d - 1)^4$

17. $(x + y)^7$

UNDERSTAND

18. **Use Structure** Expand $(3x + 4y)^3$ using Pascal's Triangle and the Binomial Theorem. ⓒ **MP.7**

19. **Error Analysis** Emma factored $625g^{16} - 25h^4$. Describe and correct the error Emma made in factoring the polynomial. ⓒ **MP.3**

$$625g^{16} - 25h^4$$
$$= (25g^4)^2 - (5h^2)^2$$
$$= (25g^4 + 5h^2)(25g^4 - 5h^2)$$

✗

20. **Higher Order Thinking** Use Pascal's Triangle and the Binomial Theorem to expand $(x + i)^4$. Justify your work.

21. **Use Structure** Expand the expression $(2x - 1)^4$. What is the sum of the coefficients? ⓒ **MP.7**

22. **Error Analysis** A student says that the expansion of the expression $(-4y + z)^7$ has seven terms. Describe and correct the error the student may have made. ⓒ **MP.3**

23. **Reason** The sum of the coefficients in the expansion of the expression $(a + b)^n$ is 64. Use Pascal's Triangle to find the value of n. ⓒ **MP.2**

24. **Use Structure** Factor $x^3 - 125y^6$ in the form $(x - A)(x^2 + Bx + C)$. What are the values of A, B, and C? ⓒ **MP.7**

25. **Generalize** How many terms will there be in the expansion of the expression $(x + 3)^n$? Explain how you know. ⓒ **MP.8**

26. **Make Sense and Persevere** How could you use polynomial identities to factor the expression $x^6 - y^6$? ⓒ **MP.1**

PRACTICE

27. Prove the polynomial identity.
$x^4 - y^4 = (x - y)(x + y)(x^2 + y^2)$
SEE EXAMPLE 1

Use polynomial identities to multiply the expressions. SEE EXAMPLE 2

28. $(x + 9)(x - 9)$

29. $(x + 6)^2$

30. $(3x - 7)^2$

31. $(2x - 5)(2x + 5)$

32. $(4x^2 + 6y^2)(4x^2 - 6y^2)$

33. $(x^2 + y^6)^2$

34. $(8 - x^2)(8 + x^2)$

35. $(6 - y^3)^2$

36. $18 \cdot 22$

37. $103 \cdot 97$

38. $(7 + 9)^2$

39. $(10 + 5)^2$

Use polynomial identities to factor the polynomials or simplify the expressions. SEE EXAMPLE 3

40. $x^8 - 9$

41. $x^9 - 8$

42. $8x^3 + y^9$

43. $x^6 - 27y^3$

44. $4x^2 - y^6$

45. $216 + 27y^{12}$

46. $64x^3 - 125y^6$

47. $\frac{1}{16}x^6 - 25y^4$

48. $9^3 + 6^3$

49. $10^3 + 5^3$

50. $10^3 - 3^3$

51. $8^3 - 2^3$

Use the Binomial Theorem to expand the expressions. SEE EXAMPLES 4 and 5

52. $(x + 3)^3$

53. $(2a - b)^5$

54. $\left(b - \frac{1}{2}\right)^4$

55. $(x^2 + 1)^4$

56. $\left(2x + \frac{1}{3}\right)^3$

57. $(x^3 + y^2)^6$

58. $(d - 3)^4$

59. $(2m + 2n)^6$

60. $(n + 5)^5$

61. $(3x - 0.2)^3$

62. $(4g + 2h)^4$

63. $\left(m^2 + \frac{1}{2}n\right)^3$

APPLY

64. Reason A medium-sized shipping box with side length s units has a volume of s^3 cubic units. **© MP.2**

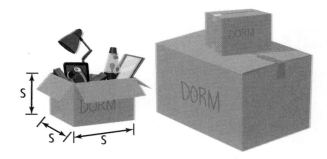

a. A large shipping box has side lengths that are 3 units longer than the medium shipping box. Write a binomial expression for the volume of the large shipping box.

b. Expand the polynomial in part a to simplify the volume of the large shipping box.

c. A small shipping box has side lengths that are 2 units shorter than the medium shipping box. Write a binomial expression for the volume of the small shipping box.

d. Expand the polynomial in part c to simplify the volume of the small shipping box.

65. Use Structure The dimensions of a rectangle are shown. Write the area of the rectangle as a sum of cubes. **© MP.7**

$x + 3$

$x^2 - 3x + 9$

66. A Pythagorean triple is a set of three positive integers a, b, and c that satisfy $a^2 + b^2 = c^2$. The identity $(x^2 - y^2)^2 + (2xy)^2 = (x^2 + y^2)^2$ can be used to generate Pythagorean triples. Use the identity to generate a Pythagorean triple when $x = 5$ and $y = 4$.

© ASSESSMENT PRACTICE

67. Are the expressions below perfect square trinomials? Select *Yes* or *No*.

	Yes	No
$x^2 + 16x + 64$	☐	☐
$4x^2 - 44x + 121$	☐	☐
$9x^2 - 15x + 25$	☐	☐

68. SAT/ACT How many terms are in the expansion of $(2x + 7y)^9$?

Ⓐ 2   Ⓑ 7   Ⓒ 8   Ⓓ 9   Ⓔ 10

69. Performance Task If an event has a probability of success p and a probability of failure q, then each term in the expansion of $(p + q)^n$ represents a probability. For example, if a basketball player makes 60% of his free throw attempts, $p = 0.6$ and $q = 0.4$. To find the probability the basketball player will make exactly h out of k free throws, find $C_{k-h}p^hq^{k-h}$, where C_{k-h} is a coefficient of row k of Pascal's Triangle, p is the probability of success, and q is the probability of failure.

$p = 0.6$ $q = 0.4$

Part A What is the probability the basketball player will make exactly 6 out of 10 free throws? Round to the nearest percent.

Part B Another basketball player makes 80% of her free throw attempts. Write an expression to find the probability of this basketball player making exactly 7 out of 10 free throws. Describe what each variable in the expression represents.

Part C Find the probability that the basketball player from Part B will make exactly 7 out of 10 free throws. Round to the nearest percent.

I CAN... divide polynomials.

VOCABULARY
- Factor Theorem
- Remainder Theorem
- synthetic division

© **Common Core State Standards** HSA.SSE.A.2, HSA.APR.B.2, HSA.APR.D.6, MP.2, MP.6, MP.7

 Activity   Assess

EXPLORE & REASON

Benson recalls how to divide whole numbers by solving a problem with 6 as the divisor and 83 as the dividend. He determines that the quotient is 13 with remainder 5.

A. Explain the process of long division using Benson's example.

B. How can you express the remainder as a fraction?

C. Use Structure Use the results of the division problem to write two expressions for 83 that include the divisor, quotient, and remainder. © MP.7

? ESSENTIAL QUESTION

How can you divide polynomials?

EXAMPLE 1 Use Long Division to Divide Polynomials

How can you use long division to divide $P(x)$ by $D(x)$? Write the polynomial $P(x)$ in terms of the quotient and remainder.

LOOK FOR RELATIONSHIPS
Compare the long division of these two polynomials to this numerical long division problem. © MP.7

$$
\begin{array}{r}
120 \\
13\overline{)1{,}569} \\
-13 \\
\hline
26 \\
-26 \\
\hline
09
\end{array}
$$

A. Let $P(x) = x^3 + 5x^2 + 6x + 9$ and $D(x) = x + 3$.

Long division of polynomials is similar to long division of numbers.

$$
\begin{array}{r}
x^2 + 2x \\
x + 3\overline{)x^3 + 5x^2 + 6x + 9} \\
-(x^3 + 3x^2) \\
\hline
2x^2 + 6x + 9 \\
-(2x^2 + 6x) \\
\hline
9
\end{array}
$$

········ Divide the leading terms: $x^3 \div x = x^2$.

········ Multiply: $x^2(x + 3) = x^3 + 3x^2$. Then subtract.

········ Divide the leading terms again: $2x^2 \div x = 2x$.

········ Multiply: $2x(x + 3) = 2x + 6x$.

········ Subtract. The remainder is 9.

When you divide polynomials, you can express the relationship of the quotient and remainder to the dividend and divisor in two ways.

$$\frac{\text{dividend}}{\text{divisor}} = \text{quotient} + \frac{\text{remainder}}{\text{divisor}}$$

$$\text{dividend} = \text{quotient} \times \text{divisor} + \text{remainder}$$

$$\frac{x^3 + 5x^2 + 6x + 9}{x + 3} = x^2 + 2x + \frac{9}{x + 3}$$ $$x^3 + 5x^2 + 6x + 9 = (x^2 + 2x)(x + 3) + 9$$

CONTINUED ON THE NEXT PAGE

EXAMPLE 1 CONTINUED

B. Let $P(x) = 8x^3 + 27$ and $D(x) = 2x + 3$.

The dividend is a cubic polynomial with no first- or second-degree term.

$$
\begin{array}{r}
4x^2 - 6x + 9 \\
2x + 3 \overline{)\,8x^3 + 0x^2 + 0x + 27} \\
-(8x^3 + 12x^2) \\
\hline
-12x^2 + 0x + 27 \\
-(-12x^2 - 18x) \\
\hline
18x + 27 \\
-(18x + 27) \\
\hline
0
\end{array}
$$

Use 0 as the coefficient for the missing 1st- and 2nd-degree terms.

The remainder is 0. This means the divisor is a factor of the dividend.

So, $\dfrac{8x^3 + 27}{2x + 3} = 4x^2 - 6x + 9$ and $8x^3 + 27 = (2x + 3)(4x^2 - 6x + 9)$.

GENERALIZE
When the remainder is 0, you can use the results of the long division to write $P(x)$ in factored form. © MP.8

✓ **Try It!**   **1.** Use long division to divide the polynomials. Then write the dividend in terms of the quotient and remainder.

a. $x^3 - 6x^2 + 11x - 6$ divided by $x^2 - 4x + 3$

b. $16x^4 - 85$ divided by $4x^2 + 9$

EXAMPLE 2   **Use Synthetic Division to Divide by $x - a$**

What is $2x^3 - 7x^2 - 4$ divided by $x - 3$? Use synthetic division.

Synthetic division is a method used to divide a polynomial by a linear expression in the form $x - a$. Note that the leading coefficient of the divisor is 1, and that a is the zero of the divisor.

Step 1 To change from long division format to synthetic division format, write only the zero of the divisor and the coefficients of the dividend.

$$x - 3\,\overline{)\,2x^3 - 7x^2 + 0x - 4}$$

zero of the divisor, a

$$3 \quad 2 \quad -7 \quad 0 \quad -4$$

coefficients of the dividend

Separate a from the dividend.

Step 2 Bring down the first coefficient. Multiply the zero of the divisor by the first coefficient. Add the result to the second coefficient.

$$
\begin{array}{r|rrrr}
3 & 2 & -7 & 0 & -4 \\
 & & 6 & & \\
\hline
 & 2 & -1 & & \\
\end{array}
$$

$3 \cdot 2 = 6$

$-7 + 6 = -1$

CONTINUED ON THE NEXT PAGE

EXAMPLE 2 CONTINUED

Step 3 Repeat the process until all the columns are complete.

$$
\begin{array}{r|rrrr}
3 & 2 & -7 & 0 & -4 \\
  &   & 6 & -3 & \\
\hline
  & 2 & -1 & -3 &
\end{array}
\qquad 3 \cdot -1 = -3
$$

$$
\begin{array}{r|rrrr}
3 & 2 & -7 & 0 & -4 \\
  &   & 6 & -3 & -9 \\
\hline
  & 2 & -1 & -3 & -13
\end{array}
\qquad 3 \cdot -3 = -9
$$

> **COMMON ERROR**
> Remember to keep track of all positive and negative signs when multiplying.

Step 4 Use the numbers in the last row to write the quotient and remainder.

$$
\begin{array}{r|rrrr}
3 & 2 & -7 & 0 & -4 \\
  &   & 6 & -3 & -9 \\
\hline
  & 2 & -1 & -3 & -13
\end{array}
$$

remainder

coefficients of the quotient

$$2x^2 - 1x - 3 - \frac{13}{x-3}$$

Since the dividend is cubic and the divisor is linear, the quotient is quadratic.

So, $\frac{2x^3 - 7x^2 - 4}{(x-3)} = 2x^2 - x - 3 - \frac{13}{x-3}$.

> **USE STRUCTURE**
> You can use the result to write the dividend $2x^3 - 7x - 4$ in the form $(2x^2 - x - 3)(x - 3) - 13$. Ⓒ **MP.7**

 Try It! **2.** Use synthetic division to divide $3x^3 - 5x + 10$ by $x - 1$.

CONCEPTUAL UNDERSTANDING

 **EXAMPLE 3** Relate $P(a)$ to the Remainder of $P(x) \div (x - a)$

How is the value of $P(a)$ related to the remainder of $P(x) \div (x - a)$?

To explore this question, let $P(x) = x^3 + 10x^2 + 29x + 24$. Use synthetic division to divide $P(x)$ by $x + 5$.

To identify the value of a, write the divisor $x + 5$ in the form $x - a$.

$$x + 5 = x - (-5) \qquad a = -5$$

$$
\begin{array}{r|rrrr}
-5 & 1 & 10 & 29 & 24 \\
   &   & -5 & -25 & -20 \\
\hline
   & 1 & 5 & 4 & 4
\end{array}
$$

The remainder is 4.

The quotient is $x^2 + 5x + 4$.

So, $P(x) = (x^2 + 5x + 4)(x + 5) + 4$. Use this form to evaluate $P(-5)$.

$$
\begin{aligned}
P(-5) &= [((-5)^2 + 5(-5) + 4)(-5 + 5)] + 4 \\
&= [(25 - 25 + 4)(0)] + 4 \\
&= 0 + 4 \\
&= 4
\end{aligned}
$$

-5 is the zero of the divisor, so the product of the quotient and the divisor is 0.

So, $P(-5)$ is the remainder, 4, of $P(x)$ divided by $x - (-5)$.

CONTINUED ON THE NEXT PAGE

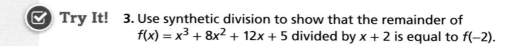
EXAMPLE 3 CONTINUED

In general, dividing $P(x)$ by $x - a$ results in a quotient $Q(x)$ and a remainder r.

$$P(x) = Q(x)(x - a) + r$$
$$P(a) = Q(x)(a - a) + r$$
$$= Q(x)(0) + r$$
$$= r$$

> Evaluating $P(x)$ at a, the zero of the divisor, shows that $P(a) = r$.

So, the for a polynomial $P(x)$ the value of $P(a)$ is equal to the remainder of the division $P(x) \div (x - a)$.

Try It! 3. Use synthetic division to show that the remainder of $f(x) = x^3 + 8x^2 + 12x + 5$ divided by $x + 2$ is equal to $f(-2)$.

CONCEPT Remainder Theorem and Factor Theorem

The **Remainder Theorem** states that if a polynomial $P(x)$ is divided by $x - a$, the remainder is $P(a)$.

When $x - a$ is a factor of $P(x)$, we can show that $P(a) = 0$.

$$P(x) = Q(x)(x - a)$$
$$P(a) = Q(x)(a - a)$$
$$P(a) = 0$$

Conversely, when $P(a) = 0$, we can show that $x - a$ is a factor.

$$P(x) = Q(x)(x - a) + r$$
$$P(x) = Q(x)(x - a) + P(a)$$
$$P(x) = Q(x)(x - a) + 0$$
$$P(x) = Q(x)(x - a)$$

> Use the Remainder Theorem.

The Factor Theorem formalizes these two points.

The **Factor Theorem** states that the expression $x - a$ is a factor of a polynomial $P(x)$ if and only if $P(a) = 0$.

APPLICATION

EXAMPLE 4 Use the Remainder Theorem to Evaluate Polynomials

The population of tortoises on an island is modeled by the function $P(x) = -x^3 + 6x^2 + 12x + 325$ where x is the number of years since 2015. Use the Remainder Theorem to estimate the population in 2023.

Use synthetic division to find $P(a)$ when $a = 8$.

$$
\begin{array}{r|rrrr}
8 & -1 & 6 & 12 & 325 \\
  &   & -8 & -16 & -32 \\
\hline
  & -1 & -2 & -4 & 293
\end{array}
$$

The estimated population in 2023 is 293 tortoises.

Try It! 4. A technology company uses the function $R(x) = -x^3 + 12x^2 + 6x + 80$ to model expected annual revenue, in thousands of dollars, for a new product, where x is the number of years after the product is released. Use the Remainder Theorem to estimate the revenue in year 5.

EXAMPLE 5 Check Whether $x - a$ is a Factor of $P(x)$

How can you use the Remainder and Factor Theorems to determine whether the given binomial is a factor of $P(x)$? If it is a factor, write the polynomial in factored form.

A. $P(x) = x^4 - 8x^3 + 16x^2 - 23x - 6$; binomial: $x - 6$

The binomial $x - 6$ is a factor of $P(x)$ if 6 is a zero of $P(x)$.

Method 1 Use synthetic substitution.

$$
\begin{array}{r|rrrrr}
6 & 1 & -8 & 16 & -23 & -6 \\
  &   & 6 & -12 & 24 & 6 \\
\hline
  & 1 & -2 & 4 & 1 & 0
\end{array}
$$

Method 2 Use direct substitution.

$P(6) = 6^4 - 8(6^3) + 16(6^2) - 23(6) - 6$

$\qquad = 1{,}296 - 1{,}728 + 576 - 138 - 6$

$\qquad = 0$

Because $P(6) = 0$, you can use the Factor Theorem to conclude that $x - 6$ is a factor of $P(x)$: $P(x) = (x^3 - 2x^2 + 4x + 1)(x - 6)$.

B. $P(x) = x^5 - 5x^3 + 9x^2 - x + 3$; binomial: $x + 3$

Method 1 Use synthetic substitution.

$$
\begin{array}{r|rrrrrr}
-3 & 1 & 0 & -5 & 9 & -1 & 3 \\
   &   & -3 & 9 & -12 & 9 & -24 \\
\hline
   & 1 & -3 & 4 & -3 & 8 & -21
\end{array}
$$

> **COMMON ERROR**
> When using synthetic division, remember to include 0 coefficients for any missing terms.

Method 2 Use direct substitution.

$P(-3) = (-3)^5 - 5((-3)^3) + 9((-3)^2) - (-3) + 3$

$P(-3) = -243 + 135 + 81 + 3 + 3$

$P(-3) = -21$

Because -3 is a not a zero of $P(x)$, you can use the Factor Theorem to conclude that $x + 3$ is not a factor of $P(x)$.

✓ **Try It!** 5. Use the Remainder and Factor Theorems to determine whether the given binomial is a factor of $P(x)$.

  a. $P(x) = x^3 - 10x^2 + 28x - 16$; binomial: $x - 4$

  b. $P(x) = 2x^4 + 9x^3 - 2x^2 + 6x - 40$; binomial: $x + 5$

CONCEPT SUMMARY Dividing Polynomials

Example: Divide $x^3 - 8x^2 - 5x - 30$ by $x - 9$.

LONG DIVISION

Can be used for any polynomial division.

$$
\begin{array}{r}
x^2 + x + 4 \\
x - 9 \overline{)\, x^3 - 8x^2 - 5x - 30} \\
\underline{-(x^3 - 9x^2)} \\
x^2 - 5x - 30 \\
\underline{-(x^2 - 9x)} \\
4x - 30 \\
\underline{-(4x - 36)} \\
6
\end{array}
$$

SYNTHETIC DIVISION

Most readily used when the divisor is linear and its leading coefficient is 1.

$$
\begin{array}{r|rrrr}
9 & 1 & -8 & -5 & -30 \\
  &   & 9 & 9 & 36 \\
\hline
  & 1 & 1 & 4 & 6
\end{array}
$$

Either method shows that $x^3 - 8x^2 - 5x - 30 = (x^2 + x + 4)(x - 9) + 6$

REMAINDER THEOREM

If a polynomial $P(x)$ is divided by a linear divisor $x - a$, the remainder is $P(a)$.

$P(x) = x^3 - 2x + 1$ divided by $x - 2$ has remainder 5.

$$
\begin{array}{r|rrrr}
2 & 1 & 0 & -2 & 1 \\
  &   & 2 & 4 & 4 \\
\hline
  & 1 & 2 & 2 & 5
\end{array}
\qquad P(2) = 5
$$

FACTOR THEOREM

The binomial $x - a$ is a factor of $P(x)$ if and only if $P(a) = 0$.

$P(x) = 2x^4 - 5x^3 - 12x^2 + x - 4$ divided by $x - 4$ has remainder 0.

$$
\begin{array}{r|rrrrr}
4 & 2 & -5 & -12 & 1 & -4 \\
  &   & 8 & 12 & 0 & 4 \\
\hline
  & 2 & 3 & 0 & 1 & 0
\end{array}
$$

Do You UNDERSTAND?

1. **ESSENTIAL QUESTION** How can you divide polynomials?

2. **Error Analysis** Ella said the remainder of $x^3 + 2x^2 - 4x + 6$ divided by $x + 5$ is 149. Is Ella correct? Explain. **© MP.3**

3. **Look for Relationships** You divide a polynomial $P(x)$ by a linear expression $D(x)$. You find a quotient $Q(x)$ and a remainder $R(x)$. How can you check your work? **© MP.7**

Do You KNOW HOW?

4. Use long division to divide $x^4 - 4x^3 + 12x^2 - 3x + 6$ by $x^2 + 8$.

5. Use synthetic division to divide $x^3 - 8x^2 + 9x - 5$ by $x - 3$.

6. Use the Remainder Theorem to find the remainder of $2x^4 + x^2 - 10x - 1$ divided by $x + 2$.

7. Is $x + 9$ a factor of the polynomial $P(x) = x^3 + 11x^2 + 15x - 27$? If so, write the polynomial as a product of two factors. If not, explain how you know.

UNDERSTAND

8. Reason Write a polynomial division problem with a quotient of $x^2 - 5x + 7$ and a remainder of 2. Explain your reasoning. How can you verify your answer? Ⓒ MP.2

9. Communicate Precisely Show that $x - 3$ and $x + 5$ are factors of $x^4 + 2x^3 - 16x^2 - 2x + 15$. Explain your reasoning. Ⓒ MP.6

10. Error Analysis Alicia divided the polynomial $2x^3 - 4x^2 + 6x + 10$ by $x^2 + x$. Describe and correct the error Alicia made in dividing the polynomials. Ⓒ MP.3

$$2x - 6 + \frac{10}{x^2 + x}$$
$$x^2 + x \overline{)2x^3 - 4x^2 + 6x + 10}$$
$$\underline{-(2x^3 + 2x^2)}$$
$$-6x^2 + 6x$$
$$\underline{-(-6x^2 - 6x)}$$
$$10$$

✗

11. Higher Order Thinking When dividing polynomial $P(x)$ by polynomial $d(x)$, the remainder is $R(x)$. The remainder can also be written as $\frac{R(x)}{d(x)}$. How can you use the degrees of $R(x)$ and $d(x)$ to determine whether you are finished dividing?

12. Look for Relationships When dividing polynomial $P(x)$ by polynomial $x - n$, the remainder is 0. When graphing $P(x)$, what is an x-intercept of the graph? Ⓒ MP.7

13. Reason When dividing $x^3 + nx^2 + 4nx - 6$ by $x + 3$, the remainder is -48. What is the value of n? Ⓒ MP.2

14. Mathematical Connections Use polynomial long division to divide $8x^3 + 27$ by $2x + 3$. How can you use multiplication to check your answer? Show your work.

PRACTICE

Use long division to divide. SEE EXAMPLE 1

15. $x^3 + 5x^2 - x - 5$ divided by $x - 1$

16. $2x^3 + 9x^2 + 10x + 3$ divided by $2x + 1$

17. $3x^3 - 2x^2 + 7x + 9$ divided by $x^2 - 3x$

18. $2x^4 - 6x^2 + 3$ divided by $2x - 6$

Use synthetic division to divide. SEE EXAMPLE 2

19. $x^4 - 25x^2 + 144$ divided by $x - 4$

20. $x^3 + 6x^2 + 3x - 10$ divided by $x + 5$

21. $x^5 + 2x^4 - 3x^3 + x - 1$ divided by $x + 2$

22. $-x^4 + 7x^3 + x^2 - 2x - 12$ divided by $x - 3$

23. Use synthetic division to show that the remainder of $f(x) = x^4 - 6x^3 - 33x^2 + 46x + 75$ divided by $x - 9$ is $P(9)$. SEE EXAMPLE 3

Use the Remainder Theorem to evaluate each polynomial for the given value of x. SEE EXAMPLE 4

24. $f(x) = x^3 + 9x^2 + 3x - 7$; $x = -5$

25. $f(x) = 2x^3 - 3x^2 + 4x + 13$; $x = 3$

26. $f(x) = -x^4 + 2x^3 - x^2 + 4x + 8$; $x = -2$

27. $f(x) = x^5 - 3x^4 - 2x^3 + x^2 - 2x - 1$; $x = 4$

Is each given binomial a factor of the given polynomial? If so, write the polynomial as a product of two factors. SEE EXAMPLE 5

28. polynomial: $P(x) = 8x^3 - 10x^2 + 28x - 16$; binomial: $x - 3$

29. polynomial: $P(x) = 4x^4 - 9x^3 - 7x^2 - 2x + 25$; binomial: $x + 4$

30. polynomial: $P(x) = -x^5 + 12x^3 + 6x^2 - 23x + 1$; binomial: $x - 2$

31. polynomial: $P(x) = 2x^3 + 3x^2 - 8x - 12$; binomial: $2x + 3$

PRACTICE & PROBLEM SOLVING

APPLY

32. Model With Mathematics Darren is placing shipping boxes in a storage unit with a floor area of $x^4 + 5x^3 + x^2 - 20x - 14$ square units. Each box has a volume of $x^3 + 10x^2 + 29x + 20$ cubic units and can hold a stack of items with a height of $x + 5$ units. **© MP.4**

a. How much floor space will each box cover?

b. What is the maximum number of boxes Darren can place on the floor of the storage unit?

c. Assume Darren places the maximum number of boxes on the floor of the storage unit, with no overlap. How much of the floor space is not covered by a box?

33. Reason Lauren wants to determine the length and height of her DVD stand. The function $f(x) = x^3 + 14x^2 + 57x + 72$ represents the volume of the DVD stand, where the width is $x + 3$ units. What are possible dimensions for the length and height of the DVD stand? Explain. **© MP.2**

34. Make Sense and Persevere A truck traveled $6x^3 + x^2 + 20x - 11$ miles in $2x - 1$ hours. At what rate did the semi-truck travel? (*Hint:* Use the formula $d = rt$, where d is the distance, r is the rate, and t is the time.) **© MP.1**

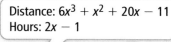

Distance: $6x^3 + x^2 + 20x - 11$
Hours: $2x - 1$

ASSESSMENT PRACTICE

35. When polynomial $P(x)$ is divided by the linear factor $x - n$, the remainder is 0. What can you conclude? Select all that apply.

Ⓐ $P(x) = 0$

Ⓑ $P(n) = 0$

Ⓒ $P(-n) = 0$

Ⓓ $x - n$ is a factor of $P(x)$.

Ⓔ $x + n$ is a factor of $P(x)$.

36. SAT/ACT $x + 3$ is a factor of the polynomial $x^3 + 2x^2 - 5x + n$. What is the value of n?

Ⓐ -6

Ⓑ -3

Ⓒ -2

Ⓓ 3

Ⓔ 6

37. Performance Task The table shows some quotients of the polynomial $x^n - 1$ divided by the linear factor $x - 1$.

Dividend	Divisor	Quotient
$x^2 - 1$	$x - 1$	$x + 1$
$x^3 - 1$	$x - 1$	$x^2 + x + 1$
$x^4 - 1$	$x - 1$	
$x^5 - 1$	$x - 1$	
$x^6 - 1$	$x - 1$	

Part A Use long division or synthetic division to find the missing quotients to complete the table.

Part B Look for a pattern. Then describe the pattern when $x^n - 1$ is divided by $x - 1$.

Part C Use the pattern to find the quotient when $x^{10} - 1$ is divided by $x - 1$.

3-5

Zeros of Polynomial Functions

SavvasRealize.com

I CAN... model and solve problems using the zeros of a polynomial function.

VOCABULARY
• multiplicity of a zero

© **Common Core State Standards** HSA.SSE.A.2, HSA.APR.B.3, HSF.IF.C.7.C, MP.1, MP.7, MP.8

  Activity Assess

MODEL & DISCUSS

Charlie and Aisha built a small rocket and launched it from their backyard. The rocket fell to the ground 10 s after it launched.

The height h, in feet, of the rocket relative to the ground at time t seconds can be modeled by the function shown.

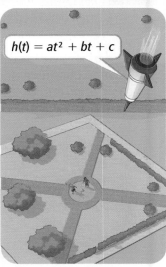

$h(t) = at^2 + bt + c$

A. How are the launch and landing times related to the modeling function?

B. What additional information about the rocket launch could you use to construct an accurate model for the rocket's height relative to the ground?

C. Construct Arguments Charlie believes that the function $h(t) = -16t^2 + 160t$ models the height of the rocket with respect to time. Do you agree? Explain your reasoning and indicate the domain of this function. © **MP.3**

? ESSENTIAL QUESTION How are the zeros of a polynomial function related to an equation and graph of the function?

CONCEPTUAL UNDERSTANDING

EXAMPLE 1 Use Zeros to Graph a Polynomial Function

What are the zeros of $f(x) = x(x - 4)(x + 3)$? Graph the function.

A *zero* of a polynomial function is a value for which the function is equal to 0. By the Zero-Product Property, the zeros of the function are –3, 0, and 4.

The zeros divide a number line into four intervals.

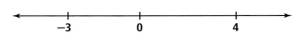

To see how the graph of the function behaves on each interval, look at the sign of each factor on each interval, and the sign of the product.

Interval	Sign			
	x	$x - 4$	$x + 3$	Product
$x < -3$	−	−	−	−
$-3 < x < 0$	−	−	+	+
$0 < x < 4$	+	−	+	−
$x > 4$	+	+	+	+

The last column shows the sign of the product of the three factors.

CONTINUED ON THE NEXT PAGE

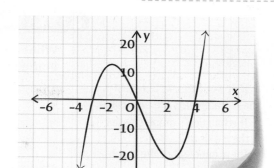
EXAMPLE 1 CONTINUED

Sketch the graph. Draw a continuous curve that passes through each zero on the *x*-axis, and is below the *x*-axis when the function is negative, and above the *x*-axis when the function is positive.

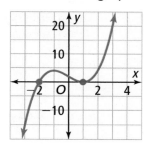

> **Try It!** 1. Factor each function. Then use the zeros to sketch its graph.
>
>   **a.** $f(x) = 4x^3 + 4x^2 - 24x$ **b.** $g(x) = x^4 - 81$

EXAMPLE 2   **Understand How a Multiple Zero Can Affect a Graph**

How does a multiple zero affect the graph of a polynomial function?

The **multiplicity of a zero** of a polynomial function is the number of times its related factor appears in the factored form of the polynomial. Notice the behavior of each graph as it approaches the *x*-axis. What can you conclude about the multiplicity of a zero and its effect on the graph of the function?

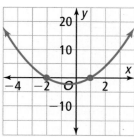

$f(x) = (x - 1)(x + 2)$

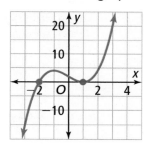

$f(x) = (x - 1)^2(x + 2)$

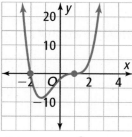

$f(x) = (x - 1)^3(x + 2)$

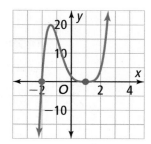

$f(x) = (x - 1)^4(x + 2)$

When the multiplicity of a zero is odd, the function crosses the *x*-axis.
When the multiplicity of a zero is even, the graph has a turning point at the *x*-axis.

> **Try It!** 2. Describe the behavior of the graph of the function at each of its zeros.
>
>   **a.** $f(x) = x(x + 4)(x - 1)^4$ **b.** $f(x) = (x^2 + 9)(x - 1)^5(x + 2)^2$

☞ **EXAMPLE 3** **Find Real and Complex Zeros**

What are all the real and complex zeros of the polynomial function shown in the graph?

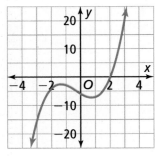

$f(x) = x^3 + x^2 - 3x - 6$

LOOK FOR RELATIONSHIPS
These statements are equivalent:
- The function's graph crosses the x-axis at 2.
- The x-intercept of the graph is 2.
- $f(2) = 0$
- 2 is a zero of the function.
- $x - 2$ is a factor of the polynomial. Ⓒ **MP.7**

Step 1 Use the graph to determine one of the zeros of the polynomial. The function appears to cross the x-axis at $x = 2$.

Confirm that 2 is a zero of the function.

$$f(2) = (2)^3 + (2)^2 - 3(2) - 6$$
$$= 0$$

So 2 is a zero of the function. By the Factor Theorem, $x - 2$ is a factor of the related polynomial.

Step 2 Use synthetic division to factor the polynomial.

$$
\begin{array}{r|rrrr}
2 & 1 & 1 & -3 & -6 \\
  &   & 2 & 6 & 6 \\
\hline
  & 1 & 3 & 3 & 0
\end{array}
$$

So $f(x) = (x - 2)(x^2 + 3x + 3)$.

Step 3 Use the Quadratic Formula to find the remaining zeros.

$$x = \frac{-3 \pm \sqrt{3^2 - 4(1)(3)}}{2(1)}$$
$$= -\frac{3}{2} \pm \frac{\sqrt{3}}{2}i$$

The zeros of the polynomial function f are 2, $-\frac{3}{2} + \frac{\sqrt{3}}{2}i$, and $-\frac{3}{2} - \frac{\sqrt{3}}{2}i$.

☑ **Try It!** **3.** What are all the real and complex zeros of the polynomial function shown in the graph?

a.

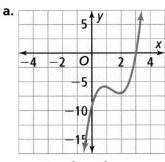

$f(x) = 2x^3 - 8x^2 + 9x - 9$

b.

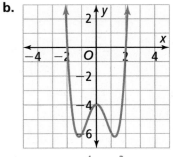

$f(x) = x^4 - 3x^2 - 4$

APPLICATION

EXAMPLE 4   **Interpret the Zeros of a Function**

Acme Innovations makes and sells lamps. Their profit P, in hundreds of dollars earned, is a function of the number of lamps sold x, in thousands.

From historical data, they know that their company's profit is modeled by the function shown.

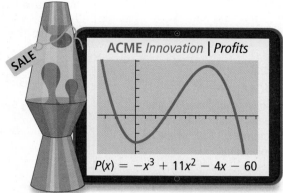

ACME *Innovation* | *Profits*

$P(x) = -x^3 + 11x^2 - 4x - 60$

What do the zeros of the function tell you about the number of lamps that Acme Innovations should produce?

Formulate ◀   A profit for the company corresponds to the portions of the graph that lie above the x-axis. Find the zeros of the function to determine where the graph crosses the x-axis.

Based on the graph, the zeros of the function appear to be –2, 3, and 10. If these are the zeros of the function, then by the Factor Theorem you can determine the factors of the related polynomial.

Zero of P	Factor of $P(x)$
–2	$x + 2$
3	$x - 3$
10	$x - 10$

Compute ◀   Multiply these factors to verify that the product is equal to the polynomial given.

$$(x + 2)(x - 3)(x - 10) = (x + 2)(x^2 - 13x + 30)$$
$$= x^3 - 13x^2 + 30x + 2x^2 - 26x + 60$$
$$= x^3 - 11x^2 + 4x + 60$$

The result is equal to $-P(x)$, not $P(x)$. But both polynomials have the same factors since $P(x) = -(x + 2)(x - 3)(x - 10)$.

So the zeros of the function are –2, 3, and 10.

Interpret ◀   When $P(x)$ is positive, Acme Innovations earns a profit. The profit is positive when $x < -2$ or $3 < x < 10$. Acme Innovations cannot produce a negative number of lamps, so disregard the interval $x < -2$. Since x represents the number of lamps in hundreds, the company should make between 3,000 and 10,000 lamps.

☑ **Try It!**   **4.** Due to a decrease in the cost of materials, the profit function for Acme Innovations has changed to $Q(x) = -x^3 + 10x^2 + 13x - 22$. How many lamps should they make in order to make a profit?

EXAMPLE 5 **Solve Polynomial Equations**

What are the solutions of $2x^3 + 5x^2 - 3x = 3x^3 + 8x^2 + 1$?

Rewrite the equation in the form $P(x) = 0$.

$$2x^3 + 5x^2 - 3x = 3x^3 + 8x^2 + 1$$

$$x^3 + 3x^2 + 3x + 1 = 0$$

> Combine like terms on one side of the equation.

VOCABULARY
A *polynomial equation* is an equation that can be written in the form $P(x) = 0$, where $P(x)$ is a polynomial.

The roots are the zeros of the function $P(x) = x^3 + 3x^2 + 3x + 1$.

$$(x + 1)^3 = 0 \quad \cdots\cdots\cdots \text{Cube of a binomial.}$$

$$x + 1 = 0 \quad \cdots\cdots\cdots \text{Zero-Product Property.}$$

$$x = -1 \quad \cdots\cdots\cdots \text{Subtract 1 from each side.}$$

To check, write each side of the equation as a separate polynomial and graph. Use the INTERSECT feature to confirm that the graphs intersect at $x = -1$.

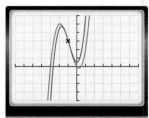

x scale: 1   *y* scale: 2

Try It! **5.** What is the solution of the equation?

a. $x^3 - 7x + 6 = x^3 + 5x^2 - 2x - 24$ **b.** $x^4 + 2x^2 = -x^3 - 2x$

EXAMPLE 6 **Solve a Polynomial Inequality by Graphing**

What are the solutions of $x^3 - 16x < 0$?

The solutions are all values of x that make the inequality true. The polynomial $x^3 - 16x$ defines a polynomial function $P(x) = x^3 - 16x$.

Factor to find the zeros of the function.

$$x^3 - 16x = 0$$

$$x(x^2 - 16) = 0 \quad \cdots\cdots\cdots \text{Factor out the greatest common factor.}$$

$$x(x - 4)(x + 4) = 0 \quad \cdots\cdots\cdots \text{Difference of squares.}$$

By the Zero-Product Property, the zeros of P are −4, 0, and 4.

Sketch the function, and use the graph to determine where $P(x) < 0$.

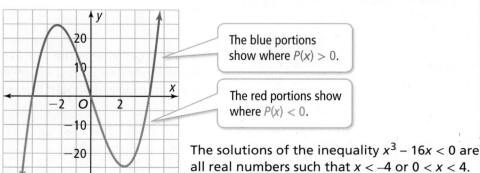

> The blue portions show where $P(x) > 0$.

> The red portions show where $P(x) < 0$.

The solutions of the inequality $x^3 - 16x < 0$ are all real numbers such that $x < -4$ or $0 < x < 4$.

CONTINUED ON THE NEXT PAGE

EXAMPLE 6 CONTINUED

☑ **Try It!**   **6.** What are the solutions of the inequality?

a. $2x^3 + 12x^2 + 12x < 0$ b. $(x^2 - 1)(x^2 - x - 6) > 0$

🔑 CONCEPT SUMMARY Zeros of Polynomials

FUNCTION ▶ $f(x) = (x - a)^2(x - b)^3(x - c)$

GRAPH ▶

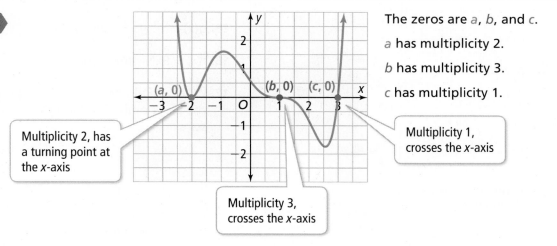

The zeros are a, b, and c.

a has multiplicity 2.

b has multiplicity 3.

c has multiplicity 1.

Multiplicity 2, has a turning point at the x-axis

Multiplicity 3, crosses the x-axis

Multiplicity 1, crosses the x-axis

☑ Do You UNDERSTAND?

1. 🔍 **ESSENTIAL QUESTION** How are the zeros of a polynomial function related to the equation and graph of a function?

2. Error Analysis In order to identify the zeros of the function, a student factored the cubic function $f(x) = x^3 - 3x^2 - 10x$ as follows:

$f(x) = x^3 - 3x^2 - 10x$
$= x(x^2 - 3x - 10)$
$= x(x - 5)(x + 2)$
$x = 0, x = -5, x = 2$

Describe and correct the error the student made. © **MP.3**

3. Make Sense and Persevere Explain how you can determine that the function $f(x) = x^3 + 3x^2 + 4x + 2$ has both real and complex zeros. © **MP.1**

Do You KNOW HOW?

4. If the graph of the function f has a multiple zero at $x = 2$, what is a possible exponent of the factor $x - 2$? Justify your reasoning.

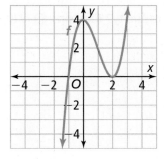

5. Energy Solutions manufactures LED light bulbs. The profit p, in thousands of dollars earned, is a function of the number of bulbs sold, x, in ten thousands. Profit is modeled by the function $-x^3 + 9x^2 - 11x - 21$.

For what number of bulbs manufactured does the company make a profit?

UNDERSTAND

6. **Reason** If you use zeros to sketch the graph of a polynomial function, how can you verify that your graph is correct? Ⓒ **MP.2**

7. **Error Analysis** Describe and resolve two errors that Tonya may have made in finding all the roots of the polynomial function, $f(x) = x^3 + 3x^2 + 7x + 5$. Ⓒ **MP.3**

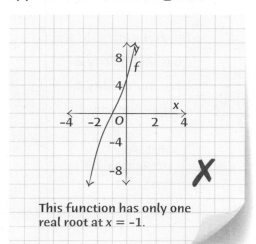

This function has only one real root at $x = -1$.

8. **Higher Order Thinking** How could you use your graphing calculator to determine that $f(x) = (x + 2)(x + 6)(x - 1)$ is not the correct factorization of $f(x) = x^3 + 7x^2 + 16x + 12$? Explain.

9. **Generalize** How can you determine that the polynomial function shown does not have any zeros with even multiplicity? Explain. Ⓒ **MP.8**

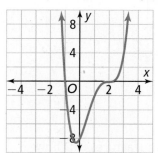

10. **Use Structure** Factor the polynomial $x^4 - 16$. How many real zeros does the function $g(x) = x^4 - 16$ have? Ⓒ **MP.7**

11. At what points do the graphs of $f(x) = x^3 - 2x^2 - 16x + 20$ and $g(x) = -12$ intersect?

PRACTICE

Sketch the graph of the function by finding the zeros. SEE EXAMPLE 1

12. $f(x) = 3x^3 - 9x^2 - 12x$

13. $g(x) = (x + 3)(x - 1)(x - 4)$

Find the zeros of the function, and describe the behavior of the graph at each zero. SEE EXAMPLE 2

14. $f(x) = x^3 - 8x^2 + 16x$

15. $g(x) = x^3 - x^2 - 25x + 25$

16. $f(x) = 9x^4 - 40x^2 + 16$

17. What are all the real and complex zeros of the polynomial function shown in the graph? SEE EXAMPLE 3

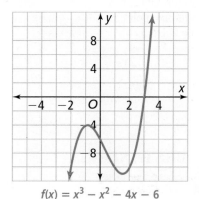

$f(x) = x^3 - x^2 - 4x - 6$

18. Waterworks is a company that manufactures and sells paddleboards. Their profit P, in hundreds of dollars earned, is a function of the number of paddleboards sold x, measured in thousands. Profit is modeled by the function $P(x) = -3x^3 + 48x^2 - 144x$. What do the zeros of the function tell you about the number of paddleboards that Waterworks should produce? SEE EXAMPLE 4

What are the solution(s) of the equation? SEE EXAMPLE 5

19. $-3x^3 - x^2 + 54x - 40 = 2x^2 + 6x + 20$

20. $2x^3 + 3x^2 - 36 = x^3 - x^2 + 9x$

21. $-5x^4 + 4x^2 - 12x = -6x^4 + 3x^3$

What are the solutions of the inequality? SEE EXAMPLE 6

22. $x^3 - 9x > 0$ 23. $0 > 4x^3 + 8x^2 - x - 2$

24. $64x^2 > -4x^3 - x - 16$

APPLY

25. Make Sense and Persevere A firework is launched vertically into the air. Its height in meters is given by the function shown, where t is measured in seconds. **© MP.1**

$h = -4.9t^2 + 49t$

a. What is a reasonable domain of the function?

b. What are the zeros of the function? Explain what they represent in this situation.

c. Use technology to find the vertex. What does it represent in this situation?

26. The height of a baseball thrown in the air can be modeled by the function $h(t) = -16t^2 + 32t + 6.5$, where $h(t)$ represents the height in feet of the baseball after t seconds. Explain why the graph of this function only shows one zero.

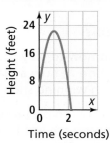

Time (seconds)

27. Model With Mathematics The height of a rectangular storage box is less than both its length and width. The function $f(x) = x^3 + 2x^2 - 3x$ represents the volume of the rectangular box, where x represents the width of the box, in feet. **© MP.4**

a. Find the factored form of $f(x)$.

b. Find the zeros of the function.

c. You know x represents the width of the box. What do the other two factors represent?

d. Find the dimensions of the box when the volume is 10 ft^3.

28. Complete each statement so it means the same as 4 is *a zero of the function*.

The graph of the function crosses the _____ at 4. _____ is a factor of the polynomial.

29. SAT/ACT Without the use of a graphing calculator, determine which of the graph of $f(x) = x^3 + x^2 - 4x$.

Ⓐ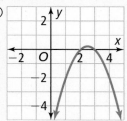

Ⓑ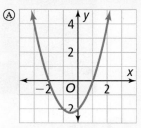

Ⓒ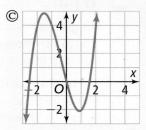

Ⓓ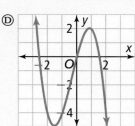

30. Performance Task Venetta opened several deli sandwich franchises in 2000. The profit P (in hundreds of dollars) of the franchises in t years (since the franchises opened) can be modeled by the function $P(t) = t^3 + t^2 - 6t$.

Part A Sketch a graph of the function.

Part B Based on the model, during what years did Venetta not make a profit?

Part C If the model is appropriate, predict the amount of profit Venetta will receive from her franchises in 2020.

MATHEMATICAL MODELING IN **3** ACTS

SavvasRealize.com

Video

What Are the Rules?

All games have rules about how to play the game. The rules outline such things as when a ball is in or out, how a player scores points, and how many points a player gets for each winning shot.

If you didn't already know how to play tennis, or some other game, could you figure out what the rules were just by watching? What clues would help you understand the game? Think about this during the Mathematical Modeling in 3-Acts lesson.

Scan for Multimedia

ACT 1 Identify the Problem

1. What is the first question that comes to mind after watching the video?

2. Write down the main question you will answer about what you saw in the video.

3. Make an initial conjecture that answers this main question.

4. Explain how you arrived at your conjecture.

5. What information will be useful to know to answer the main question? How can you get it? How will you use that information?

ACT 2 Develop a Model

6. Use the math that you have learned in this Topic to refine your conjecture.

ACT 3 Interpret the Results

7. Did your refined conjecture match the actual answer exactly? If not, what might explain the difference?

3-6

Theorems About Roots of Polynomial Equations

SavvasRealize.com

I CAN... use roots of a polynomial equation to find other roots.

© **Common Core State Standards** HSN.CN.C.8 (+), HSN.CN.C.9 (+), HSA.APR.B.2, HSA.APR.B.3, MP.2, MP.5, MP.7

Activity   Assess

👆 CRITIQUE & EXPLAIN

Look at the polynomial functions shown.

$$g(x) = x^2 - 7x - 18$$

$$h(x) = 5x^2 + 24x + 16$$

A. Avery has a conjecture that the zeros of a polynomial function have to be positive or negative factors of its constant term. Factor $g(x)$ completely. Are the zeros of g factors of -18?

B. **Look for Relationships** Now test Avery's conjecture by factoring $h(x)$. Does Avery's conjecture hold? If so, explain why. If not, make a new conjecture. © **MP.7**

❓ ESSENTIAL QUESTION

How are the roots of a polynomial equation related to the coefficients and degree of the polynomial?

CONCEPT The Rational Root Theorem

Let $P(x) = a_n x^n + a_{n-1} x^n + \ldots + a_1 x + a_0$ be a polynomial with integer coefficients.

If the polynomial equation $P(x) = 0$ has any rational roots, then each rational root is of the form $\frac{p}{q}$, where p is a factor of the constant term, a_0, and q is a factor of the leading coefficient, a_n.

👆 EXAMPLE 1   Identify Possible Rational Solutions

From the graph it appears that 4 is a zero of the function $P(x) = 8x^5 - 32x^4 + x^2 - 4$. Without substituting, how can you determine if 4 is a possible solution to $P(x) = 0$?

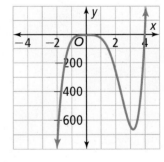

List all the factors of the leading coefficient and the constant term of $P(x)$.

constant term $= -4$ factors: $\pm 1, \pm 2, \pm 4$

leading coefficient $= 8$ factors: $\pm 1, \pm 2, \pm 4, \pm 8$

COMMON ERROR
These are *possible* roots of the equation. You still need to test them to determine whether they are *actual* roots.

The Rational Root Theorem states that the possible rational roots of $P(x) = 0$ are

$$\pm\frac{1}{1}, \pm\frac{1}{2}, \pm\frac{1}{4}, \pm\frac{1}{8}, \pm\frac{2}{1}, \pm\frac{2}{2}, \pm\frac{2}{4}, \pm\frac{2}{8}, \pm\frac{4}{1}, \pm\frac{4}{2}, \pm\frac{4}{4}, \pm\frac{4}{8}$$

Values in the numerator are factors of the constant term.

$\frac{4}{1}$ is equal to 4, so it is a possible solution to $8x^5 - 32x^4 + x^2 - 4 = 0$ according to the Rational Roots Theorem.

Values in the denominator are factors of the leading coefficient.

☑ Try It!   1. List all the possible rational solutions for each equation.

a. $4x^4 + 13x^3 - 124x^2 + 212x - 8 = 0$

b. $7x^4 + 13x^3 - 124x^2 + 212x - 45 = 0$

APPLICATION

👆 **EXAMPLE 2**   Use the Rational Root Theorem

A storage company is designing a new storage unit. Based on the dimensions shown, the volume of a container is modeled by the polynomial $v(x) = 2x^3 - 7x^2 + 6x$, where x is the width in feet. What are the dimensions of the container in feet if the volume of the unit is 154 ft³?

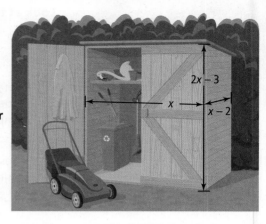

$2x - 3$
x
$x - 2$

Formulate ◀ The volume is 154 ft³, so find solutions to the equation $2x^3 - 7x^2 + 6x = 154$.

The zeros of the polynomial will be rational roots of the equation in standard form: $2x^3 - 7x^2 + 6x - 154 = 0$.

Compute ◀ List the factors of the constant term and the leading coefficient.

constant term $= -154$

factors: $\pm 1, \pm 2, \pm 7, \pm 11, \pm 14, \pm 22, \pm 77, \pm 154$

leading coefficient $= 2$

factors: $\pm 1, \pm 2$

List all possible rational roots, eliminating repeated values.

> Use a spreadsheet or a programmable calculator to test the possible roots.

$$\pm \frac{1}{1}, \pm \frac{2}{1}, \pm \frac{7}{1}, \pm \frac{11}{1}, \pm \frac{14}{1}, \pm \frac{22}{1}, \pm \frac{77}{1}, \pm \frac{154}{1}, \pm \frac{1}{2}, \pm \frac{7}{2}, \pm \frac{11}{2}, \pm \frac{77}{2}$$

Look for an x-value where $2x^3 - 7x^2 + 6x - 154 = 0$.

Testing shows that $\frac{11}{2}$ is a solution to the equation. Once you find one root, you can use synthetic division to find the other factor.

$$
\begin{array}{r|rrrr}
\frac{11}{2} & 2 & -7 & 6 & -154 \\
  &   & 11 & 22 & 154 \\
\hline
  & 2 & 4 & 28 & 0 \\
\end{array}
$$

The factored form of the equation is $\left(x - \frac{11}{2} \right)(2x^2 + 4x + 28) = 0$.

The discriminant of the quadratic factor is -208, so there are no real zeros for this factor. Therefore $\frac{11}{2}$ is the only real solution to the original equation.

Interpret ◀ The width of the container is $\frac{11}{2}$, or 5.5 ft; its length is $\frac{11}{2} - 2$, or 3.5 ft; and its height is $2\left(\frac{11}{2} \right) - 3$, or 8 ft.

✅ **Try It!** **2.** A jewelry box measures $2x + 1$ in. long, $2x - 6$ in. wide, and x in. tall. The volume of the box is given by the function $v(x) = 4x^3 - 10x^2 - 6x$. What is the height of the box, in inches, if its volume is 28 in.³?

CONCEPT Fundamental Theorem of Algebra

If $P(x)$ is a polynomial of degree $n \geq 1$, then $P(x) = 0$ has exactly n solutions in the set of complex numbers.

If $P(x)$ has any factor of multiplicity m, count the solution associated with that factor m times. For example, the equation $(x - 3)^4 = 0$ has four solutions, each equal to 3.

EXAMPLE 3 Find All Complex Roots

What are all the complex roots of the polynomial equation?

$$3x^4 + 4x^3 + 2x^2 - x - 2 = 0$$

Step 1 List the factors of the constant term and leading coefficient

constant term $= -2$ factors: $\pm 1, \pm 2$

leading coefficient $= 3$ factors: $\pm 1, \pm 3$

Step 2 List the possible rational roots.

$$\pm \tfrac{1}{3}, \pm \tfrac{2}{3}, \pm 1, \pm 2$$

> **STUDY TIP**
> Remember that if you use synthetic division to test for factors, the result also tells you the quotient after division by the factor.

Step 3 Testing with synthetic division reveals that $\tfrac{2}{3}$ and -1 are roots.

Divide $3x^4 + 4x^3 + 2x^2 - x - 2$ by $x - \tfrac{2}{3}$.

$$
\begin{array}{c|ccccc}
\tfrac{2}{3} & 3 & 4 & 2 & -1 & -2 \\
  &   & 2 & 4 & 4 & 2 \\
\hline
  & 3 & 6 & 6 & 3 & 0
\end{array}
$$

So $3x^4 + 4x^3 + 2x^2 - x - 2 = \left(x - \tfrac{2}{3}\right)(3x^3 + 6x^2 + 6x + 3)$.

Now divide the cubic factor by $x - (-1)$.

$$
\begin{array}{c|cccc}
-1 & 3 & 6 & 6 & 3 \\
   &   & -3 & -3 & -3 \\
\hline
   & 3 & 3 & 3 & 0
\end{array}
$$

After factoring out 3 from the final quotient, the polynomial equation can be written as $3(x - \tfrac{2}{3})(x + 1)(x^2 + x + 1) = 0$.

Step 4 Use the Quadratic Formula to find the last two roots.

If $x^2 + x + 1 = 0$, then $x = \dfrac{-1 \pm \sqrt{1^2 - 4(1)(1)}}{2(1)}$

$$= \dfrac{-1 \pm i\sqrt{3}}{2}$$

The complex numbers $\tfrac{2}{3}$, -1, $\dfrac{-1 - i\sqrt{3}}{2}$, and $\dfrac{-1 + i\sqrt{3}}{2}$ are all roots of the equation. Since the polynomial has degree 4, the Fundamental Theorem of Algebra states that these are the only four roots of the equation.

 Try It! **3.** What are all the complex roots of the equation
$x^3 - 2x^2 + 5x - 10 = 0$?

CONCEPTUAL
UNDERSTANDING   **EXAMPLE 4**   Irrational Roots and the Coefficients of a Polynomial

How are the types of zeros of a polynomial function related to the coefficients of the polynomial?

A. Suppose a quadratic polynomial function P has one rational zero c and one irrational zero $a + \sqrt{b}$ where a and b are rational numbers. Are all the coefficients of P rational?

> **LOOK FOR RELATIONSHIPS**
> Remember that if r is a zero of a polynomial, then $x - r$ is a factor of the polynomial. **© MP.7**

Write $P(x)$ in terms of its factors.

$$P(x) = (x - c)(x - (a + \sqrt{b}))$$
$$= x^2 - (a + \sqrt{b} + c)x + (a + \sqrt{b})c$$

> Multiply and collect like terms.

No, the function P has two irrational coefficients.

B. Suppose a quadratic polynomial function R has two irrational zeros: a conjugate pair $a + \sqrt{b}$ and $a - \sqrt{b}$ (where a and b are rational numbers). Are all the coefficients of R rational?

$$R(x) = (x - (a + \sqrt{b}))\,(x - (a - \sqrt{b})) \quad \cdots\cdots\cdots \text{Write } R(x) \text{ in terms of its factors.}$$
$$= (x - a - \sqrt{b})(x - a + \sqrt{b}) \quad \cdots\cdots\cdots \text{Distribute.}$$
$$= ((x - a) - \sqrt{b})((x - a) + \sqrt{b}) \quad \cdots\cdots \text{Regroup the factors.}$$
$$= (x - a)^2 - (\sqrt{b})^2 \quad \cdots\cdots\cdots\cdots \text{Rewrite as the difference of squares.}$$
$$= x^2 - 2ax + (a^2 - b) \quad \cdots\cdots\cdots \text{Expand.}$$

> rational numbers

Yes, R has only rational coefficients.

So a quadratic function with one rational zero and one irrational zero $a + \sqrt{b}$ (where a and b are rational) will have some irrational coefficients. But a quadratic with a conjugate pair of irrational zeros $a + \sqrt{b}$ and $a - \sqrt{b}$ (where a and b are rational) will have only rational coefficients.

✓ **Try It!**   **4.** Suppose a quadratic polynomial function f has two complex zeros which are a conjugate pair, $a - bi$ and $a + bi$ (where a and b are real numbers). Are all the coefficients of f real? Explain.

CONCEPT Conjugate Root Theorems

- Let P be a polynomial function with rational coefficients and let a and b be real numbers. Then if $a + \sqrt{b}$ is a root of $P(x) = 0$, then $a - \sqrt{b}$ is also a root of $P(x) = 0$.
- Let P be a polynomial function with real coefficients and let a and b be real numbers. Then if $a + bi$ is a root of $P(x) = 0$, then $a - bi$ is also a root of $P(x) = 0$.

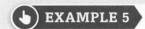 **EXAMPLE 5**   Write Polynomial Functions Using Conjugates

A. What is a quadratic function _P_ with rational coefficients in standard form such that $P(x) = 0$ has $2 + 5i$ as a root?

By the Fundamental Theorem of Algebra, you know that a quadratic equation has two complex roots. Since $2 + 5i$ is one root, its complex conjugate, $2 - 5i$, must be the other.

Use the Factor Theorem to write the quadratic function using the two roots.

$$P(x) = (x - (2 + 5i))(x - (2 - 5i)) \quad\cdots\cdots \text{Write } P \text{ in factored form.}$$

$$= (x - 2 - 5i)(x - 2 + 5i) \quad\cdots\cdots \text{Distribute.}$$

$$= ((x - 2) - 5i)((x - 2) + 5i) \quad\cdots\cdots \text{Associative Property.}$$

$$= (x - 2)^2 - (5i)^2 \quad\cdots\cdots \text{Rewrite as the difference of squares.}$$

$$= x^2 - 4x + 4 - (-25) \quad\cdots\cdots \text{Simplify.}$$

$$= x^2 - 4x + 29$$

> **STUDY TIP**
> Any equation of the form $cP(x) = 0$, where $c \neq 0$, is another equation with the same roots.

So the equation $x^2 - 4x + 29$ is a quadratic equation with $2 + 5i$ as root.

B. A polynomial function _Q_ of degree 4 with rational coefficients has zeros $3 - \sqrt{7}$ and $4i$. What is a polynomial equation in standard form with these roots?

The zeros of Q are the same as the roots of $Q(x) = 0$. Since one root is irrational and the other is complex with a non-zero imaginary component, their conjugates are also roots.

Factors of $Q(x)$: $x - (3 - \sqrt{7})$ and $x - (3 + \sqrt{7})$

$$x - 4i \text{ and } x - (-4i)$$

Multiply the four factors of $Q(x)$.

$$Q(x) = (x - (3 - \sqrt{7}))(x - (3 + \sqrt{7}))(x - 4i)(x - (-4i))$$

$$= ((x - 3) + \sqrt{7})((x - 3) - \sqrt{7})(x - 4i)(x + 4i) \quad\cdots\cdots \text{Distribute and regroup.}$$

$$= ((x - 3)^2 - (\sqrt{7})^2)(x^2 - (4i)^2) \quad\cdots\cdots \text{Rewrite as the difference of squares.}$$

$$= (x^2 - 6x + 2)(x^2 + 16) \quad\cdots\cdots \text{Simplify.}$$

$$= x^4 - 6x^3 + 18x^2 - 96x + 32$$

The polynomial equation $x^4 - 6x^3 + 18x^2 - 96x + 32 = 0$ has roots $3 - \sqrt{7}$ and $4i$.

 Try It! **5a.** What is a quadratic equation in standard form with rational coefficients that has a root of $5 + 4i$?

     b. What is a polynomial function _Q_ of degree 4 with rational coefficients such that $Q(x) = 0$ has roots $2 - \sqrt{3}$ and $5i$?

CONCEPT SUMMARY Theorems About Roots of Polynomial Equations

	Words	Example
RATIONAL ROOT THEOREM	For the polynomial equation $0 = a_nx^n + a_{n-1}x^{n-1} + \ldots + a_1x^1 + a_0$, there are a limited number of possible rational roots.	$2x^3 + 3x^2 - 10x - 15 = 0$ $p = -15$; Factors of p: $\pm 1, \pm 3, \pm 5, \pm 1$ $q = 2$; Factors of q: $\pm 1, \pm 2$
	Rational roots must have reduced form $\frac{p}{q}$ where p is an integer factor of a_0 and q is an integer factor of a_n. Use substitution or synthetic division to check roots.	Possible rational roots: $\pm 1, \pm 3, \pm 5, \pm 15, \pm\frac{1}{2}, \pm\frac{3}{2}, \pm\frac{5}{2}, \pm\frac{15}{2}$ $-\frac{3}{2}$ is a root of the equation.
FUNDAMENTAL THEOREM OF ALGEBRA	If $P(x)$ is a polynomial of degree $n \geq 1$, then $P(x) = 0$ has exactly n solutions in the set of complex numbers.	
CONJUGATE ROOT THEOREMS	**Irrational Conjugates** Let P be a polynomial function with rational coefficients and let a and b be real numbers. Then if $a + \sqrt{b}$ is a root of $P(x) = 0$, then $a - \sqrt{b}$ is also a root of $P(x) = 0$.	**Complex Conjugates** Let P be a polynomial function with real coefficients and let a and b be re numbers. Then if $a + bi$ is a root of $P(x) = 0$, then $a - bi$ is also a root of $P(x) = 0$.

Do You UNDERSTAND?

1. **ESSENTIAL QUESTION** How are the roots of a polynomial equation related to the coefficients and degree of the polynomial?

2. **Error Analysis** Renaldo said that a polynomial equation with rational coefficients that has zeros $-1 + 2i$ and $3 + \sqrt{5}$ has a degree of 4. Is Renaldo correct? Explain. Ⓒ MP.3

3. **Use Structure** A fifth degree polynomial $P(x)$ with rational coefficients has zeros $2i$ and $\sqrt{7}$. What other zeros does $P(x)$ have? Explain. Ⓒ MP.7

4. **Construct Arguments** If one root of a polynomial equation with real coefficients is $4 + 2i$, is it certain that $4 - 2i$ is also a root of the equation? Explain. Ⓒ MP.3

Do You KNOW HOW?

List all the possible rational solutions for each equation according to the Rational Roots Theorem. Then find all of the rational roots.

5. $0 = x^3 + 4x^2 - 9x - 36$

6. $0 = x^4 - 2x^3 - 7x^2 + 8x + 12$

7. $0 = 4x^3 + 8x^2 - x - 2$

8. $0 = 9x^4 - 40x^2 + 16$

A polynomial equation with rational coefficients has the given roots. List two more roots of each equation.

9. $1 + \sqrt{11}$ and $-3 + \sqrt{17}$

10. $5 + 12i$ and $-9 - 7i$

11. $12 + 5i$ and $6 - \sqrt{13}$

12. $5 - 15i$ and $17 + \sqrt{23}$

UNDERSTAND

13. Construct Arguments Consider the polynomial $P(x) = 5x^3 + mx^2 + nx + 6$, where m and n are rational coefficients. Is 3 *sometimes, always,* or *never* a root? Explain. **MP.3**

14. Use Structure Write a fourth-degree polynomial function Q with roots -1, 0, and $2i$. **MP.7**

15. Error Analysis A student says that a fifth-degree polynomial equation with rational coefficients has roots -5, -3, 1, 2, and $\sqrt{3}$. Describe possible errors the student may have made. **MP.3**

16. Reason Write a third-degree polynomial with rational coefficients that has the following possible roots. Explain your reasoning. **MP.2**

$$\pm\frac{1}{1}, \pm\frac{1}{2}, \pm\frac{2}{1}, \pm\frac{2}{2}, \pm\frac{5}{1}, \pm\frac{5}{2}, \pm\frac{10}{1}, \pm\frac{10}{2}$$

17. Error Analysis Describe and correct the error a student made in finding the roots of the polynomial equation $2x^3 - x^2 - 10x + 5 = 0$. **MP.3**

List all possible rational roots.

$$\pm 1, \pm\frac{1}{2}, \pm 5, \pm\frac{5}{2}$$

Testing reveals that $\frac{1}{2}$ is a root.
Dividing the polynomial by the binomial $x - \frac{1}{2}$ results in the factored form

$$f(x) = \left(x - \frac{1}{2}\right)(2x^2 - 10)$$

The equation $2x^2 - 10 = 0$ has two irrational roots, $\sqrt{10}$ and $-\sqrt{10}$.

The complete set of roots is $\{\frac{1}{2}, \sqrt{10}, -\sqrt{10}\}$.

18. Higher Order Thinking What is the least number of terms a fifth-degree polynomial with root $3i$ can have? Give an example of such a polynomial equation. Explain.

19. Use Structure Show that the Fundamental Theorem of Algebra is true for all quadratic equations with real coefficients. (*Hint*: Use the Quadratic Formula and examine the possibilities for the value of the discriminant.) **MP.7**

PRACTICE

List all the possible rational solutions for each equation. SEE EXAMPLE 1

20. $0 = x^3 - 3x^2 + 4x - 12$

21. $0 = 2x^4 + 13x^3 - 47x^2 - 13x + 45$

22. $0 = 4x^3 + 64x^2 - x - 16$

23. $0 = 8x^3 + 11x^2 - 13x - 6$

24. A closet in the shape of a rectangular prism has the measurements shown. What is the height of the closet, in feet, if its volume is 220 ft³? SEE EXAMPLE 2

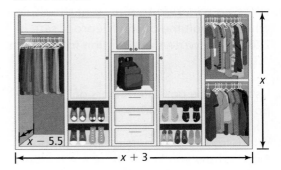

What are all real and complex roots of the following functions? SEE EXAMPLE 3

25. $0 = x^3 - 3x - 52$

26. $0 = x^3 + 9x^2 - 7x - 63$

27. $0 = x^4 + 34x^2 - 72$

28. $0 = x^6 + 4x^4 - 41x^2 + 36$

29. Suppose a cubic polynomial f has one rational zero c and two irrational zeros which are a conjugate pair $a + \sqrt{b}$ and $a - \sqrt{b}$, where a and b are rational numbers. Does f have rational coefficients? SEE EXAMPLE 4

Find a polynomial function $P(x)$ such that P has the degree and $P(x) = 0$ has the root(s) listed. SEE EXAMPLE 5

30. degree of $P = 2$;
zero: $1 + 6i$

31. degree of $P = 4$;
zeros: $3 - \sqrt{11}$ and $-9i$

32. degree of $P = 3$;
zeros: -5 and $4 - 8i$

APPLY

33. Make Sense and Persevere A fireproof safe has the measurements shown. © MP.1

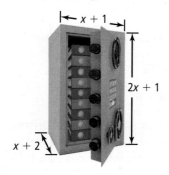

$x + 1$

$2x + 1$

$x + 2$

a. Write an equation to represent the situation when the volume of the fireproof safe is 270 in.^{3}. Rewrite the equation in the form $P(x) = 0$.

b. List all of the possible factors of the polynomial expression.

c. What are the real roots of the equation? Explain how you know these are the only real roots.

d. What are the length, width, and height of the fireproof safe?

34. Reason What are the dimensions of the fish tank, in feet, if its volume is 176 ft^3? © MP.2

$x - 3$

$x + \sqrt{5}$ $x - \sqrt{5}$

35. Reason The cost of producing x video game consoles is modeled by the function $C(x) = x^4 - 5x^3 - 12x^2 - 22x - 40$. If a company spent \$1,706 to produce video game consoles, how many consoles were made? © MP.2

ASSESSMENT PRACTICE

36. A fifth-degree polynomial equation with rational coefficients has the roots 3, 8i, and $7 - \sqrt{5}$. Which are also roots of the polynomial equation? Select all that apply.

Ⓐ −3

Ⓑ −8i

Ⓒ 1 − 8i

Ⓓ −7 − √5

Ⓔ 7 + √5

37. SAT/ACT Which is a third-degree polynomial equation with rational coefficients that has roots −2 and 6i?

Ⓐ $x^3 + 2x^2 + 36x + 72$

Ⓑ $x^3 - 2x^2 + 36x - 72$

Ⓒ $x^3 + 2x^2 - 36x - 72$

Ⓓ $x^2 + (6i - 2)x - 12$

Ⓔ $x^2 - (6i - 2)x - 12$

38. Performance Task The table shows the number of possible real and imaginary roots for an nth degree polynomial equation with rational coefficients.

Degree	Real Roots	Imaginary Roots
3	3	0
3	1	2
5	5	0
5	3	2
5	1	4

Part A List all of the possible combinations of real and imaginary roots for a seventh-degree polynomial equation.

Part B What do you notice about the number of real roots of a polynomial equation with an odd degree?

Activity  Assess

3-7

Transformations of Polynomial Functions

 SavvasRealize.com

I CAN... identify symmetry in and transform polynomial functions.

VOCABULARY
- even function
- odd function

👆 **EXPLORE & REASON**

Look at the polynomial graphs below.

$f(x) = x^2$

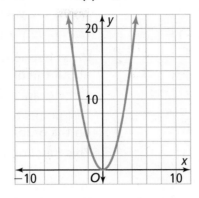

$g(x) = x^3$

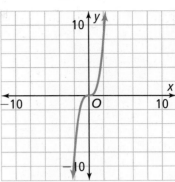

A. Is the graph of *f* or *g* symmetric about the *y*-axis? Is the graph of *f* or *g* symmetric about the origin? Explain.

B. **Look for Relationships** Graph more functions of the form $y = x^n$ where *n* is a natural number. Which of these functions are symmetric about the origin? Which are symmetric about the *y*-axis? What conjectures can you make? © **MP.7**

? **ESSENTIAL QUESTION**

How are symmetry and transformations represented in the graph and equation of a polynomial function?

CONCEPT Odd and Even Functions

A polynomial function $P(x) = a_nx^n + a_{n-1}x^{n-1} + \cdots + a_1x^1 + a_0$ is an **even function** if it is symmetric about the *y*-axis and an **odd function** if it is symmetric about the origin.

Other types of functions can also be classified as odd or even. For example, the function $y = |x|$ is an even function.

Even Function	**Odd Function**	**Neither**

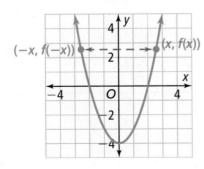 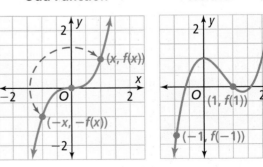

For all *x* in the domain,

$f(x) = f(-x)$.

For all *x* in the domain,

$f(-x) = -f(x)$.

$f(1) \neq f(-1)$ (not even)

$f(-1) \neq -f(1)$ (not odd)

EXAMPLE 1 **Identify Even and Odd Functions From Their Graphs**

Use the graph to classify the polynomial function. Is it even, odd, or neither?

A.

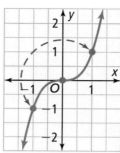

What happens when you reflect the graph across the *y*-axis?

New graph – not even.

What happens when you rotate the graph 180° about the origin?

Same graph – odd

Test points to confirm: (1, 1) and (−1, −1) are both on the graph.

This function is odd.

B.

What happens when you reflect the graph across the *y*-axis?

Same graph – even

Test points to confirm: (1, 2) and (−1, 2) are both on the graph.

This function is even.

COMMON ERROR
An odd degree polynomial function may have rotational symmetry around a point other than (0, 0). It is only an odd function if the symmetry is around the origin.

C.

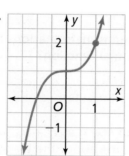

What happens when you reflect the graph across the *y*-axis?

New graph – not even

What happens when you rotate the graph 180° about the origin?

New graph – not odd

Test points to confirm: (1, 2) is on the graph, but (−1, 2) and (−1, −2) are not.

This function is neither even nor odd.

Try It! **1.** Classify the polynomial functions as even or odd based on the graphs.

a.

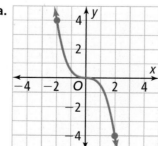

b.

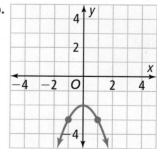

 **EXAMPLE 2** Identify Even and Odd Functions From Their Equations

Is the function odd, even, or neither?

A. $f(x) = 4x^4 + 5$

$f(-x) = 4(-x)^4 + 5$ ⋯⋯ Replace x with $-x$.

$f(-x) = 4x^4 + 5$ ⋯⋯ Simplify.

Since $f(x) = f(-x)$, $f(x) = 4x^4 + 5$ is an even function.

B. $g(x) = 2x^3 + 3x$

$g(-x) = 2(-x)^3 + 3(-x)$ ⋯⋯ Replace x with $-x$.

$g(-x) = -2x^3 - 3x = -(2x^3 + 3x)$ ⋯⋯ Simplify.

Since $g(-x) = -g(x)$, $g(x) = 2x^3 + 3x$ is an odd function.

CONSTRUCT ARGUMENTS
Why use a variable rather than a specific value? You must show that $f(x) = f(-x)$ or that $-f(x) = f(-x)$ for all x in the domain, not just one value. **Ⓒ MP.3**

 Try It! 2. Is the function odd, even, or neither?

a. $f(x) = 7x^5 - 2x^2 + 4$　　b. $f(x) = x^6 - 2$

 **EXAMPLE 3** Graph Transformations of Cubic and Quartic Parent Functions

How do transformed graphs compare to the graph of the parent function?

A. $g(x) = 3x^4 - 18$

Identify the transformations: $g(x) = 3x^4 - 18$.

Parent function: $f(x) = x^4$

Leading coefficient, 3, stretches the graph vertically, making it narrower than the graph of the parent function.

Subtracting 18 translates the graph down 18 units.

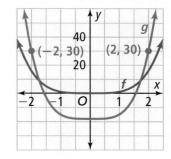

USE APPROPRIATE TOOLS
The graph of the parent function is a valuable tool, because it provides the foundation for sketching the graphs of related functions using transformations. **Ⓒ MP.5**

B. $h(x) = 5(x - 2)^3 + 4$

Identify the transformations: $h(x) = 5(x - 2)^3 + 4$.

Parent function: $f(x) = x^3$

Subtracting 2 (before calculating the cube) shifts the parent graph to the right 2 units.

Multiplying by 5 stretches the translated graph vertically, making it narrower than the graph of the parent function.

Adding 4 translates the stretched graph up 4 units.

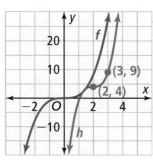

 Try It! 3. How does the graph of the function $g(x) = 2x^3 - 5$ differ from the graph of its parent function?

CONCEPTUAL
UNDERSTANDING   👆 **EXAMPLE 4**   **Identify a Transformation**

VOCABULARY
A cubic function is 3rd degree. A quartic function is 4th degree.

Each of the given graphs is a transformation of the parent cubic function or parent quartic function. How can you determine the equation of the graph?

A.
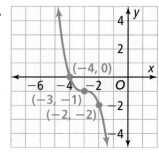

B.
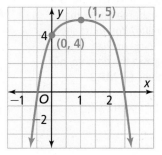

Since the ends extend in opposite directions, the end behavior shows that the parent function has odd degree: $y = x^3$.

The end behavior indicates a negative leading coefficient so this graph is a reflection across the x-axis, such as $y = -x^3$.

The point (0, 0) has shifted to (−3, −1), which shows that the graph has been translated:

Left 3 units

$$y = -(x + 3)^3$$

Down 1 unit

$$y = -(x + 3)^3 - 1$$

The function is
$f(x) = -(x + 3)^3 - 1$.

Since the ends extend in the same direction, the end behavior shows that the parent function has even degree: $y = x^4$.

The end behavior indicates a negative leading coefficient so this graph is a reflection across the x-axis, such as $y = -x^4$.

The point (0, 0) has shifted to (1, 5), which shows that the graph has been translated:

Right 1 unit

$$y = -(x - 1)^4$$

Up 5 units

$$y = -(x - 1)^4 + 5$$

The function is
$f(x) = -(x - 1)^4 + 5$.

 Try It!   **4.** Determine the equation of each graph as it relates to its parent cubic function or quartic function.

a.
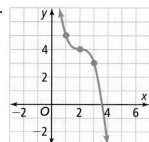

b.
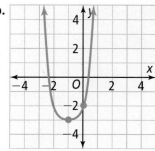

APPLICATION **EXAMPLE 5** Apply a Transformation of a Cubic Function

A. The volume of a box, in cubic yards, is given by the function $V(x) = x^3$. The post office lists permissible shipping volumes in cubic feet. Write a function for the volume in cubic feet if x is the edge length in yards.

Replace x with $3x$ .... Convert yards to feet.

$V(3x) = (3x)^3$ .... Evaluate $V(x)$ for the value $3x$.

$V(x) = 27x^3$ .... Simplify to write the function in units of cubic feet.

The function that represents the volume of the box, in cubic feet, is $V(x) = 27x^3$.

COMMON ERROR
Remember to apply exponents correctly: $(3x)^3 \neq 3x^3$.

B. A terrarium is in the shape of a rectangular prism. The volume of the tank is given by $V(x) = (x)(2x)(x + 5) = 2x^3 + 10x^2$, where x is measured in inches. The manufacturer wants to compare the volume of this tank with one that has a width 2 inches shorter but maintains the relationships between the width and the other dimensions. Write a new function for the volume of this smaller tank.

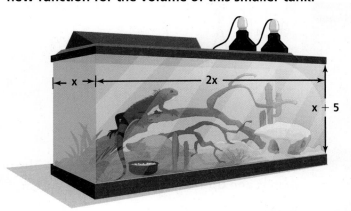

$V(x - 2) = (x - 2)[2(x - 2)][(x - 2) + 5]$ ◁—— Replace x with $x - 2$.

$= (x - 2)(2x - 4)(x + 3)$

$= (2x^2 - 8x + 8)(x + 3)$

$= 2x^3 - 2x^2 - 16x + 24$

The function that represents the volume of the smaller tank is $V(x - 2) = 2x^3 - 2x^2 - 16x + 24$.

✓ **Try It!** **5a.** The volume of a cube, in cubic feet, is given by the function $V(x) = x^3$. Write a function for the volume of the cube in cubic inches if x is the edge length in feet.

b. A storage unit is in the shape of a rectangular prism. The volume of the storage unit is given by $V(x) = (x)(x)(x - 1) = x^3 - x^2$, where x is measured in feet. A potential customer wants to compare the volume of this storage unit with that of another storage unit that is 1 foot longer in every dimension. Write a function for the volume of this larger unit.

Even Function	Odd Function
DEFINITION Line of symmetry: y-axis For all x, $f(x) = f(-x)$.	Point of symmetry: origin For all x, $f(-x) = -f(x)$.
PARENT FUNCTION Has even degree: $y = x^2$, $y = x^4$, $y = x^6$,...	Has odd degree: $y = x$, $y = x^3$, $y = x^5$,...

END BEHAVIOR

(positive leading coefficient)
(negative leading coefficient)

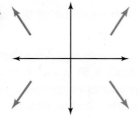   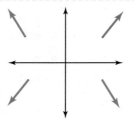

TRANSLATION

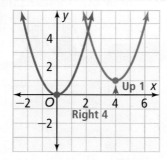

The vertex moves to the right 4 units and up 1 unit.

$y = x^2 \rightarrow y = (x - 4)^2 + 1$

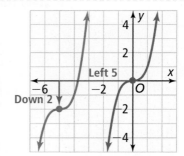

The graph of the function moves to the left 5 units and down 2 units.

$y = x^3 \rightarrow y = (x + 5)^3 - 2$

Do You UNDERSTAND?

1. **ESSENTIAL QUESTION** How are symmetry and transformations represented in the graph and equation of a polynomial function?

2. **Vocabulary** What is the difference between the graph of an even function and the graph of an odd function?

3. **Error Analysis** A student identified the transformations of the polynomial function $f(x) = 3(x - 1)^3 - 6$ as follows:

   The function shifted to the left 1 unit, stretched vertically, and shifted downward 6 units.

   Describe and correct the error the student made. © MP.3

Do You KNOW HOW?

4. Classify the function on the graph as odd, even, or neither.

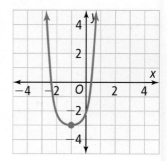

5. Use the equation to classify the function as odd, even, or neither.
$$g(x) = 4x^3 - x$$

6. The volume of a cardboard box is given by the function $V(x) = x(x - 2)(x) = x^3 - 2x^2$. Write a new function for the volume of a cardboard box that is 2 units longer in every dimension.

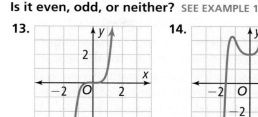
PRACTICE & PROBLEM SOLVING

UNDERSTAND

7. Make Sense and Persevere If you use a graph to determine the equation of a function, explain how to check that your equation is correct. **© MP.1**

8. Error Analysis Describe the error Terrence made in graphing the transformation of the cubic function $g(x) = x^3$ to $f(x) = -\frac{1}{2}x^3 + 10$. **© MP.3**

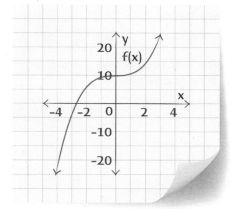

9. Higher Order Thinking Explain how to identify a transformation of the function $y = x^3$ by looking at a graph. What do you look for to determine a translation? A reflection? A stretch or compression?

10. Use Structure Describe the steps used to determine the equation of the graph of the transformed parent quartic function. **© MP.7**

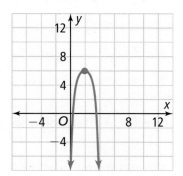

11. Construct Arguments Explain why the function $g(x) = 2x^5 + 3x^4 + 1$ is neither even nor odd. **© MP.3**

12. Construct Arguments Provide an example that demonstrates the following statement is not true.

If the degree of a function is an even number, then the function is an even function. **© MP.3**

PRACTICE

Use the graph to classify the polynomial function. Is it even, odd, or neither? SEE EXAMPLE 1

13.
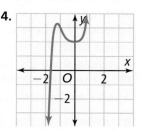

14.

Use the equation to classify the polynomial function. Is it even, odd, or neither? SEE EXAMPLE 2

15. $f(x) = 2x^5 + 4x^2$ **16.** $g(x) = 6x^4 + 2x^2$

How do the graphs of transformations compare to the graph of the parent function? SEE EXAMPLE 3

17. $f(x) = 3(x + 1)^3 - 2$ **18.** $g(x) = -x^4 - 8$

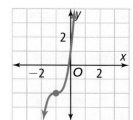   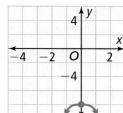

Each graph is a transformation of the parent cubic function or quartic function. Determine the equation of the graph. SEE EXAMPLE 4

19.
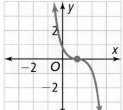

20.
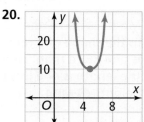

21. The volume of a rectangular room, in cubic yards, is given by the function shown. Write a function for the volume in cubic feet if x is in yards. SEE EXAMPLE 5

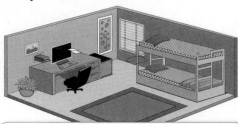

Volume in cubic yards: $(x) = x(3x)(x + 4) = 3x^3 + 12x^2$

APPLY

22. Make Sense and Persevere Last season the approximate number of guests in week x at an amusement park could be modeled by the function, f, where x represents the number of weeks since the park opened for the season. This year, since the park opened its new water slide, the approximate number of guests in week x at the park can be modeled by g. ⓒ **MP.1**

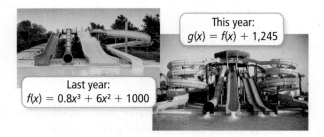

This year:
$g(x) = f(x) + 1,245$

Last year:
$f(x) = 0.8x^3 + 6x^2 + 1000$

a. Write the function g in terms of x.

b. Describe the transformation of the graph of g compared to f.

c. Compare the number of weekly visitors from last year to this year.

23. Generalize The volume of a storage box, in cubic feet, is given by the function $V(x) = (x)(x + 1)^2$. A freight company lists the shipping rates of items in cubic inches. Write a function for the volume of the box in cubic inches if x is its width in feet. ⓒ **MP.8**

24. Model With Mathematics A swimming pool is in the shape of a rectangular prism. The width is one more than five times the height, and the length is one less than eleven times the height. ⓒ **MP.4**

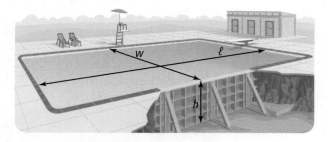

a. Using x for the height, write a function $V(x)$ to represent the volume of the pool.

b. Compare the volume of this pool with a larger one that is the same height, but twice the length and twice the width of this pool. Write a function $Z(x)$ for the volume of this larger pool.

ASSESSMENT PRACTICE

25. Match the number in each function with its effect on the parent function.
$f(x) = 2(x - 1)^4 + 5$
$g(x) = (x + 3)^6 - 7$

I   vertical stretch   **A.** 7
II shift to the left   **B.** 5
III shift to the right   **C.** 3
IV shift upward   **D.** 2
V   shift downward   **E.** 1

26. SAT/ACT Which of the following functions is neither even nor odd?

Ⓐ $f(x) = x^4 + 3x^2$

Ⓑ $g(x) = 5x^3 - x$

Ⓒ $h(x) = x^5 + 4x^3 + x^2$

Ⓓ $k(x) = 9 - 8x^2$

Ⓔ $p(x) = 5$

27. Performance Task The height of a ball thrown in the air can be modeled by the function $h(x) = -16t^2 + 32t + 6$, where $h(x)$ represents the height in feet of the ball after t seconds. The graph of this function is shown below.

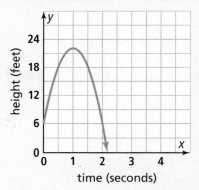

Part A What do the vertex, y-intercept, and x-intercept represent?

Part B If the ball is thrown from a height of 10 ft, how will this transform the graph?

Part C About how much longer will the ball be in the air when it is thrown from 10 ft compared to when it was thrown from 6 ft? (Hint: You may want to use your graphing calculator to compare the two graphs.)

Topic Review

? TOPIC ESSENTIAL QUESTION

1. What can the rule for a polynomial function reveal about its graph, and what can the graphs of polynomial functions reveal about the solutions of polynomial equations?

Vocabulary Review

Choose the correct term to complete each sentence.

2. The _____ is the greatest power of the variable in a polynomial expression.

3. The _____ is the non-zero constant multiplied by the greatest power of the variable in a polynomial expression.

4. The _____ of a function describes what happens to its graph as x approaches positive and negative infinity.

5. _____ is the triangular pattern of numbers where each number is the sum of two numbers above it.

6. The _____ determines whether the graph of the function will cross the x-axis at the point or merely touch it.

7. The _____ is a formula that can be used to expand powers of binomial expressions.

8. _____ is a method to divide a polynomial by a linear factor whose leading coefficient is 1.

- Binomial Theorem
- degree of a polynomial
- end behavior
- even function
- Factor Theorem
- identity
- leading coefficient
- multiplicity of a zero
- Pascal's Triangle
- synthetic division

Concepts & Skills Review

LESSON 3-1 **Graphing Polynomial Functions**

Quick Review

A **polynomial** can be either a monomial or a sum of monomials. When a polynomial has more than one monomial, the monomials are also referred to as **terms**.

Example

Graph the function $f(x) = 2x^3 - x^2 - 13x - 6$.

There are zeros at $x = -2$, $x = -0.5$, and $x = 3$.

There are turning points between -2 and -0.5 and between -0.5 and 3.

As $x \to -\infty$, $y \to -\infty$.

As $x \to +\infty$, $y \to +\infty$.

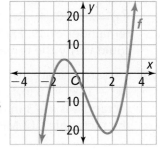

Practice & Problem Solving

Graph the polynomial function. Estimate the zeros and the turning points of the graph.

9. $f(x) = x^5 + 2x^4 - 10x^3 - 20x^2 + 9x + 18$

10. $f(x) = x^4 + x^3 - 16x^2 - 4x + 48$

11. **Reason** A polynomial function has the following end behavior: As $x \to -\infty$, $y \to +\infty$. As $x \to +\infty$, $y \to -\infty$. Describe the degree and leading coefficient of the polynomial function. **© MP.2**

12. **Make Sense and Persevere** After x hours of hiking, Sadie's elevation is $p(x) = -x^3 + 11x^2 - 34x + 24$, in meters. After how many hours will Sadie's elevation be 18 m below sea level? What do the x- and y-intercepts of the graph mean in this context? **© MP.1**

Quick Review

To add or subtract polynomials, add or subtract like terms. To multiply polynomials, use the Distributive Property.

Polynomial identities can be used to factor or multiply polynomials.

Example

Add $(-2x^3 + 5x^2 + 2x - 3) + (x^3 - 6x^2 + x + 12)$.

Use the Commutative and Associative Properties. Then combine like terms.

$(-2x^3 + 5x^2 + 2x - 3) + (x^3 - 6x^2 + x - 12)$

$= (-2x^3 + x^3) + (5x^2 - 6x^2) + (2x + x) + (-3 + 12)$

$= -x^3 - x^2 + 3x + 9$

Example

Use polynomial identities to factor $8x^3 + 27y^3$.

Use the Sum of Cubes Identity. Express each term as a square. Then write the factors.

$a^3 + b^3 = (a + b)(a^2 - ab + b^2)$

$8x^3 + 27y^3 = (2x)^3 + (3y)^3$

$\qquad = (2x + 3y)(4x^2 - 6xy + 9y^2)$

Practice & Problem Solving

Add or subtract the polynomials.

13. $(-8x^3 + 7x^2 + x - 9) + (5x^3 + 3x^2 - 2x - 1)$

14. $(9y^4 - y^3 + 4y^2 + y - 2) - (2y^4 - 3y^3 + 6y - 7)$

Multiply the polynomials.

15. $(9x - 1)(x + 5)(7x + 2)$

Use polynomial identities to multiply each polynomial.

16. $(5x + 8)^2$　　　　17. $(7x - 4)(7x + 4)$

Factor the polynomial.

18. $x^6 - 64$　　　　19. $27x^3 + y^6$

Use Pascal's Triangle or the Binomial Theorem to expand the expressions.

20. $(x - 2)^4$　　　　21. $(x + 5y)^5$

22. **Communicate Precisely** Explain why the set of polynomials is closed under subtraction. Ⓒ **MP.6**

23. **Reason** The length of a rectangle is represented by $3x^3 - 2x^2 + 10x - 4$, and the width is represented by $-x^3 + 6x^2 - x + 8$. What is the perimeter of the rectangle? Ⓒ **MP.2**

LESSON 3-4 ▸ Dividing Polynomials

Quick Review

Polynomials can be divided using long division or synthetic division. **Synthetic division** is a method to divide a polynomial by a linear factor whose leading coefficient is 1.

Example

Use synthetic division to divide $x^4 - 5x^3 - 6x^2 + 2x - 8$ by $x + 3$.

$$
\begin{array}{r|rrrrr}
-3 & 1 & -5 & -6 & 2 & -8 \\
   &   & -3 & 24 & -54 & 156 \\
\hline
   & 1 & -8 & 18 & -52 & 148 \\
   & \downarrow & \downarrow & \downarrow & \downarrow & \downarrow \\
   & x^3 & -8x^2 & +18x & -52 & +\dfrac{148}{x+3}
\end{array}
$$

The quotient is $x^3 - 8x^2 + 18x - 52$, and the remainder is 148.

Practice & Problem Solving

Use long division to divide.

24. $x^4 + 2x^3 - 8x^2 - 3x + 1$ divided by $x + 2$

Use synthetic division to divide.

25. $x^4 + 5x^3 + 7x^2 - 2x + 17$ divided by $x - 3$

26. **Make Sense and Persevere** A student divided $f(x) = x^3 + 8x^2 - 9x - 3$ by $x - 2$ and got a remainder of 19. Explain how the student could verify the remainder is correct. Ⓒ **MP.1**

27. **Reason** The area of a rectangle is $4x^3 + 14x^2 - 18$ in.^{2}. The length of the rectangle is $x + 3$ in. What is the width of the rectangle? Ⓒ **MP.2**

Zeros of Polynomial Functions and Theorems about Roots of Polynomial Equations

Quick Review

You can factor and use synthetic division to find zeros of polynomial functions. Then you can use the zeros to sketch a graph of the function.

The **Rational Root Theorem** states that the possible rational roots, or zeros, of a polynomial equation with integer coefficients come from the list of numbers of the form: $\pm\dfrac{\text{factor of } a_0}{\text{factor of } a_n}$.

Example

List all the possible rational solutions for the equation $0 = 2x^3 + x^2 - 7x - 6$. Then find all of the rational roots.

$\pm 1, \pm 2, \pm 3, \pm 6$ Factors of the constant term

$\pm 1, \pm 2$ Factors of the leading coefficient

List the possible roots, eliminating duplicates.

$\pm\dfrac{1}{1}, \pm\dfrac{1}{2}, \pm\dfrac{2}{1}, \pm\dfrac{3}{1}, \pm\dfrac{3}{2}, \pm\dfrac{6}{1}$

Use synthetic division to find that the roots are $-\dfrac{3}{2}, -1$, and 2.

Practice & Problem Solving

Sketch the graph of the function.

28. $f(x) = 2x^4 - x^3 - 32x^2 + 31x + 60$

29. $g(x) = x^3 - x^2 - 20x$

30. What x-values are solutions to the equation $x^3 + 2x^2 - 4x + 8 = x^2 - x + 4$?

31. What values of x are solutions to the inequality $x^3 + 3x^2 - 4x - 12 > 0$?

32. What are all of the real and complex roots of the function $f(x) = x^4 - 4x^3 + 4x^2 - 36x - 45$?

33. A polynomial function Q of degree 4 with rational coefficients has zeros $1 + \sqrt{5}$ and $-7i$. What is an equation for Q?

34. **Reason** What does the graph of a function tell you about the multiplicity of a zero? Ⓒ **MP.2**

35. **Make Sense and Persevere** A storage unit in the shape of a rectangular prism measures $2x$ ft long, $x + 8$ ft wide, and $x + 9$ ft tall. What are the dimensions of the storage unit, in feet, if its volume is 792 ft^3? Ⓒ **MP.1**

Transformations of Polynomial Functions

Quick Review

Polynomial functions can be translated, reflected, and stretched in similar ways to other functions you have studied.

Example

How does the graph of $f(x) = 2(x + 1)^3 - 3$ compare to the graph of the parent function?

Parent function: $y = x^3$

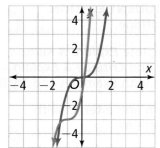

Adding 1 shifts the graph to the left 1 unit.

Multiplying by 2 stretches the graph vertically.

Subtracting 3 shifts the graph down 3 units.

Practice & Problem Solving

Classify each function as even, odd, or neither.

36.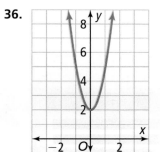

37.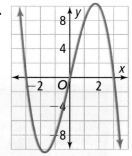

38. **Error Analysis** A student says the graph of $f(x) = 0.5x^4 + 1$ is a vertical stretch and a translation up 1 unit of the parent function. Explain the student's error. Ⓒ **MP.3**

39. **Make Sense and Persevere** The volume of a refrigerator, in cubic centimeters, is given by the function $V(x) = (x)(x + 1)(x - 2)$. Write a new function for the volume of the refrigerator in cubic millimeters if x is in centimeters. Ⓒ **MP.1**

Try It! **1.** Determine if each table of values represents an inverse variation.

a.

x	1	2	3	5	6	15
y	25.5	12.75	8.50	5.10	4.25	1.70

b.

x	6.6	5.5	4.4	3.3	2.2	1.1
y	3	5	7	9	11	13

CONCEPT Inverse Variation

When a relation between x and y is an inverse variation, we say that x varies inversely as y. Inverse variation is modeled by the equation $y = \frac{k}{x}$, or with an equivalent form $x = \frac{k}{y}$ or $xy = k$, where $k \neq 0$. The variable k represents the **constant of variation**, the number that relates the two variables in an inverse variation.

In this table, the constant of variation is 24.

x	1	2	3	4	6	8	12	24
y	24	12	8	6	4	3	2	1

Notice how as x doubles in value from 1 to 2 to 4 to 8, . . .

. . . the value of y is halved from 24 to 12 to 6 to 3.

 EXAMPLE 2 **Use Inverse Variation**

In an inverse variation, $x = 10$ when $y = 3$. Write an equation to represent the inverse variation. Then find the value of y when $x = -6$.

$y = \frac{k}{x}$ ⸺⸺ Write the equation for an inverse variation.

$3 = \frac{k}{10}$ ⸺⸺ Substitute 10 and 3 for x and y.

$30 = k$ ⸺⸺ Multiply both sides by 10 to solve for k.

After solving for k, write an equation for the inverse variation.

$y = \frac{30}{x}$ ⸺⸺ Write the equation to represent the inverse variation.

$y = \frac{30}{-6}$ ⸺⸺ Substitute −6 for x in the equation.

$y = -5$ ⸺⸺ Divide.

COMMON ERROR
Remember to keep track of any negative signs when substituting into equations and performing calculations.

The equation that represents the inverse relation is $y = \frac{30}{x}$. When $x = -6$, $y = -5$.

 Try It! **2.** In an inverse variation, $x = 6$ and $y = \frac{1}{2}$.

a. What is the equation that represents the inverse variation?

b. What is the value of y when $x = 15$?

 Go Online | SavvasRealize.com

APPLICATION

 EXAMPLE 3 **Use an Inverse Variation Model**

On a guitar, the string length, *s*, varies inversely with the frequency, *f*, of its vibrations.

MAKE SENSE AND PERSEVERE
Use what you know about inverse variation to mentally compute an approximate value of your answer. © MP.1

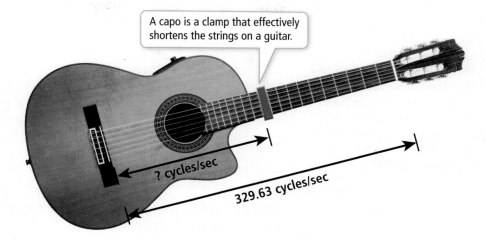

A capo is a clamp that effectively shortens the strings on a guitar.

? cycles/sec

329.63 cycles/sec

The frequency of a 26-inch E-string is 329.63 cycles per second. What is the frequency when the string length is 13 inches?

$$s = \frac{k}{f}$$ .... Write the equation for an inverse variation.

$$26 = \frac{k}{329.63}$$ .... Substitute 26 and 329.63 for *s* and *f*.

$$8{,}570.38 = k$$ .... Multiply by 329.63 to solve for *k*.

After solving for *k*, write an equation for the inverse variation.

$$s = \frac{8{,}570.38}{f}$$ .... Substitute 8,570.38 for *k* in the equation.

$$13 = \frac{8{,}570.38}{f}$$ .... Substitute 13 for *s* in the equation.

$$f = 659.26$$ .... Solve for *f*.

So the frequency of the 13-inch string is 659.26 cycles per second.

☑ **Try It!** **3.** The amount of time it takes for an ice cube to melt varies inversely to the air temperature, in degrees. At 20° Celsius, the ice will melt in 20 minutes. How long will it take the ice to melt if the temperature is 30° Celsius?

CONCEPTUAL UNDERSTANDING

 EXAMPLE 4 **Graph the Reciprocal Function**

How do you graph the reciprocal function, $y = \frac{1}{x}$?

The **reciprocal function** maps every non-zero real number to its reciprocal.

Step 1: Consider the domain and range of the function.

Domain: $\{x \mid x \neq 0\}$

Range: $\{y \mid y \neq 0\}$

If $x = 0$ that will result in an undefined expression, so $x \neq 0$.

CONTINUED ON THE NEXT PAGE

EXAMPLE 4 CONTINUED

Step 2: Graph the function.

x	−3	−2	−1	−$\frac{1}{2}$	−$\frac{1}{3}$	0	$\frac{1}{3}$	$\frac{1}{2}$	1	2	3
f(x)	−$\frac{1}{3}$	−$\frac{1}{2}$	−1	−2	−3	Undefined	3	2	1	$\frac{1}{2}$	$\frac{1}{3}$

> **USE APPROPRIATE TOOLS**
> For an equation such as this one, that does not involve a lot of parameters, graphing by hand makes sense. As you encounter more complex equations, it may be appropriate to graph with technology. © **MP.5**

Use a table of values or technology to graph the function.

Step 3: Observe the graph of $y = \frac{1}{x}$ as it approaches positive infinity and negative infinity.

x	1	10	100	1,000	10,000
f(x)	1	$\frac{1}{10}$	$\frac{1}{100}$	$\frac{1}{1,000}$	$\frac{1}{10,000}$

As x gets larger, the denominator gets larger and the value of the function approaches zero.

An **asymptote** is a line that a graph approaches. Asymptotes guide the end behavior of a function.

As x approaches infinity, f(x) approaches 0. The same is true as x-values approach negative infinity, so the line $y = 0$ is a *horizontal asymptote*.

Step 4: Observe the graph of $y = \frac{1}{x}$ as x approaches 0 for positive and negative x-values.

x	1	$\frac{1}{10}$	$\frac{1}{100}$	$\frac{1}{1,000}$	$\frac{1}{10,000}$
f(x)	1	10	100	1,000	10,000

As x gets closer to 0, the value of the function gets larger and larger.

For positive values of x, as x approaches 0, f(x) approaches positive infinity.

x	−1	−$\frac{1}{10}$	−$\frac{1}{100}$	−$\frac{1}{1,000}$	−$\frac{1}{10,000}$
f(x)	−1	−10	−100	−1,000	−10,000

As x gets closer to 0, the value of the function approaches negative infinity.

For negative values of x, as x approaches 0, f(x) approaches negative infinity. The domain of the function excludes 0, so the graph will never touch the line $x = 0$. The line $x = 0$ is a *vertical asymptote*.

 Try It! **4.** Graph the function $y = \frac{10}{x}$. What are the domain, range, and asymptotes of the function?

EXAMPLE 5 ▶ Graph Translations of the Reciprocal Function

Graph $g(x) = \frac{1}{x-3} + 2$. What are the equations of the asymptotes? What are the domain and range?

Start with the graph of the parent function, $f(x) = \frac{1}{x}$.

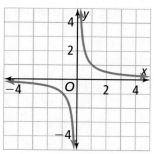

Recall that adding h to x in the definition of f translates the graph of f horizontally. Adding k to $f(x)$ translates the graph of f vertically.

The function $q(x) = \frac{1}{x-h} + k$ is a transformation of the parent function f that shifts the graph of f horizontally by h units and then shifts the graph of f vertically by k units.

The graph of $g(x) = \frac{1}{x-3} + 2$ is a translation of the graph of the parent function 3 units right and 2 units up.

MAKE SENSE AND PERSEVERE
Not only are the points of the graph translated, but the asymptotes are translated as well. © MP.1

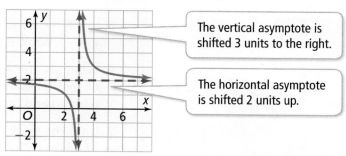

The vertical asymptote is shifted 3 units to the right.

The horizontal asymptote is shifted 2 units up.

The line $x = 3$ is a vertical asymptote. The line $y = 2$ is a horizontal asymptote.

The domain is $\{x \mid x \neq 3\}$.

The range is $\{y \mid y \neq 2\}$.

Try It! 5. Graph $g(x) = \frac{1}{x+2} - 4$. What are the equations of the asymptotes? What are the domain and range?

🔑 CONCEPT SUMMARY Inverse Variation and the Reciprocal Function

	Inverse Variation	Transformations of the Reciprocal Function
WORDS	An inverse variation is a relation between two variables such that as one variable increases, the other decreases proportionally.	The reciprocal function models the inverse variation, $y = \frac{1}{x}$. Like other functions, it can be transformed.
ALGEBRA	$y = \frac{k}{x}$, where $k \neq 0$	$y = \frac{a}{x - h} + k$
EXAMPLES	$y = \frac{1}{x}$ asymptotes: $x = 0$ $y = 0$ 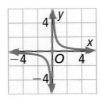	$y = \frac{1}{x - 4} - 2$ $h = 4$ $k = -2$ Parent is transformed down 2 and right 4. asymptotes: $x = 4$ $y = -2$ 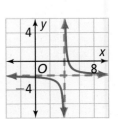

☑ Do You UNDERSTAND?

1. **? ESSENTIAL QUESTION** How are inverse variations related to the reciprocal function?

2. **Construct Arguments** Explain why the amount of propane in a grill's tank and the time spent grilling could represent an inverse variation.
   © **MP.3**

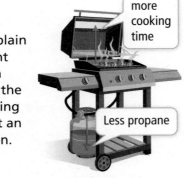
more cooking time

Less propane

3. **Vocabulary** Why is it impossible for the graph of the function $y = \frac{1}{x}$ to intersect the horizontal asymptote at the x-axis?

4. **Error Analysis** Carmen said the table of values shown represents an inverse variation. Explain why Carmen is mistaken. © **MP.3**

x	1	2	3	4	8	16
y	24	12	8	6	3	2

Do You KNOW HOW?

5. In an inverse variation, $x = -8$ when $y = -\frac{1}{4}$. What is the value of y when $x = 4$?

6. What are the equations of the asymptotes of the function $f(x) = \frac{1}{x - 5} + 3$? What are the domain and range?

7. Until the truck runs out of gas, the amount of gas in its fuel tank varies inversely with the number of miles traveled. Model a relationship between the amount of gas in a fuel tank of a truck and the number of miles traveled by the truck as an inverse variation.

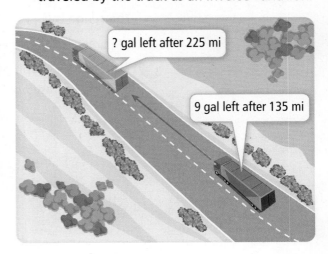
? gal left after 225 mi
9 gal left after 135 mi

PRACTICE & PROBLEM SOLVING

UNDERSTAND

8. Communicate Precisely Explain the difference between the graphs of inverse variation functions when $k > 0$ and when $k < 0$. ⓒ **MP.6**

9. Generalize Just from looking at the table of values, how can you determine that the data do *not* represent an inverse variation? ⓒ **MP.8**

x	−2	2	4	6	8	10
y	−6	6	12	18	24	30

10. Construct Arguments Explain why zero cannot be in the domain of an inverse variation. ⓒ **MP.3**

11. Error Analysis Describe and correct the error a student made in graphing the function $y = \frac{5}{x}$. ⓒ **MP.3**

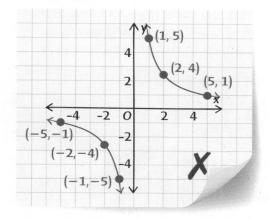

12. Higher Order Thinking The cost to rent a condominium at the beach is $1,500 per week. If two people share the cost, they each have to pay $750. Explain why the relationship between the cost per person varies inversely with the number of persons sharing the cost. Then write an inverse variation function that can be used to calculate the cost per person, c, of p persons sharing the rental fee.

13. Generalize For an inverse variation, write an equation that gives the value of k in terms of x and y. ⓒ **MP.8**

PRACTICE

Do the tables of values represent inverse variations? Explain. SEE EXAMPLE 1

14.

x	$-\frac{1}{4}$	$-\frac{1}{2}$	$\frac{1}{3}$	2	5	11
y	$-\frac{9}{2}$	−9	6	36	90	198

15.

x	1	2	3	4	5	6
y	60	30	20	15	12	10

16. If x and y vary inversely and $x = 3$ when $y = \frac{2}{3}$, what is the value of y when $x = -1$? SEE EXAMPLE 2

17. The wavelength, w, of a radio wave varies inversely to its frequency, f, as shown in the graph.

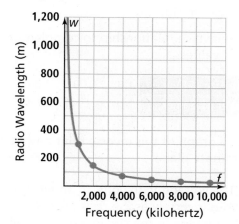

A radio wave with a frequency of 1,000 kilohertz has a length of 300 m. What is the frequency when the wave-length is 375 m? SEE EXAMPLE 3

18. Graph the function $y = \frac{-2}{x}$. What are the domain, range, and asymptotes of the function? SEE EXAMPLE 4

19. Graph $g(x) = \frac{1}{x-2} + 6$. What are the equations of the asymptotes? What are the domain and range? SEE EXAMPLE 5

APPLY

20. Model With Mathematics The time t required to empty a water tank varies inversely as the rate of pumping p. A pump can empty a water tank in 40 min at the rate of 120 gal/min. Write the equation of the inverse variation. How long it will take the pump to empty the water tank at the rate of 200 gal/min? Ⓒ **MP.4**

21. Use Structure The number of downloaded games that can be stored on a video game system varies inversely with the average size of a video game. A certain video game system can store 160 games when the average size of a game is 2.0 gigabytes (GB). Ⓒ **MP.7**

   a. Write an inverse equation that relates the number of games n that will fit on the video game system as a function of the average game size s in GB.

   b. Use the inverse relationship to complete the table of values.

Game Size (GB), s	1.0	2.5	3.0	4.0
Number of Games, n	▦	▦	▦	▦

   c. Sketch a graph of this inverse relationship on a coordinate plane.

22. Reason The voltage V, in volts, in an electrical circuit varies inversely as the resistance R in ohms. The voltage in the circuit is 15 volts when the resistance is 192 ohms.

   a. Write the equation of the inverse variation.

   b. Find the voltage in the circuit when the resistance is 144 ohms. Ⓒ **MP.2**

23. Boyle's Law states that the pressure exerted by fixed quantity of a gas, P, varies inversely with the volume the gas occupies, V, assuming constant temperature.

   The volume and air pressure of a volleyball are 300 in.³ and 4.5 psi. The volume and air pressure of a basketball are 415 in.³ and 8 psi. How much smaller would the volleyball have to be to equal the air pressure of the basketball?

ASSESSMENT PRACTICE

24. Given that $\frac{A}{B} = k$, which of the following is true?

   Ⓐ k varies inversely with A.

   Ⓑ k varies inversely with B.

   Ⓒ A varies inversely with k.

   Ⓓ A varies inversely with B.

25. SAT/ACT Suppose y varies inversely as the square of x. If x is multiplied by 4, which of the following is true for the value of y?

   Ⓐ It is multiplied by 4.

   Ⓑ It is multiplied by 16.

   Ⓒ It is multiplied by $\frac{1}{4}$.

   Ⓓ It is multiplied by $\frac{1}{16}$.

26. Performance Task Suppose Cameron takes a road trip. He starts from his home in the suburbs of Cleveland, OH and travels to Pittsburgh, PA to visit his aunt and uncle.

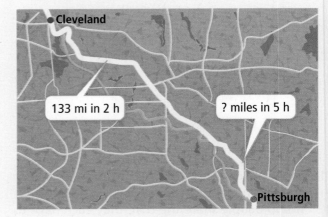

Part A The distance Cameron drives from Cleveland to Pittsburgh is 133 miles. The trip takes him 2 hours. The distance d in miles that Cameron drives varies directly with the amount of time t in hours, he spends driving. Write the equation of the direct variation. Use the given relationship and the equation to find the number of miles Cameron would travel if he continues on for 5 more hours.

Part B The amount of gas in Cameron's car is 9 gal after he drives for 2 h. The amount of gas g in gallons in his tank varies inversely with the amount of time t, in hours, he spends driving. Write the equation of the inverse variation. Use the given relationship and the equation to find the number of gallons in Cameron's tank after 5 more hours of driving.

4-2

Graphing Rational Functions

I CAN... graph rational functions.

VOCABULARY
• rational expression
• rational function

Common Core State Standards HSF.IF.C.7.D (+), HSA.APR.D.6, HSA.REI.D.11, MP.2, MP.6, MP.7

  Activity  Assess

👆 EXPLORE & REASON

Look at the three functions shown.

A. **Look for Relationships** Graph each function. Determine which of the functions are linear. Find the y-intercept of each function and the slope, if appropriate. © **MP.7**

B. What is the effect on the graph of f when dividing x − 1 by 2?

C. What happens to the graph of h as x approaches 2?

D. **Communicate Precisely** What is the effect on the graph of f(x) when dividing x − 1 by x − 2? (Hint: Compare it to what you found in part (B).) © **MP.6**

$f(x) = x - 1$

$g(x) = \frac{x-1}{2}$

$h(x) = \frac{x-1}{x-2}$

❓ ESSENTIAL QUESTION | How can you graph a rational function?

👆 EXAMPLE 1 | Rewrite a Rational Function to Identify Asymptotes

Rewrite $g(x) = \frac{4x}{x-3}$ using long division. How is the quotient related to the reciprocal function, $f(x) = \frac{1}{x}$? Sketch the graph.

$g(x) = \dfrac{4x}{x-3}$ .... Write the equation.

$= x - 3 \overline{)\begin{array}{c} 4 \\ 4x \end{array}}$ .... Divide $4x$ by x.

$\dfrac{-(4x - 12)}{12}$ .... Multiply $x - 3$ by 4 and subtract from $4x$.

$g(x) = 4 + \dfrac{12}{x-3}$ .... Write the remainder as a fraction in the quotient.

Rewrite g in the form $g(x) = \dfrac{a}{x-h} + k$ to identify the transformation of the parent function, $f(x) = \dfrac{1}{x}$.

$g(x) = 4 + \dfrac{12}{x-3}$

USE STRUCTURE
Rewriting g in this way is similar to rewriting an improper fraction as a mixed number. © **MP.7**

In the graph, the parent function f has been shifted up 4 units and then right 3 units. The resulting graph has been stretched vertically by a factor of 12.

There is a vertical asymptote at $x = 3$ and a horizontal asymptote at $y = 4$.

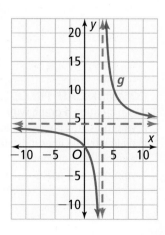

✓ Try It!

1. Use long division to rewrite each rational function. Find the asymptotes of f and sketch the graph.

a. $f(x) = \dfrac{6x}{2x+1}$

b. $f(x) = \dfrac{x}{x-6}$

CONCEPT Rational Functions

Just as a rational number is a number that can be expressed as the ratio of two integers, a **rational expression** is an expression that can be expressed as the ratio of two polynomials, such as $\frac{P(x)}{Q(x)}$, where the value of $Q(x) \neq 0$.

A **rational function** is any function defined by a rational expression, such as $R(x) = \frac{P(x)}{Q(x)}$. The domain of $R(x)$ is all values of x for which $Q(x) \neq 0$.

The function $g(x) = \frac{4x}{x-3}$ is a rational function.

CONCEPTUAL UNDERSTANDING

① **EXAMPLE 2** Find Asymptotes of a Rational Function

How do you find vertical and horizontal asymptotes of a rational function?

A. **What are the vertical asymptotes for the graph of** $f(x) = \dfrac{3x-2}{x^2+7x+12}$?

Vertical asymptotes can occur at the x-values where the function is undefined. Determine where the denominator of the rational function is equal to 0.

$$x^2 + 7x + 12 = 0 \qquad \text{Set the denominator equal to 0.}$$
$$(x+3)(x+4) = 0 \qquad \text{Factor.}$$
$$x + 3 = 0 \text{ or } x + 4 = 0 \qquad \text{Use the Zero Product Property.}$$
$$x = -3 \quad \text{or} \quad x = -4 \qquad \text{Solve using the Addition Property of Equality.}$$

The possible vertical asymptotes are $x = -3$ and $x = -4$.

Graph the function to determine if there are asymptotes at $x = -3$ or $x = -4$.

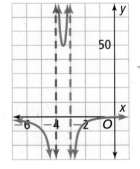

Use the TRACE feature on the graphing calculator to confirm that the graph is not defined at $x = -3$ or $x = -4$.

COMMUNICATE PRECISELY
When creating a graph with asymptotes, it is important to explain why the lines indicated are vertical or horizontal asymptotes. ⓒ **MP.6**

The graph is not defined at $x = -3$ or $x = -4$. These lines are vertical asymptotes.

CONTINUED ON THE NEXT PAGE

EXAMPLE 2 CONTINUED

B. What are the horizontal asymptotes for the graph $f(x) = \dfrac{3x - 2}{x^2 + 7x + 12}$?

To identify *horizontal asymptotes*, we have to consider three cases.

Case 1: The degree of the numerator is less than the degree of the denominator.

Consider $g(x) = \dfrac{x + 4}{x^2 + 1}$

> As the value of x increases, the value of the denominator gets very large in relation to the numerator. The value of the function gets closer and closer to 0.

When the degree of the numerator is less than the degree of the denominator, there exists a horizontal asymptote at $y = 0$.

Case 2: The degree of the numerator is greater than the degree of the denominator.

Consider $h(x) = \dfrac{x^2 + 1}{x + 2}$

> As the value of x increases, the value of the numerator gets very large in relation to the denominator. The value of the function continues to increase.

When the degree of the numerator is greater than the degree of the denominator, there are no horizontal asymptotes.

Case 3: The degree of the numerator and the denominator are the same.

Consider $k(x) = \dfrac{2x^2 + x + 1}{x^2 - 1}$

Using long division, we can rewrite this as $k(x) = 2 + \dfrac{x + 3}{x^2 - 1}$.

> As the value of x increases, the value of the rational part of the quotient approaches 0, so the value of the function approaches 2.

$k(x) = \dfrac{2x^2 + x + 1}{x^2 - 1}$ has a horizontal asymptote at $y = 2$.

When the degree of the numerator is equal to the degree of the denominator, the horizontal asymptote is the ratio of the leading coefficients.

For the function $k(x) = \dfrac{3x - 2}{x^2 + 7x + 12}$, the degree of the numerator is less than the degree of the denominator.

It has a horizontal asymptote at $y = 0$.

STUDY TIP

The vertical asymptote(s) are found by factoring the denominator of the function.

The horizontal asymptote(s) are found using the relationship between the degree of the numerator and the degree of the denominator.

MAKE SENSE AND PERSEVERE

To show that the horizontal asymptote is accurate, try substituting different values for x and see if the values for y approach the asymptote(s). ⒸMP.1

 Try It! **2.** What are the vertical and horizontal asymptotes of the graph of each function?

a. $g(x) = \dfrac{2x^2 + x - 9}{x^2 - 2x - 8}$ **b.** $\dfrac{x^2 + 5x + 4}{3x^2 - 12}$

EXAMPLE 3 > Graph a Function of the Form $\frac{ax + b}{cx + d}$

What is the graph of the function $f(x) = \frac{2x + 1}{3x - 4}$**?**

Step 1: Determine if there is a vertical asymptote.

$3x - 4 = 0$ ·············· Set the denominator equal to 0.

$3x = 4$ ·············· Solve.

$x = \frac{4}{3}$ ·············· Divide to isolate the variable.

At $x = \frac{4}{3}$, the value of the denominator is 0. There is a vertical asymptote at $x = \frac{4}{3}$.

Step 2: Determine if there is a horizontal asymptote.

$y \approx \frac{2x}{3x}$ ·············· Approximate f with ratio of leading terms.

$y \approx \frac{2}{3}$ ·············· Simplify.

As $x \to \pm\infty$, $y \to \frac{2}{3}$.

There is a horizontal asymptote at $y = \frac{2}{3}$.

COMMON ERROR
The ratio of the leading terms cannot be used as an approximation unless x is approaching positive or negative infinity.

Step 3: Graph the function.

- Indicate the asymptotes.
- Choose x-values on either side of the vertical asymptote, and evaluate the function for those x-values to create coordinate points.
- Plot the points.

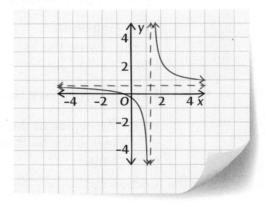

 Try It! **3.** Graph each function.

a. $f(x) = \frac{4x - 3}{x + 8}$

b. $g(x) = \frac{3x + 2}{x - 1}$

APPLICATION   **EXAMPLE 4**   **Use a Rational Function Model**

The cost of removing a pollutant is modeled by the given function where $f(p)$ is the cost, in millions of dollars, of removing p percent of the pollutant. What percent of the pollutant can be removed for $78.3 million?

$$f(p) = \frac{8.7p}{100 - p}$$

Formulate   Since p is a percent, you know that $0 \le p \le 100$.

Compute   Find the vertical asymptote by solving $100 - p = 0$:

$p = 100$.

Refine the domain: $0 \le p < 100$.

Graph $y = 78.3$ and $y = \frac{8.7p}{100 - p}$.

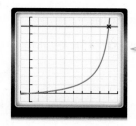

Use graphing technology to find the point of intersection.

The point $(90, 78.3)$ lies on both graphs.

Interpret   90% of the pollutant can be removed for $78.3 million.

 Try It!   **4.** New techniques have changed the cost function. For the new function $g(p) = \frac{3.2p + 1}{100 - p}$, what percent of the pollutant can be removed for $50 million?

👆 **EXAMPLE 5** Graph a Rational Function

What is the graph of $f(x) = \dfrac{4x^2 - 9}{x^2 + 2x - 15}$**?**

Step 1 Determine if there are any vertical asymptotes.

$$x^2 + 2x - 15 = 0 \quad \text{·····} \quad \text{Set the denominator equal to 0.}$$

$$(x + 5)(x - 3) = 0 \quad \text{·····} \quad \text{Factor.}$$

$$x + 5 = 0 \text{ or } x - 3 = 0 \quad \text{·····} \quad \text{Use the Zero Product Property.}$$

$$x = -5 \quad \text{or} \quad x = 3$$

Neither of these values makes the numerator equal to 0, but they each make the denominator equal to 0.

Vertical asymptotes: $x = -5$ and $x = 3$

Step 2 Determine if there is a horizontal asymptote.

$$y \approx \frac{4x^2}{x^2} \quad \text{·····} \quad \text{Approximate } f \text{ with ratio of leading terms.}$$

$$\approx 4 \quad \text{·····} \quad \text{Simplify.}$$

As $x \to \pm\infty$, $y \to 4$.

There is a horizontal asymptote at $y = 4$.

> **COMMUNICATE PRECISELY**
> When graphing, it is important to indicate and clearly label both horizontal and vertical asymptotes. © **MP.6**

Step 3 Sketch the graph.

Indicate the asymptotes.

Plot points, choosing some x-values from each area of the graph.

x	f(x)
−20	4.61
−15	4.95
−10	6.02
−4	−7.86
0	0.60
4	6.11
7	3.90
13	3.71
20	3.74

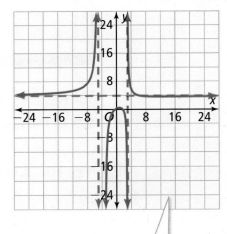

For $x > 3$ as the x values get larger, this graph drops below the horizontal asymptote and then approaches it from below.

✓ **Try It!** **5.** Identify the asymptotes and sketch the graph of $g(x) = \dfrac{x^2 - 5x + 6}{2x^2 - 10}$.

CONCEPT SUMMARY Graphing Rational Functions

| RATIONAL FUNCTION | A function that is expressible as a fraction with polynomials in the numerator and the denominator |

ASYMPTOTES

Vertical

Vertical asymptotes are guides for the behavior of a graph as it approaches a vertical line.

- The line $x = a$ is a vertical asymptote of $\frac{P(x)}{Q(x)}$, if $Q(a) = 0$ and $P(a) \neq 0$.

- The up or down behavior of the function as it approaches the asymptote can be determined by substituting values close to a on either side of the asymptote.

Horizontal

Horizontal asymptotes are guides for the end behavior of a graph as it approaches a horizontal line.

If the degree of the numerator is

- less than the degree of the denominator, the horizontal asymptote is at $y = 0$.

- greater than the denominator, there is no horizontal asymptote.

- equal to the degree of the denominator, set y equal to the ratio of the leading coefficients. The graph of this line is the horizontal asymptote.

ALGEBRA

$f(x) = \frac{8x - 3}{4x + 1}$

Vertical Asymptote: Let $4x + 1 = 0$ and solve.

$x = -\frac{1}{4}$

Horizontal Asymptote: Find the ratio of the leading coefficients $\left(\frac{8}{4}\right)$.

$y = 2$

GRAPH

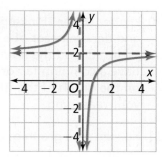

✓ Do You UNDERSTAND?

1. **ESSENTIAL QUESTION** How can you graph a rational function?

2. **Vocabulary** Why does it make sense to call the expressions in this lesson *rational* functions?

3. **Error Analysis** Ashton said the graph of $f(x) = \frac{x + 2}{2x^2 + 4x - 6}$ has a horizontal asymptote at $y = \frac{1}{2}$. Describe and correct Ashton's error. Ⓒ MP.3

4. **Reason** When will the graph of a rational function have no vertical asymptotes? Give an example of such a function. Ⓒ MP.2

Do You KNOW HOW?

Find the vertical asymptote(s) and horizontal asymptote(s) of the rational function. Then graph the function.

5. $f(x) = \frac{x + 2}{x - 3}$

6. $f(x) = \frac{x - 1}{2x + 1}$

7. A trainer mixed water with an electrolyte solution. The concentration of electrolytes can be modeled by $f(x) = \frac{3}{x + 12}$. Graph the function.

x gal of water

12 gal of 25% electrolyte solution

✎ **PRACTICE & PROBLEM SOLVING**

UNDERSTAND ▶

8. **Communicate Precisely** What is the horizontal asymptote of the rational function $f(x) = \frac{ax^2 + bx + c}{dx^2 + ex + f}$? Explain. ⓒ MP.6

9. **Error Analysis** Juanita is trying to determine the vertical and horizontal asymptotes for the graph of the function $f(x) = \frac{x^2 + 3x - 4}{x^2 - x - 12}$. Describe and correct the error Juanita made in determining the vertical and horizontal asymptotes. ⓒ MP.3

$$f(x) = \frac{x^2 + 3x - 4}{x^2 - x - 12}$$
$$= \frac{(x + 4)(x - 1)}{(x + 3)(x - 4)}$$

vertical asymptote: $x = -3$, $x = 4$
horizontal asymptote: $y = -4$, $y = 1$ ✗

10. **Higher Order Thinking** Suppose the numerator and denominator of a rational function are factored, and the numerator and denominator have a common factor of $x + a$. What happens on the graph of the function at $x = -a$? Explain your reasoning.

11. **Reason** The graph of a rational function has vertical asymptotes at $x = -3$ and $x = 1$ and a horizontal asymptote at $y = 3$.

   a. Write a function that has these attributes.

   b. Graph your function to verify it is correct. ⓒ MP.2

   c. Is it possible to have a different graph with the same attributes? Explain.

12. **Communicate Precisely** Explain how to use the end behavior of the function $f(x) = \frac{x^2 + 6}{4x^2 - 3x - 1}$ to determine the horizontal asymptote of the graph. Then explain why using end behavior for finding the horizontal asymptote works the same as using the ratio of the leading terms. ⓒ MP.6

PRACTICE ▶

Use long division to rewrite each rational function. What are the asymptotes of f? Sketch the graph. SEE EXAMPLE 1

13. $f(x) = \frac{2x}{x + 4}$

14. $f(x) = \frac{5x}{x - 2}$

15. $f(x) = \frac{6x^2}{3x^2 + 1}$

16. $f(x) = \frac{x^2}{2x^2 - 2}$

Identify the vertical and horizontal asymptotes of each rational function. SEE EXAMPLE 2

17. $f(x) = \frac{3x^2}{4x^2 - 1}$

18. $f(x) = \frac{5x + 6}{x^2 - 9x + 18}$

19. $f(x) = \frac{4x + 3}{x^2 - 4}$

20. $f(x) = \frac{5x^2 - 19x - 4}{2x^2 - 2}$

Graph each function. SEE EXAMPLE 3

21. $f(x) = \frac{-1}{x + 3}$

22. $f(x) = \frac{3x}{x - 1}$

23. $f(x) = \frac{x + 2}{-x + 1}$

24. $f(x) = \frac{2x - 3}{3x + 4}$

25. An owner tracks her sales each day since opening her marketing company. The daily sales, in dollars, after day x is given by the function $f(x) = \frac{200,000x}{x^2 + 150}$. On approximately which day(s) will the daily sales be \$3,000? SEE EXAMPLE 4

DAILY SALES TRACKER	
DAYS	**SALES**
1	\$1,324.50
2	\$2,597.40
3	\$3,773.58
4	\$4,819.28

AC
ADVERTISING COMPANY

Graph each function, labeling all horizontal or vertical asymptotes of the form $x = a$ or $y = b$. SEE EXAMPLE 5

26. $f(x) = \frac{x + 4}{2x^2 - 13x - 7}$

27. $f(x) = \frac{2x - 1}{x^2 - 3x - 10}$

28. $f(x) = \frac{x^2 + x - 2}{2x^2 - 9x - 18}$

29. $f(x) = \frac{6x^2 - 12x}{x^2 + 5x - 24}$

Go Online | SavvasRealize.com

APPLY

30. **Make Sense and Persevere** Amaya made 10 three-point shots out of 25 attempts. If she then goes on to make x consecutive three-point shots, her success would be given by the function $f(x) = \frac{x + 10}{x + 25}$. © **MP.1**

SHOTS MADE
10
SHOTS ATTEMPTED
25

a. Identify the vertical asymptote(s) and horizontal asymptote(s).

b. Graph the function.

31. **Model With Mathematics** A software CD can be manufactured for $0.10 each. The development cost to produce the software is $500,000. The first 200 CDs were used by testers to test the functionality of the software and were not sold. © **MP.4**

a. Write a function f for the average cost, in dollars, of a salable software CD where x is the number of salable software CDs.

b. What are the vertical asymptotes of the graph?

c. What are the horizontal asymptotes of the graph?

d. Graph the function.

e. What do the asymptotes mean?

32. **Reason** After diluting salt water, the concentration of salt in the water is given by the function $f(x) = \frac{0.5x}{x^2 - 1}$, where x is the time in hours since the dilution.

a. What is the concentration of salt in the water after 4 hours?

b. After how many hours will the concentration of salt in the water be 0.2? Round to the nearest hundredth. © **MP.2**

ASSESSMENT PRACTICE

33. Which function has a graph with a vertical asymptote at $x = 3$? Select all that apply.

Ⓐ $f(x) = \frac{x - 2}{x^2 + 2x - 15}$

Ⓑ $f(x) = \frac{x - 3}{x^2 + 7x + 12}$

Ⓒ $f(x) = \frac{x^2 - 9}{x + 9}$

Ⓓ $f(x) = \frac{x^2 + 6x + 5}{x^2 - 9}$

34. **SAT/ACT** Which function has a graph with a horizontal asymptote at $y = -1$?

Ⓐ $f(x) = \frac{x + 5}{x - 3}$

Ⓑ $f(x) = \frac{-x + 9}{x - 8}$

Ⓒ $f(x) = \frac{x^2 + 4}{x^2 - 1}$

Ⓓ $f(x) = \frac{2x^2}{x^2 - x - 2}$

35. **Performance Task** There is a relationship between the degree of the numerator and denominator of a rational function and the function's horizontal asymptote.

Function	Horizontal Asymptote
$f(x) = \frac{2x}{x^2}$	
$f(x) = \frac{5x^2}{2x^3}$	
$f(x) = \frac{9x^6}{7x}$	
$f(x) = \frac{-3x^7}{4x^4}$	

Part A Complete the right column of the table.

Part B What is the relationship between the degree of the numerator and denominator when the horizontal asymptote is $y = 0$?

Part C What is the relationship between the degree of the numerator and denominator when there is no a horizontal asymptote?

4-3

Multiplying and Dividing Rational Expressions

 SavvasRealize.com

I CAN... find the product and the quotient of rational expressions.

VOCABULARY
• simplified form of a rational expression

👆 EXPLORE & REASON

Consider the following graph of the function $y = x + 2$.

A. What is the domain of this function?

B. Sketch a function that resembles the graph, but restrict its domain to exclude 2.

C. Use Structure Consider the function you have sketched.
What kind of function might have a graph like this? Explain. © **MP.7**

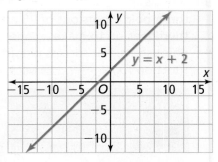

❓ ESSENTIAL QUESTION

How does understanding operations with fractions help you multiply and divide rational expressions?

CONCEPT Rational Expression

A *rational expression* is the quotient of two polynomials. The domain is all real numbers except those for which the denominator is equal to 0.

$\frac{x^2}{x^2 - 9}$ is an example of a rational expression.

Since the denominator cannot equal 0, $x^2 - 9 \neq 0$.

$x^2 \neq 9 \rightarrow x \neq 3$ or -3.

So the domain of $\frac{x^2}{x^2 - 9}$ is all real numbers except 3 and -3.

CONCEPTUAL UNDERSTANDING →

👆 EXAMPLE 1   Write Equivalent Rational Expressions

When are two rational expressions equivalent?

Rational expressions can be simplified in a process that is similar to the process for simplifying rational numbers.

$$\frac{12}{16} = \frac{3 \cdot 2 \cdot 2}{2 \cdot 2 \cdot 2 \cdot 2} = \frac{3}{2 \cdot 2} \cdot \frac{2}{2} \cdot \frac{2}{2} = \frac{3}{2 \cdot 2} \cdot 1 \cdot 1 = \frac{3}{4}$$

By replacing quotients of common factors between the numerator and denominator with 1, you learn that $\frac{12}{16}$ is equivalent to $\frac{3}{4}$.

Write an expression that is equivalent to $\frac{x^3 - 5x^2 - 24x}{x^3 + x^2 - 72x}$.

Step 1 Factor the numerator and the denominator.

$$\frac{x^3 - 5x^2 - 24x}{x^3 + x^2 - 72x} = \frac{x(x^2 - 5x - 24)}{x(x^2 + x - 72)} = \frac{x(x - 8)(x + 3)}{x(x - 8)(x + 9)}$$

Step 2 Find the domain of the rational expression.

The domain is all real numbers except 0, 8, and -9.

Both $\frac{x^3 - 5x^2 - 24x}{x^3 + x^2 - 72x}$ and $\frac{x(x - 8)(x + 3)}{x(x - 8)(x + 9)}$ have the same domain.

CONTINUED ON THE NEXT PAGE

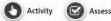
EXAMPLE 1 CONTINUED

Step 3 Recognize that the ratio of the common factors in the numerator and denominator are equal to 1.

$$\frac{x(x-8)(x+3)}{x(x-8)(x+9)} = \frac{x}{x} \cdot \frac{(x-8)}{(x-8)} \cdot \frac{(x+3)}{(x+9)} = 1 \cdot 1 \cdot \frac{(x+3)}{(x+9)} = \frac{x+3}{x+9}$$

So $\frac{x^3 - 5x^2 - 24x}{x^3 + x^2 - 72x}$ is equivalent to $\frac{x+3}{x+9}$ for all x except -9, 0, and 8.

> Like the original expression, the domain of $\frac{x+3}{x+9}$ excludes -9. But the domain of the original expression also excludes 0 and 8.

COMMUNICATE PRECISELY
A statement of equivalence between two expressions is an identity. The identity is only valid where both expressions are defined. © MP.6

Try It! 1. Write an expression equivalent to $\frac{3x^5 - 18x^4 - 21x^3}{2x^6 - 98x^4}$. Remember to give the domain for your expression.

EXAMPLE 2 Simplify a Rational Expression

What is the simplified form of the rational expression? What is the domain for which the identity between the two expressions is valid?

$$\frac{4-x^2}{x^2 + 3x - 10}$$

The **simplified form of a rational expression** has no common factors, other than 1, in the numerator and the denominator.

$$\frac{4-x^2}{x^2 + 3x - 10} = \frac{(2-x)(2+x)}{(x-2)(x+5)}$$ .... Factor the polynomials.

The domain is all real numbers ..... Identify the domain from
except 2 and -5.   the original expression.

$$= \frac{-(x-2)(x+2)}{(x-2)(x+5)}$$ .... Divide out common factors.

The simplified form of $\frac{4-x^2}{x^2 + 3x - 10}$ is $-\frac{x+2}{x+5}$ for all real numbers except 2 and -5.

COMMON ERROR
Be sure to factor out -1 from $2 - x$ before dividing out common factors: $2 - x = -(x - 2)$

Try It! 2. Simplify each expression and state the domain.

a. $\frac{x^2 + 2x + 1}{x^3 - 2x^2 - 3x}$ b. $\frac{x^3 + 4x^2 - x - 4}{x^2 + 3x - 4}$

EXAMPLE 3 Multiply Rational Expressions

A. What is the product of $\frac{2xy}{z}$ and $\frac{3x^2}{4yz}$?

To multiply rational expressions, follow a similar method to that for multiplying two numerical fractions.

The domain is $z \neq 0$ and $y \neq 0$.

$$\frac{2xy}{z} \cdot \frac{3x^2}{4yz} = \frac{(2xy)(3x^2)}{z(4yz)}$$ .... Multiply the expressions.

$$= \frac{z \cdot 3 \cdot x^3 \cdot y}{z \cdot 2 \cdot y \cdot z^2}$$ .... Divide out common factors.

$$= \frac{3x^3}{2z^2}$$

The product of $\frac{2xy}{z}$ and $\frac{3x^2}{4yz}$ is $\frac{3x^3}{2z^2}$ for $y \neq 0$ and $z \neq 0$.

USE STRUCTURE
Recall that when multiplying $\frac{a}{b} \times \frac{c}{d}$ you can often simplify by dividing both a and d (or both b and c) by the greatest common factor. © MP.7

CONTINUED ON THE NEXT PAGE

EXAMPLE 3 CONTINUED

B. What is the simplified form of $\dfrac{5x}{x+3} \cdot \dfrac{x^2+x-6}{x^2+2x+1} \cdot \dfrac{x^2+x}{5x-10}$?

STUDY TIP
It is easier to find the domain after factoring the denominator. Use the Zero Product Property to find values that will make the expression undefined. In this example, x cannot be -3, -1, or 2.

$$\dfrac{5x}{x+3} \cdot \dfrac{x^2+x-6}{x^2+2x+1} \cdot \dfrac{x^2+x}{5x-10} = \dfrac{5x(x+3)(x-2)x(x+1)}{(x+3)(x+1)^2 5(x-2)}$$ ⋯⋯ Multiply and factor the expressions.

$$= \dfrac{5x(x+3)(x-2)x(x+1)}{(x+3)(x+1)(x+1)5(x-2)}$$ ⋯⋯ Divide out common factors.

$$= \dfrac{x^2}{x+1}$$ ⋯⋯⋯⋯⋯⋯⋯⋯⋯⋯ Simplify.

So $\dfrac{5x}{x+3} \cdot \dfrac{x^2+x-6}{x^2+2x+1} \cdot \dfrac{x^2+x}{5x-10} = \dfrac{x^2}{x+1}$ for $x \neq -3$, -1, or 2.

✅ **Try It!**   **3.** Find the simplified form of each product, and give the domain.

  a. $\dfrac{x^2-16}{9-x} \cdot \dfrac{x^2+x-90}{x^2+14x+40}$

  b. $\dfrac{x+3}{4x} \cdot \dfrac{3x-18}{6x+18} \cdot \dfrac{x^2}{4x+12}$

👆 **EXAMPLE 4**   **Multiply a Rational Expression by a Polynomial**

What is the product of $\dfrac{x+2}{x^4-16}$ **and** x^3+4x^2-12x?

STUDY TIP
This process is similar to writing a whole number with a denominator of 1 when multiplying a fraction and a whole number.

$$\dfrac{x+2}{x^4-16} \cdot (x^3+4x^2-12x) = \dfrac{x+2}{x^4-16} \cdot \dfrac{x^3+4x^2-12x}{1}$$

$$= \dfrac{(x+2)x(x^2+4x-12)}{1(x^2+4)(x^2-4)}$$

$$= \dfrac{(x+2)x(x+6)(x-2)}{1(x^2+4)(x+2)(x-2)}$$ The domain is $x \neq -2$ or 2.

So $\dfrac{x+2}{x^4-16} \cdot (x^3+4x^2-12x) = \dfrac{x(x+6)}{x^2+4}$ for $x \neq -2$ or 2.

✅ **Try It!**   **4.** Find the simplified form of each product and the domain.

  a. $\dfrac{x^3-4x}{6x^2-13x-5} \cdot (2x^3-3x^2-5x)$

  b. $\dfrac{3x^2+6x}{x^2-49} \cdot (x^2+9x+14)$

👆 **EXAMPLE 5**   **Divide Rational Expressions**

What is the quotient of $\dfrac{x^3+3x^2+3x+1}{1-x^2}$ **and** $\dfrac{x^2+5x+4}{x^2+3x-4}$?

Multiply by the reciprocal of the divisor.

$$\dfrac{x^3+3x^2+3x+1}{1-x^2} \div \dfrac{x^2+5x+4}{x^2+3x-4} = \dfrac{x^3+3x^2+3x+1}{1-x^2} \cdot \dfrac{x^2+3x-4}{x^2+5x+4}$$

The domain is $x \neq -4, -1,$ or 1.

$$= \dfrac{(x+1)(x+1)(x+1)(x+4)(x-1)}{-(x-1)(x+1)(x+1)(x+4)}$$

$$= \dfrac{(x+1)}{-1} \cdot \dfrac{(x+1)}{(x+1)} \cdot \dfrac{(x+1)}{(x+1)} \cdot \dfrac{(x-1)}{(x-1)} \cdot \dfrac{(x+4)}{(x+4)}$$

$$= -(x+1)$$

COMMON ERROR
Remember to include the factor of -1!

The quotient is $-(x+1)$, $x \neq -4$, -1, or 1.

CONTINUED ON THE NEXT PAGE

Go Online | SavvasRealize.com

EXAMPLE 5 CONTINUED

 Try It! **5.** Find the simplified quotient and the domain of each expression.

      a. $\dfrac{1}{x^2 + 9x} \div \left(\dfrac{6 - x}{3x^2 - 18x}\right)$ **b.** $\dfrac{2x^2 - 12x}{x + 5} \div \left(\dfrac{x - 6}{x + 5}\right)$

APPLICATION    **EXAMPLE 6**   **Use Division of Rational Expressions**

A company is evaluating two packaging options for its product line. The more efficient design will have the lesser ratio of surface area to volume. Should the company use packages that are cylinders or rectangular prisms?

Option 1: A rectangular prism with a square base

Option 2: A cylinder with the same height as the prism, and diameter equal to the side length of the prism's base

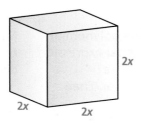

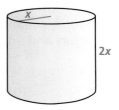

Surface Area: $2(2x)^2 + 4(2x)^2$
Volume: $(2x)^3$

Surface Area: $2\pi x^2 + 2\pi x(2x)$
Volume: $\pi x^2(2x)$

The efficiency ratio is $\dfrac{SA}{V}$, where SA represents surface area and V represents volume.

Option 1:

$$\dfrac{SA}{V} = \dfrac{2(4x^2) + 4(4x^2)}{8x^3}$$

$$= \dfrac{24x^2}{8x^3}$$

$$= \dfrac{3}{x}$$

Option 2:

$$\dfrac{SA}{V} = \dfrac{2\pi x^2 + 4\pi x^2}{2\pi x^3}$$

$$= \dfrac{6\pi x^2}{2\pi x^3}$$

$$= \dfrac{3}{x}$$

The company can now compare the efficiency ratio of the package designs.

Prism: $\dfrac{3}{x}$ Cylinder: $\dfrac{3}{x}$

In this example, the efficiency ratio of the cylinder is equal to that of the prism. So the company should choose their package design based on other criteria.

> Regardless of what positive value is selected for x, the efficiency ratios for these two package designs will be the same.

CONTINUED ON THE NEXT PAGE

EXAMPLE 6 CONTINUED

Try It! 6. The company compares the ratios of surface area to volume for two more containers. One is a rectangular prism with a square base. The other is a rectangular prism with a rectangular base. One side of the base is equal to the side-length of the first container, and the other side is twice as long. The surface area of this second container is $4x^2 + 6xh$. The heights of the two containers are equal. Which has the smaller surface area-to-volume ratio?

CONCEPT SUMMARY Products and Quotients of Rational Expressions

	Multiply	Multiply an Integer or a Polynomial	Divide
RATIONAL EXPRESSIONS	$\dfrac{3x}{x+1} \cdot \dfrac{x^2+x}{3x-6}$ The domain is $x \neq -1$ or 2.	$\dfrac{x+2}{x^2-4} \cdot (x^2 - 2x)$ $= \dfrac{x+2}{x^2-4} \cdot \dfrac{x^2-2x}{1}$ The domain is $x \neq -2$ or 2.	$\dfrac{1-x^2}{x^2+3x-4} \div \dfrac{x+1}{x+4}$ $= \dfrac{1-x^2}{x^2+3x-4} \cdot \dfrac{x+4}{x+1}$ The domain is $x \neq -4$, -1, or 1.
WORDS	Identify common factors and simplify.	Write the polynomial as a rational expression with 1 in the denominator. Then multiply.	Multiply by the reciprocal of the divisor.

Do You UNDERSTAND?

1. **ESSENTIAL QUESTION** How does understanding operations with fractions help you multiply and divide rational expressions?

2. **Vocabulary** In your own words, define *rational expression* and provide an example of a rational expression.

3. **Error Analysis** A student divided the rational expressions as follows:

$$\dfrac{4x}{5y} \div \dfrac{20x^2}{25y^2} = \dfrac{4x}{\cancel{5}y} \div \dfrac{\overset{4}{\cancel{20x^2}}}{25y^2} = \dfrac{16x^3}{25y^3}.$$

Describe and correct the errors the student made. Ⓒ MP.3

4. **Communicate Precisely** Why do you have to state the domain when simplifying rational expressions? Ⓒ MP.6

Do You KNOW HOW?

5. What is the simplified form of the rational expression $\dfrac{x^2-36}{x^2+3x-18}$? What is the domain?

6. Find the product and give the domain of $\dfrac{y+3}{y+2} \cdot \dfrac{y^2+4y+4}{y^2-9}$.

7. Find and simplify the ratio of the volume of Figure A to the volume of Figure B.

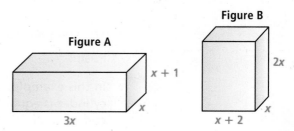

Figure A

Figure B

Go Online | SavvasRealize.com

UNDERSTAND

8. **Reason** Explain why $\frac{4x^2 - 7}{4x^2 - 7} = 1$ is a valid identity under the domain of all real numbers except $\pm\frac{\sqrt{7}}{2}$. © MP.2

9. **Error Analysis** Describe the error a student made in multiplying and simplifying $\frac{x + 2}{x - 2} \cdot \frac{x^2 - 4}{x^2 + x - 2}$. © MP.3

$$\frac{x + 2}{x - 2} \cdot \frac{x^2 - 4}{x^2 + x - 2}$$

$$= \frac{\cancel{x} + 2}{\cancel{x} - 2} \cdot \frac{\cancel{(x + 2)}(x - 2)}{\cancel{(x + 2)}(x - 1)}$$

$$= \frac{2}{-1} \qquad \times$$

10. **Higher Order Thinking** Explain why the process of dividing by a rational number is the same as multiplying by its reciprocal.

11. **Use Appropriate Tools** Explain how you can use your graphing calculator to show that the rational expressions $\frac{-6x^2 + 21x}{3x}$ and $-2x + 7$ are equivalent under a given domain. What is true about the graph at $x = 0$ and why? © MP.5

12. **Generalize** Explain the similarities between rational numbers and rational expressions. © MP.8

13. **Use Structure** Determine whether $\frac{5x + 11}{6x + 11} = \frac{5}{6}$ is *sometimes, always,* or *never* true. Justify your reasoning. © MP.7

14. **Construct Arguments** Explain how you can tell whether a rational expression is in simplest form. © MP.3

15. **Communicate Precisely** When multiplying $\frac{15}{x} \cdot \frac{x}{3} = 5$, is it necessary to make the restriction $x \neq 0$? Why or why not? © MP.6

16. **Reason** If the denominator of a rational expression is $x^3 + 3x^2 - 10x$, what value(s) must be restricted from the domain for x? © MP.2

PRACTICE

Write an equivalent expression. State the domain. SEE EXAMPLE 1

17. $\dfrac{x^3 + 4x^2 - 12x}{x^2 + x - 30}$

18. $\dfrac{3x^2 + 15x}{x^2 + 3x - 10}$

What is the simplified form of each rational expression? What is the domain? SEE EXAMPLE 2

19. $\dfrac{y^2 - 5y - 24}{y^2 + 3y}$

20. $\dfrac{ab^3 - 9ab}{12ab^2 + 12ab - 144a}$

21. $\dfrac{x^2 + 8x + 15}{x^2 - x - 12}$

22. $\dfrac{x^3 + 9x^2 - 10x}{x^3 - 9x^2 - 10x}$

Find the product and the domain. SEE EXAMPLE 3

23. $\dfrac{x^2 + 6x + 8}{x^2 + 4x + 3} \cdot \dfrac{x + 3}{x + 2}$ 24. $\dfrac{(x - y)^2}{x + y} \cdot \dfrac{3x + 3y}{x^2 - y^2}$

Find the product and the domain. SEE EXAMPLE 4

25. $\dfrac{(x + 5)}{(x^3 - 25x)} \cdot (2x^3 - 11x^2 + 5x)$

26. $\dfrac{(2x^2 - 10x)}{(x - 5)(x^2 - 1)} \cdot (3x^2 + 4x + 1)$

Find the quotient and the domain. SEE EXAMPLE 5

27. $\dfrac{y^2 - 16}{y^2 - 10y + 25} \div \dfrac{3y - 12}{y^2 - 3y - 10}$

28. $\dfrac{(x - y)^2}{x + y} \div \dfrac{3x + 3y}{x^2 - y^2}$

29. $\dfrac{25x^2 - 4}{x^2 - 9} \div \dfrac{5x - 2}{x + 3}$

30. $\dfrac{x^4 + x^3 - 30x^2}{x^2 - 3x - 18} \div \dfrac{x^3 + x^2 - 30x}{x^2 - 36}$

31. A rectangular prism with a volume of $3x^3 + 7x^2 + 2x$ cubic units has a base area of $x^2 + 2x$ square units. Find the height of the rectangular prism. SEE EXAMPLE 6

APPLY

32. Make Sense and Persevere An engineering firm wants to construct a cylindrical structure that will maximize the volume for a given surface area. Compare the ratios of the volume to surface area of each of the cylindrical structures shown, using the following formulas for volume and surface area of cylinders. Ⓒ **MP.1**

Volume $(V) = \pi r^2 h$

Surface Area $(SA) = 2\pi rh + 2\pi r^2$

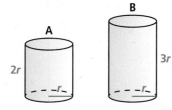

a. Calculate the ratio of volume to surface area for cylinder A.

b. Calculate the ratio of volume to surface area for cylinder B.

c. Which of these cylinders has a greater ratio of volume to surface area?

33. Look for Relationships A parallelogram with an area of $\frac{3x + 12}{10x + 25}$ square units has a height shown. Find the length of the base of the parallelogram. Ⓒ **MP.7**

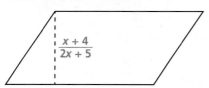

34. Model With Mathematics Brie designed a carnival game that involves tossing a beanbag into the box shown. In order to win a prize, the beanbag must fall inside the black rectangle. The probability of winning is equal to the ratio of the area of the black rectangle to the total area of the face of the box shown. Find this probability in simplified form. Ⓒ **MP.4**

35. Which of the following rational expressions simplify to $\frac{y}{y + 3}$? Select all that apply.

Ⓐ $\dfrac{(2y^2 + y)(y + 3)}{(4y + 2)(y + 3)^2}$

Ⓑ $\dfrac{3y^2 + y}{3y^2 + 10y + 3}$

Ⓒ $\dfrac{2y^3 + 3y^2 + y}{(2y + 1)(y^2 + 4y + 3)}$

Ⓓ $\dfrac{y^2 + 2y}{y^2 + 4y + 3}$

Ⓔ $\dfrac{\frac{1}{y}}{y + 3}$

36. SAT/ACT For what value of x is $\dfrac{2x^2 + 8x}{(x + 4)(x^2 - 9)}$ undefined?

Ⓐ -8

Ⓑ -3

Ⓒ 0

Ⓓ 4

Ⓔ 9

37. Performance Task The approximate annual interest rate r of a monthly installment loan is given by the formula:

$$r = \frac{\left[\frac{24(nm - p)}{n}\right]}{\left(p + \frac{nm}{12}\right)},$$

where n is the total number of payments, m is the monthly payment, and p is the amount financed.

Part A Find the approximate annual interest rate (to the nearest percent) for a four-year signature loan of $20,000 that has monthly payments of $500.

Part B Find the approximate annual interest rate (to the nearest tenth percent) for a five-year auto loan of $40,000 that has monthly payments of $750.

4-4

Adding and Subtracting Rational Expressions

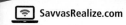 SavvasRealize.com

I CAN... find the sum or difference of rational expressions.

VOCABULARY
• compound fraction

CRITIQUE & EXPLAIN

Teo and Shannon find the following exercise in their homework:

$$\frac{1}{2} + \frac{1}{3} + \frac{1}{9}$$

A. Teo claims that a common denominator of the sum is $2 + 3 + 9 = 14$. Shannon claims that it is $2 \cdot 3 \cdot 9 = 54$. Is either student correct? Explain why or why not.

B. Find the sum, explaining the method you use.

C. Construct Arguments Timothy states that the quickest way to find the sum of any two fractions with unlike denominators is to multiply their denominators to find a common denominator, and then rewrite each fraction with that denominator. Do you agree? **© MP.3**

? ESSENTIAL QUESTION   **How do you rewrite rational expressions to find sums and differences?**

EXAMPLE 1   Add Rational Expressions With Like Denominators

USE STRUCTURE
Compare addition of numerical and algebraic fractions:

$$\frac{1}{5} + \frac{3}{5} = \frac{1+3}{5} = \frac{4}{5}$$

In the same way,

$$\frac{x}{x+4} + \frac{5}{x+4} = \frac{x+5}{x+4}. \quad © MP.7$$

What is the sum?

A. $\dfrac{x}{x+4} + \dfrac{5}{x+4}$

$= \dfrac{x+5}{x+4}$ .... When denominators are the same, add the numerators.

So $\dfrac{x}{x+4} + \dfrac{5}{x+4} = \dfrac{x+5}{x+4}$

B. $\dfrac{2x+1}{x^2+3x} + \dfrac{3x-8}{x(x+3)}$

$= \dfrac{(2x+1)+(3x-8)}{x^2+3x}$ .... Add the numerators.

$= \dfrac{(2x+3x)+(1-8)}{x^2+3x}$ .... Use the Commutative and Associative Properties.

$= \dfrac{5x-7}{x^2+3x}$ .... Combine like terms.

So $\dfrac{2x+1}{x^2+3x} + \dfrac{3x-8}{x(x+3)} = \dfrac{5x-7}{x^2+3x}$

Try It! **1.** Find the sum.

   a. $\dfrac{10x-5}{2x+3} + \dfrac{8-4x}{2x+3}$

   b. $\dfrac{x-5}{x+5} + \dfrac{3x-21}{x+5}$

CONCEPTUAL UNDERSTANDING

 EXAMPLE 2   Identify the Least Common Multiple of Polynomials

How can you find the least common multiple (LCM) of polynomials?

A. $(x + 2)^2$, $x^2 + 5x + 6$

Factor each polynomial.

$(x + 2)^2 = (x + 2)(x + 2)$

$x^2 + 5x + 6 = (x + 2)(x + 3)$

The LCM is the product of the factors. Duplicate factors are raised to the greatest power represented.

LCM: $(x + 2)(x + 2)(x + 3)$ or $(x + 2)^2(x + 3)$

B. $x^3 - 9x$, $x^2 - 2x - 15$, $x^2 - 5x$

Factor each polynomial.

$x^3 - 9x = x(x^2 - 9) = x(x + 3)(x - 3)$

$x^2 - 2x - 15 = (x + 3)(x - 5)$

$x^2 - 5x = x(x - 5)$

LCM: $x(x + 3)(x - 3)(x - 5)$

> Each original polynomial is a factor of the LCM.

> **STUDY TIP**
> Using the LCM of the denominators can mean less work simplifying later.

Try It! **2.** Find the LCM for each set of expressions.

    a. $x^3 + 9x^2 + 27x + 27$, $x^2 - 4x - 21$

    b. $10x^2 - 10y^2$, $15x^2 - 30xy + 15y^2$, $x^2 + 3xy + 2y^2$

EXAMPLE 3   Add Rational Expressions With Unlike Denominators

What is the sum of $\frac{x + 3}{x^2 - 1}$ and $\frac{2}{x^2 - 3x + 2}$?

Follow a similar procedure to the one you use to add numerical fractions with unlike denominators.

$\dfrac{x + 3}{x^2 - 1} + \dfrac{2}{x^2 - 3x + 2} = \dfrac{x + 3}{(x + 1)(x - 1)} + \dfrac{2}{(x - 1)(x - 2)}$ Factor each denominator.

$= \dfrac{(x + 3)(x - 2)}{(x + 1)(x - 1)(x - 2)} + \dfrac{2(x + 1)}{(x + 1)(x - 1)(x - 2)}$ Use the LCM as the least common denominator (LCD).

$= \dfrac{(x + 3)(x - 2) + 2(x + 1)}{(x + 1)(x - 1)(x - 2)}$ Add the numerators.

$= \dfrac{(x^2 + x - 6) + (2x + 2)}{(x + 1)(x - 1)(x - 2)}$ Distribute.

$= \dfrac{x^2 + 3x - 4}{(x + 1)(x - 1)(x - 2)}$ Combine like terms.

$= \dfrac{(x + 4)(x - 1)}{(x + 1)(x - 1)(x - 2)}$ Factor.

$= \dfrac{(x + 4)}{(x + 1)(x - 2)} \cdot \dfrac{(x - 1)}{(x - 1)}$ Rewrite to identify unit factors.

$= \dfrac{x + 4}{(x + 1)(x - 2)}$ for $x \neq -1$, 1, and 2   Simplify and state the domain.

The sum of $\frac{x + 3}{x^2 - 1}$ and $\frac{2}{x^2 - 3x + 2}$ is $\frac{x + 4}{(x + 1)(x - 2)}$ for $x \neq -1$, 1, and 2.

> **USE STRUCTURE**
> The LCM of 6 and 15 is 30, not 90.
> $\frac{1}{6} + \frac{1}{15} = \frac{1}{2 \cdot 3} + \frac{1}{3 \cdot 5} = \frac{1 \cdot 5 + 1 \cdot 2}{2 \cdot 3 \cdot 5}$
> The LCM does not contain the common factor 3 twice. In the example problem, the common factor $(x - 1)$ is not used twice. **© MP.7**

Try It! **3.** Find the sum.

    a. $\dfrac{x + 6}{x^2 - 4} + \dfrac{2}{x^2 - 5x + 6}$

    b. $\dfrac{2x}{3x + 4} + \dfrac{4x^2 - 11x - 12}{6x^2 + 5x - 4}$

👆 **EXAMPLE 4**   **Subtract Rational Expressions**

What is the difference between $\dfrac{x+1}{x^2-6x-16}$ **and** $\dfrac{x+1}{x^2+6x+8}$**?**

> The LCD is $(x-8)(x+2)$ $(x+4)$.

$$\frac{x+1}{x^2-6x-16}-\frac{x+1}{x^2+6x+8}=\frac{x+1}{(x-8)(x+2)}-\frac{x+1}{(x+2)(x+4)}$$

$$=\frac{(x+1)(x+4)}{(x-8)(x+2)(x+4)}-\frac{(x-8)(x+1)}{(x-8)(x+2)(x+4)}$$

$$=\frac{(x^2+5x+4)-(x^2-7x-8)}{(x-8)(x+2)(x+4)}$$

$$=\frac{x^2+5x+4-x^2+7x+8}{(x-8)(x+2)(x+4)}$$

$$=\frac{12x+12}{(x-8)(x+2)(x+4)}$$

$$=\frac{12(x+1)}{(x-8)(x+2)(x+4)}$$

> Check for common factors in the numerator and denominator and simplify, if possible.

COMMON ERROR
When subtracting polynomials, remember to distribute -1 when removing the parentheses.

The difference between $\dfrac{x+1}{x^2-6x-16}$ and $\dfrac{x+1}{x^2+6x+8}$ is $\dfrac{12(x+1)}{(x-8)(x+2)(x+4)}$ for $x\neq-4,-2,$ and 8.

☑️ **Try It!**   **4.** Simplify.

   a. $\dfrac{1}{3x}+\dfrac{1}{6x}-\dfrac{1}{x^2}$ **b.** $\dfrac{3x-5}{x^2-25}-\dfrac{2}{x+5}$

APPLICATION

👆 **EXAMPLE 5**   **Find a Rate**

Leah drives her car to the mechanic, then she takes the commuter rail train back to her neighborhood. The average speed for the 10-mile trip is 15 miles per hour faster on the train. Find an expression for Leah's total travel time. If she drove 30 mph, how long did this take?

Speed = $r + 15$ Speed = r

USE APPROPRIATE TOOLS
Use a table to organize information and help create an accurate model of the situation. Ⓒ **MP.5**

	Distance	Rate	Time
Car	10	r	$\dfrac{10}{r}$
Commuter Rail	10	$r+15$	$\dfrac{10}{r+15}$

> Remember: distance = rate • time, so time = $\dfrac{\text{distance}}{\text{rate}}$.

Total time for the trip:

$$\frac{10}{r}+\frac{10}{r+15}=\frac{10(r+15)}{r(r+15)}+\frac{10r}{r(r+15)}$$

> Add the times for each part of the trip.

$$=\frac{10r+150+10r}{r(r+15)}$$

$$=\frac{20r+150}{r(r+15)}$$

CONTINUED ON THE NEXT PAGE

EXAMPLE 5 CONTINUED

At a driving rate of 30 mph, you can find the total time.

$$\frac{20r + 150}{r(r + 15)} = \frac{20(30) + 150}{30(30 + 15)}$$

> Substitute 30 mph for the rate, and simplify.

$$= \frac{750}{1,350}$$

$$= \frac{5}{9}$$

The expression for Leah's total travel time is $\frac{20r + 150}{r(r + 15)}$. The total time is $\frac{5}{9}$ h, or about 33 min.

☑ **Try It!**   **5.** On the way to work Juan carpools with a fellow co-worker, then takes the city bus back home in the evening. The average speed of the 20-mile trip is 5 miles per hour faster in the carpool. Write an expression that represents Juan's total travel time.

👆 **EXAMPLE 6**   **Simplify a Compound Fraction**

A **compound fraction** is in the form of a fraction and has one or more fractions in the numerator and/or the denominator. How can you write a simpler form of a compound fraction?

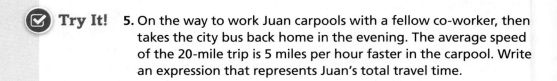

Method 1 Find the Least Common Multiple (LCM) of the fractions in the numerator and denominator. Multiply the numerator and the denominator by the LCM.

$$\frac{\frac{1}{x} + \frac{2}{x + 1}}{\frac{1}{y}} = \frac{\left[\frac{1}{x} + \frac{2}{x + 1}\right] \cdot [x(x + 1)y]}{\frac{1}{y} \cdot [x(x + 1)y]}$$ ···· Multiply the numerator and the denominator by the LCD.

$$= \frac{(x + 1)y + 2xy}{x(x + 1)}$$ ············· Use the Distributive Property to eliminate the fractions.

$$= \frac{xy + y + 2xy}{x(x + 1)}$$ ············· Simplify.

$$= \frac{(3x + 1)y}{x(x + 1)}$$ ············· Factor.

Method 2 Express the numerator and denominator as single fractions. Then multiply the numerator by the reciprocal of the denominator.

$$\frac{\frac{1}{x} + \frac{2}{x + 1}}{\frac{1}{y}} = \frac{\frac{1}{x} \cdot \frac{x + 1}{x + 1} + \frac{2}{x + 1} \cdot \frac{x}{x}}{\frac{1}{y}}$$ ·········· Multiply the numerator by the LCD.

$$= \frac{\frac{(x + 1) + 2x}{x(x + 1)}}{\frac{1}{y}}$$ ············· Simplify.

$$= \frac{3x + 1}{x(x + 1)} \cdot \frac{y}{1}$$ ············· Multiply the numerator by the reciprocal of the denominator.

$$= \frac{(3x + 1)y}{x(x + 1)}$$ ············· Simplify.

Using either method, $\frac{\frac{1}{x} + \frac{2}{x + 1}}{\frac{1}{y}}$ is equal to $\frac{(3x + 1)y}{x(x + 1)}$ when $x \neq -1, 0$ and $y \neq 0$.

USE STRUCTURE
Remember that the fraction bar separating the numerator and denominator represents division.
© **MP.7**

☑ **Try It!**   **6.** Simplify each compound fraction.

a. $\dfrac{\frac{1}{x - 1}}{\frac{x + 1}{3} + \frac{4}{x - 1}}$

b. $\dfrac{2 - \frac{1}{x}}{x + \frac{2}{x}}$

CONCEPT SUMMARY Find Sums and Differences of Rational Expressions

WORDS	To add or subtract rational expressions with common denominators, add the numerators and keep the denominator the same.	To add or subtract rational expressions with different denominators, rewrite each expression so that its denominator is the LCD, then add or subtract the numerators.
NUMBERS	$\dfrac{1}{5} + \dfrac{3}{5} = \dfrac{1+3}{5} = \dfrac{4}{5}$	$\dfrac{1}{6} + \dfrac{1}{15} = \dfrac{1}{2 \cdot 3} + \dfrac{1}{3 \cdot 5}$ $= \dfrac{1 \cdot 5 + 1 \cdot 2}{2 \cdot 3 \cdot 5}$
ALGEBRA	$\dfrac{x}{x+4} + \dfrac{5}{x+4} = \dfrac{x+5}{x+4}$	$\dfrac{x+3}{x^2 - 1} + \dfrac{2}{x^2 - 3x + 2}$ $= \dfrac{x+3}{(x+1)(x-1)} + \dfrac{2}{(x-1)(x-2)}$ $= \dfrac{(x+3)(x-2)}{(x+1)(x-1)(x-2)} + \dfrac{2(x+1)}{(x+1)(x-1)(x-2)}$

Rewrite the rational expressions using the LCD.

Do You UNDERSTAND?

1. **ESSENTIAL QUESTION** How do you rewrite rational expressions to find sums and differences?

2. **Vocabulary** In your own words, define **compound fraction** and provide an example of one.

3. **Error Analysis** A student added the rational expressions as follows:

$$\frac{5x}{x+7} + \frac{7}{x} = \frac{5x}{x+7} + \frac{7(7)}{x+7} = \frac{5x+49}{x+7}$$

Describe and correct the error the student made. © MP.3

4. **Construct Arguments** Explain why, when stating the domain of a sum or difference of rational expressions, not only should the simplified sum or difference be considered but the original expression should also be considered. © MP.3

5. **Make Sense and Persevere** In adding or subtracting rational expressions, why is the L in LCD significant? © MP.1

Do You KNOW HOW?

6. Find the sum of $\dfrac{3}{x+1} + \dfrac{11}{x+1}$.

Find the LCM of the polynomials.

7. $x^2 - y^2$ and $x^2 - 2xy + y^2$

8. $5x^3y$ and $15x^2y^2$

Find the sum or difference.

9. $\dfrac{3x}{4y^2} - \dfrac{y}{10x}$

10. $\dfrac{9y+2}{3y^2 - 2y - 8} + \dfrac{7}{3y^2 + y - 4}$

11. Find the perimeter of the quadrilateral in simplest form.

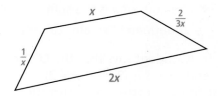

UNDERSTAND

12. Generalize Explain how addition and subtraction of rational expressions is similar to and different from addition and subtraction of rational numbers. **© MP.8**

13. Error Analysis Describe and correct the error a student made in adding the rational expressions. **© MP.3**

$$\frac{1}{x^2 + 3x + 2} + \frac{x^2 + 4x}{4x + 8} = \frac{1}{(x+1)(x+2)} + \frac{x(x+4)}{4(x+2)}$$

$$= \frac{4}{4(x+1)(x+2)} + \frac{x(x+4)}{4(x+1)(x+2)}$$

$$= \frac{4 + x^2 + 4x}{4(x+1)(x+2)}$$

$$= \frac{x^2 + 4x + 4}{4(x+1)(x+2)}$$

$$= \frac{(x+2)(x+2)}{4(x+1)(x+2)}$$

$$= \frac{x+2}{4(x+1)} \cdot \frac{(x+2)}{(x+2)}$$

$$= \frac{x+2}{4(x+1)} \quad ✗$$

14. Higher Order Thinking Find the slope of the line that passes through the points shown. Express in simplest form.

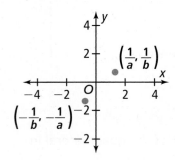

15. Reason For what values of x is the sum of $\frac{x-5y}{x+y}$ and $\frac{x+7y}{x+y}$ undefined? Explain. **© MP.2**

16. Error Analysis A student says that the LCM of $3x^2 + 7x + 2$ and $9x + 3$ is $(3x^2 + 7x + 2)(9x + 3)$. Describe and correct the error the student made. **© MP.3**

PRACTICE

Find the sum. SEE EXAMPLE 1

17. $\dfrac{4x}{x+7} + \dfrac{9}{x+7}$

18. $\dfrac{3y-1}{y^2+4y} + \dfrac{9y+6}{y(y+4)}$

Find the LCM for each group of expressions. SEE EXAMPLE 2

19. $x^2 - 7x + 6,\ x^2 - 5x - 6$

20. $y^2 + 2y - 24,\ y^2 - 16,\ 2y$

Find the sum. SEE EXAMPLE 3

21. $\dfrac{6x}{x^2-8x} + \dfrac{4}{2x-16}$

22. $\dfrac{3y}{2y^2-y} + \dfrac{2}{2y}$

Find the difference. SEE EXAMPLE 4

23. $\dfrac{4x}{x^2-1} - \dfrac{4}{x-1}$

24. $\dfrac{y-1}{3y+15} - \dfrac{y+3}{5y+25}$

25 On Saturday morning, Ahmed decided to take a bike ride from one end of the 15-mile bike trail to the other end of the bike trail and back. His average speed the first half of the ride was 2 mph faster than his speed on the second half. Find an expression for Ahmed's total travel time. If his average speed for the first half of the ride was 12 mph, how long was Ahmed's bike ride? SEE EXAMPLE 5

Speed $x + 2$

Trail length 15 miles

Speed x

Rewrite as a rational expression. SEE EXAMPLE 6

26. $\dfrac{1 + \frac{1}{x}}{x - \frac{1}{x}}$

27. $\dfrac{\frac{3}{y} + \frac{7}{x}}{\frac{1}{y} - \frac{2}{x}}$

28. $\dfrac{\frac{1}{a} + \frac{1}{b}}{\frac{a^2 - b^2}{ab}}$

29. $\dfrac{\frac{z^2 - z - 12}{z^2 - 2z - 15}}{\frac{z^2 + 8z + 12}{z^2 - 5z - 14}}$

APPLY

30. Use Structure Aisha paddles a kayak 5 miles downstream at a rate 3 mph faster than the river's current. She then travels 4 miles back upstream at a rate 1 mph slower than the river's current. Hint: Let x represent the rate of the river current. Ⓒ **MP.7**

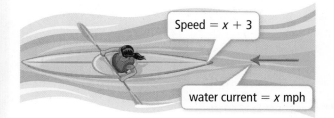

Speed = $x + 3$

water current = x mph

a. Write and simplify an expression to represent the total time it takes Aisha to paddle the kayak 5 miles downstream and 4 miles upstream.

b. If the rate of the river current, x, is 2 mph, how long was Aisha's entire kayak trip?

31. Model With Mathematics Rectangles A and B are similar. An expression that represents the width of each rectangle is shown. Find the scale factor of rectangle A to rectangle B in simplest form. Ⓒ **MP.4**

$\dfrac{x^2 - 25}{x - 4}$ **A**

B $\dfrac{x + 5}{x^2 - 16}$

32. Reason The Taylor family drives 180 miles (round trip) to a professional basketball game. On the way to the game, their average speed is approximately 8 mph faster than their speed on the return trip home. Ⓒ **MP.2**

a. Let x represent their average speed on the way home. Write and simplify an expression to represent the total time it took them to drive to and from the game.

b. If their average speed going to the game was 72 mph, how long did it take them to drive to the game and back?

Ⓒ **ASSESSMENT PRACTICE**

33. Which of the following compound fractions simplifies to $\dfrac{x + 1}{x - 3}$? Select all that apply.

Ⓐ $\dfrac{\dfrac{x^2 + 5x + 4}{x^2 + 2x - 8}}{\dfrac{x^2 - 4x + 3}{x^2 - 3x + 2}}$

Ⓑ $\dfrac{\dfrac{x^2 - 1}{x^2 - 4}}{\dfrac{x^2 + x - 7}{x^2 + 5x + 6}}$

Ⓒ $\dfrac{\dfrac{x^2 + 3x - 10}{x^2 - 16}}{\dfrac{x^2 - 4x - 5}{x^2 - 1}}$

Ⓓ $\dfrac{\dfrac{x^2 + 3x - 10}{x^2 - 5x + 6}}{\dfrac{x^2 - 25}{x^2 - 4x - 5}}$

34. SAT/ACT What is the difference between $\dfrac{x}{9}$ and $\dfrac{x - y}{6}$?

Ⓐ $\dfrac{5x - y}{18}$

Ⓑ $\dfrac{5x + y}{18}$

Ⓒ $\dfrac{-x + 3y}{18}$

Ⓓ $\dfrac{-x - 3y}{18}$

35. Performance Task The lens equation $\dfrac{1}{f} = \dfrac{1}{d_i} + \dfrac{1}{d_o}$ represents the relationship between f, the focal length of a camera lens, d_i, the distance from the lens to the film, and d_o, the distance from the lens to the object.

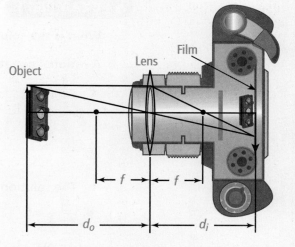

Part A Find the focal length of a camera lens if an object that is 12 cm from a camera lens is in focus on the film when the lens is 6 cm from the film.

Part B Suppose the focal length of another camera lens is 3 inches, and the object to be photographed is 5 feet away. What distance (to the nearest tenth inch) should the lens be from the film?

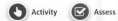
4-5

Solving Rational Equations

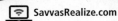 SavvasRealize.com

I CAN... solve rational equations and identify extraneous solutions.

VOCABULARY
- rational equation
- extraneous solution

CRITIQUE & EXPLAIN

Nicky and Tavon used different methods to solve the equation $\frac{1}{2}x + \frac{2}{5} = \frac{9}{10}$.

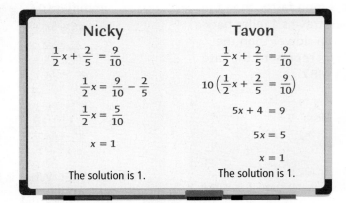

Nicky

$$\frac{1}{2}x + \frac{2}{5} = \frac{9}{10}$$

$$\frac{1}{2}x = \frac{9}{10} - \frac{2}{5}$$

$$\frac{1}{2}x = \frac{5}{10}$$

$$x = 1$$

The solution is 1.

Tavon

$$\frac{1}{2}x + \frac{2}{5} = \frac{9}{10}$$

$$10\left(\frac{1}{2}x + \frac{2}{5} = \frac{9}{10}\right)$$

$$5x + 4 = 9$$

$$5x = 5$$

$$x = 1$$

The solution is 1.

A. Explain the different strategies that Nicky and Tavon used and the advantages or disadvantages of each.

B. Did Nicky use a correct method to solve the equation? Did Tavon?

C. Use Structure Why might Tavon have chosen to multiply both sides of the equation by 10? Could he have used another number? Explain. © **MP.7**

? ESSENTIAL QUESTION

How can you solve rational equations and identify extraneous solutions?

EXAMPLE 1   Solve a Rational Equation

What is the solution to each rational equation?

A **rational equation** is an equation that contains a rational expression.

A. $\frac{1}{x+4} = 2$

$$(x+4)\left(\frac{1}{x+4}\right) = 2(x+4)$$

$$1 = 2x + 8$$

$$x = -\frac{7}{2}$$

The solution is $x = -\frac{7}{2}$.

> Multiply both sides of the equation by the common denominator to eliminate the fractions. Then solve. Confirm that the solution is valid in the original equation.

B. $\frac{1}{x-3} = 5$

$$(x-3)\left(\frac{1}{x-3}\right) = 5(x-3)$$

$$1 = 5x - 15$$

$$x = \frac{16}{5}$$

The solution is $x = \frac{16}{5}$.

STUDY TIP
A fraction with a denominator equal to zero is undefined.

✓ Try It!   1. What is the solution to each equation?

a. $\frac{2}{x+5} = 4$

b. $\frac{1}{x-7} = 2$

APPLICATION   **EXAMPLE 2** Solve a Work-Rate Problem

Arthur and Cheyenne can paint a wall in 6 hours when working together. Cheyenne works twice as fast as Arthur. How long would it take Cheyenne to paint the wall if she were working alone?

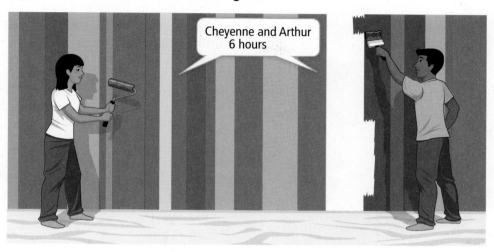

Cheyenne and Arthur
6 hours

Step 1 Determine the work-rates of Arthur and Cheyenne.

Let x represent the number of hours Arthur needs to paint the wall himself.

> The fraction of a job completed *per hour* is the work-rate.

Arthur can paint 1 wall in x hours, or $\frac{1}{x}$ of a wall in 1 hour.

Cheyenne is twice as fast, so Cheyenne paints $\frac{2}{x}$ of a wall in 1 hour.

Together they paint 1 wall in 6 hours, or $\frac{1}{6}$ of a wall in 1 hour.

COMMON ERROR
You might have multiplied x by 2 because Cheyenne works twice as fast. However, it takes Cheyenne *half* the time to paint the wall.

Step 2 Write the equation for their rates working together.

$$\frac{1}{x} + \frac{2}{x} = \frac{1}{6}$$

$$6x\left(\frac{1}{x} + \frac{2}{x}\right) = 6x\left(\frac{1}{6}\right)$$

$$6 + 12 = x$$

$$18 = x$$

> Write the equation for their rates working together. Then solve.

It takes Arthur 18 hours to paint the wall alone. Since Cheyenne works twice as fast as Arthur, it would take her 9 hours to paint the wall alone.

☑ **Try It!**   **2.** It takes 12 hours to fill a pool with two pipes, where the water in one pipe flows three times as fast as the other pipe. How long will it take the slower pipe to fill the pool by itself?

CONCEPTUAL
UNDERSTANDING ➔  **EXAMPLE 3** Identify an Extraneous Solution

What is the solution of the equation $\frac{1}{x-5} + \frac{x}{x-3} = \frac{2}{x^2-8x+15}$?

Step 1 Multiply each side of the equation by the common denominator, $(x-5)(x-3)$.

$$(x-5)(x-3)\left(\frac{1}{x-5} + \frac{x}{x-3}\right) = \frac{2(x-5)(x-3)}{x^2-8x+15}$$

Step 2 Continue to simplify.

$$\frac{(x-5)(x-3)}{x-5} + \frac{x(x-5)(x-3)}{x-3} = \frac{2(x-5)(x-3)}{x^2-8x+15}$$

Step 3 Divide out common factors in the numerator and the denominator.

$$\frac{(x-5)(x-3)}{x-5} + \frac{x(x-5)(x-3)}{x-3} = \frac{2(x-5)(x-3)}{x^2-8x+15}$$

Step 4 Solve the equation.

$$(x-3) + x(x-5) = 2$$
$$x - 3 + x^2 - 5x = 2$$
$$x^2 - 4x - 3 = 2$$
$$x^2 - 4x - 5 = 0$$
$$(x-5)(x+1) = 0$$
$$x = 5 \text{ and } x = -1$$

> You can divide out common factors under the assumption that $\frac{(x-5)}{(x-5)} = 1$ and $\frac{(x-3)}{(x-3)} = 1$. This is only true if $x \neq 5$ or 3.

> Consider both solutions. If either solution makes the value of the denominator 0, it is not valid.

The solution $x = 5$ is an **extraneous solution** because it makes the value of a denominator in the original equation equal to 0.

The solution of the equation $\frac{1}{x-5} + \frac{x}{x-3} = \frac{2}{x^2-8x+15}$ is -1.

Confirm with a graph.

Consider the graphs of $\frac{1}{x-5} + \frac{x}{x-3}$ and $\frac{2}{x^2-8x+15}$.

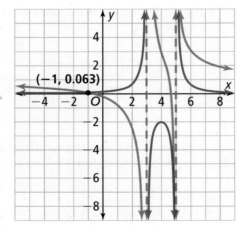

$(-1, 0.063)$

LOOK FOR RELATIONSHIPS
How are an extraneous solution and an asymptote related? Is this always true? Ⓖ **MP.7**

Note that each graph has a vertical asymptote at $x = 3$ and $x = 5$. Therefore, neither graph has a value at $x = 5$. The graphs only intersect in one point, at $x = -1$.

 Try It! **3.** What is the solution to the equation $\frac{1}{x+2} + \frac{1}{x-2} = \frac{4}{(x+2)(x-2)}$?

👆 **EXAMPLE 4**   Solve Problems With Extraneous Solutions

What are the solutions to the following equations?

A. $\dfrac{5x}{x-2} = 7 + \dfrac{10}{x-2}$

<table>
<tr><td>$\dfrac{5x}{x-2} = 7 + \dfrac{10}{x-2}$</td><td>Write the original equation.</td></tr>
<tr><td>$(x-2)\left(\dfrac{5x}{x-2}\right) = \left(7 + \dfrac{10}{x-2}\right)(x-2)$</td><td>Multiply by the LCD.</td></tr>
<tr><td>$5x = 7(x-2) + 10$</td><td>Distributive Property</td></tr>
<tr><td>$5x = 7x - 14 + 10$</td><td>Distributive Property</td></tr>
<tr><td>$-2x = -4$</td><td>Collect terms and simplify.</td></tr>
<tr><td>$x = 2$</td><td>Solve for x.</td></tr>
</table>

Check the solution in the original equation. The value 2 is an extraneous solution because it would cause the denominator in the original equation to be equal to 0. This equation has no solution.

B. $\dfrac{3}{x-3} = \dfrac{x}{x-3} - \dfrac{x}{4}$

<table>
<tr><td>$\dfrac{3}{x-3} = \dfrac{x}{x-3} - \dfrac{x}{4}$</td><td>Write original equation.</td></tr>
<tr><td>$(4)(x-3)\left(\dfrac{3}{x-3}\right) = \left(\dfrac{x}{x-3} - \dfrac{x}{4}\right)(4)(x-3)$</td><td>Multiply by LCD.</td></tr>
<tr><td>$4(3) = 4(x) - x(x-3)$</td><td>Distributive Property</td></tr>
<tr><td>$12 = 4x - x^2 + 3x$</td><td>Simplify.</td></tr>
<tr><td>$x^2 - 7x + 12 = 0$</td><td>Write in standard form</td></tr>
<tr><td>$(x-3)(x-4) = 0$</td><td>Factor.</td></tr>
<tr><td>$x - 3 = 0 \text{ or } x - 4 = 0$</td><td>Solve using the Zero Product Property.</td></tr>
<tr><td>$x = 3 \text{ or } x = 4$</td><td>Solve for x.</td></tr>
</table>

Check the solutions in the original equation. The value 3 is an extraneous solution because it would cause the denominator of the original equation to be equal to zero. The only solution to the equation is $x = 4$.

 Try It!   4. What are the solutions to the following equations?

     a. $x + \dfrac{6}{x-3} = \dfrac{2x}{x-3}$ **b.** $\dfrac{x^2}{x+5} = \dfrac{25}{x+5}$

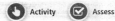
APPLICATION 👆 **EXAMPLE 5** ▸ Solve a Rate Problem

Paddling with the current in a river, Jake traveled 16 miles. Even though he paddled upstream for an hour longer than the amount of time he paddled downstream, Jake could only travel 6 miles against the current. In still water, Jake paddles at a rate of 5 mph. What is the speed of the current in the river?

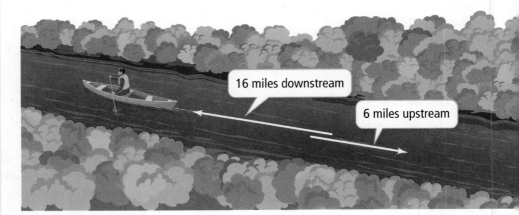

16 miles downstream

6 miles upstream

Formulate ◂ Let c be the rate of the river's current.

Recall that distance = rate • time so time = $\frac{\text{distance}}{\text{rate}}$.

$$\frac{16}{5+c} + 1 = \frac{6}{5-c}$$

Jake's paddle rate in still water + the rate of the current

Jake paddles 1 h longer upstream than downstream.

Jake's paddle rate in still water − the rate of the current

Compute ◂ Solve the equation for c.

$$\frac{16}{5+c} + 1 = \frac{6}{5-c}$$

$(5+c)(5-c)\left(\frac{16}{5+c} + 1\right) = \left(\frac{6}{5-c}\right)(5+c)(5-c)$ .... Multiply both sides by a common denominator.

$80 - 16c + 25 - c^2 = 30 + 6c$ .... Combine like terms.

$0 = c^2 + 22c - 75$ .... Write in standard form.

$0 = (c+25)(c-3)$ .... Factor.

$0 = c + 25 \quad 0 = c - 3$ .... Use the Zero Product Property.

$c = -25 \quad c = 3$ .... Solve.

Interpret ◂ The solution $c = -25$ is extraneous because the speed of the current cannot be negative.

The speed of the current is 3 mph.

☑ **Try It!** **5.** Three people are planting tomatoes in a community garden. Marta takes 50 minutes to plant the garden alone, Benito takes x minutes and Tyler takes $x + 15$ minutes. If the three of them take 20 minutes to finish the garden, how long would it have taken Tyler alone?

CONCEPT SUMMARY Solving Rational Equations

WORDS ▷ A rational equation is an equation that contains a rational expression. To solve, identify the domain for the variable. Then multiply both sides of the equation by a common denominator and solve. An extraneous solution is a solution that is not valid because that value is excluded from the domain of the original equation.

ALGEBRA ▷

$$\frac{1}{x} + \frac{2}{x} = \frac{1}{6}$$ Domain: $x \neq 0$

$$6x\left(\frac{1}{x} + \frac{2}{x}\right) = 6x\left(\frac{1}{6}\right)$$

$$6 + 12 = x$$

$$18 = x$$

The domain includes $x = 18$, so the solution to the equation is 18.

$$\frac{x^2 + 4}{x - 1} = \frac{5}{x - 1}$$ Domain: $x \neq 1$

$$(x - 1)\left(\frac{x^2 + 4}{x - 1}\right) = (x - 1)\left(\frac{5}{x - 1}\right)$$

$$x^2 + 4 = 5$$

$$x^2 = 1$$

$$x = \pm 1$$

The domain does not include $x = 1$, so 1 is an extraneous solution. It does include $x = -1$, so the solution to the equation is -1.

☑ Do You UNDERSTAND?

1. **ESSENTIAL QUESTION** How can you solve rational equations and identify extraneous solutions?

2. **Vocabulary** Write your own example of a rational equation that, when solved, has at least one **extraneous solution**.

3. **Error Analysis** A student solved the rational equation as follows:

   $$\frac{1}{2x} - \frac{2}{5x} = \frac{1}{10x} - 3; \ x = 0$$

   Describe and correct the error the student made. © **MP.3**

4. **Construct Arguments** Yuki says, "*You can check the solution(s) of rational equations in any of the steps of the solution process.*" Explain why her reasoning is incorrect. © **MP.3**

Do You KNOW HOW?

Solve.

5. $\dfrac{4}{x + 6} = 2$

6. $\dfrac{x^2}{x + 3} = \dfrac{9}{x + 3}$

7. Organizing given information into a table can be helpful when solving rate problems. Use this table to solve the following problem.

	Distance	Rate	Time
Upstream			
Downstream			

The speed of a stream is 4 km/h. A boat can travel 6 km upstream in the same time it takes to travel 12 km downstream. Find the speed of the boat in still water.

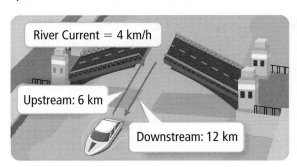

River Current = 4 km/h

Upstream: 6 km

Downstream: 12 km

PRACTICE & PROBLEM SOLVING

UNDERSTAND

8. **Reason** If you solve a work-rate problem and your solution, which represents the amount of time it would take *working together,* exceeds the individual *working alone* times that are given, then how do you know your solution is unreasonable? Explain. Ⓒ **MP.2**

9. **Construct Arguments** Explain why a negative solution must be eliminated as an extraneous solution when solving a rational equation for an unknown rate. Ⓒ **MP.3**

10. **Error Analysis** Describe and correct the error Miranda made in solving the rational equation. Ⓒ **MP.3**

$$\frac{1}{x-2} + \frac{x-2}{x+2} = \frac{x-4}{x-2}$$

$$(x+2)(x-2)\left(\frac{1}{x-2} + \frac{x-2}{x+2}\right) = \left(\frac{x-4}{x-2}\right)(x+2)(x-2)$$

$$(x+2)(1) + (x-2)(x-2) = (x+4)(x+2)$$

$$x+2 + \cancel{x^2} - 4x + 4 = \cancel{x^2} + 6x + 8$$

$$-3x + 6 = 6x + 8$$

$$-2 = 9x; \text{ or } x = -\frac{2}{9} \quad ✗$$

11. **Generalize** In addition to identifying extraneous solutions, why else is it important to substitute your solution into the original equation? Ⓒ **MP.8**

12. **Mathematical Connections** Explain how solving rational equations is related to solving linear and quadratic equations.

13. **Higher Order Thinking** Write a rational equation that cannot have 2 or −6 as solutions.

14. **Make Sense and Persevere** Solve the rational equation shown. Explain what is unique about the solution. Ⓒ **MP.1**

$$\frac{x^2 - 7x - 18}{x+2} = x - 9$$

PRACTICE

Solve the equation. SEE EXAMPLE 1

15. $\frac{1}{x-3} = 10$

16. $\frac{15}{x+3} = 3$

17. $\frac{12}{x-4} = 9$

18. $\frac{5}{3-x} = 1$

Solve the problem. SEE EXAMPLE 2

19. Paige can complete a landscaping job in 6 hours. Malia can complete the same job in 4 hours. Working together, how long would it take them to complete the job?

Malia 4 hours

Paige 6 hours

20. Russel and Aaron can build a shed in 8 hours when working together. Aaron works three times as fast as Russel. How long would it take Russel to build the shed if he were to work alone?

Aaron and Russel 8 hours

Solve the equation. SEE EXAMPLE 3

21. $\frac{x}{x-3} - 4 = \frac{3}{x-3}$

22. $\frac{x^2}{x-10} = \frac{100}{x-10} - 10$

Solve the equation. SEE EXAMPLE 4

23. $\frac{4}{3(x+1)} = \frac{12}{x^2 - 1}$

24. $\frac{x}{x-3} + \frac{2x}{x+3} = \frac{18}{(x+3)(x-3)}$

Solve the problem. SEE EXAMPLE 5

25. A boat travels 8 miles upstream in the same amount of time it can travel 12 miles downstream. In still water the speed of the boat is 5 mi/h. What is the speed of the current?

PRACTICE & PROBLEM SOLVING

APPLY

26. Make Sense and Persevere Kenji can finish a puzzle in 2 hours working alone. Oscar can finish the same puzzle in 3 hours working alone. How long would it take Oscar and Kenji to finish the puzzle if they worked on it together? © **MP.1**

27. Use Structure A commercial jet flies 1,500 miles with the wind. In the same amount of time it can fly 1,000 miles against the wind. The speed of the jet in still air is 550 mph. Find the speed of the wind. © **MP.7**

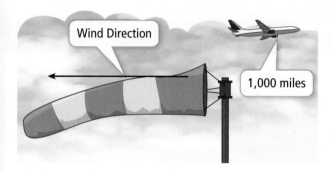

Wind Direction

1,000 miles

a. Organize the given information and what you need to find in a table.

b. Write and solve a rational equation to find the wind speed.

28. Reason During their day at the beach, Jae and his friends rent a Jet Ski. They split the $120 rental fee evenly among themselves. Then Jae, with only his friend Morgan, share the cost of a $16 pizza. If Jae spends a total of $48 for both, then find the number of friends, n, with whom he shared the cost of the Jet Ski rental. © **MP.2**

29. Make Sense and Persevere When driving to their family reunion, River's mom drove 10 miles at a rate of x mph and then 25 miles at a rate of $x + 10$ mph. The total driving time was 45 minutes. What were the two driving speeds at which River's mom drove? © **MP.1**

30. Generalize So far this baseball season, Philip has gotten a hit 8 times out of 40 at-bats. He wants to increase his batting average to 0.333. Calculate the number of consecutive hits, h, he would need in order to achieve this goal. Round your answer to the nearest whole number. © **MP.8**

31. Which of the following rational equations have at least one extraneous solution? Select all that apply.

Ⓐ $\frac{2}{x} = \frac{3}{x-4}$

Ⓑ $\frac{x^2}{x-3} = \frac{9}{x-3}$

Ⓒ $\frac{x-1}{x-5} = \frac{9}{x-5}$

Ⓓ $x + \frac{3}{x} = 4$

Ⓔ $\frac{x}{x-3} - \frac{3}{2} = \frac{3}{x-3}$

32. SAT/ACT Which of the following is the solution of $\frac{3}{x+1} = \frac{2}{x-3}$?

Ⓐ $x = -11$

Ⓑ $x = -\frac{7}{5}$

Ⓒ $x = \frac{7}{5}$

Ⓓ $x = 11$

33. Performance Task A chemist needs alcohol solution in the correct concentration for her experiment. She adds a 6% alcohol solution to 50 gallons of solution that is 2% alcohol. The function that represents the percent of alcohol in the resulting solution is $f(x) = \frac{50(0.02) + x(0.06)}{50 + x}$, where x is the amount of 6% solution added.

6% alcohol

50 gal
2% alcohol

Part A How much 6% solution should be added to create a solution that is 5% alcohol?

Part B Use Appropriate Tools Explain the steps you could take to use your graphing calculator to verify the correctness of your answer to part (A). © **MP.5**

© **Common Core State Standards** HSA.CED.A.1, HSA.REI.A.1, HSA.REI.B.3, MP.4

Video

▶ Real Cool Waters

Nothing feels better on a hot day than jumping into a pool! Many cities have swimming pools that people can go to for a small fee. Some people have swimming pools in their backyards that they can enjoy any time.

If neither of these options are available, you can always create your own beach paradise! Get a kiddie pool, a lawn chair, and a beach umbrella. Think about your beach paradise during the Mathematical Modeling in 3 Acts lesson.

Scan for
Multimedia

ACT 1   Identify the Problem

1. What is the first question that comes to mind after watching the video?

2. Write down the main question you will answer about what you saw in the video.

3. Make an initial conjecture that answers this main question.

4. Explain how you arrived at your conjecture.

5. Write a number that you know is too small.

6. Write a number that you know is too large.

7. What information will be useful to know to answer the main question? How can you get it? How will you use that information?

ACT 2   Develop a Model

8. Use the math that you have learned in this Topic to refine your conjecture.

ACT 3   Interpret the Results

9. Is your refined conjecture between the highs and lows you set up earlier?

10. Did your refined conjecture match the actual answer exactly? If not, what might explain the difference?

Topic Review

1. How do you calculate with functions defined as quotients of polynomials, and what are the key features of their graphs?

Vocabulary Review

Choose the correct term to complete each sentence.

2. The _____ can be represented by the equation $y = \frac{1}{x}$.

3. A(n) _____ is any function $R(x) = \frac{P(x)}{Q(x)}$ where $P(x)$ and $Q(x)$ are polynomials and $Q(x) \neq 0$.

4. _____ can be modeled by the equation $y = \frac{k}{x}$.

5. A(n) _____ is the quotient of two polynomials.

6. A(n) _____ is a line that a graph approaches but may not touch.

7. A(n) _____ is a fraction that has one or more fractions in the numerator and/or the denominator.

8. A(n) _____ is a value that is a solution to an equation that is derived from an original equation but does not satisfy the original equation.

- inverse variation
- constant of variation
- reciprocal function
- asymptote
- rational function
- extraneous solution
- rational expression
- compound fraction

Concepts & Skills Review

LESSON 4-1	Inverse Variation and the Reciprocal Function

Quick Review

The equation $y = \frac{k}{x}$, or $xy = k$, $k \neq 0$, represents an **inverse variation**, where k is the **constant of variation**. The parent **reciprocal function** is $y = \frac{1}{x}$.

Example

In an inverse variation, $x = 9$ when $y = 2$. What is the value of y when $x = 3$?

$2 = \frac{k}{9}$ .... Substitute 9 and 2 for x and y.

$18 = k$ .... Solve for k.

$y = \frac{18}{3}$ .... Substitute 18 and 3 for k and x, respectively.

$y = 6$ .... Divide.

Practice & Problem Solving

9. In an inverse variation, $x = 2$ when $y = -4$. What is the value of y when $x = 16$?

10. In an inverse variation, $x = 6$ when $y = \frac{1}{12}$. What is the value of x when $y = 2$?

11. Graph the function $y = \frac{5}{x}$. What are the domain, range, and asymptotes of the function?

12. **Look for Relationships** How is the parent reciprocal function related to an inverse variation? ⓒ **MP.7**

13. **Make Sense and Persevere** The volume, V, of a gas varies inversely with pressure, P. If the volume of a gas is 6 cm^3 with pressure 25 kg/cm^2, what is the volume of a gas with pressure 15 kg/cm^2? ⓒ **MP.1**

Graphing Rational Functions

Quick Review

Vertical asymptotes may occur when the denominator of a rational function is equal to 0.

Horizontal asymptotes guide the end behavior of a graph and depend on the degrees of the numerator and denominator.

Example

What is the graph of $f(x) = \dfrac{9x^2 - 25}{x^2 - 5x - 6}$?

Find vertical asymptotes.

$x^2 - 5x - 6 = 0$ .... Set denominator equal to 0.

$(x + 1)(x - 6) = 0$ .... Factor.

$x = -1 \qquad x = 6$ .... Solve.

Find horizontal asymptotes.

Find the ratio of leading terms.

$f(x) = \dfrac{9x^2}{x^2} = 9$

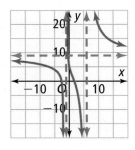

Practice & Problem Solving

Identify the vertical and horizontal asymptotes of each rational function.

14. $f(x) = \dfrac{x - 8}{x^2 + 9x + 14}$

15. $f(x) = \dfrac{2x + 1}{x^2 + 5x - 6}$

16. $f(x) = \dfrac{x^2 - 9}{2x^2 + 25}$

17. $f(x) = \dfrac{16x^2 - 1}{x^2 - 6x - 16}$

Graph each function and identify the horizontal and vertical asymptotes.

18. $f(x) = \dfrac{x}{x^2 - 1}$

19. $f(x) = \dfrac{3}{x - 2}$

20. $f(x) = \dfrac{2x^2 + 7}{x^2 + 2x + 1}$

21. $f(x) = \dfrac{3x^2 - 11x - 4}{4x^2 - 25}$

22. **Reason** The daily attendance at an amusement park after day x is given by the function $f(x) = \dfrac{3{,}000x}{x^2 - 1}$. On approximately which day will the attendance be 1,125 people? **ⓒ MP.2**

Multiplying and Dividing Rational Expressions

Quick Review

To multiply **rational expressions**, divide out common factors and simplify. To divide rational expressions, multiply by the reciprocal of the divisor.

Example

What is the quotient of $\dfrac{x^2 + x - 2}{x + 3}$ and $\dfrac{x^2 + 3x - 4}{2x + 6}$?

$= \dfrac{x^2 + x - 2}{x + 3} \cdot \dfrac{2x + 6}{x^2 + 3x - 4}$ .... Multiply by reciprocal.

$= \dfrac{(x + 2)(x - 1)}{x + 3} \cdot \dfrac{2(x + 3)}{(x + 4)(x - 1)}$ .... Divide out common factors.

$= \dfrac{2(x + 2)}{x + 4}$ .... Simplify.

Practice & Problem Solving

Find the simplified product, and state the domain.

23. $\dfrac{x^2 + x - 12}{x^2 - x - 6} \cdot \dfrac{x + 2}{x + 4}$

24. $\dfrac{x^2 + 8x}{x^3 + 5x^2 - 24x} \cdot (x^3 + 2x^2 - 15x)$

Find the simplified quotient, and state the domain.

25. $\dfrac{x^2 - 36}{x^2 - 3x - 18} \div \dfrac{x^2 + 2x - 24}{x^2 + 7x + 12}$

26. $\dfrac{2x^2 + 5x - 3}{x^2 - 4x - 21} \div \dfrac{2x^2 + 5x - 3}{3x + 9}$

27. **Reason** The volume, in cubic units, of a rectangular prism with a square base can be represented by $25x^3 + 200x^2$. The height, in units, can be represented by $x + 8$. What is the side length of the base of the rectangular prism, in units? **ⓒ MP.2**

Adding and Subtracting Rational Expressions

Quick Review

To add or subtract rational expressions, multiply each expression in both the numerator and denominator by a common denominator. Add or subtract the numerators. Then simplify.

Example

What is the sum of $\frac{x-2}{x^2-25}$ and $\frac{3}{x+5}$?

$\frac{x-2}{(x+5)(x-5)} + \frac{3}{x+5}$ .... Factor denominators.

$= \frac{x-2}{(x+5)(x-5)} + \frac{3(x-5)}{(x+5)(x-5)}$ .... Find common denominator.

$= \frac{x-2+3(x-5)}{(x+5)(x-5)}$ .... Add numerators.

$= \frac{x-2+3x-15}{(x+5)(x-5)}$ .... Multiply.

$= \frac{4x-17}{(x+5)(x-5)}$ .... Simplify.

Practice & Problem Solving

Find the sum or difference.

28. $\frac{2x}{x+6} + \frac{3}{x-1}$

29. $\frac{x}{x^2-4} - \frac{5}{x-2}$

Simplify.

30. $\frac{2+\frac{2}{x}}{2-\frac{2}{x}}$

31. $\frac{\frac{-1}{x}+\frac{3}{y}}{\frac{4}{x}-\frac{5}{y}}$

32. Communicate Precisely Why is it necessary to consider the domain when adding and subtracting rational expressions? Ⓒ **MP.6**

33. Make Sense and Persevere Mia paddles a kayak 6 miles downstream at a rate 4 mph faster than the river's current. She then travels 6 miles back upstream at a rate 2 mph faster than the river's current. Write and simplify an expression for the time it takes her to make the round trip in terms of the river's current c. Ⓒ **MP.1**

Solving Rational Equations

Quick Review

A **rational equation** is an equation relating rational expressions. An **extraneous solution** is a value that is a solution to an equation that is derived from an original equation but does not satisfy the original equation.

Example

What are the solutions to the equation $\frac{2}{x-2} = \frac{x}{x-2} - \frac{x}{4}$?

$(4)(x-2)\left(\frac{2}{x-2}\right)$

$= \left(\frac{x}{x-2} - \frac{x}{4}\right)(4)(x-2)$ .... Multiply by the LCD.

$8 = 4x - x^2 + 2x$ .... Multiply.

$x^2 - 6x + 8 = 0$ .... Write in standard form.

$(x-2)(x-4) = 0$ .... Factor.

$x-2 = 0$ or $x-4 = 0$ .... Zero Product Property

$x = 2$ or $x = 4$ .... Solve to identify possible solutions.

The solution $x = 2$ is extraneous. The only solution to the equation is $x = 4$.

Practice & Problem Solving

Solve the equation.

34. $\frac{18}{x+4} = 6$

35. $\frac{9}{x-1} = 3$

36. $-\frac{4}{3} + \frac{2}{x} = 8$

37. $\frac{2x}{x+3} = 5 + \frac{6x}{x+3}$

38. $-8 + \frac{64}{x-8} = \frac{x^2}{x-8}$

39. $\frac{9}{x^2-9} = \frac{3}{6(x-3)}$

40. Communicate Precisely Explain how to check if a solution to a rational equation is an extraneous solution. Ⓒ **MP.6**

41. Reason Diego and Stacy can paint a doghouse in 5 hours when working together. Diego works twice as fast as Stacy. Let x be the number of hours it would take Diego to paint the doghouse and y be the number of hours it would take Stacy to paint the doghouse. How long would it take Stacy to paint the doghouse if she was working alone? How long would it take Diego to paint the doghouse if he was working alone? Ⓒ **MP.2**

TOPIC 5

Rational Exponents and Radical Functions

? TOPIC ESSENTIAL QUESTION

How are rational exponents and radical equations used to solve real-world problems?

Topic Overview

enVision™ STEM Project:
Tune a Piano

5-1 *n*th Roots, Radicals, and Rational Exponents

5-2 Properties of Exponents and Radicals

5-3 Graphing Radical Functions

5-4 Solving Radical Equations

Mathematical Modeling in 3 Acts:
The Snack Shack

5-5 Function Operations

5-6 Inverse Relations and Functions

Topic Vocabulary

- composite function
- composition of functions
- extraneous solution
- index
- inverse function
- inverse relation
- like radicals
- *n*th root
- radical function
- radical symbol
- radicand
- reduced radical form

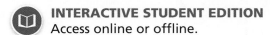

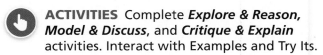

Digital Experience

INTERACTIVE STUDENT EDITION
Access online or offline.

ACTIVITIES Complete *Explore & Reason, Model & Discuss*, and *Critique & Explain* activities. Interact with Examples and Try Its.

ANIMATION View and interact with real-world applications.

PRACTICE Practice what you've learned.

 Go online | SavvasRealize.com

▶ The Snack Shack

Many Americans love the beach! When visiting the beach, some people bring coolers packed with food and drinks. Others prefer to take advantage of snack bars and shops set up along the beach.

Some beachside communities have built long wooden walkways, or boardwalks, to make it easier for beachgoers to walk to the snack bars and stores. How easy do you find walking in the sand? Think about this during the Mathematical Modeling in 3 Acts lesson.

VIDEOS Watch clips to support *Mathematical Modeling in 3 Acts Lessons* and **enVision™ STEM Projects.**

CONCEPT SUMMARY Review key lesson content through multiple representations.

ASSESSMENT Show what you've learned.

GLOSSARY Read and listen to English and Spanish definitions.

TUTORIALS Get help from *Virtual Nerd,* right when you need it.

MATH TOOLS Explore math with digital tools and manipulatives.

enVision™ STEM

Video

Did You Know?

The size of an instrument can affect the range of pitches it can produce.

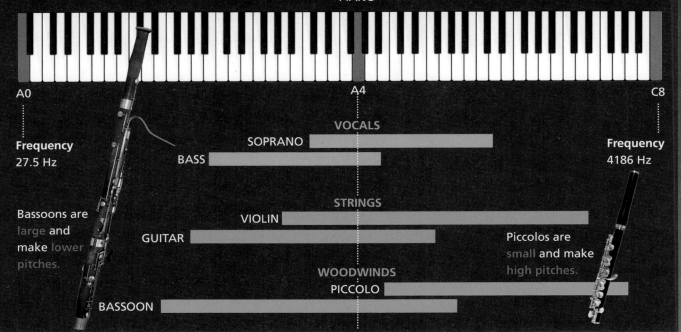

PIANO

A0

A4

C8

Frequency
27.5 Hz

Frequency
4186 Hz

VOCALS
SOPRANO
BASS

Bassoons are large and make lower pitches.

STRINGS
VIOLIN
GUITAR

Piccolos are small and make high pitches.

WOODWINDS
PICCOLO
BASSOON

Digital music programs allow musicians, audio technicians, and music producers to alter a tone or pitch, edit music, and visualize sounds.

1 : 1
1 : 2

Where you press down on a guitar string affects the pitch of the string when plucked. Pressing halfway down the string produces a pitch an octave higher than pressing the top of the string.

▶ Your Task: Tune a Piano

You and your classmates will investigate different ways to tune a piano. You will select a musical piece and then decide what tuning sounds best for it.

5-1

nth Roots, Radicals, and Rational Exponents

I CAN... relate roots and rational exponents and use them to simplify expressions and solve equations.

VOCABULARY
- index
- nth root
- radical symbol
- radicand

Common Core State Standards HSN.RN.A.1, HSN.RN.A.2, HSA.REI.A.1, MP.1, MP.4, MP.5

 Activity   Assess

👆 EXPLORE & REASON

The graph shows $y = x^2$.

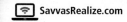

A. Find *all* possible values of x or y so that the point is on the graph.

(a) (2, ___)   (b) (3, ___)

(c) (−3, ___)   (d) (5, ___)

(e) (___ , 4)   (f) (___, −16)

(g) (___ , 7)   (h) (___, 5)

B. Communicate Precisely Write a precise set of instructions that show how to find an approximate value of $\sqrt{13}$ using the graph. © **MP.6**

C. Draw a graph of $y = x^3$. Use the graph to approximate each value.

(a) $\sqrt[3]{5}$ (b) $\sqrt[3]{-5}$

(c) $\sqrt[3]{8}$ (d) A solution to $x^3 = 5$

(e) A solution to $x^3 = -5$ (f) A solution to $x^3 = 8$

❓ ESSENTIAL QUESTION   How are exponents and radicals used to represent roots of real numbers?

👆 EXAMPLE 1   Find All Real nth Roots

A. What are all the real cube roots of 125?

An **nth root** of a number c is x, such that $x^n = c$. An nth root can be denoted by a **radical symbol** with an **index** of n: $\sqrt[n]{c}$; c is called the **radicand.**

To represent the real cube root of 125, write $x = \sqrt[3]{125}$.

Find the value of x such that $x^3 = 125$.

To solve $x^3 = 125$, note that $5^3 = 125$, so 5 is a root.

Consider if there are others. To determine this, set the expression equal to 0 and factor.

$x^3 - 125 = 0$

$(x - 5)(x^2 + 5x + 25)$

$x - 5 = 0$ gives the root 5

$x^2 + 5x + 25 = 0$

The discriminant of the expression is $5^2 - 4(1)(25)$, or -75. The roots are not real.

Therefore, 5 is the only real cube root of 125.

> Recall that complex solutions to polynomial equations come in pairs. The number of real roots depends on the degree of the equation.
> - odd degree → odd number of real roots
> - even degree → even number of real roots

MAKE SENSE AND PERSEVERE
Recall that third degree equations have three solutions; here, one solution is real and two are complex. © **MP.1**

CONTINUED ON THE NEXT PAGE

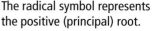
EXAMPLE 1 CONTINUED

B. What are all the real fourth roots of 16?

The index is 4 and the radicand is 16. Write $x = \sqrt[4]{16}$.

Find the value of x such that $x^4 = 16$.

Set the expression equal to 0 and factor.

$$x^4 - 16 = 0$$
$$(x^2 - 4)(x^2 + 4) = 0$$
$$(x + 2)(x - 2)(x^2 + 4) = 0$$
$$x = 2, -2$$

$x^2 + 4 = 0$ leads to imaginary roots.

The real roots of $x^4 = 16$ are 2 and -2.

> The radical symbol represents the positive (principal) root.

 Try It!   **1.** Find the specified roots of each number.

a. real fourth roots of 81   **b.** real cube roots of 64

CONCEPTUAL UNDERSTANDING

👆 **EXAMPLE 2**   **Understand Rational Exponents**

A. What is the meaning of the exponent in the expression $16^{\frac{1}{4}}$?

To interpret a rational exponent, look at what happens if you extend the properties of *integer* exponents to *rational* exponents.

Assume the Power of a Power Property applies to exponents in the form $\frac{1}{n}$.

$$\left(16^{\frac{1}{4}}\right) = (2^4)^{\frac{1}{4}} = 2 = \sqrt[4]{16}$$

> $16^{\frac{1}{4}}$ is a number you raise to the 4th power to get 16.

STUDY TIP
It is important to recognize multiple representations of the same value so you can select the form that is most efficient for a given situation.

This means you can define $16^{\frac{1}{4}}$ to be $\sqrt[4]{16}$, or 2.

In general, for positive integer n, $x^{\frac{1}{n}}$ is defined to be $\sqrt[n]{x}$.

$$x^{\frac{1}{n}} = \sqrt[n]{x}$$

> Both the exponent $\frac{1}{n}$ and the radical symbol $\sqrt[n]{x}$ indicate the principal nth root.

B. What is the meaning of the exponent in the expression $27^{\frac{2}{3}}$?

$$27^{\frac{2}{3}} = \left(27^{\frac{1}{3}}\right)^2 \quad \cdots\cdots\cdots \text{Rewrite using the Power of a Power Property.}$$

$$= \left(\sqrt[3]{27}\right)^2 \quad \cdots\cdots\cdots \text{Use the definition of the exponent } \frac{1}{n}, x = \sqrt[n]{x}.$$

$$= 3^2$$

$$= 9$$

This means that you can define $27^{\frac{2}{3}}$ to be the $\left(\sqrt[3]{27}\right)^2$, or 9.

 Try It!   **2.** Explain what each fractional exponent means, then evaluate.

a. $25^{\frac{1}{2}}$ **b.** $32^{\frac{2}{5}}$

CONCEPT Interpreting Fractional Exponents

The index of a radical is equivalent to the denominator of a fractional exponent.

In general, if the nth root of c is a real number, $\sqrt[n]{c} = c^{\frac{1}{n}}$.

Furthermore, if m is an integer and $\frac{m}{n}$ is in lowest terms, then

$$c^{\frac{m}{n}} = (c^{\frac{1}{n}})^m = (\sqrt[n]{c})^m \text{ and } \sqrt[n]{c^m} = (c^m)^{\frac{1}{n}} = c^{\frac{m}{n}}.$$

APPLICATION ➔

 EXAMPLE 3 **Evaluate Expressions With Rational Exponents**

A. Evaluate the expressions $32^{\frac{3}{5}}$, $27^{-\frac{2}{3}}$, $50^{\frac{3}{4}}$.

USE APPROPRIATE TOOLS
Many expressions with integer roots can be evaluated using mental math. However, when the root is not an integer, it can be efficient to use the power function of a calculator to compute rational roots. Ⓖ **MP.5**

$$32^{\frac{3}{5}} = \left(32^{\frac{1}{5}}\right)^3$$
$$= 2^3$$
$$= 8$$

$$27^{-\frac{2}{3}} = \left(27^{\frac{1}{3}}\right)^{-2}$$
$$= (3)^{-2}$$
$$= \frac{1}{9}$$

Since 50 does not have a perfect 4th root, use a calculator to approximate:
$$50^{\frac{3}{4}} \approx 18.80$$

B. The Fujita scale rating, F, of a tornado is represented by $F = \sqrt[3]{\left(\frac{W}{14.1}\right)^2} - 2$, where W is the estimated wind speed of the tornado in miles per hour. What is the Fujita scale rating of a tornado with estimated wind speeds of 100 mph?

Wind: 100 mph

$F = \sqrt[3]{\left(\frac{100}{14.1}\right)^2} - 2$ ········· Substitute 100 for W in the formula.

$= \left(\frac{100}{14.1}\right)^{\frac{2}{3}} - 2$ ·········· Rewrite the radical using an exponent.

$\approx (7.09)^{\frac{2}{3}} - 2$ ··········· Divide 100 by 14.1.

$\approx 3.69 - 2$ ··············· Evaluate the exponent.

≈ 1.69 ···················· Subtract.

A tornado with estimated wind speeds of 100 mph is classified as F1 according to the Fujita scale.

☑ **Try It!** **3.** What is the value of each expression? Round to the nearest hundredth if necessary.

    a. $-\left(16^{\frac{3}{4}}\right)$ **b.** $\sqrt[5]{3.5^4}$

EXAMPLE 4   **Simplify *n*th Roots**

Simplify each expression.

A. $\sqrt[5]{32m^{15}}$

> Write the radicand as an expression to the 5th power.

$$\sqrt[5]{2^5 m^{15}} = \sqrt[5]{(2m^3)^5}$$

$$= 2m^3$$

So, $\sqrt[5]{32m^{15}} = 2m^3$.

LOOK FOR RELATIONSHIPS
Why do even roots sometimes require absolute value symbols, while odd roots do not?

B. $\sqrt[4]{x^{20}y^8}$

> Write the radicand as an expression to the 4th power.

$$\sqrt[4]{x^{20}y^8} = \sqrt[4]{(x^5 y^2)^4}$$

> Use absolute value to indicate that the principal 4th root is nonnegative.

$$= |x^5 y^2|$$

$$= |x^5| y^2$$

> The square of a number is always nonnegative, so y^2 can be written outside the absolute value.

So, $\sqrt[4]{x^{20}y^8} = |x^5| y^2$.

 Try It!   **4.** Simplify each expression.

a. $\sqrt[3]{-8a^3 b^9}$ **b.** $\sqrt[4]{256x^{12}y^{24}}$

 EXAMPLE 5   **Use *n*th Roots to Solve Equations**

Solve the equation $2x^5 = 64$.

$$2x^5 = 64$$

> Raise each side of the equation to the $\frac{1}{5}$ power.

$$x^5 = 32$$

$$(x^5)^{\frac{1}{5}} = 32^{\frac{1}{5}}$$

> Use Power of a Power Property on the left, and simplify the rational exponent on the right.

$$x = 2$$

GENERALIZE
Raise both sides of the equation to a power so that the exponent of the variable becomes 1. Using the Power of a Power Property, $(x^n)^{\frac{1}{n}} = x^1$. **MP.8**

The solution to the equation is $x = 2$.

 Try It!   **5. a.** Solve the equation $5x^3 = 320$.

        b. Solve the equation $2p^4 = 162$.

CONCEPT Solving an Equation in the Form $x^n = c$

To solve an equation in the form $x^n = c$, find the nth root of both sides by raising each expression to the $\frac{1}{n}$ power.

$$(x^n)^{\frac{1}{n}} = (c)^{\frac{1}{n}}$$

APPLICATION **EXAMPLE 6** Use nth Roots to Solve Problems

One cube-shaped container has an edge length 2 cm longer than the edge length of a second cube. The volume of the larger cube is 729 cm³. When the larger cube empties into the smaller cube, how much water will spill?

729 cm³

MODEL WITH MATHEMATICS
Use the information in the problem to write an equation that models the situation. © MP.4

$(x + 2)^3 = 729$

$[(x + 2)^3]^{\frac{1}{3}} = (729)^{\frac{1}{3}}$ ← Raise both sides to the $\frac{1}{3}$ power and solve.

$x + 2 = 9$

$x = 7$

The volume of the smaller cube is 7^3, or 343 cm³.

The volume of the larger cube is 729 cm³.

The amount of water that spills is $729 - 343 = 386$.

When the larger cube empties into the smaller cube, 386 cm³ of water will spill out.

☑ **Try It!** 6. One cube has an edge length 3 cm shorter than the edge length of a second cube. The volume of the smaller cube is 200 cm³. What is the volume of the larger cube?

	Relating Radical and Exponential Forms	Solving an Equation in the Form $x^n = c$
WORDS	The index of a radical is equivalent to the denominator of a fractional exponent. The exponent of the radicand is equivalent to the numerator of a fractional exponent.	To solve an equation in the form $x^n = c$, find the *n*th root of both sides of the equation by raising each expression to the $\frac{1}{n}$ power.
NUMBERS Radical Form	$\sqrt[5]{32^4} = (32^4)^{\frac{1}{5}} = 32^{\frac{4}{5}}$	$x^3 = 1{,}728$ $(x^3)^{\frac{1}{3}} = (1{,}728)^{\frac{1}{3}}$
Exponential Form	$729^{\frac{5}{6}} = \left(729^{\frac{1}{6}}\right)^5 = (\sqrt[6]{729})^5$	$x = 12$
ALGEBRA Radical Form	$\sqrt[n]{c^m} = (c^m)^{\frac{1}{n}} = c^{\frac{m}{n}}$	$x^n = c$ $(x^n)^{\frac{1}{n}} = (c)^{\frac{1}{n}}$
Exponential Form	$c^{\frac{m}{n}} = \left(c^{\frac{1}{n}}\right)^m = \sqrt[n]{c^m}$	$x = c^{\frac{1}{n}}$

☑ Do You UNDERSTAND?

1. **ESSENTIAL QUESTION** How are exponents and radicals used to represent roots of real numbers?

2. **Error Analysis** Kaitlyn said $\sqrt[3]{10} = 10^3$. Explain Kaitlyn's error. © **MP.3**

3. **Vocabulary** In the radical expression $\sqrt[5]{125}$, what is the index? What is the radicand?

4. **Use Structure** Why is $75^{\frac{3}{5}}$ equal to $\left(75^{\frac{1}{5}}\right)^3$? © **MP.7**

5. **Construct Arguments** Anastasia said that $(x^8)^{\frac{1}{4}} = \frac{x^8}{x^4} = x^4$. Is Anastasia correct? Explain. © **MP.3**

6. **Make Sense and Persevere** Is it possible for a rational exponent to be an improper fraction? Explain how $27^{\frac{4}{3}}$ is evaluated or why it cannot be evaluated. © **MP.1**

Do You KNOW HOW?

Write each expression in radical form.

7. $a^{\frac{1}{5}}$

8. $7^{\frac{2}{3}}$

Write each expression in exponential form.

9. $\sqrt[3]{b}$

10. $\sqrt[4]{p^7}$

11. How many real third roots does 1,728 have?

12. How many real sixth roots does 15,625 have?

13. Solve the equation $4x^3 = 324$.

14. Solve the equation $2x^4 = 2{,}500$.

Simplify each expression.

15. $\sqrt[3]{27x^{12}y^6}$

16. $\sqrt[5]{-32x^5y^{30}}$

17. A snow globe is packaged in a cubic container that has volume 64 in.³ A large shipping container is also a cube, and its edge length is 8 inches longer than the edge length of the snow globe container. How many snow globes can fit into the larger shipping container?

UNDERSTAND

18. Construct Arguments Justice found that the fifth root of $243x^{15}y^5$ is $3x^3y$. Is Justice correct? Explain your reasoning. **© MP.3**

19. Make Sense and Persevere For a show, each sphere was inflated to have a volume of $4{,}186\frac{2}{3}$ in.^{3} Explain how to find the radius r of one of the inflated spheres. Use technology to compute your answer. **© MP.1**

$V = \frac{4}{3}\pi r^3$

20. Error Analysis Describe and correct the error a student made in writing this exponential expression in radical form. **© MP.3**

$$x^{\frac{4}{3}} = (x^4)^{\frac{1}{3}}$$
$$(x^4)^{\frac{1}{3}} = \sqrt[4]{x^3} \quad \times$$

21. Construct Arguments Determine whether $\sqrt[3]{x^2}$ is equal to $(\sqrt[3]{x})^2$. Explain your reasoning. **© MP.3**

22. Use Structure How many third roots does -512 have? Explain your reasoning. **© MP.7**

23. Higher Order Thinking The annual interest formula below calculates the final balance of an account, F, given a starting balance, S, and an interest rate, r, after 10 years.

$$F = S(1 + r)^{10}$$

When solving for r, why can the negative root be ignored?

24. Mathematical Connections The lengths of the two legs of a right triangle are 4 and 8. What is the length of the hypotenuse, in simplest radical form?

PRACTICE

Find the specified roots of each number.
SEE EXAMPLE 1

25. the real fourth roots of 81

26. the real third roots of 343

27. the real fifth roots of 1,024

28. the real square roots of 25

Rewrite each expression using a fractional exponent. SEE EXAMPLE 2

29. $\sqrt[4]{16^2}$ **30.** $\sqrt[6]{729}$

31. $\sqrt[7]{x^2}$ **32.** $\sqrt[4]{ab}$

What is the value of each expression? Round to the nearest hundredth if necessary. SEE EXAMPLE 3

33. $\sqrt[4]{25^2}$ **34.** $-\sqrt[3]{125^5}$

Simplify each expression. SEE EXAMPLE 4

35. $\sqrt[3]{8y^9}$ **36.** $\sqrt[4]{q^{12}z^4}$

37. $\sqrt[6]{729a^{24}b^{18}}$ **38.** $\sqrt[8]{v^8g^{40}}$

Solve each equation. SEE EXAMPLE 5

39. $1{,}125 = 9x^3$ **40.** $6{,}480 = 5w^4$

41. $270 = 10q^3$ **42.** $256 = 4h^6$

43. A small cube has the volume shown. Its side length is 1.5 in. less than a second, larger cube. What is the volume of the larger cube? SEE EXAMPLE 6

Volume: 85 in.^{3}

APPLY

44. Model With Mathematics A water-walking ball has a volume of approximately 4.19 m³. What is the radius, r, of the ball? Ⓒ **MP.4**

$$V = \frac{4}{3}\pi r^3$$

45. Make Sense and Persevere Ahmed received a box of gifts. The box is a rectangular prism with the same height and width, and the length is twice the width. The volume of the box is 3,456 in.³. What is the height of the box? Ⓒ **MP.1**

2x in.   x in.

x in.

46. Make Sense and Persevere Amelia's bank account earns interest annually. The equation shows her starting balance of $200 and her balance at the end of four years, $220.82. At what rate, r, did Amelia earn interest? Ⓒ **MP.1**

$$220.82 = 200(1 + r)^4$$

47. Model With Mathematics One measure of a patient's body surface area is found using the expression $\sqrt{\frac{H \cdot W}{3,600}}$. Write this with a fractional exponent. Ⓒ **MP.4**

Ⓒ **ASSESSMENT PRACTICE**

48. Determine if each expression is another way to write $b^{\frac{3}{4}}$. Select *Yes* or *No*.

	Yes	No
a. $\sqrt[4]{b^3}$	☐	☐
b. $(b^3)^{\frac{1}{4}}$	☐	☐
c. $b^{\frac{4}{3}}$	☐	☐
d. $\sqrt[3]{b^4}$	☐	☐
e. $\frac{b^3}{b^4}$	☐	☐

49. SAT/ACT Which of the following is equivalent to $\sqrt[6]{4{,}096x^{18}y^{30}}$, where $x > 0$ and $y > 0$?

Ⓐ $682.7x^{15}y^{24}$

Ⓑ $4x^{1.6}y^{1.8}$

Ⓒ $4{,}096x^3y^5$

Ⓓ $4x^3y^5$

Ⓔ $682.7x^3y^5$

50. Performance Task A milk processing company uses cylindrical-shaped containers. The height of the container is equal to the diameter of the base.

Volume
169.65 ft³

Part A The volume of one container is about 169.65 ft³. How much material is needed to make the lateral surface of the shipping container?

Part B The cargo hold of a ship is 20 ft high. What is the largest number of these shipping containers that could be stacked on top of each other inside the cargo hold?

5-2

Properties of Exponents and Radicals

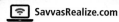
I CAN... use properties of exponents and radicals to simplify radical expressions.

VOCABULARY
- like radicals
- reduced radical form

👆 **CRITIQUE & EXPLAIN**

Olivia was practicing evaluating and simplifying expressions. Her work for three expressions is shown.

1. $24^2 = 400 + 16 = 416$

2. $3^6 = 9(27) = 270 - 27 = 243$

3. $\sqrt{625} = \sqrt{400} + \sqrt{225} = 20 + 15 = 35$

A. Is Olivia's work in the first example correct? Explain your thinking.

B. Is Olivia's work in the second example correct? Explain your thinking.

C. Is Olivia's work in the third example correct? Explain your thinking.

D. Make Sense and Persevere What advice would you give Olivia on simplifying expressions? © **MP.1**

❓ **ESSENTIAL QUESTION**   How can properties of exponents and radicals be used to rewrite radical expressions?

CONCEPT Properties of Rational Exponents

The properties of exponents apply not only to integer exponents, but to *rational* exponents as well. Now let m and n represent *rational* numbers, with a, b nonnegative real numbers.

	Property	**Example**
Product of Powers	$a^m \cdot a^n = a^{m+n}$	$4^{\frac{2}{3}} \cdot 4^{-\frac{1}{3}} = 4^{\frac{1}{3}}$
Quotient of Powers	$\dfrac{a^m}{a^n} = a^{m-n}$	$\dfrac{3^4}{3^2} = 3^{4-2} = 3^2 = 9$
Power of Power	$(a^m)^n = a^{mn}$	$(7^3)^{\frac{2}{3}} = 7^2$
Power of Product	$(ab)^m = a^m b^m$	$(16x)^{\frac{1}{2}} = (16^{\frac{1}{2}} x^{\frac{1}{2}}) = 4x^{\frac{1}{2}}$
Negative Exponent	$a^{-m} = \dfrac{1}{a^m}$	$5^{-\frac{1}{2}} = \dfrac{1}{5^{\frac{1}{2}}}$

👆 **EXAMPLE 1**   Use Properties of Exponents

USE STRUCTURE
When multiplying numbers with the same base, adding a negative exponent gives the same result as subtracting its opposite. © **MP.7**

How can you rewrite each expression using the properties of exponents?

A. $81^{\frac{5}{6}} \cdot 81^{-\frac{1}{3}}$

$81^{\frac{5}{6}} \cdot 81^{-\frac{1}{3}} = 81^{\frac{5}{6} - \frac{1}{3}}$ .... Use the Product of Powers Property.

$= 81^{\frac{1}{2}}$ .... Simplify the exponent.

$= 9$ .... Evaluate.

You can rewrite $81^{\frac{5}{6}} \cdot 81^{-\frac{1}{3}}$ as 9.

CONTINUED ON THE NEXT PAGE

EXAMPLE 1 CONTINUED

B. $\left(\dfrac{xy^3}{x^{\frac{1}{2}}}\right)^{\frac{2}{3}}$

$\left(\dfrac{xy^3}{x^{\frac{1}{2}}}\right)^{\frac{2}{3}} = \left(x^{1-\frac{1}{2}}\,y^3\right)^{\frac{2}{3}}$ ⋯⋯ Use the Quotient of Powers Property.

$= \left(x^{\frac{1}{2}}\,y^3\right)^{\frac{2}{3}}$ ⋯⋯⋯ Simplify.

$= x^{\frac{1}{3}}\,y^2$ ⋯⋯⋯ Use the Power of Product and Power of Power Properties.

$= y^2\,\sqrt[3]{x}$ ⋯⋯⋯ Write in radical form.

You can rewrite $\left(\dfrac{xy^3}{x^{\frac{1}{2}}}\right)^{\frac{2}{3}}$ as $y^2\,\sqrt[3]{x}$.

 Try It! **1.** How can you rewrite each expression using the properties of exponents?

a. $\left(\dfrac{3}{32^{\frac{2}{5}}}\right)^{\frac{1}{2}}$ **b.** $2a^{\frac{1}{3}}\left(ab^{\frac{1}{2}}\right)^{\frac{2}{3}}$

CONCEPTUAL UNDERSTANDING

 EXAMPLE 2 Use Properties of Exponents to Rewrite Radicals

How can you extend the properties of exponents to derive the properties of radicals?

A. How can you rewrite $\sqrt[n]{ab}$ using the properties of exponents?

$\sqrt[n]{ab} = (ab)^{\frac{1}{n}}$ ⋯⋯⋯ Rewrite the radical as a rational exponent.

$= a^{\frac{1}{n}}\,b^{\frac{1}{n}}$ ⋯⋯⋯ Rewrite using the Power of a Product Property.

$= \sqrt[n]{a}\,\sqrt[n]{b}$ ⋯⋯⋯ Rewrite the rational exponents as radicals.

So, $\sqrt[n]{ab} = \sqrt[n]{a}\,\sqrt[n]{b}$.

You can use a similar method to show that $\sqrt[n]{\dfrac{a}{b}} = \dfrac{\sqrt[n]{a}}{\sqrt[n]{b}}$.

B. How can you rewrite $\sqrt[3]{16x^5}$ using the properties of exponents?

$\sqrt[3]{16x^5} = \sqrt[3]{8x^3 \cdot 2x^2}$

Factors of 16 and x^5 that are perfect cubes

Remaining factors of 16 and x^5 that are not perfect cubes

$= \sqrt[3]{8x^3} \cdot \sqrt[3]{2x^2}$

$= 2x\sqrt[3]{2x^2}$

So, $\sqrt[3]{16x^5} = 2x\sqrt[3]{2x^2}$.

Writing the expression as $2x\sqrt[3]{2x^2}$ may be referred to as the **reduced radical form** of the expression because all nth roots of perfect nth powers in the radicand have been simplified, and no radicals remain in the denominator.

 Try It! **2.** How can you rewrite each expression?

a. $\sqrt[4]{81a^8b^5}$ **b.** $\sqrt[3]{\dfrac{x^4y^2}{125x}}$

CONCEPT Properties of Radicals

Product Property of Radicals
The nth root of a product of nonnegative real numbers is equal to the product of the nth roots of those numbers.

$$\sqrt[n]{ab} = \sqrt[n]{a}\,\sqrt[n]{b} \qquad (ab)^{\frac{1}{n}} = a^{\frac{1}{n}}b^{\frac{1}{n}}$$

Quotient Property of Radicals
The nth root of a quotient of nonnegative real numbers is equal to the quotient of the nth roots of those numbers.

$$\sqrt[n]{\frac{a}{b}} = \frac{\sqrt[n]{a}}{\sqrt[n]{b}} \qquad \left(\frac{a}{b}\right)^{\frac{1}{n}} = \frac{a^{\frac{1}{n}}}{b^{\frac{1}{n}}}$$

👆 **EXAMPLE 3** **Rewrite the Product or Quotient of a Radical**

A. What is $\sqrt[5]{16} \cdot \sqrt[5]{8}$ in reduced radical form?

$$\sqrt[5]{16} \cdot \sqrt[5]{8} = \sqrt[5]{16 \cdot 8} \qquad \text{Use the Product Property of Radicals.}$$

$$= \sqrt[5]{128} \qquad \text{Multiply radicands.}$$

$$= \sqrt[5]{32} \cdot \sqrt[5]{4} \qquad \text{Use the Product Property of Radicals.}$$

$$= 2\sqrt[5]{4} \qquad \text{Simplify.}$$

In reduced radical form $\sqrt[5]{16} \cdot \sqrt[5]{8}$ is $2\sqrt[5]{4}$.

B. What is $\sqrt[6]{8x} \cdot \sqrt[3]{2x}$ in reduced radical form?

Use rational exponents.

$$\sqrt[6]{8x} \cdot \sqrt[3]{2x} = (8x)^{\frac{1}{6}} \cdot (2x)^{\frac{1}{3}} \qquad \text{Rewrite using rational exponents.}$$

$$= (8x)^{\frac{1}{6}} \cdot (2x)^{\frac{2}{6}} \qquad \text{Write with common index (denominator).}$$

$$= \left(8x \cdot (2x)^2\right)^{\frac{1}{6}} \qquad \text{Use the Product Property of Radicals.}$$

$$= \sqrt[6]{32x^3} \qquad \text{Simplify.}$$

In reduced radical form $\sqrt[6]{8x} \cdot \sqrt[3]{2x}$ is $\sqrt[6]{32x^3}$.

C. What is $\sqrt[3]{\dfrac{2n}{9m}}$ in reduced radical form?

To rationalize the denominator of an expression, rewrite it so there are no radicals in any denominator and no denominators in any radical.

$$\sqrt[3]{\frac{2n}{9m}} = \frac{\sqrt[3]{2n}}{\sqrt[3]{9m}}$$

> To rationalize the denominator, find a factor so that a cube root of a perfect cube is created.

$$= \frac{\sqrt[3]{2n}}{\sqrt[3]{9m}} \cdot \frac{\sqrt[3]{3m^2}}{\sqrt[3]{3m^2}}$$

$$= \frac{\sqrt[3]{6nm^2}}{\sqrt[3]{27m^3}}$$

> 9 is a factor of the perfect cube 27, and m^1 is a factor of m^3. Multiply the denominator and numerator by $\sqrt[3]{3m^2}$ to create a perfect cube.

$$= \frac{\sqrt[3]{6nm^2}}{3m}$$

In reduced radical form $\sqrt[3]{\dfrac{2n}{9m}}$ is $\dfrac{\sqrt[3]{6nm^2}}{3m}$.

 Try It! **3. What is the reduced radical form of each expression?**

a. $\sqrt[5]{\dfrac{7}{16x^3}}$

b. $\sqrt[4]{27x^2} \cdot \sqrt{3x}$

 EXAMPLE 4 **Add and Subtract Radical Expressions**

A. What is the sum of $\sqrt{20} - \sqrt[3]{16} + \sqrt[3]{250} - \sqrt{5}$?

Like radicals have the same index and the same radicand. Only like radicals can be combined with addition and subtraction.

$$\sqrt{20} - \sqrt[3]{16} + \sqrt[3]{250} - \sqrt{5}$$

$$\sqrt{20} - \sqrt{5} - \sqrt[3]{16} + \sqrt[3]{250}$$ .... Group radical terms with like indices.

$$2\sqrt{5} - \sqrt{5} - 2\sqrt[3]{2} + 5\sqrt[3]{2}$$ .... Simplify each radical term.

$$(2-1)\sqrt{5} + (-2+5)\sqrt[3]{2}$$ .... Factor out the radicals with the inverse of the Distributive Property.

$$\sqrt{5} + 3\sqrt[3]{2}$$ .... Combine like radical terms.

The expression $\sqrt{20} - \sqrt[3]{16} + \sqrt[3]{250} - \sqrt{5}$ is equivalent to $\sqrt{5} + 3\sqrt[3]{2}$.

> **STUDY TIP**
> Use the inverse of the Distributive Property to combine like radicals in the same way that you would combine like terms.

APPLICATION

B. The design shows the boards needed for bracing the back of some set scenery. Will 75 ft of wood be enough for all of the bracing?

Let a represent the length of the diagonal for the smaller square and b represent the length of the diagonal for the larger square. Determine the lengths of the diagonals:

$$4^2 + 4^2 = a^2 \qquad 7^2 + 7^2 = b^2$$
$$32 = a^2 \qquad 98 = b^2$$
$$4\sqrt{2} = a \qquad 7\sqrt{2} = b$$

> Take the square root of both sides of the equation and simplify the radical. Since the context is length, the negative solution may be disregarded.

There are 3 edges that are 4 ft, 4 edges that are 7 ft, and 2 diagonals each of $4\sqrt{2}$ ft and $7\sqrt{2}$ ft in length. Determine the total length of the boards:

$$3(4) + 4(7) + 2(4\sqrt{2}) + 2(7\sqrt{2}) = 40 + 22\sqrt{2}$$

Evaluating the expression, $40 + 22\sqrt{2} \approx 71.1$.
So 75 ft of wood is enough to make the bracing for the set scenery.

✅ **Try It!** **4.** How can you rewrite each expression in a simpler form?

  a. $\sqrt[3]{2,000} + \sqrt{2} - \sqrt[3]{128}$ **b.** $\sqrt{20} - \sqrt{600} - \sqrt{125}$

 EXAMPLE 5 **Multiply Binomial Radical Expressions**

What is the reduced radical form of each product?

A. $\sqrt[3]{7}(2 - \sqrt[3]{49})$

$\sqrt[3]{7}(2) - \sqrt[3]{7}\sqrt[3]{49}$ ············· Use the Distributive Property.

$\sqrt[3]{7}(2) - \sqrt[3]{343}$ ············· Multiply radicands with like indices.

$2\sqrt[3]{7} - 7$ ············· Simplify each radical term.

The product is $2\sqrt[3]{7} - 7$.

B. $(2x - \sqrt{3})(2x - \sqrt{3})$

$4x^2 - 2x\sqrt{3} - 2x\sqrt{3} + \sqrt{9}$ ············· Expand the product.

$4x^2 - 4x\sqrt{3} + 3$ ············· Combine like terms.

The product is $4x^2 - 4x\sqrt{3} + 3$.

STUDY TIP
Recall that there are different methods for expanding the product of binomial factors.

 Try It! **5.** Multiply.

a. $(x - \sqrt{10})(x + \sqrt{10})$ **b.** $\sqrt{6}(5 + \sqrt{3})$

 EXAMPLE 6 **Rationalize a Binomial Denominator**

How can you rewrite $\dfrac{1}{2 + \sqrt{5}}$ without a radical in the denominator?

To rationalize a denominator that has a binomial denominator, multiply by the conjugate of the denominator.

STUDY TIP
The product of conjugates is $a^2 - b^2$, which eliminates radicals from the denominator.

$\dfrac{1}{2 + \sqrt{5}} \cdot \dfrac{2 - \sqrt{5}}{2 - \sqrt{5}}$ ············· Multiply the numerator and denominator by the conjugate of the denominator.

$\dfrac{2 - \sqrt{5}}{4 - 5}$ ············· Multiply the numerators and the denominators.

$\dfrac{2 - \sqrt{5}}{-1}$ ············· Subtract the terms in the denominators.

$\sqrt{5} - 2$ ············· Simplify.

$\dfrac{1}{2 + \sqrt{5}}$ can be rewritten as $\sqrt{5} - 2$.

Try It! **6.** What is the reduced radical form of each expression?

a. $\dfrac{5 - \sqrt{2}}{2 - \sqrt{3}}$ **b.** $\dfrac{-4x}{1 - \sqrt{x}}$

CONCEPT SUMMARY Properties of Radicals

	Product Property of Radicals	Quotient Property of Radicals	Rationalize the Denominator
WORDS	The nth root of a product is equal to the product of the nth roots of the factors.	The nth root of a quotient is equal to the quotient of the nth roots of the factors.	To rationalize the denominator of an expression, multiply by the conjugate of the denominator.
ALGEBRA	$\sqrt[n]{ab} = \sqrt[n]{a} \cdot \sqrt[n]{b}$	$\sqrt[n]{\dfrac{a}{b}} = \dfrac{\sqrt[n]{a}}{\sqrt[n]{b}}$	$\dfrac{3}{\sqrt{x}} \cdot \dfrac{\sqrt{x}}{\sqrt{x}} = \dfrac{3\sqrt{x}}{x}$
NUMBERS	$\sqrt[3]{2} \cdot \sqrt[3]{20} = \sqrt[3]{40}$ $\sqrt[3]{40} = \sqrt[3]{8} \cdot \sqrt[3]{5} = 2\sqrt[3]{5}$	$\sqrt{\dfrac{8}{9}} = \dfrac{\sqrt{8}}{\sqrt{9}} = \dfrac{2\sqrt{2}}{3}$	$\dfrac{2}{\sqrt{5}} \cdot \dfrac{\sqrt{5}}{\sqrt{5}} = \dfrac{2\sqrt{5}}{5}$

Using Properties of Radicals

SIMPLIFY

$\sqrt[4]{32x^9} = \sqrt[4]{16x^8} \cdot \sqrt[4]{2x}$
$= 2x^2\sqrt[4]{2x}$

Find factors that have a perfect 4th root.

$\dfrac{5}{x-\sqrt{8}} \cdot \dfrac{x+\sqrt{8}}{x+\sqrt{8}} = \dfrac{5(x+\sqrt{8})}{x^2 + x\sqrt{8} - x\sqrt{8} - 8} = \dfrac{5x+5\sqrt{8}}{x^2 - 8}$

Since the denominator is a binomial, multiply the numerator and the denominator by the conjugate of the denominator.

Do You UNDERSTAND?

1. **ESSENTIAL QUESTION** How can properties of exponents and radicals be used to rewrite radical expressions?

2. **Vocabulary** How can you determine if a radical expression is in reduced form?

3. **Use Structure** Explain why $(-64)^{\frac{1}{3}}$ equals $-64^{\frac{1}{3}}$ but $(-64)^{\frac{1}{2}}$ does not equal $-64^{\frac{1}{2}}$. **MP.7**

4. **Error Analysis** Explain the error in Julie's work in rewriting the radical expression. **MP.3**
$\sqrt{-3} \cdot \sqrt{-12} = \sqrt{-3(-12)} = \sqrt{36} = 6$

Do You KNOW HOW?

What is the reduced radical form of each expression?

5. $49^{\frac{3}{4}} \cdot 49^{\frac{-1}{4}}$

6. $\left(\dfrac{a^2b^8}{a^{\frac{1}{3}}}\right)^{\frac{3}{4}}$

7. $\sqrt[4]{1{,}024x^9y^{12}}$

8. $\sqrt[3]{\dfrac{4}{9m^2}}$

9. $\sqrt{63} - \sqrt{700} - \sqrt{112}$

10. $\sqrt{5}(6 + \sqrt{2})$

11. $\dfrac{3}{\sqrt{6}}$

12. $\dfrac{\sqrt{7}}{\sqrt{5} + 3}$

UNDERSTAND

13. Model With Mathematics In the expression $PV^{\frac{4}{3}}$, P represents the pressure and V represents the volume of a sample of a gas. Evaluate the expression for $P = 7$ and $V = 8$. ⓒ **MP.4**

14. Reason Describe the possible values of k such that $\sqrt{32} + \sqrt{k}$ can be rewritten as a single term. ⓒ **MP.2**

15. Error Analysis Explain why the following work is incorrect. Find the correct answer. ⓒ **MP.3**

$$5\left(4 - 5^{\frac{1}{2}}\right) = 5(4) - 5\left(5^{\frac{1}{2}}\right)$$
$$= 20 - 25^{\frac{1}{2}}$$
$$= 15 \quad ✗$$

16. Communicate Precisely Discuss the advantages and disadvantages of first rewriting $\sqrt{27} + \sqrt{48} + \sqrt{147}$ in order to estimate its decimal value. ⓒ **MP.6**

17. Higher Order Thinking Write $\sqrt{\frac{4}{5}}$ in two different ways, one where the numerator is simplified and another where the denominator is rationalized.

18. Construct Arguments Justify each step used in simplifying the expression below. ⓒ **MP.3**

$$\left(\frac{a^2}{a^{\frac{3}{4}}}\right)^{\frac{1}{5}} = \left(a^{2-\frac{3}{4}}\right)^{\frac{1}{5}}$$
$$= \left(a^{\frac{5}{4}}\right)^{\frac{1}{5}}$$
$$= a^{\frac{1}{4}}$$
$$= \sqrt[4]{a}$$

PRACTICE

What is the reduced radical form of each expression? SEE EXAMPLE 1

19. $\left(3x^{\frac{1}{2}}\right)\left(4x^{\frac{2}{3}}\right)$

20. $2b^{\frac{1}{2}}\left(3b^{\frac{1}{2}}c^{\frac{1}{3}}\right)^2$

21. $\left(x^{\frac{1}{2}} \cdot x^{\frac{5}{12}}\right)^4 \div x^{\frac{2}{3}}$

22. $\left(\frac{16c^{14}}{81d^{18}}\right)^{\frac{1}{2}}$

What is the reduced radical form of each expression? SEE EXAMPLE 2

23. $\sqrt[3]{250y^2z^4}$

24. $\sqrt[4]{256v^7w^{12}}$

25. $\sqrt{\frac{48x^3}{3xy^2}}$

26. $\sqrt{\frac{56x^5y^5}{7xy}}$

27. $\sqrt[3]{216m}$

28. $\sqrt[3]{\frac{250f^7g^3}{2f^2g}}$

What is the reduced radical form of each expression? SEE EXAMPLE 3

29. $\sqrt{x^5y^5} \cdot 3\sqrt{2x^7y^6}$

30. $\sqrt[3]{\frac{18n^2}{24n}}$

31. $\sqrt[3]{3x^2} \cdot \sqrt[3]{x^2} \cdot \sqrt[3]{9x^3}$

32. $\sqrt{\frac{162a}{6a^3}}$

33. $\sqrt[5]{2pq^6} \cdot 2\sqrt{2p^3q}$

34. $\sqrt[3]{\frac{x^2}{9y}}$

35. $\sqrt[3]{6} \cdot \sqrt[3]{16}$

36. $\sqrt[4]{\frac{2}{5x}}$

What is the reduced radical form of each expression? SEE EXAMPLE 4

37. $4\sqrt[3]{81} - 2\sqrt[3]{72} - \sqrt[3]{24}$

38. $6\sqrt{45y^2} - 4\sqrt{20y^2}$

39. $3\sqrt{12} - \sqrt{54} + 7\sqrt{75}$

40. $\sqrt{32h} + 4\sqrt{98h} - 3\sqrt{50h}$

Multiply. SEE EXAMPLE 5

41. $(3\sqrt{p} - \sqrt{5})(\sqrt{p} + 5\sqrt{5})$

42. $(4m - \sqrt{3})(4m - \sqrt{3})$

43. $(3\sqrt{2} + 8)(3\sqrt{2} - 8)$

44. $\sqrt[3]{3}(5\sqrt[3]{9} - 4)$

What is the reduced radical form of each expression? SEE EXAMPLE 6

45. $\frac{4}{1 - \sqrt{3}}$

46. $\frac{20}{3 + \sqrt{2}}$

47. $\frac{3 + \sqrt{8}}{2 - 2\sqrt{8}}$

48. $\frac{-2x}{3 + \sqrt{x}}$

PRACTICE & PROBLEM SOLVING

APPLY

ASSESSMENT PRACTICE

49. Model With Mathematics A triangular swimming area is marked off by a rope. **MP.4**

   a. If a woman swims around the perimeter of the swimming area, how far will she swim?

   b. What is the area of the roped off section?

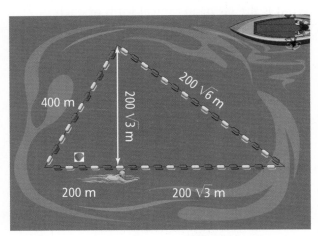

50. Use Structure The interest rate r required to increase your investment p to the amount a in m months is found by $r = \left(\frac{a}{p}\right)^{\frac{1}{m}} - 1$. What interest rate would be required to increase your investment of \$3,600 to \$6,400 over 7 months? Round your answer to the nearest tenth of a percent. **MP.7**

51. Use Structure The length of a rectangle is $(2 + \sqrt{5})y$. The width is $(4 + 3\sqrt{5})z$. What is the area of the rectangle? **MP.7**

52. Model With Mathematics A rectangular boardroom table is $\sqrt{440}$ ft by $\sqrt{20}$ ft. Find its area. **MP.4**

53. Aaron is rewriting $\frac{1 + \sqrt{3}}{5 - \sqrt{3}}$ into reduced radical form. Determine if Aaron would have written the steps below to show his work. Select *Yes* or *No*.

	Yes	No
$\dfrac{6 + 4\sqrt{3} - 3}{25 + 9}$	❑	❑
$\dfrac{5 + \sqrt{3} + 5\sqrt{3} + \sqrt{9}}{25 + 5\sqrt{3} - 5\sqrt{3} - \sqrt{9}}$	❑	❑
$\dfrac{4 + 3\sqrt{3}}{11}$	❑	❑
$\dfrac{8 + 6\sqrt{3}}{28}$	❑	❑
$\dfrac{5 + 6\sqrt{3} + 3}{25 - 3}$	❑	❑

54. SAT/ACT Which expression cannot be rewritten as -10?

   Ⓐ $\sqrt{25} \cdot \sqrt[3]{-8}$ Ⓑ $\sqrt[3]{-125} \cdot \sqrt[4]{16}$

   Ⓒ $-\sqrt[3]{1,000}$ Ⓓ $-\sqrt{25} \cdot \sqrt[5]{-32}$

   Ⓔ $\sqrt{4} \cdot -\sqrt[3]{125}$

55. Performance Task The volume of a sphere of radius r is $V = \frac{4}{3}\pi r^3$.

   Part A Use the formula to find r in terms of V. Rationalize the denominator.

   Part B A snowman is made using three spherical snowballs. The top snowball for the head has a volume of 500 in.^{3}. What is the diameter of the top snowball?

   Part C The volumes of the other two snowballs are 750 in.^{3} and 1,000 in.^{3}. How tall is the snowman?

5-3

Graphing Radical Functions

I CAN... graph and transform radical functions.

VOCABULARY
• radical function

  Activity  Assess

EXPLORE & REASON

Consider the formula for the area of a square: $A = s^2$

A. Graph the function that represents area as a function of side length.

B. On the same set of axes, graph the function that represents side length as a function of area.

C. Look for Relationships How are the two graphs related? **MP.7**

ESSENTIAL QUESTION How can you use what you know about transformations of functions to graph radical functions?

EXAMPLE 1   Graph Square Root and Cube Root Functions

Graph the following functions. What are the domain and range of each function? Is the function increasing or decreasing?

A. $f(x) = \sqrt{3x}$

Make a table of values and graph.

x	0	3	12	27
y	0	3	6	9

> For ease, choose x-values that make the radicand a perfect square.

For a square root function, the radicand cannot be negative, so the domain of the function is $\{x \mid x \geq 0\}$.

LOOK FOR RELATIONSHIPS
How does the graph of the function shown compare to the graph of its parent function? **MP.7**

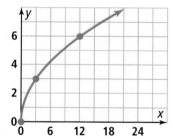

> Radical functions do not have a horizontal asymptote; they grow without limit.

The solution to a square root function always returns a positive value or 0, so the range is $\{y \mid y \geq 0\}$. As x increases, y increases, so the function is increasing.

B. $g(x) = \sqrt[3]{2x}$

Make a table of values, and graph.

x	−13.5	−4	0	4	13.5
y	−3	−2	0	2	3

> The radicand in a cube root function can be positive or negative.

CONTINUED ON THE NEXT PAGE

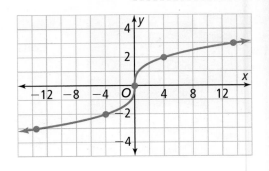
EXAMPLE 1 CONTINUED

There are no restrictions on the radicand of a cube root function, so the domain and range of the function is all real numbers.

The function is increasing over the entire domain.

LOOK FOR RELATIONSHIPS
Odd functions are symmetric about the origin. The cube root parent is an odd function. *Even functions* are symmetric about the *y*-axis. © **MP.7**

 Try It!   **1.** Graph the following functions. What are the domain and range of each function? Is the function increasing or decreasing?

  a. $f(x) = \sqrt{x - 5}$ **b.** $g(x) = \sqrt[3]{x + 1}$

CONCEPT Radical Function

A **radical function** is a function of the form $f(x) = a\sqrt[n]{x - h} + k$, where

| *a* determines a vertical stretch or compression. | *h* determines a horizontal translation. | *k* determines a vertical translation. |

EXAMPLE 2   **Graph a Transformation of a Radical Function**

Graph $g(x) = 2\sqrt{(x + 3)} + 5$. What transformations map the graph of $f(x) = \sqrt{x}$ to the graph of *g*? How do the domain and range of *g* differ from those of *f*?

Step 1 Identify the parameters in $g(x) = 2\sqrt{(x + 3)} + 5$.

$$g(x) = 2\sqrt{x - (-3)} + 5$$

a = 2, so the function is stretched vertically by a factor of 2.

h = −3, so the graph is translated left 3 units.

k = 5, so the graph is translated up 5 units.

STUDY TIP
The radicand $x + 3$ can be written as $x - (-3)$, which relates more directly to the general form of a radical function. The horizontal translation, *h*, is −3, so the graph of the function will shift (or translate) *left* 3 units.

Step 2 Graph the parent function *f*, and use it as a guide to graph *g*.

x	0	1	4	9	16
f(x)	0	1	2	3	4

This stretched graph is then translated 3 units left and 5 units up to show the graph of *g*.

The graph of *f* is stretched vertically by a factor of 2, so each *y*-value is twice as far from the *x*-axis.

The domain of *f* is $\{x \mid x \geq 0\}$, while the domain of *g* is $\{x \mid x \geq -3\}$.
The range of *f* is $\{y \mid y \geq 0\}$, while the range of *g* is $\{y \mid y \geq 5\}$.

CONTINUED ON THE NEXT PAGE

EXAMPLE 2 CONTINUED

 Try It!   **2.** Graph $g(x) = \frac{1}{2}\sqrt{x-1} - 3$. What transformations of the graph of $f(x) = \sqrt{x}$ produce the graph of g? What is the effect of the transformations on the domain and range of g?

EXAMPLE 3   **Rewrite Radical Functions to Identify Transformations**

How can you rewrite the following radical functions to identify their transformations from the parent graph of $f(x) = \sqrt{x}$?

A. $g(x) = \sqrt{9x}$

Use the properties of radicals to rewrite the function and identify a vertical change.

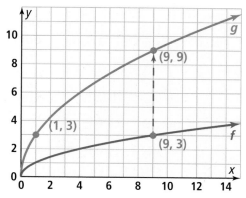

$g(x) = \sqrt{9x}$ .... Write the original equation.

$= \sqrt{9} \cdot \sqrt{x}$ .... Use the Product Property of Radicals.

$= 3\sqrt{x}$ .... Simplify.

$a = 3$, so the graph of g is stretched vertically by a factor of 3 from the parent graph. Both h and k are 0, so there is no translation of the graph.

B. $h(x) = \sqrt{4x + 16} + 7$

Rewrite the function in the form $h(x) = a\sqrt{x - h} + k$.

$h(x) = \sqrt{4x + 16} + 7$ .... Write the original equation.

$= \sqrt{4(x + 4)} + 7$ .... Factor the radicand.

$= \sqrt{4} \cdot \sqrt{x + 4} + 7$ .... Use the Product Property of Radicals.

$= 2\sqrt{x + 4} + 7$ .... Simplify.

The graph of $h(x)$ is a vertical stretch of the parent function by a factor of 2, followed by a translation of 4 units to the left, and a translation of 7 units up.

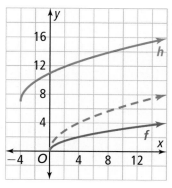

STUDY TIP
You may recall that the parameter k in $f(kx)$ determines horizontal stretch or compression. In this example, $g(x)$ can be described as either a horizontal compression or a vertical stretch. Both transformations of the parent function result in the same graph.

CONCEPTUAL UNDERSTANDING

 Try It!   **3.** What transformations of the parent graph of $f(x) = \sqrt{x}$ produce the graphs of the following functions?

a. $m(x) = \sqrt{7x - 3.5} - 10$ **b.** $j(x) = -2\sqrt{12x} + 4$

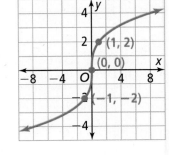
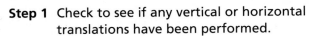

EXAMPLE 4   Write an Equation of a Transformation

What radical function is represented in the graph?

Compare the graph to the parent graph of $f(x) = \sqrt[3]{x}$.

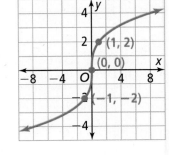

Step 1 Check to see if any vertical or horizontal translations have been performed.

Since $f(-x) = -f(x)$, you know that the function is odd. Like the graph of the parent function, the graph of this function is symmetric about the origin, so no translation has been performed.

Step 2 Check for a vertical and horizontal stretch.

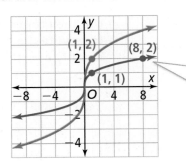

The function has either been vertically stretched by a factor of 2 or horizontally compressed by a factor of 8.

Either transformation maps the initial graph to the same resulting graph.

Step 3 Identify the transformation.

The function g can be written as $g(x) = 2\sqrt[3]{x}$ or $g(x) = \sqrt[3]{8x}$.

Try It!   4. What radical function is represented in each graph below?

a.

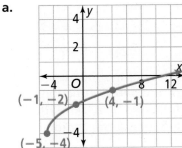

b.

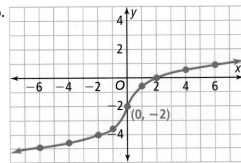

APPLICATION   **EXAMPLE 5**   Interpret a Radical Function Model

Looking out to the sea, the visibility in miles from a certain spot on a cliff can be calculated using the function $d(x) = \sqrt{1.5x}$, where x is the height in feet above sea level. Sasha walks through elevations ranging from 5 ft to 40 ft above sea level. What are the minimum and maximum distances that she can see?

USE STRUCTURE
Think about the shape of the radical function's graph. It is always increasing or decreasing, so the maximum and minimum points will always be the endpoints of the context's domain. © MP.7

Step 1 Graph the function over the given domain.

Step 2 Look for the minimum and maximum points on the graph. Notice they are the endpoints of the graph of the function along the given domain.

Step 3 Find the value of the function at the minimum and maximum value of the domain to determine the minimum and maximum distances that Sasha can see.

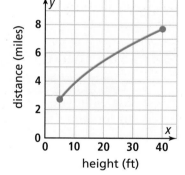

$$d(5) = \sqrt{(1.5)(5)} \approx 2.74$$
$$d(40) = \sqrt{(1.5)(40)} \approx 7.75$$

The minimum and maximum distances that Sasha can see are approximately 2.74 mi and 7.75 mi.

 Try It!   5. Use the same function as in Example 5. Suppose Sasha's brother walks through elevations ranging from 8 ft to 48 ft. What are the minimum and maximum distances that he can see?

🔍 CONCEPT SUMMARY Use Transformations to Graph Radical Functions

ALGEBRA Understand how the values of a radical function transform the graph of the parent function.

$$f(x) = a\sqrt[n]{x - h} + k$$

a determines a vertical stretch or compression.

h determines a horizontal translation.

k determines a vertical translation.

GRAPHS Understand the relationship between the graph of the parent function and the graph of the radical function.

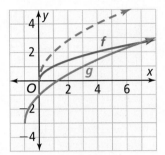

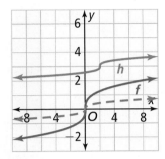

$f(x) = \sqrt{x}$ is the parent square root function.

$g(x) = 2\sqrt{x + 1} - 3$ is the result of a vertical stretch by a factor of 2, a translation 1 unit left, and a translation 3 units down from the parent function.

$f(x) = \sqrt[3]{x}$ is the parent cube root function.

$h(x) = \frac{1}{3}\sqrt[3]{x - 2} + 3$ is the result of a vertical compression by a factor of 3, a translation 2 units right, and a translation 3 units up from the parent function.

☑ Do You UNDERSTAND?

1. 🤔 **ESSENTIAL QUESTION** How can you use what you know about transformations of functions to graph radical functions?

2. **Error Analysis** Parker said the graph of the radical function $g(x) = -\sqrt{x + 2} - 1$ is a translation 2 units left and 1 unit down from the parent function $f(x) = \sqrt{x}$. Describe and correct the error. Ⓒ **MP.3**

3. **Reason** What effect does *a* have on the graph of $f(x) = a\sqrt{x}$? Ⓒ **MP.2**

Do You KNOW HOW?

Graph each function. Then identify its domain and range.

4. $f(x) = \sqrt{x - 2}$

5. $f(x) = \sqrt[3]{x + 2}$

6. $f(x) = \sqrt{x + 1} - 2$

7. $f(x) = \sqrt[3]{x - 3} + 2$

8. $f(x) = 3\sqrt{x - 5}$

9. $f(x) = \frac{1}{2}\sqrt[3]{x} + 1$

10. The volume of a cube is a function of the cube's side length. The function can be written as $V(s) = s^3$, where *s* is the length of the cube's edge and *V* is the volume.

   a. Express a cube's edge length as a function of its volume, *s(V)*.

   b. Graph *V(s)* and *s(V)*. What are the domain and range of the functions? Explain.

UNDERSTAND

11. Communicate Precisely What is the domain and range of the radical function $h(x) = \sqrt{x + a} + b$? Is the function increasing or decreasing? Explain. Ⓒ **MP.6**

12. Model with Mathematics The graph of a cube root function has a horizontal translation that is three times the vertical translation. The vertical translation is negative. Ⓒ **MP.4**

    a. Write a function, g, that has these attributes.

    b. Graph your function and the parent function, f, to verify it is correct.

13. Error Analysis Helena is trying to write a radical function that is represented by the graph below. Describe and correct the error Helena made in writing the radical function. Ⓒ **MP.3**

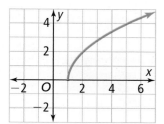

$$f(x) = \sqrt{x - 1} \quad \textbf{✗}$$

14. Higher Order Thinking Rewrite the radical function $g(x) = \sqrt[3]{8x + 64} - 3$ to identify the transformations from the parent graph of $f(x) = \sqrt[3]{x}$. Explain how you rewrote the radical function.

15. Reason The parent function $f(x) = \sqrt{x}$ and a transformation of the parent function, $g(x)$, are reflections of each other over the x-axis. Write the function $g(x)$. Ⓒ **MP.2**

16. Mathematical Connections How do the transformations of a radical function compare to the transformations of an absolute value function?

PRACTICE

Graph the following functions. State the domain and range. Is the function increasing or decreasing? SEE EXAMPLE 1

17. $f(x) = \sqrt{x} + 2$ **18.** $f(x) = \sqrt[3]{x} - 4$

19. $f(x) = \sqrt[3]{x - 8}$ **20.** $f(x) = \sqrt{x + 6}$

21. Graph $f(x) = \sqrt[3]{x}$ and $g(x) = 3\sqrt[3]{x + 9} - 8$. What transformations of the graph of f produce the graph of g? What effect do the transformations have on the domain and range of g?
SEE EXAMPLE 2

Rewrite the following radical functions to identify their transformations from the parent graph $f(x) = \sqrt{x}$. SEE EXAMPLE 3

22. $f(x) = \sqrt{16x}$ **23.** $f(x) = \sqrt{25x + 75}$

24. $f(x) = \sqrt{9x - 45}$ **25.** $f(x) = \sqrt{4x - 24} - 6$

What radical function is represented in each graph? SEE EXAMPLE 4

26.

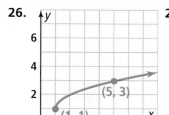

27.

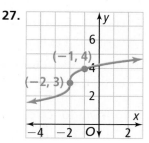

28. The hull speed, y, measured in knots, of a sailboat can be estimated by the function $y = 1.34\sqrt{x}$, where x is the waterline length of the sailboat, in feet. Luis works at a sailboat rental business with boats that have a waterline length between 25 ft and 64 ft. SEE EXAMPLE 5

    a. Graph the relationship between the hull speed of a sailboat and its waterline length.

    b. What are the minimum and maximum hull speeds of the sailboats at the rental business?

PRACTICE & PROBLEM SOLVING

APPLY

29. Make Sense and Persevere The radius of a sphere can be found using the function $r = \sqrt[3]{\frac{3V}{4\pi}}$, where V is the volume of the sphere. Heather filled a basketball with 448.92 in.^{3} of air. © MP.1

$V = 448.92$ in.^{3}

a. Graph the function.

b. Identify the domain and range of the graph.

c. Do the domain and range make sense in this context? Explain.

d. What is the length of the radius of the basketball?

30. A formula for calculating the distance to the horizon is $d = \sqrt{\frac{h}{0.57}}$, where d is the distance to the horizon, in miles, and h is the height above the surface, in feet.

Horizon 5 mi

a. Graph the function.

b. **Reason** What is your height above the surface if you can see a distance of 5 mi to the horizon? © MP.2

ASSESSMENT PRACTICE

31. Choose yes or no to tell whether the function is an odd function.

a. $f(x) = 5\sqrt{x - 10} - 12$ ○ Yes ○ No

b. $f(x) = \frac{1}{4}\sqrt[3]{x}$ ○ Yes ○ No

c. $f(x) = \frac{1}{2}\sqrt{x + 8} - 1$ ○ Yes ○ No

d. $f(x) = 6\sqrt[3]{x}$ ○ Yes ○ No

e. $f(x) = 9\sqrt[3]{x - 7} + 8$ ○ Yes ○ No

32. SAT/ACT Which function has a graph with domain $x \geq -1$ and range $y \geq -2$?

Ⓐ $f(x) = \sqrt{x - 1} + 2$ Ⓑ $f(x) = \sqrt[3]{x + 1} - 2$

Ⓒ $f(x) = \sqrt[3]{x - 1} + 2$ Ⓓ $f(x) = \sqrt{x + 1} - 2$

33. Performance Task The table shows the domain and range of the function $f(x) = \sqrt[n]{x}$ for different values of n, where x is a positive real number.

n	Domain of $f(x) = \sqrt[n]{x}$	Range of $f(x) = \sqrt[n]{x}$
1	All real numbers	All real numbers
2	$x \geq 0$	$y \geq 0$
3	All real numbers	All real numbers
4		
5		
6		
7		
8		

Part A Identify the domain and range of the function $f(x) = \sqrt[n]{x}$ when $n = 4, 5, 6, 7,$ and 8.

Part B Make a conjecture about the values of n that gives a domain and range of all real numbers.

Part C Make a conjecture about the values of n that gives a domain of $x \geq 0$ and a range of $y \geq 0$.

5-4

Solving Radical Equations

SavvasRealize.com

  Activity  Assess

👆 EXPLORE & REASON

A. Solve $3(a + 1)^2 + 2 = 11$. Use at least two different methods.

B. Try each of the methods you used in part (a) to solve $3\sqrt{(a + 1)} + 2 = 11$.

C. Generalize Which of the methods is better suited for solving an equation with a radical? What problems arise when using the other method? © **MP.8**

I CAN...solve radical equations and inequalities.

VOCABULARY
• extraneous solution

LOOK FOR RELATIONSHIPS
When you square both sides of an equation, you are multiplying each side by the same quantity. The expression for the quantity differs, but $\sqrt{x + 5}$ and 4 are equal. © **MP.7**

❓ ESSENTIAL QUESTION

How can you solve equations that include radicals or rational exponents?

👆 EXAMPLE 1 · Solve an Equation With One Radical

A. Solve the radical equation $\sqrt{x + 5} - 1 = 3$.

To solve this equation, you can isolate the radical. Then you can square both sides of the equation to eliminate the radical and solve for x.

$\sqrt{x + 5} - 1 = 3$ ·········· Write the original equation.

$\sqrt{x + 5} = 4$ ·········· Add 1 to each side.

$(\sqrt{x + 5})^2 = 4^2$ ·········· Square both sides to eliminate the radical.

$x + 5 = 16$ ·········· Simplify.

$x = 11$ ·········· Subtract 5 from each side.

So the solution to the radical equation is $x = 11$.

Check your answer by substituting 11 for x in the original equation:
$\sqrt{11 + 5} - 1 = \sqrt{16} - 1 = 4 - 1 = 3$ ✓
You can also check by graphing
$y = \sqrt{x + 5} - 1$ and $y = 3$ on the same coordinate axes. The graphs of the equations intersect at (11, 3).

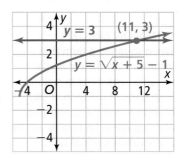

B. Solve the radical equation $\sqrt[3]{x} + 2 = 4$.

$\sqrt[3]{x} + 2 = 4$ ·········· Write the original equation.

$\sqrt[3]{x} = 2$ ·········· Subtract 2 from each side to isolate the radical.

$(\sqrt[3]{x})^3 = 2^3$ ·········· Cube both sides to eliminate the cube root.

$x = 8$ ·········· Simplify.

So the solution to the radical equation is $x = 8$.

Check your answer by substituting 8 for x in the original equation:
$\sqrt[3]{8} + 2 = 2 + 2 = 4$ ✓

☑ Try It! 1. Solve each radical equation.

a. $\sqrt{x - 2} + 3 = 5$

b. $\sqrt[3]{x - 1} = 2$

LESSON 5-4 Solving Radical Equations **263**

 **EXAMPLE 4** **Solve Equations With Rational Exponents**

A. What are the solutions to the equation $(x^2 + 5x + 5)^{\frac{5}{2}} = 1$?

APPLICATION → **EXAMPLE 6** **Solve a Radical Inequality**

The body surface area (BSA) of a human being is used to determine doses of medication. The formula for finding BSA is $BSA = \sqrt{\dfrac{H \cdot M}{3,600}}$, where H is the height in centimeters and M is the mass in kilograms.

A doctor calculates a particular dose of medicine for a patient whose BSA is less than 1.9. If the patient is 160 cm tall, what must the mass of the person be for the dose to be appropriate?

BSA < 1.9
Height = 160cm

LOOK FOR RELATIONSHIPS
Recall that you solve an inequality just as you do an equation, using an inequality sign instead of an equal sign. © **MP.7**

$$BSA = \sqrt{\dfrac{H \cdot M}{3,600}}$$ .... Write the BSA model.

$$\sqrt{\dfrac{160 \cdot M}{3,600}} < 1.9$$ .... Write an inequality to represent the situation. Substitute 160 for H.

$$\left(\sqrt{\dfrac{160 \cdot M}{3,600}}\right)^2 < (1.9)^2$$ .... Square both sides to remove the radical sign.

$$\dfrac{160 \cdot M}{3,600} < 3.61$$ .... Simplify.

$$160 \cdot M < 12,996$$ .... Multiply both sides by 3,600.

$$M < 81.225$$ .... Divide both sides by 160.

The mass of the individual must be less than 81.225 kg for the dose to be appropriate.

The graph of the inequality $y < \sqrt{\dfrac{160 \cdot M}{3,600}}$ shows that when the BSA is 1.9, the mass of the individual must be less than approximately 81 kg.

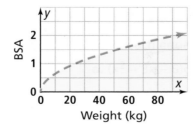

Weight (kg)

 Try It! **6.** A doctor calculates that a particular dose of medicine is appropriate for an individual whose BSA is less than 1.8. If the mass of the individual is 75 kg, how many cm tall can he or she be for the dose to be appropriate?

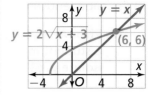

CONCEPT SUMMARY Solving Radical Equations

	WORDS	ALGEBRA	GRAPH
Step 1	Isolate the radical term.	$2\sqrt{x+3} - x = 0$ $2\sqrt{x+3} = x$	
Step 2	Square both sides to remove the radical.	$\left(2\sqrt{x+3}\right)^2 = (x)^2$	
Step 3	Solve the equation.	$4(x+3) = x^2$ $x^2 - 4x - 12 = 0$ $(x-6)(x+2) = 0$ $x = 6$ or $x = -2$	
Step 4	Eliminate extraneous solutions.	$2\sqrt{6+3} - 6 \overset{?}{=} 0 \qquad 2\sqrt{-2+3} - (-2) \overset{?}{=} 0$ $2\sqrt{9} \overset{?}{=} 6 \qquad\qquad 2\sqrt{1} \overset{?}{=} -2$ $6 \overset{?}{=} 6 \qquad\qquad\quad 2 \overset{?}{=} -2$ $6 = 6 \checkmark \qquad\qquad 2 \neq -2$ ✗	

Graph in Step 3–4: shows $y = x$, $y = 2\sqrt{x+3}$, point $(6, 6)$, axes from -4 to 8.

Do You UNDERSTAND?

1. **ESSENTIAL QUESTION** How can you solve equations that include radicals or rational exponents?

2. **Construct Arguments** How can you use a graph to show that the solution to $\sqrt[3]{84x + 8} = 8$ is 6? **Ⓒ MP.3**

3. **Vocabulary** Why does solving a radical equation sometimes result in an extraneous solution?

4. **Error Analysis** Neil said that -3 and 6 are the solutions to $\sqrt{3x + 18} = x$. What error did Neil make? **Ⓒ MP.3**

5. **Communicate Precisely** Describe how you would solve the equation $x^{\frac{2}{3}} = n$. How is this solution method to be interpreted if the equation had been written in radical form instead? **Ⓒ MP.6**

Do You KNOW HOW?

Solve for x.

6. $3\sqrt{x + 22} = 21$

7. $\sqrt[3]{5x} = 25$

In 8 and 9, find the extraneous solution.

8. $\sqrt{8x + 9} = x$

9. $x = \sqrt{24 - 2x}$

10. Rewrite the equation $y = \sqrt{\dfrac{x - 48}{6}}$ to isolate x.

11. Use a graph to find the solution to the equation $9 = \sqrt{3x + 11}$.

Solve each equation.

12. $(3x + 2)^{\frac{2}{5}} = 4$

13. $\sqrt{2x - 5} - \sqrt{x - 3} = 1$

14. $\sqrt{x + 2} + \sqrt{3x + 4} = 2$

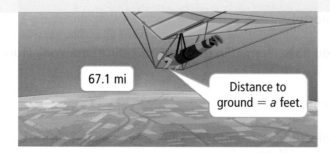

67.1 mi

Distance to ground = *a* feet.

Part A Rewrite the equation to solve for mass.

Part B The escape velocity of Earth is 11,200 m/s and its radius is 6,371,000 m. The gravitational constant is 6.67×10^{-11}. What is Earth's mass in kilograms?

PRACTICE & PROBLEM SOLVING

UNDERSTAND

15. Generalize Explain how to identify an extraneous solution for an equation containing a radical expression. @ **MP.8**

16. Look for Relationships Write a radical equation that relates a square's perimeter to its area. Explain your reasoning. Use *s* to represent the side length of the square.

PRACTICE

Solve each radical equation. SEE EXAMPLE 1

21. $\sqrt[3]{x} + 8 = 13$

22. $\sqrt{4x} = 11$

23. $\sqrt{75 + x} - 6 = 14$

24. $25 - \sqrt[4]{x} = 22$

Solve for *y*. SEE EXAMPLE 2

25. $y - 3(\sqrt[3]{15 + y})$

26. $y = \sqrt{2y}$

EXAMPLE 1 CONTINUED

B. What is the difference of $f(x) = 3x + 4$ and $g(x) = x^2 - 5x + 2$?

PRACTICE & PROBLEM SOLVING

EXAMPLE 1 CONTINUED

✓ **Try It!** **1.** Identify the inverse relation. Is it a function?

x	−1	0	1	2	3	4
y	9	7	5	3	1	−1

▶ **EXAMPLE 2** **Find an Equation of an Inverse Relation**

Let $f(x) = x^2$.

A. How can you represent the inverse relation of f algebraically?

$$f(x) = x^2 \rightarrow y = x^2$$

$$x = y^2 \quad \text{Switch the roles of } x \text{ and } y.$$

$$y = \pm\sqrt{x} \quad \text{Solve for } y.$$

The inverse of f can be represented algebraically by the equation $y = \pm\sqrt{x}$.

B. How are the graphs of $y = x^2$ and $y = \pm\sqrt{x}$ related?

LOOK FOR RELATIONSHIPS
The domain of a relation becomes the range of its inverse, and the range of a relation becomes the domain of its inverse. @ **MP.7**

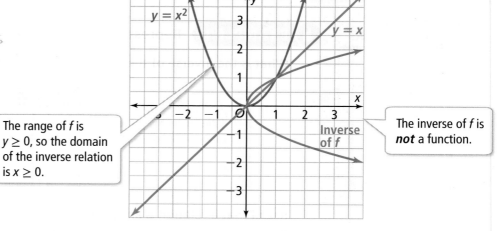

The range of f is $y \geq 0$, so the domain of the inverse relation is $x \geq 0$.

$y = x^2$

$y = x$

Inverse of f

The inverse of f is **not** a function.

The graph of the inverse of f is the reflection of the graph of $y = x^2$ across the line $y = x$.

✓ **Try It!** **2.** Let $f(x) = 2x + 1$.

    a. Write an equation to represent the inverse of f.

    b. How can you use the graph of f to determine if the inverse of f is a function? Explain your answer.

👆 **EXAMPLE 3**   **Restrict a Domain to Produce an Inverse Function**

Consider again the function $f(x) = x^2$. Under what domain will the inverse relation be a function?

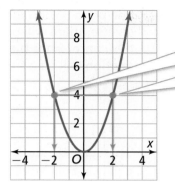

The inverse relation is not a function since it would contain the inverse of these two points, $(4, -2)$ and $(4, 2)$.

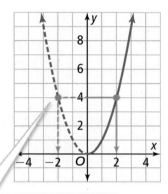

For the inverse to be a function, all of the duplicate y-values would have to be eliminated from the original function.

Restrict the domain of f to be $x \geq 0$.

If a function has two x-values for the same y-value, its inverse will not be a function. You can restrict the domain in many different ways to create a function that will have an inverse that is a function.

STUDY TIP
There is more than one way to restrict the domain of a function. The context of a situation often influences the choice of domain.

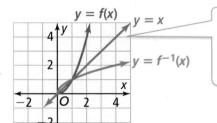

The graph of the inverse function of f is the reflection of the graph of $f(x)$ across the line $y = x$.

The inverse relation of $f(x) = x^2$ is $y = \pm \sqrt{x}$. If the domain of $f(x) = x^2$ is restricted to $x \geq 0$, then the inverse is the function defined as $f^{-1}(x) = \sqrt{x}$.

✓ **Try It!**   **3.** Find the inverse of each function by identifying an appropriate restriction of its domain.

a. $f(x) = x^2 + 8x + 16$

b. $f(x) = x^2 - 9$

A. Find an equation of the inverse function of $f(x) = \sqrt{x-2}$.

The graph shows that no horizontal line intersects the graph in more than one point. When the graph is reflected over the line $y = x$ to produce an inverse, there will be no vertical line that will intersect the graph more than once. Since the inverse will pass the vertical line test, the inverse relation will be a function.

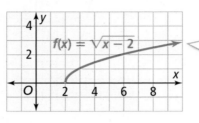

Use the graph to identify the domain and range of f and f^{-1}.

	domain	range
f	$x \geq 2$	$y \geq 0$
f^{-1}	$x \geq 0$	$y \geq 2$

$y = \sqrt{x-2}$

$x = \sqrt{y-2}$ ◁ Switch the roles of x and y and solve for y.

$x^2 = y - 2$

$x^2 + 2 = y$

COMMON ERROR
Don't apply f^{-1} notation too quickly. This notation is only used when the inverse of f is a function.

So the inverse of $f(x) = \sqrt{x-2}$ is a function, $f^{-1}(x) = x^2 + 2$, $x \geq 0$. You can verify this on a graph.

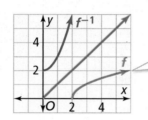

The graphs of f and f^{-1} are both functions and are reflections over the line $y = x$.

B. Find an equation of the inverse function of $f(x) = -\sqrt[3]{4x}$.

The graph shows that no horizontal line intersects the graph in more than one point, so the inverse relation will be a function.

$y = -\sqrt[3]{4x}$

$x = -\sqrt[3]{4y}$

$x^3 = -4y$

$\dfrac{-x^3}{4} = y$

Since the inverse is a function, $f^{-1}(x) = \dfrac{-x^3}{4}$ for all real x. You can verify this on a graph.

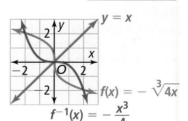

$f(x) = -\sqrt[3]{4x}$

$f^{-1}(x) = -\dfrac{x^3}{4}$

 Try It! **4.** Let $f(x) = 2 - \sqrt[3]{x+1}$.

    a. Sketch the graph of f.

    b. Verify that the inverse will be a function and write an equation for $f^{-1}(x)$.

👆 **EXAMPLE 5** **Use Composition to Verify Inverse Functions**

A. What is the inverse of $f(x) = 2x + 5$, and how can you verify this?

$y = 2x + 5 \rightarrow x = 2y + 5$ .... Switch x and y.

$2y = x - 5$ .... Isolate y-term.

$y = \frac{1}{2}x - \frac{5}{2}$ .... Divide by 2.

So the inverse of f is $g(x) = \frac{1}{2}x - \frac{5}{2}$. You can verify this with function composition: To be inverse functions, $(f \circ g)(x) = x$ and $(g \circ f)(x) = x$.

LOOK FOR RELATIONSHIPS
Because a function's inverse reverses the action of the original function, the composition of the two (in either order) simplifies to the identity function. Ⓒ **MP.7**

$(f \circ g)(x) = f(g(x))$

$= 2(g(x)) + 5$

$= 2\left(\frac{1}{2}x - \frac{5}{2}\right) + 5$

$= x - 5 + 5$

$= x$

$(g \circ f)(x) = g(f(x))$

$= \frac{1}{2}(f(x)) - \frac{5}{2}$

$= \frac{1}{2}(2x + 5) - \frac{5}{2}$

$= x + \frac{5}{2} - \frac{5}{2}$

$= x$

Since $(f \circ g)(x) = x$ and $(g \circ f)(x) = x$, the functions $f(x) = 2x + 5$ and $g(x) = \frac{1}{2}x - \frac{5}{2}$ are inverses.

You can also verify $g(x)$ is the inverse of $f(x)$ by graphing.

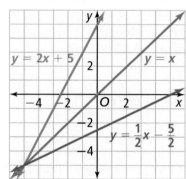

The graph of $y = \frac{1}{2}x - \frac{5}{2}$ is a reflection of the graph of $y = 2x + 5$ across the line $y = x$.

B. Are the two functions $f(x) = x^2 + 5$ and $g(x) = \sqrt{x} - 5$ inverses of each other?

To be inverse functions, $(f \circ g)(x) = x$ and $(g \circ f)(x) = x$.

$(f \circ g)(x) = f(g(x))$

$= (g(x))^2 + 5$

$= (\sqrt{x} - 5)^2 + 5$

$= x - 10\sqrt{x} + 25 + 5$

$= x - 10\sqrt{x} + 30$

$(g \circ f)(x) = g(f(x))$

$= \sqrt{f(x)} - 5$

$= \sqrt{x^2 + 5} - 5$

Since neither $(f \circ g)(x)$ nor $(g \circ f)(x)$ simplify to the identity function, the functions are not inverses.

☑ **Try It!** 5. Use composition to determine whether f and g are inverse functions.

a. $f(x) = \frac{1}{4}x + 7$, $g(x) = 4x - 7$

b. $f(x) = \sqrt[3]{x - 1}$, $g(x) = x^3 + 1$

 **EXAMPLE 6** Rewrite a Formula

A sculpture artist is making an ice sculpture of Earth for a display. He created a mold that can hold 4.5 L of ice. What will the radius of the ice sculpture be if he fills the mold all of the way?

4.5 liters of ice

The volume of a sphere is calculated using the formula $V = \frac{4}{3}\pi r^3$.

Rewrite the formula to find the length of the radius.

$$\frac{4}{3}\pi r^3 = V$$

$$\pi r^3 = \frac{3}{4}V$$

$$r^3 = \frac{3}{4\pi}V$$

$$r = \sqrt[3]{\frac{3}{4\pi}V}$$

Since a liter is a measure of capacity, or volume, it can be expressed using cubic units of length. When you take the cube root of an expression involving volume in cubic units of length, the units of the result will be in the correct units to describe length. One liter is equivalent to 1,000 cm^3, so 4.5 L is equivalent to 4,500 cm^3.

$$r = \sqrt[3]{\frac{3}{4\pi}V}$$

$$= \sqrt[3]{\frac{3}{4\pi} \cdot 4{,}500 \text{ cm}^3}$$

Substitute 4,500 cm^3 for V.

$$\approx 10.2 \text{ cm}$$

MAKE SENSE AND PERSEVERE
If this seems smaller than expected, remember that this is the radius—the diameter of the ice sculpture mold is about 20.4 cm. Ⓒ **MP.1**

Rewriting the equation to show r in terms of V is similar to finding the inverse. In effect, you are exchanging the roles of the dependent and independent variables.

$$V = \frac{4}{3}\pi r^3 \qquad\qquad r = \sqrt[3]{\frac{3V}{4\pi}}$$

In the original equation, you can see how the value of V *depends* on the value of r.

In this form of the equation, you can see how the value of r can be determined by, and depends on, a given value of V.

The ice sculpture mold will have a radius of about 10 cm.

 Try It! 6. The manufacturer of a gift box designs a box with length and width each twice as long as its height. Find a formula that gives the height h of the box in terms of its volume V. Then give the length of the box if the volume is 640 cm^3.

TOPIC 5 Rational Exponents and Radical Functions

Go Online | SavvasRealize.com

CONCEPT SUMMARY Inverse Functions

To find the **inverse** of a function, exchange the roles of the independent and dependent variables.

TABLES Switch the columns.

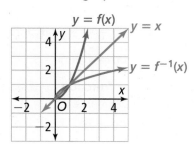

f	
x	y
0	2
1	4
2	6
3	8
4	10

f^{-1}	
x	y
2	0
4	1
6	2
8	3
10	4

ALGEBRA

Exchange the roles of the independent and dependent variables. Solve for the new dependent variable.

$$y = x + 9$$
$$x = y + 9$$
$$x - 9 = y$$
$$y = x - 9$$

GRAPHS

Reflect the graph across the line $y = x$.

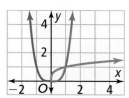

$y = f(x)$
$y = x$
$y = f^{-1}(x)$

If needed, **restrict the domain** of the original function to find an appropriate inverse for the function.

Restrict the domain of $y = x^4$ to $x \geq 0$.

Composition verifies inverses: $f(f^{-1}(x)) = x$ and $f^{-1}(f(x)) = x$.

Do You UNDERSTAND?

1. **ESSENTIAL QUESTION** How can you find the inverse of a function and verify the two functions are inverses?

2. **Error Analysis** Abi said the inverse of $f(x) = 3x + 1$ is $f^{-1}(x) = \frac{1}{3}x - 1$. Is she correct? Explain. © **MP.3**

3. **Construct Arguments** Is the inverse of a function always a function? Explain. © **MP.3**

Do You KNOW HOW?

Consider the function $f(x) = -\frac{1}{2}x + 5$.

4. Write an equation for the inverse of f.

5. Use composition to show that f and the equation you wrote are inverses.

6. Sketch a graph of f and its inverse.

7. How can you verify by the graph of f and its inverse that they are indeed inverses?

8. Is the inverse of f a function? Explain.

UNDERSTAND

9. **Reason** Explain how to find the range of the inverse of $f(x) = \sqrt{2x - 3}$ without finding $f^{-1}(x)$. Ⓒ **MP.2**

10. **Error Analysis** Describe and correct the error a student made in finding the inverse of the function $f(x) = x^2 - 4$. Ⓒ **MP.3**

$$f(x) = x^2 - 4$$
$$x = y^2 - 4$$
$$\sqrt{x} = \sqrt{y^2 - 4}$$
$$\sqrt{x} = y - 2$$
$$\sqrt{x} + 2 = y$$
$$f^{-1}(x) = \sqrt{x} + 2 \quad ✗$$

11. **Higher Order Thinking** What is the inverse operation of raising a number to the 4th power? How can you use the inverse operation of a number raised to the 4th power to find the inverse of the function $f(x) = x^4 - 1$? Is the inverse of f a function? Explain.

12. **Communicate Precisely** A function has the ordered pairs (1, 3), (7, 4), (8, 6), and (9, y). What restrictions are there on the value of y so that the inverse of the function is also a function? Explain. Ⓒ **MP.6**

13. **Construct Arguments** What is the inverse of the function $a(b) = \frac{1}{4}b^2$? Show how to use composition of functions to prove you found the correct inverse. Ⓒ **MP.3**

14. **Construct Arguments** A relation has one element in its domain and two elements in its range. Is the relation a function? Is the inverse of the relation a function? Explain. Ⓒ **MP.3**

15. **Mathematical Connections** Find the x- and y-intercepts of the function $y = 2x + 1$. What are the intercepts of the inverse function? How are the intercepts related?

PRACTICE

Identify the inverse relation. Is it a function?
SEE EXAMPLE 1

16.

x	−2	−1	0	1	2	3
y	9	3	−4	8	−6	3

17.

x	−2	1	0	1	2	3
y	−7	6	8	−1	3	7

Write an equation to represent the inverse of f. Sketch the graphs of f, $y = x$, and the inverse of f on the same coordinate axes. Is the inverse of f a function? SEE EXAMPLE 2

18. Let $f(x) = x + 3$.

19. Let $f(x) = 4x - 1$.

20. Let $f(x) = x^2 + 1$.

21. Let $f(x) = \sqrt{x + 5}$.

Find the inverse of the function by identifying an appropriate restriction of its domain. SEE EXAMPLE 3

22. $f(x) = x^2 + 4x + 4$

23. $f(x) = x^2 - 6x + 9$

24. $f(x) = x^2 - 2$

25. $f(x) = x^2 + 5$

Find an equation of the inverse function, and state the domain of the inverse. SEE EXAMPLE 4

26. $f(x) = 2x^2 - 5$

27. $f(x) = \sqrt{x + 6}$

28. $f(x) = 3x + 10$

29. $f(x) = \sqrt{x - 9}$

Use composition to determine whether f and g are inverse functions. SEE EXAMPLE 5

30. $f(x) = 2x - 9$, $g(x) = \frac{1}{2}x + 9$

31. $f(x) = \sqrt{\frac{x + 4}{3}}$, $g(x) = 3x^2 - 4$

32. A manager purchased cones for ice cream. Find a formula for the length of the radius, r, of a cone in terms of its volume, V. Then find the length of the radius of a cone if the volume is 290π cm^3 and the height is 15 cm. SEE EXAMPLE 6

V of cone = 290π cm³

APPLY

33. Model With Mathematics The formula for converting Celsius to Fahrenheit is $F = \frac{9}{5}C + 32$. Find the inverse formula, and use it to find the Celsius temperature when the Fahrenheit temperature is 59° F. © **MP.4**

34. Reason A DJ charges an hourly fee and an equipment setup fee. © **MP.2**

a. Write a function for the cost, C, of hiring a DJ for n hours.

b. Find the inverse of the cost function. What does the function represent?

c. If the DJ charged $550, for how many hours was she hired? Use the inverse function.

35. Reason A coffee can is in the shape of a cylinder. © **MP.2**

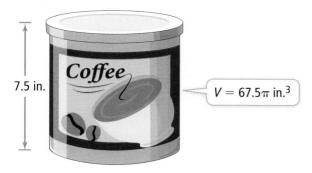

7.5 in.

$V = 67.5\pi$ in.^{3}

a. Find the formula that gives the radius of the coffee can r in terms of the volume V and height h.

b. Describe any restrictions on the formula.

c. What is the radius of a coffee can given the volume is 67.5π in.^{3} and the height is 7.5 in.?

© **ASSESSMENT PRACTICE**

36. Choose Yes or No to tell whether each function has an inverse that is a function.

	Yes	No
a. $f(x) = 2x - 9$	☐	☐
b. $f(x) = x^2 + 4$	☐	☐
c. $f(x) = x^3 - 6$	☐	☐
d. $f(x) = \sqrt{2x + 7}$	☐	☐
e. $f(x) = x^2 - 10x + 25$	☐	☐

37. SAT/ACT What is the range of the inverse of $f(x) = \sqrt{-ax + b} - c$, where a, b, and c are real numbers?

Ⓐ $y \geq \frac{a}{b}$

Ⓑ $y \leq \frac{b}{a}$

Ⓒ $y \geq -\frac{a}{b}$

Ⓓ $y \geq -\frac{b}{a}$

Ⓔ $y \geq c$

38. Performance Task The table shows several functions and some of the inverses of those functions. The table also shows whether some of the inverses are functions.

Function	Inverse	Is the inverse a function?
$f(x) = x$	$f^{-1}(x) = x$	yes
$g(x) = x^2$	$g^{-1}(x) = \pm\sqrt{x}$	no
$h(x) = x^3$	$h^{-1}(x) = \sqrt[3]{x}$	yes
$k(x) = x^4$		
$m(x) = x^5$		
$n(x) = x^6$		

Part A Determine the inverses of the remaining functions in the table.

Part B Determine if the inverses of the remaining functions in the table are functions.

Part C Make a conjecture about the power of a function if the inverse of that function is a function.

Topic Review

1. How are rational exponents and radical equations used to solve real-world problems?

Vocabulary Review

Choose the correct term to complete each sentence.

2. In the expression $\sqrt[n]{c}$, n is the _____.

3. In the expression $\sqrt[n]{c}$, c is the _____.

4. Radicals with the same index and the same radicand are _____.

5. A(n) _____ is a function defined by a radical expression.

6. A(n) _____ of a number c is x, such that $x^n = c$.

7. A(n) _____ is a potential solution that must be rejected because it does not satisfy the original equation.

8. When all nth roots of perfect nth powers have been simplified and no radicals remain in the denominator, an expression is in _____.

9. A(n) _____ results from the application of one function to the output of another function.

- composite function
- extraneous solution
- index
- inverse function
- like radicals
- *n*th root
- radical function
- radicand
- reduced radical form

Concepts & Skills Review

> **LESSON 5-1** | *n*th Roots, Radicals, and Rational Exponents

Quick Review

An **nth root** of a number c is x, such that $x^n = c$. The nth root of c can be represented as $\sqrt[n]{c}$, where n is the **index** and c is the **radicand**.

Example

Solve the equation $2x^4 = 162$.

$2x^4 = 162$ ········· Write the original equation.

$x^4 = 81$ ········· Divide both sides by 2.

$(x^4)^{\frac{1}{4}} = (81)^{\frac{1}{4}}$ ········· Raise both sides to the reciprocal of the exponent of x.

$x = \pm 3$ ········· Use the Power of a Power Property.

Practice & Problem Solving

What is the value of each expression? Round to the nearest hundredth, if necessary.

10. $\sqrt[4]{16^2}$

11. $-\sqrt[3]{25^6}$

Simplify each expression.

12. $\sqrt[3]{27x^{12}}$

13. $\sqrt[4]{16a^{24}b^8}$

Solve each equation.

14. $750 = 6y^3$

15. $1{,}280 = 5z^4$

16. **Communicate Precisely** Describe the relationship between a rational exponent and a root of a number x. ⓒ **MP.6**

17. **Make Sense and Persevere** The function $d(t) = 9.8t^2$ represents how far an object falls, in meters, in t seconds. How long would it take a rock to fall from a height of 300 m? Round to the nearest hundredth of a second. ⓒ **MP.1**

Properties of Exponents and Radicals

Quick Review

To simplify radical expressions, look for factors that are perfect nth power factors.

The Product Property of Radicals and Quotient Property of Radicals can also be used to rewrite radical expressions.

Product Property of Radicals $\sqrt[n]{ab} = \sqrt[n]{a} \cdot \sqrt[n]{b}$

Quotient Property of Radicals $\sqrt[n]{\frac{a}{b}} = \frac{\sqrt[n]{a}}{\sqrt[n]{b}}$

Example

What is $\sqrt[4]{64} \cdot \sqrt[4]{2}$ in reduced radical form?

$\sqrt[4]{64} \cdot \sqrt[4]{2}$ .... Write the original expression.

$\sqrt[4]{64 \cdot 2}$ .... Use the Product Property of Radicals.

$\sqrt[4]{128}$ .... Multiply.

$\sqrt[4]{16} \cdot \sqrt[4]{8}$ .... Rewrite using the Product Property of Radicals.

$2\sqrt[4]{8}$ .... Simplify.

Practice & Problem Solving

What is the reduced radical form of each expression?

18. $\sqrt{x^6 y^4} \cdot \sqrt{x^8 y^6}$

19. $\sqrt[3]{\dfrac{243 m^4}{3m}}$

20. $\sqrt[3]{5x^4} \cdot \sqrt[3]{x^2} \cdot \sqrt[3]{25x^3}$

21. $\sqrt{\dfrac{98 a^{10}}{2a^4}}$

Multiply.

22. $(\sqrt{n} - \sqrt{7})(\sqrt{n} + 3\sqrt{7})$

23. $(9x + \sqrt{2})(9x + \sqrt{2})$

24. $(5\sqrt{3} + 6)(5\sqrt{3} - 6)$

25. $\sqrt[3]{4}\,(6\sqrt[3]{2} - 1)$

How can you rewrite each expression so there are no radicals in the denominator?

26. $\dfrac{6}{1 + \sqrt{2}}$

27. $\dfrac{5}{2 - \sqrt{5}}$

28. $\dfrac{4 + \sqrt{6}}{3 - 3\sqrt{6}}$

29. $\dfrac{-9x}{\sqrt{x}}$

30. **Error Analysis** Describe and correct the error made in rewriting the radical expression. © **MP.3**
$$5\sqrt{18} - \sqrt{27} = 7\sqrt{2}$$

31. **Reason** A rectangular wall is $\sqrt{240}$ ft by $\sqrt{50}$ ft. You need to paint the wall twice to cover the area with two coats of paint. If each can of paint can cover 60 square feet, how many cans of paint will you need? © **MP.2**

Graphing Radical Functions

Quick Review

A **radical function** is a function defined by a radical expression. To determine transformations of a radical function, write the radical function in the form $h(x) = \sqrt[n]{a x - h} + k$ and compare it to the parent function.

Example

Graph $g(x) = 2\sqrt{x - 1} + 3$.

$g(x) = 2\sqrt{x - 1} + 3$ is a vertical stretch by a factor of 2, a horizontal shift 1 unit to the right, and a vertical shift 3 units up from the parent function $f(x) = \sqrt{x}$.

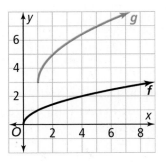

Practice & Problem Solving

Graph the following functions. What are the domain and range? Is the function increasing or decreasing?

32. $f(x) = \sqrt{x} - 1$

33. $f(x) = \sqrt[3]{x} + 2$

34. $f(x) = \frac{1}{2}\sqrt{x + 1}$

35. $f(x) = 2\sqrt[3]{x} - 1$

36. $f(x) = \sqrt[3]{x - 3}$

37. $f(x) = \sqrt{x + 4} - 2$

38. Communicate Precisely Explain how to rewrite the function $g(x) = \sqrt[3]{8x - 24} + 1$ to identify the transformations from the parent graph $f(x) = \sqrt[3]{x}$. © **MP.6**

39. Reason The speed s, in miles per hour, of a car when it starts to skid can be estimated using the formula $s = \sqrt{30 \cdot 0.5d}$, where d is the length of the skid marks, in feet. Graph the function. If a car's skid marks measure 40 ft in a zone where the speed limit is 25 mph, was the car speeding? Explain. © **MP.2**

Solving Radical Equations

Quick Review

To solve a radical equation, isolate the radical. Raise both sides of the equation to the appropriate power to eliminate the radical and solve for x. Then check for **extraneous solutions**. If the equation includes more than one radical, eliminate one radical at a time using a similar process.

Example

Solve the radical equation $\sqrt{6 - x} = x$.

$\sqrt{6 - x} = x$ ·········· Write the original equation.

$(\sqrt{6 - x})^2 = (x)^2$ ·········· Square both sides.

$6 - x = x^2$ ·········· Simplify.

$0 = x^2 + x - 6$ ·········· Write in standard form.

$0 = (x + 3)(x - 2)$ ·········· Factor.

$x = -3$ or $x = 2$ ·········· Use the Zero-Product Property.

Check the solutions to see if they both make the original equation true.

Practice & Problem Solving

Solve each radical equation. Check for extraneous solutions.

40. $\sqrt[3]{x} - 2 = 7$

41. $\sqrt{2x} = 12$

42. $\sqrt{25 + x} + 5 = 9$

43. $13 - \sqrt[4]{x} = 10$

44. $\sqrt{5x + 1} + 1 = x$

45. $\sqrt{6x - 20} - x = -6$

46. Construct Arguments Give an example of a radical equation that has no real solutions. Explain your reasoning. © **MP.3**

47. Make Sense and Persevere The formula $d = \frac{\sqrt{15w}}{3.14}$ gives the diameter d, in inches, of a rope needed to lift a weight of w, in tons. How much weight can be lifted with a rope that has a diameter of 4 in? © **MP.1**

Function Operations

Quick Review

You can add, subtract, multiply, or divide functions. When adding, subtracting, and multiplying functions, the domain is the intersection of the domains of the two functions. When dividing functions, the domain is the set of all real numbers for which both original functions and the new function are defined. You can also compose functions, by using one function as the input for another function. These are called **composite functions**.

Example

Let $f(x) = 5x$ and $g(x) = 3x - 1$. What is the rule for the composition $f \circ g$?

$f \circ g = f(g(x))$ ⋯⋯⋯ Apply the definition.

$= f(3x - 1)$ ⋯⋯⋯ Apply the rule for g.

$= 5(3x - 1)$ ⋯⋯⋯ Apply the rule for f.

$= 15x - 5$ ⋯⋯⋯ Distribute.

Practice & Problem Solving

Let $f(x) = -x + 6$ and $g(x) = 5x$. Identify the rule for the following functions.

48. $f + g$

49. $f - g$

50. $g(f(2))$

51. $f(g(-1))$

52. Reason For the functions f and g, what is the domain of $f \circ g$? $\frac{f}{g}$? $\frac{g}{f}$? ⓒ **MP.2**

53. Make Sense and Persevere A test has a bonus problem. If you get the bonus problem correct, you will receive 2 bonus points and your test score will increase by 3% of your score. Let $f(x) = x + 2$ and $g(x) = 1.03x$, where x is the test score without the bonus problem. Find $g(f(78))$. What does $g(f(78))$ represent? ⓒ **MP.1**

Inverse Relations and Functions

Quick Review

An **inverse relation** is formed when the roles of the independent and dependent variables are reversed. If an inverse relation of a function, f, is itself a function, it is called the **inverse function** of f, which is written $f^{-1}(x)$.

Example

What is the inverse of the relation represented in the table?

x	y
-2	0
-1	6
0	5
1	3
3	-1

Switch the values of x and y. Then reorder the ordered pairs.

x	y
-1	3
0	-2
3	1
5	0
6	-1

Practice & Problem Solving

Find an equation of the inverse function.

54. $f(x) = -4x^2 + 3$

55. $f(x) = \sqrt{x - 4}$

56. $f(x) = 9x + 5$

57. $f(x) = \sqrt{x + 7} - 1$

58. Error Analysis Jamie said the inverse of $f(x) = \sqrt{x - 9}$ is $f^{-1}(x) = (x + 9)^2$. Is Jamie correct? Explain. ⓒ **MP.3**

59. Make Sense and Persevere An electrician charges $50 for a house visit plus $40 per hour. Write a function for the cost C of an electrician charging for h hours. Find the inverse of the function. If the bill is $150, how long did the electrician work? ⓒ **MP.1**

? TOPIC ESSENTIAL QUESTION

How do you use exponential and logarithmic functions to model situations and solve problems?

Topic Overview

Topic Vocabulary

- Change of Base Formula
- common logarithm
- compound interest
- continuously compounded interest
- decay factor
- exponential equation
- exponential function
- exponential decay function
- exponential growth function
- growth factor
- logarithm
- logarithmic equation
- logarithmic function
- natural base e
- natural logarithm

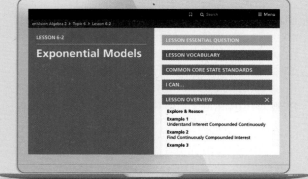

Digital Experience

 INTERACTIVE STUDENT EDITION Access online or offline.

 ACTIVITIES Complete *Explore & Reason, Model & Discuss,* and *Critique & Explain* activities. Interact with Examples and Try Its.

 ANIMATION View and interact with real-world applications.

 PRACTICE Practice what you've learned.

 Go online | SavvasRealize.com

▶ The Crazy Conditioning

Like all sports, soccer requires its players to be well trained. That is why players often have to run sprints in practice.

To make sprint drills more interesting, many coaches set up competitions. Coaches might split the players into teams and have them run relay races against each other. Or they might have the players sprint around cones and over barriers. What other ways would make doing sprints more fun? Think about this during the Mathematical Modeling in 3 Acts lesson.

TOPIC 6

VIDEOS Watch clips to support *Mathematical Modeling in 3 Acts Lessons* and **enVision™** *STEM Projects.*

CONCEPT SUMMARY Review key lesson content through multiple representations.

ASSESSMENT Show what you've learned.

GLOSSARY Read and listen to English and Spanish definitions.

TUTORIALS Get help from *Virtual Nerd*, right when you need it.

MATH TOOLS Explore math with digital tools and manipulatives.

Video

enVision™ STEM

Did You Know?

While you might expect the digits 1 through 9 to lead off the numbers in a data set with equal frequency, Benford's Law shows that they do not. **Benford's Law** states that, in real-world data, the leading digit is 1 more than 30% of the time, while the leading digit is 9 less than 5% of the time.

Data Sets That Follow Benford's Law

| Bacterial growth | Expansion of 2^n | Price × Quantity |

Data Sets That Do Not Follow Benford's Law

000-55-5555

| Price | Quantity | Zip Codes | Social Security numbers |

Bacteria (plural of bacterium) exist in soil, water, plants, glaciers, hot springs, and the oceans. Bacteria grow by duplicating themselves, so a population grows by doubling. In a laboratory, a population can double at regular intervals. These intervals vary from about 12 minutes to as much as 24 hours.

▶ Your Task: Analyze Elections

You and your classmates will use Benford's law to analyze election results and determine which, if any, may be fraudulent.

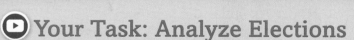 Go Online | SavvasRealize.com

6-1

Key Features of Exponential Functions

SavvasRealize.com

I CAN... recognize the key features of exponential functions.

VOCABULARY
- decay factor
- exponential decay function
- exponential function
- exponential growth function
- growth factor

Common Core State Standards HSF.IF.B.4, HSF.IF.B.5, HSF.IF.C.7.E, HSF.IF.C.9, HSF.BF.B.3, HSF.LE.A.2, HSF.LE.B.5, MP.2, MP.4, MP.7

  Activity Assess

✋ EXPLORE & REASON

Margaret investigates three functions: $y = 3x$, $y = x^3$, and $y = 3^x$. She is interested in the differences and ratios between consecutive y-values. Here is the table she started for $y = 3x$.

Investigating $y = 3x$			
x	y	Difference between y-values	Ratio between y-values
1	3		
2	6	$6 - 3 = 3$	$\frac{6}{3} = 2$
3	9	$9 - 6 = 3$	$\frac{9}{6} = 1.5$
4	12	$12 - 9 = 3$	$\frac{12}{9} \approx 1.33$

A. Create tables like Margaret's for all three functions and fill in more rows.

B. Which functions have a constant difference between consecutive y-values? Constant ratio?

C. **Use Structure** Which of these three functions will have y-values that increase the fastest as x increases? Why? ⓒ **MP.7**

❓ ESSENTIAL QUESTION

How do graphs and equations reveal key features of exponential growth and decay functions?

✋ EXAMPLE 1   Identify Key Features of Exponential Functions

What are the key features of each function? Include domain, range, intercepts, asymptotes, and end behavior.

An **exponential function** is any function of the form $y = a \cdot b^x$ where a and b are constants with $a \neq 0$, and $b > 0$, $b \neq 1$.

A. $f(x) = 2^x$

STUDY TIP
Recall your investigation of the ratios of consecutive y-values in the Explore & Reason activity. That ratio, which was 3 for the function $y = 3^x$, is equal to the value of b in the equation $y = a \cdot b^x$.

Graphing $y = a \cdot b^x$	
x	$f(x) = 2^x$
-2	0.25
-1	0.5
0	1
1	2
2	4

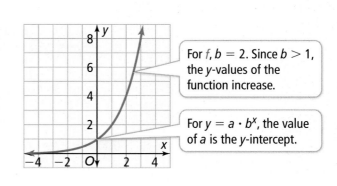

For f, $b = 2$. Since $b > 1$, the y-values of the function increase.

For $y = a \cdot b^x$, the value of a is the y-intercept.

Domain: all real numbers
Range: $\{y \mid y > 0\}$
y-intercept: 1;

Asymptote: x-axis
End Behavior:
As $x \to -\infty$, $y \to 0$. As $x \to \infty$, $y \to \infty$.

CONTINUED ON THE NEXT PAGE

EXAMPLE 1 CONTINUED

B. $g(x) = 5\left(\frac{1}{2}\right)^x$

Graphing $y = a \cdot b^x$	
x	$g(x) = 5\left(\frac{1}{2}\right)^x$
-2	20
-1	10
0	5
1	2.5
2	1.25

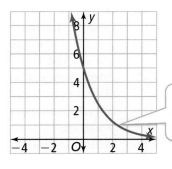

For g, $b = \frac{1}{2}$. Since $b < 1$, the y-values of the function decrease.

Domain: all real numbers   **Asymptote:** x-axis
Range: $\{y \mid y > 0\}$ **End Behavior:** As $x \to -\infty$, $y \to \infty$.
y-intercept: 5;   As $x \to \infty$, $y \to 0$.

 Try It!   **1.** Graph $f(x) = 4(0.5)^x$. What are the domain, range, intercepts, asymptote, and the end behavior for this function?

EXAMPLE 2   **Graph Transformations of Exponential Functions**

Graph each function. Describe the graph in terms of transformations of the parent function $f(x) = 3^x$. How do the asymptote and intercept of the given function compare to the asymptote and intercept of the parent function?

A. $g(x) = -3^x$

When the sign of a changes, the function is reflected across the x-axis.

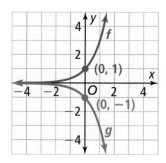

B. $h(x) = 3^x - 4$

When adding a constant k, the function shifts vertically by k units.

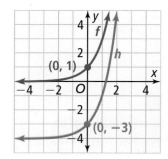

COMMON ERROR
You may confuse reflection across the axes. Recall that if the y-value is multiplied by -1 (as in this case, with $g(x) = -3^x$), the reflection is across the x-axis. Each y-value is replaced by its opposite.

$g(x) = -3^x = -f(x)$

The intercept changes from a to $-a$.

The asymptote of the function does not change. It is still the x-axis.

$h(x) = 3^x - 4 = f(x) - 4$

The intercept changes from 1 to $1 + K$.

The asymptote of the function also changes. It is $y = k$ or $y = -4$.

 Try It!   **2.** How do the asymptote and intercept of the given function compare to the asymptote and intercept of the function $f(x) = 5^x$?

  a. $g(x) = 5^{x+3}$ **b.** $h(x) = 5^{-x}$

CONCEPTUAL
UNDERSTANDING   👆 **EXAMPLE 3** ▸ **Model with Exponential Functions**

The population of a large city was about 4.6 million in the year 2010 and grew at a rate of 1.3% for the next four years.

A. What exponential function models the population of the city over that 4-year period?

Compute the population for the first few years to look for a pattern.

USE STRUCTURE
Exponential functions of the form $y = a \cdot b^x$ involve repeated multiplication by the factor b. To understand how to model population with an exponential function, look for repeated multiplication in your computations. ©️ **MP.7**

t (years since 2010)   *p* (population in millions)

In 2011, there are 4.6 million people, and another 1.3% of 4.6 million are added.

0 — 4.6

1 — $4.6 + 4.6(0.013) = 4.6(1.013)$

The process repeats each year. The 1 in 1.013 represents the current population and the 0.013 represents the yearly increase.

2 — $4.6(1.013)(1.013) = 4.6(1.013)^2$

3 — $4.6(1.013)^3$

4 — $4.6(1.013)^4$

The exponent is the number of years since 2010.

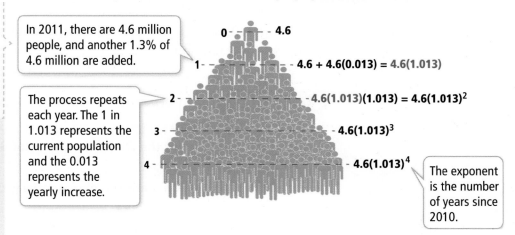

The population can be modeled by the exponential function:

| population after *t* years | population in 2010 | growth factor | years since 2010 |

$$P = 4.6(1.013)^t$$

B. If the population continues to grow at the same rate, what will the population be in 2040?

To find the population in 2040, solve the equation for $t = 30$:

$$P = 4.6(1.013)^{30} \approx 6.78.$$

In 2040, the population will be about 6.78 million.

☑️ **Try It!**   **3.** A factory purchased a 3D printer in 2010. The value of the printer is modeled by the function $f(x) = 30(0.93)^x$, where x is the number of years since 2010.

   a. What is the value of the printer after 10 years?

   b. Does the printer lose more of its value in the first 10 years or in the second 10 years after it was purchased?

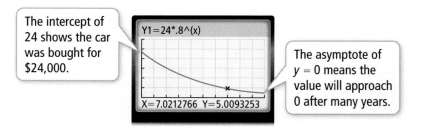

CONCEPT Exponential Growth and Decay Models

Exponential growth and **exponential decay** functions model quantities that increase or decrease by a fixed percent during each time period. Given an initial amount a and the rate of increase or decrease r, the amount $A(t)$ after t time periods is given by:

Exponential Growth Model

$$A(t) = a(1 + r)^t$$
$$a > 0, b > 1, b = 1 + r$$

Exponential Decay Model

$$A(t) = a(1 - r)^t$$
$$a > 0, 0 < b < 1, b = 1 - r$$

The **growth or decay factor** is equal to b, and is the ratio between two consecutive y-values.

EXAMPLE 4   Interpret an Exponential Function

A car was purchased for \$24,000. The function $y = 24 \cdot 0.8^x$ can be used to model the value of the car (in thousands of dollars) x years after it was purchased.

A. Does the function represent exponential growth or decay?

$$y = 24 \cdot 0.8^x$$

$b = 0.8$, so $b < 1$ and the function represents exponential decay.

B. What is the rate of decay for this function? What does it mean?

$$b = 1 - r$$
$$0.8 = 1 - r$$
$$r = 0.2$$

The rate of decay is 0.2, or 20%. This means that the value of the car decreases by 20% each year.

C. Graph the function on a reasonable domain. What do the y-intercept and asymptote represent? When will the value of the car be about \$5,000?

The intercept of 24 shows the car was bought for \$24,000.

Y1=24*.8^(x)

X=7.0212766 Y=5.0093253

The asymptote of $y = 0$ means the value will approach 0 after many years.

Find the value of x when $y = 5$.

The graph (approximately) passes through the point (7, 5). This means that the value of the car will be about \$5,000 after 7 years.

CONTINUED ON THE NEXT PAGE

EXAMPLE 4 CONTINUED

 Try It! **4.** Two-hundred twenty hawks were released into a region on January 2, 2016. The function $f(x) = 220(1.05)^x$ can be used to model the number of hawks in the region x years after 2016.

  a. Is the population increasing or decreasing? Explain.

  b. In what year will the number of hawks reach 280?

APPLICATION  **EXAMPLE 5** **Compare Two Exponential Functions**

A museum purchased a painting and a sculpture in the same year. Their changing values are modeled as shown. Find the average rate of change of the value of each art work over the 5-year period. Which art work's value is increasing more quickly?

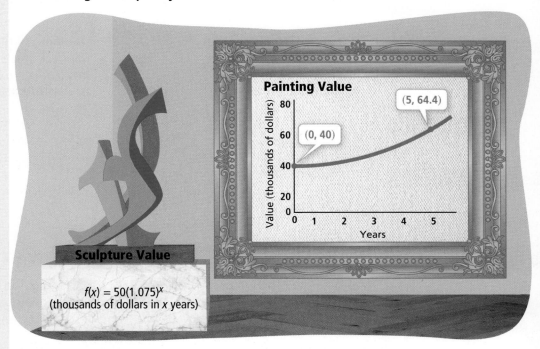

Painting Value
(5, 64.4)
(0, 40)
Value (thousands of dollars)
Years

Sculpture Value

$f(x) = 50(1.075)^x$
(thousands of dollars in x years)

Sculpture

$$f(0) = 50(1.075)^0 = 50$$

$$f(5) = 50(1.075)^5 \approx 71.78$$

$$\frac{y_2 - y_1}{x_2 - x_1} = \frac{71.78 - 50}{5 - 0} = \frac{21.78}{5} = 4.356$$

The sculpture's value increased at an average of $4,356 per year.

Painting

$$\frac{y_2 - y_1}{x_2 - x_1} = \frac{64.4 - 40}{5 - 0} = \frac{24.4}{5} = 4.88$$

The painting's value increased at an average of $4,880 per year.

MODEL WITH MATHEMATICS
The average rate of change of $f(x)$ from x_1 to x_2 is the slope of the line containing the points $(x_1, f(x_1))$ and $(x_2, (f(x_2))$. Ⓖ **MP.4**

Over the 5-year period, the value of the painting increased at a greater average rate than the value of the sculpture.

 Try It! **5.** In Example 5, will the value of the painting ever surpass the value of the sculpture according to the models? Explain.

	Exponential Growth	Exponential Decay
GRAPHS	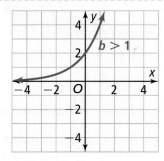 $b > 1$ Growth factor: $1 + r$	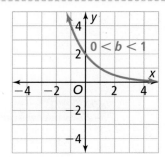 $0 < b < 1$ Decay factor: $1 - r$
EQUATIONS	$y = a \cdot b^x$, for $b > 1$	$y = a \cdot b^x$, for $0 < b < 1$
KEY FEATURES	Domain: All real numbers Range: $\{y \mid y \geq 0\}$ Intercepts: $(0, a)$ Asymptote: x-axis	Domain: All real numbers Range: $\{y \mid y \geq 0\}$ Intercepts: $(0, a)$ Asymptote: x-axis
END BEHAVIOR	As $x \to -\infty$, $y \to 0$ As $x \to \infty$, $y \to \infty$	As $x \to -\infty$, $y \to \infty$ As $x \to \infty$, $y \to 0$
MODELS	Growth: $A(t) = a(1 + r)^t$	Decay: $A(t) = a(1 - r)^t$

☑ Do You UNDERSTAND?

1. **ESSENTIAL QUESTION** How do graphs and equations reveal key features of exponential growth and decay functions?

2. **Vocabulary** How do *exponential functions* differ from polynomial and rational functions?

3. **Error Analysis** Charles claimed the function $f(x) = \left(\frac{3}{2}\right)^x$ represents exponential decay. Explain the error Charles made. © MP.3

4. **Communicate Precisely** How are exponential growth functions similar to exponential decay functions? How are they different? © MP.6

Do You KNOW HOW?

5. Graph the function $f(x) = 4 \times 3^x$. Identify the domain, range, intercept, and asymptote, and describe the end behavior.

6. The exponential function $f(x) = 2500(0.4)^x$ models the amount of money in Zachary's savings account over the last 10 years. Is Zachary's account balance increasing or decreasing? Write the base in terms of the rate of growth or decay.

7. Describe how the graph of $g(x) = 4(0.5)^{x-3}$ compares to the graph of $f(x) = 4(0.5)^x$.

8. Two trucks were purchased by a landscaping company in 2016. Their values are modeled by the functions $f(x) = 35(0.85)^x$ and $g(x) = 46(0.75)^x$ where x is the number of years since 2016. Which function models the truck that is worth the most after 5 years? Explain.

UNDERSTAND

9. Use Structure What value of a completes the equation $y = a \cdot 2^x$ for the exponential growth function shown below? © **MP.7**

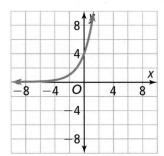

10. Make Sense and Persevere Cindy found a collection of baseball cards in her attic worth $8,000. The collection is estimated to increase in value by 1.5% per year. Write an exponential growth function and find the value of the collection after 7 years. © **MP.1**

11. Error Analysis Describe and correct the error a student made in identifying the growth or decay factor for the function $y = 2.55(0.7)^x$. © **MP.3**

Step 1   The base of the function is 0.7, so it represents exponential decay.
Step 2   The function in the form $y = a(1 - r)^x$ is $y = 2.55(1 - 0.7)^x$.
Step 3   The decay factor is 0.3.

12. Reason In 2000, the population of St. Louis was 346,904, and it decreased to 319,257 in 2010. If this population decrease were modeled by an exponential decay function, what value would represent the y-intercept? Explain your reasoning. © **MP.2**

13. Mathematical Connections Describe how the graph of $g(x) = 6 \cdot 2^{x+1} - 4$ compares to the graph of $f(x) = 6 \cdot 2^x$.

PRACTICE

Identify the domain, range, intercept, and asymptote of each exponential function. Then describe the end behavior. SEE EXAMPLE 1

14. $f(x) = 5 \cdot 3^x$

15. $f(x) = 0.75\left(\dfrac{2}{3}\right)^x$

16. $f(x) = 4\left(\dfrac{1}{2}\right)^x$

17. $f(x) = 7 \cdot 2^x$

Determine whether each function represents exponential growth or decay. Write the base in terms of the rate of growth or decay, identify r, and interpret the rate of growth or decay. SEE EXAMPLES 3 AND 4

18. $y = 100 \cdot 2.5^x$

19. $f(x) = 10{,}200\left(\dfrac{3}{5}\right)^x$

20. $f(x) = 12{,}000\left(\dfrac{7}{10}\right)^x$

21. $y = 450 \cdot 2^x$

22. The function $f(x)$, shown in the graph, represents an exponential growth function. Compare the average rate of change of $f(x)$ to the average rate of change of the exponential growth function $g(x) = 25\,(1.4)^x$. Use the interval [0, 4]. SEE EXAMPLE 5

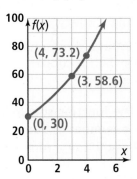

23. Write a function $g(x)$ that represents the exponential function $f(x) = 2^x$ after a vertical stretch of 6 and a reflection across the x-axis. Graph both functions. SEE EXAMPLE 2

24. The population of Medway, Ohio, was 4,007 in 2000. It is expected to decrease by about 0.36% per year. Write an exponential decay function and use it to approximate the population in 2020. SEE EXAMPLE 4

APPLY

25. Model With Mathematics A colony of bacteria starts with 50 organisms and quadruples each day. Write an exponential function, $P(t)$, that represents the population of the bacteria after t days. Then find the number of bacteria that will be in the colony after 5 days. **© MP.4**

DAY 0: 50   DAY 5: ?

26. Higher Order Thinking The number of teams y remaining in a single elimination tournament can be found using the exponential function $y = 128\left(\frac{1}{2}\right)^x$, where x is the number of rounds played in the tournament.

  a. Determine whether the function represents exponential growth or decay. Explain.

  b. What does 128 represent in the function?

  c. What percent of the teams are eliminated after each round? Explain how you know.

  d. Graph the function. What is a reasonable domain and range for the function? Explain.

27. Construct Arguments The function shown in the graph represents the number of lions in a region after x years, where the rate of decay is 20%. The number of zebras in that same region after x years can be modeled by the function $f(x) = 300(0.95)^x$. A representative for a conservationist group claims there will be fewer lions than zebras within 2 years. Is the representative correct? Justify your answer. **© MP.3**

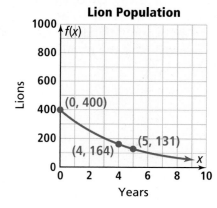

Lion Population

(0, 400)

(4, 164) (5, 131)

Lions / Years

ASSESSMENT PRACTICE

28. The exponential function $g(x) = 3^{x-1} + 6$ is a transformation of the function $f(x) = 3^x$. Does each statement accurately describe how the graph of $g(x)$ compares to the graph of $f(x)$? Select yes or no.

	Yes	No
a. $g(x)$ is translated 6 units up.	❑	❑
b. $g(x)$ is translated 6 units down.	❑	❑
c. $g(x)$ is translated 6 units to the right.	❑	❑
d. $g(x)$ is translated 1 unit to the right.	❑	❑
e. $g(x)$ is translated 1 unit to the left.	❑	❑
f. The horizontal asymptote shifts 1 unit down.	❑	❑

29. SAT/ACT Which of the functions defined below could be the one shown in this graph?

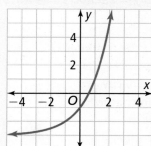

  Ⓐ $f(x) = 4(2)^{x-1} + 3$ Ⓒ $f(x) = 4(2)^{x-1} - 3$

  Ⓑ $f(x) = 4(2)^{x+1} + 3$ Ⓓ $f(x) = 4(2)^{x+1} - 3$

30. Performance Task A radioactive isotope of the element osmium Os-182 has a half-life of 21.5 hours. This means that if there are 100 grams of Os-182 in a sample, after 21.5 hours there will only be 50 grams of that isotope remaining.

Part A Write an exponential decay function to model the amount of Os-182 in a sample over time. Use A_0 for the initial amount and A for the amount after time t in hours.

Part B Use your model to predict how long it would take a sample containing 500 g of Os-182 to decay to the point where it contained only 5 g of Os-182.

© **Common Core State Standards** HSA.SSE.A.1.B, HSA.SSE.A.2, HSA.SSE.B.3.C, HSF.IF.C.8, HSF.IF.C.8.B, HSF.LE.A.2, HSF.LE.B.5, HSS.ID.B.6, HSS.ID.B.6.A, MP.1, MP.4, MP.7

  Activity Assess

6-2

Exponential Models

 SavvasRealize.com

I CAN... write exponential models in different ways to solve problems.

VOCABULARY

- compound interest formula
- continuously compounded interest formula
- natural base e

👆 **EXPLORE & REASON**

Juan is studying exponential growth of bacteria cultures. Each is carefully controlled to maintain a specific growth rate. Copy and complete the table to find the number of bacteria cells in each culture.

Culture	Initial Number of Bacteria	Growth Rate per Day	Time (days)	Final Number of Bacteria
A	10,000	8%	1	
B	10,000	4%	2	
C	10,000	2%	4	
D	10,000	1%	8	

A. What is the relationship between the daily growth rate and the time in days for each culture?

B. **Look for Relationships** Would you expect a culture with a growth rate of $\frac{1}{2}$% and a time of 16 days to have more or fewer cells than the others in the table? Explain. © **MP.7**

❓ **ESSENTIAL QUESTION** ▶ How can you develop exponential models to represent and interpret situations?

👆 **EXAMPLE 1** ▶ Rewrite an Exponential Function to Identify a Rate

In 2015, the population of a small town was 8,000. The population is increasing at a rate of 2.5% per year. Rewrite an exponential growth function to find the monthly growth rate.

Write an exponential growth function using the annual rate to model the town's population y, in t years after 2015.

initial population   annual growth rate

$$y = 8{,}000(1 + 0.025)^t$$

years after 2015

$$y = 8{,}000(1.025)^t$$

To identify the monthly growth rate, you need the exponent to be the number of months in t years, or $12t$.

$$y = 8{,}000(1.025)^{\frac{12t}{12}}$$

Multiply the exponent by $\frac{12}{12}$ so that $12t$ represents the number of months.

$$y = 8{,}000(1.025^{\frac{1}{12}})^{12t}$$

$$y \approx 8{,}000(1.00206)^{12t}$$

Applying the Power of a Power rule helps to reveal the monthly growth rate by producing an expression with the exponent $12t$.

COMMON ERROR
Dividing the annual growth rate by 12 does not give the exact monthly growth rate. This Example shows how to find an expression for the exact monthly rate: $1.025^{\frac{1}{12}} - 1$.

The monthly growth rate is about $1.00206 - 1 = 0.00206$. The population is increasing about 0.206% per month.

☑ **Try It!** **1.** The population in a small town is increasing annually by 1.8%. What is the quarterly rate of population increase?

CONCEPT Compound Interest

When interest is paid monthly, the interest earned after the first month becomes part of the new principal for the second month, and so on. Interest is earned on interest already earned. This is compound interest.

The **compound interest formula** is an exponential model that is used to calculate the value of an investment when interest is compounded.

$$A = P\left(1 + \frac{r}{n}\right)^{nt}$$

$P =$ the initial principal invested

$r =$ annual interest rate, written as a decimal

$n =$ number of compounding periods per year

$A =$ the value of the account after t years

 EXAMPLE 2 Understand Compound Interest

Tamira invests $5,000 in an account that pays 4% annual interest. How much will there be in the account after 3 years if the interest is compounded annually, semi-annually, quarterly, or monthly?

Use the Compound Interest formula to find the amount in Tamira's account after 3 years.

	Compound Interest Formula	Amount After 3 Years ($)
Annually	$A = 5000\left(1 + \frac{0.04}{1}\right)^{3(1)}$	5,624.32
Semi-Annually	$A = 5000\left(1 + \frac{0.04}{2}\right)^{3(2)}$	5,630.81
Quarterly	$A = 5000\left(1 + \frac{0.04}{4}\right)^{3(4)}$	5,634.13
Monthly	$A = 5000\left(1 + \frac{0.04}{12}\right)^{3(12)}$	5,636.36

As the number of compounding periods increases, the amount in the account also increases.

REASON
The more frequently interest is added to the account, the earlier that interest generates more interest. This reasoning supports the trend shown in the table.
Ⓒ **MP.2**

✓ **Try It!**   **2.** $3,000 is invested in an account that earns 3% annual interest, compounded monthly.

     a. What is the value of the account after 10 years?

     b. What is the value of the account after 100 years?

CONCEPTUAL
UNDERSTANDING

 EXAMPLE 3 Understanding Continuously Compounded Interest

Consider an investment of $1 in an account that pays a 100% annual interest rate for one year. The equation $A = 1\left(1 + \frac{1}{n}\right)^{n(1)} = \left(1 + \frac{1}{n}\right)^{n}$ gives the amount in the account after one year for the number of compounding periods n. Find the value of the account for the number of periods given in the table.

Number of Periods, n	Value of $\left(1 + \frac{1}{n}\right)^{n}$
1	$\left(1 + \frac{1}{1}\right)^{1} = 2$
10	$\left(1 + \frac{1}{10}\right)^{10} = 2.59374246$
100	$\left(1 + \frac{1}{100}\right)^{100} = 2.704813829$
1000	$\left(1 + \frac{1}{1,000}\right)^{1,000} = 2.716923932$
10000	$\left(1 + \frac{1}{10,000}\right)^{10,000} = 2.718145927$
100000	$\left(1 + \frac{1}{100,000}\right)^{100,000} = 2.718268237$

Notice that as n continues to increase, the value of the account remains very close to 2.718. This special number is called the *natural base*.

The **natural base e** is defined as the value that the expression $\left(1 + \frac{1}{x}\right)^{x}$ approaches as $x \rightarrow +\infty$. The number e is an irrational number.

$$e = 2.718281828459\ldots$$

The number e is the base in the **continuously compounded interest formula**.

$$A = Pe^{rt}$$ $P =$ the initial principal invested
$e =$ the natural base
$r =$ annual interest rate, written as a decimal
$A =$ the value of the account after t years

 Try It! 3. If you continued the table for $n = 1,000,000$, would the value in the account increase or decrease? How do you know?

 EXAMPLE 4 Find Continuously Compounded Interest

Regina invests $12,600 in an account that earns 3.2% annual interest, compounded continuously. What is the value of the account after 12 years? Round your answer to the nearest dollar.

Use the continuously compounded interest formula with $P = 12,600$, $r = 0.032$, and $t = 12$.

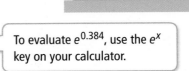

3.2% interest rate
12-year term

$A = Pe^{rt}$

$= 12,600e^{0.032(12)}$

$= 12,600e^{0.384}$ ← To evaluate $e^{0.384}$, use the e^x key on your calculator.

$\approx 18,498.63$

To the nearest dollar, the value of the account after 12 years is $18,499.

COMMON ERROR
Be sure that when you evaluate $e^{0.032(12)}$ you either simplify 0.032(12) as 0.384 first, or use parentheses to ensure that e is raised to the entire product, rather than just the first factor.

CONTINUED ON THE NEXT PAGE

Try It! **4.** You invest $125,000 in an account that earns 4.75% annual interest, compounded continuously.

a. What is the value of the account after 15 years?

b. What is the value of the account after 30 years?

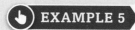 APPLICATION

EXAMPLE 5 **Use Two Points to Find an Exponential Model**

Tia knew that the number of e-mails she sent was growing exponentially. She generated a record of the number of e-mails she sent each year since 2009. What is an exponential model that describes the data?

Write an exponential model in the form $y = a \cdot b^x$, with y equal to the number of e-mails in hundreds and x equal to the number of years since 2009. Use the data to find the values of the constants a and b.

COMMON ERROR
Remember that the growth factor $(1 + r)$ is different from the growth rate (r). In this example, the growth factor is 1.4 while the growth rate is 0.4, or 40%.

The growth factor for Tia's e-mails in the two consecutive years was $\frac{14}{10}$, or 1.4.

> When data points have consecutive x-values, the growth factor, b, is the ratio of their y-values.

Use the value of b and one of the data points to find the initial value, a.

$y = a \cdot b^x$	Write an exponential growth equation.
$14 = a(1.4)^7$	Substitute 1.4 for b, 7 for x, and 14 for y.
$\frac{14}{(1.4)^7} = a$	Division Property of Equality
$1.33 \approx a$	Simplify.

So, the function $y = 1.33(1.4)^x$ models the number of e-mails (in hundreds) Tia sends x years after 2009.

 Try It! **5.** A surveyor determined the value of an area of land over a period of several years since 1950. The land was worth $31,000 in 1954 and $35,000 in 1955. Use the data to determine an exponential model that describes the value of the land.

APPLICATION ⟶

EXAMPLE 6 Use Regression to Find an Exponential Model

Randy is making soup. The soup reaches the boiling point and then, as shown by the data, begins to cool off. Randy wants to serve the soup when it is about 80°F, or about 10 degrees above room temperature (68°F).

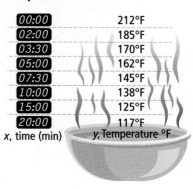

00:00	212°F
02:00	185°F
03:30	170°F
05:00	162°F
07:30	145°F
10:00	138°F
15:00	125°F
20:00	117°F

x, time (min)   y, Temperature °F

A. Explain why the temperature might follow an exponential decay curve as it approaches room temperature.

A scatter plot of the data shows the soup cooling toward room temperature. The graph is not a line.

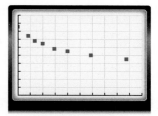

The rate of cooling appears to slow as the graph approaches room temperature, around 68° F. This indicates exponential decay toward an asymptote of $y = 68$.

B. Find an exponential model for the data. Use your model to determine when Randy should serve the soup.

Step 1 Enter the data as lists in a graphing calculator. Because the temperature values approach 68°F, subtract 68 from each temperature value.

> Most graphing calculators will only calculate exponential regressions for data values that approach 0. You can subtract 68 so your data will approach 0. Then you can undo the adjustment in **Step 3** below.

L1	L2	L3 2
2	117	
3.5	102	
5	94	
7.5	77	
10	70	
15	57	
20	49	

L2(8)=49

STUDY TIP
The procedure for determining an exponential regression model for data may be slightly different on your graphing calculator, but the steps should be very similar.

Step 2 Use the calculator to find an exponential regression equation. The exponential model that best fits the data is $y = 126.35(0.9492)^x$.

Step 3 Translate this function up vertically by 68 units.

The translated model is
$y = 126.35(0.9492)^x + 68$.

Use the translated model to find when the soup has a temperature of about 80°F.

X	Y1
42	82.142
43	82.424
44	80.742
45	80.094
46	79.48
47	78.897
48	78.343

X=45

The soup has a temperature of about 80°F after 45 minutes.

So, Randy should serve the soup about 45 minutes after it begins to cool.

 Try It! **6.** According to the model in Example 6, what was the approximate temperature 35 minutes after cooling started?

🔧 CONCEPT SUMMARY Writing Exponential Models

	General Exponential Model	Compound Interest	Continuously Compounded Interest
ALGEBRA	$y = a \cdot b^x$	$A = P\left(1 + \frac{r}{n}\right)^{nt}$	$A = Pe^{rt}$
NUMBERS	A necklace costs \$250 and increases in value by 2% per year. $a =$ initial amount \$250 $b =$ growth factor 1.02 $x =$ number of years $y = 250(1.02)^x$	A principal of \$3,000 is invested at 5% annual interest, compounded monthly, for 4 years. $P = 3,000$ $r = 5\%$ $n = 12$ compounding periods per year $t = 4$ years $A = 3000\left(1 + \frac{0.05}{12}\right)^{(12)(4)}$	A principal of \$3,000 is invested at 5% continuously compounded interest for 4 years. $P = 3,000$ $r = 5\%$ $t = 4$ years $A = 3000e^{(0.05)(4)}$

✅ Do You UNDERSTAND?

1. **❓ ESSENTIAL QUESTION** Why do you develop exponential models to represent and interpret situations?

2. **Error Analysis** The exponential model $y = 5,000(1.05)^t$ represents the amount Yori earns in an account after t years when \$5,000 is invested. Yori said the monthly interest rate of the exponential model is 5%. Explain Yori's error. **ⓒ MP.3**

3. **Vocabulary** Explain the similarities and differences between compound interest and continuously compounded interest.

4. **Communicate Precisely** Kylee is using a calculator to find an exponential regression model. How would you explain to Kylee what the variables in the model $y = a \cdot b^x$ represent? **ⓒ MP.6**

Do You KNOW HOW?

The exponential function models the annual rate of increase. Find the monthly and quarterly rates.

5. $f(t) = 2,000(1.03)^t$

6. $f(t) = 500(1.055)^t$

Find the total amount of money in an account at the end of the given time period.

7. compounded monthly, $P = \$2,000$, $r = 3\%$, $t = 5$ years

8. continuously compounded, $P = \$1,500$, $r = 1.5\%$, $t = 6$ years

Write an exponential model given two points.

9. (3, 55) and (4, 70)

10. (7, 12) and (8, 25)

11. Paul invests \$6,450 in an account that earns continuously compounded interest at an annual rate of 2.8%. What is the value of the account after 8 years?

UNDERSTAND

12. Error Analysis Suppose $6,500 is invested in an account that earns interest at a rate of 2% compounded quarterly for 10 years. Describe and correct the error a student made when finding the value of the account. Ⓒ **MP.3**

$$A = 6500\left(1 + \frac{0.02}{12}\right)^{12(10)}$$

$$A = 7937.80 \quad ✗$$

13. Communicate Precisely The points (2, 54.61) and (4, 403.48) are points on the graph of an exponential model in the form $y = a \cdot e^x$. Ⓒ **MP.6**

a. Explain how to write the exponential model, and then write the model.

b. How can you use the exponential model to find the value of y when $x = 8$?

14. Model with Mathematics Use the points listed in the table for years 7 and 8 to find an exponential model. Then use a calculator to find an exponential model for the data. Explain how to find each model. Predict the amount in the account after 15 years. Ⓒ **MP.4**

Time (yr)	Amount ($)
1	3,225
2	3,500
3	3,754
4	4,042
5	4,368
6	4,702
7	5,063
8	5,456

15. Higher Order Thinking A power model is a type of function in the form $y = a \cdot x^b$. Use the points (1, 4), (2, 8), (3, 16) and (4, 64) and a calculator to find an exponential model and a power model for the data. Then use each model to predict the value of y when $x = 6$. Graph the points and models in the same window. What do you notice?

PRACTICE

Find the amount in the account for the given principal, interest rate, time, and compounding period. SEE EXAMPLES 2 AND 4

16. $P = 800$, $r = 6\%$, $t = 9$ years; compounded quarterly

17. $P = 3,750$, $r = 3.5\%$, $t = 20$ years; compounded monthly

18. $P = 2,400$, $r = 5.25\%$, $t = 12$ years; compounded semi-annually

19. $P = 1,500$, $r = 4.5\%$, $t = 3$ years; compounded daily

20. $P = \$1,000$, $r = 2.8\%$, $t = 5$ years; compounded continuously

21. $P = \$16,000$, $r = 4\%$, $t = 25$ years; compounded continuously

Write an exponential model given two points.
SEE EXAMPLE 5

22. (9, 140) and (10, 250)

23. (6, 85) and (7, 92)

24. (10, 43) and (11, 67)

25. In 2012, the population of a small town was 3,560. The population is decreasing at a rate of 1.7% per year. How can you rewrite an exponential growth function to find the quarterly decay rate? SEE EXAMPLE 1

26. Selena took a pizza out of the oven and it started to cool to room temperature (68°F). She will serve the pizza when it reaches 150°F. She took the pizza out of the oven at 5:00 P.M. When can she serve it? SEE EXAMPLE 6

Time (min)	Temperature (°F)
5	310
8	264
10	238
15	202
20	186
25	175

APPLY

27. **Reason** Adam invests $8,000 in an account that earns 1.25% interest, compounded quarterly for 20 years. On the same date, Jacinta invests $8,000 in an account that earns continuous compounded interest at a rate of 1.25% for 20 years. Who do you predict will have more money in their account after 20 years? Explain your reasoning. ⓒ **MP.2**

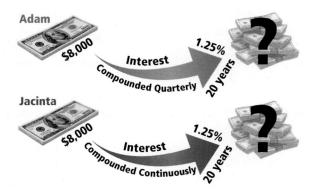

28. **Make Sense and Persevere** A blogger found that the number of visits to her Web site increases 5.6% annually. The Web site had 80,000 visits this year. Write an exponential model to represent this situation. By what percent does the number of visits increase daily? Explain how you found the daily rate. ⓒ **MP.1**

29. **Use Structure** Jae invested $3,500 at a rate of 2.25% compounded continuously in 2010. How much will be in the account in 2025? How much interest will the account have earned by 2025? ⓒ **MP.7**

30. **Model with Mathematics** A scientist is conducting an experiment with a pesticide. Use a calculator to find an exponential model for the data in the table. Use the model to determine how much pesticide remains after 180 days. ⓒ **MP.4**

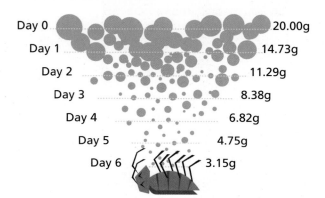

Day 0	20.00g
Day 1	14.73g
Day 2	11.29g
Day 3	8.38g
Day 4	6.82g
Day 5	4.75g
Day 6	3.15g

ⓒ ASSESSMENT PRACTICE

31. The table shows the account information of five investors. Which of the following are true, assuming no withdrawals are made? Select all that apply.

Employee	P	r	t(years)	Compound
Anna	4000	1.5%	12	Quarterly
Nick	2500	3%	8	Monthly
Lori	7200	5%	15	Annually
Tara	2100	4.5%	6	Continuously
Steve	3800	3.5%	20	Semi-annually

Ⓐ After 12 years, Anna will have about $4,788.33 in her account.

Ⓑ After 8 years, Nick will have about $3,177.17 in his account.

Ⓒ After 15 years, Lori will have about $15,218.67 in her account.

Ⓓ After 6 years, Tara will have about $2,750.93 in her account.

Ⓔ After 20 years, Steve will have about $7,629.00 in his account.

32. **SAT/ACT** Rick invested money in a continuous compound account with an interest rate of 3%. How long will it take Rick's account to double?

Ⓐ about 2 years

Ⓑ about 10 years

Ⓒ about 23 years

Ⓓ about 46 years

Ⓔ about 67 years

33. **Performance Task** Cassie is financing a $2,400 treadmill. She is going to use her credit card for the purchase. Her card charges 17.5% interest compounded monthly. She is not required to make minimum monthly payments.

Part A How much will Cassie pay in interest if she waits a full year before paying the full balance?

Part B How much additional interest will Cassie pay if she waits two full years before paying the full balance?

Part C If both answers represent a single year of interest, why is the answer in B greater than the answer in A?

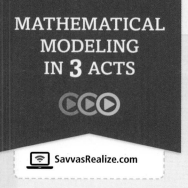
© **Common Core State Standards** HSF.LE.B.5, HSS.ID.B.6.A, MP.4

Video

▶ **The Crazy Conditioning**

Like all sports, soccer requires its players to be well-trained. That is why players often have to run sprints in practice.

To make sprint drills more interesting, many coaches set up competitions. Coaches might split the players into teams and have them run relay races against each other. Or they might have the players sprint around cones and over barriers. What other ways would make doing sprints more fun? Think about this during this Mathematical Modeling in 3 Acts lesson.

Scan for Multimedia

ACT 1 > **Identify the Problem**

1. Write down the Main Question you will answer.

2. Make an initial conjecture that answers this Main Question.

3. Explain how you arrived at your conjecture.

4. Write a number that you know is too small.

5. Write a number that you know is too high.

6. What information do you need to know to answer the main question? How can you get it? How will you use that information?

ACT 2 > **Develop a Model**

1. Use the math that you have learned in this Topic to refine your conjecture.

2. Is your refined conjecture between the high and low estimates you came up with earlier?

ACT 3 > **Interpret the Results**

1. Did your refined conjecture match the actual answer exactly? If not, what might explain the difference?

Common Core State Standards HSF.BF.B.4.A, HSF.BF.B.5 (+), HSF.LE.A.4, MP.2, MP.4, MP.7

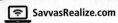 SavvasRealize.com

Activity   Assess

CRITIQUE & EXPLAIN

Earthquakes make seismic waves through the ground. The equation $y = 10^x$ relates the height, or amplitude, in microns, of a seismic wave, y, and the power, or magnitude, x, of the ground-shaking it can cause.

Magnitude, x	Amplitude, y
2	100
3	1,000
?	5,500
4	10,000

I CAN... evaluate and simplify logarithms.

VOCABULARY
• common logarithm
• logarithm
• logarithmic function
• natural logarithm

Taylor and Chen used different methods to find the magnitude of the earthquake with amplitude 5,500.

Taylor
5,500 is halfway between 1,000 and 10,000.

3.5 is halfway between 3 and 4.

The magnitude is about 3.5.

Chen
$y = 10^x$

$10^3 = 1,000$
$10^4 = 10,000$
$10^{3.5} \approx 3,162$
$10^{3.7} \approx 5,012$
$10^{3.8} \approx 6,310$
$10^{3.74} \approx 5,500$

The magnitude is about 3.74.

A. What is the magnitude of an earthquake with amplitude 100,000? How do you know?

B. Construct Arguments Critique Taylor's and Chen's work. Is each method valid? Could either method be improved? Ⓒ **MP.3**

C. Describe how to express the exact value of the desired magnitude.

ESSENTIAL QUESTION

What are logarithms and how are they evaluated?

CONCEPTUAL UNDERSTANDING

EXAMPLE 1   Understand Logarithms

Solve the equations $2x = 8$ and $2^x = 8$.

You can use inverse operations to solve the first equation.

$$\frac{2x}{2} = \frac{8}{2}$$
$$x = 4$$

> Division is the inverse of multiplication, so you can divide both sides by 2 to solve the equation.

The operation in $2^x = 8$ is exponentiation. To solve this equation, you need an inverse for exponentiation that answers the question, "To what exponent would you raise the base 2 to get 8?"

USE STRUCTURE

Creating the notation $\log_2 x$ to represent the exponent to which you raise 2 to get x is similar to creating the radical notation $\sqrt{x}$ to represent one number you can square to get x. Ⓒ **MP.7**

The inverse of exponentiation is called a *logarithm*. To solve the equation $2^x = 8$, you can write $\log_2 8 = x$.
Solving this gives $\log_2 8 = 3$ because $2^3 = 8$.

> This is read "logarithm base 2 of 8" or "log base 2 of 8."

CONTINUED ON THE NEXT PAGE

Go Online | SavvasRealize.com

EXAMPLE 1 CONTINUED

The **logarithm** base b of x is defined as follows.

$$\log_b x = y \text{ if and only if } b^y = x, \text{ for } b > 0, b \neq 1, \text{ and } x > 0.$$

The **logarithmic function** $y = \log_b x$ is the inverse of the exponential function $y = b^x$.

 Try It! **1.** Write the logarithmic form of $y = 8^x$.

CONCEPT Exponential and Logarithmic Forms

Exponential form shows that a base raised to an exponent equals the result.

$$a^b = c$$

Logarithmic form shows that the log of the result with the given base equals the exponent.

$$\log_a c = b$$

> When written in logarithmic form, the number that was the result of the exponential equation is often called the argument.

 EXAMPLE 2 Convert Between Exponential and Logarithmic Forms

STUDY TIP
Do you remember writing *fact families* for related operations like addition and subtraction? Think of exponential and logarithmic forms as a *fact family* for the three numbers given.

A. What is the logarithmic form of $3^4 = 81$?

The base is 3, the exponent is 4, and the result is 81.

So, in logarithmic form,

$$3^4 = 81 \rightarrow \log_3 81 = 4.$$

The logarithmic form of $3^4 = 81$ is $\log_3 81 = 4$.

B. What is the exponential form of $\log_{10} 1,000 = 3$?

The base is 10, the exponent is 3, and the result (or argument) is 1,000.

So, in exponential form,

$$\log_{10} 1,000 = 3 \rightarrow 10^3 = 1,000.$$

The exponential form of $\log_{10} 1,000 = 3$ is $10^3 = 1,000$.

 Try It! **2. a.** What is the logarithmic form of $7^3 = 343$?

b. What is the exponential form of $\log_4 16 = 2$?

EXAMPLE 3 **Evaluate Logarithms**

GENERALIZE

The output of any exponential function of the form $y = b^x$, with $b > 0$, is always a positive number. Therefore, the input of a logarithmic function must also be a positive number. © **MP.8**

What is the value of each logarithmic expression?

A. $\log_5 125$	**B. $\log_{\frac{1}{4}} 16$**
THINK: $5^? = 125$	THINK: $\left(\frac{1}{4}\right)^? = 16$
Since $5^3 = 125$, $\log_5 125 = 3$.	Since $\left(\frac{1}{4}\right)^{-2} = 16$, $\log_{\frac{1}{4}} 16 = -2$.
C. $\log_3 0$	**D. $\log_2 2^8$**
THINK: $3^? = 0$	THINK: $2^? = 2^8$
There is no such power, so $\log_3 0$ is undefined.	Since $2^8 = 2^8$, $\log_2 2^8 = 8$.

 Try It! **3.** What is the value of each logarithmic expression?

   a. $\log_3\left(\frac{1}{81}\right)$ **b.** $\log_7(-7)$ **c.** $\log_5 5^9$

CONCEPT Common Logarithms and Natural Logarithms

The base 10 logarithm is called the **common logarithm** and is written as $\log x$ with the base of 10 implied.

The base e logarithm is called the **natural logarithm** and is written as $\ln x$.

The expressions $\log_{10} x$ and $\log x$ mean the same thing, as do $\ln_e x$ and $\ln x$.

EXAMPLE 4 **Evaluate Common and Natural Logarithms**

STUDY TIP

Most calculators have keys for the common logarithm (LOG) and the natural logarithm (LN).

What is the value of each logarithmic expression to the nearest ten-thousandth?

A. $\log 900$

   $\log 900 \approx 2.9542$ $10^{2.9542} \approx 900$

> Check by writing the expression in exponential form and evaluating.

B. $\ln e$

   $\ln e = 1$ $e^1 = e$

C. $\ln(-1.87)$

   $\ln(-1.87)$ $e^? = -1.87$

```
log(900)
              2.954242509
ln(e)
                        1
ln(-1.87)
                    Error
```

There is no exponent to which e can be raised in order to get a negative number, so $\ln(-1.87)$ is undefined.

 Try It! **4.** What is the value of each logarithmic expression to the nearest ten-thousandth?

   a. $\log 321$ **b.** $\ln 1{,}215$ **c.** $\log 0.17$

EXAMPLE 5 **Solve Equations With Logarithms**

What is the solution to each equation? Round to the nearest thousandth.

A. $25 = 10^{x-1}$

$$25 = 10^{x-1}$$

$$\log 25 = x - 1 \quad \cdots\cdots\cdots \text{ Convert to logarithmic form.}$$

$$1 + \log 25 = x \quad \cdots\cdots\cdots \text{ Addition Property}$$

$$2.398 \approx x \quad \cdots\cdots\cdots \text{ Use calculator to evaluate.}$$

B. $\ln(2x + 3) = 4$

$$\ln(2x + 3) = 4$$

$$2x + 3 = e^4 \quad \cdots\cdots\cdots \text{ Convert to exponential form.}$$

$$2x + 3 \approx 54.598 \quad \cdots\cdots\cdots \text{ Use calculator to evaluate.}$$

$$2x \approx 51.598 \quad \cdots\cdots\cdots \text{ Addition Property}$$

$$x \approx 25.799 \quad \cdots\cdots\cdots \text{ Multiplication Property}$$

✓ Try It! **5.** Solve each equation. Round to the nearest thousandth.

a. $\log(3x - 2) = 2$ **b.** $e^{x+2} = 8$

APPLICATION **EXAMPLE 6** **Use Logarithms to Solve Problems**

The seismic energy, x, in joules can be estimated based on the magnitude, m, of an earthquake by the formula $x = 10^{1.5m+12}$. What is the magnitude of an earthquake with a seismic energy of 4.2×10^{20} joules?

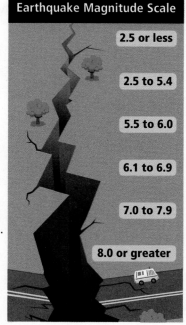

Earthquake Magnitude Scale

2.5 or less

2.5 to 5.4

5.5 to 6.0

6.1 to 6.9

7.0 to 7.9

8.0 or greater

Formulate ◄ Substitute 4.2×10^{20} for x in the formula.

$$4.2 \times 10^{20} = 10^{1.5m+12}$$

Compute ◄ Solve the equation for m.

$$4.2 \times 10^{20} = 10^{1.5m+12} \quad \cdots\cdots\cdots \text{ Write the original equation.}$$

$$\log(4.2 \times 10^{20}) = 1.5m + 12 \quad \cdots\cdots \text{ Write the equation in logarithmic form.}$$

$$20.6 \approx 1.5m + 12 \quad \cdots\cdots\cdots \text{ Evaluate the logarithm.}$$

$$5.75 \approx m \quad \cdots\cdots\cdots \text{ Solve for } m.$$

Interpret ◄ The magnitude of the earthquake is about 5.75.
Verify the answer: $10^{1.5(5.75)+12} \approx 4.2 \times 10^{20}$

✓ Try It! **6.** What is the magnitude of an earthquake with a seismic energy of 1.8×10^{23} joules?

CONCEPT SUMMARY Logarithms

	Exponential Form		Logarithmic Form
ALGEBRA	$b^x = y$	⟷	$\log_b y = x$
WORDS	The base raised to the exponent is equal to a result.		The logarithm with a base b of the result (or argument) is equal to the exponent.
NUMBERS	$3^4 = 81$	⟷	$\log_3 81 = 4$

 Do You UNDERSTAND?

1. **ESSENTIAL QUESTION** What are logarithms and how are they evaluated?

2. **Error Analysis** Amir said the expression $\log_5(-25)$ simplifies to -2. Explain Amir's possible error. © **MP.3**

3. **Vocabulary** Explain the difference between the common logarithm and the natural logarithm.

4. **Make Sense and Persevere** How can logarithms help to solve an equation such as $10^t = 656$? © **MP.1**

Do You KNOW HOW?

Write each equation in logarithmic form.

5. $2^{-6} = \frac{1}{64}$ 6. $e^4 \approx 54.6$

Write each equation in exponential form.

7. $\log 200 \approx 2.301$ 8. $\ln 25 \approx 3.22$

Evaluate the expression.

9. $\log_4 64$

10. $\log\frac{1}{100}$

11. $\ln e^5$

12. Solve for x. $4e^x = 7$.

Go Online | SavvasRealize.com

UNDERSTAND

13. Make Sense and Persevere If the LN button on your calculator were broken, how could you still use your calculator to find the value of the expression ln 65? ⓒ **MP.1**

14. Error Analysis Describe and correct the error a student made in solving an exponential equation. ⓒ **MP.3**

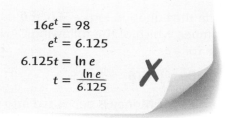

$$16e^t = 98$$
$$e^t = 6.125$$
$$6.125t = \ln e$$
$$t = \frac{\ln e}{6.125}$$

15. Higher Order Thinking Use the graph of $y = 3^x$ to estimate the value of $\log_3 50$. Explain your reasoning.

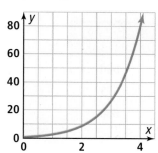

16. Generalize For what values of x is the expression $\log_4 x < 0$ true? ⓒ **MP.8**

17. Use Structure A student says that $\log_3\left(\frac{1}{27}\right)$ simplifies to -3. Is the student correct? Explain. ⓒ **MP.7**

18. Use Structure Explain why the expression ln 1,000 is not equal to 3. ⓒ **MP.7**

PRACTICE

Write the inverse of each exponential function.
SEE EXAMPLE 1

19. $y = 4^x$

20. $y = 10^x$

21. $y = 7^x$

22. $y = a^x$

Write each equation in logarithmic form.
SEE EXAMPLE 2

23. $3^8 = 6{,}561$

24. $e^{-3} \approx 0.0498$

25. $5^0 = 1$

26. $7^3 = 343$

Write each equation in exponential form.
SEE EXAMPLE 2

27. $\log\frac{1}{100} = -2$

28. $\log_8 64 = 2$

29. $\ln 148.41 \approx 5$

30. $\log_2 \frac{1}{32} = -5$

Evaluate each logarithmic expression. SEE EXAMPLE 3

31. $\log_5 \frac{1}{125}$

32. $\log_6 (-216)$

33. $\log_3 3^4$

34. $\log_2 32$

35. $\log_9 729$

36. $\log_8 \frac{1}{64}$

37. $\log_7 0$

38. $\log_7 7^a$

Use a calculator to evaluate each expression. Round to the nearest ten-thousandth. SEE EXAMPLE 4

39. $\log 78.5$

40. $\log 0.24$

41. $\ln(-37)$

42. $\ln 41.5$

43. $\log 12$

44. $\ln 3$

Solve each equation. Round answers to the nearest ten-thousandth. SEE EXAMPLES 5 AND 6

45. $\log(7x + 6) = 3$

46. $2.75e^t = 38.6$

47. $\ln(3x - 1) = 2$

48. $10^{t+1} = 50$

49. $1.5e^t = 27$

50. $\log(x - 3) = -1$

51. How long does it take for $250 to grow to $600 at 4% annual percentage rate compounded continuously? Round to the nearest year.

PRACTICE & PROBLEM SOLVING

APPLY

52. Model with Mathematics Michael invests $1,000 in an account that earns a 4.75% annual percentage rate compounded continuously. Peter invests $1,200 in an account that earns a 4.25% annual percentage rate compounded continuously. Which person's account will grow to $1,800 first? **MP.4**

53. Reason The Richter magnitude of an earthquake is $R = 0.67\log(0.37E) + 1.46$, where E is the energy (in kilowatt-hours) released by the earthquake. **MP.2**

   a. What is the magnitude of an earthquake that releases 11,800,000,000 kilowatt-hours of energy? Round to the nearest tenth.

   b. How many kilowatt-hours of energy would an earthquake have to release in order to be an 8.2 on the Richter scale? Round to the nearest whole number.

   c. What number of kilowatt-hours of energy would an earthquake have to release in order for walls to crack? Round to the nearest whole number.

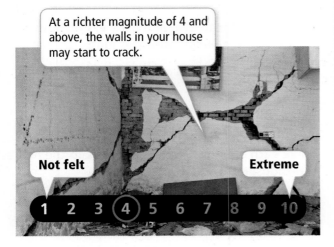

At a richter magnitude of 4 and above, the walls in your house may start to crack.

Not felt   Extreme

1   2   3   ④   5   6   7   8   9   10

54. Reason The function $c(t) = 108e^{-0.08t} + 75$ calculates the temperature, in degrees Fahrenheit, of a cup of coffee that was handed out a drive-thru window t minutes ago. **MP.2**

   a. What is the temperature of the coffee in the instant that it is handed out the window?

   b. After how many minutes is the coffee in the cup 98 degrees Fahrenheit? Round to the nearest whole minute.

ASSESSMENT PRACTICE

55. Given that $\log_b x < 0$, which of the following are true? Select all that apply.

   Ⓐ $b < 0$

   Ⓑ $x < 0$

   Ⓒ $b > 0$

   Ⓓ $x > 0$

   Ⓔ $x < 1$

56. SAT/ACT In the equation $\log_3 a = b$, if b is a whole number, which of the following CANNOT be a value for a?

   Ⓐ 1   Ⓑ 3   Ⓒ 6   Ⓓ 9   Ⓔ 81

57. Performance Task Money is deposited into two separate accounts. The money in one account is compounded continuously. The money in the other account is not compounded continuously. Neither account has any money withdrawn in the first 6 years.

Year	Account 1 Balance ($)	Account 2 Balance ($)
0	400	500
1	433.31	575
2	469.40	650
3	508.50	725
4	550.85	800
5	596.72	875

Part A Write a function to calculate the amount of money in each account given t, the number of years since the account was opened. Describe the growth in each account.

Part B Will the amount of money in Account 1 ever exceed the amount of money in Account 2? Explain. If so, when will that occur?

6-4

Logarithmic Functions

I CAN... graph logarithmic functions and find equations of the inverses of exponential and logarithmic functions.

Ⓒ **Common Core State Standards** HSF.BF.B.3, HSF.BF.B.4, HSF.BF.B.4.A, HSF.BF.B.4.C (+), HSF.IF.B.5, HSF.IF.B.6, HSF.IF.C.7.E, HSF.IF.C.9, MP.3, MP.4, MP.7

  🖐 Activity   ✓ Assess

🖐 EXPLORE & REASON

Compare the graphs.

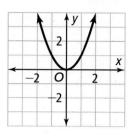 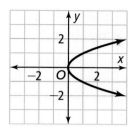 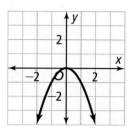

A. Which two graphs represent the inverse of each other? Explain.

B. Look for Relationships What is the relationship between the domain and the range of the two inverse relations? Ⓒ **MP.7**

❓ ESSENTIAL QUESTION

How is the relationship between logarithmic and exponential functions revealed in the key features of their graphs?

🖐 EXAMPLE 1   Identify Key Features of Logarithmic Functions

Graph $y = \log_2 x$. What are the domain, range, x-intercept, and asymptote? What is the end behavior of the graph?

Create a table of values for $y = 2^x$.

x	−2	−1	0	1	2
y	0.25	0.5	1	2	4

> $y = \log_2 x$ and $y = 2^x$ are inverse functions, so start by making a table of values for $y = 2^x$.

Interchange the corresponding x- and y-values. These ordered pairs represent $y = \log_2 x$.

x	0.25	0.5	1	2	4
y	−2	−1	0	1	2

Graph the ordered pairs.

USE STRUCTURE
The functions $y = \log_2 x$ and $y = 2^x$ are inverse functions. The graphs are reflections of each other across the line $y = x$. Ⓒ **MP.7**

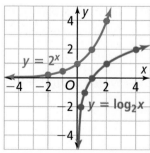

domain: $\{x \mid x > 0\}$

range: all real numbers

x-intercept: 1

asymptote: y-axis

> The logarithmic function accepts only positive input values.

> The graph of the logarithmic function approaches $x = 0$ but does not touch it.

end behavior: As $x \to 0$, $y \to -\infty$.
As $x \to \infty$, $y \to \infty$.

✓ Try It!

1. Graph each function and identify the domain and range. List any intercepts or asymptotes. Describe the end behavior.

a. $y = \ln x$ **b.** $y = \log_{\frac{1}{2}} x$

EXAMPLE 2 Graph Transformations of Logarithmic Functions

Graph the function. How do the asymptote and *x*-intercept of the given function compare to those of the parent function?

$g(x) = \log_2 (x + 3)$

In g, the value of h is –3, so the logarithmic function is translated 3 units to the left.

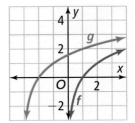

$$f(x) = \log_2 x$$
$$g(x) = \log_2 (x + 3) = f(x -(-3))$$

The vertical asymptote and the *x*-intercept each shift 3 units to the left.

COMMON ERROR
With exponential functions, the value of *k* dictates the shift of the horizontal asymptote. With logarithmic functions, the asymptote is vertical. So the value of *h* determines the shift of the asymptote.

☑ **Try It!** **2.** Describe how each graph compares to the graph of $f(x) = \ln x$.

a. $g(x) = \ln x + 4$ **b.** $h(x) = 5 \ln x$

CONCEPTUAL
UNDERSTANDING

 EXAMPLE 3 Inverses of Exponential and Logarithmic Functions

What is the equation of the inverse of the functions?
A. $f(x) = 10^{x+1}$

Write the function in $y = f(x)$ form and then interchange *x* and *y*.

$y = 10^{x+1}$ .... Write the function in $y = f(x)$ form.
$x = 10^{y+1}$ .... Interchange *x* and *y*.
$y + 1 = \log x$ .... Write in log form.
$y = \log x - 1$ .... Solve for *y*.

The equation of the inverse of $f(x) = 10^{x+1}$ is $f^{-1} (x) = \log x - 1$.

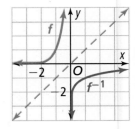

LOOK FOR RELATIONSHIPS
$f(x)$ is a translation of the parent function $y = 10^x$ one unit left. $f^{-1}(x)$ is a translation of the parent function $y = \log x$ one unit down. Graphical translations of a function and its inverse are directly related, with horizontal and vertical effects switching places. Ⓒ **MP.7**

B. $g(x) = \log_7 (x + 5)$

Write the function in $y = g(x)$ form and then interchange *x* and *y*.

$y = \log_7 (x + 5)$ ···· Write the function in $y = g(x)$ form.
$x = \log_7 (y + 5)$ ···· Interchange *x* and *y*.
$y + 5 = 7^x$ .... Write in exponential form.
$y = 7^x - 5$ .... Solve for *y*.

The equation of the inverse of $g(x) = \log_7 (x + 5)$ is $g^{-1}(x) = 7^x - 5$.

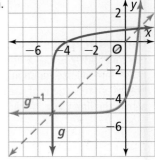

☑ **Try It!** **3.** Find the inverse of each function.

a. $f(x) = 3^{x+2}$ **b.** $g(x) = \log_7 x - 2$

 EXAMPLE 4   Interpret the Inverse of a Formula Involving Logarithms

A company uses this function to relate sales revenue R and advertising costs, a:

> R is revenue in thousands of dollars. a is advertising costs in thousands of dollars.

$$R = 12 \log(a + 1) + 25$$

STUDY TIP
To find the inverse formula do not interchange the variables. Instead, solve for a in terms of R. The variables a and R have a particular meaning in this context and are not interchangeable.

What is the equation of the inverse of the formula? Which equation would be easier to use to find a value of a for a particular value of R?

$R = 12 \log(a + 1) + 25$	Write the equation in $R = f(a)$ form.
$R - 25 = 12 \log(a + 1)$	Subtract 25 from each side.
$\dfrac{R - 25}{12} = \log(a + 1)$	Divide each side by 12.
$a + 1 = 10^{\frac{R-25}{12}}$	Rewrite in exponential form.
$a = 10^{\frac{R-25}{12}} - 1$	Subtract 1 from each side.

The inverse of the formula is $a = 10^{\frac{R-25}{12}} - 1$. It would be easier to use the inverse to find a when R is known.

✓ **Try It!**   4. Describe what happens to the amount of monthly revenue as the cost of advertising increases. How might you determine the optimal advertising budget? Explain.

 EXAMPLE 5   Compare Two Logarithmic Functions

Logarithmic functions can approximate the altitude of a plane over time. Which plane's altitude shows the greater rate of change over the interval $10 \le t \le 15$?

Plane A

Altitude is approximated by following the function:

$$A = 9{,}200 \ln t + 10{,}000$$

t is time in minutes after takeoff.

A is altitude in feet.

Plane B

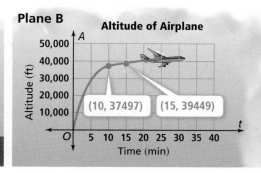

Altitude of Airplane

(10, 37497)   (15, 39449)

STUDY TIP
The average rate of change is a ratio of the change in altitude to the change in time over the interval.

Step 1 Determine the average rate of change for Plane A.

$$\frac{34{,}914 - 31{,}184}{15 - 10} = \frac{3{,}730}{5} = 746 \text{ ft per min}$$

> Find $A(15)$ and $A(10)$ using the function given for Plane A.

Step 2 Determine the average rate of change for Plane B.

$$\frac{39{,}449 - 37{,}497}{15 - 10} = \frac{1{,}952}{5} = 390 \text{ ft per min}$$

> Use the points given in the graph for Plane B.

Between 10 and 15 min after takeoff, the average rate of change of the altitude of Plane A is greater than the average rate of change for Plane B.

✓ **Try It!**   5. For which plane do you think the altitude will change more quickly over the interval $15 \le t \le 20$? Explain your reasoning.

CONCEPT SUMMARY Logarithmic Functions

GRAPH

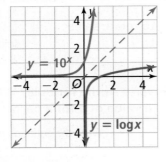

The functions are inverses so their graphs are reflections of each other across the line with equation $y = x$.

EQUATIONS

$y = \log x$

$y = 10^x$

KEY FEATURES

Domain: $\{x \mid x > 0\}$

Range: all real numbers

x-intercept: 1

Asymptote: y-axis

Domain: all real numbers

Range: $\{y \mid y > 0\}$

y-intercept: 1

Asymptote: x-axis

END BEHAVIOR

As $x \to 0$, $y \to -\infty$

As $x \to \infty$, $y \to \infty$

As $x \to -\infty$, $y \to 0$

As $x \to \infty$, $y \to \infty$

Do You UNDERSTAND?

1. **ESSENTIAL QUESTION** How is the relationship between logarithmic and exponential functions revealed in the key features of their graphs?

2. **Error Analysis** Raynard claims the domain of the function $y = \log_3 x$ is all real numbers. Explain the error Raynard made. © **MP.3**

3. **Communicate Precisely** How are the graphs of $f(x) = \log_5 x$ and $g(x) = -\log_5 x$ related? © **MP.6**

Do You KNOW HOW?

4. Graph the function $y = \log_4 x$ and identify the domain and range. List any intercepts or asymptotes. Describe the end behavior.

5. Write the equation for the function $g(x)$, which can be described as a vertical shift $1\frac{1}{2}$ units up from the function $f(x) = \ln x - 1$.

6. The function $y = 5 \ln(x + 1)$ gives y, the number of downloads, in hundreds, x minutes after the release of a song. Find the equation of the inverse and interpret its meaning.

UNDERSTAND

7. Look for Relationships Are the logarithmic and exponential functions shown inverses of each other? Explain. **© MP.7**

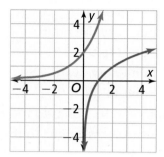

8. Communicate Precisely How is the graph of the logarithmic function $g(x) = \log_2 (x - 7)$ related to the graph of the function $f(x) = \log_2 x$? Explain your reasoning. **© MP.6**

9. Error Analysis Describe and correct the error a student made in finding the inverse of the exponential function $f(x) = 5^{x-6} + 2$. **© MP.3**

$y = 5^{x-6} + 2$	Write in $y = f(x)$ form.
$x = 5^{y-6} + 2$	Interchange x and y.
$x - 2 = 5^{y-6}$	Subtract 2 from each side.
$y - 6 = \log_5 x - 2$	Rewrite in logarithmic form.
$y = \log_5 x - 2 + 6$	Add 6 to each side.
$y = \log_5 x + 4$	Simplify.
$f'(x) = \log_5 x + 4$	

10. Make Sense and Persevere The number of members m who joined a new workout center w weeks after opening is modeled by the equation $m = 1.6^{\,w+2}$, where $0 \le w \le 10$. Find the inverse of the function and explain what the inverse tells you. **© MP.1**

11. Use Structure The graph shows a transformation of the parent graph $f(x) = \log_3 x$. Write an equation for the graph. **© MP.7**

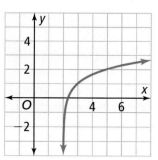

PRACTICE

Graph each function and identify the domain and range. List any intercepts or asymptotes. Describe the end behavior. SEE EXAMPLE 1

12. $y = \log_5 x$

13. $y = \log_8 x$

14. $y = \log_{\frac{3}{10}} x$

15. $y = \log_{0.1} x$

Describe the graph in terms of transformations of the parent function $f(x) = \log_6 x$. Compare the asymptote and x-intercept of the given function to the parent function. SEE EXAMPLE 2

16. $g(x) = \frac{1}{2} \log_6 x$

17. $g(x) = \log_6 (-x)$

18. Describe how the graph of $g(x) = -\ln(x + 0.5)$ is related to the graph of $f(x) = \ln x$. SEE EXAMPLE 2

Find the equation of the inverse of each function. SEE EXAMPLE 3

19. $f(x) = 5^{x-3}$

20. $f(x) = \left(\frac{1}{2}\right)^{x-1}$

21. $f(x) = 6^{x+7}$

22. $f(x) = \log_2 (8x)$

23. $f(x) = \ln (x + 3) - 1$

24. $f(x) = 4 \log_2 (x - 3) + 2$

25. The altitude y, in feet, of a plane t minutes after takeoff is approximated by the function $y = 5,000 \ln(.05t) + 8,000$. Solve for t in terms of y. What is a situation in which it would be easier to use your new equation rather than the original? SEE EXAMPLE 4

26. Find the average rate of change of the function graphed below over the interval $10 \le x \le 50$. Compare it to the average rate of change of $y = 3 \log x + 12$ over the same interval. SEE EXAMPLE 5

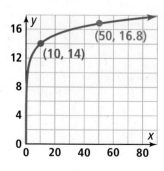

APPLY

27. Model with Mathematics The equation $r = 90 - 25 \log(t + 1)$ is to model a student's retention r after taking a physics course where r represents a student's test score (as a percent), and t represents the number of months since taking the course. **MP.4**

a. Make a table of values for ordered pairs that represent $r = 90 - 25 \log(t + 1)$, rounding to the nearest tenth. Then sketch the graph of the function on a coordinate plane through those ordered pairs. (You may use a graphing calculator to check.)

b. Find the equation of the inverse. Interpret the meaning of this function.

28. Higher Order Thinking As shown by the diagram, an earthquake occurs below Earth's surface at point F (the focus). Point E, on the surface above the focus, is called the *epicenter*. A seismograph station at point S records the waves of energy generated by the earthquake. The surface wave magnitude M of the earthquake is given by this formula:

$$M = \log\left(\frac{A}{T}\right) + 1.66(\log D) + 3.3$$

In the formula, A is the amplitude of the ground motion in micrometers, T is the period in seconds, and D is the measure of ES in degrees.

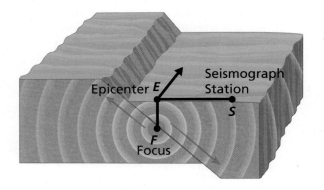

a. Find surface wave magnitude of an earthquake with $A = 700$ micrometers, $T = 2$ and $D = 100°$.

b. In the formula, $20° < D \leq 160°$. By how much can the size of arc ES affect the surface wave magnitude? Explain.

ASSESSMENT PRACTICE

29. The logarithmic function $g(x) = \ln x$ is transformed to $h(x) = \ln(x + 2) - 1$. Which of the following are true? Select **all** that apply.

Ⓐ $g(x)$ is translated 2 units upward.

Ⓑ $g(x)$ is translated 2 units to the right.

Ⓒ $g(x)$ is translated 2 units to the left.

Ⓓ $g(x)$ is translated 1 unit downward.

Ⓔ $g(x)$ is translated 1 unit to the left.

Ⓕ The vertical asymptote shifts 2 units to the left.

Ⓖ The vertical asymptote shifts 2 units to the right.

30. SAT/ACT The graph shows the exponential function $f(x) = 5^{x+1}$. Which of the following functions represents its inverse, $f^{-1}(x)$?

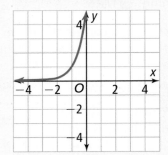

Ⓐ $f^{-1}(x) = 1 + \log_5 x$ Ⓒ $f^{-1}(x) = \log_5 (x - 1)$

Ⓑ $f^{-1}(x) = \log_5 x - 1$ Ⓓ $f^{-1}(x) = \log_5 (x + 1)$

31. Performance Task The logarithmic function $M(d) = 5 \log d + 2$ is used to find the limiting magnitude of a telescope, where d represents the diameter of the lens of the telescope (mm) that is being used for the observation.

Part A Find the limiting magnitude of a telescope having a lens diameter of 40 mm.

Part B Find the equation of the inverse of this function.

Part C Interpret why astronomers may wish to use the inverse of this function. Justify your reasoning.

Part D Using the inverse function, find the diameter of the lens that has a limiting magnitude of 13.5. Check your answer with the table function of your graphing calculator.

6-5

Properties of Logarithms

I CAN...
use properties of logarithms to rewrite expressions.

VOCABULARY
• Change of Base Formula

EXPLORE & REASON

Look at the graph of $y = \log x$ and the ordered pairs shown.

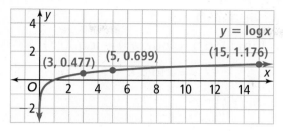

A. Complete the table shown.

x	3	5	15
$\log x$			

B. Look for Relationships What is the relationship between the numbers 3, 5, and 15? What is the relationship between the logarithms of 3, 5, and 15? **MP.7**

C. What is your prediction for the value of $\log 45$? $\log 75$? Explain.

? ESSENTIAL QUESTION

How are the properties of logarithms used to simplify expressions and solve logarithmic equations?

CONCEPT Properties of Logarithms

For positive numbers b, m, and n with $b \neq 1$, the following properties hold.

$$\log_b mn = \log_b m + \log_b n \quad \text{ .... Product Property of Logarithms}$$

$$\log_b \frac{m}{n} = \log_b m - \log_b n \quad \text{ .... Quotient Property of Logarithms}$$

$$\log_b m^n = n \log_b m \quad \text{ .... Power Property of Logarithms}$$

EXAMPLE 1   Prove a Property of Logarithms

How can you prove the Product Property of Logarithms?

Let $x = \log_b m$ and $y = \log_b n$. Then $b^x = m$ and $b^y = n$.

$$b^x \cdot b^y = m \cdot n \quad \text{ .... Multiply the expressions } b^x \text{ and } b^y.$$

$$b^{x+y} = mn \quad \text{ .... Product Property of Exponents}$$

$$x + y = \log_b mn \quad \text{ .... Rewrite the equation in logarithmic form.}$$

$$\log_b m + \log_b n = \log_b mn \quad \text{ .... Substitute.}$$

☑ Try It!   1. Prove the Quotient Property of Logarithms.

EXAMPLE 2 **Expand Logarithmic Expressions**

MAKE SENSE AND PERSEVERE
Expanding logarithmic expressions requires the use of a variety of properties. Look at the whole expression first to determine the sequence of properties that will be used. © **MP.1**

How can you use the properties of logarithms to expand each expression?

A. $\log_5(a^2b^7)$

$$\log_5(a^2b^7) = \log_5(a^2) + \log_5(b^7) \quad \cdots \text{Product Property of Logarithms}$$

$$= 2\log_5 a + 7\log_5 b \quad \cdots \text{Power Property of Logarithms}$$

B. $\ln\left(\frac{25}{3}\right)$

$$\ln\left(\frac{25}{3}\right) = \ln\left(\frac{5^2}{3}\right) \quad \cdots \text{Rewrite the numerator as a power.}$$

$$= \ln(5^2) - \ln 3 \quad \cdots \text{Quotient Property of Logarithms}$$

$$= 2\ln 5 - \ln 3 \quad \cdots \text{Power Property of Logarithms}$$

Try It! **2.** Use the properties of logarithms to expand each expression.

a. $\log_7\left(\frac{r^3t^4}{v}\right)$ **b.** $\ln\left(\frac{7}{225}\right)$

 EXAMPLE 3 **Write Expressions as Single Logarithms**

STUDY TIP
Recall that the Properties of Logarithms are each associated with a different operation. Addition signals the Product Property, subtraction signals the Quotient Property, and multiplication by a constant signals the Power Property.

What is each expression written as a single logarithm?

A. $4\log_4 m + 3\log_4 n - \log_4 p$

$$4\log_4 m + 3\log_4 n - \log_4 p$$

$$= \log_4(m^4) + \log_4(n^3) - \log_4 p \quad \cdots \text{Power Property of Logarithms}$$

$$= \log_4(m^4 n^3) - \log_4 p \quad \cdots \text{Product Property of Logarithms}$$

$$= \log_4\left(\frac{m^4 n^3}{p}\right) \quad \cdots \text{Quotient Property of Logarithms}$$

B. $3\ln 2 - 2\ln 5$

$$3\ln 2 - 2\ln 5 = \ln(2^3) - \ln(5^2) \quad \cdots \text{Power Property of Logarithms}$$

$$= \ln\left(\frac{2^3}{5^2}\right) \quad \cdots \text{Quotient Property of Logarithms}$$

$$= \ln\left(\frac{8}{25}\right) \quad \cdots \text{Simplify exponents}$$

Try It! **3.** Write each expression as a single logarithm.

a. $5\log_2 c - 7\log_2 n$ **b.** $2\ln 7 + \ln 2$

APPLICATION

 EXAMPLE 4 Apply Properties of Logarithms

The pH of a solution is a measure of its concentration of hydrogen ions. This concentration (measured in moles per liter) is written $[H^+]$ and is given by the formula

$$pH = \log\frac{1}{[H^+]}.$$

pH OF A SOLUTION			
Orange juice pH = 3	Acid rain pH = 4.5	Clear rain pH = 5.6	Healthy lake pH = 6.5

What is the concentration of hydrogen ions in the acid rainfall?

$$4.5 = \log\frac{1}{[H^+]} \quad\text{............... Substitute 4.5 for pH.}$$

$$4.5 = \log 1 - \log[H^+] \quad\text{............... Quotient Property}$$

$$-4.5 = \log[H^+] \quad\text{............... Solve for } \log[H^+]$$

$$10^{-4.5} = H^+ \quad\text{............... Write in exponential form.}$$

The concentration of hydrogen ions in the acid rainfall is $10^{-4.5} \approx 0.0000316$ moles per liter.

COMMON ERROR
The expression $\log\frac{1}{[H^+]}$ is equal to $\log 1 - \log[H^+]$, not $\log[1 - H^+]$.

 Try It! 4. What is the concentration of hydrogen ions in a liter of orange juice?

CONCEPTUAL UNDERSTANDING

 EXAMPLE 5 Evaluate Logarithmic Expressions by Changing the Base

How can you use base 10 logarithms to evaluate base 2 logarithms?

To evaluate $\log_2 3$ with a calculator, you need to express $\log_2 3$ in terms of base 10 logarithms.

$$\log_2 3 = \frac{\log_2 3 \cdot \log 2}{\log 2} \quad\text{....... Multiply } \log_2 3 \text{ by 1 in the form of } \frac{\log 2}{\log 2}.$$

$$= \frac{\log 2^{\log_2 3}}{\log 2} \quad\text{....... Power Property of Logarithms.}$$

$$= \frac{\log 3}{\log 2} \quad\text{....... Since } 2^{\log_2 3} = 3, \text{ the numerator simplifies to } \log 3.$$

> Remember that exponents and logarithms are inverse operations, so they undo one another.

$$= \frac{0.477}{0.301} \approx 1.585 \quad\text{..... Use a calculator to evaluate.}$$

STUDY TIP
To divide logs with a calculator using one expression, be sure to include parentheses in the correct places. To evaluate $\log_2 3$, press [LOG] [3] [÷] [(] [LOG] [2] [)] [ENTER.]

This illustrates the **Change of Base Formula**:

For positive numbers m, b, and a, with $b \neq 1$ and $a \neq 1$, $\log_b m = \frac{\log_a m}{\log_a b}$.

 Try It! 5. Estimate the value of each logarithm. Then use a calculator to find the value of each logarithm to the nearest thousandth.

    a. $\log_2 7$ **b.** $\log_5 3$

 **EXAMPLE 6**   Use the Change of Base Formula

What is the solution of the equation $2^x = 7$? Express the solution as a logarithm and then evaluate. Round to the nearest thousandth.

$2^x = 7$	Write the equation.
$x = \log_2 7$	Rewrite in logarithmic form.
$x = \dfrac{\log 7}{\log 2}$	Use the Change of Base Formula.
$x \approx 2.807$	Use a calculator.

Check $2^{2.807} \approx 7$

STUDY TIP
The equation $2^x = 7$ can also be solved using natural logarithms.

☑ **Try It!**   **6.** What is the solution to the equation $3^x = 15$? Express the solution as a logarithm, make an estimate, and then evaluate. Round to the nearest thousandth.

CONCEPT SUMMARY Properties of Logarithms

	Product Property	Quotient Property	Power Property	Change of Base
ALGEBRA	$\log_b (mn) =$ $\log_b m + \log_b n$	$\log_b \left(\dfrac{m}{n}\right) =$ $\log_b m - \log_b n$	$\log_b (m^n) =$ $n \cdot \log_b m$	$\log_b m = \dfrac{\log_a m}{\log_a b}$
WORDS	The log of a product is the sum of the logs.	The log of a quotient is the difference of the logs.	The log of a number raised to a power is the power multiplied by the log of the number.	The log base b of a number is equal to the log base a of the number divided by the log base a of b.
NUMBERS	$\log_2 (20) =$ $\log_2 (4) + \log_2 (5)$	$\log_{10} \left(\dfrac{2}{3}\right) =$ $\log_{10} 2 - \log_{10} 3$	$\log_3 (16) = 4 \cdot \log_3 2$	$\log_5 7 = \dfrac{\log 7}{\log 5}$

☑ Do You UNDERSTAND?

1.  **ESSENTIAL QUESTION** How are the properties of logarithms used to simplify expressions and solve logarithmic equations?

2. **Vocabulary** While it is not necessary to change to base 10 when applying the Change of Base Formula, why is it common to do so?

3. **Error Analysis** Amanda claimed the expanded form of the expression $\log_4 (c^2 d^5)$ is $5 \log_4 c + 5 \log_4 d$. Explain the error Amanda made. ⊙ **MP.3**

Do You KNOW HOW?

4. Use the properties of logarithms to expand the expression $\log_6 \left(\dfrac{49}{5}\right)$.

5. Use the properties of logarithms to write the expression $5 \ln s + 6 \ln t$ as a single logarithm.

6. Use the formula $\text{pH} = \log \dfrac{1}{[H^+]}$ to write an expression for the concentration of hydrogen ions, $[H^+]$, in a container of baking soda with a pH of 8.9.

UNDERSTAND

7. **Use Structure** Without applying the Change of Base Formula, explain how to use $\log_3 2 \approx 0.631$ and $\log_3 5 \approx 1.465$ to approximate $\log_3\left(\frac{2}{5}\right)$. ⓒ **MP.7**

8. **Communicate Precisely** Explain what is meant by *expanding a logarithmic expression*. How are the processes of *expanding logarithmic expressions* and *writing logarithmic expressions as a single logarithm* related? ⓒ **MP.6**

9. **Higher Order Thinking** The graph of $y = \log\left(\frac{1}{x}\right)$ and $y = -\log x$ are shown. Notice the graph is the same for both equations. Use properties of logarithms to explain why the graphs are the same.

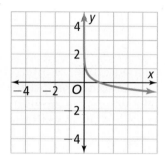

10. **Communicate Precisely** Emma used the Change of Base Formula to solve the equation $6^x = 72$ and found that $x = 2.387$. How can Emma check her solution? ⓒ **MP.6**

11. **Error Analysis** Describe and correct the error a student made in writing the logarithmic expression in terms of a single logarithm. ⓒ **MP.3**

$$\log_3 2 + \frac{1}{2}\log_3 y = \log_3 2y^2 \quad \text{✗}$$

12. **Error Analysis** A student wants to approximate $\log_2 9$ with her calculator. She enters the equivalent expression $\frac{\ln 2}{\ln 9}$, but the decimal value is not close to her estimate of 3. What happened? ⓒ **MP.3**

$$\log_2 9 = \frac{\ln 2}{\ln 9} \quad \text{✗}$$

PRACTICE

13. Use the properties of exponents to prove the Power Property of Logarithms. **SEE EXAMPLE 1**

Use the properties of logarithms to expand each expression. **SEE EXAMPLE 2**

14. $\log_5\left(\frac{2}{3}\right)$ 15. $\log_6\left(2m^5n^3\right)$

16. $\ln 2x^5$ 17. $\log_2\left(\frac{x}{5y}\right)$

Use the properties of logarithms to write each expression as a single logarithm. **SEE EXAMPLE 3**

18. $9\ln x - 6\ln y$ 19. $\log_5 6 + \frac{1}{2}\log_5 y$

20. $2\log 10 + 4\log(3x)$ 21. $\frac{1}{3}\ln 27 - 3\ln(2y)$

22. $8\log_3 2 + 5\log_3 c + 7\log_3 d$

23. Use properties of logarithms to show that $pH = \log\frac{1}{[H^+]}$ can be written as $pH = -\log[H^+]$.
SEE EXAMPLE 4

Use the Change of Base Formula to evaluate each logarithm. Round to the nearest thousandth.
SEE EXAMPLE 5

24. $\log_4 9$ 25. $\log_6 5$

26. $\ln 3$ 27. $\log_2 7$

28. $\log_9 12$ 29. $\ln 23$

Use the Change of Base Formula to solve each equation for x. Give an exact solution as a logarithm and an approximate solution rounded to the nearest thousandth. **SEE EXAMPLE 6**

30. $3^x = 4$ 31. $5^x = 11$

32. $8^x = 10$ 33. $2^x = 30$

34. $7^x = 100$ 35. $4^x = 55$

APPLY

36. **Make Sense and Persevere** The loudness of sound is measured in decibels. For a sound with intensity I (in watts per square meter), its loudness $L(I)$ (in decibels) is modeled by the function $L(I) = 10 \log \frac{I}{I_0}$, where I_0 represents the intensity of a barely audible sound (approximately 10^{-12} watts per square meter). © **MP.1**

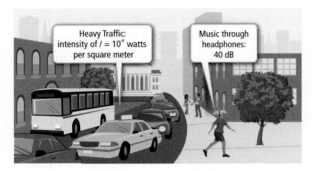

Heavy Traffic: intensity of $I = 10^4$ watts per square meter

Music through headphones: 40 dB

a. Find the decibel level of the sound made by the heavy traffic.

b. Find the intensity of the sound that is made by music playing at 40 decibels.

c. How many times as great is the intensity of the traffic than the intensity of the music?

37. **Model with Mathematics** Miguel collected data on the attendance at an amusement park and the daily high temperature. He found that the model $A = 2 \log t + \log 5$ approximated the attendance A, in thousands of people, at the amusement park, when the daily high temperature is t degrees Fahrenheit. © **MP.4**

a. Use properties of logarithms to simplify Miguel's formula.

b. The daily high temperatures for the week are below.

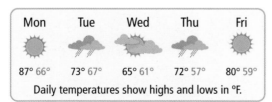

Mon	Tue	Wed	Thu	Fri
87° 66°	73° 67°	65° 61°	72° 57°	80° 59°

Daily temperatures show highs and lows in °F.

What is the expected attendance on Wednesday? Round to the nearest person.

ASSESSMENT PRACTICE

38. Match each expression with an equivalent expression.

I. $\log_4 20$
II. $2 \log_2 5$
III. $\log_2 5$
VI. $4 \log_4 2$

Ⓐ $\log_2 20 - \log_2 4$
Ⓑ $\log_4 2 + \log_4 10$
Ⓒ $\frac{\log 25}{\log 2}$
Ⓓ $\log_2 4$

39. **SAT/ACT** Use the properties of logarithms to write the following expression in terms of a single logarithm.

$$2(\log_3 20 - \log_3 4) + 0.5 \log_3 4$$

Ⓐ $\log_3 4$
Ⓑ $\log_3 5$
Ⓒ $\log_3 25$
Ⓓ $\log_3 50$

40. **Performance Task** The magnitude, or intensity, of an earthquake is measured on the Richter scale. For an earthquake where the amplitude of its seismographic trace is A, its magnitude is modeled by the function:

$$R(A) = \log \frac{A}{A_0},$$

where A_0 represents the amplitude of the smallest detectable earthquake.

Part A An earthquake occurs with an amplitude 200 times greater than the amplitude of the smallest detectable earthquake, A_0. What is the magnitude of this earthquake on the Richter scale?

Part B Approximately how many times as great is the amplitude of an earthquake measuring 6.8 on the Richter scale than the amplitude of an earthquake measuring 5.9 on the Richter scale?

Part C Suppose the intensity of one earthquake is 150 times as great as that of another. How much greater is the magnitude of the more intense earthquake than the less intense earthquake?

6-6

Exponential and Logarithmic Equations

SavvasRealize.com

I CAN... solve exponential and logarithmic equations.

VOCABULARY
- exponential equation
- logarithmic equation

MODEL & DISCUSS

A store introduces two new models of fitness trackers to its product line. A glance at the data is enough to see that sales of both types of fitness trackers are increasing. Unfortunately, the store has limited space for the merchandise. The manager decides that the store will sell both models until sales of TrackSmart exceed those of FitTracker.

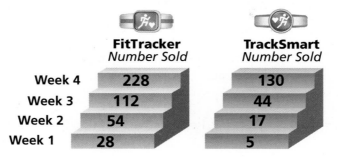

	FitTracker Number Sold	**TrackSmart** Number Sold
Week 4	228	130
Week 3	112	44
Week 2	54	17
Week 1	28	5

A. Model With Mathematics Find an equation of an exponential function that models the sales for each fitness tracker. Describe your method. © **MP.4**

B. Based on the equations that you wrote, determine when the store will stop selling FitTracker.

ESSENTIAL QUESTION

How do properties of exponents and logarithms help you solve equations?

CONCEPT Property of Equality for Exponential Equations

VOCABULARY
An **exponential equation** is an equation that contains variables in the exponents.

Symbols	Suppose $b > 0$ and $b \neq 1$, then $b^x = b^y$ if and only if $x = y$.
Words	If two powers of the same base are equal, then their exponents are equal; if two exponents are equal, then the powers with the same base are equal.

EXAMPLE 1   Solve Exponential Equations Using a Common Base

What is the solution to $\left(\frac{1}{2}\right)^{x+7} = 4^{3x}$?

$\left(\frac{1}{2}\right)^{x+7} = 4^{3x}$	Write the original equation.
$(2^{-1})^{x+7} = (2^2)^{3x}$	Rewrite each side with a common base.
$2^{-x-7} = 2^{6x}$	Power of a Power Property
$-x - 7 = 6x$	Property of Equality for Exponential Equations
$-7 = 7x$	Add x to each side.
$-1 = x$	Divide each side by 7.

✓ Try It!   1. Solve each equation using a common base.

     a. $25^{3x} = 125^{x+2}$ **b.** $0.001 = 10^{6x}$

CONCEPTUAL
UNDERSTANDING

 EXAMPLE 2 **Rewrite Exponential Equations Using Logarithms**

How can you rewrite the equation $17 = 4^x$ using logarithms?

There is no common base for 17 and 4. Write each number as a power of 10.

$$17 = 4^x$$ .... Write the original equation.

$$10^{\log 17} = 10^{\log 4^x}$$ .... Write the equation using the powers of 10.

$$\log 17 = \log 4^x$$ .... Property of Equality for Exponential Equations

Rewriting expressions using logarithms can help you solve many types
of problems.

 Try It! **2.** Rewrite the equation $5^x = 12$ using logarithms.

CONCEPT Property of Equality for Logarithmic Equations

Symbols If $x > 0$, then $\log_b x = \log_b y$ if and only if $x = y$.

Words If two logarithms (exponents) of the same base are equal, then
the quantities are equal; if two quantities are equal, and the
bases are the same, then the logarithms (exponents) are equal.

 EXAMPLE 3 **Solve Exponential Equations Using Logarithms**

What is the solution to $3^{x+1} = 5^x$?

$$3^{x+1} = 5^x$$ .... Write the original equation.

$$\log(3^{x+1}) = \log(5^x)$$ .... Property of Equality for Logarithmic Equations

$$(x + 1) \log 3 = x \log 5$$ .... Power Property of Logarithms

$$x \log 3 + \log 3 = x \log 5$$ .... Use the Distributive Property.

$$x(\log 3 - \log 5) = -\log 3$$ .... Move terms and factor out x.

$$x = \frac{-\log 3}{\log 3 - \log 5}$$ .... Divide.

$$x \approx 2.15$$ .... Evaluate.

> **COMMON ERROR**
> The entire quantity of $x + 1$ is the
> exponent, so it must be written as
> a quantity to be multiplied by the
> logarithmic expression.

Check

Substitute 2.15 into the equation:

$$3^{x+1} = 3^{2.15+1} \approx 31.8$$

$$5^x = 5^{2.15} \approx 31.8$$

The point of intersection of the graphs is about (2.15, 31.8).

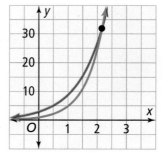

 Try It! **3.** What is the solution to $2^{3x} = 7^{x+1}$?

APPLICATION

EXAMPLE 4   **Use an Exponential Model**

The diagram shows how a forest fire grows over time. The fire department can contain a 160-acre fire without needing additional resources. About how many minutes does it take for a fire to become too big for the fire department to contain without additional resources? Round to the nearest minute.

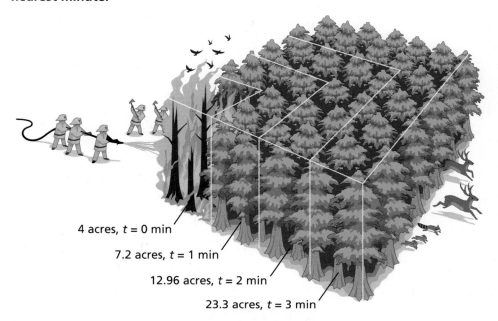

4 acres, $t = 0$ min

7.2 acres, $t = 1$ min

12.96 acres, $t = 2$ min

23.3 acres, $t = 3$ min

Formulate ◀ Because the ratios of the number of acres from the diagram are all 1.8, the exponential growth model uses $b = 1.8$. The model is $160 = 4(1.8)^t$.

> Use the model $y = ab^t$ where y represents the number of acres, a is the initial number of acres, b is the growth rate of the fire, and t is the number of minutes the fire has raged.

Compute ◀ Solve the equation for t.

$160 = 4(1.8)^t$ .... Write the original equation.

$40 = (1.8)^t$ .... Divide each side by 4.

$\log 40 = \log(1.8)^t$ .... Property of Equality for Logarithmic Equations

$\log 40 = t \log 1.8$ .... Power Property of Logarithms

$\dfrac{\log 40}{\log 1.8} = t$ .... Isolate the variable t.

$6.276 \approx t$ .... Evaluate.

Interpret ◀ Verify the answer by evaluating the expression $4(1.8)^{6.276}$.

$4(1.8)^{6.276} \approx 160.01$

The fire department has a little more than 6 minutes to contain the fire before they will require additional resources.

 Try It!   **4.** About how many minutes does it take the fire to spread to cover 100 acres?

VOCABULARY
A **logarithmic equation** contains one or more logarithms of variable expressions.

 EXAMPLE 5   Solve Logarithmic Equations

What is the solution to $\ln (x^2 - 16) = \ln (6x)$?

$$\ln (x^2 - 16) = \ln (6x) \quad \text{.............. Write the original equation.}$$

$$x^2 - 16 = 6x \quad \text{.............. Property of Equality for Logarithmic Equations}$$

$$x^2 - 6x - 16 = 0 \quad \text{.............. Set quadratic equation equal to 0.}$$

$$(x - 8)(x + 2) = 0 \quad \text{.............. Factor.}$$

$$x = 8 \text{ or } -2 \quad \text{.............. Apply the Zero Product Property.}$$

Check   Substitute each value into the original equation.

$x = 8$	$x = -2$
$\ln (8^2 - 16) = \ln (6 \cdot 8)$	$\ln ((-2)^2 - 16) = \ln (6 \cdot (-2))$
$\ln (48) = \ln (48)$ ✔	$\ln (-12) = \ln (-12)$ ✘

Because logarithms are not defined for negative values, only $x = 8$ is a solution. The value $x = -2$ is an extraneous solution.

 Try It!   **5.** Solve each equation.

a. $\log_5 (x^2 - 45) = \log_5 (4x)$ **b.** $\ln (-4x - 1) = \ln (4x^2)$

EXAMPLE 6   Solve Logarithmic and Exponential Equations by Graphing

What is the solution to $\log (2x + 1)^5 = x - 2$?

USE APPROPRIATE TOOLS
When typing this equation into a calculator, it is helpful to write the equation using the Power Property of Logarithms rather than risking incorrect input of the exponent. Ⓒ **MP.5**

Let $y_1 = 5 \log (2x + 1)$ and $y_2 = x - 2$.

Graph both equations.

Use the INTERSECT feature to find the point(s) of intersection.

The points of intersection, to the nearest thousandth, are $(-0.329, -2.329)$ and $(8.204, 6.204)$.

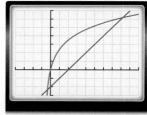

x scale: 1   y scale: 1

Check

$$\log (2(-0.329) + 1)^5 = -0.329 - 2 \qquad \log (2(8.204) + 1)^5 = 8.204 - 2$$

$$\log (0.342)^5 = -2.329 \qquad\qquad \log (17.408)^5 = 6.204$$

$$-2.329 = -2.329 \text{ ✔} \qquad\qquad 6.204 = 6.204 \text{ ✔}$$

The solutions are $x \approx -0.329$ and $x \approx 8.204$.

Try It!   **6.** Solve each equation by graphing. Round to the nearest thousandth.

a. $3(2)^{x+2} - 1 = 3 - x$ **b.** $\ln (3x - 1) = x - 5$

CONCEPT SUMMARY Exponential and Logarithmic Equations

Property of Equality for Exponential Equations		Property of Equality for Logarithmic Equations	
ALGEBRA	If b is a positive number other than 1, $b^x = b^y$ if and only if $x = y$.		If b is a positive number other than 1, $\log_b x = \log_b y$ if and only if $x = y$.
WORDS	If two powers of the same base are equal, then their exponents are equal.	If two exponents are equal, then the powers with the same base are equal.	If two logarithms of the same base are equal, then the arguments are equal.	If two arguments are equal and the bases are the same, then the logarithms are equal.
NUMBERS	If $2^x = 2^4$, then $x = 4$.	If $x = 4$, then $2^x = 2^4$.	If $\log_3 x = \log_3 8$, then $x = 8$.	If $x = 8$, then $\log_3 x = \log_3 8$.

 Do You UNDERSTAND?

1. **ESSENTIAL QUESTION** How do properties of exponents and logarithms help you solve equations?

2. **Vocabulary** Jordan claims that $x^2 + 3 = 12$ is an exponential equation. Is Jordan correct? Explain your thinking.

3. **Communicate Precisely** How can properties of logarithms help to solve an equation such as $\log_6 (8x - 2)^3 = 12$? © **MP.6**

Do You KNOW HOW?

Solve. Round to the nearest hundredth, if necessary. List any extraneous solutions.

4. $16^{3x} = 256^{x+1}$

5. $6^{x+2} = 4^x$

6. $\log_5 (x^2 - 44) = \log_5 (7x)$

7. $\log_2 (3x - 2) = 4$

8. $4^{2x} = 9^{x-1}$

9. A rabbit farm had 200 rabbits in 2015. The number of rabbits increases by 30% every year. How many rabbits are on the farm in 2031?

PRACTICE & PROBLEM SOLVING

UNDERSTAND

10. Use Structure Would you use the natural log or the common log when solving the equation $10^{x+2} = 78$? Is it possible to use either the natural log or common log? Explain. **MP.7**

11. Make Sense and Persevere Explain why logarithms are necessary to solve the equation $3^{x+2} = 8$, but are not necessary to solve the equation $3^{x+2} = 27^{4x}$. **MP.1**

12. Reason Tristen solved the equation $\log_3(x + 1) - \log_3(x - 6) = \log_3(2x + 2)$. Justify each step of solving the equation in Tristen's work. Are both numbers solutions to the equation? Explain. **MP.2**

$$\log_3(x + 1) - \log_3(x - 6) = \log_3(2x + 2)$$
$$\log_3(x + 1) = \log_3(2x + 2) + \log_3(x - 6)$$
$$\log_3(x + 1) = \log_3(2x + 2)(x - 6)$$
$$(x + 1) = (2x + 2)(x - 6)$$
$$x + 1 = 2x^2 - 10x - 12$$
$$0 = 2x^2 - 11x - 13$$
$$x = 6.5 \text{ or } x = -1$$

13. Error Analysis The number of milligrams of medicine in a person's system after t hours is given by the function $A = 20e^{-0.40t}$. Thomas sets $A = 0$ to find the number of hours it takes for all of the medicine to be removed from a person's system. What mistake did Thomas make? Explain. **MP.3**

14. Mathematical Connections Explain the importance of the Power Property of Logarithms when solving exponential equations.

15. Error Analysis Find the student error in the solution of the logarithmic equation. **MP.3**

$$\log(x + 3) + \log x = 1$$
$$\log x(x + 3) = 1$$
$$x(x + 3) = 10^1$$
$$x^2 + 3x - 10 = 0$$
$$(x - 2)(x + 5) = 0$$
$$x = 2, -5 \quad ✗$$

PRACTICE

Find all solutions of the equation. Round answers to the nearest ten-thousandth. SEE EXAMPLE 1

16. $3^{2-3x} = 3^{5x-6}$

17. $7^{3x} = 54$

18. $25^{x^2} = 125^{x+3}$

19. $4^{3x-1} = \left(\dfrac{1}{2}\right)^{x+5}$

20. $4^{2x+1} = 4^{3x-5}$

21. $6^{x-2} = 216$

Find all solutions of the equation. Round answers to the nearest ten-thousandth. SEE EXAMPLES 2 AND 3

22. $2^{3x-2} = 5$

23. $4 + 5^{6-x} = 15$

24. $6^{3x+1} = 9^x$

25. $-3 = \left(\dfrac{1}{2}\right)^x - 12$

26. $3^{2x-3} = 4^x$

27. $4^{x+2} = 8^{x-1}$

28. Dale has \$1,000 to invest. He has a goal to have \$2,500 in this investment in 10 years. At what annual rate compounded continuously will Dale reach his goal? Round to the nearest hundredth. SEE EXAMPLE 4

Find all solutions of the equation. Round answers to the nearest thousandth. SEE EXAMPLE 5

29. $\log_2(4x + 5) = \log_2 x^2$

30. $2\ln(3x - 2) = \ln(5x + 6)$

31. $\log_4(x^2 - 2x) = \log_4(3x + 8)$

32. $\ln(5x - 2) = \ln(x - 1)$

33. $\ln(2x^2 + 5x) = \ln(2x + 7)$

34. $2\log(x + 1) = \log(x + 1)$

35. $\log_2 x + \log_2(x - 3) = 2$

36. $\log_2(3x - 2) = \log_2(x - 1) + 4$

37. $\log_6(x^2 - 2x) = \log_6(2x - 3) + \log_6(x + 1)$

Solve by graphing. Round answers to the nearest thousandth. SEE EXAMPLE 6

38. $\log(5x - 3)^2 = x - 4$

39. $\ln(2x) = 3x - 5$

40. $\log(4x) = x + \log x$

APPLY

41. Model With Mathematics The population of a city is modeled by the function $P = 250{,}000e^{0.013t}$, where t is the number of years since 2000. In what year, to the nearest year, will the population reach 450,000? **© MP.4**

42. Use Structure Felix invested $10,000 into a retirement account in 2010. He then projected the amount of money that would be in the account for several years assuming that interest would compound continuously at an annual rate. Later, when he looked back the data, he could not recall the annual rate that he used for the projections. Use the data below to determine the annual rate. **© MP.7**

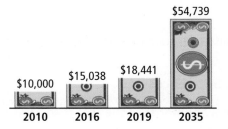

$54,739

$10,000 $15,038 $18,441

2010   2016   2019   2035

43. Higher Order Thinking A biologist is using the logarithmic model $n = k\log(A)$ to determine the number of a species n, that can live on a land mass of area A. The constant k varies according to the species.

a. Use the graph to determine the constant k for the species that the scientist is studying.

b. Determine the land mass in acres that is needed to support 3,000 of the species.

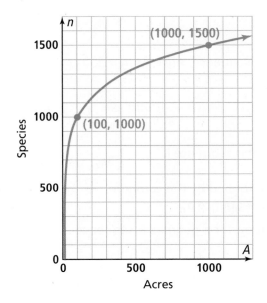

ASSESSMENT PRACTICE

44. Which of the following have the same solution? Select all that apply.

Ⓐ $\log_8(x^2 - 15) = \log_8(2x)$

Ⓑ $\ln(12x + 2) = \ln(2x - 3)$

Ⓒ $\log_2 x + \log_2(x + 4) = 5$

Ⓓ $\log_3(15x + 6)^2 = 8$

Ⓔ $\log_4(3x - 5) = 2$

45. SAT/ACT The graph shows the function $y = 4^x$. Determine when the function shown in the graph is greater than the function $y = 2^{3x-1}$.

Ⓐ $x > 1$

Ⓑ $x < 1$

Ⓒ $x > -1$

Ⓓ $x < -1$

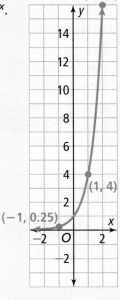

(2, 16)

(1, 4)

(−1, 0.25)

46. Performance Task A professor conducted an experiment to find the relationship between time and memory. The professor determined the model $f(t) = t_0 - 15\log(t + 1.1)$ gives the memory score after t months when a student had an initial memory score of t_0.

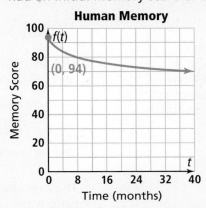

Human Memory

(0, 94)

Part A Write a model for a student with the given initial memory score.

Part B After about how many years will the student have a memory score of 65?

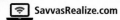

👆 **EXPLORE & REASON**

A store offered customers two plans for getting bonus points:

A. What expression represents the number of points received each day for Plan A?

B. What expression represents the number of points received each day for Plan B?

C. **Reason** On the 7th day, which plan would offer the most bonus points? Explain. © **MP.2**

PLAN A

10 POINTS TODAY!

Following days =
2X AS MANY POINTS
as the day before

PLAN B

1 POINT TODAY!

Following days =
3X AS MANY POINTS
as the day before

I CAN... identify, write, and use geometric sequences and series.

VOCABULARY
• common ratio
• geometric sequence
• geometric series

❓ **ESSENTIAL QUESTION**   How can you represent and use geometric sequences and series?

👆 **EXAMPLE 1**   **Identify Geometric Sequences**

A. Is the sequence shown in the table a geometric sequence? If so, write a recursive definition for the sequence.

A **geometric sequence** is a sequence with a constant ratio between consecutive terms. This ratio is called the **common ratio**, r.

Notice the relationship between the terms in this sequence:

Term Number (n)	Term (a_n)
1	4
2	12
3	36
4	108
5	324

⟩×3
⟩×3

Each term is 3 times the preceding term.

STUDY TIP
Notice that r serves in a similiar capacity as d in an arithmetic sequence. Where d is added to each preceding term, r is multiplied by each preceding term.

This sequence is a geometric sequence, since for $n = 1$, $a_1 = 4$, $r = 3$, and $a_2 = a_1 \cdot 3$

$a_3 = a_2 \cdot 3$

$a_n = a_{n-1} \cdot 3$

The recursive definition for this sequence is $a_n = \begin{cases} 4, & n = 1 \\ 3a_{n-1}, & n > 1. \end{cases}$

First term   Term number

common ratio

The preceding term a_{n-1} multiplied by the common ratio is the next term in the sequence a_n.

The general recursive defintion for a geometric sequence is $a_n = \begin{cases} a_1, & n = 1 \\ a_{n-1} \cdot r, & n > 1 \end{cases}$

CONTINUED ON THE NEXT PAGE

EXAMPLE 1 CONTINUED

B. Is the sequence 12, 9.6, 7.68, 6.144, ... a geometric sequence? If so, write the recursive definition for the sequence.

Find the ratio between consecutive terms.

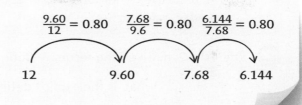

$$\frac{9.60}{12} = 0.80 \quad \frac{7.68}{9.6} = 0.80 \quad \frac{6.144}{7.68} = 0.80$$

12   9.60   7.68   6.144

The ratio between the consecutive terms is constant. This is a geometric sequence with $a_1 = 12$ and $r = 0.8$.

The recursive definition for the sequence is $a_n = \begin{cases} 12, & n = 1 \\ 0.8\, a_{n-1}, & n > 1 \end{cases}$

 Try It!   **1. Is the sequence a geometric sequence? If so, write a recursive definition for the sequence.**

     a. 1.22, 1.45, 1.68, 1.91, ...

     b. −1.5, 0.75, −0.375, 0.1875, ...

EXAMPLE 2   **Translate Between Recursive and Explicit Definitions**

A. Given the recursive definition $a_n = \begin{cases} 5, & n = 1 \\ \frac{1}{2}\, a_{n-1}, & n > 1 \end{cases}$

what is the explicit definition for the geometric sequence?

The first term is 5, and the common ratio is $\frac{1}{2}$.

The recursive definition is $a_n = \frac{1}{2} a_{n-1}$. Use this definition to find a pattern:

$a_1 = 5$ .... Identify the first term.

$a_2 = 5\left(\frac{1}{2}\right)$ .... 1 common ratio multiplied to the first term

$a_3 = a_2 \cdot \left(\frac{1}{2}\right) = (5)\left(\frac{1}{2}\right)\left(\frac{1}{2}\right) = (5)\left(\frac{1}{2}\right)^2$ ...... 2 common ratios multiplied to the first term

$a_4 = a_3 \cdot \left(\frac{1}{2}\right) = (5)\left(\frac{1}{2}\right)^2\left(\frac{1}{2}\right) = (5)\left(\frac{1}{2}\right)^3$ ...... 3 common ratios multiplied to the first term

The pattern reveals the explicit definition for the sequence: $a_n = (5)\left(\frac{1}{2}\right)^{n-1}$.

The general explicit definition for any geometric sequence is: $a_n = a_1 r^{n-1}$.

VOCABULARY
Recall that an explicit definition allows you to find any term in the sequence without knowing the previous term.

CONTINUED ON THE NEXT PAGE

EXAMPLE 2 CONTINUED

B. Given the explicit definition $a_n = 3(2)^{n-1}$, what is the recursive definition for the geometric sequence?

From the explicit definition, $a_1 = 3$ and $r = 2$.

The recursive definition for the sequence is $a_n = \begin{cases} 3, & n = 1 \\ 2a_{n-1}, & n > 1 \end{cases}$.

Try It! **2. a.** Given the recursive definition $a_n = \begin{cases} 12, & n = 1 \\ \frac{1}{3}a_{n-1}, & n > 1 \end{cases}$
what is the explicit definition for the sequence?

b. Given the explicit definition $a_n = 6(1.2)^{n-1}$, what is the recursive definition?

APPLICATION  **EXAMPLE 3** **Solve Problems With Geometric Sequences**

A phone tree is when one person calls a certain number of people, then those people each call the same number of people, and so on. In the fifth round of calls, 243 people were called.

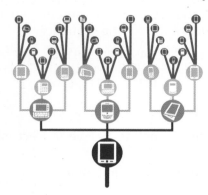

A. Write an explicit definition to find the number of people called in each round.

So $a_1 = 3$ and $a_5 = 243$. Use the explicit definition to find r.

$a_n = a_1 r^{n-1}$ .... Write the general explicit formula.

$243 = 3r^{5-1}$ .... Substitute 243 for a_5, 3 for a_1, and 5 for n.

$81 = r^4$ .... Isolate the power.

$3 = r$ .... Solve. Disregard the negative solution.

The explicit definition is $a_n = 3(3)^{n-1}$.

CONTINUED ON THE NEXT PAGE

LOOK FOR RELATIONSHIPS
Notice that the equation for an explicit definition is in the same form as the equation for an exponential function. **MP.7**

EXAMPLE 3 CONTINUED

B. How many people were called in the eighth round of the phone tree?

Use the explicit definition and solve for $n = 8$.

$a_r = a_1 r^{n-1}$

$a_8 = 3(3)^{8-1}$ — Substitute 8 for n and simplify.

$a_8 = 3(3)^7$

$a_8 = 6{,}561$

On the eighth round, 6,561 people were called.

 Try It! **3.** A geometric sequence can be used to describe the growth of bacteria in an experiment. On the first day of the experiment there were 9 bacteria in a Petri dish. On the 10th day, there are 3^{20} bacteria in the dish. How many bacteria were in the dish on the 7th day of the experiment?

CONCEPTUAL UNDERSTANDING

EXAMPLE 4 **Formula for the Sum of a Finite Geometric Series**

A. How can you find the sum of a finite geometric series?

A **geometric series** is the sum of the terms of a geometric sequence. S_n represents the sum of a geometric sequence with n terms.

$S_n = a_1 + a_1 r + a_1 r^2 + a_1 r^3 + \ldots + a_1 r^{n-1}$ ⋯⋯ Write the equation for a geometric series.

$r S_n = a_1 r + a_1 r^2 + a_1 r^3 + \ldots + a_1 r^{n-1} + a_1 r^n$ ⋯ Multiply each side by r.

$S_n - r S_n = a_1 - a_1 r^n$ ⋯⋯⋯⋯⋯⋯⋯⋯⋯⋯⋯ Subtract the second equation from the first equation.

$S_n(1 - r) = a_1(1 - r^n)$ ⋯⋯⋯⋯⋯⋯⋯⋯⋯⋯⋯ Factor.

$S_n = \dfrac{a_1(1 - r^n)}{(1 - r)}$ for $r \neq 1$ ⋯⋯⋯⋯⋯⋯ Solve for S_n.

MAKE SENSE AND PERSEVERE
Notice that multiplying each side by r gives you a second equation with many of the same terms as the original equation. How does this help you eliminate terms to find an expression for the sum of a finite geometric series? ⒼMP.1

B. Write the expanded form of the series $\displaystyle\sum_{n=1}^{7} 3\left(\dfrac{2}{3}\right)^{n-1}$. What is the sum?

Recall how to use sigma ($\sum$) notation to represent a series.

$\displaystyle\sum_{m=1}^{n} a_1 r^{m-1} = a_1 + a_1 r + a_1 r^2 + a_1 r^3 + \ldots + a_1 r^{n-1} = \dfrac{a_1(1 - r^n)}{(1 - r)}$.

The series is $3 + 2 + \dfrac{4}{3} + \dfrac{8}{9} + \dfrac{16}{27} + \dfrac{32}{81} + \dfrac{64}{243}$. To find the sum, use the sum of a finite geometric series formula with $a_1 = 3$, $r = \dfrac{2}{3}$, and $n = 7$.

$s_7 = \dfrac{3\left(1 - \left(\frac{2}{3}\right)^7\right)}{1 - \frac{2}{3}} = \dfrac{2{,}059}{243}$

The sum is $\dfrac{2{,}059}{243}$.

You can check by finding the sum of the terms directly:

$3 + 2 + \dfrac{4}{3} + \dfrac{8}{9} + \dfrac{16}{27} + \dfrac{32}{81} + \dfrac{64}{243} = \dfrac{2{,}059}{243}$.

CONTINUED ON THE NEXT PAGE

Try It! **4. a.** Write the expanded form of the series $\sum_{n=1}^{5} \frac{1}{2}(3)^{n-1}$. What is the sum?

b. Write the series $-2 + \left(\frac{-2}{3}\right) + \dots \left(\frac{-2}{243}\right)$ using sigma notation. What is the sum?

EXAMPLE 5 **Number of Terms in a Finite Geometric Series**

A. How many terms are in the geometric series 200 + 300 + 450 + ... + 7,688.7?

COMMON ERROR
Be careful to calculate the common ratio as a term divided by the previous term, not the next term.

Since the series is geometric, you can find that $r = 1.5$. Use the explicit definition to find n, the number of terms.

$$7{,}688.7 = 200(1.5)^{n-1}$$

$$38.4435 = (1.5)^{n-1}$$

> Substitute the last term in the series into the explicit definition to determine n.

$$\log 38.4435 = \log (1.5)^{n-1}$$

$$\log 38.4435 = (n - 1)\log (1.5)$$

$$\frac{\log 38.4435}{\log 1.5} = n - 1$$

$$n = \frac{\log 38.4435}{\log 1.5} + 1$$

$$n \approx 10$$

There are 10 terms in the geometric series.

B. The sum of a geometric series is 11,718. The first term of the series is 3, and its common ratio is 5. How many terms are in the series?

$$S_n = \frac{a_1(1 - r^n)}{(1 - r)}$$

> Substitute for S_n, a_1, and r in the formula for the sum of a geometric series to find n.

$$11{,}718 = \frac{3(1 - 5^n)}{(1 - 5)}$$

$$-46{,}872 = 3(1 - 5^n)$$

$$-15{,}624 = 1 - 5^n$$

$$5^n = 1 + 15{,}624$$

$$\log (5^n) = \log 15{,}625$$

> Once you have isolated the term with the exponent, take the logarithm of both sides.

$$n\log 5 = \log 15{,}625$$

$$n = \frac{\log 15{,}625}{\log 5}$$

$$n = 6$$

There are 6 terms in the series.

 Try It! **5a.** How many terms are in the geometric series $3 + 6 + 12 + \dots + 768$?

b. The sum of a geometric series is 155. The first term of the series is 5, and its common ratio is 2. How many terms are in the series?

APPLICATION

EXAMPLE 6 **Use a Finite Geometric Series**

Isabel wants to borrow $24,000 for 6 years with an annual interest rate of 4.5% to purchase a share in a food truck business. What will be her monthly payment?

$24,000
for
6 years

ANNUAL
Interest
Rate 4.5%

The formula to calculate a monthly payment is $A = \dfrac{P}{\sum\limits_{k=1}^{n}\left(\frac{1}{1+i}\right)^k}$, where A is the

monthly amount, P is the principal, or amount of the loan, n is the number of months, and i is the monthly interest rate.

For Isabel's loan, $P = 24{,}000$, $n = 72$, and $i = 0.00375$. Substitute the values into the formula.

> The annual interest rate is 4.5%, so you must divide that by 12 to get the monthly interest rate.

USE APPROPRIATE TOOLS
You can use your calculator's memory feature to use more precise values rather than the estimates used here. **ⓒ MP.5**

$$A = \dfrac{24{,}000}{\sum\limits_{k=1}^{72}\left(\dfrac{1}{1 + 0.00375}\right)^k}$$

> The denominator is a finite geometric series with $a_1 \approx 0.996$ and $r \approx 0.996$.

Find the sum.

$$\sum_{k=1}^{72}\left(\dfrac{1}{1 + 0.00375}\right)^k \approx \dfrac{0.996(1 - 0.996^{72})}{(1 - 0.996)} \approx 62.417$$

Now calculate the amount of the monthly payment:

$$A \approx \dfrac{24{,}000}{62.417} \approx 384.51$$

Isabel's monthly payment for the loan would be about $384.51.

 Try It! **6.** What is the monthly payment for a $40,000 loan for 4 years with an annual interest rate of 4.8%?

CONCEPT SUMMARY Geometric Sequences and Series

In a geometric sequence, the ratio defined by a term divided by the previous term is a constant, r. Alternately, any term in a geometric sequence multiplied by r gives the next term.

The sequence 1, 5, 25, 125, 625, ... is a geometric sequence, since $r = 5$.

WORDS	ALGEBRA	EXAMPLE
Each term in the sequence is r times the previous term.	The recursive definition for a geometric sequence is $$a_n = \begin{cases} a_1, & n = 1 \\ a_{n-1} \cdot r, & n > 1 \end{cases}$$	$$a_n = \begin{cases} 1 & n = 1 \\ 5a_{n-1}, & n > 1 \end{cases}$$
The fourth term in a sequence is the first term multiplied by three common ratios.	The explicit definition is $$a_n = a_1 r^{n-1}$$	$$a_n = 1(5)^{n-1}$$
You can find the sum of a certain number of terms in a geometric series.	For a finite geometric series with $r \neq 1$ $$\sum_{m=1}^{n} a_1 r^{m-1} = \frac{a_1(1 - r^n)}{(1 - r)}.$$	The sum of the first five terms is $$\frac{1(1 - 5^5)}{1 - 5} = \frac{-3,124}{-4} = 781$$

☑ Do You UNDERSTAND?

1. **❓ ESSENTIAL QUESTION** How can you represent and use geometric sequences and series?

2. **Error Analysis** Denzel claims the sequence 0, 7, 49, 343, ... is a geometric sequence and the next number is 2,401. What error did he make? **ⓒ MP.3**

3. **Vocabulary** Describe the similarities and differences between a common difference and a common ratio.

4. **Use Structure** What happens to the terms of a sequence if a_1 is positive and $r > 1$? What happens if $0 < r < 1$? Explain. **ⓒ MP.7**

Do You KNOW HOW?

Find the common ratio and the next three terms of each geometric sequence.

5. 2, −4, 8, −16, ...

6. −64, −16, −4, −1, ...

7. 0.8, 2.4, 7.2, 21.6, ...

8. 2, −10, 50, −250, ...

9. 100, 50, 25, 12.5, ...

10. In a video game, players earn 10 points for finishing the first level and twice as many points for each additional level. How many points does a player earn for finishing the fifth level? How many points will the player have earned in the game up to that point?

PRACTICE & PROBLEM SOLVING

UNDERSTAND

11. Reason True or False: If the first two terms of a geometric sequence are positive, then the third term is positive. Explain your reasoning. © MP.2

12. Error Analysis The first term of a geometric sequence is 4 and grows exponentially by a factor of 3. Murphy writes out the terms and says that the sum of the 4th and 5th terms is 1,296. Explain Murphy's error and correct it. © MP.3

13. Construct Arguments Write a geometric sequence with at least four terms and describe it using both an explicit and recursive definitions. How can you confirm that your sequence is geometric? © MP.3

14. Higher Order Thinking Adam drops a ball from a height of 12 feet. Each bounce is 50% as high as the previous bounce. What is the total vertical distance the ball has traveled when it hits the ground for the 4th time?

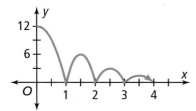

15. Model with Mathematics The Sierpinski Triangle is a fractal made by cutting an equilateral triangle into four congruent pieces and removing the center piece, leaving three smaller triangles. The process is repeated on each triangle, creating more triangles that are even smaller. Continuing this pattern, how many triangles would there be after the tenth step in the process? © MP.4

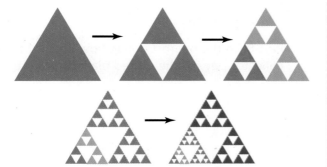

PRACTICE

Is the sequence geometric? If so, write a recursive definition for the sequence. SEE EXAMPLE 1

16. 1, −3, 9, −27, …   **17.** 3, −15, 75, −375, …

18. 4, 5, 6, 7, …   **19.** 24, 8, $\frac{8}{3}$, $\frac{8}{9}$, …

20. 2, 4, 6, 8, …   **21.** 10, 40, 160, 640, …

Translate between the recursive and explicit definitions for each sequence. SEE EXAMPLE 2

22. $a_n = 1{,}024\left(\frac{1}{2}\right)^{n-1}$

23. $a_n = \begin{cases} 2, & n = 1 \\ -2a^{n-1}, & n > 1 \end{cases}$

24. $a_n = 35(2)^{n-1}$

25. $a_n = -6(-3)^{n-1}$

26. $a_n = \begin{cases} 1, & n = 1 \\ \frac{2}{3}a_{n-1}, & n > 1 \end{cases}$

27. In an experiment, the number of bacteria present each day form a geometric sequence. On the first day, there were 100 bacteria. On the eighth day, there were 12,800 bacteria. How many bacteria were there on the fourth day? SEE EXAMPLE 3

Write the expansion of each series. What is the sum? SEE EXAMPLE 4

28. $\sum_{n=1}^{6} 4(2)^{n-1}$ **29.** $\sum_{n=1}^{20} 6(2)^{n-1}$

30. $\sum_{n=1}^{7} -4(3)^{n-1}$ **31.** $\sum_{n=1}^{12} (-4)^{n-1}$

Write each series using sigma notation. Find the sum. SEE EXAMPLE 4

32. 8 + 16 + 32 + … + 1,024

33. −7 − 42 − 252 − … − 54,432

34. $\frac{1}{5} + \frac{1}{10} + \frac{1}{20} + … + \frac{1}{80}$

35. 4 − 12 + 36 − … + 2,916

36. The sum of a geometric series is 31.75. The first term of the series is 16, and its common ratio is 0.5. How many terms are in the series? SEE EXAMPLE 5

37. What is the monthly payment for a $12,000 loan for 7 years with an annual interest rate of 2.7%? SEE EXAMPLE 6

APPLY

38. Model With Mathematics Kelley opens a bank account to save for a down payment on a car. Her initial deposit is $250, and she plans to deposit 10% more each month. Kelley's goal is to have $2,000 in the account after six months. Will she meet her goal? **© MP.4**

39. Make Sense and Persevere Henry just started his own cleaning business. He is using word-of-mouth from his current clients to promote his business. He currently has seven clients. **© MP.1**

  a. Five of his clients really like Henry's work and each told two friends the following month. This group each told two friends the following month, and so on for a total of five months. Assuming no one heard twice, how many people have had or heard of a positive experience with Henry's cleaning business?

  b. The two unhappy clients each told five people the following month. This group each told five people, and so on, for five months. Assuming no one heard twice, how many people have had or heard of a negative experience with Henry's cleaning business?

40. Model with Mathematics Ricardo bought a motorcycle for $15,000. The value depreciates 15% at the start of every year. What is the value of the motorcycle after three years? **© MP.4**

Time	Value
0 Yr	$15,000
1 Yr	
2 Yr	
3 Yr	

ASSESSMENT PRACTICE

41. The first term of a geometric series is −1, and the common ratio is −2. Fill in the number to complete the sentence.

If the sum of the series is −43, there are ___?___ terms in the series.

42. SAT/ACT What is the value of the 11th term in the following geometric sequence?

$$\frac{1}{27}, \frac{1}{9}, \frac{1}{3}, \cdots$$

  Ⓐ 3^4

  Ⓑ 3^5

  Ⓒ 3^6

  Ⓓ 3^7

  Ⓔ 3^8

43. Performance Task An avid collector wants to purchase a signed basketball from a particular playoff game. He plans to put away 4% more money each year, in a safe at his home, to save up for the basketball. In the sixth year, he puts $580 in the safe and realizes that he has exactly enough money to purchase the basketball.

Price = Year 5 savings + $580.00

Part A How much money did the collector put into the safe the first year?

Part B To the nearest dollar, how much did the collector pay for the signed playoff basketball?

Topic Review

? TOPIC ESSENTIAL QUESTION

1. How do you use exponential and logarithmic functions to model situations and solve problems?

Vocabulary Review

Choose the correct term to complete each sentence.

2. A(n) _____ has base e.

3. A(n) _____ has the form $f(x) = a \cdot b^x$.

4. In an exponential function, when $0 < b < 1$, b is a(n) _____.

5. The _____ allows logarithms with a base other than 10 or e to be evaluated.

6. A(n) _____ has base 10.

7. The inverse of an exponential function is a(n) _____.

- decay factor
- exponential function
- logarithmic function
- growth factor
- common logarithm
- natural logarithm
- Change of Base Formula

Concepts & Skills Review

LESSON 6-1   Key Features of Exponential Functions

Quick Review

An **exponential function** has the form $f(x) = a \cdot b^x$. When $a > 0$ and $b > 1$, the function is an **exponential growth function**. When $a > 0$ and $0 < b < 1$, the function is an **exponential decay function**.

Example

Paul invests $4,000 in an account that pays 2.5% interest annually. How much money will be in the account after 5 years?

Write and use the exponential growth function model.

$A(t) = a(1 + r)^n$

$A(5) = 4{,}000(1 + 0.025)^5$

$A(5) = 4{,}000(1.025)^5$

$A(5) = 4{,}525.63$

There will be about $4,525.63 in Paul's account after 5 years.

Practice & Problem Solving

Identify the domain, range, intercept, and asymptote of each exponential function. Then describe the end behavior.

8. $f(x) = 400 \cdot \left(\frac{1}{2}\right)^x$

9. $f(x) = 2 \cdot (3)^x$

10. **Reason** Seth invests $1,400 at 1.8% annual interest for 6 years. How much will Seth have at the end of the sixth year? Ⓒ **MP.2**

11. **Model With Mathematics** Bailey buys a car for $25,000. The car depreciates in value 18% per year. How much will the car be worth after 3 years? Ⓒ **MP.4**

12. Identify the domain, range, intercept, and asymptote.

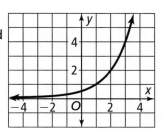

Quick Review

Interest may be compounded over different time periods, such as quarterly, monthly, or daily. The formula $A = P\left(1 + \frac{r}{n}\right)^{nt}$ is used to calculate the amount of money available after it has been invested for an amount of time. Interest may also be compounded continuously. The formula $A = Pe^{rt}$ is used to calculate the amount of money available in an account that is compounded continuously. The calculator can be used to find an exponential model for a set of data.

Example

Jenny invests $2,500 in an account that pays 2.4% interest annually. The interest is compounded quarterly. How much will Jenny have in the account after 6 years?

Use the formula $A = P\left(1 + \frac{r}{n}\right)^{nt}$.

$A = 2,500\left(1 + \frac{0.024}{4}\right)^{4(6)}$ ⋯⋯⋯ Substitute for A, P, n, and r.

$A = 2,500(1.006)^{24}$ ⋯⋯⋯⋯ Simplify.

$A = 2,885.97$ ⋯⋯⋯⋯⋯⋯ Use a calculator.

Jenny will have about $2,885.97.

Practice & Problem Solving

Find the total amount of money in the account after the given amount of time.

13. Compounded quarterly, $P = \$12,000$, $r = 3.6\%$, $t = 4$ years

14. Compounded monthly, $P = \$5,000$, $r = 2.4\%$, $t = 8$ years

15. Continuously compounded, $P = \$7,500$, $r = 1.6\%$, $t = 10$ years

Write an exponential model given two points.

16. (12, 256) and (13, 302)

17. (3, 54) and (4, 74)

18. **Model With Mathematics** Jason's parents invested some money for Jason's education when Jason was born. The table shows how the account has grown.

Number of Years	Amount ($)
1	2,250
3	2,525
6	3,480
7	4,400
9	6,000
13	9,250

Predict how much will be in the account after 18 years. ⓒ **MP.4**

Quick Review

A logarithm is an exponent. Common logarithms have base 10 and natural logarithms have base e. Exponential expressions can be rewritten in logarithmic form, and logarithmic expressions can be converted to exponential form.

$5^3 = 125$ can be rewritten as $\log_5 125 = 3$.

$\log 100 = 2$ can be rewritten as $10^2 = 100$.

Example

Evaluate $\log_2 \frac{1}{8}$.

$\log_2 \frac{1}{8} = x$ Write an equation.

$2^x = \frac{1}{8}$ Rewrite the equation in exponential form.

$2^x = 2^{-3}$ Rewrite the equation with a common base.

$x = -3$ Since the two expressions have a common base, the exponents are equal.

Practice & Problem Solving

Use Structure If an equation is given in exponential form, write the logarithmic form. If an equation is given in logarithmic form, write the exponential form. **© MP.7**

19. $4^3 = 64$ **20.** $10^2 = 100$

21. $\log_6 216 = 3$ **22.** $\ln 20 = x$

Evaluate each logarithmic expression.

23. $\log_8 \frac{1}{64}$ **24.** $\log_3 81$

Use Appropriate Tools Evaluate each logarithmic expression using a calculator. Round answers to the nearest thousandth. **© MP.5**

25. $\log 628$ **26.** $\ln 0.55$

Evaluate each logarithmic expression.

27. $\log_5 5^9$ **28.** $7^{\log_7 49}$

Quick Review

A logarithmic function is the inverse of an exponential function.

Example

Find the inverse of $f(x) = 10^{x-2}$. Identify any intercepts or asymptotes.

$y = 10^{x-2}$ Write in $y = f(x)$ form.

$x = 10^{y-2}$ Interchange x and y.

$y - 2 = \log x$ Write in log form.

$y = \log x + 2$ Solve for y.

The equation of the inverse is $f^{-1}(x) = \log x + 2$. It has an x-intercept at $x = \frac{1}{100}$ and a vertical asymptote at the y-axis.

Practice & Problem Solving

Look for Relationships Graph each function and identify the domain and range. List any intercepts or asymptotes. Describe the end behavior. **© MP.7**

29. $f(x) = \log_4 x$ **30.** $f(x) = \ln(x - 2)$

Use Structure Find the equation of the inverse of each function. **© MP.7**

31. $f(x) = 8^{x-2}$ **32.** $f(x) = \frac{5^{x-2}}{8}$

Properties of Logarithms

Quick Review

Properties of logarithms can be used to either expand a single logarithmic expression into individual logarithms or condense several logarithmic expressions into a single logarithm.

The Change of Base Formula can be used to find logarithms of numbers with bases other than 10 or e.

Example

Use the properties of logarithms to expand the expression $\log_6 \frac{x^3 y^5}{z}$.

$\log_6 \frac{x^3 y^5}{z}$

$= \log_6 x^3 y^5 - \log_6 z$ ·········· Quotient Property of Logarithms

$= \log_6 x^3 + \log_6 y^5 - \log_6 z$ ····· Product Property of Logarithms

$= 3\log_6 x + 5\log_6 y - \log_6 z$ ····· Power Property of Logarithms

Practice & Problem Solving

Use Structure Use the properties of logarithms to write each as a single logarithm. @ MP.7

33. $3\log r - 2\log s + \log t$

34. $2\ln 3 + 4\ln 2 - \ln 36$

Evaluate each logarithm.

35. $\log_4 12$ **36.** $\log_7 70$

Make Sense and Persevere Solve each equation for x. Give an exact solution written as a logarithm and use the Change of Base Formula to provide an approximated solution rounded to the nearest thousandth. @ MP.1

37. $5^x = 200$ **38.** $7^x = 486$

Exponential and Logarithmic Equations

Quick Review

You can solve exponential equations by taking the logarithm of both sides. You can solve a logarithmic equation by combining the logarithmic terms into one logarithm and then converting to exponential form.

Example

Solve $7^{2x} = 10^{x+1}$.

$7^{2x} = 10^{x+1}$

$\log 7^{2x} = \log 10^{x+1}$ ·········· Take the common log of each side.

$2x \log 7 = (x + 1) \log 10$ ···· Power Property of Logarithms

$2x \log 7 = x + 1$ ············· Since $\log 10 = 1$

$2x \log 7 - x = 1$ ············· Subtract x from each side.

$x(2 \log 7 - 1) = 1$ ············· Factor out x.

$x = \frac{1}{2 \log 7 - 1}$ ············· Divide each side by $2 \log 7 - 1$.

$x \approx 1.449$ ·········· Use a calculator.

Practice & Problem Solving

Find all solutions of the equation. Round answers to the nearest ten-thousandth.

39. $2^{5x+1} = 8^{x-1}$

40. $9^{2x+3} = 27^{x+2}$

41. $3^{x-2} = 5^{x-1}$

42. $7^{x+1} = 12^{x-1}$

Find all solutions of the equation.

43. $\log_5 (3x - 2)^4 = 8$

44. $\ln (x^2 - 32) = \ln (4x)$

45. $\log_6 (2x - 1) = 2 - \log_6 x$

46. Model With Mathematics Geri has $1,500 to invest. He has a goal to have $3,000 in this investment in 10 years. At what annual rate, compounded continuously, will Geri reach his goal? Round the answer to the nearest tenth. **@ MP.4**

Quick Review

A geometric sequence is defined by a common ratio between consecutive terms. It can be defined explicitly or recursively. A geometric series is the sum of the terms of a geometric sequence.

Example

A geometric sequence is defined by
$a_n = \begin{cases} \frac{1}{9}, & n = 1 \\ 3a_{n-1}, & n > 1 \end{cases}$. **What is the sum of the first 10 terms of this sequence?**

$a_n = \frac{1}{9}(3)^{n-1}$ — Write the explicit definition.

$a_{10} = \frac{1}{9}(3)^9 = 2187$ — Find the 10th term.

$S_{10} = \frac{\frac{1}{9}(1 - 3^{10})}{(1 - 3)} = 3280\frac{4}{9}$ — Calculate the sum.

Practice & Problem Solving

Determine whether or not each sequence is geometric.

47. 2, 4, 6, 8, 10, 12, …

48. 2, 4, 8, 16, 32, 64, …

Convert between recursive and explicit forms.

49. $a_n = \begin{cases} \frac{1}{8}, & n = 1 \\ \frac{3}{2}a_{n-1}, & n > 1 \end{cases}$

50. $a_n = -2(5)^{n-1}$

Find the sum for each geometric series.

51. $\sum\limits_{n=1}^{8} 6(2)^{n-1}$

52. $\sum\limits_{n=1}^{9} 81\left(\frac{1}{3}\right)^{n-1}$

53. Look for Relationships Find the difference $\sum\limits_{n=1}^{10} 10(2)^{n-1} - \sum\limits_{k=2}^{11} 10(2)^{k-1}$. Explain how you found your answer. **©** **MP.7**

54. Make Sense and Persevere The half-life of carbon-14 is 5,730 years. This is the amount of time it takes for half of a sample to decay. From a sample of 24 grams of carbon 14, how long will it take until only 3 grams of the sample remains? **©** **MP.1**

TOPIC 7

Trigonometric Functions

? TOPIC ESSENTIAL QUESTION

How are trigonometric functions used to solve real-world problems?

Topic Overview

enVision™ STEM Project:
Space Goggles

7-1 Trigonometric Functions and Acute Angles

7-2 Angles and the Unit Circle

7-3 Trigonometric Functions and Real Numbers

7-4 Graphing Sine and Cosine Functions

Mathematical Modeling in 3 Acts:
What Note Was That?

7-5 Graphing Other Trigonometric Functions

7-6 Translating Trigonometric Functions

Topic Vocabulary

- amplitude
- cofunction
- cofunction identities
- cosecant
- cosine
- cotangent
- coterminal angles
- frequency
- initial side
- midline
- period
- periodic function
- phase shift
- radian
- radian measure
- reciprocal trigonometric functions
- reference angle
- reference triangle
- secant
- sine
- standard position
- tangent
- terminal side
- unit circle

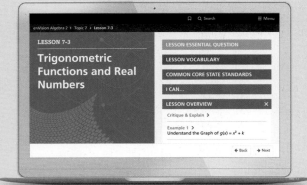

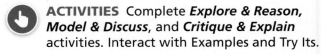

Digital Experience

INTERACTIVE STUDENT EDITION Access online or offline.

ACTIVITIES Complete *Explore & Reason*, *Model & Discuss*, and *Critique & Explain* activities. Interact with Examples and Try Its.

ANIMATION View and interact with real-world applications.

PRACTICE Practice what you've learned.

 Go online | SavvasRealize.com

▶ What Note Was That?

Sounds are created by vibrations. As the vibrations travel through the air, they create sound waves. The frequency of a sound is the measurement of the number of cycles of that wave per second, in a unit called hertz (Hz). Music notes can be identified by their frequency.

What information do you need to determine the frequency of a note? How accurate does your data need to be? Think about this during the Mathematical Modeling in 3 Acts lesson.

VIDEOS Watch clips to support *Mathematical Modeling in 3 Acts Lessons* and enVision™ *STEM Projects.*

CONCEPT SUMMARY Review key lesson content through multiple representations.

ASSESSMENT Show what you've learned.

GLOSSARY Read and listen to English and Spanish definitions.

TUTORIALS Get help from *Virtual Nerd*, right when you need it.

MATH TOOLS Explore math with digital tools and manipulatives.

Did You Know?

In space, all **electromagnetic waves** move at the same speed: the speed of light, which is 299,792,458 meters per second. The length of 1 meter is defined to be the distance light travels in space in 1/299,792,458 of a second.

Light travels from Earth to the Moon in 1.255 seconds.

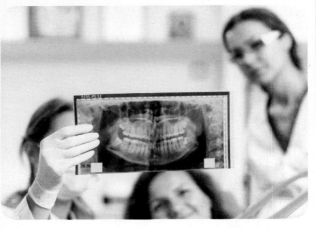

The **frequency of an electromagnetic wave** is proportional to its energy. X-ray machines range in strength from the **low-frequency machines** used to examine teeth and bones to the **high-frequency machines** used to kill cancer cells.

The **spectrum of visible light** is a very small portion of the electromagnetic spectrum, which includes gamma rays, x-rays, ultraviolet light, infrared radiation, microwaves, and radio waves.

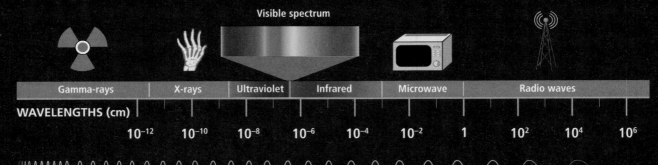

Visible spectrum

| Gamma-rays | X-rays | Ultraviolet | Infrared | Microwave | Radio waves |

WAVELENGTHS (cm)

10^{-12} 10^{-10} 10^{-8} 10^{-6} 10^{-4} 10^{-2} 1 10^2 10^4 10^6

FREQUENCY (Hz)

⊙ Your Task: Design Space Goggles

You and your classmates will investigate different electromagnetic waves, including the relative energy and dangers of each. Then you will designs space goggles to protect a space traveler's vision.

7-1

Trigonometric Functions and Acute Angles

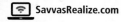

I CAN... use trigonometric functions.

VOCABULARY

- cofunction
- cofunction identities
- cosecant
- cosine
- cotangent
- reciprocal trigonometric functions
- secant
- sine
- tangent

  Activity Assess

👆 EXPLORE & REASON

In the figure below, △ABC ~ △DEF.

A. Write as many ratios as you can using two side lengths from △ABC.

B. Write as many ratios as you can using two side lengths from △DEF.

C. Look for Relationships What do the results from parts (a) and (b) suggest about the ratios of side lengths in similar right triangles? Ⓒ **MP.7**

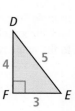

❓ ESSENTIAL QUESTION

How can ratios of lengths of sides within right triangles help determine other lengths and angle measures in the triangles?

CONCEPT Trigonometric Ratios

The three sides of a right triangle are referred to as the hypotenuse and two legs.

The Greek letter θ, read "theta", is often used to represent an acute angle in a right triangle. Angle θ is an abbreviation for "angle with measure θ".

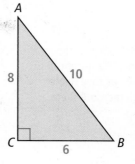

The *adjacent* side forms the given acute angle with the hypotenuse.

The *hypotenuse* is the side across from the right angle.

The *opposite* side is across from the given acute angle.

These are the six basic trigonometric functions of the angle θ.

Sine

$$\sin \theta = \frac{\text{opposite}}{\text{hypotenuse}}$$

Cosine

$$\cos \theta = \frac{\text{adjacent}}{\text{hypotenuse}}$$

Tangent

$$\tan \theta = \frac{\text{opposite}}{\text{adjacent}}$$

The **reciprocal trigonometric functions** of the angle θ are formed by exchanging the terms in each ratio.

Cosecant

$$\csc \theta = \frac{\text{hypotenuse}}{\text{opposite}}$$

Secant

$$\sec \theta = \frac{\text{hypotenuse}}{\text{adjacent}}$$

Cotangent

$$\cot \theta = \frac{\text{adjacent}}{\text{opposite}}$$

EXAMPLE 1   Write Trigonometric Ratios

Given the right triangle below, write the six trigonometric ratios for the given angle with measure θ.

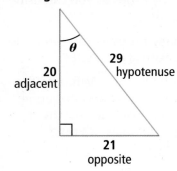

$$\sin \theta = \frac{21}{29} \qquad \csc \theta = \frac{29}{21}$$

$$\cos \theta = \frac{20}{29} \qquad \sec \theta = \frac{29}{20}$$

$$\tan \theta = \frac{21}{20} \qquad \cot \theta = \frac{20}{21}$$

✓ **Try It!**   **1.** Write the six trigonometric ratios for the given angle with measure θ.

a.

b.
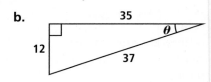

EXAMPLE 2   Use One Trigonometric Ratio to Find Another

Knowing that $\tan \theta = \frac{15}{8}$, what are the other trigonometric ratios for θ?

You can use one trigonometric ratio to find the other five trigonometric ratios.

Step 1 Use the definition of the tangent ratio to draw a right triangle with angle θ.

$$\tan \theta = \frac{15}{8} = \frac{\text{opposite}}{\text{adjacent}}$$

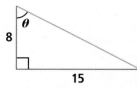

Step 2 Use the Pythagorean Theorem to find the hypotenuse.

$$a^2 + b^2 = c^2$$

$$(8)^2 + (15)^2 = c^2$$

$$17 = c$$

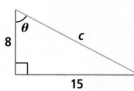

Step 3 Use the side lengths to write the other trigonometric ratios.

Substitute the side lengths into the formulas. For example, since $\sin \theta = \frac{\text{opposite}}{\text{hypotenuse}}$, $\sin \theta = \frac{15}{17}$. Now write the rest of the trigonometric ratios.

$$\sin \theta = \frac{15}{17}, \ \cos \theta = \frac{8}{17}, \ \csc \theta = \frac{17}{15}, \ \sec \theta = \frac{17}{8}, \cot \theta = \frac{8}{15}$$

✓ **Try It!**   **2.** What are the trigonometric ratios of an angle with measure θ in a right triangle in which $\sin \theta = \frac{24}{25}$?

APPLICATION

EXAMPLE 3   **Find a Missing Side Length**

A fire truck has an 84 ft ladder extended against a building forming a 55° angle with the top of the truck. The truck is 8 ft tall. The firefighters are trying to reach a window that is 75 ft above the ground. Will they be able to reach the window using the ladder set at this angle?

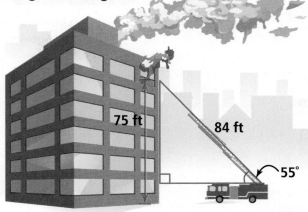

75 ft

84 ft

55°

Step 1   Sketch a diagram to represent the situation. Label the sides and angles of your diagram with all of the known information.

Step 2   Decide which trigonometric function to use. You are given the hypotenuse, and you are trying to find the length opposite the angle with a measure of 55°. The ratio that relates the opposite side of an angle to the hypotenuse of the right triangle is the sine ratio.

wall   ladder 84 ft

55°

8 ft

ground

Step 3   Let x represent the length of the side opposite the 55° angle and write an equation.

$$\sin 55° = \frac{x}{84}$$

COMMON ERROR
Make sure that your calculator is set to degrees when you calculate the value of sine.

Step 4   Solve for x.

$$x = 84 \sin 55$$

$$\approx 68.8 \text{ ft}$$

Step 5   Find the height on the building that the ladder will reach.

$$68.8 + 8 = 76.8 \text{ ft}$$

The height the ladder will reach is the side length of the triangle plus 8 ft for the height of the truck.

The ladder will extend to a height of about 76.8, which is longer than 75. The firefighters will be able to reach the window 75 ft above the ground.

 Try It!   **3.** The sun shines at a 60° angle to the ground. How long is the shadow cast by a 20 ft tall flagpole?

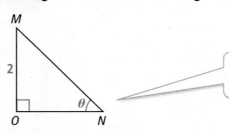

EXAMPLE 4 | **Evaluate Trigonometric Ratios in Special Triangles**

A. △*MNO* is a 45°-45°-90° triangle with side length *OM* = 2. What are the six trigonometric ratios for angle *N* with measure *θ*?

> This is an isosceles right triangle so the legs are congruent.

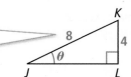

Find the hypotenuse using the Pythagorean Theorem:

$$a^2 + b^2 = c^2$$
$$(2)^2 + (2)^2 = c^2$$
$$c = \sqrt{8} = 2\sqrt{2}$$

The side lengths are *MO* = 2, *NM* = $2\sqrt{2}$, and *ON* = 2.

The trigonometric ratios for *θ* in △*MNO* are:

$\sin \theta = \frac{2}{2\sqrt{2}} = \frac{\sqrt{2}}{2}$ $\qquad$ $\cos \theta = \frac{2}{2\sqrt{2}} = \frac{\sqrt{2}}{2}$ $\qquad$ $\tan \theta = \frac{2}{2} = 1$

$\csc \theta = \frac{2\sqrt{2}}{2} = \sqrt{2}$ $\qquad$ $\sec \theta = \frac{2\sqrt{2}}{2} = \sqrt{2}$ $\qquad$ $\cot \theta = \frac{2}{2} = 1$

Check your calculations. Use a calculator to evaluate both sin 45° and $\frac{\sqrt{2}}{2}$. They should both be approximately equal to 0.7071.

B. △*JKL* is a 30°-60°-90° right triangle with side length *LK* = 4 and *m∠J* = 30°. What are the six trigonometric ratios for angle *J* with measure *θ*?

> This triangle is half of an equilateral triangle, so the length of the hypotenuse is twice the length of the shortest leg.

Use the Pythagorean Theorem to find the length of the third side:

$$a^2 + b^2 = c^2$$
$$(4)^2 + b^2 = (8)^2$$
$$b^2 = 48$$
$$b = 4\sqrt{3}$$

The side lengths are *JL* = $4\sqrt{3}$, *KJ* = 8, and *LK* = 4.

The trigonometric ratios for *θ* in △*JKL* are:

$\sin \theta = \frac{4}{8} = \frac{1}{2}$ $\qquad$ $\cos \theta = \frac{4\sqrt{3}}{8} = \frac{\sqrt{3}}{2}$ $\qquad$ $\tan \theta = \frac{4}{4\sqrt{3}} = \frac{\sqrt{3}}{3}$

$\csc \theta = \frac{8}{4} = 2$ $\qquad$ $\sec \theta = \frac{2}{\sqrt{3}} = \frac{2\sqrt{3}}{3}$ $\qquad$ $\cot \theta = \sqrt{3}$

STUDY TIP
Recall that in every 45°-45°-90° triangle, the sides lengths can be expressed as *x*, *x*, and $x\sqrt{2}$.

GENERALIZE
Recall that in a 45°-45°-90° right triangle, since the two legs are equal, $\sin \theta = \cos \theta$, $\csc \theta = \sec \theta$, and $\tan \theta = \cot \theta = 1$. **© MP.8**

STUDY TIP
Recall that in every 30°-60°-90° triangle, the sides lengths can be expressed as *x*, 2*x*, and $x\sqrt{3}$.

Try It! **4.** The length of the hypotenuse in a 45°-45°-90° triangle is $5\sqrt{2}$. What are the sine and secant ratios for a 45° angle?

CONCEPTUAL
UNDERSTANDING ⟶ 👆 **EXAMPLE 5** **Explain Trigonometric Identities**

A. **Which trigonometric ratios are reciprocals of each other?**

An **identity** is an equation that is true for all values of the variable for which all expressions in the equation are defined. You have seen that some trigonometric functions include ratios that are reciprocals. One example:

$$\sin \theta = \frac{\text{opposite}}{\text{hypotenuse}} \qquad \csc \theta = \frac{\text{hypotenuse}}{\text{opposite}}$$

Show that the following reciprocal identity is true for all values of θ that measure an acute angle: $\sin \theta = \frac{1}{\csc \theta}$.

Confirm that the equation is true algebraically by using substitution:

$$\sin \theta = \frac{1}{\csc \theta} = \frac{1}{\left(\frac{\text{hypotenuse}}{\text{opposite}}\right)} = \frac{\text{opposite}}{\text{hypotenuse}}$$

> **STUDY TIP**
> In a right triangle, the sum of the measures of the two acute angles is 90°, so these angles are complementary.

B. **How are the trigonometric ratios of the two non-right angles in a right triangle related to each other?**

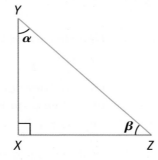

α and β are complementary angles.

$\alpha + \beta = 90°$, so

$\alpha = 90° - \beta$

$\beta = 90° - \alpha$

> The Greek letters α (alpha) and β (beta) are often used to represent angles in trigonometry.

Compare sine and cosine for α and β:

$$\sin \alpha = \frac{ZX}{YZ} \qquad \sin \beta = \frac{XY}{YZ}$$

$$\cos \alpha = \frac{XY}{YZ} \qquad \cos \beta = \frac{ZX}{YZ}$$

If $\beta = 90° - \alpha$, then $\sin \alpha = \cos \beta$ and $\cos \alpha = \sin \beta$. The trigonometric function for the complement of an angle is called a **cofunction**, so these are the **cofunction identities** for sine and cosine.

C. **Triangle *DEF* has right angle, *F*. The $m\angle D = \alpha$ and $m\angle E = \beta$. If $\sin \alpha = \frac{8}{17}$ and $\cos \alpha = \frac{15}{17}$, find $\sin \beta$ and $\cos \beta$.**

In a right triangle, where α and β are complementary angles, $\sin \alpha = \cos \beta$ and $\cos \alpha = \sin \beta$.

You are given $\sin \alpha = \frac{8}{17}$ and $\cos \alpha = \frac{15}{17}$.

Use this information to determine that $\sin \beta = \frac{15}{17}$ and $\cos \beta = \frac{8}{17}$.

You may confirm your findings by sketching one possible triangle that represents the situation.

In this example, the hypotenuse is 17, the side opposite α is 8, and the side adjacent α is 15.

From this information, you can confirm that $\sin \beta = \frac{15}{17}$ and $\cos \beta = \frac{8}{17}$.

 Try It! **5.** What are the cofunction identities for tangent and cotangent?

🔧 CONCEPT SUMMARY Trigonometric Functions and Acute Angles

WORDS ▶ The ratios of the sides of any right triangle are always the same for a given angle θ. These ratios define the six basic trigonometric functions.

DEFINITIONS ▶

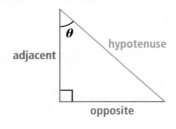

Sine	Cosine	Tangent
$\sin \theta = \dfrac{\text{opposite}}{\text{hypotenuse}}$	$\cos \theta = \dfrac{\text{adjacent}}{\text{hypotenuse}}$	$\tan \theta = \dfrac{\text{opposite}}{\text{adjacent}}$
Cosecant	**Secant**	**Cotangent**
$\csc \theta = \dfrac{\text{hypotenuse}}{\text{opposite}}$	$\sec \theta = \dfrac{\text{hypotenuse}}{\text{adjacent}}$	$\cot \theta = \dfrac{\text{adjacent}}{\text{opposite}}$

☑ Do You UNDERSTAND?

1. **ESSENTIAL QUESTION** How can ratios of lengths of sides within right triangles help determine other lengths and angle measures in the triangles?

2. **Error Analysis** Terrell said that $\cos \theta$ is the reciprocal of $\sin \theta$. Explain and correct Terrell's error. ⓒ **MP.3**

3. **Vocabulary** Explain what it means to say that $\tan \theta = \dfrac{1}{\cot \theta}$ is an identity.

4. **Construct Arguments** Why are the cofunction identities true for all right triangles? ⓒ **MP.3**

5. **Generalize** How does knowing one trigonometric ratio allow you to find the other five trigonometric ratios? ⓒ **MP.8**

6. **Look for Relationships** Why do secant and cosecant always have to be greater than 1 or less than −1? ⓒ **MP.7**

Do You KNOW HOW?

Find $\sin \theta$ using the given trigonometric ratio.

7. $\csc \theta = \dfrac{7}{3}$ 8. $\tan \theta = \dfrac{5}{12}$

Use the trigonometric ratio given to write the other five trigonometric ratios for θ.

9. $\cos \theta = \dfrac{5}{13}$ 10. $\tan \theta = \dfrac{3}{4}$

Write the reciprocal identity of the given trigonometric ratio.

11. $\cos \theta$ 12. $\sec \theta$

Write the cofunction identity of the given trigonometric ratio.

13. $\csc \theta$ 14. $\sec \theta$

15. A right triangle has a side of 16 m adjacent to an angle of 37°. What is the length of the hypotenuse rounded to the nearest whole meter?

16. A flagpole is 24 ft tall. A support wire runs from the top of the flagpole to an anchor in the ground. The wire makes a 73° angle with the ground. To the nearest tenth of a foot, how far from the base of the flagpole is the anchor?

UNDERSTAND

17. Construct Arguments Yama said you can find any side length or angle measure of a right triangle if you know at least 1 side length and 1 non-right angle measure, or 2 side lengths. Is Yama correct? Explain your reasoning. ⓒ **MP.3**

18. Look for Relationships The sine of an acute angle must be greater than 0 and less than 1. Explain why. ⓒ **MP.7**

19. Error Analysis Describe and correct the error a student made in solving for the length of the hypotenuse in the triangle shown. ⓒ **MP.3**

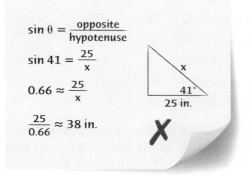

$$\sin \theta = \frac{\text{opposite}}{\text{hypotenuse}}$$

$$\sin 41 = \frac{25}{x}$$

$$0.66 \approx \frac{25}{x}$$

$$\frac{25}{0.66} \approx 38 \text{ in.}$$

20. Construct Arguments Show that the reciprocal identity $\sec \theta = \frac{1}{\cos \theta}$ is true. ⓒ **MP.3**

21. Generalize Knowing all three angle measures of a right triangle does not determine the exact side lengths. However, knowing all three side lengths of a right triangle does determine the exact angle measures. Explain why. ⓒ **MP.8**

22. Reason The sun shines at a 75° angle to the ground. How long is the shadow cast by a 15 ft tall cactus? Round to the nearest foot. ⓒ **MP.2**

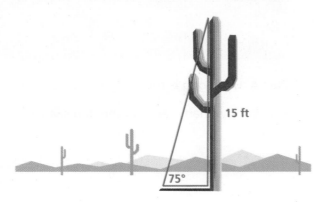

PRACTICE

Write the six trigonometric ratios for θ.
SEE EXAMPLE 1

23.

24.

What are the trigonometric ratios of θ in a right triangle with the given value?
SEE EXAMPLE 2

25. $\cos \theta = \frac{4}{5}$

26. $\cot \theta = \frac{12}{16}$

27. $\csc \theta = \frac{17}{15}$

28. $\sec \theta = \frac{52}{20}$

29. A closed umbrella casts a shadow when the sun shines at a 16.3° angle to the ground. How tall is the top of the umbrella to the nearest foot? SEE EXAMPLE 3

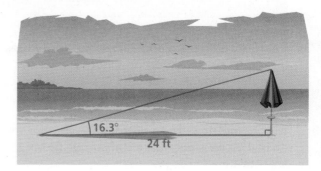

What are the sine and cosine ratios for the special triangles described? SEE EXAMPLE 4

30. A 45°-45°-90° triangle with a leg of 9

31. A 30°-60°-90° triangle with a hypotenuse of 14, when $\theta = 30°$

What is the cofunction identity for the given trigonometric ratio? SEE EXAMPLE 5

32. secant

33. cosine

PRACTICE & PROBLEM SOLVING

APPLY

34. Make Sense and Persevere Roshaun sees two rock formations on the other side of a canyon from where he is hiking. One is directly across the canyon, and the other is across at an angle of 27°. How far apart are the two rock formations? Round your answer to the nearest tenth. ⓒ **MP.1**

35. Reason The Health and Safety Authority uses a "1 in 4" rule for judging whether a ladder is angled enough to be safe (1 unit out for every 4 units up). The angle measure that is the maximum angle for safety is 75°. Use a trigonometric ratio to determine whether the "1 in 4" rule is adequate for safety. ⓒ **MP.2**

36. Model With Mathematics An inflatable figure is a decoration on Gabriella's lawn. A rope 42 in. long secures the top of the figure to the ground at an angle of 80°. About how tall is the figure? ⓒ **MP.4**

37. Make Sense and Persevere A zip line starts 28 feet in the air and ends 11 feet in the air. The zip line drops at an angle of 85°. How long is the zip line cable when completely taut (no rider)? Round your answer to the nearest whole number. ⓒ **MP.1**

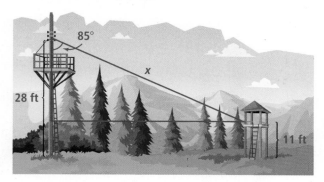

ASSESSMENT PRACTICE

38. Match each trigonometric ratio in the left column with its reciprocal expression in the right column.

   I. $\sin \theta$ **A.** $\frac{1}{\cos \theta}$

   II. $\sec \theta$ **B.** $\frac{1}{\sin \theta}$

   III. $\tan \theta$ **C.** $\frac{1}{\cot \theta}$

   IV. $\cos \theta$ **D.** $\frac{1}{\sec \theta}$

   V. $\csc \theta$ **E.** $\frac{1}{\tan \theta}$

   VI. $\cot \theta$ **F.** $\frac{1}{\csc \theta}$

39. SAT/ACT Which of the following is true?

Ⓐ $\sin \theta = \csc(90° - \theta)$

Ⓑ $\sec \theta = \cos(90° - \theta)$

Ⓒ $\tan \theta = \cos(90° - \theta)$

Ⓓ $\sec \theta = \sin(90° - \theta)$

Ⓔ $\tan \theta = \cot(90° - \theta)$

40. Performance Task Simon's dog jumped into a stream at a 68° angle from the corner of a bridge. Simon crossed the bridge and walked downstream to meet the dog.

Part A How long is the bridge, in feet?

Part B How many feet did the dog swim?

7-2

Angles and the Unit Circle

 SavvasRealize.com

I CAN... understand angles in standard position.

VOCABULARY

- coterminal angles
- initial side
- radian
- radian measure
- reference angle
- reference triangle
- standard position
- terminal side
- unit circle

👍 **EXPLORE & REASON**

A bug is placed at the point (1, 0) of the coordinate plane shown. It starts walking counterclockwise along a circle with radius 1.

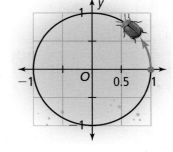

A. Model With Mathematics How can you calculate the distance along the circle the bug has traveled? How can you determine the measure of the central angle? Ⓒ **MP.4**

B. When the bug has traveled $\frac{1}{8}$ of the way along the circle, how far has it traveled? What central angle does its path travel through?

C. What are the distances shown traveled and the central angles when the bug has traveled $\frac{1}{6}$ of the way around the circle and $\frac{4}{5}$ of the way around the circle?

❓ **ESSENTIAL QUESTION**   How can we extend the trigonometric ratios to angles greater than 90°?

👍 **EXAMPLE 1**   Find the Measure of an Angle in Standard Position

What is the measure of the angle shown?

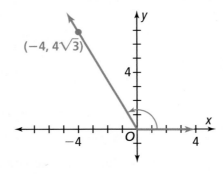

The angle represented by θ is in **standard position**. The vertex is at the origin, and the **initial side** of the angle is the positive x-axis. The **terminal side** is the other ray that forms the angle.

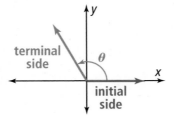

CONTINUED ON THE NEXT PAGE

EXAMPLE 1 CONTINUED

To find the measure of an angle in standard position, create a right triangle and use right triangle trigonometry. Draw a vertical line from the given point to the x-axis to form a right triangle.

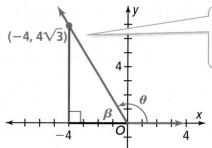

The lengths of the legs are 4 and $4\sqrt{3}$ units. Use the Pythagorean Theorem to find that the hypotenuse is 8.

STUDY TIP
It is helpful to label key angles in the figure so you can easily refer to them while working through the problem.

LOOK FOR RELATIONSHIPS
Recall that in a 30°-60°-90° right triangle, if the length of the shorter leg is *x*, then the length of the hypotenuse is 2*x*, and the length of the longer leg is $x\sqrt{3}$.
© **MP.7**

Examine the lengths of the sides of the right triangle. The dimensions fit the pattern of a 30°-60°-90° triangle, so $\beta = 60°$. Since β is supplementary to θ, we can can solve for $\theta = 180° - 60°$. Therefore $\theta = 120°$.

An angle in standard position can have its measure described in different ways.

As a positive angle measure	As a negative angle measure	As a positive angle measure greater than 360°
(−4, 4√3), 120°	(−4, 4√3), −240°	(−4, 4√3), 480°
$0 \le \theta < 360$	$-360 \le \theta < 0$	$\theta + 360k$, where *k* is a natural number representing the number of rotations

Because all three of the angles in this exercise are in standard position and share a terminal side, they are **coterminal angles**.

In standard position, the measure of the angle could be 120°, −240°, or 120 + 360*k*°, where *k* is an integer.

CONTINUED ON THE NEXT PAGE

EXAMPLE 1 CONTINUED

☑ Try It! **1.** Given the initial and terminal sides, find a positive angle measure, a negative angle measure, and an angle measure greater than 360° for each angle below.

a.

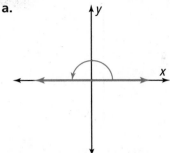

b.

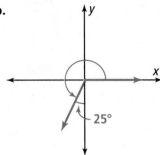

25°

⟡ EXAMPLE 2 **Find Reference Angles**

A. What is the reference angle for a 130° angle?

When an angle is in standard position, the **reference angle** is the acute angle formed between the terminal side of the angle and the *x*-axis.

To find the reference angle for any angle, first sketch the angle by considering the quadrant in which the terminal side lies.

Quadrant II $90° < \theta < 180°$ $-270° < \theta < -180°$	**Quadrant I** $0° < \theta < 90°$ $-360° < \theta < -270°$
Quadrant III $180° < \theta < 270°$ $-180° < \theta < -90°$	**Quadrant IV** $270° < \theta < 360°$ $-90° < \theta < 0°$

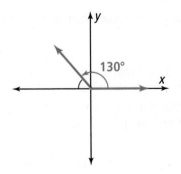

130°

A 130° angle in standard position has its terminal side in Quardrant II. The reference angle is: $180° - 130° = 50°$. When the given angle is greater than 90° and less than 180°, it is supplementary to its reference angle.

COMMON ERROR
Make sure you are always using the *x*-axis to locate the reference angle, not the *y*-axis.

CONTINUED ON THE NEXT PAGE

EXAMPLE 2 CONTINUED

B. What is the reference angle for a 210° angle?

Sketch the angle to determine in which Quadrant the terminal side lies.

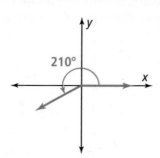

A 210° angle in standard position has its terminal side in Quadrant III. The measure of the reference angle is 180° less than the measure of the given angle: 210° − 180° = 30°.

C. A reference angle is 45°, and its terminal side lies in Quadrant IV. What are a possible positive measure and negative measure for the angle?

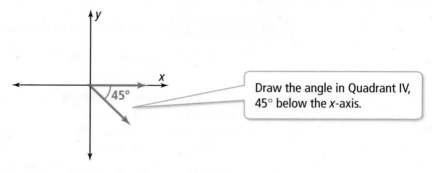

Draw the angle in Quadrant IV, 45° below the x-axis.

A positive angle measure is 360° − 45° = 315°.
A negative angle measure is −45°.

STUDY TIP
Notice that the sum of the positive angle of measure and the absolute value of the negative angle measure is 360°. This is because, taken together, the two rotations combine to make one full rotation around the circle.

 Try It! **2.** Give a possible positive angle measure and a possible negative angle measure for each reference angle.

a. 10° in Quadrant III   **b.** 15° in Quadrant I

CONCEPT The Unit Circle

The unit circle is a circle that has its center at the origin and has a radius of 1.

In any right triangle formed with the radius as the hypotenuse, the length of the hypotenuse is 1.

Based on right triangle trigonometry

$$\sin \theta = \frac{y}{1}, \text{ or } y \qquad \cos \theta = \frac{x}{1}, \text{ or } x$$

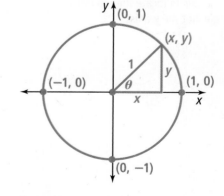

⏺ **EXAMPLE 3** ▶ **Find the Coordinates of a Point on the Unit Circle**

An angle, θ, has a measure of 60° and a terminal side that intercepts the unit circle at (x, y). What are the values of x and y?

Sketch a figure to represent the problem.

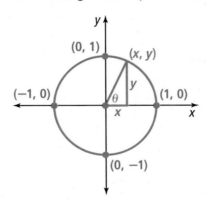

This figure represents the unit circle, so the radius is 1. Draw a **reference triangle**, formed by drawing a perpendicular line from the terminal point of an angle θ in standard position to the x-axis. The length of the hypotenuse of this triangle is 1.

$$\sin \theta = \frac{y}{1} = y \quad \cos \theta = \frac{x}{1} = x$$

The reference triangle formed is a 30°-60°-90° triangle, so you can use the relationship between the sides to find the value of x and y. The side across from the 30° angle is

half of the hypotenuse, or $\frac{1}{2}$. The side across from the 60° angle is $\sqrt{3}$ times the shorter side, or $\frac{\sqrt{3}}{2}$. So, $\sin 60° = \frac{\sqrt{3}}{2}$ and $\cos 60° = \frac{1}{2}$, and the coordinate (x, y) is $\left(\frac{1}{2}, \frac{\sqrt{3}}{2} \right)$.

☑ **Try It!**   **3.** An angle, θ, has a measure of 45° and a terminal side that intercepts the unit circle at (x, y). What are the values of x and y?

⏺ **EXAMPLE 4** ▶ **Understand Radian Measure on the Unit Circle**

A. What is the radian measure of an angle?

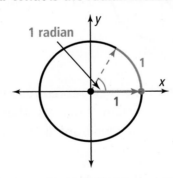

The **radian measure** of a central angle is equal to the length of the arc on the unit circle subtended by that angle.

An angle measure of 1 **radian** subtends an arc on the unit circle with length 1.

The radius of the **unit circle** is 1, so the circumference of the unit circle is $C = 2\pi r = 2\pi(1) = 2\pi$. This implies that a 360° angle, or one complete rotation of the circle, measures 2π radians.

The x- and y-axis divide the unit circle into four congruent arcs, each representing $\frac{\pi}{2}$ radians.

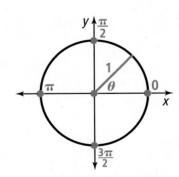

CONTINUED ON THE NEXT PAGE

EXAMPLE 4 CONTINUED

In general, the radian measure, θ, of an angle is the length of the intercepted arc measured in radius units.

$$\theta = \frac{\text{length of intercepted arc}}{\text{radius}}.$$

Since the radius of the unit circle is 1, the radian measure of, θ, of an angle is equal to the length of its intercepted arc on the unit circle.

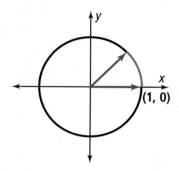

STUDY TIP
The circumference of the unit circle is 2π, and $\frac{2\pi}{8} = \frac{\pi}{4}$, so $\frac{\pi}{4}$ is $\frac{1}{8}$ of the circumference.

For example, if an angle measures $\frac{\pi}{4}$ radians, its intercepted arc is also $\frac{\pi}{4}$ radians. The angle lies in Quadrant I, with a terminal side halfway between 0 and $\frac{\pi}{2}$.

B. How can you use radian measure to sketch an angle?

Suppose an angle measures $\frac{4\pi}{3}$ radians. Its intercepted arc on the unit circle is also $\frac{4\pi}{3}$ radians.

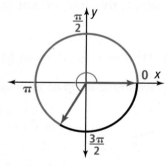

The top half of the circle represents π radians. $\frac{4\pi}{3}$ radians is greater than π radians but less than $\frac{3\pi}{2}$ radians. Therefore an angle with a measure of $\frac{4\pi}{3}$ radians lies in Quadrant III and has a reference angle of $\frac{\pi}{3}$.

 Try It! 4. Sketch the graph of an angle that measures $-\frac{5\pi}{6}$ in standard position.

👆 **EXAMPLE 5** **Convert Between Degrees and Radians**

A. How do you convert between degrees and radians?

One full rotation, or 360°, is the same as 2π radians. Half a rotation, or 180°, is the same as π radians.

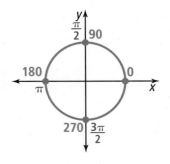

Radian	0	$\frac{\pi}{2}$	π	$\frac{3\pi}{2}$	2π
Degrees	0	90	180	270	360

2π radians = 360°

π radians = 180°

> To find the value of 1 radian in terms of degrees, divide both sides by π.

1 radian = $\frac{180°}{\pi}$

For example, if an angle measures $\frac{\pi}{2}$ radians, what is its measure in degrees?

$\frac{\pi}{2} \cdot \frac{180°}{\pi} = 90°$

> To convert any number of radians to degrees, multiply the number of radians by $\frac{180°}{\pi}$.

π radians = 180°

> To find the value of 1 degree in terms of radians, divide both sides by 180°.

1 degree = $\frac{\pi}{180°}$ radians

For example, if an angle measures 120°, what is its measure in radians?

$120° \cdot \frac{\pi}{180°}$ radians = $\frac{2\pi}{3}$ radians

> To convert any number of degrees to radians, multiply the number of degrees by $\frac{\pi}{180°}$.

USE APPROPRIATE TOOLS
Your calculator is able to work with both radians and degrees. Be sure that it is set properly for your calculations. ⓒ **MP.5**

B. How can you convert each angle measure from radians to degrees or degrees to radians?

$\frac{\pi}{7}$ radians   75°

$\frac{\pi}{7} \cdot \frac{180°}{\pi} \approx 25.7°$ $75° \cdot \frac{\pi}{180°} = \frac{5\pi}{12}$ radians

☑ **Try It!** **5.** Convert the angle measures.

a. 112° to radians   **b.** $\frac{\pi}{6}$ radians to degrees

APPLICATION   👆 **EXAMPLE 6** > **Use Radians to Find Arc Length**

NASA is tracking a satellite traveling in a circular orbit above Earth. It can only be tracked while it orbits through a $\frac{\pi}{6}$ angle. The radius of Earth is 6,400 km. What is the distance the satellite travels while it is being tracked?

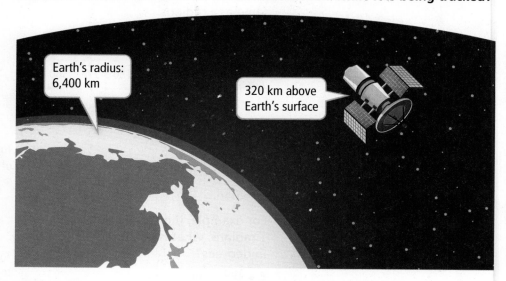

Earth's radius: 6,400 km

320 km above Earth's surface

The satellite travels through an arc surrounding Earth.

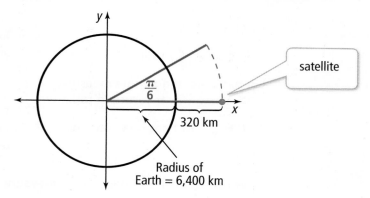

satellite

$\frac{\pi}{6}$

320 km

Radius of Earth = 6,400 km

The total distance from the center of Earth to the satellite is 6,400 km + 320 km, or 6,720 km.

Use the formula for the radian measure of an arc to find the distance through which the satellite can be tracked.

$$\text{Radian Measure} = \frac{\text{length of intercepted arc}}{\text{Radius}}$$

Length of Intercepted Arc = Radian Measure × Radius

Length of Intercepted Arc = $\left(\frac{\pi}{6}\right)$(6,720 km)

≈ 3,519 km

The satellite can be tracked for about 3,519 km.

STUDY TIP
Make sure that the units are the same for the radius and the arc length.

☑ **Try It!**   **6.** If the satellite could be tracked for 5,000 km, what angle in radians would it pass through?

 Go Online | SavvasRealize.com

CONCEPT SUMMARY Angles and the Unit Circle

STANDARD POSITION

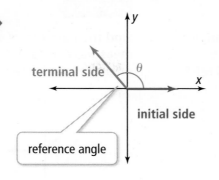

terminal side

θ

initial side

reference angle

An angle is in standard position when its initial side is the positive *x*-axis and its vertex is at the origin.

The reference angle is the acute angle formed by the terminal side and the *x*-axis.

DEGREES AND RADIANS

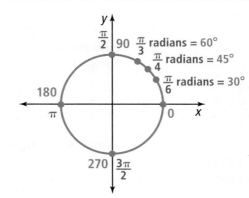

$\frac{\pi}{2}$ 90 $\frac{\pi}{3}$ radians = 60°

$\frac{\pi}{4}$ radians = 45°

$\frac{\pi}{6}$ radians = 30°

180

π

270 $\frac{3\pi}{2}$

$$radians = \frac{\pi}{180} \cdot degrees$$

$$degrees = \frac{180}{\pi} \cdot radians$$

Do You UNDERSTAND?

1. **ESSENTIAL QUESTION** How can we extend the trigonometric ratios to angles greater than 90°?

2. **Error Analysis** Camilla said that θ and its reference angle are always supplementary angles. Explain and correct Camilla's error. **© MP.3**

3. **Vocabulary** What two features distinguish a circle as the unit circle?

4. **Reason** If given an angle measure in radians, how can you determine in which quadrant its terminal side will be, without converting to degrees? **© MP.2**

5. **Make Sense And Persevere** If you are using a calculator to find the measure of an angle in degrees, what type of measure might make you question whether your calculator is actually in radian mode? Explain. **© MP.1**

Do You KNOW HOW?

The angles given are in standard position. What is the reference angle for each given angle?

6. 65°

7. 145°

In what quadrant does the angle, given in radians, lie?

8. $\frac{\pi}{6}$

9. $\frac{5\pi}{3}$

What is the negative angle of rotation for the angle with given positive angle of rotation?

10. 270°

11. 110°

Convert each radian measure to a degree measure.

12. $\frac{\pi}{3}$

13. $\frac{7\pi}{4}$

Convert each degree measure to a radian measure.

14. −30°

15. 480°

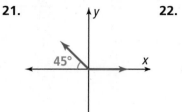
UNDERSTAND

16. Make Sense and Persevere If the given angle were drawn in standard position, in what quadrant would the terminal side be? Ⓒ **MP.1**

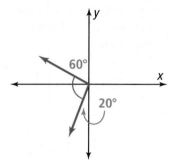

17. Look for Relationships Explain why the length of an intercepted arc on the unit circle always equals the corresponding central angle measure in radians. Ⓒ **MP.7**

18. Error Analysis Describe and correct the error a student made in converting $\frac{\pi}{2}$ radians to degrees. Ⓒ **MP.3**

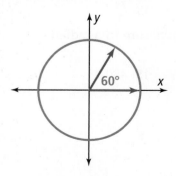

$$\frac{\pi}{2} \text{ radians} = x°$$
$$\frac{\pi}{2} \times \frac{\pi}{180} = x°$$
$$\frac{\pi^2}{360} = x°$$
$$\frac{25}{0.66} \approx 0.03° \quad ✗$$

19. Generalize What is the relationship between a positive angle and a negative angle that share a common terminal side? Write a formula that relates the two measures. Ⓒ **MP.8**

20. Higher Order Thinking At what coordinates does the terminal side of a 60° angle intersect the unit circle?

PRACTICE

Find the measure of each angle as a positive angle measure, a negative angle measure, and an angle measure that is greater than 360°. SEE EXAMPLE 1

21.

22.

Find the measure of an angle in standard position for each reference angle. SEE EXAMPLE 2

23. 15° in Quadrant II   **24.** 75° in Quadrant IV

25. 8° in Quadrant III   **26.** 56° in Quadrant I

Sketch each angle in standard position.
SEE EXAMPLE 3

27. 30°   **28.** −45°

29. −210°   **30.** 130°

Sketch each angle in standard position.
SEE EXAMPLE 4

31. $\frac{3\pi}{4}$ **32.** $\frac{\pi}{3}$

33. $\frac{-2\pi}{3}$ **34.** $\frac{3\pi}{2}$

Convert each angle measure to radians. Round to the nearest hundredth. SEE EXAMPLE 5

35. 148°   **36.** 20°

Convert each angle measure to degrees.
SEE EXAMPLE 5

37. $\frac{2\pi}{3}$ **38.** $\frac{5\pi}{6}$

Solve using the formula given. SEE EXAMPLE 6

39. Earth's radius is 6,400 km. If a satellite is orbiting at 200 km above Earth's surface and can be tracked while it orbits through a $\frac{\pi}{3}$ radian angle, what is the distance the satellite travels while being tracked? Round your answer to the nearest tenth.

APPLY

40. Make Sense and Persevere Physicists use the Large Hadron Collider in France and Switzerland to observe particle collisions. A circular chamber with beam pipes to track the particles circular path has a radius of 4.3 km. One beam pipe tracks a particle's movement over an angle of $\frac{\pi}{4}$ radians. What is the distance traveled by the particle being tracked by the one beam pipe? **© MP.1**

4.3 km

$\frac{\pi}{4}$

41. Reason The steps into a hot tub need to span a 60° section of the tub. How can you modify the formula for finding the intercepted arc length from an angle in radians to use degrees instead? **© MP.2**

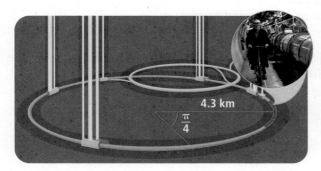

60°

42. Make Sense and Persevere Riders on a Ferris wheel get on a seat, then the Ferris wheel turns and stops to load the next seat. The radius of the Ferris wheel is 18 m. The riders travel 5.5 m in a circular path before stopping. What angle is the Ferris wheel turning between stops?

© MP.1

ASSESSMENT PRACTICE

43. Match each angle measure in degrees in the left column with its corresponding measure in radians in the right column.

I. 60°	**A.** $\frac{\pi}{8}$
II. −15°	**B.** $-\frac{\pi}{12}$
III. −200°	**C.** $\frac{4\pi}{3}$
IV. −108°	**D.** $-\frac{10\pi}{9}$
V. 22.5°	**E.** $-\frac{3\pi}{5}$
VI. 240°	**F.** $\frac{\pi}{3}$

44. SAT/ACT What is another way to represent an angle in standard position that has a measure of 530°?

Ⓐ 370°

Ⓑ 170°

Ⓒ 10°

Ⓓ −10°

Ⓔ −170°

45. Performance Task A center-pivot circular irrigator has sprayers that follow concentric circular paths as the irrigator rotates. The radius of the innermost path is 20 m and to the outermost path is 420 m more.

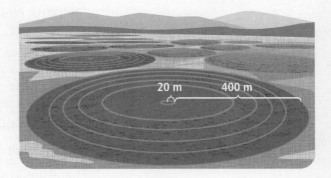

20 m   400 m

Part A What is the length of the path covered by the innermost sprayer when the irrigator rotates through an angle of $\frac{3\pi}{2}$ radians?

Part B What angle must the irrigator rotate through for the outermost sprayer to cover a path of the same length?

Activity Assess

7-3

Trigonometric Functions and Real Numbers

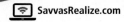
SavvasRealize.com

I CAN... use the unit circle to evaluate the trigonometric functions of any angle.

👆 **EXPLORE & REASON**

The graph shows the terminal sides of an angle with measure θ and its supplement, $180 - \theta$, on the unit circle.

A. How are the coordinates of the intersection of the terminal side of an angle with measure θ and the unit circle related to the sine and cosine of the angle?

B. What do you notice about θ and the measure of the acute angle formed by the terminal side of $180 - \theta$ and the x-axis?

C. Draw the terminal sides of angles in Quadrants III and IV that form the same acute angle with the x-axis as the angles in Quadrants I and II. How are these angles related to θ?

D. **Communicate Precisely** How are all four terminal sides related geometrically on the coordinate plane? ⓒ **MP.6**

❓ **ESSENTIAL QUESTION**   How is the unit circle related to trigonometric functions?

CONCEPTUAL
UNDERSTANDING

👆 **EXAMPLE 1**   Use Reference Triangles to Evaluate Sine and Cosine

A. What are the sine and cosine of the angle $\frac{2\pi}{3}$?

Recall that a reference triangle for an angle θ in standard position includes the acute angle formed by the x-axis and the terminal side of θ, and a right angle that is formed by connecting the terminal point of θ to the x-axis.

The reference triangle for $\frac{2\pi}{3}$ includes the reference angle $\frac{\pi}{3}$, (which is $\pi - \frac{2\pi}{3}$). The coordinates of the terminal point of the reference angle $\frac{\pi}{3}$ are $\left(\cos\frac{\pi}{3}, \sin\frac{\pi}{3}\right)$, or $\left(\frac{1}{2}, \frac{\sqrt{3}}{2}\right)$.

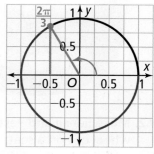

The reference triangle and the triangle with the reference angle in standard position are congruent. So once the values of sine and cosine of the reference angle are found, only the signs of the values are left to be determined.

Since the terminal point of $\frac{2\pi}{3}$ lies in Quadrant II, the coordinates of the terminal point are $\left(-\frac{1}{2}, \frac{\sqrt{3}}{2}\right)$.

Therefore, $\cos\frac{2\pi}{3} = -\frac{1}{2}$ and $\sin\frac{2\pi}{3} = \frac{\sqrt{3}}{2}$.

CONTINUED ON THE NEXT PAGE

📶 Go Online | SavvasRealize.com

EXAMPLE 1 CONTINUED

B. What are the sine and cosine of a −45° angle?

REASON

When working on the unit circle, how do you know if the sine and cosine of an angle are positive or negative? **© MP.2**

A −45° angle has a reference triangle that includes a 45° reference angle. The coordinates of the terminal point of 45° are $\left(\frac{\sqrt{2}}{2}, \frac{\sqrt{2}}{2}\right)$. This reference triangle is congruent to the triangle in standard position with the reference angle 45°. Since the −45° angle lies in Quadrant IV, the point on the unit circle is $\left(\frac{\sqrt{2}}{2}, -\frac{\sqrt{2}}{2}\right)$.

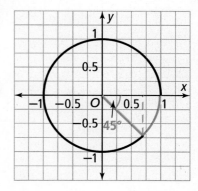

Therefore, $\cos -45° = \frac{\sqrt{2}}{2}$ and $\sin -45° = -\frac{\sqrt{2}}{2}$.

✅ **Try It!**   **1. What are the sine and cosine of each angle?**

　　　　a. $\frac{4\pi}{3}$ 　　　　　　**b.** $\frac{3\pi}{4}$

👆 **EXAMPLE 2**   **Use the Pythagorean Identity $\sin^2\theta + \cos^2\theta = 1$**

What is $\sin\theta$ if $\cos\theta = -\frac{3}{5}$ and the angle with measure θ is in Quadrant III?

Sketch the angle with measure θ and its reference triangle on the unit circle, as shown.

The coordinates of the point where the terminal side of the angle intersects the unit circle are $(\cos\theta, \sin\theta)$. The reference triangle has sides of length $|\cos\theta|$ and $|\sin\theta|$.

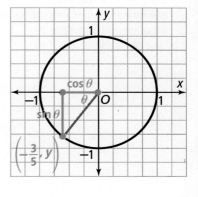

STUDY TIP

Note the absolute value signs: the *coordinates* sin θ and cos θ might be positive or negative, but the *lengths* of the sides of the triangle are always positive.

The hypotenuse of the reference triangle has length 1. The length of the side of the triangle opposite θ is $\sin\theta$. The length of the side of the triangle adjacent to θ is $\cos\theta$, or in this case, $\left|\frac{-3}{5}\right|$, or $\frac{3}{5}$.

Relate these values to those used in the Pythagorean Theorem to find the third side of the triangle. This will give you the *y*-coordinate of the terminal point, or $\sin\theta$.

COMMON ERROR

Be careful not to interpret the notation $\sin^2\theta$ as $\sin(\theta^2)$ or $\sin(\theta \cdot \theta)$. The notation $\sin^2\theta$ means $(\sin\theta)(\sin\theta)$.

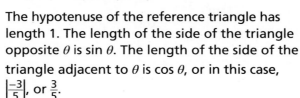

$\sin^2\theta + \cos^2\theta = 1$　— This equation is called The Pythagorean Identity.

Given $\cos\theta = -\frac{3}{5}$, you can solve for $\sin\theta$:

$\sin^2\theta + \cos^2\theta = 1$ ·········· Write the Pythagorean Identity.

$\sin^2\theta + \left(-\frac{3}{5}\right)^2 = 1$ ·········· Substitute $-\frac{3}{5}$ for $\cos\theta$.

$\sin^2\theta + \frac{9}{25} = 1$ ·········· Evaluate $\left(-\frac{3}{5}\right)^2$.

$\sin^2\theta = \frac{16}{25}$ ·········· Subtract $\frac{9}{25}$ from both sides.

$\sin\theta = \pm\frac{4}{5}$ ·········· Take the square root of both sides.

Since the angle is in Quadrant III, the *y*-coordinate $\sin\theta$ must be negative. Therefore, $\sin\theta = -\frac{4}{5}$.

CONTINUED ON THE NEXT PAGE

EXAMPLE 2 CONTINUED

 Try It! **2. a.** What is $\sin \theta$ if $\cos \theta = \frac{\sqrt{2}}{2}$ and $0 < \theta < \frac{\pi}{2}$?

b. What is $\cos \theta$ if $\sin \theta = -0.8$ and θ is in Quadrant IV?

 EXAMPLE 3   **Use the Unit Circle to Evaluate Tangents**

A. What is $\tan\left(-\frac{5\pi}{6}\right)$?

To find $\tan\left(-\frac{5\pi}{6}\right)$, start by finding $\sin\left(-\frac{5\pi}{6}\right)$ and $\cos\left(-\frac{5\pi}{6}\right)$, then use the identity $\tan \theta = \frac{\sin \theta}{\cos \theta}$ to find $\tan\left(-\frac{5\pi}{6}\right)$.

The angle with measure $-\frac{5\pi}{6}$ is in Quadrant III. Its reference angle is $\frac{\pi}{6}$, or 30°.

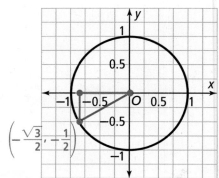

The reference triangle is a 30°-60°-90° triangle.

The length of the hypotenuse is 1, the length of the shorter leg is $\frac{1}{2}$, and the length of the longer leg is $\frac{\sqrt{3}}{2}$.

By considering the signs of a point in Quadrant III, you can determine that the coordinate of the point where the terminal side of the angle meets the unit circle is $\left(-\frac{\sqrt{3}}{2}, -\frac{1}{2}\right)$.

Use the reciprocal identity for tangent:

$$\tan\left(-\frac{5\pi}{6}\right) = \frac{\sin\left(-\frac{5\pi}{6}\right)}{\cos\left(-\frac{5\pi}{6}\right)}$$

$$= \frac{-\frac{1}{2}}{-\frac{\sqrt{3}}{2}}$$

$$= \frac{\sqrt{3}}{3}$$

So the tangent of $-\frac{5\pi}{6}$ is $\frac{\sqrt{3}}{3}$.

B. What is $\tan(3\pi)$?

$3\pi = 2\pi + \pi$, so 3π is coterminal with π. The terminal point of π has coordinates $(-1, 0)$.

Since $\tan \theta = \frac{\sin \theta}{\cos \theta}$, $\tan \theta = \frac{y}{x}$.

From this you can conclude that $\tan(3\pi) = \frac{0}{-1} = 0$.

> **STUDY TIP**
> Consider rationalizing the denominator when evaluating trigonometric functions of special angles.

 Try It! **3.** What is the tangent of each angle?

a. $-\frac{3\pi}{2}$ **b.** 675°

EXAMPLE 4 Evaluate the Reciprocal Functions

Evaluate the secant, cosecant, and cotangent of a 135° angle.

The coordinates of the terminal point on the unit circle are $\left(-\frac{\sqrt{2}}{2}, \frac{\sqrt{2}}{2}\right)$.

$\sec \theta = \frac{1}{\cos \theta}$ $\sec 135° = \frac{1}{-\frac{\sqrt{2}}{2}}$

$= -\frac{2}{\sqrt{2}} = -\sqrt{2}$

$\csc \theta = \frac{1}{\sin \theta}$ $\csc 135° = \frac{1}{\frac{\sqrt{2}}{2}} = \sqrt{2}$

$\cot \theta = \frac{1}{\tan \theta}$ $\cot 135° = \frac{1}{-1} = -1$

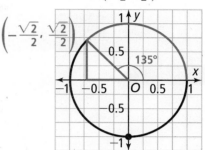

Try It! **4.** What are the secant, cosecant, and cotangent for each angle?

a. 210° b. $-\frac{10\pi}{4}$

APPLICATION

EXAMPLE 5 Use Any Circle Centered at the Origin

A rescue team is searching a circular area in a 4-mi radius around their camp. The team travels on a path 30° east of south from the camp. What is their final position relative to their camp?

Formulate ◄ Draw a circle with radius 4 to represent the search perimeter with the camp as the origin. Show the path of the team by drawing a radius at 30° east of south. This corresponds to an angle of 300°.

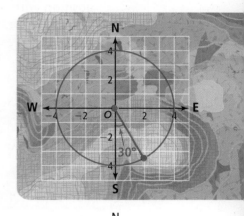

Compute ◄ Draw a perpendicular line from the team's final position to the x-axis, creating a right triangle with hypotenuse 4.

This triangle is similar to a triangle on the unit circle. The scale factor between the triangles is 4, since your triangle has hypotenuse 4 and the unit circle triangle has hypotenuse 1.

The team's final position will have coordinates 4 times those of the terminal point of 300° on the unit circle. On the unit circle, the terminal point of 300° is $\left(\frac{1}{2}, -\frac{\sqrt{3}}{2}\right)$. So the team's final

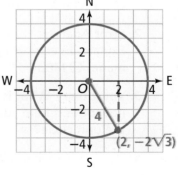

position on the search perimeter circle will be at $4\left(\frac{1}{2}, -\frac{\sqrt{3}}{2}\right)$, or $(2, -2\sqrt{3})$.

Interpret ◄ The point $(2, -2\sqrt{3})$ represents a position that is 2 mi east and about 3.5 mi south of the camp.

Try It! **5.** What is the final position of a search team relative to the camp if they walk 30° north of due west for 5 mi from their base camp?

🔑 **CONCEPT SUMMARY** Trigonometric Functions and the Unit Circle

A reference triangle is formed using the terminal side of an angle and a perpendicular segment from the terminal point to the *x*-axis. This can help you find the coordinates of the terminal point on the unit circle.

Trigonometric Functions on the Unit Circle	Trigonometric Functions on Any Circle

GRAPHS

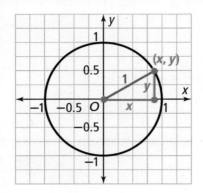

WORDS

For an angle with measure θ in standard position with terminal point (x, y) on the unit circle:

$$\sin \theta = y \qquad \csc \theta = \frac{1}{y}$$

$$\cos \theta = x \qquad \sec \theta = \frac{1}{x}$$

$$\tan \theta = \frac{y}{x} \qquad \cot \theta = \frac{x}{y}$$

For an angle with measure θ in standard position with terminal point (x, y) on any circle:

$$\sin \theta = \frac{y}{r} \qquad \csc \theta = r \cdot \frac{1}{y}$$

$$\cos \theta = \frac{x}{r} \qquad \sec \theta = r \cdot \frac{1}{x}$$

$$\tan \theta = \frac{y}{x} \qquad \cot \theta = \frac{x}{y}$$

✅ Do You UNDERSTAND?

1. **ESSENTIAL QUESTION** How is the unit circle related to trigonometric functions?

2. **Error Analysis** Hugo said $\sin \frac{5\pi}{2} = -1$. Explain an error Hugo could have made. © **MP.3**

3. **Vocabulary** What is a reference triangle and how does it help you work with angles on the unit circle?

4. **Reason** Why is $\cos 30° = \cos (-30°)$? © **MP.2**

Do You KNOW HOW?

Find the sine and cosine of each angle.

5. $\frac{5\pi}{4}$

6. $120°$

7. What is $\sin \theta$ if $\cos \theta = \frac{4}{5}$ and θ is in Quadrant II?

8. What is $\cos \theta$ if $\sin \theta = -\frac{1}{2}$ and θ is in Quadrant III?

Find the tangent of each angle.

9. $\frac{\pi}{6}$

10. $-45°$

11. Evaluate the secant, cosecant, and tangent of a 135° angle.

UNDERSTAND

PRACTICE

12. Reason Nadeem said the tangent of 270° is 0. Is he correct? Explain your reasoning. © **MP.2**

13. Make Sense and Persevere In your own words explain how you can convert an angle measured in radians to an angle measured in degrees. © **MP.1**

14. Error Analysis Describe and correct the error a student made in evaluating the secant of a 135° angle. © **MP.3**

> The coordinates of the terminal point on the unit circle are
>
> $\left(-\frac{\sqrt{2}}{2}, \frac{\sqrt{2}}{2}\right)$.
>
> $\sec 135° = \dfrac{-\frac{\sqrt{2}}{2}}{1} = -\frac{\sqrt{2}}{2}$ ✗

15. Generalize In which quadrant(s) are all six trigonometric functions positive? Explain. © **MP.8**

16. Construct Arguments Can a reference angle have a negative measure? Justify your reasoning. © **MP.3**

17. Communicate Precisely How many coterminal angles does a given angle have? Explain. © **MP.6**

18. Model With Mathematics Through how many radians does the minute hand of an analog clock rotate in 50 min? © **MP.4**

19. Error Analysis If the coordinates of the terminal point of an angle θ on the unit circle are $(-3, 4)$, describe and correct the error a student made in finding $\tan \theta$. © **MP.3**

> $\tan \theta = \dfrac{x}{y} = -\dfrac{3}{4}$ ✗

Find the sine and cosine of each angle.
SEE EXAMPLE 1

20. $\dfrac{5\pi}{6}$ **21.** 225°

22. 270°   **23.** $\dfrac{29\pi}{4}$

24. What is $\sin \theta$ if $\cos \theta = \dfrac{8}{17}$ and θ is in Quadrant I?
SEE EXAMPLE 2

25. What is $\cos \theta$ if $\sin \theta = -\dfrac{24}{25}$ and θ is in Quadrant IV? SEE EXAMPLE 2

Find the tangent of each angle. SEE EXAMPLE 3

26. $\dfrac{7\pi}{3}$ **27.** 405°

Find the secant, cosecant, and cotangent for each angle. SEE EXAMPLE 4

28. −315°   **29.** $\dfrac{13\pi}{4}$

30. 750°   **31.** $-\dfrac{2\pi}{3}$

32. Scientists are making an aerial study of a volcano. Their helicopter is circling at an 8 km radius around the volcano's crater, and one of the scientists notices a new vent that is 45° east of due north from the crater. What is the position of the new vent relative to the crater? SEE EXAMPLE 5

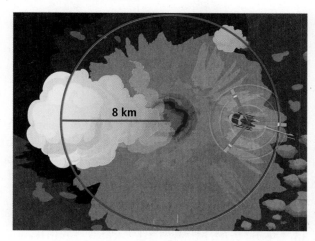

8 km

33. Model With Mathematics The horizontal distance d (in feet) traveled by a projectile launched at an angle θ and with an initial speed v (in feet per second) is given by the formula: $d = \frac{v^2}{32}\sin 2\theta$. Suppose you kick a soccer ball with an initial speed of 35 ft/sec projected at an angle of 45°. How many feet will the soccer ball travel horizontally before hitting the ground? Round to the nearest foot. © **MP.4**

34. Make Sense and Persevere A circular carnival ride has a diameter of 120 ft. Suppose you board a gondola at the bottom of the circular ride, which is 6 ft above the ground, and rotate 240° counterclockwise before the ride temporarily stops. How many feet above ground are you when the ride stops? © **MP.1**

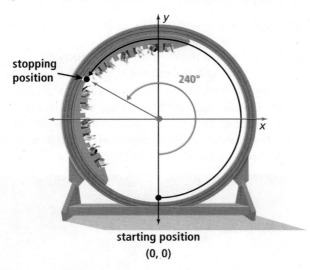

starting position
(0, 0)

35. Make Sense and Persevere Twelve people sit at a round table. Alani, in the five o'clock seat, passes a piece of paper to Carla, at nine o'clock. What are the degree and radian measures of the angle through which the piece of paper passes? © **MP.1**

36. Model With Mathematics Kelsey boards one of the outer horses of a carousel that has a 32 ft diameter. She represents her starting position at the point (16, 0) on a coordinate plane. The carousel rotates 300° and stops. © **MP.4**

   a. Find the coordinates (x, y) of Kelsey's horse when the ride stopped.

   b. How far from her starting position was she when the ride stopped?

37. What is $\sin\theta$ if $\cos\theta = -\frac{5}{13}$ and θ is in Quadrant II?

  Ⓐ $-\frac{12}{13}$

  Ⓑ $-\frac{8}{13}$

  Ⓒ $\frac{8}{13}$

  Ⓓ $\frac{12}{13}$

38. SAT/ACT Which of the following is $\tan\left(\frac{4\pi}{6}\right)$?

  Ⓐ $-\sqrt{3}$

  Ⓑ $-\frac{\sqrt{3}}{2}$

  Ⓒ $-\frac{\sqrt{3}}{3}$

  Ⓓ $-\frac{1}{2}$

39. Performance Task In navigation, the term *bearing* is used to describe the location of an object, or the clockwise-directed measure of the angle from due north. Suppose a ship's bearing is 30° from a lighthouse, as shown.

Part A Sketch the diagram on a coordinate plane, placing the lighthouse at the origin.

Part B What is the measure of the angle in standard position that describes the ship's location?

Part C If the distance from the lighthouse to the ship is 20 mi, find the coordinates of the point that represent its position on the coordinate plane.

7-4

Graphing Sine and Cosine Functions

 SavvasRealize.com

I CAN… create and use graphs of sine and cosine functions.

VOCABULARY
- amplitude
- frequency
- midline
- period
- periodic function

👆 **EXPLORE & REASON**

The graph shows a rider's height above the platform when riding a Ferris wheel *t* minutes after entering the Ferris wheel car.

A. Sketch a graph of a rider's height if the Ferris wheel is twice as high. How does the graph represent the change in height?

B. Sketch a graph of a rider's height if the Ferris wheel is the same height as the first but goes twice as fast. How does the graph represent the change in speed?

C. Communicate Precisely How are the three graphs similar? How are they different? © MP.6

<table>
<tr><th>?</th><th>ESSENTIAL QUESTION</th><th>How can you identify key features of sine and cosine functions?</th></tr>
</table>

CONCEPTUAL
UNDERSTANDING

👆 **EXAMPLE 1**   **Understand the Graph of a Periodic Function**

LOOK FOR RELATIONSHIPS
Notice that the function values that repeat occur at coterminal angles in the circle. © MP.7

A. What is the period of the graph of $f(x) = \sin x$?

A **periodic function** is a function for which the outputs repeat at regular intervals. When a function is periodic, $f(x) = f(x + p)$, for some real number p. The smallest such value of p is called the **period**.

To understand the period of the function, you could use a table of values with radian measures on the unit circle to graph $f(x) = \sin x$.

x	0	$\frac{\pi}{6}$	$\frac{\pi}{4}$	$\frac{\pi}{3}$	$\frac{\pi}{2}$	$\frac{2\pi}{3}$	π	$\frac{5\pi}{4}$	$\frac{3\pi}{2}$	$\frac{11\pi}{6}$	2π	$\frac{13\pi}{6}$	$\frac{9\pi}{4}$
$f(x)$	0	$\frac{1}{2}$	$\frac{\sqrt{2}}{2}$	$\frac{\sqrt{3}}{2}$	1	$\frac{\sqrt{3}}{2}$	0	$-\frac{\sqrt{2}}{2}$	-1	$-\frac{1}{2}$	0	$\frac{1}{2}$	$\frac{\sqrt{2}}{2}$

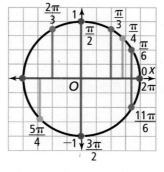
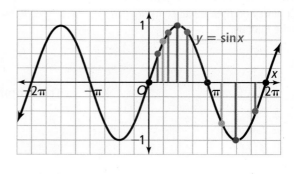

Notice that the *y*-values begin to repeat themselves after $x = 2\pi$. For this periodic function, $\sin(x + 2\pi) = \sin x$, for all *x*

The period of the function $f(x) = \sin x$ is 2π.

CONTINUED ON THE NEXT PAGE

EXAMPLE 1 CONTINUED

B. What are the other key features of the graph of $f(x) = \sin x$?

The **midline** is the horizontal line halfway between the maximum and minimum points of the graph. The **amplitude** is the distance from the midline to the minimum or maximum value of the graph.

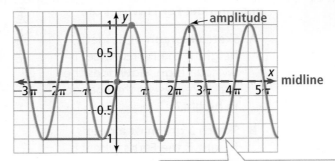

The minimum and maximum values of -1 and 1 occur at $\frac{3\pi}{2} + 2\pi k$ and $\frac{\pi}{2} + 2\pi k$, respectively, for all integers k.

The domain is $(-\infty, \infty)$ and there are infinitely many zeros, occurring at every integer multiple of π. The range is $[-1, 1]$.

The graph of $f(x) = \sin x$ has a midline at $y = 0$ and amplitude of 1.

✓ **Try It!** **1. a.** What is the period of the function $f(x) = \cos x$?

b. What are the other key features of the function?

 EXAMPLE 2 **Identify Amplitude and Period**

A. What are the amplitude and period of $f(x) = 3\cos x$?

Graph both $f(x) = 3\cos x$ and the parent function $f(x) = \cos x$.

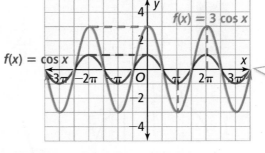

The midline is $y = 0$ and there are minimum values at -3 and maximum values at 3, which are 3 times those of $f(x) = \cos x$.

The amplitude of $f(x) = 3\cos x$ is 3, and the period is 2π.

CONTINUED ON THE NEXT PAGE

STUDY TIP
When looking for the amplitude of a sine or cosine function, find the minimum and maximum points and their distance from the midline.

EXAMPLE 2 CONTINUED

B. What are the amplitude and period of $y = -\sin 2x$?

$$y = -\sin 2x$$

As with other functions, the graph of $y = -f(x)$ is a reflection of the graph of the parent function over the x-axis.

As with other functions, the graph of $y = f(2x)$ is a horizontal compression of the graph of the parent function by a factor of $\frac{1}{2}$.

Neither of these transformations changes the amplitude, so the amplitude of $y = -\sin 2x$ is 1.

The period is compressed by a factor of $\frac{1}{2}$. Since $\frac{1}{2}(2\pi) = \pi$, the period of $y = -\sin 2x$ is π.

STUDY TIP
Since the period of the graph of $y = \sin x$ is 2π, multiplying the x by 2 will make the graph repeat itself twice as often, so the period of the graph of $y = \sin 2x$ is half the period of the graph of $y = \sin x$.

Check with a graph:

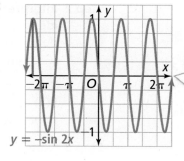

The function has an amplitude of 1, and the values of the function repeat at multiples of π.

$y = -\sin 2x$

 Try It! 2. What are the amplitude and period of each function?

a. $y = \frac{1}{3} \cos \frac{1}{2}x$ b. $y = 2 \sin \pi x$

CONCEPT: Frequency

Frequency is the reciprocal of the period.

$y = \sin x$ and $y = \cos x$ each have a period of 2π and a frequency of $\frac{1}{2\pi}$. The function repeats itself one time from 0 to 2π.

$y = -\sin 2x$ has a period of π, and a frequency of $\frac{1}{\pi}$. The function repeats itself one time from 0 to π.

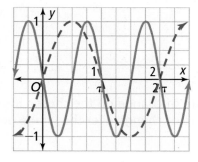

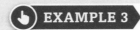
EXAMPLE 3 ▷ Graph $y = a \sin bx$ and $y = a \cos bx$

A. What is the frequency of the graph of $y = 5 \sin \frac{1}{2}x$?

Step 1 Identify transformations to the parent function $y = \sin x$.

$$y = 5 \sin \frac{1}{2}x$$

In an equation of the form $y = a \sin bx$ the parameter a indicates a vertical stretch or compression.

The parameter b indicates a horizontal stretch or compression.

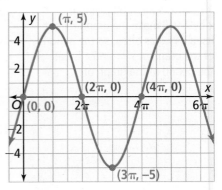

Step 2 Interpret the parameters to identify the amplitude and period of the graph of $y = 5 \sin \frac{1}{2}x$.

The amplitude is stretched to $5(1) = 5$. The period is stretched to $2(2\pi) = 4\pi$.

COMMON ERROR
Use key points to determine if a graph's appearance is different because of a change in the viewing window or a change in the period of a function.

Step 3 Sketch the graph. Divide one period into fourths. Plot in order, a zero, a maximum, a zero, a minimum, and a zero.

The frequency of the graph is $\frac{1}{4\pi}$. The graph goes through one period every 4π units.

B. How does the average rate of change differ within one period of the function $y = 5 \sin \frac{1}{2}x$?

Choose different intervals in $[0, 4\pi]$, and determine each average rate of change:

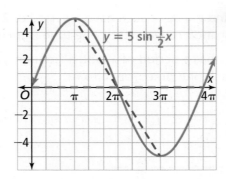

Interval	Endpoints	Average Rate of Change
$[0, \pi]$	$(0, 0)$ to $(\pi, 5)$	$\frac{5-0}{\pi-0} = \frac{5}{\pi}$
$[\pi, 2\pi]$	$(\pi, 5)$ to $(2\pi, 0)$	$\frac{0-5}{2\pi-\pi} = \frac{-5}{\pi}$
$[0, 2\pi]$	$(0, 0)$ to $(2\pi, 0)$	$\frac{0-0}{2\pi-0} = 0$
$[2\pi, 3\pi]$	$(2\pi, 0)$ to $(3\pi, -5)$	$\frac{-5-0}{3\pi-2\pi} = \frac{-5}{\pi}$
$[0, 4\pi]$	$(0, 0)$ to $(4\pi, 0)$	$\frac{0-0}{4\pi-0} = 0$

The average rate of change on the chosen intervals varies between $\frac{-5}{\pi}$ and $\frac{5}{\pi}$. The average rate of change over the whole period $[0, 4\pi]$ is 0.

 Try It! **3. a.** Graph $y = \frac{3}{2} \cos 3\pi x$. What is the frequency?

b. What is the average rate of change over the interval $[0, 1]$?

APPLICATION   👆 **EXAMPLE 4**   **Develop a Graph and an Equation From a Description**

A math teacher has a clock centered at the origin of a coordinate system. The hour hand of the clock is 5 in. long. Graph the relationship between *x*, in hours, and *y*, in inches between the horizontal axis and the tip of the hour hand. Let midnight represent 0 h, and graph the relationship for the time between midnight and 11:59 P.M. Write the equation describing the relationship you graphed.

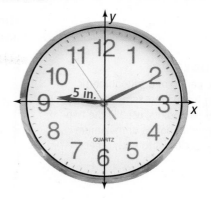

Formulate ◀   Construct a diagram to represent the clock:

Think of the horizontal axis as the midline.

The tip of the hour hand starts 5 in. above the horizontal axis at midnight.

3 h later it reaches the horizontal axis.

At 6:00 A.M. it is 5 in. below the horizontal axis.

At 9:00 A.M. it is back to the horizontal axis.

At noon, after 12 h, the cycle starts over again.

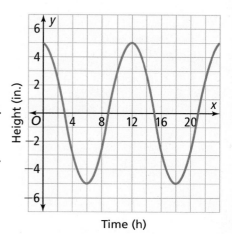

Time (h)

Compute ◀   The function starts at (0, 5) for midnight, then crosses (3, 0) at 3 A.M. and (6, −5) at 6 A.M. The hour hand travels back up to (9, 0) and then at noon is at (12, 5) before repeating the cycle again to end at (24, 5) at midnight the next day.

Interpret ◀   The graph has a *y*-intercept at the maximum value, so the equation is $y = a \cos bx$.

The minimum and maximum values occur at −5 and 5 respectively, so the midline is $y = 0$ and the amplitude is $a = 5$.

The minimum value repeats after 12 h, so the period is 12.

$$12 = \frac{2\pi}{b}, \text{ so } b = \frac{\pi}{6}.$$

The equation describing the relationship is $y = 5 \cos \frac{\pi}{6}x$.

✅ **Try It!**   **4.** Construct a graph over 3 h for the tip of the minute hand *t* minutes after noon if the minute hand is 8 in. long. What is the period?

EXAMPLE 5 Compare Key Features of Two Periodic Functions

The equation for *f* and the graph of *g* are given below. How do the period and amplitude of the functions compare?

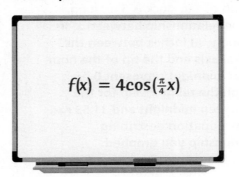

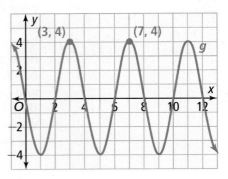

STUDY TIP
The period of a trigonometric graph can be determined using any two points, usually the two minimum points or maximum points closest to each other.

$$f(x) = 4\cos\left(\tfrac{\pi}{4}x\right)$$

Find the period of *f* by dividing the period of the parent function by the parameter $\frac{\pi}{4}$.

The period of *f* is $\frac{2\pi}{\frac{\pi}{4}}$, or 8.

Find the amplitude of *f* by multiplying the amplitude of the parent function by the parameter 4.

The amplitude of *f* is 1(4), or 4.

Find the period of *g* by measuring the distance from one maximum to the next.

The period of *g* is 4.

Find the amplitude of *g* by measuring the distance from the midline to a maximum or minimum.

The midline of *g* is the line with equation $y = 0$, so the distance to a maximum is 4.

The amplitude of *g* is 4.

The two functions have the same amplitude, but the period of *f* is twice as long as the period of *g*.

 Try It! **5. a.** How do the frequencies of *f* and *g* compare?

b. What else is different about the two functions? Explain.

CONCEPT SUMMARY Key Features of Sine and Cosine Graphs

WORDS

The general equation for a sine function is $y = a \sin bx$, just as the general equation for a cosine function is $y = a \cos bx$. In both cases, the amplitude is $|a|$ and the frequency is $\frac{b}{2\pi}$.

The equation for the graph below is $y = \frac{1}{2} \sin 4x$.

GRAPH

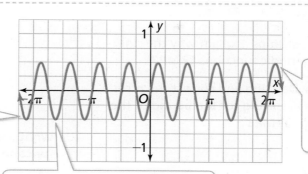

The amplitude is the distance between a minimum or maximum point and the midline, or $\frac{1}{2}$.

The x-axis, or $y = 0$, is the midline, which is halfway between the maximum points and minimum points.

The period is $\frac{\pi}{2}$, or the length of one cycle. The frequency is $\frac{2}{\pi}$, because the function repeats 2 times from 0 to π.

☑ Do You UNDERSTAND?

1. ❓ **ESSENTIAL QUESTION** How can you identify key features of sine and cosine functions?

2. **Error Analysis** Christy said that the function $y = 3 \cos 4x$ has an amplitude of 3 and a period of $\frac{\pi}{4}$. Explain and correct Christy's error. ⓒ **MP.3**

3. **Vocabulary** Explain the difference between the period and the amplitude of a periodic function.

4. **Reason** What is the range of the cosine function? How does the range compare to the amplitude of the function? ⓒ **MP.2**

Do You KNOW HOW?

Find the period and amplitude of each function.

5.

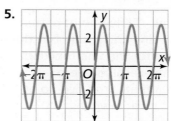

6.

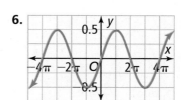

7. Use the graph from Exercise 6. How many cycles does the function have in the interval from 0 to 2π?

UNDERSTAND

8. Use Structure Write the equations of three cosine functions that have an amplitude of $\frac{1}{2}$ and that have periods of $\frac{1}{2}$, 2, and 4. Then graph and label all three equations on the same coordinate plane. © **MP.7**

9. Look for Relationships Explain why the sine function is a periodic function. © **MP.7**

10. Error Analysis Describe and correct the error a student made in solving for the period of the given function. © **MP.3**

$$y = \frac{1}{4} \sin \frac{2}{3}x$$

$$\text{period} = \frac{2\pi}{\frac{1}{4}}$$

$$\text{period} = \frac{2\pi}{1} \times \frac{4}{1}$$

$$\text{period} = 8\pi \quad \bf{X}$$

11. Look for Relationships A "five-point pattern" can be used to graph sine and cosine functions. The five-point pattern for the sine function when $a > 0$ is zero-max-zero-min-zero, as shown on the graph. What is the five-point pattern for the sine function when $a < 0$? © **MP.7**

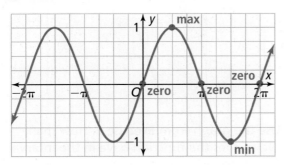

12. Higher Order Thinking Use a graphing calculator to graph $y = \sin x$ and $y = \csc x$. What do you notice about the graph of $y = \csc x$ where $y = 0$ on the graph of $y = \sin x$? (*Hint*: $y = \csc x$ is equivalent to $y = \frac{1}{\sin x}$.)

PRACTICE

13. Identify the domain, range, and period of the function $y = \cos x$. SEE EXAMPLE 1

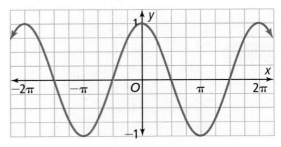

What are the amplitude and period of each function? SEE EXAMPLE 2

14. $y = \frac{1}{2} \cos \frac{1}{8}x$ **15.** $y = 5 \sin \frac{1}{4}x$

16. Use technology to graph $y = \frac{3}{4} \sin 2x$. What is the frequency? What is the average rate of change on the interval $[0, \pi]$? SEE EXAMPLE 3

17. A particle in the ocean moves with a wave. The motion of the particle can be modeled by the cosine function. If a 14 in. wave occurs every 6 s, write a function that models the height of the particle in inches y as it moves in seconds x. What is the period of the function? SEE EXAMPLE 4

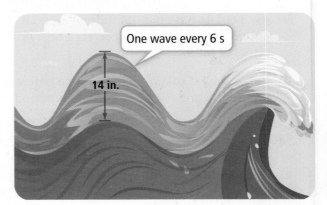

One wave every 6 s

14 in.

18. How do the periods of the two functions compare? SEE EXAMPLE 5

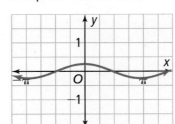

$$f(x) = \frac{1}{4} \cos \frac{\pi}{3}x$$

PRACTICE & PROBLEM SOLVING

APPLY

19. Make Sense and Persevere The relationship between the height of a point on a unicycle wheel, in feet, and time, in seconds, can be modeled by the sine function. A unicycle wheel has a diameter of 2 ft. A marker was placed on the wheel at time $t = 0$ s with a height of $h = 0$ ft. When Esteban is riding the unicycle, it takes $\frac{\pi}{2}$ s for the unicycle wheel to make one complete revolution. © **MP.1**

2 ft

marker
$t = 0$

a. What is the period of the function?

b. What is the amplitude of the function?

c. Write an equation to represent this situation.

d. Graph the function.

e. How many revolutions will the unicycle wheel make in 4π s when Esteban is riding the unicycle?

20. Model With Mathematics A solar day is 24 h and a lunar day is 24 h 50 min. A lunar day is 50 min longer than a solar day because the moon revolves around Earth, and Earth rotates around its axis in the same direction. This means it takes Earth 50 min longer to catch up with the moon. Each lunar day, two high tides and two low tides occur. High tides occur 12 h 25 min apart. Yesterday, high tide was measured at 8 ft above sea level and low tide was measured at 2 ft above sea level. A cosine function models the depth of the water in feet, D, at time t in hours. © **MP.4**

a. What is the period of the function?

b. The amplitude is the difference between the depth of the water at high tide and the average depth of the water. What is the amplitude?

c. Write an equation to represent D as a function of t.

© **ASSESSMENT PRACTICE**

21. Find the key features of the function $y = 8\cos\left(\frac{\pi}{6}x\right)$. Write the correct value from the box next to each key feature.

amplitude =

period =

frequency =

midline =

3	8	12
$\frac{1}{8}$	$\frac{1}{12}$	$\frac{\pi}{3}$
$x = 0$		$y = 0$

22. SAT/ACT What is the equation of the graph?

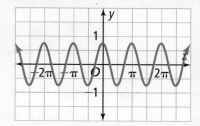

Ⓐ $y = \frac{3}{4}\cos(2x)$ Ⓒ $y = \frac{3}{4}\sin(2x)$

Ⓑ $y = \frac{3}{2}\cos x$ Ⓓ $y = \frac{3}{2}\sin x$

23. Performance Task Danielle is investigating how the signs of the parameters a and b create transformations of the sine function.

Part A Graph $y = (\sin 2x)$ and $y = -\sin(2x)$ on the same coordinate plane.

Part B How are the graphs of $y = \sin(2x)$ and $y = -\sin(2x)$ related?

Part C Graph $y = \sin(2x)$ and $y = \sin(-2x)$ on the same coordinate plane.

Part D How are the graphs of $y = \sin 2x$ and $y = \sin(-2x)$ related?

Part E How is the graph of $y = a\sin(bx)$ affected when a or b is replaced with its opposite? Explain.

⚞Ⓒ **Common Core State Standards** HSF.IF.C.7.E, HSF.IF.B.4, MP.4

▶ ## What Note Was That?

Sounds are created by vibrations. As the vibrations travel through the air, they create sound waves. The frequency of a sound is the measurement of the number of cycles of that wave per second, in a unit called hertz (Hz). Music notes can be identified by their frequency.

What information do you need to determine the frequency of a note? How accurate does your data need to be? Think about this during the Mathematical Modeling in 3 Acts lesson.

Scan for
Multimedia

ACT 1 ⟩ Identify the Problem

1. What is the first question that comes to mind after watching the video?

2. Write down the main question you will answer about what you saw in the video.

3. Make an initial conjecture that answers this main question.

4. Explain how you arrived at your conjecture.

5. What information will be useful to know to answer the main question? How can you get it? How will you use that information?

ACT 2 ⟩ Develop a Model

6. Use the math that you have learned in this Topic to refine your conjecture.

ACT 3 ⟩ Interpret the Results

7. Did your refined conjecture match the actual answer exactly? If not, what might explain the difference?

7-5

Graphing Other Trigonometric Functions

SavvasRealize.com

I CAN... sketch the graphs of the ratio and reciprocal trigonometric functions.

Common Core State Standards HSF.IF.B.4, HSF.BF.B.3, HSF.TF.B.5, MP.1, MP.7, MP.8

  Activity  Assess

👆 EXPLORE & REASON

Use the graphs of $f(x) = x + 3$ and $g(x) = \frac{1}{x+3}$ to compare these reciprocal functions.

A. Identify the zeros of each function.

B. Identify the asymptotes of $y = g(x)$. Describe how the rule for g can be used to predict the horizontal and vertical asymptotes of its graph.

C. **Look for Relationships** How can you use the graph of f to predict a vertical asymptote in the graph of g? © **MP.7**

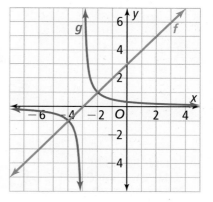

❓ ESSENTIAL QUESTION

How do key features of one trigonometric function relate to key features of other trigonometric functions?

👆 EXAMPLE 1 ▸ Graph $y = \tan x$

How can the unit circle help you sketch the graph of $y = \tan x$?

Use what you know about the unit circle to create a table of values.

LOOK FOR RELATIONSHIPS
How does the unit circle relate to the graph of the function $y = \tan x$? A semicircle on the unit circle corresponds to one period of the function's graph. © **MP.7**

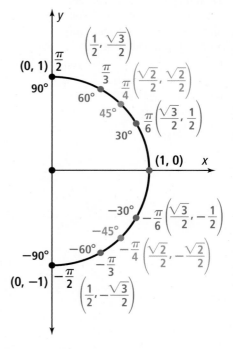

x	$-\frac{\pi}{2}$	$-\frac{\pi}{3}$	$-\frac{\pi}{4}$	$-\frac{\pi}{6}$	0	$\frac{\pi}{6}$	$\frac{\pi}{4}$	$\frac{\pi}{3}$	$\frac{\pi}{2}$
$\tan x$	undefined	$-\sqrt{3}$	-1	$-\frac{\sqrt{3}}{3}$	0	$\frac{\sqrt{3}}{3}$	1	$\sqrt{3}$	undefined

The graph of $y = \tan x$ goes through one complete cycle from $-\frac{\pi}{2} < x < \frac{\pi}{2}$. Over this interval the range is all real numbers.

CONTINUED ON THE NEXT PAGE

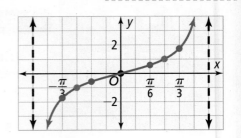
EXAMPLE 1 CONTINUED

Notice that at the boundaries of this interval, $y = \tan x$ is undefined: these are the values where $\cos x = 0$. Since $\tan x = \frac{\sin x}{\cos x}$, the graph of $y = \tan x$ will have vertical asymptotes at these values.

Try It! 1. Create a table of values, and use the unit circle to help you sketch the graph of $y = \cot x$. Plot the function's zeros and asymptotes in your sketch.

CONCEPTUAL
UNDERSTANDING

EXAMPLE 2 **Describe Key Features of Tangent Functions**

What are the key features (domain, range, period, zeros, and asymptotes) of the graph of $y = \tan x$?

Refer back to the table of values and sketch you made in Example 1.

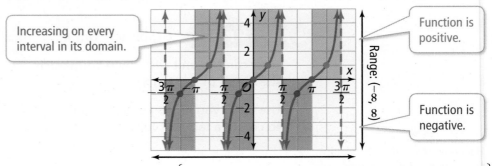

Increasing on every interval in its domain.

Function is positive.

Range: $(-\infty, \infty)$

Function is negative.

GENERALIZE
What do you notice about the key features of the graph? Points and characteristics repeat every π units. If you understand the graph for $-\frac{\pi}{2} < x < \frac{\pi}{2}$, then you understand the graph everywhere. Ⓒ **MP.8**

Domain: $\left\{ x: x \neq \frac{\pi}{2} + n\pi, \text{ where } x \text{ is a real number and } n \text{ is an integer} \right\}$;

Range: $(-\infty, \infty)$

Period: π

$y = \tan x = \frac{\sin x}{\cos x}$ → Function has zeros whenever $\sin x = 0$.

→ Function has vertical asymptotes whenever $\cos x = 0$.

The function is increasing everywhere.

The function is positive for every interval $\left(0 + n\pi, \frac{\pi}{2} + n\pi \right)$ where n is an integer: these correspond to the green shaded regions on the graph.

The function is negative for every interval $\left(-\frac{\pi}{2} + n\pi, n\pi \right)$ where n is an integer. These correspond to the purple shaded regions on the graph.

Try It! 2. Describe the key features of the graph of the function $y = \cot x$. Refer to your graph from Example 1, Try It!

👆 **EXAMPLE 3**   Graph $y = a \tan bx$

How can you use transformations to sketch the graph of the function $y = a \tan bx$?

To sketch a graph using transformations, first consider how the parameters a and b change the graph of the parent function.

$$y = 2 \tan 4x$$

$a = 2$; the coefficient of the tangent function stretches the graph of the function vertically.

$b = 4$; a larger coefficient of x corresponds to a smaller period, so the graph appears to be the parent graph compressed horizontally.

The vertical stretch makes the graph of $y = 2 \tan 4x$ rise more steeply than the graph of $y = \tan x$.

The horizontal compression changes the period of the function:

The period of the graph of $y = \tan x$ is π.

The period of the graph of $y = 2 \tan 4x$ is $\frac{\pi}{4}$.

COMMON ERROR
Since the function $y = 2 \cos x$ has an amplitude of 2, you may think that the function $y = 2 \tan 4x$ has an amplitude of 2. The tangent function, however, has no maximum or minimum values, so it has no amplitude.

$y = 2 \tan 4x$ $y = \tan x$

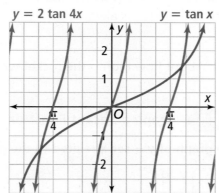

✓ **Try It!**   **3.** Sketch the graph of the function $y = \frac{1}{2} \cot 3x$.

APPLICATION   👆 **EXAMPLE 4**   **Model With a Trigonometric Function**

MODEL WITH MATHEMATICS
Why does the function involve the tangent? Could you use a sine or cosine function to model this problem instead? ⓒ **MP.4**

Seth is observing today's rocket launch at Cape Canaveral from the viewing area about 3 mi away. Write a function to model the height h of the rocket as a function of the angle of inclination θ, from Seth's position in the viewing area to the rocket. Identify an appropriate domain, and use the function to describe the motion of the rocket.

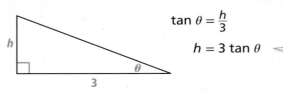

$$\tan \theta = \frac{h}{3}$$

$$h = 3 \tan \theta$$

The rocket will never be directly overhead, because there is always a horizontal distance of 3 mi.

In this context, the domain of the function is $\left\{\theta \mid 0 < \theta < \frac{\pi}{2}\right\}$ because the rocket will never be directly overhead. The range is $\{h \mid h > 0\}$, because the height of the rocket is always positive.

☑ **Try It!**   **4.** About how high is the rocket when the angle of inclination is $\frac{\pi}{3}$?

👆 **EXAMPLE 5**   **Graph a Secant Function**

STUDY TIP
Use the unit circle to help you learn the values of sine and cosine for key angle measures. You can then use this knowledge to find values and sketch the graphs of the remaining trigonometric functions.

How is the graph of $y = \sec x$ related to the graph of $y = \cos x$?

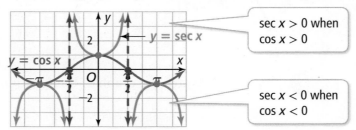

$\sec x > 0$ when $\cos x > 0$

$\sec x < 0$ when $\cos x < 0$

The domain of $y = \sec x$ is $\left\{x : x \neq \frac{\pi}{2} + n\pi, \text{ integer } n\right\}$. The graph of $y = \sec x$ has a vertical asymptote wherever $x = \frac{\pi}{2} + n\pi$ for any integer n. This makes sense, since $\sec x = \frac{1}{\cos x}$ and $\cos x$ is 0 for any $\frac{\pi}{2} + n\pi$. Since the graph of $y = \cos x$ changes sign at those values, the graph of $y = \sec x$ approaches $+\infty$ on one side of the asymptote and $-\infty$ on the other.

☑ **Try It!**   **5.** How is the graph of $y = \csc x$ related to the graph of $y = \sin x$?

CONCEPT SUMMARY Graph Ratios and Reciprocals of Sine and Cosine

	Tangent and Cotangent		Secant and Cosecant	
ALGEBRA	$y = \tan x = \dfrac{\sin x}{\cos x}$	$y = \cot x = \dfrac{\cos x}{\sin x}$	$y = \sec x = \dfrac{1}{\cos x}$	$y = \csc x = \dfrac{1}{\sin x}$
GRAPHS	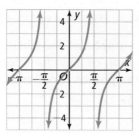	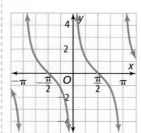	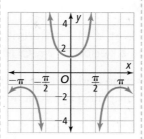	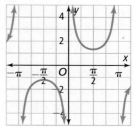

KEY FEATURES

- Zeros in denominators ⇔ vertical asymptotes

- tan x increasing; cot x decreasing

- Period $= \pi$

- Zeros in denominators ⇔ vertical asymptotes

- Sign of reciprocal matches sign of denominator

- Period $= 2\pi$

Do You UNDERSTAND?

1. **ESSENTIAL QUESTION** How do key features of one trigonometric function relate to key features of other trigonometric functions?

2. **Error Analysis** Mia said the period of the tangent function is 2π. Explain an error that Mia could have made. ⓒ **MP.3**

3. **Reason** Explain why the graph of $y = \tan x$ does not have an amplitude. ⓒ **MP.2**

Do You KNOW HOW?

4. Sketch the graph of the function $y = \frac{1}{2}\tan x$ over the interval $-\frac{\pi}{2} < x < \frac{\pi}{2}$. How does this graph differ from the graph of $y = \tan x$?

5. Find the period of the function $y = \tan 3x$.

UNDERSTAND

6. Look for Relationships Describe the relationship between the ranges of the sine and cosine graphs and the ranges of the secant and cosecant graphs. What values do all their ranges share? Ⓒ **MP.7**

7. Use Structure Write at least 2 different tangent functions that have a period of 2π. Ⓒ **MP.7**

8. Error Analysis Describe and correct the error a student made in graphing the function $y = \sec x$. Ⓒ **MP.3**

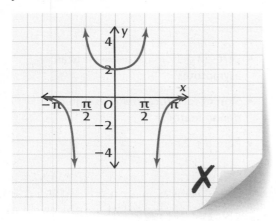

9. Construct Arguments Explain why the cosecant function is undefined at multiples of π radians or 180°. Ⓒ **MP.3**

10. Generalize For what values of x is the function $y = \tan x$ undefined? Explain. Ⓒ **MP.8**

11. Look for Relationships Explain how the periods of the tangent and cotangent functions differ from the periods of the other four trigonometric functions. Ⓒ **MP.7**

12. Generalize Identify all the asymptotes of the graph of $y = \sec x$. Ⓒ **MP.8**

13. Use Structure Write a tangent function that has a period of $\frac{\pi}{3}$. Graph the function. Ⓒ **MP.7**

14. Higher Order Thinking A function f is considered even if $f(-x) = f(x)$ for all x in the domain of f; a function is odd if $f(-x) = -f(x)$ for all x in the domain of f. Which of the six trigonometric functions are even, and which are odd?

PRACTICE

15. Sketch the graph of $y = \tan x$ over the domain $-\pi$ to π. SEE EXAMPLE 1

16. Describe the domain, range, period, zeros, and asymptotes of the function $y = \tan x$. SEE EXAMPLE 2

Sketch the graphs of the functions. Then describe how the graph of each function compares to the graph of the parent function. SEE EXAMPLE 3

17. $y = \frac{1}{2} \tan 3x$

18. $y = 2 \cot \frac{1}{2}x$

19. Stacy is observing a glass elevator from a bench 20 ft away from the elevator's entrance. SEE EXAMPLE 4

   a. Write a function to model the height h of the elevator as a function of the angle of inclination θ from Stacy's position to the elevator.

   b. Identify an appropriate domain, and use the function to graph and describe the motion of the elevator.

   c. About how high is the elevator when the angle of inclination is $\frac{\pi}{4}$?

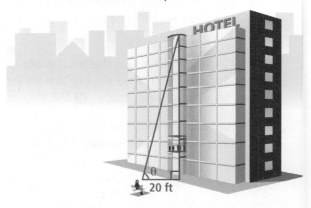

20. Graph the function $y = \csc x$. Describe how the graph of $y = \csc x$ is related to the graph of $y = \sin x$. SEE EXAMPLE 5

APPLY

21. Make Sense and Persevere An architect is designing a sloped rooftop that is triangular from the side view. **© MP.1**

θ

12ft

a. Write a function that models the height of the triangle where θ is the angle indicated.

b. Graph the function over the domain $\left[0, \frac{\pi}{4}\right]$.

c. What is the height of the triangle if θ is $\frac{\pi}{10}$? Round to the nearest tenth of a foot. **© MP.1**

22. Make Sense and Persevere A carpenter is constructing a hexagonal floor for a treehouse. The floor will be made of six isosceles triangles placed together as shown. **© MP.1**

16 ft

θ

a. Write a function that models the height of one of the triangles where θ is the measure of one of the base angles and the base of the triangle is 16 ft in length.

b. Graph the function over the domain (0, 60°).

ASSESSMENT PRACTICE

23. Fill in the blanks to complete each statement regarding the properties of the tangent function.

a. The domain is the set of all real numbers, except odd multiples of _____ .

b. The range is the set of _____ .

c. The x-intercepts are {..., −2π, _____ , 0, π, 2π, _____ ...}; the y-intercept is 0.

d. Vertical asymptotes occur at x = ..., _____ , $-\frac{\pi}{2}$, _____ $\frac{3\pi}{2}$, ...

24. SAT/ACT Which equation is represented by the graph?

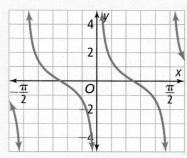

Ⓐ y = 2 cot x

Ⓑ y = cot 2x

Ⓒ y = 2 tan x

Ⓓ y = tan 2x

25. Performance Task A homeowner wants to move a flat screen television around the corner of two hallways that meet at a right angle as shown. One hallway is 6 ft wide, and the other hallway is only 4 ft wide. The length L of the diagonal through which the television must pass, as a function of θ, is $L(\theta) = \frac{4}{\sin \theta} + \frac{6}{\cos \theta}$.

Part A Write the function in terms of csc θ and sec θ.

Part B Use your graphing calculator to graph the function for 0 < θ < 90° in order to determine the greatest length the television could have to the nearest foot.

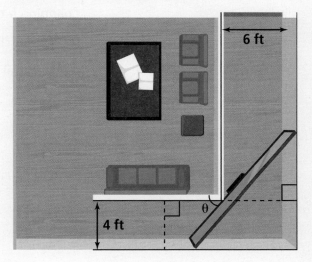

6 ft

θ

4 ft

7-6

Translating Trigonometric Functions

 SavvasRealize.com

I CAN... use transformations to analyze and sketch graphs of trigonometric functions.

VOCABULARY
• phase shift

CONCEPTUAL UNDERSTANDING

LOOK FOR RELATIONSHIPS
Just as with other functions you have studied, adding or subtracting a constant value from x shifts the graph of the function *horizontally*. Adding or subtracting a constant value from y shifts the graph of the function *vertically*. © MP.7

© **Common Core State Standards** HSF.BF.B.3, HSF.IF.B.4, HSF.TF.B.5, MP.3, MP.7, MP.8

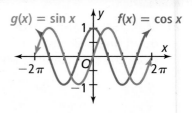

CRITIQUE & EXPLAIN

Sadie and Zhang use translations to relate the graphs of sine and cosine.

Sadie claims that $\sin x = \cos\left(x - \frac{\pi}{2}\right)$.

Zhang insists that $\cos x = \sin\left(x + \frac{\pi}{2}\right)$.

A. Who is correct? How do you know?

B. Communicate Precisely Victor claims that knowing $\sin 0 = \cos\frac{\pi}{2}$ can be used to determine who is correct. Is Victor's suggestion helpful? If so, explain why. If not, explain why not. © **MP.6**

? ESSENTIAL QUESTION   How can you find and use translations of graphs of trigonometric functions?

EXAMPLE 1   Understand Phase Shift as a Horizontal Translation

How can you identify a horizontal translation from the rule of a trigonometric function?

A. How does changing the value of h affect the graph of $y = 2\sin(x - h)$?

Sketch the graphs:

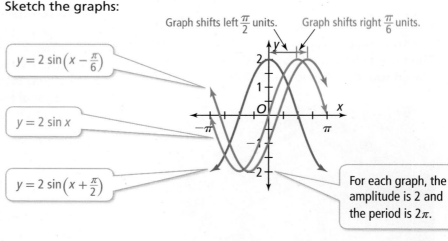

Changing h translates the graph left or right.

It does not change the amplitude or period.

A horizontal translation of a periodic function is called a **phase shift**.

CONTINUED ON THE NEXT PAGE

EXAMPLE 1 CONTINUED

B. How does changing the value of *h* affect the graph of $y = \sin 2 (x - h)$?

Sketch the graphs:

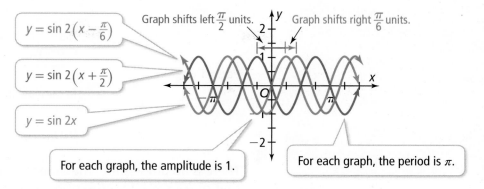

$y = \sin 2\left(x - \frac{\pi}{6}\right)$

$y = \sin 2\left(x + \frac{\pi}{2}\right)$

$y = \sin 2x$

Graph shifts left $\frac{\pi}{2}$ units. Graph shifts right $\frac{\pi}{6}$ units.

For each graph, the amplitude is 1.   For each graph, the period is π.

Changing *h* shifts the graph left or right as before.

The amplitude and period are the same for all three graphs.

Try It!   **1.** Sketch the graph.

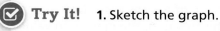

a. $y = 3 \cos \left(x + \frac{\pi}{4}\right)$ **b.** $y = \cos \left(3x + \frac{3\pi}{4}\right)$.

EXAMPLE 2   **Graph a Sine or Cosine Function**

How can knowledge of transformations help you sketch the graph of $y = 2 \sin \frac{x}{2} + 3$?

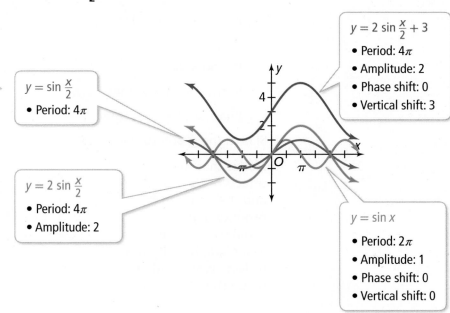

$y = \sin \frac{x}{2}$
• Period: 4π

$y = 2 \sin \frac{x}{2}$
• Period: 4π
• Amplitude: 2

$y = 2 \sin \frac{x}{2} + 3$
• Period: 4π
• Amplitude: 2
• Phase shift: 0
• Vertical shift: 3

$y = \sin x$
• Period: 2π
• Amplitude: 1
• Phase shift: 0
• Vertical shift: 0

Try It!   **2.** Sketch the graph of the function $y = \frac{2}{3} \cos \left(x - \frac{\pi}{2}\right) + 1$.

EXAMPLE 3 Analyze a Sine or Cosine Function

A. What are the key features of the graph of the function $y = 4\cos(3x) + 1$?

$y = 4\cos 3x + 1$

Amplitude $= |4| = 4$ ◄──── The amplitude is the absolute value of the coefficient of cosine.

Period $= \frac{2\pi}{3}$

To calculate the period, divide 2π by the coefficient of x.

Vertical shift $= 1$

The graph of $y = 4\cos 3x$ has been shifted up 1 unit.

There is no phase shift. The graph has not been shifted horizontally from that of $y = \cos x$. In terms of the general form, $y = a\cos[b(x - c)] + d$, $c = 0$.

Sketching the graph can help make sense of these parameters.

The amplitude of $y = \cos x$ is 1. Notice that, for this function, the maximum value is $4 + 1$, or 5, and the minimum value is $-4 + 1$, or -3.

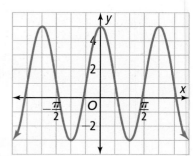

USE APPROPRIATE TOOLS
Why is it important to identify the key features of a function, even if you intend to graph it on a calculator? © **MP.5**

B. What are the key features of the graph of the function $y = -3\sin\left(x + \frac{\pi}{2}\right) - 2$?

$y = -3\sin\left(x + \frac{\pi}{2}\right) - 2$ ◄──── Since the coefficient of the sine function is negative, this graph is a reflection over the x-axis of the parent function.

Amplitude $= |-3| = 3$

Period $= 2\pi$

Vertical shift $= 2$ units down

Phase shift $= \frac{\pi}{2}$ units left

Sketch the graph to check.

Notice that the combined effects of the reflection and the phase shift produce a graph that could be interpreted as a sine graph without a reflection and with a phase shift $\frac{\pi}{2}$ units right.

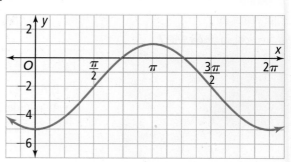

☑ **Try It!**   **3.** Identify the amplitude, period, phase shift, vertical shift, and the maximum and minimum values of each function.

a. $y = \frac{1}{2}\sin\left(x - \frac{\pi}{3}\right) - 4$ **b.** $y = 2\cos\left(2x + \frac{\pi}{4}\right) + 2$

APPLICATION ⟶   👆 **EXAMPLE 4**   **Write the Equation of a Translation**

An assembly-line machine stamps a company's logo on each product coming down the line. The graph models the stamp's height from the machine's axle, *y*, at time *x* seconds since the machine turns on. What is an equation that models this motion? Interpret the graph's *y*-intercept in terms of the context.

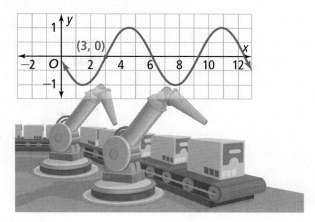

STUDY TIP
Because sine and cosine are simply phase shifts of each other, you can build the equation using either function.

The sine function has a general form

$$y = a \sin b(x - c) + d.$$

The amplitude here is 1, so $a = 1$.

The period is 2π, so $b = 1$ also.

There is no vertical shift—the midline is the *y*-axis, just like the midline of $y = \sin x$. So $d = 0$.

This graph contains the point (3, 0), where the corresponding point on $y = \sin (x)$ would be (0, 0).

There is a horizontal shift of 3, so $c = 3$.

So an equation for the graph is $y = \sin (x - 3)$.

At $x = 0$, when the equipment is turned on, the equipment is near the midline of its cycle, moving down.

✅ **Try It!**   **4.** Write an equation that models the function represented by the graph.

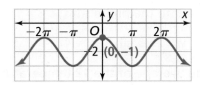

APPLICATION   👆 **EXAMPLE 5**   Find a Trigonometric Model

The table shows the average high temperature by month for Washington, DC. How can these temperatures be modeled with a trigonometric graph? How does the midline function value compare with the average of the 12 temperatures?

Month	Jan.	Feb.	Mar.	April	May	June	July	Aug.	Sept.	Oct.	Nov.	Dec.
High (°F)	43	47	56	67	75	84	88	87	80	68	58	47

Formulate ◀ Assign numbers to represent the months of the year, and create a scatter plot to show the pattern of temperatures in the table repeating over a span of two years.

Washington D.C. Average High Temperature (°F)

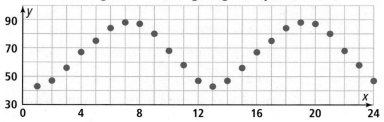

The temperatures can be modeled by a function in the form $y = a \sin b(x - c) + d$.

Compute ◀ Average the maximum and minimum temperatures to find the midline (vertical shift). $\frac{88 + 43}{2} = 65.5$, so the vertical shift is $d = 65.5$.

Find the amplitude.

$$\text{amplitude} = \frac{\text{max} - \text{min}}{2} = \frac{88 - 43}{2} = 22.5$$
so the amplitude $a = 22.5$

The period is 12 months, so $b = \frac{2\pi}{12} = \frac{\pi}{6}$.

Estimate the phase shift: $c \approx 4$

$$y = 22.5 \sin\left[\frac{\pi}{6}(x - 4)\right] + 65.5$$

> Determine the phase shift by looking for the point where the graph crosses the midline. In the parent function, there is a zero exactly at the origin.

Interpret ◀ The average of the 12 temperatures, 66.7°F, is close to the midline value, 65.5°F.

☑ **Try It!**   5. Write a trigonometric function to model the average high temperatures for Philadelphia, Pennsylvania. How does the midline value compare with the average of the 12 temperatures?

Month	Jan.	Feb.	Mar.	Apr.	May	June	July	Aug.	Sept.	Oct.	Nov.	Dec.
High (°F)	40	44	53	64	74	83	87	85	78	67	56	45

CONCEPT SUMMARY Transformations of Trigonometric Functions

GRAPH

$$y = 2 \sin\left[\frac{1}{2}\left(x - \frac{\pi}{2}\right)\right] + 1$$

$y = \sin x$

WORDS AND SYMBOLS

$$y = a \sin b \, (x - c) + d$$

$$y = 2 \sin\left[\frac{1}{2}\left(x - \frac{\pi}{2}\right)\right] + 1$$

Amplitude $= |a| = |2| = 2$

Stretches the graph by a factor of 2

Period $= \frac{2\pi}{b} = \frac{2\pi}{\frac{1}{2}} = 4\pi$

Cycle repeats every 4π units.

Phase Shift $= c = \frac{\pi}{2}$

Graph is shifted $\frac{\pi}{2}$ units to the right.

Vertical Shift $= d = 1$

Graph is shifted up one unit.

Do You UNDERSTAND?

1. **ESSENTIAL QUESTION** How can you find and use translations of graphs of trigonometric functions?

2. **Vocabulary** What is a *phase shift*?

3. **Error Analysis** Felipe said the function $y = \frac{1}{2} \cos\left[3\left(x + \frac{\pi}{4}\right)\right] - 3$ has a phase shift $\frac{\pi}{4}$ units to the right and a vertical shift 3 units down. Describe and correct the error Felipe made. **Ⓒ MP.3**

4. **Use Structure** Write a sine function that has an amplitude of $\frac{1}{6}$, a period of $\frac{8\pi}{3}$, a phase shift of 2π units to the right, and a vertical shift of 5 units up. **Ⓒ MP.7**

Do You KNOW HOW?

Identify the amplitude, period, phase shift, and vertical shift of the function.

5. $y = 4 \sin\left(x - \frac{\pi}{6}\right) + 2$

6. $y = \frac{1}{3} \cos\left[2\left(x + \frac{\pi}{2}\right)\right] - 1$

7. Write an equation for the function represented by the graph using the cosine function.

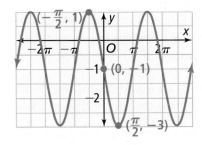

8. Sketch a graph of the function $y = \sin\left[2\left(x + \frac{\pi}{2}\right)\right] + 1.$

UNDERSTAND

9. Use Structure Write a sine function and a cosine function for the graph. © MP.7

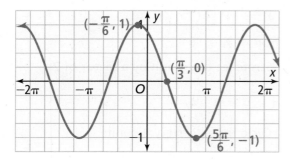

10. Error Analysis Describe and correct the error a student made in finding the phase shift of the given function. © MP.3

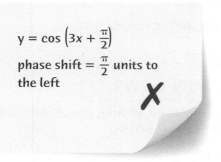

$$y = \cos\left(3x + \frac{\pi}{2}\right)$$

phase shift = $\frac{\pi}{2}$ units to the left

11. Generalize Describe the phase shift and vertical shift of a function in the form $y = a \sin[b(x - c)] + d$. © MP.8

12. Higher Order Thinking How are the domain and range of the function $y = \frac{1}{4}\cos\left[3\left(x - \frac{2\pi}{3}\right)\right] + 2$ related to the domain and range of the parent function $y = \cos x$? Explain your reasoning.

13. Generalize Write an equation for the midline of the function $y = a \cos[b(x - c)] + d$. © MP.8

14. Reason How are the zeros of the function $y = \sin\left(x + \frac{\pi}{3}\right)$ related to the zeros of the parent function $y = \sin x$? © MP.2

15. Mathematical Connections In the equation $y = a \sin[b(x - c)] + d$, which of the parameters a, b, c, and d can have an effect on the y-intercept of the graph? Explain.

PRACTICE

Sketch the graph of the function. SEE EXAMPLE 1

16. $y = \cos\left(x - \frac{\pi}{4}\right)$ **17.** $y = 2\sin\left(x + \frac{3\pi}{4}\right)$

Sketch the graph of the function. SEE EXAMPLE 2

18. $y = \frac{1}{3}\cos\left(x + \frac{\pi}{2}\right) - 2$ **19.** $y = 3\sin\left(x - \frac{\pi}{6}\right) + 1$

Identify the amplitude, period, phase shift, vertical shift, and the maximum and minimum values of the function. SEE EXAMPLE 3

20. $y = \frac{2}{3}\sin\left(x + \frac{\pi}{3}\right) + 3$ **21.** $y = \frac{1}{2}\cos\left[2\left(x - \frac{\pi}{4}\right)\right] - 1$

22. Write an equation for the function represented by the graph using the sine function. SEE EXAMPLE 4

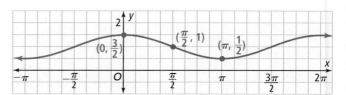

23. The table shows the brightness of the moon at the end of eight consecutive weeks. How can you model this with a trigonometric function? How does the midline of the function compare with the average of the 8 visibility levels? SEE EXAMPLE 5

Week	Percent Visible	
1	50%	
2	0%	
3	48%	
4	100%	
5	67%	
6	5%	
7	34%	
8	95%	

PRACTICE & PROBLEM SOLVING

APPLY

24. Model With Mathematics Alternating current is the flow of charge that periodically changes direction. Alternating current is used to deliver power. The function $V(t) = E \cos\left(wt + \frac{\pi}{2}\right)$ gives the voltage in amps for t seconds. Ⓒ **MP.4**

a. Edgar wants to find the voltage when $E = 40$ volts and $w = 188$ radians per second. Write a function to represent this situation.

b. Rewrite the function so that the coefficient of t is 1.

c. What is the amplitude of the function?

d. What is the period of the function?

e. What is the phase shift of the function?

f. Graph the function.

25. Make Sense and Persevere The table shows the average amount of rainfall in inches by month for Junction City, California. Ⓒ **MP.1**

Month	Rainfall (in.)
January	6.46
February	5.83
March	4.84
April	2.52
May	1.81
June	0.79
July	0.29
August	0.16
September	0.59
October	2.28
November	5.39
December	7.87

a. How can these rainfall amounts be modeled with a trigonometric graph?

b. How does the midline function value compare with the average of the 12 rainfall amounts?

c. Graph the function.

ASSESSMENT PRACTICE

26. Determine if each statement about the function $y = \frac{3}{4} \cos\left[3\left(x + \frac{\pi}{6}\right)\right] - 5$ is true. Write *yes* or *no*.

A. The amplitude is $\frac{3}{4}$.

B. The period is 3.

C. The phase shift is $\frac{\pi}{6}$ units to the right.

D. The vertical shift is 5 units down.

27. SAT/ACT Kathryn graphed the function $y = 2 \sin\left(x + \frac{\pi}{2}\right) - 1$ but forgot to label the x-axis. What is the value of d on the x-axis?

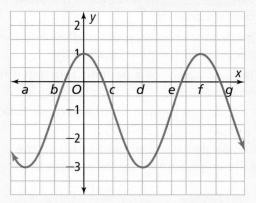

Ⓐ $\frac{\pi}{2}$ Ⓑ π Ⓒ $\frac{3\pi}{2}$ Ⓓ 2π

28. Performance Task Micah is investigating phase shifts of the parent sine function, $y = \sin x$. He wants to map the sine function onto itself.

Part A Write an equation of a function that has an identical graph but includes a phase shift.

Part B Write an equation that will map the parent sine function onto itself by shifting the parent function to the right.

Part C What do the equations in part (a) and part (b) tell you about the period of the sine function?

Part D How many equations can you write to map the parent sine function onto itself? Explain.

Topic Review

1. How are trigonometric functions used to solve real-world problems?

Vocabulary Review

Choose the correct term to complete each sentence.

2. The _____ of an angle in standard position is along the positive *x*-axis.

3. The _____ of an angle is the other side of an angle in standard position.

4. The distance between the midline and the minimum or maximum of a periodic function is called the _____.

5. The _____ of a periodic function is the reciprocal of the period.

6. A horizontal translation of a periodic function is often called a _____.

7. If an angle θ is in standard position, the _____ for θ is the acute angle formed by the *x*-axis and the terminal side of θ.

- amplitude
- frequency
- initial side
- phase shift
- reference angle
- terminal side

Concepts & Skills Review

LESSON 7-1 **Trigonometric Functions and Acute Angles**

Quick Review

$$\sin \theta = \frac{\text{opposite}}{\text{hypotenuse}} \qquad \csc \theta = \frac{\text{hypotenuse}}{\text{opposite}}$$

$$\cos \theta = \frac{\text{adjacent}}{\text{hypotenuse}} \qquad \sec \theta = \frac{\text{hypotenuse}}{\text{adjacent}}$$

$$\tan \theta = \frac{\text{opposite}}{\text{adjacent}} \qquad \cot \theta = \frac{\text{adjacent}}{\text{opposite}}$$

Example

Write the six trigonometric ratios for the angle θ in the given triangle.

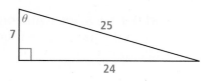

$$\sin \theta = \frac{24}{25} \qquad \csc \theta = \frac{25}{24}$$

$$\cos \theta = \frac{7}{25} \qquad \sec \theta = \frac{25}{7}$$

$$\tan \theta = \frac{24}{7} \qquad \cot \theta = \frac{7}{24}$$

Practice & Problem Solving

Write the six trigonometric ratios for the angle θ in each given triangle.

8.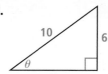

9.

What are the trigonometric ratios of θ in a right triangle with the given value?

10. $\sin \theta = \frac{5}{13}$

11. $\cot \theta = \frac{56}{33}$

12. **Look for Relationships** What trigonometric ratio is given by the cofunction identity $\sec (90° - \theta)$? **Ⓒ MP.7**

13. **Make Sense and Persevere** A 15-foot ladder is leaning against the side of a house at a 65° angle. What is the distance from the house to the base of the ladder? Round to the nearest hundredth. **Ⓒ MP.1**

Angles and the Unit Circle

Quick Review

An angle is in **standard position** when its vertex is at the origin and the initial side lies on the *x*-axis. Angles in standard position may be named with positive values or negative values.

The **unit circle** is a circle that has its center at the origin and has a radius of 1. An angle of full circle rotation, or 360°, has a measure of 2π radians.

Example

What is the measure of this angle as a positive number of degrees and in radians? As a negative number of degrees and in radians?

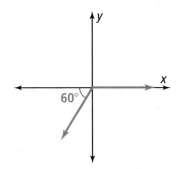

$$m\angle\theta = 180° + 60° = 240°$$
$$m\angle\theta = 240°\left(\frac{\pi}{180°}\right) = \frac{4\pi}{3}$$
$$m\angle\theta = 240° - 360° = -120°$$
$$m\angle\theta = -120°\left(\frac{\pi}{180°}\right) = -\frac{2\pi}{3}$$

Practice & Problem Solving

Find a positive angle measure for each reference angle.

14. 67° in Quadrant I   **15.** 63° in Quadrant IV

16. 25° in Quadrant II   **17.** 14° in Quadrant III

Convert the angle measures.

18. 136° to radians   **19.** $\frac{2\pi}{3}$ radians to degrees

20. 80° to radians   **21.** $-\frac{\pi}{3}$ radians to degrees

For each angle give the reference angle and Quadrant.

22. $-\frac{3\pi}{4}$ radians   **23.** 330°

24. Communicate Precisely Why is it convenient to express an angle in radians when you want to compute arc length? ⓒ **MP.6**

25. Model With Mathematics The radius of a pond is about 840 feet. After walking around the pond through an angle of $\frac{2\pi}{3}$, you pick up a plastic bottle. You carry it to a recycle bin at a point where you have walked through an angle of $\frac{5\pi}{4}$. How far did you carry the bottle? ⓒ **MP.4**

LESSON 7-3 ▸ Trigonometric Functions and Real Numbers

Quick Review

The domains of the sine and cosine functions are extended to all real numbers using the unit circle. The coordinates of the point where the terminal side of an angle in standard position intersects the unit circle are (cos θ, sin θ). The values of the other trigonometric functions can be calculated from this result.

Example

Use the unit circle to evaluate tan $\frac{\pi}{6}$.

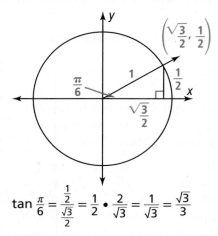

$$\tan \frac{\pi}{6} = \frac{\frac{1}{2}}{\frac{\sqrt{3}}{2}} = \frac{1}{2} \cdot \frac{2}{\sqrt{3}} = \frac{1}{\sqrt{3}} = \frac{\sqrt{3}}{3}$$

Practice & Problem Solving

Find the sine and cosine for each angle.

26. $\frac{4\pi}{3}$

27. 135°

28. $\frac{5\pi}{6}$

29. 420°

Find the tangent for each angle.

30. 120°

31. $-\frac{\pi}{4}$

Find the secant, cosecant, and cotangent for each angle.

32. −135°

33. $\frac{8\pi}{3}$

34. **Use Structure** What is sin θ if cos $\theta = \frac{3}{5}$ and θ is in Quadrant IV? ⓒ **MP.7**

35. **Reason** A scout team is searching a circular region in a 6-mile radius around a camp. Two of the scouts travel on a route that is 45° east of south from the camp. What is their final position, relative to the camp? ⓒ **MP.2**

LESSON 7-4 ▸ Graphing Sine and Cosine Functions

Quick Review

The distance between the midline and the minimum or maximum point is the **amplitude**. The **period** is the interval of the domain for which the function does not repeat. **Frequency** is the reciprocal of the period.

Example

What are the amplitude, period, and frequency of $y = 2 \sin x$?

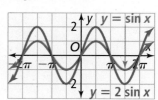

The distance between the midline and maximum point is 2, so the amplitude is 2. The period is 2π. The frequency is $\frac{1}{2\pi}$.

Practice & Problem Solving

What are the amplitude, period, and frequency of each function?

36. $y = \frac{1}{4} \cos (4x)$

37. $y = 3 \sin \left(\frac{1}{2}\right)x$

38. $y = 4 \sin 2x$

39. $y = -2 \cos 6x$

40. **Use Structure** What equation represents the graph? ⓒ **MP.7**

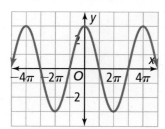

Quick Review

When graphing $y = a \tan bx$, a stretches the graph of the parent function vertically and b compresses the graph of the parent function horizontally. The period of the tangent function can be found using period $= \frac{\pi}{|b|}$.

Example

How can you use transformations of the parent function to sketch the graph of the function $y = 2 \tan \frac{1}{4} x$?

$a = 2$, so stretch the graph vertically by a factor of 2.

$b = \frac{1}{4}$, so stretch the graph horizontally by a factor of 4.

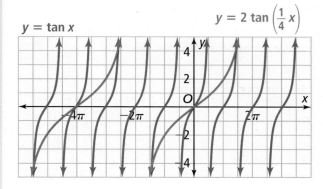

$y = \tan x$

$y = 2 \tan \left(\frac{1}{4} x\right)$

Practice & Problem Solving

Sketch the graph of the function. Then describe how the parent graph of the function was affected by the transformations.

41. $y = \frac{1}{4} \tan 4x$ **42.** $y = \frac{1}{2} \cot 6x$

43. Use Structure Describe the domain, range, period, zeros, and asymptotes of the function $y = \cot x$. ⓒ **MP.7**

44. Reason Write a function that represents the height, h, of the triangle where θ is the angle indicated. Graph the function over the domain $[0, \frac{\pi}{2}]$. ⓒ **MP.2**

10 ft

45. Make Sense and Persevere The function $y = 3 \sec \theta$ models the length of a pole leaning against a wall as a function of the measure of the angle θ formed by the pole and the horizontal when the bottom of the pole is 3 ft from the wall. Graph the function and find the length the pole when $\theta = 62°$. Round to the nearest hundredth. ⓒ **MP.1**

Quick Review

A horizontal translation of a periodic function is the **phase shift**. When graphing $y = a \sin b(x - c) + d$ or $y = a \cos b(x - c) + d$, $|a|$ is the amplitude, $\frac{|b|}{2\pi}$ is the frequency, c is the phase shift, and d is the vertical shift.

Example

What are the key features of the function $y = 5 \cos 2(x - 1) + 6$.

$a = 5$, so the amplitude is 5.

$b = 2$, so the frequency is 2, which means the period is $\frac{2\pi}{2} = \pi$.

$c = 1$, so the phase shift is 1 unit to the right.

$d = 6$, so the vertical shift is 6 units up.

Practice & Problem Solving

Identify the amplitude, period, phase shift, and vertical shift of the function.

46. $y = -4 \sin (x + 4\pi) - 8$

47. $y = \frac{1}{4} \cos\left[6\left(x + \frac{\pi}{2}\right)\right] + 2$

48. Use Structure Write an equation that models the function represented by the graph using the cosine function. ⓒ **MP.7**

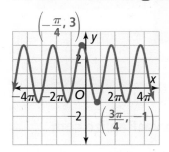

$\left(-\frac{\pi}{4}, 3\right)$

$\left(\frac{3\pi}{4}, -1\right)$

? TOPIC ESSENTIAL QUESTION

How do trigonometric identities and equations help you solve problems involving real or complex numbers?

Topic Overview

Topic Vocabulary

- argument
- complex plane
- imaginary axis
- Law of Cosines
- Law of Sines
- modulus of a complex number
- polar form of a complex number
- real axis
- trigonometric identity

 Go online | **SavvasRealize.com**

Digital Experience

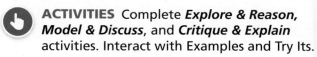

INTERACTIVE STUDENT EDITION Access online or offline.

ACTIVITIES Complete *Explore & Reason, Model & Discuss*, and *Critique & Explain* activities. Interact with Examples and Try Its.

ANIMATION View and interact with real-world applications.

PRACTICE Practice what you've learned.

Ramp Up Your Design

Wheelchair users and others with mobility challenges require ramps or elevators to access buildings and other public spaces. Most public buildings are required to have accessible ramps through the Americans with Disabilities Act. However, most homes do not have such ramps. Wheelchair users who move into a home with steps will have to have a new ramp installed.

The construction of accessibility ramps must follow strict guidelines. If ramps are not accurately built to follow these guidelines, they can be dangerous to use. Think about this during the Mathematical Modeling in 3 Acts lesson.

VIDEOS Watch clips to support *Mathematical Modeling in 3 Acts Lessons* and **enVision™** *STEM Projects.*

CONCEPT SUMMARY Review key lesson content through multiple representations.

ASSESSMENT Show what you've learned.

GLOSSARY Read and listen to English and Spanish definitions.

TUTORIALS Get help from *Virtual Nerd*, right when you need it.

MATH TOOLS Explore math with digital tools and manipulatives.

TOPIC 8

Did You Know?

A roller coaster has no engine. The first car in the train is pulled to the top of the first hill, after which gravity and momentum take over.

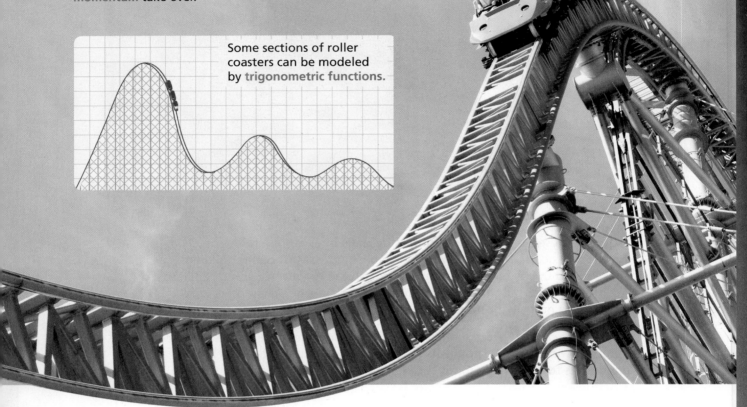

Some sections of roller coasters can be modeled by trigonometric functions.

Materials used to build **Big One steel roller coaster** =  +  +  +

1,270
pilings

2,212
tons of steel

60,000
bolts

42,000
square feet of paint

▶ Your Task: Design a Roller Coaster

You and your classmates will design a roller coaster following a track modeled on trigonometric functions.

Go Online | SavvasRealize.com

© Common Core State Standards HSF.TF.B.6 (+), HSF.TF.B.7 (+), HSF.BF.B.4.D (+), MP.3, MP.5, MP.7

  Activity Assess

CRITIQUE & EXPLAIN

Marisol and Nadia are both asked to find θ given $\sin \theta = \frac{\sqrt{3}}{2}$.

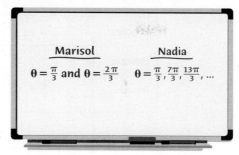

$$\underline{\text{Marisol}} \qquad \underline{\text{Nadia}}$$
$$\theta = \frac{\pi}{3} \text{ and } \theta = \frac{2\pi}{3} \qquad \theta = \frac{\pi}{3}, \frac{7\pi}{3}, \frac{13\pi}{3}, \cdots$$

A. Is either student correct? Explain.

B. Make Sense and Persevere What are all of the correct solutions for θ? **© MP.1**

? ESSENTIAL QUESTION   How can you use an inverse function to find all the solutions of a trigonometric equation?

CONCEPTUAL UNDERSTANDING

EXAMPLE 1   Define Inverse Trigonometric Functions

How can we derive inverse trigonometric functions? Why use an inverse function?

For a relation to be a function, each value in the domain can have only one output. For an inverse relation to be a function, it must map each value in the range of the original function to only one value in the domain of the original function.

By definition, the sine function is periodic so the values of the range repeat throughout the domain. To create a valid inverse function, restrict the domain of $y = \sin x$.

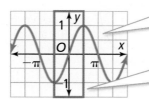

Choose a portion of the graph where the function is always increasing (or decreasing) and includes 0.

Every value in the range from −1 to 1 is represented exactly once, and none are missing.

The inverse function can be defined as $y = \sin^{-1} x$ where $x = \sin y$ for $-\frac{\pi}{2} \le y \le \frac{\pi}{2}$.

Given an angle, the sine function outputs the y-coordinate where the terminal side of the angle, in standard position, intersects the unit circle. The inverse sine function allows you to input the value of the output of the original function from a limited range of the sine function and obtain the measure of the angle.

LOOK FOR RELATIONSHIPS
How do the domain and range of the sine function relate to those of its inverse function? **© MP.7**

 Try It!   **1.** How should the domain of $y = \cos x$ be restricted to define the inverse cosine function?

CONCEPT Inverse Trigonometric Functions

	Inverse sine	Inverse cosine	Inverse tangent
Function	$y = \sin^{-1} x$	$y = \cos^{-1} x$	$y = \tan^{-1} x$
Domain	$[-1, 1]$	$[-1, 1]$	$(-\infty, \infty)$
Range	$\left[\frac{-\pi}{2}, \frac{\pi}{2}\right]$	$[0, \pi]$	$\left(\frac{-\pi}{2}, \frac{\pi}{2}\right)$
Graph			

EXAMPLE 2   **Evaluate Inverse Trigonometric Functions**

COMMUNICATE PRECISELY
The expression $\sin^{-1} x$ asks for the angle measure that has x for its sine. © MP.6

What is $\sin^{-1}\left(\frac{1}{2}\right)$?

Recall that the range of the inverse sine function is $\frac{-\pi}{2} \leq x \leq \frac{\pi}{2}$, or $-90°$ to $90°$. The expression $\sin^{-1}\left(\frac{1}{2}\right)$ represents the angle in the given range that has a sine value of $\frac{1}{2}$. Consider the unit circle. The sine function of an angle is positive in Quadrant I and Quadrant II, but the range of the inverse sine function does not include Quadrant II.

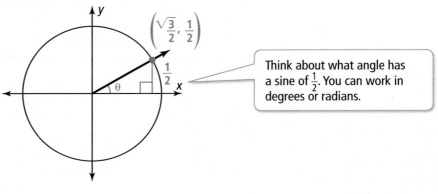

Think about what angle has a sine of $\frac{1}{2}$. You can work in degrees or radians.

$$\sin^{-1}\left(\frac{1}{2}\right) = \theta$$
$$\theta = 30°$$

$30° \times \frac{\pi}{180°} = \frac{\pi}{6}$ radians

 Try It!   **2. a.** What is $\cos^{-1}\left(\frac{\sqrt{2}}{2}\right)$?   **b.** What is $\tan^{-1}(-\sqrt{3})$?

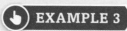
EXAMPLE 3 Find All Angles With a Given Trigonometric Value

A. What are all of the angles that have a cosine value of 0.57?

Step 1 Write the inverse cosine function $\cos^{-1}(0.57) = \theta$.

Step 2 Use the inverse cosine function on your calculator to find the value for θ, $\cos^{-1}(0.57) = 55.25°$, or 0.96 radians.

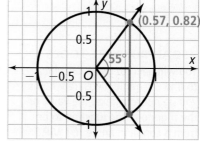

Step 3 Draw the angle on a unit circle. Look for all angles that have an x-coordinate equal to 0.57.

The x-coordinate is positive in Quadrants I and IV, so $-55.25°$, or -0.96 radians, also has a cosine of 0.57.

Step 4 Identify all coterminal angles.

$55.25°$ is coterminal with $55.25° + (360°)k$, or $0.96 + (2\pi)k$, where k is an integer.

$-55.25°$ is coterminal with $-55.25° + (360°)k$, or $-0.96 + (2\pi)k$, where k is an integer.

So the angle measures that have a cosine value of 0.57 are $55.25° + (360°)k$ and $-55.25° + (360°)k$, where k is an integer.

B. What are all of the angles that have a tangent value of -0.35?

Step 1 Write the inverse tangent function $\tan^{-1}(-0.35) = \theta$.

Step 2 Use the inverse tangent function on your calculator to find the value for θ: $\tan^{-1}(-0.35) = -19.29°$, or -0.34 radians.

Step 3 Draw the angle on a unit circle. An angle of $-19.29°$ is in Quadrant IV. The tangent function is also negative in Quadrant II. The angle in Quadrant II with the same value of tangent is $180° - 19.29° = 160.71°$, or 2.80 radians.

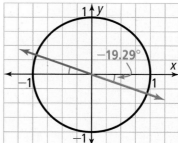

Step 4 Identify all coterminal angles. Since the two angles are on the same line, each angle coterminal with $-19.29°$ is 180° from angles coterminal with 160.71°. So all of the angles are given by $-19.29° + (180°)k$, where k is an integer, or $-0.34 + \pi k$, where k is an integer.

So the angles that have a tangent value of -0.35 are $-19.29° + (180°)k$, where k is an integer.

 Try It! **3. a.** What are all of the angles that have a sine value of 0.95?

b. What are all of the angles that have a cosine value of 0.54?

EXAMPLE 4 Solve a Trigonometric Equation

How can you solve the trigonometric equation $6 \sin \theta = 3 \sin \theta + 2$ for values between 0 and 2π?

$6 \sin \theta = 3 \sin \theta + 2$	Write the original equation.
$3 \sin \theta = 2$	Subtract $3 \sin \theta$ from both sides of the equation.
$\sin \theta = \frac{2}{3}$	Isolate the sine function.
$\theta = \sin^{-1}\left(\frac{2}{3}\right)$	Apply inverse sine function.
$\theta \approx 0.73$ radians or $41.81°$	Use technology to find θ.

USE APPROPRIATE TOOLS
You will need to use a calculator to find the angle measure when you do not recognize the value of the trigonometric function to be from a common angle. **© MP.5**

If you reflect the terminal side of an angle with measure 0.73 radians across the y-axis, that angle will also have a sine of $\frac{2}{3}$. That angle is $\pi - 0.73 \approx 2.41$ radians, or $138.19°$.

 **Try It!** 4. **a.** What is the value for θ when $0.25 \cos \theta + 1 = 1.5 \cos \theta$ for values between 0 and 2π?

b. What is the value for θ when $3 \tan \theta - 4 = \tan \theta$ for values between 0 and π?

APPLICATION **EXAMPLE 5** Use a Trigonometric Model

The average monthly temperature in New Zealand is modeled by the function $T = 4 \cos\left(\frac{\pi x}{6}\right) + 14$, where T is the temperature in °C, and x is the month, with the beginning of January being 1. In what months will the average temperature be less than 15°C?

CONTINUED ON THE NEXT PAGE

EXAMPLE 5 CONTINUED

To determine the months during which the temperature is less than 15°C, find the values of x that make the value of the function less than 15. Start by considering the period of the function.

Recall that you can find the period of the function $f(x) = \cos(bx)$ by dividing 2π by b. In this example, $b = \frac{\pi}{6}$.

$$\text{Period} = 2\pi \div \frac{\pi}{6}, \text{ or } 12$$

> Since we are looking at the temperature over one year, a period of 12 (or 12 months) makes sense.

Now, solve for x to find the points over the period when the temperature is equal to 15°C.

$T = 4 \cos\left(\frac{\pi x}{6}\right) + 14$ .... Write the original equation.

$15 = 4 \cos\left(\frac{\pi x}{6}\right) + 14$ .... Substitute 15 for T.

$1 = 4 \cos\left(\frac{\pi x}{6}\right)$ .... Subtract 14 from both sides.

$\frac{1}{4} = \cos\left(\frac{\pi x}{6}\right)$ .... Isolate the cosine function.

$\cos^{-1}\left(\frac{1}{4}\right) = \frac{\pi x}{6}$ .... Rewrite as an inverse cosine function.

$\frac{6 \cos^{-1}\left(\frac{1}{4}\right)}{\pi} = x$ .... Multiply both sides by $\frac{6}{\pi}$ to isolate x.

$x \approx 2.5$ .... Use technology to find x.

One solution for x is about 2.5. However, the cosine function is periodic so the value of the function will equal 15 at another point over the 12-month period. Graph the function to find the second point and then determine over which interval the value of the function is less than 15.

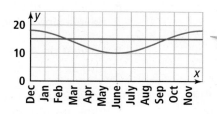

> Using technology, you can see that, in addition to x = 2.5 (or mid February), the temperature function has a value of 15 at x = 9.5 (or mid September).

The graph of $y = 4 \cos \frac{\pi x}{6} + 14$ is less than the graph of $y = 15$ between 2.5 and 9.5. This interval represent the months from mid-February to mid-September.

So, the average monthly temperature is below 15°C from mid-February to mid-September.

 Try It!   5. The average monthly high temperature in a city is modeled by the function $T = 30 \sin\left(\frac{\pi}{6}x - 1.8\right) + 61$, where T is the temperature in °F, x is the month, and x = 1 corresponds to January. Use this function to determine the months that have a monthly high temperature of 54°.

CONCEPT SUMMARY   Inverse Trigonometric Functions

	Inverse sine	Inverse cosine	Inverse tangent
FUNCTION	$y = \sin^{-1} x$	$y = \cos^{-1} x$	$y = \tan^{-1} x$
DOMAIN	$[-1, 1]$	$[-1, 1]$	$(-\infty, \infty)$
RANGE	$\left[\dfrac{-\pi}{2}, \dfrac{\pi}{2}\right]$	$[0, \pi]$	$\left(\dfrac{-\pi}{2}, \dfrac{\pi}{2}\right)$
GRAPHS	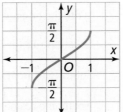	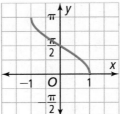	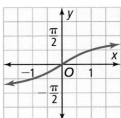

✓ Do You UNDERSTAND?

1. **ESSENTIAL QUESTION** How can you use an inverse function to find all the solutions of a trigonometric equation?

2. **Error Analysis** Luis said that the inverse of $y = \cos x$ is a function. Explain and correct Luis's error. Ⓒ MP.3

3. **Use Structure** What are the radian measures of the angles whose sine is 1? Ⓒ MP.7

4. **Error Analysis** Describe and correct the error a student made when asked to find the radian measures of the angles whose sine is 1. Ⓒ MP.3

> Let n be an integer.
> $\sin(0 + 2\pi n) = 1$
>
> ✗

Do You KNOW HOW?

5. What is $\sin^{-1}\left(\dfrac{\sqrt{2}}{2}\right)$?

6. What is $\tan^{-1}(\sqrt{3})$?

7. What are all of the angles (in degrees) that have a cosine value of 0.74?

8. What are all of the angles (in degrees) that have a sine value of 0.83?

9. Solve $4 \sin \theta - 1 = 0$ for values between 0 and 2π.

10. Solve $2 \tan \theta + 3 = 0$ for values from $0°$ to $360°$. Round angle measures to the nearest degree.

UNDERSTAND

PRACTICE

11. Use Structure Find the radian measures of the angles θ whose cosine is -1.5. Explain your reasoning. © **MP.7**

12. Communicate Precisely In order to define the inverse sine, inverse cosine, and inverse tangent functions, the domains of the sine, cosine, and tangent functions must be restricted. Explain why. © **MP.6**

13. Error Analysis Describe and correct the error a student made in solving the following trigonometric equation for θ. © **MP.3**

$$2 \sin \theta + 3 = 4$$
$$2 \sin \theta = 1$$
$$\sin \theta = \frac{1}{2}$$
$$\theta = \sin^{-1}\left(\frac{1}{2}\right)$$
$$\theta = \frac{\pi}{3} + 2\pi n \text{ or } \frac{5\pi}{3} + 2\pi n$$
✗

14. Construct Arguments Explain why there is no solution for $\theta = \cos^{-1} 3.75$. © **MP.3**

15. Generalize Find $\sec^{-1}\left(\frac{1}{2}\right)$. Justify your answer. © **MP.8**

16. Higher Order Thinking Evaluate or simplify.

a. $\cos^{-1}\left(\cos\left(\frac{\pi}{8}\right)\right)$

b. $\tan\left(\tan^{-1}(-3.6)\right)$

c. $\sin^{-1}\left(\tan\left(-\frac{\pi}{4}\right)\right)$

17. Generalize Find the value(s) of $\sin \theta$, if $\sin^2 \theta = 1$. © **MP.8**

18. Mathematical Connections Write a trigonometric equation with solutions of $240°$ and $300°$ in the domain $[0, 360°]$.

19. How would you restrict the domain of the cotangent function to define the inverse cotangent function? SEE EXAMPLE 1

Evaluate the inverse trigonometric functions at the given value. Keep the angle values within the range of each inverse function. Give answers in both radian and degree measures. SEE EXAMPLE 2

20. $\tan^{-1}\left(\frac{\sqrt{3}}{3}\right)$

21. $\sin^{-1}\left(\frac{\sqrt{3}}{2}\right)$

22. $\tan^{-1}(-1)$

23. $\cos^{-1}\left(-\frac{1}{2}\right)$

Find all the angle values of the trigonometric functions that have the given values. Give answers in degree measures rounded to the nearest tenth. SEE EXAMPLE 3

24. $\sin x = 0.64$

25. $\cos x = -0.6293$

26. $\sin x = -0.39$

27. $\tan x = -0.6293$

Solve each trigonometric equation for values between 0 and 2π. SEE EXAMPLE 4

28. $\sqrt{3} \tan x + 1 = 0$

29. $2 \sin x + \sqrt{3} = 0$

30. $2 \cos^2 \theta - 1 = 0$

31. $2 \sin^2 \theta + \sin \theta - 1 = 0$ (*Hint*: Factor the trinomial).

32. A sprint car with a loud engine is racing around a track. The engine's volume V, in dB, is defined as $V = -12 \sin\left(\frac{2\pi}{15}t\right) + 70$, where t is the time in minutes since the sprint car has passed your position. When will the sound of the sprint car first be below 65 dB?

< 65 dB at time __?__

PRACTICE & PROBLEM SOLVING

APPLY

33. Make Sense and Persevere A pendulum is pulled away from its resting position and released. The equation $h = 2\cos(\pi t) + 6$ models the height h in inches as a function of time at t seconds. **© MP.1**

a. Solve the equation for t.

b. Find the first time at which the pendulum is at a height of 5 in. Round to the nearest hundredth second.

34. Model With Mathematics Air traffic controllers at LaGuardia Airport have asked an aircraft to maintain a holding pattern near the airport. The function $d(x) = 70\sin(0.60x) + 120$ represents the horizontal distance d, in miles, of the aircraft from the airport at time x, in minutes. **© MP.4**

a. When the aircraft enters the holding pattern, $x = 0$, how far is it from LaGuardia Airport?

b. During the first 15 min after the aircraft enters the holding pattern, at what time, x, is the aircraft exactly 187 mi from the airport?

35. Make Sense and Persevere A photographer stands 60 ft from the White House, which is, 60 ft, 4 in. tall, and photographs a bird sitting on the roof. Provided the line of sight of the photographer is 6 ft above the ground, find the angle of elevation of the line of sight of the photographer to the roof of the White House. Round the angle measure to the nearest degree. **© MP.1**

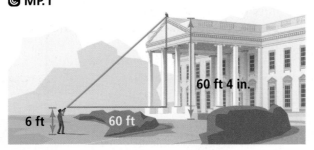

36. Model With Mathematics The tides at a particular North Carolina beach could be modeled by $h = 4.5\cos\frac{3\pi}{17}t$, where h is the height of the tide in feet above the mean water level and t is the number of hours past midnight. At what time will the tide be about $2\frac{1}{2}$ ft above the mean water level? **© MP.4**

ASSESSMENT PRACTICE

37. Solve the equation $4\sin^2\theta - 3 = 0$ for θ measured in radians. Determine if each of the following are part of the solution set. Select *Yes* or *No*.

	Yes	No
a. $\frac{\pi}{6} + 2k\pi$, where k is an integer	❑	❑
b. $\frac{\pi}{3} + k\pi$, where k is an integer	❑	❑
c. $\frac{\pi}{3} + 2k\pi$, where k is an integer	❑	❑
d. $\frac{2\pi}{3} + 2k\pi$, where k is an integer	❑	❑
e. $\frac{2\pi}{3} + k\pi$, where k is an integer	❑	❑
f. $\frac{5\pi}{6} + k\pi$, where k is an integer	❑	❑

38. SAT/ACT What is the approximate measure of the angle θ in the triangle shown?

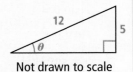

Not drawn to scale

Ⓐ $\theta = 22.6°$ Ⓑ $\theta = 24.6°$

Ⓒ $\theta = 65.4°$ Ⓓ $\theta = 67.4°$

39. Performance Task The Washington Monument is 555 ft tall. The angle of elevation from the end of the monument's shadow to the top of the monument has a cosecant of 1.10.

Part A What is the measure of the angle θ?

Part B What is the distance d from the end of the monument's shadow to the top of the monument? Round to the nearest tenth of a foot.

Part C What is the length l of the monument's shadow? Round to the nearest tenth of a foot.

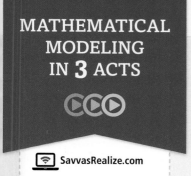

MATHEMATICAL
MODELING
IN **3** ACTS

SavvasRealize.com

⬚ Video

▶ Ramp Up Your Design

Wheelchair users and others with mobility challenges require ramps or elevators to access buildings and other public spaces. Most public buildings are required to have accessible ramps through the Americans with Disabilities Act. However, most homes do not have such ramps. Wheelchair users who move into a home with steps will have to have a new ramp installed.

The construction of accessibility ramps must follow strict guidelines. If ramps are not accurately built to follow these guidelines, they can be dangerous to use. Think about this during the Mathematical Modeling in 3 Acts lesson.

Scan for
Multimedia

ACT 1 ▸ Identify the Problem

1. What is the first question that comes to mind after watching the video?

2. Write down the main question you will answer about what you saw in the video.

3. Make an initial conjecture that answers this main question.

4. Explain how you arrived at your conjecture.

5. What information will be useful to know to answer the main question? How can you get it? How will you use that information?

ACT 2 ▸ Develop a Model

6. Use the math that you have learned in this Topic to refine your conjecture.

ACT 3 ▸ Interpret the Results

7. Did your refined conjecture match the actual answer exactly? If not, what might explain the difference?

8-2

Law of Sines and Law of Cosines

I CAN... use the Law of Sines and the Law of Cosines to solve for unknown angles and sides of a triangle.

VOCABULARY
• Law of Cosines
• Law of Sines

✋ **MODEL & DISCUSS**

A biologist measures the slant height of a conical termite mound to be about 32 ft. The angle from the ground to the top of the mound is 51°. The base of the mound has a diameter of about 40 ft.

A. Draw a model to help the biologist.

B. Make Sense and Persevere What is the height of the mound? Ⓒ **MP.1**

❓ **ESSENTIAL QUESTION** How can you use the sine and cosine functions with non-right triangles?

CONCEPT Law of Sines and Law of Cosines

The Law of Sines and the Law of Cosines allow you to apply trigonometric functions to non-right triangles. Given $\triangle ABC$, with angles A, B, and C and opposite-side lengths a, b, and c:

Law of Sines: $\dfrac{\sin A}{a} = \dfrac{\sin B}{b} = \dfrac{\sin C}{c}$

Law of Cosines:

$a^2 = b^2 + c^2 - 2bc(\cos A)$

$b^2 = a^2 + c^2 - 2ac(\cos B)$

$c^2 = a^2 + b^2 - 2ab(\cos C)$

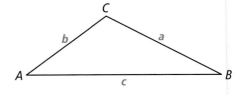

✋ **EXAMPLE 1** Prove the Law of Sines

How can you derive the Law of Sines?

STUDY TIP
Drawing an altitude allows you to create two right triangles and apply trigonometric functions.

Step 1 Draw $\triangle ABC$ with an altitude from C to side c with length x.

Step 2 Write the sine function for angles A and B.

$$\sin A = \frac{x}{b} \text{ or } x = b \sin A$$

$$\sin B = \frac{x}{a} \text{ or } x = a \sin B$$

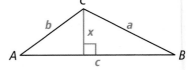

Step 3 Since you have two statements that are both equal to x, you can set them equal to each other.

$$b \sin A = a \sin B$$

Step 4 Divide both sides of the equation by ab.

$$\frac{\sin A}{a} = \frac{\sin B}{b}$$

The ratio of the sine of an angle to its opposite side is the same for all angles in the same triangle.

✓ **Try It!** **1.** How can you derive the Law of Sines for angles B and C?

APPLICATION   **EXAMPLE 2** | **Use the Law of Sines**

A. Nicholas is walking along an obstacle course that begins at point *X*. He starts going straight on the path. It then takes a wide right turn onto a second path (at point *Y*) and continues for 1,000 feet before turning on to the final path (at point *Z*). What is the angle between the second path and the final path (point *Z*)? Round to the nearest tenth of a degree.

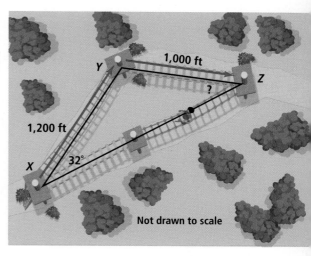

Not drawn to scale

$$\frac{\sin A}{a} = \frac{\sin B}{b}$$ .... Use Law of Sines, since an angle and its opposite side length are given.

$$\frac{\sin 32°}{1,000} = \frac{\sin Z}{1,200}$$ .... Substitute.

$$\frac{6 \sin 32°}{5} = \sin Z$$ .... Isolate the sine function.

$$\sin^{-1}\left(\frac{6 \sin 32°}{5}\right) = m\angle Z$$ .... Use the inverse sine function.

$$m\angle Z \approx 39.5°$$ .... Solve.

Since the turn at ∠*Y* is described as wide, ∠*Y* must be an obtuse angle, and ∠*Z* must be acute. This means you do not need to check for other angles with the same sine value.

The angle between the second path and the trail is about 39.5°.

B. Amaya is flying her zeppelin balloon. The string is 90 ft long, and the angle of elevation to the balloon from the ground is 60°. Across the park, Rochelle is watching the balloon which is between Rochelle and Amaya. The angle of elevation from Rochelle's feet to the balloon is 75°. How far apart are Amaya and Rochelle standing? Round to the nearest tenth of a foot.

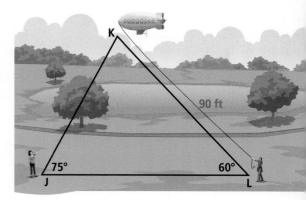

To use the Law of Sines to find *JL*, you need to know the measure of the angle opposite *JL*.

Find *m∠K* using the measures of the other two angles in the triangle.

$$m\angle K = 180° - 75° - 60° = 45°.$$

CONTINUED ON THE NEXT PAGE

EXAMPLE 2 CONTINUED

$$\frac{\sin A}{a} = \frac{\sin B}{b}$$ .... Use the Law of Sines.

$$\frac{\sin 45°}{k} = \frac{\sin 75°}{90}$$ .... Substitute.

$$\frac{90 \sin 45°}{\sin 75°} = k$$ .... Isolate the variable.

$$k \approx 65.9 \text{ ft}$$ .... Solve.

Amaya and Rochelle are standing about 65.9 ft apart.

 Try It! **2.** In $\triangle NPQ$, $m\angle N = 105°$, $n = 12$, and $p = 10$.

　a. To the nearest degree, what is $m\angle Q$?

　b. What is the length of side q? Round to the nearest tenth of a unit.

CONCEPTUAL UNDERSTANDING

 **EXAMPLE 3** **Understand the Ambiguous Case**

In $\triangle CDE$, $CD = 8$, $DE = 6$, and $m\angle C = 30°$. What is $m\angle E$ in $\triangle CDE$? Round to the nearest degree.

Start by drawing a sketch of the given information. It is not necessary to try to make your sketch to scale as you will not be relying on measurements of the sketch to find the missing information.

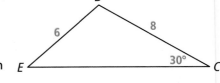

Because you know one side and the angle opposite that side, you can use the Law of Sines to find a second angle.

$$\frac{\sin A}{a} = \frac{\sin B}{b}$$ .... Use the Law of Sines.

$$\frac{\sin 30°}{6} = \frac{\sin E}{8}$$ .... Substitute.

$$\frac{8 \sin 30°}{6} = \sin E$$ .... Isolate the variable.

$$\sin^{-1}\left(\frac{4 \sin 30°}{3}\right) = m\angle E$$ .... Use the inverse sine function.

$$m\angle E \approx 42°$$ .... Solve.

LOOK FOR RELATIONSHIPS
If a triangle has one obtuse angle given, there is only one possible triangle. If one acute angle is given, then *two* triangles may be possible. © **MP.7**

So you could conclude that the angles in the triangle measure 30°, 42°, and 108°. However, there is another angle which has the same sine value as the 42° angle.

Using the unit circle, you can see that an angle with measure 138° has the same sine value.

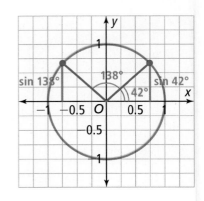

CONTINUED ON THE NEXT PAGE

EXAMPLE 3 CONTINUED

So the angles in the triangle could also measure 30°, 138°, and 12°. The triangle would look quite different than the original sketch, but it does match all of the information given in the problem.

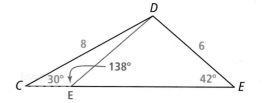

There are two possible triangles that could have the given information, one where $m\angle E = 42°$ and one where $m\angle E = 138°$.

 Try It! 3. In $\triangle ABC$, $m\angle A = 30°$, $a = 5$, and $b = 8$. Find $m\angle B$. How many possible triangles are there?

EXAMPLE 4 Prove the Law of Cosines

Prove the Law of Cosines $a^2 = b^2 + c^2 - 2bc(\cos A)$ for an acute angle A.

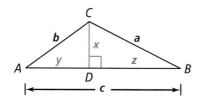

Step 1 The Law of Cosines resembles the Pythagorean Theorem. To prove the Law of Cosines, start by thinking of a right triangle in which a is the hypotenuse.

The drawing shows $\triangle ABC$ with an altitude of length x that divides length c into y and z at point D, so that two right triangles are formed.

Step 2 Since z is in the right triangle with hypotenuse a, find an expression for z using b, c, and $\angle A$, the variables on the right side of the Law of Cosines equation.

$$\cos A = \frac{y}{b} \text{ or } y = b \cos A$$

$$c = y + z \text{ or } z = c - y$$

$$z = c - b \cos A \quad \boxed{\text{Substitute } b \cos A \text{ for } y.}$$

Step 3 Now you need an expression for x in terms of b, c, and $\angle A$. You can get one by finding $\sin A$.

$$\sin A = \frac{x}{b} \text{ or } x = b \sin A$$

CONTINUED ON THE NEXT PAGE

EXAMPLE 4 CONTINUED

Step 4 Use the Pythagorean Theorem for $\triangle BCD$, and substitute to obtain an equation relating a, b, c, and $\angle A$. Simplify.

COMMON ERROR
Be careful to square both quantities correctly. The first quantity is a monomial while the second is a binomial.

$$a^2 = x^2 + z^2$$
$$a^2 = (b \sin A)^2 + (c - y)^2$$
$$a^2 = (b \sin A)^2 + c^2 - 2cy + y^2$$

$y = b \cos A$

$$a^2 = b^2 \sin^2 A + c^2 - 2bc(\cos A) + b^2 \cos^2 A$$
$$a^2 = b^2(\sin^2 A + \cos^2 A) + c^2 - 2bc(\cos A)$$
$$a^2 = b^2 + c^2 - 2bc(\cos A)$$

This result is the Law of Cosines for $\angle A$.

 Try It! **4. a.** How can you derive the Law of Cosines for an obtuse angle C?

b. How does the equation compare to the equation for an acute angle?

EXAMPLE 5 Use the Law of Cosines

What is t? Round to the nearest tenth.

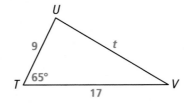

COMMON ERROR
Make sure to assign the correct values for a, b, and c based on their relationship to the given angle.

$$a^2 = b^2 + c^2 - 2bc(\cos A) \quad \cdots\cdots\cdots\cdots\cdots \text{Write the original equation.}$$

$$t^2 = 9^2 + 17^2 - 2(9)(17) \cos 65° \quad \cdots\cdots\cdots \text{Substitute.}$$

$$t^2 = 81 + 289 - 306 \cos 65° \quad \cdots\cdots\cdots \text{Simplify.}$$

$$t^2 \approx 240.68 \quad \cdots\cdots\cdots\cdots\cdots\cdots\cdots\cdots \text{Compute using technology.}$$

$$t \approx \sqrt{240.68} \quad \cdots\cdots\cdots\cdots\cdots\cdots \text{Take the square root of both sides.}$$

$$t \approx 15.5 \quad \cdots\cdots\cdots\cdots\cdots\cdots\cdots\cdots\cdots \text{Solve.}$$

To the nearest tenth, $t \approx 15.5$.

 Try It! **5. a.** In $\triangle JKL$, $j = 15$, $k = 13$, and $l = 12$. What is $m\angle J$?

b. In $\triangle ABC$, $a = 11$, $b = 17$, and $m\angle C = 42°$. What is c?

APPLICATION · **EXAMPLE 6** Use the Law of Cosines and the Law of Sines

A wire 5.3 m long is attached to the top of a flagpole that leans to the left in a strong wind. The wire is anchored to the ground 1.2 m to the right of the pole. The wire forms a 68° angle with the ground. What angle does the wire form with the top of the flagpole? Round to the nearest degree.

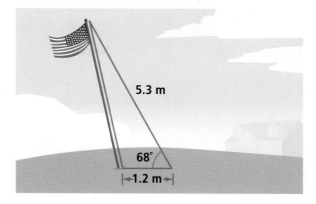

5.3 m

68°

|←1.2 m→|

Since the lengths of two sides and the measure of the included angle are given, use the Law of Cosines to find the length *h* of the flagpole.

$a^2 = b^2 + c^2 - 2bc \, (\cos A)$ .... Write the original equation.

$h^2 = 1.2^2 + 5.3^2 - 2(1.2)(5.3) \cos 68°$ .... Substitute.

$h^2 = 1.44 + 28.09 - 12.72 \cos 68°$ .... Simplify.

$h^2 \approx 24.77$ .... Compute using technology.

$h \approx \pm\sqrt{24.77}$ .... Take the square root of both sides.

$h \approx 4.98$ m .... Solve.

Now that an angle and its opposite length are known, use the Law of Sines to find the angle θ that the wire forms with the flagpole.

$\dfrac{\sin A}{a} = \dfrac{\sin B}{b}$ .... Use the Law of Sines.

$\dfrac{\sin 68°}{4.98} = \dfrac{\sin \theta}{1.2}$ .... Substitute.

$\dfrac{1.2 \sin 68°}{4.98} = \sin \theta$ .... Isolate the sine function.

$\sin^{-1}\left(\dfrac{1.2 \sin 68°}{4.98}\right) = \theta$ .... Take the inverse sine.

$12.9° \approx \theta$ .... Solve.

The angle formed by the wire and the flagpole is about 13°.

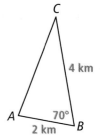 **Try It!** 6. A bike race follows a triangular path, represented by triangle *ABC*. If *A* is the starting point and the measure of the angle at point *B* is 70°, what is the measure of the angle formed by path *BC* and path *CA*?

C

4 km

A   70°

2 km   B

🔍 **CONCEPT SUMMARY** Law of Sines and Law of Cosines

Law of Sines	Law of Cosines

ALGEBRA

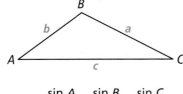

$$\frac{\sin A}{a} = \frac{\sin B}{b} = \frac{\sin C}{c}$$

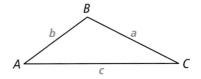

$$a^2 = b^2 + c^2 - 2bc(\cos A)$$
$$b^2 = a^2 + c^2 - 2ac(\cos B)$$
$$c^2 = a^2 + b^2 - 2ab(\cos C)$$

NUMBERS

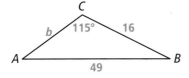

Find the measure of ∠A.

$$\frac{\sin A}{a} = \frac{\sin C}{c} \text{ so } \frac{\sin A}{16} = \frac{\sin 115°}{49}$$

$$\frac{\sin A}{16} = \frac{\sin 115°}{49}$$

$$\sin A \approx 0.2959$$

$$A \approx \sin^{-1} 0.2959; \ m\angle A \approx 17.2°$$

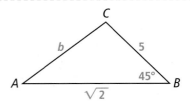

Find b.

$$b^2 = a^2 + c^2 - 2ac(\cos B)$$
$$b^2 = 5^2 + (\sqrt{2})^2 - 2(5)(\sqrt{2})(\cos 45°)$$
$$b^2 = 25 + 2 - 10(\sqrt{2})\left(\frac{\sqrt{2}}{2}\right)$$
$$b^2 = 17; \ b \approx 4.1$$

☑ Do You UNDERSTAND?

1. **ESSENTIAL QUESTION** How can you use the sine and cosine functions with non-right triangles?

2. **Error Analysis** Alejandro said the Law of Sines always gives one answer. Explain and correct Alejandro's error. © **MP.3**

3. **Construct Arguments** Consider the Law of Cosines as $a^2 = b^2 + c^2 - 2bc(\cos A)$. Explain why the negative square root of a is not a valid solution. © **MP.3**

4. **Reason** In what situations do you use the Law of Sines? Law of Cosines? © **MP.2**

Do You KNOW HOW?

Use the Law of Sines or the Law of Cosines to find the indicated measure in △ABC.

5. $m\angle A = 50°$, $a = 4.5$, $b = 3.8$; find $m\angle B$.

6. $m\angle A = 72°$, $a = 61$, $c = 58$; find $m\angle C$.

7. $m\angle A = 18°$, $m\angle C = 75°$, $c = 101$; find a.

8. $m\angle B = 112°$, $m\angle C = 20°$, $c = 1.6$; find b.

9. $m\angle C = 45°$, $a = 15$, $b = 8$; find c.

10. $m\angle A = 82°$, $b = 2.5$, $c = 6.8$; find a.

11. $a = 14$, $b = 12$, $c = 5.8$; find $m\angle A$.

PRACTICE & PROBLEM SOLVING

UNDERSTAND

12. Construct Arguments Lourdes said that you can use the Law of Sines if you have any two angles and any side, or any two sides and any angle. Is Lourdes correct? Explain your reasoning. © **MP.3**

13. Generalize Knowing a particular combination of the sides and/or angles in a triangle leads to the ambiguous case. What is that combination? © **MP.8**

14. Error Analysis Describe and correct the error a student made in using the Law of Cosines to find a. © **MP.3**

$$a^2 = 14^2 + 9^2 - 2(14)(9)(\cos 140)$$
$$a^2 = 196 + 81 - 252(-.766)$$
$$a^2 = 277 - 193.03$$
$$a^2 = 83.97$$
$$a \approx 9.16$$

✗

15. Communicate Precisely Two students are solving for d in the triangle shown, using the Law of Cosines. One says the answer is 20 in., and the other says the answer is 20.3 in. Is either student incorrect? Explain your reasoning. © **MP.6**

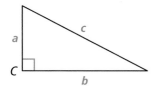

16. Look for Relationships Show that the Law of Cosines is equivalent to the Pythagorean Theorem when the given angle is 90°. © **MP.7**

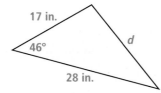

17. Higher Order Thinking The ambiguous case only causes a problem when the given angle is acute, not when an obtuse angle is given. Explain why.

PRACTICE

How can you derive the Law of Sines for the given angles? SEE EXAMPLE 1

18. *E* and *F*

19. *F* and *G*

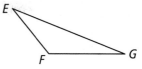

Use the Law of Sines to solve. SEE EXAMPLE 2

20. In △HJK, m∠J = 122°, j = 17, and k = 8. What is m∠K?

21. In △RST, m∠R = 45°, m∠S = 19°, and r = 15. What is s?

Find the number of possible triangles for each set of measures. Then find the angle measure(s).
SEE EXAMPLE 3

22. In △WXY, m∠X = 104°, x = 7, and y = 2. Find m∠Y.

23. In △DEF, m∠D = 28°, d = 8, and e = 15. Find m∠E.

24. In △RST, m∠R = 30°, r = 14, and t = 32. Find m∠T.

How can you derive the Law of Cosines for obtuse angle *K*? SEE EXAMPLE 4

25.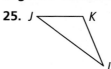

In △PQR, find m∠P. SEE EXAMPLE 5

26. p = 5, q = 8, r = 9

27. p = 14, q = 6, r = 12

What is the measure of angle *Z*? SEE EXAMPLE 6

28. 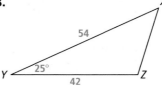 **29.**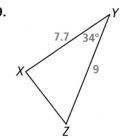

APPLY

30. Model with Mathematics The head sail for Melissa's sailboat is a triangle with the three sides having lengths of 24 ft, 23 ft, and 12 ft. What is the measure of the sail's greatest angle? Ⓒ **MP.4**

31. Use Structure
An art sculpture is made of rotated scalene triangles, as shown. The triangles are all congruent. What is the length of the longest side of each triangle? Ⓒ **MP.7**

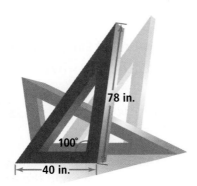

78 in.

100°

40 in.

32. Make Sense and Persevere The course for a race follows three roads as shown. How far do the runners travel along Jappa Road? Ⓒ **MP.1**

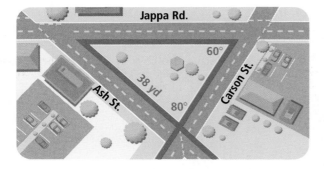

Jappa Rd.

60°

38 yd

Ash St.

80°

Carson St.

33. Model With Mathematics Noemi throws a ball to Parker, who is 6 m away. When Parker catches the ball, he turns 50°, and then throws the ball 7 m to Shandra. What angle does Shandra turn to throw back to Noemi? Ⓒ **MP.4**

34. Make Sense and Persevere Tamika parked her car and walked 300 yd down a path. She then made a 135° turn onto a new path. She walked another 40 yd along a river to her fishing spot. If Tamika turns to face the direction of her car, what angle does she need to turn? Ⓒ **MP.1**

35. In $\triangle EFG$, $m\angle E = 35°$, $e = 5.8$, and $f = 10$. Choose *Yes* or *No* to tell whether each is a possible value for $m\angle F$.

	Yes	No
There are no possible values.	☐	☐
6.2°	☐	☐
60.3°	☐	☐
81.5°	☐	☐
98.5°	☐	☐
119.7°	☐	☐

36. SAT/ACT In $\triangle ABC$, $a = 29.7$, $b = 48.5$, and $B = 92°$. What is $m\angle A$?

Ⓐ There is no possible value.

Ⓑ 37.7°

Ⓒ 56.3°

Ⓓ 123.7°

Ⓔ 142.3°

37. Performance Task Teo is standing 80 yd from the base of a Mayan pyramid. The side of the pyramid is 100 ft from base to peak.

20°   x   P

Teo

80 yd   100 ft

Part A How many feet from the base of the pyramid is Teo?

Part B What is the measure of angle *P* formed by the side of the pyramid and Teo's line of sight?

Part C What is the distance in a straight line from Teo to the peak *x*?

Activity   Assess

8-3
Trigonometric Identities

SavvasRealize.com

I CAN... verify and use trigonometric identities.

VOCABULARY
• trigonometric identity

EXPLORE & REASON

Two right triangles share the same base leg length.

A. Is the ratio between the base angles the same as the ratio between the vertical heights? Explain.

B. How do the values of sin(2(30°)) and 2 sin 30° compare?

C. Look for Relationships Graph $y = \sin 2x$ and $y = 2 \sin x$ on the same coordinate plane. How do the two graphs help explain your answer to part (b)? **© MP.7**

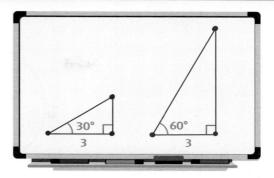

ESSENTIAL QUESTION   How can you verify and apply relationships between trigonometric functions?

CONCEPTUAL UNDERSTANDING

EXAMPLE 1   Use the Unit Circle to Verify Trigonometric Identities

A. What does the relationship between sin(−θ) and −sin θ indicate about the function $f(x) = \sin x$?

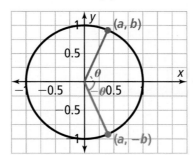

The coordinate (a, b) may represent any point on the unit circle. Therefore, this justification holds true for any angle, θ.

Graph terminal sides representing angles θ and $-\theta$ intersecting the unit circle.

If the terminal side of θ intersects the circle at some point (a, b), the terminal side of $-\theta$ intersects the circle at $(a, -b)$. Since this is the unit circle, $\sin \theta = b$ and $\sin(-\theta) = -b$. Therefore, $\sin(-\theta) = -\sin \theta$.

The equation $\sin(-x) = -\sin x$ is a **trigonometric identity**, or a trigonometric equation that is true for all values of the variable for which both sides of the equation are defined.

Since $f(-x) = -f(x)$, $f(x) = \sin x$ is an odd function.

REASON
Think about how transformations of the graph of $y = \sin x$ can be used to show the equivalence of $\sin(-x)$ and $-\sin x$. **© MP.2**

CONTINUED ON THE NEXT PAGE

EXAMPLE 1 CONTINUED

B. How are cos($\theta + \pi$) and cos($2\pi - \theta$) related to cos θ?

Graph the terminal sides of θ, $\theta + \pi$, and $2\pi - \theta$ on the unit circle.

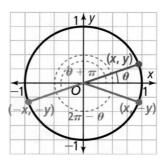

The x-coordinates of θ and $\theta + \pi$ have their signs reversed. Therefore, cos($\theta + \pi$) = $-$cos θ.

The x-coordinates of θ and $2\pi - \theta$ are the same. Therefore, cos($2\pi - \theta$) = cos θ.

 Try It!   **1. a.** Verify that for $f(x) = \cos x$, $f(-x) = f(x)$.

   b. How are sin($x + \pi$) and sin($2\pi - x$) related to sin x?

CONCEPT Trigonometric Identities

Quotient Identity	**Pythagorean Identity**
$\tan x = \dfrac{\sin x}{\cos x}$	$\sin^2 x + \cos^2 x = 1$

Cofunction Identities	**Odd-Even Identities**
$\sin\left(\dfrac{\pi}{2} - x\right) = \cos x$	$\sin(-x) = -\sin x$
$\cos\left(\dfrac{\pi}{2} - x\right) = \sin x$	$\cos(-x) = \cos x$
$\tan\left(\dfrac{\pi}{2} - x\right) = \cot x$	$\tan(-x) = -\tan x$

EXAMPLE 2   **Use Identities to Rewrite Expressions**

A. What is an equivalent form of [tan($-x$)](cos x)?

COMMON ERROR
Be careful not to replace tan ($-x$) with $\frac{\sin x}{\cos x}$. When replacing a trigonometric expression with an equivalent one, be sure to use the same angle expression in the substitution.

$[\tan(-x)](\cos x) = \dfrac{\sin(-x)}{\cos(-x)} \cdot \cos(x)$ ········· Apply the Quotient Identity.

$= \dfrac{-\sin(x)}{\cos x} \cdot \cos x$ ········· Apply the Odd-Even Identities.

$= -\sin x$ ········· Simplify.

So $[\tan(-x)](\cos x) = -\sin x$.

CONTINUED ON THE NEXT PAGE

EXAMPLE 2 CONTINUED

B. What is a simplified form of $1 - \sin x \cos\left(x - \frac{\pi}{2}\right)$?

$$1 - \sin x \cos\left(x - \tfrac{\pi}{2}\right) = 1 - \sin x \cos\left[-\left(\tfrac{\pi}{2} - x\right)\right] \quad \cdots\cdots \text{ Factor out } -1.$$

$$= 1 - \sin x \cos\left(\tfrac{\pi}{2} - x\right) \quad \cdots\cdots \text{ Apply the Odd-Even Identity.}$$

$$= 1 - \sin x \cdot \sin x \quad \cdots\cdots\cdots\cdots \text{ Apply a Cofunction Identity.}$$

$$= 1 - \sin^2 x \quad \cdots\cdots\cdots\cdots\cdots\cdots \text{ Simplify.}$$

$$= \cos^2 x \quad \cdots\cdots\cdots\cdots\cdots\cdots\cdots \text{ Apply the Pythagorean Identity.}$$

The simplified form of $1 - \sin x \cos\left(x - \frac{\pi}{2}\right)$ is $\cos^2 x$.

 Try It!   **2. What is a simplified form of each expression?**

a. $\tan\left(x - \frac{\pi}{2}\right)$ **b.** $\sin(-x) \tan(-x) + \cos x$

CONCEPT Sum and Difference Formulas

Sum Formulas	Difference Formulas
$\sin(\alpha + \beta) = \sin \alpha \cos \beta + \cos \alpha \sin \beta$	$\sin(\alpha - \beta) = \sin \alpha \cos \beta - \cos \alpha \sin \beta$
$\cos(\alpha + \beta) = \cos \alpha \cos \beta - \sin \alpha \sin \beta$	$\cos(\alpha - \beta) = \cos \alpha \cos \beta + \sin \alpha \sin \beta$
$\tan(\alpha + \beta) = \dfrac{\tan \alpha + \tan \beta}{1 - \tan \alpha \tan \beta}$	$\tan(\alpha - \beta) = \dfrac{\tan \alpha - \tan \beta}{1 + \tan \alpha \tan \beta}$

EXAMPLE 3   **Prove Sum and Difference Formulas**

A. Prove the cosine difference formula.

Draw the terminal sides of an angle α and an angle β on the unit circle. Connect the terminal points A and B to create $\triangle AOB$.

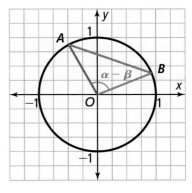

Thus, $OA = 1$, $OB = 1$, and $m\angle AOB = \alpha - \beta$.

Determine $(AB)^2$ using the Law of Cosines.

$$(AB)^2 = 1^2 + 1^2 - 2(1)(1)\cos(\alpha - \beta)$$

$$(AB)^2 = 2 - 2\cos(\alpha - \beta)$$

STUDY TIP
Often the clue that the Pythagorean Identity might be useful is an expression like $\sin^2 x + \cos^2 x$, or the expressions $1 - \sin^2 x$ and $1 - \cos^2 x$.

Determine $(AB)^2$ using the Distance Formula.

If $A = (x_2, y_2)$ and $B = (x_1, y_1)$, then $(AB)^2 = (x_2 - x_1)^2 + (y_2 - y_1)^2$

$$= (\cos \alpha - \cos \beta)^2 + (\sin \alpha - \sin \beta)^2$$

$$= [\cos^2\alpha - 2\cos \alpha \cos \beta + \cos^2\beta] + [\sin^2\alpha - 2\sin \alpha \sin \beta + \sin^2\beta]$$

$$= 2 - 2\cos \alpha \cos \beta - 2\sin \alpha \sin \beta$$

> Use the Pythagorean Identity to simplify.

CONTINUED ON THE NEXT PAGE

EXAMPLE 3 CONTINUED

By the Transitive Property, $2 - 2\cos(\alpha - \beta) = 2 - 2\cos\alpha\cos\beta - 2\sin\alpha\sin\beta$.

Solve for $\cos(\alpha - \beta)$.

$$2 - 2\cos(\alpha - \beta) = 2 - 2\cos\alpha\cos\beta - 2\sin\alpha\sin\beta$$
$$-2\cos(\alpha - \beta) = -2\cos\alpha\cos\beta - 2\sin\alpha\sin\beta$$
$$\cos(\alpha - \beta) = \cos\alpha\cos\beta + \sin\alpha\sin\beta$$

Thus, $\cos(\alpha - \beta) = \cos\alpha\cos\beta + \sin\alpha\sin\beta$.

B. Prove the cosine sum formula.

$\cos(\alpha + \beta) = \cos(\alpha - (-\beta))$ ⋯⋯⋯⋯⋯⋯⋯ Rewrite the angle sum as a difference.

$\qquad = \cos\alpha\cos(-\beta) + \sin\alpha\sin(-\beta)$ ⋯⋯⋯⋯ Apply the difference formula.

$\qquad = \cos\alpha\cos\beta + \sin\alpha(-\sin\beta)$ ⋯⋯⋯⋯ Apply the Odd-Even Identities.

$\qquad = \cos\alpha\cos\beta - \sin\alpha\sin\beta$ ⋯⋯⋯⋯⋯ Simplify.

Thus, $\cos(\alpha + \beta) = \cos\alpha\cos\beta - \sin\alpha\sin\beta$.

✓ Try It! **3. a.** Use the cosine difference formula and the fact that

$$\sin(\alpha + \beta) = \cos\left(\tfrac{\pi}{2} - (\alpha + \beta)\right)$$
$$= \cos\left(\left(\tfrac{\pi}{2} - \alpha\right) - \beta\right)$$

to prove the sine sum formula.

b. Prove the sine difference formula.

✋ EXAMPLE 4 **Use a Sum or Difference Formula to Find a Value**

What is the exact value of sin 75°?

Although 75° is not a familiar angle, it can be written as the sum of two special angle measures.

$\sin 75° = \sin(30° + 45°)$

$\qquad = \sin 30° \cos 45° + \cos 30° \sin 45°$

$\qquad = \dfrac{1}{2}\left(\dfrac{\sqrt{2}}{2}\right) + \dfrac{\sqrt{3}}{2}\left(\dfrac{\sqrt{2}}{2}\right)$

$\qquad = \dfrac{\sqrt{2} + \sqrt{6}}{4}$

So $\sin 75° = \dfrac{\sqrt{2} + \sqrt{6}}{4}$.

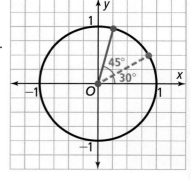

> **STUDY TIP**
> There is often more than one way to rewrite an angle measure as a sum or difference of common reference angles.

Check: Evaluate sin 75° on your calculator, and compare the value to your calculator's approximation for $\dfrac{\sqrt{2} + \sqrt{6}}{4}$. Both expressions are approximately equal to 0.9659. ✓

✓ Try It! **4.** What is the exact value of each expression?

a. tan 15° **b.** $\sin\left(-\tfrac{\pi}{12}\right)$

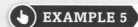
APPLICATION   ☞ **EXAMPLE 5**   Model With Sum and Difference Formulas

Noise-reducing headphones create a sound wave that effectively cancels out other noises around you. Does a noise with a sound wave modeled by $y = \sin(1{,}100\pi x)$ get cancelled out by another noise with a sound wave modeled by $y = \sin\left[1{,}100\pi\left(x - \frac{1}{220}\right)\right]$?

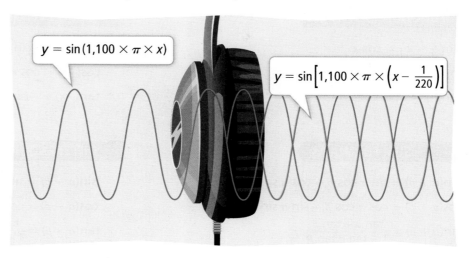

$y = \sin(1{,}100 \times \pi \times x)$

$y = \sin\left[1{,}100 \times \pi \times \left(x - \frac{1}{220}\right)\right]$

Formulate ◀   Add the sound waves together to combine the noises. If the two waves do, in fact, cancel each other out, their sum will be 0.

Compute ◀ $\sin(1{,}100\pi x) + \sin\left[1{,}100\pi\left(x - \frac{1}{220}\right)\right]$

$= \sin(1{,}100\pi x) + \sin[1{,}100\pi x - 5\pi]$

$= \sin(1{,}100\pi x) + \sin(1{,}100\pi x)[\cos(5\pi)] - \cos(1{,}100\pi x)[\sin(5\pi)]$

$= \sin(1{,}100\pi x) + \sin(1{,}100\pi x)(-1) - \cos(1{,}100\pi x)(0)$

$= 0$

Interpret ◀   Since the sum of the sound waves is 0 for all values of x, the noises cancel each other out.

☑ **Try It!**   **5.** The sound wave for a musical note of A is modeled by $y = \sin(880\pi x)$. The sound wave for a different A note is modeled by $y = \sin\left[880\pi\left(x + \frac{1}{440}\right)\right]$. What is the simplified form of an equation that models the sound wave if the two notes are played at the same time?

QUOTIENT IDENTITY

$$\tan x = \frac{\sin x}{\cos x}$$

PYTHAGOREAN IDENTITY

$$\sin^2 x + \cos^2 x = 1$$

COFUNCTION IDENTITIES

$$\sin\left(\frac{\pi}{2} - x\right) = \cos x$$

$$\cos\left(\frac{\pi}{2} - x\right) = \sin x$$

$$\tan\left(\frac{\pi}{2} - x\right) = \cot x$$

ODD-EVEN IDENTITIES

$$\sin(-x) = -\sin x$$

$$\cos(-x) = \cos x$$

$$\tan(-x) = -\tan x$$

SUM FORMULAS

$$\sin(\alpha + \beta) = \sin\alpha\cos\beta + \cos\alpha\sin\beta$$

$$\cos(\alpha + \beta) = \cos\alpha\cos\beta - \sin\alpha\sin\beta$$

$$\tan(\alpha + \beta) = \frac{\tan\alpha + \tan\beta}{1 - \tan\alpha\tan\beta}$$

DIFFERENCE FORMULAS

$$\sin(\alpha - \beta) = \sin\alpha\cos\beta - \cos\alpha\sin\beta$$

$$\cos(\alpha - \beta) = \cos\alpha\cos\beta + \sin\alpha\sin\beta$$

$$\tan(\alpha - \beta) = \frac{\tan\alpha - \tan\beta}{1 + \tan\alpha\tan\beta}$$

Do You UNDERSTAND?

1. **ESSENTIAL QUESTION** How can you verify and apply relationships between trigonometric functions?

2. **Error Analysis** Sarah said that because of the odd-even identities, both the sine and cosine functions are odd functions. Explain and correct Sarah's error. **© MP.3**

3. **Vocabulary** Explain what it means to say that $\cos(-x) = \cos x$ is a trigonometric identity.

4. **Reason** Why do the cofunction identities apply to an angle θ of any size? **© MP.2**

5. **Make Sense and Persevere** How can the quotient identity help you to identify angles for which the tangent is undefined? **© MP.1**

Do You KNOW HOW?

Verify each identity.

6. $\sin\theta\sec\theta\cot\theta = 1$

7. $\sec\theta\cot\theta = \csc\theta$

Find a simplified form of each expression.

8. $\dfrac{\tan\theta}{\sin\theta}$

9. $\dfrac{\sec\theta}{\sin\theta}(1 - \cos^2\theta)$

Use a sum or difference formula to find the exact value of each of the following.

10. $\sin 15°$

11. $\cos 105°$

UNDERSTAND

12. Generalize Explain the process that is used to verify that a trigonometric equation is an identity. © MP.8

13. Construct Arguments Benjamin said that he had worked out a trigonometric identity: $\cos 2\theta = \cos^2 \theta - \sin^2 \theta$. Is Benjamin correct? Explain. © MP.3

14. Mathematical Connections Show that $f(x) = \tan x$ is an odd function by verifying that $\tan(-x) = -\tan x$.

15. Error Analysis Describe and correct the error a student made in applying the cosine difference formula to find the exact value of $\cos 15°$. © MP.3

$$\cos 15° = \cos(45° - 30°)$$
$$= \cos 45°\cos 30° - \sin 45°\sin 30°$$
$$= \frac{\sqrt{2}}{2} \cdot \frac{\sqrt{3}}{2} - \frac{\sqrt{2}}{2} \cdot \frac{1}{2}$$
$$= \frac{\sqrt{6}}{4} - \frac{\sqrt{2}}{4}$$
$$= \frac{\sqrt{6} - \sqrt{2}}{4}$$ ✗

16. Construct Arguments Show that the quotient identity $\cot \theta = \frac{\cos \theta}{\sin \theta}$ is true algebraically. © MP.3

17. Higher Order Thinking Use the Pythagorean Identity $\sin^2 x + \cos^2 x = 1$ to algebraically derive each of the following identities.

a. $1 + \tan^2 x = \sec^2 x$

b. $1 + \cot^2 x = \csc^2 x$

18. Look for Relationships Using the Pythagorean Identity, express $\sin \theta$ in terms of $\cos \theta$. © MP.7

19. Use Structure Restate the Cofunction Identities using degrees instead of radians. What can you conclude about $\sin 15°$? $\cos 60°$? © MP.7

PRACTICE

20. Does the relationship between $\csc(-\theta)$ and $-\csc \theta$ indicate whether $\csc \theta$ is odd or even? SEE EXAMPLE 1

21. Does the relationship between $\sec(-\theta)$ and $-\sec \theta$ indicate whether $\sec \theta$ is odd or even? SEE EXAMPLE 1

22. Does the relationship between $\cot(-\theta)$ and $-\cot \theta$ indicate whether $\cot \theta$ is odd or even? SEE EXAMPLE 1

Find a simplified form of each expression.
SEE EXAMPLE 2

23. $\frac{\cos \theta}{\sin \theta \cot \theta}$

24. $[\cot(-x)](\sin x)$

Prove each of the following sum and difference formulas. SEE EXAMPLE 3

25. $\tan(\alpha + \beta) = \frac{\tan \alpha + \tan \beta}{1 - \tan \alpha \tan \beta}$

26. $\tan(\alpha - \beta) = \frac{\tan \alpha - \tan \beta}{1 + \tan \alpha \tan \beta}$

Find the exact value of each expression. Then evaluate the function on your calculator, comparing the calculator value to the approximation for your exact value. SEE EXAMPLE 4

27. $\tan 105°$

28. $\sin\left(\frac{3\pi}{4} + \frac{5\pi}{6}\right)$

29. $\cos 225°$

30. $\sin 75°$

31. Does a noise with a sound wave modeled by $y = \sin(660\pi x)$ get cancelled out by another noise with a sound wave modeled by $y = \sin\left[660\pi\left(x - \frac{1}{220}\right)\right]$? Explain. SEE EXAMPLE 5

32. The sound wave for a musical note is modeled by $y = \sin(1,320\pi x)$. The sound wave for a different note is modeled by $y = \sin\left[1,320\pi\left(x + \frac{1}{220}\right)\right]$. What is the simplified form of an equation that models the sound wave if the two notes are played simultaneously? SEE EXAMPLE 5

APPLY

33. Make Sense and Persevere The diagram shows a gear with a radius of 5 in. Point Q represents a 30° counterclockwise rotation of point $P(5, 0)$. Point R represents a further θ-degree rotation. The coordinates of R are $(5 \cos(\theta + 30°), 5 \sin(\theta + 30°))$. Express these coordinates in terms of $\cos \theta$ and $\sin \theta$. Ⓒ **MP.1**

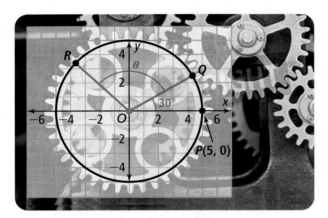

34. Look for Relationships The force required to push an object at a certain angle from its resting position can be modeled by $F = Mg \tan \theta$, where F is the force, M is the mass of the object, g is the acceleration due to gravity, and θ is the angle at which the object is being pushed. Write an equivalent equation for this formula in terms of $\sin \theta$ and $\sec \theta$. Ⓒ **MP.7**

35. Reason The length s of a shadow cast by a vertical *gnomon* (the column or shaft on a sundial that projects a shadow) of height h when the angle of the sun above the horizon is θ can be modeled by the equation $s = \dfrac{h \sin(90° - \theta)}{\sin \theta}$. Show that this equation is equivalent to $s = h \cot \theta$. (*Hint*: Convert degrees to radians and use a cofunction identity). Ⓒ **MP.2**

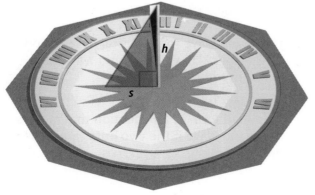

36. Fill in each blank to complete an expression equivalent to $\dfrac{\csc x(\sin^2 x + \cos^2 x \tan x)}{\sin x + \cos x}$.

a. $\sin^2 x +$ _____

b. _____ $- \cos^2 x$

37. SAT/ACT Find the exact value of $\tan 75°$.

Ⓐ $2 + \sqrt{3}$

Ⓑ $2 - \sqrt{3}$

Ⓒ $-2 + \sqrt{3}$

Ⓓ $-2 - \sqrt{3}$

38. Performance Task In order for motor vehicles to negotiate a curve in the road without skidding or running off of it, the angle of incline of the road must be determined. The angle of incline, or *angle of inclination,* is the nonnegative acute angle that the vehicle makes with the horizontal, and it is represented by the equation $\tan \theta = \dfrac{v^2}{gR}$, where R is the radius of the circular path, v is the speed that the vehicle is traveling in meters per second, and g is the acceleration due to gravity, 9.8 m/s².

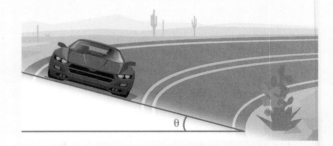

Part A Find the angle of inclination of a curve with a 120-m radius, when a vehicle is traveling at 60 km/h (16.7 m/s) around the curve. Round to the nearest tenth of a degree.

Part B Write an equivalent equation in terms of $\sin \theta$, rather than $\tan \theta$.

© **Common Core State Standards** HSN.CN.A.3 (+), HSN.CN.B.5 (+),
HSN.CN.B.6 (+), MP.3, MP.7, MP.8

  Activity  Assess

CRITIQUE & EXPLAIN

A group of students is asked to simplify the following complex
number expressions:

$$6 + 4i - (-3 + 7i)$$
$$(3 + 5i)(3 - 5i)$$

A. How would you simplify $6 + 4i - (-3 + 7i)$? Explain.

B. One student simplified the second expression this way:

$$(3 + 5i)(3 - 5i) = 3^2 - 3(5i) + 3(5i) - 5^2(i)^2$$
$$= 9 - 25i^2$$

Is the student's answer correct? Explain why or why not.

C. Use Structure What is $(a + bi)(a - bi)$? © **MP.7**

I CAN... use the complex
plane to show complex
numbers and operations on
them.

VOCABULARY
• complex plane
• imaginary axis
• modulus of a complex
  number
• real axis

? ESSENTIAL QUESTION

How can you represent complex numbers and their relationships
on a graph?

EXAMPLE 1   Represent Numbers in the Complex Plane

A. What point in the complex plane represents $5 - 3i$?

The **complex plane** has two axes, like the coordinate plane. The
horizontal axis, called the **real axis,** is for the real part of a complex
number. The vertical axis, called the **imaginary axis,** is for the imaginary
part of a complex number.

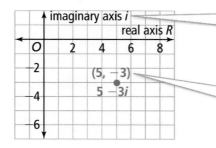

Real numbers fall on the real axis,
and purely imaginary numbers like
$-3i$ fall on the imaginary axis.

The point $(5, -3)$ corresponds
to the complex number $5 - 3i$.

COMMUNICATE PRECISELY
In both the xy-plane and the
complex plane, a point can be
labeled with an ordered pair
(a, b). In the complex plane, a
point can be labeled as a complex
number $a + bi$. © **MP.6**

CONTINUED ON THE NEXT PAGE

EXAMPLE 1 CONTINUED

B. Graph −6 + 2i and −6 − 2i. What is their relationship?

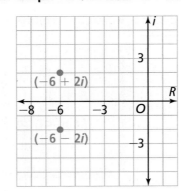

On the graph, −6 + 2i corresponds to the point (−6, 2), and −6 − 2i corresponds to the point (−6, −2).

The two numbers are complex conjugates. On the complex plane, complex conjugates are images of each other in a reflection over the real x-axis.

Try It! **1. a.** What point in the complex plane represents −3 + 4i?

b. Graph 4 + i and its complex conjugate.

EXAMPLE 2 **Find Midpoint of a Segment in the Complex Plane**

What is the midpoint of the segment joining the points representing 3 + 4i and 6 − 2i?

A. How can you find the midpoint of the segment by using the Midpoint Formula?

The Midpoint Formula states that the midpoint of the segment joining

(x_1, y_1) and (x_2, y_2) is $\left(\frac{x_1 + x_2}{2}, \frac{y_1 + y_2}{2}\right)$.

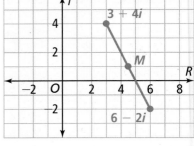

The complex numbers 3 + 4i and 6 − 2i correspond to (3, 4) and (6, −2).

Their midpoint is $\left(\frac{3 + 6}{2}, \frac{4 + (-2)}{2}\right) = (4.5, 1)$.

This point in the complex plane corresponds to the complex number 4.5 + i.

LOOK FOR RELATIONSHIPS
Notice the similarity between the result of 1) using the Midpoint Formula on two points (a, b) and (c, d), and 2) taking their average as complex numbers:

1) $\left(\frac{a + c}{2}, \frac{b + d}{2}\right)$

2) $\frac{(a + c)}{2} + \frac{(b + d)i}{2}$ © MP.7

B. How can you find the midpoint of the segment by taking the average of the complex numbers?

The average of the complex numbers 3 + 4i and 6 − 2i is

$$\frac{(3 + 4i) + (6 - 2i)}{2} = \frac{(3 + 6) + (4 - 2)i}{2} = \frac{9 + 2i}{2} = 4.5 + i.$$

So 4.5 + i is the midpoint of the segment. You can find the midpoint of any segment in the complex plane by finding the average of the complex numbers.

This number corresponds to the ordered pair (4.5, 1) in the complex plane— the same midpoint you found above.

Try It! **2. a.** Find the midpoint of the segment that joins the complex numbers 15 − 4i and −11 − 7i.

b. Find the average of the complex numbers (−4 + 6i) and (1 − 4i). What is the midpoint of the line segment they form when graphed in the complex plane?

👆 **EXAMPLE 3** Find the Modulus of a Complex Number

What is the modulus of $5 - 8i$?

The **modulus of a complex number** is the distance from the point in the complex plane to the origin. Calculating the modulus of a complex number is just like using the Distance Formula to find the distance between its corresponding point and the origin.

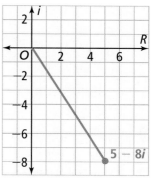

The point $5 - 8i$ corresponds to $(5, -8)$. Its distance to the origin $(0, 0)$ is

$$d = \sqrt{(x_2 - x_1)^2 + (y_2 - y_1)^2} = \sqrt{(5 - 0)^2 + (-8 - 0)^2} = \sqrt{25 + 64} = \sqrt{89}.$$

You can get the same result using the complex number and its complex conjugate.

$$5 - 8i = \sqrt{(5 - 8i)(5 + 8i)} = \sqrt{25 - 64i^2} = \sqrt{25 + 64} = \sqrt{89}$$

The modulus of $5 - 8i$ is $\sqrt{89}$. In general,

$$z = \sqrt{z \cdot \overline{z}} = \sqrt{(a + bi)(a - bi)} = \sqrt{a^2 + b^2}.$$

> The modulus of a complex number $z = a + bi$ is $\sqrt{(a^2 + b^2)}$.

STUDY TIP
Just as the absolute value of a real number gives its distance from zero on the number line, the modulus of a complex number gives the distance from its corresponding points to the origin in the complex plane.

☑ **Try It!** **3.** Find the modulus of each complex number.

a. $-5 - 12i$ b. $\frac{1}{2} - \frac{1}{4}i$

CONCEPTUAL UNDERSTANDING

👆 **EXAMPLE 4** Add and Subtract Complex Numbers Geometrically

How can you use parallelograms to represent addition and subtraction of complex numbers?

A. **How can you use a parallelogram in the complex plane to represent $(-3 + 5i) + (5 + i)$?**

Plot two points in the complex plane: P at $(-3, 5)$ to represent $-3 + 5i$ and N at $(5, 1)$ to represent $5 + i$. Then draw OP and ON by connecting the points to the origin.

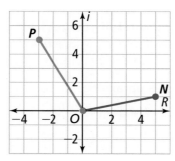

CONTINUED ON THE NEXT PAGE

EXAMPLE 4 CONTINUED

Begin at point *N*. Then add *P* to *N* by adding the real and imaginary parts.

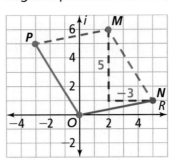

Adding −3 to 5 results in a translation 3 units to the left.

Adding 5*i* to *i* results in a translation 5 units up.

STUDY TIP
Just as with real numbers, subtracting is the same as adding the opposite. Therefore, when subtracting two complex numbers geometrically, draw the opposite of the subtrahend and add.

This results in a segment *NM* that has the same length and same slope as *OP*. Since opposite sides of *MNOP* have the same length and are parallel, *MNOP* is a parallelogram. The fourth point of this parallelogram, *M* located at (2, 6) represents the complex number 2 + 6*i*. This is the same result you get from adding the numbers algebraically.

$$(-3 + 5i) + (5 + i) = (-3 + 5) + (5i + i) = 2 + 6i$$

B. Use a parallelogram in the complex plane to represent $(-3 + 5i) - (5 + i)$.

Step 1 Find the opposite of $(5 + i)$: $(-1)(5 + i) = -5 - i$.

Step 2 Represent $(-3 + 5i) - (5 + i)$ as $(-3 + 5i) + (-5 - i)$.

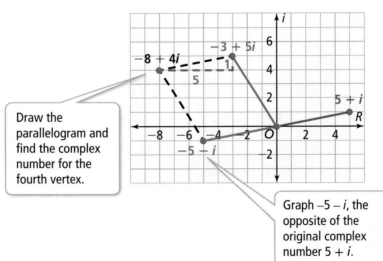

Draw the parallelogram and find the complex number for the fourth vertex.

Graph −5 − *i*, the opposite of the original complex number 5 + *i*.

Step 3 Find the fourth vertex by translating the segment −5 − *i* so that the origin corresponds to −3 + 5*i*. By moving left 5 and down 1, you end at −8 + 4*i*.

This is the same result you get from subtracting the complex numbers algebraically: $(-3 + 5i) - (5 + i) = -3 + 5i - 5 - i = -8 + 4i$.

 Try It! **4.** Use a parallelogram to determine each sum or difference.

　　a. $(-2 + i) + (-5 - 3i)$

　　b. $(-8 + 3i) - (-2 - 3i)$

EXAMPLE 5 Find the Distance Between Two Complex Numbers

For two complex numbers $r = -7 + 3i$ and $s = 2 - 8i$, how can you show that the modulus of the difference $r - s$ is the same as the *distance* between their corresponding points?

Step 1 Use the method in Example 4 to find the difference $(-7 + 3i) - (2 - 8i)$.

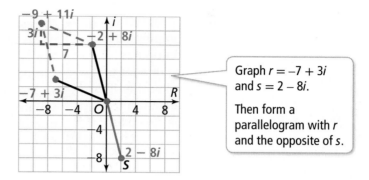

Graph $r = -7 + 3i$ and $s = 2 - 8i$.

Then form a parallelogram with r and the opposite of s.

The graph shows that $r - s = -9 + 11i$.

Step 2 Use the formula $z = \sqrt{z \cdot \bar{z}}$ to find the modulus for the complex number $-9 + 11i$.

$$|-9 + 11i| = \sqrt{(-9 + 11i)(-9 - 11i)}$$
$$= \sqrt{81 - 121i^2}$$
$$= \sqrt{81 + 121}$$
$$= \sqrt{202}$$

The modulus of the difference $r - s$ is $\sqrt{202}$.

The distance between r and s is the same as the modulus of $r - s$.

Step 3 Find the distance between $(-7, 3)$ and $(2, -8)$.

$$d = \sqrt{(-7 - 2)^2 + (3 - (-8))^2}$$
$$= \sqrt{(-9)^2 + 11^2}$$
$$= \sqrt{202}$$

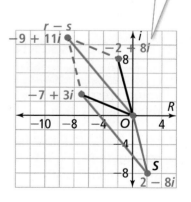

 Try It! 5. Find the distance between the complex numbers.

a. $r = 4 - 3i$, $s = 10 + 2i$

b. $r = -3 - i$, $s = -5 - 4i$

CONCEPT SUMMARY Represent Complex Numbers in the Complex Plane

	The Complex Plane and Complex Numbers	Complex Conjugate	Modulus	Distance and Difference
WORDS	The complex plane has a vertical imaginary axis and a horizontal real axis. A complex number of the form $a + bi$ corresponds to the point (a, b).	On the complex plane, points representing complex conjugates are images of each other in a reflection over the real axis.	The modulus $|z|$ of a complex number corresponds to its distance from the origin on the complex plane. The modulus is the square root of the number times its conjugate: $|z| = \sqrt{z \cdot \bar{z}}$	The *distance* between points representing two complex numbers in the complex plane is the modulus of the *difference* between the two numbers.

GRAPHS

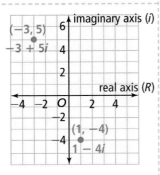

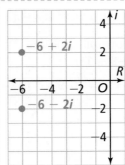

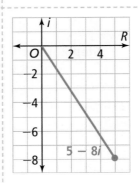

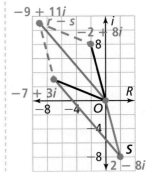

Do You UNDERSTAND?

1. **ESSENTIAL QUESTION** How can you represent complex numbers and their relationships on a graph?

2. **Error Analysis** Casey found the complex conjugate of $7 + 3i$ to be $-7 - 3i$. Explain and correct Casey's error. **© MP.3**

3. **Vocabulary** Explain how the complex plane is similar to and different from the Cartesian plane.

4. **Use Structure** How does a parallelogram demonstrate that the distance between two points is the same as the modulus of their difference? **© MP.7**

Do You KNOW HOW?

Write the ordered pair that corresponds to the complex number.

5. $14 - 7i$ 6. $-6 + 2i$

Find the modulus of the complex number.

7. $3 + i$ 8. $-5 - 4i$

Find the average of the complex numbers.

9. $8 + i$ and $5 - 6i$

10. $-2 + 3i$ and $-7 - 4i$

11. What point, S, completes the parallelogram $PTSR$ that has points P at $(0, 0)$, R at $(-4, -5)$, and T at $(8, -1)$?

UNDERSTAND

12. Construct Arguments LaTanya needed to find the fourth point in the parallelogram shown. She found the slope of $\overline{RP}$ to be -3 and used that slope to find that the missing point, T, is at $(6, 8)$. Is LaTanya correct? Explain your reasoning. Ⓖ **MP.3**

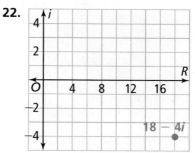

13. Error Analysis Describe and correct the error a student made in finding the midpoint of the segment joining $5 + 8i$ and $4 - 4i$. Ⓖ **MP.3**

$$\text{midpoint} = \frac{(5 + 8i) + (4 - 4i)}{2}$$

$$\text{midpoint} = \frac{(5 + 4) + (8 - 4)i}{2}$$

$$\text{midpoint} = \frac{9 + 4i}{2}$$

$$\text{midpoint} = \frac{13i}{2} = 6.5i \quad ✗$$

14. Construct Arguments Show that finding the modulus of a complex number $a + bi$ gives you the same result as using the Distance Formula to find the distance between (a, b) and the origin. Ⓖ **MP.3**

15. Generalize Is the modulus of a complex number the same as the modulus of its complex conjugate? Explain. Ⓖ **MP.8**

16. Higher Order Thinking When using a parallelogram to represent a subtraction of two complex numbers, you plot the opposite of the subtrahend. Why?

PRACTICE

Graph the complex number and its conjugate.
SEE EXAMPLE 1

17. $9 + i$

18. $-3 + 2i$

Find the midpoint of the segment that joins the points corresponding to the complex numbers. SEE EXAMPLE 2

19. $-4 + 2i$ and $2 + (-8i)$

20. $1 + i$ and $3 - 5i$

21. $-12 + 6i$ and $-5 - 5i$

Find the modulus of each complex number.
SEE EXAMPLE 3

22.

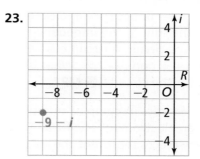

23.

Use a parallelogram to represent each operation.
SEE EXAMPLE 4

24. Add $11 + 6i$ and $7 - 4i$.

25. Add $7 + 5i$ and $4 - 3i$.

26. Subtract $-8 + 3i$ from $15 + i$.

27. Subtract $3 - 9i$ from $10 - 7i$.

Find the distance between the points representing the complex numbers. SEE EXAMPLE 5

28. $r = 4 + 6i, s = 7 - 10i$

29. $r = -12 + 2i, s = -2 + i$

30. $r = -5 - 7i, s = 1 + 4i$

APPLY

31. Make Sense and Persevere Start with a complex number c. Square it and add c to get a new complex number. Then square that and add c again. Keep going. If, for your number c, your results never get larger than 2, then c is part of a collection of points called the Mandelbrot set. $-1 + \frac{1}{8}i$ and $\frac{1}{8} - \frac{1}{4}i$ are both in the Mandelbrot set. What is the distance between them? **Ⓒ MP.1**

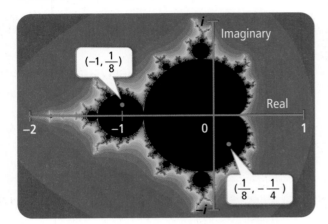

32. Reason Alternating current (AC) circuits use complex numbers to represent impedance in ohms. To find the total impedance in a circuit, you need to find the sum of the impedances from each part of the circuit. A circuit has partial impedances of $4.2 + 3i$ and $5 - 2.2i$. What is the total impedance for the circuit? **Ⓒ MP.2**

33. Model With Mathematics A complex number is used to describe an electromagnetic field. The real and imaginary pieces represent the electric and magnetic components, respectively, that result from the motion of an electric charge or electric current. What ordered pair on the complex plane represents the electromagnetic field described below? **Ⓒ MP.4**

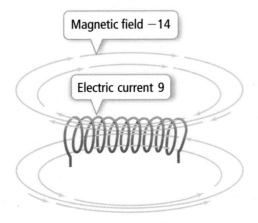

ASSESSMENT PRACTICE

34. Fill in the blanks to complete the statements about midpoints of segments.

   I. The midpoint of the segment joining $-6 - 8i$ and $7 - 9i$ is _____.

   II. The midpoint of the segment joining $-4i$ and _____ is $2 + 5i$.

   III. The midpoint of the segment joining _____ and $-3 + 3i$ is $-7 + 5.5i$.

35. SAT/ACT What is the modulus of the complex number $1 + 8i$?

   Ⓐ $\sqrt{63}$

   Ⓑ 8

   Ⓒ $\sqrt{65}$

   Ⓓ $\sqrt{66}$

   Ⓔ 9

36. Performance Task Deon is practicing with coordinates in the complex plane by determining the coordinates needed to draw a capital "A." He wants the horizontal bar of his "A" to connect the midpoints of the sides. He has chosen the top point of the "A" to be represented by $6i$ and the bottom left point to be represented by $-4 + i$.

A

Part A What complex number represents the bottom right point of the "A"?

Part B What complex numbers represent the points where the horizontal bar connects the sides of the "A"?

Part C What are the lengths (in units) of the three segments that make up the "A"?

8-5

Polar Form of Complex Numbers

I CAN... use the polar form of complex numbers to calculate products and powers.

VOCABULARY
- argument
- polar form of a complex number

👆 **EXPLORE & REASON**

Paxton's Pizza delivers via scooter. Orders are delivered only within a few blocks from the pizzeria. One afternoon, Paxton's receives orders from the places marked on the map. Paxton's is located at point *P*.

A. Paxton's limits its delivery persons to riding five blocks total to get to the delivery spot. Will the riders be able to ride to each location on the map? Explain.

B. Suppose instead that Paxton's limits its riders to delivering only within a five-block *radius* of the pizzeria. Will the riders be able to deliver to each location on the map? Explain.

C. Communicate Precisely Each block on the map is 400 ft long. How can you describe the locations of points 1, 2, and 3 in terms of how far they are from *P* in a straight line? © **MP.6**

❓ **ESSENTIAL QUESTION**   How can you use trigonometry to represent and multiply complex numbers?

👆 **EXAMPLE 1**   Represent a Complex Number in Polar Form

How can you use modulus and direction to locate a number in the complex plane?

Consider the segment connecting the complex number $z = a + bi$ to the origin. The length of the segment r is the modulus of z. The angle θ measured counterclockwise from the positive real axis to the segment is called the **argument** of z. You can use r and θ to correspond to z in the complex plane.

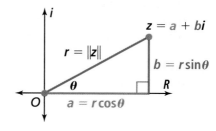

LOOK FOR RELATIONSHIPS
Just as the sign (positive or negative) of a real number on the number line tells you its direction from 0, the argument of a complex number in the complex plane tells you its direction from the origin. © **MP.7**

$z = a + bi$

$\quad = r \cos \theta + (r \sin \theta)i$ .... Using trigonometry, you know that the length $a = r \cos \theta$ and the length $b = r \sin \theta$.

$\quad = r(\cos \theta + i \sin \theta)$ .... Factor out r.

$\quad = r \operatorname{cis} \theta$ .... cis is shorthand for $\cos \theta + i \sin \theta$.

So $z = r \operatorname{cis} \theta$. This is the **polar form of a complex number** for z.

✓ **Try It!**   **1.** Graph the complex numbers.

   a. $\operatorname{cis} \dfrac{\pi}{4}$ **b.** $2 \operatorname{cis} \pi$

EXAMPLE 2 **Convert Between Rectangular Form and Polar Form**

How are the polar form and the rectangular form of a complex number related?

A. How do you express $z = 5$ cis $\frac{3\pi}{4}$ in rectangular coordinates?

Identify the values of r and θ. In this example, $r = 5$ and $\theta = \frac{3\pi}{4}$.

$z = a + bi;\ a = r\cos\theta,\ b = r\sin\theta$

$a = 5\cos\frac{3\pi}{4}$ $\qquad b = 5\sin\frac{3\pi}{4}$

$= 5\left(-\frac{\sqrt{2}}{2}\right)$ $\qquad = 5\left(\frac{\sqrt{2}}{2}\right)$

$= -\frac{5\sqrt{2}}{2}$ $\qquad\quad = \frac{5\sqrt{2}}{2}$

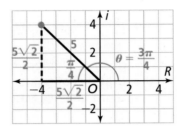

So, expressed in rectangular coordinates, $z = -\frac{5\sqrt{2}}{2} + \frac{5\sqrt{2}}{2}i$.

B. How do you express $z = -7 - 4i$ in polar form?

Graph z on the complex plane to help you find the polar form. Then find the modulus.

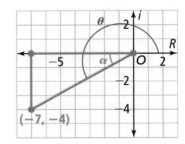

$r = |z|$

$= \sqrt{(-7)^2 + (-4)^2}$

$= \sqrt{65}$

≈ 8.06

To find θ, use the reference angle α, where $\tan\alpha = \frac{-4}{-7}$, or $\frac{4}{7}$.

So $\alpha = \tan^{-1}\frac{4}{7} \approx 0.52$ rad. Since the terminal side of θ is in Quadrant III, $\pi < \theta < \frac{3\pi}{2}$, so $\theta = \pi + \alpha \approx 3.66$ rad.

So the polar form of $z = -7 - 4i$ is about 8.06 cis 3.66.

REASON

The inverse tangent function has a restricted range $\left(-\frac{\pi}{2}, \frac{\pi}{2}\right)$.

Evaluating the inverse tangent functions, you will always get an angle in the first or fourth quadrant. Since the angle θ you are looking for is in Quadrant III, you have to add π to 0.52 to get θ. **© MP.2**

☑ **Try It!** **2. a.** Express 4 cis $\frac{\pi}{3}$ in rectangular form.

b. Express $5 - 5i$ in polar form.

CONCEPTUAL
UNDERSTANDING ⟩ **EXAMPLE 3** **Use the Sum and Difference Formulas**

A. What patterns do you notice when multiplying complex numbers in polar form?

Multiply a few example numbers to find a pattern.

Suppose $z_1 = 2 \text{ cis } \frac{\pi}{4}$, $z_2 = 2 \text{ cis}\left(-\frac{\pi}{4}\right)$, and $z_3 = 3 \text{ cis}\left(\frac{\pi}{2}\right)$.

First, multiply $z_1 z_2$.

$$z_1 z_2 = \left(2 \text{ cis }\left(\frac{\pi}{4}\right)\right)\left(2 \text{ cis}\left(-\frac{\pi}{4}\right)\right)$$

$$= (2)(2)\left(\cos \frac{\pi}{4} + i \sin \frac{\pi}{4}\right)\left(\cos\left(-\frac{\pi}{4}\right) + i \sin\left(-\frac{\pi}{4}\right)\right)$$

$$= 4\left(\frac{\sqrt{2}}{2} + i \frac{\sqrt{2}}{2}\right)\left(\frac{\sqrt{2}}{2} - i \frac{\sqrt{2}}{2}\right)$$

$$= 4\left(\frac{1}{2} + \frac{1}{2}\right)$$

$$= 4$$

Since 4 is on the real axis, $\theta = 0$. So $z_1 z_2 = 4 \text{ cis } 0$.

Next, multiply $z_2 z_3$.

$$z_2 z_3 = 6\left(\cos\left(-\frac{\pi}{4}\right) + i \sin\left(-\frac{\pi}{4}\right)\right)\left(\cos \frac{\pi}{2} + i \sin \frac{\pi}{2}\right)$$

$$= 6\left(\frac{\sqrt{2}}{2} - i \frac{\sqrt{2}}{2}\right)(0 + i)$$

$$= 6\left(\frac{\sqrt{2}}{2}i + \frac{\sqrt{2}}{2}\right)$$

$$= 6\left(\frac{\sqrt{2}}{2} + \frac{\sqrt{2}}{2}i\right)$$

$$= 6\left(\cos \frac{\pi}{4} + i \sin \frac{\pi}{4}\right)$$

$$= 6 \text{ cis } \frac{\pi}{4}$$

So $z_2 z_3 = 6 \text{ cis } \frac{\pi}{4}$.

Notice for $z_2 = 2 \text{ cis}\left(\frac{-\pi}{4}\right)$ and $z_3 = 3 \text{ cis}\left(\frac{\pi}{2}\right)$, $z_2 z_3 = 6 \text{ cis } \frac{\pi}{4}$.

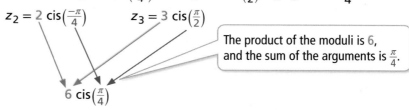

$z_2 = 2 \text{ cis}\left(\frac{-\pi}{4}\right)$ $z_3 = 3 \text{ cis}\left(\frac{\pi}{2}\right)$

The product of the moduli is 6, and the sum of the arguments is $\frac{\pi}{4}$.

$6 \text{ cis}\left(\frac{\pi}{4}\right)$

Similarly, $z_1 z_2$ is $\left(2 \text{ cis}\left(\frac{\pi}{4}\right)\right)\left(2 \text{ cis}\left(\frac{-\pi}{4}\right)\right)$ is $(2)(2)\text{cis}\left(\frac{\pi}{4} + \frac{-\pi}{4}\right)$, or $4 \text{ cis } 0$.

In both cases, multiplying the moduli and adding the arguments of the two numbers give you the same result as multiplying the two numbers themselves.

You can do the same calculations to find $z_1 z_3$.

$$\left(2 \text{ cis}\left(\frac{\pi}{4}\right)\right)\left(3 \text{ cis}\left(\frac{\pi}{2}\right)\right) = 6 \text{ cis}\left(\frac{3\pi}{4}\right)$$

CONTINUED ON THE NEXT PAGE

COMMON ERROR
Remember to multiply i by the right term when using $r \text{ cis } \theta$. The term *cis* means *cosine, then i times sine*.

EXAMPLE 3 CONTINUED

B. How can you prove that your pattern holds for every pair of complex numbers?

Multiply two complex numbers r cis α and s cis β to see if this pattern holds.

$(r \text{ cis } \alpha)(s \text{ cis } \beta) = [r (\cos \alpha + i \sin \alpha)] \bullet [s (\cos \beta + i \sin \beta)]$ ⟶ Apply the meaning of cis.

$= r \bullet (\cos \alpha + i \sin \alpha) \bullet s \bullet (\cos \beta + i \sin \beta)$ ⟶ Use the Associative Property.

$= rs \bullet (\cos \alpha + i \sin \alpha)(\cos \beta + i \sin \beta)$ ⟶ Use the Commutative Property.

$= rs \bullet (\cos \alpha \cos \beta + i \cos \alpha \sin \beta$ ⟶ Use the Distributive $+ i \sin \alpha \cos \beta + i^2 \sin \alpha \sin \beta)$ Property.

$= rs \bullet [(\cos \alpha \cos \beta - \sin \alpha \sin \beta)$ ⟶ Combine like terms. $+ i(\cos \alpha \sin \beta + \sin \alpha \cos \beta)]$

$= rs \bullet [\cos(\alpha + \beta) + i \sin(\alpha + \beta)]$ ⟶ Use the sum formulas.

$= rs \text{ cis}(\alpha + \beta)$ ⟶ Apply the meaning of cis.

So $(r \text{ cis } \alpha)(s \text{ cis } \beta) = rs \text{ cis}(\alpha + \beta)$.

 Try It! 3. Find the product of $7 \text{ cis } \frac{\pi}{3}$ and $2 \text{ cis}\left(-\frac{5\pi}{6}\right)$ in polar and rectangular form.

👆 **EXAMPLE 4** **Use Polar Form to Multiply Complex Numbers**

What is the product of $z_1 = -1 + i\sqrt{3}$ and $z_2 = \frac{5\sqrt{3}}{2} - \frac{5}{2}i$?

Step 1 Express each complex number in polar form.

$z_1 = -1 + i\sqrt{3}$

$|z_1| = \sqrt{(-1)^2 + (\sqrt{3})^2} = 2$

$\tan \theta_1 = -\sqrt{3}$

$\tan^{-1} -\sqrt{3} = -\frac{\pi}{3}$

Since $-1 + i\sqrt{3}$ is in Quadrant II, add π to that result to obtain

$\theta_1 = \frac{2\pi}{3}$.

$z_1 = 2 \text{ cis } \frac{2\pi}{3}$

$z_2 = \frac{5\sqrt{3}}{2} - \frac{5}{2}i$

$|z_2| = \sqrt{\left(\frac{5\sqrt{3}}{2}\right)^2 + \left(-\frac{5}{2}\right)^2} = 5$

$\tan \theta_1 = -\frac{1}{\sqrt{3}} = -\frac{\sqrt{3}}{3}$

$\tan^{-1}\left(-\frac{\sqrt{3}}{3}\right) = -\frac{\pi}{6}$

Since $\frac{5\sqrt{3}}{2} - \frac{5}{2}i$ is in Quadrant IV, within the domain of $\tan^{-1}$, $\theta_1 = -\frac{\pi}{6}$.

$z_2 = 5 \text{ cis}\left(-\frac{\pi}{6}\right)$

USE STRUCTURE
The equations $x = r \cos \theta$ and $y = r \sin \theta$ can also be used to find the measure of the angle. ⓒ **MP.7**

CONTINUED ON THE NEXT PAGE

EXAMPLE 4 CONTINUED

Step 2 Multiply using the formula

$$(r \text{ cis } \alpha)(s \text{ cis } \beta) = rs \text{ cis}(\alpha + \beta).$$

$$z_1 z_2 = \left(2 \text{ cis } \frac{2\pi}{3}\right)\left(5 \text{ cis}\left(-\frac{\pi}{6}\right)\right)$$

$$= (2)(5) \text{ cis}\left(\frac{2\pi}{3} - \frac{\pi}{6}\right)$$

$$= 10 \text{ cis } \frac{\pi}{2}$$

In rectangular form, $z_1 z_2 = 10i$.

STUDY TIP
You can verify your answer by multiplying the rectangular forms of z_1 and z_2.

[Graph showing $z_1 z_2 = 10 \text{ cis } \frac{\pi}{2}$, $z_1 = 2 \text{ cis } \frac{2\pi}{3}$, and $z_2 = 5 \text{ cis}\left(-\frac{\pi}{6}\right)$ on a coordinate plane]

 Try It! **4.** Use the complex numbers $z_1 = i\sqrt{2}$ and $z_2 = -1 + i$.

    a. Express each number in polar form.

    b. Find the product $z_1 z_2$ in both polar form and rectangular form.

👆 **EXAMPLE 5**   Use Polar Form to Raise a Number to a Power

What is an efficient way to calculate a power of a complex number?

Calculating powers using rectangular coordinates can take many

steps: $(a + bi)^n = (a + bi)(a + bi) \ldots (a + bi).$ ⟶ Multiply $(a + bi)$ together n times.

But using polar coordinates, you can identify a pattern.

$$z = r \text{ cis } \theta$$

$$z^2 = (r \text{ cis } \theta)(r \text{ cis } \theta) = r^2 \text{ cis } 2\theta$$

$$z^3 = (r^2 \text{ cis } 2\theta)(r \text{ cis } \theta) = r^3 \text{ cis } 3\theta$$ ⟵ Multiply Moduli and Add Arguments. Note that $z^3 = z^2 \cdot z$.

$$\vdots$$

$$z^n = r^n \text{ cis } n\theta$$

USE APPROPRIATE TOOLS
Changing the way a quantity is expressed can simplify calculations. The formula $z^n = r^n \text{ cis } n\theta$ where n is an integer, known as DeMoivre's Theorem, is an example of this.
© **MP.5**

Find z^4 where $z = 4 - 4i$.

$$z^4 = (4 - 4i)^4 \quad \cdots\cdots\cdots\cdots \text{ Substitute the value of } z.$$

$$= \left(4\sqrt{2} \text{ cis}\left(-\frac{\pi}{4}\right)\right)^4 \quad \cdots\cdots\cdots \text{ Convert to polar form.}$$

$$= (4\sqrt{2})^4 \text{ cis } 4\left(-\frac{\pi}{4}\right) \quad \cdots\cdots \text{ Apply the power formula.}$$

$$= 1{,}024 \text{ cis}(-\pi) \quad \cdots\cdots\cdots\cdots \text{ Simplify.}$$

In rectangular form, $z^4 = -1{,}024$.

Using polar coordinates can be the most efficient way to calculate the power of a complex number.

 Try It! **5.** Use the polar form to find $(\sqrt{3} - i)^8$.

    a. Write the power in polar form.

    b. Write the power in rectangular form.

 **CONCEPT SUMMARY** Using The Polar Form of Complex Numbers

EQUATIONS	Rectangular Form: $z = a + bi$	Polar Form: $z = r \operatorname{cis} \theta$
	Convert to polar: $r = |z| = \sqrt{a^2 + b^2}$ $\tan \theta = \frac{b}{a}$ so $\theta = \tan^{-1}\left(\frac{b}{a}\right)$	Convert to rectangular: $a = r \cos \theta$ $b = r \sin \theta$
FORMULAS	Product Formula: $(r \operatorname{cis} \alpha)(s \operatorname{cis} \beta) = rs \operatorname{cis}(\alpha + \beta)$	Power Formula: $z^n = r^n \operatorname{cis} n\theta$

GRAPH

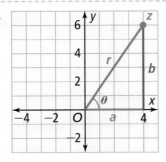

Do You UNDERSTAND?

1. **ESSENTIAL QUESTION** How can you use trigonometry to represent and multiply complex numbers?

2. **Error Analysis** Lucas said that $\left(2 \operatorname{cis} \frac{7\pi}{4}\right)\left(3 \operatorname{cis} \frac{3\pi}{4}\right) = 6 \operatorname{cis} \pi$. Explain an error Lucas may have made. **© MP.3**

3. **Vocabulary** Explain how to find the argument of a complex number.

4. **Communicate Precisely** What information about the graph of a number in the complex plane does the argument of a complex number give you? **© MP.6**

Do You KNOW HOW?

Express each complex number in polar form.

5. $2\sqrt{3} + 2i$

6. $-10 + 10i$

Express each complex number in rectangular form.

7. $5 \operatorname{cis} \pi$

8. $6 \operatorname{cis} \frac{2\pi}{3}$

Find the product of each set of complex numbers in polar form.

9. $2 \operatorname{cis} \frac{\pi}{4}$ and $6 \operatorname{cis} \frac{3\pi}{4}$

10. $7 \operatorname{cis} \frac{\pi}{2}$ and $3 \operatorname{cis} \frac{\pi}{4}$

11. $2 \operatorname{cis} \left(-\frac{\pi}{3}\right)$ and $3 \operatorname{cis} \frac{5\pi}{6}$

12. $3 \operatorname{cis} \frac{4\pi}{3}$ and $7 \operatorname{cis} \frac{\pi}{3}$

Use the polar form to find each power. Write the power in rectangular form.

13. $\left(\sqrt{2} + i\sqrt{2}\right)^4$

14. $\left(\sqrt{3} - i\right)^3$

UNDERSTAND

15. Mathematical Connections Evaluate the expression $(2 + i)(2 + i)(2 + i)(2 + i)$ using traditional multiplication. Compare the results with the results using polar coordinates and $(2 + i)^4$. Which method do you prefer and why?

16. Look for Relationships Explain how to apply an exponent as a power of an expression with a complex number. © MP.7

17. Error Analysis Describe and correct the error a student made in writing the complex number $z = \sqrt{3} - i$ in polar form. © MP.3

$r = \sqrt{x^2 + y^2} = \sqrt{(\sqrt{3})^2 + (-1)^2} = \sqrt{4} = 2$

So, $\sin\theta = \frac{y}{r} = \frac{-1}{2}$ and $\cos\theta = \frac{x}{r} = \frac{\sqrt{3}}{2}$,

for $0 \le \theta \le 2\pi$.

$\theta = \frac{5\pi}{6}$ and $r = 2$,

So $\sqrt{3} - i = 2\text{cis}\left(\frac{5\pi}{6}\right)$.

18. Communicate Precisely Explain how to graph the complex number $3 \text{ cis } \frac{5\pi}{6}$ in the complex plane. © MP.6

19. Use Structure Similar to the product formula, there is a quotient formula for two complex numbers in polar form. This formula is given by $\frac{(r \text{ cis } \alpha)}{(s \text{ cis } \beta)} = \frac{r}{s} \text{ cis } (\alpha - \beta)$. Use this formula to find $\dfrac{24 \text{ cis } \frac{5\pi}{3}}{8 \text{ cis } \frac{5\pi}{12}}$. Find the quotient in rectangular form. © MP.7

20. Higher Order Thinking Explain why the polar coordinates $\left(4, -\frac{\pi}{6}\right)$ and $\left(4, \frac{11\pi}{6}\right)$ correspond to each other on the complex plane.

PRACTICE

Graph each complex number on the complex plane. SEE EXAMPLE 1

21. $4 \text{ cis}\left(\frac{\pi}{3}\right)$

22. $2 \text{ cis}\left(\frac{5\pi}{6}\right)$

23. $3 \text{ cis}(-\pi)$

24. $1 \text{ cis}\left(\frac{2\pi}{3}\right)$

Express each complex number in rectangular form. SEE EXAMPLE 2

25. $2 \text{ cis}\left(\frac{\pi}{2}\right)$

26. $1 \text{ cis}\left(-\frac{\pi}{3}\right)$

27. $4 \text{ cis}\left(\frac{11\pi}{6}\right)$

28. $3 \text{ cis}\left(\frac{\pi}{4}\right)$

Express each complex number in polar form.
SEE EXAMPLE 2

29. $-\sqrt{3} + i$

30. $2 - 3i$

31. $4 + 5i$

32. $-3 - 3i$

Find the product of each set of complex numbers in polar and rectangular form. SEE EXAMPLE 3

33. $3 \text{ cis}\left(\frac{7\pi}{6}\right)$ and $2 \text{ cis}\left(\frac{2\pi}{3}\right)$

34. $6 \text{ cis}\left(\frac{\pi}{3}\right)$ and $4 \text{ cis}\left(\frac{2\pi}{3}\right)$

Express each number in polar form. Then find the product $z_1 z_2$ in both polar and rectangular form. SEE EXAMPLE 4

35. $z_1 = 2 - 2i; z_2 = -3 + 3i$

36. $z_1 = \sqrt{3} + i; z_2 = 2 - 2i\sqrt{3}$

Use the polar form to find each power. Write the power in both polar and rectangular form.
SEE EXAMPLE 5

37. $(-2 + 2i)^3$

38. $(1 + i\sqrt{3})^5$

APPLY

39. Use Structure Determine the voltage in a circuit when there is a current of 2 cis $\frac{\pi}{3}$ amps and an impedance of 3 cis $\frac{11\pi}{6}$ ohms. (*Hint*: Use $E = I \cdot Z$, where E is voltage, I is current, and Z is impedance.) **© MP.7**

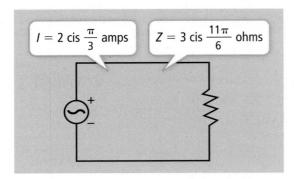

$I = 2$ cis $\frac{\pi}{3}$ amps $Z = 3$ cis $\frac{11\pi}{6}$ ohms

40. Use Structure Determine the current in a circuit when there is a voltage of 8 cis $\frac{7\pi}{6}$ volts and an impedance of 4 cis $\frac{\pi}{3}$ ohms. **© MP.7**

41. Use Appropriate Tools A coding class is using the polar form of complex numbers to develop a program to draw a flower. Based on the graphs below, what is an equation a coder could use to draw a flower with nine petals? Explain your answer. (*Hint*: You may want to use graphing technology to check your answer.) **© MP.5**

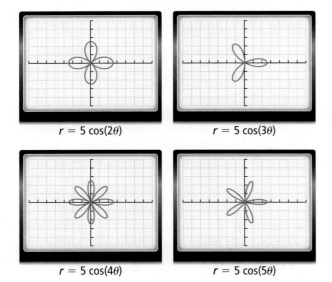

$r = 5 \cos(2\theta)$ $r = 5 \cos(3\theta)$

$r = 5 \cos(4\theta)$ $r = 5 \cos(5\theta)$

ASSESSMENT PRACTICE

42. The rectangular form of the complex number 4 cis $\left(\frac{7\pi}{4}\right)$ is _____ _____ _____ i.

43. SAT/ACT Find the polar form of the complex number $4 - 4i$.

Ⓐ $4\sqrt{2}$ cis $\left(\frac{7\pi}{4}\right)$

Ⓑ $2\sqrt{2}$ cis $\left(\frac{7\pi}{4}\right)$

Ⓒ $4\sqrt{2}$ cis $\left(\frac{5\pi}{4}\right)$

Ⓓ 4 cis $\left(\frac{5\pi}{4}\right)$

44. Performance Task Either the Distance Formula or the Law of Cosines can be used to generate a formula to find the distance between two points in the complex plane.

Part A Use the Distance Formula to find the distance between two points r_1 cis θ_1 and r_2 cis θ_2 in the complex plane. (*Hint*: Remember that for $z = r$ cis $\theta = a + bi$, $a = r\cos\theta$ and $b = r\sin\theta$.)

Part B Use the Law of Cosines to calculate the same distance. Compare the result to the result for part (a).

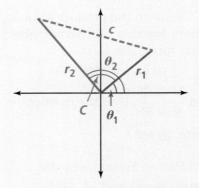

Part C Use your formula to find the distance between 3 cis $\frac{\pi}{6}$ and 5 cis π. Round to the nearest hundredth.

Topic Review

? TOPIC ESSENTIAL QUESTION

1. How do trigonometric identities and equations help you solve problems involving real or complex numbers?

Vocabulary Review

Choose the correct term to complete each sentence.

2. A(n) _____ is a trigonometric equation that is true for all values of the variable for which both sides of the equation are defined.

3. The _____ has two axes, like the Cartesian coordinate plane, which are the real axis and the imaginary axis.

4. The horizontal axis, also called the _____, is for the real part of a complex number.

5. The vertical axis, also called the _____, is for the imaginary part of a complex number.

6. The _____ is the length of the segment from the point that corresponds to the complex number to the origin.

7. The angle θ measured counterclockwise from the positive real axis to the segment is the _____.

- Law of Sines
- Law of Cosines
- trigonometric identity
- complex plane
- real axis
- imaginary axis
- modulus of a complex number
- argument
- polar form of a complex number

Concepts & Skills Review

LESSON 8-1 ▶ Solving Trigonometric Equations Using Inverses

Quick Review

An inverse trigonometric function allows you to input the values in a limited range of a trigonometric function and find the corresponding measure of an angle in the domain of the trigonometric function.

Example

Solve the trigonometric equation
5 sin θ = 3 sin θ + 1 for values between 0 and 2π.

$5 \sin \theta = 3 \sin \theta + 1$ ········ Write the original equation.

$2 \sin \theta = 1$ ········ Subtract 3 sin θ.

$\sin \theta = \frac{1}{2}$ ········ Divide by 2.

$\theta = \sin^{-1}\left(\frac{1}{2}\right)$ ········ Find the sine inverse.

$\theta = \frac{\pi}{6}$ ········ Solve.

Reflect the angle $\frac{\pi}{6}$ across the y-axis; that angle will also have a sine of $\frac{1}{2}$. That angle is $\pi - \frac{\pi}{6} = \frac{5\pi}{6}$.

Practice & Problem Solving

Evaluate each function. Angle values must be within the range of each inverse function. Give answers in radians and in degrees.

8. $\tan^{-1}(\sqrt{3})$

9. $\sin^{-1}\left(\frac{\sqrt{2}}{2}\right)$

10. $\tan^{-1}(-1)$

11. $\cos^{-1}\left(-\frac{1}{2}\right)$

Solve each trigonometric equation for values between 0 and 2π.

12. $3 \tan x - \sqrt{3} = 0$

13. $2 \cos x + \sqrt{2} = 0$

14. **Reason** Why is the domain of the inverse sine function restricted to the interval $[-1, 1]$? Ⓒ MP.2

15. **Make Sense and Persevere** A bird flies 78 ft from the top of a 4 ft tall bird feeder to the top of a 65 ft tree. To the nearest degree, find the angle of elevation of the line of sight from the top of the bird feeder to the top of the tree. Ⓒ MP.1

Quick Review

The Law of Sines and the Law of Cosines allow you to apply trigonometric functions to non-right triangles.

Law of Sines: $\frac{\sin A}{a} = \frac{\sin B}{b} = \frac{\sin C}{c}$

Law of Cosines: $a^2 = b^2 + c^2 - 2bc(\cos A)$

Example

In $\triangle ABC$, $m\angle A = 93°$, $a = 15$, and $b = 11$. To the nearest degree, what is $m\angle B$?

$\frac{\sin A}{a} = \frac{\sin B}{b}$ ····· Use the Law of Sines.

$\frac{\sin 93}{15} = \frac{\sin B}{11}$ ····· Substitute.

$\frac{11 \sin 93}{15} = \sin B$ ····· Isolate the sine function.

$\sin^{-1}\left(\frac{11 \sin 93}{15}\right) = B$ ····· Use the inverse sine function.

$m\angle B \approx 47°$ ········ Solve.

Practice & Problem Solving

Use the Law of Sines to solve.

16. In $\triangle MNP$, $m\angle N = 112°$, $n = 14$, and $p = 6$. What is $m\angle P$?

17. In $\triangle XYZ$, $m\angle X = 40°$, $m\angle Y = 25°$, and $x = 13$. What is y?

In $\triangle QRS$, find $m\angle Q$.

18. $q = 7$, $r = 6$, $s = 10$

19. $q = 8$, $r = 5$, $s = 6$

20. **Look for Relationships** How do you know whether to use the Law of Sines or the Law of Cosines to solve a problem? © **MP.7**

21. **Make Sense and Persevere** Mark went to the beach, parked his car, and walked 500 yd down a path toward the beach. Mark then turned onto a boardwalk at a 125° angle to his path and walked another 140 yd along the boardwalk to a pier. If Mark turns to face his car, what angle does he turn? © **MP.1**

Quick Review

Quotient Identity: $\tan x = \frac{\sin x}{\cos x}$

Pythagorean Identity: $\sin^2 x + \cos^2 x = 1$

Cofunction Identities: $\sin\left(\frac{\pi}{2} - x\right) = \cos x$

$\cos\left(\frac{\pi}{2} - x\right) = \sin x$

Odd-Even Identities: $\sin(-x) = -\sin x$

$\cos(-x) = \cos x$

Sum and Difference Formulas:

$\sin(\alpha \pm \beta) = \sin\alpha\cos\beta \pm \cos\alpha\sin\beta$

$\cos(\alpha \pm \beta) = \cos\alpha\cos\beta \mp \sin\alpha\sin\beta$

$\tan(\alpha \pm \beta) = \frac{\tan\alpha \pm \tan\beta}{1 \mp \tan\alpha\tan\beta}$

Example

What is the simplified form of $\frac{\csc^2 x - 1}{\csc^2 x}$?

$\frac{\csc^2 x - 1}{\csc^2 x} = \frac{\csc^2 x}{\csc^2 x} - \frac{1}{\csc^2 x}$ ····· Rewrite the fraction.

$= 1 - \sin^2 x$ ····· Use the definition of sine.

$= \cos^2 x$ ····· Apply the Pythagorean Identity.

Practice & Problem Solving

Use a trigonometric identity to write a different form of each expression.

22. $\tan^2 x + 1$

23. $\tan x + \cot x$

24. $\frac{1 + \tan^2 x}{1 - \tan^2 x}$

25. $\frac{\sec x - 1}{\sec x + 1}$

Find the exact value of each expression. Then evaluate the function on your calculator. Compare the calculator value to your exact value.

26. $\sin 15°$

27. $\cos 105°$

28. $\tan\left(\frac{\pi}{4} + \frac{\pi}{3}\right)$

29. $\cos\left(\frac{\pi}{4} - \frac{\pi}{6}\right)$

30. **Use Structure** Find expressions for $\sin 2\theta$ and $\cos 2\theta$. © **MP.7**

31. **Model With Mathematics** Is a noise with a sound wave modeled by $y = \sin(1{,}500\pi x)$ cancelled out by another noise with a sound wave modeled by $y = \sin\left[1{,}500\pi\left(x - \frac{1}{250}\right)\right]$? Explain. © **MP.4**

The Complex Plane

Quick Review

A complex number has the form $a + bi$, where a and b are real numbers. The **complex plane** has two axes. The horizontal axis, or **real axis,** is for the real part of a complex number. The vertical axis, or **imaginary axis,** is for the imaginary part of a complex number. The **modulus of a complex number** is the distance from the point representing the complex number to the origin. The *distance* between two complex numbers is the modulus of the *difference* between the two numbers.

Example

What is the modulus of $4 - 3i$?

$$|z| = \sqrt{z \bullet \bar{z}}$$
$$= \sqrt{(4 + 3i)(4 - 3i)}$$
$$= \sqrt{16 - 9i^2}$$
$$= \sqrt{16 + 9}$$
$$= \sqrt{25}$$
$$= 5$$

Practice & Problem Solving

Find the midpoint of the segment that joins the complex numbers.

32. $-7 + 5i$, $3 - 15i$ **33.** $1 + 9i$, $11 - i$

Find the modulus of each complex number.

34. $13 + 8i$ **35.** $-3 + i$

Find the distance between the complex numbers.

36. $r = -14 + 4i$, $s = -8 + i$

37. $r = 7 + 16i$, $s = -3 - 13i$

38. Look for Relationships What is the relationship between the modulus of a complex number and the modulus of its complex conjugate? Explain. **© MP.7**

39. Make Sense and Persevere On a complex plane, a library is located at $-5 + 9i$. The fire station is located at $7 - 7i$. The school is halfway between the library and the fire station. Where is the school located? **© MP.1**

Polar Form of Complex Numbers

Quick Review

Rectangular form of a complex number: $z = a + bi$
Polar form of a complex number: $z = r \text{ cis } \theta$

$$r = |z| = \sqrt{a^2 + b^2}$$
$$a = r \cos \theta \qquad b = r \sin \theta$$

Convert to polar form: $\tan \theta = \frac{b}{a}$ so $\theta = \tan^{-1}\left(\frac{b}{a}\right)$
Convert to rectangular form: $a = r \cos \theta$, $b = r \sin \theta$
Product Formula: $(r \text{ cis } \alpha)(s \text{ cis } \beta) = rs \text{ cis } (\alpha + \beta)$
Power Formula: $z^n = r^n \text{ cis } n\theta$

Example

Express $z = 4 \text{ cis } \frac{\pi}{3}$ in rectangular form.

$$a = r \cos \theta \qquad b = r \sin \theta$$
$$a = 4 \cos \frac{\pi}{3} \qquad b = 4 \sin \frac{\pi}{3}$$
$$a = 2 \qquad b = 2\sqrt{3}$$
$$z = a + bi = 2 + 2i\sqrt{3}$$

Practice & Problem Solving

Write each expression in rectangular form.

40. $z = 3 \text{ cis } \frac{\pi}{6}$ **41.** $z = 6 \text{ cis } \frac{2\pi}{3}$

Write each expression in polar form.

42. $z = 3 + 5i$ **43.** $z = -1 - 2i$

44. Find the product of z_1 and z_2 when $z_1 = 2 \text{ cis } \frac{\pi}{12}$ and $z_2 = 3 \text{ cis } \frac{3\pi}{4}$.

45. Find z^8 where $z = -1 - i$ in rectangular form.

46. Reason What complex number can you square to get $4 \text{ cis } \frac{\pi}{2}$? Explain. **© MP.2**

47. Use Structure Determine the voltage in a circuit when there is a current of $3 \text{ cis } \frac{\pi}{4}$ amps and an impedance of $2 \text{ cis } \frac{2\pi}{3}$ ohms. (*Hint*: Use $E = I \bullet Z$, where E is voltage, I is current, and Z is impedance.) **© MP.7**

TOPIC 9

Conic Sections

? TOPIC ESSENTIAL QUESTION

How do the geometric properties of conic sections relate to their algebraic representations?

Topic Overview

enVision™ STEM Project:
  Design a Whispering Gallery

9-1 Parabolas

9-2 Circles

Mathematical Modeling in 3 Acts:
  Watering the Lawn

9-3 Ellipses

9-4 Hyperbolas

Topic Vocabulary

- center of an ellipse
- center of a hyperbola
- conic section
- conjugate axis
- co-vertices
- directrix
- ellipse
- focal length
- foci of an ellipse
- foci of a hyperbola
- focus of a parabola
- general form of a second-degree equation
- hyperbola
- major axis
- minor axis
- parabola
- standard form of the equation of a circle
- standard form of the equation of an ellipse
- standard form of the equation of a hyperbola
- transverse axis
- vertices of an ellipse
- vertices of a hyperbola

Digital Experience

 INTERACTIVE STUDENT EDITION Access online or offline.

 ACTIVITIES Complete *Explore & Reason, Model & Discuss*, and *Critique & Explain* activities. Interact with Examples and Try Its.

 ANIMATION View and interact with real-world applications.

 PRACTICE Practice what you've learned.

 Go online | SavvasRealize.com

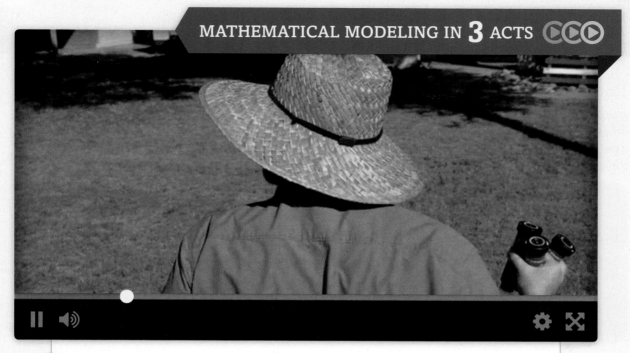

▶ **Watering the Lawn**

Like all plants, grass must receive water regularly to survive. When local rainfall is not enough to keep the grass healthy, it needs to be watered. To make the watering process easier, some property owners have sprinkler systems designed and installed to automate the watering process.

What should be considered while designing a sprinkler system? Think about this during the Mathematical Modeling in 3 Acts lesson.

TOPIC 9

VIDEOS Watch clips to support *Mathematical Modeling in 3 Acts Lessons* and **enVision™ STEM Projects.**

CONCEPT SUMMARY Review key lesson content through multiple representations.

ASSESSMENT Show what you've learned.

GLOSSARY Read and listen to English and Spanish definitions.

TUTORIALS Get help from *Virtual Nerd*, right when you need it.

MATH TOOLS Explore math with digital tools and manipulatives.

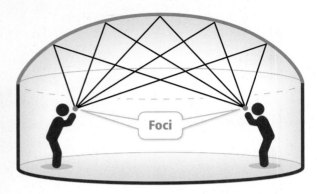

Video

Did You Know?

A **whispering gallery** is a room with geometric properties of parabolas, ellipses, and circles that allows a person in one spot in the room to hear clearly what someone else says in another spot in the room.

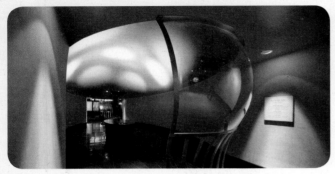

Foci

Some whispering galleries use an **elliptical ceiling** to direct sound from one focus to the other.

The **Mapparium** is a three-story, stained-glass globe and spherical whispering gallery at the Mary Baker Eddy Library in Boston, Massachusetts.

▶ Your Task: Design a Whispering Gallery

You and your classmates will use conic sections to design a whispering gallery.

Go Online | SavvasRealize.com

9-1

Parabolas

I CAN... understand and apply the geometric properties of a parabola.

VOCABULARY

• conic section
• directrix
• focal length
• focus of a parabola
• general form of a second-degree equation

👆 EXPLORE & REASON

Consider the square pyramid and the cylinder shown.

A. What shapes can be created by intersecting a vertical plane with each figure? What shapes can be created by intersecting a horizontal plane with each figure?

B. Make Sense and Persevere What shapes can be created by intersecting a diagonal plane with each figure? © MP.1

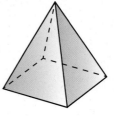

❓ ESSENTIAL QUESTION

What are the geometric properties of a parabola, and how do they relate to algebraic representations of a parabola?

CONCEPT Conic Sections

A **conic section** is a curve formed by the intersection of a plane and a double right cone.

Parabola	Circle	Ellipse	Hyperbola
The intersecting plane cuts through one side of one cone.	The intersecting plane is perpendicular to the axis.	The intersecting plane cuts through both sides of a cone.	The intersecting plane cuts through both cones.

Each conic section has a geometric definition that describes a property of every point on the curve. The conic sections covered in this topic can be graphed in a coordinate plane and can be represented by a second-degree equation in two variables.

The **general form of a second-degree equation** is

$Ax^2 + Bxy + Cy^2 + Dx + Ey + F = 0$.

All of the conic sections covered in this topic will have equations where the coefficient of the xy-term is zero. A nonzero xy-term results in conics with an axis of symmetry that is neither horizontal nor vertical.

EXAMPLE 1 **Derive an Equation of a Parabola**

How do you write an equation of a parabola?

A. What is an equation for the parabola with focus (0, 2) and directrix $y = -2$? Use the definition of a parabola to write and simplify the equation.

A parabola is the set of all points in a plane equidistant from a given point called the **focus of a parabola** and a given line called the **directrix**.

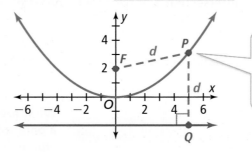

For this parabola, the focus, F, is (0, 2), the directrix is $y = -2$, a point P on the parabola is (x, y), and the closest point Q on the directrix is $(x, -2)$.

By the definition of a parabola, the distance from P to F must equal the distance from P to Q.

$$\sqrt{(x-0)^2+(y-2)^2} = \sqrt{(x-x)^2+(y+2)^2}$$
$$x^2+(y-2)^2 = (y+2)^2$$
$$x^2+y^2-4y+4 = y^2+4y+4$$
$$x^2 = 8y$$
$$\tfrac{1}{8}x^2 = y$$

The equation for a parabola with focus (0, 2) and directrix $y = -2$ is $y = \tfrac{1}{8}x^2$.

LOOK FOR RELATIONSHIPS
What are the vertex and axis of symmetry for the parabola with equation $y = \tfrac{1}{8}x^2$? © MP.7

B. What is an equation for the parabola with focus (4, 0) and directrix $x = -4$?

By sketching the parabola based on the given information, you can see that this parabola opens to the right.

As with the previous example, use the Distance Formula to set $PF = PD$.

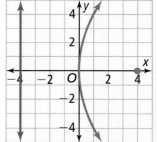

$P(x, y)$ $F(4, 0)$ $D(-4, y)$
$$\sqrt{(x-4)^2+(y-0)^2} = \sqrt{(x+4)^2+(y-y)^2}$$
$$(x-4)^2+y^2 = (x+4)^2$$
$$x^2-8x+16+y^2 = x^2+8x+16$$
$$y^2 = 16x$$
$$x = \tfrac{1}{16}y^2$$

The equation for a parabola with focus (4, 0) and directrix $x = -4$ is $x = \tfrac{1}{16}y^2$.

Try It! **1.** What is an equation for the parabola with the given focus and directrix?

  a. focus (0, −3) and directrix $y = 3$

  b. focus (−2, 0) and directrix $x = 2$

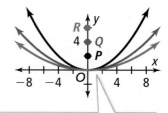

EXAMPLE 2   Relate the Focal Length of a Parabola to Its Equation

A. How does the distance between the focus and vertex affect the shape of a parabola?

The **focal length** of a parabola c is the distance between the focus and the vertex, measured along the axis of symmetry. For parabolas that open upward or to the right, $c > 0$. For parabolas that open downward or to the left, $c < 0$.

As the focal length increases from 2 to 4 to 6, the graph of the parabola becomes more vertically compressed.

> Notice that as the focus changes from (0, 2) to (0, 4) to (0, 6), the shape of the parabola changes.

B. How does the focal length relate to the equation of a vertical parabola?

Consider a parabola that opens upward with vertex at the origin, focal length c, and containing the point $P(x, y)$.

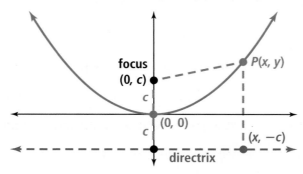

Based on the definition of a parabola, point $P(x, y)$ must be equidistant from the focus and the directrix.

$$\sqrt{(x-0)^2 + (y-c)^2} = \sqrt{(x-x)^2 + (y+c)^2}$$
$$x^2 + (y-c)^2 = (y+c)^2$$
$$x^2 + y^2 - 2cy + c^2 = y^2 + 2cy + c^2$$
$$x^2 = 4cy$$
$$\frac{1}{4c}x^2 = y$$

So the equation for a vertical parabola with vertex at the origin with focal length c is $y = \frac{1}{4c}x^2$.

Using this equation, you can see how the focal length affects the value of a in the equation $y = ax^2$.

COMMUNICATE PRECISELY
How could you write an equation for the directrix in terms of c? Ⓖ MP.6

 Try It!   **2.** A parabola has a focus of (4, 0) and a directrix at $x = -4$.

   a. What is the vertex of the parabola?

   b. Is the equation in the form $y = ax^2$ or $x = ay^2$?

   c. What is the focal length?

   d. What is the equation of the parabola?

EXAMPLE 3 Write an Equation of a Parabola

What is the equation of each parabola?

A. A parabola with vertex (0, 0) and focus (0, −0.5)

Start by sketching the parabola based on the information you are given.

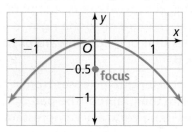

It is helpful to sketch a graph to visualize the parabola as you are writing an equation.

STUDY TIP
Be sure to determine if the parabola has a vertical or horizontal axis of symmetry. Note that the focus is always inside the parabola.

By looking at the graph, you see that the parabola has a vertical axis of symmetry, so its equation has the form $y = ax^2$.

The coordinates of the focus are $\left(0, -\frac{1}{2}\right)$, so $c = -\frac{1}{2}$. Substitute into the equation $y = \frac{1}{4c}x^2$.

$$y = \frac{1}{4\left(-\frac{1}{2}\right)}x^2 = -\frac{1}{2}x^2$$

This parabola has the equation $y = -\frac{1}{2}x^2$.

B. A parabola with vertex (0, 0) and directrix x = 5

Start by sketching the parabola based on the given information.

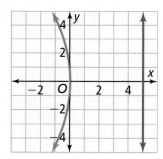

To write an equation for the parabola, first determine the focus. The vertex is equidistant between the directrix and the focus, so if the vertex is at the origin and the directrix is at $x = 5$, the focus must be at $(-5, 0)$. Then $c = -5$.

The parabola has a horizontal axis of symmetry, so use the equation $x = \frac{1}{4c}y^2$, where $c = -5$.

$$x = \frac{1}{4c}y^2 = \frac{1}{4(-5)}y^2 = -\frac{1}{20}y^2$$

The equation for this parabola is $x = -\frac{1}{20}y^2$.

 Try It! **3. a.** What is the equation of a parabola with focus (0, 6) and directrix $y = -6$?

   b. What is the equation of a parabola with focus $\left(\frac{1}{5}, 0\right)$ and vertex (0, 0)?

APPLICATION ◀ 🔘 **EXAMPLE 4** Use a Parabola to Model a Real-World Situation

One type of solar cooker is a reflective parabolic dish. Its cross section is a parabola modeled by the equation $y = \frac{1}{108}x^2$, with distances measured in inches. The bracket that holds the pan for the cooker needs to be placed at the focus. Assuming that the vertex of the parabolic dish is at the point (0, 0), at what coordinates should the bracket be placed?

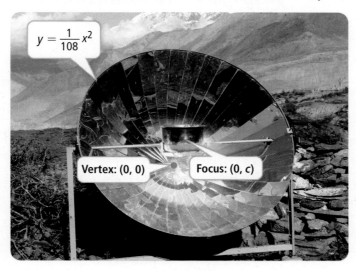

$y = \frac{1}{108}x^2$

Vertex: (0, 0)   Focus: (0, c)

Formulate ◀ Consider a cross-section of the parabolic dish.

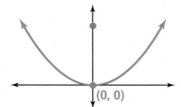

(0, 0)

The distance from the focus to the vertex is the focal length, c.

The given equation is in the form $y = \frac{1}{4c}x^2$, so $\frac{1}{108} = \frac{1}{4c}$.

Compute ◀ Solve for c.

$$\frac{1}{108} = \frac{1}{4c}$$
$$4c = 108$$
$$c = 27$$

Interpret ◀ In this example, the focal length is 27. The vertex is at (0, 0), so the focus is at (0, 27). The bracket should be placed 27 in. from the vertex.

✓ **Try It!** **4.** If the dish in Example 1 has a depth of 30 in., what is the diameter of the cooker?

👆 **EXAMPLE 5** ▷ Complete the Square to Find the Focus and Directrix

The equation for a parabola is given by $0 = y^2 - 8y + x + 14$. What is the equation in vertex form? Use the vertex form to identify the vertex, focus, and directrix.

The vertex form of a vertical parabola is $y = a(x - h)^2 + k$ and the vertex form of a horizontal parabola is $x = a(y - k)^2 + h$.

> Notice that h is always associated with x and that k is always associated with y.

Write the equation in vertex form by completing the square.

$$0 = y^2 - 8y + x + 14 \quad \cdots\cdots \text{Standard form}$$

$$-x - 14 = y^2 - 8y \quad \cdots\cdots \text{Isolate the quadratic expression.}$$

$$-x - 14 + 16 = y^2 - 8y + 16 \quad \cdots\cdots \text{Complete the square.}$$

$$2 - x = (y - 4)^2 \quad \cdots\cdots \text{Factor.}$$

$$x = -1(y - 4)^2 + 2 \quad \cdots\cdots \text{Solve for } x.$$

COMMON ERROR
You may think that $k = -4$. However, remember that the term has the form $(y - k)$, so in this case, $k = 4$, not -4.

The vertex is (h, k) where $h = 2$ and $k = 4$.

Use the value for a to find the focal length. In this equation, $a = -1$. In previous examples, you have seen that $a = \frac{1}{4c}$.

So $-1 = \frac{1}{4c}$ and $c = -\frac{1}{4}$.

The equation indicates that the parabola is horizontal and opens left or right. In this example, c is negative, so the parabola opens to the left.

The vertex is $(2, 4)$, so the focus is $(2 - 0.25, 4)$, or $(1.75, 4)$.

The directrix is the same distance to the right of the vertex, so the equation is $x = 2.25$.

You can graph the parabola to confirm that the vertex, focus, and directrix you found are correct.

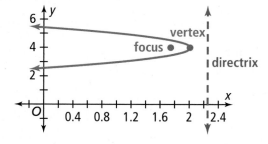

☑ **Try It!**   5. Use the vertex form to identify the vertex, focus, and directrix of the parabola with each equation.

     a. $0 = -y + 2x^2 - 4x + 6$

     b. $0 = x^2 + 6x + 4y + 5$

CONCEPT SUMMARY Parabolas

DEFINITION A parabola is the set of points on a plane that are equidistant from a given point, the *focus*, and a given line, the *directrix*.

GRAPHS The parabolas below have vertex (0, 0). Parabolas can also be translated anywhere in the coordinate plane.

Vertical

Axis of symmetry: $x = 0$
Focus $(0, c)$
Directrix $y = -c$

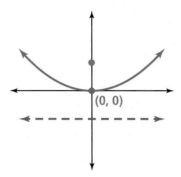

Horizontal

Axis of symmetry: $y = 0$
Focus $(c, 0)$
Directrix $x = -c$

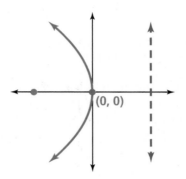

EQUATIONS For a parabola with vertex at the origin and focal length c,

$$y = \frac{1}{4c}x^2 \qquad\qquad x = \frac{1}{4c}y^2$$

Do You UNDERSTAND?

1. **ESSENTIAL QUESTION** What are the geometric properties of a parabola, and how do they relate to algebraic representations of a parabola?

2. **Vocabulary** Explain what is meant by a *conic section*.

3. **Error Analysis** Nicky said that a parabola with the equation $y^2 = -9x$ has the y-axis as its line of symmetry and opens downward. Explain and correct Nicky's error. **MP.3**

4. **Reason** What is the focus and directrix of the parabola $y = -4x^2$? Explain how you know. **MP.2**

5. **Generalize** Explain how the distance from a point to a line is measured. **MP.8**

Do You KNOW HOW?

Write an equation for the parabola with the given focus and directrix.

6. focus (0, 2) and directrix $y = -2$

7. focus (−1, 0) and directrix $x = 1$

8. A parabola has a focus of (0, 3) and a directrix at $y = -3$.

   a. What is the vertex of the parabola?

   b. Is the equation in the form $y = ax^2$ or $x = ay^2$?

   c. What is the focal length?

   d. What is the equation of the parabola?

9. Find the focus and directrix of the parabola that has equation $0 = x^2 - 6x - y + 8$.

UNDERSTAND

10. Use Structure Write an equation of the parabola shown in the graph. **MP.7**

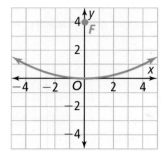

11. Generalize What determines the type, size, and shape of a conic section? **MP.8**

12. Error Analysis Describe and correct the error a student made in identifying the vertex and directrix of the parabola with equation $0 = 2x + y^2 - 8y + 16$. **MP.3**

$$0 = 2x + y^2 - 8y + 16$$
$$-2x = (y - 4)^2$$
$$x = -\frac{1}{2}(y - 4)^2$$
Vertex: $(4, 0)$; directrix: $x = -2$

✗

13. Look for Relationships What is the shape of a parabola whose focus is very near the directrix? **MP.7**

14. Reason The equation of a parabola is $(x + 2)^2 = 12y$. What are the y-intercept(s), if any, of the parabola? **MP.2**

15. Higher Order Thinking The parabola with equation $y = (x + 3)^2 - 5$ has its vertex at $(-3, -5)$ and passes through $(1, 11)$.

   a. Identify the focus and directrix of the parabola.

   b. Name the line of symmetry.

   c. Find another point through which the parabola passes that is the same distance from the line of symmetry as $(1, 11)$.

PRACTICE

Write an equation for all points equidistant from the given point and line. SEE EXAMPLE 1

16. point $(0, -2)$ and line $y = 2$

17. focus $\left(\frac{1}{4}, 0\right)$ and directrix $x = -\frac{1}{4}$

18. A parabola has a focus of $(-5, 0)$ and a directrix at $x = 5$. SEE EXAMPLE 2

   a. What is the vertex of the parabola?

   b. Is the equation in the form $y = ax^2$ or $x = ay^2$?

   c. What is the focal length?

   d. What is the equation of the parabola?

19. What is the equation of the parabola shown in the graph? SEE EXAMPLE 3

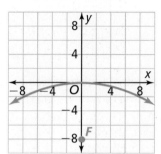

20. The cross section of a newer solar cooker is a parabola modeled by the equation $y = \frac{1}{160}x^2$, with distances measured in centimeters. The bracket that holds the pan for the cooker needs to be placed at the focus. Assuming that the vertex of the parabolic dish is at the point $(0, 0)$, at what coordinates should the bracket be placed? SEE EXAMPLE 4

21. Complete the square to find the vertex form, and identify the vertex, focus, and directrix of the parabola with the given equation. SEE EXAMPLE 5

   a. $0 = -x + 2y^2 - 12y + 19$

   b. $x^2 + 24y - 8x = -16$

APPLY

22. Make Sense and Persevere The graphs of the equations $0 = y^2 - 8y - 12x + 28$ and $0 = y^2 - 8y + 8x + 48$ have the same directrix. **© MP.1**

a. What is the equation of the directrix?

b. What is the distance between the foci?

23. Model With Mathematics

A parabolic mirror has a focus that is located above the vertex of the mirror at the distance shown below. Assume the vertex is at the origin. Write an equation of the parabola that models the cross section of the mirror. **© MP.4**

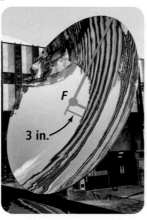

24. Reason The EuroDish was developed to provide electricity in remote areas, collecting sunlight with a parabolic reflector, which, in turn, powers the engine located at the focus. Assume that a cross section of the parabolic reflector has its vertex at (0, 0). The engine is 12 ft from the vertex. **© MP.2**

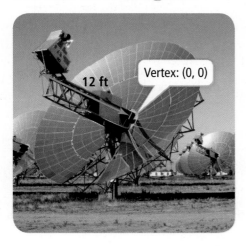

a. Write an equation for the parabola.

b. Suppose the diameter of the dish is 24 ft. How deep is the dish?

25. Which of the following are true about the graph of the parabolic equation $x + y^2 = 2y - 1$? Select all that apply.

Ⓐ opens downward   Ⓑ vertex (1, 0)

Ⓒ directrix $x = \frac{1}{4}$ Ⓓ focus $\left(-\frac{1}{4}, 1\right)$

26. SAT/ACT Which graph could have a focus at $(h, 0)$ and directrix $x = -h$, for $h < 0$?

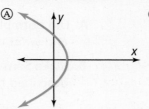

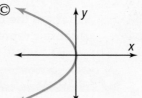

27. Performance Task The cross section of a flashlight reflector is parabolic. It has an axis of symmetry that is horizontal, and the measure of the widest part of the parabola has the measure shown. The light bulb is at the focus of the parabolic cross section, and the distance from the vertex to the light bulb measures 1 cm.

Part A What is the equation of the parabolic cross section of the reflector?

Part B How many centimeters deep is the reflector?

© **Common Core State Standards** HSG.GPE.A.1, HSA.REI.C.7, HSA.SSE.B.3, MP.2, MP.4, MP.7

  Activity Assess

I CAN... write, graph, and apply the equation of a circle.

VOCABULARY
• standard form of the equation of a circle

CRITIQUE & EXPLAIN

Latoya and Jason are lawn bowling. Each player tries to toss his or her ball closer to the target ball than his or her opponent's ball.

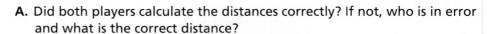

The graph shows the locations of their first attempts.

Latoya calculates the distance her ball is from the target ball: $d^2 = (4 - 1)^2 + (3 - 2)^2 = 10$, so $d \approx 3.2$ ft.

Jason calculates the distance his ball is from the target ball:
$\sqrt{(1 - (-1))^2} + \sqrt{(2 - 0)^2} = 2 + 2 = 4$.

A. Did both players calculate the distances correctly? If not, who is in error and what is the correct distance?

B. **Make Sense and Persevere** Latoya's next ball stops at a position described by (−2, 1). Is she now ahead? Explain. © **MP.1**

? **ESSENTIAL QUESTION**

What are the geometric properties of a circle, and how do they relate to algebraic representations of a circle?

CONCEPTUAL
UNDERSTANDING

EXAMPLE 1 **Derive the Equation of a Circle**

How can you write an equation in standard form that describes the circle with center (2, −1) and radius 3?

Recall that a circle is a set of points that are a fixed distance, called the *radius*, from a fixed point, called the *center*. It is the cross section of a cone cut by a plane perpendicular to the cone's axis.

This circle is the set of all points that lie 3 units from the point (2, −1).

REASON
The four points on the circle directly above, below, left, and right of the center cannot form a right triangle with the center. You can, however, verify that these points satisfy the equation of the circle as well. © **MP.2**

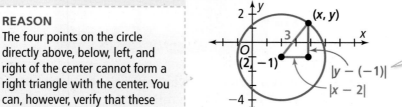

Use absolute value to find the lengths of the legs, since length must be positive.

Squaring each term eliminates the need for absolute value.

By the Pythagorean Theorem, $|x - 2|^2 + |y - (-1)|^2 = 3^2$, or $(x - 2)^2 + (y + 1)^2 = 9$.

The **standard form of the equation of a circle** with center (h, k) and radius r is $(x - h)^2 + (y - k)^2 = r^2$.

Notice that the equation that was given as the solution was expressed in standard form.

The equation of the circle is $(x - 2)^2 + (y + 1)^2 = 9$.

CONTINUED ON THE NEXT PAGE

Go Online | SavvasRealize.com

EXAMPLE 1 CONTINUED

 Activity · Assess

Try It! **1. a.** Write the equation of a circle with radius 1.8 and center at the origin.

    b. What would be the equation if the center was at $(-4, 5)$?

EXAMPLE 2 Write and Graph an Equation of a Circle

Write an equation of each circle, and sketch its graph. What are the domain and range of the relation?

A. The circle centered at the origin with radius $\sqrt{3}$

$h = 0$, $k = 0$, and $r = \sqrt{3}$ ········ Identify the values of h, k, and r.

$(x - h)^2 + (y - k)^2 = r^2$ ········ Write the standard form of the equation of a circle.

$(x - 0)^2 + (y - 0)^2 = (\sqrt{3})^2$ ···· Substitute values.

$x^2 + y^2 = 3$

The equation of the circle is $x^2 + y^2 = 3$.

To sketch the circle, first plot points on the axes that are $\sqrt{3}$ units, or about 1.7 units, away from the origin.

Although this is not the graph of a function, you can determine that both the domain and range of the graph are $[-\sqrt{3}, \sqrt{3}]$.

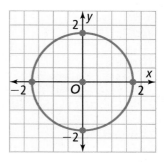

USE APPROPRIATE TOOLS
To create a sketch of the circle, the easiest points to plot are those that lie on the horizontal and vertical lines of symmetry for the circle. **ⓒ MP.5**

B. The circle centered at $(-3, 5)$ with radius $\frac{5}{2}$

$h = -3$, $k = 5$, and $r = \frac{5}{2}$ ········ Identify the values of h, k, and r.

$(x - h)^2 + (y - k)^2 = r^2$ ······ Write the standard form of the equation of a circle.

$(x - (-3))^2 + (y - 5)^2 = \left(\frac{5}{2}\right)^2$ ···· Substitute values.

$(x + 3)^2 + (y - 5)^2 = \frac{25}{4}$

Plot the center. Then plot points that are $\frac{5}{2}$ units away horizontally and vertically. This graph is also not the graph of a function, but you can determine that the domain is $\left[-\frac{11}{2}, -\frac{1}{2}\right]$ and the range is $\left[\frac{5}{2}, \frac{15}{2}\right]$.

The equation of the circle is $(x + 3)^2 + (y - 5)^2 = \frac{25}{4}$.

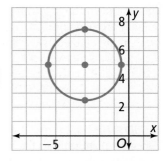

Try It! **2.** Find an equation of each circle described. Sketch the graph.

    a. center $(0, 0)$ and radius 4

    b. center $(8, -3)$ and radius 1

APPLICATION   **EXAMPLE 3**   Use a Circle to Model a Real-World Situation

A city wants to honor hometown veterans with a new memorial statue in a local park. A grid map of the park shows the statue centered inside a circular fence of radius 5. Two spotlights are shown at points (2, 2) and (10, 8) on the map. They are at the endpoints of a diameter of the circular fence.

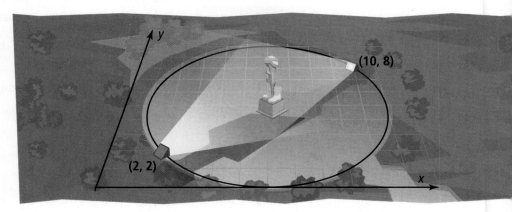

A. **What equation represents the graph of the fence on the grid map?**

To find the equation of the circle, first find its center. The center of the circle is at the midpoint of the diameter.

$$\text{Midpoint} = \left(\frac{x_1 + x_2}{2}, \frac{y_1 + y_2}{2}\right)$$
$$= \left(\frac{10 + 2}{2}, \frac{8 + 2}{2}\right)$$
$$= (6, 5)$$

The center of the circle is at (6, 5) on the grid map. (This is where the statue should be placed).

Now write the equation of the circle with center (6, 5) and radius 5.
$(x - 6)^2 + (y - 5)^2 = 25$

B. **An information kiosk is planned. One possible location is represented by the point (9, 1) on the map. Should the kiosk be here, or should it be moved so as to not interfere with the fence? Support your answer.**

Substitute 9 for x and 1 for y in the equation.

$$(9 - 6)^2 + (1 - 5)^2 \stackrel{?}{=} 25$$
$$(3)^2 + (-4)^2 \stackrel{?}{=} 25$$
$$9 + 16 \stackrel{?}{=} 25$$
$$25 = 25$$

Yes. The point (9, 1) is directly in the path of the fence, so the kiosk should be relocated.

STUDY TIP
Since the point satisfies the equation of the circle, it lies on the circle.

 Try It!   **3.** A second information kiosk is planned for the location represented by the point (3, 9). Should the kiosk be moved so as to not interfere with the fence?

👆 **EXAMPLE 4**   **Complete the Square to Find the Center and Radius of a Circle**

How can you rewrite the equation $x^2 + y^2 + 4x - 8y + 4 = 0$ to show that it is the equation of a circle and to identify its center and radius?

$$x^2 + y^2 + 4x - 8y + 4 = 0 \quad\text{.......}\quad \text{Write the given equation.}$$

$$(x^2 + 4x) + (y^2 - 8y) = -4 \quad\text{.......}\quad \text{Rearrange terms to keep } x \text{ and } y \text{ terms together.}$$

$$(x^2 + 4x + 4) + (y^2 - 8y + 16) = -4 + 4 + 16 \quad\text{...}\quad \text{Complete the squares and add to each side.}$$

$$(x + 2)^2 + (y - 4)^2 = 16 \quad\text{.......}\quad \text{Rewrite expressions as perfect square binomials.}$$

$$(x - (-2))^2 + (y - 4)^2 = 4^2 \quad\text{.......}\quad \text{Express the equation in standard form.}$$

Center: $(-2, 4)$ Radius: 4

The equation $(x + 2)^2 + (y - 4)^2 = 16$ shows radius 4 and center $(-2, 4)$.

COMMON ERROR
Remember that the number subtracted from the variable is the coordinate of the center.

☑ **Try It!**   **4.** Verify that $x^2 + y^2 + 10x - 6y - 2 = 0$ is an equation of a circle. Identify its center and radius.

👆 **EXAMPLE 5**   **Solve a Linear-Quadratic System**

What is the solution of the system of equations?

$$3x - y - 5 = 0$$
$$x^2 + y^2 - 25 = 0$$

$$y = 3x - 5 \quad\text{.......}\quad \text{Solve the linear equation for } y.$$

$$x^2 + (3x - 5)^2 - 25 = 0 \quad\text{.......}\quad \text{Substitute into the equation of the circle.}$$

$$x^2 + 9x^2 - 30x + 25 - 25 = 0 \quad\text{.......}\quad \text{Expand the perfect square binomial.}$$

$$10x^2 - 30x = 0 \quad\text{.......}\quad \text{Combine like terms.}$$

$$10x(x - 3) = 0 \quad\text{.......}\quad \text{Factor the equation.}$$

$$x = 0 \text{ or } x = 3 \quad\text{.......}\quad \text{Use the Zero Product Property.}$$

LOOK FOR RELATIONSHIPS
It is possible that a line and a circle do not intersect or intersect in just one point. If there is no intersection, what might the solutions look like? ⓒ MP.7

$y = 3x - 5$	$y = 3x - 5$
$y = 3(0) - 5$	$y = 3(3) - 5$
$y = -5$	$y = 4$
$(0, -5)$	$(3, 4)$

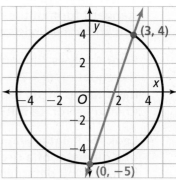

Verify the solutions $(0, -5)$ and $(3, 4)$ by substituting the values into the original equations or by graphing the system.

☑ **Try It!**   **5.** Solve the linear-quadratic system of equations.
$$2x + y = 3$$
$$x^2 + y^2 = 9$$

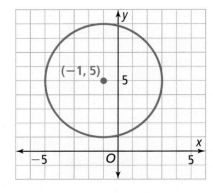

CONCEPT SUMMARY Circles

DEFINITION ▶ A circle is a set of points that are a fixed distance, called the *radius*, from a fixed point, called the *center*.

The **standard form of an equation of a circle** with center (h, k) and radius r is:

$(x - h)^2 + (y - k)^2 = r^2$.

GRAPH ▶ Graph of $(x + 1)^2 + (y - 5)^2 = 4^2$

EQUATION ▶ Complete the square to express the equation of a circle in standard form.

$$x^2 + y^2 + 2x - 10y + 10 = 0$$

$$(x^2 + 2x + 1) + (y^2 - 10y + 25) = -10 + 1 + 25$$

$$(x + 1)^2 + (y - 5)^2 = 4^2$$

Center: $(-1, 5)$, radius: 4

✓ Do You UNDERSTAND?

1. **? ESSENTIAL QUESTION** What are the geometric properties of a circle, and how do they relate to algebraic representations of a circle?

2. **Vocabulary** Explain how to find the standard form of the equation of a circle if you know the circle's center and radius.

3. **Error Analysis** Chiang said that a circle with the equation $(x + 2)^2 + (y - 5)^2 = 6$ has a radius of 36. Explain and correct Chiang's error. Ⓒ **MP.3**

4. **Look for Relationships** If the coordinates of a diameter of a circle are known, how can you determine the center of the circle? Ⓒ **MP.7**

Do You KNOW HOW?

Find the center and the radius of each circle.

5. $x^2 + y^2 = 25$

6. $(x + 3)^2 + (y + 7)^2 = 49$

7. $(x - 1)^2 + (y + 6)^2 = 5$

8. $(x - 9)^2 + (y - 4)^2 = 11$

Find an equation of each circle described.

9. center $(0, 0)$ and radius 8

10. center $(-3, 9)$ and radius 4

UNDERSTAND

11. Use Structure Write an equation of the circle shown in the graph. Ⓒ **MP.7**

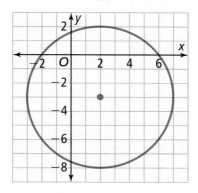

12. Look for Relationships The equation of a circle is $(x + 9)^2 + (y - 4)^2 = 17$. What is the area of the circle, in terms of π? Ⓒ **MP.7**

13. Error Analysis Describe and correct the error a student made in describing the translation of the circle. Ⓒ **MP.3**

> original equation: $x^2 + y^2 = 3$
> translated equation: $(x + 2)^2 + (y - 2)^2 = 3$
>
> translations:
> 2 units right
> 2 units down   ✗

14. Use Structure Write an equation of a circle with center $(-4, 5)$ and diameter of length $4\sqrt{3}$. Ⓒ **MP.7**

15. Reason The equation of a circle is $x^2 + y^2 = 36$. Ⓒ **MP.2**

a. What are the x-intercepts of the circle?

b. What are the y-intercepts of the circle?

16. Higher Order Thinking Write an equation of a circle that is tangent to the x-axis at $(4, 0)$ and the y-axis at $(0, 4)$.

17. Look for Relationships Does the equation $x^2 + y^2 = 0$ represent a circle? Why or why not? Ⓒ **MP.7**

PRACTICE

18. Write the equation of a circle with radius 2.2 and center at the origin. SEE EXAMPLE 1

Find an equation of each circle described. Sketch the graph. SEE EXAMPLE 2

19. center $(0, 0)$ and radius 2

20. center $(2, 4)$ and radius 3

21. center $(-1, 3)$ and radius 5

22. center $(-5, -3)$ and radius 4

23. center $(0, -3)$ and radius $\sqrt{7}$

24. center $(-4, 1)$ and radius $\frac{3}{2}$

25. Diego wants to place a circular pool in his backyard. He has already decided the pool wall will include the endpoints of a diameter, $(-3, 13)$ and $(9, -3)$, on the grid of his backyard. What equation describes the location of the swimming pool wall? SEE EXAMPLE 3

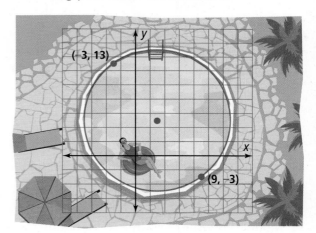

Verify that the equation is an equation of a circle. Identify its center and radius. SEE EXAMPLE 4

26. $x^2 + y^2 + 6x + 4y + 9 = 0$

27. $x^2 + y^2 + 10x - 2y + 1 = 0$

28. $x^2 + y^2 - 12x + 8y + 3 = 0$

29. $x^2 + y^2 - 4x - 8y - 5 = 0$

Solve the linear-quadratic system of equations. SEE EXAMPLE 5

30.
$y = x$
$x^2 + y^2 = 8$

31.
$y = \frac{3}{2}x$
$x^2 + y^2 = 13$

32.
$7y + x = -25$
$x^2 + y^2 = 25$

33.
$x + 2y = 0$
$x^2 + y^2 = 20$

APPLY

34. Model With Mathematics Keenan sketches a circular stone patio on grid paper. Write an equation to model the circular outline of the patio. © MP.4

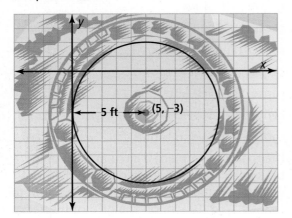

5 ft — (5, –3)

35. Reason A driving instructor showed students where they should place their hands on a steering wheel while driving a car. © MP.2

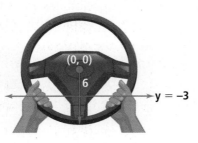

(0, 0)

6

y = –3

a. Write an equation that represents the steering wheel.

b. At what coordinates should a driver place the center of their hands on a steering wheel?

36. Model With Mathematics A cell phone tower is 32 mi east and 20 mi north of Talisha's house, represented by the point (0, 0) on a coordinate plane. A typical cell phone can be reached by the signal from a cell phone tower that has a 40 mi radius. © MP.4

a. What point represents the cell phone tower?

b. Write an equation that represents the farthest points the signal from the cell phone tower can reach.

c. Graph the location of Talisha's house, the cell phone tower, and the range of the cell phone tower.

d. Does Talisha live within the range to receive the signal from the cell phone tower? Explain.

ASSESSMENT PRACTICE

37. Write the equation of the circle given by the equation $x^2 + y^2 + 2x - 14y - 6 = 8$ in standard form. Identify the center and radius. Then sketch the graph.

Standard form: $(x - \underline{\quad})^2 + (y - \underline{\quad})^2 = \underline{\quad}$

Center: (___, ___)

Radius: ___

38. SAT/ACT The equation of a circle is $(x + 2)^2 + (y - 8)^2 = 81$. What is the circumference of the circle?

Ⓐ 3π

Ⓑ 6π

Ⓒ 9π

Ⓓ 18π

Ⓔ 81π

39. Performance Task Venetta wants to write the standard form of the equation of a circle given the circle's diameter d. The table shows the center and diameter of four different circles.

Circle	Center (h, k)	Diameter, d
1	(0, 0)	8
2	(1, −2)	10
3	(−3, 6)	12
4	(−4, −7)	32

Part A Write an equation of each of the four circles.

Part B Write the standard form of the equation of a circle with center (h, k) and diameter d.

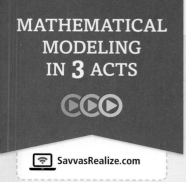
SavvasRealize.com

Common Core State Standards HSG.GPE.A.1, MP.4

Video

▶ Watering the Lawn

Like all plants, grass must receive water regularly to survive. When local rainfall is not enough to keep the grass healthy, it needs to be watered. To make the watering process easier, some property owners have sprinkler systems designed and installed to automate the watering process.

What should be considered while designing a sprinkler system? Think about this during the Mathematical Modeling in 3 Acts lesson.

Scan for Multimedia

ACT 1 ▶ **Identify the Problem**

1. What is the first question that comes to mind after watching the video?

2. Write down the main question you will answer about what you saw in the video.

3. Make an initial conjecture that answers this main question.

4. Explain how you arrived at your conjecture.

5. What information will be useful to know to answer the main question? How can you get it? How will you use that information?

ACT 2 ▶ **Develop a Model**

6. Use the math that you have learned in this Topic to refine your conjecture.

ACT 3 ▶ **Interpret the Results**

7. Did your refined conjecture match the actual answer exactly? If not, what might explain the difference?

Common Core State Standards HSG.GPE.A.3 (+), HSA.SSE.A.2, HSA.SSE.B.3, MP.2, MP.4, MP.8

 Assess

Activity

I CAN... describe the features of an ellipse given its equation or graph.

VOCABULARY
- center of an ellipse
- co-vertices
- ellipse
- foci of an ellipse
- major axis
- minor axis
- standard form of the equation of an ellipse
- vertices of an ellipse

MODEL & DISCUSS

A dog's harness can be attached to a 40 ft tether. The tether runs freely through the harness. The dog has an area to run that is related to the length of the tether. The ends of the tether can be anchored at the same point or different points.

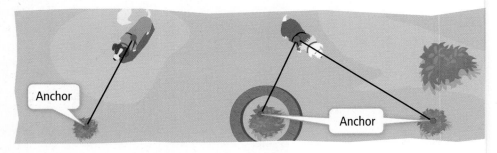

Anchor

Anchor

A. Sketch a graph of the area a dog can run if the two ends of the tether are attached at the same point. What is the relationship between the length of the tether and the shape you graphed?

B. Sketch a graph of the area a dog can run if the two ends are attached at different points. How is the shape similar to and different from the first shape you graphed?

C. Reason What is the relationship between the length of the tether and the distances of the dogs to their anchors? **MP.2**

ESSENTIAL QUESTION

How does the equation of an ellipse relate to the features of its graph?

CONCEPT Features of an Ellipse

An **ellipse** is the set of points P in a plane such that the sum of the distances from P to two fixed points F_1 and F_2 is a constant. The fixed points are the **foci** (singular: "focus").

$PF_1 + PF_2 = k$

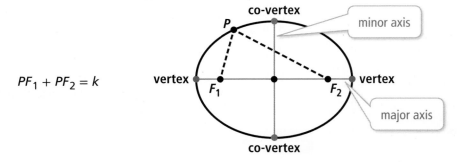

The **major axis** is the segment passing through the foci with endpoints on the ellipse. The endpoints of the major axis are called the **vertices** (singular: "vertex") of the ellipse.

The **minor axis** is the segment perpendicular to the major axis at the center with endpoints on the ellipse. The endpoints of the minor axis are called the **co-vertices** of the ellipse.

The **center of an ellipse** is the midpoint of the major or minor axis.

CONCEPTUAL
UNDERSTANDING

EXAMPLE 1   Derive the Equation of an Ellipse

The graph of the ellipse passes through the points (0, 5) and (0, −5) and has foci at (0, −4) and (0, 4). Write the equation of the ellipse.

Notice that the point (0, 5) lies on the ellipse, and that it is 1 unit from the focus, (0, 4). Point (0, 5) is 9 units from the focus (0, −4). The sum of those distances from the point (0, 5) to each focus is 10. The definition of an ellipse states that the sum of the distances from the foci to any point (x, y) on the ellipse must be a constant, in this case 10. Use this fact and the Distance Formula to write an equation.

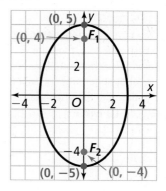

Distance from (x, y) to F_1 + Distance from (x, y) to $F_2 = 10$

$$\sqrt{(x - x_1)^2 + (y - y_1)^2} + \sqrt{(x - x_2)^2 + (y - y_2)^2} = 10$$

$$\sqrt{(x - 0)^2 + (y - 4)^2} + \sqrt{(x - 0)^2 + (y + 4)^2} = 10$$

$$x^2 + (y + 4)^2 = 100 - 20\sqrt{x^2 + (y - 4)^2} + x^2 + (y - 4)^2$$

$$x^2 + y^2 + 8y + 16 = 100 - 20\sqrt{x^2 + (y - 4)^2} + x^2 + y^2 - 8y + 16$$

$$20\sqrt{x^2 + (y - 4)^2} = 100 - 16y$$

$$\sqrt{x^2 + (y - 4)^2} = 5 - \frac{4}{5}y$$

$$x^2 + y^2 - 8y + 16 = 25 - 8y + \frac{16}{25}y^2$$

$$x^2 + \frac{9}{25}y^2 = 9$$

Notice that this equation looks similar to that of a circle. If we complete one more step to make the constant term 1, the equation contains certain features evident in the ellipse.

$$\frac{x^2}{9} + \frac{y^2}{25} = 1$$

COMMUNICATE PRECISELY

In the equation in standard form, *a* represents the distance between the center and each vertex, and *b* represents the distance between the center and each co-vertex.

Ⓒ MP.6

The **standard form of the equation of an ellipse** centered at the origin is $\frac{x^2}{b^2} + \frac{y^2}{a^2} = 1$ when the major axis is vertical and $\frac{x^2}{a^2} + \frac{y^2}{b^2} = 1$ when the major axis is horizontal.

✓ **Try It!**   **1.** What is the equation of the ellipse in standard form which has foci at (−2, 0) and (2, 0) and for which the sum of the distances from the foci to any point on the ellipse is 8?

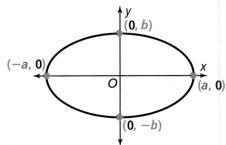

EXAMPLE 2 ▶ Graph an Ellipse

Graph the ellipse that has the equation $\frac{x^2}{45} + \frac{y^2}{36} = 1$. What are the coordinates of the foci?

USE STRUCTURE
If the largest denominator corresponds to x, then the major axis is horizontal. If the largest denominator corresponds to y, then the major axis is vertical. ⓒ MP.7

The major axis is determined by the variable component of the fraction with the largest denominator. For this ellipse, the larger numerator corresponds with x, so the major axis is horizontal. Based on the general equation, $a^2 = 45$ and $b^2 = 36$, so $a = 3\sqrt{5}$ and $b = 6$.

Since the ellipse is centered at the origin, the vertices are $(-3\sqrt{5}, 0)$ and $(3\sqrt{5}, 0)$.

The minor axis is vertical, so the co-vertices are $(0, -6)$ and $(0, 6)$.

To find the foci, let c represent the distance from the foci to the center. The Pythagorean Theorem shows that the distance from $(0, b)$ to each focus is $\sqrt{b^2 + c^2}$.

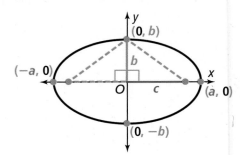

By the definition of an ellipse, the sum of those distances, $2\sqrt{b^2 + c^2}$, will be the same as the sum of the distances from $(a, 0)$ to the foci, $a - c$ and $a - (-c) = a + c$. Set the sums equal to each other.

$$2\sqrt{b^2 + c^2} = (a - c) + [a - (-c)]$$

$$2\sqrt{b^2 + c^2} = 2a$$

$$\sqrt{b^2 + c^2} = a$$

$$b^2 + c^2 = a^2$$

To find the foci in this ellipse, solve for c.

$$b^2 + c^2 = a^2$$

$$36 + c^2 = 45$$

$$c^2 = 9$$

$$c = 3$$

So the coordinates of the foci are $(-3, 0)$ and $(3, 0)$.

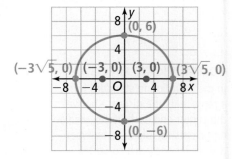

Try It! 2. Graph the ellipse represented by each equation. Then find the coordinates of the foci.

a. $\frac{x^2}{64} + \frac{y^2}{100} = 1$

b. $\frac{x^2}{16} + \frac{y^2}{8} = 1$

EXAMPLE 3 Write the Equation of an Ellipse

How can you write the equation of an ellipse?

A. What is the equation of an ellipse centered at the origin that has a horizontal axis 10 units long and a vertical axis 16 units long?

The horizontal axis is 10 units long. In order to find the distance from the co-vertex to the center, divide the axis in half. The co-vertices are each $\frac{10}{2} = 5$ units from the center, so $b = 5$.

The vertical axis is 16 units long. The vertices are each $\frac{16}{2} = 8$ units from the center, so $a = 8$.

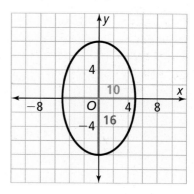

The equation representing the ellipse is $\frac{x^2}{25} + \frac{y^2}{64} = 1$.

B. What is the equation of an ellipse with foci at $(-3, 0)$ and $(3, 0)$ and that passes through the points $(0, -4)$ and $(0, 4)$?

The foci are each 3 units from the center on the horizontal axis, so $c = 3$ and the center is the origin.

The points $(0, -4)$ and $(0, 4)$ are on the vertical axis, so they are the co-vertices and $b = 4$.

Solve for a, the distance between each vertex and the center along the major axis.

$$a^2 = b^2 + c^2$$
$$a^2 = 4^2 + 3^2$$
$$a^2 = 25$$
$$a = 5$$

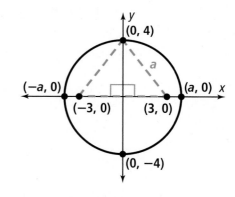

The equation of the ellipse is $\frac{x^2}{25} + \frac{y^2}{16} = 1$.

GENERALIZE

As in the previous example, you know this equation is true because the distance from the center to each vertex (a) is the same as the distance between the foci and the co-vertices $\left(\sqrt{b^2 + c^2}\right)$. ⓒ **MP.8**

Try It! **3. a** What is the equation of an ellipse with foci at $(0, -12)$ and $(0, 12)$ and that passes through the points $(-5, 0)$ and $(5, 0)$?

b What is the equation of an ellipse centered at the origin if the sum of the distances to the foci from any point is 30 units and the vertical minor axis is 24 units long?

APPLICATION → 👆 **EXAMPLE 4** Use an Ellipse to Model a Real-World Situation

A whispering gallery is an elliptical room where a soft sound at one focus in the room can be heard clearly at the other focus. A museum has a whispering gallery that is 40 ft on its longest axis, with foci 20 ft apart. The doors are located at the co-vertices. Find the equation of the ellipse representing the shape of the room. How far are the doors from the center of the room?

Formulate ◄ Put the center of the ellipse at the origin with its foci on the *x*-axis.

The vertices are each 20 ft from the center (*a* = 20) since the longest axis is 40 ft.

The foci are each 10 ft (*c* = 10) from the center since they are 20 ft apart.

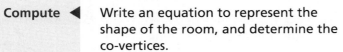

Compute ◄ Write an equation to represent the shape of the room, and determine the co-vertices.

$$b^2 + c^2 = a^2$$
$$b^2 + 10^2 = 20^2$$
$$b^2 + 100 = 400$$
$$b^2 = 300$$
$$b = \sqrt{300} = 10\sqrt{3}$$

> You do not need to consider $b = -10\sqrt{3}$ as a solution, since *b* is a distance which is always positive.

Interpret ◄ The equation representing the model room is $\frac{x^2}{400} + \frac{y^2}{300} = 1$. The co-vertices are located at $(0, \pm 10\sqrt{3})$, so the doors are about 17.3 ft from the center of the room.

☑ **Try It!** 4. Consider a whispering gallery like the one above, but 30 m east to west and 34 m north to south. Find the equation of the ellipse representing the shape of the room. How far are the whispering points from the center of the room?

EXAMPLE 5   Graph a Translated Ellipse

The equation $2x^2 - 12x + y^2 - 2y + 15 = 0$ represents an ellipse. Graph the ellipse. What are its key features?

$$2x^2 - 12x + y^2 - 2y + 15 = 0$$

$$2(x^2 - 6x) + (y^2 - 2y) = -15$$

> Group the variable terms and constants to use completing the square to rewrite the equation with perfect square factors.

$$2(x^2 - 6x + 9) + (y^2 - 2y + 1) = -15 + 2(9) + 1$$

$$2(x - 3)^2 + (y - 1)^2 = 4$$

$$\frac{(x - 3)^2}{2} + \frac{(y - 1)^2}{4} = 1$$

COMMON ERROR
Be careful not to lose track of the 2 after factoring. You have to add 2(9) to both sides of the equation when completing the square here, not just 9.

The standard form of the equation of an ellipse with a vertical major axis is $\frac{(x - h)^2}{b^2} + \frac{(y - k)^2}{a^2} = 1$. When the major axis is horizontal, the standard form of the equation is $\frac{(x - h)^2}{a^2} + \frac{(y - k)^2}{b^2} = 1$. The ellipse with equation $\frac{(x - 3)^2}{2} + \frac{(y - 1)^2}{4} = 1$ is an ellipse with a vertical axis that is a translation of the graph of $\frac{x^2}{2} + \frac{y^2}{4} = 1$. The center is translated 3 units right and 1 unit up.

The major axis is vertical, since $4 > 2$. Since $a = 2$, the vertices are $(3, -1)$ and $(3, 3)$.

The minor axis is horizontal and $b = \sqrt{2}$, so the co-vertices are at $(3 \pm \sqrt{2}, 1)$, or about $(4.4, 1)$ and $(1.6, 1)$.

Find the foci.

$$b^2 + c^2 = a^2$$

$$c^2 = a^2 - b^2$$

$$c^2 = (2)^2 - (\sqrt{2})^2$$

$$c^2 = 4 - 2 = 2$$

$$c = \sqrt{2}$$

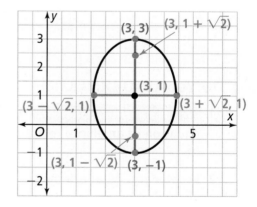

The foci are each $\sqrt{2}$ units from the center on the major axis. Their coordinates are $(3, 1 \pm \sqrt{2})$ or about $(3, 2.4)$ and $(3, -0.4)$.

 Try It!   **5. a** Graph the ellipse represented by $10x^2 + 40x + 2y^2 + 30 = 0$. Label the coordinates of the center, vertices, co-vertices, and foci.

      b Graph the ellipse represented by $x^2 + 3y^2 - 8x + 6y + 10 = 0$. Label the coordinates of the center, vertices, co-vertices, and foci.

CONCEPT SUMMARY Ellipses

DEFINITION An ellipse is the set of points P in a plane such that the sum of the distances from $P(x, y)$ to two fixed points F_1 and F_2 is a constant.

GRAPHS

Horizontal Major Axis

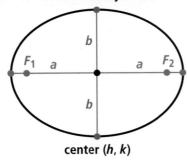

center (h, k)

Vertical Major Axis

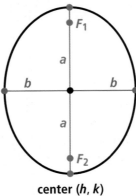

center (h, k)

EQUATIONS

$$\frac{(x - h)^2}{a^2} + \frac{(y - k)^2}{b^2} = 1$$

$$\frac{(x - h)^2}{b^2} + \frac{(y - k)^2}{a^2} = 1$$

If the major axis is horizontal, $(h \pm a, k)$ are the vertices, $(h, k \pm b)$ are the co-vertices, and $(h \pm c, k)$ are the foci where $a^2 = c^2 + b^2$.

If the major axis is vertical, $(h, k \pm a)$ are the vertices, $(h \pm b, k)$ are the co-vertices, and $(h, k \pm c)$ are the foci where $a^2 = c^2 + b^2$.

☑ Do You UNDERSTAND?

1. **ESSENTIAL QUESTION** How does the equation of an ellipse relate to the features of its graph?

2. **Vocabulary** What are the co-vertices of an ellipse?

3. **Error Analysis** Darren said that an ellipse with the equation $\frac{(x - 4)^2}{25} + \frac{(y + 1)^2}{9} = 1$ has vertices at (4, 2) and (4, −4). Explain and correct Darren's error. © **MP.3**

4. **Generalize** For any ellipse, which measure is greatest, a, b, or c? Explain. © **MP.8**

Do You KNOW HOW?

Find the vertices and co-vertices of each ellipse.

5. $\frac{x^2}{49} + \frac{y^2}{64} = 1$

6. $\frac{(x - 1)^2}{16} + \frac{(y + 5)^2}{4} = 1$

Find the foci of each ellipse.

7. $\frac{x^2}{2} + \frac{y^2}{8} = 1$

8. $\frac{(x + 5)^2}{16} + \frac{(y - 9)^2}{4} = 1$

UNDERSTAND

9. Look for Relationships When would an equation of an ellipse, with center at the origin, be in the shape of a circle? Explain how you know. Ⓒ MP.7

10. Use Appropriate Tools The equation of an ellipse is $\frac{x^2}{36} + \frac{y^2}{4} = 1$. Write two equations you can type in $Y1$ and $Y2$ on your graphing calculator to graph the ellipse. Ⓒ MP.5

11. Error Analysis Kendall wants to find the key features of an ellipse. Describe and correct the error Kendall made in finding the vertices, co-vertices, and foci of the ellipse. Ⓒ MP.3

> original equation: $\frac{(x-4)^2}{9} + \frac{(y-6)^2}{25} = 1$
>
> vertices: $(0, -5)$ and $(0, 5)$
>
> co-vertices: $(-3, 0)$ and $(3, 0)$
>
> foci: $(0, -4)$ and $(0, 4)$ ✗

12. Reason The equation of an ellipse is $\frac{x^2}{25} + \frac{y^2}{49} = 1$. Ⓒ MP.2

 a. Is the major axis of this ellipse vertical or horizontal?

 b. What are the x-intercepts of the ellipse?

 c. What are the y-intercepts of the ellipse?

13. Higher Order Thinking The area of a circle is given by the formula $A = \pi r^2$, where r is the radius. The area of an ellipse is given by the formula $A = \pi ab$, where a is half the length of the horizontal axis and b is half the length of the vertical axis. Explain the connection between the two formulas.

14. Construct Arguments Nora claims that an ellipse has vertices at $(-3, 0)$ and $(3, 0)$ and co-vertices at $(-7, 0)$ and $(7, 0)$. Is this possible? Explain. Ⓒ MP.3

PRACTICE

15. What is the equation in the form $\frac{x^2}{a^2} + \frac{y^2}{b^2} = 1$ of the ellipse which has foci at $(-3, 0)$ and $(3, 0)$ and for which the sum of the distances from the foci to any point on the ellipse is 12? SEE EXAMPLE 1

Graph the ellipse represented by each equation.
SEE EXAMPLE 2

16. $\frac{x^2}{4} + \frac{y^2}{9} = 1$

17. $\frac{(x-1)^2}{9} + \frac{(y+2)^2}{36} = 1$

18. $\frac{x^2}{25} + \frac{y^2}{16} = 1$

19. $\frac{(x+3)^2}{49} + \frac{(y-1)^2}{16} = 1$

20. What is the equation of an ellipse centered at the origin that has a horizontal axis 12 units long and a vertical axis 22 units long? SEE EXAMPLE 3

21. What is the equation of an ellipse with foci at $(-8, 0)$ and $(8, 0)$ that passes through the points $(0, -3)$ and $(0, 3)$? SEE EXAMPLE 3

22. An elliptical dining table is 60 in. on its longer axis, with foci 50 in. apart. Two chairs are located at the co-vertices. Find the equation of the ellipse representing the shape of the table. To the nearest inch, how far apart are the chairs? SEE EXAMPLE 4

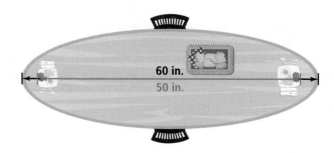

23. Graph each ellipse. Label the coordinates of the center, vertices, co-vertices, and foci.
SEE EXAMPLE 5

 a. $2x^2 + 4x + 3y^2 - 6y - 7 = 0$

 b. $4x^2 + y^2 - 16x - 6y + 9 = 0$

APPLY

24. **Model With Mathematics** The wind tunnel at Langley Research Center in Hampton, Virginia is 30 ft tall and 60 ft wide. The entrance to the tunnel is in the shape of an ellipse that can be modeled by the equation $\frac{x^2}{a^2} + \frac{y}{b^2} = 1$.

a. Find the value of a. Explain.

b. Find the value of b. Explain.

c. Write an equation of the ellipse that represents the entrance to the tunnel, assuming the center of the ellipse is at the origin.

25. **Reason** A scale drawing of an elliptical hot tub is shown. Write an equation to represent the scale drawing of the hot tub. © **MP.2**

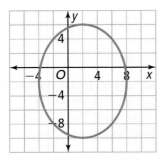

26. **Make Sense and Persevere** The Colosseum which is 188 m long and 156 m wide is an elliptical amphitheater located at the center of Rome, Italy. A backstage entrance is located at one vertex. A stage is erected at a location that corresponds to the focus that is closest to the backstage entrance. How far from the entrance is the stage? © **MP.1**

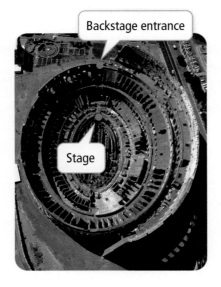

Backstage entrance

Stage

ASSESSMENT PRACTICE

27. Which equation of an ellipse has a vertical major axis? Select all that apply.

Ⓐ $\frac{x^2}{12} + \frac{y^2}{55} = 1$

Ⓑ $\frac{x^2}{53} + \frac{y^2}{25} = 1$

Ⓒ $\frac{(x-9)^2}{82} + \frac{(y-10)^2}{120} = 1$

Ⓓ $\frac{(x+7)^2}{92} + \frac{(y+16)^2}{88} = 1$

Ⓔ $\frac{(x-6)^2}{35} + \frac{(y+11)^2}{53} = 1$

28. **SAT/ACT** What is the length of the minor axis of an ellipse with equation $\frac{(x-5)^2}{64} + \frac{(y+8)^2}{16} = 1$?

Ⓐ 4   Ⓑ 8   Ⓒ 16   Ⓓ 32   Ⓔ 64

29. **Performance Task** The Oval Office in the White House in Washington, DC, is actually elliptical. Its major axis is 35 ft 10 in. long, and its minor axis is 29 ft long.

Part A Suppose that the president's desk chair is placed at one focus of the ellipse. How far is the chair from the wall behind it?

Part B If the president were to throw a tennis ball and bounce it off a wall in the Oval Office to the vice president, seated in a chair at the other focus of the ellipse, how far would the ball travel? (Assume that the path of the ball is level.)

29 ft

35 ft 10 in.

9-4

Hyperbolas

SavvasRealize.com

I CAN... understand the geometric properties of a hyperbola.

VOCABULARY

- center of a hyperbola
- conjugate axis
- foci of a hyperbola
- hyperbola
- standard form of the equation of a hyperbola
- transverse axis
- vertices of a hyperbola

© **Common Core State Standards** HSG.GPE.A.3 (+), HSA.SSE.A.2, HSA.SSE.B.3, MP.1, MP.4, MP.7

  Activity Assess

👆 **EXPLORE & REASON**

An ellipse is the set of all points where the sum of the distance of any point to two set points called foci is a constant.

A. Describe how the length of d_1 and d_2 in the ellipse relate to each other. What happens to d_2 as d_1 gets larger?

B. Imagine that instead of the *sum* of the distances being a constant, the *difference* of the distances was a constant. What would happen to d_2 as d_1 gets larger?

C. Make Sense and Persevere Imagine what the graph of those points would look like. Where would the points lie in relation to the foci? How would it compare to the graph of an ellipse? © **MP.1**

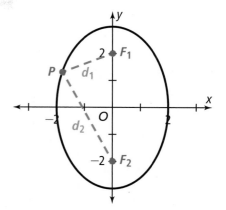

ESSENTIAL QUESTION   How does the equation of a hyperbola relate to the features of its graph?

CONCEPT Hyperbolas

A **Hyperbola** is the set of all points P such that the difference of the distances from any point P to two fixed points, or **foci** (singular: focus) **of a hyperbola**, is constant. A hyperbola has two branches and two asymptotes.

A line drawn through the foci intersects the hyperbola at two points called the **vertices of a hyperbola**.

The foci and the vertices lie along the **transverse axis**. The **conjugate axis** is perpendicular to the transverse axis and passes through the **center of a hyperbola**.

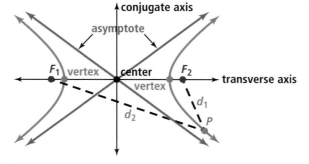

A hyperbola is the intersection of a plane with an infinite double right cone such that the plane intersects both of the cones.

👆 **EXAMPLE 1**   **Derive an Equation of a Hyperbola**

How can you derive an equation for the graph of a hyperbola?

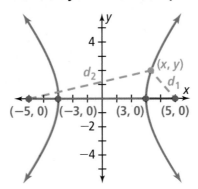

LOOK FOR RELATIONSHIPS
What is the relationship between deriving an equation for an ellipse and deriving an equation for a hyperbola? © MP.7

By definition, the difference of the distances between any point (x, y) on the hyperbola and the foci is constant. The vertices $(-3, 0)$ and $(3, 0)$ lie on the hyperbola so you can use one of those points to find the constant difference.

The distance from $(3, 0)$ to the focus $(-5, 0)$ is 8.

The distance from $(3, 0)$ to the focus $(5, 0)$ is 2.

$$8 - 2 = 6$$

The difference of these distances is 6.

So by definition, $|d_2 - d_1| = 6$ for any point (x, y) on the hyperbola.

> Use absolute value here to make sure the result is positive.

Using the Distance Formula, define the distances d_2 and d_1. From the graph you can see that $d_2 > d_1$, so the absolute value sign is not needed.

$$d_2 = \sqrt{(x + 5)^2 + y^2}, \, d_1 = \sqrt{(x - 5)^2 + y^2}$$

$$\sqrt{(x + 5)^2 + y^2} - \sqrt{(x - 5)^2 + y^2} = 6$$

$$\sqrt{(x + 5)^2 + y^2} = 6 + \sqrt{(x - 5)^2 + y^2}$$

$$(x + 5)^2 + y^2 = 36 + 12\sqrt{(x - 5)^2 + y^2} + ((x - 5)^2 + y^2)$$

$$x^2 + 10x + 25 + y^2 = 36 + 12\sqrt{(x - 5)^2 + y^2} + x^2 - 10x + 25 + y^2$$

$$20x - 36 = 12\sqrt{(x - 5)^2 + y^2}$$

$$\frac{5}{3}x - 3 = \sqrt{(x - 5)^2 + y^2}$$

$$\frac{25}{9}x^2 - 10x + 9 = x^2 - 10x + 25 + y^2$$

$$\frac{16}{9}x^2 - y^2 = 16$$

> Divide by 16 so that the equation is set equal to 1.

$$\frac{x^2}{9} - \frac{y^2}{16} = 1$$

So the equation for this hyperbola is $\frac{x^2}{9} - \frac{y^2}{16} = 1$.

☑ **Try It!**   **1.** What is the equation for the hyperbola with foci at $(10, 0)$ and $(-10, 0)$ and a constant difference of 16?

CONCEPTUAL
UNDERSTANDING

EXAMPLE 2   **Understand the Graph of a Hyperbola**

How does the equation of a hyperbola help you to understand the graph of the hyperbola?

Use the equation derived in Example 1, $\frac{x^2}{9} - \frac{y^2}{16} = 1$. The **standard form of the equation for a hyperbola** centered at the origin that opens horizontally is $\frac{x^2}{a^2} - \frac{y^2}{b^2} = 1$.

In this example, $a^2 = 9$ and $b^2 = 16$, so $a = 3$ and $b = 4$.

The first step in graphing a hyperbola is to find the asymptotes. Start with the equation for the hyperbola and isolate the y^2-term. Then you can solve for y.

$$\frac{x^2}{9} - \frac{y^2}{16} = 1$$

$$-\frac{y^2}{16} = 1 - \frac{x^2}{9}$$

$$y^2 = -16 + \frac{16}{9}x^2$$

$$y^2 = \frac{16}{9}(x^2 - 9)$$

$$\sqrt{y^2} = \sqrt{\frac{16}{9}(x^2 - 9)}$$

$$y = \pm\frac{4}{3}\sqrt{(x^2 - 9)}$$

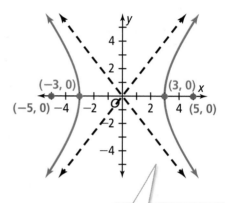

Draw the asymptotes to help you graph the hyperbola. The graph of the hyperbola will approach, but not touch, the asymptotes.

> **MAKE SENSE AND PERSEVERE**
> The vertices of a horizontal hyperbola centered at the origin are on the x-axis. So you can also find them by substituting $y = 0$ into the equation of the hyperbola and solving for the x-coordinates. **ⓒ MP.1**

As x^2 gets larger, the effect of -9 becomes negligible. So as x gets infinitely large, $\sqrt{x^2 - 9}$ will approach $\sqrt{x^2} = x$. The equation becomes approximately equal to $y = \pm\frac{4}{3}x$. This represents two lines through the origin with slopes of $\frac{4}{3}$ and $-\frac{4}{3}$. These are the asymptotes for the hyperbola.

A horizontal hyperbola $\frac{x^2}{a^2} - \frac{y^2}{b^2} = 1$ has asymptotes $y = \pm\left(\frac{b}{a}\right)x$.

The vertices of this hyperbola are $(\pm 3, 0)$.

If $c^2 = a^2 + b^2$, then the the foci of a hyperbola in standard form are $(\pm c, 0)$ if it opens horizontally, or $(0, \pm c)$ if it opens vertically. So the foci of this hyperbola are $(\pm 5, 0)$.

The form of the equation found above, $y = \pm\frac{4}{3}\sqrt{(x^2 - 9)}$, reveals the domain. The radicand cannot be negative, so $|x| \geq 3$. Thus the domain of the equation is $(-\infty, -3]$ and $[3, \infty)$. You can see why the graph is "split" into two parts—there are no points on the graph between the vertices $x = -3$ and $x = 3$, because this interval is outside the domain.

The range is not restricted—it is all real numbers.

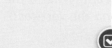 **Try It!**   **2.** Graph the hyperbola $\frac{y^2}{64} - \frac{x^2}{36} = 1$. (*Hint:* Notice that in this equation the x-term is being subtracted from the y-term, so this hyperbola will open vertically rather than horizontally.)

EXAMPLE 3 Write an Equation of a Hyperbola

How do you write the equation of a hyperbola?

A. What is the equation of a hyperbola with vertices (0, −3) and (0, 3) and asymptotes $y = \pm\frac{1}{2}x$?

Step 1 The vertices are on the y-axis, so this is a vertical hyperbola with an equation of the form
$$\frac{y^2}{a^2} - \frac{x^2}{b^2} = 1.$$

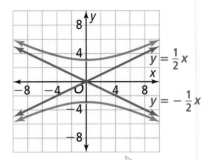

Step 2 Find a and b. The vertices are $(0, \pm 3)$, so $a = 3$.

A vertical hyperbola has asymptotes $y = \pm\frac{a}{b}x$.

In this example, the asymptotes are $y = \pm\frac{1}{2}x$, so $\frac{1}{2} = \frac{3}{b}$ and $b = 6$.

While it is not essential to sketch the graph, it may help guide your writing of the equation for a hyperbola.

Step 3 Substitute a and b into the equation to get $\frac{y^2}{9} - \frac{x^2}{36} = 1$.

The equation of the hyperbola is $\frac{y^2}{9} - \frac{x^2}{36} = 1$.

B. What is the equation of a hyperbola with foci at (−3, 0) and (3, 0) and vertices at (2, 0) and (−2, 0)?

The vertices of this hyperbola are on the x-axis so this is a horizontal hyperbola with an equation in the form $\frac{x^2}{a^2} - \frac{y^2}{b^2} = 1$.

The vertices are $(\pm 2, 0)$, so $a = 2$.

The foci are at $(\pm 3, 0)$, so $c = 3$.

Use $c^2 = a^2 + b^2$ to find b^2.

$$3^2 = 2^2 + b^2$$
$$9 = 4 + b^2$$
$$5 = b^2$$

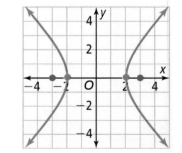

Use this information to write the equation of the hyperbola in standard form.

$$\frac{x^2}{4} - \frac{y^2}{5} = 1$$

The equation of a hyperbola with foci (−3, 0) and (3, 0) and vertices (2, 0) and (−2, 0) is $\frac{x^2}{4} - \frac{y^2}{5} = 1$.

☑ **Try It!** **3.** What is the equation of a hyperbola with foci $(-\sqrt{5}, 0)$ and $(\sqrt{5}, 0)$ and constant difference 2? (*Hint:* What is the relationship between the constant difference and the vertices?)

APPLICATION   **EXAMPLE 4**   **Use a Hyperbola to Model a Real-World Situation**

Some telescopes use a hyperbolic mirror. Light is directed inward at the hyperbolic mirror. It is reflected through a hole in the parabolic mirror toward a focus, where it can be captured by a detector. A hyperbolic mirror is shown on a coordinate plane. What equation can be used to represent the mirror? How far must the detector be placed from the mirror?

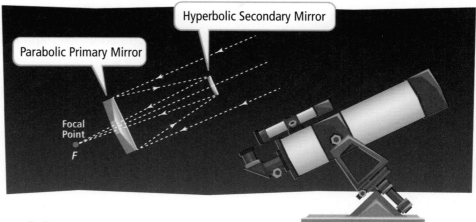

Hyperbolic Secondary Mirror

Parabolic Primary Mirror

Focal Point

F

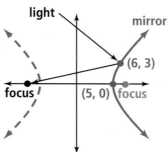

light   mirror

(6, 3)

focus   (5, 0)   focus

One of the vertices is at (5, 0), so $a = 5$. A given point on the hyperbola is (6, 3).

$$\frac{x^2}{a^2} - \frac{y^2}{b^2} = 1$$

$$\frac{6^2}{5^2} - \frac{3^2}{b^2} = 1$$

$$\frac{36}{25} - \frac{9}{b^2} = 1$$

The foci are on the x-axis, so this is a horizontal hyperbola. Use the form $\frac{x^2}{a^2} - \frac{y^2}{b^2} = 1$.

$$36b^2 - 225 = 25b^2$$

$$11b^2 = 225$$

$$b^2 = 20.5$$

STUDY TIP
You are looking for b^2 here, so you don't need to take the square root.

The equation that models this hyperbolic mirror is $\frac{x^2}{25} - \frac{y^2}{20.5} = 1$.

The detector would have to be placed at the focus of the other branch of the hyperbola, at the point $(-c, 0)$. Since $c^2 = a^2 + b^2$, the coordinates for the detector are $(-\sqrt{45.5}, 0)$ or about $(-6.7, 0)$ which is about 11.7 units away from the mirror.

 Try It!   **4.** How far from the vertex of the hyperbolic mirror is the second focus?

EXAMPLE 5 **Classify a Second-Degree Equation**

What conic section is represented by the equation?

A. $3x^2 - 12x - y + 17 = 0$

There is no y^2 term. Solve for y in terms of x^2 and x.

$$3x^2 - 12x - y + 17 = 0$$
$$y = 3x^2 - 12x + 17$$

This is a quadratic function. Its graph is a parabola.

B. $x^2 + y^2 - 2x - 8y + 8 = 0$

When there are quadratic and linear terms for both x and y, complete the square for each variable.

$$x^2 + y^2 - 2x - 8y + 8 = 0$$
$$x^2 - 2x + y^2 - 8y = -8$$
$$x^2 - 2x + 1 + y^2 - 8y + 16 = -8 + 1 + 16$$
$$(x - 1)^2 + (y - 4)^2 = 9$$

The result is the equation of a circle.

C. $4x^2 + 9y^2 - 36 = 0$

When the coefficients of x^2 or y^2 are not equal to 1, divide each side of the equation by their least common multiple.

$$4x^2 + 9y^2 - 36 = 0$$
$$4x^2 + 9y^2 = 36$$
$$\frac{x^2}{9} + \frac{y^2}{4} = 1$$

The result is the equation of an ellipse.

D. $8x^2 - 9y^2 + 16x - 64 = 0$

You may need to complete the square in one or both variables before dividing by the least common multiple of the x^2 and y^2 terms.

$$8x^2 - 9y^2 + 16x - 64 = 0$$
$$(8x^2 + 16x) - 9y^2 = 64$$
$$8(x^2 + 2x) - 9y^2 = 64$$
$$8(x^2 + 2x + 1) - 9y^2 = 64 + 8$$
$$8(x + 1)^2 - 9y^2 = 72$$
$$\frac{(x + 1)^2}{9} - \frac{y^2}{8} = 1$$

The result is the equation of a hyperbola.

USE STRUCTURE

By using algebra to transform equations, you can put some 2nd-degree equations into standard form for the four conic sections. © **MP.7**

 Try It! **5.** Which conic section is represented by each equation?

a. $x^2 + y^2 + 4x - 6y + 9 = 0$ **b.** $6y^2 - 3x^2 - 18 = 0$

CONCEPT SUMMARY Hyperbolas

DEFINITION A hyperbola is the set of all points P such that the difference of the distances from any point P to two fixed points is constant.

GRAPHS

Horizontal Hyperbola

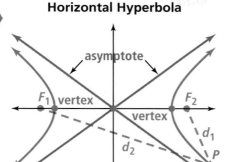

Vertical Hyperbola

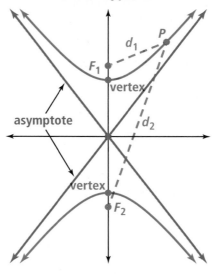

EQUATION

Horizontal: $\frac{x^2}{a^2} - \frac{y^2}{b^2} = 1$

vertices: $(\pm a, 0)$

asymptotes: $y = \pm\frac{b}{a}x$

Foci: $(\pm c, 0)$, where $c = \sqrt{a^2 + b^2}$

Vertical: $\frac{y^2}{a^2} - \frac{x^2}{b^2} = 1$

vertices: $(0, \pm a)$

asymptotes: $y = \pm\frac{a}{b}x$

foci: $(0, \pm c)$, where $c = \sqrt{a^2 + b^2}$

Do You UNDERSTAND?

1. **ESSENTIAL QUESTION** How does the equation of a hyperbola relate to the features of its graph?

2. **Error Analysis** Alberto said that a hyperbola is two parabolas opening in opposite directions. Explain his error. **ⓒ MP.3**

3. **Vocabulary** Describe the transverse axis of a horizontal and a vertical hyperbola.

4. **Look for Relationships** Describe the position of the asymptotes in the graph of a hyperbola. How do the equations of the asymptotes help you sketch a graph of a hyperbola? **ⓒ MP.7**

5. **Communicate Precisely** Explain how to determine which conic section is represented by a second degree equation in x and y with no xy-term. **ⓒ MP.6**

Do You KNOW HOW?

Find the vertices of the hyperbola.

6. $\frac{y^2}{144} - \frac{x^2}{56} = 1$

7. $\frac{x^2}{121} - \frac{y^2}{12} = 1$

Find the foci of the hyperbola.

8. $\frac{x^2}{64} - \frac{y^2}{36} = 1$

9. $\frac{y^2}{9} - \frac{x^2}{16} = 1$

Write an equation for the asymptotes of the hyperbola.

10. $\frac{x^2}{9} - \frac{y^2}{100} = 1$

11. $\frac{y^2}{4} - \frac{x^2}{36} = 1$

12. **Look for Relationships** Explain how to find the value of b in the equation of a hyperbola, given one focus at $(0, 1)$ and one vertex at $(0, 0.5)$. **ⓒ MP.7**

UNDERSTAND

13. Look for Relationships Jordan wants to graph the equation $25x^2 - 9y^2 = 225$. **MP.7**

   a. What kind of conic section could the equation represent? Explain.

   b. Explain how to write the equation in standard form. Then write the equation in standard form.

   c. What are the vertices?

   d. What are the asymptotes?

   e. What are the foci?

   f. Is the transverse axis horizontal or vertical? Explain.

   g. Graph the equation.

14. Use Structure Write the equation of the hyperbola that has its center at the origin, vertices on the y-axis 8 units apart, and asymptotes $y = \pm\frac{4}{3}x$. Then graph the hyperbola. **MP.7**

15. Error Analysis Describe and correct the error Elaine made in determining the vertices, asymptotes, and foci of a hyperbola. **MP.3**

hyperbola: $\frac{y^2}{144} - \frac{x^2}{256} = 1$

vertices: $(-12, 0)$ and $(12, 0)$

asymptotes: $y = \pm\frac{4}{3}x$

foci: $(0, -400)$ and $(0, 400)$

 ✗

16. Higher Order Thinking The square of the distance from the center of a hyperbola to a focus is 78. The intersections of the hyperbola with the transverse axis are $(-\sqrt{20}, 0)$ and $(\sqrt{20}, 0)$. Write the equation of the hyperbola.

17. Construct Arguments Determine whether the equation $\frac{x^2}{18} - \frac{y^2}{32} = -2$ represents a hyperbola. Explain. **MP.3**

PRACTICE

Write an equation for the hyperbola. SEE EXAMPLE 1

18. foci at $(5, 0)$ and $(-5, 0)$ and a constant difference of 8

19. foci at $(0, 15)$ and $(0, -15)$ and a constant difference of 18

Graph the hyperbola. SEE EXAMPLE 2

20. $\frac{y^2}{4} - \frac{x^2}{9} = 1$ **21.** $\frac{x^2}{1} - \frac{y^2}{25} = 1$

22. $\frac{x^2}{16} - \frac{y^2}{36} = 1$ **23.** $\frac{y^2}{49} - \frac{x^2}{25} = 1$

Write an equation for the hyperbola with the given information. SEE EXAMPLE 3

24. vertices $(0, -6)$ and $(0, 6)$ and asymptotes $y = \pm\frac{2}{3}x$

25. vertices $(-9, 0)$ and $(9, 0)$ and asymptotes $y = \pm\frac{4}{3}x$

26. A telescope is made with a hyperbolic mirror, shown graphed on the coordinate plane. To assemble the telescope correctly, the manufacturer needs to know the distance to the focus on the same side as the reflective side of the mirror. What is this distance? What equation represents the location of the mirror? SEE EXAMPLE 4

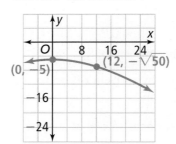

Which conic section is represented by each equation? SEE EXAMPLE 5

27. $16x^2 + 25y^2 - 64 = 0$

28. $-49x^2 + 36y^2 - 48 = 0$

29. $4y^2 + 8y - x - 16 = 0$

30. $-x^2 - y^2 + 5x - 10y + 15 = 0$

PRACTICE & PROBLEM SOLVING

APPLY

31. Model With Mathematics When the light from a lamp shines on a wall, a hyperbola is formed. What is the equation of the hyperbola with asymptotes $y = \pm\frac{2}{5}x$? Ⓒ **MP.4**

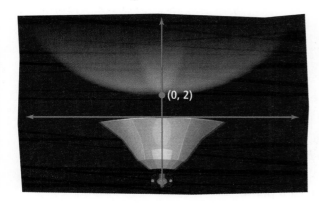

(0, 2)

32. Model With Mathematics In order to take a panoramic photograph, a camera must have a hyperbolic mirror. The graphic shows that the camera is below the mirror. The lens is at one focus of the camera, and the mirror is at one vertex. Write an equation for the cross section of the mirror. Ⓒ **MP.4**

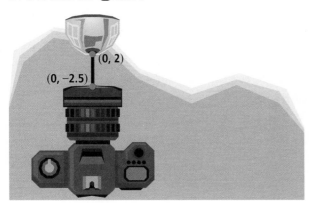

(0, 2)

(0, −2.5)

33. Reason Jupiter's gravity changes a spacecraft's path to a hyperbola as it approaches. The focus of the hyperbola nearest the spacecraft's path is the center of Jupiter. The diameter of the planet is 139,822 km. Suppose the path of an approaching spacecraft has an equation with $a = 80{,}000$ km and $c = 170{,}000$ km. Assuming the transverse axis is horizontal, write the equation that models the path of the spacecraft as it approaches Jupiter. What is the distance from the spacecraft to the planet at the vertex of the hyperbola? Ⓒ **MP.2**

ⒸASSESSMENT PRACTICE

34. Write an equation of the hyperbola shown in the graph.

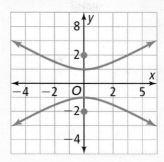

35. SAT/ACT Which equation represents a hyperbola?

Ⓐ $4x^2 + 81y^2 + 12 = 0$

Ⓑ $9x^2 + 16y^2 - 4x - 24y + 18 = 0$

Ⓒ $49y^2 + 7y - 2x + 14 = 0$

Ⓓ $-36x^2 - 36y^2 + 6x - 13y + 20 = 0$

Ⓔ $25x^2 - 121y^2 + 64 = 0$

36. Performance Task Libby wants to graph a hyperbola with the equation $y^2 - x^2 + 16 = 0$. The function $y = \sqrt{x^2 - 16}$ represents part of the hyperbola. Libby used the TABLE feature on her graphing calculator to show several points on the graph of $y = \sqrt{x^2 - 16}$.

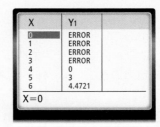

X	Y1
0	ERROR
1	ERROR
2	ERROR
3	ERROR
4	0
5	3
6	4.4721

X=0

Part A Explain why some entries show ERROR.

Part B Using the information in the table, what can you conclude about the vertices of the equation $y^2 - x^2 + 16 = 0$?

Part C Write the equation $y^2 - x^2 + 16 = 0$ in standard form to prove you correctly found the vertices from the table.

? TOPIC ESSENTIAL QUESTION

1. How do the geometric properties of conic sections relate to their algebraic representations?

Vocabulary Review

Choose the correct term to complete each sentence.

2. The foci and the vertices of a hyperbola lie along the _____.

3. The _____ of the ellipse is the midpoint of the major axis.

4. A(n) _____ is the set of points P in a plane such that the sum of the distances from $P(x, y)$ to two fixed points F_1 and F_2 is a constant.

5. A(n) _____ is a curve formed by the intersection of a plane and a double right cone.

6. A(n) _____ is the set of all points in a plane equidistant from a given point called the focus and a given line called the directrix.

- center
- conic section
- ellipse
- hyperbola
- parabola
- transverse axis

Concepts & Skills Review

LESSON 9-1   **Parabolas**

Quick Review

Vertical Parabola
$$y = \pm\tfrac{1}{4c}x^2$$

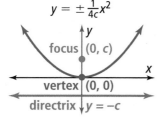

Horizontal Parabola
$$x = \pm\tfrac{1}{4c}y^2$$

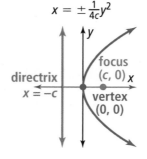

Example

Find the equation of a parabola with vertex (0, 0) and directrix $y = 3$.

Since the vertex is at the origin and the directrix is at $y = 3$, the focus is at $(0, -3)$. Therefore $c = -3$, and the parabola opens down.

The parabola has a vertical axis of symmetry, so use the equation $y = \tfrac{1}{4c}x^2$, where $c = -3$.

$$y = \tfrac{1}{4c}x^2 = \tfrac{1}{4(-3)}x^2 = -\tfrac{1}{12}x^2$$

Practice & Problem Solving

Write an equation of the parabola given the focus and directrix.

7. focus (0, 1) and directrix $y = -1$

8. focus (−4, 0) and directrix $x = 4$

9. What is the equation of the parabola?

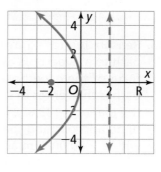

10. **Look for Relationships** How can you tell the direction a parabola opens when the focus and directrix are given? **© MP.7**

11. **Make Sense and Persevere** A flashlight reflector has a cross section of a parabola. The bulb is at the focus and is 0.75 in. from the vertex of the reflector. Write an equation of a parabola that models this cross section. **© MP.1**

LESSON 9-2 — Circles

Quick Review

A circle is a set of points equidistant from a center point. Standard form of an equation of a circle is

$(x - h)^2 + (y - k)^2 = r^2$.

radius
r

center
(h, k)

Example

Find an equation of a circle with center (−1, 2) and radius 3.

$h = -1$, $k = 2$, $r = 3$ ·········· Identify h, k, and r.

$(x - (-1))^2 + (y - 2)^2 = 3^2$ ····· Substitute.

$(x + 1)^2 + (y - 2)^2 = 9$ ·········· Simplify.

Practice & Problem Solving

Find an equation of each circle described. Sketch the graph.

12. center (2, −4) and radius 3

13. center (−4, 1) and radius 2.5

14. **Reason** The equation of a circle is $(x - 3)^2 + (y + 7)^2 = 23$. What is the length of the diameter of the circle? Ⓒ **MP.2**

15. **Make Sense and Persevere** A cross section of a tennis ball is graphed on a coordinate plane where the endpoints of a diameter are (1, 1.5) and (3, 3.3). What equation describes the cross section of the tennis ball? Ⓒ **MP.1**

LESSONS 9-3 & 9-4 — Ellipses and Hyperbolas

Quick Review

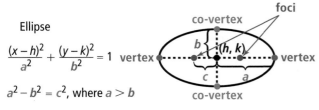

Ellipse

$\dfrac{(x - h)^2}{a^2} + \dfrac{(y - k)^2}{b^2} = 1$

$a^2 - b^2 = c^2$, where $a > b$

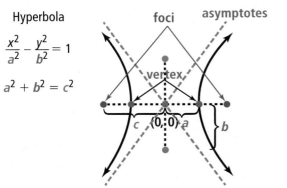

Hyperbola

$\dfrac{x^2}{a^2} - \dfrac{y^2}{b^2} = 1$

$a^2 + b^2 = c^2$

Example

What is the equation of an ellipse with foci at (−6, 0) and (6, 0) that passes through the points (0, −8) and (0, 8)?

The foci are each 6 units from the center so $c = 6$ and the center is the origin. The points (0, −8) and (0, 8) are the co-vertices and $b = 8$.

The equation is $\dfrac{x^2}{100} + \dfrac{y^2}{64} = 1$.

Practice & Problem Solving

16. What is the equation of an ellipse with foci at (−8, 0) and (8, 0) and that passes through the points (0, −3) and (0, 3)?

17. What is the equation of a hyperbola with vertices (0, −3) and (0, 3) and asymptotes $y = \pm \dfrac{1}{8}x$?

Determine the type of conic section represented by each equation.

18. $x^2 - 2y^2 - 2x - 8y - 11 = 0$

19. $3x^2 + 5y^2 - 18x + 40y - 28 = 0$

20. $y^2 - 2x + 12y + 6 = 0$

21. $-2x^2 - 2y^2 + 16y - 22 = 0$

22. **Model With Mathematics** An ice skating rink is an elliptical shape that is 80 ft on its longest axis. The foci are 60 ft apart. The entrances are located at the co-vertices. Find the equation of the ellipse representing the shape of the rink. How far are the entrances, to the nearest tenth foot, from the center of the rink? Ⓒ **MP.4**

TOPIC 10

Matrices

? TOPIC ESSENTIAL QUESTION

How can you use matrices to help you solve problems?

Topic Overview

Topic Vocabulary

- component form
- constant matrix
- determinant of a 2×2 matrix
- direction
- equal matrices
- identity matrix
- initial point
- inverse matrix
- magnitude
- scalar
- scalar multiplication
- square matrix
- terminal point
- variable matrix
- vector
- zero matrix

Digital Experience

 INTERACTIVE STUDENT EDITION
Access online or offline.

 ACTIVITIES Complete *Explore & Reason, Model & Discuss*, and *Critique & Explain* activities. Interact with Examples and Try Its.

 ANIMATION View and interact with real-world applications.

 PRACTICE Practice what you've learned.

 Go online | SavvasRealize.com

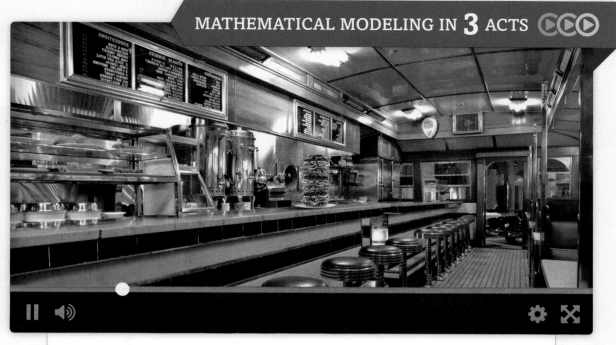

⊙ The Big Burger

For many people, hamburgers are a hallmark of American food. Nearly every restaurant, from fast food chains, to diners, to fine dining establishments, offers some kind of hamburger on their menu. Some restaurants offer various types of burgers: beef, turkey, and veggie burgers are all quite popular. You can also often choose extras to add to your burger: double patties of beef, cheese, pickles, onions, lettuce, tomatoes . . . The options are endless! Think about this during the Mathematical Modeling in 3 Acts lesson.

VIDEOS Watch clips to support Mathematical Modeling in 3 Acts Lessons and **enVision™** STEM Projects.

CONCEPT SUMMARY Review key lesson content through multiple representations.

ASSESSMENT Show what you've learned.

GLOSSARY Read and listen to English and Spanish definitions.

TUTORIALS Get help from *Virtual Nerd*, right when you need it.

MATH TOOLS Explore math with digital tools and manipulatives.

Did You Know?

A **Markov chain** is a mathematical system that explores the probabilities of changing from one state to another. A diagram can be used to represent a Markov chain, such as **weather conditions**.

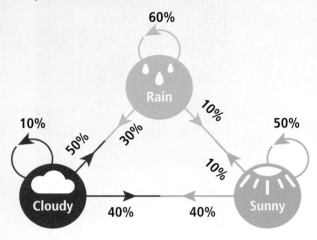

Markov chains and probability matrices are used in many fields, including **weather analysis, the outcomes of sporting events,** and **predictive texting.**

A **large matrix** can represent all the connections between roads in a city. Powers of this matrix can be used to **estimate traffic patterns,** including the effects of closing or expanding a road.

▶ Your Task: Analyzing Traffic With Markov Chains

You and your classmates will create a matrix to represent a map, then test the effects of road closures or expansion.

Activity Assess

10-1

Operations With Matrices

SavvasRealize.com

I CAN... interpret the parts of a matrix and use matrices for addition, subtraction, and scalar multiplication.

VOCABULARY

- equal matrices
- scalar
- scalar multiplication
- zero matrix

👆 MODEL & DISCUSS

This screen shows the number of Small, Medium, Large, and Extra Large limited-edition silkscreen shirts on sale at an online boutique.

| CATEGORIES ⌄ | SEARCH | 🔍 | Cart (0) |

Online Shopping Club
Exclusive Edition T-Shirts on Sale!

Size	S	M	L	XL
In Stock	23	53	21	32

Size	S	M	L	XL
In Stock	11	45	25	28

A. Construct a table to summarize the inventory that is on sale.

B. At the end of the day, the boutique has sold this many of each T-shirt from the sale items: red: 4 S, 6 M, 3 L, 5 XL; blue: 2 S, 8 M, 4 L, 0 XL. Make two new tables, one showing the merchandise sold and one showing the inventory that is left.

C. Look for Relationships What relationships did you use in creating the two tables in Part B? Ⓒ **MP.7**

❓ ESSENTIAL QUESTION

How can you interpret matrices and operate with matrices?

👆 EXAMPLE 1 — Represent Data With a Matrix

A. What could the data values in the matrix represent?

$$\begin{bmatrix} 5 & 3 & 0 \\ 2 & 1 & 4 \end{bmatrix}$$

Matrices help organize information. For example, if the columns of this matrix represent sizes (Small, Medium, Large) and the rows represent clothing items (Shirts, Sweaters), then "4" can represent 4 large sweaters.

	S	M	L
Shirts	5	3	0
Sweaters	2	1	4

COMMUNICATE PRECISELY
Recall that the dimensions of a matrix are given in the form of row × column. What are the dimensions of this matrix? Ⓒ **MP.6**

B. How can you refer to an entire matrix or to the elements of the matrix?

$$A = \begin{bmatrix} 7 & 5 \\ -2 & 0 \\ 4 & 8 \end{bmatrix}$$

A capital letter is used to refer to the entire matrix. This matrix is referred to as Matrix A, or just A.

A specific element can be referred to using subscripts to indicate the row and column where the element is located. In general, a_{ij} indicates the element in row i and column j.

	j	k
g	a_{gj}	a_{gk}
h	a_{hj}	a_{hk}
i	a_{ij}	a_{ik}

The subscript lists the row number, then the column number. In this matrix, a_{32} refers to the element in row 3, column 2, which is the number 8.

CONTINUED ON THE NEXT PAGE

EXAMPLE 1 CONTINUED

C. What are the values of the variables in the matrix equation?

$$\begin{bmatrix} 12 & 0 \\ 2x & 10 \end{bmatrix} = \begin{bmatrix} 12 & y \\ 14 & 10 \end{bmatrix}$$

Equal matrices have the same dimensions, and corresponding elements are equal.

a_{11}, 12 = 12. $\qquad\qquad$ a_{12}, 0 = y, so y = 0.

a_{21}, 2x = 14, so x = 7. $\qquad$ a_{22}, 10 = 10.

The matrices are equal for y = 0 and x = 7.

 Try It! **1.** In matrix C, the entries are the numbers of students on a committee. Column 1 lists girls, column 2 lists boys, row 1 lists sophomores, and row 2 lists juniors. Find a_{12}, a_{21}, and a_{22}, and tell what each number represents.

$$C = \begin{bmatrix} 7 & 5 \\ 8 & 10 \end{bmatrix}$$

APPLICATION  **EXAMPLE 2** **Apply Scalar Multiplication**

Cool Threads, a clothing store, uses a matrix C to represent the prices of women's clothes.

$$C = \begin{bmatrix} 320 & 210 & 160 \\ 240 & 110 & 65 \end{bmatrix}$$

The columns represent the brands Vintage, Casual, and Distressed, and the rows represent jeans and jackets. If the sales tax rate is 5%, how can you use a matrix operation to find the amount of sales tax on each item?

Formulate ◄ If the sales tax rate is 5%, you can multiply each element in the matrix by 0.05 to get S, the matrix of sales tax amounts.

Scalar multiplication is the multiplication of each element in a matrix by a single real number, called a **scalar**.

$S = 0.05 \cdot C$

Compute ◄
$$= 0.05 \cdot \begin{bmatrix} 320 & 210 & 160 \\ 240 & 110 & 65 \end{bmatrix}$$

> Scalar multiplication does not change the dimensions or the headings of the rows and columns of the original matrix.

$$= \begin{bmatrix} (320)(0.05) & (210)(0.05) & (160)(0.05) \\ (240)(0.05) & (110)(0.05) & (65)(0.05) \end{bmatrix} = \begin{bmatrix} 16 & 10.50 & 8 \\ 12 & 5.50 & 3.25 \end{bmatrix}$$

Interpret ◄ This scalar product represents the sales tax amounts for each item of clothing.

 Try It! **2.** In this matrix C, the rows represent prices for shirts and khakis. The columns have the same meaning as in Example 2. If the sales tax rate is 6%, use scalar multiplication to find the sales tax for each item.

$$C = \begin{bmatrix} 75 & 40 & 25 \\ 100 & 60 & 30 \end{bmatrix}$$

APPLICATION

 EXAMPLE 3   Add and Subtract Matrices

Cool Threads uses matrices to keep track of monthly sales. In matrices A and B, Row 1 represents the sale of jeans and Row 2 represents the sale of jackets, with the columns representing Vintage, Casual, and Distressed brands, respectively, during two consecutive months.

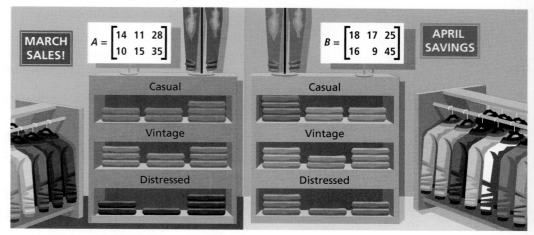

MARCH SALES! $A = \begin{bmatrix} 14 & 11 & 28 \\ 10 & 15 & 35 \end{bmatrix}$ $B = \begin{bmatrix} 18 & 17 & 25 \\ 16 & 9 & 45 \end{bmatrix}$ APRIL SAVINGS

Casual   Casual
Vintage   Vintage
Distressed   Distressed

A. What is the sales total for the two months?

The sum $A + B$ represents the totals sold during the two months. Add corresponding elements of the two matrices.

> The entry "25" means that 25 pairs of distressed jeans were sold in the second month.

$$A + B = \begin{bmatrix} 14 & 11 & 28 \\ 10 & 15 & 35 \end{bmatrix} + \begin{bmatrix} 18 & 17 & 25 \\ 16 & 9 & 45 \end{bmatrix} = \begin{bmatrix} 14 + 18 & 11 + 17 & 28 + 25 \\ 10 + 16 & 15 + 9 & 35 + 45 \end{bmatrix}$$

$$= \begin{bmatrix} 32 & 28 & 53 \\ 26 & 24 & 80 \end{bmatrix}$$

> The entry "26" means that in these two months, 26 Vintage jackets were sold.

B. What is the difference in the number of items sold each month?

The difference $A - B$ represents the differences in the monthly sales. Subtract corresponding elements of the two matrices.

$$A - B = \begin{bmatrix} 14 & 11 & 28 \\ 10 & 15 & 35 \end{bmatrix} - \begin{bmatrix} 18 & 17 & 25 \\ 16 & 9 & 45 \end{bmatrix} = \begin{bmatrix} 14 - 18 & 11 - 17 & 28 - 25 \\ 10 - 16 & 15 - 9 & 35 - 45 \end{bmatrix}$$

$$= \begin{bmatrix} -4 & -6 & 3 \\ -6 & 6 & -10 \end{bmatrix}$$

In the matrix $A - B$, a positive number means more of this type were sold in the first month. A negative number means that more were sold in the second month.

Try It!   **3.** Consider matrices M and N.

$$M = \begin{bmatrix} -3 & 5 \\ 2 & 0 \end{bmatrix}, N = \begin{bmatrix} 6 & 5 \\ -8 & 0.2 \end{bmatrix}$$

a. What are matrices $M + N$ and $N + M$?

b. What are matrices $M - N$ and $N - M$?

CONCEPTUAL
UNDERSTANDING

 EXAMPLE 4 **Understand Matrix Addition and Subtraction**

Consider the matrices below. How can you add and subtract these matrices?

$$A = \begin{bmatrix} 5 & -7 & 3 \\ 4 & 8 & -2 \end{bmatrix}, B = \begin{bmatrix} 6 & 5 \\ -2 & 0 \\ 3 & -4 \end{bmatrix}, C = \begin{bmatrix} 12 & 0 & 0 \\ 0 & 15 & -9 \end{bmatrix}, D = \begin{bmatrix} -5 & 7 & -3 \\ -4 & -8 & 2 \end{bmatrix}$$

A. Which matrices can be combined using addition or subtraction?

Adding (or subtracting) matrices involves adding (or subtracting) corresponding pairs of elements. To have corresponding pairs of elements, the matrices must have the same dimensions.

The matrices A, C, and D are 2×3 matrices, so they can be added or subtracted in any order, but matrix B is a 3×2 matrix so it cannot be combined with A, C, or D using addition or subtraction.

> **COMMON ERROR**
> The dimensions of a matrix, $r \times c$, always give the number of rows first and number of columns second.

B. How can you interpret a matrix of zeros?

$$A + D = \begin{bmatrix} 5 & -7 & 3 \\ 4 & 8 & -2 \end{bmatrix} + \begin{bmatrix} -5 & 7 & -3 \\ -4 & -8 & 2 \end{bmatrix} = \begin{bmatrix} 0 & 0 & 0 \\ 0 & 0 & 0 \end{bmatrix}$$

Every element in $A + D$ is zero. A matrix with all zeros is a **zero matrix.** When the sum of two matrices is a zero matrix, the matrices are additive inverses.

> This is the zero 2×3 matrix. A zero 3×2 matrix would also have all zeros, but it would have 3 rows and 2 columns.

C. What is the additive inverse of matrix B?

Solve the equation $B + X = 0$, so that X is the additive inverse of B.

$$\begin{bmatrix} 6 & 5 \\ -2 & 0 \\ 3 & 4 \end{bmatrix} + \begin{bmatrix} -6 & -5 \\ 2 & 0 \\ -3 & -4 \end{bmatrix} = \begin{bmatrix} 0 & 0 \\ 0 & 0 \\ 0 & 0 \end{bmatrix}$$

> Think about what elements of Matrix X will make every element of the sum matrix equal to 0.

$$X = \begin{bmatrix} -6 & -5 \\ 2 & 0 \\ -3 & -4 \end{bmatrix}$$

> The additive inverse of a matrix is the scalar multiple of –1 times the matrix.

D. How does $A + C$ relate to $C + A$?

$$A + C = \begin{bmatrix} 5 & -7 & 3 \\ 4 & 8 & -2 \end{bmatrix} + \begin{bmatrix} 12 & 0 & 0 \\ 0 & 15 & -9 \end{bmatrix} = \begin{bmatrix} 17 & -7 & 3 \\ 4 & 23 & -11 \end{bmatrix}$$

$$C + A = \begin{bmatrix} 12 & 0 & 0 \\ 0 & 15 & -9 \end{bmatrix} + \begin{bmatrix} 5 & -7 & 3 \\ 4 & 8 & -2 \end{bmatrix} = \begin{bmatrix} 17 & -7 & 3 \\ 4 & 23 & -11 \end{bmatrix}$$

In this example, $A + C = C + A$. Matrix addition is real number addition of corresponding elements. Because real number addition is commutative, a Commutative Property of Addition holds for matrices.

Try It! **4.** Consider the matrices below.

$$P = \begin{bmatrix} 5 & 2 & -3 \\ 7 & 0 & -5 \end{bmatrix}, Q = \begin{bmatrix} 2 & -2 \\ 5 & -5 \\ -7 & 7 \end{bmatrix}, R = \begin{bmatrix} 6 & 0.5 \\ -3 & 0 \\ -2 & -2 \end{bmatrix}$$

a. Find $R - Q$. What other matrix sums or differences can be calculated?

b. Find the additive inverses of P, Q, and R.

EXAMPLE 5   Use Matrices to Translate and Dilate Figures

In this diagram $\overline{AB}$ is translated 4 units right and 2 units up to $\overline{PQ}$. Also, $\overline{XY}$ is a dilation of $\overline{AB}$ by a factor of $\frac{1}{2}$, centered at the origin.

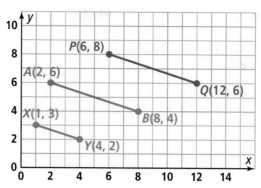

How can you use matrices to show a translation and a dilation?

GENERALIZE

The coordinates of the vertices of an n-sided polygon can be represented as a 2 × n matrix, with 2 rows and n columns. ⓒ **MP.8**

A. Show the translation of $\overline{AB}$ to $\overline{PQ}$ using matrices.

A matrix with one column can represent an ordered pair. A matrix with two columns can represent two ordered pairs, where the first row gives the x-coordinates and the second row gives the y-coordinates.

Point A: $\begin{bmatrix} 2 \\ 6 \end{bmatrix}$ endpoints of $\overline{AB}$: $\begin{bmatrix} 2 & 8 \\ 6 & 4 \end{bmatrix}$

A translation can be represented as a matrix. The matrix for $\overline{AB}$ has two columns, so a matrix for a translation of $\overline{AB}$ also has two columns.

Since the translation results in the x-coordinates increasing by 4 and the y-coordinates increasing by 2, add the matrix $\begin{bmatrix} 4 & 4 \\ 2 & 2 \end{bmatrix}$ to the matrix representing $\overline{AB}$.

To show the translation of $\overline{AB}$, use matrix addition:

$$\underset{\text{preimage}}{\begin{bmatrix} 2 & 8 \\ 6 & 4 \end{bmatrix}} + \underset{\text{translation}}{\begin{bmatrix} 4 & 4 \\ 2 & 2 \end{bmatrix}} = \underset{\text{image}}{\begin{bmatrix} 6 & 12 \\ 8 & 6 \end{bmatrix}}$$

The sum represents the endpoints $P(6, 8)$ and $Q(12, 6)$.

B. Show the dilation of $\overline{AB}$ by a scale factor of $\frac{1}{2}$.

Use scalar multiplication:

$$\underset{\text{scalar}}{\frac{1}{2}} \cdot \underset{\text{preimage}}{\begin{bmatrix} 2 & 8 \\ 6 & 4 \end{bmatrix}} = \underset{\text{image}}{\begin{bmatrix} 1 & 4 \\ 3 & 2 \end{bmatrix}}$$

This method can be used only for a dilation centered at the origin.

☑ **Try It!**   **5.** A segment has endpoints $M(8, -7)$ and $N(1, 2)$.

a. Use matrices to represent a translation of $\overline{MN}$ to $\overline{RS}$ by 6 units left and 3 units down. What are the coordinates of R and S?

b. Use matrices to represent a dilation of $\overline{MN}$ to $\overline{DE}$ by a scale factor of 3, centered at the origin. What are the coordinates of D and E?

CONCEPT SUMMARY Operating With and Interpreting Matrices

DIMENSIONS The dimensions of a matrix are stated as the number of rows (r) by the number of columns (c).

$$A = \begin{bmatrix} t & u & v \\ x & y & z \end{bmatrix}$$

The dimensions of this matrix are 2×3, because it has 2 rows and 3 columns. $a_{13} = v$, because v is in the 1st row and 3rd column.

OPERATIONS To multiply a matrix by a scalar, multiply each element in the matrix by the scalar.

$$k \cdot \begin{bmatrix} w & x \\ y & z \end{bmatrix} = \begin{bmatrix} kw & kx \\ ky & kz \end{bmatrix}$$

To add matrices, add the corresponding elements.

$$\begin{bmatrix} a & b \\ c & d \end{bmatrix} + \begin{bmatrix} e & f \\ g & h \end{bmatrix} = \begin{bmatrix} a+e & b+f \\ c+g & d+h \end{bmatrix}$$

To subtract matrices, subtract the corresponding elements.

$$\begin{bmatrix} p & q \\ r & s \end{bmatrix} - \begin{bmatrix} w & x \\ y & z \end{bmatrix} = \begin{bmatrix} p-w & q-x \\ r-y & s-z \end{bmatrix}$$

DILATIONS A matrix can represent the transformation of a figure such as a dilation, centered at the origin, of a quadrilateral.

$$3\begin{bmatrix} 5 & -3 & 0 & -8 \\ 6 & 5 & -2 & 7 \end{bmatrix} = \begin{bmatrix} 15 & -9 & 0 & -24 \\ 18 & 15 & -6 & 21 \end{bmatrix}$$

Do You UNDERSTAND?

1. **ESSENTIAL QUESTION** How can you interpret matrices and operate with matrices?

2. **Error Analysis** Tonya says $\begin{bmatrix} 3 & 2 \\ -4 & 1 \end{bmatrix} - \begin{bmatrix} 3 & 2 \\ 4 & 1 \end{bmatrix}$ would produce a zero matrix. Explain her error. **ⓒ MP.3**

3. **Communicate Precisely** Explain how you know if two matrices can be added. Then explain how to add them. **ⓒ MP.6**

4. **Vocabulary** What are equal matrices? Give an example of equal matrices.

Do You KNOW HOW?

Identify the element for each matrix.

5. $\begin{bmatrix} 4 & 1 & 0 \\ 7 & 3 & 5 \end{bmatrix}$; a_{23}

6. $\begin{bmatrix} -6 \\ 2 \end{bmatrix}$; a_{11}

Given $A = \begin{bmatrix} 3 & -2 \\ 7 & 1 \end{bmatrix}$ and $B = \begin{bmatrix} 0 & 7 \\ -4 & 12 \end{bmatrix}$, calculate each of the following.

7. $A + B$

8. $B - A$

9. $4A$

10. $A - B$

11. The endpoints of $\overline{AB}$ are represented by the matrix $\begin{bmatrix} 3 & 7 \\ 1 & 5 \end{bmatrix}$.

Find the image of the segment after a dilation, centered at the origin, by a scale factor of 2.

UNDERSTAND

12. Communicate Precisely Explain how you would solve for each variable. Then find the value of each variable. $\begin{bmatrix} a & b-3 \\ c & d+5 \end{bmatrix} = \begin{bmatrix} 4 & -3 \\ 6 & 4 \end{bmatrix}$ Ⓒ MP.6

13. Make Sense and Persevere Find the sum of $A = \begin{bmatrix} 5 \\ 3 \\ 8 \end{bmatrix}$ and the additive inverse of $P = \begin{bmatrix} -2 \\ 1 \\ 7 \end{bmatrix}$ Ⓒ MP.1

14. Error Analysis Describe and correct the error a student made in translating the points $A(1, -3)$, $B(2, 1)$ and $C(-3, -2)$ 3 units left and 1 unit up. Ⓒ MP.3

Original points $\begin{pmatrix} 1 & 2 & -3 \\ -3 & 1 & -2 \end{pmatrix}$

Translation matrix $\begin{pmatrix} -3 & -3 & -3 \\ -1 & -1 & -1 \end{pmatrix}$

Answer matrix $\begin{pmatrix} -2 & -1 & -6 \\ -4 & 0 & -3 \end{pmatrix}$ ✗

15. Construct Arguments Suppose A and B are two matrices with the same dimensions. Explain how to find $A + B$, $A - B$, and matrix C such that $A + C$ is the zero matrix. Ⓒ MP.3

16. Higher Order Thinking Explain why $A = \begin{bmatrix} 0.5 \\ 4 \end{bmatrix}$ and $B = \begin{bmatrix} \frac{1}{2} \\ 1+3 \end{bmatrix}$ have the same additive inverse.

17. Mathematical Connections For the set of real numbers, if the sum of two numbers is the additive identity element, then the two numbers are additive inverses of each other. How does this property relate to matrix addition?

18. Reason The coordinates of the vertices of a square are represented in a matrix. The matrix is then multiplied by the scalar 3. How does the area of the new square compare to the area of the original square? Ⓒ MP.2

PRACTICE

19. In matrix D, the entries are the number of students playing volleyball at a high school. Column 1 lists boys, column 2 lists girls, row 1 lists juniors, and row 2 lists seniors. Find d_{22}, d_{12}, and d_{11}, and tell what each number represents. $D = \begin{bmatrix} 4 & 5 \\ 7 & 6 \end{bmatrix}$ SEE EXAMPLE 1

20. In the price matrix P, the rows represent prices for sweatshirts and sweatpants. The columns represent the color scheme of the items: white, red, and tie-dye. If the sales tax rate is 7%, find the sales tax of each item. $P = \begin{bmatrix} 30 & 40 & 50 \\ 25 & 35 & 55 \end{bmatrix}$ SEE EXAMPLE 2

Given matrices $X = \begin{bmatrix} 7 & 2 & 1 \\ 4 & -3 & 6 \end{bmatrix}$, $Y = \begin{bmatrix} -2 & 4 \\ 3 & 8 \end{bmatrix}$, and $Z = \begin{bmatrix} 0 & 3 & 7 \\ 1 & -2 & 6 \end{bmatrix}$, calculate each of the following. If not possible, state so. SEE EXAMPLE 3

21. $X + Y$

22. $Z - X$

23. $X + Z$

24. $X - Z$

Find the additive inverse of each matrix.
SEE EXAMPLE 4

25. $Q = \begin{bmatrix} 3 \\ 2 \end{bmatrix}$

26. $R = \begin{bmatrix} 2 & 0 \\ 6 & -5 \\ -4 & 11 \end{bmatrix}$

27. $S = \begin{bmatrix} 4 & -7 & -8 & 9 \end{bmatrix}$

28. $T = \begin{bmatrix} 9 & -1 \\ 4 & 10 \\ 3 & -7 \end{bmatrix}$

A segment has endpoints $E(5, -1)$ and $F(6, 11)$.
SEE EXAMPLE 5

29. Use matrices to represent a translation of $\overline{EF}$ to $\overline{YZ}$ by 5 units right and 1 unit down. What are the coordinates of Y and Z?

30. Use matrices to represent a dilation of $\overline{EF}$ to $\overline{UV}$ by a scale factor of 4, centered at the origin. What are the coordinates of U and V?

APPLY

31. Model With Mathematics Using a 10×10 grid, create a battleship game board with 5 ships placed. Write a matrix B for your battleship board. Use a 1 for a space a ship is placed and a 0 for a space no ship exists. © **MP.4**

32. Model With Mathematics The table shows some of the men's running records in seconds.

Distance (meters)	World record	American record	Olympic record
100	9.58	9.69	9.63
200	19.19	19.32	19.30
400	43.03	43.18	43.03
1,500	206	209.3	212.07

a. Write a matrix that represents the difference between the Olympic and World records for each race distance expressed as a column matrix.

b. If all of the records in the table are expressed in seconds and are represented by a matrix B, what matrix expression could be used to convert all data to minutes? © **MP.4**

33. Use Structure A matrix can be used to represent which towns are connected by a single road to each other on a map. Use a 1 to represent two towns connected to each other and a 0 to represent two towns not connected to each other. Use a 0 to show that the indicated row and column both represent the same town. Create a matrix C to represent this situation. © **MP.7**

34. Use these matrices to complete the statements.

$$A = \begin{bmatrix} 0 & 9 & 6 \\ 1 & 2 & 4 \\ 7 & -3 & 1 \end{bmatrix} \qquad B = \begin{bmatrix} 2 & -7 & -2 \\ 0 & 5 & 8 \\ -3 & 1 & 1 \end{bmatrix}$$

In matrix A, the value of a_{31} is _____ the value of a_{12}. In matrix B, the value of b_{31} is _____ the value of b_{12}.

Ⓐ less than; less than

Ⓑ less than; greater than

Ⓒ greater than; less than

Ⓓ greater than; greater than

35. SAT/ACT If $5\begin{bmatrix} a \\ b \end{bmatrix} = 14\begin{bmatrix} 20 \\ 12 \end{bmatrix}$, then what is the value of $a + b$?

Ⓐ 29   Ⓑ $\frac{148}{5}$ Ⓒ $\frac{448}{5}$ Ⓓ $\frac{191}{4}$ Ⓔ $\frac{41}{5}$

36. Performance Task A computer animator uses a screen that is 1,000 pixels wide and 800 pixels tall. The animator uses matrix columns to represent three locator points on an avatar. The top row represents the horizontal coordinate of each point, and the bottom row represents the vertical coordinate. Let $P = \begin{bmatrix} 100 & 150 & 200 \\ 50 & 150 & 50 \end{bmatrix}$ represent the initial position of the avatar.

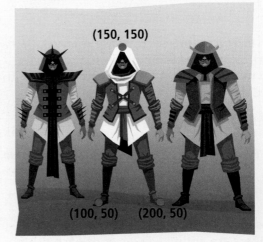

(150, 150)

(100, 50)   (200, 50)

Part A The animator wants the avatar to move up at a rate of 100 pixels per second. Use addition of matrices to show the position of the avatar after 2 seconds and after 5 seconds.

Part B The animator wants the avatar to move right at a rate of 50 pixels per second. Use addition of matrices to show the position of the avatar after 3 seconds and after 8 seconds.

Part C How could the animator use scalar multiplication and matrix addition to show how the avatar moves across the screen?

10-2

Matrix Multiplication

© Common Core State Standards HSN.VM.C.8 (+), HSN.VM.C.9 (+), HSN.VM.C.10 (+), MP.2, MP.3, MP.7

Activity   Assess

📶 SavvasRealize.com

I CAN... find the product of matrices or explain why the product does not exist.

VOCABULARY
• identity matrix
• square matrix

👆 **EXPLORE & REASON**

Two stores, Quick Repair and TechRite, buy and sell pre-owned phones, tablets, and computers. The matrices below represent their average revenue *R*, purchase costs *C*, and repair expenses *E* for each item:

R			
Quick Repair	$150	$100	$400
TechRite	$200	$250	$500

C			
Quick Repair	$100	$50	$200
TechRite	$125	$75	$300

E			
Quick Repair	$25	$20	$50
TechRite	$10	$50	$50

A. Would it make sense to find the sum and/or difference of any two of the three matrices? Explain.

B. Make Sense and Persevere Quick Repair and TechRite both need to estimate their total purchase and repair costs. They each predict that they will need to purchase 100 phones, 100 tablets, and 100 computers, and that they will need to repair 50% of them. Explain what you would do to find the total costs. **© MP.1**

❓ **ESSENTIAL QUESTION**   What does it mean to multiply a matrix by another matrix?

CONCEPTUAL UNDERSTANDING

👆 **EXAMPLE 1**   Understand Matrix Multiplication

A teacher assigns final grades based on a weighted system. Students are graded on unit assessments, a semester project, and the final exam, each with a different weight. The matrices given below represent the weights for each kind of work and the grades for two students Oscar and Reagan.

Weighting

$$W = \begin{array}{ccc} \text{unit} & \text{project} & \text{final} \\ [0.50 & 0.30 & 0.20] \end{array}$$

Grades

$$G = \begin{array}{c} \\ \text{unit} \\ \text{project} \\ \text{final} \end{array} \begin{array}{c} \text{O} \quad\ \text{R} \\ \begin{bmatrix} 90 & 80 \\ 95 & 70 \\ 75 & 85 \end{bmatrix} \end{array}$$

What are the final grades for each student?

The final grade is the sum of the weighted averages.

Final grade = 0.5(unit grade) + 0.3(project grade) + 0.2(final exam grade)

This equation shows that computing the final grade for each student is like multiplying the elements of row 1 of *W* (weights) by the corresponding elements of each student's column and finding the sum of the products. This method is similar to multiplying two matrices.

COMMUNICATE PRECISELY
Grades that are weighted aren't simply averaged but, instead, are multiplied by their weight, then added. **© MP.6**

CONTINUED ON THE NEXT PAGE

EXAMPLE 1 CONTINUED

To find each student's final grade, multiply the elements of the 1×3 matrix with the elements of the 3×1 matrix, then add.

Oscar's Final Grade

Weight Matrix • Grade Matrix

$$= [0.50 \ 0.30 \ 0.20] \begin{bmatrix} 90 \\ 95 \\ 75 \end{bmatrix}$$

$$= 0.50(90) + 0.30(95) + 0.20(75)$$

$$= 88.5$$

Reagan's Final Grade

Weight Matrix • Grade Matrix

$$= [0.50 \ 0.30 \ 0.20] \begin{bmatrix} 80 \\ 70 \\ 85 \end{bmatrix}$$

$$= 0.50(80) + 0.30(70) + 0.20(85)$$

$$= 78$$

So, Oscar's final grade is 88.5, and Reagan's final grade is 78.

> **COMMON ERROR**
> Scalar multiplication is often confused with matrix multiplication. Remember that matrix multiplication considers the product of two matrices while scalar multiplication considers the product of a matrix and a number.

These can be represented in a matrix F. Each element in matrix F is the sum of the products of the corresponding row elements in W, multiplied by the corresponding column elements in G.

$$F = WG = [0.50 \ \ 0.30 \ \ 0.20] \begin{bmatrix} 90 & 80 \\ 95 & 70 \\ 75 & 85 \end{bmatrix} = [88.5 \ \ 78]$$

Since you are multiplying elements of the rows of W by elements of the columns of G, it is important that the number of elements in each row of W is equal to the number of elements in each column of G.

In general, the product matrix QR has the same number of rows, r_Q, as Q, and the same number of columns, c_R, as R.

$$\begin{array}{ccccc} Q & \bullet & R & = & QR \\ r_Q \times c_Q & & r_R \times c_R & & r_Q \times c_R \end{array}$$

If the number of columns in the first matrix does not match the number of rows in the second matrix ($c_Q \neq r_R$) then the product matrix does not exist.

Since 88.5 results from row 1 of W by the element in column 1 of G, it is element a_{11} of F. Similarly, 78 results from multiplying the element in multiplying the element in row 1 of W by the element in column 2 of G, so it is element a_{12} of F. Then F will be a 1×2 matrix.

The matrix that shows the final average for each student is $F = \begin{matrix} Q & R \\ [88.5 & 78] \end{matrix}$.

 Try It!   **1.** How could you organize the weighting and grade information differently so that Oscar's and Reagan's final grades are given by GW?

 EXAMPLE 2 **Examine Multiplication of Square Matrices**

Below are square matrices A and B. Determine if the given equations are true for A and B. What conclusions can we make about the Commutative and Distributive Properties for multiplying square matrices?

$$A = \begin{bmatrix} -2 & 1 \\ -1 & 0 \end{bmatrix} \qquad B = \begin{bmatrix} -1 & -5 \\ 0 & 4 \end{bmatrix}$$

> The element $AB_{12} = 14$ is found by multiplying the elements in the first row of A by the elements of the second column of B.

A. Is $AB = BA$?

Find the product on each side of the equation.

$$AB = \begin{bmatrix} -2 & 1 \\ -1 & 0 \end{bmatrix} \begin{bmatrix} -1 & -5 \\ 0 & 4 \end{bmatrix} = \begin{bmatrix} -2(-1) + 1(0) & -2(-5) + 1(4) \\ -1(-1) + 0(0) & -1(-5) + 0(4) \end{bmatrix} = \begin{bmatrix} 2 & 14 \\ 1 & 5 \end{bmatrix}$$

$$BA = \begin{bmatrix} -1 & -5 \\ 0 & 4 \end{bmatrix} \begin{bmatrix} -2 & 1 \\ -1 & 0 \end{bmatrix} = \begin{bmatrix} -1(-2) + (-5)(-1) & -1(1) + (-5)(0) \\ 0(-2) + 4(-1) & 0(1) + 4(0) \end{bmatrix} = \begin{bmatrix} 7 & -1 \\ -4 & 0 \end{bmatrix}$$

$$\begin{bmatrix} 2 & 14 \\ 1 & 5 \end{bmatrix} \neq \begin{bmatrix} 7 & -1 \\ -4 & 0 \end{bmatrix}$$

CONSTRUCT ARGUMENTS
Explain why the Commutative Property does not hold for matrix multiplication. **© MP.3**

A **square matrix** is a matrix that has the same number of rows as columns. Since $AB \neq BA$ above, the Commutative Property does NOT hold for all square matrices.

B. Is $A(A + B) = AA + AB$?

What is the product on each side of the equation?

$$A(A + B) = \begin{bmatrix} -2 & 1 \\ -1 & 0 \end{bmatrix} \left(\begin{bmatrix} -2 & 1 \\ -1 & 0 \end{bmatrix} + \begin{bmatrix} -1 & -5 \\ 0 & 4 \end{bmatrix} \right) = \begin{bmatrix} -2 & 1 \\ -1 & 0 \end{bmatrix} \begin{bmatrix} -3 & -4 \\ -1 & 4 \end{bmatrix}$$

$$= \begin{bmatrix} -2(-3) + 1(-1) & -2(-4) + 1(4) \\ -1(-3) + 0(-1) & -1(-4) + 0(4) \end{bmatrix} = \begin{bmatrix} 5 & 12 \\ 3 & 4 \end{bmatrix}$$

> The product of two square matrices with the same dimensions will always exist, because the number of rows in the first equals the number of columns in the second.

$$AA + AB = \begin{bmatrix} -2 & 1 \\ -1 & 0 \end{bmatrix} \begin{bmatrix} -2 & 1 \\ -1 & 0 \end{bmatrix} + \begin{bmatrix} -2 & 1 \\ -1 & 0 \end{bmatrix} \begin{bmatrix} -1 & -5 \\ 0 & 4 \end{bmatrix}$$

$$= \begin{bmatrix} -2(-2) + 1(-1) & -2(1) + 1(0) \\ -1(-2) + 0(-1) & -1(1) + 0(0) \end{bmatrix} + \begin{bmatrix} -2(-1) + 1(0) & -2(-5) + 1(4) \\ -1(-1) + 0(0) & -1(-5) + 0(4) \end{bmatrix}$$

$$= \begin{bmatrix} 3 & -2 \\ 2 & -1 \end{bmatrix} + \begin{bmatrix} 2 & 14 \\ 1 & 5 \end{bmatrix} = \begin{bmatrix} 5 & 12 \\ 3 & 4 \end{bmatrix}$$

Since $A(A + B) = AA + AB$, the Distributive Property is true for this case.

> Proving the equation for a specific example is not sufficient to prove that the equation is true for all matrices.

Try It! **2.** Determine whether each equation may be true for the following matrices.

$$A = \begin{bmatrix} 3 & 0 \\ -1 & -2 \end{bmatrix}, B = \begin{bmatrix} -2 & 1 \\ 3 & -4 \end{bmatrix}, C = \begin{bmatrix} 6 & 2 \\ 4 & 8 \end{bmatrix}$$

a. $(AB)C = A(BC)$ **b.** $(A + B)C = AC + BC$

EXAMPLE 3   Understand Identity Matrices

What is the product of the 3-by-3 matrices $I = \begin{bmatrix} 1 & 0 & 0 \\ 0 & 1 & 0 \\ 0 & 0 & 1 \end{bmatrix}$ **and**

$A = \begin{bmatrix} 1 & -3 & 2 \\ -4 & 5 & -6 \\ 9 & -7 & 8 \end{bmatrix}$?

Multiply the matrices, and compare IA and AI.

$$IA = \begin{bmatrix} 1 & 0 & 0 \\ 0 & 1 & 0 \\ 0 & 0 & 1 \end{bmatrix} \begin{bmatrix} 1 & -3 & 2 \\ -4 & 5 & -6 \\ 9 & -7 & 8 \end{bmatrix}$$

$$IA = \begin{bmatrix} 1(1) + 0(-4) + 0(9) & 1(-3) + 0(5) + 0(-7) & 1(2) + 0(-6) + 0(8) \\ 0(1) + 1(-4) + 0(9) & 0(-3) + 1(5) + 0(-7) & 0(2) + 1(-6) + 0(8) \\ 0(1) + 0(-4) + 1(9) & 0(-3) + 0(5) + 1(-7) & 0(2) + 0(-6) + 1(8) \end{bmatrix}$$

$$IA = \begin{bmatrix} 1 & -3 & 2 \\ -4 & 5 & -6 \\ 9 & -7 & 8 \end{bmatrix}$$

> When you multiply 3×3 matrices, use the same process as with 2×2 matrices.

$$AI = \begin{bmatrix} 1 & -3 & 2 \\ -4 & 5 & -6 \\ 9 & -7 & 8 \end{bmatrix} \begin{bmatrix} 1 & 0 & 0 \\ 0 & 1 & 0 \\ 0 & 0 & 1 \end{bmatrix}$$

$$AI = \begin{bmatrix} 1(1) + (-4)(0) + 9(0) & -3(1) + 5(0) + (-7)(0) & 2(1) + (-6)(0) + 8(0) \\ 1(0) + (-4)(1) + 9(0) & -3(0) + 5(1) + (-7)(0) & 2(0) + (-6)(1) + 8(0) \\ 1(0) + (-4)(0) + 9(1) & -3(0) + 5(0) + (-7)(1) & 2(0) + (-6)(0) + 8(1) \end{bmatrix}$$

$$AI = \begin{bmatrix} 1 & -3 & 2 \\ -4 & 5 & -6 \\ 9 & -7 & 8 \end{bmatrix}$$

So the product matrices IA and AI are both equal to A.

STUDY TIP
When multiplying a matrix by 1, as in $1A = A$, you are using scalar multiplication. The identity for multiplication of matrices must be a matrix where $AI = A$ and $IA = A$.

$$A = AI = IA = \begin{bmatrix} 1 & -3 & 2 \\ -4 & 5 & -6 \\ 9 & -7 & 8 \end{bmatrix}$$

> Although the identity matrix commutes with any matrix, matrix multiplication is not commutative in general.

The matrix I is an **identity matrix,** because $M = MI = IM$ for every 3×3 matrix M. Identity matrices are always square matrices with a 1 as each element of the main diagonal and zeros for all other elements.

 Try It!   **3. a.** What is the product of $\begin{bmatrix} a & b \\ c & d \end{bmatrix} \begin{bmatrix} 1 & 0 \\ 0 & 1 \end{bmatrix}$?

b. What is the product of $\begin{bmatrix} a & b \\ c & d \end{bmatrix} \begin{bmatrix} -1 & 0 \\ 0 & -1 \end{bmatrix}$?

CONCEPT SUMMARY Products of Matrices

MATRIX MULTIPLICATION The product of two matrices is a new matrix. The elements of the new matrix are the sums of the products of the corresponding row and column elements.

$$\begin{bmatrix} a & b \\ c & d \end{bmatrix} \begin{bmatrix} w & x \\ y & z \end{bmatrix} = \begin{bmatrix} aw + by & ax + bz \\ cw + dy & cx + dz \end{bmatrix}$$

THE IDENTITY MATRIX For the $n \times n$ matrix A, the multiplicative identity matrix I is an $n \times n$ square matrix with 1s on the main diagonal and 0s for all other elements: $AI = IA = A$

$$\begin{bmatrix} a & b & c \\ d & e & f \\ g & h & j \end{bmatrix} \begin{bmatrix} 1 & 0 & 0 \\ 0 & 1 & 0 \\ 0 & 0 & 1 \end{bmatrix} = \begin{bmatrix} a & b & c \\ d & e & f \\ g & h & j \end{bmatrix}$$

Do You UNDERSTAND?

1. **ESSENTIAL QUESTION** What does it mean to multiply a matrix by another matrix?

2. **Use Structure** Would it be possible to multiply $A_{3 \times 5}$ and $B_{4 \times 5}$? Explain your reasoning. **MP.7**

3. **Vocabulary** Explain why a matrix with ones on the main diagonal and zeros for all the other elements is called the *identity matrix*.

4. **Construct Arguments** A student thought that the product of $A_{1 \times 5}$ and $B_{5 \times 1}$ should have five elements in the answer. Is the student correct? If not, how many elements will there be? **MP.3**

Do You KNOW HOW?

Let $A = \begin{bmatrix} 3 & 0 \\ -1 & -2 \end{bmatrix}$ and $B = \begin{bmatrix} -2 & 1 \\ 3 & -4 \end{bmatrix}$.

5. Find AB and BA to demonstrate that matrix multiplication is not commutative. Show your work.

Find each product.

6. $\begin{bmatrix} 4 & 7 \\ 1 & -2 \end{bmatrix} \begin{bmatrix} 1 & 0 \\ 0 & 1 \end{bmatrix}$

7. $\begin{bmatrix} 1 & 0 \\ 0 & 1 \end{bmatrix} \begin{bmatrix} 5 & 0 \\ 8 & 2 \end{bmatrix}$

8. The coordinates of the vertices of a triangle are $A(-2, 3)$, $B(1, 1)$, and $C(2, -1)$. The coordinate are multiplied by the matrix $\begin{bmatrix} 1 & 0 \\ 0 & -1 \end{bmatrix}$. Find the coordinates of the image of the triangle after the transformation.

PRACTICE & PROBLEM SOLVING

UNDERSTAND

9. **Generalize** Suppose square matrices A and B have dimensions $n \times n$, where n is a positive integer greater than or equal to 2. What are the dimensions of their product $A \times B$ © MP.8

10. **Use Structure** If you wanted to find a product of the two matrices shown below, explain why it is necessary to write them in this order. © MP.7

$$\begin{bmatrix} 10 & 15 & 12 \\ 7 & 11 & 20 \end{bmatrix} \begin{bmatrix} 50 \\ 14 \\ 38 \end{bmatrix}$$

11. **Error Analysis** Describe and correct the error a student made in mulitiplying matrix A by matrix B. © MP.3

$$\begin{matrix} A & B \\ \begin{pmatrix} 6 & 2 \\ -3 & 5 \end{pmatrix} & \begin{pmatrix} -1 & 0 \\ 4 & -2 \end{pmatrix} \end{matrix}$$

$$\begin{pmatrix} 6 & 2 \\ -3 & 5 \end{pmatrix} \begin{pmatrix} -1 & 0 \\ 4 & -2 \end{pmatrix} = \begin{pmatrix} -6 & 0 \\ -12 & -10 \end{pmatrix}$$

✗

12. **Higher Order Thinking** The triangle shown is transformed using two matrices, $A = \begin{bmatrix} 1 & 0 \\ 0 & -1 \end{bmatrix}$ and $B = \begin{bmatrix} 0 & 1 \\ -1 & 0 \end{bmatrix}$, in that order.

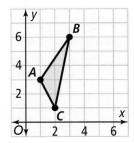

a. What transformation occurs as a result of multiplication by matrix A?

b. What transformation occurs as a result of multiplication by matrix B?

PRACTICE

13. A math teacher assigns final grades based on a weighted system. Matrix W represents the weights of each type of assignment, and matrix G represents the grades for two students, Jacob and Lucy. Use matrix multiplication to find matrix F that represents the final class grades for these two students. **SEE EXAMPLE 1**

$$W = \begin{matrix} \text{hw} & \text{tests} & \text{exam} \\ [0.20 & 0.50 & 0.30] \end{matrix}$$

$$G = \begin{matrix} & \text{Jacob} & \text{Lucy} \\ \text{hw} & \begin{bmatrix} 95 & 85 \\ \text{tests} & 80 & 90 \\ \text{exam} & 75 & 85 \end{bmatrix} \end{matrix}$$

Determine whether each equation is true for the following matrices. **SEE EXAMPLE 2**

$$A = \begin{bmatrix} 1 & 2 \\ 0 & -2 \end{bmatrix}, \ B = \begin{bmatrix} -4 & 0 \\ -1 & 8 \end{bmatrix}, \ C = \begin{bmatrix} 5 & 1 \\ 7 & -2 \end{bmatrix}$$

14. $(A + B)C = AC + BC$

15. $A(BC) = (AB)C$

16. Find IQ, if

$$I = \begin{bmatrix} 1 & 0 & 0 \\ 0 & 1 & 0 \\ 0 & 0 & 1 \end{bmatrix} \text{ and } Q = \begin{bmatrix} 1 & -3 & 2 \\ -4 & 5 & -6 \\ 9 & -7 & 8 \end{bmatrix}.$$

SEE EXAMPLE 3

17. Create matrix A to represent the coordinates of quadrilateral *EFGH*.

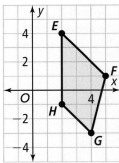

a. Multiply matrix A by $\begin{bmatrix} 0 & -1 \\ -1 & 0 \end{bmatrix}$

b. Graph the quadrilateral represented by the resulting matrix, and describe the movement of the quadrilateral in the coordinate plane.

APPLY

18. Reason The following matrix represents the inventory of the three snack bars at a state park.

	fish taco	veggie burger	burger	chicken teriyaki
Snack Bar A	20	15	7	11
Snack Bar B	22	18	6	8
Snack Bar C	15	19	10	5

MENU

Fish taco $10

Veggie burger $5

Burger $4

Chicken teriyaki ... $12

Use matrix multiplication to find the total value of the inventory for each snack bar. © MP.2

19. Model With Mathematics Raul owns and operates two souvenir stands. At his baseball park stand, sweatshirts cost $45 and T-shirts cost $20. At his football stadium stand, sweatshirts cost $50 and T-shirts cost $15. Today Raul sold 20 sweatshirts and 25 T-shirts at each stand. Use matrix multiplication to find the total amount in daily sales at each souvenir stand. © MP.4

20. Reason A drama teacher assigns final grades in her class based on the weighted system shown below. The matrix G represents the grades for Kiyo and his two friends, Rachel and Leo. © MP.2

$$G = \begin{array}{c} \text{tests} \\ \text{proj} \\ \text{part} \end{array} \begin{bmatrix} 90 & 83 & 78 \\ 94 & 88 & 96 \\ 98 & 94 & 89 \end{bmatrix}$$

(Kiyo Rachel Leo)

Drama Syllabus
Tests 45%
Projects 30%
Participation 25%

a. Write matrix W as a 1×3 matrix to represent the weighted grading system.

b. Perform matrix multiplication to find the final grades for each of the three students.

21. Find the product of the two matrices.

$$\begin{bmatrix} 1 & 0 \\ 2 & -3 \end{bmatrix} \begin{bmatrix} -3 & 4 \\ 5 & 2 \end{bmatrix} = \begin{bmatrix} \square & \square \\ \square & \square \end{bmatrix}$$

22. SAT/ACT Select the undefined matrix product.

Ⓐ $\begin{bmatrix} 1 & 2 \\ 3 & 6 \end{bmatrix} \begin{bmatrix} 5 & 0 \\ 0 & 2 \end{bmatrix}$ Ⓑ $\begin{bmatrix} 1 & 4 \\ 2 & -1 \end{bmatrix} \begin{bmatrix} 2 \\ 5 \end{bmatrix}$

Ⓒ $\begin{bmatrix} 2 & -1 \\ 2 & 4 \end{bmatrix} \begin{bmatrix} 1 & 1 & -1 \\ -2 & 0 & -4 \end{bmatrix}$ Ⓓ $\begin{bmatrix} 1 & -2 & -1 \\ -2 & 3 & 0 \end{bmatrix} \begin{bmatrix} 1 & -1 \\ 1 & 0 \end{bmatrix}$

23. Performance Task Paula has a candle-making business. The candles come in four different types. The cost of making each type of candle is $0.50, $1, $5, and $7, in order of size. Paula's candle sales for her first three years of business are shown in the table below.

	Tea $1	Floating $2	Jar $12	Pillar $15
Year 1	20	15	40	30
Year 2	25	20	50	35
Year 3	15	20	60	45

Part A Write matrix C as a 4×1 matrix to represent the cost of making each type of candle, write matrix P as a 4×1 matrix to represent the selling price of each candle, and write matrix S as a 3×4 matrix to represent Paula's candle sales for the first three years.

Part B Use matrix subtraction to find a matrix, X, that represents the amount of profit that Paula makes per candle.

Part C Use matrix multiplication to find the product of matrices S and X. Explain what the elements of this product represent.

I CAN... interpret and use vectors for addition, subtraction, and scalar multiplication.

VOCABULARY

• component form
• direction
• initial point
• magnitude
• terminal point
• vector

Common Core State Standards HSN.VM.A.1 (+), HSN.VM.A.2 (+), HSM.VM.A.3 (+), HSN.VM.B.4 (+), HSN.VM.B.5 (+), HSN.VM.C.11 (+), MP.2, MP.7, MP.8

 Activity   Assess

CRITIQUE & EXPLAIN

Olivia and Benito are taking part in a scavenger hunt. They are given a map that shows the start and finish line. They are also given a list of directions on how to get to the finish line. They get to choose how they want to follow the directions, so they took different paths.

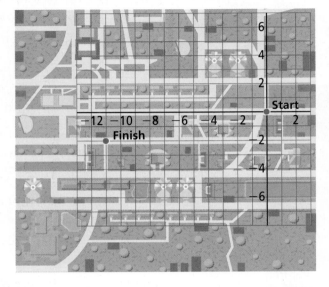

Olivia's path:
5 blocks south
7 blocks west
3 blocks north
4 blocks west

Benito's path:
7 blocks west
3 blocks north
4 blocks west
5 blocks south

A. Will both Olivia and Benito reach the finish line? Explain.

B. Create a different set of directions that would get someone to the finish line.

C. Communicate Precisely Does the order of the instructions that pair distance and direction affect the outcome? Explain. Ⓒ **MP.6**

? ESSENTIAL QUESTION How does including a direction with a quantity affect how you carry out operations on quantities?

CONCEPT Vectors

A **vector,** written as $\vec{a}$, is a quantity with both direction and magnitude.

The **direction** of a vector is considered from the **initial point** to the **terminal point.**

The **magnitude** is the length of the vector and is written as $|\vec{a}|$.

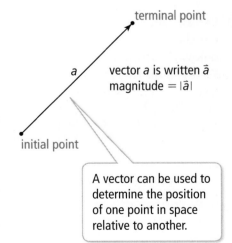

terminal point

a

vector a is written $\vec{a}$
magnitude $= |\vec{a}|$

initial point

A vector can be used to determine the position of one point in space relative to another.

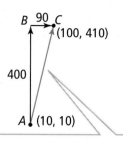

EXAMPLE 1 ▸ Represent Vector Quantities

A plane is flying due north, but it is pushed off course by a crosswind blowing east. At 1 P.M. the plane is at the point (10, 10), and at 2 P.M. the plane is at (100, 410).

A. **Find the speed of the wind and the speed of the plane due to its engine. How can you represent the change in the plane's location as a vector written in component and matrix form?**

The wind is responsible for the eastward change in the plane's location. Subtract the x-coordinates to find the amount of change.

> Because the plane's path has both distance and direction, it is a vector.

$$100 - 10 = 90$$

The plane travels 90 mi east in 1 h. The windspeed is 90 mph.

The plane's engine is responsible for the northward change in the plane's location. Subtract the y-coordinates to find the amount of change.

$$410 - 10 = 400$$

The plane travels 400 mi north in 1 h, so the speed of the plane due to its engine is 400 mph.

The **component form** of a vector is represented by the coordinates $\langle x, y \rangle$. They describe the horizontal and vertical change of position from the initial point to the terminal point. In this case, the vector includes both eastward and northward changes.

The vector $\overrightarrow{AC}$ represents a horizontal change of 90 mi and a vertical change of 400 mi.

The change in the plane's location is $\langle 90, 400 \rangle$ in component form and $\begin{bmatrix} 90 \\ 400 \end{bmatrix}$ in matrix form.

B. **How can you describe the direction the plane is heading? How fast is the plane moving with respect to the ground?**

The direction of the vector can be defined using an angle.

$$\theta = \tan^{-1}\left(\frac{90}{400}\right) \approx 12.7°$$

Calculate the magnitude of $\overrightarrow{AC}$ using the distance formula.

$$|\overrightarrow{AC}| = \sqrt{(x_2 - x_1)^2 + (y_2 - y_1)^2}$$
$$= \sqrt{90^2 + 400^2}$$
$$= 410 \text{ mph}$$

> Remember that $\tan \theta = \frac{opposite}{adjacent}$.

The plane is traveling at about 12.7° east of north at a speed of 410 mph in that direction.

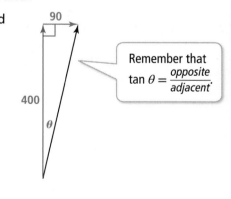

 Try It! 1. A vector has an initial point at (8, 2) and a terminal point at (5, 6). What is the vector in component form, and what are its magnitude and direction?

👆 **EXAMPLE 2** **Understand Vector Addition**

How can you add vectors $\vec{v} = \langle 4, 8 \rangle$ and $\vec{w} = \langle 3, -6 \rangle$ graphically and algebraically?

To add two vectors graphically, draw both vectors with an initial point at the origin.

Create a parallelogram by drawing a copy of one of the vectors using the terminal point of the other vector as its initial point.

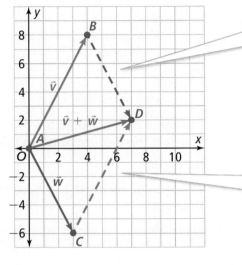

Locate the fourth point D with a copy of $\vec{w}$ with initial point at the terminal point of $\vec{v}$.

A copy of $\vec{v}$ with initial point at the terminal point of $\vec{w}$ leads to the same location for point D.

The terminal point of this copy is the fourth point D of the parallelogram, $(7, 2)$.

The Parallelogram Rule states that if two vectors represent adjacent sides of a parallelogram, then the sum of the vectors is equal to the vector that is the diagonal of the parallelogram with the same initial point.

The initial point of $\overrightarrow{AD}$ is the origin, and its terminal point is $(7, 2)$. So, the sum of vectors $\vec{v}$ and $\vec{w}$ is the vector $\overrightarrow{AD}$ with the component form $\langle 7, 2 \rangle$.

The components of $\overrightarrow{AD}$ can also be found algebraically by adding the components of $\vec{v} = \langle 4, 8 \rangle$ and $\vec{w} = \langle 3, -6 \rangle$.

$$\vec{v} + \vec{w} = \langle 4 + 3, 8 + (-6) \rangle$$
$$= \langle 7, 2 \rangle$$

Adding the vectors together graphically or algebraically results in the same sum, $\overrightarrow{AD} = \langle 7, 2 \rangle$.

COMMON ERROR
Remember to keep track of the *x*- and *y*-terms when adding vectors. Add the *x*-terms together and the *y*-terms together.

 Try It! **2. a.** If $\overrightarrow{MN} = \langle 9, 12 \rangle$ and $\overrightarrow{NO} = \langle 2, 7 \rangle$, what is $\overrightarrow{MN} + \overrightarrow{NO}$?

b. If $\vec{v} = \langle -3, 4 \rangle$ and $\vec{w} = \langle 5, -8 \rangle$, what is $\vec{v} + \vec{w}$?

APPLICATION   **EXAMPLE 3** Find the Magnitude and Direction of a Sum

Paige is operating a boat across a river with engine speed set at 12 mph headed 30° south of east. The current of the river is 2 mph at a direction that is 30° west of south. What are the magnitude and direction of the path of her boat as she operates it across the river?

Step 1 Use trigonometry to find the component form of the vectors.

The boat engine $\vec{e}$ is going 12 mph (magnitude) at 30° south of east.

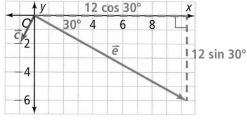

$12 \sin 30° = 6$

$12 \cos 30° = 6\sqrt{3} \approx 10.39$

Since the vertical component is in the negative direction, $\vec{e} \approx \langle 10.39, -6 \rangle$.

The current $\vec{c}$ is 2 mph (magnitude) at 30° west of south. This vector makes a 60° angle with the horizontal axis. Find its component form in the same way.

$2 \sin 60° = \sqrt{3} \approx 1.73$

$2 \cos 60° = 1$

Since both components are in the negative direction, $\vec{c} \approx \langle -1, -1.73 \rangle$.

Step 2 Find the sum of the vectors that represent the boat's speed and the current of the river.

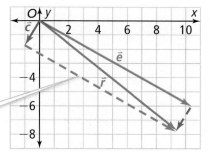

$\vec{r} = \vec{e} + \vec{c}$

$= \langle 10.39 + (-1), -6 + (-1.73) \rangle$

$= \langle 9.39, -7.73 \rangle$

> Paige's actual speed is the sum of the two vectors, which is the diagonal of the parallelogram.

LOOK FOR RELATIONSHIPS
The magnitude of the sum of the vectors is not the same as the sum of the magnitudes of those vectors. In this problem, $|\vec{r}| \neq |\vec{e} + \vec{c}|$. © MP.7

Step 3 Find the magnitude of $\vec{r}$ using the Pythagorean Theorem.

$|\vec{r}| = \sqrt{9.39^2 + (7.73)^2} \approx 12.2$

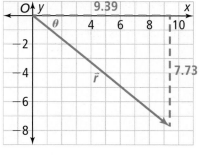

Step 4 Use the components of $\vec{r}$ to find its direction as an angle.

Direction of $\vec{r}$: $\theta = \tan^{-1}\left(\dfrac{7.73}{9.39}\right) \approx 39.5°$

Recall that the first component of the vector sum is positive and the second component is negative. Therefore the vector that represents direction of Paige's boat is in Quandrant IV. Paige's boat went at a speed of about 12.2 mph in the direction of about 40° south of east.

☑ **Try It!** **3.** If the engine speed was 9 mph northwest at 135° with the same current, what would be the magnitude and direction of the boat's speed? Round the magnitude and angle of direction to the nearest tenth.

EXAMPLE 4   Understand Vector Subtraction

How can you subtract $\vec{v} - \vec{w}$ graphically and algebraically, when $\vec{v} = \langle 6, 2 \rangle$ and $\vec{w} = \langle 0, -4 \rangle$? What are the components, magnitude, and direction of $\vec{v} - \vec{w}$?

The graph of $\vec{v} - \vec{w}$ can be found in a similar way to the graph of the sum of two vectors.

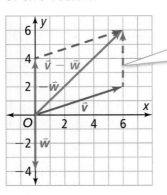

In order to subtract $\vec{w}$, add its additive inverse, $-\vec{w}$, a vector with the same magnitude but opposite direction.

The terminal point of $\vec{v} - \vec{w}$ is (6, 6), so its component form is $\langle 6, 6 \rangle$.

COMMON ERROR
When you are finding the direction using the inverse tangent, make sure your angle is in the correct quadrant. The possible outputs of $\tan^{-1} \theta$ are $-90° < \theta < 90°$.

The components of $\vec{v} - \vec{w}$ can also be found algebraically by subtracting the components of $\vec{v} = \langle 6, 2 \rangle$ and $\vec{w} = \langle 0, -4 \rangle$.

$$\vec{v} - \vec{w} = \vec{v} + (-\vec{w}) = \langle 6 + 0, 2 + 4 \rangle = \langle 6, 6 \rangle$$

The direction of the difference is $\theta = \tan^{-1} \frac{6}{6} = 45°$.

The magnitude of $\vec{v} - \vec{w}$ is $\sqrt{6^2 + 6^2} = \sqrt{72} \approx 8.5$.

Subtracting the vectors graphically or algebraically results in the same difference, $\vec{v} - \vec{w} = \langle 6, 6 \rangle$. The magnitude of $\vec{v} - \vec{w}$ is about 8.5, and its direction is 45°.

Try It!   **4. a.** What are the components, magnitude, and direction of $\vec{s} - \vec{t}$, where $\vec{s} = \langle 6, -3 \rangle$ and $\vec{t} = \langle 3, 2 \rangle$?

b. For $\vec{m} = \langle 1, -3 \rangle$ and $\vec{n} = \langle -2, 7 \rangle$, what is $\vec{m} - \vec{n}$?

EXAMPLE 5   Multiply a Vector by a Scalar

Multiply each vector by the given scalar. How do the magnitude and direction of the product compare to the original vector?

A. $\vec{r} = \langle 9, 3 \rangle$; scalar = 5

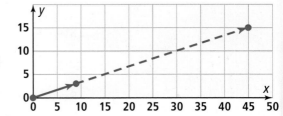

USE STRUCTURE
What have you learned about matrices and dilations that might apply to this problem? **MP.7**

To multiply a vector by a scalar, multiply each of the components of the vector by the scalar:

Note that the new vector has the same direction as $\vec{r}$.

$$5 \cdot \vec{r} = 5 \cdot \langle 9, 3 \rangle = \langle 5 \cdot 9, 5 \cdot 3 \rangle = \langle 45, 15 \rangle$$

CONTINUED ON THE NEXT PAGE

EXAMPLE 5 CONTINUED

While the direction does not change, the magnitude is increased by a factor of the scalar. Check that this works algebraically.

$$5\,|\vec{r}| = 5\sqrt{9^2 + 3^2} = 5\sqrt{90} \approx 47.4$$

$$|5\vec{r}| = \sqrt{45^2 + 15^2} = \sqrt{2{,}250} \approx 47.4$$

$$\theta_r = \tan^{-1}\frac{3}{9} \approx 18.4° \text{ and } \theta_{5r} = \tan^{-1}\frac{15}{45} \approx 18.4°$$

The scalar product $5\vec{r} = \langle 45, 15 \rangle$ has the same direction and 5 times the magnitude of $\vec{r}$.

B. $\vec{s} = \langle 4, 5 \rangle$; scalar $= -3$

Find the new vector components.

$$-3 \cdot \vec{s} = -3 \cdot \langle 4, 5 \rangle = \langle -3 \cdot 4, -3 \cdot 5 \rangle = \langle -12, -15 \rangle$$

Compare the magnitude and direction.

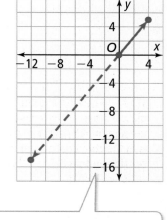

$$|-3||\vec{s}| = 3\sqrt{4^2 + 5^2} = 3\sqrt{41} \approx 19.2$$

$$|-3\vec{s}| = \sqrt{(-12)^2 + (-15)^2} = \sqrt{369} \approx 19.2$$

$$|\vec{s}| = \sqrt{4^2 + 5^2} = \sqrt{41} \approx 6.4$$

$$|-3||\vec{s}| \approx 3(6.4) = 19.2$$

$$\theta_s = \tan^{-1}\frac{5}{4} \approx 51.3° \text{ and } \theta_{-3s}$$
$$= \tan^{-1}\frac{-15}{-12} \approx 231.3°$$

> **STUDY TIP**
> The resulting vector after the scalar multiplication is in the third quadrant, so its direction is 180° greater than the inverse tangent of its components.

The scalar product $-3\vec{s} = \langle -12, -15 \rangle$ has the opposite direction and 3 times the magnitude of $\vec{s}$.

> Because the scalar is negative, the new vector has the opposite direction as $\vec{s}$.

The magnitude of the resulting vector after scalar multiplication is the product of the magnitude of the original vector and the absolute value of the scalar. The direction of the resulting vector is the same unless the sign of the scalar is negative, and then the resulting vector differs by 180°.

 Try It!   **5. a.** If $\vec{t} = \langle -5, -7 \rangle$, what are the components, magnitude, and direction of $-4(\vec{t})$?

b. What are the components, magnitude, and direction of $2t$?

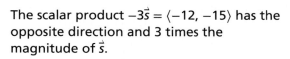

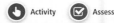

 EXAMPLE 6 Use Matrices to Transform a Vector

How can you use matrix multiplication to transform each vector by the given transformation?

A. Rotate $\overrightarrow{AB} = \langle 7, 9 \rangle$ 180° around the origin using matrices.

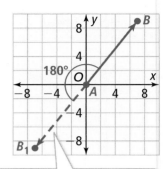

The matrix used to rotate a vector 180° around the origin will change each point (x, y) to $(-x, -y)$. The matrix that does this is

$$T = \begin{bmatrix} -1 & 0 \\ 0 & -1 \end{bmatrix}.$$

$$T \cdot \overrightarrow{AB} = \begin{bmatrix} -1 & 0 \\ 0 & -1 \end{bmatrix} \begin{bmatrix} 7 \\ 9 \end{bmatrix} = \begin{bmatrix} -7 + 0 \\ 0 + (-9) \end{bmatrix} = \begin{bmatrix} -7 \\ -9 \end{bmatrix}$$

Notice that the effect of multiplying $[7 \quad 9]$ by the matrix $\begin{bmatrix} -1 & 0 \\ 0 & -1 \end{bmatrix}$ is to multiply the each component of the vector by -1. This results in another vector equal in magnitude, but with opposite direction.

> The magnitude of the image is the same and the direction is the opposite of the direction of the original vector.

B. Reflect $\overrightarrow{CD} = \langle 6, 2 \rangle$ across the x-axis using matrices.

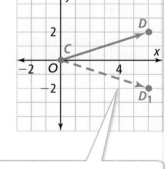

The matrix that will reflect a vector across the x-axis will change each point (x, y) to $(x, -y)$. The matrix that does this is

$$T = \begin{bmatrix} 1 & 0 \\ 0 & -1 \end{bmatrix}.$$

$$T \cdot \overrightarrow{CD} = \begin{bmatrix} 1 & 0 \\ 0 & -1 \end{bmatrix} \begin{bmatrix} 6 \\ 2 \end{bmatrix} = \begin{bmatrix} 6 + 0 \\ 0 + (-2) \end{bmatrix} = \begin{bmatrix} 6 \\ -2 \end{bmatrix}.$$

Notice that the effect of multiplying $[6 \quad 2]$ by the matrix $\begin{bmatrix} 1 & 0 \\ 0 & -1 \end{bmatrix}$ is to multiply the second component of the vector by -1.

> The magnitude of the image is the same, but the direction of the vector is changed by a reflection across the x-axis.

This results in another vector equal in magnitude, but reflected over the x-axis.

LOOK FOR RELATIONSHIPS
Recall what you know about the effects of these transformations from Geometry. How does a reflection affect magnitude and direction? Ⓒ **MP.7**

✓ **Try It!** **6. a.** Let $\overrightarrow{EF} = \langle 5, 10 \rangle$. How is $\overrightarrow{EF}$ transformed when it is multiplied by the matrix $\begin{bmatrix} -1 & 0 \\ 0 & 1 \end{bmatrix}$?

b. How is $\overrightarrow{EF}$ transformed when it is multiplied by the matrix $\begin{bmatrix} 0 & -1 \\ 1 & 0 \end{bmatrix}$?

CONCEPT SUMMARY Vectors

WORDS

A vector is a quantity that has both magnitude and direction.

Vectors may be labeled as $\vec{v}$ or $\overrightarrow{AB}$.

The components of a vector are x and y, noted $\vec{v} = \langle x, y \rangle$.

GRAPH

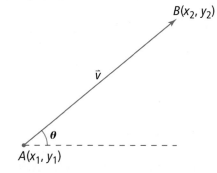

Magnitude
$$|\vec{v}| = \sqrt{x^2 + y^2}$$

Direction
$$\theta = \tan^{-1}\left(\frac{y_2 - y_1}{x_2 - x_1}\right) = \tan^{-1}\frac{y}{x},$$

OPERATIONS

Scalar Multiplication

For $\vec{t} = \langle c, d \rangle$, $a \cdot \vec{t} = \langle a \cdot c, a \cdot d \rangle$
$$|a \cdot \vec{t}| = |a| \cdot |\vec{t}|$$

Addition

For $\vec{r} = \langle j, k \rangle$ and $\vec{s} = \langle m, n \rangle$,
$\vec{r} + \vec{s} = \langle j + m, k + n \rangle$.

Subtraction

For $\vec{r} = \langle j, k \rangle$ and $\vec{s} = \langle m, n \rangle$,
$\vec{r} - \vec{s} = \vec{r} + (-\vec{s}) = \langle j + (-m), k + (-n) \rangle$
or $\vec{r} - \vec{s} = \langle j - m, k - n \rangle$.

Do You UNDERSTAND?

1. **ESSENTIAL QUESTION** How does including a direction with a quantity affect how you carry out operations on quantities?

2. **Error Analysis** Drew says the sum of the vectors $\overrightarrow{AB} = \langle 5, 11 \rangle$ and $\overrightarrow{BC} = \langle 2, -4 \rangle$ is $\overrightarrow{AC} = \langle 7, 13 \rangle$. Explain and correct Drew's error. **MP.3**

3. **Communicate Precisely** Explain the process for vector subtraction. **MP.6**

4. **Look for Relationships** Explain why you can use matrix multiplication to perform transformations on vectors. **MP.7**

5. **Reason** A boat is at the origin and headed 60° north of west. In which quadrant is the vector representing the boat's movement? **MP.2**

Do You KNOW HOW?

Write the component form of the vector, given its initial and terminal points.

6. initial point (6, 2); terminal point (3, −5)

7. initial point (4, −1); terminal point (−8, 0)

8. A vector has an initial point at (6, 13) and a terminal point at (3, 2). What is the vector in component form, and what are its magnitude and direction?

9. A vector has a direction of 235° and magnitude of 6. What is the component form of the vector? Express your answer to the nearest tenth of a unit.

10. Find $\overrightarrow{MN} + \overrightarrow{NO}$ and $\overrightarrow{MN} - \overrightarrow{NO}$ if $\overrightarrow{MN} = \langle 6, 10 \rangle$ and $\overrightarrow{NO} = \langle -3, 0 \rangle$.

UNDERSTAND

11. **Communicate Precisely** Explain two ways in which you can find the magnitude of vectors. © MP.6

12. **Error Analysis** Describe and correct the error a student made in graphically adding the vectors $\overrightarrow{AB} = \langle 2, 5 \rangle$ and $\overrightarrow{BC} \langle 4, -1 \rangle$. © MP.3

The Sum is the dotted diagonal line.

13. **Generalize** Why is the magnitude of a vector always represented by a positive value? © MP.8

14. **Construct Arguments** Is $\overrightarrow{MN}$ the same as $\overrightarrow{NM}$? Justify your answer with an explanation. © MP.3

15. **Make Sense and Persevere** If $\overrightarrow{EF} = \langle -2, 6 \rangle$, write the component form of a vector with the same magnitude but in the opposite direction. © MP.1

16. **Higher Order Thinking** The sum of two vector forces operating on an object gives the total net force on the object. Use the Law of Cosines to find the magnitude of $\vec{v}$ when two forces of 15 and 22 kg act on a point P in the plane.

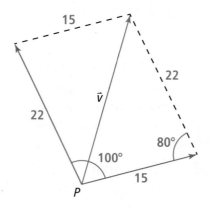

PRACTICE

Write each vector in component form. Identify its magnitude and direction. SEE EXAMPLE 1

17. initial point at (9, 5); terminal point at (4, 3)

18. initial point at (0, 6); terminal point at (−1, 2)

19. initial point at (0, 0); terminal point at (7, 3)

20. initial point at (2, −2); terminal point at (1, 8)

Add each vector pair. SEE EXAMPLE 2

21. $\overrightarrow{MN} = \langle 12, 4 \rangle$ and $\overrightarrow{NO} = \langle -5, 0 \rangle$

22. $\overrightarrow{MN} = \langle 2, 13 \rangle$ and $\overrightarrow{NO} = \langle -10, 6 \rangle$

23. $\overrightarrow{MN} = \langle -7, 10 \rangle$ and $\overrightarrow{NO} = \langle 14, -9 \rangle$

24. Yumiko is operating a boat across a river with engine speed set at 15 mph headed 45° south of west. The current of the river is 3 mph at a direction that is 45° east of south. What are the magnitude and direction of the path of her boat as she operates it across the river? SEE EXAMPLE 3

Find the components, magnitude, and direction of $\vec{s} - \vec{t}$ for each given vector pair. SEE EXAMPLE 4

25. $\vec{s} = \langle 6, 5 \rangle$ and $\vec{t} = \langle -8, 1 \rangle$

26. $\vec{s} = \langle -1, 10 \rangle$ and $\vec{t} = \langle 1, 1 \rangle$

27. $\vec{s} = \langle -3, 7 \rangle$ and $\vec{t} = \langle 0, 0 \rangle$

Multiply each vector by the given scalar. SEE EXAMPLE 5

28. $\vec{t} = \langle -7, -9 \rangle$; scalar = 4

29. $\vec{t} = \langle 4, 12 \rangle$; scalar = −6

30. $\vec{t} = \langle 6, -1 \rangle$; scalar = 2

31. $\overrightarrow{EF} = \langle 8, 4 \rangle$. How can you reflect $\overrightarrow{EF}$ across the *y*-axis using matrices? SEE EXAMPLE 6

APPLY

32. Reason A ball is thrown with an initial speed of 20 mph in a direction that makes an angle of 30° with the positive *x*-axis. Express the velocity vector $\vec{v}$ in terms of the horizontal movement along the *x*-axis $\overrightarrow{AP}$ and the vertical movement along the *y*-axis $\overrightarrow{AQ}$. © MP.2

33. Model With Mathematics A plane is flying due south, but it is pushed off course by a crosswind blowing east. At 7 A.M. the plane is located at point *A*, and at 8 A.M. the plane is located at point *C*. The diagram below shows the movement of the plane and the coordinates of the locations. © MP.4

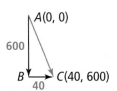

A(0, 0)

600

B →
40 C(40, 600)

a. What is the component form of vector $\overrightarrow{AC}$?

b. What does each of the components of vector $\overrightarrow{AC}$ represent?

c. Find and interpret the magnitude of $\overrightarrow{AC}$.

d. To what degree did the crosswind change the plane's original course?

34. Make Sense and Persevere You are pushing a 350 lb sofa on wheels onto a ramp that inclines 10°. Find the component form and magnitude of the blue vector in the diagram to determine how much force you need to apply to keep the sofa from rolling down the ramp. © MP.1

ASSESSMENT PRACTICE

35. Which of the following vectors have the same magnitude? Select all that apply.

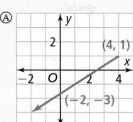

Ⓐ
(4, 1)
(−2, −3)

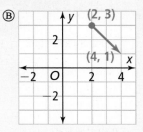

Ⓑ
(2, 3)
(4, 1)

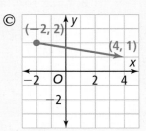

Ⓒ
(−2, 2)
(4, 1)

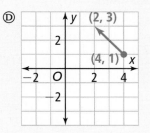

Ⓓ
(2, 3)
(4, 1)

36. SAT/ACT If $\vec{s} = \langle -2, 8 \rangle$ and $\vec{t} = \langle 7, 11 \rangle$, find $\vec{s} + \vec{t}$.

Ⓐ $\langle -5, 3 \rangle$ Ⓑ $\langle 9, 19 \rangle$ Ⓒ $\langle 9, 3 \rangle$ Ⓓ $\langle 5, 19 \rangle$

37. Performance Task Starting from her cabin, Marta hikes 2 mi east to a cove and then turns 60° toward the north to hike 6 mi to a waterfall. The component form, $\vec{v}$, of Marta's hike to the cove is $\langle 2, 0 \rangle$. Let $\vec{u}$ represent Marta's hike from the cove to the waterfall.

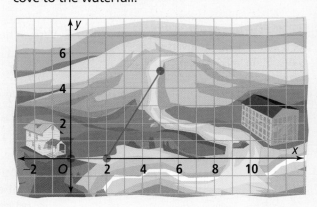

Part A Find the component form of $\vec{u}$.

Part B Use vector addition to find the component form of the vector that represents the straight distance from Marta's current location back to her cabin.

Part C Find Marta's actual straight distance from her cabin by finding the magnitude of the vector in part (b).

10-4

Inverses and Determinants

 SavvasRealize.com

I CAN... find and use the inverse of a matrix.

VOCABULARY
- determinant of a 2×2 matrix
- inverse matrix

Common Core State Standards HSA.REI.C.9 (+), HSN.VM.C.10 (+), HSN.VM.C.12 (+), MP.2, MP.5, MP.7

👆 EXPLORE & REASON

A teacher writes these three equations on the board.

A. Carolina notices that the solution to the first equation is given by $\frac{3}{2}$, and she hypothesizes that

$p + qi = \frac{1}{2+3i}$ and $\begin{bmatrix} w & x \\ y & z \end{bmatrix} = \frac{\begin{bmatrix} 1 & 0 \\ 0 & 1 \end{bmatrix}}{\begin{bmatrix} 2 & 0 \\ 0 & 2 \end{bmatrix}}$.

Is Carolina correct?

B. Look for Relationships What do the methods for solving these equations have in common? © MP.7

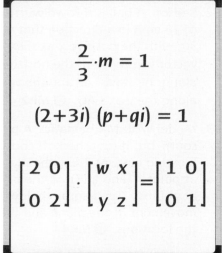

$$\frac{2}{3} \cdot m = 1$$

$$(2+3i)(p+qi) = 1$$

$$\begin{bmatrix} 2 & 0 \\ 0 & 2 \end{bmatrix} \cdot \begin{bmatrix} w & x \\ y & z \end{bmatrix} = \begin{bmatrix} 1 & 0 \\ 0 & 1 \end{bmatrix}$$

❓ ESSENTIAL QUESTION

How do you find and use an inverse matrix?

CONCEPTUAL UNDERSTANDING

👆 EXAMPLE 1 Explore Inverses of 2 × 2 Matrices

A. What is the inverse matrix of $\begin{bmatrix} 2 & 1 \\ 3 & 0 \end{bmatrix}$?

An **inverse matrix** of a matrix $\begin{bmatrix} a & b \\ c & d \end{bmatrix}$ is a matrix $\begin{bmatrix} w & x \\ y & z \end{bmatrix}$ such that the product of the two matrices is the identity matrix. $\begin{bmatrix} a & b \\ c & d \end{bmatrix} \cdot \begin{bmatrix} w & x \\ y & z \end{bmatrix} = \begin{bmatrix} 1 & 0 \\ 0 & 1 \end{bmatrix}$

LOOK FOR RELATIONSHIPS
For a matrix A and its inverse matrix B, $AB = BA = I$, where I is the identity matrix. © MP.7

Step 1 Write the equation for the inverse.

$$\begin{bmatrix} 2 & 1 \\ 3 & 0 \end{bmatrix} \cdot \begin{bmatrix} w & x \\ y & z \end{bmatrix} = \begin{bmatrix} 1 & 0 \\ 0 & 1 \end{bmatrix}$$

Step 2 Multiply the matrices on the left side of the equation.

$$\begin{bmatrix} 2w + y & 2x + z \\ 3w + 0y & 3x + 0z \end{bmatrix} = \begin{bmatrix} 1 & 0 \\ 0 & 1 \end{bmatrix}$$

Step 3 Solve the equations that result from the matrix multiplication. Set each element of the first matrix equal to the corresponding element in the second matrix. This results in a system of four equations:

$$2w + y = 1 \qquad\qquad 2x + z = 0$$

$$3w + 0y = 0 \qquad\qquad 3x + 0z = 1$$

Solve the equations that involve only one variable first.

$$3w + 0y = 0 \qquad\qquad 3x + 0z = 1$$

$$3w = 0 \qquad\qquad 3x = 1$$

$$w = 0 \qquad\qquad x = \frac{1}{3}$$

CONTINUED ON THE NEXT PAGE

EXAMPLE 1 CONTINUED

Substituting w and x into the first two equations yields the following.

$$2w + y = 1 \qquad\qquad 2x + z = 0$$

$$2(0) + y = 1 \qquad\quad 2\left(\tfrac{1}{3}\right) + z = 0$$

$$y = 1 \qquad\qquad\qquad z = -\tfrac{2}{3}$$

$$\begin{bmatrix} w & x \\ y & z \end{bmatrix} = \begin{bmatrix} 0 & \tfrac{1}{3} \\ 1 & -\tfrac{2}{3} \end{bmatrix}$$

Step 4 Verify the solution:

$$\begin{bmatrix} 0 & \tfrac{1}{3} \\ 1 & -\tfrac{2}{3} \end{bmatrix} \cdot \begin{bmatrix} 2 & 1 \\ 3 & 0 \end{bmatrix} = \begin{bmatrix} 0(2) + \tfrac{1}{3}(3) & 0(1) + \tfrac{1}{3}(0) \\ 1(2) - \tfrac{2}{3}(3) & 1(1) - \tfrac{2}{3}(0) \end{bmatrix} = \begin{bmatrix} 1 & 0 \\ 0 & 1 \end{bmatrix}.$$

The inverse matrix of $\begin{bmatrix} 2 & 1 \\ 3 & 0 \end{bmatrix}$ is $\begin{bmatrix} 0 & \tfrac{1}{3} \\ 1 & -\tfrac{2}{3} \end{bmatrix}$.

B. What is the inverse matrix of $\begin{bmatrix} 1 & -1 \\ -1 & 1 \end{bmatrix}$?

Find a matrix $\begin{bmatrix} w & x \\ y & z \end{bmatrix}$, so that $\begin{bmatrix} 1 & -1 \\ -1 & 1 \end{bmatrix} \cdot \begin{bmatrix} w & x \\ y & z \end{bmatrix} = \begin{bmatrix} 1 & 0 \\ 0 & 1 \end{bmatrix}$.

Multiplying the matrices on the left of the equation yields

$$\begin{bmatrix} w - y & x - z \\ -w + y & -x + z \end{bmatrix} = \begin{bmatrix} 1 & 0 \\ 0 & 1 \end{bmatrix}$$

Create a system of four equations from the equal matrices.

$$w - y = 1 \qquad\qquad x - z = 0$$

$$-w + y = 0 \qquad\quad -x + z = 1$$

> Combining these equations to solve for x and z leads to the contradiction $0 = 1$.

LOOK FOR RELATIONSHIPS
Do all real numbers have a multiplicative inverse? Ⓖ **MP.7**

To solve, combine two equations that contain the same variables.

This system has no solution. Some matrices *do not have* inverses.

The matrix $\begin{bmatrix} 1 & -1 \\ -1 & 1 \end{bmatrix}$ does not have an inverse.

 Try It!   **1.** What is the inverse matrix of $\begin{bmatrix} 1 & 5 \\ 1 & 3 \end{bmatrix}$?

CONCEPT The Inverse of a 2 × 2 Matrix

For $A = \begin{bmatrix} a & b \\ c & d \end{bmatrix}$, the **determinant of a 2 × 2 matrix A**, denoted det A, is the value $ad - bc$.

The inverse of A is denoted A^{-1} and exists if and only if det $A \neq 0$.

If $A = \begin{bmatrix} a & b \\ c & d \end{bmatrix}$ and A has an inverse, then $A^{-1} = \dfrac{1}{\det A} \begin{bmatrix} d & -b \\ -c & a \end{bmatrix}$.

EXAMPLE 2 ▶ Find Inverses of Square Matrices

A. What is the inverse of $A = \begin{bmatrix} 4 & 1 \\ -1 & 2 \end{bmatrix}$?

The matrix is a square matrix, 2×2. The inverse exists because
$\det A = ad - bc = 4(2) - 1(-1) = 9$.

$$A^{-1} = \frac{1}{\det A} \begin{bmatrix} 2 & -1 \\ 1 & 4 \end{bmatrix}$$

$$A^{-1} = \frac{1}{9} \begin{bmatrix} 2 & -1 \\ 1 & 4 \end{bmatrix} = \begin{bmatrix} \frac{2}{9} & -\frac{1}{9} \\ \frac{1}{9} & \frac{4}{9} \end{bmatrix}$$

The inverse of $A = \begin{bmatrix} 4 & 1 \\ -1 & 2 \end{bmatrix}$ is $\begin{bmatrix} \frac{2}{9} & -\frac{1}{9} \\ \frac{1}{9} & \frac{4}{9} \end{bmatrix}$.

Check your work by using your calculator to multiply A by the matrix you found for A^{-1}. If your answer is correct, the product will be the identity matrix.

B. What is the inverse of $B = \begin{bmatrix} 6 & 8 \\ 3 & 4 \end{bmatrix}$?

The matrix is a square matrix, 2×2.
Since $\det B = ad - bc = 6(4) - 8(3) = 0$, the inverse matrix does not exist.

C. What is the inverse of $C = \begin{bmatrix} 1 & 2 & 1 \\ 0 & -1 & 0 \\ 2 & 1 & 4 \end{bmatrix}$?

The matrix is a square matrix, 3×3. The formulas that we have shown you for finding the determinant and inverse matrix apply only to matrices that are 2×2. Use a calculator to find the determinant and inverse of a 3×3 matrix.

Since $\det C = -2$, the inverse exists.

The calculator shows that the inverse matrix is

$$C^{-1} = \begin{bmatrix} 2 & \frac{7}{2} & -\frac{1}{2} \\ 0 & -1 & 0 \\ -1 & -\frac{3}{2} & \frac{1}{2} \end{bmatrix}.$$

```
det C = -2
[C]^-1
[[2       3.5     -.5]
 [0       -1       0]
 [-1     -1.5      .5]]
```

> **VOCABULARY**
> A *determinant* is a number associated with a square matrix that *determines* whether or not the matrix has an inverse.

Try It!   **2.** Does each given matrix have an inverse? If so, find it.

a. $P = \begin{bmatrix} -4 & 2 \\ -6 & 3 \end{bmatrix}$ b. $Q = \begin{bmatrix} 7 & 3 \\ 2 & 1 \end{bmatrix}$ c. $R = \begin{bmatrix} 5 & 1 & -1 \\ 2 & 0 & 5 \\ 1 & 0 & 2 \end{bmatrix}$

EXAMPLE 3 Use a Matrix Inverse

Use matrices to encode and decode the message WE COME IN PEACE.

Matrix multiplication can be used to encode and decode messages.

Step 1 Convert the message into a string of numbers.

Assign every letter in the alphabet a number, from $A = 1$ to $Z = 26$. Let 27 represent a space between words.

Write the message, and translate each letter into its corresponding number.

W	E	*	C	O	M	E	*	I	N	*	P	E	A	C	E
23	5	27	3	15	13	5	27	9	14	27	16	5	1	3	5

Step 2 Choose a matrix that has an inverse to encode the message, such as

$$A = \begin{bmatrix} 2 & 2 & 3 \\ 1 & -3 & -1 \\ 2 & -1 & 1 \end{bmatrix}.$$

The encoding matrix is a 3×3 matrix, so break the message into three-digit strings.

$$\begin{bmatrix} 23 \\ 5 \\ 27 \end{bmatrix}, \begin{bmatrix} 3 \\ 15 \\ 13 \end{bmatrix}, \begin{bmatrix} 5 \\ 27 \\ 9 \end{bmatrix}, \begin{bmatrix} 14 \\ 27 \\ 16 \end{bmatrix}, \begin{bmatrix} 5 \\ 1 \\ 3 \end{bmatrix}, \begin{bmatrix} 5 \\ 27 \\ 27 \end{bmatrix}$$

> Insert spaces at the end to complete the string.

Create a matrix from these strings, and multiply by the encoding matrix.

USE APPROPRIATE TOOLS
Use technology to perform the matrix multiplications and to find the inverse matrix. ⓒ **MP.5**

Encoding Matrix   **Matrix representation of message**

$$\begin{bmatrix} 2 & 2 & 3 \\ 1 & -3 & -1 \\ 2 & -1 & 1 \end{bmatrix} \begin{bmatrix} 23 & 3 & 5 & 14 & 5 & 5 \\ 5 & 15 & 27 & 27 & 1 & 27 \\ 27 & 13 & 9 & 16 & 3 & 27 \end{bmatrix} =$$

$$\begin{bmatrix} 137 & 75 & 91 & 130 & 21 & 145 \\ -19 & -55 & -85 & -83 & -1 & -103 \\ 68 & 4 & -8 & 17 & 12 & 10 \end{bmatrix}$$

Step 3 Multiply by the inverse of A to decode the message.

The inverse matrix is $A^{-1} = \begin{bmatrix} -4 & -5 & 7 \\ -3 & -4 & 5 \\ 5 & 6 & -8 \end{bmatrix}.$

> Try decoding the matrix by making a chart of letters to convert the matrix product back into the message.

$$\begin{bmatrix} -4 & -5 & 7 \\ -3 & -4 & 5 \\ 5 & 6 & -8 \end{bmatrix} \begin{bmatrix} 137 & 75 & 91 & 130 & 21 & 145 \\ -19 & -55 & -85 & -83 & -1 & -103 \\ 68 & 4 & -8 & 17 & 12 & 10 \end{bmatrix} =$$

$$\begin{bmatrix} 23 & 3 & 5 & 14 & 5 & 5 \\ 5 & 15 & 27 & 27 & 1 & 27 \\ 27 & 13 & 9 & 16 & 3 & 27 \end{bmatrix}$$

Now, this matrix can be reorganized into a string of numbers that represents the letter in the message.

CONTINUED ON THE NEXT PAGE

EXAMPLE 3 CONTINUED

✅ **Try It!** **3.** The matrix $\begin{bmatrix} -3 & -5 & 11 & 6 \\ 130 & 105 & 106 & 65 \\ 323 & 269 & 205 & 128 \end{bmatrix}$ was encoded using the matrix

$A = \begin{bmatrix} 2 & 1 & -2 \\ 5 & 3 & 0 \\ 4 & 3 & 8 \end{bmatrix}$. What is the message?

👆 **EXAMPLE 4**   **Use Determinants to Find the Area of a Triangle**

A. How can you use vectors and determinants to find the area of a triangle?

Orient the triangle so that one vertex is at the origin. Use the vectors $\langle a, b \rangle$ and $\langle c, d \rangle$ that result from the two sides of the triangle, so that each side has an endpoint at the origin.

Use the vectors to form a matrix, placing one point in each column.

$$T = \begin{bmatrix} a & c \\ b & d \end{bmatrix}$$

The area of the triangle can be found by subtracting the areas of the surrounding triangles from the area of the rectangle.

USE APPROPRIATE TOOLS
Determinants can be used for more than determining the existence of an inverse matrix. You can also use them to find the areas of triangles in the coordinate plane. Ⓖ **MP.5**

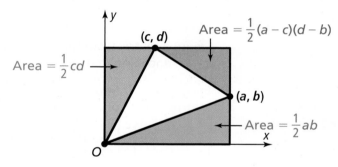

If you compute the area this way, the result is that the area of the triangle is half the absolute value of the determinant:

$$\text{area of } T = \frac{1}{2}(ad - bc) = \frac{1}{2}|\det T|$$

B. What is the area of the triangle defined by the vectors $\langle 3, 4 \rangle$ and $\langle -1, 2 \rangle$?

The vector matrix is $T = \begin{bmatrix} 3 & -1 \\ 4 & 2 \end{bmatrix}$.

Then $|\det T| = |3(2) - (4)(-1)| = 10$.

Area of the triangle $= \frac{1}{2}|\text{determinant}| = \frac{1}{2}(10) = 5$

The area of the triangle is 5 square units.

✅ **Try It!** **4. a.** Find the area of the triangle determined by the vectors $\langle -2, 10 \rangle$ and $\langle -1, -5 \rangle$.

     b. Find the area of the triangle determined by the vectors $\langle 8, 4 \rangle$ and $\langle 7, -3 \rangle$.

EXAMPLE 5 Use a Determinant to Find the Area of a Parallelogram

A. What is the area of a parallelogram with one vertex at the origin and defined by the vectors $\langle 5, 7 \rangle$ and $\langle 2, -5 \rangle$?

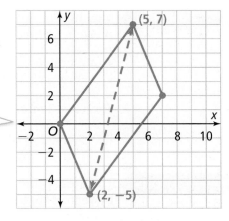

Use the origin as the initial point for both given vectors. Then graph a copy of each vector starting at the terminal point of the other to complete the parallelogram.

COMMON ERROR
The sign of the determinant changes based on the order of vectors in your matrix. Remember to use absolute value when calculating area.

The area of the parallelogram formed by the vectors is twice the area of the triangle, so area of $P = |\det T|$.

Using the matrix $T = \begin{bmatrix} 5 & 2 \\ 7 & -5 \end{bmatrix}$, the area of the parallelogram is $|\det T|$.

$|\det T| = |5(-5) - 7(2)| = 39$

The area of the parallelogram is 39 square units.

B. A parallelogram has one vertex at the origin, is defined by the vectors $\langle -2, 1 \rangle$ and $\langle 1, a \rangle$, and has an area of 5 square units. What are the possible value(s) of a?

$T = \begin{bmatrix} -2 & 1 \\ 1 & a \end{bmatrix}$ .... Write the matrix defined by the two vectors.

$|-2a - 1(1)| = 5$ .... Find the absolute value of the determinant, and set it equal to the area of the parallelogram.

$|-2a - 1| = 5$ .... Simplify.

$-2a - 1 = 5$ or $-2a - 1 = -5$ .... Rewrite using definition of absolute value.

$-2a = 6$ or $\quad -2a = -4$ .... Solve.

$a = -3$ or $\quad a = 2$

Check the solutions.

$\left| \det \begin{bmatrix} -2 & 1 \\ 1 & -3 \end{bmatrix} \right| = 5 \qquad \left| \det \begin{bmatrix} -2 & 1 \\ 1 & 2 \end{bmatrix} \right| = 5$

$|(-2)(-3) - (1)(1)| = 5 \qquad |(-2)(2) - (1)(1)| = 5$

$5 = 5 \checkmark \qquad\qquad\qquad 5 = 5 \checkmark$

The possible values for a are -3 and 2.

 Try It! **5.** Find the area of the parallelogram defined by the vectors $\langle 3, 8 \rangle$ and $\langle 1, 4 \rangle$.

CONCEPT SUMMARY Matrix Inverses and Determinants

DETERMINANT The determinant of a 2×2 matrix, $A = \begin{bmatrix} a & b \\ c & d \end{bmatrix}$, is denoted det A and is equal to $ad - bc$. If A is an $n \times n$ matrix with $n \geq 3$, use technology to calculate the determinant.

INVERSE The multiplicative inverse of a square matrix A, denoted A^{-1}, exists if and only if det $A \neq 0$. It is the unique matrix such that:

- $A \cdot A^{-1} = I$
- $A^{-1} \cdot A = I$.

For a 2×2 matrix $A = \begin{bmatrix} a & b \\ c & d \end{bmatrix}$, the inverse matrix is $A^{-1} = \frac{1}{\det A} \begin{bmatrix} d & -b \\ -c & a \end{bmatrix}$.

If A is an $n \times n$ matrix with $n \geq 3$, use technology to calculate the inverse matrix.

APPLICATIONS The area of the parallelogram defined by vectors $\langle a, b \rangle$ and $\langle c, d \rangle$ and the matrix

$P = \begin{bmatrix} a & c \\ b & d \end{bmatrix}$ is given by $|\det P|$.

For vectors $\langle 4, -3 \rangle$ and $\langle 6, 7 \rangle$,

$P = \begin{bmatrix} 4 & 6 \\ -3 & 7 \end{bmatrix}$; det $P = \begin{vmatrix} 4 & 6 \\ -3 & 7 \end{vmatrix} = |28 - (-18)| = 46$

The area of the parallelogram is 46 square units.

The area of the triangle defined by vectors $\langle a, b \rangle$ and $\langle c, d \rangle$ and the matrix $T = \begin{bmatrix} a & c \\ b & d \end{bmatrix}$ is $\frac{1}{2} |\det T|$.

For vectors $\langle 2, 3 \rangle$ and $\langle 6, -2 \rangle$,

$T = \begin{bmatrix} 2 & 6 \\ 3 & -2 \end{bmatrix}$

det $T = \begin{vmatrix} 2 & 6 \\ 3 & -2 \end{vmatrix} = \frac{1}{2} |-4 - 18| = \frac{1}{2} (22) = 11$

The area of the triangle is 11 square units.

Do You UNDERSTAND?

1. **ESSENTIAL QUESTION** How do you find and use an inverse matrix?

2. **Vocabulary** What is the determinant of a 2×2 matrix?

3. **Error Analysis** Enrique says the matrix $\begin{bmatrix} 3 & 4 \\ 6 & 8 \end{bmatrix}$ has an inverse. Explain his error. Ⓒ MP.3

4. **Communicate Precisely** Explain how to use the determinant of a matrix to find the area of a triangle. Ⓒ MP.6

Do You KNOW HOW?

Find the inverse of each matrix, if it exists.

5. $\begin{bmatrix} -2 & -4 \\ 2 & 3 \end{bmatrix}$
6. $\begin{bmatrix} -1 & 3 \\ -3 & 9 \end{bmatrix}$

7. $\begin{bmatrix} -3 & -2 & 1 \\ 5 & 4 & -3 \\ 6 & -4 & 2 \end{bmatrix}$
8. $\begin{bmatrix} 2 & 0 & -4 \\ 0 & 6 & 3 \\ -1 & 1 & 3 \end{bmatrix}$

9. **Make Sense and Persevere** What is the area of a triangle determined by the vectors $\langle 2, 3 \rangle$ and $\langle 6, -1 \rangle$? Ⓒ MP.1

10. What is the area of a parallelogram determined by the vectors $\langle 5, 2 \rangle$ and $\langle -1, -10 \rangle$?

UNDERSTAND

11. Use Structure Write a 2 × 2 matrix that does not have an inverse. Explain how you can tell that it does not have an inverse. © MP.7

12. Construct Arguments Can a 2 × 3 matrix have an inverse? Explain. © MP.3

13. Error Analysis Leah wants to find the area of a parallelogram with one vertex at the origin and defined by the vectors $\langle 3, 6 \rangle$ and $\langle -4, -10 \rangle$. Explain and correct Leah's error in finding the area of the parallelogram. © MP.3

Let $T = \begin{bmatrix} 3 & -4 \\ 6 & -10 \end{bmatrix}$.

$A = \frac{1}{2} |\det T|$

$A = \frac{1}{2} |-6| = 3$

The area of the parallelogram is 3 square units. ✗

14. Reason Are $\begin{bmatrix} 8 & 4 \\ 4 & -2 \end{bmatrix}$ and $\begin{bmatrix} \frac{1}{16} & \frac{1}{8} \\ \frac{1}{8} & -\frac{1}{4} \end{bmatrix}$ inverses?

Explain how you know. © MP.2

15. Higher Order Thinking Let $A = \begin{bmatrix} a & b \\ c & d \end{bmatrix}$. Find values of a, b, c, and d, where $A = A^{-1}$. (*Hint:* There are four distinct possible values.)

16. Construct Arguments Monisha said that to find det B, where $B = \begin{bmatrix} a & b \\ c & d \end{bmatrix}$, you can use the expression $ad - bc$ or the expression $bc - ad$. Is Monisha correct? Explain. © MP.3

17. Reason Matrix A does not have an inverse. Find the value of b and explain how you know that this value for b is correct. © MP.2

$A = \begin{bmatrix} -1 & b \\ 3 & 6 \end{bmatrix}$

PRACTICE

Find the inverse of each matrix. SEE EXAMPLE 1

18. $\begin{bmatrix} 10 & 2 \\ -5 & -3 \end{bmatrix}$

19. $\begin{bmatrix} \frac{1}{2} & \frac{1}{4} \\ \frac{1}{2} & \frac{3}{4} \end{bmatrix}$

Does each given matrix have an inverse? If so, find it. SEE EXAMPLE 2

20. $P = \begin{bmatrix} 1 & -3 \\ -1 & 4 \end{bmatrix}$

21. $R = \begin{bmatrix} -2 & 8 & -5 \\ 3 & -11 & 7 \\ 9 & -34 & 21 \end{bmatrix}$

22. $Q = \begin{bmatrix} -6 & -9 \\ -4 & -6 \end{bmatrix}$

23. $S = \begin{bmatrix} -24 & 18 & 5 \\ 20 & -15 & -4 \\ -5 & 4 & 1 \end{bmatrix}$

24. The matrix $\begin{bmatrix} 30 & 15 & 106 & 63 & 33 & 121 \\ 18 & 120 & 80 & 102 & 102 & 164 \\ 101 & 24 & 154 & 43 & 111 & 162 \end{bmatrix}$

was encoded using the matrix $A = \begin{bmatrix} -1 & 3 & 2 \\ 4 & 6 & -2 \\ 0 & 1 & 5 \end{bmatrix}$.

What is the message? SEE EXAMPLE 3

25. The matrix $\begin{bmatrix} 49 & 145 & 173 & 124 & 76 & 215 \\ 18 & 50 & 62 & 46 & 30 & 78 \end{bmatrix}$ was

encoded using the matrix $\begin{bmatrix} 6 & 5 \\ 2 & 2 \end{bmatrix}$. What is the secret word?

Find the area of the triangle defined by the given vectors. SEE EXAMPLE 4

26. vectors $\langle 2, 10 \rangle$ and $\langle -1, 5 \rangle$

27. vectors $\langle 9, -3 \rangle$ and $\langle -6, -1 \rangle$

What is the area of a parallelogram with one vertex at the origin and defined by the given vectors? SEE EXAMPLE 5

28. vectors $\langle -4, 16 \rangle$ and $\langle -2, 12 \rangle$

29. vectors $\langle -5, 3 \rangle$ and $\langle 7, -1 \rangle$

APPLY

30. Reason A job title was hidden in the matrix
$$\begin{bmatrix} -34 & -29 & -35 & -23 & -19 & -92 \\ 123 & 93 & 114 & 219 & 66 & 153 \\ 97 & 26 & -137 & -83 & 11 & 16 \end{bmatrix}$$
using the encoding matrix $A = \begin{bmatrix} -4 & -2 & 1 \\ 0 & 3 & 6 \\ 5 & -8 & 2 \end{bmatrix}$.

Only those who discovered the title could apply. What job title was advertised? **Ⓒ MP.2**

31. Model With Mathematics The coordinate plane shows the location of a triangular park, where each unit on the grid represents 10 ft. **Ⓒ MP.4**

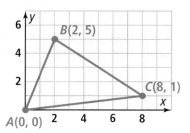

a. Use the vectors to write a matrix that represents the coordinates of the vertices of the triangular park.

b. What is the area of the triangular park?

c. A five-pound bag of grass seed covers about 300 square feet and costs $17.98. How much will it cost to cover the park with grass seed? Explain.

32. Make Sense and Persevere A city planner uses a coordinate plane to plan out a new neighborhood. Each grid square represents 4,000 square feet. A park, roughly in the shape of a parallelogram, is to be built so that one vertex of the parallelogram is located at (3, 7) on the planner's coordinate plane. Using this as an initial point, the points (10, 9) and (1, 10) are the terminal points of the two vectors that determine the parallelogram. What is the area of the park? **Ⓒ MP.1**

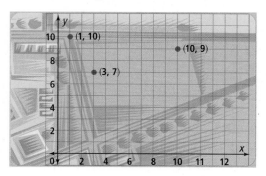

ASSESSMENT PRACTICE

33. Does the matrix have an inverse? Write *Yes* or *No*.

a. $\begin{bmatrix} -5 & 10 \\ -2 & -3 \end{bmatrix}$ b. $\begin{bmatrix} 15 & 2 \\ -12 & -3 \end{bmatrix}$

c. $\begin{bmatrix} 9 & -6 \\ 12 & 8 \end{bmatrix}$ d. $\begin{bmatrix} -3 & -6 \\ -6 & -12 \end{bmatrix}$

34. SAT/ACT The area of a triangle defined by the vectors $\langle 2, y \rangle$ and $\langle 4, 7 \rangle$ is 11 square units. What are the possible values of *y*?

Ⓐ 2 and 9   Ⓑ −2 and −9   Ⓒ −9 and 2   Ⓓ −2 and 9

35. Performance Task A credit card company encodes its issued credit card numbers when transmitting them electronically so that a customer's number is more secure. The company uses a 2 × 8 matrix to represent the 16 digits in the card number. The first column represents the first two digits, and so on.

Part A The matrix
$$\begin{bmatrix} 450 & 450 & 280 & 30 & 10 & 330 & 100 & 370 \\ 945 & 945 & 580 & 75 & 25 & 685 & 210 & 765 \end{bmatrix}$$
was encoded using the matrix $\begin{bmatrix} 10 & 40 \\ 25 & 80 \end{bmatrix}$.
What was the customer's credit card number?

Part B Create your own 16-digit credit card number and an encoding matrix, and encode your card number. Trade encoded card number matrices and the encoding matrix you used with a partner, and decode each other's numbers.

Part C The head of the company decides that a 2 × 2 encoding matrix is not secure enough and wants to institute a policy of using 3 × 3 encoding matrices. How will this affect the encoding process?

10-5

Inverse Matrices and Systems of Equations

 SavvasRealize.com

I CAN... use matrices to represent and solve systems of equations.

VOCABULARY
- constant matrix
- variable matrix

CRITIQUE & EXPLAIN

This augmented matrix represents a system of linear equations in three variables. Students are asked to identify possible values of *a* and *b* for which the system has an infinite number of solutions.

$$\begin{bmatrix} 1 & 1 & 2 & | & -1 \\ 0 & 2 & 0 & | & 8 \\ 0 & 0 & a & | & b \end{bmatrix}$$

> Recall that an augmented matrix for a system of equations has a row for each equation showing its coefficients and constants.

Here are the answers that three students wrote:

Deshawn: $a = 0$, $b = 1$; Jacy: $a = 0$, $b = 0$; Avery: $a = 1$, $b = 0$

A. Which student, if any, is correct? Explain your reasoning.

B. For each student you think has an incorrect response, explain how many solutions their suggested values generate.

C. **Look for Relationships** Which of the coefficient matrices that the three students wrote has an inverse? Is the number of solutions related to the existence of an inverse? **MP.7**

 ESSENTIAL QUESTION   How can matrix inverses be used to simplify the process of solving a system of linear equations?

EXAMPLE 1 Solve a Matrix Equation

How can you solve the matrix equation $\begin{bmatrix} 2 & -1 \\ 0 & 2 \end{bmatrix} \cdot \begin{bmatrix} x \\ y \end{bmatrix} = \begin{bmatrix} 2 \\ 8 \end{bmatrix}$?

Let A represent the matrix $\begin{bmatrix} 2 & -1 \\ 0 & 2 \end{bmatrix}$, and let A^{-1} represent the inverse of the matrix. The goal is to isolate the variable matrix to determine the values of x and y.

LOOK FOR RELATIONSHIPS
Multiplying by an inverse matrix is like multiplying by the reciprocal of a real number. **MP.7**

$A \cdot X = B$ $\begin{bmatrix} 2 & -1 \\ 0 & 2 \end{bmatrix} \cdot \begin{bmatrix} x \\ y \end{bmatrix} = \begin{bmatrix} 2 \\ 8 \end{bmatrix}$

$A^{-1} \cdot A \cdot X = A^{-1} \cdot B$ $\begin{bmatrix} \frac{1}{2} & \frac{1}{4} \\ 0 & \frac{1}{2} \end{bmatrix} \cdot \begin{bmatrix} 2 & -1 \\ 0 & 2 \end{bmatrix} \cdot \begin{bmatrix} x \\ y \end{bmatrix} = \begin{bmatrix} \frac{1}{2} & \frac{1}{4} \\ 0 & \frac{1}{2} \end{bmatrix} \cdot \begin{bmatrix} 2 \\ 8 \end{bmatrix}$

$I \cdot X = A^{-1} \cdot B$ $\begin{bmatrix} 1 & 0 \\ 0 & 1 \end{bmatrix} \cdot \begin{bmatrix} x \\ y \end{bmatrix} = \begin{bmatrix} 3 \\ 4 \end{bmatrix}$

$X = A^{-1} \cdot B$ $\begin{bmatrix} x \\ y \end{bmatrix} = \begin{bmatrix} 3 \\ 4 \end{bmatrix}$

So the solution to the equation is $\begin{bmatrix} x \\ y \end{bmatrix} = \begin{bmatrix} 3 \\ 4 \end{bmatrix}$.

You can check your work by multiplying A by the solution matrix to be sure the product is B.

Try It!   **1.** Solve the matrix equation $A \cdot X = B$ for

$$A = \begin{bmatrix} -1 & 4 & -2 \\ 2 & -1 & 0 \\ -1 & -4 & 2 \end{bmatrix} \text{ and } B = \begin{bmatrix} 6 \\ 8 \\ 2 \end{bmatrix}.$$

EXAMPLE 2   Write a System of Linear Equations as a Matrix Equation

How can each system of linear equations be represented as a matrix equation?

A. $\begin{cases} 3x - 5y = 7 \\ 2x + y = 4 \end{cases}$

$\begin{bmatrix} 3 & -5 \\ 2 & 1 \end{bmatrix} \begin{bmatrix} x \\ y \end{bmatrix} = \begin{bmatrix} 7 \\ 4 \end{bmatrix}$ ⟵ The coefficient of y in the second equation is 1.

The coefficient matrix has rows which contain the coefficients from a single equation. Each column contains all coefficients of a single variable.

The **variable matrix** has one column that represents all the variables in the system of equations.

> The variable matrix is sometimes called the "variable vector."

Use the constant values from the *right-hand side* of the equations to make the **constant matrix**.

B. $\begin{cases} x - 2y + 4z = 9 \\ 2x - 8z = -24 \\ 3x + y - 2z = -1 \end{cases}$

$\begin{bmatrix} 1 & -2 & 4 \\ 2 & 0 & -8 \\ 3 & 1 & -2 \end{bmatrix} \begin{bmatrix} x \\ y \\ z \end{bmatrix} = \begin{bmatrix} 9 \\ -24 \\ -1 \end{bmatrix}$

USE STRUCTURE
Multiply the matrices on the left-hand side and use properties of equivalent matrices to recover the original system of linear equations from the matrix equation. © **MP.7**

✓ **Try It!**   **2.** Express each system of linear equations as a matrix equation.

a. $10x - 9y = 1$
$7x + 6y = 13$

b. $4x + 2y - z = 14$
$2x - 3y + 5z = 20$
$3x - 6y \quad = 8$

CONCEPTUAL UNDERSTANDING ⟶ **EXAMPLE 3**   Solve a System of Linear Equations Using an Inverse Matrix

How can you use matrix inverses to solve a system of linear equations?

A. If possible, use inverse matrices to solve $\begin{cases} -3x + z = -9 \\ -x + 2z = 2 \\ 2x - y = 10 \end{cases}$

Step 1 Express the system of linear equations as a matrix equation.

$\begin{cases} -3x + z = -9 \\ -x + 2z = 2 \\ 2x - y = 10 \end{cases}$ ⟶ $\begin{bmatrix} -3 & 0 & 1 \\ -1 & 0 & 2 \\ 2 & -1 & 0 \end{bmatrix} \cdot \begin{bmatrix} x \\ y \\ z \end{bmatrix} = \begin{bmatrix} -9 \\ 2 \\ 10 \end{bmatrix}$

Step 2 Find the inverse of the 3×3 coefficient matrix using technology.

STUDY TIP
Notice the original matrix has to be invertible for this method to work.

The inverse of $\begin{bmatrix} -3 & 0 & 1 \\ -1 & 0 & 2 \\ 2 & -1 & 0 \end{bmatrix}$ is $\begin{bmatrix} -0.4 & 0.2 & 0 \\ -0.8 & 0.4 & -1 \\ -0.2 & 0.6 & 0 \end{bmatrix}$.

CONTINUED ON THE NEXT PAGE

EXAMPLE 3 CONTINUED

Step 3 Multiply each side of the matrix equation by the inverse matrix.

$$\begin{bmatrix} -0.4 & 0.2 & 0 \\ -0.8 & 0.4 & -1 \\ -0.2 & 0.6 & 0 \end{bmatrix} \cdot \begin{bmatrix} -3 & 0 & 1 \\ -1 & 0 & 2 \\ 2 & -1 & 0 \end{bmatrix} \cdot \begin{bmatrix} x \\ y \\ z \end{bmatrix} = \begin{bmatrix} -0.4 & 0.2 & 0 \\ -0.8 & 0.4 & -1 \\ -0.2 & 0.6 & 0 \end{bmatrix} \cdot \begin{bmatrix} -9 \\ 2 \\ 10 \end{bmatrix}$$

$$\begin{bmatrix} 1 & 0 & 0 \\ 0 & 1 & 0 \\ 0 & 0 & 1 \end{bmatrix} \begin{bmatrix} x \\ y \\ z \end{bmatrix} = \begin{bmatrix} -0.4(-9) + 0.2(2) + 0(10) \\ -0.8(-9) + 0.4(2) - 1(10) \\ -0.2(-9) + 0.6(2) + 0(10) \end{bmatrix}$$

Multiplying a matrix by its inverse results in an identity matrix.

Multiplying the inverse matrix by the constant matrix gives the solution matrix.

Step 4 Multiply by the identity matrix, and write your solution.

$$\begin{bmatrix} 1 & 0 & 0 \\ 0 & 1 & 0 \\ 0 & 0 & 1 \end{bmatrix} \cdot \begin{bmatrix} x \\ y \\ z \end{bmatrix} = \begin{bmatrix} 4 \\ -2 \\ 3 \end{bmatrix} \longrightarrow \begin{bmatrix} x \\ y \\ z \end{bmatrix} = \begin{bmatrix} 4 \\ -2 \\ 3 \end{bmatrix}$$

The solution to the original system of equations is $(4, -2, 3)$.

B. If possible, use inverse matrices to solve $\begin{cases} \frac{1}{4}x - \frac{5}{8}y = \frac{1}{2} \\ -2x + 5y = -4 \end{cases}$

Express the system of linear equations as a matrix equation, $CX = D$.

$$\begin{bmatrix} \frac{1}{4} & -\frac{5}{8} \\ -2 & 5 \end{bmatrix} \cdot \begin{bmatrix} x \\ y \end{bmatrix} = \begin{bmatrix} \frac{1}{2} \\ -4 \end{bmatrix}$$

COMMON ERROR
The matrix is not invertible, so this system of equations has no unique solution.

To use the method from part (a), you need an invertible matrix. Find the determinant of the coefficient matrix C to see if it has an inverse.

$$\det(C) = \frac{1}{4}(5) - \left(-\frac{5}{8}\right)(-2) = \frac{5}{4} - \frac{5}{4} = 0$$

The determinant of the coefficient matrix is 0, so this matrix does not have an inverse. You will have to solve this system using a different method, such as substitution, elimination, or matrix row reduction.

$$8\left(\frac{1}{4}x - \frac{5}{8}y = \frac{1}{2}\right) \longrightarrow 2x - 5y = 4$$

$$\begin{array}{r} 2x - 5y = 4 \\ +(-2x + 5y = -4) \\ \hline 0 + 0 = 0 \end{array}$$

Using elimination results in the equation $0 = 0$, so the system of linear equations has infinitely many solutions.

 Try It! **3.** Solve the following systems of linear equations using inverse matrices, if possible.

a. $\begin{cases} 3x + 4y = 8 \\ \frac{3}{2}x + 2y = 5 \end{cases}$

b. $\begin{cases} x + 2y - 4z = 4 \\ x - 2y + 2z = -10 \\ -x - y + z = 4 \end{cases}$

APPLICATION 👆 **EXAMPLE 4** Solve a Real-World System of Equations With an Inverse

A company makes men's and women's sneakers. Last week, the company spent $340 on labor and $420 on materials. How many sneakers of each type did the company produce?

WOMEN'S SNEAKERS	MEN'S SNEAKERS
Labor: $10	Labor: $14
Materials: $12	Materials: $18

Formulate ◀ To find a solution using a matrix inverse, first define the variables. Then write a system of equations to model the situation. Finally express the system as a matrix equation.

w = the number of pairs of women's sneakers produced

m = the number of pairs of men's sneakers produced

The first equation represents the *labor* costs.

The second equation represents the *materials* costs.

$$10w + 14m = 340$$
$$12w + 18m = 420$$

$$\begin{bmatrix} 10 & 14 \\ 12 & 18 \end{bmatrix} \begin{bmatrix} w \\ m \end{bmatrix} = \begin{bmatrix} 340 \\ 420 \end{bmatrix}$$

Compute ◀ Now solve the system of equations by multiplying by an inverse matrix.

Use technology to find that the inverse of $\begin{bmatrix} 10 & 14 \\ 12 & 18 \end{bmatrix}$ is $\begin{bmatrix} \frac{3}{2} & -\frac{7}{6} \\ -1 & \frac{5}{6} \end{bmatrix}$.

Multiply each side of the matrix equation by the inverse matrix.

$$\begin{bmatrix} \frac{3}{2} & -\frac{7}{6} \\ -1 & \frac{5}{6} \end{bmatrix} \begin{bmatrix} 10 & 14 \\ 12 & 18 \end{bmatrix} \begin{bmatrix} w \\ m \end{bmatrix} = \begin{bmatrix} \frac{3}{2} & -\frac{7}{6} \\ -1 & \frac{5}{6} \end{bmatrix} \begin{bmatrix} 340 \\ 420 \end{bmatrix}$$

$$\begin{bmatrix} 1 & 0 \\ 0 & 1 \end{bmatrix} \begin{bmatrix} w \\ m \end{bmatrix} = \begin{bmatrix} \frac{3}{2}(340) + \left(-\frac{7}{6}\right)(420) \\ -1(340) + \left(\frac{5}{6}\right)(420) \end{bmatrix}$$

Recall that a matrix multiplied by its inverse gives the identity matrix.

$$\begin{bmatrix} w \\ m \end{bmatrix} = \begin{bmatrix} 20 \\ 10 \end{bmatrix}$$

Interpret ◀ The solution is (20, 10). So the company made 20 pairs of women's sneakers and 10 pairs of men's sneakers.

☑ **Try It!** 4. For a three-week period, the same company budgets $860 for labor and $1,080 for materials. How many pairs of men's and women's sneakers can they make in three weeks?

CONCEPT SUMMARY Solving Systems of Linear Equations With Matrices

LINEAR SYSTEMS ▶ • Express the linear system of equations as a matrix equation.

$$\begin{cases} x + 2y + 3z = 4 \\ 3x - 2y + z = -1 \\ x + y - 2z = 6 \end{cases} \longrightarrow \begin{bmatrix} 1 & 2 & 3 \\ 3 & -2 & 1 \\ 1 & 1 & -2 \end{bmatrix} \cdot \begin{bmatrix} x \\ y \\ z \end{bmatrix} = \begin{bmatrix} 4 \\ -1 \\ 6 \end{bmatrix}$$

• For a 2 × 2 matrix, find the determinant of the coefficient matrix, A. If det $A \neq 0$, solve the matrix equation using the inverse of the coefficient matrix. If det $A = 0$, solve the original system with an alternative method. Use substitution, elimination, or matrix row reduction.

• For an $n \times n$ matrix, where $n \geq 3$, use technology to find the inverse of the matrix. Then multiply each side of the equation by the inverse matrix to find the solution.

MATRIX EQUATIONS ▶

$$AX = B$$
$$A^{-1} \cdot AX = A^{-1} \cdot B$$
$$I \cdot X = A^{-1} \cdot B$$
$$X = A^{-1} \cdot B$$

> Multiply by the inverse matrix (A^{-1}) on the left to isolate the variable matrix.

✓ Do You UNDERSTAND?

1. **ESSENTIAL QUESTION** How can matrix inverses be used to simplify the process of solving a system of linear equations?

2. **Error Analysis** Corey says the matrix equation $\begin{bmatrix} 3 & 2 \\ -1 & 4 \\ 2 & 6 \end{bmatrix} \begin{bmatrix} x \\ y \\ z \end{bmatrix} = \begin{bmatrix} 8 \\ 13 \\ 22 \end{bmatrix}$ represents the system of linear equations $\begin{cases} 3x + 2y = 8 \\ -y + 4z = 13 \\ 2x + 6z = 22 \end{cases}$. Explain Corey's error. ⓒ **MP.3**

3. **Vocabulary** How do you determine the coefficient matrix for a particular system of linear equations?

4. **Communicate Precisely** Explain how to solve a system of linear equations using an inverse matrix. ⓒ **MP.6**

Do You KNOW HOW?

Express the system of linear equations as a matrix equation.

5. $\begin{cases} 5x + 3y = -21 \\ 2x - 4y = -24 \end{cases}$ 6. $\begin{cases} 6x - 8y + 2z = -46 \\ -x + 5y + 3z = 29 \\ 9x - 4z = -35 \end{cases}$

7. Given the matrix equation $A \cdot X = B$ for $A = \begin{bmatrix} 1 & 3 & -4 \\ 2 & -2 & 3 \\ -4 & -6 & -1 \end{bmatrix}$ and $B = \begin{bmatrix} 0 \\ -5 \\ -5 \end{bmatrix}$, find A^{-1}. Then use A^{-1} to solve the matrix equation for X.

8. Write an equation that shows what your next step would be in solving this matrix equation for x, y, and z.
$$\begin{bmatrix} -1 & 2 & -3 \\ 2 & -13 & 9 \\ -4 & 12 & -6 \end{bmatrix} \cdot \begin{bmatrix} x \\ y \\ z \end{bmatrix} = \begin{bmatrix} 2 \\ -7 \\ 2 \end{bmatrix}$$

UNDERSTAND

9. **Construct Arguments** Explain why the equation $X = BA^{-1}$ cannot be used to solve this matrix equation in the form $AX = B$. © MP.3

$$\begin{bmatrix} -1 & 2 & -3 \\ 2 & -13 & 9 \\ -4 & 12 & -6 \end{bmatrix} \cdot \begin{bmatrix} x \\ y \\ z \end{bmatrix} = \begin{bmatrix} 2 \\ -7 \\ 2 \end{bmatrix}$$

10. **Communicate Precisely** Give an advantage of solving a system of linear equations using matrices instead of using the substitution or elimination method. (Assume you use technology to find the inverse matrix.) © MP.6

11. **Error Analysis** Describe and correct the error a student made in solving the matrix equation

$$\begin{bmatrix} 5 & 9 \\ 2 & -3 \end{bmatrix} \cdot \begin{bmatrix} x \\ y \end{bmatrix} = \begin{bmatrix} -26 \\ 16 \end{bmatrix}. © MP.3$$

$$\begin{bmatrix} 5 & 9 \\ 2 & -3 \end{bmatrix} \cdot \begin{bmatrix} x \\ y \end{bmatrix} = \begin{bmatrix} -26 \\ 16 \end{bmatrix}$$

$$\begin{bmatrix} x \\ y \end{bmatrix} = \begin{bmatrix} 5 & 9 \\ 2 & -3 \end{bmatrix} \cdot \begin{bmatrix} -26 \\ 16 \end{bmatrix}$$

$$\begin{bmatrix} x \\ y \end{bmatrix} = \begin{bmatrix} 14 \\ -100 \end{bmatrix} \quad ✗$$

12. **Look for Relationships** Assume $a = c$ and $b = d$ for the matrix equation $\begin{bmatrix} a & b \\ c & d \end{bmatrix} \cdot \begin{bmatrix} x \\ y \end{bmatrix} = \begin{bmatrix} e \\ f \end{bmatrix}$. What is the relationship between e and f when there are infinitely many solutions? What is the relationship between e and f when there are no solutions? © MP.7

13. **Higher Order Thinking** Write a system of linear equations in four variables, w, x, y, and z that has integer solutions. Then write a matrix equation to represent your system of equations. Finally, solve the matrix equation using technology to verify the integer solutions.

PRACTICE

Solve the matrix equation $A \cdot X = B$ for the given matrices. SEE EXAMPLE 1

14. $A = \begin{bmatrix} 8 & -7 \\ -6 & 4 \end{bmatrix}$ and $B = \begin{bmatrix} 11 \\ -12 \end{bmatrix}$

15. $A = \begin{bmatrix} 2 & 8 & 4 \\ 1 & -1 & -3 \\ -3 & 2 & -9 \end{bmatrix}$ and $B = \begin{bmatrix} 26 \\ -2 \\ 37 \end{bmatrix}$

Express the system of linear equations as a matrix equation. SEE EXAMPLE 2

16. $8x + y = -1$
    $-12x - 2y = 6$

17. $2x + 3y + 7z = 4$
    $10x + 8y - 2z = -12$
    $6x - y = 30$

Solve the following systems of linear equations using inverse matrices, if possible. SEE EXAMPLE 3

18. $-x + 2y = 8$
    $-3x + 6y = -12$

19. $9x + 2y + 3z = 1$
    $-8x - 3y - 4z = 1$
    $12x + y - 2z = -17$

20. $-3x + 4y = -4$
    $\frac{1}{2}x - 3y = -11$

21. $2x + \frac{2}{3}y + z = -8$
    $x + 2y - \frac{1}{3}z = 6$
    $-\frac{1}{2}x + 3y - 2z = 22$

22. Katrina makes bracelets and necklaces. Last week, she made 5 bracelets and 2 necklaces. This week, she made 3 bracelets and 5 necklaces. How many hours does it take Katrina to make one bracelet? How many hours does it take Katrina to make one necklace? SEE EXAMPLE 4

APPLY

23. Use Structure Luke had some quarters and dimes in his pocket. The quarters and dimes are worth $2.55. He has 3 times as many quarters as dimes. © MP.7

a. Write a matrix equation to find the number of quarters, x, and dimes, y, Luke has.

b. How many quarters and dimes does Luke have?

24. Make Sense and Persevere Malia is training for a triathlon. The table shows the number of hours she swam, biked, and ran and the total distance traveled on three different days. Write and solve a matrix equation to find Malia's average speed while swimming, biking, and running. © MP.1

DAY				Total Distance (mi.)
1	$\frac{1}{3}$	1	2	32
2	$\frac{2}{3}$	$\frac{4}{5}$	1	22
3	1	2	$\frac{1}{2}$	37

25. Model With Mathematics Steve wants to mix three different types of cereal to create a mixture with 3,400 calories, 90 grams of protein, and 90 grams of fiber. The boxes of cereal show the number of calories, grams of protein, and grams of fiber in one serving of cereal A, B, and C. Write a matrix equation to represent this situation. How many servings of each type of cereal does Steve need to include in the mixture? © MP.4

Cereal A
Calories: 300
Protein: 11g
Fiber: 8g

Cereal B
Calories: 300
Protein: 7g
Fiber: 6g

Cereal C
Calories: 320
Protein: 8g
Fiber: 10g

ASSESSMENT PRACTICE

26. Which matrix equation has a unique solution? Select all that apply.

Ⓐ $\begin{bmatrix} 6 & 2 \\ 9 & 3 \end{bmatrix} \cdot \begin{bmatrix} x \\ y \end{bmatrix} = \begin{bmatrix} 12 \\ 18 \end{bmatrix}$

Ⓑ $\begin{bmatrix} 2 & 9 \\ -3 & -8 \end{bmatrix} \cdot \begin{bmatrix} x \\ y \end{bmatrix} = \begin{bmatrix} -46 \\ 36 \end{bmatrix}$

Ⓒ $\begin{bmatrix} 1 & 1 \\ -1 & -1 \end{bmatrix} \cdot \begin{bmatrix} x \\ y \end{bmatrix} = \begin{bmatrix} 4 \\ -4 \end{bmatrix}$

Ⓓ $\begin{bmatrix} -4 & 2 \\ -14 & 7 \end{bmatrix} \cdot \begin{bmatrix} x \\ y \end{bmatrix} = \begin{bmatrix} 10 \\ -7 \end{bmatrix}$

27. SAT/ACT The coordinates (x, y) of a point in a plane are the solution of the matrix equation $\begin{bmatrix} -1 & 2 \\ 3 & 4 \end{bmatrix} \begin{bmatrix} x \\ y \end{bmatrix} = \begin{bmatrix} -5 \\ 2 \end{bmatrix}$. In what quadrant is the point located?

Ⓐ I   Ⓑ II   Ⓒ III   Ⓓ IV

28. Performance Task Nitrogen (N_2) and hydrogen (H_2) can react to form ammonia (NH_3). To write an equation for the reaction, the number of molecules of each element that are combined must equal the number of molecules of each element in the result. You can use matrices to figure out the coefficients that will balance the reaction. $a(N_2) + b(H_2) \rightarrow c(NH_3)$

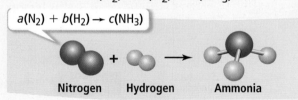

$a(N_2) + b(H_2) \rightarrow c(NH_3)$

Nitrogen   Hydrogen   Ammonia

Part A Let $c = 1$. Write a system of equations in a and b for this reaction. Make one equation to represent N and one equation to represent H, and think of the reaction arrow as an equal sign.

Part B Rewrite your system of equations as a matrix equation, and solve for a and b.

Part C Substitute the coefficients into the reaction equation. Multiply the equation by the least common denominator of all fractions so that all coefficients are whole numbers. Check that it is balanced.

Part D Use the same process to balance the reaction $a(Cr) + b(O_2) \rightarrow c(Cr_2O_3)$.

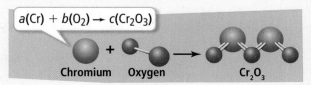

$a(Cr) + b(O_2) \rightarrow c(Cr_2O_3)$

Chromium   Oxygen Cr_2O_3

MATHEMATICAL MODELING IN **3** ACTS

© **Common Core State Standards** HSN.VM.C.6, HSA.REI.C.8, MP.4

Video

The Big Burger

For many people, hamburgers are a hallmark of American food. Nearly every restaurant, from fast food chains, to diners, to fine dining establishments, offers some kind of hamburger on their menu.

Some restaurants offer various types of burgers: beef, turkey, and veggie burgers are all quite popular. You can also often choose extras to add to your burger: double patties of beef, cheese, pickles, onions, lettuce, tomatoes . . . The options are endless! Think about this during the Mathematical Modeling in 3 Acts lesson.

Scan for Multimedia

ACT 1 ▶ Identify the Problem

1. What is the first question that comes to mind after watching the video?

2. Write down the main question you will answer about what you saw in the video.

3. Make an initial conjecture that answers this main question.

4. Explain how you arrived at your conjecture.

5. What information will be useful to know to answer the main question? How can you get it? How will you use that information?

ACT 2 ▶ Develop a Model

6. Use the math that you have learned in this Topic to refine your conjecture.

ACT 3 ▶ Interpret the Results

7. Did your refined conjecture match the actual answer exactly? If not, what might explain the difference?

Topic Review

1. How can you use matrices to help you solve problems?

Vocabulary Review

Choose the correct term to complete each sentence.

2. The _____ has one column that represents all the variables in the system of equations.

3. The _____ is a square matrix with ones on the main diagonal and zeros for all other elements.

4. _____ means the multiplication of each element of a matrix by a single real number.

5. The _____ is the length of the vector.

6. The product of a matrix and its _____ is the identity matrix.

7. The _____ has one column that contains the constants from the right-hand side of the system of equations.

8. A(n) _____ is a matrix that has the same number of rows as columns.

- constant matrix
- identity matrix
- inverse matrix
- magnitude
- scalar multiplication
- square matrix
- variable matrix
- vector
- zero matrix

Concepts & Skills Review

LESSON 10-1 **Operations With Matrices**

Quick Review

To multiply a matrix by a scalar, multiply each element in the matrix by the scalar.

To add (or subtract) matrices, add (or subtract) the corresponding elements.

Example

Add matrices A and B.

$A = \begin{bmatrix} 9 & 2 & 11 \\ -3 & 5 & 6 \end{bmatrix}$ $B = \begin{bmatrix} 4 & -1 & 7 \\ 8 & 12 & 0 \end{bmatrix}$

Add corresponding elements of the two matrices.

$A + B = \begin{bmatrix} 9 & 2 & 11 \\ -3 & 5 & 6 \end{bmatrix} + \begin{bmatrix} 4 & -1 & 7 \\ 8 & 12 & 0 \end{bmatrix}$

$= \begin{bmatrix} 9+4 & 2+(-1) & 11+7 \\ -3+8 & 5+12 & 6+0 \end{bmatrix}$

$= \begin{bmatrix} 13 & 1 & 18 \\ 5 & 17 & 6 \end{bmatrix}$

Practice & Problem Solving

Given matrices $C = \begin{bmatrix} 9 & -5 \\ 3 & 6 \end{bmatrix}$ and $D = \begin{bmatrix} -7 & 1 \\ 8 & 2 \end{bmatrix}$,

calculate each of the following.

9. $D - C$ 10. $5D$

11. A segment has endpoints $A(5, -3)$ and $B(2, 4)$. Use matrices to represent a translation of $\overline{AB}$ to $\overline{YZ}$ by 3 units right and 7 units down. What are the coordinates of Y and Z?

12. **Communicate Precisely** Suppose N is a 3×3 matrix. Explain how to find matrix P so that $N + P$ is the zero matrix. **© MP.6**

13. **Make Sense and Persevere** A seminar has 6 women and 8 men register early. Then 18 women and 12 men register in class. Use matrix addition to find the total number of men and women in the seminar. **© MP.1**

Quick Review

The product of two matrices is a new matrix with the sums of the products of corresponding row and column elements.

$$\begin{bmatrix} a & b \\ c & d \end{bmatrix} \begin{bmatrix} w & x \\ y & z \end{bmatrix} = \begin{bmatrix} aw + by & ax + bz \\ cw + dy & cx + dz \end{bmatrix}$$

For an $n \times n$ matrix A, the multiplicative **identity matrix** I is an $n \times n$ square matrix with 1s on the main diagonal and 0s for all other elements: $AI = IA = A$.

Example

Multiply matrices A and B.

$$A = \begin{bmatrix} 3 & -2 \\ 1 & -4 \end{bmatrix} \qquad B = \begin{bmatrix} -1 & 6 \\ 0 & 5 \end{bmatrix}$$

Find the sums of products of corresponding row and column elements.

$$AB = \begin{bmatrix} 3 & -2 \\ 1 & -4 \end{bmatrix} \begin{bmatrix} -1 & 6 \\ 0 & 5 \end{bmatrix}$$

$$= \begin{bmatrix} (3)(-1) + (-2)(0) & (3)(6) + (-2)(5) \\ (1)(-1) + (-4)(0) & (1)(6) + (-4)(5) \end{bmatrix}$$

$$= \begin{bmatrix} -3 & 8 \\ -1 & -14 \end{bmatrix}$$

Practice & Problem Solving

Given matrices $A = \begin{bmatrix} 4 & -3 \\ 0 & 9 \end{bmatrix}$, $B = \begin{bmatrix} -7 & 8 \\ -5 & 1 \end{bmatrix}$, **and** $C = \begin{bmatrix} 6 & -1 \\ 2 & -2 \end{bmatrix}$, **find each of the following.**

14. AB **15.** AC **16.** BC

17. BA **18.** CA **19.** CB

20. Represent the coordinates of the triangle as a matrix. Then multiply by $\begin{bmatrix} 1 & 0 \\ 0 & -1 \end{bmatrix}$ to find the coordinates of the image of triangle ABC after a reflection across the x-axis.

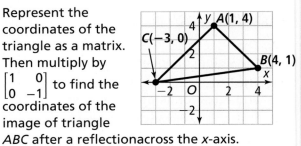

21. **Look for Relationships** Explain how to determine whether two matrices can be multiplied. ⓒ **MP.7**

22. **Make Sense and Persevere** At Store X, Television A costs \$800 and Television B costs \$500. At Store Y, Television A costs \$750 and Television B costs \$550. Last month, each store sold 25 of Television A and 20 of Television B. Write and solve a matrix equation to find the total amount in sales at each store. ⓒ **MP.1**

Quick Review

For vectors $\vec{u} = \langle a, b \rangle$ and $\vec{v} = \langle c, d \rangle$, the magnitude of $\vec{u}$ is $|\vec{u}| = \sqrt{a^2 + b^2}$, and the direction of $\vec{u}$ is $\theta = \tan^{-1}\left(\frac{b}{a}\right)$.

For a scalar k, $k \cdot \vec{u} = \langle k \cdot a, k \cdot b \rangle$, $|k \cdot \vec{u}| = |k| \cdot |\vec{u}|$. $\vec{u} + \vec{v} = \langle a + c, b + d \rangle$ and $\vec{u} - \vec{v} = \vec{u} + (-\vec{v}) = \langle a - c, b - d \rangle$.

Example

Add vectors $\overrightarrow{AB} = \langle 6, -2 \rangle$ and $\overrightarrow{CD} = \langle 3, 7 \rangle$.

$$\overrightarrow{AB} + \overrightarrow{CD} = \langle 6, -2 \rangle + \langle 3, 7 \rangle$$
$$= \langle 6 + 3, -2 + 7 \rangle$$
$$= \langle 9, 5 \rangle$$

Practice & Problem Solving

Add and subtract each vector pair.

23. $\overrightarrow{AB} = \langle 8, 10 \rangle$ and $\overrightarrow{CD} = \langle -3, 2 \rangle$

24. $\overrightarrow{RS} = \langle -7, 9 \rangle$ and $\overrightarrow{TU} = \langle 11, -5 \rangle$

25. Multiply the vector $\vec{t} = \langle 13, -3 \rangle$ by the scalar 4.

26. **Communicate Precisely** Describe how $\overrightarrow{MN} = \langle -2, 9 \rangle$ is transformed when it is multiplied by the matrix $\begin{bmatrix} -1 & 0 \\ 0 & -1 \end{bmatrix}$. ⓒ **MP.6**

27. **Reason** A blimp flying due north is pushed off course by a crosswind blowing west. By how many degrees did the crosswind change the blimp's original course? ⓒ **MP.2**

LESSON 10-4 Inverses and Determinants

Quick Review

The determinant of a **2 × 2 matrix** $A = \begin{bmatrix} a & b \\ c & d \end{bmatrix}$ is denoted det A and is equal to $ad - bc$.

The **inverse matrix** is $A^{-1} = \frac{1}{\det A} \begin{bmatrix} d & -b \\ -c & a \end{bmatrix}$.

Example

Find the inverse of matrix $A = \begin{bmatrix} 4 & 8 \\ 2 & 6 \end{bmatrix}$.

det $A = ad - bc = (4)(6) - (2)(8) = 24 - 16 = 8$

Because the determinant does not equal 0, there is an inverse.

$A^{-1} = \frac{1}{8} \begin{bmatrix} 6 & -8 \\ -2 & 4 \end{bmatrix} = \begin{bmatrix} \frac{3}{4} & -1 \\ -\frac{1}{4} & \frac{1}{2} \end{bmatrix}$

Practice & Problem Solving

Find the determinant of each matrix.

28. $\begin{bmatrix} 12 & -6 \\ 8 & -3 \end{bmatrix}$ **29.** $\begin{bmatrix} 14 & -3 \\ 2 & 0 \end{bmatrix}$

Does each given matrix have an inverse? If so, find it.

30. $A = \begin{bmatrix} 2 & -1 \\ 4 & 1 \end{bmatrix}$ **31.** $B = \begin{bmatrix} 1 & 3 & 2 \\ -2 & -4 & 0 \\ -1 & -3 & 5 \end{bmatrix}$

32. Error Analysis Carla said the inverse of matrix $A = \begin{bmatrix} 8 & 2 \\ 2 & 1 \end{bmatrix}$ is $\begin{bmatrix} 2 & \frac{1}{2} \\ \frac{1}{2} & \frac{1}{4} \end{bmatrix}$. Describe and correct Carla's error. ⒸMP.3

33. Use Structure Find the area of the triangle defined by vectors $\langle 8, 6 \rangle$ and $\langle 2, -4 \rangle$. ⒸMP.7

LESSON 10-5 Inverse Matrices and Systems of Equations

Quick Review

Matrices can be used to solve systems of equations.

The coefficient matrix has rows which contain the coefficients from a single equation. Each column contains all coefficients of a single variable.

The **variable matrix** has one column that represents all the variables in the system of equations.

The constant values from the right-hand side of the equations are used to make the **constant matrix**.

$\begin{aligned} ax + by + cz &= k \\ dx + ey + fz &= m \\ gx + hy + jz &= n \end{aligned} \Rightarrow \begin{bmatrix} a & b & c \\ d & e & f \\ g & h & j \end{bmatrix} \cdot \begin{bmatrix} x \\ y \\ z \end{bmatrix} = \begin{bmatrix} k \\ m \\ n \end{bmatrix}$

Example

Solve the system of equations $\begin{cases} 3x + 6y = 0 \\ -2x + 3y = -7 \end{cases}$ using matrices.

$\begin{aligned} 3x + 6y &= 0 \\ -2x + 3y &= -7 \end{aligned} \Rightarrow \begin{bmatrix} 3 & 6 \\ -2 & 3 \end{bmatrix} \cdot \begin{bmatrix} x \\ y \end{bmatrix} = \begin{bmatrix} 0 \\ -7 \end{bmatrix}$

$\begin{bmatrix} 3 & 6 \\ -2 & 3 \end{bmatrix}^{-1} \cdot \begin{bmatrix} 3 & 6 \\ -2 & 3 \end{bmatrix} \cdot \begin{bmatrix} x \\ y \end{bmatrix} = \begin{bmatrix} 3 & 6 \\ -2 & 3 \end{bmatrix}^{-1} \cdot \begin{bmatrix} 0 \\ -7 \end{bmatrix}$

$\begin{bmatrix} x \\ y \end{bmatrix} = \begin{bmatrix} \frac{1}{7} & -\frac{2}{7} \\ \frac{2}{21} & \frac{1}{7} \end{bmatrix} \cdot \begin{bmatrix} 0 \\ -7 \end{bmatrix}$

$\begin{bmatrix} x \\ y \end{bmatrix} = \begin{bmatrix} 2 \\ -1 \end{bmatrix}$

Practice & Problem Solving

Solve the following systems of equations using inverse matrices.

34. $\begin{cases} 2x + 4y = 4 \\ -3x - 7y = -4 \end{cases}$ **35.** $\begin{cases} -2x + 3y + 3z = 6 \\ 6x - 8y - 2z = -4 \\ 2x - 2y - 3z = -13 \end{cases}$

36. Communicate Precisely Explain how to write a system of equations given the matrix equation $\begin{bmatrix} 4 & 9 & 1 \\ 8 & -2 & 0 \\ -7 & 3 & 2 \end{bmatrix} \cdot \begin{bmatrix} x \\ y \\ z \end{bmatrix} = \begin{bmatrix} 3 \\ 10 \\ 6 \end{bmatrix}$. ⒸMP.6

37. Reason Two students visited the school store to buy supplies for the school year. One student purchased 8 folders and 6 notebooks for a total price of $38. The other student purchased 2 folders and 9 notebooks for a total of $47. If each folder is the same price and each notebook is the same price, how much does each folder and each notebook cost? ⒸMP.2

TOPIC 11

Data Analysis and Statistics

 TOPIC ESSENTIAL QUESTION

What questions can you answer by using statistics and normal distributions?

Topic Overview

enVision™ STEM Project:
   Plan a Public Space

Mathematical Modeling in 3 Acts:
   Mark and Recapture

Topic Vocabulary

- alternative hypothesis
- bias
- control group
- experiment
- experimental group
- margin of error
- normal distribution
- null hypothesis
- observational study
- parameter
- random sample
- sample survey
- sampling distribution
- standard deviation
- statistic
- *z*-score

Digital Experience

 INTERACTIVE STUDENT EDITION Access online or offline.

 ACTIVITIES Complete *Explore & Reason*, *Model & Discuss*, and *Critique & Explain* activities. Interact with Examples and Try Its.

 ANIMATION View and interact with real-world applications.

 PRACTICE Practice what you've learned.

 Go online | SavvasRealize.com

▶ Mark and Recapture

It wouldn't take very long for you to count the number of people who live in your home or the number of socks in your drawer. How about the number of deer in Yellowstone National Park or the number of sharks in the waters around Hawaii?

The mark and recapture method is a popular way researchers can estimate an animal population. You will see an example of this method in the Mathematical Modeling in 3 Acts lesson.

TOPIC 11

▶ VIDEOS Watch clips to support *Mathematical Modeling in 3 Acts Lessons* and **enVision™ STEM Projects.**

CONCEPT SUMMARY Review key lesson content through multiple representations.

ASSESSMENT Show what you've learned.

A-Z GLOSSARY Read and listen to English and Spanish definitions.

TUTORIALS Get help from *Virtual Nerd*, right when you need it.

MATH TOOLS Explore math with digital tools and manipulatives.

enVision™ STEM

Did You Know?

Community officials and planners use **surveys and statistics** to decide how best to use public spaces.

How Would You Use Your Park?

Camping   Cycling   Picnicking   Hiking

Public spaces come in different shapes and sizes. The many uses of public spaces include **ice-skating, bicycling, and skateboarding.**

Dog parks are the fastest-growing type of urban park in the United States. Off-leash dog parks encourage **physical activity** and **social interaction.**

▶ Your Task: Plan a Public Space

You and your classmates will draft a survey about preferred uses of a public space and poll your community. You will analyze and present the data along with your conclusions.

Go Online | SavvasRealize.com

11-1

Statistical Questions and Variables

SavvasRealize.com

I CAN... use vocabulary related to statistical questions and variables.

VOCABULARY

- categorical variable
- parameter
- population
- quantitative variable
- sample
- statistic
- statistical question
- statistical variable

EXPLORE & REASON

A state questioned some of its high schools about the price they were charging for prom tickets. The results are summarized in the histogram.

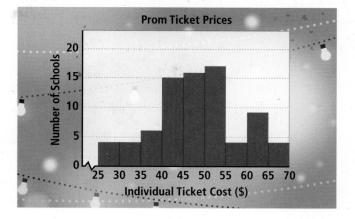

A. What questions can be answered using the data in this histogram?

B. Who might be interested in the answers to these questions? Explain.

C. Construct Arguments Anastasia is surprised that the median cost of a prom ticket is not higher, given that her school is charging $60 per ticket. What are some possible reasons for the data not conforming to her expectations? **MP.3**

ESSENTIAL QUESTION

What kinds of questions about quantities and relationships among quantities can be answered with statistics?

APPLICATION

EXAMPLE 1   Understand Statistical Questions

A. Consider the following questions.

I. *"In what month is your birthday?"*

II. *"What month has the most birthdays of students at your school?"*

What is the difference between the two questions?

Question I can be answered using one piece of information.

> Question I could be asked as *part* of an investigation into Question II. But a specific interview question is different from the general statistical question the investigation is trying to answer.

Question II can be answered by collecting many pieces of information and summarizing them.

STUDY TIP
The answers to statistical questions can be summarized in different types of displays such as bar graphs, line graphs, scatter plots, and frequency charts.

Question II is a **statistical question** because it can be answered by collecting many pieces of information, or data, and summarizing the data.

CONTINUED ON THE NEXT PAGE

EXAMPLE 1 CONTINUED

B. Does each graph represent the answer to a statistical question?

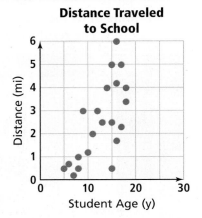

Distance Traveled to School

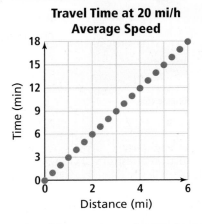

Travel Time at 20 mi/h Average Speed

The graph of distance traveled to school is a scatter plot and represents some students' answers to the question *"How far do you travel to get to school?"* This is a statistical question because it is answered by gathering and summarizing varying data about many students.

The graph of travel time is a function model and represents answers to the question *"How long does it take to travel x miles at 20 mi/h?"* This is a question that has a predetermined answer. The answer varies predictably with x, so it is not a statistical question.

 Try It! 1. Is the given question a statistical question?

 a. "Which is the most popular visual art form: photography, painting, sculpting, or drawing?"

 b. "How many lithographs were created by the artist M.C. Escher?"

CONCEPTUAL UNDERSTANDING

EXAMPLE 2 Understand Statistical Variables

A. What type of statistical variable is represented by the following question and corresponding chart?

"What is your favorite Summer Olympic sport?"

A **statistical variable** is a quantity or quality that can be measured or counted, and for which data are expected to differ from one observation to another. Two main types are categorical and quantitative.

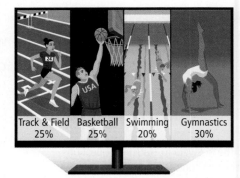

Track & Field 25% | Basketball 25% | Swimming 20% | Gymnastics 30%

Answers to the question above will be different Olympic sports, as shown by the chart summarizing the various responses. Data that fall into categories, or that indicate a qualitative rather than quantitative attribute, represent a **categorical variable**. "Favorite Olympic sport"

CONTINUED ON THE NEXT PAGE

EXAMPLE 2 CONTINUED

is a categorical variable because the values belong to a limited set of possible categories.

B. What type of statistical variable is represented by the following question and corresponding graph?

"What is the typical number of apps a teenager has on a smartphone?"

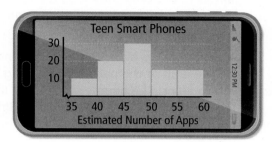

Responses to this question are *quantities* representing the number of apps on a phone. Numerical data like these, that in the context of the data can be compared, added, subtracted or otherwise operated on, represent a second type of statistical variable, a **quantitative variable.** "Number of apps on a phone" is a quantitative variable because the values are numbers that you could meaningfully count, add, subtract and so on.

STUDY TIP
Some variables, such as month or semester grade, can be categorical or quantitative depending on the context.

 Try It! **2.** What is the statistical variable represented by each of the following questions, and is it categorical or quantitative?

a. *"What breed of dog is most likely to be adopted from an animal shelter?"*

b. *"What is the average number of students per activity participating in after-school activities at Jefferson High School?"*

APPLICATION **EXAMPLE 3** **Distinguish Between Populations and Samples**

A. A school newspaper randomly selects 30 students from each grade level to participate in a survey to determine the opinions of students at the school. What is the relationship between the sophomores surveyed, all the students surveyed, and all the students at the school?

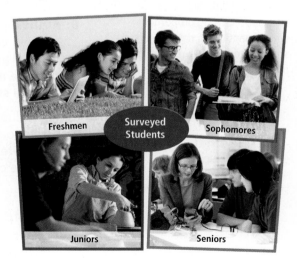

In statistics, the set of all members of a group that you want to know something about is called a **population**. The group of all the students at the school is the population that the school newspaper is studying in their survey.

COMMON ERROR
In statistics, a "population" does not have to be made up of people. The population is whatever whole group that is under statistical study—it could be a group of corporations, a group of bodies of water, or a group of cars of different models.

CONTINUED ON THE NEXT PAGE

EXAMPLE 3 CONTINUED

A **sample** is a subset of the population that is being studied to answer a statistical question about the population. The group of all the students who were surveyed is a sample of all the students at the school, as is the group of sophomores who were surveyed.

B. A polling organization randomly chose eligible voters in the state of Illinois to ask who they would vote for in an upcoming election for governor, to determine who will win the election. What are the sample and the population in this scenario?

The population is all the voters in Illinois who are eligible to vote. The sample is all of the people the polling organization asked about their voting plans. The people selected by the polling organization are a subset of the voting population of Illinois.

 Try It! **3.** A city worker collects five vials of water from each of ten randomly selected locations all over the city to test the levels of bacteria in the city water supply.

    a. What is the sample in this experiment?

    b. What is the population?

APPLICATION  **EXAMPLE 4** **Distinguish Between Parameters and Statistics**

Is each quantity a statistic or a parameter?

A. A high school has three lunch periods. In a randomly selected lunch period, 24% of students brought lunch from home.

A **parameter** is a measure that describes a population. A **statistic** is a measure that describes a sample of the population. In this situation, the population is the set of all students in the school. The figure 24% describes a sample of that population, the students who were in the selected lunch period. Therefore, it is a statistic.

GENERALIZE
Categorical data are often summarized using proportions while quantitative data are often summarized using a median or a mean. © **MP.8**

B. At the end of its first year of business, a movie theater collected data on how well its concession stand operated that year. The theater used its total yearly concessions sales and number of tickets sold to calculate that the mean amount spent at concessions by a moviegoer was $8.14. Is this a statistic or a parameter?

The value $8.14 describes the concession purchases of all of the moviegoers who attended the theater that year. This value is a parameter since the theater included all moviegoers to determine how well the concession stand is doing.

 Try It! **4.** Is the given data summary a parameter or statistic?

    a. 53.2% of a district's eligible voters voted for the sitting U.S. House Representative.

    b. The median age of a car in 20 randomly selected spaces in the school parking lot is 7 years.

A statistical question is a question that can be answered by collecting many pieces of information, or data.

"What is the average number of pets owned by students at your school?"

"What is the most popular type of pet owned by students at your school?"

The value of a statistical variable will vary from one observation to another.

Number of Pets	Types of Pets		
	Dog	Cat	Other
3	X	X	
0			
1			X
⋮	⋮	⋮	⋮

A quantitative variable has numerical values that can be meaningfully compared, added, subtracted, or otherwise operated upon.

A categorical variable has a limited number of possible responses that are not quantitative.

A parameter is a piece of information about a variable that is based on the entire population, or group of people or things that is being studied.

A statistic is a piece of information about a variable that is based on a sample or subgroup chosen from the population.

Do You UNDERSTAND?

1. **ESSENTIAL QUESTION** What kinds of questions about quantities and relationships among quantities can be answered with statistics?

2. **Error Analysis** Dyani says she identified a quantitative variable and conducted a survey when she asked her fellow classmates in her homeroom about their favorite style of sweatshirt from the categories: hoodie, pullover, or zip-up. Explain her error. © MP.3

3. **Vocabulary** Explain the difference between a categorical variable and a quantitative variable.

4. **Communicate Precisely** Suppose Hana wants to find out the most commonly driven type of vehicle among the students at her high school. Since 1,560 students attend her high school, she asks every tenth student who enters the building one morning what kind of vehicle he or she drives. What is the population in this scenario? © MP.6

Do You KNOW HOW?

5. Is the following question a statistical question?

   "During which month did your family take a vacation?"

6. What is the statistical variable represented by the following question, and is it categorical or quantitative?

   "How many TV sets are owned by families?"

7. Forty randomly-selected members of a high school music program were asked to report the number of hours they spend practicing each week. If you were to compute the mean number of hours, would your answer be a parameter or a statistic? Explain.

UNDERSTAND

8. Communicate Precisely Does the scatterplot below relate to a statistical question? Explain. ⒸMP.6

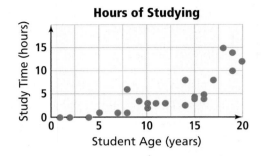

Hours of Studying

Study Time (hours) vs *Student Age (years)*

9. Make Sense and Persevere At the end of the month, a restaurant manager used the total food sales for the month and the total number of customers for the month to calculate that the mean amount spent per customer during that month was $12.59. Is this value a statistic or a parameter? Explain. ⒸMP.1

10. Error Analysis Describe and correct the error a student made in responding to the question regarding the following scenario. ⒸMP.3

A Detroit, Michigan, radio station polled its listeners about whether they supported a citywide tax increase to renovate the city's professional football stadium to determine whether city residents support the increase. What are the sample and the population in this scenario?

> The sample is the listeners of the radio station.
> The population is all the registered voters in the state of Michigan.
> ✗

11. Higher Order Thinking Write a response to the following items regarding statistical variables.

a. Write a statistical question that uses a categorical variable.

b. Write a statistical question that uses a quantitative variable.

PRACTICE

12. Is the given question a statistical question? Explain. SEE EXAMPLE 1

a. *"What is the tallest building in Chicago, Illinois?"*

b. *"What is the most popular store in the Turtlecreek Mall among teenagers?"*

13. What type of statistical variable is represented by the graph shown? SEE EXAMPLE 2

Most Popular H.S. Sport to Watch

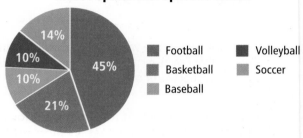

- Football
- Basketball
- Baseball
- Volleyball
- Soccer

45%, 21%, 14%, 10%, 10%

14. A biology teacher wants to know which dissection his students liked best this semester, so he randomly selects eight students from each of his five classes to participate in a survey.

a. What is the sample in this situation?

b. What is the population? SEE EXAMPLE 3

15. The data below were collected from all race participants to answer the question, "What is the average age of runners in the Fall Harvest 5K?" Does this histogram represent data related to a parameter or statistic? Explain your response. SEE EXAMPLE 4

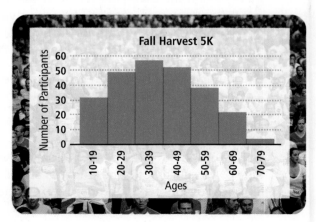

Fall Harvest 5K — Number of Participants vs Ages (10-19, 20-29, 30-39, 40-49, 50-59, 60-69, 70-79)

PRACTICE & PROBLEM SOLVING

APPLY

16. Is the given question a statistical question? Explain.

    a. *"Which is the most popular category of children's literature: biography, science fiction, fantasy, or mystery?"*

    b. *"For which category of children's literature is J.K. Rowling best known?"*

17. **Make Sense and Persevere** Can the graph below be helpful in answering a statistical question? Explain. **© MP.1**

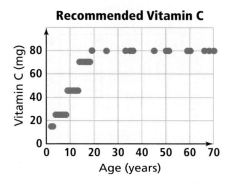

Recommended Vitamin C

18. **Use Structure** What type of statistical variable is represented by the following question and corresponding graph? **© MP.7**

"How many pets does your family own?"

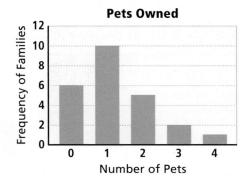

Pets Owned

19. **Look For Relationships** Ms. Lee wants to know what kinds of things her students do to prepare for her tests. Ms. Lee placed the names of her students into a box. To determine who she would ask about their study habits she asked a student to draw names from the box. **© MP.7**

    a. What is the sample in this situation?

    b. What is the population?

ASSESSMENT PRACTICE

20. The average length of all the trout in a river is 60 cm. This data summary represents a _____. (parameter/statistic)

21. **SAT/ACT** If the Hamilton High School freshmen class is the sample in a statistical study, then which is **not** a possible population for the study?

    Ⓐ the student body of Hamilton High School

    Ⓑ the students in Hamilton High School's district

    Ⓒ the students in Ms. Anderson's science class

    Ⓓ all freshmen students in the state

22. **Performance Task** A state randomly questioned some of its high schools about the average percentages of their students who attend home football games. The results are summarized in the histogram below.

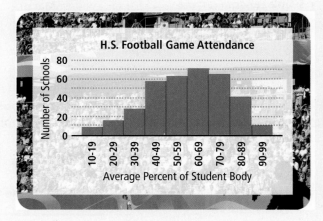

Part A Describe the population and the sample for these data. Are these data quantitative or categorical? Explain.

Part B What is an example of a statistical question that could be answered with these data?

Part C Joshua was surprised that the median of the data was not a much lower number. What is a possible reason that Joshua could be surprised by these results?

Activity Assess

11-2

Statistical Studies and Sampling Methods

 SavvasRealize.com

I CAN... design a statistical study.

VOCABULARY
- bias
- control group
- experiment
- experimental group
- observational study
- sample survey
- simple random sample

👆 **CRITIQUE & EXPLAIN**

Jacinta and Felix were each asked to design a study to answer the question: "What proportion of students at this school listen to music while studying?"

A. What group did Jacinta select from to conduct her study? What group did Felix select from?

B. How did Jacinta choose which members of her group to question? How did Felix choose which members from his group to observe?

C. **Look for Relationships** Who designed a better study, Jacinta or Felix? Explain. © **MP.7**

Jacinta Friends in Gym Class	yes	no
Cameron	✗	
Dana	✗	
Emma		✗
Henry		✗
Jung	✗	
Keisha		✗
Marisol		✗

Felix

Students listening to music in the library

卌 卌 卌 卌
卌 卌 卌
卌 ‖‖

Total students = 100

43%

? **ESSENTIAL QUESTION**

How can you choose the best type of study to answer a given statistical question and choose a reasonable sample?

👆 **EXAMPLE 1** ▶ **Choose a Type of Study**

A. Which of the three main types of study is shown in each example below?

A newspaper polls randomly selected residents in a town about which mayoral candidate they prefer.

This is a **sample survey**. A sample survey asks every member of a sample the same set of questions and records the answers.

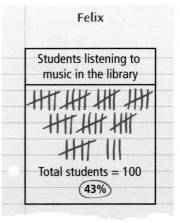

LOOK FOR RELATIONSHIPS
In which type of study might a person be unaware that he or she is a participant? © **MP.7**

A doctor conducts a clinical trial of a new blood pressure medicine by prescribing it to half the patients in the study and measuring the effect it has on their blood pressure.

This is an **experiment**. An experiment involves applying a treatment to some group or groups and measuring the effects of the treatments.

A grocery store wonders how many customers bring reusable grocery bags to the store. They have an employee stand at the checkout and count the number of people using reusable bags.

This is an **observational study**. In an observational study, you measure or observe members of a sample in such a way that they are not affected by the study.

CONTINUED ON THE NEXT PAGE

 Go Online | SavvasRealize.com

EXAMPLE 1 CONTINUED

B. What type of study could you use to answer the following questions?

Question	Study
Does urban pollution have an effect on rates of asthma?	Observational study: observe residents of urban and non-urban areas, and compare the rates of asthma over a long period of time.
How many students in a school would like the cafeteria to serve breakfast?	Sample survey: ask randomly chosen students in the school their opinion and record the results.
A group of plants is not growing well compared to the rest. What should you change to improve their growth?	Experiment: split the plants into groups randomly, and give each group different conditions such as more light, more water, or different fertilizer. Leave one group under the current conditions to see if the new treatments show improvement.

COMMON ERROR
Conducting an experiment might be the most efficient way to answer a question, but it may be unethical to do so. For example, you would not intentionally expose people to pollution to test its affect on asthma rates. In these cases, an observational study is more appropriate.

Try It! **1.** What type of study is described?

a. A gym asks its customers if they would prefer the gym to open earlier in the morning.

b. A gym tries out a new weightlifting method to see if it will build muscle for their customers faster than their current method.

c. A gym counts the customers who come before 8 A.M.

CONCEPTUAL UNDERSTANDING

EXAMPLE 2 Determine Sources of Bias

In the following situations, are the differences between groups potentially due to bias?

A. A psychologist is conducting surveys to study the happiness levels of people who live in a neighborhood. She asks the same questions to the two samples below chosen from the population of the neighborhood.

100 people surveyed
Sunny Saturday afternoon
65% people happy

100 people surveyed
Monday morning
35% people happy

The difference between the results of these surveys is due to bias, because the circumstances when the two samples were surveyed may influence their responses. A study has **bias** if it systematically produces results that misrepresent a population.

STUDY TIP
Personal bias, or a personal inclination for or against something, and statistical bias are different. While personal bias can lead to statistical bias, statistical bias has many other possible causes.

CONTINUED ON THE NEXT PAGE

EXAMPLE 2 CONTINUED

Bias might also arise if a sample is more likely to include a certain category of the population than another. For example, a poll on a website is more likely to select frequent Internet users than those who do not go online often.

> Bias can be introduced in other ways. For example, a survey might have questions that influence the answers in some way.

B. A school wants to know the average height of its students. The school randomly chooses some students and measures their height. Some students are under 5 feet tall and some are over 6 feet, 5 inches tall.

The fact that some of the data collected are either very high or very low is not necessarily the result of bias. A population like students in a high school will naturally have people with a wide variety of heights. A true random sample may have members from both extremes.

 Try It! **2.** A soft drink company calls 500 people at random and asks, "Is our product or our rival's product the best soft drink on the market?" Why is this question a potential source of bias?

MAKE SENSE AND PERSEVERE
Why should you determine whether any differences in the collected data are due to a biased study or from natural variability in a population? **© MP.1**

CONCEPT Sampling Methods

In order to select a sample that is likely to be representative of the population, you need to choose members of the sample using randomness. The simplest way to use randomness is with a **simple random sample**. In a simple random sample, each member of the population is equally likely to chosen, and each possible sample of the size you want is equally likely to be chosen.

> Some sampling methods can involve randomness in other ways to select a sample. Some sampling methods do not use enough randomness to give reliable results.

Care must be taken to avoid bias.			High Risk of Bias	
Stratified sampling is when a population is divided into groups with similar characteristics and a sample is randomly chosen from each group.	Cluster sampling is when a population is divided into convenient clusters, and entire clusters are chosen at random as the sample.	Systematic sampling is when you start with one member chosen at random then use a rule, such as "every 3rd member of the population," to select members of the sample.	Convenience sampling is only choosing subjects that are in close proximity or easy to get to.	Self-selected sampling is using a sample made up of volunteers.

EXAMPLE 3 Identify a Sampling Method

What sampling method is used in the following examples? Is the method likely to be biased?

Study	Sampling Method
A. Starting with a randomly chosen ID number, every fifth student ID number was chosen and that student was asked to fill out a survey.	This is systematic sampling. The rule is that every fifth number was chosen. This method unlikely to be biased.
B. A retailer put feedback cards at the front of its store. They got responses from 22% of their customers.	This is a self-selected sample, which only includes people who decided to respond to the survey. This method is not random and likely biased.
C. A city wants to know what percent of people in the city own a dog or a cat. A city worker goes door to door in the neighborhood around city hall to ask people about their pets.	This is convenience sampling because only the neighborhood around city hall was sampled. The process is likely to be biased because pets may be more or less common in other parts of the city.

CONSTRUCT ARGUMENTS
How could you redesign the biased studies here so that the samples are not biased? **ⓒ MP.3**

 Try It! **3.** What sampling method is used in the following examples? Is the method likely to be biased or not?

a. The population is grouped according to age and a random sample is chosen from each group.

b. A number of hospitals around the country were randomly chosen. Within each hospital, all of the nurses were chosen.

 APPLICATION

 EXAMPLE 4 Randomize Experiments

Describe a design for a controlled experiment to test a new drug for treating the flu on mice. How does randomization apply to your design?

In a simple controlled experiment, randomly assign mice to one of two groups. One group, the **experimental group**, receives the treatment. The other group, the **control group**, does not. Then use statistics to compare the effect of the treatment to the effect of no treatment.

Mice are assigned randomly to either group, and all mice are infected with the flu. The control group does not receive the drug. The experimental group receives the new drug. The results are analyzed to see whether the new drug affects the progression of flu in a way that is significantly different from receiving no treatment. The random assignment to experimental and control groups should ensure that the difference between the two groups is due to the drug rather than some other cause.

STUDY TIP
Some experiments can have more than two groups, especially if you are testing multiple variables. Some experiments do not have a control group and just compare different treatments.

 Try It! **4.** Design an experiment to test whether drinking coffee improves memory. How will you choose the experimental and control groups?

TYPES OF STUDIES

- An **experiment** involves randomly dividing a population into two groups, applying a different treatment to each group, and measuring the difference between the treatments.

- A **sample survey** asks every member of a randomly selected sample the same set of questions and records the answers to try to draw a conclusion about the population.

- In an **observational study,** you do not assign treatments to the subjects being studied. The subjects are already affected by the treatments under investigation.

TYPES OF SAMPLING

Care must be taken to avoid bias.			High Risk of Bias	
Stratified sampling is when a population is divided into groups with similar characteristics and a sample is randomly chosen from each group.	Cluster sampling is when a population is divided into convenient clusters, and entire clusters are chosen at random as the sample.	Systematic sampling is when you start with one member chosen at random then use a rule, such as "every 3rd member of the population," to select members of the sample.	Convenience sampling is only choosing subjects that are in close proximity or easy to get to.	Self-selected sampling is using a sample made up of volunteers.

Do You UNDERSTAND?

1. **ESSENTIAL QUESTION** How can you choose the best type of study to answer given statistical question and choose a reasonable sample?

2. **Vocabulary** A city is weighing whether to increase fares for public transit, or to provide more funding to public transit through the city's general fund, which is primarily funded by local property taxes. A survey of public transit riders was conducted to determine popular opinion. What is this sampling method an example of?

3. **Error Analysis** When Lila conducted an experiment on citywide pond water, all of her samples came from the pond in her uncle's backyard. Explain her error. **ⓒ MP.3**

Do You KNOW HOW?

4. An ice cream shop asks its customers if they would like the shop to offer containers of ice cream to take home. What type of study does this describe?

5. A television news program asks its viewers to call in to give their opinions on an upcoming ballot question. What type of sampling method does this represent?

6. A doctor assigns people to treatment groups based on data from their medical records. Is this method of selecting treatment groups biased or unbiased? Explain.

UNDERSTAND

7. Reason Suppose a civic engineer wants to conduct a survey to find out if residents of a city would be in favor of widening one of the city's roadways for increased traffic flow. **Ⓒ MP.2**

a. Would a sample consisting of residents who utilize that roadway to travel to work each morning be representative? Explain.

b. Would a sample consisting of residents who live along that roadway be representative? Explain.

c. Would a random sample of homeowners in the city be representative? Explain.

8. Make Sense and Persevere A pharmaceutical company is developing a new oral medication for the treatment of psoriasis, a skin disease marked by red, itchy, scaly patches. Describe how you could design a controlled experiment to test the effect of the medication. How could you keep participants from knowing whether or not they were in the treatment group? **Ⓒ MP.1**

9. Error Analysis Describe and correct the error a student made when responding to the following question. **Ⓒ MP.3**

A website wants to post a blog about the most popular type of pet in the Seattle area. Would a sample consisting of every tenth ticket holder to the local dog show be representative? Explain.

Yes; since the sample is a systematic random sample, it would be representative of the population.

10. Higher Order Thinking Suppose a grocery store manager wishes to survey the store's employees in order to determine whether they prefer expanding the existing break room or building an outdoor patio for the employees.

a. How could the manager conduct an unbiased stratified sampling?

b. How could the manager conduct an unbiased systematic sampling?

PRACTICE

11. What type of study is described? SEE EXAMPLE 1

a. Managers of a forest preserve want to know what percent of the visitors with dogs keep their dogs on a leash. The park assigns an employee to count the numbers of visitors that do and do not use a leash.

b. A local newspaper polls citizens of a city about whether they support a local tax levy.

12. A researcher wants to know the average growth of a certain plant one week after germination. The greenhouse where he grows the plants has 12 trays with 36 plants on each tray. He picks one tray from the greenhouse and measures the heights of each plant. The results are shown in the dot plot.

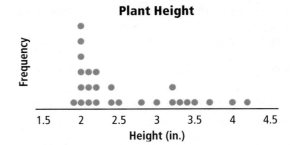

Plant Height

When analyzing the data, he sees that the heights of the plants are clustered around 2 in. Could this be the result of bias in his sampling method? Explain. SEE EXAMPLE 2

13. What sampling method is used in the following examples? Is the method biased or not? SEE EXAMPLE 3

a. A clothing manufacturing company divided its employees up by units, and then they randomly selected three employees from each unit to represent the company at a convention in Las Vegas.

b. Mr. Yotsey put names of all students at his school on identical slips of paper in a box and distributed surveys to the students whose names he pulled.

14. Researchers want to find out if warm water therapy increases muscle strength in people 65 years of age and older. Describe a design for a controlled study of this question. What are some potential sources of bias in your study? SEE EXAMPLE 4

APPLY

ASSESSMENT PRACTICE

15. **Make Sense and Persevere** Suppose a major oil company hired a survey organization to conduct a study of citizens living within 5 mi of the coast. ⒸMP.1

The survey question is, *"Do you want to save money at the gas pump? Well then you would be in favor of off shore drilling, right?"*

Explain the bias that exists in this scenario.

16. **Communicate Precisely** A group of farmers wants to test a new fertilizer being produced for soybean crops. Explain how the farmers could set up the control group and the experimental group for this study. ⒸMP.6

17. **Make Sense and Persevere** At Miami University in Oxford, OH, there is a university seal located in the heart of campus. There is a long-standing tradition that claims if you step on the seal you will fail your next exam.

Natalie spends several hours over several different days, at varying times, counting the number of students who pass along the walkway and the number of students who step on the seal. Which of the three main types of study does Natalie use in her project? ⒸMP.1

18. **Model With Mathematics** A commercial developer hires a market research company to determine the mean household income of those who live within a 10 mi radius of the site of a proposed upscale shopping center. ⒸMP.4

   a. Explain why the commercial developer would do this.

   b. How might the market research company get the information?

19. A newspaper hires a polling company to determine the level of support in the county for raising property taxes in order to increase funding for local schools. The polling company calls phone numbers chosen at random from a phone number registry between the hours of 5:00 P.M. and 7:00 P.M. What are some potential sources of bias in this sampling method?

20. Choose Yes or No to tell whether each of the following describes a convenience sampling method.

	Yes	No
A manager surveys every fourth customer about their level of satisfaction with their shopping experience.	❑	❑
When a school district wishes to get feedback on the district's new webpage, they survey the entire population of randomly selected schools.	❑	❑
When Sheila wanted to find out what type of music was most popular among the students in her history class, she asked the two students who sat on either side of her.	❑	❑
The quality control officer of a ladder manufacturer walked into the shop, pulled the five closest ladders, and gave them several stress tests checking for potential defects.	❑	❑

21. **SAT/ACT** A researcher studies differences in career goals between boys and girls in middle school. All of the students in the seventh grade schools in a particular county answer a list of questions. What type of study is this?

   Ⓐ experiment   Ⓒ observational study

   Ⓑ sample survey   Ⓓ random trial

22. **Performance Task** A grocery store surveys every fifth customer to determine whether it should consider expanding its organic foods department. The results of the 500 customers surveyed are shown in the table.

In favor of expanded organic dept.?	
Yes	378
No	97
Indifferent	25

Part A What type of sampling method was used? Does it seem valid?

Part B Based upon the results of this survey, about what percent of the store's customers would favor the expansion?

Part C What is the statistical variable in this study? Is this a quantitative or categorical variable?

11-3
Data Distributions

I CAN... evaluate data distributions

VOCABULARY
- normal distribution
- skewed distribution
- standard deviation
- symmetrical distribution

  Activity Assess

CRITIQUE & EXPLAIN

Chen and Dakota were asked to estimate the mean and median of the following data set. Chen said, "The middle value is 11. Both the mean and median are approximately 11." Dakota said, "Most of the data are the left. I think the mean and median will be about 9, with the mean slightly larger."

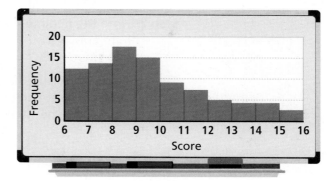

A. Is either Chen or Dakota correct? Explain.

B. What strategies could you use to approximate the exact mean and median?

C. Reason Which measure of center is more representative in this case, the mean or the median? Explain. © **MP.2**

? ESSENTIAL QUESTION

How can you interpret the distribution of data in a data set?

EXAMPLE 1 Find Measures of Center and Spread

A. What are the mean and standard deviation of the following data set?

4, 12, 15, 9, 14, 16, 13, 6, 7, 6, 25, 3, 13, 17, 22, 4

The mean, or average, of a data set is the sum of the values in the data set divided by the number of values in the data set. The **standard deviation** is a measure of how much the values in a data set vary, or deviate, from the mean. It is a measure of the variability or spread of the data.

> The mean and the standard deviation are used together to measure the center and spread of the data.

STUDY TIP
Most technology has the ability to calculate mean and standard deviation.

You can use a spreadsheet to calculate the mean and standard deviation.

	A	B	C	D	E	F	G	H	I	J	K	L	M	N	O	P	Q	R
1																		
2	4	12	15	9	14	16	13	6	7	6	25	3	13	17	22	4	Mean	11.625
3																	SD	6.313
4																		

The mean is $\bar{x} \approx 11.6$, and the standard deviation is $\sigma \approx 6.3$.

CONTINUED ON THE NEXT PAGE

EXAMPLE 1 CONTINUED

B. What is the five-number summary of the data set?

The five-number summary includes the minimum value, first quartile, median, third quartile, and maximum value.

Step 1 Rearrange the data in ascending numerical order.

3, 4, 4, 6, 6, 7, 9, 12, 13, 13, 14, 15, 16, 17, 22, 25

Step 2 Note the minimum and maximum values:
minimum = 3
maximum = 25

Step 3 Calculate the median, the number in the middle of the data set. Since there are an even number of values, the median is the average of the two middle values, or 12.5.

{3, 4, 4, 6, 6, 7, 9, 12,}   {13, 13, 14, 15, 16, 17, 22, 25}

    1st quartile   median   3rd quartile

Step 4 Calculate the first and third quartiles. The quartiles show how the data are distributed. The first quartile is the median of the lower half of the data, 6. The third quartile is the median of the upper half of the data, 15.5.

These data can be represented in a box-and-whisker plot. Notice that the one quartile is closer to the median than the other.

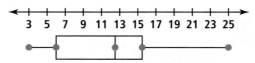

The five-number summary of this data set is: minimum = 3, 1st quartile = 6, median = 12.5, 3rd quartile = 15.5, maximum = 25

> **COMMON ERROR**
> Remember that for a data set that has an odd number of values, the median IS the middle value. Do not consider this value when finding the quartiles.

 Try It!   **1.** List the mean, standard deviation, and five-number summary of the following data set.
3 4 9 12 12 14 15 19 25 30 32 33 34 34 35

EXAMPLE 2   **Use Appropriate Statistics to Compare Data Sets**

A. How can you describe different types of distributions?

To compare the different types of distributions, look at the shape, the center, and the spread of the distributions.

The standard deviation, range, and the interquartile range are three measures of spread. The range of a data set is the difference between the maximum and minimum values. The interquartile range is the difference between the third quartile and the first quartile.

> When measuring center and spread, median and interquartile range are used together, and mean and standard deviation are used together.

A **skewed distribution** is one with a shape that is stretched out in either the positive or negative direction. A **symmetrical distribution** has a shape that, when reflected across the mean, the display is roughly the same.

CONTINUED ON THE NEXT PAGE

EXAMPLE 2 CONTINUED

The shape of a distribution can affect the measures of center and spread and determine which measures of center and spread best describe the data.

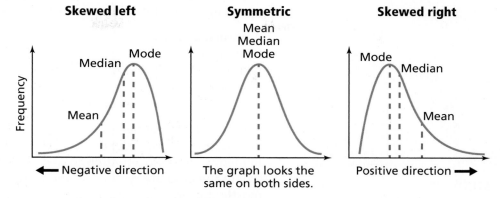

The mean, median, and mode are all about the same in a symmetric distribution. You can use the mean and the standard deviation to describe the center and spread.

B. What measures of center and spread would you use for the following data set?

10 13 16 21 22 26 29 29 30 32 33 33 33 35 37

You can use a histogram to determine the shape.

Since the mean is more affected than the median by a data distribution that is skewed, it is better to use the median and interquartile range as the measures of center and spread. Also, the quartiles show how the data are distributed differently on either side of the center.

USE APPROPRIATE TOOLS
What are some other ways you can determine the shape of the distribution of these data? © MP.5

The data are already in numerical order.

{10 13 16 21 22 26 29} 29 {30 32 33 33 33 35 37}

   1st quartile   median   3rd quartile

The range is 37 − 10 = 27, and the interquartile range is 33 − 21 = 12.

 Try It! 2. What are the better measures of center and spread of the following data sets?

   a. 55 55 57 57 57 58 58 59 59 59 61 61

   b. 110 110 110 120 120 130 140 150 160 170 180 190

CONCEPTUAL
UNDERSTANDING   👆 **EXAMPLE 3**   Recognize a Normal Distribution

Are the following variables likely to have a normal distribution?

A. The heights of all the people in a large group

A **normal distribution** can
be modeled by a particular
bell-shaped curve that is
symmetric about the mean.
This is called a normal curve.

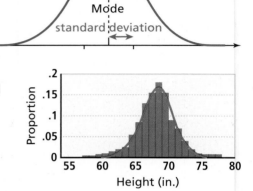

Approximately normal
distributions can be found
in many real-world situations
where the data are symmetric and
mostly clustered near the mean.

The heights of people in a large
group are likely to be normally
distributed.

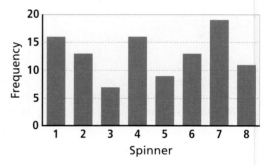

STUDY TIP
Notice that for real-world
examples, the data in a normal
distribution might not be perfectly
normally distributed but can be
modeled by a normal curve.

B. The probability of landing on each of 8 equal parts of a spinner

This data set is not normally
distributed because each
outcome has the same
probability of occurring as
any other.

C. The scores on an easy test

The scores on an easy test
are often skewed left and
not normally distributed,
because more students will
receive higher scores.

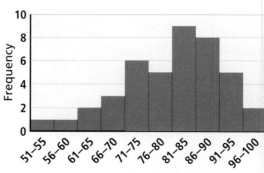

CONTINUED ON THE NEXT PAGE

EXAMPLE 3 CONTINUED

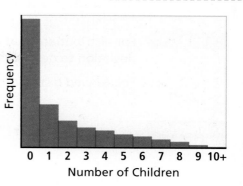

D. The number of children in a family

The number of children in a family is not normally distributed. The distribution is skewed right because many families have 0, 1, 2, or 3 children, but very few families have 10 or more children.

 Try It! 3. Is each situation likely to be normally distributed? Explain.

    a. weight of individuals in a population

    b. the scores on a difficult test

EXAMPLE 4   **Classify a Data Distribution**

How would you classify the following data set? Describe the shape of the distribution and the center and spread of the data.

106, 96, 86, 120, 98, 76, 112, 64, 99, 72, 119, 115, 76, 120, 97

Step 1 Make a histogram of the data.

Step 2 Analyze the shape of the histogram.

Since the data are bunched to the right and have a long tail to the left, the data are skewed left.

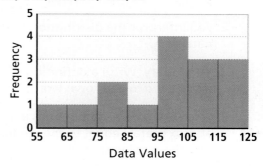

> **STUDY TIP**
> If the median and the mean are equal or very close, then the data are likely to be symmetric.

Step 3 Determine the center and spread of the data. Use the median and interquartile range.

    64 72 76 76 86 96 97 98 99 106 112 115 119 120 120

    1st quartile = 76, median = 98, 3rd quartile = 115

The interquartile range is 115 − 76 = 39. Notice that the 3rd quartile is closer to the median than the 1st quartile is. This is characteristic of a distribution that is skewed left.

The distribution is skewed left with median 98 and interquartile range 39.

 Try It! 4. What is the type of distribution and the center and spread of the data? 20, 17, 17, 12, 18, 21, 19, 18, 13, 14, 17, 23, 25

CONCEPT SUMMARY Data Distributions

SHADES For distributions that are approximately normal, use mean and standard deviation to describe the data.

For skewed distributions, use median and quartiles to describe the data.

GRAPHS

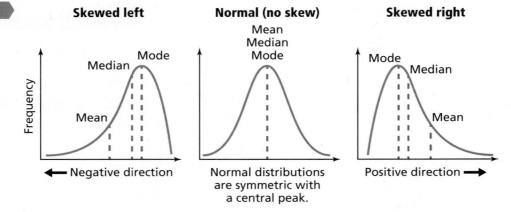

| Skewed left | Normal (no skew) | Skewed right |

Negative direction ← | Normal distributions are symmetric with a central peak. | Positive direction →

Do You UNDERSTAND?

1. **ESSENTIAL QUESTION** How can you interpret the distribution of data in a data set?

2. **Vocabulary** Write a definition for *normally distributed* in your own words.

3. **Error Analysis** A data set has a mean that is approximately equal to the median. Ralph says the median should be used to describe the measure of center, and the quartiles should be used to describe the measure of spread. Explain his error. **ⓒ MP.3**

4. **Communicate Precisely** Explain how to determine if the data distribution shown is skewed left, right, or is symmetric. **ⓒ MP.6**

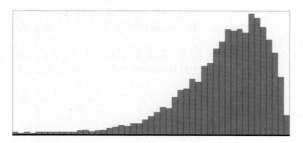

Do You KNOW HOW?

Determine the mean, standard deviation, and five-number summary of each data set. Round to the nearest hundredth, if necessary.

5. 5, 8, 5, 9, 6, 14, 9, 3, 8, 7, 10, 12

6. 10.5, 2.25, 7.75, 8.8, 3.4, 9.2, 6.5, 4.3, 3.9, 6.4

Describe the shape of the data summarized in the histograms.

7.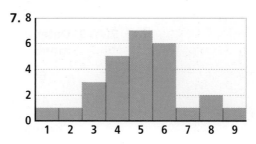

8.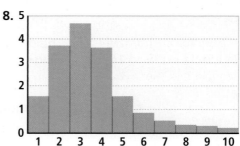

UNDERSTAND

9. **Communicate Precisely** Describe a situation that is likely to produce the following data distribution. © MP.6

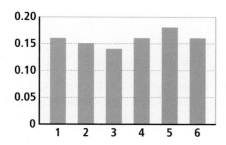

10. **Error Analysis** Maurice's teacher asked him to compare the mean and median of the data distribution. Explain and correct Maurice's error in comparing the mean and median. © MP.3

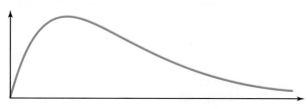

The distribution is skewed right.

This implies the mean is less than the median. ✗

11. **Higher Order Thinking** Dale drew the following box plot to represent a data set.

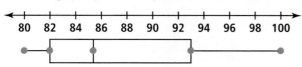

a. Identify the five-number summary of the data.

b. Explain how to use the five-number summary to write a data set with 14 data values to match the box plot. Then write such a data set.

PRACTICE

Find the mean, standard deviation, and five-number summary of each data set. Round to the nearest tenth, if necessary. SEE EXAMPLE 1

12. 9, 15, 17, 21, 23, 31, 33, 39, 46, 50

13. 35, 12, 25, 33, 27, 48, 30, 34, 35, 41, 14

14. 9, 24, 10, 11, 5, 16, 18, 30, 19, 22, 12, 28, 9, 33

For each set of data, describe the shape of the distribution and determine which measures of center and spread best represent the data. SEE EXAMPLE 2

15. 28, 13, 23, 34, 55, 38, 44, 65, 49, 33, 50, 59, 67, 45

16. 3.1, 2.3, 8.8, 2.8, 3.2, 3.5, 3.9, 4.3, 4.5, 2.9, 3.9, 5.5

17. 12, 2, 14, 4, 1, 6, 11, 7, 8, 5, 9, 10, 8, 15

Determine if each situation is likely to be uniformly distributed, normally distributed, skewed left, or skewed right. SEE EXAMPLE 3

18. The age at which people die in the United States

19. number of pets owned by students at your school

20. Selling price of cars in 2018

21. The height of all adult females in Connecticut

Determine the type of distribution and the best measure of center and spread of each data set. Round to the nearest hundredth, if necessary. SEE EXAMPLE 4

22. 3, 6, 12, 14, 17, 17, 18, 21, 21, 22, 23, 28

23. 17, 9, 27, 13, 15, 19, 19, 21, 11, 23, 17, 25

24. 7.8, 4.9, 5.7, 24.2, 3.3, 6.2, 9.1, 10.6, 11.9, 3.9, 12.3, 17.2, 18

25. 53, 24, 65, 26, 60, 32, 41, 7, 44, 49, 50, 52, 55, 46

APPLY

26. **Make Sense and Persevere** The test scores from a history test are 88, 95, 92, 60, 86, 78, 95, 98, 92, 96, 70, 80, 89, and 96. ©**MP.1**

   a. Find the mean and standard deviation of the test scores.

   b. Find the five-number summary of the test scores.

   c. Describe the type of distribution. Explain.

   d. Do you think the test was an easy test or a hard test for these students? Explain.

27. **Reason** The salaries of some employees at a company are shown. ©**MP.2**

Employee Salary

$40,000

$50,000

$75,000

$175,000

$55,000

$90,000

$100,000

$60,000

   a. Describe the type of distribution.

   b. Find an appropriate measure of center and measure of spread. Explain your choice.

28. A real estate agent wants to convince a client to raise the asking price on his home so she can earn a higher commission. Based on the data shown, should she tell her client the mean or median home price? Explain.

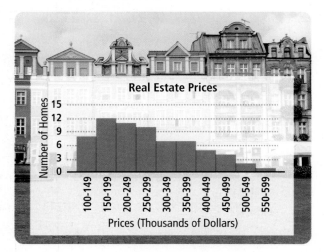

Real Estate Prices

ASSESSMENT PRACTICE

29. Select all five-number summaries that represent a data distribution that is normally distributed.

   Ⓐ 2, 7, 8, 9, 10

   Ⓑ 2, 4.6, 6, 7.4, 10

   Ⓒ 2, 2, 2, 2, 2

   Ⓓ 1, 2.3, 3, 3.7, 5

30. **SAT/ACT** How are the data representing the age of people who purchased movie tickets at a senior citizen discount likely to be distributed?

   Ⓐ uniformly distributed   Ⓑ skewed right

   Ⓒ normally distributed   Ⓓ skewed left

31. **Performance Task** A voice coach looks up the ages of all the contestants on a popular singing competition and creates two graphs by grouping the data differently.

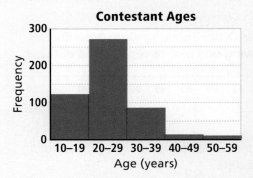

Contestant Ages

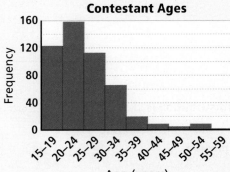

Contestant Ages

Part A Describe the shape of the data. How would you expect the mean and median to compare?

Part B Which graph would be better to convince students that they should continue singing lessons into 20s? Which graph would be better to convince students to continue lessons into their 30s?

11-4

Normal Distributions

 SavvasRealize.com

I CAN... understand where a data value falls in relation to other values in a normal distribution.

VOCABULARY
• percentile
• standard normal distribution
• z-score

Common Core State Standards HSS.ID.A.4, HSS.IC.B.6, MP.3, MP.5, MP.7

EXPLORE & REASON

The owner of an apple orchard and the owner of an orange grove create histograms to display fruit production data.

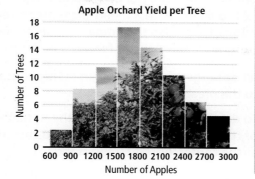

Apple Orchard Yield per Tree

mean = 1,750
standard deviation = 296

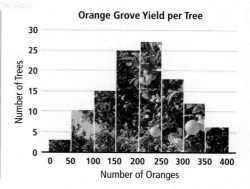

Orange Grove Yield per Tree

mean = 210
standard deviation = 47

A. Describe the shape of each distribution. Discuss how the distributions are alike and how they are different.

B. Use Structure Explain how you could estimate the mean from the graphs. The standard deviation measures spread from the mean. Which data values are within a standard deviation of the mean on each graph? © **MP.7**

ESSENTIAL QUESTION

How can you use the normal distribution to explain where data values fall within a population?

CONCEPT The Empirical Rule

The normal distribution has a special property called The Empirical Rule. The approximate percentage of data values falling in any interval of the range of the data can be determined using just the mean and the standard deviation.

> For a population, the mean is denoted by μ and the standard deviation by σ.

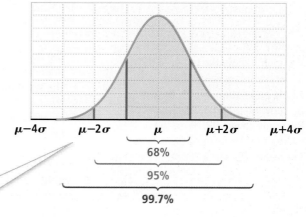

How far from the mean does a value in a normal distribution fall?

- About 68% of all values fall within 1 standard deviation.
- About 95% of all values fall within 2 standard deviations.
- About 99.7% of all values fall within 3 standard deviations.

> The rule applies *only* to normal distributions.

👆 **EXAMPLE 1** Find Population Intervals

An example of an early application of statistics was in the year 1817. A study of chest circumference among a group of Scottish men exhibited an approximately normal distribution. Their chest circumferences ranged from 33 to 48 in., with a mean chest measurement of 40 in. and a standard deviation of 2 in. Use the Empirical Rule to help you understand the distribution of chest circumferences in the study.

A. **What range of chest measurements contains the 68% which fall closest to the mean?**

To draw the graph, first draw the horizontal axis. Draw the "bell curve" of the normal distribution and add the labels to the axis with the mean at the center. Count by the standard deviation to each end of the curve.

Distribution of Chest Circumferences

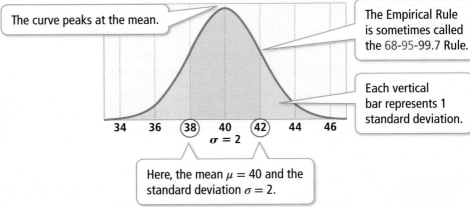

The curve peaks at the mean.

The Empirical Rule is sometimes called the 68-95-99.7 Rule.

Each vertical bar represents 1 standard deviation.

Here, the mean $\mu = 40$ and the standard deviation $\sigma = 2$.

You would expect approximately 68% of the men in the population had chest measurements between 38 and 42 in.

B. **What would you expect the chest measurements to be for the 2.5% of the men with the smallest chest measurements in the population?**

Distribution of Chest Circumferences

The question asks for the *smallest* 2.5% of measurements. The symmetry of the curve means that the largest 2.5% of measurements will be equally far from the mean.

After subtracting 5%, 95% remains. The Empirical Rule says that 95% of all values in a normal distribution fall within 2 standard deviations of the mean.

You would expect 2.5% of the men in the population to have chests measuring less than 36 in.

CONTINUED ON THE NEXT PAGE

LOOK FOR RELATIONSHIPS
One standard deviation from the mean is where the curve changes from opening upward to downward (left of mean), and from opening downward to upward (right of mean). Ⓒ MP.7

STUDY TIP
You won't know the upper and lower boundary values for a whole population in a study just by knowing μ and σ. The Empirical Rule only covers 99.7% of the values, not the farthest 0.3% from the mean. Ⓒ MP.5

EXAMPLE 1 CONTINUED
  Activity Assess

 Try It! **1. a.** What would you expect to be the smallest and largest chest measurements of the "middle" 95% of the men?

b. What would you expect to be the measurements of the 16% of the men with the largest chests in the population?

 EXAMPLE 2 **Use The Empirical Rule**

Recent SAT scores for college-bound seniors are normally distributed with mean score 508 and standard deviation 121. How does the Empirical Rule help you understand the performances of individual students?

A. What proportion of students received scores between 387 and 629?

Sketch the graph to see where the numbers 387 and 629 fall in terms of the distribution.

Distribution of SAT Math Scores

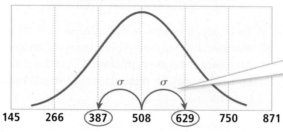

When you compute the numbers for the horizontal scale, 387 and 629 are each 1 standard deviation from the mean.

According to the Empirical Rule, 68% of scores are within 1 standard deviation of the mean. That means that approximately 68% of students received SAT Math scores between 387 and 629.

B. What proportion of students received scores greater than 387?

Distribution of SAT Math Scores

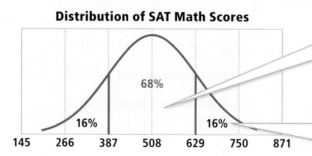

100% − 68% = 32% of students earned scores either greater than 629 or less than 387.

The symmetry of the curve means half, or 16%, of the remaining 32% of scores are greater than 629, and half are less than 387.

So 68% + 16% = 84% of students received scores greater than 387.

USE APPROPRIATE TOOLS
Consulting an accurate sketch of the distribution under consideration will help tell you determine whether the Empirical Rule applies. © MP.5

 Try It! **2.** Find the proportion of students who earned SAT Math scores in the following ranges.

a. between 266 and 750

b. between 266 and 629

CONCEPTUAL UNDERSTANDING **EXAMPLE 3** Compare Values Using *z*-Scores

Ella and Alicia are comparing scores on their college entrance exams. Ella's SAT score is 1380. Alicia's ACT score is 32. The mean SAT score is 1000 with a standard deviation of 200. The mean ACT score is 21 with a standard deviation of 5. Who has the better score?

You cannot compare their scores directly, but you can compare their relative position within each distribution.

Distribution of SAT Scores

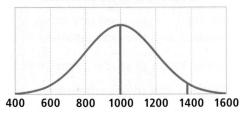

400 600 800 1000 1200 1400 1600

Ella's score is *less than* 2 standard deviations greater than the mean.

Distribution of ACT Scores

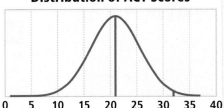

0   5   10   15   20   25   30   35   40

Alicia's score is *more than* 2 standard deviations greater than the mean.

To analyze where a data value falls in the distribution, find how many standard deviations it is above or below the mean. Most data values are not an exact integer number of standard deviations from the mean, so we need to find a way to describe fractional numbers of standard deviations from the mean.

The **z-score** counts how many standard deviations a data value is above or below the mean, because it divides the difference from the mean by the distance of a standard deviation. These distributions are normal, but you can use z-scores with any distribution.

COMMON ERROR
You may think that a positive z-score is always better than a negative one. Be careful to consider the context, though.
- Test scores: higher is better
- Golf scores: lower is better
- Height: no "better" score

$$z = \frac{\text{data value} - \text{mean}}{\text{standard deviation}}$$

Ella's z-score is: $z_E = \frac{1380 - 1000}{200} = 1.9$

Alicia's z-score is: $z_A = \frac{32 - 21}{5} = 2.2$

Alicia's score is better than Ella's.

> Ella's score: 1380
> Mean SAT score: 1000
> Standard deviation of scores: 200

> Alicia's score: 32
> Mean ACT score: 21
> Standard deviation of scores: 5

✓ **Try It!**   **3.** How does an SAT score of 1120 compare to an ACT score of 23?

APPLICATION → **EXAMPLE 4** Use a *z*-Score to Compute Percentage

The weight of captive adult female lowland gorillas is normally distributed with a mean of $\mu = 82.30$ kg and standard deviation of $\sigma = 15.33$ kg. Calculate a *z*-score for Sasha. How can you use this score to find the percentage of captive adult female lowland gorillas whose weights are less than or equal to Sasha's?

Sasha
61.8 kg

Sasha's weight of 61.8 kg gives her a *z*-score of $\frac{61.8 - 82.3}{15.33} \approx -1.34$.

When you calculate the *z*-score for a data value, you are finding its corresponding value on the *standard normal distribution*. The **standard normal distribution** is the normal distribution with mean $\mu = 0$ and standard deviation $\sigma = 1$.

LOOK FOR RELATIONSHIPS
$z = \frac{x - \mu}{\sigma}$

The formula for the *z*-score can be used to determine part of the transformation of the standard normal distribution into the normal distribution with mean μ and standard deviation σ. For example, there is a horizontal translation of μ units. Ⓒ **MP.7**

The total area under the curve of the standard normal distribution is equal to 1, and represents 100% of the data values.

Standard Normal Distribution

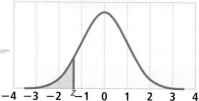

$-4 \ -3 \ -2 \ ^z\!-1 \ 0 \ 1 \ 2 \ 3 \ 4$

The percentage of values less than or equal to a particular data value is equal to the percentage of the total area under the distribution curve for that population to the left of that data value. This percentage is called the **percentile** of the data value. The percentage of area to the left of a data value is equal to the area to the left of the value's *z*-score under the standard normal distribution.

To calculate the area under the curve of the standard normal distribution to the left of $z = -1.34$, use a spreadsheet program or a calculator.

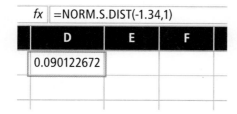

	D	E	F
	0.090122672		

fx =NORM.S.DIST(-1.34,1)

```
normalcdf(-1E99,
-1.34,0,1)
        .0901227339
```

The percentile of Sasha's weight or of a *z*-score of -1.34 is approximately 9%. This means that about 9% of all captive adult female lowland gorillas have a weight less than or equal to Sasha's weight.

☑ **Try It!** **4.** Find the percentage of all values in a normal distribution with $z \leq 1.85$.

CONCEPT SUMMARY Using Normal Distributions in the Real World

EMPIRICAL RULE

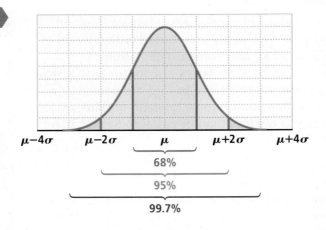

Approximately 68% of data values in a normal distribution fall within 1 standard deviation of the mean.

Approximately 95% of data values in a normal distribution fall within 2 standard deviations of the mean.

Approximately 99.7% of data values in a normal distribution fall within 3 standard deviations of the mean.

z-SCORES $z = \dfrac{\text{data value} - \text{mean}}{\text{standard deviation}}$

z tells how many standard deviations a data value is above or below the mean.

STANDARD NORMAL DISTRIBUTION

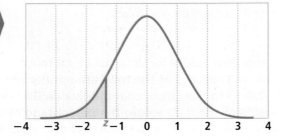

Mean: 0
Standard Deviation: 1

Along with z-scores, the standard normal distribution allows you to compare values across different population distributions.

Normal distributions are predictable, allowing you to calculate percentiles using tables, calculators, or spreadsheets.

Do You UNDERSTAND?

1. **ESSENTIAL QUESTION** How can you use the normal distribution to explain where data values fall within a population?

2. **Vocabulary** Write a definition for *z-score* using your own words.

3. **Look for Relationships** Why is it useful to compare a normal distribution to the standard normal distribution? Ⓒ **MP.7**

Do You KNOW HOW?

A data set with a mean of 75 and a standard deviation of 3.8 is normally distributed.

4. What value is three standard deviations above the mean?

5. What percent of the data is from 67.4 to 82.6?

6. What is the *z*-score for a data value of 69.3? Ⓒ **MP.4**

PRACTICE & PROBLEM SOLVING

UNDERSTAND

7. Communicate Precisely Explain how to use the Empirical Rule to find the percentage of the population that falls in a given interval of values. **© MP.6**

8. Mathematical Connections How could you use the standard normal curve to verify the Empirical Rule? Show your computations.

9. Error Analysis The cost of movie tickets at several movie theaters is normally distributed with a mean ticket price of $10 and a standard deviation of $0.50. Kenji bought a movie ticket for $9.25. Explain and correct the error in finding the z-score. **© MP.3**

$$z = \frac{\text{mean} - \text{data value}}{\text{standard deviation}}$$
$$z = \frac{\$10 - \$9.25}{\$0.5} = 1.5 \quad \text{✗}$$

10. Higher Order Thinking Skyler took an English test and a French test. The mean score for both tests was 84. Skyler got an 88 on the English test and a 92 on the French test. What condition would have to exist so that Skyler's score on the English test was more impressive relative to her classmates' scores than on the French test?

11. Use Structure The graph of normally distributed data is shown. What are the mean and standard deviation of the data? Explain how you know. **© MP.7**

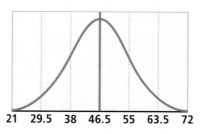

21 29.5 38 46.5 55 63.5 72

12. Reason The monthly cost of joining a gym is normally distributed with a mean of $50 and a standard deviation of $5. The cost of the gym Tyler joined was exactly two standard deviations away from the mean. **© MP.2**

a. What are possible z-scores of Tyler's cost?

b. Suppose the cost of Tyler's gym stays the same, but other gyms change their prices. How would your answer to part (a) be affected?

PRACTICE

The lifespan of a certain brand of car tires is approximately normally distributed. The car tires have a mean lifespan of 50,000 miles and a standard deviation of 7,500 miles. SEE EXAMPLE 1

13. What range of car tire lifespan contains the 95% closest to the mean?

14. What would the lifespan be for the 2.5% of the tires with the greatest lifespan in the population?

The price of a certain brand of printers is normally distributed with mean cost of $215 and standard deviation $35. SEE EXAMPLE 2

15. What proportion of printers cost between $110 and $320?

16. What proportion of printers cost less than $145?

17. What proportion of printers cost more than $250?

18. In their last basketball game, Holly scored 25 points and Juanita scored 16 points. The mean number of points Holly scores is 20 with a standard deviation of 2. The mean number of points Juanita scores is 12 with a standard deviation of 1.25. Whose score is better relative to her average number of points per game? SEE EXAMPLE 3

Find the percentage of all values in a normal distribution for each z-score.
SEE EXAMPLE 4

19. $z \leq 2.15$ **20.** $z \leq 1.25$

21. $z \geq 0.62$ **22.** $z \leq 0.48$

23. $z \geq -1.39$ **24.** $z \leq -2.26$

Given the mean μ and standard deviation σ, find the z-score for each data point x.

25. $\mu = 0;\ \sigma = 2;\ x = 3$

26. $\mu = 1;\ \sigma = 0.15;\ x = 0.70$

27. $\mu = 100;\ \sigma = 15;\ x = 70$

28. $\mu = 2.7;\ \sigma = 0.5;\ x = 3.0$

APPLY

29. Make Sense and Persevere Mrs. Burleson surveyed the students in her class to find the number of minutes they spent doing homework each night. She found that the data was normally distributed with $\mu = 30$ min and $\sigma = 10$ min. © **MP.1**

   a. What range of time spent doing homework contains the 68% closest to the mean?

   b. How much time spent on homework would you expect from the 2.5% of the students with the least time spent on homework?

   c. Jeffrey studied 25 min last night. What percent of the students studied fewer minutes than Jeffrey? Round to the nearest hundredth.

30. Reason A random sample of attendance numbers for last year's soccer matches for a local team are shown. © **MP.2**

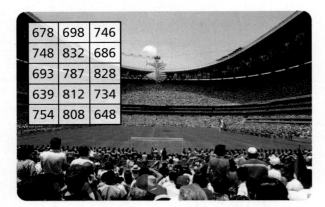

678	698	746
748	832	686
693	787	828
639	812	734
754	808	648

   a. Find the mean and standard deviation of the attendance numbers to the nearest tenth.

   b. Use the data given in the problem to find what percent of last year's games had at least 808 people in attendance. Round to the nearest tenth of a percent.

   c. Given that the data is normally distributed, estimate the percent of games that will have at least 808 people in attendance.

31. Anna scored an 89 on an exam with $\mu = 68$ points and $\sigma = 10$ points. Damian scored a 95 on an exam with $\mu = 76$ points and $\sigma = 12$ points. If both exams had normally distributed scores, what was the z-score for each student? Who did better on their exam? Explain.

ASSESSMENT PRACTICE

32. A normally distributed data set has a mean of 35 and a standard deviation of 5.23. Complete the table to find the probability that a randomly selected value is in the given interval. Round to the nearest hundredth percent, if necessary.

Interval	Probability (%)
at most 43	
at least 48	
between 32 and 38	
at least 41.6	
between 30.2 and 42.6	
at most 36.25	

33. SAT/ACT In a set of data that is normally distributed, the value that is 1 standard deviation above the mean is 93. The value that is 2 standard deviations below the mean is 39. What is the mean of the set of data?

   Ⓐ 3   Ⓑ 18   Ⓒ 57   Ⓓ 75

34. Performance Task Outliers can be identified using the interquartile method. Multiply the interquartile range by 1.5. If a data value has a distance below the first quartile or above the third quartile greater than this product, it is an outlier. Another way is to use the z-score method. If a data value falls more than 3 standard deviations from the mean, the data value is an outlier. The table shows the high temperature for 14 days.

| 81°F | 78°F | 77°F | 75°F | 80°F | 81°F | 80°F |
| 77°F | 74°F | 75°F | 49°F | 71°F | 72°F | 80°F |

Part A Identify the mean, standard deviation, first quartile, third quartile, and interquartile range of the data.

Part B Which data values, if any, are outliers using the interquartile method? Explain your reasoning.

Part C Which data values, if any, are outliers using the z-score method? Explain your reasoning.

11-5
Margin of Error

I CAN... use margin of error to estimate a population parameter accurately.

VOCABULARY
• margin of error
• sampling distribution

👆 MODEL & DISCUSS

With a partner or a group, toss a number cube 30 times and record the number showing on each toss.

A. Compute the means of the numbers in the first five tosses, the first ten tosses, and all thirty tosses.

B. Use Appropriate Tools Compile the results for your entire class in three sets of data: the means of the first five tosses, the means of the first ten tosses, and the means of all thirty tosses. Create a histogram for each data set. © **MP.5**

C. Compare the histograms. Describe how the distribution of the mean changes as the number of tosses increases.

❓ ESSENTIAL QUESTION
How can you determine how far a statistic is likely to be from a parameter?

APPLICATION ➤

👆 EXAMPLE 1   Estimate a Population Parameter

Seth selects a random sample of students from a local college. He asks students their year in college and how far the college is from their home in miles. How can Seth's sample estimate the proportion of freshmen in the population? How accurate is the estimate likely to be?

Seth's Data

Sophomore	5	Senior	60
Junior	50	Senior	20
Freshman	65	Junior	10
Sophomore	200	Sophomore	110
Junior	120	Sophomore	75
Junior	2	Junior	30
Sophomore	180	Senior	15
Freshman	800	Freshman	45
Junior	100	Sophomore	15
Freshman	90	Sophomore	25

You can use sample statistics, such as proportion and mean, to estimate the corresponding population parameters. The proportion of freshmen in a sample can be used to estimate the proportion of freshmen in the population.

COMMUNICATE PRECISELY
Different samples include different individuals with different characteristics. Results should be reported clearly, explaining how measures were obtained. © **MP.6**

$$\text{Ratio of freshmen to students in the population} = \frac{\text{number of freshmen in sample}}{\text{number of participants in sample}}$$

$$= \frac{4}{20}$$

$$= \frac{1}{5} \text{ or } 0.20$$

0.20 of the sample, or 20%, are freshmen.

The accuracy of this estimate depends on the number of participants in the sample and how well the sample represents the population.

> If by chance the sample clusters away from the true mean, estimates will not be very accurate.

> Larger samples usually provide more accurate estimates than smaller samples.

CONTINUED ON THE NEXT PAGE

EXAMPLE 1 CONTINUED

 Try It! **1.** Use the sample data to estimate the mean distance from home. Estimate the proportion of seniors to the total population at the college.

APPLICATION ⟶ 👆 **EXAMPLE 2** **Make an Inference Using Multiple Samples**

Tia is contributing to the same project as Seth and has sampled a different group of students. The proportion of freshmen in her sample is 0.40 or 40%. How can Seth and Tia determine whose result is a better representation of the population?

Tia and Seth decide to examine more samples. Everyone in their class completed the same survey. They compared the 50 total samples of 20 college students. Seth and Tia create a histogram of the proportion of freshmen in each sample.

Tia's Data

Junior	120	Freshman	60
Sophomore	320	Freshman	200
Senior	240	Sophomore	130
Freshman	150	Freshman	120
Freshman	20	Junior	15
Sophomore	25	Freshman	30
Senior	5	Junior	70
Freshman	30	Sophomore	60
Sophomore	20	Freshman	10
Senior	100	Junior	15

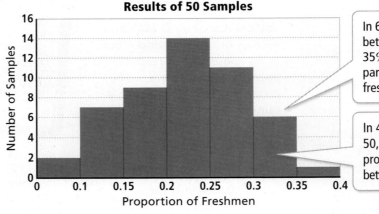

Results of 50 Samples

In 6 samples out of 50, between 30% and 35% of the sample participants are freshmen.

In 47 samples out of 50, the sample proportion falls between 0.1 and 0.35.

GENERALIZE
Most samples provide a reasonable estimate of the parameter. The average value of a set of sample statistics will approximate the population parameter with high precision. © **MP.8**

The distribution of sample results is approximately normal. There is natural variability among the samples, but most of the samples return statistics between 0.1 and 0.35. It is reasonable to predict that the actual proportion of freshmen at the college is between 0.1 and 0.35.

Seth's result of 0.20 is in the middle of the range and is likely a good representation of the population proportion. Tia's result of 0.40 falls outside the range of most of the results, so it is more likely that her estimate is further away from the true mean.

CONTINUED ON THE NEXT PAGE

EXAMPLE 2 CONTINUED

 Try It! 2. Each classmate calculates the mean distance from home in miles reported by participants. Seth and Tia create this histogram to investigate the sample statistics. How many samples reported an average distance from home between 101 and 125 mi? Use the histogram to suggest a reasonable interval to estimate the population parameter.

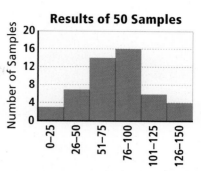

Results of 50 Samples

Mean Distance From Home (mi)

CONCEPTUAL DEVELOPMENT

EXAMPLE 3 Use a Simulation to Evaluate a Claim

Gabriela wants proof of Alex's claim that he is a 75% free-throw shooter. She observes Alex shoot 50 free throws, of which he makes 30. Gabriela notes his 60% success rate, but Alex points out that this is a reasonable result due to the natural variability that happens from sample to sample. Is he correct?

A. How can you use random numbers to investigate Alex's claim?

Assume Alex does make 75% of his free throws. Use a random number generator on a calculator or spreadsheet to simulate the outcome of a random sample of shots.

Create a list of 50 random numbers ranging from 1–100. Numbers 1–75 represent successful free throws, and numbers 76–100 represent missed shots.

USE APPROPRIATE TOOLS
A random number generator allows you to generate many samples based on a possible population parameter. These samples will provide a collection of statistics with natural variability. You can evaluate a statistic by comparing it to this collection. © MP.5

fx =RANDBETWEEN(1,100)

A formula like this generates a random number between 1 and 100.

D	E	F	G	H	I
50	10	66	61	15	
9	82	50	22	78	
49	13	26	76	48	
19	12	11	35	4	
95	18	15	16	17	
61	55	86	58	22	
74	78	100	40	58	
65	25	89	82	84	
35	22	57	66	22	
1	64	88	65	30	

In this sample, 39 out of 50 shots, or 0.78, are successful.

While the simulated proportion 0.78 is much higher than 0.60 or 60%, this one simulation does not refute Alex's reasoning about natural variability. Gabriela needs more evidence.

CONTINUED ON THE NEXT PAGE

EXAMPLE 3 CONTINUED

Continue the simulation, analyzing 100 samples of 50 shots each. The distribution of sample statistics, such as means or proportions from different samples of the same population, is called the **sampling distribution.**

This sampling distribution of the number of successes in 50 shots for 100 simulated samples is approximately normal.

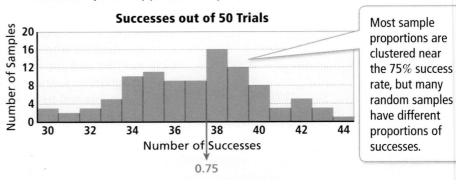

Most sample proportions are clustered near the 75% success rate, but many random samples have different proportions of successes.

As the number of samples increases, the distribution will more accurately reflect the population parameter.

B. How can you interpret the sampling distribution?

This simulated sampling distribution is based on the assumption that Alex makes 75% of his free throws.

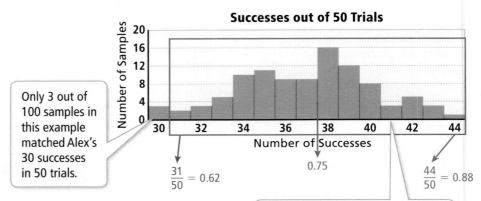

Only 3 out of 100 samples in this example matched Alex's 30 successes in 50 trials.

$\frac{31}{50} = 0.62$

0.75

$\frac{44}{50} = 0.88$

Select a range of data that is centered on the mean and includes about 95% of the samples.

Most samples (47 of 50, or 0.94) have a proportion of success between 0.62 and 0.88. This is as much as 0.13 above or below the central value of 0.75.

You can say that 0.13 or 13% represents a reasonable difference from the target that could appear through natural variability.

Based on the simulation, a basketball player who actually shoots free throws with 75% accuracy can reliably be expected to make 62%–88% of free throws in a 50-shot trial.

It would be very unusual for a real 75%-shooter to make only 30 shots out of 50. It is likely that Alex's low performance shows that he does not make 75% of his free throws overall.

CONTINUED ON THE NEXT PAGE

COMMON ERROR
Do not assume that Alex's "true" free-throw percentage *must* be less than 75%. It is unlikely, but it is still possible that his lower actual success rate of 60% is due to chance, or other adverse factors.

EXAMPLE 3 CONTINUED

 Activity   Assess

 Try It! **3.** How would your conclusion in Example 3 differ if you did 100 simulations of 10 shots each? How would it differ if you did 100 simulations of 1,000 shots each?

CONCEPT Margin of Error

The sampling distributions of means and proportions tend to be normal. The mean of such a sampling distribution is the population parameter, and the standard deviation decreases as the sample size increases.

According to the Empirical Rule, 95% of values in a normal distribution fall within two standard deviations of the mean.

So, 95% of all sample results fall within two standard deviations of the population parameter being evaluated.

The **margin of error** gives the maximum expected difference between the sample result and the population parameter.

> These formulas give the maximum difference between the parameter and the statistic for 95% of samples.

Quantitative Data

Margin of Error $\approx \dfrac{2\sigma}{\sqrt{n}}$

σ = population standard deviation

n = sample size.

Categorical Data

Margin of Error $\approx \dfrac{1}{\sqrt{n}}$

for samples of size n.

EXAMPLE 4 Use a Margin of Error for a Mean

The College Board recently reported that the mean score on the SAT mathematics exam is 508, with standard deviation 121. Washington High believes that its seniors score considerably higher than the national average, so the school randomly sampled scores from 200 seniors, finding a mean score of 550. Is Washington High correct in its belief?

STUDY TIP
Before calculating margin of error, identify the type of data being analyzed. Formulas are different for categorical and quantitative values.

Since the data in this example is quantitative, the margin of error for SAT data is $\dfrac{2\sigma}{\sqrt{n}} = \dfrac{2(121)}{\sqrt{200}} \approx 17$.

So, about 95% of random samples with 200 participants will have mean values within 17 points of the population parameter, $\mu = 508$. Find the range of reasonable means.

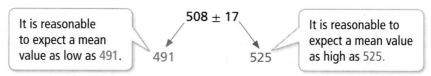

It is reasonable to expect a mean value as low as 491.

508 ± 17

491   525

It is reasonable to expect a mean value as high as 525.

Washington High's sample mean score of 550 is above the range of reasonable means, so they can conclude that their seniors perfom better than the national average.

CONTINUED ON THE NEXT PAGE

EXAMPLE 3 CONTINUED

 Try It! **4.** A random sample of 100 Washington High seniors reveals that 40% plan to take the SAT this year. Use the margin of error to predict the actual proportion of seniors planning to take the exam.

 CONCEPT SUMMARY Understanding Sampling Distributions

| SAMPLING DISTRIBUTION | Sample statistics tend to be normally distributed (for samples of the same size). |

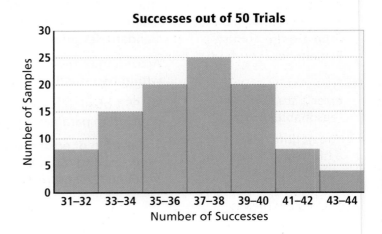

Successes out of 50 Trials

| MARGIN OF ERROR | **Quantitative Data** | **Categorical Data** |

Quantitative Data

Margin of Error $\approx \frac{2\sigma}{\sqrt{n}}$

σ = population standard deviation

n = sample size

Categorical Data

Margin of Error $\approx \frac{1}{\sqrt{n}}$

n = sample size

 Do You UNDERSTAND?

1. **ESSENTIAL QUESTION** How can you determine how far a statistic is likely to be from a parameter?

2. **Error Analysis** In a sample of 16 students from a teacher's physical education classes, students attempted to do as many sit-ups as possible in one minute. The mean was 10 with a standard deviation of 2. The teacher said that the margin of error was $\frac{1}{4}$. What is the teacher's error? Ⓒ **MP.3**

3. **Vocabulary** Explain what a sampling distribution is in your own words.

4. **Communicate Precisely** Suppose you want to find the margin of error for a certain sample. Explain when to use the formula Margin of Error $= \frac{2\sigma}{\sqrt{n}}$ and when to use the formula Margin of Error $= \frac{1}{\sqrt{n}}$. Ⓒ **MP.6**

Do You KNOW HOW?

Suppose an event occurs x times in a sample size of n. Find the sample proportion and the margin of error to the nearest percent.

5. $x = 80$ and $n = 700$

6. $x = 45$ and $n = 1,200$

Suppose a sample has a standard deviation of σ and a sample size of n. Find the margin of error to the nearest tenth.

7. $\sigma = 21.26$ and $n = 500$

8. $\sigma = 122.18$ and $n = 850$

9. **Model With Mathematics** In a sample of 400 adults, 348 have never been to Australia. Find the sample proportion for those who have never been to Australia. Write the answer as a percent. Ⓒ **MP.4**

UNDERSTAND

10. Reason Erin found the margin of error of a certain random sample. Suppose she triples the sample size. How is the margin of error affected? © MP.2

11. Make Sense and Persevere A poll reports that 48% of voters are going to vote for Candidate A. The poll reports a margin of error of ±4%. Estimate the number of voters in the poll. Explain how you found your answer. © MP.1

12. Error Analysis Describe and correct the error a student made in finding the range of reasonable means. © MP.3

The nationwide mean height of players on a high school basketball team is 71 in., with standard deviation of 5 in. A random sample of 150 players was used to determine the range of reasonable means.

Margin of Error = $\frac{1}{\sqrt{150}} \approx 0.08$

Range of Means:

between 71 − 0.08 = 70.92 in.

and 71 + 0.08 = 71.08 in. ✗

13. Higher Order Thinking The students in Mr. Morrison's science class measured the heights of flowers in the school's playground area. The class took six random samples by measuring a group of flowers. The table shows the standard deviation of each sample. Use the information in the table to determine which was likely the smallest sample. Explain your reasoning.

Sample	Standard Deviation
A	1.45
B	2.03
C	1.12
D	1.35
E	2.78
F	1.84

PRACTICE

14. Ryan selects a random sample of students from a high school. Students were asked how long it takes them to get ready for school. Use the sample data in the table to estimate the mean time to get ready for school. Estimate the proportion of juniors at the school. SEE EXAMPLE 1

Junior	45 min
Sophomore	30 min
Junior	15 min
Senior	25 min
Sophomore	60 min
Freshman	10 min
Sophomore	35 min
Junior	40 min
Senior	10 min
Freshman	30 min

15. Ryan's classmates each calculated the mean time it takes to get ready for school reported by a sample of 100 participants. Ryan created this histogram of the sample means. How many samples reported an average time to get ready between 11 and 20 min? Suggest a reasonable interval to estimate the population parameter. SEE EXAMPLE 2

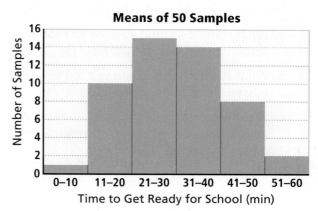

16. Jake makes 80% of the field goals he attempts. Suppose Jake attempts 100 field goals. Use technology to simulate 50 trials with 100 field goals each. Identify the range that contains the middle 95% of results. SEE EXAMPLE 3

17. The mean score on a statewide science test is 72, with standard deviation 12. Hailey believes that the scores in her school are considerably higher than the state average. A random sample of 100 students from Hailey's school showed a mean score of 76. Is Hailey correct in her belief? Explain. SEE EXAMPLE 4

APPLY

18. **Reason** A survey of 2,390 employees found that 7% are left-handed. **© MP.2**

   a. Find the margin of error for the sample. Round to the nearest percent.

   b. Use the margin of error to find an interval that will likely include the population proportion of the employees that are left-handed.

19. **Model With Mathematics** Lydia wants proof of Mike's claim that he is a 40% three-point shooter in basketball. She observes him make 17 out of 50 three-point shots. Lydia used a random number generator to simulate the outcome of a random sample of shots. **© MP.4**

16	22	53	51	62	81	69	68	59	29
69	71	29	83	79	34	67	82	64	50
30	79	68	94	33	24	6	28	91	59
33	59	42	89	13	56	15	6	75	97
83	6	89	55	39	61	69	17	20	89

   a. What numbers could you use to represent successful three-point shots?

   b. What numbers could you use to represent missed three-point shots?

   c. What proportion of the random numbers generated were successful? Explain what this means regarding Mike's claim.

20. **Make Sense and Persevere** An app estimates phone usage by counting the number of times a phone screen is unlocked during the course of a day. A sample of 25 users is shown. **© MP.1**

123	65	119	145	114
125	114	91	113	125
88	141	105	116	121
186	136	65	128	107
97	126	101	90	10

   a. What is the mean and standard deviation?

   b. Assuming the sample standard deviation matches the population standard deviation, what is the margin of error?

   c. When Isabel says, "I check my phone at least 100 times a day," is she exaggerating, or could her claim be reasonable? Explain.

ASSESSMENT PRACTICE

21. In a random survey of 60 customers, 46 prefer Cracker A. Fill in the blank with the correct value.

   a. The sample proportion is about _____.

   b. The margin of error is about _____.

   c. The interval likely to contain the true population proportion is between _____ and _____.

22. **SAT/ACT** A manufacturing company wants to randomly sample customers about their satisfaction rating on products. The company will give a gift certificate worth $25 to every customer who completes the survey. How much will it cost the company to obtain a margin of error of ±5%?

   Ⓐ $400   Ⓒ $4,000
   Ⓑ $1,000   Ⓓ $10,000

23. **Performance Task** The population of songbirds is often calculated using a *capture-tag-recapture* technique. This means birds are captured and then tagged. After being tagged, the birds are released. A group of researchers is investigating a ranger's claim about the percentage of songbirds that are tagged. They recapture 10 birds, and only 3 have tags.

In one forest, a ranger claims that 50% of songbirds are tagged.

   Part A Use a calculator or spreadsheet to simulate 25 samples with 10 birds recaptured by selecting 10 random numbers.

   Part B After simulating 25 trials, analyze the proportion of successes in each trial and create a histogram to display the sampling distribution.

   Part C Identify the range of values that contains the middle 95% of results. Does the ranger's claim seem reasonable?

11-6

Introduction to Hypothesis Testing

SavvasRealize.com

I CAN... state two hypotheses for a statistics question and decide if the data support one of the hypotheses.

VOCABULARY
- alternative hypothesis
- hypothesis
- null hypothesis

👆 EXPLORE & REASON

The tables below each show the results of flipping a coin 30 times.

Coin 1					
H	H	H	H	H	T
H	T	T	H	H	T
T	T	H	H	T	H
H	H	T	T	T	H
H	T	T	H	T	H

Coin 2					
T	T	H	T	H	H
H	T	T	T	H	T
T	T	H	T	T	T
H	T	T	T	T	T
T	T	T	H	T	T

A. How many heads and how many tails resulted from flipping each coin 30 times?

B. How many heads and how many tails would you expect from flipping a fair coin 30 times? Are either of these coins close to what you would expect?

C. Construct Arguments Can you conclude with certainty that either of the coins is fair? Can you conclude that either of the coins is unfair? © **MP.3**

? ESSENTIAL QUESTION

How do you formulate and test a hypothesis using statistics?

CONCEPTUAL UNDERSTANDING

👆 EXAMPLE 1 Write Hypotheses

A car has been getting 34.6 miles per gallon. With a fuel additive, the car gets 35.3 miles per gallon. What hypotheses would you test to determine whether the increase in mileage is due to the additive?

The first step in determining whether the additive is effective is to formulate *hypotheses* to test using statistical methods.

COMMUNICATE PRECISELY
Exactly one of the hypotheses can be true. Data from an experiment will provide evidence to help you argue for which hypothesis is more likely true. © **MP.6**

Step 1 Determine what your question means in terms of a parameter.

The additive works if a car gets a higher mean gas mileage when using the additive than the mean gas mileage when not using the additive.

Step 2 State this information about the parameter mathematically.

Let μ represent the mean gas mileage for the car with the additive. You want to know if $\mu > 34.6$. This is a **hypothesis**, a possible explanation of one or more observed occurrences.

Step 3 State what would happen if this hypothesis is not true.

If the fuel additive does not cause an increase in gas mileage, then $\mu = 34.6$. This is also a hypothesis.

CONTINUED ON THE NEXT PAGE

EXAMPLE 1 CONTINUED

Step 4 Write the *null hypothesis* and *alternative hypothesis*.

The hypothesis that there is no increase with the additive is the **null hypothesis** and is denoted H_0. In this case you would write H_0 as $\mu = 34.6$.

The **alternative hypothesis** is H_a: $\mu > 34.6$ because it includes only the possibility of difference between the quantities of interest.

Stating hypotheses is useful because it gives you two possibilities to test using statistics. The hypotheses used to determine whether the fuel additive causes an increase in gas mileage are:

$$H_0: \mu = 34.6$$
$$H_a: \mu > 34.6.$$

 Try It! **1.** A soccer goalie saved 46.4% of her opponents' tiebreaker attempts. After her coach adjusted her position in the goal, she saved 47.3% of the attempts. Write the null hypothesis and alternative hypothesis for a statistical study to evaluate the population parameter P, the proportion of tiebreaker goals she saves after working with her coach.

APPLICATION    **EXAMPLE 2** **Examine Data from an Experiment**

A car company performed an experiment to determine whether the fuel additive from Example 1 increases a particular type of car's gas mileage.

The company recorded the gas mileage of ten identical cars all driven under the same conditions with and without the use of the fuel additive.

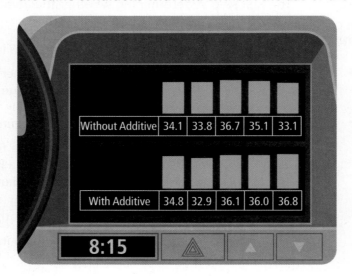

| Without Additive | 34.1 | 33.8 | 36.7 | 35.1 | 33.1 |

| With Additive | 34.8 | 32.9 | 36.1 | 36.0 | 36.8 |

8:15

CONTINUED ON THE NEXT PAGE

EXAMPLE 2 CONTINUED

How can you use the data to compare the effectiveness of the additive?

If there were no difference in the gas mileages with or without the additive, the means of the gas mileages would be equal and their difference would be 0. If the additive increases gas mileage, the difference of the means would be greater than 0.

Let μ_1 be the mean of the gas mileage with the additive and let μ_2 be the mean of the gas mileage without the additive. The null hypothesis and alternative hypothesis for this situation are,

$$H_0: \mu_1 - \mu_2 = 0$$
$$H_A: \mu_1 - \mu_2 > 0$$

The sample means are $\bar{x}_1 = 34.56$ and $\bar{x}_2 = 35.32$.

The difference of the sample means is $35.32 - 34.56 = 0.76$.

> Recall that the notation $\bar{x}$ represents the sample mean. Note that the hypotheses use the population mean μ.

The average gas mileage with the additive was *0.76 miles per gallon greater* than the average without it. But is this due to the additive, or to random variation?

It is extremely unlikely that all ten cars will have exactly the same gas mileage, even if the additive has no effect. There will always be some amount of variation. It is possible that by chance alone the cars with the higher gas mileage were grouped together and the cars with the lower gas mileage were grouped together.

One way to test the hypotheses is to randomly assign the data to two new groups many times and look at the variability of the differences of the means. The table shows one such assignment.

USE APPROPRIATE TOOLS
You can use technology or draw slips of paper from a container to sort the data randomly into two new groups. © MP.5

| New Group 1 | 34.8 | 33.8 | 36.7 | 36.1 | 33.1 |
| New Group 2 | 34.1 | 35.1 | 36.0 | 32.9 | 36.8 |

Mean of New Group 1 = 34.9
Mean of New Group 2 = 34.98

If there is no difference in mileage between the groups with or without the additive, reassigning the data into two groups repeatedly will likely result in differences closely distributed around zero. If there is a difference in mileage, there is likely to be large variability in the distribution of differences.

In this regrouping of the data, the difference of the sample means is 0.08, which is closer to 0 than the original difference of sample means, 0.76.

While this provides one basis of comparison for testing the null hypothesis, many more resamples and many more comparisons are needed before you can possibly reject the null hypothesis. You will see this in Example 3.

 Try It! 2. In one particular randomization one group has these data values: 34.1, 36.7, 35.1, 36.1, 36.8.

    a. Identify the data values for the other group.

    b. Calculate the difference of the means for the two groups.

EXAMPLE 3 Use Simulation Results to Test Hypotheses

How can continued randomization of the gas mileage data be used to test the hypotheses in Example 2?

In Example 2, you randomly reassigned the data into two new groups to make a comparison. If you randomize the data many times, you can create a distribution that you can use to evaluate the hypotheses. To do this, follow these steps.

- Pool all data values into a single set.
- Create two new groups of data values at random from the pool. Each data value must be used exactly once.
- Calculate the difference of the means for the new groups.
- Repeat. The histogram below shows the result of 200 randomizations.

When data values were assigned to new groups at random, the differences of the means were greater than 0.76 almost a quarter of the time.

COMMON ERROR
The initial experiment relied on a very small sample. It is difficult to establish definitive results with a small sample. Repeat the experiment with a greater number of trials.

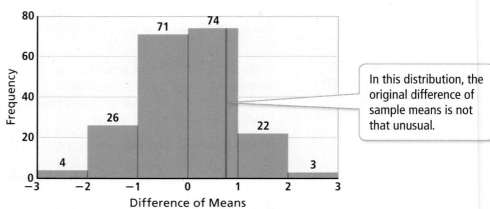

In this distribution, the original difference of sample means is not that unusual.

The initial difference of means could reasonably be attributed to the variability inherent in random sampling.

This small experiment *does not* give convincing evidence that the fuel additive improved the car's gas mileage. More testing, possibly with larger samples, is needed. For now, we cannot reject the null hypothesis, that there is no difference in the means of the gas mileage with and without the additive, and that any variation is due to chance alone.

 Try It! 3. The fuel additive was tested again, resulting in the data displayed below. Use a simulation to randomly assign the data into two new groups. Find the difference of the means of the original sample and the new groups you just created. How do they differ? Explain what additional information you need to be able to test the hypotheses from Example 2.

Without Additive	34.1	32.8	33.8	30.9	36.7
	33.4	35.1	32.1	30.4	33.1
With Additive	34.8	35.1	32.9	35.3	36.1
	36.9	36.0	37.2	36.3	36.8

APPLICATION

EXAMPLE 4 Evaluate a Report Based on Data

Best Bet Mac & Cheese reports that the average price for a box of their product is $1.45. A marketing company selects a national sample of 100 retail prices. The standard deviation of prices nationally is $0.20 and the mean of the prices of the sample is $1.65. Does this study provide strong evidence that Best Bet's claim is false?

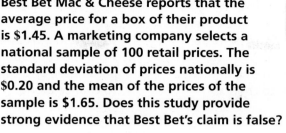

$\bar{x} = \$1.65$
$\sigma = \$0.20$

Step 1 Write the null hypothesis and alternative hypothesis for this study.

$H_0: \mu = 1.45$ The mean price of Best Bet Mac & Cheese is $1.45.

$H_A: \mu \neq 1.45$ The mean price of Best Bet Mac & Cheese is NOT $1.45.

Step 2 Calculate the margin of error for the new sample.

Use the formula $m = \frac{2\sigma}{\sqrt{n}}$, where σ is the population standard deviation of $0.20, and n is 100, the number of prices sampled.

$$m = \frac{2(0.20)}{\sqrt{100}} = 0.04$$

Step 3 Use the sample statistic and margin of error to predict a range of reasonable values estimating the population parameter.

Sample mean $\pm$ margin of error

$1.65 \pm 0.04 = 1.61$ to 1.69

Based on sampling, we would predict the value of the mean price to fall between $1.61 and $1.69.

Step 4 Compare the claim to the predicted interval.

The claim falls outside the range of reasonable values predicted by the statistical study. This evidence suggests you should reject the null hyothesis.

 Try It! 4. Best Bet revises their claim and reports an average retail price of $1.60. A second marketing study sampled 300 prices for Best Bet Mac & Cheese finding a mean price of $1.64.

     a. What is the margin of error for the new sample?

     b. Is Best Bet's revised claim supported by this new study? Explain why or why not.

CONCEPT SUMMARY Using Statistical Data to Test Claims

SET UP — Write two statements.

Null hypothesis, H_0: The observed statistic in a treatment group is equal to the corresponding population parameter, and any variation is due to chance.

Alternative hypothesis, H_a: The observed statistic in a treatment group differs from the corresponding population parameter, and the variation is not due to chance alone.

COMPARE — Compare two groups by comparing their distributions, means, standard deviations, proportions, or other statistics.

Analyze the data to determine how likely it is that differences between the two groups occurred by chance.

DECIDE — Decide whether the differences could be attributed to natural variability.

Likely to have occurred by chance?

Then there is no reason to reject the null hypothesis.

Too different to be coincidence?

Strong evidence that the difference is not due to chance points to the truth of the alternative hypothesis.

Do You UNDERSTAND?

1. **ESSENTIAL QUESTION** How do you formulate and test a hypothesis using statistics?

2. **Error Analysis** When presented with an experiment about teeth whitening strips claiming to deliver visibly whiter teeth within two weeks, Mercedes said the null hypothesis of the experiment was that the teeth would become significantly whiter after two weeks of using the whitening strips. Explain Mercedes' error. **© MP.3**

3. **Vocabulary** Explain the difference between a *null hypothesis* and an *alternative hypothesis*.

4. **Communicate Precisely** If the null hypothesis of an experiment is $H_0: \mu \leq 10.8$, then what is the alternative hypothesis H_a? **© MP.6**

Do You KNOW HOW?

5. A baseball player's career batting average was .278. After working with a new coach, the player batted .315. Write the null hypothesis and alternative hypothesis for a study of the effect of the change.

6. A lumber company claims that at least 80% of its plywood is made from recycled materials. It tests 25 pieces of the plywood and finds that the mean of the percentage of recycled material in the sample is 78%. The standard deviation of the population is 3%. Give an interval of reasonable values for the percentage of recycled material in the plywood. Is the company's claim likely true?

7. Terrence grows two varieties of tomatoes, TomTom and Hugemato. Hugemato claims to grow 10% heavier tomatoes. Find the difference of sample means for the samples shown. Resample randomly and find the new difference of sample means. How do they compare?

TomTom	10.1	10.5	9.9	10.4	11.2
Hugemato	13.1	11	12.1	11.4	12.9

PRACTICE & PROBLEM SOLVING

UNDERSTAND

8. Communicate Precisely Becky buys a new hybrid grass seed that is supposed to require only a small amount of water to grow. After Becky plants the new seed, it rains every other day for a two-week period, and the grass grows well. Explain why this particular situation cannot be used to support the claim about the water required to grow the seed. © MP.6

9. Error Analysis Jake's average bowling score was 230. Jake bought a new bowling ball. Since using the new bowling ball Jake's average score has improved to 250. He wrote the null hypothesis and alternative hypothesis for a statistical study to evaluate the effect of the new ball on his bowling sscore. Explain his error. © MP.3

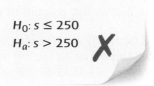

$$H_0: s \le 250$$
$$H_a: s > 250$$

10. Generalize Using the formula for margin of error, $m = \frac{2\sigma}{\sqrt{n}}$, explain why the larger a sample size is, the smaller the margin of error should be. © MP.8

11. Reason Answer the following questions about randomizing samples. © MP.2

  a. Why is the method of randomizing samples used when working with experimental data sets?

  b. If the red vertical line in the histogram shown represents the difference in the means of the original samples, then how does it compare to the differences of the means in the randomly generated samples?

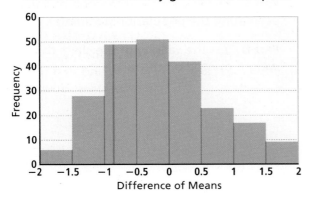

Difference of Means

PRACTICE

12. Tavon had an average time for the 100-yd dash of 18 seconds. Since starting a strength-training program, he has been running the 100-yd dash in an average time of 15 seconds. Write the null hypothesis and alternative hypothesis for a statistical study to evaluate the effect of the training on Tavon's time in the 100-yd dash.
SEE EXAMPLE 1

13. The coach wants to perform an experiment to determine whether strength training impacts a runner's speed. The coach completed several trials and recorded the speeds of the 100-yd dash (in seconds) of a sample of five track athletes both before and after they tried strength training. SEE EXAMPLE 2

Without Training	18	20	16	15	14
With Training	15	19	17	16	14

  a. Find the sample means and their difference. Resample the data so that one group has these data values: 15, 20, 17, 15, 14.

  b. Identify the data values for the other group.

  c. Calculate the difference of the means for the two resample groups.

14. The training regimen was tested again, resulting in the data displayed below. Use a simulation to randomize the data without replacement, creating 50 new groupings. Create a histogram of the differences between group means to display your results. Use the data to draw a conclusion about the initial hypothesis. SEE EXAMPLE 3

Without Vitamins	14	12	18	19	15
With Vitamins	15	12	16	18	14

15. Grain Goodness reports the average price for a box of their granola is $3.87. A marketing company selects a national sample of 100 retail prices and states the mean price was $4.42. The standard deviation was $0.60. What is the margin of error for this new sample? SEE EXAMPLE 4

APPLY

16. Model with Mathematics A botanist is doing an experimental research study to determine whether a certain fertilizer will increase the yield of soybean plants. The botanist included several soybean farmers in his study. The average yield of soybeans for each farmer (in bushels per acre) of the crops with and without fertilizer are recorded in the table shown.

Without Fertilizer	40	42	45	50	47
With Fertilizer	42	40	46	49	48

Find the means of both samples and their difference. State how the average yield of the soybean crops with the fertilizer compares to the average yield of the soybean crops without fertilizer. **© MP.4**

17. Communicate Precisely A randomization of the data from Exercise 16, placed into two new random groups, is shown in the table. **© MP.6**

New Group 1	46	50	40	42	47
New Group 2	40	49	42	48	45

a. Find the difference between the sample means of the new groups.

b. Does it provide evidence that the difference in the original two sample means is due to the effects of the fertilizer or just due to chance?

18. Make Sense and Persevere The rules state that a baseball must have a certain circumference. What hypotheses would you test to determine whether the baseballs made on a new machine are within the specifications? **© MP.1**

Circumference within 3 mm of 232 mm.

© ASSESSMENT PRACTICE

19. What are the different types of hypotheses used in a statistical study? Select all that apply

Ⓐ experimental   Ⓑ supported

Ⓒ alternative   Ⓓ strategic

Ⓔ null

20. SAT/ACT A survey found that 72% of freshmen planned to take at least one spring break trip while in college with a margin of error of ±3.5%. Central U claims that 75% of freshman plan trips. Is their claim reasonable?

Ⓐ No, their claim is not within the margin of error.

Ⓑ No, their claim is within the margin of error.

Ⓒ Yes, their claim is not within the margin of error.

Ⓓ Yes, their claim is within the margin of error.

21. Performance Task Loaves of a particular brand of wheat bread are labeled as weighing at least 16 oz. A consumer advocate studies the weights of 500 loaves of this bread.

$\bar{x} = 15.6$ oz
$\sigma = 0.8$ oz

Part A Find H_0 and H_a.

Part B Calculate the margin of error.

Part C Predict a range of reasonable values estimating the population parameter.

Part D Test the validity of the claim of the weight printed on the labels.

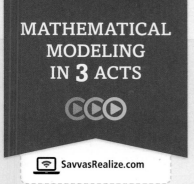

MATHEMATICAL MODELING IN 3 ACTS

© **Common Core State Standards** HSS.IC.A.1, HSS.IC.A.2, HSS.IC.B.4, MP.4

▢ ▶ Video

▶ Mark and Recapture

It wouldn't take very long for you to count the number of people who live in your home or the number of socks in your drawer. How about the number of deer in Yellowstone National Park or the number of sharks in the waters around Hawaii?

The mark and recapture method is a popular way researchers can estimate an animal population. You will see an example of this method in the Mathematical Modeling in 3 Acts lesson.

Scan for
Multimedia

ACT 1 ▸ Identify the Problem

1. What is the first question that comes to mind after watching the video?

2. Write down the main question you will answer about what you saw in the video.

3. Make an initial conjecture that answers this main question.

4. Explain how you arrived at your conjecture.

5. What information will be useful to know to answer the main question? How can you get it? How will you use that information?

ACT 2 ▸ Develop a Model

6. Use the math that you have learned in this Topic to refine your conjecture.

ACT 3 ▸ Interpret the Results

7. Did your refined conjecture match the actual answer exactly? If not, what might explain the difference?

Topic Review

1. What questions can you answer by using statistics and normal distributions?

Vocabulary Review

Choose the correct term to complete each sentence.

2. _____ is used to find a range of reasonable values used to estimate the population parameter based on a sample statistic.

3. A(n) _____ involves applying a treatment to some group or groups and measuring the effects of the treatment.

4. The _____ is a statement that expresses that there is no difference between the parameter and the benchmark.

5. A(n) _____ can be answered by collecting many pieces of information, or data, and summarizing the data.

6. The _____ counts how many standard deviations a data value is from the mean.

- experiment
- margin of error
- null hypothesis
- statistical question
- *z*-score

Concepts & Skills Review

> **LESSON 11-1** Statistical Questions and Variables

Quick Review

A **statistical variable** is a quantity or quality for which data are expected to differ. A **categorical variable** has values that belong to a limited set of possible qualitative responses. A **quantitative variable** has values that are numbers that you could meaningfully compare, add, subtract, and so on.

A **population** represents all the members of a group studied by a statistical question. A **sample** is a subset of the population—one that is being studied to answer a statistical question about the population.

Example

A political volunteer asked passersby about who they would vote for in an upcoming election for city council to try to determine who would win. What are the sample and the population in this scenario?

The population is all the voters in the city who plan to vote in the election. The sample is all of the passersby who responded.

Practice & Problem Solving

Is the given question a statistical question?

7. How many days are in September?

8. Do football coaches generally get paid more than swimming coaches?

9. **Communicate Precisely** Explain how to determine if a quantity is a statistic or a parameter. Ⓒ MP.6

10. **Make Sense and Persevere** What type of statistical variable is represented by the graph? Ⓒ MP.1

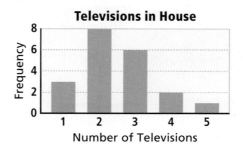

Televisions in House

Ⓢ **Go Online** | SavvasRealize.com

Statistical Studies and Sampling Methods

Quick Review

An **experiment** is a statistical study where a researcher applies treatment(s) to the sample. In an **observational study** researchers observe the sample without intentionally affecting it. Researchers use **sample surveys** to ask sample members the same set of questions.

Example

What sampling method is used in the following example? Is the method biased?

The first ten students who enter the school are sampled.

This is convenience sampling because only the first ten students were sampled. The method is biased.

Practice & Problem Solving

In Exercises 11–12, describe what king of study you would conduct to answer each statistical question.

11. Is the lifespan of giraffes affected by the number of offspring they produce?

12. Do employees at a company want vending machines with healthy snacks?

13. Communicate Precisely Explain the difference between an experimental group and a control group. ⓒ **MP.6**

14. Look for Relationships What sampling method is used below? Is the method biased? ⓒ **MP.7**

Every 10th person in line was chosen to fill out a survey.

Data Distributions

Quick Review

The **standard deviation** is a measure of how much the values in a data set vary, or deviate, from the mean.

For **skewed distributions**, use the median and interquartile range to describe the data. For distributions that are symmetric, use the mean and standard deviation to describe the data.

Example

Which measures of center and spread are best for describing this set of data?

9 2 17 12 3 20 5 22 7 11 6 14 3 15 10 19

Draw a histogram of the data.

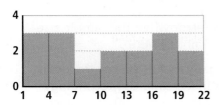

Since the data are not skewed, the best measures of center and spread and the mean and standard deviation.

Practice & Problem Solving

Find the mean, standard deviation, and five-number summary of the data set. Round to the nearest tenth, if necessary.

15. 23 35 19 27 33 24 18 26 38 29

16. 82 77 88 65 68 73 81 74 68 83 80

Which measures of center and spread describe each data set best?

17. 13 28 14 30 18 22 29 24 26 12 20 16

18. 45 56 38 48 41 35 59 46 52 79 62

19. Communicate Precisely Describe a situation that could produce a data distribution similar to this one. ⓒ **MP.6**

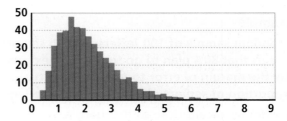

20. Use Structure A data set has a mean that is equal to the median. What is the likely shape of the distribution of the data? Explain. ⓒ **MP.7**

Quick Review

The Empirical Rule gives the percentage of data values falling near the mean.

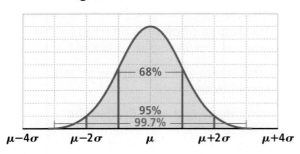

Example

Suppose test scores are normally distributed with mean score 78 and standard deviation 3. What portion of the students scored between 72 and 84?

The interval between 72 and 84 includes all the scores within two standard deviations of the mean.

According to the Empirical Rule, 95% of students scored between 72 and 84.

Practice & Problem Solving

Find the percentage of all values in a normal distribution for each z-score.

21. $z \leq 0.29$

22. $z \leq 1.45$

23. $z \leq 0.89$

24. $z \geq 2.11$

25. $z \geq -0.67$

26. $z \leq -1.55$

27. The heart rate of a random sample of people is approximately normally distributed. The mean heart rate is 73 beats per minutes and the standard deviation is 6 beats per minute. What range of heart rates contains the 95% closest to the mean?

28. Error Analysis Hana said the percentage of all values in a normal distribution with $z \geq 1.05$ is 85.31%. Describe and correct Hana's error. Ⓒ **MP.3**

29. Reason Suppose travel times of employees at a company are normally distributed with mean travel time of 18 min and standard deviation of 3.25 min. What portion of the employees have a travel time between 14.75 and 22.5 min? Ⓒ **MP.2**

Quick Review

Margin of Error (ME)	
Quantitative Data	Categorical Data
$ME \approx \dfrac{2\sigma}{\sqrt{n}}$	$ME \approx \dfrac{1}{\sqrt{n}}$
σ = standard deviation n = sample size	n = sample size

Example

A random sample of 100 Jefferson High seniors reveals that 80% plan to go to college next year. Use the margin of error to predict the actual proportion of seniors planning to go to college.

The data is categorical, so the margin of error is $\dfrac{1}{\sqrt{100}} = 0.1 = 10\%$.

Range: $80\% - 10\% = 70\%$ and $80\% + 10\% = 90\%$

The proportion of seniors planning to go to college next year is between 70% and 90%.

Practice & Problem Solving

30. Find the sample proportion and margin of error to the nearest percent for an event that occurs 67 times in a sample size of 400.

31. Suppose a population has standard deviation 32.5 and the sample size is 350. Find the margin of error to the nearest tenth.

32. Communicate Precisely What happens to the margin of error when the sample size increases? Explain. Ⓒ **MP.6**

33. Reason Kimberly makes 20% of the goals she attempts in lacrosse. Use technology to simulate 50 trials with 100 goals each. Identify the range that contains the middle 95% of results. Ⓒ **MP.2**

Quick Review

The **null hypothesis** H_0 is a statement that expresses that there is no difference between the quantities of interest. The **alternative hypothesis** H_a is the statement that expresses that there is a difference between the quantities.

Example

Keen Beenz reports that the average price for a can of their beans is $0.85. A sample of 100 retail prices of their beans has a mean price of $1.15. The standard deviation of prices nationally is $0.25. Does this study provide strong evidence that Keen Beenz' claim is true or false?

Write the hypotheses: H_0: $\mu = 0.85$; H_a: $\mu \neq 0.85$

Calculate the margin of error: $\frac{2\sigma}{\sqrt{n}} = \frac{2(0.25)}{\sqrt{100}} = 0.05$

Predict a range of reasonable values:
sample mean $\pm$ margin of error $= 1.15 \pm 0.05$

The range of values is 1.10 to 1.20.

The claim falls outside the range of reasonable values predicted by the statistical study. This evidence suggests that the claim is false.

Practice & Problem Solving

34. A baseball player got a hit in 30.5% of his attempts. After his coach attempted to improve his swing, he got a hit in 32.8% of the attempts. Write the null hypothesis and alternative hypothesis for a statistical study to evaluate the effect of the change on the player's percentage of getting a hit.

35. Scores from students chosen randomly for a study group had a sample mean 2.8 points higher than that for students who studied alone. The data were randomized 50 times, producing this histogram. Can you conclude that the study group improved scores? Explain.

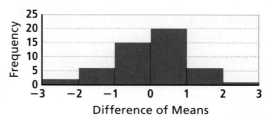

36. Make Sense and Persevere SportORiffic reports that they sell a daily average of 25 athletic tops per day. A national sample of 100 SportORiffic stores is selected, and mean number of athletic tops sold was 23 per day. The standard deviation is 12 per day. Does this study provide strong evidence that SportORiffic's claim is true or false? Explain. Ⓒ **MP.1**

TOPIC 12

Probability

? TOPIC ESSENTIAL QUESTION

How can you find the probability of events and combinations of events?

Topic Overview

enVision™ STEM Project:
Simulate Weather Conditions

12-1 Probability Events

12-2 Conditional Probability

Mathematical Modeling in 3 Acts:
Place Your Guess

12-3 Permutations and Combinations

12-4 Probability Distributions

12-5 Expected Value

12-6 Probability and Decision Making

Topic Vocabulary

- binomial distribution
- binomial experiment
- binomial probability
- combination
- complement
- conditional probability
- dependent events
- expected value
- factorial
- Fundamental Counting Principle
- independent events
- mutually exclusive
- permutation
- probability distribution
- uniform probability distribution

Digital Experience

 INTERACTIVE STUDENT EDITION
Access online or offline.

 ACTIVITIES Complete *Explore & Reason*, *Model & Discuss*, and *Critique & Explain* activities. Interact with Examples and Try Its.

ANIMATION View and interact with real-world applications.

 PRACTICE Practice what you've learned.

 Go online | SavvasRealize.com

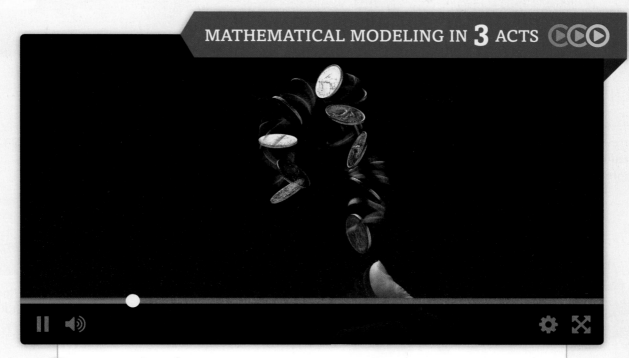

⊙ Place Your Guess

A coin toss is a popular way to decide between two options or settle a dispute. The coin toss is popular because it is a simple and unbiased way of deciding. Assuming the coin being tossed is a fair coin, both parties have an equally likely chance of winning.

What other methods could you use to decide between two choices fairly? Think about this during the Mathematical Modeling in 3 Acts lesson.

VIDEOS Watch clips to support *Mathematical Modeling in 3 Acts Lessons* and **enVision™ STEM Projects.**

CONCEPT SUMMARY Review key lesson content through multiple representations.

ASSESSMENT Show what you've learned.

GLOSSARY Read and listen to English and Spanish definitions.

TUTORIALS Get help from *Virtual Nerd*, right when you need it.

MATH TOOLS Explore math with digital tools and manipulatives.

Did You Know?

Meteorologists use past climate data for a particular location and date as well as **weather models** to make weather predictions. Some regions in the U.S. are more predictable than others.

The **greatest temperature change** in a one-day period occurred in Loma, Montana, in 1972. The temperature rose an incredible **103 degrees**, from –54 to 49 °F, in 24 hours.

Weather events can surprise experts, and can vary greatly even within a few miles.

Climate is the long-term average of weather conditions. So the difference between weather and climate is a measure of time.

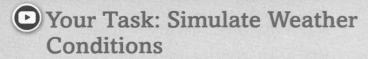

▶ Your Task: Simulate Weather Conditions

You and your classmates will research climate data for a specific location for one month. You'll use probability to simulate a plausible set of weather conditions for each day of February, including temperature and precipitation, and whether the precipitation will be rain or snow.

12-1

Probability Events

🛜 SavvasRealize.com

I CAN... use relationships among events to find probabilities.

VOCABULARY
- complement
- independent events
- mutually exclusive

© **Common Core State Standards** HSS.CP.A.1, HSS.CP.A.2, HSS.CP.A.5, HSS.CP.B.7, MP.2, MP.3, MP.7

👆 **EXPLORE & REASON**

Allie spins the spinner and draws one card without looking. She gets a 3 on the spinner and the 3 card. Then she sets the card aside, spins again, and draws another card.

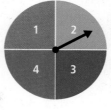

A. Is it possible for Allie to get a 3 on her second spin? On her second card? Explain.

B. Construct Arguments How does getting the 3 card on her first draw affect the probability of getting the 2 card on her second draw? Explain. © **MP.3**

❓ **ESSENTIAL QUESTION**   How does describing events as mutually exclusive or independent affect how you find probabilities?

👆 **EXAMPLE 1**   Find Probabilities of Mutually Exclusive Events

You roll a standard number cube once. Let *E* represent the event "roll an even number." Let *T* represent the event "roll a 3 or 5."

A. What is the probability that you roll an even number or roll a 3 or 5?

Show the outcomes of events *E* and *T* as a subset of the sample space *S*.

Events *E* and *T* are **mutually exclusive** because there is no outcome in both sets.

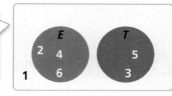

There are 5 outcomes that are even numbers or a 3 or 5.
{2, 3, 4, 5, 6}
There are a total of 6 possible outcomes in the sample space.

$$P(E \text{ or } T) = \frac{\text{number of favorable outcomes}}{\text{number of total possible outcomes}}$$

$$= \frac{3 + 2}{6}$$ There are 3 outcomes in event *E* and 2 outcomes in event *T*.

$$= \frac{3}{6} + \frac{2}{6}$$ This is equivalent to $P(E) + P(T)$.

$$= \frac{5}{6}$$

The probability of rolling an even number or rolling a 3 or a 5 is $\frac{5}{6}$.

VOCABULARY
A *favorable* outcome is an outcome that is being tested or observed and not necessarily a desirable result. A "favorable" outcome may be a loss for the home team or testing positive for a disease.

B. You roll a standard number cube once. What is the probability that you roll an even number and a 3 or 5?

$$P(E \text{ and } T) = \frac{\text{number of favorable outcomes}}{\text{number of total possible outcomes}}$$

$$= \frac{0}{6}$$ Because events *E* and *T* are mutually exclusive, there are no outcomes that are in both sets.

$$= 0$$

The probability of rolling an even number and rolling a 3 or a 5 is 0.

CONTINUED ON THE NEXT PAGE

EXAMPLE 1 CONTINUED

GENERALIZE

Notice that E and *not E* are mutually exclusive events. What would the sum of $P(E)$ and $P(\text{not } E)$ be equal to? © **MP.8**

C. You roll a standard number cube once. What is the probability that you do *not* roll an even number?

$$P(\text{not } E) = \frac{3}{6} \text{ or } \frac{1}{2}$$

There are 3 outcomes that are not even numbers.

The probability of not rolling an even number is $\frac{1}{2}$.

 Try It! **1.** A box contains 100 balls. Thirty of the balls are purple and 10 are orange. If you select one of the balls at random, what is the probability of each of the following events?

a. The ball is purple or orange.

b. The ball is not purple and not orange.

CONCEPT Probabilities of Mutually Exclusive Events

If A and B are mutually exclusive events, then

- $P(A \text{ or } B) = P(A) + P(B)$
- $P(A \text{ and } B) = 0$

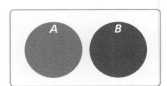

The **complement** of an event is the set of all outcomes in a sample space that are not included in the event.

If C is the event that A does not occur, then

$$P(C) = 1 - P(A).$$

APPLICATION  **EXAMPLE 2** **Find the Probabilities of Non-Mutually Exclusive Events**

A student-made target includes two overlapping squares. Assume that a sticky ball thrown at the target is equally likely to land anywhere on the target. What is the probability that the ball lands inside one or both of the squares?

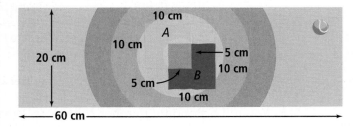

Step 1 Find the area of the squares, and their overlapping area.

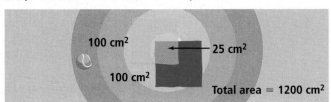

CONTINUED ON THE NEXT PAGE

EXAMPLE 2 CONTINUED

Step 2 Find the probabilities.

One method: $75 \text{ cm}^2 + 25 \text{ cm}^2 + 75 \text{ cm}^2 = 175 \text{ cm}^2$

$$P(A \text{ or } B) = \frac{175}{1,200} = \frac{7}{12}$$

Another method: $P(A \text{ or } B) = \frac{100}{1,200} + \frac{100}{1,200} - \frac{25}{1,200}$

> Subtract the probability of the overlapping area because it was included twice, once for each large square.

$$= \frac{175}{1,200} = \frac{7}{48}$$

The probability that the ball will land inside one or both squares is $\frac{7}{48}$, or about 15%.

 Try It!   **2.** A video game screen is a rectangle with dimensions 34 cm and 20 cm. A starship on the screen is made of two circles with radius 6 cm, and overlapping area of 20 cm². A black hole appears randomly on the screen. What is the probability that it appears within the starship?

CONCEPT Probabilities of Non-Mutually Exclusive Events

If A and B are not mutually exclusive events, then
$P(A \text{ or } B) = P(A) + P(B) - P(A \text{ and } B)$.

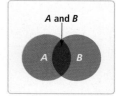

CONCEPTUAL UNDERSTANDING

EXAMPLE 3 Identify Independent Events

A jar contains 12 green marbles and 8 violet marbles.

A. A marble is chosen at random from the jar and replaced. Another marble is chosen at random from the jar. Does the color of the first marble chosen affect the possible outcomes for the second marble chosen?

Determine the probabilities for each choice to decide whether the first marble chosen affects the possibilities for the second marble.

First Choice-Sample Space
12 Green
8 Violet

Second Choice-Sample Space
12 Green
8 Violet

$P(G) = \frac{12}{20} = \frac{3}{5}$ $P(G) = \frac{12}{20} = \frac{3}{5}$

$P(V) = \frac{8}{20} = \frac{2}{5}$ $P(V) = \frac{8}{20} = \frac{2}{5}$

> The probabilities are the same.

The color of the first marble chosen does not affect the possible outcomes for the second marble chosen.

Two events are **independent events** if and only if the occurrence of one event does not affect the probability of a second event.

CONTINUED ON THE NEXT PAGE

EXAMPLE 3 CONTINUED

B. A marble is chosen at random from the jar and not replaced. Another marble is chosen at random from the jar. Does the color of the first marble chosen affect the possible outcomes for the second marble chosen?

Determine whether the events are independent.

First Choice-Sample Space
12 Green
8 Violet

$P(G) = \frac{12}{20} = \frac{3}{5}$ $P(V) = \frac{8}{20} = \frac{2}{5}$

Assume a green marble was chosen first.

Assume a violet marble is chosen first.

Second Choice-Sample Space
11 Green
8 Violet

Second Choice-Sample Space
12 Green
7 Violet

$P(G) = \frac{11}{19}$ $P(V) = \frac{8}{19}$

$P(G) = \frac{12}{19}$ $P(V) = \frac{7}{19}$

When the first marble is not replaced in the jar, the color of the first marble chosen does affect the possible outcomes for the second marble chosen. These events are not independent.

> **COMMON ERROR**
> When two or more items are selected from the same set, you must determine whether the first item(s) is replaced before the next item is selected. Then find the probabilities.

 Try It!   **3.** There are 10 cards in a box, 5 black and 5 red. Two cards are selected from the box, one at a time.

    a. A card is chosen at random and then replaced. Another card is chosen. Does the color of the first card chosen affect the possibilities of the second card chosen? Explain.

    b. A card is chosen at random and *not* replaced. Another card is chosen. Does the color of the first card chosen affect the possibilities of the second card chosen? Explain.

CONCEPT Probability of Independent Events

If *A* and *B* are independent events, then $P(A \text{ and } B) = P(A) \cdot P(B)$.

If $P(A \text{ and } B) = P(A) \cdot P(B)$, then *A* and *B* are independent events.

Example: When rolling a die and tossing a coin, the result of the die roll and the result of the coin toss are independent events.

$P(4) = \frac{1}{6}$ $P(H) = \frac{1}{2}$

$P(4 \text{ and } H) = \frac{1}{6} \cdot \frac{1}{2} = \frac{1}{12}$

APPLICATION   👍 **EXAMPLE 4**   Find Probabilities of Independent Events

Alex cannot decide which shirt to wear today, so she chooses one at random.

The probability of rain today is 40%, or $\frac{2}{5}$.

A. What is the probability that Alex chooses a yellow shirt and it does not rain today?

Let Y represent the event "yellow shirt." Let N represent "no rain."

Y and N are independent because Alex's choice of shirt does not affect the weather, and the weather does not affect Alex's choice of shirt. Use the formula to find $P(Y \text{ and } N)$.

Step 1 Find $P(N)$ and $P(Y)$.

> Subtract the probability that it will rain, $\frac{2}{5}$, from 1 to find the probability that it will *not* rain.

$$P(N) = 1 - \frac{2}{5} = \frac{3}{5}.$$

$$P(Y) = \frac{\text{number of favorable outcomes}}{\text{total number of outcomes}} = \frac{2}{4} \text{ or } \frac{1}{2}$$

Step 2 Apply the formula and multiply the probabilities of Y and N.

$$P(Y \text{ and } N) = P(Y) \cdot P(N) = \frac{1}{2} \cdot \frac{3}{5} = \frac{3}{10} = 30\%$$

> Use the rule for the probability of independent events.

The probability that Alex chooses a yellow shirt and it does not rain is 30%.

B. What is the probability that Alex chooses a yellow shirt and it does not rain today or that Alex chooses a green shirt and it rains today?

Let G represent "green shirt."   Let R represent "rain."

The events "Y and N" and "G and R" are mutually exclusive because no outcomes are in both events.

Step 1 Find $P(G \text{ and } R)$

$$P(G \text{ and } R) = P(G) \cdot P(R) = \frac{1}{4} \cdot \frac{2}{5} = \frac{2}{20} = \frac{1}{10} = 10\%$$

Step 2 Find $P((Y \text{ and } N) \text{ or } (G \text{ and } R))$

> Add to find the probability that either event will occur.

$$P((Y \text{ and } N) \text{ or } (G \text{ and } R)) = P(Y \text{ and } N) + P(G \text{ and } R)$$

$$= 30\% + 10\% = 40\%$$

The probability that Alex chooses a yellow shirt and it does not rain or that Alex chooses a green shirt and it rains is 40%.

✅ **Try It!**   **4.** You spin the spinner two times. Assume that the probability of Blue each spin is $\frac{1}{3}$ and the probability of Orange each spin is $\frac{2}{3}$. What is the probability of getting the same color both times? Explain.

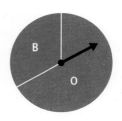

	Mutually Exclusive Events	Independent Events
WORDS	A and B are mutually exclusive because no outcome is in both A and B.	D and M are independent because the occurrence of one does not affect the probability of the other.
ALGEBRA	If A and B are mutually exclusive events, then $P(A \text{ or } B) = P(A) + P(B)$. If C is the event that A does not occur, then $P(C) = 1 - P(A)$.	If D and M are independent events, then $P(D \text{ and } M) = P(D) \cdot P(M)$. If $P(D \text{ and } M) = P(D) \cdot P(M)$, then D and M are independent events.
EXAMPLES	Experiment: spin the spinner.  Event A: number less than 3 Event B: number greater than 5 $P(A \text{ or } B) = P(A) + P(B) = \dfrac{2}{6} + \dfrac{1}{6} = \dfrac{1}{2}$	Experiment: spin the spinner and roll a number cube Event D: odd number on spinner Event M: number greater than 4 on number cube $P(D \text{ and } M) = P(D) \cdot P(M) = \dfrac{1}{2} \cdot \dfrac{1}{3} = \dfrac{1}{6}$

☑ Do You UNDERSTAND?

1. **ESSENTIAL QUESTION** How does describing events as independent or mutually exclusive affect how you find probabilities?

2. **Reason** Two marbles are chosen, one at a time, from a bag containing 6 marbles, 4 red marbles and 2 green marbles. Suppose the first marble chosen is green. Is the probability that the second marble will be red greater if the first marble is returned to the bag or if it is not returned to the bag? Explain. ⓒ **MP.2**

3. **Error Analysis** The probability that Deshawn plays basketball (event B) after school is 20%. The probability that he talks to friends (event T) after school is 45%. He says that $P(B \text{ or } T)$ is 65%. Explain Deshawn's error. ⓒ **MP.3**

4. **Vocabulary** What is the difference between mutually exclusive events and independent events?

Do You KNOW HOW?

5. A bag contains 40 marbles. Eight are green and 2 are blue. You select one marble at random. What is the probability of each event?

   a. The marble is green or blue.

   b. The marble is not green and not blue.

6. A robot at a carnival booth randomly tosses a dart at a square target with 8 inch sides and circle with a 3 inch radius in the middle. To the nearest whole percent, what is the probability that the dart will land in the circle?

For Exercises 7 and 8, assume that you roll a standard number cube two times.

7. What is the probability of rolling an even number on the first roll and a number less than 3 on the second roll?

8. What is the probability of rolling an odd number on the first roll and a number greater than 3 on the second roll?

UNDERSTAND

9. Construct Arguments Let *S* be a sample space for an experiment in which every outcome is both equally likely and mutually exclusive. What can you conclude about the sum of the probabilities for all of the outcomes? Give an example. © **MP.3**

10. Error Analysis At Lincoln High School, 6 students are members of both the Chess Club and the Math Club. There are 20 students in the Math Club, 12 students in the Chess Club, and 400 students in the entire school.

Danielle calculated the probability that a student chosen at random belongs to the Chess Club or the Math Club. Explain her error. © **MP.3**

Event *C*: Student is in Chess Club
Event *M*: Student is in Math Club

$$P(C \text{ or } M) = P(C) + P(M)$$
$$= \frac{12}{400} + \frac{20}{400}$$
$$= \frac{32}{400} = 0.08$$

11. Higher Order Thinking Murphy's math teacher sometimes wears scarves to class. Murphy has been documenting the relationship between his teacher wearing a scarf and when the class has a math quiz. The probabilities are as follows:

- *P*(wearing a scarf) = 10%
- *P*(math quiz) = 15%
- *P*(wearing a scarf and math quiz) = 5%

Are the events "the teacher is wearing a scarf" and "there will be a quiz" independent events? Explain.

Reason A card is drawn from a box containing 5 cards, each showing a different number from 1 to 5. Consider the events "even number," "odd number," "less than 3," and "greater than 3." Determine whether each pair of events mutually exclusive. © **MP.2**

12. < 3, > 3   **13.** even, > 3

14. odd, > 3   **15.** odd, even

PRACTICE

16. Hana is playing a virtual reality game in which she must toss a disc to land on the largest triangular section of the board. If the disc is equally likely to land anywhere on the board, what is the probability that she will succeed? Explain. SEE EXAMPLE 1

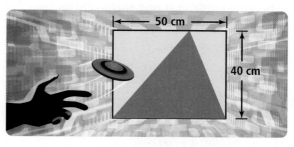

In a class of 25 students, 8 students have heights less than 65 inches and 10 students have heights of 69 inches or more. For Exercises 17–19, find the probabilities described. SEE EXAMPLE 1

17. *P*(less than 65 inches or greater than 69 inches)

18. *P*(greater than or equal to 65 inches)

19. *P*(greater than or equal to 65 inches and less than or equal to 69 inches)

20. A skydiver is equally likely to land at any point on a rectangular field. Two overlapping circular targets of radius 5 meters are marked on the field. To the nearest percent, what is the probability that the sky diver will land in one or both of the circles? SEE EXAMPLE 2

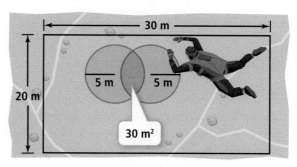

21. Two marbles are chosen at random, one at a time from a box that contains 7 marbles, 5 red and 2 green. SEE EXAMPLES 3 AND 4

a. Find the probability of drawing 2 red marbles when the first marble is replaced before the second marble is chosen.

b. Determine whether the situation described is independent.

APPLY

22. Mathematical Connections For a science fair project, Paige wants to test whether ants prefer certain colors. She releases ants on the colored surface shown. If the ants are randomly distributed across the entire surface, what is the probability that any given ant will be within the blue circle, but not within the yellow circle? Round to the nearest whole percent.

15 in.

9 in.

Y
3 in.

B

W

23. Use Structure A city issues 3-digit license plates for motorized scooters. The digits 0–9 are chosen at random by a computer program. What is the probability that a license plate issued meets each set of criteria? ⓒ MP.7

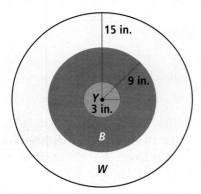

???

   a. The three-digit number formed is even.

   b. The first number is not 7.

   c. The first two digits are the same.

   d. All three digits are the same.

24. Model With Mathematics During a football game, a kicker is called in twice to kick a field goal from the 30 yard line. Suppose that for each attempt, the probability that he will make the field goal is 0.8. ⓒ MP.4

   a. What is the probability that he will make both field goals?

   b. What is the probability that he will make neither field goal?

ⓒ ASSESSMENT PRACTICE

25. The probability of events A and B both occurring is 15%. The probability of event A or B occurring is 60%. The probability of B occurring is 50%. What is the probability of A occurring?

26. SAT/ACT A robot spins the spinner shown twice. Assume that the outcomes 1, 2, 3, and 4 are equally likely for each spin. What is the probability that the sum of the two outcomes will be 6?

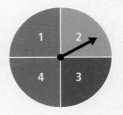

1   2

4   3

  Ⓐ $\frac{1}{16}$　　　　Ⓓ $\frac{1}{4}$

  Ⓑ $\frac{1}{8}$　　　　Ⓔ $\frac{3}{4}$

  Ⓒ $\frac{3}{16}$

27. Performance Task Paula is packing to visit a friend in another city for a long weekend. She looks at the weather forecast shown below to find the chance of rain. Assume that whether it rains on each day is independent of whether it rains on any other day.

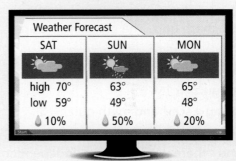

Weather Forecast		
SAT	SUN	MON
high 70°	63°	65°
low 59°	49°	48°
💧 10%	💧 50%	💧 20%

Part A What is the probability that it will not rain on any of the three days to the nearest percent?

Part B What is the probability that it will rain at least one of the three days to the nearest percent?

Part C Do you think Paula should pack an umbrella? Explain.

Common Core State Standards HSS.CP.A.3, HSS.CP.A.5, HSS.CP.B.6, MP.1, MP.3, MP.7

  Activity Assess

I CAN... find the probability of an event given that another event has occurred.

VOCABULARY
- conditional probability
- dependent events

EXPLORE & REASON

At Central High School, 85% of all senior girls attended and 65% of all senior boys attended the Spring Dance. Of all attendees, 20% won a prize.

A. Assuming that the number of senior girls at Central High School is about equal to the number of senior boys, estimate the probability that a randomly selected senior won a prize at the dance. Explain.

B. **Construct Arguments** If you knew whether the selected student was a boy or a girl, would your estimate change? Explain. **MP.3**

? ESSENTIAL QUESTION

How are conditional probability and independence related in real-world experiments?

EXAMPLE 1 Understand Conditional Probability

A student committee is being formed to decide how after-school activities will be funded. The committee members are selected at random from current club members. The frequency table shows the current club membership data.

Monday Club Memberships by Grade

	Drama	Science	Art	Total
Sophomore	3	9	24	36
Junior	6	18	16	40
Senior	8	13	18	39
Total	17	40	58	115

What is the probability that a member of the art club selected at random is a junior?

One Method Use the frequency table to find the probability that the student chosen is a junior given that the student is a member of the art club.

> The probability that an event B will occur given that another event A has already occurred is called a **conditional probability** and is written as $P(B \mid A)$.

COMMON ERROR
Avoid confusing $P(A \mid B)$ with $P(B \mid A)$. In the first case the prior event is B, but in the second case the prior event is A.

$$P(\text{junior} \mid \text{member of the art club}) = \frac{\text{number of juniors in art club}}{\text{total number of art club members}}$$

$$= \frac{16}{58} = \frac{8}{29}$$

Another Method Use the formula for conditional probability.

For any two events A and B, with $P(A) \neq 0$, $P(B \mid A) = \frac{P(B \text{ and } A)}{P(A)}$.

$$P(\text{junior} \mid \text{art}) = \frac{P(\text{junior and art})}{P(\text{art})} = \frac{\frac{16}{115}}{\frac{58}{115}} = \frac{8}{29}$$

> Of the 115 Monday club members and 58 art club members, 16 are juniors and in the art club.

The probability that the student chosen is a junior member from the art club is $\frac{8}{29}$.

CONTINUED ON THE NEXT PAGE

EXAMPLE 1 CONTINUED

 Try It! **1. a.** What is the probability that a member of the drama club is a sophomore, $P(\text{sophomore} \mid \text{drama})$?

b. What is the probability that a sophomore is a member of the drama club, $P(\text{drama} \mid \text{sophomore})$? Is $P(\text{sophomore} \mid \text{drama})$ the same as $P(\text{drama} \mid \text{sophomore})$? Explain.

CONCEPT Conditional Probability and Independent Events

Let A and B be events with $P(A) \neq 0$ and $P(B) \neq 0$.

If events A and B are independent, then the conditional probability of B given A equals the probability of B and the conditional probability of A given B equals the probability of A.

If events A and B are independent, then $P(B \mid A) = P(B)$ and $P(A \mid B) = P(A)$.

If the conditional probability of B given A equals the probability of B and the conditional probability of A given B equals the probability of A, then events A and B are independent.

If $P(B \mid A) = P(B)$ and $P(A \mid B) = P(A)$, then events A and B are independent.

CONCEPTUAL UNDERSTANDING

👆 **EXAMPLE 2** Use the Test for Independence

The table below shows the vehicles in a parking garage one afternoon. A vehicle in the garage will be selected at random. Let B represent "the vehicle is black" and V represent "the vehicle is a van." Are the events B and V independent or dependent?

STUDY TIP
When looking at a table of probabilities, consider events that are impossible or guaranteed to occur. For example, it is impossible to select a red van.

	Car	Van	Pickup	Totals
Red	5	0	2	7
White	0	0	2	2
Black	6	3	4	13
Totals	11	3	8	22

One Method

Since $P(B) = \frac{13}{22} \neq 0$ and $P(V \text{ and } B) = \frac{3}{22}$,

$$P(V \mid B) = \frac{P(V \text{ and } B)}{P(B)} = \frac{\frac{3}{22}}{\frac{13}{22}} = \frac{3}{13}$$

Since $P(V \mid B) \neq P(V)$, B and V are not independent events, they are **dependent events**.

CONTINUED ON THE NEXT PAGE

EXAMPLE 2 CONTINUED

Another Method

Since $P(V) = \frac{3}{22} \neq 0$ and $P(B \text{ and } V) = P(V \text{ and } B)$,

$$P(B \mid V) = \frac{P(B \text{ and } V)}{P(V)}$$

$$= \frac{\frac{3}{22}}{\frac{3}{22}} = 1$$

A probability of 1, or 100%, indicates that the event is certain. Given that a van is selected, it must be black.

Again, Since $P(B \mid V) \neq P(B)$, the events B and V are dependent events.

☑ **Try It!** 2. Let R represent "the vehicle is red" and C represent "the vehicle is a car." Are the events R and C independent or dependent? Explain.

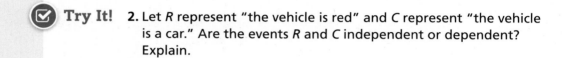 **EXAMPLE 3** **Apply the Conditional Probability Formula**

A band's marketing agent conducted a survey to determine how many high school fans the band has. What is the probability that a surveyed student plans to attend the band's concert and is a fan of the group?

Concert Survey Results

Students who plan to attend concert

- 70% of students plan to attend,
- 80% of students who plan to attend are fans of the band.

Students who do not plan to attend

- 30% of students do not plan to attend,
- 25% are fans of the band.

Use the conditional probability formula to find the combined probability.

Rewrite $P(B \mid A) = \frac{P(A \text{ and } B)}{P(A)}$ as $P(A \text{ and } B) = P(A) \cdot P(B \mid A)$.

$$P(A \text{ and } B) = P(A) \cdot P(B \mid A)$$

$$P(\text{attend and fan}) = P(\text{attend}) \cdot P(\text{fan} \mid \text{attend})$$

Event A is "attend." Event B is "fan."

$$= 0.7 \cdot 0.8$$

Substitute 0.7 for $P(\text{attend})$ and 0.8 for $P(\text{fan} \mid \text{attend})$.

$$= 0.56, \text{ or } 56\%$$

LOOK FOR RELATIONSHIPS
Why might $P(\text{fan} \mid \text{attend})$ not equal $P(\text{attend} \mid \text{fan})$ in this situation? ⒸMP.7

The probability that a surveyed student plans to attend the concert and is a fan of the group is 0.56, or 56%.

☑ **Try It!** 3. What is the probability that a surveyed student plans to attend but is not a fan of the group?

APPLICATION → **EXAMPLE 4** > **Use Conditional Probability to Make a Decision**

A marketer is looking at mobile phone statistics to help plan an online advertising campaign. She wants to find out which of her company's products is most likely to be purchased after a related search after a search for that product on a mobile phone.

Mobile Phone Search and Buying Behavior		
Product	Search(S)	Search & Buy (S and B)
W	46%	16%
X	32%	14%
Y	35%	12%
Z	40%	15%

Find the probability a mobile phone customer buys, given that they performed a related search. Use the formula $P(B \mid S) = \dfrac{P(S \text{ and } B)}{P(S)}$.

MAKE SENSE AND PERSEVERE
Product W has the highest $P(S \text{ and } B)$ of 16% but not the highest $P(B \mid S)$. Can you explain why? **©** **MP.1**

Product	$P(B \mid S)$
W	$\frac{0.16}{0.46} \approx 0.348$ or about 34.8%
X	$\frac{0.14}{0.32} = 0.4375$ or 43.75%
Y	$\frac{0.12}{0.35} \approx 0.343$ or 34.3%
Z	$\frac{0.15}{0.40} = 0.375$ or 37.5%

Product X has the highest probability of being purchased given that a related search was performed.

 Try It! 4. The marketer also has data from desktop computers. Which product is most likely to be purchased after a related search?

Computer Search and Buying Behavior
(% of computer-based site visitors)

Product	Search	Search & Buy
J	35%	10%
K	28%	9%
L	26%	8%
M	24%	5%

Conditional Probability Formula	Conditional Probability and Independent Events
WORDS The probability that an event B will occur given that another event A has already occurred is called a **conditional probability**.	Events A and B are independent events if and only if the conditional probability of A given B is the same as the probability of A, and the conditional probability of B given A is the same as the probability of B.
ALGEBRA For any two events A and B, with $P(A) \neq 0$, $$P(B \mid A) = \frac{P(A \text{ and } B)}{P(A)}$$	For any events A and B with $P(A) \neq 0$ and $P(B) \neq 0$, A and B are independent if and only if $P(B \mid A) = P(B)$ and $P(A \mid B) = P(A)$.

✓ Do You UNDERSTAND?

1. **ESSENTIAL QUESTION** How are conditional probability and independence related in experiments?

2. **Vocabulary** How is the sample space for $P(B \mid A)$ different from the sample space for $P(B)$?

3. **Vocabulary** Why does the definition of $P(B \mid A)$ have the condition that $P(A) \neq 0$?

4. **Use Structure** Why is $P(A) \cdot P(B \mid A) = P(B) \cdot P(A \mid B)$? ⓒ MP.7

5. **Error Analysis** Taylor knows that $P(R) = 0.8$, $P(B) = 0.2$, and $P(R \text{ and } B) = 0.05$. Explain Taylor's error. ⓒ MP.3

$$P(B \mid R) = \frac{0.05}{0.2}$$
$$= 0.25 \quad ✗$$

6. **Reason** At a sports camp, a coach wants to find the probability that a soccer player is a local camper. Because 40% of the students in the camp are local, the coach reasons that the probability is 0.4. Is his conclusion justified? Explain. ⓒ MP.2

Do You KNOW HOW?

7. Let $P(A) = \frac{3}{4}$, $P(B) = \frac{2}{3}$, and $P(A \text{ and } B) = \frac{1}{2}$. Find each probability.

   a. What is $P(B \mid A)$?

   b. What is $P(A \mid B)$?

8. Students randomly generate two digits from 0 to 9 to create a number between 0 and 99. Are the events "first digit 5" and "second digit 6" independent or dependent in each case? What is $P(56)$ in each experiment?

   a. The digits may not be repeated.

   b. The digits may be repeated.

9. Suppose that you select one card at random from the set of 6 cards below.

| W2 | B3 | W4 | B3 | B2 | W3 |

   Let B represent the event "select a blue card" and T represent the event "select a card with a 3." Are B and T independent events? Explain your reasoning.

PRACTICE & PROBLEM SOLVING

UNDERSTAND

10. **Mathematical Connections** How can the formula $P(A \text{ and } B) = P(A) \cdot P(B \mid A)$ be simplified to find the probability of A and B when the events are independent? Explain.

11. **Error Analysis** From a bag containing 3 red marbles and 7 blue marbles, 2 marbles are selected without replacement. Esteban calculated the probability that two red marbles are selected. Explain Esteban's error. © MP.3

$$P(\text{red}) = 0.3$$
$$P(\text{red and red}) = P(\text{red}) \cdot P(\text{red})$$
$$= 0.3 \cdot 0.3$$
$$= 0.09 \quad ✗$$

12. **Generalize** Kiyo is creating a table using mosaic tiles chosen and placed randomly. She is picking tiles without looking. How does P(yellow second | blue first) compare to P(yellow second | yellow first) if the tiles are selected without replacement? If the tiles are selected and returned to the pile because Kiyo wants a different color? © MP.8

13. **Use Structure** At a fundraiser, a participant is asked to guess what is inside an unlabeled can for a possible prize. If there are two crates of cans to choose from, each having a mixture of vegetables and soup, what is the probability that the first participant will select a vegetable can from the left crate given each situation? © MP.7

   a. The left crate has 2 cans of vegetables and 8 cans of soup, and the right crate has 7 cans of vegetables and 3 cans of soup.

   b. The left crate has 8 cans of vegetables and 2 cans of soup, and the right crate has 5 cans of vegetables and 5 cans of soup.

PRACTICE

For Exercises 14–18, use the data in the table to find the probability of each event. SEE EXAMPLE 1

Technology Class Enrollment by Year

	Sophomore	Junior
Robotics	16	24
Game Design	18	22

14. P(Junior | Robotics)

15. P(Robotics | Junior)

16. P(Game Design | Sophomore)

17. P(Sophomore | Game Design)

18. Are year and technology class enrollment dependent or independent events? Explain. SEE EXAMPLE 2

19. At a high school, 40% of the students play an instrument. Of those students, 20% are freshmen. Of the students who do not play an instrument, 30% are freshmen. What is the probability that a student selected at random is a freshman who plays an instrument? SEE EXAMPLE 3

In a study of an experimental medication, patients were randomly assigned to take either the medication or a placebo.

Effectiveness of New Medication As Compared to a Placebo

	Medication	Placebo
Health Improved	53	47
Health Did Not Improve	65	35

20. What is the probability that a patient taking the medication showed improvement? Round to the nearest whole percent. SEE EXAMPLE 1

21. Are taking the medication and having improved health independent or dependent events? SEE EXAMPLE 2

22. Based on the data in the table, would you recommend that the medication be made available to doctors? Explain. SEE EXAMPLE 4

APPLY

ASSESSMENT PRACTICE

23. **Reason** In a recreation center with 1,500 members, 200 are high school students. Of the members, 300 regularly swim. The 45 students of the high school swim team are all members and practice at the pool every week. What is the probability that a high school member selected at random is on the swim team? Ⓒ **MP.2**

24. **Use Structure** At the school fair, 5% of students will win a prize. A winner has an equally likely chance to win each prize type shown. What is the probability that a student at the fair will win a comic book? Explain. Ⓒ **MP.7**

PRIZES

25. **Make Sense and Persevere** A box contains 50 batteries, of which 10 are dead and 5 are weak. Suppose you select batteries at random from the box and set them aside for recycling if they are dead or weak. If the first battery you select is dead and the second one is weak, what is the probability that the next battery you select will be weak? Ⓒ **MP.1**

26. **Higher Order Thinking** An inspector at a factory has determined that 1% of the flash drives produced by the plant are defective. If assembly line A produces 20% of all the flash drives, what is the probability that a defective flash drive chosen at random is from the corresponding conveyor belt A? Explain.

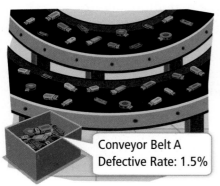

Conveyor Belt A
Defective Rate: 1.5%

27. Which of the following pairs of events are independent? Select all that apply.

Ⓐ A student selected at random has a backpack. A student selected at random has brown hair.

Ⓑ Events A and B, where $P(B \mid A) = \frac{1}{3}$, $P(A) = \frac{3}{5}$ and $P(B) = \frac{5}{9}$

Ⓒ A student selected at random is a junior. A student selected at random is a freshman.

Ⓓ Events A and B, where $P(A) = 0.30$, $P(B) = 0.25$ and $P(A \text{ and } B) = 0.075$

Ⓔ Events A and B, where $P(A) = 0.40$, $P(B) = 0.3$ and $P(A \text{ and } B) = 0.012$

28. **SAT/ACT** The table shows student participation in the newspaper and yearbook by year. A student on the newspaper staff is selected at random to attend a symposium. What is the probability that the selected student is a senior?

Journalism Club Members

	Junior	Senior
Newspaper	16	9
Yearbook	8	17

Ⓐ $\frac{9}{50}$ Ⓓ $\frac{9}{17}$

Ⓑ $\frac{9}{26}$ Ⓔ $\frac{9}{16}$

Ⓒ $\frac{9}{25}$

29. **Performance Task** In a survey of 50 male and 50 female high school students, 60 students said they exercise daily. Of those students, 32 were female.

Part A Use the data to make a two-way frequency table.

Part B What is the probability that a surveyed student who exercises daily is female? What is the probability that a surveyed student who exercises regularly is male?

Part C Based on the survey, what can you conclude about the relationship between exercise and gender? Explain.

MATHEMATICAL MODELING IN **3** ACTS

Ⓒ **Common Core State Standards** HSS.CP.A.1, HSS.CP.A.2, MP.4

Video

▶ Place Your Guess

A coin toss is a popular way to decide between two options or settle a dispute. The coin toss is popular because it is a simple and unbiased way of deciding. Assuming the coin being tossed is a fair coin, both parties have an equally likely chance of winning.

What other methods could you use to decide between two choices fairly? Think about this during the Mathematical Modeling in 3 Acts lesson.

Scan for Multimedia

ACT 1 ▶ Identify the Problem

1. What is the first question that comes to mind after watching the video?

2. Write down the main question you will answer about what you saw in the video.

3. Make an initial conjecture that answers this main question.

4. Explain how you arrived at your conjecture.

5. What information will be useful to know to answer the main question? How can you get it? How will you use that information?

ACT 2 ▶ Develop a Model

6. Use the math that you have learned in this Topic to refine your conjecture.

ACT 3 ▶ Interpret the Results

7. Did your refined conjecture match the actual answer exactly? If not, what might explain the difference?

12-3

Permutations and Combinations

📶 SavvasRealize.com

I CAN... use permutations and combinations to find the number of outcomes in a probability experiment.

VOCABULARY

- combination
- factorial
- Fundamental Counting Principle
- permutation

✋ EXPLORE & REASON

Holly, Tia, Kenji, and Nate are eligible to be officers of the Honor Society. Two of the four students will be chosen at random as president and vice-president. The table summarizes the possible outcomes.

Honor Society Officers

		Vice-President			
		Holly	**Tia**	**Kenji**	**Nate**
President	**Holly**	–	HT	HK	HN
	Tia	TH	–	TK	TN
	Kenji	KH	KT	–	KN
	Nate	NH	NT	NK	–

A. Holly wants to be an officer with her best friend Tia. How many outcomes make up this event?

B. How many outcomes show Holly as president and Tia as vice-president?

C. **Generalize** How many outcomes have only one of them as an officer? Explain. © **MP.8**

❓ ESSENTIAL QUESTION

How are permutations and combinations useful when finding probabilities?

✋ EXAMPLE 1   Use the Fundamental Counting Principle

Manuel wants to advertise the number of one-topping pizzas he offers to his customers. How many different one-topping pizzas are available at Manuel's Pizzeria?

MANUEL'S PIZZERIA
Choose a Size:
large, medium
Choose a Crust:
deep dish or thin
Choose One Topping:
sausage, pepperoni, cheese

Make a tree diagram to find the number of pizzas.

COMMON ERROR

When you compare a tree diagram to the Fundamental Counting Principle, remember to count the total number of paths from the beginning to the end of the tree diagram, not the number of branches in each section.

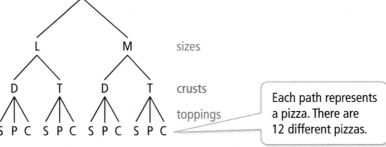

Each path represents a pizza. There are 12 different pizzas.

sizes × crusts × toppings = number of pizzas

2 × 2 × 3 = 12

This example illustrates the **Fundamental Counting Principle**. If there are m ways to make the first selection and n ways to make the second selection, then there are $m \times n$ ways to make the two selections. If a third selection with p choices is added, then there are $m \times n \times p$ to make all three selections, and so on.

CONTINUED ON THE NEXT PAGE

EXAMPLE 1 CONTINUED

  Activity Assess

 Try It! **1.** The car that Ms. Garcia is buying comes with a choice of 3 trim lines (standard, sport, or luxury), 2 types of transmission (automatic or manual), and 8 colors. How many different option packages does Ms. Garcia have to choose from? Explain.

CONCEPTUAL UNDERSTANDING ➞

EXAMPLE 2 **Find the Number of Permutations**

A. Gabriela is making a playlist with her 3 favorite songs. How many possible orders are there for the songs?

Method 1 Use an organized list.

Let A, B, and C represent the 3 songs.
There are 6 different possible orders for the songs.

ABC	ACB
BAC	BCA
CAB	CBA

Method 2 Use the Fundamental Counting Principle.

$3 \cdot 2 \cdot 1$ ⟵ There are 3 choices for the first song, 2 choices for the second song, and 1 choice for the third song.

The **factorial** of a positive integer n is the product of all positive integers less than or equal to n. It is written $n!$ and is read as n *factorial*. By definition, $0!$ equals 1.

$$n! = n \cdot (n - 1) \cdot (n - 2) \cdot \ldots \cdot 2 \cdot 1$$

The number of different possible orders for the songs is $3!$.

$$3! = 3 \cdot 2 \cdot 1 = 6$$

There are 6 different possible orders for the 3 songs.

> **REASON**
> How many ways are there to create a playlist with 0 songs?
> Ⓒ **MP.2**

B. Gabriela wants to make another playlist using 5 of the 8 songs from her favorite artist's latest album. How many playlists are possible?

Method 1 Use the Fundamental Counting Principle.

There are 8 choices for the first song, 7 choices for the second song, and so on.

$$8 \cdot 7 \cdot 6 \cdot 5 \cdot 4 = 6,720$$

There are 6,720 possible playlists with 5 of the 8 songs.

Method 2 Use factorials.

To count the number of ways to order 5 songs from A, B, C, D, E, F, G, and H, consider the list ABCDE. The diagram shows all the possible ways that sequence appears among the 8! ways to list all songs.

For any sequence of 5 songs, there are $(8 - 5)! = 3!$ ways that sequence appears as the first 5 songs when listing all 8! lists. So divide 8! by 3! to find the number of 5-song playlists.

ABCDEFGH	ABCDEFHG
ABCDEGFH	ABCDEGHF
ABCDEHFG	ABCDEHGF

$$\frac{8!}{3!} = \frac{8 \cdot 7 \cdot 6 \cdot 5 \cdot 4 \cdot 3 \cdot 2 \cdot 1}{3 \cdot 2 \cdot 1} = 6,720$$

There are 6,720 possible playlists with 5 of the 8 songs.

CONTINUED ON THE NEXT PAGE

EXAMPLE 2 CONTINUED

 Try It!   **2.** How many possibilities are there for each playlist?

        a. Gabriela's 4 favorite songs   **b.** 5 of the 10 most popular songs

---

CONCEPT Permutations

A **permutation** is an arrangement of objects in a specific order.

The number of permutations of r objects taken from a set of n objects is

$$_nP_r = \frac{n!}{(n-r)!} \text{ for } 0 \le r \le n.$$

CONCEPTUAL UNDERSTANDING →

 **EXAMPLE 3**   **Find the Number of Combinations**

Marisol is planning to be a counselor at summer camp. She can choose 3 activities for her session. How many different combinations of 3 activities are possible?

Use the formula to write an expression for the number of permutations of 3 objects chosen from a group of 10.

$$_{10}P_3 = \frac{10!}{(10-3)!} = 720$$

However, in this situation, the order of the 3 chosen activities does not matter, so you must adjust the formula.

A **combination** is a set of objects with no specific order.

3! Permutations   1 Combination

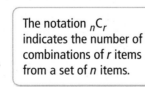

$\{A, B, C\}$

A group of 3 items can be arranged in 3! ways, so you must divide the the number of permutations, $_{10}P_3$, by the number of arrangements of each group of 3 items, 3!.

USE APPROPRIATE TOOLS
Most scientific and graphing calculators can calculate permutations ($_nP_r$) and combinations ($_nC_r$). They often use the notation P(n,r) and C(n,r).
 MP.5

The notation $_nC_r$ indicates the number of combinations of r items from a set of n items.

$$_{10}C_3 = \frac{_{10}P_3}{3!} = \frac{10!}{3!(10-3)!}$$
$$= \frac{720}{6}$$
$$= 120$$

$_{10}C_3$ denotes the number of combinations of 3 items from a set of 10 items.

There are 120 different combinations of activities that Marisol can choose.

 Try It!   **3.** How many ways can a camper choose 5 activities from the 10 available activities at the summer camp?

A **combination** is a set of objects with no specific order.

The number of combinations of r objects taken from a set of n objects is

$$_nC_r = \frac{n!}{r!(n-r)!} \text{ for } 0 \le r \le n.$$

 APPLICATION 👆 **EXAMPLE 4**   **Use Permutations and Combinations to Find Probabilities**

A teacher chooses 5 students at random from the names shown to work together on a group project. What is the probability that the 5 students' names begin with a consonant?

Formulate ◄ Determine if the problem is about permutations or combinations.

Since the order in which the students are chosen does not matter, use combinations to find the numbers of possible outcomes and desirable outcomes to calculate the probability.

Compute ◄ **Step 1** Find the total number of possible outcomes.

$$_{18}C_5 = \frac{18!}{5!(18-5)!} = 8{,}568$$

There are 8,568 ways the teacher could choose 5 students.

Step 2 Find the number of possible outcomes in which all the names begin with a consonant and none of the names begin with a vowel.

$$_{13}C_5 = \frac{13!}{5!(13-5)!} = 1{,}287 \qquad _5C_0 = \frac{5!}{0!(5-0)!} = 1$$

Choose 5 out of 13 names.   Choose 0 out of 5 names.

Use the Fundamental Counting Principle. Multiply the number of possible outcomes for the two subsets to find the total number of outcomes.

$$_{13}C_5 \cdot {}_5C_0 = 1{,}287 \cdot 1 = 1{,}287$$

There are 1,287 outcomes with all the names beginning with consonants.

Step 3 Find the probability.

$$P(\text{all consonants}) = \frac{\text{number of outcomes with all consonants}}{\text{total number of possible outcomes}}$$
$$= \frac{1{,}287}{8{,}568} \approx 0.15$$

Interpret ◄ The probability that all 5 names begin with a consonant is about 0.15, or 15%.

☑ **Try It!**   **4.** Using the data from Example 4, what is the probability that the 5 students' names end with a vowel?

Go Online | SavvasRealize.com

CONCEPT SUMMARY Permutations and Combinations

	Permutation	Combination
WORDS	A selection of items in which the order of the items is important. $_nP_r$ represents the number of permutations of r objects taken from a set of n objects.	A selection of items in which the order of the items is not important. $_nC_r$ represents the number of combinations of r objects taken from a set of n objects.
ALGEBRA	$_nP_r = \dfrac{n!}{(n-r)!}$ for $0 \le r \le n$	$_nC_r = \dfrac{n!}{r!(n-r)!}$ for $0 \le r \le n$
NUMBERS	The number of permutations of 3 objects taken from a set of 6 objects is $$_6P_3 = \frac{6!}{3!} = \frac{6 \cdot 5 \cdot 4 \cdot 3 \cdot 2 \cdot 1}{3 \cdot 2 \cdot 1} = 120$$	The number of combinations of 3 objects taken from a set of 6 objects is $$_6C_3 = \frac{6!}{3!3!} = \frac{6 \cdot 5 \cdot 4 \cdot 3 \cdot 2 \cdot 1}{(3 \cdot 2 \cdot 1)(3 \cdot 2 \cdot 1)} = 20$$

Do You UNDERSTAND?

1. **ESSENTIAL QUESTION** How are permutations and combinations useful when finding probabilities?

2. **Use Structure** How is the formula for combinations related to the formula for permutations? **© MP.7**

3. **Vocabulary** Why is it important to distinguish between a *permutation* and a *combination* when counting possible outcomes?

4. **Look for Relationships** How is $_9C_2$ related to $_9C_7$? Explain. How can you generalize this observation for any values of n and r? **© MP.7**

5. **Error Analysis** Explain Beth's error. **© MP.3**

$$\frac{_3P_3}{_5P_3} = \frac{3!}{\dfrac{5!}{(5-3)!}} = \frac{3!}{5!2!} = \frac{1}{40} \quad \textbf{✗}$$

6. **Construct Arguments** A company wants to form a committee of 4 people from its 12 employees. How can you use combinations to find the probability that the 4 people newest to the company will be selected? **© MP.3**

Do You KNOW HOW?

Do the possible outcomes represent permutations or combinations?

7. Jennifer will invite 3 of her 10 friends to a concert.

8. Jennifer must decide how she and her 3 friends will sit at the concert.

Find the number of permutations.

9. How many ways can 12 runners in a race finish first, second, and third?

Find the number of combinations.

10. In how many ways can 11 contestants for an award be narrowed down to 3 finalists?

11. How many different ways can a 4-person team be chosen from a group of 8 people?

Students will be chosen at random for school spirit awards. There are 6 athletes and 8 non-athletes who are eligible for 2 possible prizes. What is each probability?

12. P(both prizes are awarded to athletes)

13. P(both prizes are awarded to non-athletes)

14. P(no prize is awarded to an athlete)

15. P(no prize is awarded to a non-athlete)

16. Explain how Exercises 12 and 13 are similar to Exercises 14 and 15.

UNDERSTAND

17. Use Structure Dwayne bought a new bike lock, and the lock came with instructions to choose 3 out of 30 numbers on a circular dial to keep his bike secure. The numbers cannot be repeated. How many possible arrangements can Dwayne choose for his lock? Do the arrangements represent permutations or combinations? Explain. © MP.7

18. Construct Arguments Sage volunteers to read and play with sick children in a hospital. She selects some erasers at random from a bag to use as prizes. There are 8 alien erasers and 10 flying saucer erasers. © MP.3

    a. How many groups of 6 erasers can be formed from the 18 erasers? Explain.

    b. In how many ways can 3 aliens be selected? Explain.

    c. In how many ways can 3 aliens and 3 flying saucers be selected? Explain.

    d. What is the probability that 3 aliens and 3 flying saucers will be selected? Explain.

19. Error Analysis There are 6 tiles numbered 1 to 6 in a box. Two tiles are selected at random without replacement to form a 2-digit number. Jeffrey found the probability that the number selected is 16. Explain his error. © MP.3

> The number of ways to select 1 and 6 is given by $_6C_2 = 15$
>
> $$P(16) = \frac{1}{_6C_2} = \frac{1}{15}$$ ✗

20. Mathematical Connections How many lines are determined by the points, *P*, *Q*, *R*, and *S*? Explain.

S•

Q•

P•

R•

21. Higher Order Thinking There are 11! different ways for a group of people to sit around a circular table. How many people are in the group? Explain.

PRACTICE

For Exercises 22–27, state if the possible arrangements represent permutations or combinations, then state the number of possible arrangements. SEE EXAMPLES 1, 2, AND 3

22. A student chooses at random 4 books from a reading list of 11 books.

23. At the end of a season, 10 soccer teams are ranked by the state.

24. A committee of 5 people is being selected from a group of 9 to choose the food for a sport's banquet.

25. Hugo displays his 8 model planes in a single row.

26. A class president, secretary, and treasurer are chosen from 12 students running for office.

27. A food truck has a lunch special on tacos. Customers choose a shell, three toppings, and two sides for one price.

Menu	
Shell:	Hard, Soft, Wheat
Toppings:	Ground Beef, Chicken, Steak, Cheese, Lettuce, Tomato, Sour Cream
Sides:	Fountain Drink, Rice, Beans, Fruit

28. There are 4 comedians and 5 musicians performing in a variety show. The order in which the performers are chosen is random. SEE EXAMPLE 4

    a. What is the probability that the first 3 performers are comedians?

    b. What is the probability that the first two performers are a comedian followed by a musician?

29. A jewelry maker chooses three beads at random from a bag with 10 beads labeled A, B, C, D, E, F, G, H, I, and J. SEE EXAMPLES 2, 3, AND 4

    a. How can you use permutations or combinations to find *P*(selected beads spell the initials DEB)? What is the probability?

    b. How can you use permutations or combinations to find *P*(selected beads are all vowels)? What is the probability?

APPLY

30. Make Sense and Persevere Amaya's wallet contains three $1 bills, two $5 bills, and three $10 bills. If she pulls 2 bills without looking, what is the probability that she draws a $1-bill and a $10-bill? Explain. **MP.1**

31. Model with Mathematics Raul's favorite restaurant is running a prize game. Five of each of the winning tickets shown are available, and a customer must collect three winning tickets to receive the prize. What is the probability Raul will receive the prize for the baseball cap with his first 3 tickets? **MP.4**

32. Look for Relationships Smart Phones, Inc. chooses a 5-digit security code at random from the digits 0–9. **MP.7**

a. Suppose the digits cannot be repeated. What is the probability that the security code is 30429? Explain.

b. Suppose the digits can be repeated. What is the probability that the security code is 30429? Explain.

33. Make Sense and Persevere Edwin randomly plays 6 different songs from his playlist. **MP.1**

a. What is the probability that Edwin hears his 6 favorite songs?

b. What is the probability that he hears the songs in order from his most favorite to his sixth most favorite?

34. Consider an arrangement of 8 items taken 3 at a time in which order is not important. Does each expression give the correct number of arrangements? Select *Yes* or *No*.

	Yes	No
$_8P_3$	❑	❑
$_8C_3$	❑	❑
$\dfrac{_8P_3}{3!}$	❑	❑
$8! \cdot 3!$	❑	❑
$\dfrac{8!}{3!}$	❑	❑
$\dfrac{8!}{5!}$	❑	❑
$\dfrac{8!}{3!5!}$	❑	❑
$8 \cdot 7$	❑	❑

35. SAT/ACT Fifteen students enter a Safety Week poster contest in which prizes will be awarded for first through fourth place. In how many ways could the prizes be given out?

Ⓐ 4

Ⓑ 60

Ⓒ 1,365

Ⓓ 32,760

Ⓔ 50,625

36. Performance Task Use the word shown on the tiles below to find each probability.

Part A Two tiles are chosen at random without replacement. Use conditional probability to find the probability that both letters are vowels. Then find the probability using permutations or combinations. Explain.

Part B Four of the tiles are chosen at random and placed in the order in which they are drawn. Use conditional probability to find the probability the tiles spell the word SURF. Then find the probability using permutations or combinations. Explain.

12-4
Probability Distributions

 SavvasRealize.com

I CAN... define probability distributions to represent experiments and solve problems.

VOCABULARY
- binomial experiment
- probability distribution
- uniform probability distribution

👆 **MODEL & DISCUSS**

Mr. and Mrs. Mason have three children. Assume that the probability of having a baby girl is 0.5 and the probability of having a baby boy is also 0.5.

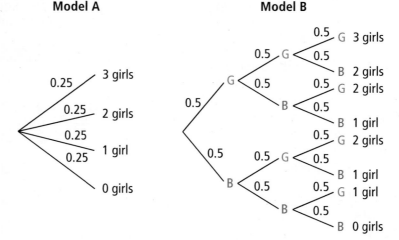

Model A   Model B

A. Reason Which model represents the situation correctly, Model A or Model B? Explain. © **MP.2**

B. What is the probability that Mr. and Mrs. Mason have 3 girls?

C. Compare the probability that the Masons' first child was a boy and they then had two girls to the probability that their first two children were girls and they then had a boy. Does the order affect the probabilities? Explain.

❓ **ESSENTIAL QUESTION**   What does a probability distribution tell you about an experiment?

CONCEPTUAL UNDERSTANDING

👆 **EXAMPLE 1**   **Develop a Theoretical Probability Distribution**

A. Teo and Henry are running for President of the Student Council. You will select a campaign button at random from the box containing 3 Teo buttons and 3 Henry buttons. You will record the number of Teo buttons that you get. What is the theoretical probability distribution for the sample space {0, 1}?

COMMUNICATE PRECISELY
The sample space {0, 1} represents how many Teo buttons you can select in one trial. © **MP.6**

A **probability distribution** for an experiment is a function that assigns a probability to each outcome of a sample space for the experiment.

Since you are selecting a button at random, you are equally likely to get 0 buttons or 1 button for Teo.

The theoretical probability distribution for this experiment is the function P, defined on the set {0, 1}, such that $P(0) = \frac{1}{2}$ and $P(1) = \frac{1}{2}$.

> A theoretical probability is based upon assumptions rather than on experimentation.

CONTINUED ON THE NEXT PAGE

EXAMPLE 1 CONTINUED

B. **Now you plan to select a button at random, put it back in the box, and then select another button at random. You will record the total number of times that you get a Teo button in the experiment. Define the theoretical probability distribution for the sample space {0, 1, 2}. How does this probability distribution differ from the distribution in Part A?**

Make a tree diagram for the experiment.

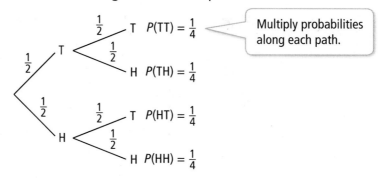

Multiply probabilities along each path.

Add the probabilities of TH and HT to find the probability of getting one Teo button.

$$P(1) = \frac{1}{4} + \frac{1}{4} = \frac{1}{2}$$

The theoretical probability distribution is the function P, defined on the set {0, 1, 2}, such that $P(0) = \frac{1}{4}$, $P(1) = \frac{1}{2}$, and $P(2) = \frac{1}{4}$.

Compare this probability distribution to the one in Part A.

A **uniform probability distribution** assigns the same probability to each outcome.

Comparing Probability Distributions		
Select one button	$P(0) = \frac{1}{2}$, $P(1) = \frac{1}{2}$.	uniform
Select two buttons	$P(0) = \frac{1}{4}$, $P(1) = \frac{1}{2}$, $P(2) = \frac{1}{4}$	not uniform

The probability distribution in Part A is a uniform probability distribution. The probability distribution in this part is not.

> **STUDY TIP**
> One way to check your work is to check that the sum of the probabilities of all the outcomes is 1.

 Try It! **1.** You select two marbles at random from the bowl. For each situation, define the theoretical probability distribution for selecting a number of red marbles on the sample space {0, 1, 2}. Is it a uniform probability distribution?

a. You select one marble and put it back in the bowl. Then you select a second marble.

b. You select one marble and do not put it back in the bowl. Then you select a second marble.

APPLICATION   **EXAMPLE 2**   Develop an Experimental Probability Distribution

A cell phone company surveyed 500 households about the number of smartphones they have that are in use.

Number of Smartphones per Household							
Number	0	1	2	3	4	5	6 or more
Frequency	10	66	120	144	79	37	44

Would you recommend that the company concentrate on selling data plans for individuals or plans for families with three or more smartphones? Explain.

Step 1   Define an experimental probability distribution on the sample space {0, 1, 2, 3, 4, 5, 6 or more}.

First divide each frequency by 500 to find each relative frequency. For convenience, round each relative frequency to the nearest whole percent.

Number of Smartphones per Household							
Number	0	1	2	3	4	5	6 or more
Frequency	10	66	120	144	79	37	44
Relative Frequency	2%	13%	24%	29%	16%	7%	9%

Each relative frequency represents the experimental probability that a household selected at random from the 500 households has a given number of smartphones.

> An experimental probability is based upon collecting real-world data and finding relative frequencies.

An experimental probability distribution for the experiment is the function *P* such that if *n* is an outcome of the sample space, then *P*(*n*) is the probability of that outcome. For example, *P*(0) = 2%.

Step 2   Graph the probability distribution.

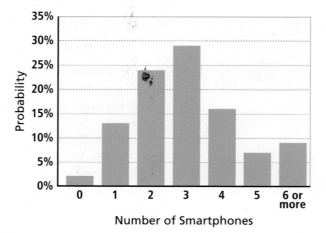

COMMON ERROR
When graphing a probability distribution, the heights of the bars represent the probabilities of each outcome, not their frequencies.

Step 3   Interpret the results.

The probability that a household has 3 or more cell phones is 61%.

Therefore, the company should probably focus on family plans rather than individual plans.

CONTINUED ON THE NEXT PAGE

EXAMPLE 2 CONTINUED

  Activity Assess

 Try It! 2. Suppose that you selected a student at random from the Drama Club and recorded the student's age.

Ages of Students in Drama Club					
Age	14	15	16	17	18
Students	4	7	10	7	9

a. Define an experimental probability distribution on the sample space {14, 15, 16, 17, 18}.

b. Graph the probability distribution you defined.

CONCEPT Binomial Experiments

A **binomial experiment** is an experiment that consists of a fixed number of trials, with the following features.

- Each trial has two possible outcomes, one of which is denoted as "success."
- The results of the trials are independent events.
- The probability of "success" is the same for every trial.

EXAMPLE 3 Binomial Experiments

Is the experiment a binomial experiment?

A. **This spinner is spun 3 times. Assume that the spinner is equally likely to stop in any of the sections. Success is landing on a section marked "Go Forward 2 Spaces."**

Compare the experiment to the requirements for a binomial experiment.

- There are two possible outcomes for each trial, landing on a section labeled "Go Forward 2 Spaces" (success) and not landing on one of those sections.
- The outcome of one spin does not affect the probability of success on any other spin.
- The probability of success is 0.25 for every trial.

The experiment is a binomial experiment.

B. **In a class of 23 students, 7 students completed the term project. Two students selected at random have to give presentations. Success is that the student has completed the project.**

The probability that the first student has completed the project is $\frac{7}{23}$.

If the first student completed the project, the probability that the second student did is $\frac{6}{22}$. If the first student is not, the probability is $\frac{7}{22}$.

Because the probabilities for each trial are different, the experiment is not a binomial experiment.

GENERALIZE
Would the experiment be a binomial experiment if there were 25 students in the class? Some other number? **MP.8**

CONTINUED ON THE NEXT PAGE

 Try It! **3.** Is the experiment a binomial experiment? If so, find the probability of success. Explain.

    a. You select one card at random from a set of 7 cards, 4 labeled A and 3 labeled B. Then you select another card at random from the cards that remain. For each selection, success is that the card is labeled A.

    b. You roll a standard number cube 4 times. Assume that each time you roll the number cube, each number is equally likely to come up. For each roll, success is getting an even number.

CONCEPT Binomial Probability Formula

For a binomial experiment consisting of n trials with the probability of success p for each trial, the probability of exactly r successes out of the n trials is given by the following formula:

    $P(r) = $ (ways to get r successes in n trials) $\cdot$ $P(r$ successes$)$ $\cdot$ $P(n–r$ failures$)$

    $P(r) = \ _nC_r \cdot p^r(1 - p)^{n-r}$

EXAMPLE 4   **Probabilities in a Binomial Experiment**

A grocery store gives away scratch-off cards with a purchase of more than $100.

Terrell has 5 scratch-off cards. What is the probability that he has exactly 3 winning cards if each card has a 30% chance of being a winner?

Step 1 Determine whether the situation is a binomial experiment.

    • Terrell's 5 cards represent 5 trials.

    • Each card is either a winning card (success) or not.

    • Whether one card is a winning card does not affect the probability that another card is a winning card.

    • The probability of success, 0.3, is the same for every trial.

So this is a binomial experiment.

REASON
In the formula for binomial probability, what probability does the term $1 - p$ represent?
© MP.2

Step 2 Find the probability of 3 successes.

The formula $P(r) = \ _nC_r \cdot p^r(1 - p)^{n-r}$ gives the probability of r successes out of n trials. Use $n = 5$, $r = 3$, and $p = 0.3$.

$$_5C_3 = \frac{5!}{3!(5 - 3)!}$$
$$= \frac{5 \cdot 4}{2 \cdot 1}$$
$$= 10$$

$$P(3) = \ _5C_3 \cdot (0.3)^3(1 - 0.3)^{5-3}$$
$$= 10(0.3)^3(0.7)^2$$
$$= 10(0.027)(0.49)$$
$$= 0.1323$$

The probability of having exactly 3 winning cards is about 13%.

 Try It! **4.** To the nearest tenth of a percent, what is the probability that Terrell has more than 3 winning cards? Explain.

A probability distribution for an experiment is a function that assigns a probability to each outcome of a sample space for the experiment.

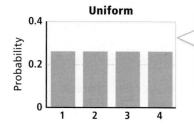

Uniform

A uniform probability distribution assigns the same probability to each outcome.

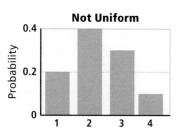

Not Uniform

A binomial experiment is an experiment that consists of a fixed number of trials, in which:

- each trial has two possible outcomes, one of which is denoted as "success";

- the results of the trials are independent events; and

- the probability of "success" is the same for every trial.

If the probability of success is p for each trial, then the probability of exactly r successes out of n trials is $P(r) = {}_nC_r \cdot p^r(1 - p)^{n-r}$.

 ## Do You UNDERSTAND?

1. **ESSENTIAL QUESTION** What does a probability distribution tell you about an experiment?

2. **Vocabulary** What are the characteristics of a *binomial experiment*?

3. **Error Analysis** A regular tetrahedron has four triangular sides, with one of the letters A, B, C, and D on each side. Assume that if you roll the tetrahedron, each of the letters is equally likely to end up on the bottom. {A, B, C, D} is a sample space for the experiment. Rochelle was asked to find the theoretical probability distribution for the experiment. Explain and correct the error. © MP.3

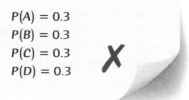

$P(A) = 0.3$
$P(B) = 0.3$
$P(C) = 0.3$
$P(D) = 0.3$ ✗

Do You KNOW HOW?

Graph the probability distribution P.

4. Theoretical probabilities from selecting a student at random from a group of 3 students, Jack, Alani, and Seth

5. Probabilities from flipping a fair coin 3 times and counting the number of heads. The sample space is the set of numbers 0, 1, 2, 3. $P(0) = 0.125$, $P(1) = 0.375$, $P(2) = 0.375$, $P(3) = 0.125$

A bag contains 5 balls: 3 green, 1 red, and 1 yellow. You select a ball at random 4 times, replacing the ball after each selection. Calculate the theoretical probability of each event to the nearest whole percent.

6. getting a green ball exactly 3 times

7. getting a green ball exactly 4 times

8. getting a green ball at least 3 times

9. getting a yellow ball twice

10. getting only red and green balls

Scan for Multimedia

Practice Tutorial

Additional Exercises Available Online

UNDERSTAND

11. Communicate Precisely Explain what it means for a coin to be a fair coin. ⓒ MP.6

12. Reason You spin the spinner shown.

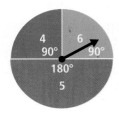

Describe a theoretical probability distribution for the experiment. ⓒ MP.2

13. Communicate Precisely Five students in a class of 27 students ate hamburgers for lunch. Suppose the teacher selects a student in the class at random and then selects another student at random. Success for each selection is selecting a student who ate a hamburger. Is this a binomial experiment? Explain. ⓒ MP.6

14. Error Analysis A standard number cube is rolled 7 times. Success for each roll is defined as getting a number less than 3. Abby tried to calculate the probability of 5 successes. Describe and correct her error. ⓒ MP.3

$$P(5) = \left(\tfrac{1}{3}\right)^5 \left(\tfrac{2}{3}\right)^2 \approx 0.002 \quad ✗$$

15. Mathematical Connections A marble is selected from the bowl shown 4 times. The marble is returned to the bowl after each selection.

a. Show that there are exactly $_4C_2$ ways to get exactly 2 green marbles.

b. How are $_5C_3$ and $_5C_2$ related? Explain.

PRACTICE

A card is chosen at random from the box containing 10 cards: 3 yellow, 4 red, 2 green, and 1 blue. SEE EXAMPLES 1 AND 2

16. Define a probability distribution for this experiment on the sample space {Y, R, G, B}.

17. Graph the probability distribution.

In a certain game, the player can score 0, 1, 2, 3, or 4 points during their turn. The table shows the number of times Kennedy scored each number of points the last time she played the game. SEE EXAMPLE 2

Score	0	1	2	3	4
Frequency	3	7	9	6	5

18. Define an experimental probability distribution based on Kennedy's scores.

19. Graph the probability distribution you defined in Exercise 18.

Is the experiment a binomial experiment? Explain. SEE EXAMPLE 3

20. A quality control specialist tests 50 LED light bulbs produced in a factory. Success is that a tested light bulb burns for at least 2,000 hours without dimming. For each light bulb, the probability of success is 0.9.

21. There are 10 black and 10 red cards face down on the table. One card is selected at random. Then another card is selected at random. Success is getting a red card.

22. A basketball player is shooting 2 free throws. The probability of her making the first free throw is 0.86. The probability of her making the second free throw is 0.92.

Each time Bailey is at bat, the probability that he gets a hit is 0.250. If he bats 10 times in the course of two games, what is the probability of each result? Round to the nearest tenth of a percent. SEE EXAMPLE 4

23. He gets no hits.

24. He gets exactly 1 hit.

25. He gets exactly 2 hits.

26. He gets fewer than 3 hits.

Go Online | SavvasRealize.com

APPLY

27. Model with Mathematics The circle graph shows the result of a survey of the most popular types of music in the U.S., based on sales, downloads, and streaming. Ⓒ MP.4

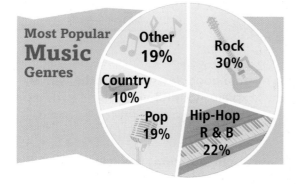

Most Popular **Music** Genres

Other 19%
Rock 30%
Country 10%
Pop 19%
Hip-Hop R & B 22%

a. Define a probability distribution for the sample space.

b. Graph the probability distribution.

c. According to the survey, which is the most popular type of music in the United States?

28. Higher Order Thinking A pharmaceutical company is testing a new version of a medication. In a clinical trial of the old version of the medication, 18% of the subjects taking the old medication experienced headaches.

a. Suppose that 18% of the people taking the new medications will experience headaches. If 8 subjects are selected at random and given the new medication, what is the probability that less than two of them will experience headaches?

b. Suppose that two of the eight subjects experience headaches after taking the new medication. Is that cause for concern? Explain your reasoning.

29. Communicate Precisely In a quiz show, a contestant is asked 6 questions. Each question has 5 answer choices. Assume that the contestant picks an answer at random for each question and the probability of guessing the correct answer is 20%. What is the probability of guessing correctly on at least 4 of the questions? Round your answer to the nearest tenth of a percent. Ⓒ MP.6

ASSESSMENT PRACTICE

30. You are going to roll a game piece two times. The game piece has 10 sides of equal area, each with one of the numbers 0 through 9. Assume that it is equally likely to land with any of the sides on top. Success is defined as getting a 3 on top.

Let P be the function defined on {0, 1, 2} such that $P(n)$ is the probability of n successes. Select all that apply.

Ⓐ This is a binomial experiment.

Ⓑ P is a probability distribution for the sample space {0, 1, 2}.

Ⓒ $P(0) = 0.81$

Ⓓ $P(1) = 0.09$

Ⓔ $P(2) = 0.01$

31. SAT/ACT A standard number cube is rolled 6 times. Success is defined as getting a number greater than 4. Rounded to the nearest percent, what is the probability of exactly 2 successes?

Ⓐ 2%   Ⓑ 8%   Ⓒ 23%   Ⓓ 33%   Ⓔ 50%

32. Performance Task Get 5 index cards. Draw a picture on one side and no picture on the other side of each card.

Part A You are going to throw all 5 cards up in the air and count the number of cards that land face up. Assume that it is equally likely that each card will land face up and face down. Define a theoretical probability distribution for the sample space {0, 1, 2, 3, 4, 5}.

Part B Perform the experiment 20 times. Each time you perform the experiment, record the number of cards that land face up. Find the experimental probability for each outcome in the sample space {0, 1, 2, 3, 4, 5} and define an experimental probability distribution the sample space.

Part C Compare the results of Part A and B. If they are different, explain why you think they are different.

SavvasRealize.com

I CAN... calculate, interpret, and apply expected value.

VOCABULARY
- binomial distribution
- expected value

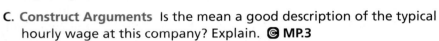
👆 **EXPLORE & REASON**

A company has 20 employees whose hourly wages are shown in the bar graph.

A. An employee is chosen at random. What is the probability that his or her hourly wage is $12? $25? $50?

B. What is the mean hourly wage? Explain your method.

C. **Construct Arguments** Is the mean a good description of the typical hourly wage at this company? Explain. © **MP.3**

Employee Hourly Wages

? **ESSENTIAL QUESTION**   What does expected value tell you about situations involving probability?

CONCEPTUAL UNDERSTANDING

👆 **EXAMPLE 1**   Evaluate and Apply Expected Value

The table shows data on sales in one month for each item on a restaurant menu. To estimate future profits, the owner evaluates the average profit from each meal.

A. Based on the data, what is the average profit that the owner can expect to make from each meal?

Meal	Profit per Serving	Percent Sold
Stew	$0.34	12%
Soup	$0.41	7%
Lasagna	$0.64	45%
Chili	$0.73	36%

Expected value is the sum of the value of each outcome multiplied by the probability of the outcome.

$$E = x_1P(x_1) + x_2P(x_2) + x_3P(x_3) + \ldots + x_nP(x_n)$$

The outcomes are the profits for each meal. The probability for each meal is the percent sold. Multiply each outcome by its probability. Then add.

$$E = 0.34(0.12) + 0.41(0.07) + 0.64(0.45) + 0.73(0.36) = 0.6203$$

> Use the expected value formula when the probability of at least one outcome differs from any of the others.

If this expected value continues, the owner can expect to earn about $0.62 per meal.

COMMON ERROR
Note that average profit from each meal is not simply the average of the cost of 1 serving of each of the 4 meals because the number of each kind of meal varies.

B. What is the expected profit for the next 200 meals ordered?

$$\$0.6203 \times 200 = \$124.06$$

The owner can expect to net about $124.06 for the next 200 meals.

CONTINUED ON THE NEXT PAGE

EXAMPLE 1 CONTINUED

 Try It! 1. a. What would happen to the expected value if fewer people ordered chili and more people ordered stew? Explain.

        b. Suppose the restaurant's profit on an order of stew increased by $0.05 and the profit on an order of chili decreased by $0.05. How would these changes affect the expected profit per meal?

EXAMPLE 2 **Find Expected Payoffs**

A charity is considering a fundraising event in which donors will pay $1 to spin the wheel 3 times. What is the expected payoff for the charity for each game?

EVEN THREES

Spin 3 times
Get 3 even numbers
Win an item worth $4

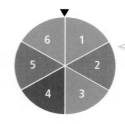

There are 6 possible outcomes. 3 of the possible outcomes are even numbers.

MAKE SENSE AND PERSEVERE
Think about methods used to find probabilities. What do you need to identify to find the probabilities for each situation? © **MP.1**

Step 1 Find the probabilities for the donor.

There are 6^3, or 216 outcomes for spinning the wheel 3 times.

There are 3^3, or 27, ways to spin 3 even numbers in a row, so the probability of a donor winning a $4 prize is $\frac{27}{216}$, or $\frac{1}{8}$.

So, the probability of a donor not winning is $1 - \frac{1}{8}$, or $\frac{7}{8}$.

Step 2 Find probabilities for the charity.

The probability that the charity gains $1 is $P(1) = \frac{7}{8}$.

The probability that the charity loses $3 is $P(-3) = \frac{1}{8}$.

Step 3 Find the expected value of each game for the charity.

$$E(x) = 1\left(\frac{7}{8}\right) + (-3)\left(\frac{1}{8}\right)$$

$$= \frac{4}{8}$$

$$= \frac{1}{2}$$

The charity can expect to earn $0.50 each game.

 Try It! 2. What is the expected payoff for the person making the donation?

APPLICATION

EXAMPLE 3 | **Use Expected Values to Evaluate Strategies**

You are considering options for an auto insurance policy. The insurance company offers new car replacement insurance, in the case your car is totaled. There is a 1% annual chance of the car being totaled.

Plan	Premium ($)	Deductible ($)
A	50	500
B	60	0

> The deductible is the portion of the cost that the car owner pays.

A. Which of the two plans has the lower expected cost?

The total expected cost is the sum of the known costs and the expected value of the unknown cost. The cost of a new car is higher than the deductible, so you would pay the full deductible if the car needs to be replaced.

	Known cost		Expected value of unknown cost		
	Premium	+	Deductible • Probability of replacement	=	Expected cost of insurance
Plan A:	$50	+	$500 • 0.01	=	$55
Plan B:	$60	+	$0 • 0.01	=	$60

Plan A has the lower expected cost.

B. How can you decide whether or not to purchase replacement insurance?

The cost of a new car is very high, so purchasing replacement insurance can be a good idea. Solve an inequality to determine when having no insurance is more costly than having insurance.

	Known cost		Expected value of unknown cost		
	Premium	+	Cost of a new car • Probability of replacement	>	Expected cost of insurance
	$0	+	x • 0.01	>	$55
			$0.01x$	>	$55
			x	>	$5,500

> With or without insurance, you have the same chance of needing a new car.

You should buy replacement insurance if the cost of a new car is greater than $5,500.

Try It! 3. The insurance company also offers safety glass coverage. There is a 50% chance of no repairs ($0), a 30% chance of minor repairs ($50), and 20% chance of full replacement ($300). Which plan for optional safety glass coverage has the lower expected cost?

Plan	Premium ($)	Deductible ($)
C	50	200
D	100	0

EXAMPLE 4   Use Binomial Probability to Find Expected Value

According to the weather app on Talisha's smartphone, there is a 40% chance of rain for each of the 5 days of her vacation. How many rainy days should Talisha expect during her vacation?

Days of Rain	Probability
0	$_5C_0(0.4)^0(0.6)^5 \approx 0.0776$
1	$_5C_1(0.4)^1(0.6)^4 = 0.2592$
2	$_5C_2(0.4)^2(0.6)^3 = 0.3456$
3	$_5C_3(0.4)^3(0.6)^2 = 0.2304$
4	$_5C_4(0.4)^4(0.6)^1 = 0.0768$
5	$_5C_5(0.4)^5(0.6)^0 \approx 0.0102$

Apply the binomial probability formula with $n = 5$, $p = 0.4$, and $1 - p = 0.6$ to find the probability of rain for each number of days of Talisha's vacation.

To find the expected number of rainy days, multiply each probability by the number of rainy days it corresponds to, and add those values together.

Expected number of rainy days

$= 0 \cdot P(0) + 1 \cdot P(1) + 2 \cdot P(2) + 3 \cdot P(3) + 4 \cdot P(4) + 5 \cdot P(5)$

$= 0(0.0776) + 1(0.2592) + 2(0.3456) + 3(0.2304) + 4(0.0768) + 5(0.0102) \approx 2$

Talisha should expect 2 rainy days during her vacation.

The table shows the probability of every outcome of a binomial experiment. This probability distribution is called a **binomial distribution**. A special relationship exists for the expected value for any binomial distribution.

$$E = np$$
$$2 = 5(0.4)$$

E expected value n trials p probability

Try It! 4. A carnival game has 4 orange lights and 1 green light that flash rapidly one at a time in a random order. When a player pushes a button, the game stops, leaving one light on. If the light is green, the player wins a prize. Copy and complete the table, then determine the number of prizes that a player can expect to win if the game is played 4 times.

Number of Green Lights	Probability
0	$_4C_0(0.2)^0(0.8)^4 = \blacksquare$
1	$_4C_\blacksquare(0.2)^\blacksquare(0.8)^\blacksquare = \blacksquare$
2	$_\blacksquare C_\blacksquare(0.2)^\blacksquare(0.8)^\blacksquare = \blacksquare$
3	$_\blacksquare C_\blacksquare(0.2)^\blacksquare(0.8)^\blacksquare = \blacksquare$
4	$_\blacksquare C_\blacksquare(0.2)^\blacksquare(0.8)^\blacksquare = \blacksquare$

🔍 CONCEPT SUMMARY Expected Value

WORDS

Expected value is the average outcome that will occur with many trials of an experiment. It is the sum of the value of each outcome times the probability of the outcome.

ALGEBRA

Let $x_1, x_2, x_3, \ldots x_n$ represent the values of the outcomes of a set of trials.

You can find the expected value, E, with this formula.

$$E = x_1 P(x_1) + x_2 P(x_2) + \ldots + x_n P(x_n)$$

☑ Do You UNDERSTAND?

1. ❓ **ESSENTIAL QUESTION** What does expected value tell you about situations involving probability?

2. **Error Analysis** Benjamin is finding the expected value of the number of heads when tossing a fair coin 10 times. What is Benjamin's error? © **MP.3**

> Toss a coin 10 times
> $E = 50\%$
> ✗

3. **Construct Arguments** A carnival game costs $1 to play. The expected payout for each play of this game is $1.12. Should the carnival operators modify the game in any way? Explain. © **MP.3**

4. **Reason** The students in Ms. Kahn's class are raising money to help earthquake victims. They expect to raise $0.52 for each raffle ticket they sell. If each raffle ticket is sold for $2, what can you conclude? © **MP.2**

5. **Reason** A spinner is divided into 6 equal-sized sectors, numbered 1, 1, 1, 4, 7, and 10. Is the expected value of a spin the same as the mean of the numbers? Explain.

Do You KNOW HOW?

6. What is the expected value when rolling a standard number cube?

7. What is the expected value of the sum when rolling two standard number cubes?

8. A travel website reports that in a particular European city, the probability of rain on any day in April is 40%. What is the expected number of rainy days in this city during the month of April?

9. You buy an airplane ticket for $900. You discover that if you cancel or rebook your vacation flight to Europe, you will be charged an extra $300. There is a 20% chance that you will have to rebook your flight.

   a. What is the expected value of the cost of the ticket?

   b. Is the expected value the amount you will pay to book the ticket whether or not you have to rebook? Explain.

10. A child-care service charges families an hourly rate based upon the age of the child. Their hourly rate per child is $20 per hour for infants less than 1 year old, $18 for toddlers 1 to 3 years old, $15 per hour children 3 or more years old. The ratios of infants : toddlers : 3+ years is 2 : 3 : 5. What is the expected charge per child per hour?

UNDERSTAND

11. Error Analysis For the dartboard shown, Deshawn calculated the expected number of points per dart. Explain Deshawn's error. What is the correct expected value? ⓒ **MP.3**

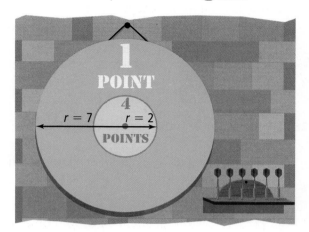

$$\text{Expected value} = \frac{2}{7}(4) + \frac{5}{7}(1)$$
$$= \frac{8}{7} + \frac{5}{7}$$
$$= \frac{13}{7} \approx 1.86 \quad ✗$$

12. Reason A nonrefundable plane ticket costs $600, while a refundable ticket costs $900. A traveler estimates there is a 20% chance he will have to cancel his upcoming trip. Should the traveler purchase a refundable or nonrefundable ticket? Explain. ⓒ **MP.2**

13. Construct Arguments A consumer determines that her expected cost for Option B is $528 per year. ⓒ **MP.3**

Option	Annual Premium	Deductible
A	$600	$0
B	$500	$1,000

a. Why might this consumer select the policy with the $1000 deductible?

b. Why might this consumer select the policy with no deductible?

14. Mathematical Connections How is expected value related to the mean?

PRACTICE

A farmer estimates her hens will produce 3,000 dozen more eggs this year than last year. She estimates the probability of her net profit or loss on each dozen eggs based on her costs. SEE EXAMPLE 1

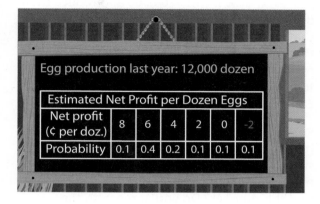

Egg production last year: 12,000 dozen

Estimated Net Profit per Dozen Eggs						
Net profit (¢ per doz.)	8	6	4	2	0	-2
Probability	0.1	0.4	0.2	0.1	0.1	0.1

15. What is her expected profit per dozen eggs?

16. What is her expected profit on the total egg production?

17. An electronics store offers students a discount of 10% on purchases of computers. They estimate that $\frac{1}{16}$ of computer sales are to students. The average sale per customer is $498 and the store's profit is $80 before the discount. What is the expected profit on the sale of a computer? SEE EXAMPLE 2

18. An insurance company offers three policy options. The probability a car will be damaged in a given year is 5%, and if a car is damaged, the cost of the repairs will be $1000. Which option has the least expected annual cost for the car owner? Explain. SEE EXAMPLE 3

Insurance Policy Options

Option	Annual Premium ($)	Deductible ($)
A	900	0
B	800	400
C	700	1000

On a tropical island, the probability of sunny weather is 90% each day. SEE EXAMPLE 4

19. What is the expected number of sunny days in a non-leap year?

20. What is the expected number of sunny days during the month of June?

APPLY

21. **Model With Mathematics** A solar panel company has found that about 1% of its panels are defective. The company's cost to replace each defective panel is $600. A consultant recommends changes to the manufacturing process that will cost $200,000 and reduce the defective rate to 0.2%. The company estimates that it will sell 30,000 panels next year and that sales will increase by 5,000 panels per year for the next 10 years. Should the company follow the consultant's recommendation? Explain. ⓒ **MP.4**

22. **Reason** A student tosses a coin 4 times and the results are heads, tails, heads, and heads. The student concludes that the expected number of heads for 100 tosses is 75. How did the student find this number? Do you agree with the student's reasoning? Explain. ⓒ **MP.2**

23. **Higher Order Thinking** Your family is going to buy a new TV set for $599. You find out that the probability that the TV set will need to be serviced in the second year is 0.05 and the probability that the TV set will need to be serviced in the third year is 0.08. A 2-year warranty costs $55, and a 3-year warranty costs $80. The average cost of repairing the TV set is $278. What would you advise your family to do, get a 2-year extended warranty, a 3-year extended warranty or not to get any extended warranty? Explain your reasoning.

24. **Make Sense and Persevere** A company makes tablets that are guaranteed for one year. On average, one out of every 200 tablets needs to be repaired or replaced within the first year. If a tablet needs to be repaired, the company loses an average of $140. If the company sells 2,600,000 of the tablets in a year, what is their net profit on the sale of the tablets in that year? ⓒ **MP.1**

If no repairs or replacement is needed for a tablet, the company makes a $24 profit on that tablet.

ASSESSMENT PRACTICE

25. A commuter recorded data on the arrival time of his morning train each weekday for 5 weeks. According to the data, he should expect the train to be 1.16 minutes late on any given day. What are the missing values in the commuter's table?

Arrival Time for Train

Minutes late	0	1	2	3	4	5
Number of days	■	5	1	■	1	3

26. **SAT/ACT** What is the expected total for 20 spins?

Ⓐ 100
Ⓑ 105
Ⓒ 110
Ⓓ 115
Ⓔ 120

27. **Performance Task** A toy company is designing a children's game in which players toss chips onto a board. The square board will contain a smaller square at its center.

20 points

Part A Write design instructions for the board so that a chip tossed randomly onto the board is 8 times more likely to land in the outer region than in the inner square. Explain your reasoning.

Part B Assign a whole number of points to the outer region so that the expected score on a single toss is as close as possible to 5. Explain your reasoning.

Part C If the area of the inner square is doubled and the overall size of the board remains the same, how does the expected score change? Is it also doubled? Explain.

12-6

Probability and Decision Making

SavvasRealize.com

I CAN... use probability to make decisions.

CRITIQUE & EXPLAIN

Your friend offers to play the following game with you "If the product of the roll of two number cubes is 10 or less, I win. If not, you win!"

A. If you were to play the game many times, what percent of the games would you expect to win?

B. Is the game fair? Should you take the offer? Explain.

C. **Make Sense and Persevere** Suggest a way to change the game from fair to unfair, or vice versa, while still using the product of the two number cubes. Explain. **© MP.1**

ESSENTIAL QUESTION

How can you use probability to make decisions?

APPLICATION

EXAMPLE 1 Use Probability to Make Fair Decisions

Sadie, Tamira, River, Victor, and Jae are candidates to represent their school at an event. How can you use random integers to select 2 students from the 5 candidates, so that each one is equally likely to be selected?

There are 5 students. Assign a number to each student.

1	2	3	4	5
Sadie	Tamira	River	Victor	Jae

To select a student, use a calculator or other random number generator to generate a random integer from 1 to 5. Repeat to select the second student.

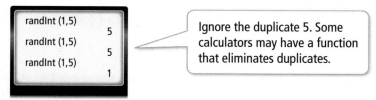

Ignore the duplicate 5. Some calculators may have a function that eliminates duplicates.

Jae (5) and Sadie (1) are selected.

MAKE SENSE AND PERSEVERE
Consider how you would assign integers from 1 to 10 among the 5 students. How do you adjust this for a random number generator that gives a number *r* from the interval $0 \leq r < 1$? **© MP.1**

 Try It! 1. Your trainer creates training programs for you. How can you use index cards to randomly choose the following: Strength training 1 day per week; Cardio training 2 days per week, with no consecutive days; Swimming 1 day per week.

CONCEPTUAL UNDERSTANDING

👍 **EXAMPLE 2** Determine Whether a Decision Is Fair or Unfair

Thato places three cards in a hat and challenges Helena to a game.

A. Thato says, "If you draw a number greater than 2, you earn 2 points. Otherwise, I earn 2 points." Is the game fair, or unfair? If it is unfair, which player has the advantage? Explain.

In each round, Thato either wins 2 points or loses 2 points.

> If Helena draws a "3" and gets 2 points, Thato considers this a loss of 2 points for himself.

COMMON ERROR
Recall that the expected value is the sum of the products of the outcomes' values by their respective probabilities. Be careful not to use the sum of the probabilities.

Find the probability of each outcome. Then find the expected value.

$$P(-2) = \frac{1}{3} \text{ and } P(+2) = \frac{2}{3}.$$

$$E = -2 \cdot \left(\frac{1}{3}\right) + 2 \cdot \left(\frac{2}{3}\right)$$

$$= \frac{2}{3}$$

> A game is considered "fair" if and only if the expected value is 0.

The game is unfair and is skewed to Thato's advantage. The probability of his scoring 2 points is twice the probability of Helena scoring 2 points.

B. Helena proposes a change to the scoring of the game. She says, "If I draw a number greater than 2, I get 2 points. Otherwise, you get 1 point." Is the game fair, or unfair? If it is unfair, which player has the advantage? Explain.

In each round, Thato either scores 1 point or he loses 2 points.

Find the probability of each outcome. Then find the expected value.

$$P(-2) = \frac{1}{3} \text{ and } P(+1) = \frac{2}{3}.$$

$$E = -2 \cdot \left(\frac{1}{3}\right) + 1 \cdot \left(\frac{2}{3}\right)$$

$$= -\frac{2}{3} + \frac{2}{3} = 0$$

This is a fair game because the expected value is 0. Neither player has an advantage over the other.

 Try It! 2. Justice and Tamika use the same 3 cards but change the game. In each round, a player draws a card and replaces it, and then the other player draws. The differences between the two cards are used to score each round. Order matters, so the difference can be negative. Is each game fair? Explain.

   a. If the difference between the first and second cards is 2, Justice gets a point. Otherwise Tamika gets a point.

   b. They take turns drawing first. Each round, the first player to draw subtracts the second player's number from her own and the result is added to her total score.

🖥 Go Online | SavvasRealize.com

APPLICATION **EXAMPLE 3** **Make a Decision Based on Expected Value**

The Silicon Valley Company manufactures tablets and computers. Their tablets are covered by a warranty for one year, so that if the tablet fails, the company replaces it. Since the failure rate of their model TAB5000 tablet is high, the head of production has a plan for replacing certain components inside the TAB5000 and calling the new model TAB5001.

Model TAB5000
- Cost to produce: $100
- Price: $150
- 5% fail within first year
- Replacement cost to company: $130

Model TAB5001
- Cost to produce: $105
- Price: $150
- 1% fail within first year (estimate)
- Replacement cost to company: $135

If you were the head of production, would you recommend switching to selling the TAB5001?

Formulate ◀ Find the expected profit for each model.

Expected profit = price − cost − (cost to replace)(failure rate)

Compute ◀ Expected profit of TAB5000 = $150 − $100 − ($130)(0.05)

$$= \$50 - \$6.50$$

$$= \$43.50$$

Expected profit of TAB5001 = $150 − $105 − ($135)(0.01)

$$= \$45 - \$1.35$$

$$= \$43.65$$

Interpret ◀ The expected profit of the TAB5001 is more than the expected profit of the TAB5000. It makes sense to sell the TAB5001 instead of the TAB5000. Also, customers who bought a tablet would be more likely to be pleased with their purchase and buy from the same company in the future.

 Try It! **3.** Additional data is collected for the TAB5000 and TAB5001. The production and replacement costs for the TAB5001 remain unchanged.

a. The production and replacement costs for the TAB5000 increased by $10. What would the expected profit be for the TAB5000?

b. The failure rate for the TAB5001 increased by 1%. What would the expected profit be for the TAB5001?

c. As a consultant for the company, what would you recommend they do to maximize their profit?

EXAMPLE 4   Use a Binomial Distribution to Make Decisions

An airport shuttle company takes 8 reservations for each trip because 25% of their reservations do not show up. Is this a reasonable policy?

Find the probability that more passengers show up than the van can carry.

For 8 reservations, the graph shows the number of possible combinations of passengers showing up.

USE APPROPRIATE TOOLS
How does the graph of the number of combinations help you think about the situation? ⓒ **MP.5**

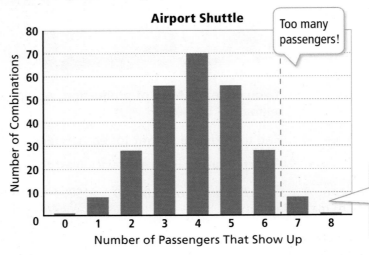

Too many passengers!

8 ways that 7 people show up ($_8C_7 = 8$)
1 way that 8 people show up ($_8C_8 = 1$)

To find the probability that too many reservations show up, compute the probability that either 7 or 8 passengers show up. Each reservation has a 75% chance of showing up and a 25% chance of not showing up. Use $P(r) = {}_nC_r\, p^r(1 - p)^{n - r}$.

Find the probability that 7 reservations show up.

$$P(7) = {}_8C_7(0.75)^7(0.25)^1 \approx 8(0.1335)(0.25) \approx 0.267$$

Find the probability that 8 reservations show up.

$$P(8) = {}_8C_8(0.75)^8(0.25)^0 \approx 1(0.1001)(1) \approx 0.100$$

The probability that more reservations will show up than the van can carry is $P(7) + P(8)$, or about $0.267 + 0.100 = 0.367$.

Over one third of the trips will have passengers who can not get a seat in the van. This will result in dissatisfied customers, so this is not a reasonable policy.

Try It! 4. A play calls for a crowd of 12 extras with non-speaking parts. Because 10% of the extras have not shown up in the past, the director selects 15 students as extras. Find the probabilities that 12 extras show up to the performance, 15 extras show up to the performance, and more than 12 extras show up to the performance.

CONCEPT SUMMARY Using Probability to Make Decisions

METHOD	DESCRIPTION	APPLICATIONS
Simple Probability	Find the probability of random events.	• Select the most favorable among random events.
Expected Value	Multiply the probability of each outcome by its value. Add to find the expected value.	• Compare expected values to choose the best of several options. • Compare expected values to decide if a game is fair.
Probability Distribution	Find the probability distribution of all possible outcomes.	• Compare probabilities of outcomes in a binomial experiment. • Create a graph of a probability distribution to present the distribution visually.

Do You UNDERSTAND?

1. **ESSENTIAL QUESTION** How can you use probability to make decisions?

2. **Reason** How can you use random numbers to simulate rolling a standard number cube? © MP.2

3. **Error Analysis** Explain the error in Diego's reasoning. © MP.3

> If a game uses random numbers, it is always fair. ✗

4. **Use Structure** Describe what conditions are needed for a fair game. © MP.7

5. **Use Appropriate Tools** Explain how you can visualize probability distributions to help you make decisions. © MP.5

6. **Reason** Why must the expected value of a fair game of chance equal zero? © MP.2

Do You KNOW HOW?

7. A teacher assigns each of 30 students a unique number from 1 to 30. The teacher uses the random numbers shown to select students for presentations. Which student was selected first? second?

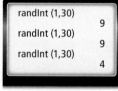

randInt (1,30)   9
randInt (1,30)   9
randInt (1,30)   4

8. Three friends are at a restaurant and they all want the last slice of pizza. Identify three methods involving probability that they can use to determine who gets the last slice. Explain mathematically why each method will guarantee a fair decision.

9. Edgar rolls one number cube and Micah rolls two. If Edgar rolls a 6, he wins a prize. If Micah rolls a sum of 7, she gets a prize. Is this game fair? Explain.

10. The 10 parking spaces in the first row of the parking lot are reserved for the 12 members of the Student Council. Usually an average of ten percent of the Student Council does not drive to school dances. What is the probability that more members of the Student Council will drive to a dance than there are reserved parking spaces?

UNDERSTAND

11. **Reason** Suppose Chris has pair of 4-sided dice, each numbered from 1 to 4, and Carolina has a pair of 10-sided dice, each numbered from 1 to 10. They decide to play a series of games against each other, using their own dice. ⓒ **MP.2**

 a. Describe a game that would be fair. Explain.

 b. Describe an unfair game. Explain.

12. **Construct Arguments** Mr. and Ms. Mitchell have 3 children, Luke, Charlie, and Aubrey. All 3 children want to sit in the front seat. Charlie suggests that they flip a coin two times to decide who will sit in the front seat. The number of heads determines who sits in the front seat. Is this a fair method? Explain. ⓒ **MP.3**

Number of Heads	Front Seat Passenger
0	Luke
1	Charlie
2	Aubrey

13. **Error Analysis** Mercedes is planning a party for 10 people. She knows from experience that about 20% of those invited will not show up. If she invites 12 people, how can she calculate the probability that more than 10 people will show up. What error did she make? What is the correct probability? ⓒ **MP.3**

> Use the binomial distribution for 12 trials, with a 20% probability, and more than 10 show up.
> $(12)(0.80)^1(0.20)^{11} +$
> $(1)(0.80)^0(0.20)^{12}$ ✗

PRACTICE

14. How can you use random integers to select 3 students from a group of 8 to serve as student body representatives, so that each student is equally likely to be selected? SEE EXAMPLE 1

Explain whether each game is fair or unfair.
SEE EXAMPLE 2

15. When it is your turn, roll a standard number cube. If the number is even, you get a point. If it is odd, you lose a point.

16. When it is your turn, roll two standard number cubes. If the product of the numbers is even, you get a point. If the product is odd, you lose a point.

Fatima is a contestant on a game show. So far, she has won $34,000. She can keep the $34,000 or spin the spinner shown below and add or subtract the amount shown from $34,000. SEE EXAMPLE 3

17. If Fatima spins the spinner, what are her expected total winnings?

18. Would you advise Fatima to keep the $34,000 or to spin the spinner? Explain your reasoning.

19. Suppose 0.5% of people who file federal tax returns with an adjusted gross income (AGI) between $50,000 and $75,000 are audited. Of 5 people in that tax bracket for whom ABC Tax Guys prepared their taxes, 2 were audited. SEE EXAMPLE 4

 a. If 5 people with an AGI between $50,000 and $75,000 are selected at random from all the people who filed federal tax returns, what is the probability that at least 2 people are audited?

 b. Would you recommend that a friend with an AGI between $50,000 and $75,000 use ABC Tax Guys to prepare her tax returns? Explain.

APPLY

20. Model With Mathematics For $5.49 per month, Ms. Corchado can buy insurance to cover the cost of repairing a leak in the natural gas lines within her house. She estimates that there is a 3% chance that she will need to have such repairs made next year. **©** MP.4

a. What is the expected cost of a gas leak, if Ms. Corchado does not buy insurance? Use the cost shown in the middle of the graph.

b. With more recent information, Ms. Corchado learns that repair costs could be as much as $1,200 dollars with an 8% probability of a leak. What is the expected cost of a gas leak with these assumptions?

c. Would you advise Ms. Corchado to buy the insurance? Explain.

21. Higher Order Thinking You are a consultant to a company that manufactures components for cell phones. One of the components the company manufactures has a 4% failure rate. Design changes have improved the quality of the component. A test of 50 of the new components found that only one of the new components is defective.

a. Before the design improvements what was the probability that among 50 of the items, at most one of the items was defective?

b. Is it reasonable to conclude that the new components have a lower failure rate than 4%?

c. Would you recommend further testing to determine whether the new parts have a lower failure rate than 4%? Explain.

© ASSESSMENT PRACTICE

22. Paula, Sasha, and Yumiko live together. They want a system to determine who will wash the dinner dishes on any given night. Select all of the methods that are fair.

Ⓐ Roll a standard number cube. If the result is 1 or 2, Paula does the dishes; if 3 or 4, Sasha; if 5 or 6, Yumiko.

Ⓑ Roll a standard number cube. If the result is 1, Paula does the dishes; if 2, Sasha; if 4, Yumiko. If the result is 3, 5, or 6, roll again.

Ⓒ Roll two standard number cubes. If the sum of the numbers that come up is less than 6, Paula washes the dishes; if the sum is 8, 9, or 12, Sasha; if the sum is 6 or 7, Yumiko. If the sum is 10 or 11, roll again.

Ⓓ Write the name of each girl on a slip of paper, place the slips in a box, mix them up, and select one at random. The person whose name is selected does the dishes.

23. SAT/ACT A fair choice among a group of students may be made by flipping three coins in sequence, and noting the sequences of heads and tails. If each student is assigned one of these sequences, how many students can be selected fairly by this method?

Ⓐ 4   Ⓑ 5   Ⓒ 6   Ⓓ 7   Ⓔ 8

24. Performance Task Acme Tire Company makes two models of steel belted radial tires, Model 1001 and Model 1002.

Model	1001
Blowouts per 200,000 tires	2
Profits before any lawsuits	$60

Model	1002
Blowouts per 200,000 tires	1
Profits before any lawsuits	$56

If one of these tires fails and the company is sued, the average settlement is $1,200,000.

Part A Find the expected profit for both models of tires after any potential lawsuits. Explain.

Part B Would you recommend that the company continue selling both models? Explain.

1. How can you find the probability of events and combinations of events?

Vocabulary Review

Choose the correct term to complete each sentence.

2. An arrangement of items in a specific order is called a(n) _____.

3. Two events are _____ if there is no outcome that is in both events.

4. Two events are _____ if the occurrence of one event affects the probability of the other event.

5. The _____ of an event is the set of all outcomes in the sample space that are not included in the event.

6. The predicted average outcome of many trials in an experiment is called the _____.

- combination
- complement
- conditional probability
- dependent events
- expected value
- independent events
- mutually exclusive
- permutation
- probability distribution

Concepts & Skills Review

LESSON 12-1 **Probability Events**

Quick Review

Two events are **mutually exclusive** if and only if there is no outcome that lies in the sample space of both events. Two events are **independent events** if and only if the occurrence of one event does not affect the probability of a second event.

Example

Let A represent the event "even number," or A = {2, 4, 6, 8}.

Let B represent the event "odd number," or B = {1, 3, 5, 7}.

Let C represent the event "divisible by 3," or C = {3, 6}.

Are A and B mutually exclusive? Explain.
　　Yes; all of their elements are different.

Are A and C mutually exclusive? Explain.
　　No; they both have a 3 in their sample space.

Practice & Problem Solving

Ten craft sticks lettered A through J are in a coffee cup. Consider the events "consonant," "vowel," "letter before D in the alphabet," "letter after A in the alphabet," and "letter after E in the alphabet." State whether each pair of events is mutually exclusive.

7. vowel, letter before D

8. letter before D, letter after E

9. letter after A, letter before D

10. **Communicate Precisely** Edward is rolling a number cube to decide on the new combination for his bicycle lock. If he only has one number to go, find the probability of each event. Use what you know about mutually exclusive events to explain your reasoning. **ⓒ MP.6**

    a. Edward rolls a number that is both even and less than 2. Explain.

    b. Edward rolls a number that is even or less than 2. Explain.

Conditional Probability

Quick Review

For any two events A and B, with $P(A) \neq 0$, $P(A \text{ and } B) = P(A) \cdot P(B \mid A)$. Events A and B are independent if and only if $P(B \mid A) = P(B)$.

Example

The table shows the number of students on different teams by grade. One of these students is selected at random for an interview. Are selecting a sophomore and selecting a member of the track team independent events?

Team Enrollment by Year

	Sophomore	Junior
Cross Country	9	6
Track	12	23

$P(\text{Soph}) = 0.42$, $P(\text{Track}) = 0.70$,

and $P(\text{Track and Soph}) = 0.24$

$P(\text{Soph}|\text{Track}) = \frac{P(\text{Track and Soph})}{P(\text{Track})} \approx 0.34$

$P(\text{Soph}|\text{Track}) \neq P(\text{Soph})$

No, selecting a sophomore and selecting a member of the track team are dependent events.

Practice & Problem Solving

Use the table in the Example for Exercises 11–15. Find each probability for a randomly-selected student.

11. $P(\text{Junior})$

12. $P(\text{Cross Country})$

13. $P(\text{Junior} \mid \text{Cross Country})$

14. $P(\text{Cross Country} \mid \text{Junior})$

15. Are selecting a junior and selecting a cross country runner dependent or independent events?

16. **Error Analysis** One card is selected at random from five cards numbered 1–5. A student says that drawing an even number and drawing a prime number are dependent events because $P(\text{prime} \mid \text{even}) = 0.5$ and $P(\text{even}) = 0.4$. Describe and correct the error the student made. Ⓒ **MP.3**

17. **Use Structure** A person entered in a raffle has a 3% chance of winning a prize. A prize winner has a 25% chance of winning two theater tickets. What is the probability that a person entered in the raffle will win the theater tickets? Ⓒ **MP.7**

Permutations and Combinations

Quick Review

The number of permutations of r items from a set of n items is $_nP_r = \frac{n!}{(n-r)!}$ for $0 \leq r \leq n$.

The number of combinations of r items from a set of n items is $_nC_r = \frac{n!}{r!(n-r)!}$ for $0 \leq r \leq n$.

Example

A bag contains 4 blue tiles and 4 yellow tiles. Three tiles are drawn from the bag at random without replacement. What is the probability all three tiles are blue?

Use combinations since order does not matter. Select 3 blue from 4 blue tiles $_4C_3$, or 4, ways.

Select 0 yellow from 4 yellow tiles $_4C_0$, or 1, way. Select 3 tiles from 8 total tiles $_8C_3$, or 56, ways.

$P(3 \text{ blue}) = \frac{4 \cdot 1}{56} = \frac{1}{14} \approx 0.07 = 7\%$

Practice & Problem Solving

In Exercises 18 and 19, determine whether the situation involves finding permutations or combinations. Then find the number.

18. How many ways can a team choose a captain and a substitute captain from 8 players?

19. How many ways can 3 numbers be selected from the digits 0–9 to set a lock code if the digits cannot be repeated?

20. **Error Analysis** A student computed $_5C_2$, and said that it is equal to 20. Describe and correct the error the student made. Ⓒ **MP.3**

21. **Look for Relationships** The formulas for permutations and combinations must always evaluate to a natural number. Explain why. Ⓒ **MP.7**

Quick Review

For a binomial experiment consisting of n trials, the probability of r successes out of n trials is given by the **binomial probability formula**:

$$P(r) = {}_nC_r \cdot p^r(1 - p)^{n-r}$$

Example

Curtis scores a touchdown 24% of the time he receives the ball. If Curtis receives the ball 7 times, what is the probability he scores a touchdown 4 of those times?

$$P(4 \text{ touchdowns}) = {}_7C_4 \cdot 0.24^4(1 - 0.24)^{7-4}$$

$$= 35 \cdot 0.24^4(0.76)^3$$

$$\approx 0.051 = 5.1\%$$

Practice & Problem Solving

Rhoda finds that every seed she plants has a 56% chance to grow to full height. If she plants 10 seeds, what is the probability each number of plants grows to full height? Round to the nearest hundredth of a percent.

22. 1 plant

23. 3 plants

24. 5 plants

25. 10 plants

26. Error Analysis Using the Example, Akasi tried to calculate Curtis' probable success rate of 3 touchdowns if he received the ball 5 times, but could not get an answer. Find and correct her mistake. ⓒ MP.3

$$P(3) = {}_3C_5 \cdot 0.24^5 (1-0.24)^{3-5}$$
$$= \,?$$

✗

Quick Review

The **expected value** E of a trial of an experiment is the sum of the value of each possible outcome times its probability or

$$E = x_1P(x_1) + x_2P(x_2) + \ldots + x_nP(x_n).$$

Example

The outer ring on a dartboard is worth 10 points, the middle ring is worth 25 points, and the bullseye is worth 100 points. When throwing darts, Ravi has a 45% chance of hitting the outer ring, a 40% chance of hitting the inner ring, a 5% chance of hitting the bullseye, and a 10% chance of missing the board. What is the expected value of a single dart throw?

$$E = 10(0.45) + 25(0.4) + 100(0.05) + 0(0.1)$$

$$= 4.5 + 10 + 5 + 0$$

$$= 19.5$$

Practice & Problem Solving

Use the information in the Example to find the expected value of 15 throws from each of the following people.

27. Rosa: 20% outer ring; 65% inner ring, 10% bullseye, 5% miss

28. Vicki: 60% outer ring; 20% inner ring, 12% bullseye, 8% miss

29. Higher Order Thinking A basketball player takes 2 shots from the 3-point line and misses them both. She calculates the expected value of taking a shot from the 3-point line is 0 points. Do you agree with the player's calculation? Her reasoning? How could the player improve the accuracy of her estimate?

Quick Review

Combined with probability, expected value can be used to help make decisions.

Example

Frederica is playing a game tossing 20 beanbags from a choice of three lines. Frederica has a 90% chance of success from the 5-point line, a 65% chance of success from the 10-point line, and a 20% chance from the 20-point line. Frederica wants to toss every beanbag from the same line, and thinks she should toss from the 5-point line since it has the highest probability of success. Is Frederica correct?

Find the expected points per toss, or expected value.

5-point line:
5 points • 0.90 = 4.5 points per toss

10-point line:
10 points • 0.65 = 6.5 points per toss

20-point line:
20 points • 0.20 = 4 points per toss

Frederica should toss the beanbag from the 10-point line.

Practice & Problem Solving

Both situations have the same expected value. Find the missing information.

30. Situation 1: Paul hits a dart target worth 15 points 45% of the time.

Situation 2: He hits a dart target worth 10 points x% of the time.

31. Situation 1: Lenora has a success rate of 25% when selling bracelets at $15 each.

Situation 2: She has a success rate of 20% when selling bracelets at $$x$ each.

32. **Make Sense of Problems** Use the information from the Example. Frederica practices her shots and increases her chances from the 20-point line to 30%. Should she now toss the beanbag from the 20-point line? Explain your reasoning. ⓒ **MP.1**

Visual Glossary

English

Alternative hypothesis   An alternative hypothesis is a statement that expresses that there is a difference between the parameter and the benchmark.

Amplitude   The amplitude of a periodic function is half the difference between the maximum and minimum values of the function.

Example   The maximum and minimum values of $y = 4 \sin x$ are 4 and -4, respectively.
amplitude $= \dfrac{4 - (-4)}{2} = 4$

Argument   In the complex plane, the argument is the angle measured counterclockwise from the positive real axis to the segment connecting the complex number to the origin.

Example

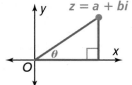

The argument is θ.

Arithmetic sequence   An arithmetic sequence is a number sequence formed by adding a fixed number to each previous term to find the next term. The fixed number is called the common difference.

Example   The arithmetic sequence 1, 5, 9, 13, . . . has a common difference of 4.

Arithmetic series   An arithmetic series is the sum of the terms in an arithmetic sequence.

Example $1 + 5 + 9 + 13 + 17 + 21$ is an arithmetic series with six terms.

Asymptote   An asymptote is a line that a graph approaches. Asymptotes guide the end behavior of a function.

Example   The function $y = \frac{x+2}{x-2}$ has $x = 2$ as a vertical asymptote and $y = 1$ as a horizontal asymptote.

Augmented matrix   An augmented matrix is a matrix that shows all coefficients and constants in a system of equations.

Example
The augmented matrix for the system $\begin{cases} x + 2y \quad\;\; = 2 \\ x - \; y + 3z = 5 \\ 2x + \; y - 4z = 10 \end{cases}$

is $\begin{bmatrix} 1 & 2 & 0 & \vdots & 2 \\ 1 & -1 & 3 & \vdots & 5 \\ 2 & 1 & -4 & \vdots & 10 \end{bmatrix}$.

Spanish

Hipótesis alternativa   Una hipótesis alternativa es un enunciado que expresa que hay una diferencia entre el parámetro y el punto de referencia.

Amplitud   La amplitud de una función periódica es la mitad de la diferencia entre los valores máximo y mínimo de la función.

Argumento   En el plano complejo, el argumento es el ángulo que se mide en el sentido contrario a las manecillas del reloj desde el eje real positivo hasta el segmento.

Secuencia aritmética   Una secuencia aritmética es una secuencia de números que se forma al sumar un número fijo a cada término para hallar el término que le sigue. El número fijo se denomina diferencia común.

Serie aritmética   Una serie aritmética es la suma de los términos de una progresión aritmética.

Asíntota   Una asíntota es una recta a la cual se acerca una gráfica. Las asíntotas actúan como guías del comportamiento extremo de una función.

Matriz aumentada   Una matriz aumentada es una matriz que muestra todos los coeficientes y las constantes en un sistema de ecuaciones.

English

Spanish

Average rate of change The average rate of change is the slope of the line segment between the points $(a, f(a))$ and $(b, f(b))$.

Tasa de cambio promedio La tasa de cambio promedio es la pendiente del segmento de recta entre los puntos $(a, f(a))$ y $(b, f(b))$.

Example For the parabola $y = x^2$, the average rate of change through the points $(2, 4)$ and $(4, 16)$ is $\frac{16 - 4}{4 - 2} = \frac{12}{2} = 6$.

B

Bias A bias is a systematic error that results in a sample that misrepresents a population.

Sesgo El sesgo es un error sistemático que produce una muestra que no representa con precisión a una población.

Binomial distribution A binomial distribution is a probability distribution that shows the probabilities of the outcomes of a binomial experiment.

Distribución binomial Una distribución binomial es una distribución de probabilidad que muestra las probabilidades de los resultados de un experimento binomial.

Binomial experiment A binomial experiment is one in which the situation involves repeated trials. Each trial has two possible outcomes (success or failure), and the probability of success is constant throughout the trials.

Experimento binomial Un experimento binomial es un experimento que requiere varios ensayos. Cada ensayo tiene dos resultados posibles (éxito o fracaso), y la probabilidad de éxito es constante durante todos los ensayos.

Binomial probability For a binomial experiment consisting of n trials with probability of success p for each trial, the binomial probability is the probability of r successes out of n trials given by the function $P(r) = {}_nC_r \cdot p^r(1 - p)^{n-r}$.

Probabilidad binomial En un experimento que incluye n ensayos con una probabilidad p de cada ensayo, la probabilidad binomial es la probabilidad de r éxitos de n ensayos dados por la función $P(r) = {}_nC_r \cdot p^r(1 - p)^{n-r}$.

Example Suppose you roll a standard number cube and that you call rolling a 1 a success. Then $p = \frac{1}{6}$. The probability of rolling nine 1s in twenty rolls is
$${}_{20}C_9 \left(\frac{1}{6}\right)^9 \left(1 - \frac{1}{6}\right)^{20-9} \approx 0.022.$$

Binomial Theorem For every positive integer n, $(a + b)^n = P_0a^n + P_1a^{n-1}b + P_2 a^{n-2}b^2 + \ldots + P_{n-1} ab^{n-1} + P_n b^n$ where $P_0, P_1, \ldots, P_n$ are the numbers in the row of Pascal's Triangle that has n as its second number.

Teorema binomial Para cada número entero positivo n, $(a + b)^n = P_0a^n + P_1a^{n-1} b + P_2a^{n-2} b^2 + \ldots + P_{n-1}ab^{n-1} + P_nb^n$, donde $P_0, P_1, \ldots, P_n$ son los números de la fila del Triángulo de Pascal cuyo segundo número es n.

Example $(x + 1)^3 = {}_3C_0(x)^3 + {}_3C_1(x)^2(1)^1$
$+ {}_3C_2(x)^1(1)^2 + {}_3C_3(1)^3$
$= x^3 + 3x^2 + 3x + 1$

C

Categorical variable A categorical variable is a variable for which the possible values belong to a limited set of qualitative responses.

Variable categórica Una variable categórica es una variable cuyos valores posibles pertenecen a un conjunto limitado de respuestas cualitativas.

Center of a hyperbola The center of a hyperbola is the midpoint between the vertices.

Centro de una hipérbola El centro de una hipérbola es el punto medio entre los vértices.

Center of an ellipse The center of an ellipse is the midpoint of the major axis.

Centro de una elipse El centro de una elipse es el punto medio del eje mayor.

English

Spanish

Center of rotation A center of rotation is the fixed point of a rotation.

Centro de rotación Un centro de rotación es el punto fijo de una rotación.

Example

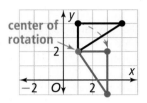

Central angle A central angle of a circle is an angle whose vertex is at the center of a circle.

Ángulo central El ángulo central de un círculo es un ángulo cuyo vértice está situado en el centro del círculo.

Example

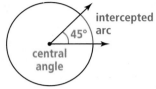

Change of Base Formula This formula allows logarithms with a base other than 10 and e to be evaluated. $\log_b m = \frac{\log_a m}{\log_a b}$, where m, b, and a are positive numbers, and $b \neq 1$ and $a \neq 1$.

Fórmula de cambio de base Esta fórmula permite evaluar logaritmos con base distinta de 10 y e. $\log_b m = \frac{\log_a m}{\log_a b}$, donde m, b, y a son números positivos y $b \neq 1$ y $a \neq 1$.

Example $\log_3 8 = \frac{\log 8}{\log 3} \approx 1.8928$

Coefficient matrix A coefficient matrix is a matrix that shows the coefficients of the variables in a system of equations.

Matriz de coeficientes Una matriz de coeficientes es una matriz que muestra los coeficientes de las variables en un sistema de ecuaciones.

Example $\begin{cases} x + 2y = 5 \\ 3x + 5y = 14 \end{cases}$

coefficient matrix $\begin{bmatrix} 1 & 2 \\ 3 & 5 \end{bmatrix}$

Cofunction A cofunction is the trigonometric function for the complement of an angle.

Cofunción Una cofunción es la función trigonométrica para el complemento de un ángulo.

Cofunction identities A cofunction identity is an equation that represents a trigonometric function with an equivalent trigonometric function related to its complement.

Identidades de cofunción Una identidad de cofunción es una ecuación que representa una función trigonométrica con una función trigonométrica equivalente relacionada con su complemento.

Combination Any unordered selection of r objects from a set of n objects is a combination. The number of combinations of n objects taken r at a time is $_nC_r = \frac{n!}{r!(n-r)!}$ for $0 \leq r \leq n$.

Combinación Cualquier selección no ordenada de r objetos tomados de un conjunto de n objetos es una combinación. El número de combinaciones de n objetos, cuando se toman r objetos cada vez, $_nC_r = \frac{n!}{r!(n-r)!}$ para $0 \leq r \leq n$.

Example The number of combinations of seven items taken four at a time is $_7C_4 = \frac{7!}{4!(7-4)!} = 35$. There are 35 ways to choose four items from seven items without regard to order.

Common difference A common difference is the difference between consecutive terms of an arithmetic sequence.

Diferencia común La diferencia común es la diferencia entre los términos consecutivos de una progresión aritmética.

Example The arithmetic sequence 1, 5, 9, 13, . . . has a common difference of 4.

English

Common logarithm   A common logarithm is a logarithm that uses base 10. You can write the common logarithm $\log_{10} y$ as $\log y$.

> **Example** $\log 1 = 0$
> $\log 10 = 1$
> $\log 50 = 1.698970004\ldots$

Common ratio   A common ratio is the ratio of consecutive terms of a geometric sequence.

> **Example**   The geometric sequence 2.5, 5, 10, 20, . . . has a common ratio of 2.

Complement of an event   All possible outcomes that are not in the event.
$P(\text{complement of event}) = 1 - P(\text{event})$

> **Example**   The complement of rolling a 1 or a 2 on a standard number cube is rolling a 3, 4, 5, or 6.

Completing the square   Completing the square is the process of adding $\left(\frac{b}{2}\right)^2$ to $x^2 + bx$ to form a perfect-square trinomial.

> **Example** $x^2 - 12x + \blacksquare$
> $x^2 - 12x + \left(\frac{-12}{2}\right)^2$
> $x^2 - 12x + 36$

Complex conjugates   Complex numbers with equivalent real parts and opposite imaginary parts are complex conjugates.

> **Example**   The complex numbers $2 - 3i$ and $2 + 3i$ are complex conjugates.

Complex number   Complex numbers are numbers that can be written in the form $a + bi$, where a and b are real numbers and i is the square root of -1.

> **Example** $6 + i$
> 7
> $2i$

Complex plane   The complex plane is similar to the coordinate plane except the horizontal axis represents the real part of a complex number and the vertical axis represents the imaginary part of a complex number.

Spanish

Logaritmo común   El logaritmo común es un logaritmo de base 10. El logaritmo común $\log_{10} y$ se expresa como $\log y$.

Razón común   Una razón común es la razón de términos consecutivos en una secuencia geométrica.

Complemento de un suceso   Todos los resultados posibles que no se dan en el suceso.
$P(\text{complemento de un suceso}) = 1 - P(\text{suceso})$

Completar el cuadrado   Completar un cuadrado es el proceso mediante el cual se suma $\left(\frac{b}{2}\right)^2$ a $x^2 + bx$ para formar un trinomio cuadrado perfecto.

Conjugados complejos   Los números complejos con partes reales equivalentes y partes imaginarias opuestas son conjugados complejos.

Número complejo   Los números complejos son los números que se pueden escribir como $a + bi$, donde a y b son números reales y donde i es la raíz cuadrada de -1.

Plano complejo   El plano complejo es similar al plano de coordenadas, a excepción de que el eje horizontal representa la parte real de un número complejo y el eje vertical representa la parte imaginaria de un número complejo.

> **Example**

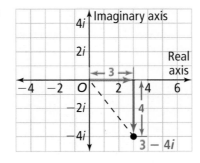

English

Component form The component form of a vector describes the horizontal and vertical change of position from the initial point to the terminal point of the vector.

> **Example** The vector $\langle 90, 400 \rangle$ could represent a change in position of 90 miles east and 400 miles north.

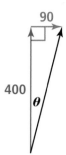

Composite function A composite function is a combination of two functions such that the output from the first function becomes the input for the second function.

> **Example** $f(x) = 2x + 1$, $g(x) = x^2 - 1$
> $(g \circ f)\,(5) = g(f(5)) = g(2(5) + 1)$
> $= g(11)$
> $= 11^2 - 1 = 120$

Composition of functions A composition of functions is the operation that forms composite functions.

> **Example** $f \circ g(x) = f(g(x))$
> $g \circ f(x) = g(f(x))$

Compound event A compound event is an event that consists of two or more events linked by the word *and* or the word *or*.

> **Example** Rolling a 5 on a standard number cube and then rolling a 4 is a compound event.

Compound fraction A compound fraction is a fraction that has one or more fractions in the numerator and/or the denominator.

> **Example** $\dfrac{\frac{x}{4} + \frac{x+2}{2}}{\frac{x-1}{3}}$

Compound inequality A combination of two or more inequalities is a compound inequality.

> **Example** $-1 < x$ and $x \le 3$
> $x < -1$ or $x \ge 3$

Compound interest Interest that is paid on both the principal and the interest that has already been paid is compound interest.

Compound interest formula This formula is an exponential model that is used to calculate the value of an investment when interest is compounded.

Spanish

Componentes de un vector Los componentes de un vector describen el cambio de posición horizontal y vertical desde el punto de inicio hasta el punto terminal del vector.

Función compuesta Una función compuesta es la combinación de dos funciones. La cantidad de salida de la primera función es la cantidad de entrada de la segunda función.

Composición de funciones Una composición de funciones es la operación que forma funciones compuestas.

Suceso compuesto Un suceso compuesto es un suceso que consiste en dos o más sucesos unidos por medio de la palabra *y* o la palabra *o*.

Fracción compuesta Una fracción compuesta está en forma de fracción y tiene una o más fracciones en el numerador o el denominador.

Desigualdad compuesta Una combinación de dos o más desigualdades es una desigualdad compuesta.

Interés compuesto El interés calculado tanto sobre el capital como sobre los intereses ya pagados es el interés compuesto.

Fórmula de interés compuesto Esta fórmula es un modelo exponencial que se usa para calcular el valor de una inversión cuando el interés es compuesto.

English

Spanish

Compression   A compression is a transformation that decreases the distance between the points of a graph and a given line by the same factor.

Compresión   La compresión es una transformación que reduce por el mismo factor la distancia entre los puntos de una gráfica y una recta dada.

Example

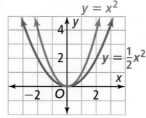

$y = x^2$

$y = \frac{1}{2}x^2$

The graph of $y = \frac{1}{2}x^2$ is a compression of the graph of $y = x^2$.

Conditional probability   A conditional probability is the probability that an event B will occur given that another event A has already occurred. The notation $P(B|A)$ is read "the probability of event B, given event A." For any two events A and B in the sample space, $P(B|A) = \frac{P(A \text{ and } B)}{P(A)}$.

Probabilidad condicional   Una probabilidad condicional es la probabilidad de que ocurra un suceso B cuando ya haya ocurrido otro suceso A. La notación $P(B|A)$ se lee "la probabilidad del suceso B, dado el suceso A". Para dos sucesos cualesquiera A y B en el espacio muestral $P(B|A) = \frac{P(A \text{ and } B)}{P(A)}$.

Example $= \frac{P(\text{departs and arrives on time})}{P(\text{departs on time})}$

$= \frac{0.75}{0.83}$

≈ 0.9

Conic section   A conic section is a curve formed by the intersection of a plane and a double cone.

Sección cónica   Una sección cónica es una curva que se forma por la intersección de un plano con un cono doble.

Example

ellipse   **hyperbola**

Conjugate axis   The conjugate axis for the hyperbola $\frac{x^2}{a^2} - \frac{y^2}{b^2} = 1$ is the vertical line passing through the center of the hyperbola. For $\frac{y^2}{a^2} - \frac{x^2}{b^2} = 1$, the conjugate axis is the horizontal line passing through the center of the hyperbola.

Eje conjugado   El eje conjugado de la hipérbola $\frac{x^2}{a^2} - \frac{y^2}{b^2} = 1$ es la recta vertical que pasa por el centro de la hipérbola. Para $\frac{x^2}{a^2} - \frac{y^2}{b^2} = 1$, el eje conjugado es la recta horizontal que pasa por el centro de la hipérbola.

Constant matrix   When representing a system of equations with a matrix equation, the matrix containing the constants of the system is the constant matrix.

Matriz de constantes   Al representar un sistema de ecuaciones con una ecuación matricial, la matriz que contiene las constantes del sistema es la matriz de constantes.

Example $x + 2y = 5$
$3x + 5y = 14$
constant matrix $\begin{bmatrix} 5 \\ 14 \end{bmatrix}$

English

Spanish

Constant of variation The constant of variation is the ratio of the two variables in a direct variation and the product of the two variables in an inverse variation.

Constante de variación La constante de variación es la razón de dos variables en una variación directa y el producto de las dos variables en una variación inversa.

Example In $y = 3.5x$, the constant of variation k is 3.5. In $xy = 5$, the constant of variation k is 5.

Continuously compounded interest formula This formula is a model for interest that has an infinitely small compounding period. The number e is the base in the formula $A = Pe^{rt}$.

Fórmula de interés compuesto continuo Esta fórmula es un modelo para calcular el interés que tiene un período de capitalización muy reducido. El número e es la base de la fórmula $A = Pe^{rt}$.

Example Suppose that $P = \$1200$, $r = 0.05$, and $t = 3$. Then
$$A = 1200e^{0.05 \cdot 3}$$
$$= 1200(2.718 \ldots)^{0.15}$$
$$\approx 1394.20$$

Control group In an experiment, the group chosen to not receive the treatment is the control group.

Grupo controlado En un experimento, el grupo no manipulado es el grupo controlado.

Cosecant function The cosecant (csc) function is the reciprocal of the sine function. For all real numbers θ except those that make $\sin \theta = 0$, $\csc \theta = \frac{1}{\sin \theta}$.

Función cosecante La función cosecante (csc) se define como el recíproco de la función seno. Para todos los números reales θ, excepto aquéllos para los que $\sin \theta = 0$, $\csc \theta = \frac{1}{\sin \theta}$.

Example If $\sin \theta = \frac{5}{13}$, then $\csc \theta = \frac{13}{5}$

Cosine In a right triangle, the cosine of an acute angle is the ratio of the length of the side adjacent to the angle to the length of the hypotenuse.

Coseno En un triángulo rectángulo, el coseno de un ángulo agudo es la razón de la longitud del cateto adyacente al ángulo a la longitud de la hipotenusa.

Example

In the triangle, $\cos \theta = \frac{3}{5}$.

Cotangent function The cotangent (cot) function is the reciprocal of the tangent function. For all real numbers θ except those that make $\tan \theta = 0$, $\cot \theta = \frac{1}{\tan \theta}$.

Función cotangente La función cotangente (cot) es el recíproco de la función tangente. Para todos los números reales θ, excepto aquéllos para los que $\tan \theta = 0$, $\cot \theta = \frac{1}{\tan \theta}$.

Example If $\tan \theta = \frac{5}{12}$, then $\cot \theta = \frac{12}{5}$.

Coterminal angles Two angles in standard position are coterminal if they have the same terminal side.

Ángulo coterminal Dos ángulos que están en posición normal son coterminales si tienen el mismo lado terminal.

Example

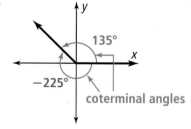

Angles that have measures 135° and −225° are coterminal.

English

Spanish

Co-vertices   The endpoints of the minor axis of an ellipse are the co-vertices of the ellipse.

Covértices   Los puntos de intersección entre una elipse y los ejes menores son los covértices de la elipse.

Example

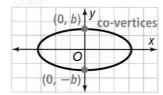

Decay factor   In an exponential function of the form $y = ab^x$, b is the decay factor if $0 < b < 1$.

Factor de decaimiento   En la función exponencial de la forma $y = ab^x$, b es el factor de decaimiento si $0 < b < 1$.

Example   In the equation $y = 0.3^x$, 0.3 is the decay factor.

Degree of a polynomial   The degree of a polynomial is the greatest degree among its monomial terms.

Grado de un polinomio   El grado de un polinomio es el grado mayor entre los términos de monomios.

Example $P(x) = x^6 + 2x^3 - 3$ has degree 6

Dependent events   When the outcome of one event affects the probability of a second event, the events are dependent events.

Sucesos dependientes   Dos sucesos son dependientes si el resultado de un suceso afecta la probabilidad del otro.

Example   You have a bag with marbles of different colors. If you pick a marble from the bag and pick another without replacing the first, the events are dependent events.

Determinant of a 2 × 2 matrix   For the matrix $\begin{bmatrix} a & b \\ c & d \end{bmatrix}$, the value $ad - bc$ is the determinant.

Determinante de una matriz de 2 × 2   Para la matriz $\begin{bmatrix} a & b \\ c & d \end{bmatrix}$, el valor $ad - bc$ es el determinante.

Example   The determinant of $\begin{bmatrix} 3 & -2 \\ 5 & 6 \end{bmatrix}$ is $3(6) - 5(-2) = 28$.

Dimensions of a matrix   The dimensions of a matrix are determined by the number of rows and columns in a matrix.

Dimensiones de una matriz   La dimensión de una matriz está determinada por la cantidad de filas y columnas de la matriz.

Example   The matrix $\begin{bmatrix} 3 & 5 & 4 \\ -2 & 1 & 6 \end{bmatrix}$ has 2 rows and 3 columns; the dimensions are 2 × 3.

Direction of a vector   The direction of a vector is the direction from the initial point to the terminal point of the vector.

Dirección de un vector   La dirección de un vector es la dirección desde el punto inicial hasta el punto terminal del vector.

Example

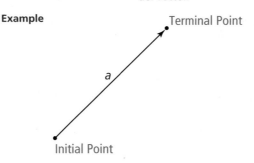

English	Spanish

Directrix The directrix of a parabola is the fixed line used to define a parabola. Each point of the parabola is the same distance from the focus and the directrix.

Directriz La directriz de una parábola es la recta fija con que se define una parábola. Cada punto de la parábola está a la misma distancia del foco y de la directriz.

Example

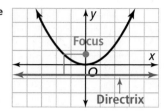

Discriminant The discriminant of a quadratic equation in the form $ax^2 + bx + c = 0$ is the value of the expression $b^2 - 4ac$. The value of the discriminant determines the number of solutions of the equation.

Discriminante El discriminante de una ecuación cuadrática en la forma $ax^2 + bx + c = 0$ es el valor de la expresión $b^2 - 4ac$. El valor del discriminante determina el número de soluciones de la ecuación.

Example $3x^2 - 6x + 1$
$$\text{discriminant} = (-6)^2 - 4(3)(1)$$
$$= 36 - 12 = 24$$

Domain The domain of a relation is the set of all inputs.

Dominio El dominio de una relación es el conjunto de todos los valores de entrada.

Examples In the relation $\{(0, 1), (0, 2), (0, 3),$ $(0, 4), (1, 3), (1, 4), (2, 1)\}$, the domain is $\{0, 1, 2\}$. In the function $f(x) = x^2 - 10$, the domain is all real numbers.

E

Ellipse An ellipse is the set of points P in a plane such that the sum of the distances from P to two fixed points F_1 and F_2 is a constant. The standard form of the equation of an ellipse with its center at the origin is $\frac{x^2}{a^2} + \frac{y^2}{b^2} = 1$ if the major axis is horizontal and $\frac{x^2}{b^2} + \frac{y^2}{a^2} = 1$ if the major axis is vertical, where $a > b$.

Elipse Una elipse es el conjunto de puntos P situados en un plano tal que la suma de las distancias entre P y dos puntos fijos F_1 y F_2 es una constante. La forma normal de la ecuación de una elipse con su centro en el origen es $\frac{x^2}{a^2} + \frac{y^2}{b^2} = 1$ si el eje mayor es horizontal y $\frac{x^2}{b^2} + \frac{y^2}{a^2} = 1$ si el eje mayor es vertical, donde $a > b$.

Example

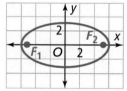

$$\frac{x^2}{36} + \frac{y^2}{9} = 1$$
$$F_1 = (-3\sqrt{3}, 0), F_2 = (3\sqrt{3}, 0)$$

End behavior End behavior of the graph of a function describes the directions of the graph as you move to the left and to the right, away from the origin.

Comportamiento extremo El comportamiento extremo de la gráfica de una función describe las direcciones de la gráfica al moverse a la izquierda y a la derecha, apartándose del origen.

Equal matrices Equal matrices are matrices with the same dimensions and equal corresponding elements.

Matrices equivalentes Dos matrices son equivalentes si y sólo si tienen las mismas dimensiones y sus elementos correspondientes son iguales.

Example Matrices A and B are equal.

$$A = \begin{bmatrix} 2 & 6 \\ \frac{9}{3} & 1 \end{bmatrix} \qquad B = \begin{bmatrix} \frac{6}{3} & 6 \\ 3 & \frac{-13}{-13} \end{bmatrix}$$

English	Spanish

Even function A function that is symmetric about the y-axis is an even function; $f(x) = f(-x)$ for all x-values.

Función par Una función que es simétrica respecto del eje y es una función par; $f(x) = f(-x)$ para todos los valores de x.

Example $f(x) = x^2$ is an even function since $f(-x) = (-x)^2 = x^2$.

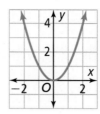

Event Any group of outcomes in a situation involving probability.

Suceso En la probabilidad, cualquier grupo de resultados.

Example When rolling a number cube, there are six possible outcomes. Rolling an even number is an event with three possible outcomes, 2, 4, and 6.

Expected value The average value you can expect for a large number of trials of an experiment; the sum of each outcome's value multiplied by its probability.

Valor esperado El valor promedio que se puede esperar para una cantidad grande de pruebas en un experimento; la suma de los valores de los resultados multiplicados cada uno por su probabilidad.

Example In a game, a player has a 25% probability of earning 10 points by spinning an even number and a 75% probability of earning 5 points by spinning an odd number.

expected value = 0.25(10) + 0.75(5) = 6.25

Experimental probability The ratio of the number of times an event actually happens to the number of times the experiment is done.

$$P(\text{event}) = \frac{\text{number of times an event happens}}{\text{number of times the experiment is done}}$$

Probabilidad experimental La razón entre el número de veces que un suceso sucede en la realidad y el número de veces que se hace el experimento.

$$P(\text{suceso}) = \frac{\text{número de veces que sucede un suceso}}{\text{número de veces que se hace el experimento}}$$

Example A baseball player's batting average shows how likely it is that a player will get a hit, based on previous times at bat.

Experiment An experiment is the application of a treatment to some group or groups and the measurement of the effects of the treatment.

Experimento Un experimento es la manipulación de un grupo o varios grupos y la medición de los efectos de esa manipulación.

Experimental group In an experiment, the group chosen to receive the treatment is the experimental group.

Grupo experimental En un experimento, el grupo manipulado es el grupo experimental.

Explicit definition An explicit definition allows any term in a sequence to be found without knowing the previous term.

Definición explícita Una definición explícita permite hallar cualquier término de una progresión aunque no se conozca el término anterior.

Example The explicit definition $a_n = 3 + 4(n - 1)$ allows the 7th term to be calculated directly:
$a_7 = 3 + 4(7 - 1) = 27$.

English

Exponential decay function Exponential decay is modeled by a function of the form $y = ab^x$ with $a > 0$ and $0 < b < 1$.

Exponential equation An exponential equation contains the form b^{cx}, with the exponent including a variable.

Example
$$5^{2x} = 270$$
$$\log 5^{2x} = \log 270$$
$$2x \log 5 = \log 270$$
$$2x = \frac{\log 270}{\log 5}$$
$$2x \approx 3.4785$$
$$x \approx 1.7392$$

Exponential function An exponential function is any function of the form $f(x) = ab^x$ where a and b are constants with $a \neq 0$, $b > 0$, and $b \neq 1$.

Example

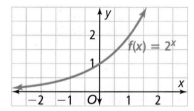

Exponential growth function Exponential growth is modeled by a function of the form $y = ab^x$ with $a > 0$ and $b > 1$.

Extraneous solution An extraneous solution is a solution of an equation derived from an original equation, but it is not a solution of the original equation.

Example $\sqrt{x - 3} = x - 5$
$$x - 3 = x^2 - 10x + 25$$
$$0 = x^2 - 11x + 28$$
$$0 = (x - 4)(x - 7)$$
$$x = 4 \text{ or } 7$$
The number 7 is a solution, but 4 is not, since $\sqrt{4 - 3} \neq 4 - 5$.

Factor Theorem The expression $x - a$ is a linear factor of a polynomial if and only if the value of a is a root of the related polynomial function.

Example The value 2 makes the polynomial $x^2 + 2x - 8$ equal to zero. So, $x - 2$ is a factor of $x^2 + 2x - 8$.

Factorial The factorial of a positive integer n is the product of all positive integers less than or equal to n and written $n!$

Example $4! = 4 \cdot 3 \cdot 2 \cdot 1 = 24$

Focal length The focal length of a parabola is the distance between the vertex and the focus.

Spanish

Función de decaimiento El decaimiento exponencial se expresa con una función $y = ab^x$ donde $a > 0$ y $0 < b < 1$.

Ecuación exponencial Una ecuación exponencial tiene la forma b^{cx}, y su exponente incluye una variable.

Función exponencial Una función exponencial es cualquier función de la forma $f(x) = ab^x$ donde a y b son constantes con $a \neq 0$, $b > 0$ y $b \neq 1$.

Función de crecimiento exponencial El crecimiento exponencial se expresa con una función de la forma $y = ab^x$ donde $a > 0$ y $b > 1$.

Solución extraña Una solución extraña es una solución de una ecuación derivada de una ecuación dada, pero que no satisface la ecuación dada.

Teorema de factores La expresión $x - a$ es un factor lineal de un polinomio si y sólo si el valor de a es una raíz de la función polinomial con la que se relaciona.

Factorial El factorial de un número entero positivo n es el producto de todos los números positivos menores que o iguales a n, y se escribe $n!$

Distancia focal La distancia focal de una parábola es la distancia entre el vértice y el foco.

English

Focus (plural: foci) of a hyperbola   A hyperbola is the set of all points P in a plane such that the difference of the distances from P to two fixed points is constant. Each of the fixed points is a focus of the hyperbola.

Focus (plural: foci) of a parabola   A parabola is the set of all points in a plane that are the same distance from a fixed line and a fixed point not on the line. The fixed point is the focus of the parabola.

Focus (plural: foci) of an ellipse   An ellipse is the set of all points P in a plane such that the sum of the distances from P to two fixed points is constant. Each of the fixed points is a focus of the ellipse.

Frequency   For a periodic function, the frequency is the reciprocal of the period.

Example   The period of $y = \sin x$ is 2π so the frequency is $\frac{1}{2\pi}$.

Frequency table   A table that groups a set of data values into intervals and shows the frequency for each interval.

Example

Interval	Frequency
0–9	5
10–19	8
20–29	4

Function   A function is a relation in which each element of the domain corresponds with exactly one element in the range.

Example   The relation $y = 3x^3 - 2x + 3$ is a function. $f(x) = 3x^3 - 2x + 3$ is the same relation written in function notation.

Fundamental Counting Principle   If there are m ways to make the first selection and n ways to make the second selection, then there are $m \cdot n$ ways to make the two selections.

Example   For 5 shirts and 8 pairs of shorts, the number of possible outfits is $5 \cdot 8 = 40$.

General form of a second-degree equation   The general form of a second-degree equation is $Ax^2 + Bxy + Cy^2 + Dx + Ey + F = 0$

Example $2x^2 + 4xy + 5y^2 + 3x + 7y + 1 = 0$

Spanish

Foco de una hipérbola   Una hipérbola es el conjunto de puntos P en un plano tal que la diferencia de las distancias desde P hasta dos puntos fijos es constante. Cada uno de los puntos fijos es el foco de la hipérbola.

Foco de una parabola   Una parábola es el conjunto de todos los puntos en un plano con la misma distancia desde una línea fija y un punto fijo que no permanece en la línea. El punto fijo es el foco de la parábola.

Foco de una elipse   Una elipse es el conjunto de todos los puntos P en un plano en el cual la suma de las distancias desde P hasta dos puntos fijos es constante. Cada uno de estos puntos fijos es un foco de la elipsis.

Frecuencia   En una función periódica, la frecuencia es el recíproco del período.

Tabla de frecuencias   Tabla que agrupa un conjunto de datos en intervalos y muestra la frecuencia de cada intervalo.

Función   Una función es una relación en la que cada elemento del dominio corresponde exactamente con un elemento del rango.

Principio fundamental de Conteo   Si hay m maneras de hacer la primera selección y n maneras de hacer la segunda selección, quiere decir que hay $m \cdot n$ maneras de hacer las dos selecciones.

Forma general de una ecuación de segundo grado   La forma general de una ecuación de segundo grado es $Ax^2 + Bxy + Cy^2 + Dx + Ey + F = 0$.

English

Geometric sequence   A geometric sequence is a sequence with a constant ratio between consecutive terms.

Example   The geometric sequence 2.5, 5, 10, 20, 40 . . . , has a common ratio of 2.

Geometric series   A geometric series is the sum of the terms in a geometric sequence.

Example   One geometric series with five terms is $2.5 + 5 + 10 + 20 + 40$.

Greatest common factor   The greatest common factor (GCF) of an expression is the common factor of each term of the expression that has the greatest coefficient and the greatest exponent.

Example   The GCF of $4x^2 + 20x - 12$ is 4.

Growth factor   In an exponential function of the form $y = ab^x$, b is the growth factor if $b > 1$.

Example   In the exponential equation $y = 2^x$, 2 is the growth factor.

H

Hyperbola   A hyperbola is a set of points P in a plane such that the difference between the distances from P to the foci F_1 and F_2 is a constant. The standard form of an equation of a hyperbola centered at (0, 0) is $\frac{x^2}{a^2} - \frac{y^2}{b^2} = 1$ if the transverse axis is horizontal and $\frac{y^2}{a^2} - \frac{x^2}{b^2} = 1$ if the transverse axis is vertical.

Spanish

Secuencia geométrica   Una secuencia geométrica es una secuencia con una razón constante entre términos consecutivos.

Serie geométrica   Una serie geométrica es la suma de términos en una progresión geométrica.

Máximo factor común   El máximo factor común de una expresión es el factor común de cada término de la expresión que tiene el mayor coeficiente y el mayor exponente.

Factor de incremento   En una función exponencial de la forma $y = ab^x$, b es el factor de incremento si $b > 1$.

Hipérbola   Una hipérbola es un conjunto de puntos P en un plano tal que la diferencia entre las distancias de P a los focos F_1 y F_2 es una constante. La forma normal de la ecuación de una hipérbola centrada en (0, 0) es $\frac{x^2}{a^2} - \frac{y^2}{b^2} = 1$, si el eje transversal es horizontal, y $\frac{y^2}{a^2} - \frac{x^2}{b^2} = 1$, si el eje transversal es vertical.

Example

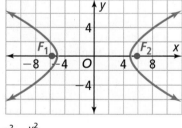

$$\frac{x^2}{5^2} - \frac{y^2}{3^2} = 1$$

I

Identity   An identity is an equation between two polynomial expressions in which one side can be transformed into the other side using defined rules of calculation.

Identidad   Una ecuación entre dos expresiones polinomiales para la cual un lado se puede transformar en el otro lado usando reglas de cálculo definidas.

Identity matrix   An identity matrix is a matrix I such that $IB = BI = B$; it is a square matrix with 1s along the main diagonal and 0 for all of the other elements.

Matriz de identidad   Una matriz de identidad es una matriz I tal que $IB = BI = B$; una matriz cuadrada con unos por la diagonal principal y ceros en los demás elementos.

Example $\begin{bmatrix} 1 & 0 \\ 0 & 1 \end{bmatrix} \begin{bmatrix} 3 & 5 \\ -2 & 4 \end{bmatrix} = \begin{bmatrix} 3 & 5 \\ -2 & 4 \end{bmatrix}$

$\begin{bmatrix} 3 & 5 \\ -2 & 4 \end{bmatrix} \begin{bmatrix} 1 & 0 \\ 0 & 1 \end{bmatrix} = \begin{bmatrix} 3 & 5 \\ -2 & 4 \end{bmatrix}$

English

Spanish

Imaginary axis   The vertical axis in the complex plane is the imaginary axis.

Eje imaginario   El eje vertical en el plano complejo es el eje imaginario.

Example

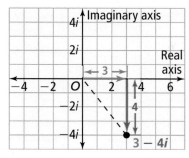

Imaginary number   An imaginary number is any number of the form *bi*, where *b* is a nonzero real number and *i* is the square root of −1.

Número imaginario   Un número imaginario es cualquier número de la forma *bi*, donde *b* es un número real distinto de cero y donde *i* es la raíz cuadrada de −1.

Example $7i$
i

Imaginary unit   The imaginary unit *i* is the complex number whose square is −1.

Unidad imaginaria   La unidad imaginaria *i* es el número complejo cuyo cuadrado es −1.

Inconsistent system   A system of equations that has no solution is an inconsistent system.

Sistema incompatible   Un sistema incompatible es un sistema de ecuaciones para el cual no hay solución.

Example $\begin{cases} y = 2x + 3 \\ -2x + y = 1 \end{cases}$ is a system of
parallel lines, so it has no solution.
It is an inconsistent system.

Independent events   When the outcome of one event does not affect the probability of a second event, the two events are independent.

Sucesos independientes   Cuando el resultado de un suceso no altera la probabilidad de otro, los dos sucesos son independientes.

Example   The results of two rolls of a number cube are independent. Getting a 5 on the first roll does not change the probability of getting a 5 on the second roll.

Index   With a radical sign, the index indicates the degree of the root.

Índice   Con un signo de radical, el índice indica el grado de la raíz.

Example   index 2   index 3   index 4
$\sqrt{16}$ $\sqrt[3]{16}$ $\sqrt[4]{16}$

Initial point   The initial point of a vector is the endpoint (not the tip) of a vector arrow.

Punto de inicio   El punto de inicio de un vector es el extremo (no la punta) de una flecha vectorial.

English

Spanish

Initial side   When an angle is in standard position, the initial side of the angle is given to be on the positive *x*-axis. The other ray is the terminal side of the angle.

Lado inicial   Cuando un ángulo está en posición normal, el lado inicial del ángulo se ubica en el eje positivo de las *x*. El otro rayo, o semirrecta, forma el lado terminal del ángulo.

Example

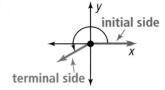

Interquartile range   The interquartile range of a set of data is the difference between the third and first quartiles.

Intervalo intercuartil   El rango intercuartil de un conjunto de datos es la diferencia entre el tercero y el primer cuartiles.

Example   The first and third quartiles of the data set {2, 3, 4, 5, 5, 6, 7, 7} are 3.5 and 6.5. The interquartile range is $6.5 - 3.5 = 3$.

Interval notation   Interval notation represents a set of real numbers with a pair of values that are its left (minimum) and right (maximum) boundaries.

Notación de intervalo   La notación de intervalo representa un conjunto de números reales con un par de valores que son sus límites a la izquierda (mínimo) y a la derecha (máximo).

Example   The interval (2, 7] represents the inequality $2 < x \leq 7$.

Inverse function   If function *f* pairs a value *b* with *a*, then its inverse, denoted f^{-1}, pairs the value *a* with *b*. If f^{-1} is also a function, then *f* and f^{-1} are inverse functions.

Funcion inversa   Si la función *f* empareja un valor *b* con *a*, entonces su inversa, cuya notación es f^{-1}, empareja el valor *a* con *b*. Si f^{-1} también es una función, entonces *f* y f^{-1} son funciones inversas.

Example   If $f(x) = x + 3$, then $f^{-1}(x) = x - 3$.

Inverse matrix   An inverse matrix is a matrix such that its product with another matrix yields the identity matrix.

Matriz inversa   Una matriz inversa es una matriz tal que su producto con otra matriz da la matriz de identidad.

Example   The inverse matrix of $\begin{bmatrix} 2 & 1 \\ 3 & 0 \end{bmatrix}$ is $\begin{bmatrix} 0 & \frac{1}{3} \\ 1 & -\frac{2}{3} \end{bmatrix}$ since $\begin{bmatrix} 2 & 1 \\ 3 & 0 \end{bmatrix} \begin{bmatrix} 0 & \frac{1}{3} \\ 1 & -\frac{2}{3} \end{bmatrix} = \begin{bmatrix} 1 & 0 \\ 0 & 1 \end{bmatrix}$.

Inverse relation   An inverse relation is formed when the roles of the independent and dependent variables are reversed.

Relación inversa   Una relación inversa se forma cuando se invierten los roles de las variables independientes y dependientes.

Inverse variation   An inverse variation is a relation represented by an equation of the form $xy = k$, $y = \frac{k}{x}$, or $x = \frac{k}{y}$, where $k \neq 0$.

Variación inversa   Una variación inversa es una relación representada por la ecuación $xy = k$, $y = \frac{k}{x}$, ó $x = \frac{k}{y}$, donde $k \neq 0$.

Example

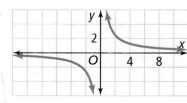

$xy = 5$, or $y = \frac{5}{x}$

Go Online | SavvasRealize.com

English

Spanish

Law of Cosines   In $\triangle ABC$, let a, b, and c represent the lengths of the sides opposite $\angle A$, $\angle B$, and $\angle C$, respectively. Then
$a^2 = b^2 + c^2 - 2bc \cos A$,
$b^2 = a^2 + c^2 - 2ac \cos B$, and
$c^2 = a^2 + b^2 - 2ab \cos C$

Ley de cosenos   En $\triangle ABC$, sean a, b y c las longitudes de los lados opuestos a $\angle A$, $\angle B$ y $\angle C$, respectivamente. Entonces
$a^2 = b^2 + c^2 - 2bc \cos A$,
$b^2 = a^2 + c^2 - 2ac \cos B$ y
$c^2 = a^2 + b^2 - 2ab \cos C$

Example

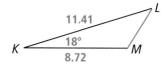

$LM^2 = 11.41^2 + 8.72^2 - 2(11.41)(8.72) \cos 18°$
$LM^2 \approx 16.9754$
$LM \approx 4.12$

Law of Sines   In $\triangle ABC$, let a, b, and c represent the lengths of the sides opposite $\angle A$, $\angle B$, and $\angle C$, respectively. Then $\frac{\sin A}{a} = \frac{\sin B}{b} = \frac{\sin C}{c}$.

Ley de senos   En $\triangle ABC$, sean a, b y c las longitudes de los lados opuestos a $\angle A$, $\angle B$ y $\angle C$, respectivamente. Entonces $\frac{\text{sen } A}{a} = \frac{\text{sen } B}{b} = \frac{\text{sen } C}{c}$.

Example

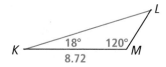

$m\angle L = 180 - (120 + 18) = 42°$
$\frac{KL}{\sin 120°} = \frac{8.72}{\sin 42°}$
$KL = \frac{8.72 \sin 120°}{\sin 42°}$
$KL \approx 11.29$

Leading coefficient   In a polynomial, the non-zero term that is multiplied by the greatest power of x is the leading coefficient.

Coeficiente principal   En un polinomio, el término distinto de cero que se multiplica por la potencia de x mayor es el coeficiente principal.

Example   In the expression $4x^5 + 3x^2 - x - 6$, 4 is the leading coefficient.

Like radicals   Like radicals are radical expressions that have the same index and the same radicand.

Radicales semejantes   Los radicales semejantes son expresiones radicales que tienen el mismo índice y el mismo radicando.

Example $4\sqrt[3]{7}$ and $\sqrt[3]{7}$ are like radicals.

Logarithm   For $b > 0$, $b \neq 1$, and $x > 0$, the logarithm base b of a positive number x is defined as follows: $\log_b x = y$, if and only if $x = b^y$.

Logaritmo   Para $b > 0$, $b \neq 1$ y $x > 0$, la base del logaritmo b de un número positivo x se define como $\log_b x = y$, si y sólo si $x = b^y$.

Example $\log_2 8 = 3$
$\log_{10} 100 = \log 100 = 2$
$\log_5 5^7 = 7$

Logarithmic equation   A logarithmic equation is an equation that includes a logarithm involving a variable.

Ecuación logarítmica   Una ecuación logarítmica es una ecuación que incluye un logaritmo con una variable.

Example $\log_3 x = 4$

English	Spanish

Logarithmic function A logarithmic function is the inverse of an exponential function.

Función logarítmica Una función logarítmica es la inversa de una función exponencial.

Example

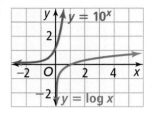

Magnitude The magnitude of a vector $\vec{v}$ is the length of the arrow.

Magnitud La magnitud de un vector $\vec{v}$ es la longitud de la flecha.

Major axis The major axis of an ellipse is the segment that contains the foci of the ellipse and has endpoints on the ellipse.

Eje mayor En una elipsis, el eje mayor es el segmento que contiene los focos de la elipsis y tiene puntos extremos sobre la elipsis.

Example

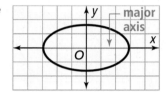

Margin of error The margin of error of a sample statistic is the maximum expected difference between the sample statistic and the population parameter.

Margen de error El margen de error de una estadística de muestreo aleatorio es la diferencia máxima que se espera entre la estadística de muestreo y el parámetro de la población.

Example The standard deviation of a sample is 5.0 and the number of trials is 30. The margin of error at a 95% confidence level is

$$ME \approx \frac{2 \cdot 5.0}{\sqrt{30}} \approx 1.8.$$

Matrix A matrix is a rectangular array of numbers written within brackets.

Matriz Una matriz es un conjunto de números encerrados en corchetes y dispuestos en forma de rectángulo.

Example $A = \begin{bmatrix} 1 & -2 & 0 & 10 \\ 9 & 7 & -3 & 8 \\ 2 & -10 & 1 & -6 \end{bmatrix}$

The number 2 is the element in the third row and first column. A is a 3×4 matrix.

Maximum The maximum of a function is the greatest value that the function attains in its domain. It is the y-coordinate of the highest point on the graph of the function.

Máximo El valor máximo de una función es el mayor valor que la función alcanza en su dominio. Es la coordenada y del punto más alto de la gráfica de la función.

Example

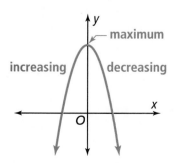

English

Spanish

Mean The mean of a data set is the sum of the data values divided by the number of data values.

Media La media de un conjunto de datos es la suma de los valores de datos dividida por el número de valores de los datos.

Example $\{1, 2, 3, 3, 6, 6\}$

$$\text{mean} = \frac{1 + 2 + 3 + 3 + 6 + 6}{6}$$

$$= \frac{21}{6} = 3.5$$

Median The median is the middle value in a data set. If the data set contains an even number of values, the median is the mean of the two middle values.

Mediana La mediana es el valor situado en el medio en un conjunto de datos. Si el conjunto de datos contiene un número par de valores, la mediana es la media de los dos valores del medio.

Example $\{1, 2, 3, 3, 4, 5, 6, 6\}$

$$\text{median} = \frac{3 + 4}{2} = \frac{7}{2} = 3.5$$

Midline The horizontal line through the average of the maximum and minimum values.

Línea media Recta horizontal que pasa a través de la media de los valores máximos y mínimos.

Example

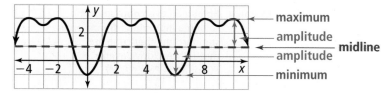

Minimum The minimum of a function is the least value that the function attains in its domain. It is the y-coordinate of the lowest point on the graph of the function.

Mínimo El valor mínimo de una función es el menor valor que la función alcanza en su dominio. Es la coordenada y del punto más bajo de la gráfica de la función.

Example

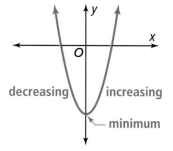

Minor axis The minor axis of an ellipse is the segment that is perpendicular to the major axis at its midpoint and has endpoints on the ellipse.

Eje menor En una elipsis, el eje menor es el segmento perpendicular al eje mayor en su punto medio y que tiene puntos extremos sobre la elipsis.

Example

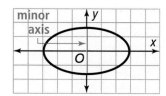

Modulus of a complex number In the complex plane, the length of the segment from a complex number to the origin is the modulus of the complex number.

Módulo de un número complejo La longitud del segmento desde el número complejo hasta el origen es el módulo del número complejo.

Example The modulus of $4 - 3i = \sqrt{4^2 + (-3)^2} = 5$.

English	Spanish

Monomial A monomial is either a real number, a variable, or a product of real numbers and variables with whole number exponents.

Monomio Un monomio es un número real, una variable o un producto de números reales y variables cuyos exponentes son números enteros.

Example $1, x, 2z, 4ab^2$

Multiplicity The multiplicity of a zero of a polynomial function is the number of times the related linear factor is repeated in the factored form of the polynomial.

Multiplicidad La multiplicidad de un cero de una función polinomial es el número de veces que el factor lineal relacionado se repite en la forma factorizada del polinomio.

Example The zeros of the function $P(x) = 2x(x-3)^2(x+1)$ are 0, 3, and −1. Since $(x-3)$ occurs twice as a factor, the zero 3 has multiplicity 2.

Mutually exclusive events When two events cannot happen at the same time, the events are mutually exclusive. If A and B are mutually exclusive events, then $P(A \text{ or } B) = P(A) + P(B)$.

Sucesos mutuamente excluyentes Cuando dos sucesos no pueden ocurrir al mismo tiempo, son mutuamente excluyentes. Si A y B son sucesos mutuamente excluyentes, entonces $P(A \text{ o } B) = P(A) + P(B)$.

Example Rolling an even number E and rolling a multiple of five M on a standard number cube are mutually exclusive events.
$$P(E \text{ or } M) = P(E) + P(M)$$
$$= \frac{3}{6} + \frac{1}{6}$$
$$= \frac{4}{6}$$
$$= \frac{2}{3}$$

N

nth root For any real numbers a and b, and any positive integer n, if $a^n = b$, then a is an nth root of b.

raíz n-ésima Para todos los números reales a y b, y todo número entero positivo n, si $a^n = b$, entonces a es la n-ésima raíz de b.

Example $\sqrt[5]{32} = 2$ because $2^5 = 32$.
$\sqrt[4]{81} = 3$ because $3^4 = 81$.

Natural base e The value that the expression $(1 + \frac{1}{x})^x$ approaches as $x \to \infty$. The value is approximately $2.7818282\ldots$

Base natural e El valor al que se acerca la expresión $(1 + \frac{1}{x})^x$ a medida que $x \to \infty$. El valor es aproximadamente igual a $2.7818282\ldots$

Natural logarithmic function A natural logarithmic function is a logarithmic function with base e. The natural logarithmic function $y = \ln x$ is $y = \log_e x$. It is the inverse of $y = e^x$.

Función logarítmica natural Una función logarítmica natural es una función logarítmica con base e. La función logarítmica natural $y = \ln x$ es $y = \log_e x$. Ésta es la función inversa de $y = e^x$.

Example

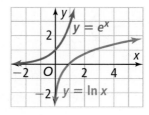

$\ln e^3 = 3$
$\ln 10 \approx 2.3026$
$\ln 36 \approx 3.5835$

English

Spanish

Normal distribution   A normal distribution shows data that vary randomly from the mean in the pattern of a bell-shaped curve.

Distribución normal   Una distribución normal muestra, con una curva en forma de campana, datos que varían alcatoriamento respecto de la media.

Example   **Distribution of Test Scores**

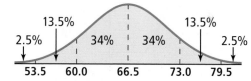

In a class of 200 students, the scores on a test were normally distributed. The mean score was 66.5 and the standard deviation was 6.5. The number of students who scored greater than 73 percent was about 13.5% + 2.5% of those who took the test.
16% of 200 = 32
About 32 students scored 73 or higher on the test.

Null hypothesis   A null hypothesis is a statement that expresses that there is no difference between the parameter and the benchmark.

Hipótesis nula   Una hipótesis nula es un enunciado que expresa que no hay diferencia entre el parámetro y el punto de referencia.

Observational study   In an observational study, you measure or observe members of a sample in such a way that they are not affected by the study.

Estudio de observación   En un estudio de observación, se miden u observan a los miembros de una muestra de tal manera que no les afecte el estudio.

Odd function   An odd function is a function that is symmetric about the origin; $f(-x) = -f(x)$ for all x-values.

Función impar   Una función impar es una función que es simétrica respecto del origen; $f(-x) = -f(x)$ para todos los valores de x.

Example $f(x) = x^3$ is an odd function since $f(-x) = (-x)^3 = -x^3$.

Outcome   An outcome is the result of a single trial in a probability experiment.

Resultado   Un resultado es que se obtiene al hacer una sola prueba en un experimento de probabilidad.

Example   The outcomes of rolling a number cube are 1, 2, 3, 4, 5, and 6.

Overlapping events   Overlapping events are events that have at least one common outcome. If A and B are overlapping events, then $P(A \text{ or } B) = P(A) + P(B) - P(A \text{ and } B)$.

Sucesos traslapados   Sucesos traslapados son sucesos que tienen por lo menos un resultado en común. Si A y B son sucesos traslapados, entonces $P(A \text{ ó } B) = P(A) + P(B) - P(A \text{ y } B)$.

Example   Rolling a multiple of 3 and rolling an odd number on a number cube are overlapping events.

$P(\text{multiple of 3 or odd}) = P(\text{multiple of 3}) + P(\text{odd}) - P(\text{multiple of 3 and odd})$
$= \frac{1}{3} + \frac{1}{2} - \frac{1}{6}$
$= \frac{2}{3}$

English

Spanish

P

Parabola   A parabola is the graph of a quadratic function. It is the set of all points *P* in a plane that are the same distance from a fixed point *F*, the focus, as they are from a line *d*, the directrix.

Parábola   La parábola es la gráfica de una función cuadrática. Es el conjunto de todos los puntos *P* situados en un plano a la misma distancia de un punto fijo *F*, o foco, y de la recta *d*, o directriz.

Example

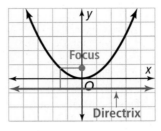

Parameter   A parameter is a piece of data from a whole population, not from a sample.

Parámetro   Un parámetro es un dato de una población completa, no de una muestra.

Pascal's Triangle   Pascal's Triangle is a triangular array of numbers in which the first and last number in each row is 1. Each of the other numbers in the row is the sum of the two numbers above it.

Triángulo de Pascal   El Triángulo de Pascal es una distribución triangular de números en la cual el primer número y el último número son 1. Cada uno de los otros números en la fila es la suma de los dos números de encima.

Example   **Pascal's Triangle**

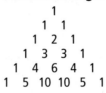

Percentile   A percentile is the percentage of values less than or equal to a particular data value. It is equal to the percentage of the total area under the distribution curve for the population to the left of that value.

Percentil   Un percentil es el porcentaje de valores que es menor que o igual a un valor de datos en particular. Es igual al porcentaje del área total bajo la curva de distribución para la población a la izquierda de ese valor.

Period   The period of a periodic function is the horizontal length of one cycle.

Período   El período de una función periódica es el intervalo horizontal de un ciclo.

Example

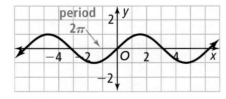

The periodic function $y = \sin x$ has period 2π.

Periodic function   A periodic function repeats a pattern of *y*-values at regular intervals.

Función periódica   Una función periódica repite un patrón de valores *y* a intervalos regulares.

Example

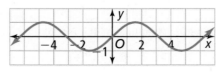

$y = \sin x$

English

Permutation   A permutation is an arrangement of some or all of a set of objects in a specific order. You can use the notation $_nP_r$ to express the number of permutations, where n equals the number of objects available and r equals the number of selections to make.

Example   How many ways can you arrange 5 objects 3 at a time?

$$_5P_3 = \frac{5!}{(5-3)!} = \frac{5!}{2!} = \frac{5 \cdot 4 \cdot 3 \cdot 2 \cdot 1}{2 \cdot 1} = 60$$

There are 60 ways to arrange 5 objects 3 at a time.

Phase shift   A horizontal translation of a periodic function is a phase shift.

Example

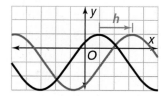

$g(x)$: horizontal translation of $f(x)$
$$g(x) = f(x - h)$$

Piecewise-defined function   A piecewise-defined function has different rules for different parts of its domain.

Polar form of a complex number   The polar form of a complex number $a + bi$ represented on the complex plane is $r(\cos \theta + i \sin \theta)$, where r is the modulus of the number and θ is the argument.

Example $-7 - 4i \approx 8.06 (\cos 3.66 + i\sin 3.66)$
$= 8.06$ cis 3.66

Polynomial   A polynomial is a monomial or the sum or difference of two or more monomials.

Example $3x^3 + 4x^2 - 2x + 5$
$8x$
$x^2 + 4x + 2$

Polynomial function   A polynomial function is a function whose rule is a polynomial.

Example $P(x) = a_n x^n + a_{n-1}x^{n-1} + \ldots + a_1x + a_0$
is a polynomial function, where n is a nonnegative integer and the coefficients $a_n, \ldots, a_0$ are real numbers.

Population   A population is all the members of a set.

Spanish

Permutación   Una permutación es una disposición de algunos o de todos los objetos de un conjunto en un orden determinado. El número de permutaciones se puede expresar con la notación $_nP_r$, donde n es igual al número total de objetos y r es igual al número de selecciones que han de hacerse.

Cambio de fase   Una traslación horizontal de una función periódica es un cambio de fase.

Función definida por partes   Una función de fragmentos tiene reglas diferentes para diferentes partes de su dominio.

Forma polar de un número complejo   La forma polar de un número complejo $a + bi$ representado en el plano complejo es $r(\cos \theta + i \sin \theta)$, donde r es el módulo del número y θ es el argumento.

Polinomio   Un polinomio es un monomio o la suma o la diferencia de dos o más monomios.

Función polinomial   Una función polinomial es una función cuya regla es un polinomio.

Población   Una población está compuesta por los miembros de un conjunto.

English

Probability   Probability is the likelihood that an event will occur (written formally as P(event)).

Example   You have 4 red marbles and 3 white marbles. The probability that you select one red marble, and then, without replacing it, randomly select another red marble is $P(\text{red}) = \frac{4}{7} \cdot \frac{3}{6} = \frac{2}{7}$.

Probability distribution   A probability distribution for an experiment is a function that assigns a probability to each outcome of a sample space for the experiment.

Example

Roll	Fr.	Prob.
1	5	0.125
2	9	0.225
3	7	0.175
4	8	0.2
5	8	0.2
6	3	0.075

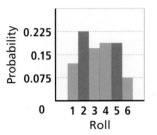

The table and graph both show the experimental probability distribution for the outcomes of 40 rolls of a standard number cube.

Q

Quadratic Formula   The Quadratic Formula is $x = \frac{-b \pm \sqrt{b^2 - 4ac}}{2a}$ for $ax^2 + bx + c = 0$ and $a \neq 0$.

Example   If $-x^2 + 3x + 2 = 0$, then

$$x = \frac{-3 \pm \sqrt{(3)^2 - 4(-1)(2)}}{2(-1)}$$

$$= \frac{-3 \pm \sqrt{17}}{-2}$$

Quadratic function   A quadratic function is a function that you can write in the form $f(x) = ax^2 + bx + c$ with $a \neq 0$.

Example

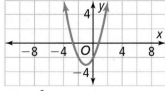

$f(x) = x^2 + 2x - 2$

Quadratic regression   Quadratic regression is a method used to find the quadratic function that best fits a set of data.

Spanish

Probabilidad   Probabilidad es la posibilidad de que un suceso ocurra, escrita formalmente P(suceso).

Distribución de probabilidades   La distribución de probabilidades de un experimento es una función que asigna una probabilidad a cada resultado de un espacio muestral del experimento.

Fórmula cuadrática   La fórmula cuadrática es $x = \frac{-b \pm \sqrt{b^2 - 4ac}}{2a}$ para $ax^2 + bx + c = 0$ y $a \neq 0$.

Función cuadrática   Una función cuadrática es una función que puedes escribir como $f(x) = ax^2 + bx + c$ con $a \neq 0$.

Regresión cuadrática   La regresión cuadrática es un método que se usa para hallar la función cuadrática que más se acerque a un conjunto de datos.

English

Quantitative variable A quantitative variable is a variable for which the possible values are numbers that can be meaningfully counted, added, subtracted, and so on.

Example "Number of apps on a phone" is a quantitative variable.

Quartile Quartiles are values that separate a finite data set into four equal parts. The second quartile (Q_2) is the median of the data. The first and third quartiles (Q_1 and Q_3) are the medians of the lower half and upper half of the data, respectively.

Example $\{2, 3, 4, 5, 5, 6, 7, 7\}$
$Q_1 = 3.5$
Q_2 (median) $= 5$
$Q_3 = 6.5$

R

Radian A radian is the measure of a central angle that intercepts an arc with length equal to the radius of the circle.

Example

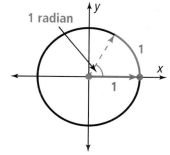

Radian measure Radian measure is the ratio of the length of an intercepted arc and the radius.

Radical function A radical function is a function that can be written in the form $f(x) = a\sqrt[n]{x - h} + k$, where $a \neq 0$. For even values of n, the domain of a radical function is the real numbers $x \geq h$.

Example $f(x) = \sqrt{x - 2}$

Radical symbol The symbol denoting a root is a radical symbol.

Example $\sqrt{}$

Radicand The number under a radical sign is the radicand.

Example The radicand in $3\sqrt[4]{7}$ is 7.

Spanish

Variable cuantitativa Una variable cuantitativa es una variable para la cual los valores posibles son números que se pueden contar, sumar, restar, y así, de manera significativa.

Cuartil Los cuartiles son valores que separan un conjunto finito de datos en cuatro partes iguales. El segundo cuartil (Q_2) es la mediana de los datos. Los cuartiles primero y tercero (Q_1 y Q_3) son las medianas de la mitad superior e inferior de los datos, respectivamente.

Radián Un radián es la medida de un ángulo central que interseca a un arco que tiene una longitud igual al radio del círculo.

Medida en radianes La medida del radián es la razón de la longitud de un arco interceptado y el radio.

Función radical Una función radical es una función quepuede expresarse como $f(x) = a\sqrt[n]{x - h} + k$, donde $a \neq 0$. Para n par, el dominio de la función radical son los números reales tales que $x \geq h$.

Símbolo de radical El símbolo que expresa una raíz es un símbolo de radical.

Radicando La expresión que aparece debajo del signo radical es el radicando.

English	Spanish

Range   The range of a relation is the set of all values of the output, or dependent, variable of a relation or function.

Rango   El rango de una relación es el conjunto de todos los valores de la salida, o variable dependiente, de una relación o una función.

Example   In the relation {(0, 1), (0, 2), (0, 3), (0, 4), (1, 3), (1, 4), (2, 1)}, the range is {1, 2, 3, 4}. In the function $f(x) = |x - 3|$, the range is the set of real numbers greater than or equal to 0.

Range of a set of data   The range of a set of data is the difference between the greatest and least values.

Rango de un conjunto de datos   El rango de un conjunto de datos es la diferencia entre el valor máximo y el valor mínimo de los datos.

Example   The range of the set {3.2, 4.1, 2.2, 3.4, 3.8, 4.0, 4.2, 2.8} is $4.2 - 2.2 = 2$.

Rational equation   A rational equation is an equation that contains a rational expression.

Ecuación racional   Una ecuación racional es una ecuación que contiene una expresión racional.

Rational expression   A rational expression is the quotient of two polynomials.

Expresión racional   Una expresión racional es el cociente de dos polinomios.

Rational function   A rational function $f(x)$ can be written as $f(x) = \frac{P(x)}{Q(x)}$, where $P(x)$ and $Q(x)$ are polynomial functions. The domain of a rational function is all real numbers except those for which $Q(x) = 0$.

Función racional   Una función racional $f(x)$ se puede expresar como $f(x) = \frac{P(x)}{Q(x)}$, donde $P(x)$ y $Q(x)$ son funciones de polinomios. El dominio de una función racional son todos los números reales excepto aquéllos para los cuales $Q(x) = 0$.

Example

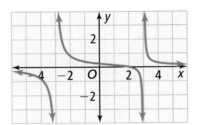

The function $y = \frac{x - 2}{x^2 - 9}$ is a rational function with three branches separated by asymptotes $x = -3$ and $x = 3$.

Real axis   The real axis is the horizontal axis in the complex plane.

Eje real   El eje real es el eje horizontal en el plano complejo.

Example

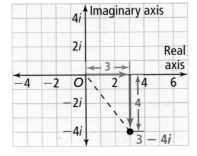

Reciprocal function   The reciprocal function maps every non-zero real number to its reciprocal.

Función recíproca   La función recíproca establece una correspondencia entre cada número real distinto de cero y su recíproco.

Example   The function $f(x) = \frac{1}{x}$ is the reciprocal function.

English

Reciprocal trigonometric functions Trigonometric functions formed by inverting the ratio of a given trigonometric function are reciprocal trigonometric functions.

Example Cosecant, secant, and cotangent are the reciprocal trigonometric functions.

Recursive definition A recursive definition of a sequence is a rule in which each term is defined by operations on the previous term.

Example Let $a_n = 2.5a_{n-1} + 3a_{n-2}$.
If $a_5 = 3$ and $a_4 = 7.5$, then
$a_6 = 2.5(3) + 3(7.5) = 30$.

Reduced radical form Reduced radical form is the form of an expression for which all nth roots of perfect nth powers in the radicand have been simplified and no radicals remain in the denominator.

Example The reduced radical form of $\sqrt{50x^7} = 5x^3\sqrt{2x}$.

Reduced row echelon form A matrix that represents the solution of a system is in reduced row echelon form. The leading 1 in each row has 0's elsewhere in its column.

Reference angle For an angle in standard position, the reference angle is the acute angle formed between the terminal side of the angle and the x-axis.

Example

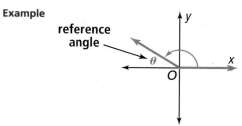

Reference triangle A reference triangle is the triangle formed by drawing a perpendicular line from the terminal point on the unit circle of an angle in standard position to the x-axis.

Example

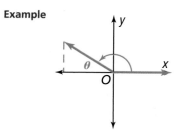

Spanish

Funcións trigonométrica recíproca Las funciones trigonométricas que se forman al invertir la razón de una función trigonométrica dada son funciones trigonométricas recíprocas.

Definición recursiva Una definición recursiva de una sucesión es una regla en la cual cada término se define por operaciones efectuadas en el término anterior.

Forma radical reducida La forma radical reducida es la forma de una expresión en la cual todas las raíces enésimas de potencias enésimas perfectas en el radicando se han simplificado y no quedan radicales en el denominador.

Forma reducida fila-escalón Una matriz que representa la solución de un sistema está en forma reducida fila-escalón. El 1 principal en cada fila tiene ceros en otras partes de la columna.

Ángulo de referencia Para un ángulo en posición estándar, el ángulo de referencia es el ángulo agudo que se forma entre el lado terminal del ángulo y el eje x.

Triángulo de referencia Un triángulo de referencia es el triángulo que se forma al trazar una recta perpendicular desde el punto terminal en el círculo unitario de un ángulo en posición estándar hasta el eje x.

English

Reflection A reflection flips the graph of a function across a line, such as the *x*- or *y*-axis. Each point on the graph of the reflected function is the same distance from the line of reflection as is the corresponding point on the graph of the original function.

Example

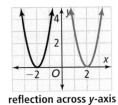

reflection across *y*-axis

Relative frequency The relative frequency of an event is the ratio of the number of times the event occurs to the total number of trials.

Example

Archery Results					
Scoring Region	Yellow	Red	Blue	Black	White
Arrow Strikes	52	25	10	8	5

$$\text{Relative frequency of striking red} = \frac{\text{frequency of striking red}}{\text{total frequencies}}$$
$$= \frac{25}{100} = \frac{1}{4}$$

Relative maximum (minimum) A relative maximum (minimum) is the value of the function at an up-to-down (down-to-up) turning point.

Example

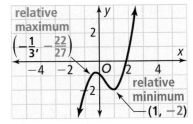

Remainder Theorem If you divide a polynomial $P(x)$ of degree $n > 1$ by $x - a$, then the remainder is $P(a)$.

Example If $P(x) = x^3 - 4x^2 + x + 6$ is divided by $x - 3$, then the remainder is $P(3) = 3^3 - 4(3)^2 + 3 + 6 = 0$ (which means that $x - 3$ is a factor of $P(x)$).

Spanish

Reflexión Una reflexión voltea la gráfica de una función sobre una línea, como el eje de las *x* o el eje de las *y*. Cada punto de la gráfica de la función reflejada está a la misma distancia del eje de reflexión que el punto correspondiente en la gráfica de la función original.

Frecuencia relativa La frecuencia relativa de un suceso es la razón del número de veces que ocurre un evento al número de eventos en el espacio muestral.

Máximo (mínimo) relativo El máximo (mínimo) relativo es el valor de la función en un punto de giro de arriba hacia abajo (de abajo hacia arriba).

Teorema del residuo Si divides un polinomio $P(x)$ con un grado $n > 1$ por $x - a$, el residuo es $P(a)$.

English

Sample   A sample from a population is some of the population.

Example   Let the set of all males between the ages of 19 and 34 be the population. A random selection of 900 males between those ages would be a sample of the population.

Sample space   A sample space is the set of all possible outcomes of a situation or experiment.

Example   When you roll a standard number cube, the sample space is {1, 2, 3, 4, 5, 6}.

Sample survey   A sample survey is a survey in which every member of a sample is asked the same set of questions.

Sampling distribution   A sampling distribution is the distribution of sample statistics from different samples of the same population.

Scalar   A real number factor in a special product, such as the 3 in the vector product $3\vec{v}$, is a scalar.

Scalar multiplication   Scalar multiplication is an operation that multiplies a matrix A by a scalar c. To find the resulting matrix cA, multiply each element of A by c.

Example $2.5 \begin{bmatrix} 1 & 0 \\ -2 & 3 \end{bmatrix} = \begin{bmatrix} 2.5(1) & 2.5(0) \\ 2.5(-2) & 2.5(3) \end{bmatrix}$

$= \begin{bmatrix} 2.5 & 0 \\ -5 & 7.5 \end{bmatrix}$

Secant function   The secant (sec) function is the reciprocal of the cosine function. For all real numbers θ except those that make $\cos \theta = 0$, $\sec \theta = \frac{1}{\cos \theta}$.

Example   If $\cos \theta = \frac{5}{13}$, then $\sec \theta = \frac{13}{5}$.

Self-selected sampling   In self-selected sampling you select only members of the population who volunteered for the sample.

Sequence   A sequence is an ordered list of numbers that often forms a pattern.

Example   1, 4, 7, 10, . . .

Series   A series is the sum of the terms of a sequence.

Example   The series 3 + 6 + 9 + 12 + 15 corresponds to the sequence 3, 6, 9, 12, 15. The sum is 45.

Set-builder notation   Set-builder notation uses a verbal description or an inequality to describe the numbers in a set.

Example $\{x \mid x$ is a real number$\}$
$\{x \mid x > 3\}$

Spanish

Muestra   Una muestra de una población es una parte de la población.

Espacio muestral   Un espacio muestral es el conjunto de todos los resultados posibles de un suceso.

Encuesta muestral   Una encuesta muestral es una encuesta en la cual a cada miembro de una muestra se le hace el mismo conjunto de preguntas.

Distribución muestral   La distribución muestral es la distribución de las estadísticas muestrales de diferentes muestras de la misma población.

Escalar   Un factor que es un número real en un producto especial, como el 3 en el producto vectorial $3\vec{v}$, es un escalar.

Multiplicación escalar   La multiplicación escalar es la que multiplica una matriz A por un número escalar c. Para hallar la matriz cA resultante, multiplica cada elemento de A por c.

Función secante   La función secante (sec) es el recíproco de la función coseno. Para todos los números reales θ, excepto aquéllos para los que $\cos \theta = 0$, $\sec \theta = \frac{1}{\cos \theta}$.

Muestra de voluntarios   En una muestra de voluntarios se seleccionan sólo a los miembros de la población que se ofrecen voluntariamente para ser parte de la muestra.

Progresión   Una progresión es una sucesión de números que suelen formar un patrón.

Serie   Una serie es la suma de los términos de una secuencia.

Notación conjuntista   La notación conjuntista usa una descripción verbal o una desigualdad para describir los números.

English

Sigma notation   Sigma notation denotes a sum of terms. The terms to be added are formed by evaluating an expression for a specified range of values.

Example $\displaystyle\sum_{n=1}^{5} 2n - 1 = 1 + 3 + 5 + 7 + 9 = 25$

Simple Random Sample   A simple random sample is a sample where each member of the population is equally likely to be chosen, and for all n, each sample of size n is equally likely to be chosen.

Simplest form of a radical expression   A radical expression with index n is in simplest form if there are no radicals in any denominator, no denominators in any radical, and any radicand has no nth power factors.

Simplified form of a rational expression   A rational expression is in simplified form if its numerator and denominator are polynomials that have no common divisor other than 1.

Example $\dfrac{x^2 - 7x + 12}{x^2 - 9} = \dfrac{(x - 4)(x - 3)}{(x + 3)(x - 3)} = \dfrac{x - 4}{x + 3}$, where $x \neq -3$

Sine   In a right triangle, the sine of an acute angle is the ratio of the length of the side opposite the angle to the length of the hypotenuse.

Example

In this triangle, $\sin \theta = \dfrac{4}{5}$.

Skewed distribution   A skewed distribution is a distribution whose shape is stretched out in either the positive or negative direction.

Example

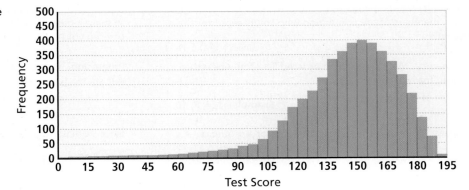

This distribution is skewed left.

Spanish

Notación sigma   La notación sigma indica una suma de sumandos. Los sumandos que se deben sumar se identifican al evaluar una expresión para un rango determinado de valores.

Muestra aleatoria simple   Una muestra aleatoria simple es una muestra donde la probabilidad de ser seleccionado es igual para todos los miembros de la población, y para todos los valores de n, la probabilidad de ser seleccionado es igual para cada muestra de tamaño n.

Mínima expresión de una expresión radical   Una expresión radical con índice n está en su mínima expresión si no tiene radicales en ningún denominador ni denominadores en ningún radical y los radicandos no tienen factores de potencia.

Forma simplificada de una expresión racional   Una expresión racional se encuentra en su mínima expresión si su numerador y su denominador son polinomios que no tienen otro divisor aparte de 1.

Seno   En un triángulo rectángulo, el seno de un ángulo agudo es la razón de la longitud del cateto opuesto al ángulo a la longitud de la hipotenusa.

Distribución asimétrica   Una distribución asimétrica es una distribución cuya forma se extiende en dirección positiva o en dirección negativa.

English

Spanish

Solution of a system of linear equations   A solution of a system of linear equations is a set of values for the variables that makes all the equations true.

Solución de un sistema de ecuaciones lineales   Una solución de un sistema de ecuaciones lineales es un conjunto de valores para las variables que hace que todas las ecuaciones sean verdaderas.

Square matrix   A square matrix is a matrix with the same number of columns as rows.

Matriz cuadrada   Una matriz cuadrada es la que tiene la misma cantidad de columnas y filas.

Example   Matrix A is a square matrix.

$$A = \begin{bmatrix} 1 & 2 & 0 \\ -1 & 0 & -2 \\ 1 & 2 & 3 \end{bmatrix}$$

Standard deviation   Standard deviation is a measure of how much the values in a data set vary, or deviate, from the mean, $\bar{x}$.

Desviación típica   La desviación típica denota cuánto los valores de un conjunto de datos varían, o se desvían, de la media, $\bar{x}$.

Example $\{0, 2, 3, 4, 6, 7, 8, 9, 10, 11\}$
$\bar{x} = 6$
standard deviation $= \sqrt{12} \approx 3.46$

Standard form of the equation of a circle   The standard form of the equation of a circle with center (h, k) and radius r is $(x - h)^2 + (y - k)^2 = r^2$.

Forma normal de la ecuación de un círculo   La forma normal de la ecuación de un círculo con centro en (h, k) y un radio r es $(x - h)^2 + (y - k)^2 = r^2$.

Example $(x - 3)^2 + (y - 4)^2 = 4$

Standard form of a polynomial function   The standard form of a polynomial function arranges the terms by degree in descending numerical order. A polynomial function, $P(x)$, in standard form is $P(x) = a_n x^n + a_{n-1} x^{n-1} + \cdots + a_1 x + a_0$, where n is a nonnegative integer and $a_n, \ldots, a_0$ are real numbers.

Forma normal de una función polinomial   La forma normal de una función polinomial organiza los términos por grado en orden numérico descendiente. Una función polinomial, $P(x)$, en forma normal es $P(x) = a_n x^n + a_{n-1} x^{n-1} + \cdots + a_1 x + a_0$, donde n es un número entero no negativo y $a_n, \ldots, a_0$ son números reales.

Example $2x^3 - 5x^2 - 2x + 5$

Standard form of a quadratic function   The standard form of a quadratic function is $f(x) = ax^2 + bx + c$ with $a \neq 0$.

Forma normal de una función cuadrática   La forma normal de una función cuadrática es $f(x) = ax^2 + bx + c$ con $a \neq 0$.

Example $f(x) = 2x^2 + 5x + 2$

Standard form of the equation of a hyperbola   The standard form of the equation of a hyperbola with the center at the origin is $\frac{x^2}{a^2} - \frac{y^2}{b^2} = 1$ when the hyperbola opens horizontally.

Forma normal de la ecuación de una hipérbola   La forma normal de la ecuación de una hipérbola con centro en el origen es $\frac{x^2}{a^2} - \frac{y^2}{b^2} = 1$ donde la hipérbola se abre de forma horizontal.

Example $\frac{x^2}{25} - \frac{y^2}{9} = 1$

Standard form of the equation of an ellipse   The standard form of the equation of an ellipse with the center at the origin is $\frac{x^2}{b^2} + \frac{y^2}{a^2} = 1$ when the major axis is vertical and $\frac{x^2}{a^2} + \frac{y^2}{b^2} = 1$ when the major axis is horizontal.

Forma normal de la ecuación de una elipse   La forma normal de la ecuación de una elipse con centro en el origen es $\frac{x^2}{b^2} + \frac{y^2}{a^2} = 1$ donde el eje mayor es vertical y $\frac{x^2}{a^2} + \frac{y^2}{b^2} = 1$ cuando el eje mayor es horizontal.

Example $\frac{x^2}{4} + \frac{y^2}{16} = 1$ or $\frac{x^2}{16} + \frac{y^2}{4} = 1$

English

Spanish

Standard normal distribution The standard normal distribution is a normal distribution with mean 0 and standard deviation 1.

Distribución normal estándar La distribución normal estándar es una distribución normal con una media de 0 y una desviación típica de 1.

Example

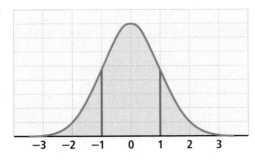

Standard position An angle in the coordinate plane is in standard position when the vertex is at the origin and one ray is on the positive *x*-axis.

Posición estándar Un ángulo en el plano de coordenadas se encuentra en posición estándar si el vértice se encuentra en el origen y una semirrecta se encuentra en el eje *x* positivo.

Example

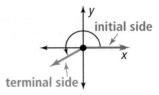

Statistic A statistic is a piece of data from a sample, not a whole population.

Estadística Una estadística es un dato tomado de una muestra, no de una población completa.

Statistical question A statistical question is a question that can be answered by collecting many pieces of information, or data, and summarizing the data.

Pregunta estadística Una pregunta estadística es una pregunta que se puede responder reuniendo mucha información, o datos, y resumiéndola.

Example "What month has the most birthdays of students at your school?"

Statistical variable A statistical variable is a quantity or quality for which data are expected to differ.

Variable estadística Una variable estadística es una cantidad o cualidad para la cual se anticipan variaciones en los datos.

Step function A step function pairs every number in an interval with a single value. The graph of a step function can look like the steps of a staircase.

Función escalón Una función escalón empareja cada número de un intervalo con un solo valor. La gráfica de una función escalón se puede parecer a los peldaños de una escalera.

English

Stretch   A stretch is a transformation that increases the distance between the points of a graph and a given line by the same factor.

Spanish

Estiramiento   Un estiramiento es una transformación que aumenta por el mismo factor la distancia entre los puntos de una gráfica y una recta dada.

Example

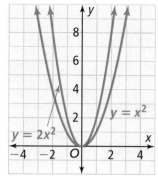

Symmetric distribution   A symmetric distribution is a distribution whose shape is evenly distributed around the mean.

Distribución simétrica   Una distribución simétrica es una distribución cuya forma está distribuida en forma pareja alrededor de la media.

Example

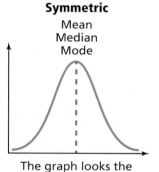

Symmetric

Mean
Median
Mode

The graph looks the same on both sides.

Synthetic division   Synthetic division is a process for dividing a polynomial by a linear expression $x - a$.

División sintética   La división sintética es un proceso para dividir un polinomio por una expresión lineal $x - a$.

Example

$$-3 \,\big|\; \begin{array}{ccccc} 2 & 5 & 0 & -2 & -8 \\ & -6 & 3 & -9 & 33 \\ \hline 2 & -1 & 3 & -11 & 25 \end{array}$$

Divide $2x^4 + 5x^3 - 2x - 8$ by $x + 3$. $2x^4 + 5x^3 - 2x - 8$ divided by $x + 3$ gives $2x^3 - x^2 + 3x - 11$ as quotient and 25 as remainder.

System of linear equations   A system of equations is a set of two or more equations using the same variables.

Sistema de ecuaciones lineales   Un sistema de ecuaciones es un conjunto de dos o más ecuaciones que contienen las mismas variables.

Example

$$\begin{cases} 2x - 3y = -13 \\ 4x + 5y = 7 \end{cases}$$

English

Spanish

System of linear inequalities   A system of linear inequalities is a set of two or more linear inequalities using the same variables.

Sistema de desigualdades lineales   Un sistema de desigualdades lineales es un conjunto de dos o más desigualdades lineales que contienen las mismas variables.

$$\text{Example} \quad x + 2y < 5$$
$$3x - 2y > -1$$

Tangent   In a right triangle, tangent of an acute angle is the ratio of the length of the side opposite the angle to the length of the side adjacent to the angle. It is also equal to the ratio of the sine of the angle to the cosine of the angle.

Tangente   En un triángulo rectángulo, la tangente de un ángulo agudo es la razón de la longitud del cateto opuesto al ángulo a la longitud del cateto adyacente a dicho ángulo. También es igual a la razón del seno del ángulo al coseno de dicho ángulo.

Term of an expression   A term is a number, a variable, or the product of a number and one or more variables.

Término de una expresión   Un término es un número, una variable o el producto de un número y una o más variables.

$$\text{Example} \quad \text{The expression } 4x^2 - 3y + 7.3$$
$$\text{has 3 terms.}$$

Terminal point   The terminal point of a vector is the tip (not the starting point) of a vector arrow.

Punto terminal   El punto terminal de un vector es la punta (no el extremo) de una flecha vectorial.

Terminal side   *See* **Initial side.**

Lado terminal   *Ver* **Initial side.**

Theoretical probability   The theoretical probability is the ratio of the number of favorable outcomes to the number of possible outcomes if all outcomes have the same chance of happening.

Probabilidad teórica   Si cada resultado tiene la misma probabilidad de darse, la probabilidad teórica de un suceso se calcula como la razón del número de resultados favorables al número de resultados posibles.

$$P(\text{event}) = \frac{\text{number of favorable outcomes}}{\text{number of possible outcomes}}$$

$$P(\text{suceso}) = \frac{\text{numero de resultados favorables}}{\text{numero de resultados posibles}}$$

Example   In tossing a coin, the events of getting heads or tails are equally likely. The likelihood of getting heads is $P(\text{heads}) = \frac{1}{2}$.

Transformation   A transformation of a function maps each point of its graph to a new location.

Transformación   Una transformación de una función desplaza cada punto de su gráfica a una ubicación nueva.

$$\text{Example} \quad g(x) = 2(x - 3) \text{ is a transformation}$$
$$\text{of } f(x) = x.$$

Translation   A translation shifts the graph of the parent function horizontally, vertically, or both.

Traslación   Una traslación desplaza la gráfica de la función madre horizontalmente, verticalmente o en ambas direcciones.

Example

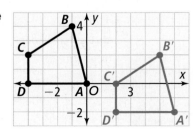

Go Online | SavvasRealize.com

English

Transverse axis   The transverse axis of a hyperbola is the segment that is on the line containing the foci and has endpoints on the hyperbola.

Example

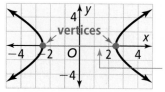

Trigonometric identity   A trigonometric identity in one variable is a trigonometric equation that is true for all values of the variable for which both sides of the equation are defined.

Example $\tan \theta = \dfrac{\sin \theta}{\cos \theta}$

Turning point   A turning point of the graph of a function is a point where the graph changes direction from upward to downward or from downward to upward.

Two-way frequency table   A two-way frequency table is a table that displays frequencies in two different categories.

Example

	Male	Female	Totals
Juniors	3	4	7
Seniors	3	2	5
Totals	6	6	12

The last column shows a total of 7 juniors and 5 seniors.
The last row shows a total of 6 males and 6 females.

U

Uniform probability distribution   A uniform probability distribution assigns the same probability to each outcome.

Unit circle   The unit circle has a radius of 1 unit and its center is at the origin of the coordinate plane.

Example

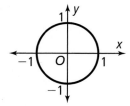

Spanish

Eje transversal   El eje transversal de una hipérbola es el segmento que se encuentra sobre la línea que contiene los focos y tiene sus puntos extremos sobre la hipérbola.

Identidad trigonométrica   Una identidad trigonométrica en una variable es una ecuación trigonométrica que es verdadera para todos los valores de la variable para los cuales se definen los dos lados de la ecuación.

Punto de giro   Un punto de giro de la gráfica de una función es un punto donde la gráfica cambia de dirección de arriba hacia abajo o vice versa.

Tabla de frecuencias de doble entrada   Una tabla de frecuencias de doble entrada es una tabla de frecuencias que contiene dos categorías de datos.

Distribución uniforme de probabilidad   Una distribución uniforme de probabilidad le asigna la misma probabilidad a cada resultado.

Círculo unitario   El círculo unitario tiene un radio de 1 unidad y el centro está situado en el origen del plano de coordenadas.

English

Spanish

Variable matrix   A variable matrix is a one-column matrix that contains the variables of a system of equations.

Matriz variable   Una matriz variable es una matriz de una sola columna que contiene las variables de un sistema de ecuaciones.

Example $\begin{cases} x + 2y = 5 \\ 3x + 5y = 14 \end{cases}$
variable matrix $\begin{bmatrix} x \\ y \end{bmatrix}$

Vector   A vector is a mathematical object that has both magnitude and direction.

Vector   Un vector es un objeto matemático que tiene tanto magnitud como dirección.

Vertex form of a quadratic function   The vertex form of a quadratic function is $f(x) = a(x - h)^2 + k$, where $a \ne 0$ and (h, k) is the vertex of the function.

Forma del vértice de una función cuadrática   La forma vértice de una función cuadrática es $f(x) = a(x - h)^2 + k$, donde $a \ne 0$ y (h, k) es el vértice de la función.

Example $f(x) = x^2 + 2x - 1 = (x + 1)^2 - 2$
The vertex is $(-1, -2)$.

Vertices of a hyperbola   The endpoints of the transverse axis of a hyperbola are the vertices of the hyperbola.

Vértices de una hipérbola   Los dos puntos de intersección de la hipérbola y su eje mayor son los vértices de la hipérbola.

Example
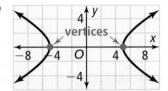

Vertices of an ellipse   The endpoints of the major axis of an ellipse are the vertices of the ellipse.

Vértices de una elipse   Los dos puntos de intersección de la elipse y su eje mayor son los vértices de la elipse.

Example
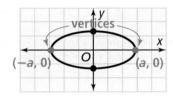

x-intercept, y-intercept   The point at which a line crosses the x-axis (or the x-coordinate of that point) is an x-intercept. The point at which a line crosses the y-axis (or the y-coordinate of that point) is a y-intercept.

Intercepto en x, intercepto en y   El punto donde una recta corta el eje x (o la coordenada x de ese punto) es el intercepto en x. El punto donde una recta cruza el eje y (o la coordenada y de ese punto) es el intercepto en y.

Example
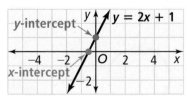

The x-intercept of $y = 2x + 1$ is $\left(-\frac{1}{2}, 0\right)$ or $-\frac{1}{2}$
The y-intercept of $y = 2x + 1$ is $(0, 1)$ or 1.

English

Z

Zero matrix   The zero matrix O, or $O_{m \times n}$, is the $m \times n$ matrix whose elements are all zeros. It is the additive identity matrix for the set of all $m \times n$ matrices.

Zero of a function   A zero of a function is an x-intercept of the graph of a function.

Zero-Product Property   If the product of two or more factors is zero, then at least one of the factors must be zero.

z-score   The z-score of a value is the number of standard deviations that the value is from the mean.

Spanish

Matriz cero   La matriz cero, O, o $O_{m \times n}$, es la matriz $m \times n$ cuyos elementos son todos ceros. Es la matriz de identidad aditiva para el conjunto de todas las matrices $m \times n$.

Example $\begin{bmatrix} 1 & 4 \\ 2 & -3 \end{bmatrix} + O = \begin{bmatrix} 1 & 4 \\ 2 & -3 \end{bmatrix}$

Cero de una función   Un cero de una función es un intercepto en x de la gráfica de una función.

Example

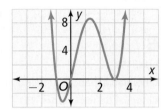

Propiedad del cero del producto   Si el producto de dos o más factores es cero, entonces al menos uno de los factores debe ser cero.

Example $(x - 3)(2x - 5) = 0$
$x - 3 = 0$ or $2x - 5 = 0$

Puntaje z   El puntaje z de un valor es el número de desviaciones normales que tiene ese valor de la media.

Example $\{0, 2, 3, 4, 6, 7, 8, 9, 10, 11\}$
$\bar{x} = 6$
standard deviation $= \sqrt{12} \approx 3.46$
For 8, z-score $= \dfrac{8 - 6}{\sqrt{12}} \approx 0.58$.

VISUAL GLOSSARY

Index

A

absolute value functions, 26

addition
- of complex numbers, 96, 443–444
- of functions, 273–274
- of matrices, 505–506
- of polynomials, 139
- of radical expressions, 250
- of rational expressions, 217, 218
- of vectors, 520

alternative hypothesis, 590

amplitude, 384

angles
- complement of, 361
- cosine of, 376–377
- coterminal, 366
- initial side, 365
- measure of, 365–366
- radian measure, 369
- reference, 367–368
- sine of, 376–377
- terminal side, 365
- unit circle and, 368–369

Application Example, 7, 19, 27, 33, 36, 41, 48, 51, 61, 75, 82, 90, 105, 113, 118, 135, 141, 142, 157, 165, 172, 183, 195, 205, 213, 225, 228, 241, 243, 250, 259, 264, 268, 274, 277, 286, 301, 308, 309, 317, 329, 335, 342, 345, 359, 372, 379, 387, 395, 403, 404, 418, 425, 429, 437, 467, 474, 484, 493, 504, 505, 521, 533, 540, 551, 553, 554, 561, 577, 581, 582, 590, 593, 606, 609, 616, 624, 630, 638, 643, 645

arc length, 372

area
- of a parallelogram, 533
- of a triangle, 532

argument, 449

arithmetic sequences
- common differences, 31
- defined, 31
- explicit definition, 33
- recursive definition, 32
- recursive formula, 33
- sum of terms, 34

arithmetic series, 34–37

asymptotes
- defined, 196
- of exponential functions, 297–298
- horizontal, 202–203
- of logarithmic functions, 321

- of rational functions, 201–204
- vertical, 202

augmented matrix, 50

average rate of change, 9

axes
- of the complex plane, 441–442
- of ellipses, 480
- of hyperbola, 489
- imaginary, 441–442
- real, 441–442

B

bias, 559

binomial, expand a power of a, 149

binomial denominators, 251

binomial experiments, 631–632

binomial probability, 632, 639

Binomial Probability Formula, 632

binomial radical expressions, 251

Binomial Theorem, 150

C

categorical variables, 552–553

center
- of circles, 475
- of hyperbola, 489

change, average rate of, 9

Change of Base, 329–330

circles
- center of, 475
- conic section, 463
- equation of, 472–473
- graphing, 473
- radius of, 475
- real-world application, 474
- standard form of the equation of, 472–473
- trigonometric functions and, 376–377
- verifying trigonometric identities, 433–434

classification
- data distributions, 569
- of polynomials, 131
- second-degree equations, 494

closure, 140

coefficient matrix, 50

cofunction, 361

cofunction identities, 361, 434

combinations, 620–621, 623–624

common difference, 31

Common Error, 8, 16, 24, 31, 41, 42, 50, 59, 75, 82, 84, 91, 97, 106, 119, 134, 148, 150, 156, 158, 171, 180, 183, 194, 204, 211, 212, 219, 225, 242, 248, 264, 267, 275, 284, 298, 305, 307, 308, 317, 322, 329, 334, 344, 359, 365, 377, 386, 394, 401, 417, 428, 434, 445, 539, 552, 553, 559, 566, 576, 584, 592, 608, 613, 621, 630, 636, 655

common logarithms, 316

common ratio (r), 340

complement
- of angles, 361
- of an event, 606

completing the square
- defined, 104
- finding center and radius of a circle, 475
- finding focus and directrix, 468
- process of, 104
- real-world application, 105–106
- solving quadratic equations by, 103, 104

complex conjugates, 97

complex numbers
- adding, 96, 443–444
- calculating powers of, 453
- on the complex plane, 441–445
- conjugates, 97
- defined, 96
- finding distance between, 445
- modulus of, 443
- multiplying, 97, 451–453
- polar form of, 449–453
- rectangular form of, 450
- simplify a quotient with, 97–98
- subtracting, 96, 443–444

complex plane
- axes of the, 441–442
- complex numbers in the, 441–445
- defined, 441
- midpoints, 442

component form of vectors, 519

composite function, 276–277

composition of functions, 276, 285

compound fractions, 220

compound interest, 306

compressions, defined, 16

equations. *see also* solving equations;
  systems of equations; systems of
  linear equations
  of circles, 472–473
  of ellipses, 481, 483
  from graphs, 19
  of hyperbola, 490–492
  identifying transformations from, 18
  of inverse functions, 284
  of parabolas, 75–76, 83, 91, 464, 466
  polynomial. *see* polynomial equations
  quadratic. *see* quadratic equations
  radical, 263, 265, 267
  rational. *see* rational equations
  second-degree, 463, 494
  in standard form, 472–473, 491
  of transformations, 76, 258

even functions, 179–181

expected value
  decision-making based on, 645
  defined, 636–639

experimental group, 561

experiments
  binomial, 631–632
  defined, 558
  randomizing, 561

explicit definition of a sequence, 32,
  341–342

Explore & Reason, 5, 13, 47, 73, 95,
  110, 117, 131, 139, 146, 154, 179,
  201, 210, 239, 255, 263, 281, 297,
  305, 321, 327, 340, 357, 365, 376,
  383, 393, 433, 449, 463, 489, 511,
  528, 551, 573, 589, 605, 613, 621,
  635, 647

Exponential Decay Model, 300

exponential equations
  defined, 333
  logarithms to rewrite, 334
  Property of Equality for Exponential
    Equations, 333
  solving by graphing, 336
  solving using a common base, 333
  solving using logarithms, 334

Exponential Form, 315

exponential functions
  comparing, 301
  defined, 297
  interpreting, 300–301
  inverses of, 322
  key features, 297–298
  transformations, 298

exponential growth, 297–298

Exponential Growth Model, 300

exponential models
  compound interest, 306
  continuously compounded
    interest, 307

exponential decay, 300
exponential growth, 300
finding using regression, 309
finding using two points, 308
general, 305

exponents
  fractional, 240
  rational, 240

expressions
  adding, 217–218, 250
  dividing, 212–214
  factoring, 88
  multiplying, 147, 211–212, 251
  quadratic, 88
  radical, 247–251
  rational. *see* rational expressions
  simplifying, 148
  subtracting, 219, 250
  trigonometric identities to rewrite,
    434–435

extraneous solutions, 226–227, 265

F

Factor Theorem, 157–158

factoring
  quadratic expressions, 88–89
  solving quadratic equations
    using, 98
  sum of squares, 98

finite arithmetic series, 34

finite series, 34

focus
  of an ellipse, 480
  of hyperbola, 489
  of a parabola, 464, 465, 468

formulas
  Binomial Probability Formula, 632
  Change of Base Formula, 329–330
  conditional probability, 615
  continuously compounded
    interest, 307
  Difference Formulas, 435–437
  Midpoint Formula, 442
  Quadratic Formula, 110–111
  Sum Formulas, 435–437
  sum of a finite geometric series,
    343–344

fractional exponents, 240

fractions, compound, 220

frequency, 385

functions
  absolute value, 26
  adding, 273–274
  average rate of change, 9
  composing, 275–277
  composite, 276
  composition of, 276, 285
  compressions of, 16

cube root, 255–256
cubic, 181–183
decreasing, 8
dividing, 275
domain, 5–6
end behavior, 297–298, 321
even, 179–181
exponential. *see* exponential
  functions
graphs of. *see* graphs of functions
increasing, 8
intervals, 8, 91
inverse, 193–195, 281–285
linear, 5–10
logarithmic, 315, 321–323
maximum values, 8
minimum values, 8
multiplying, 274–275
odd, 179–181
periodic, 383–385, 388
piecewise-defined, 23–26
polynomial. *see* polynomial
  functions
quadratic. *see* quadratic functions
quartic, 181–182
radical, 256–258
range of, 5–6
rational, 201–205, 206
reciprocal, 193–197, 379
reflections, 14
square root, 255–256
step, 27
stretches of, 15–16
subtracting, 273–274
transformations of, 13–20, 74, 76,
  181–183, 256–258, 298, 322
translations of, 13–14
trigonometric. *see* trigonometric
  functions
zeros of, 7, 89–90, 162–165

Fundamental Counting Principle,
620–621

Fundamental Theorem of Algebra, 173

G

geometric sequence
  common ratio (*r*) in, 340
  defined, 340
  explicit definition, 341–342
  recursive definition, 341–342

geometric series
  defined, 343
  finite, number of terms in, 344
  formula for the sum of a finite,
    343–344

Glossary, G2–G33

graphs
  amplitude, 384
  circles on, 473
  of ellipses, 482, 485

random sample, 560

range
  exponential functions, 297–298
  logarithmic functions, 321

rate of change, 9

rational equations
  defined, 224
  with extraneous solutions, 226–227
  solving, 224–227

rational exponents
  interpreting, 240
  properties of, 247–248
  solving equations with, 266

rational expressions
  adding, 217, 218
  defined, 202, 210
  dividing, 212–214
  equivalent, 210–211
  multiplying, 211–212
  simplified form of, 211
  subtracting, 219

rational functions
  asymptotes of, 201–204
  defined, 202
  graphing, 201–204, 206

Rational Root Theorem, 172

ratios, trigonometric, 357–361

real axis, 441–442

reciprocal functions, 193–197, 379

reciprocals, 357, 361

rectangular form of complex
  numbers, 450

recursive definition of a sequence, 32,
  341–342

recursive formula, 33

reduced row echelon form of a matrix,
  57–58, 60

reference angles, 367–368

reference triangle, 368, 376–377

reflections, 14

regression
  finding exponential models
    using, 309
  quadratic, 84

relative maximum, 133

relative minimum, 133

Remainder Theorem, 157–158

resampling, 591

roots
  nth, 239, 242–243
  of polynomials, 171–175

row operations, matrix, 56–57

S

sample survey, 558

samples
  defined, 553
  populations vs., 553–554

sampling distributions, 581–586

sampling methods, 560–561

scalar, 504

scalar multiplication, 504, 522–523

secant, 357, 396

sequences
  arithmetic, 31–37
  defined, 31
  geometric, 340–342
  writing sum of terms in, 35

series
  arithmetic, 34–37
  finite, 34
  finite arithmetic, 34
  geometric, 343–344

set-builder notation, 5–6

sigma notation, 35

simple random sample, 560

simplified form of rational
  expressions, 211

simulations
  evaluating hypotheses using, 592
  finding margin of error, 583–585

sine, 357, 376–377, 383–388, 401–402

skewed distribution, 566

solving equations
  by completing the square, 103, 104
  exponential equations, 333, 334, 336
  extraneous solutions, 226–227, 265
  by factoring, 89, 98
  linear equations, 47, 49, 56–62,
    537–540
  linear-quadratic systems, 118,
    120, 475
  logarithmic equations, 336
  polynomial equations, 166
  quadratic equations, 89, 95, 98,
    103–104, 110–112
  radical equations, 263, 265–267
  rational equations, 224–225
  systems of linear equations, 56–62,
    537–540
  trigonometric, 418
  using a common base, 333
  using circles, 475
  using graphs, 40–43, 120, 336
  using logarithms, 317, 334
  using matrices, 56–62, 537–540
  using rational exponents, 266
  using square roots, 95, 103

using substitution, 118
using tables, 42–43
using the quadratic formula,
  110–112
with infinitely many solutions, 60
with one radical, 263
with three variables, 49, 61
with two radicals, 267

solving inequalities
  linear, 48
  linear-quadratic, 119–120
  with one variable, 41–42
  polynomial, 166–167
  using graphs, 40–42, 166–167

Spanish vocabulary, G2–G33

square matrices, 512–513

square root, 95, 103

square root functions, 255–256

squares, factoring a sum of, 98

standard deviation, 565

standard form
  of the equation for a hyperbola, 491
  of the equation of a circle, 472
  of the equation of an ellipse, 481
  of polynomials, 131
  of quadratic functions, 80–81

standard normal distribution, 577

standard position, 365

statistical questions
  defined, 551
  graphing, 552

statistical studies
  bias in, 559–560
  choosing, 558–559
  experiment, 558
  observational study, 558
  sample survey, 558

statistical variables, 552

statistics
  defined, 554
  parameters vs., 554

STEM
  Analyze Elections, 296
  Analyzing Traffic with Markov
    Chains, 502
  Design a Roller Coaster, 414
  Design a Stadium, 130
  Design a Whispering Gallery, 462
  Design Space Goggles, 356
  Fuel efficiency, 4
  Hit a Home Run, 72
  Manufacturing Costs, 192
  Plan a Public Space, 550
  Simulate Weather Conditions, 604
  Tune a Piano, 238

W

writing
    polynomial functions, 141
    radical expressions, 247–249
    sum of terms in sequences, 35

writing equations
    of circles, 473
    of ellipses, 483
    exponential, 334
    from graphs, 19, 75–76
    of hyperbolas, 492
    of parabolas, 75–76, 83, 91
    from points, 83

X

***x*-axis, reflections,** 14–15
***x*-intercept,** 6, 298, 321

Y

***y*-axis, reflections,** 14–15
***y*-intercept,** 6, 298, 321

Z

zero matrix, 506
Zero Product Property, 89
zeros
    complex, 164
    multiplicity of, 163
    real, 164

zeros of a function
    defined, 7
    factors related to, 89–90
    polynomial functions, 162–165
    quadratic, 90

***z*-scores,** 576–577

Acknowledgments

Photographs

Cover
Kennethbarker/Moment/Getty Images

Topic 01
003 Dibas99/Fotolia; **006** The lefty/Fotolia; **007** Steve Lovegrove/Fotolia; **019** Jan Gorzynik/123RF; **046** Artazum/Shutterstock; **055** Dibas99/Fotolia; **063** Tomasz Nieweglowski/Shutterstock

Topic 02
071 Aksonov/E+/Getty Images; **079** Historic American Engineering Record, creator/Library of Congress Prints and Photographs Division; **087** Westend61/Getty Images; **102** Aksonov/E+/Getty Images

Topic 03
129 Danmorgan12/Fotolia; **170** Danmorgan12/Fotolia; **178T** Roger Costa morera/123RF; **178B** Mkos83/Fotolia; **186TL** Stratos Giannikos/Fotolia; **186TR** Georgiy Pashin/Fotolia

Topic 04
191 Aerogondo/iStock/Getty Images; **195** AlexMaster/Shutterstock; **205** Urbanhearts/Fotolia; **232** Aerogondo/iStock/Getty Images

Topic 05
237 Christian Fallini/Fotolia; **241** Willoughby Owen/Moment/Getty Images; **245** Paul A. Hebert/Invision/AP Images; **261** Netfalls/Fotolia; **264** Kris Wiktor/Shutterstock; **272** Willoughby Owen/Moment/Getty Images

Topic 06
295 Fuse/Corbis/Getty Images; **313** Fuse/Corbis/Getty Images; **320** John Henshall/Alamy Stock Photo

Topic 07
355 Pearson Education inc; **375** Epa European Pressphoto Agency b.v./Alamy Stock Photo; **392** Pearson Education inc

Topic 08
413 Pearson Education inc; **418** Kovgabor/Shutterstock; **422** Hisham Ibrahim/The Image Bank/Getty Images; **355** Pearson Education inc; **432** Premium Collection/Fotolia; **440** Zhao Jiankang/123RF; **448** Scott Camazine/Alamy Stock Photo

Topic 09
461 Pearson Education inc; **467** Dinodia Photos/Alamy Stock Photo; **471B** DOE Photo/Alamy Stock Photo; **471T** Heather Drake/Alamy Stock Photo; **479** Pearson Education inc; **484** Peter Barritt/Robertharding/Alamy Stock Photo; **488L** G.A. Rossi/Arco Images GmbH/Alamy Stock Photo; **488R** WDC Photos/Alamy Stock Photo

Topic 10
501 Gerald McDonald/Alamy Stock Photo; **536** Destina/Fotolia; **544** Gerald McDonald/Alamy Stock Photo

Topic 11
549 Animal Stock/Alamy Stock Photo; **553TL** Blue Jean Images/Alamy Stock Photo; **553TR** David Schaffer/Caia Image/Alamy Stock Photo; **553BL** H.Mark Weidman Photography/Alamy Stock Photo; **553BR** Phil Boorman/Cultura Creative (RF)/Alamy Stock Photo; **556** Imagebroker/Alamy Stock Photo; **557** Jonathan Larsen/Diadem Images/Alamy Stock Photo; **558T** Koji Niino/Mixa/Alamy Stock Photo; **558B** Richard Levine/Alamy Stock Photo; **558C** Hybrid Images/Cultura Creative (RF)/Alamy Stock Photo; **559L** Andy Dean Photography/Shutterstock/Asset Library; **559R** David Grossman/Alamy Stock Photo; **572** Neirfy/Fotolia; **573L** Budimir Jevtic/Fotolia; **573R** Olaf Speier/Fotolia; **577** Andrew Bignell/ShutterStock; **580** Aflo Co., Ltd./Alamy Stock Photo; **597** Animal Stock/Alamy Stock Photo

Acknowledgments

Topic 12

603 Jacques Beauchamp/Glow Images; **620** Jacques Beauchamp/Glow Images;
648 Blackregis/123RF

STEM

004B 3DDock/Shutterstock; **004BR** PhoelixDE/Shutterstock; **004C** Kolopach/Shutterstock;
004CR gorbovoi81/Fotolia; **004ML** Jaochainoi/Shutterstock; **004TC** National Motor Museum/
Motoring Picture Library/Alamy Stock Photo; **004TC** Denebola_h/Fotolia; 004TL EV_Korobov/
Fotolia; **004TR** eVox/Drive Images/Alamy Stock Photo; **072** Chuck Franklin/Alamy Stock Photo;
072 Dejan Popovic/Shutterstock; **072** Tim Sharp/Reuters/Alamy Stock Photo;
072 Chingachgook/Shutterstock; **072** learchitecto/Fotolia; **156B** Andrejco/Fotolia;
156C Mark Herreid/Alamy Stock Photo; **156TL** Peter Tsai Photography/Alamy Stock Photo;
156TR Fotokostic/Shutterstock; **192B** Minerva Studio/Fotolia; **192C** Roger Bacon/Reuters/
Alamy Stock Photo; **192T** Monty Rakusen/Cultura Creative/Alamy Stock Photo;
238 Chris Stock /Lebrecht Music & Arts/Lebrecht Music and Arts Photo Library/Alamy Stock
Photo; **238** Furtseff/Fotolia; **238** PrinceOfLove/Shutterstock; **238** 32 pixels/Fotolia;
238 Fosin/Shutterstock; **238** Scanrail1/Shutterstock; **296** Denis Rozhnovsky/Shutterstock;
296 ImageFlow/Shutterstock; **296** RedlineVector/Shutterstock; **296** Nobelus/Shutterstock;
296 Blan-k/Shutterstock; **296** Castaldostudio/Shutterstock; **296** Africa Studio/Shutterstock;
296BL Andrii Gorulko/Shutterstock; **296BR** Aksonov/E+/Getty Images; **296C** Andrew
Orlemann/Shutterstock; **296T** Alexander Y/Shutterstock; **356** Studio023/Fotolia; **356** Designua/
Fotolia; **356** ShutterDivision/Shutterstock; **356** Andrey Armyagov/Shutterstock; **414** David
Kleyn/Alamy Stock Photo; **414** littleny/Fotolia; **414** 3desc/Fotolia; **414** Angelo.Gi/Fotolia;
414 Stevecuk/Fotolia; **414** Megastocker/Fotolia; **462** John Nordell/The Christian Science
Monitor/Getty Images; **462** Museum of Science and Industry, Chicago/Archive Photos/Getty
Images; **462** Rui Santos/Alamy Stock Photo; **502** Harvepino/Shutterstock; **502** David Lee/
Shutterstock; **502** ImYanis/Shutterstock; **502** Guitar Photographer/Shutterstock; **502** J.D.S/
Shutterstock; **550** Heather Drake/Alamy Stock Photo; **550** Greg Gard/Alamy Stock Photo;
550 Kumar Sriskandan/Alamy Stock Photo; **550** Michael Ventura/Alamy Stock Photo;
550 MaxAlex/Fotolia